DATE DUE

PRINTED IN U.S.A.

International Encyclopedia of the
Social Sciences, 2nd edition

International Encyclopedia of the Social Sciences, 2nd edition

VOLUME 3
ETHNIC CONFLICT–INEQUALITY, GENDER

William A. Darity Jr.
EDITOR IN CHIEF

MACMILLAN REFERENCE USA
A part of Gale, Cengage Learning

Detroit • New York • San Francisco • New Haven, Conn • Waterville, Maine • London

International Encyclopedia of the Social Sciences, 2nd edition
William A. Darity Jr., Editor in Chief

LIBRARY OF CONGRESS CATALOGING-IN-PUBLICATION DATA

International encyclopedia of the social sciences / William A. Darity, Jr., editor in chief.—2nd ed. v. cm. Rev. ed. of: International encyclopedia of the social sciences / David L. Sills, editor. c1968–c1991.
Includes bibliographical references and index.
ISBN 978-0-02-865965-7 (set hardcover : alk. paper)—ISBN 978-0-02-865966-4 (v. 1 hardcover : alk. paper)—ISBN 978-0-02-865967-1 (v. 2 hardcover : alk. paper)—ISBN 978-0-02-865968-8 (v. 3 hardcover : alk. paper)—ISBN 978-0-02-865969-5 (v. 4 hardcover : alk. paper)—ISBN 978-0-02-865970-1 (v. 5 hardcover : alk. paper)—ISBN 978-0-02-865971-8 (v. 6 hardcover : alk. paper)—ISBN 978-0-02-865972-5 (v. 7 hardcover : alk. paper)—ISBN 978-0-02-865973-2 (v. 8 hardcover : alk. paper)—ISBN 978-0-02-866141-4 (v. 9 hardcover : alk. paper)—ISBN 978-0-02-866117-9 (ebook : alk. paper)
1. Social sciences—Dictionaries. 2. Social sciences—Encyclopedias. I. Darity, William A., 1953– II. Title: Encyclopedia of the social sciences.
H40.A2I5 2008
300.3–dc22
2007031829

0-02-865965-1 (set)   0-02-865970-8 (v. 5)
0-02-865966-X (v. 1)   0-02-865971-6 (v. 6)
0-02-865967-8 (v. 2)   0-02-865972-4 (v. 7)
0-02-865968-6 (v. 3)   0-02-865973-2 (v. 8)
0-02-865969-4 (v. 4)   0-02-866141-9 (v. 9)

This title is also available as an e-book.
ISBN 978-0-02-866117-9; 0-02-866117-6
Contact your Gale representative for ordering information.

Printed in the United States of America
3 4 5 6 7 8 14 13 12 11 10 09 08

Editorial Board

Contents

Contents

E

ETHNIC CONFLICT

Ethnicity culturally differentiates groups from one another based on each group's prominent characteristics, including a common history, ancestry, language, as well as other kinds of symbols, dress, religion, and traditions. Ethnic affiliations do not necessarily fragment ethnically diverse societies but the context tends to influence how individuals organize and define themselves as well as how others regard them. Ethnic differences can generate ethnic conflict when these differences are used to promote prejudice and discrimination against a group that has been marked or stigmatized. Stigmatization of groups can occur within and between countries. It may manifest itself in various forms and to different degrees. But the pertinent literature diverges on the root causes of ethnic conflict, from riots to genocide. Broadly speaking there are two contending perspectives, the cultural and structural paradigm. Both perspectives implicitly or explicitly implicate the role of social institutions.

The cultural paradigm regards ethnic conflict as a social identity issue prompted by real or perceived threat to group boundaries and a familiar way of life. In this case resorting to group identity represents a fallback position for the frightened, alienated, and the angry as the ethnic group becomes the magna mater. Structural changes, for example, rapid, often imposed modernization or dramatic regime change, both accompanied by institutional failures, may evoke reactions expressed in cultural terms in triggering the closing of ethnic group boundaries.

The structural paradigm postulates that ethnic conflict is not about ethnicity at all but rather involves economic and political factors, including territory. Ethnicity may be manipulated to gain economic and political power, and for stratifying societies or nation-states within the world system. Stratification usually involves exploitation of the less powerful groups.

When diverse ethnic groups share a common territory they may resort to segregation as one type of ethnic conflict. Segregation inhibits a group's contact with other groups, as was practiced in Europe, beginning in Venice, Italy, in 1516 with the confinement of Jews to areas of towns or ghettos. Other examples include blacks in the United States between the end of slavery and desegregation, and blacks in South Africa under apartheid. During World War II (1939–1945) the U.S. government confined Japanese Americans to internment camps. Generally, forced segregation renders the ghettoized group vulnerable to individual and institutionalized harassment by the other group and sexual relations between groups as well as intermarriage are punishable by law. One of the unintended consequences of segregation is for the forcibly isolated group to further accentuate its distinctive cultural characteristics. This is one area where race and ethnicity intersect. Segregation may avert ethnic riots, a type of ethnic conflict, which involves sudden, often brutal violence inflicted on members of one ethnic group by members of another ethnic group.

Expulsion is another strategy of ethnic conflict, when the dominant group forces a less powerful group to relocate. One historical example is that of European colonists in the Americas, who conquered territories inhabited by Native Americans, displacing the indigenous population from its ancestral lands. Another example is the case of the Palestinians, who were expelled from Israel to make room for the Jewish State in 1948. An additional case, rarely discussed although it constitutes the largest forced migration of modern times, is the expulsion of 14.5 million Germans from East Central Europe between 1944 and 1950. Expulsion is a type of ethnic cleansing. Usually the perpetrators want to achieve simultaneous goals: wipe the region clean of the expelled ethnic groups and decimate it in the process.

Ethnic conflict in the former Yugoslavia attracted world attention and international intervention largely because it involved ethnic cleansing. Yugoslavia had been under the iron fist of communism. With the demise of communism latent ethnic tensions erupted into open ethnic conflict in a civil war in 1991. Yugoslavia disintegrated as a nation-state, splintering into smaller states with populations of numeric majority and minority ethnic groups, some of which vied for political power. Croatia asserted state autonomy by forcibly expelling a substantial number of Serbs that formerly coexisted with Croats. The Bosnian conflict between Serbs, Croats, and Muslims erupted into a war in 1992. Serbs attempted to ethnically cleanse Bosnia of the Muslim population. Serbs' strategies of ethnic cleansing involved the internment in concentration camps of large numbers of Muslim men, as well as their torture and murder, and the systematic mass rapes of their women. In addition to harassment, these are widely used practices of ethnic cleansers toward survivors of the targeted group, regularly accompanying expulsion. The former Yugoslavia also generated the 1999 Kosovo War, in which Serbs attempted to ethnically cleanse the province of Kosovar Albanian Muslims. Following NATO's military intervention, the process of ethnic cleansing reversed itself; Kosovar Albanian Muslims turned on Serbs. The region has remained volatile despite new borders representing ethnic nationalism and the presence of a United Nations contingent.

The most extreme form of ethnic cleansing is genocide, the intent to systematically destroy an entire national or ethnic group. The term *genocide* was first applied to the attempted extermination of Jews by the National Socialists or Nazis in Germany. Millions of Jews and others deemed unfit or dangerous to Adolf Hitler's regime were murdered in concentration camps during World War II, in the context of a well-orchestrated campaign of virulent anti-Semitic propaganda. History witnessed additional instances of attempted genocide, including the Turkish Ottoman Empire's massacre of more than 1 million Armenians between 1915 and 1923, the killing fields of the Khmer Rouge in the 1970s where 2 million Cambodians perished, and the Hutu's slaughter of the Tutsis during the 1990s in Rwanda, Africa. The structural school of thought views the Rwandan case as a class war instead of ethnic cleansing. Some regard the forced migration of 14.5 million Germans from East Central Europe, resulting in more than 2 million civilian deaths, and the

fire bombing of Dresden at the close of World War II, additionally killing several hundred thousand civilians, as attempted genocide. Scholars disagree, however, on which cases besides the Jewish case constitute genocide.

If one applies the structural lens to the ethnic conflict in Iraq that erupted since the U.S. war on that country and the removal of Saddam Hussein's dictatorial regime, one can explain the conflict between Shi'is, Sunnis, and Kurds as an attempt by elites to gain political and economic power by appealing to the respective ethnic group. The absence of strong institutions able to mediate exacerbates this conflict. Similar to the former Yugoslavia, each power broker tries to capitalize from long-standing tensions between the groups. The international context and external powers are implicated as well.

SEE ALSO *Ethnic Fractionalization; Ethnocentrism; Genocide*

BIBLIOGRAPHY

Bardhan, Pranab. 1997. Method in Madness? A Political-Economy Analysis of Ethnic Conflicts in Less Developed Countries. *World Development* 25 (9): 1381–1398.

Horowitz, Donald L. 1985. *Ethnic Groups in Conflict*. Berkeley: University of California Press.

Horowitz, Donald L. 2001. *The Deadly Ethnic Riot*. Berkeley: University of California Press.

Rudolph, Joseph R., ed. 2003. *Encyclopedia of Modern Ethnic Conflicts*. Westport, CT: Greenwood Press.

Van den Berghe, Pierre. 1981. *Ethnic Phenomenon*. New York: Elsevier North Holland.

Várdy, Steven Béla, and T. Hunt Tooley, eds. 2003. *Ethnic Cleansing in Twentieth Century Europe*. New York: Columbia University Press.

Brigitte U. Neary

ETHNIC ENCLAVE

The term *ethnic enclave* first emerged in the contemporary sociological literature in 1967 (Hanna and Hanna 1967). However, Alejandro Portes and his colleagues (Portes and Bach 1985; Portes and Manning 1985; and Portes and Stepick 1985; but see also Model 1985) are credited with developing the concept theoretically and bringing it to the forefront in our understanding of the labor market experiences of marginalized workers, particularly immigrants. A review of the literature shows that while the ethnic enclave concept gained popularity during the 1985–1994 period, it continued to receive attention in the 1995–2005 period.

THEORETICAL ORIGINS OF THE ETHNIC ENCLAVE CONCEPT

The origins of the ethnic enclave concept can be traced to the segmented labor market perspective (Sanders and Nee 1987), which is an extension of dual economy theory (Averitt 1968; Galbraith 1971). According to this perspective, the labor market is segmented in advanced capitalistic societies into at least two labor markets (Edwards 1975; Gordon 1972). Primary labor markets are characterized by stable working conditions, high wages, scarce skill specifications, internal labor markets, and high returns to human capital investments for workers. In contrast, secondary labor markets are characterized by high turnover rates, low wages, low skills, lack of opportunities for promotion, and lower returns to human capital. Given that advanced capitalism requires the continual flow of low-wage and relatively unskilled labor to fill undesirable jobs (Burawoy 1976; Piore 1979; Sassen-Koob 1978), minorities, women, and immigrants are disproportionately clustered in secondary labor markets (Light and Gold 2000; Sanders and Nee 1987; Tolbert et al. 1980).

However, Kenneth Wilson and Portes (1980) shifted the focus from "ethnic" to "immigrant" enclaves in one of the earliest recalibrations of the ethnic enclave concept. Subsequently, Portes defined the enclave economy as involving "immigrant groups which concentrate in a distinct spatial location and organize a variety of enterprises serving their own ethnic market and/or the general population. Their basic characteristic is that a significant proportion of the immigrant workforce is employed in enterprises owned by other immigrants" (1981, p. 291).

Hence, Portes's (1981) "immigrant enclave" concept has two characteristics: (1) a critical mass of immigrant-owned business firms that employ a critical mass of co-ethnic workers; and (2) spatial clustering of enterprises. Although Portes and his associates (Portes and Jensen 1992; Portes and Bach 1985) have altered the definition, it has basically followed the general conceptualization of immigrant enclaves.

The term *ethnic enclave economy* has come to stand for the economic advantage of location clustering (Light and Gold 2000). Some argue that one of the benefits of ethnic enclaves is protection from discrimination (Portes and Bach 1985; Zhou 1992). Accordingly, ethnic enclaves allow workers from discriminated groups to overcome the barriers for which they are punished in mainstream labor markets. As such, the process of ethnic enclave formation compensates for background deficits and discrimination that ethnic groups encounter in the general labor market. Examples of successful groups in ethnic enclaves include Japanese Americans in the early twentieth century (Bonacich and Modell 1980) and Cubans in contemporary Miami (Portes and Jensen 1992).

In contrast, some argue that ethnic enclaves are used to maintain and enforce sweatshop conditions, including low-wages and restrictions against union organizing (Sanders and Nee 1987). Additionally, ethnic enclaves may fuel paternalistic ethnic assistantship in which immigrants who depend on kinship or ethnic-group assistance in the initial stage of adaptation to a host society may become caught in a web of obligations that interfere with rational pursuits of economic opportunities (Li 1977). Furthermore, as long as immigrant and minority workers are restricted to ethnic enclaves, entrepreneurs can profit from the surplus of cheap labor (Schrover 2001) and impede upward mobility by restricting the accumulation of skills (e.g., proficiency in English) to compete in general labor markets (Sanders and Nee 1987). Indeed, in a study of Cuban and Chinese immigrants, Jimmy Sanders and Victor Nee (1987) observed that the positive economic rewards of the ethnic enclave apply only to entrepreneurs but not to their workers.

In sum, immigrants, and their native-born counterparts to a lesser extent, participate in ethnic enclaves because of their limited human capital, their exclusion from mainstream labor markets, and as a protective mechanism from discrimination. However, there is no agreement about the benefits of these ethnic enclaves, particularly in light of the characteristics often associated with them—unsafe working conditions, low-wages particularly for rank-and-file laborers, workers being overburdened with obligations, and the entrapment of workers that impedes their acquisition of the human-capital resources needed to gain greater economic rewards.

SEE ALSO *Assimilation; Ethnic Enterprises; Immigrants to North America; Networks*

BIBLIOGRAPHY

Averitt, Robert T. 1968. *The Dual Economy: The Dynamics of American Industry Structure.* New York: Norton.

Bonacich, Edna, and John Modell. 1980. *The Economic Basis of Ethnic Solidarity: Small Business in the Japanese American Community.* Berkeley: University of California Press.

Burawoy, Michael. 1976. The Functions and Reproduction of Migrant Labor: Comparative Material from Southern Africa and the United States. *American Journal of Sociology* 81: 1050–1087.

Edwards, Richard C. 1975. The Social Relations on Production in the Firm and Labor Market Structure. In *Labor Market Segmentation*, eds. Richard C. Edwards, Michael Reich, and David M. Gordon, 3–26. Lexington, MA: D.C. Heath.

Galbraith, John Kenneth. 1971. *The New Industrial State.* New York: Mentor.

Gordon, David. 1972. *Theories of Poverty and Underemployment: Orthodox, Radical, and Dual Labor Market.* Lexington, MA: Lexington Books.

Hanna, W. J., and J. L. Hanna. 1967. The Integrative Role of Urban Africa's Middleplaces and Middlemen. *Civilisation* 17 (1–2): 12–39.

Li, Peter S. 1977. Occupational Achievement and Kinship Assistance among Chinese Immigrants in Chicago. *The Sociological Quarterly* 18: 478–489.

Light, Ivan, and Steven Gold. 2000. *Ethnic Economies.* San Diego, CA: Academic Press.

Model, Suzanne W. 1985. A Comparative Perspective on the Ethnic Enclave: Blacks, Italians, and Jews in New York City. *International Migration Review* 19 (1): 64–81.

Piore, Michael J. 1979. *Birds of Passage: Migrant Labor and Industrial Societies.* New York: Cambridge University Press.

Portes, Alejandro. 1981. Modes of Structural Incorporation and Present Theories of Labor Immigration. In *Global Trends in Migration: Theory and Research on International Population Movements*, eds. Mary Kritz, Charles B. Keely, and Silvano Tomasi, 20–33. New York: Center for Migration Studies.

Portes, Alejandro, and Robert Bach. 1985. *Latin Journey: Cuban and Mexican Immigrants in the United States.* Berkeley: University of California Press.

Portes, Alejandro, and Leif Jensen. 1992. Disproving the Enclave Hypothesis. *American Sociological Review* 57: 418–420.

Portes, Alejandro, and Robert D. Manning. 1985. The Ethnic Enclave: Theoretical and Empirical Examples. *International Review of Community Development* 14 (Autumn): 45–61.

Portes, Alejandro, and Alex Stepick. 1985. Unwelcome Immigrants: The Labor Experience of 1980 (Mariel) Cuban and Haitian Refugees in South Florida. *American Sociological Review* 50 (4): 493–514.

Sanders, Jimmy M., and Victor Nee. 1987. Limits of Ethnic Solidarity in the Enclave Economy. *American Sociological Review* 52: 745–767.

Sassen-Koob, Saskia. 1978. The International Circulation of Resources and Development: The Case of Migration Labor. *Development and Change* 9: 509–545.

Schrover, Marlou. 2001. Immigrant Business and Niche Formation in Historical Perspective: The Netherlands in the Nineteenth Century. *Journal of Ethnic and Migration Studies* 27: 295–311.

Tolbert, Charles M., Patrick M. Horan, and E. M. Beck. 1980. The Structure of Economic Segmentation: A Dual Economy Approach. *American Journal of Sociology* 85: 1095–1116.

Wilson, Kenneth L., and Alejandro Portes. 1980. Immigrant Enclaves: An Analysis of the Labor Market Experiences of Cubans in Miami. *American Journal of Sociology* 86: 295–319.

Zhou, Min. 1992. *Chinatown: The Socioeconomic Potential of an Urban Enclave.* Philadelphia: Temple University Press.

M. Cristina Morales
Rogelio Saenz

ETHNIC ENTERPRISES

Ethnic enterprises, which often result from voluntary or involuntary segregation or segmented economic systems, are economic entities tied to specific cultural groups. They provide goods and services both within and external to the specific group. Ethnic enterprises that are associated with ethnic communities provide avenues for social mobility, socialization, and acculturation for group members. There are several factors, occurring both internal and external to the specific community, that account for the viability of ethnic enterprises. For example, among some immigrant communities (such as Koreans), ethnic enterprises appear to be more vibrant and produce significantly higher rates of self-employment than in the rest of the United States. Alternatively, some racialized groups, such as blacks, appear to have markedly lower rates of enterprise viability and self-employment.

The success or failure of ethnic enterprises cannot be viewed in a vacuum. The road to success has much to do not only with entrepreneurial skill and motivation, but also with the business climate in which the enterprise operates. The relative success of Koreans in the United States, for example, had a lot to do with the U.S. government's influence in creating cheap labor in South Korea, the economic interests of the South Korean government, the decline of U.S. labor standards, and the positive response of U.S. corporations to Korean small business development. As pointed out by Ivan Light and Edna Bonacich, in *Immigrant Entrepreneurs* (1988), business enterprises among Korean immigrants were positively influenced by a decades-long international process that was stimulated by U.S. governmental policies encouraging the development of capital, technology, and military power in Korea. The ability of Korean businesses to take advantage of these external stimuli was greatly influenced by their use of kin labor networks and the traditional Korean revolving credit association, or "kye." Thus, external and internal factors produced a situation that enhanced the viability of Korean ethnic enterprises. With time and success, the Korean economic sphere grew beyond their enclave economy. However, other ethnic and racial groups have at times responded to the Koreans' success with antagonism. Consequently—as exemplified by the 1992 Los Angeles riots, in which several Korean businesses were targeted—such success is not without its costs.

Similar positive results have also been witnessed among Japanese and Chinese immigrant enterprises. One should not, however, assume that their immigration experience has not been fraught with significant loss, nor should one look upon these success stories as indicative of the failure of other groups. The experiences of some groups, such as blacks, have been drastically different, suggesting alternative (and often negative) development. The involuntary migration of blacks, followed by centuries of oppressive slavery, racial segregation, and an economic system hostile to black economic development, has severely restricted the development of African American enterprise.

Nonetheless, a continual record of black enterprise development can be identified in the United States from as far back as 1736. Significant developments have always been associated with external and internal factors. For example, in both the Revolutionary War and the Civil War, black business flourished as a direct result of blacks taking advantage of enhanced business climates in the U.S. The 1920s, for example, is often described as the golden era for black business development. Over 100,000 black business enterprises were observed by 1932. Another period of black economic success followed World War II, and a final boom in black enterprise development was associated with the 1960s civil rights and affirmative action initiatives. Thus, by 1969, approximately 1,603,000 black enterprises, generating annual receipts of 4.5 billion dollars, were concentrated in five states (California, Illinois, New York, Ohio, and Texas). The leading businesses, in terms of revenue, were automotive dealers, service stations, and food retailers. These successes belie the hardships, setbacks, and failures along the way.

As pointed out by Manning Marable, both dominant corporations and the public in the United States have met each period of black business success with significant retrenchment, racial hostility, and racially exclusionary practices. Vandalism targeting black enterprises occurred during and immediately after each of the above periods, leading to a significant decline in black businesses in each instance. In 1919 alone, twenty-six race riots were identified. In cities like Tulsa, Oklahoma, and Cincinnati, Ohio, blacks were uprooted and forced to leave.

Another example occurred in California in association with the gold rush of the mid-1800s. Originally, blacks were encouraged to develop a wide range of businesses. But with the eventual decline of opportunities, white racial preferences began to restrict black business operations to the service trades, such as tonsorial, bootblack, livery, restaurant and catering, and drayage businesses. Blacks restricted to the tonsorial trade developed a monopoly. This monopoly however was short-lived, as white patrons began expressing a preference for white barbers. Restrictive ordinances, city covenants, real estate and business redlining, and racially exclusionary business and labor practices served to curtail black enterprise development from 1910 to the mid-1960s. The 1960s civil rights movement, and its associated affirmative action programs, marshaled in what many thought would be a new day for black business development. This fifteen-year period,

unprecedented in U.S. history, witnessed the development of a large, diverse middle class working in the public sector. Accompanying this was the growth of a new black elite in such areas as media, politics, sports, and entertainment.

Conservative backlashes to the civil rights movement, starting in the mid-1980s, served to stymie black economic enterprise development in the black community. These conservative backlashes took the form of (1) conservative attacks against affirmative action, (2) continual bias in banking and lending programs, and (3) a reluctance on the part of corporate America to fully encourage or utilize products and services.

Contrary to popular belief (or mythology), white ethnicity is alive and well in America. While the illusion of a monolithic white world serves specific political and cultural purposes, the reality of specific white enclaves serves very real and continuous economic needs. Thus, white ethnic enterprises associated with Italians, Irish, Germans, Poles, Jews, and others are easily identifiable throughout the United States. Throughout much of America, major white ethnic holidays not only celebrate white ethnicity but also tend to feature white ethnic enterprises. Such ethnic celebrations include Oktoberfest (German), St. Patrick's Day (Irish), and Columbus Day (Italian), though the fact that these celebrations take on a national character does much to hide the fact that they are indeed ethnic in nature. Since the 1960s, a tremendous amount of scholarship has been produced documenting the emergence and the continuance of ethnic communities and identity—as well as the resultant white ethnic enterprises.

White ethnic communities persist because they continue to provide for the special needs of specific communities. The principal ways in which these needs are satisfied are through the perpetuation and creation of ethnic enterprises. While these enterprises and communities were once located mainly in urban areas, they are now also associated with suburban growth. What this suggests is that as these white ethnic communities gave way to urban migrants, they were able to continue their existence in suburbia.

The economic viability, diversity, and independence an ethnic enterprise enjoys is dependent upon such things as the perceived status of the immigrant community in the host society, the availability and types of financial resources, and the size, longevity, and history of the ethnic group (and other ethnic groups) in the host society. Larger and more financially secure ethnic enterprises are typically able to operate more independently of a particular ethnic community. Alternatively, smaller and less financially secure enterprises are more likely to be dependent upon constituent ethnic communities for survival. For these latter types, growth and development of ethnic enterprises are more likely to be dependent upon the capacity of the ethnic entrepreneur to accumulate start up capital.

Postcolonial situations may provide the most fertile environments in which unique hybrid ethnic enterprises can develop. Richard Werbner documented this hybridism in Botswana in the early years of the twenty-first century. He calls it a "cosmopolitan ethnicity" that "builds inter-ethnic alliances from intra-ethnic ones and constructs differences while transcending it" (Werbner 2002, pp. 731–732). This approach maintains traditional intra-ethnic identity while also seeking to identify with a national ethnic elite identity. Such transcendence is most appropriate in those situations in which an ethnic elite is able to promote a set of national economic and political agendas through its various enterprises. Thus, the Kalanga elites, originating in the borderland of Botswana and Zimbabwe, are able to utilize a form of super-tribalism to foster nation-building in Botswana.

Although ethnic enterprises facilitate the economic stability of ethnic elites in specific host countries, they may also facilitate the economic stability of the countries of origin. By tracking remittance and capital flow data to developing countries, researchers have demonstrated that these transfers can mean the difference between economic stability and financial crisis. Billions of dollars go from primarily Western host countries to developing countries in the form of remittances. (Remittances to developing countries were estimated by the World Bank to be US$72 billion in 2001 and US$93 billion in 2003, which was significantly higher then the global foreign aid in those years of US$52 billion and US$69 billion, respectively.) Between 2001 and 2006, such remittances doubled, as countries became more aggressive in documenting and encouraging the transfer of funds. Unfortunately, activities that may account for even more transfers—illegal drugs and organized crime—often still go under the radar. Regardless, such remittances provide the basis of considerable reinvestment, capital transfer, and economic investment in third world countries. While Latin America (specifically Mexico) accounts for the largest share of such remittances, the amount going to Asia, the Middle East, Israel, and Africa cannot be discounted.

SEE ALSO *Ethnic Enclave; Immigrants to North America*

BIBLIOGRAPHY

Alba, Robert D., John R. Logan, and Kyle Crowder. 1997. White Ethnic Neighborhoods and Assimilation: The Greater New York Region, 1980–1990. *Social Forces* 75 (3): 883–912.

Lieberson, Stanley, and Mary Waters. 1988. *From Many Strands: Ethnic and Racial Groups in Contemporary America.* New York: Russell Sage Foundation.

Light, Ivan, and Edna Bonacich. 1988. *Immigrant Entrepreneurs: Koreans in Los Angeles, 1965–1982.* Berkeley: University of California Press.

Marable, Manning. 2000. *How Capitalism Underdeveloped Black America.* 2nd ed. Cambridge, MA: South End.

Marger, Martin N., and Constance A. Hoffman. 1992. Ethnic Enterprise in Ontario: Immigrant Participation in the Small Business Sector. *International Migration Review* 26 (3): 968–981.

Werbner, Richard. 2002. Cosmopolitan Ethnicity, Entrepreneurship and the Nation: Minority Elites in Botswana. *Journal of Southern African Studies* 28 (4): 731–753.

World Bank. 2003. *Global Development Finance Report 2003: Striving for Stability in Development Finance.* Washington, DC: World Bank Group. http://web.worldbank.org.

Rodney D. Coates

ETHNIC FRACTIONALIZATION

Ethnic fractionalization (EF) deals with the number, sizes, socioeconomic distribution, and geographical location of distinct cultural groups, usually in a state or some otherwise delineated territory. The specific cultural features might refer to language, skin color, religion, ethnicity, customs and tradition, history, or another distinctive criterion, alone or in combination. Frequently these features are used for social exclusion and the monopolization of power.

A crucial distinction is whether there is a commonly accepted value order above each distinct subculture (as in the "melting pot" idea) or each culture stands for itself (the "salad bowl" image). In addition one culture may be dominant in a relatively benign way (as in the British and Roman Empires, which had second-class citizens but with access to some public goods) or in a harmful way (the Tutsis and Hutus reciprocally, the Germans and Poles or Czechs, the Russians and the peoples in Caucasia and the Baltic States).

The distinction between majorities and minorities is important, though frequently some minorities are better off socioeconomically (Basques, Jews, the Indians in East Africa, the Chinese in Southeast Asia) or even rule over majorities. The conflict potential due to EF increases if disputed borders are involved (as in irredenta) or if the state collapses (as in sub-Saharan African examples) or does not exist at all (Palestine, the Kurdish state). Then there is a temptation either to exit into the other bordering state or to attack from there (Carment and James 2004).

Because ethnic or other cultural minorities often have suffered from other (majoritarian) groups in the past, they have vivid memories of their tragedies and fears for the future. Structurally they cannot trust the state as a benevolent mediator because there is always the possibility that it might command private information (information withheld from the opponent) to be used against the subgroup, thus wiping out any consociational arrangements. Such arrangements (as in Switzerland, the Netherlands, the European Union) usually follow the proportional rule of representation and engage in broad-based collective decision making. In cultural matters (e.g., language use, schooling, cultural symbols) there is even allowance for veto rights by cultural subgroups. Yet few of these arrangements have survived (Lijphart 1977).

All variations in numbers and sizes of EF seem possible. In theory two large groups equal in size could balance each other perfectly (consider the Israelis and Palestinians) or could provide ground for perennial self-reinforcing conflict. Likewise a small number of groups of equal size could balance each other but also provide sources of intergroup conflict, particularly if coalitions are considered (the *tertius gaudens* phenomenon, that is, the third party that is winning from a conflict of the other two parties). "Measures of polarization are more appropriate to capture the intensity of disagreements across groups" (Alesina et al. 2003, p. 164), reaching their maximum when two equally sized groups confront each other.

Three basic arguments explain how and in part why ethnic heterogeneity creates a potential for social cleavage and conflict. First, following Georg Simmel (1908), the "stranger" is considered untrustworthy and in possession of hidden knowledge. He or she can compare his or her past knowledge and experiences with his or her present ones. He or she comes from unknown places and may leave for unknown ones. In knowing less about the local rules and values, he or she intensifies *we* and *they* feelings, which carry mostly negative and threatening stereotypes. Second, group experiments show that these distinctions arise even when characteristics differ minimally (see minimal group theory, Tajfel 1981). Third, cultural groups reduce social costs within groups in daily interactions (with lower rates of misunderstanding and conflict), they give protection, and they produce a public good of shared norms. On this basis, EF will persist. Thus Michael Hechter (2000) recommends granting autonomy to distinct cultural groups and shunning centralism. Cultural autonomy and decentralization can buy off conflict. The paradigm at the macro and micro levels is the Roman Empire or the Islamic millet system.

When identities become politically salient in an ethnically diverse area can be explained (partially) by a number of theories, the most prominent being resource mobilization theory, which stresses entrepreneurism on the part of leaders and resource accumulation and collective action on the part of followers (Tilly and Tarrow 2006); relative deprivation theory; and more directly to the timely circumstances, the theory of political opportunity structure, which, for example, involves the collapse of a repressive multicultural empire such as the Soviet Union with ethnic strife in the Caucasus and the Baltics, external warfare, and shelter with groups beyond the national border (Carment and James 2004).

Karl Deutsch (1966) adds an important macro perspective, emphasizing that modernization of one ethnocultural group usually leads to more integration via social mobilization. In case of different ethnocultural groups, however, massive conflict results, paradoxically at higher levels of overall economic development. In each subgroup, social movement entrepreneurs employ the forces of communication and indigenous integration for the benefit of cultural distinction (e.g., in Northern Ireland, Palestine, and Iraq). Forms of conflict resulting from EF include coups d'état, interethnic rioting and war, and even external warfare (Hibbs 1973; Carment and James 2004). States that have suffered from violent ethnocultural fractionalization and conflict usually exhibit lower overall levels of socioeconomic development and attract little foreign investment (Collier and Hoeffler 2004). The breakdown of the state monopoly of violence and territorial borders looms large, contributing to and ending in state failure (Rotberg 2004).

EF usually is measured as 1 minus the Herfindahl concentration index of ethnolinguistic group shares, which reproduces the probability that two randomly drawn individuals from the population belong to different groups. The theoretical maximum of EF at 1 means that each person belongs to a different group. Alberto Alesina and colleagues (2003) employ this measure separately for ethnic, linguistic, and religious fractionalization (with data mainly from the *Encyclopedia Britannica*). EF correlates negatively with economic growth and government quality (from 1960s onward, n=190 countries), although its effects decline with intermediating channels, such as schooling, financial depth, fiscal surplus, and the use of telephones controlled (Easterly and Levine 1997). According to Alesina: "The thirteen most ethnically diverse countries are all in Sub-Saharan Africa, followed by Yugoslavia and seven more Sub-Saharan African countries. The least ethnically fractionalized countries are South Korea, Japan, and North Korea" (Alesina et al. 2003, p. 163).

EF may, however, be endogenously affected, for example by changes in different group fertilities, by the definition of groups, and by individual self-definitions. James Fearon and David Laitin (1999) point to reverse causalities (e.g., cases of rebellion leading to the inclusion of groups in the dataset or large-scale ethnic violence causing low gross domestic product [GDP]) in suggesting improvements in the minorities at risk data (Gurr 1993), another of the major datasets on EF. Groups included in countries with more than one million inhabitants and comprising at least 1 percent of the population had to meet at least one of four "risks":

the group suffers "discrimination";

it is "disadvantaged from past discrimination";

it is an "advantaged minority being challenged"; or

the group is "mobilized," meaning that "the group (in whole or part) supports one or more political organizations that advocates greater group rights, privileges, or autonomy." (Gurr 1993, pp. 7, 65)

Fearon and Laitin provide numerous examples of dubious classifications on the basis of language or culture alone. The third and oldest measure is the ethnolinguistic classification from the Soviet *Atlas Narodov Mira* (Atlas of peoples of the world, 1964), which relies on linguistic distinctions and thus obscures other aspects of ethnicity, such as racial origin, skin color, and cultural traits (see Fearon 2003 for a further dataset).

Fearon and Laitin also report results on geographic concentration, "with widely dispersed and mainly urban groups being unlikely to be involved in ethnic violence"; on relative group size, "with a weak tendency for larger groups to be more disposed to violence"; and "degree of ethnic heterogeneity of the country, with greater heterogeneity associated with less violence once we control for GDP and other factors" (Fearon and Laitin 1999). Intermixing as such, and thus the alleged "security dilemma" (Posen, in Cederman 2002), is not enough to dispose ethnic groups to violent conflict.

The question remains why are some minorities engaged in large-scale separatist or autonomy-related violence while others are not? "Ecological" data must be supplemented by perceptual data on the deepness and unbargainability of conflict to go further in explaining the virulence of EF and participant groups and to avoid the logical pitfalls of sampling on the dependent variable.

SEE ALSO *Coalition; Contact Hypothesis; Democracy, Consociational; Development and Ethnic Diversity; Ethnic Conflict; Ethnicity; Ethnocentrism; Identities, Deadly; Identity; Majorities; Minorities; Quotas; Secession; Separatism; Violence; Violence, Frantz Fanon on*

BIBLIOGRAPHY

Alesina, Alberto, Arnaud Devleeschauwer, William Easterly, et al. 2003. Fractionalization. *Journal of Economic Growth* 8: 155–194.

Carment, David, and Patrick James. 2004. Third-Party States in Ethnic Conflict: Identifying the Domestic Determinants of Intervention. In *Ethnic Conflict and International Politics: Explaining Diffusion and Escalation*, eds. Steven E. Lobell and Philip Mauceri, 11–34. New York: Palgrave.

Cederman, Lars-Erik. 2002. Nationalism and Ethnicity. In *Handbook of International Relations*, eds. Walter Carlsnaes, Thomas Risse, and Beth A. Simmons, 409–428. London: Sage.

Collier, Paul, and Anke Hoeffler. 2004. Conflict. In *Global Crises, Global Solutions*, ed. Bjørn Lomborg, 129–156. New York: Cambridge University Press.

Deutsch, Karl W. 1966. *Nationalism and Social Communication: An Inquiry into the Foundations of Nationality*. Cambridge, MA: MIT Press.

Easterly, William, and Ross Levine. 1997. Africa's Growth Tragedy: Policies and Ethnic Divisions. *Quarterly Journal of Economics* 111 (4): 1203–1250.

Fearon, James D. 2003. Ethnic Structure and Cultural Diversity by Country. *Journal of Economic Growth* 8 (2): 195–222.

Fearon, James D., and David D. Laitin. 1999. Collaborative Project: "Minorities at Risk" Data Base and Explaining Ethnic Violence. National Science Foundation Grant Proposal. Mimeo.

Fearon, James D., and David D. Laitin. 2003. Ethnicity, Insurgency, and Civil War. *American Political Science Review* 97 (1): 75–90.

Gurr, Ted Robert. 1993. *Minorities at Risk: A Global View of Ethnopolitical Conflicts*. Washington, DC: U.S. Institute of Peace Press.

Hechter, Michael. 2000. *Containing Nationalism*. Oxford: Oxford University Press.

Hibbs, Douglas A. 1973. *Mass Political Violence*. New York: Wiley.

Lijphart, Arend. 1977. *Democracy in Plural Societies: A Comparative Exploration*. New Haven, CT: Yale University Press.

Rotberg, Robert I., ed. 2004. *When States Fail: Causes and Consequences*. Princeton, NJ: Princeton University Press.

Simmel, Georg. 1908. *Soziologie: Untersuchungen über die Formen der Vergesellschaftung* [Sociology: Investigations on the forms of socialization]. Leipzig: Dunker and Humblot.

Tajfel, Henri. 1981. *Human Groups and Social Categories*. Cambridge, U.K.: Cambridge University Press.

Tilly, Charles, and Sidney Tarrow. 2006. *Contentious Politics*. Boulder, CO: Paradigm Publishers.

Ekkart Zimmermann

ETHNICITY

Ethnicity refers to the differentiation of groups of people who have shared cultural meanings, memories, and descent produced through social interaction. In classical Greek, the terms *ethnos* and *ethnikos* were used in a number of ways to refer to a collectivity that shares similar cultural or biological characteristics—for example, a tribe of people or a band of friends—and who were not Greek, came from outside the nation, were foreign and different, and were also considered inferior, barbarian, and less civilized. This distinction between ethnically marked "others" and nonethnically marked "us" persists in modern popular usage with references to ethnic fashion or food.

Sociological accounts of ethnicity are highly varied but tend to break the classical linkage between ethnicity and "other" in asserting that all people are ethnically located in that their subjectivity and identity are contextualized by history, language, descent, and culture. Ethnicity usually refers to the differentiation of social groups on the basis of the following distinct criteria. First, a notion of a "homeland" or place of common origin is a key element. It is often linked to the idea of a diaspora, where an ethnic group has migrated from the homeland to form communities elsewhere whose members identify with their place of origin. Second, a common language, either distinctive in itself or a distinct dialect of a language shared with others, may be central to the construction of shared memories and affective belonging. Identification with a distinct religion—for example, Sikhism—or a religion shared with others can be a central feature of many ethnic groups. A common culture with distinctive social institutions and behavior, diet, and dress, as well as a common tradition or shared history of one's own "people" or nation are other criteria used in specifying ethnic groups.

Ethnicities may be highly durable over millennia and space, and they can also be formed from new conjunctions of social contexts. This occurs, for example, when migrants shape a new backward-looking sense of ethnic belonging with the construction of national context to produce hyphenated forms, such as British-Asian or Hispanic-American. Ethnic solidarity can provide a deep sense of physical and psychological security, allowing individuals to identify and find a sense of common purpose with a great and long-lasting tradition of people. But if fictive shared beliefs underlie ethnic differentiation, then the boundaries of ethnic groups are inevitably unclear and caution is required in assessing the extent to which external categories accurately reflect social meanings, social roles, and wider social inequalities. There may often be a poor fit between the state and bureaucratic constructions of ethnic categories and dynamic forms of intersubjective ethnic identities.

Scholars have made various attempts to develop global typologies of ethnicity, including those by Thomas Eriksen (1993) and Stephen Castles (2000). These typologies include indigenous peoples dispossessed and over-whelmed by colonizers. The United States, Canada, Australia, and New Zealand have similar histories in this respect and contain indigenous minorities—Aborigines, Maoris, Native Americans, and Native Canadians—who remain in unequal marginalized positions. Indigenous groups are also found in Latin America, where there have been massacres, for example, in Guatemala in the 1980s, and in most Asian countries, where native groups may be categorized as "tribal peoples" or "hill tribes" (Castles 2000). Other categories and contexts include: migrant workers and their descendants forming strong ethnic communities—for example, Turks in Germany or Pakistanis in the United Kingdom; ethno-nations—for example, the Quebecois in Canada or the Basques in Spain—with regional ethnic groups contesting national control; postslavery groups in, for example, Brazil, the United States, and the Caribbean; and people living in postcolonial and postcommunist contexts, as in, for example, Uganda, Zimbabwe, Chechnya, or the former Yugoslavia, where ethnic loyalties have had grave consequences in terms of conflict and violence.

UNDERSTANDING ETHNICITY

Ethnic hostility, discrimination, and exclusion take many forms, but three broad categories can be identified. The first category includes the most severe acts involving mass societal aggression, such as the annihilation of native peoples in North America, South Africa, and Australia from the seventeenth to the twentieth centuries; the Nazi Holocaust during World War II (1939–1945); plantation slavery from the late seventeenth to the mid-nineteenth centuries; or the massacres of Tutsi by Hutu in Rwanda in 1994 and ethnic cleansing of Kosovar Albanians by Serbs in the 1990s. The second category of ethnic exclusion and discrimination involves denial of access to societal opportunities and rewards in such areas as employment, education, housing, health care, and justice. Many instances of such discrimination have been documented in Europe by the European Monitoring Centre on Racism and Xenophobia, mostly affecting Roma, Sinti, Gypsy, and Traveller groups. Poor mental and physical health, lower levels of educational attainment, restricted access to work, and lower income levels have been linked to poor housing conditions for many of these groups. The lack of social rights has also constrained their opportunities for political participation. A third category of ethnic discrimination includes the use of derogatory or abusive language or forms of representation that are felt to be offensive (e.g., the anti-Muslim Danish cartoons that circulated in 2005 and 2006). Such derogatory expressions, together with racist jokes, the use of Nazi insignia, and unwitting stereotyping and pejorative phrases, may constitute lesser forms of ethnic hostility. Explanations for ethnic conflict must encompass micropsychological processes, individual and group experiences, and competition and socialization, together with structural power relations and aspects of globalization.

Sociological approaches to conceptualizing ethnicity fall into two camps. *Primordial* approaches, first suggested by Edward Shils in 1957, regard ties of blood, race, language, region, and custom as exterior, coercive, and given. This approach has been criticized as static and naturalistic, and as failing to account for the impact of immigration and intermarriage. In contrast, *instrumentalist* approaches, represented, for example, by Michael Banton's work on ethnic competition (1993), view ethnicity as a social, political, and cultural resource that can be used in competition for resources or as a motivation for conflict. This approach has been criticized for underplaying durable, affective, and persisting constructions of ethnic identity. The *transactionalist* mode of enquiry advocated by Fredrik Barth is seen as making a vital contribution to the instrumentalist approach in arguing that "the critical focus of investigation from this point of view becomes the ethnic boundary that defines the group, not the cultural stuff which it encloses" (Barth 1969, p.15). The conceptual separation of culture and ethnicity and the focus on processes of interaction and boundary-maintenance have been highly influential.

As with culture, the concepts of race and nation crosscut the specification of ethnicity. As Steve Fenton (2003) has argued, the word *nation* also refers to groups of people with common descent, culture, and a shared sense of territory. But what differentiates a *nation* from an ethnic group is its members' construction as a state or a state-like political form. Also, ethnic groups are more frequently conceived as a subset of the nation-state, particularly where states do not have a pure monoethnic form. The word *race* also refers to groups with a common descent and culture, but race carries an explicit reference to physical or visible difference. Race may operate as a subset of ethnicity, being one of the many markers used to differentiate a particular ethnic group. On the other hand, ethnicity may operate as a subset of a race, where one racial group is seen as encompassing many ethnic groups—for example, the community of black British within which Caribbean ethnicities have been erased.

Competing sociological accounts of ethnicity have been classified and critically differentiated by Siniša Malešević (2004). Classical sociology, neo-Marxism, functionalism, symbolic interactionism, sociobiology, rational-choice theory, elite theory, neo-Weberian approaches, and antifoundationalist positions have all been used to theorize ethnicity. Malešević illustrates how each position can be used to provide an explanation of the 1994 Rwandan genocide, and he highlights key epistemological tensions.

Differing approaches prioritize different determining factors, ranging from the legacy of German and Belgian colonial divide-and-rule policies in the region; the downfall of the Rwandan economy; the lack of a common cultural system; the primordial ethnic differentiation between shorter, darker Hutus and taller, light-skinned Tutsi; the individual self-interest of those involved; the motives and behavior of Hutu power holders; status differentiation between Tutsi aristocracy and Hutu farmers; and the rationalist urge to impose order on difference using modernist methods. Central factors in such cases also include, as Helen Fein (1993) has argued in relation to Armenian genocide during World War I (1914–1918) and the Nazi Holocaust, the rise of new elites in declining states who see their idealized political vision as exclusive and who position minorities as outside moral obligation, and where extermination is less visible and operates with little fear of sanction.

ETHNIC RELATIONS

Ethnic relations encompass highly varied, complex forms of social relations where attachment to cultural difference is paramount. Milton Esman (2004) has identified differing categories of ethnic relations. *Exclusionary domination* involves enforcing an ethnically stratified system of unequal rights, status, and opportunities. This was common in European colonial societies on all continents, in apartheid-era South Africa, and in many of the more extreme cases previously noted. *Inclusionary domination* or *assimilation* involves dismantling ethnic cultures, languages, and attachments by facilitating acculturation to the nation. The classic French republican model of aggressive assimilation, the Thai government's approach to its Chinese minority, and the Turkish government's approach to Turkey's large Kurdish minority are all examples of this form of ethnic relations.

Granting rights to minority groups can also ensure their domination. Limited rights have been granted to Arab Palestinian citizens in Israel, but these rights serve to confirm their second-class status, and there remains entrenched opposition to equal rights with Jewish Israelis. In Malaysia, domination with significant but unequal rights for Chinese and Indian citizens is well established. Power-sharing solutions have been developed in many national contexts where ethnic divisions have not produced conflict or separation. Belgium, India, and Switzerland provide examples where forms of federalism and consociationalism have enabled the establishment of multiethnic states. This approach supports ethnic pluralism, while the final position, integration, foresees its decline with the gradual building of social and cultural cohesion. This position is strongly advocated in the United Kingdom, where multiculturalism was officially abandoned in 2004 due to its perceived effect as ethnically divisive, in favor of policies concerned with community cohesion ad integration. Here, integration is seen as encompassing the goals of ethnic equality and ethnic interaction, with strong concern over ethnic groups that lead parallel and separated lives.

The strength of ethnic loyalties and their practical adequacy for many people in making sense of their position in the world in premodern, modern, and contemporary times indicates the likelihood that ethnic conflict will continue, despite international declarations and interventions, creative national policies, and interethnic mixing. Ethnic conflict is "a world-wide phenomenon that has become the leading source of lethal violence in international affairs" (Esman 2004, p. 26). In the context of insecure national states and global inequalities, population mobility and international migration will lead to greater cultural diversification of national populations. New technologies and changing patterns of consumption are driving the construction of larger regional and global cultures. These globalizing, cosmopolitan forces are also stimulating new forms of ethnic defensiveness and hostility toward new migrants, as is occurring in the United States, as well as toward long-established minorities, as evident in the development of anti-Semitic movements and anti-minority hate speech in Russia. Nevertheless, social science failed to predict the demise of apartheid in South Africa in the 1990s, as John Stone and Rutledge Dennis (2003) remind us, and this one example indicates the importance of theorizing and understanding the potential for constructive conflict resolution.

SEE ALSO *Assimilation; Immigrants to North America; Multiculturalism; Race*

BIBLIOGRAPHY

Banton, Michael. 1993. *Racial and Ethnic Competition.* Cambridge, U.K.: Cambridge University Press.

Barth, Fredrik, ed. 1969. *Ethnic Groups and Boundaries: The Social Organization of Cultural Difference.* London: Allen and Unwin.

Castles, Stephen. 2000. *Ethnicity and Globalization: From Migrant Worker to Transnational Citizen.* London and Thousand Oaks, CA: Sage.

Eriksen, Thomas. 1993. *Ethnicity and Nationalism: Anthropological Perspectives.* London and Boulder, CO: Pluto.

Esman, Milton J. 2004. *An Introduction to Ethnic Conflict.* Cambridge, U.K.: Polity.

Fein, Helen. 1990. *Genocide: A Sociological Perspective.* London and Newbury Park, CA: Sage.

Fenton, Steve. 2003. *Ethnicity.* Cambridge, U.K.: Polity

Malešević, Siniša. 2004. *The Sociology of Ethnicity.* London and Thousand Oaks, CA: Sage.

Shils, Edward. 1957. Primordial, Personal, Sacred, and Civil Ties. *British Journal of Sociology* 8 (2): 130–145.

Stone, John, and Rutledge Dennis, eds. 2003. *Race and Ethnicity: Comparative and Theoretical Approaches.* Oxford: Blackwell.

Ian Law

ETHNOCENTRISM

Ethnocentrism is a basic attitude expressing the belief that one's own ethnic group or one's own culture is superior to other ethnic groups or cultures, and that one's cultural standards can be applied in a universal manner. The term was first used by the American sociologist William Graham Sumner (1840–1910) to describe the view that one's own culture can be considered central, while other cultures or religious traditions are reduced to a less prominent role. Ethnocentrism is closely related to other attitudinal indicators for racism, xenophobia, prejudice, mental closure, and, more generally, an authoritarian personality structure. Ethnocentrism is widely used in research on social and political attitudes because it proves to be a very powerful and easily identifiable attitude that can be measured in a valid manner with a limited number of variables. Although ethnocentric prejudice can be directed toward one specific outsider group, empirical research reveals that usually ethnocentrism is generalized toward all outsider groups.

Although ethnocentrism is closely related to racism, it can be distinguished from racism because it does not involve necessarily a negative vision toward other races. Any culturally distinct outsider group (whether the distinction involves language, religion, color, or descent) can be targeted by ethnocentric attitudes. In practice, European researchers often tend to avoid using the term *racism* because they are reluctant to apply the concept of race to human beings. In a U.S. context, the use of the term *racism* is not considered a problem. Given the fact that ethnocentrism is such a powerful attitude and is associated strongly with various behavioral patterns, ethnocentrism measurements are routinely included in almost all major survey projects. Ethnocentrism leads to in-group favoritism with regard to contact and cooperation, and accompanies outsider-group hostility, sometimes even leading to intergroup conflict, violence, or support for discriminatory behavior. There is also an abundant research literature on consumer ethnocentrism, that is, the tendency of consumers to prefer goods and services produced in one's own society.

CAUSES OF ETHNOCENTRISM

Various explanations have been suggested for ethnocentrism. Social identity approaches assume that ethnocentrism is the result of a strong identification with the in-group of the actor, which almost automatically leads to negative feelings toward and stereotyping of members of the out-group. Because some personality types are more clearly dependent on this strong form of group identification, these personality types are also more vulnerable to adopting ethnocentric prejudice. Experimental research has demonstrated that even if groups are assigned on a purely random basis, processes of in-group identification and polarization with outsider-group members still occur. Social scientists also have speculated that a lack of real-life contact with members of outsider groups might enhance stereotyping, as the outsider group can be seen as homogeneous, but the empirical evidence about the allegedly beneficial effects of contact tends to be mixed.

Realistic conflict theory, in contrast, assumes that ethnocentrism is triggered by a real or perceived conflict between various ethnic groups competing for scarce resources in society. The originally dominant groups in a territory will develop antagonistic feelings toward newly arriving outsiders when they perceive these outsiders as a threat to their own social position (e.g., in the labor or housing markets). In practice, however, empirical research has demonstrated quite convincingly that even groups whose positions are not threatened by ethnic competition still develop ethnocentric prejudice.

Survey research routinely reveals strong individual-level determinants of ethnocentrism: for example, high education levels effectively reduce ethnocentrism, and in general, men are more willing to express ethnocentrism than women. It is believed that actors with fewer individual resources (e.g., lower socioeconomic status, cognitive ability, or self-esteem) are more dependent on in-group confirmation of their identity, thus strengthening prejudice toward members of outsider groups. There is no consensus, however, on the impact of religion on ethnocentrism. Several authors have argued that this relation can be considered as curvilinear, with the highest ethnocentrism levels among believers that are only marginally connected to organized religion. Ethnocentrism is also clearly associated with distrust and with authoritarian and right-wing ideologies, and is the single most powerful determinant of extreme-right voting behavior.

ELEMENTS OF ETHNOCENTRISM

Research distinguishes two major components of ethnocentrism that are closely related but still can be empirically distinguished. Cultural ethnocentrism finds its origin in the belief that one's own cultural norms and attitudes are superior to the cultures of other societies or groups. Furthermore, cultural ethnocentrists believe that this cultural order is threatened by the arrival of new groups (with their own cultural norms) to the territory that is claimed as their own. Cultural ethnocentrism often expresses itself in a symbolic manner, for instance, in disagreements about the public presence of cultural markers of identity such as clothing, religious symbols, or other visible elements of minority cultures. Economic ethnocentrism is tied more closely to the perception that other groups can be seen as economic competitors and therefore should be limited in their capacity as economic actors. Economic ethnocentrism can express itself in discriminatory measures on the labor market, and in boycotts or other consumer actions expressing a clear preference for goods and services associated with one's own culture.

Some researchers have also distinguished between explicit and implicit ethnocentrism. In the explicit condition, respondents are willing to express negative stereotypes toward outsider groups; the implicit condition is characterized by an inhibition to express these sentiments despite the fact that other responses clearly indicate that the respondent is unwilling to grant the same rights and legal protections to members of outsider groups. Implicit ethnocentrism can lead to calls for segregation with regard to education, housing, or cultural participation, or to a negative attitude toward affirmative action.

Although throughout the world, various government agencies and education systems have developed social and legal strategies to reduce ethnocentrism, thus far no universally successful strategies have been documented. Avoiding stereotyping seems to be a necessary prerequisite, and mass media and other socialization agents clearly play an important role in this respect.

SEE ALSO *Ethnic Conflict; Ethnic Fractionalization; Ethnicity; Jingoism; Nationalism and Nationality; Prejudice*

BIBLIOGRAPHY

Allport, Gordon. 1954. *The Nature of Prejudice*. Cambridge, MA: Addison-Wesley.

LeVine, Robert, and Donald Campbell. 1972. *Ethnocentrism*. New York: Wiley.

Sniderman, Paul, Philip Tetlock, and Edward Carmines, eds. 1993. *Prejudice, Politics, and the American Dilemma*. Stanford, CA: Stanford University Press.

Tajfel, Henri, ed. 1982. *Social Identity and Intergroup Relations*. Cambridge, U.K.: Cambridge University Press.

Marc Hooghe

ETHNO-EPIDEMIOLOGICAL METHODOLOGY

The term *ethno-epidemiology* has acquired two different but intertwined meanings in the social sciences. On the one hand, it refers to an emergent cross-disciplinary health research methodology that combines the strengths of direct participant observation and other qualitative methods for understanding social meanings and contexts as practiced in medical anthropology with the design, sampling, data collection, and analytical strategies focusing on risk factors and disease outcomes developed in epidemiology. This use is referred to here as *ethno-epidemiological methodology*. On the other hand, as Michael Agar notes in "Recasting the 'Ethno' in 'Epidemiology'" (1996), the term is also used in the literature to refer to *emic* (i.e., insider) or folk systems of disease understanding and response. This usage is referred to as the *ethno-epidemiological explanatory model*. Together, these constitute important tools for conducting and targeting public health research.

ETHNO-EPIDEMIOLOGICAL METHODOLOGY

When *medical anthropology* emerged as a field, it was concerned primarily with folk illness conceptions and related indigenous healing behaviors. On this foundation, it has evolved into a robust subdiscipline focused on studying the immediate cultural and broader social factors involved in the experience, understanding, and behavior of illness. Medical anthropologists use this information to contribute to empirically grounded public health development. *Epidemiology* developed as the scientific arm of public health centered on emergent disease causation, trends in disease occurrence, and assessment of the effectiveness of intervention. Since the mid-1970s, the boundary between medical anthropology and epidemiology has witnessed a growing number of conceptual and programmatic exchanges. Some contacts have been fraught with tensions, as occurred in the medical anthropological critique of epidemiological construction of "risk groups" in the HIV/AIDS epidemic, or when epidemiologists express wariness about small, nonrepresentative anthropological studies. Other points of contact have been highly collaborative and productive, such as various successful oral rehydration projects internationally. Although both disciplines bring a distinct approach to the study of the intersection of disease and behavior, epidemiology traditionally has taken the formal road of statistical and quantitative methods, whereas medical anthropology has favored qualitative strategies that allow access to on-the-ground behaviors and insider understandings. Ethno-epidemiological methodology is a direct product of efforts to build collaborative approaches between these two health-related research disciplines.

The development of ethno-epidemiological methodology reflects several trends in public health and medical anthropology, including: (1) a growing reliance on mixed-method research designs and multidisciplinary research teams in the investigation of health risks; (2) an increasing emphasis in medical anthropology on systematic data collection and analytic strategies and a corresponding decline among quantitative researchers in criticism of ethnography as being unscientific; and (3) a growing understanding of strategies for the triangulation or integration of different types of data. All of these changes are seen, for example, in the study of drug-related risks for the spread of HIV disease. Research in this arena now typically involves teams of experts from diverse disciplines; the integration of ethnographical, epidemiological, and other approaches to data collection; and achievement of enhanced outcomes based on the comparison of qualitative and quantitative findings.

More recently, there has been a push for an even greater integration of medical anthropology and epidemiology through the creation of *cultural epidemiology*. According to Jim Trostle (2005), cultural epidemiology promotes the study of diseases and their causes in terms of the contribution to health trends made by culture. Modeled after social epidemiology, which examines the health-related effects of social inequalities, cultural epidemiology would extend the variables under consideration to include folk systems of disease classification, meaning systems, culturally constituted risk patterns and conceptions, and other behaviors commonly analyzed as cultural in origin by medical anthropologists. These factors, Trostle maintains, should be critically important to epidemiology because people's conceptions and behaviors impact their health. Raymond Massé (2001) introduced the term *critical ethnoepidemiology* to refer to the linking of an interpretativist analysis of local illness meaning and a critical analysis of asymmetric social and economic relationships.

ETHNO-EPIDEMIOLOGICAL EXPLANATORY MODEL

Arthur Kleinman (1980) introduced the term *explanatory model* to label the ideas activated during an episode of sickness and treatment by all those involved in the clinical process. Explanatory models provide culturally meaningful explanations of sickness (e.g., its nature and causes) and treatment (e.g., best practices) that are used in health decision-making. For example, in *The Spirit Catches You and You Fall Down* (1997), Anne Fadiman recounts the story of Lia Lee, a Hmong child who began having intense seizures, which were interpreted as signs of "soul loss" by her parents and a Hmong shaman, but diagnosed by physicians as epilepsy. Convinced that Lia's parents were not administering the medicines they prescribed because of their faith in Hmong ethnomedicine, Lia's doctors launched a successful effort to have her removed to foster care.

As Kleinman recognized, different parties active in a sickness incident—including professional healers, folk healers, and the wider social group of the patient—can embrace differing conceptions or models of illness, treatment, and recovery. Of interest to Kleinman, and many medical anthropologists ever since, are the relationship of explanatory models to the wider cultural systems of which they are a part and the nature of the interactions that unfold when alternative explanatory models meet (and perhaps clash) during sickness episodes in diverse sociogeographic settings.

Ethno-epidemiology in this sense, as an indigenous explanatory model of disease causation, spread, prevention, and treatment, reflects the growing medical and public-health understanding of the significant influence of patient attitude, experience, and behavior in sickness and recovery. D. Lee and coworkers (2004), for example, demonstrated that the Chinese cultural practice of *peiyue*—a postpartum custom of mandated family support—is associated with a lower risk of postnatal depression.

The two meanings of the term *ethno-epidemiology* described above are unified in their recognition of the fundamental importance of culture in health, with ethno-epidemiological methodology referring to approaches for its in-depth and systematic study, and ethno-epidemiological explanatory models labeling the local cultural conceptions of disease now recognized as a significant influence on disease expression and response.

SEE ALSO *Anthropology, Medical; Disease; Public Health*

BIBLIOGRAPHY

Agar, Michael. 1996. Recasting the "Ethno" in "Epidemiology." *Medical Anthropology* 16 (4): 391–403.

Fadiman, Anne. 1997. *The Spirit Catches You and You Fall Down: A Hmong Child, Her American Doctors, and the Collision of Two Cultures.* New York: Farrar, Straus, and Giroux.

Kleinman, Arthur. 1980. *Patients and Healers in the Context of Culture.* Berkeley: University of California Press.

Lee, D., Chan, S., Sahota, D., et al. 2004. A Prevalence Study of Antenatal Depression among Chinese Women. *Journal of Affective Disorders* 82 (1): 93–99.

Massé, Raymond. 2001. Towards a Critical Ethnoepidemiology of Social Suffering in Postcolonial Martinique. *Sciences sociales et santé* 19 (1): 45–54.

Reisinger, Heather. 2004. Counting Apples as Oranges: Epidemiology and Ethnography in Adolescent Substance Abuse Treatment. *Qualitative Health Research* 14 (2): 241–258.

Trostle, James. 2005. *Epidemiology and Culture.* Cambridge, U.K.: Cambridge University Press.

Merrill Singer

ETHNOGRAPHY

The Greek etymology of the term *ethnography* is deceptively simple: writing about a people, where both writing and cultural difference are, respectively, explicit or strongly implied. Ethnography has had a long and complex relationship with its parent discipline, anthropology, and has come to mean more than writing alone, because the written record had to be based on knowledge of another culture acquired by the writer. *Ethnography* is thus a term that is used both as reference to the written product of the research process, usually assumed to be descriptive, and the research process itself. Ethnography, as a research process, is based on fieldwork. Since at least the time of Bronislaw Malinowski (1884–1942), fieldwork has meant living with a people for an extended period of time, learning their language, becoming immersed in their everyday life, understanding their whole cultural system and how the parts interrelate, and trying to understand the native point of view. The process of sharing in the daily life of one's hosts while making a detailed record of their lives in the form of field notes is known as "participant observation." Not all fieldwork is ethnographic—it becomes ethnographic based on the relationship one has with hosts or collaborators, and the intimate immersion in their way of life, with a keen concern for understanding how they act in the world and see the world in their terms.

Although fieldwork is often qualitative, it can and has included quantitative research as well (Bernard 2000, 2005). In the classic and standard works of the anthropological discipline, ethnographies were holistic accounts in that they strove to present comprehensive accounts of another society and its culture, showing the interrelation of elements such as political organization, religion, law, kinship, mythology, and subsistence practices. Often the unit of analysis was as small as a single village, and the society in question was a tribal one. Ethnographies contained little or nothing in the way of a historical perspective. Today, ethnographies written by anthropologists take a much sharper focus, addressing a specific research question rather than cataloging another way of life, and they tend to do so in a reflexive and often very theoretical manner as well. They also engage in research across multiple sites, including the anthropologist's home society. Yet, ethnographers still do not deal with large samples of people, focusing on smaller environments and more intimate interactions.

Given the unique nature of ethnographic research, which distinguishes it from impersonal archival work, mass-administered questionnaires and number crunching, public surveillance, and more remote ways of interpreting people's behaviors and their meanings, many fields and diverse interests have become attracted to ethnography, from corporations and market research firms to other disciplines in the social sciences and the humanities. Although ethnography is associated with anthropology primarily, there is an important tradition of ethnography in sociology, particularly in the Chicago school of sociology, which produced prominent ethnographies by distinguished sociologists such as William Foote Whyte (1994). However, unlike in anthropology, ethnographic fieldwork is not a requirement for a doctorate in sociology.

PROBLEMS OF EXPRESSION

Ethnography presents special challenges to the anthropologist and collaborators, and to the discipline's status in the academy and wider society. Intimate, face-to-face research can be politically sensitive and can heighten the self-consciousness of all parties involved. The experiential and subjective nature of this mode of research opens anthropological reflections to the humanities and to ways of becoming involved in social issues. Anthropological self-questioning concerning the conditions and outcomes of knowledge production are especially acute where ethnography is concerned.

In the introduction to a controversial collection edited with George Marcus, James Clifford argued that ethnographic accounts are at best incomplete and partial truths, much like fictional works (Clifford and Marcus 1986, pp. 6–7). Clifford Geertz (1988) also interpreted anthropology as a kind of writing, a literary creation. Interest in the writing of ethnography focused attention on the rhetoric, metaphors, and tropes used by anthropologists to assert their expertise, authority, and credibility, especially when objectivist science had once held such sway in the discipline. A growing concern with narrative styles, acts of interpretation, and issues of cultural translation in ethnography began to turn the discipline in on itself, and led to the erosion of confidence in realist approaches. Expression seemed to overtake explanation as the focus of these critiques of realism that have been labeled "postmodernist." The attention to how ethnographic texts are constructed was accompanied by an interest in the subjective and personal conditions of knowledge production, by critically examining the ways the anthropologist becomes part of and shapes the situation that is being studied. *Reflexivity* became a key term, prompting many anthropologists to reflect on how their

personal biographies led them to certain subjects and to ways of understanding those subjects. Ethnographic filmmakers such as Jean Rouch (1917–2004) deepened and extended discussions of reflexivity, of anthropology as a humanistic art, and of ethnography as fiction, well before it became popularized as "postmodern" in the late 1980s. The question that remains open is a philosophical one: Is the mission of the ethnographer primarily to uncover truth, or to explain reality?

ETHICAL AND POLITICAL CONSIDERATIONS

The act of writing about persons is based on actual interactions, and anthropologists have been keen to elaborate ethical guidelines for fair and proper relationships with their collaborators. The basics of most anthropological guidelines stress the principles of seeking informed consent, not causing harm to individuals, leaving the field situation in the way one found it, and safeguarding confidentiality (e.g., American Anthropological Association 1998), and much wider debates have raged since the 1970s (Rynkiewich and Spradley 1976). Revelations that some anthropologists had spied for the U.S. government during counterinsurgency campaigns in the 1960s in Asia and Latin America shook the discipline. Intellectuals, media, and political leaders in recently decolonized countries, as well as indigenous peoples, charged that anthropology functioned as an imperial discipline of surveillance, and researchers became concerned with how to decolonize anthropology. New ethical guidelines have stressed the need for collaboration, coproduction, and multiple authorship, and for ongoing negotiation of the terms of access to research data. Much controversy has emerged over the status of "practicing" anthropology—anthropology done outside of the academy, in the service of governments and private firms—especially as ethical guidelines produced in the 1970s have been tempered by a concern of "practicing anthropologists" for the rights of those funding their research, such as commercial stakeholders.

Politics have been intimately tied up with issues of research, ethics, and writing. Since the 1970s more attention has been devoted to the politics of ethnography as a dominating knowledge that posits a different "other." The rise of indigenous anthropology (Medicine 2001), feminist anthropology, and anthropology "at home" have all sought to confront and contest the colonial origins of anthropology (Biolsi and Zimmerman 1997; Brettell 1993; Deloria 1988; Harrison 1991). New approaches to ethnography call into question the older scientific "gaze" of anthropology as a kind of imperial vision that manifested itself in imperious writing—that is, writing in the "voice of god" as an unseen, authoritative, and trustworthy observer. More attention has been paid to how gender, class, ethnicity, and nationality condition one's rapport with hosts, delimit access to spheres of life, and determine what kind of data can be recorded. Reinterpreting ethnography as premised on humanistic, face-to-face, intimate relationships; delving into intersubjective understandings; and not placing oneself outside of the research context as a remote analyst or, worse, as a spectator of zoological phenomena, have worked to produce more self-conscious and politically sensitive ethnographies (Rabinow 1977). Dialogic exchanges (Crapanzano 1980) challenged the previous, sportscaster-like narrations of what people were doing.

NEW TRENDS

Self-reflection has been acute in anthropology, at times bordering on paralyzing angst. The prolonged immersion in other cultures, the everyday and intimate interactions with one's hosts, arriving as an outsider and becoming an insider, the questions of one's own identity and the status of one's involvements with others almost inevitably heighten self-consciousness. Hortense Powdermaker was aware of how involvement and detachment, art and science, worked in tension with one another in ethnography (Powdermaker 1967). Currently, the relationship between theory and ethnography is tense, too, and there is a greater tendency to produce theoretically heavy accounts that seemingly render ethnographic description as secondary in importance, or as ornamentation in predetermined exercises. Debates about writing styles in anthropology were conducted largely in private, among and for other professional anthropologists, with little or no impact on the social standing and public engagement of the discipline. Some have noted the limits to discussions of reflexivity, arguing that the result has bordered on narcissism and a failure to reflect on broader-than-personal conditions of knowledge production (Bourdieu 2000). Although ethnography still addresses the impacts of postmodern and postcolonial critiques, there are new trends emerging: fieldwork in one's home society; feminist and indigenous anthropology; autoethnography; experimental writing, including fiction in the regular sense (Bowen 1954); and militant advocate approaches. In terms of the politics of writing, there are more dialogic and multivocal texts rather than authoritative, univocal accounts. Some scholars are questioning how anthropologists conceptually constitute "the field" at the heart of their ethnographies, with increased sensitivity to the realization that there is no definite beginning and end to fieldwork, no clear "home" and "away" (Amit 2000). Revised ethnographic realism—understanding the differences between experience and reality—has led some to admit that what ethnography can capture is limited, with the resulting admission of multi-method approaches involving research in archives, media analysis, and use of statistics. Understanding how cultures are delinked from territories, with greater concern for globalization and transnational movements, has led some anthropologists to elaborate frameworks for multisited ethnography (Marcus 1995) premised on traveling cultures, on the movements of money, persons, metaphors, narratives, and biographies. As much as anthropology has been riven by debate about its ethnographic core, very few anthropologists have argued for abandoning ethnography. As Nancy Scheper-Hughes put it: "Not to look, not to touch, not to record can be the hostile act, an act of indifference and of turning away" (1995, p. 418).

SEE ALSO *Anthropology; Bourdieu, Pierre; Culture; Ethnology and Folklore; Gaze, Colonial; Gaze, The; Geertz, Clifford; Methods, Qualitative; Narratives; Observation; Observation, Participant; Social Science; Sociology; Sociology, Urban; Street Culture*

BIBLIOGRAPHY

American Anthropological Association. 1998. Code of Ethics of the American Anthropological Association. http://www.aaanet.org/committees/ethics/ethcode.htm.

Amit, Vered, ed. 2000. *Constructing the Field: Ethnographic Fieldwork in the Contemporary World.* London: Routledge.

Bernard, H. Russell, ed. 2000. *Handbook of Methods in Cultural Anthropology.* Walnut Creek, CA: AltaMira Press.

Bernard, H. Russell. 2005. *Research Methods in Anthropology: Qualitative and Quantitative Approaches.* 4th ed. Walnut Creek, CA: AltaMira Press.

Biolsi, Thomas, and Larry J. Zimmerman. 1997. *Indians and Anthropologists: Vine Deloria Jr. and the Critique of Anthropology.* Tucson: University of Arizona Press.

Boas, Franz. 1920. The Methods of Ethnology. *American Anthropologist* 22 (4): 311–321.

Bourdieu, Pierre. 2000. Participant Objectivation. Huxley Memorial Lecture, Royal Anthropological Institute, December 6.

Bowen, Elenore Smith. 1954. *Return to Laughter.* New York: Doubleday Anchor.

Brettell, Caroline B., ed. 1993. *When They Read What We Write: The Politics of Ethnography.* Westport, CT: Bergin and Garvey.

Clifford, James, and George E. Marcus, eds. 1986. *Writing Culture: The Poetics and Politics of Ethnography.* Berkeley: University of California Press.

Crapanzano, Vincent. 1980. *Tuhami: Portrait of a Moroccan.* Chicago: University of Chicago Press.

Deloria, Vine, Jr. 1988. *Custer Died for Your Sins: An Indian Manifesto.* Norman: University of Oklahoma Press.

DeWalt, Kathleen M., and Billie R. DeWalt. 2002. *Participant Observation: A Guide for Fieldworkers.* Walnut Creek, CA: AltaMira Press.

Geertz, Clifford. 1988. *Works and Lives: The Anthropologist as Author.* Stanford, CA: Stanford University Press.

Harrison, Faye V., ed. 1991. *Decolonizing Anthropology: Moving Further Toward an Anthropology for Liberation.* Washington, DC: American Anthropological Association.

Hume, Lynne, and Jane Mulcock, eds. 2004. *Anthropologists in the Field: Cases in Participant Observation.* New York: Columbia University Press.

Malinowski, Bronislaw. [1922] 1984. *Argonauts of the Western Pacific.* Prospect Heights, IL: Waveland Press.

Marcus, George E. 1995. Ethnography in/of the World System: The Emergence of Multi-Sited Ethnography. *Annual Review of Anthropology* 24: 95–117.

Medicine, Beatrice. 2001. *Learning To Be an Anthropologist and Remaining "Native."* Urbana: University of Illinois Press.

Powdermaker, Hortense. 1967. *Stranger and Friend: The Way of an Anthropologist.* London: Secker and Warburg.

Rabinow, Paul. 1977. *Reflections on Fieldwork in Morocco.* Berkeley: University of California Press.

Ruby, Jay. 1996. Visual Anthropology. In *Encyclopedia of Cultural Anthropology*, vol. 4, eds. David Levinson and Melvin Ember, 1345–1351. New York: Henry Holt.

Rynkiewich, Michael A., and James P. Spradley, eds. 1976. *Ethics and Anthropology: Dilemmas in Fieldwork.* New York: John Wiley and Sons.

Scheper-Hughes, Nancy. 1995. The Primacy of the Ethical: Propositions for a Militant Anthropology. *Current Anthropology* 36 (3): 409–420.

Stocking, George W., ed. 1983. *Observers Observed: Essays on Ethnographic Fieldwork.* Madison: University of Wisconsin Press.

Van Maanen, John. 1988. *Tales of the Field: On Writing Ethnography.* Chicago: University of Chicago Press.

Wax, Rosalie H. 1971. *Doing Fieldwork: Warnings and Advice.* Chicago: University of Chicago Press.

Whyte, William Foote. 1993. *Street Corner Society: The Social Structure of an Italian Slum.* 4th ed. Chicago: University of Chicago Press.

Maximilian C. Forte

ETHNOLOGY AND FOLKLORE

Ethnology and folklore emerged as the "science of tradition" during the nineteenth century and during the twentieth as a discipline concerned with "expressive culture" and cultural identities, particularly within modernizing societies. Professionals in these fields may call themselves *folklorists* or *ethnologists*. Whereas anthropologists frequently sought out homogeneous societies separated from the modern world, folklorists and ethnologists theorized about the persistence, adaptation, and function of tradition within complex societies.

Folklore and ethnology are related, sometimes linked, concepts for the way that individuals and groups use tradition to express values, beliefs, and ideas in a number of forms, including art, architecture, story, song, speech, and custom. Both terms refer to the process of tradition that results from informal learning: word of mouth, imitation and demonstration, and custom. The concept of folklore, however, has roots in the literary appreciation of oral and customary tradition (especially in Great Britain and America), whereas ethnology has a legacy of anthropological attention to the social and material basis of tradition, particularly in rural and peasant societies (especially in Scandinavia and Germany where holistic terms *folkiv* and *Volkskunde*, respectively, circulated).

As the fields developed, however, they came together into a broad inquiry of tradition, usually spanning categories of oral, social, and material culture. Into the twenty-first century, the term *ethnology* is still generally used in continental Europe, broadened to include urban and emergent traditions, and *folklore* in Great Britain and America. *Ethnology*, when used in the Americas, frequently refers to the social study of native tribal groups rather than to the cultural traditions of ethnic, occupational, and other groups, as in Europe. One learned society bridging the transatlantic tendencies is the International Society for Ethnology and Folklore, based in the Netherlands.

Related terms vying for wider usage include *folklife* and *folk culture*, representing concerns for the social and material life of tradition-centered groups. In addition to The Folklore Society, Great Britain has a Society for Folklife Studies, whose journal is *Folklife: Journal of Ethnological Studies.* Likewise the Archive of Folk Culture in the American Folklife Center of the Library of Congress in the United States has been a national repository for field-collected materials since 1928, and national centers for "folk culture" were established in the twentieth century in India, Lithuania, Estonia, Flanders, and the Netherlands, among others. Also vying for wider usage is the term *folkloristics* (*folkloristik* in German), often implying, like its cognate of *linguistics*, a distinction between the material under study—language and folklore—and the scientific branch of study. Use of folkloristics often implies an analytical emphasis on structure, communication, and performance of traditional behavior.

The scholarly inquiry into tradition, often traced to the field research of German intellectuals Jacob Grimm (1785–1863) and his brother Wilhelm Grimm (1786–1859), who published a collection of folktales with comparative notes as *Kinder-und Hausmärchen* (Children's and Household Tales) in 1812, signaled significant international intellectual movements that influenced the social sciences (e.g., romantic nationalism, comparative anthropology, "etic" narrative analysis). The Grimms celebrated the verbal artistry of German peasantry, or *Volk*, as the soul of the culture. This usage inspired British antiquarian W. J. Thoms (1803–1885) in 1846 to suggest the name "folk-lore" as a replacement for popular literature and antiquities. The implication was that *folk* was a noun for a level or class of culture that retained superstition and storytelling while the surrounding society modernized. The Victorian folklorists produced comparative studies on a global scale, applying Darwinistic ideas of evolution to culture to explain the survival of beliefs and customs in modern society. A "Finnish School" was promoted in the United States by Stith Thompson, who revised the Finnish typologies of Antti Aarne and methodology of Kaarle Krohn. This "Finnish School" developed "historic-geographic" approaches to explain the universality (codified as "tale types") and localization (called "oikotypes") of narratives by identifying global distributions of tales and reconstructing their origins and diffusion. A lasting result of this approach was the creation of standard reference works of tale-type and motif indices.

In the twentieth century, the influential American anthropologist Franz Boas (1858–1942), as editor of the *Journal of American Folklore* from 1908 to 1925, emphasized folklore as essential cultural evidence of an individual society. This approach signaled a shift away from global Darwinian models to a cultural relativism and historical particularism driven by a field-based ethnography of cultural distinctions and settings. Several of Boas's students took over the editorship of *Journal of American Folklore* through the mid-twentieth century. The work of Boas and students such as Ruth Benedict, A. L. Kroeber, Melville Herskovits, and Martha Beckwith (who has the historical distinction of holding the first chair in folklore at Vassar College in the 1920s) in recording and interpreting texts among diverse groups including Native Americans, African Americans, and college women emphasized the idea of folklore as a reflection, or symbolic autobiography, of a culture, and the analysis of folklore's functions within a particular society and setting.

As folklore and ethnological studies developed with a social focus, more attention was given to *folk* as an adjective for traditional learning that everyone participates in. Alan Dundes (1934–2005) in *The Study of Folklore* presented an influential definition of *folk group* that applied to "any group of people whatsoever who share at least one common factor" (1965, pp. 1-2). In this modern perspective, folklore, the logical, functional outcome of such a common grouping, becomes a popular, necessary expression instead of a rare find or survival. It need not even be old. As a special kind of knowledge (e.g., jokes, gestures, dress, nicknames, slang) serving the purposes of the group

(expanded beyond ethnic and occupational categories to include, for example, family, deaf, gay, children's, organizational, corporate, and Internet communities), folklore is ever changing and, indeed, can be created anew. The expressions can be analyzed functionally not only to bond the group, but also to provide psychological outlets to deal with disturbing issues and adaptive strategies to conflicts and human development. Generations of professionals with doctorates in folklore developed its study as a separate discipline with distinctive approaches. American folklorists such as Michael Owen Jones, Roger Abrahams, Dan Ben-Amos, Richard Bauman, David Hufford, and Barbara Kirshenblatt-Gimblett were instrumental in developing behavioral or performance-centered theories of folklore as "artistic communication in small groups," while others such as Alan Dundes, Jay Mechling, Gary Alan Fine, Simon Bronner, Elliott Oring, and Henry Glassie explored the social structural and cognitive dimensions of human expressiveness.

In the twenty-first century, folklore is viewed as a dynamic process of cultural communication by which individuals discover or establish their identities. Individuals in contemporary society are understood as having multiple, often overlapping, identities that are recognized by different folkloric repertoires. Social-scientific research in folklore emphasizes field work and ethnography—the observation of "cultural scenes" in which symbolic communication and behavior occur. No longer content to collect folkloric "texts" like natural history specimens, folklorists and ethnologists interpret for the social sciences the relation of folklore to cultural "contexts." To be sure, historical perspectives are still evident in the analysis of precedents and variations of tradition, and there is often a social-psychological consideration of the function and enactment of cultural expression in the formation of identity, both group and individual. Folklore and ethnology contribute to the social sciences by theorizing the roles of expressions in binding and differentiating groups and their identities, sustaining values and beliefs from one generation to another, and understanding the artistic components of everyday life. The folkloristic purview of groups and genres has greatly expanded since the nineteenth century, but the inquiry into tradition's role in mind, society, and behavior remains.

SEE ALSO *Boas, Franz*

BIBLIOGRAPHY

Abrahams, Roger D. 2005. *Everyday Life: A Poetics of Vernacular Practices.* Philadelphia: University of Pennsylvania Press.

Briggs, Charles, and Amy Shuman, eds. 1993. *Theorizing Folklore: Toward New Perspectives on the Politics of Culture.* Los Angeles: California Folklore Society.

Bronner, Simon J. 1998. *Following Tradition: Folklore in the Discourse of American Culture.* Logan: Utah State University Press.

Dundes, Alan, ed. 1965. *The Study of Folklore.* Englewood Cliffs, NJ: Prentice-Hall.

Dundes, Alan. 1980. *Interpreting Folklore.* Bloomington: Indiana University Press.

Dundes, Alan, ed. 1999. *International Folkloristics: Classic Contributions by the Founders of Folklore.* Lanham, MD: Rowman & Littlefield.

Feintuch, Burt, ed. 2003. *Eight Words for the Study of Expressive Culture.* Urbana: University of Illinois Press.

Georges, Robert A., and Michael Owen Jones. 1995. *Folkloristics: An Introduction.* Bloomington: Indiana University Press.

Oring, Elliott, ed. 1986. *Folk Groups and Folklore Genres: An Introduction.* Logan: Utah State University Press.

Toelken, Barre. 1996. *The Dynamics of Folklore.* Rev. ed. Logan: Utah State University Press.

Simon J. Bronner

ETHNOMETHODOLOGY

Ethnomethodology is an approach to the study of everyday life with a particular emphasis on the construction of cultural meanings amongst minority groups. The term incorporates the prefix *ethno-* to refer to cultural context, including language and jargon, myths, symbols, and codes of behavior, and the word *methodology*, which refers to the means, rationale, and philosophical assumptions involved in the approach to investigating such phenomena.

Developed by Harold Garfinkel in 1967, ethnomethodology was initially dismissed by prominent social theorists of the time, such as Alvin W. Gouldner (1920–1981), who described Garfinkel's work as "mere Californian sociology" (cited in Garfinkel 2002, p. 3). In spite of this early disinterest, ethnomethodology continues to influence empirical social science research in a diverse range of fields, most notably in the areas of education, health, gender, media, and criminal justice.

Specifically, ethnomethodology investigates the functioning of common sense within cultural contexts, stressing the active, reasoned, and informed character of human social behavior. Put simply, ethnomethodology is the study of how individuals maintain a sense of reality in a given social situation through the means of social interaction with other individuals. That is, a conversation is a social process of interaction that has certain requirements in order for individual participants to identify it as a conversation and keep it going as such. For example, people will look at one another, nod, murmur, take turns in speaking, and in asking and responding to questions. If these requirements are not met, or are employed in ways that

deviate from the expectations attached to the perceived reality of a conversation, then the interaction breaks down to be replaced by an alternative social process.

Garfinkel's work was thus a development of the phenomenological insights of Alfred Schutz (1899–1959), who had argued that commonsense knowledge is patchy and incomplete and that shared understandings between individuals are contingent achievements based upon this revisable and approximate knowledge. Garfinkel conducted a series of quasi-experimental procedures that exposed the tacit assumptions and presuppositions that underpin shared understandings during social interaction, which he argued had to be understood as an "event-in-context." That is, linkages are assembled between a process of social interaction and the cultural context within which the interaction takes place.

Crucially, therefore, changes in the understanding of an event's context will evoke some shift or elaboration in an individual's ability to grasp the meaning and reality of the interaction itself. Put simply, to make sense of social interaction between individuals it is necessary to grasp the cultural context in which it takes place. Individuals frequently design their interaction so as to make use of localized contexts in order to elaborate and particularize the sense of their talk and actions. A useful example here is how the cultural products of the poor and minority groups, such as rap lyrics, can be misunderstood if the cultural context in which they are produced is not fully grasped.

Ethnomethodology remains a highly influential approach in the international social sciences, continuing to open up innovative areas of analysis in sociology, social psychology, and linguistics in particular.

SEE ALSO *Communication; Conversational Analysis; Cultural Relativism; Culture; Culture of Poverty; Ethnicity; Minorities; Nonverbal Communication*

BIBLIOGRAPHY

Garfinkel, Harold. 1967. *Studies in Ethnomethodology.* Englewood Cliffs, NJ: Prentice-Hall.

Garfinkel, Harold. 2002. *Ethnomethodology's Program: Working Out Durkheim's Aphorism.* Lanham, MD: Rowman & Littlefield.

Heritage, John. 1984. *Garfinkel and Ethnomethodology.* Cambridge, U.K.: Polity.

Mark Davis

ETHNOMUSICOLOGY

Although there is no universally accepted definition of *ethnomusicology,* a few words stand out in most definitions: "sound," "music," "performance," "context," and "culture." Ethnomusicology is "humanly organized sound" (John Blacking, in Byron 1995), "the study of music in culture" (Merriam 1964, p. 7), or more broadly, sound in context. Ethnomusicology also touches on other disciplines, such as linguistics, history, sociology, and the study of dance.

Bruno Nettl nicely skims over the befuddlement of defining *ethnomusicology* in *The Study of Ethnomusicology* (2005). By about 1950, ethnomusicologists studied what was then called "primitive," "folk," or "ancient" music. The first term was used to describe "unschooled" music, especially music from indigenous, colonial peoples. The second term referred to the music of nonliterate or semi-literate people in Europe or the European diaspora, the so-called peasants or the remnants of peasant populations of earlier eras. The third term referred to the focus for European musicologists who studied the roots of European classical music, especially in the Middle Ages, before modern musical transcription was as full as it has become.

Traditionally, ethnomusicology may involve learning to play what a North American novice might think of as "exotic" music, or it may focus on any music or sound whatsoever in a cultural context. An ethnomusicologist may view music sui generis. She may use music as a metaphor for something outside the music, or focus on an event of which music is a small part. As one moves from the study of music as such to music in context, one tends to move from scholars who are musicians and have training in transcription, toward ethnographers. Most scholars who study music in the field have musical training, but today they also have knowledge of local languages and/or linguistic theory, as well as participant observation skills. All these academic attributes combine in the ground-breaking work of Steven Feld, who examined sound in a cultural context, especially birdsongs that formed a springboard of meaning for the songs of the Kaluli people of Papua New Guinea (1990).

In the nineteenth century and early in the twentieth century some European composers and musicologists began to look at peasant music of their own countries, as well as the "primitive" music of the people in European colonies. They documented that music, either to enhance their own compositions or just to extend the range of musical styles with which they were familiar. At about the same time, other scholars in folklore and anthropology were beginning to document festivals, rituals, and other customs, many of which had musical or dance components. Working independently from one another, for the most part, these disparate scholars developed the roots of what later (around 1950) came to be called "ethnomusicology" in the United States.

In the 1890s aural recordings, first on cylinder records and then on discs, were made "in the field" or in recording studios such as at the Library of Congress. Early recordings supplemented written transcriptions of "exotic" music. Together with filmed musical events, aural and visual documents opened up the study of music in cultural context to a wider group of researchers. This led to a broad division in the field, between early ethnomusicologists who recorded in many different cultures in many parts of the world (Alan Lomax is a good example—see Cohen 2003) and more recent scholars who record in a few places throughout their careers and then write in depth on those few areas (Stone 2002). In keeping with a humanistic bent, which has challenged social science approaches to the field, most ethnomusicologists have become self-reflective and have subjectively inserted themselves into the musical and cultural context they study. However, whether or not ethnomusicology remains a social science, most ethnomusicologists hold a humanistic value that the music of ordinary people in their own cultural settings—as opposed to music by and for elites only—should be the focus of the discipline.

SEE ALSO *Anthropology; Anthropology, Linguistic; Culture; Ethnography; Ethnology and Folklore; Ethnomethodology; Exoticism; Music; Performance; Rituals; Vinyl Recordings*

BIBLIOGRAPHY

Byron, Reginald, ed. 1995. *Music, Culture, and Experience: Selected Papers of John Blacking.* Chicago: University of Chicago Press.

Cohen, Ronald D. 2003. *Alan Lomax: Selected Writings, 1937–1997.* New York: Routledge.

Feld, Steven. 1990. *Sound and Sentiment: Birds, Weeping, Poetics, and Song in Kaluli Expression.* 2nd ed. Philadelphia: University of Pennsylvania Press.

Merriam, Alan P. 1964. *The Anthropology of Music.* Chicago: Northwestern University Press.

Nettl, Bruno. 2005. The Harmless Drudge: Defining Ethnomusicology. In *The Study of Ethnomusicology: Thirty-one Issues and Concepts,* ed. Bruno Nettl, 3–15. Urbana: University of Illinois Press.

Stone, Ruth M., ed. 2002. *The World's Music: General Perspectives and Reference Tools.* Vol. 10 of *The Garland Encyclopedia of World Music.* New York: Routledge.

Donald R. Hill

ETHNONATIONALISM

SEE *Ethnocentrism; Liberation Movements; Nationalism and Nationality.*

ETHOLOGICAL ATTACHMENT THEORY

SEE *Attachment Theory; Separation Anxiety.*

EUGENICS

Although ideas concerning the mutability of so-called natural human traits have been a part of Western civilization since antiquity, the science of eugenics emerged out of a particular nineteenth-century discourse that had its roots in social Darwinism and scientific racism. Throughout the second half of the nineteenth century, the English scientist Sir Francis Galton used statistical studies of British families to argue that heredity governed physical ability, talent, and character, and that "reputable" families were much more likely than ordinary families to produce superior offspring. He argued, moreover, that humans possessed the ability—through a system of selective breeding—to guide the course of human evolution and ultimately improve the race. In 1883, Galton named his new science *eugenics*, which he derived from the Greek word *eugenes*, meaning "good in birth" or "noble in heredity."

Following the publication of his famous cousin Charles Darwin's *On the Origin of Species* in 1859, Sir Francis Galton began his inquiry into human heredity and the use of science to improve the human race. His first attempt to articulate his thoughts concerning the power of nature in determining human ability came in the form of a two-part article entitled "Hereditary Talent and Character," which was published in a popular English magazine in 1865. In another article entitled, "Hereditary Improvement," published in 1873, Galton established his method for improving the quality of the human race. He declared that his goal was to "improve the race of man by a system which shall be perfectly in accordance with the moral sense of the present time" (Gillham 2001, pp. 195–197). To implement his plan, Galton envisioned the creation of a state agency that would gather, analyze, and distribute important pedigree data, accompanied by photographs and physical measurements, to all Englishmen interested in improving the race. This information would then be used to encourage the reproduction of those families perceived to have talent, and to discourage the reproduction of the masses of individuals perceived to be of inferior quality. Programs designed to encourage "fit" individuals to reproduce came to be known as positive or productive eugenics, and those programs designed to prohibit "unfit" individuals from reproducing came to be known as negative or selectionist eugenics.

By the beginning of the twentieth century, eugenics had become very popular among a broad array of Americans eager to remedy the social, cultural, and political upheaval caused by decades of massive industrialization, urbanization, and immigration. Men such as Charles B. Davenport and Harry Laughlin of the Eugenics Record Office at Cold Spring Harbor, New York, embraced the new science. Women reformers such as Margaret Sanger also extolled the benefits of controlled breeding. In the 1920s, eugenicists created the American Eugenics Society, and the Eugenics Research Association. American eugenicists played a critical role in the passage of a 1924 immigration law known as the National Origins Act (or the Johnson-Reed Act), which greatly reduced the number of southern and eastern Europeans entering the United States. Harry Laughlin and other eugenicists wrote the Virginia sterilization law that became the focus of a 1927 Supreme Court decision in *Buck v. Bell*. The court voted to uphold forced sterilization, ultimately resulting in the sterilization of over 65,000 individuals throughout the United States. Eugenic ideology also made possible studies such as the controversial Tuskegee syphilis study, which focused on African American males and lasted forty years, from 1932 to 1972.

Eugenics was not limited to England and the United States. Societies across the globe embraced the new scientific thinking. In Germany, Alfred Ploetz and other scientists applied American eugenics to the new science of race hygiene, resulting in the creation of the Society for Racial Hygiene and the eventual Nazi extermination of millions of Jews, Gypsies, persons with disabilities, and other "unfit" individuals during World War II. Throughout the twentieth century, Scandinavian countries coerced large populations, consisting mostly of women welfare recipients, to be sterilized in an effort to reduce the number of genetic "flaws" among their offspring. In places such as Argentina, Brazil, and Mexico, eugenics greatly influenced biological and cultural definitions of race and gender, as well as popular notions of national "fitness." In Latin America, the state regulated reproduction through different legal restrictions imposed on marriage.

Eugenic thought has loomed large in the public discourse and social policy of numerous countries throughout the world since the late nineteenth century. It has assumed many forms; it has spanned the geopolitical spectrum; and although it fell into disfavor after World War II, it has experienced a resurgence in the late-twentieth and early twenty-first centuries. The advent of the Human Genome Project and other advances in genetic science has ushered in new concerns about the moral, ethical, and racial implications of selective breeding. In his recent best-selling book *Freakonomics*, the University of Chicago economist Steven D. Levitt caused a tremendous stir when he argued that abortion has been the most dominant factor in declining crime rates in the United States. Put simply, Levitt argued that unwanted children are more likely to become criminals, and that since the 1973 *Roe v. Wade* decision fewer unwanted children have been born, resulting in a reduction in American crime rates. Critics have since charged Levitt with being a eugenicist who advocates the selective extermination of "at-risk" offspring. Although this was not his intent, Levitt has subsequently been forced to defend his abortion hypothesis in a number of popular media outlets. Clearly, and understandably, anything that even remotely smacks of eugenics continues to create a firestorm of controversy.

SEE ALSO *Genocide; Nazism; Population Control; Racism*

BIBLIOGRAPHY

Gillham, Nicholas Wright. 2001. *A Life of Sir Francis Galton: From African Exploration to the Birth of Eugenics.* Oxford, U.K.: Oxford University Press.

Kevles. Daniel J. 1985. *In the Name of Eugenics: Genetics and the Uses of Human Heredity.* New York: Knopf.

Paul, Diane B. 1995. *Controlling Human Heredity, 1865 to the Present.* Atlantic Highlands, NJ: Humanities Press.

Proctor, Robert. 1988. *Racial Hygiene: Medicine under the Nazis.* Cambridge, MA: Harvard University Press.

Stepan, Nancy. 1991. *The Hour of Eugenics: Race, Gender, and Nation in Latin America.* Ithaca, NY: Cornell University Press.

Michael A. Rembis

EURO, THE

The euro regime is an epochal economic paradigm of supranational macroeconomics, based on a common continental economy with a common currency. On January 1, 1999, eleven of the original fifteen European Union (EU) members (Austria, Belgium, Finland, France, Germany, Ireland, Italy, Luxembourg, Netherlands, Portugal, and Spain) elected to voluntarily surrender their monetary sovereignty and adopt the euro as a common currency, which would be managed by a common central bank, The European Central Bank (ECB). Greece joined the following year. This group of nations, known as the EU12, became the euro regime. Denmark, Sweden, and the United Kingdom have thus far not adopted the euro and each continue to use its own currency. Ten new members were admitted to EU membership in May 2004, and they will join the euro regime when they meet the guidelines of the Maastricht Treaty adopted by the ECB.

The euro began as an accounting unit and came to be a medium of exchange on January 1, 2002. For another twelve months, each member economy was allowed to have joint circulation of their national currency along with the euro. Thereafter, the euro became the exclusive medium of exchange of the euro regime. The new currency soon became the store of value not only for the euro regime, but also for the rest of the world. Holding a part of the GDP (gross domestic product) of an economic unit in money, the most liquid form of asset, is a familiar practice. Because the nation-state economies of the world at the present time hold their international reserves in dollar and euro, each of the two currencies represents overwhelming shares of world output and trade. The competitive shares of official holdings of euros and dollars merit attention. In 1999, the dollar had a 71 percent share of official world holdings of foreign exchange, while the euro began with a nearly 18 percent share. By 2004, reserve values of dollars and euros had been climbing steadily. However, the world share of dollar holdings had fallen by 6.5 percent by 2004, while that of euro shot up by more than 39 percent.

On January 1, 1999, the euro was launched at a 17 percent premium over the dollar, based on the market quotation of the day. Within a year, the euro depreciated to converge with the dollar, and it continued to fluctuate below the value of the dollar until 2002. A psychological attachment to national currencies, as well as their joint circulation with the euro, prevented a significant strengthening of the euro. Soon after the euro became the exclusive medium of exchange of the EU12, it appreciated over the dollar. International uncertainty and terrorism, as well as the mounting national debt and budget and trade deficits of the United States, compromised the competitive value of the dollar vis-à-vis the euro. In addition, fluctuations in the price of both petroleum and gold in the world market (based on and quoted in dollars) have had an impact on the relative strength of the euro. Meanwhile, successive interest rate increases by the U.S. Federal Reserve Bank beginning in 2004 contributed to an increasing demand for the dollar. The ECB responded by raising its core interest rate at the end of 2005. In December 2004, the dollar reached a record low against the euro, falling some 36 percent from its high against the euro in June 2001.

As the EU share of world output and trade has become competitively large, the euro has progressively become a global currency. In 2004, the gross domestic product of the EU12 stood at US$8.2 trillion, compared with US$11.0 trillion in the United States (OECD 2005). In shares of world trade (exports and imports), the euro regime leads the United States by substantive margins. The comparative strength of a currency must relate directly to its shares of world output and trade. Given this criteria, the euro will continue to be a dominant currency. It has been suggested that Denmark, Sweden, and Great Britain will eventually join the euro regime, as will the ten new members of the EU. Then these twenty-five members of the EU (the EU25) will have more competitive shares of world output and trade than the EU12 now has, which will have a significant impact on the euro-dollar exchange rate. In the 1960s, the U.S. dollar, based on a fixed gold value, was king, and its acceptance was global, at least within the free-market economies. Today, the euro and the dollar are the only two competitive global currencies.

The concept of geo-economics has replaced the cold-war concept of geopolitics. Based on the principle of competition, the euro and dollar currency regimes will contribute to the global optimization of economic gains for all micro units (households as units of consumption and businesses as units for investment). The European Union will be a learning model for other continents, and the Asian Economic Community, the African Economic Union, the American Hemispheric Economic Union, and the Free Trade Area of the Americas (FTAA) will increasingly command attention (Dutta 2005, 2007). The African Union has been formally instituted and others are in advanced preparatory stages.

To fully appreciate the role of the euro, one must have a comprehensive understanding of Jean Monnet's vision of Europe as one common European family (1978). An integrated economy in a continental geographic unit, with well-specified intraregional micro- and macroeconomic parameters, both transparent and judicially enforceable, is now in place. The Free Trade Area of the EU, with one common membership and one vote in the World Trade Organization (WTO), is unique. The euro is common currency for the euro regime, and it will therefore eventually lead to one Europe, to one political union (Issing 1996; Vanthoor 2002).

SEE ALSO *Common Market, The; Exchange Rates; Policy, Monetary*

BIBLIOGRAPHY

Dutta, Manoranjan. 2005. The Theory of Optimum Currency Area Revisited: Lessons from the Euro/Dollar Competitive Currency Regimes. *Journal of Asian Economics* 16 (3) 352–375.

Dutta, Manoranjan. 2007. *European Union and the Euro Revolution.* Amsterdam: Elsevier.

Issing, Otmar. 1996. *Europe: Political Union through Common Money.* Occasional Paper 98. London: Institute of Economic Affairs.

Monnet, Jean. 1978. *Memoirs.* London: Collins.

Mundell, Robert 1961. A Theory of Optimum Currency Areas. *American Economic Review* 51(4), 657–665.

Organisation for Economic Co-operation and Development (OECD). 2005. *Economic Survey of the Euro Area, 2005.* Paris: OECD.

Vanthoor, Wim F. V. 2002. *European Monetary Union since 1848: A Political and Historical Analysis.* Cheltenham, U.K.: Edward Elgar.

Manoranjan Dutta

EURO BAROMETER
SEE *Pollsters.*

EUROPEAN CONVENTION OF HUMAN RIGHTS
SEE *Civil Liberties.*

EUROPEAN UNION

The European Union (EU) is a cooperative entity that has qualities of both a federal nation-state and an international organization. It is neither, but falls somewhere in between. The EU is comprised of twenty-five member-states with around 460 million citizens. All member-states are democratic countries, which have agreed to cede some of their sovereignty to the institutions of the EU by participating in the common market, making their domestic laws conform to EU laws, adopting the Euro as a common currency, and allowing free movement of goods, capital, and persons, among other things. Social scientists attempt to explain why the EU came about, the role of its institutions in promoting cooperation, and its future trajectory. Will it continue to become more federal or will it reach policy gridlock? Will it continue to enlarge or will it reach its absorption capacity?

FORMATION OF THE EU

The earliest precursor to the EU was the European Coal and Steel Community (ECSC), formed in the wake of World War II as European countries sought a way to prevent such destruction from happening again. They believed if they became economically interdependent, they would be less likely to repeat the mistakes of the past. In addition, ECSC would make economic recovery and industrial modernization possible. For West Germany in particular, Chancellor Konrad Adenauer saw it as an opportunity for rapprochement with France and new ties with the West.

It was the 1950 Schuman Declaration that unveiled Jean Monnet's idea of the ECSC. Six member-states (Italy, France, Belgium, Luxembourg, The Netherlands, and West Germany) signed it into being with the 1951 Treaty of Paris. The ECSC was so successful in the early 1950s that it led to the 1957 Treaties of Rome, establishing the European Economic Community (EEC), which was a customs union, and the European Atomic Energy Community (Euratom). The 1967 Merger Treaty merged the executive bodies of the three treaties, thereby creating the institutions that continue to exist in the twenty-first century. In addition, ECSC, EEC (later EC), and Euratom became known together as the European Communities. The 1987 Single European Act replaced the Treaty of Paris and the Treaties of Rome as the EC's policy domain grew into new areas not encompassed by the original treaties. It remained the European Communities until member-states signed and ratified the 1992 Maastricht Treaty, officially creating the European Union, which established the economic, monetary, and political union.

The basic evolution of these treaties embodies not only structural and institutional changes, but an increasing recognition of Europeans' common values, goals, and even identity, as well as a willingness to vest more authority in EU institutions. Besides economic integration—the largest area of common jurisdiction—there are common policies on agriculture, culture, energy, the environment, transportation, crime, and defense, among other things. Moreover, the EU has become increasingly political over time. In addition to increasing areas of jurisdiction, the EU has experienced successive enlargements, and the treaties have also attempted to accommodate its growing size. Membership in the EU has been so attractive that many European countries have voluntarily undergone extensive measures to democratize and develop economically so that they meet the criteria to begin accession negotiations.

EU INSTITUTIONS

At the core of the EU are its institutions, which are located in Brussels, Strasbourg, and Luxembourg. The European Parliament is the only representative institution as its members are directly elected, and belong to European political parties of which there are seven. It shares some decision-making authority with the Council of the European Union, which is an intergovernmental institution comprised of ministers and ambassadors from the member-states. The Council presidency, which sets the agenda for the EU, rotates every six months. Through the co-decision procedure, the Parliament and Council together take policy decisions, pass laws, and approve the EU's €100 billion annual budget. However, it is only the European Commission that can initiate new laws. The Commission, unlike the Council, represents EU interests as a whole, rather than the interests of individual member-states. Commissioners are required to swear an oath of loyalty to this effect. There is one Commissioner from every member-state, chosen by their national governments, and only the European Parliament has the ability to approve the College of Commissioners or dissolve it. Still, the parliament is rather weak compared to the Council and Commission, and this is problematic given that it is the only directly elected body.

Besides these three major EU institutions, the European Court of Justice (ECJ) has played a significant role in the operations of the EU, and in pushing integration forward. The ECJ is comprised of one judge from each member-state, and its primary role is to ensure that national law is compatible with EU law. In their 1993 article "Europe before the Court: A Political Theory of Legal Integration" Anne-Marie Burley and Walter Mattli argue that the judicial legitimacy of the ECJ has enabled it to take on more jurisdiction than had been intended, and to create precedents that assert the primacy of EU law over domestic law. Consequently, many individuals and local judges bring cases directly to the ECJ instead of to their national courts. Other important institutions are the European Central Bank, Court of Auditors, the European Economic and Social Committee, and the Committee of the Regions.

HOW IT WORKS

Besides the business of initiating and approving new laws, the EU has undergone major changes to its treaties. Member-states have willingly ceded increasing levels of sovereignty in numerous policy areas, but their control of the treaties is fundamentally intergovernmental. In order to change the jurisdiction of the EU fundamentally, statesmen must negotiate a new treaty at an Intergovernmental Conference (IGC). However, as argued in Mai'a K. Davis Cross's *The European Diplomatic Corps* (2007), the process of negotiation is much more complex than just the IGC summit, which is typically a highly publicized two-day event. Personal representatives of the statesmen, who are usually ambassadors based in Brussels, take years to prepare a draft treaty in advance of the IGC. Ultimately, agreement must be unanimous, and member-states can choose their own method of ratification, either through a parliamentary vote or popular referendum.

The last extensive revision to the EU was the 1992 Maastricht Treaty, which created the so-called "pillar system." All of the policy areas that used to fall under the EC became the first pillar, which is governed by the "community method." That is, in these policy areas the EU has full control at the supranational level, above the level of national governments. The second two pillars are intergovernmental, with the Common Foreign and Security Policy as the second pillar, and Justice and Home Affairs as the third.

A major part of the first pillar is the Single Market, which removed trade barriers among member-states, as well as establishing free movement of goods and a common tariff for imports from outside of the EU. The Single Market was part of the Treaty of Rome, but it was not fully completed until 1993. The Maastricht Treaty introduced the single currency, the Euro, which went into circulation on January 1, 2002. The benefits of a single currency are that it makes economic transactions easier, encourages investment, and completely eliminates exchange rate fluctuations. All member-states, including the ten new ones, have adopted the Euro, with the exception of the United Kingdom, Denmark, and Sweden. The European Central Bank, established in 1993, is completely independent of member-states and interests groups, and is charged with managing the Euro and Single Market, setting the EU's external exchange rate policy, and ensuring price stability and low inflation within the EU.

In addition to free movement of goods, the Maastricht Treaty also established free movement of persons, capital, and services, although certain restrictions still apply. Free labor mobility is of particular importance as it clearly distinguishes the EU from other free trade areas like the North American Free Trade Agreement (NAFTA). Europeans actually have citizenship in the EU, and can move, study, travel, and work within an internally borderless EU.

The Treaty Establishing a Constitution for Europe—negotiated between June and October 2004 and signed by all EU governments on October 29—was an attempt to revise the EU Treaty. But the ongoing national ratification process resulted in failure when the French and Dutch referenda in May and June 2005 rejected it. Nevertheless, the ratification process continued in 2006 even as efforts were underway to devise a new version.

THE FUTURE OF THE EU

There are numerous scholarly debates over why the EU has continued to deepen its policies, and what its future holds. Functionalists have argued that the process of EU integration has proceeded based on functional need, and on an ad-hoc basis. Neo-functionalists have argued that once the six member-states founded the ECSC a spillover effect ensued, in which one policy area necessitated integration in other, related policy areas. For example, economic cooperation spilled over into political cooperation.

Since the 1990s the major debate has typically been between rationalists and constructivists. Rationalists argue that integration proceeded based on cost-benefit calculations. At each juncture, leaders only agreed to more integration if it directly benefited their own states' economic and power interests. Rationalists deny that any significant political integration can ever take place. On the other hand, the constructivist approach argues that the EU is a product of shared norms, which grow over time through deliberation, persuasion, and socialization. There is a certain idea of Europe that many Europeans believe is a worthwhile goal, and they comply with EU rules because they know it is in the long-term benefit of everyone. Depending on the approach, predictions about the future of the EU vary.

The question of how far enlargement can continue is also an area of attention. With the addition of ten new member-states in 2004, many scholars and politicians argue that the EU has reached its absorption capacity in the near term, and will have to wait many years before it is ready to undergo further enlargement. If the EU enlarges too quickly, it may be impossible for Europeans to continue to deepen integration, or deal with problems of democratic accountability at the supranational level.

Finally, scholars and policy practitioners debate the future role of the EU as an international actor. The strength and cohesion of the EU internally has a direct impact on its relations with the United States, its growing global security role, and its ability to be economically competitive. The EU has played a strong role in facilitating the ongoing Middle East peace process. Its policy is to favor the creation of two states to resolve the Israel Palestinian conflict, and to find a solution to the Palestinian refugee crisis. The EU participates in numerous diplomatic and humanitarian assistance efforts to ensure the success of the roadmap to peace. The EU is the largest trading, scientific, and research partner with Israel, and provides the greatest amount of aid to the Palestinians and United Nations Relief and Works Agency. The EU responded to the 2006 crisis in Lebanon with numerous high-level diplomatic meetings with both Lebanese and Israel governments, the international community, and the United States. It also devised evacuation and humanitarian corridors to assist victims in escaping the violence, or to get supplies into the region.

Besides extensive aid to the Middle East, EU member-states as a whole give about $30 billion per year in development cooperation or aid to the third world more generally. Recipient countries include seventy-seven African, Caribbean, and Pacific countries. The EU seeks to reduce poverty in the third world by slowing the spread of HIV/AIDS, increasing education, providing debt relief, and improving the coherence between development and trade policies. To that end, the EU supports a number of associated territories, giving them preferential treatment and access to the European Development Fund for financing projects.

Overall, the EU leads the world in environmental protection and humanitarian aid, its economy is roughly the same size as that of the United States, and it has a high level of soft power or influence. While there are many areas of controversy and hurdles to cooperation in the foreseeable future, the EU has repeatedly proven itself to be a viable world player with much potential.

SEE ALSO *Euro, The*

BIBLIOGRAPHY

Burley, Anne-Marie, and Walter Mattli. 1993. Europe before the Court: A Political Theory of Legal Integration. *International Organization* 47 (1): 41–76.

Cross, Mai'a K. Davis. 2007 *The European Diplomatic Corps: Diplomats and International Cooperation from Westphalia to Maastricht.* Houndmills: Palgrave.

Dinan, Desmond. 2003. *Ever Closer Union: An Introduction to European Integration.* Boulder, CO: Lynne Rienner Publishers.

McCormick, John. *Understanding the European Union.* New York: Palgrave Macmillan.

Moravcsik, Andrew. 1999. A New Statecraft? Supranational Entrepreneurs and International Cooperation. *International Organization* 53 (2): 267–303.

Nelson, Brent F., and Alexander Stubb. 2003. *The European Union: Readings on the Theory and Practice of European Integration.* New York: Palgrave Macmillan.

Mai'a K. Davis Cross

EUTHANASIA AND ASSISTED SUICIDE

The twentieth century has seen great strides in the advancement of medicine and life-sustaining technology, resulting in improved life expectancy and quality of life for people around the world. Improvements in medicine, however, raise questions about the appropriateness of life-sustaining treatments in the case of people who are terminally ill and experiencing acute pain and suffering. In the late twentieth century, end-of-life issues came to the forefront of public attention, resulting in an ongoing discussion about ethical, legal, and political implications of physician-assisted suicide (PAS) and euthanasia.

ISSUES SURROUNDING CONTROVERSIAL END-OF-LIFE DECISIONS

Part of the controversy surrounding end-of-life decisions such as PAS and euthanasia results from a lack of clear communication as to what these actions entail. *Euthanasia* refers to someone (often a physician) intentionally taking an action that ends another person's life with the stated intent of alleviating or preventing perceived suffering. Euthanasia involves the direct administration of lethal medication by a person other than the terminally ill patient. "Assisted suicide is the deliberate and knowing provisions of information, the means, and/or help to another person for the act of suicide" (American Association of Suicidology 1996, p. 6). In PAS, the assister is a medical doctor. Such assistance is typically in the form of a prescription for a lethal dose of medication that the terminally ill patient may use as a means to end his or her life. The critical distinction between these practices is that in euthanasia the physician (or somebody else) actively administers the lethal medication, while in PAS the patient is given the means to bring about his or her own death.

There are various types of euthanasia, including voluntary, nonvoluntary, and involuntary. *Voluntary euthanasia* refers to deliberate termination of a patient's life upon that person's explicit and direct request. Nonvoluntary euthanasia occurs when the patient is unconscious or incompetent and is thus unable to make a decision. Involuntary euthanasia takes place when the patient is competent and aware but his or her consent is not obtained. It should be noted that involuntary euthanasia is not an acceptable practice even in countries where voluntary euthanasia is currently legalized. The involuntary termination of a patient's life is not supported by legislation and is considered homicide around the world. This distinction has led several authors to argue that euthanasia is by definition voluntary and that terms such as *nonvoluntary* and *involuntary euthanasia* are contradictory and misleading (Materstvedt Clark, Ellershaw, et al., 2003).

In addition, distinction has been made between active and passive euthanasia. *Active euthanasia* is the procedure whereby a physician (or someone else) shortens a person's life, usually through the administration of a lethal dose of medication. *Passive euthanasia* refers to the practice of withholding or withdrawing a futile or ineffective treatment upon the patient's request (American Association of Suicidology 1996). Several researchers have argued against the use of this latter term by pointing out that practices such as withholding and withdrawing treatment are ethically and legally distinct from active euthanasia (Materstvedt, Clark, Ellershaw, et al. 2003). This view is consistent with practices in countries such as the United States and Israel where euthanasia is illegal, but withholding and withdrawing treatment are acceptable medical practices (Ganz, Benbenishty, Hersch, et al. 2006). However, in other countries the term *passive euthanasia* is still used. Similarly, providing high doses of pain-relieving medication, even if this may shorten a patient's life, is seen as distinct from euthanasia (Materstvedt, Clark, Ellershaw, et al. 2003). This is also the case with terminal sedation, a practice whereby pain medication is used to bring about unconsciousness, after which life-support equipment is withdrawn (Parpa, Mystajudou, Tsilika, et al. 2006).

ARGUMENTS REGARDING PAS AND EUTHANASIA

A firm grasp on the definitions of *PAS* and *euthanasia* as well as on the alternatives that exist to these practices is essential for an informed understanding of the debate surrounding end-of-life decision-making. As of the early twenty-first century, more empirical data are necessary in order to evaluate the accuracy of arguments in favor of and against PAS and euthanasia.

Proponents of assisted suicide and euthanasia claim the practices exist but are hidden, and legalizing such acts would allow for stricter government regulation and control (Quill and Battin 2004). In addition, involving medical practitioners in the decision-making process would allow for professional and expert judgment to be made regarding the validity of end-of-life decisions. Another fundamental argument in favor of legalizing PAS and euthanasia is maximizing personal autonomy and self-determination. According to this view, a terminally ill patient who is enduring unbearable pain or suffering is entitled to the right of choosing death with dignity and peace. Alleviation of unnecessary suffering and maintaining the quality of life of terminally ill patients are the paramount goals behind PAS and euthanasia. Some proponents of PAS claim that this practice is ethically different from euthanasia, as in PAS the patient is the one who performs the act of ending his or her life.

Opponents of euthanasia and PAS point out the potential for abuse if these practices are granted legal recognition (Foley and Hendin 2002). Critics of PAS and euthanasia often refer to the threat of a slippery slope. They fear that once voluntary euthanasia or PAS for terminally ill patients becomes legally permissible, other forms of medicalized killing, such as involuntary euthanasia for mentally incompetent and/or disabled individuals would increase. Many medical professionals state that euthanasia and PAS are prohibited under the Hippocratic Oath and violate the fundamental ethical principles of nonmaleficence and beneficence. Furthermore, these professionals argue that the need for such end-of-life decisions can be eliminated with the provision of appropriate palliative care and the effective use of pain control medication.

Questions have also been raised about the stability and rationality of end-of-life requests (Foley and Hendin, 2002). In addition, patients may request PAS or euthanasia as a result of experiencing hopelessness and depression rather than acute physical pain or suffering. Alternatively, the patients may feel obligated to alleviate their families from unnecessary burden and thus feel pressured to end their lives. Finally, many opponents claim that the sanctity of human life overrules concerns of personal autonomy and that the protection of human life should be of paramount importance in end-of-life medical cares.

INTERNATIONAL VIEWS OF PAS AND EUTHANASIA

Both euthanasia and PAS were legalized in the Netherlands in 2002 after they had been tolerated for

more than 30 years (Materstvedt, Clark, Ellershaw, et al. 2003). Belgium legalized euthanasia in September 2002, and did not legalize PAS (Adams and Nys 2003). Physician-assisted suicide, but not euthanasia, was legalized in Oregon in 1994 with the Death with Dignity Act, and began to be in use in 1997 (Materstvedt, Clark, Ellershaw, et al. 2003). In 2006, the Oregon Department of Human Services announced that it will no longer use the term "physician-assisted suicide" to describe deaths under the Death with Dignity Act (Colburn 2006) because the act itself specifies that deaths that occur following the provisions of the law are not to be considered suicide. Although active euthanasia is illegal in Switzerland, assisting in the suicide of a terminally ill patient is considered a crime only if the death, and therefore the motive behind the assistance, benefits the person who assists the suicide (Schildmann, Herrmann, Burchardi, et al. 2006). Although Australia's Northern Territory was the first jurisdiction to legalize euthanasia in 1995, the Rights of the Terminally Ill Act was repealed nine months later by an act of the Commonwealth (Materstvedt, Clark, Ellershaw, et al. 2003).

The legalization of PAS and euthanasia in several nations signals changes in public awareness of end-of-life issues. However, countries with legal endorsement of these interventions are the exception rather than the rule. A 2001 survey conducted by the Council of Europe (2003) revealed that a majority of European nations do not have laws concerning assisted suicide and euthanasia. Of those nations that do have laws, the overwhelming majority oppose the practices. A 1999 study by Luigi Grassi, Katia Magnani, and Mauro Ercolani, published in the *Journal of Pain & Symptom Management*, found that only 15 percent of Italian physicians favored euthanasia and assisted suicide. In Ireland, where suicide was considered a crime until 1993, discussions of euthanasia and assisted suicide have been taboo (Phillips 1997).

Euthanasia is not a legal option in Germany and physicians are obligated to prevent harm, which may also include cases of attempted suicide. However, suicide and assisted suicide are not considered criminal acts because of an artifact of German law (Schildmann, Herrmann, Burchardi, et al. 2006). This creates a precarious situation in which assisted suicide is theoretically an option for German physicians but may lead to legal sanctions if an argument is made that there was a duty to protect the patient's life. As of 2003, open discussion on PAS and euthanasia does not exist in Bosnia-Herzegovina (Haračić 2003), and Estonia has not engaged in a public debate surrounding end-of-life issues (Koorits 2003). In Greece, only 8.1 percent of the general public and 2.1 percent of physicians favor PAS, although 56.7 percent of the surveyed medical doctors had administered terminal sedation (Parpa, Mystajudou, Tsilika, et al. 2006). In Russia, euthanasia is seen as contrary to the physician's duty to preserve and promote human life and is therefore considered unethical and illegal (Leenaars and Connolly 2001). In contrast, a large percentage of physicians in China may approve of euthanasia, although such acts are not officially legalized (Leenaars and Connolly 2001). In India, 50 percent of medical students favor euthanasia (Leenaars and Connolly 2001). Israeli medical doctors view euthanasia, PAS, and withdrawing of treatment as being forbidden by Jewish ethics and law; however, withholding of treatment is an accepted practice (Ganz, Benbenishty, Hersch, et al. 2006).

Issues of culture, religion, and national history are critical when attempting to explain the observed differences in beliefs about end-of-life decision-making. Several authors have hypothesized that positive attitudes toward PAS and euthanasia are the product of highly industrialized, individualistic societies (Kemmelmeier, Wieczorkowska, Erb, and Burnstein 2002). For example, an increase in positive attitudes regarding autonomy in the United States beginning in the late twentieth century has been correlated with a shift toward more positive attitudes regarding assisted suicide (Kemmelmeier, Wieczorkowska, Erb, and Burnstein 2002). In collectivistic societies such as Japan, arguments about the right to self-determination hold less appeal and end-of-life decisions are seen as prerogatives of the family as well as of the individual patient (Konishi and Davis 2001).

This picture is complicated by differences in religion. Most religions of the world uphold the sanctity of human life and prohibit actions that intentionally hasten death. Catholicism officially disapproves of euthanasia and PAS, as does the Christian Eastern Orthodox Church (Parpa, Mystajudou, Tsilika, et al. 2006). There are a variety of branches of Judaism, some of which oppose the active shortening of human life but deem interventions that artificially extend the agony of terminally ill patients unnecessary, therefore allowing withholding and withdrawing treatment (Gesundheit, Steinberg, Glick, et al. 2006). Islam does not recognize a patient's right to die but allows for non-treatment decisions such as withholding and withdrawal of treatment to be made by the patient's family and community (Sachedina 2005). Islamic law also condones the use of pain-reducing medication at the risk of shortening the life of a terminally ill patient (Sachedina 2005).

Views about euthanasia and PAS are further affected by national history. The term *euthanasia*, for example, evokes negative memories in many German-speaking countries where the term was used during the Nazi regime to refer to the systematic extermination of six million Jews and more than 200,000 mentally ill and physically disadvantaged people, as well as the Roma (Schildmann,

Herrmann, Burchardi, et al. 2006) and other groups. Such historical experiences have prohibited public discussions of euthanasia in Germany (Schildmann, Herrmann, Burchardi, et al. 2006).

CONCLUSION

Given the advances in life-sustaining technology and medical treatments, the controversy surrounding end-of-life decision-making is likely to continue, at least in technologically advanced countries. Open discussion of PAS and euthanasia is complicated by a constantly evolving terminology and differing cultural, religious, and national ideals. People need to stay informed of current developments and research on these issues in order to be prepared to face the end-of-life dilemmas of the future.

SEE ALSO *Death and Dying; Morbidity and Mortality; Suicide*

BIBLIOGRAPHY

Adams, Maurice, and Herman Nys. 2003. Comparative Reflections on the Belgian Euthanasia Act 2002. *Medical Law Review* 11: 353–376.

American Association of Suicidology. 1996. Report of the Committee on Physician-Assisted Suicide and Euthanasia. *Suicide and Life-Threatening Behavior* 26 (suppl.): 1–19.

Colburn, Don. 2006. Death Act's Alias Has State Tongue-Tied. *The Oregonian.* November 11. http://www.oregonlive.com/.

Council of Europe, Steering Committee on Bioethics. 2003. *Replies to the Questionnaire for Member States Relating to Euthanasia.* Strasbourg, France: Council of Europe. http://www.coe.int/t/e/legal_affairs/legal_co-operation/bioethics/activities/euthanasia/1INF(2003)8e_replies_euthanasia.pdf.

Foley, Kathleen, and Herbert Hendin, eds. 2002. *The Case Against Assisted Suicide: For the Right to End-of-Life Care.* Baltimore, MD: Johns Hopkins University Press.

Ganz, F. D., J. Benbenishty, M. Hersch, et al. 2006. The Impact of Regional Culture on Intensive Care End of Life Decision Making: An Israeli Perspective from the ETHICUS Study. *Journal of Medical Ethics* 32: 196–199.

Gesundheit, Benjamin, Avraham Steinberg, Shimon Glick, et al. 2006. Euthanasia: An Overview of the Jewish Perspective. *Cancer Investigation* 24: 621–629.

Grassi, Luigi, Katia Magnani, and Mauro Ercolani. 1999. Attitudes toward Euthanasia and Physician-Assisted Auicide among Italian Primary Care Physicians. *Journal of Pain & Symptom Management* 17: 188–196.

Haračić, Midhat. 2003. From Bosnia-Herzegovina. *Palliative Medicine* 17: 128.

Kemmelmeier, Markus, Grazyna Wieczorkowska, Hans-Peter Erb, and Eugene Burnstein. 2002. Individualism, Authoritarianism, and Attitudes toward Assisted Death: Cross-Cultural, Cross-Regional, and Experimental Evidence. *Journal of Applied Social Psychology* 32: 60–85.

Konishi, Emiko, and A. J. Davis. 2001. The Right-to-Die and the Duty-to-Die: Perceptions of Nurses in the West and in Japan. *International Nursing Review* 48: 17–28.

Koorits, Ursula. 2003. From Estonia. *Palliative Medicine* 17: 127.

Leenaars, Antoon, and John Connolly. 2001. Suicide, Assisted Suicide and Euthanasia: International Perspectives. *Irish Journal of Psychological Medicine* 18: 33–37.

Materstvedt, Lars, David Clark, John Ellershaw, et al. 2003. Euthanasia and Physician-Assisted Suicide: A View from an AEPC Ethics Task Force. *Palliative Medicine* 17: 97–101.

Parpa, Efi, Kyriaki Mystajudou, Eleni Tsilika, et al. 2006. The Attitudes of Greek Physicians and Lay People on Euthanasia and Physician-Assisted Suicide in Terminally Ill Cancer Patients. *American Journal of Hospice and Palliative Medicine* 23: 297–303.

Phillips, Pat. 1997. Views of Assisted Suicide from Several Nations. *Journal of the American Medical Association* 278: 969–971.

Quill, Timothy E., and Margaret P. Battin, eds. 2004. *Physician-Assisted Dying: The Case for Palliative Care and Patient Choice.* Baltimore, MD: Johns Hopkins University Press.

Sachedina, Abdulaziz. 2005. End-of-Life: The Islamic View. *The Lancet* 366: 774–779.

Schildmann, Jan, Eva Herrmann, Nicole Burchardi, et al. 2006. Physician-Assisted Suicide: Knowledge and Views of Fifth-Year Medical Students in Germany. *Death Studies* 30: 29–39.

Elena Yakunina
Jessica Richmond
James L. Werth Jr.

EVALUATION RESEARCH

SEE *Methods, Research (in Sociology).*

EVANS-PRITCHARD, E. E.
1902–1973

E. E. Evans-Pritchard was one of the world's leading social anthropologists from the 1940s to the 1960s, his work marking a transition from structural-functionalism to cultural interpretation and history. His theoretical statements on the aims of anthropology and his ethnographic writings on African societies were equally influential.

As an undergraduate, Evans-Pritchard studied history at Oxford University. For his postgraduate studies in anthropology, he moved to the London School of Economics (LSE) to work with the English ethnologist Charles G. Seligman (1873–1940). Another strong influence on Evans-Pritchard during his LSE years was the

British anthropologist Bronislaw Malinowski, despite an intense mutual dislike between them. Evans-Pritchard received his Ph.D. in 1927 for a thesis on the Azande. Along with Raymond Firth, Isaac Schapera, Audrey Richards, Siegfried Frederick Nadel, and others, Evans-Pritchard was part of a group of students trained by Malinowski who came to occupy key positions in social anthropology from the mid-1940s to the 1970s. Evans-Pritchard did extensive ethnographic fieldwork among several African societies, most notably among the Azande and Nuer (both in the southern Sudan). He stayed in Africa during World War II to fight for Britain against Italian troops. He converted to Roman Catholicism in 1944, and his religiosity subtly colored his writings on belief systems. After World War II, Evans-Pritchard settled down as professor at Oxford University (1946–1970) where he attracted a large number of students from around the world. He was president of the Royal Anthropological Institute (1949–1951), co-founder of the Association of Social Anthropologists (ASA), and was knighted in 1971.

Evans-Pritchard was a prolific writer, with more than 400 publications to his credit. In *Witchcraft, Oracles and Magic among the Azande* (1937), he developed an ethnographic perspective on apparently irrational modes of thought. This work on the internal coherence of witchcraft beliefs fascinated philosophers such as Robin George Collingwood and Michael Polanyi, and remains one of anthropology's most acclaimed monographs. In *The Nuer* (1940), the first of several books on this cattle-farming society, Evans-Pritchard pioneered an approach to social ecology. His analysis of how the Nuer derive their modes of time-reckoning from kinship relations and economic activities is a classic reading in the anthropology of time. The edited volume *African Political Systems* (1940) develops a comparative perspective on African political traditions, with a view to facilitating British colonial governance. Evans-Pritchard often acknowledged Alfred Reginald Radcliffe-Brown as his main inspiration, but his BBC lectures on *Social Anthropology* (1951) make a noticeable shift from structural-functionalism to ethnohistorical interpretation. Placing anthropology among the humanities, he argued that "social anthropology is best regarded as an art and not as a natural science" (1951, p. 84) and that the "translation" of cultural concepts is at the core of the discipline. A fruitful combination of anthropology and history informs many of his works. In *The Sanusi of Cyrenaica* (1949), he retraced the history of this North African Sufi order from 1837 to 1942 and provided a grim assessment of Italian colonialism in the region. Later works, such as *The Azande: History and Political Institutions* (1971), further confirm his rejection of synchronic perspectives (typical of both structural-functionalism and structuralism) toward interpreting historical change.

Evans-Pritchard's early works were always widely acclaimed. His later turn to history and interpretation initially received hostile reactions, but laid the groundwork for many developments in anthropology since the 1980s. In the early twenty-first century Evans-Pritchard's status as a classic of social anthropology is undisputed.

SEE ALSO *Anthropology; Malinowski, Bronislaw*

BIBLIOGRAPHY

PRIMARY WORKS

Evans-Pritchard, Edward Evan. 1937. *Witchcraft, Oracles and Magic among the Azande.* Oxford: Clarendon Press.

Evans-Pritchard, Edward Evan. 1940. *African Political Systems.* Ed. M. Fortes and E. E. Evans-Pritchard. London: Humphrey Milford (for Oxford University Press).

Evans-Pritchard, Edward Evan. 1940. *The Nuer: A Description of the Modes of Livelihood and Political Institutions of a Nilotic People.* Oxford: Clarendon Press.

Evans-Pritchard, Edward Evan. 1949. *The Sanusi of Cyrenaica.* Oxford: Clarendon Press.

Evans-Pritchard, Edward Evan. 1951. *Social Anthropology.* London: Routledge and Kegan Paul.

Evans-Pritchard, Edward Evan. 1956. *Nuer Religion.* Oxford: Clarendon Press.

Evans-Pritchard, Edward Evan. 1971. *The Azande: History and Political Institutions.* Oxford: Clarendon Press.

Evans-Pritchard, Edward Evan. 1974. *A Bibliography of the Writings of E. E. Evans-Pritchard.* Comp. E. E. Evans-Pritchard. Amended and corrected by T. O. Beidelman. London: Tavistock Publications.

Stefan Ecks

EVENT STUDIES

In the social sciences, there are instances where it is necessary to statistically assess the impact of an event on the value of the firm. In this instance, event studies are a viable tool to quantitatively assess the effectiveness of an "announced event" on the stock returns of firms. The announced event is an unanticipated event, which may have political, economic, legal, or historical implications for select firms. The stock returns of the firm are often referred to as *shareholder wealth* or the *welfare of the firm;* and assuming efficient markets, the market reaction to an announced event will be immediately reflected in the security prices (or share returns) of the firm.

DESCRIPTION OF AN EVENT STUDY

To construct an event study, a specific event and the date of the announced event, called the *event date*, must be identified. The event date may be found in prominent media outlets such as the *New York Times, Wall Street Journal,* the Associated Press, or other media outlets. Thereafter, the event window must be constructed, which is typically the event date. The event window may be extended to include the day before and the day after the actual announcement, as some announcements may occur when the stock market has closed and/or the information was leaked the day before. Alternatively, an anticipatory window may be constructed that includes days before the actual announcement to account for potential leakages prior to the actual announcement.

After the event window is constructed, the stock returns of the firm must be collected to construct an estimation window, which represents the stock returns under "normal" conditions (no confounding events have occurred such as annual report announcements, restructuring announcements, etc.). The estimation window is typically before the event window, and therefore does not include days in the event window to avoid influencing the estimation of returns under normal conditions. A selection criterion must also be determined for the inclusion of firms in the event study such as industry membership and/or data availability. Further, any potential biases during the firm selection must be disclosed.

To determine the market reaction to a specific event, the abnormal returns are constructed, which determines, on average, if the firm observed above or below average returns in response to an announced event. Specifically, assuming efficient markets, abnormal returns represent the market's valuation of the change in the firm's current and future expected profitability due to an announced event.

APPLICATIONS OF EVENT STUDIES IN THE SOCIAL SCIENCES

There have been many applications of event studies in the social sciences. Event studies have been used to determine the impact of presidential elections on the stock market. Srinivas Nippani and Bobby Medlin examined the impact of the delay in the declaration of a winner in the 2000 U.S. presidential election on the performance of the stock market and found a negative reaction to the delay in election results. Nippani and Augustine Arize also found evidence that the delay in the U.S. election results impacted the stock markets in other countries like Mexico and Canada. Sara Ellison and Wallace Mullin analyzed President Bill Clinton's 1990s health care reform proposal on pharmaceutical stock prices and found that investors reacted negatively to health care reform, estimating that shareholder wealth fell by approximately 52 percent.

Event studies are also used to determine the impact of trade policy announcements on the value of the firm. John Hughes, Stefanie Lenway, and Judy Rayburn examined the stock price reactions for the semiconductor producers and downstream consumers (electronic and computer firms) affected by a subset of events starting with the filing of a Section 301 petition by the U.S. semiconductor industry alleging unfair practices by the Japanese and culminating in the 1986 Trade Agreement. Empirical evidence suggests that U.S. semiconductor producers and consumers benefited from the trade agreement. In previous trade studies, statistical results have shown that U.S. firms observed positive abnormal returns in response to the announcement of U.S. trade protection. Bruce Blonigen, Wesley Wilson, and Kasaundra Tomlin note that the studies of trade policy on the welfare of the firm ignore the possibility that foreign firms can use foreign direct investment to mitigate the positive gains to domestic producers, also known as "tariff-jumping." Using event study methodology, the statistical results suggest that affirmative U.S. antidumping decisions yield positive abnormal returns; moreover tariff-jumping in the form of new plants or plant expansions by foreign firms has a negative impact on the welfare of U.S. domestic firms that previously received trade protection.

Issues related to human resources and human rights have also been evaluated using event study methodology. Michelle Arthur and Alison Cook examined the share price reactions to 231 work-family human resource policies adopted by Fortune 500 companies, which were announced in the *Wall Street Journal* from 1971 to 1996. The results suggest that firm announcements of work-family initiatives positively affected the shareholder wealth of firms that implemented them. With respect to human rights issues, Judith Posnikoff analyzed the effects of announcing disinvestment or withdrawal of U.S. firms from South Africa during the 1980s on those firms' shareholder wealth and found a significant positive announcement effect.

STRENGTHS AND LIMITATIONS

Event studies are a valuable tool, in that across many disciplines in the social sciences one can assess the effects of new information on the shareholder wealth of specific firms; and in some cases perform industry-level analysis. There are some limitations in the methodology. For example, it is difficult to identify the exact date of a specific event. In addition, there are some estimation issues, which Craig MacKinlay discussed in a 1997 survey article on event studies that outlines the issues and remedies. In sum, assuming efficient markets, event study methodology is a valuable statistical tool to evaluate issues in the social sciences.

SEE ALSO *Efficient Market Hypothesis; Expectations, Rational; Information, Economics of; Random Samples; Speculation; Stock Exchanges; Stock Exchanges in Developing Countries*

BIBLIOGRAPHY

Arthur, Michelle M., and Alison Cook. 2004. Taking Stock of Work-Family Initiatives: How Announcements of "Family-Friendly" Human Resource Decisions Affect Shareholder Value. *Industrial and Labor Relations Review* 57 (4): 599–613.

Blonigen, Bruce B., Wesley Wilson, and Kasaundra Tomlin. 2004. Tariff-jumping FDI and Domestic Firms Profits. *Canadian Journal of Economics* 37 (3): 656–677.

Ellison, Sara Fisher, and Wallace P. Mullin. 2001. Gradual Incorporation of Information: Pharmaceutical Stocks and the Evolution of President Clinton's Health Care Reform. *Journal of Law and Economics* 44 (1): 89–129.

Hughes, John S., Stefanie Lenway, and Judy Rayburn. 1997. Stock Price Effects of U.S. Trade Policy Responses to Japanese Trading Practices in Semi-Conductors. *Canadian Journal of Economics* 30 (4a): 922–942.

MacKinlay, Craig A. 1997. Event Studies in Economics and Finance. *Journal of Economic Literature* 35 (1): 13–39.

Nippani, Srinivas, and Augustine Arize. 2005. U.S. Presidential Election Impact on Canadian and Mexican Stock Markets. *Journal of Economics and Finance* 29 (2): 271–279.

Nippani, Srinivas, and W. Bobby Medlin. 2002. The 2000 Presidential Election and the Stock Market. *Journal of Economics and Finance* 26 (2): 162–169.

Posnikoff, Judith F. Disinvestment from South Africa: They Did Well by Doing Good. *Contemporary Economic Policy* 15 (1): 76–86.

Kasaundra M. Tomlin

EVOLUTIONARY GAMES

The modeling of evolutionary games has established itself as an important theoretical tool in the social sciences. Evolutionary games have proven useful in deriving descriptively accurate models of human behavior in an economic context, and they have provided important insights regarding the origins of conventions and other social behavior. Indeed, it is a testament to the power of evolutionary games that they have been used productively not only in the social sciences but in biological and philosophical research as well.

The best way to understand the general idea of evolutionary games is by contrasting them with the rational choice methodology in game theory. In a rational choice model, one assumes that people are perfectly rational and self-interested, acting only to increase their own payoffs. These payoffs may be understood as financial rewards or any other positive outcomes.

Although rational choice models are powerful, and often appropriate, it is now known that humans often do not behave in a perfectly rational and self-interested manner. Instead, they often lack the cognitive sophistication required to compute their optimal behavior, while at other times they are motivated by emotional or other "irrational" factors. In such cases, it often turns out that the correct explanation of a particular behavior is etiological—that is, the behavior is the result of short-sighted evolutionary processes or trial-and-error learning, rather than a deliberate rational calculation. Thus, in the context of discussing evolutionary games, the term "evolution" refers generally to any process by which a group of individuals change their behavior in a strategic context.

Accordingly, evolutionary games typically dispense with the assumption that people are rational. Instead, the typical evolutionary game-theoretic model assumes that the agents being examined are myopic, cognitively simple, and not motivated by any self-interest at all. In the most common type of evolutionary game, the agents are simply "hard-wired" to behave in a particular way. The model generates predictions by imposing a dynamic in which the most successful strategies are reproduced according to how successful they are.

The evolutionary game that is undoubtedly the most well known is Robert Axelrod's famous Prisoner's Dilemma tournament, in which people were invited to submit strategies for playing the Iterated Prisoner's Dilemma (1984). This is a game of tremendous importance in the social sciences because it is the simplest nontrivial model of situations in which there is a conflict between self-interested behavior and cooperation with another person. At the conclusion of the tournament, Axelrod considered what would happen in a population containing many copies of the submitted strategies if he introduced a dynamic in which the individuals in the population reproduced, with the most successful individuals having the most offspring, and where each offspring displayed the same behavior as their parent. There is now a large body of formal literature that has extended this idea, of which the best known is the "replicator dynamics" of Peter Taylor and Leo Jonker (1978).

In the replicator dynamics, one mathematically models the evolution of strategies by considering a population that is initially populated, in some arbitrary proportion, by at least two different strategies. In this model, it is assumed that any arbitrary pair of individuals is equally likely to interact. When they do, each will receive a payoff that is defined by the underlying game. Thus, if both the proportion of strategies in the population and the structure of the game are known, then the expected payoff that each strategy will receive in an interaction can be calculated. In the replicator dynamics, it is assumed that if a particular strategy has an expected payoff that is less than the average payoff in the population, the number of individuals using that strategy will gradually diminish. Conversely, if a particular strategy has a higher than aver-

age expected payoff, then the number of individuals using that strategy will gradually increase. This behavior is usually represented by a system of differential equations, which is solved to yield a description of the state of the population at any time in its evolution.

In the replicator dynamics, it is often the case that there is some proportion of strategies at which each strategy has the same expected payoff in the population. If this is the case, then the replicator-dynamics model implies that the representation of each strategy in the population will not change. Similarly, it is possible that one strategy will come to predominate in the population, while the other strategies gradually disappear.

Evolutionary games are most explanatory when such stable configurations of strategies exist. Typically, the explanatory strategy is to note that, unless there are powerful external influences on the population, one is most likely to observe a real-world population in a stable state, or approaching a stable state. In this way, an evolutionary model is capable of yielding specific predictions, without the use of the rationality assumptions of rational choice theory.

It is possible, of course, to derive different dynamical models that are best interpreted as models of learning processes, or that employ different assumptions. The best known of these is the "aspiration-imitation" model, which specifically represents the dynamic as a learning process that has various parameters that can be adjusted for the specific model.

Although the term *evolutionary game* is often used in a way that makes it synonymous with the replicator dynamics, it is more accurate to think of evolutionary game theory as a general framework that contains a large variety of different models. These models vary, not only in the specific parameters that define their behavior, but in more dramatic ways as well. The learning process, the cognitive sophistication of the agents, the size of the population, and the speed with which the population evolves are just some of the variables that may be taken into account in an evolutionary game (see Samuelson 1997 for an excellent survey). Evolutionary game theory is thus a flexible tool, and its study is rewarded by the large number of applications to which it can be put.

SEE ALSO *Dynamic Games; Game Theory; Noncooperative Games; Prisoner's Dilemma (Economics); Rationality; Replicator Dynamics*

BIBLIOGRAPHY

Axelrod, Robert. 1984. *The Evolution of Cooperation.* New York: Basic Books.

Samuelson, Larry. 1997. *Evolutionary Games and Equilibrium Selection.* Cambridge, MA: MIT Press.

Taylor, Peter, and Leo D. Jonker. 1978. Evolutionarily Stable Strategies and Game Dynamics. *Mathematical Biosciences* 40: 145–156.

Zachary Ernst

EVOLUTIONARY PSYCHOLOGY

Evolutionary psychology proposes a set of evolved psychological mechanisms to account for much, if not all, human behavior. The research program is one among many in the social sciences that argues for the relevance of evolutionary biology in understanding human behavior. Evolutionary psychologists argue that explanations in psychology, and social science in general, are inadequate to the extent that they ignore human evolution. Evolutionary psychologists aim to unify psychology and other social sciences and improve their explanatory capabilities. Evolutionary psychology is related to human sociobiology but evolutionary psychologists present an important criticism of human sociobiology: sociobiologists ignore the psychological mechanisms that produce human behavior. To this extent, evolutionary psychology is seen as an advance over human sociobiology because it is consistent with cognitivism in psychology. Evolutionary psychologists share cognitive psychologists' view that humans' internal psychological mechanisms are contentful representational states, sometimes referring to these mechanisms as "Darwinian algorithms." Behavioral psychologists argue that humans have no content internal representational states, which is in stark contrast to the cognitive perspective.

Evolutionary psychologists' key contribution to the social sciences is the idea that the human mind consists of many separate psychological mechanisms, each of which was formed by natural selection. An analogy with organs illustrates this key insight: Many human organs are adaptations—direct descendents of organs that helped our ancestors survive and reproduce. Keeping with the analogy, these researchers point out that although all psychological mechanisms are adaptations, they need not all be currently adaptive, just as humans' appendices are adaptations but are not currently adaptive. Similar to human organs, the relevant adapted mental mechanisms are distinct and evolved independently of one another; they are modular.

A large number of experimental projects gave weight to evolutionary psychologists' theoretical claims. Psychologist David Buss's 1990 study of human mate selection found large numbers of cross-cultural commonalities in mate choices. These commonalities were attributed to various underlying psychological adaptations that drive human mate choices. Leda Cosmides's work during the 1980s in the psychology of reasoning presented a new way of dealing with a type of reasoning puzzle called Wason selection task results. Wason selection tasks are presented in the context of psychological experimentation on human reasoning. In the earliest of these, test subjects were presented with abstract tasks that could be solved correctly by use of deductive logic. Most subjects fail to deal with such tasks correctly and subsequent researchers introduced versions of the tasks with the same logical structure but presented in a context that subjects understood. These versions of the task produced a huge improvement in performance. Much of the psychology of reasoning has focused on explaining this performance difference. Cosmides proposed that performance goes up on Wason selection tasks when they are construed in terms of social exchange because humans are deploying an evolved psychological mechanism for social exchange to carry out the selection task.

Other experimental results reported by evolutionary psychologists include controversial work on rape and murder, as well as work on many aspects of reasoning, moral judgment, sexual attractiveness, parenting, taste, aggression, cooperation, and mental health. *The Handbook of Evolutionary Psychology* details the theoretical underpinnings of the field and introduces many of the key results from empirical work. This book develops and advances upon the program announced in an earlier work, *The Adapted Mind.*

Evolutionary psychology is an extremely productive research program. Evolutionary psychologists produce a large body of both academic and popular work. This work simultaneously advances a research program and provides responses to the various critics of the program. The first broad type of criticism is mounted by social scientists who view evolutionary psychology as a kind of biological determinism. Evolutionary psychologists reply that neither biological determinism nor cultural determinism is a viable explanatory strategy in the social sciences if pursued exclusively. Critics respond that the reductionist goals of evolutionary psychology imply that they are not as ecumenical as their response would indicate.

There are two other types of criticism of evolutionary psychology. One critique comes from researchers in other biologically based social sciences, such as evolutionary anthropology, who argue that evolutionary psychologists' presuppositions about human evolution are mistaken and that their hypotheses are not subjected to the testing procedure that analogous hypotheses undergo in evolutionary biology. This debate is about how to develop and test hypotheses about adaptation. Much of this discussion has centered on the issue of whether to test for adaptive behavior or to attempt to ascertain whether a certain behavior is the result of a particular adaptation. Evolutionary anthropologists adopt their methodology from behavioral ecologists. This approach emphasizes producing models to test the extent that animal or human behavior is adaptive. Evolutionary psychologists argue that ascertaining whether or not a trait is currently adaptive for the animal or human is not the same as ascertaining whether the trait is an adaptation or whether the behavior results from an adaptation. Evolutionary anthropologists counter the hypotheses that the extent to which behavior is adaptive can be rigorously tested and is relevant with the question of whether or not behavior is an adaptation or results from an adaptation.

The other type of criticism comes from philosophers of science, who place almost every aspect of the research program under critical scrutiny. Such critics reject both the theoretical tenets of the program, such as the modularity assumption, and the viability of experimental results.

Many philosophers of science, including philosopher of biology David Buller, have argued that evolutionary psychologists are mistaken in claiming that human minds are massively modular. Such arguments are derived from work in biology and from alternate views about human mental architecture defended in the cognitive sciences and neurosciences. Philosophers also argue that evolutionary psychologists are committed to an untenable version of adaptationism. Buller's version of this latter criticism is developed along similar lines to the criticisms presented by evolutionary anthropologists. One idea here is that not all adaptationist hypotheses should be considered equal and only those that are susceptible to rigorous empirical test should be pursued. Philosophers present another version of this point arguing that evolutionary psychologists' version of adaptationism is not consistent with evolutionary biologists' adaptationism and is therefore suspect. It is important to emphasize that critics from evolutionary anthropology and philosophy of science share evolutionary psychologists' view that evolutionary biology is crucial in the overall project of understanding human behavior. The critics disagree with evolutionary psychologists about the way in which biology should be brought to bear in the study of human behavior.

There is broad agreement among some social scientists that much of human behavior will only satisfactorily be accounted for by using biological based explanatory models. Such agreement does not commit these researchers to the view that evolutionary psychologists have isolated the one correct way in which biology should be brought into social science. There is still a great deal of theoretical and experimental work to be done at the intersection of biology and the social sciences. This is an exciting growth area to which evolutionary psychology makes one prominent contribution.

SEE ALSO *Anthropology, Biological; Darwin, Charles; Natural Selection; Philosophy; Psychology; Social Science; Sociobiology*

BIBLIOGRAPHY

Barkow, Jerome H., Leda Cosmides, and John Tobby, eds. 1992. *The Adapted Mind: Evolutionary Psychology and the Generation of Culture.* New York: Oxford University Press.

Buller, David. 2005. *Adapting Minds: Evolutionary Psychology and the Persistent Quest for Human Nature.* Cambridge, MA: MIT Press.

Buss, David M., ed. 2005. *The Handbook of Evolutionary Psychology.* Hoboken, NJ: John Wiley & Sons.

Buss, David M. 2005. *The Murderer Next Door: Why the Mind Is Designed to Kill.* New York: Penguin.

Buss, David M., Max Abbott, and Alois Angleitner, et al. 1990. International Preferences in Selecting Mates: A Study of 37 Cultures. *Journal of Cross Cultural Psychology* 21: 5–47.

Cosmides, Leda. 1989. The Logic of Social Exchange: Has Natural Selection Shaped How Humans Reason? Studies with the Wason Selection Task. *Cognition* 31: 187–276.

Hrdy, Sarah B. 1999. *Mother Nature: Maternal Instincts and How They Shape the Human Species.* New York: Ballantine Books.

Pinker, Steven. 2002. *The Blank Slate: The Modern Denial of Human Nature.* New York: Viking.

Wason, Peter C. 1960. On the Failure to Eliminate Hypotheses in a Conceptual Task. *Quarterly Journal of Experimental Psychology* 12: 129–140.

Stephen M. Downes

EXCESS DEMAND

Intuitively speaking, *excess demand* (ED) refers to a condition where, in a neoclassical framework without externalities, demand and supply do not match. In particular, there is ED when, in a certain market and for a given demand-and-supply curve, a certain price level p' generates insufficient domestic production to offset the corresponding domestic demand. Analytically speaking, excess demand can be considered from both a microeconomic and macroeconomic point of view. In microeconomics, ED can be analyzed in a partial or in a general equilibrium framework.

The easiest way to illustrate ED is to start from a partial equilibrium analysis. Let's assume that in a certain market the (inverse) demand-and-supply curves are represented by the following linear functions:

Demand (D): $p = a - bq$

Supply (S): $p = c + dq$

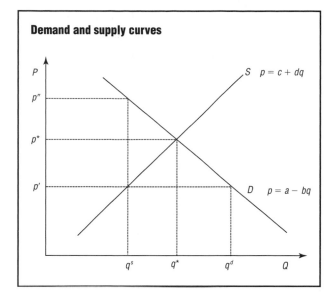

Demand and supply curves

Figure 1

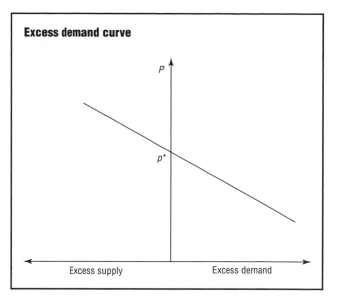

Excess demand curve

Figure 2

where p and q represent price and quantity respectively, and a, b, c, and d are real positive numbers. Clearly, the equilibrium occurs when the two schedules intersect. Therefore, we get:

$$\begin{cases} q^* = \dfrac{a - c}{b + d} \\ p^* = \dfrac{ad + bc}{b + d} \end{cases}$$

In practice, when the price level is exactly p^*, consumers demand the precise quantity that producers want to supply—that is, q^*. Hence, ED is zero.

Let's now suppose that for whatever reason the price is below its optimal value, that is, $p' < p^*$. When this happens, as seen in Figure 1, consumers demand q^d, but producers want to supply q^s only, with $q^s < q^d$. Consequently, ED may be defined as:

$$ED \equiv q^d - q^s = \frac{ad - bc}{b + d} + \frac{b - c}{bc} p'$$

Note that for a given value of a, b, c, and d, ED is increasing when p' is getting smaller, while, needless to say, when $p' \equiv p^*$, ED is zero.

In a closed competitive economy, ED is an unstable equilibrium. In fact, since consumers cannot buy the precise amount they desire at p', some of them are willing to offer a higher price. (Note that if producers supply q_s only, consumers might be willing to pay up to p'', with $p'' > p'$; see Figure 1.) However, when consumers start offering a higher price, producers have an incentive to increase their supply. In this way, the lack of balance is reduced; when the price is p^*, demand equals supply, and eventually ED becomes zero.

In terms of social welfare—that is, in terms of consumer and producer surplus—when there is ED, one cannot draw any definitive conclusions for the economy as a whole, or for consumers and producers. If international commerce is allowed, if the goods are tradable, if there are no trade barriers, and if the economy is small—that is, domestic demand for foreign production does not affect international prices—consumers could fill up ED with imports. In this case, consumers would gain, while producers would be worse off. However, the economy as a whole would be better off, because gains would overcome losses.

In a general equilibrium framework, ED in a single market would imply that there must be a symmetric excess supply in other market(s). The simplest way to demonstrate this is to use the Edgeworth box. Let's assume that in the economy there are only two goods, x and y, with p_x and p_y the price of x and y respectively. If the optimal consumption bundle—x^d and y^d—does not coincide with the production/endowment of the economy—x^s and y^s—then the value of the ED of x, $p_x(x^d - x^s)$, must be equal to the value of excess supply of y, $p_y(y^s - y^d)$, or vice versa.

Finally, in macroeconomics, ED indicates a condition where the aggregate demand (AD) exceeds the aggregate supply (AS). That is a condition that potentially stimulates both output and prices to rise. However, once full employment is reached, excess AD will only result in rising prices. In this case in fact, the increase of the price level P, implies that the real demand shifts back, and the economy returns to full employment equilibrium again.

SEE ALSO *Excess Supply; Welfare Analysis*

BIBLIOGRAPHY

Appleyard, Dennis, and Alfred Field. 2002. *International Economics*. 4th ed. Boston: Irwin.

Besanko, David A., and Ronald Braeutigam, 2005. *Microeconomics*. 2nd ed. Hoboken, NJ: Wiley.

Blanchard, Olivier. 2005. *Macroeconomics*. 4th ed. Upper Saddle River, NJ: Prentice Hall.

Jehle, Geoffrey A., and Philip J. Reny. 2001. *Advanced Microeconomic Theory*. 2nd. ed. Boston: Addison-Wesley.

Varian, Hal R. 2006. *Intermediate Microeconomics: A Modern Approach*. 7th ed. New York: Norton.

Alberto Rigoni

EXCESS SUPPLY

In simple terms, *excess supply* means that there is a surplus of unsold goods in a market. Technically speaking, excess supply refers to a situation in which the quantity supplied of a good or service exceeds the quantity demanded for that good or service.

A graph may be helpful in understanding this concept. In the figure below, price (P) is plotted on the vertical axis and quantity (Q) is plotted on the horizontal axis. The curve labeled "supply" shows a positive relationship between the price and the quantity supplied. In other words, if the price goes up, firms are willing and able to produce more of the good. The curve labeled "demand" shows a negative or inverse relationship between price and the quantity demanded: If the price goes down, consumers are willing and able to buy more. The price labeled "P_e" equates the quantity supplied and the quantity demanded; there is no excess supply in this market. At the price labeled "P_f" the quantity supplied (Q_s) exceeds the

quantity demanded (Q_d), and thus there is a surplus or excess supply in amount $Q_s - Q_d$.

According to economic theory, if prices are sufficiently flexible, then excess supply should not persist in the long run. Faced with excess supply, firms will simply cut their prices in order to sell any unwanted inventory. However, government price controls can result in persistent excess supply. According to standard economic theory, a minimum wage may result in excess supply. If the minimum wage is set above the equilibrium wage (labeled "P_e" in the figure), the result is excess supply in the labor market or unemployment. If, however, the minimum wage is set below P_e, the minimum wage will have no effect on employment. To be effective, a minimum wage must be set above the equilibrium price.

Of course, governments can and do impose price controls in all sorts of markets. For example, governments often establish minimum prices for crops such as wheat, corn, and so on. To the extent that these price floors are effective, the result is excess supply, and governments find themselves storing large quantities of crops as a result. The European Union and the United States are often accused by developing countries of dumping the resulting surpluses on world markets, depressing the prices of such commodities and, as a result, lowering the incomes of farmers in developing countries.

Do minimum wages cause unemployment? In a seminal paper on the effect of the minimum wage, David Card and Alan B. Krueger (1994) use evidence from the fast-food industry and changes in the federal minimum wage in the United States to gauge the effect of the minimum wage on employment. In contrast to the predictions of the standard model that a minimum wage results in unemployment, they find no evidence that the minimum wages create unemployment. This paper has spawned a substantial literature attempting to replicate these results. Although the evidence is mixed, the general consensus appears to be that modest changes in the minimum wage do not appear to result in dramatic changes in employment, as perhaps economic theory may lead some to conclude.

SEE ALSO *Barro-Grossman Model; Excess Demand; Flexibility; Market Clearing; Minimum Wage; Price vs. Quantity Adjustment; Supply;* Tâtonnement

BIBLIOGRAPHY

Card, David, and Alan B. Krueger. 1994. Minimum Wages and Employment: A Case Study of the Fast-Food Industry in New Jersey and Pennsylvania. *The American Economic Review* 84 (4): 772–793.

Mark Rider

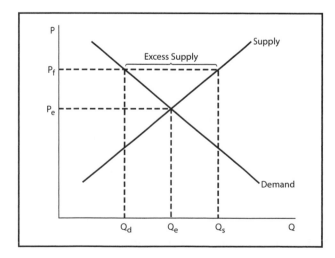

EXCHANGE, UNEQUAL

SEE *Unequal Exchange.*

EXCHANGE RATES

An *exchange rate* represents the price of a national currency valued as a foreign currency. The exchange rate plays a significant role in the economy. Because exchange rate fluctuations influence the whole economy, the exchange rate is a major economic factor for growth, stability, and economic development. In addition, the exchange rate directly influences the unemployment rate and the inflation level, and it is an indicator of external competitiveness (Madura 2003). The exchange rate also affects trade flows and investments, which in turn influence the balance of payments. Generally, the exchange rate is considered the most important price in the economy.

The exchange rate has direct practical importance to those engaged in foreign transactions, whether for trade or investment. It affects the price of imports when expressed in domestic currency, as well as the price of exports when converted into a foreign currency. The exchange rate therefore has a link to inflation. Consequently, the exchange rate is above all a monetary indicator and occupies a central position in monetary policy, where it may serve as a target or an instrument as well as simply an indicator.

The exchange rate system used by a country is called its *exchange rate regime.* Countries can choose which exchange rate regime to follow, depending on their goals. Countries may either fix or float their exchange rate, but there are a number of other exchange rate systems between these two extremes. There are four main types of exchange rate regimes: *freely floating, fixed, pegged* (also known as *adjustable peg, crawling peg, basket peg,* or *target zone* or *bands*), and *managed float.* Within these four systems there are modified or intermediate regimes, such as *currency board, dollarization,* and *monetary union* regimes. The following entry analyzes each type of exchange rate regime, highlighting advantages and disadvantages.

FREELY FLOATING EXCHANGE RATE

A freely (clean) floating (or flexible) exchange rate regime, where the monetary authorities refuse any intervention in the exchange rate market, is the simplest type of system. The rate is then freely determined by market forces and can fluctuate by any amount at any moment. More precisely, a *pure float* is an exchange rate that is determined in the market without any intervention. Flexible exchange rates are determined daily in the markets for foreign exchange by the forces of demand and supply, without restrictions imposed by governmental policy on the extent to which rates can change. Supporters of free floating argue that the foreign exchange market is a highly transparent and efficient market because market forces are left unimpeded. Monetary policy is set autonomously, as deemed appropriate in the domestic context, and the exchange rate is allowed to follow whatever path transpires, consistent with monetary policy.

The advantages of a freely floating exchange rate regime are: (1) markets efficiently allocate resources (including financial capital) since there are no capital flow restrictions; (2) changes in the nominal exchange rate carry the bulk of adjustments to foreign and domestic shocks; (3) there are no opportunities for speculators to profit at the expense of the country's central bank; (4) demand and supply for domestic currency will be balanced in the market; (5) there is no obligation on the part of the central bank to intervene; and (6) the requirement for a country to hold large reserves is eliminated. Moreover, the monetary authority sets monetary policy, but it has no exchange rate policy since the exchange rate is determined by market forces. Thus, the monetary base is determined and in the control of the monetary authority of the country in question. This implies another advantage, which is that no conflicts can arise between monetary policy and the exchange rate; thus, a crisis in the balance of payments cannot occur because market forces automatically rebalance financial flows and avert balance-of-payment crises. In the absence of balance-of-payment reasons for interfering in international trade and payments, and given the autonomy of domestic policy, another benefit of a freely floating exchange rate regime is the exploitation of the economies of international specialization and labor.

Following a freely floating exchange rate system also brings disadvantages. High nominal and real exchange rate volatility may distort resource allocation, as many resources will be devoted to hedging the exposure of exchange rate fluctuations. Furthermore, the future path of the exchange rate will be uncertain, which may create difficulties for businesses in planning and pricing, and the freedom to operate an independent domestic monetary policy may be abused when, for instance, the government, not being compelled to prevent exchange rate depreciation, may be tempted into inflationary budgetary and monetary policies. In addition, there is a chance of overshooting, which will result in the exchange rate settling at a level not warranted by the country's financial position, perhaps for a considerable period (Aziz and Caramazza 1998; Kenen 2000).

FIXED EXCHANGE RATE

In a fixed exchange rate regime, exchange rates are held constant or allowed to fluctuate within very narrow boundaries, perhaps 1 percent above or below the initial set of rates. When a country chooses to fix its exchange rate, local currency is assigned a par value in terms of gold, another currency, or a basket of currencies. When the exchange rate begins to move too much, the government intervenes with the devaluation or revaluation of its own currency against other currencies in order to maintain the exchange rate within the specified boundaries. In this case, the monetary authority has to defend the fixed parity: Such government intervention can be direct or indirect. Direct intervention requires a change in international reserves. Indirect intervention, in contrast, is affected by influencing the factors that determine exchange rates through increasing or decreasing interest rates or other economic indicators (income, inflation, etc.), a move that does not involve a change in reserves. There are two types of direct intervention. *Sterilized direct intervention* occurs when the central bank intervenes in the foreign exchange market while making adjustments to avoid a change in money supply; in other words, the central bank transacts simultaneously in foreign exchange markets and treasury securities markets. In *nonsterilized direct intervention*, the central bank changes the money supply by selling or buying foreign reserves in the foreign exchange markets.

Examples of fixed exchange regimes include the systems established by the Bretton Woods Agreement from 1944 to 1971 and the Euro zone between 1999 and 2002. Fixed but adjustable exchange rate regimes are similar, with the difference that they allow more fluctuation in the exchange rate. In such a regime, the exchange rate is fixed for extended periods or within very narrow margins, but adjustable if there is disequilibrium.

The advantages of a fixed exchange rate regime include: (1) the fixed exchange provides a stable basis for planning and pricing, and helps to increase investment and international trade; (2) it imposes discipline for monetary policy, restraining inflation; (3) it restrains competitive devaluation of the domestic currency, thus contributing to the stability of the world trade system; and (4) it reduces the risk of price fluctuations and lowers the risk premiums imposed on interest rates. The disadvantages of such a regime include the following: (1) governments cannot definitely determine if the chosen fixed exchange rate is optimal or sustainable; (2) a fixed exchange rate regime could be vulnerable to speculative attacks that may damage the monetary stability of the economy or the exchange rate reserves; (3) maintaining a fixed nominal exchange rate carries the risk of an excessive appreciation of the real exchange rate, which results in a loss of competitiveness and, ultimately, to a speculative run on an overvalued cur-

rency; (4) economies suffering from real shocks and having adopted a fixed exchange rate face the risk of a further deepening of the downturn; and (5) a fixed exchange rate regime requires the monetary authority to hold more foreign exchange reserves than other exchange rate regimes (Aziz and Caramazza 1998; Kenen 2000).

PEGGED EXCHANGE RATE

Countries operating under a pegged exchange rate regime "peg" their currency's value to a foreign currency or some unit of account (e.g., gold, the European currency unit, etc.). Hence, while bilateral parity is maintained, the home currency's value fluctuates against other currencies in line with the anchor country's currency (Madura 2003, p. 174). There are a variety of different types of pegged regimes defined by Jeffrey Frankel (1999) as intermediate arrangements or "soft pegs." These include the adjustable peg, crawling peg, basket peg, and target zone or bands. Under adjustable peg systems, the bands are narrow (up to ± 2.25%) and the target rate is adjusted less frequently and by large amounts. Under a crawling peg, the bands are wider and the peg is regularly reset, sometimes weekly, in a series of minidevaluations. Under a basket peg arrangement, the exchange rate is fixed to a weighted basket of currencies that usually reflects the country's major trade partners. The target zone or band involves setting wide prescribed margins (bands) within which the government intervenes to maintain the exchange rate. Under this type of regime, a country or a group of countries hold their currencies within a predetermined range, and government intervention occurs only when the exchange rate exceeds this range. In this system, market forces determine the exchange rate. If the exchange rate moves above or below the predetermined limits, the government will intervene to move the price of the currency back within the tolerable zone. If the range is sufficiently narrow, the target zone approaches a fixed rate; if it is sufficiently wide, it approaches a freely floating regime.

Some countries favor a pegged exchange rate because it enhances the credibility of the government's commitment to low inflation. There is a tradeoff between credibility and flexibility. Other advantages of a pegged exchange rate system are: (1) the country can mitigate pressures for domestic price fluctuations and indicate a signal of responsible monetary policy; (2) the country can reduce inflationary expectations and (3) stabilize the prices of imports and exports; (4) the government can devaluate its home currency in response to large shocks; and (5) inflation is limited because such an exchange rate regime limits the government's ability to issue money when there are no foreign exchange reserves. The disadvantages of a pegged exchange rate are: (1) when a nation links its monetary policy to some other nation, monetary policy and fluctuations in that other nation will create fluctuations in the home nation's monetary condition; (2) the country's central bank loses its monetary independence; (3) a peg system may lead to persistent misalignments if inflation is higher compared to the pegged country, causing a situation in which the home currency could be overvalued and uncompetitive; (4) in order for this policy to be credible, additional institutional measures are required; (5) pegged systems are often targets for speculative attacks; (6) such a regime is not sustainable in small countries with huge capital flows leading to a balance-of-payment crisis; and (7) a pegged system is unlikely to be sustainable when there is full capital mobility.

MANAGED FLOAT EXCHANGE RATE

In a managed float (or dirty float) exchange rate regime, the monetary authority influences the movements of the exchange rate through active intervention in the foreign market without specifying, or recommitting to, a preannounced path for the exchange rate. Although market conditions determine the exchange rate, this type of exchange rate regime also involves certain less-specified central bank interventions with various objectives. A managed float exchange rate regime belongs with the so-called intermediate methods because it stands between the extremes of perfectly flexible and fixed regimes. It resembles the freely floating exchange rate in the sense that exchange rates can fluctuate on a daily basis and official boundaries do not exist. The difference is that the government can intervene in order to prevent the currency rate from fluctuating too much in a certain direction. Under a managed float, the goal of intervention is to prevent sharp fluctuations in the short run, but intervention does not target any particular rate over the long run. Generally, the central bank intervenes only to smooth fluctuations. Some governments impose bands within which the exchange rate can fluctuate, which is one of the reasons for calling this approach "dirty."

Unlike the free float approach, the dirty float protects investors against rapid exchange rate fluctuations. It also provides a more stable investment environment, protects the country from the risk of large exchange rate movements, and mixes market-determined exchange rates with a non-rule-based stabilizing intervention by the central bank, which helps avoid potential crises. The dirty float approach has disadvantages in that the government may manipulate the exchange rate for the benefit of its own country at the expense of another currency merely because this exchange rate regime does not offer transparency. In addition, the dirty float system requires cooperation between exchange rate policy and monetary policy that may lead to conflict; the country's central bank often cannot determine whether a movement in the rate is short

term or long term, thus whether an intervention is warranted; there are no definite rules giving credibility to the monetary authorities to intervene; and such a system may not place constraints on monetary and fiscal policy, resulting in a clash with the exchange rate policy.

OTHER EXCHANGE RATE SYSTEMS

The *currency board* is a type of fixed regime, but it is more restrictive and also includes a requirement for minimum domestic reserves in foreign currency and a monetary institution that issues notes and coins fully backed by a foreign reserve currency and convertible into the reserve currency at a fixed exchange rate. This institution cannot act as a lender of last resort, does not regulate reserve requirements for commercial banks, only earns seignorage from interest on reserves, and does not engage in forward exchange operations (Hanke 1999, p. 341). The advantage of a currency board system is that it reduces the real exchange rate volatility. There are drawbacks, however, in the country's loss of an independent monetary policy, and such a system is often a target of speculative attacks and requires very high reserves of foreign currency (Bell 2001).

A country with a *dollarization* regime replaces its own currency with another foreign currency, usually the U.S. dollar. Such an approach may reduce exchange rate volatility, but it poses the drawback that the home monetary policy is dependent on a foreign country's policy. This approach amounts to a complete replacement of a local currency with a foreign one, which is a step beyond a currency board. Dollarization, a type of unified currency regime, is no guarantee for growth but can provide macroeconomic stability.

Monetary union or a *currency union* occurs when a group of countries use a common currency issued by a common central bank, as do the twelve European countries in the Euro zone. This type of system reduces real exchange rate volatility, but the member countries lose the stabilization tool of an independent monetary policy. Jeffrey Frankel and Andrew Rose (2002, p. 11), analyzing data for more than two hundred countries, determined that by belonging to a currency union a country triples its trade with other union members. Furthermore, the results suggest that for every percentage of increase in a country's trade relative to its gross domestic product, membership in a currency union raises income per capita by at least 0.33 percent.

In conclusion, different types of exchange rate regimes have various advantages and disadvantages. Governments must determine which system is the most appropriate for a particular country and for the specified time period. No one system exploits all the advantages without any disadvantages, and no system can be applicable for all countries, which have different goals and political structures in different periods (Frankel 1999).

SEE ALSO *Banking Industry; Currency; Currency Appreciation and Depreciation; Currency Devaluation and Revaluation; Dirty Float; Money; Mundell-Fleming Model; Policy, Monetary; Purchasing Power Parity; Trade*

BIBLIOGRAPHY

Aziz, Jahangir, and Francesco Caramazza. 1998. Fixed or Flexible? Getting the Exchange Rate Right in the 1990s. *IMF Economic Issues* 13: 1–18.

Bell, Stephanie. 2001. *Exchange Rate Regimes and Policy Choices: Why Do Nations Choose Currency Boards?* Unpublished manuscript. http://cas.umkc.edu/econ/Seminars/CBoardSeminar.doc.

Calvo, Guillermo, and Frederic S. Mishkin. 2003. The Mirage of Exchange Rate Regimes for Emerging Market Countries. *Journal of Economic Perspectives* 17 (4): 99–118.

Fischer, Stanley. 2001. Exchange Rate Regimes: Is the Bipolar View Correct? *Journal of Economic Perspectives* 15 (2): 3–24.

Frankel, Jeffrey. 1999. No Single Currency Regime is Right for All Countries or at All Times. NBER Working Paper No. 7338. New York: National Bureau of Economic Research.

Frankel, Jeffrey, and Andrew Rose. 2002. An Estimate of the Effect of Common Currencies on Trade and Income. *Quarterly Journal of Economics* 117 (2): 437–467.

Hanke, Steve H. 1999. Reflections on Exchange Rate Regimes. *Cato Journal* 18 (3): 335–344.

Kenen, Peter B. 2000. Fixed versus Floating Exchange Rates. *Cato Journal* 20 (1): 109–113.

Levy-Yeyati, Eduardo, and Federico Sturzenegger. 2001. Exchange Rate Regimes and Economic Performance. *IMF Staff Papers* 47: 62–98.

Madura, Jeff. 2003. *International Financial Management.* 7th ed. Mason, OH: Thomson/South-Western.

Aristidis Bitzenis
John Marangos

EXCHANGE VALUE

Exchange value refers to "the power of purchasing other goods which the possession of [an] object conveys" (Smith [1776] 1960, p. 32); in other words, it expresses the relative price of a good in terms of other goods. Although the concept of exchange value has always played an important role in economic thought, the analysis of how it is determined has been the subject of much controversy.

For Adam Smith, David Ricardo, and Karl Marx it was important to distinguish *exchange value* from *use value*. Use value was the utility or the value in the use of a commodity, and was seen as necessary but not sufficient

for a commodity to have exchange value. This is illustrated by the paradox of value, whereby things that had the greatest use value, such as air and water, had the lowest exchange value compared to (for example) diamonds, which had a low use value but high exchange value.

According to David Ricardo, commodities derive their exchange value from two sources. First, "from their scarcity," where commodities cannot be reproduced (e.g., rare paintings, coins, pictures, etc.). These commodities are, by their very nature, a very minor part of what is exchanged in any economy. Second, the majority of commodities are produced by "the exertion of human industry: and these commodities have their exchangeable value determined by the quantity of labour embodied in their production" (Ricardo [1817] 1951, p. 12). This labor theory of value, which was present in a more ambiguous form in Adam Smith's writings, played an important role in the works of both Ricardo and Karl Marx. The relationship between labor values and prices has been a source of much controversy.

In discussing these three economists, it is also important to distinguish between values that are determined in this way, that is, natural values or prices and market prices. Market prices may diverge from their natural values owing to "accidental" or "temporary deviations" (Ricardo [1817] 1951, p. 89). However, competition in the form of capital seeking the most profitable activity will ensure that the deviation is temporary and will establish a long-run tendency toward uniform profit rates through the economy. "The natural price, therefore, is, as it were, the central price, to which the prices of all commodities are continually gravitating" (Smith [1776] 1960, p. 65).

It is important to note that the factors that determine the natural price are different from the factors that bring market price toward natural prices. This is important because it means that the natural prices will not be influenced by the path taken by market prices as they adjust to their natural levels (Kriesler 2003).

For Marx, the essence of a commodity is that it is produced for its exchange value; in other words, it is produced specifically in order to be sold. It is the generalization of commodity production into all spheres of society that he saw as one of the important results of capitalism. According to Marx, exchange value reflects the underlying social relations and "is in reality only an outward form of the *social* relation between the ... producers themselves" (Sweezy 1968, p. 27, emphasis in original). So the market expression of exchange values reflected deeper social relations. This view should be compared with that of John Stuart Mill, for whom exchange value did not arise "from the nature of things," but was "created by social arrangements" (Mill [1848] 1994, p. 54).

From the 1870s a new version of economics, sometimes referred to as "neoclassical theory," came into favor, and has since become the dominant orthodoxy. The essence of this new theory was a subjective theory of value, where exchange value is determined by utility at the margin. In neoclassical economics, the distinction between use value and exchange value is abolished, as exchange value is now determined by use value at the margins, and the distinction between market and natural prices also disappears. In place of the latter is a distinction between short-run and long-run price determination, with both involving the determination of equilibrium values by the same forces—supply and demand. However, as the forces of supply and demand both determine the equilibrium position of prices in the short and long runs, and push the economy to those equilibria if it deviates, the problem of path determinacy arises. As a result, equilibrium exchange values cannot be determined, in neoclassical theory, independent of the adjustment path of the economy.

SEE ALSO *Economics, Classical; Economics, Neoclassical; Equilibrium in Economics; Labor Theory of Value; Marx, Karl; Prices; Ricardo, David; Scarcity; Smith, Adam; Utility Function; Value*

BIBLIOGRAPHY

Kriesler, Peter. 2003. The Traverse. In *The Elgar Companion to Post-Keynesian Economics*, ed. John Edward King, 355–359. Cheltenham, U.K.: Edward Elgar.

Marx, Karl. [1867] 1990. *Capital, Volume 1*. London: Penguin.

Mill, John Stuart. [1848] 1994. *Principles of Political Economy*, ed. Jonathan Riley. Oxford: Oxford University Press.

Ricardo, David. [1817] 1951. *On the Principles of Political Economy and Taxation*, ed. Piero Sraffa with the collaboration of M. H. Dobb. Cambridge, U.K.: Cambridge University Press.

Smith, Adam. [1776] 1960. *An Inquiry into the Nature and Causes of the Wealth of Nations*, Vol. 1, ed. Edwin Cannan. London: Methuen.

Sweezy, Paul. 1968. *The Theory of Capitalist Development*. New York: Monthly Review Press.

Peter Kriesler

EXCHANGE VALUE COMMODITY

SEE *Exchange Value.*

EXCHANGEABILITY

In constructing statistical models, social scientists are nearly universally required to incorporate residual terms to capture those aspects of a phenomenon that the model under analysis cannot explain. Linear models are a leading case, where a dependent variable y_i is assumed to be explained by a vector of observables x_i as well as an unobservable residual ϵ_i via the equation $y_i = x_i\beta + \epsilon_i$, $i = 1, ..., I$. Estimation and inference concerning the model parameters comprised by the vector β, in turn, requires a researcher to make assumptions about ϵ_i. Examples of assumptions include independence of the residuals across I, and homoskedasticity (constant variance) of the residuals. Such assumptions are employed because they allow one to construct precise inferential statements such as asymptotic distributions under a null hypothesis, but not because they correspond to any substantive social-scientific ideas.

From the social-scientific perspective, one way to think about what it means to specify a model is to place enough structure on the variable of interest, say y_i, so that, from the perspective of the modeler, the residuals are indistinguishable. In other words, a modeler should have no reason to believe that the probability description of ϵ_i differs from that of ϵ_j. If the modeler does believe that these residuals differ, then it would seem that the model needs to be reassessed to see whether these differences call into question the purpose of the model.

To understand the import of this claim, suppose that one is attempting to explain the differences in economic growth between Japan and the United States since World War II and is using a model that does not account for differences in the savings rates between the two countries. For the researcher using the model to find it interpretable as reflecting a causal relation, he presumably must believe that Japan's much higher average rate of saving versus the United States has no bearing on the residuals associated with the two countries. If he believes that this difference in savings rates induces a difference in the probability descriptions of the two residuals, then he needs to determine how the model may be interpreted in this light.

Exchangeability is a mathematical formalization of the idea that random variables are, from the perspective of their probability description, indistinguishable. A sequence of I random variables ϵ_i is exchangeable if $\mu(\epsilon_1, ..., \epsilon_I) = \mu(\epsilon_{\rho(1)}, ..., \epsilon_{\rho(I)})$, where $\rho()$ is an operator that permutes the I indices. Note that I may be infinite. The concept of exchangeability originated in the writings of the Italian probabilist Bruno DeFinetti (see DeFinetti 1972 for a wide-ranging statement of his views in English).

Infinite exchangeable sequences have the important property that they may be interpreted as independent and identically distributed (i.i.d.) sequences. This is known as DeFinetti's theorem. Formally, the theorem says that the probability measure describing any infinite exchangeable sequence can be written as a mixture of i.i.d. probability measures. Each sample path realization will obey one of the probability measures, so each sample path will behave as an i.i.d. sequence. DeFinetti's theorem thus provides a basis for the i.i.d. assumption: the interchangeability of errors. A proof of DeFinetti's theorem along with many related results may be found in Olav Kallenberg's work *Probabilistic Symmetries and Invariance Principles* (2005). DeFinetti's theorem does not apply to finite exchangeable sequences.

To be clear, exchangeability is not necessary for a statistical model to be interpretable as a behavioral structure. Heteroskedastic regression errors (regression errors of varying variance) violate exchangeability, but do not affect the interpretability of a regression per se. Rather, exchangeability represents a criterion by which a researcher can evaluate his modeling choices. If a researcher believes that the errors in his model are not exchangeable, then good empirical practice requires that he consider whether the violations invalidate the substantive claims for which the model will be used. This inevitably requires judgment, but judgments are part of any substantive empirical exercise. Draper et al. (1993) place judgments of exchangeability at the heart of empirical analysis and discuss how data may be used to assess these judgments. Brock and Durlauf (2001) place exchangeability judgments at the center of a general critique of empirical research on growth. This emphasis on judgment helps explain why exchangeability notions are more common in Bayesian contexts than in frequentist contexts; exchangeability captures the notion of what is meant by a researcher's subjective beliefs that a sequence is a random sample from a population (see Lindley and Novick 1981 for elaboration and links to DeFinetti's original thinking).

Exchangeability has recently been shown to have important uses in econometric theory. Donald Andrews (2005) developed a theory for asymptotic inference in cross-sections that addresses the long-standing problem of cross-sectional residual correlations. Unlike the time-series case, a cross-sectional index does not provide a natural ordering across random terms, so there is no reason to think that dependence across residuals diminishes as the difference between their respective indices grows. Andrews shows that if this dependence is generated by a set of common shocks so that, conditional on the shocks, the errors are independent, one can develop a range of asymptotic results. This independence is motivated in turn by exchangeability arguments. This mode of analysis suggests that exchangeability may play an increasingly prominent role in econometric theory.

SEE ALSO *Bayes' Theorem; Bayesian Econometrics; Probability Theory*

BIBLIOGRAPHY

Andrews, Donald. 2005. Cross-Section Regression with Common Shocks. *Econometrica* 73: 1551–1585.

Brock, William, and Steven Durlauf. 2001. Growth Empirics and Reality. *World Bank Economic Review* 15 (2): 229–272.

DeFinetti, Bruno. 1972. *Probability, Induction, and Statistics.* New York: Wiley.

Draper, David, James Hodges, Colin Mallows, and Daryl Pregibon. 1993. Exchangeability and Data Analysis (with Discussion). *Journal of the Royal Statistical Society*, series A, 156: 9–37.

Kallenberg, Olav. 2005. *Probabilistic Symmetries and Invariance Principles.* New York: Springer-Verlag.

Lindley, David, and Melvin Novick. 1981. The Role of Exchangeability in Inference. *Annals of Statistics* 9: 45–58.

William A. Brock
Steven N. Durlauf

EXCLUSION, SOCIAL

SEE *Social Exclusion.*

EXCLUSION ACTS

SEE *Immigrants, Asian.*

EXHILARATION

SEE *Stagnation.*

EXISTENTIALISM

"Existentialism" refers to a loosely knit movement holding, in the words of Jean-Paul Sartre, that "existence comes before essence." This proposition should be understood in opposition to both rationalism and empiricism. Both philosophies, existentialism argues, overlook the unique character of being human, of being an "existent" thrown into a world without pregiven meaning or significance. Moreover, the human condition is such that it does not fit into even the most exhaustive system of objective concepts. Instead, it calls for a new language of analysis that finds its expression in the works of not only Sartre but also Simone de Beauvoir, Albert Camus, Maurice Merleau-Ponty, Jean Wahl, Karl Jaspers, Martin Buber, Gabriel Marcel, Miguel de Unamuno, José Ortega y Gasset, Nicholai Berdyaev, and Lev Shestov.

These thinkers—some of whom rejected the label "existentialist"—found inspiration in the philosophies of a long list of forerunners. The most important ones are Søren Kierkegaard's anti-Hegelian philosophy and Martin Heidegger's phenomenological ontology. Common to both philosophies is the idea that being human is an "issue" for itself, that is, that the specter of death (finitude) makes it all-important how we interpret the primal nature of our own being—what Heidegger refers to as *Dasein*. The condition of *Dasein* is an ecstatic and angst-inducing one. To begin with, it discloses the historicity of our beliefs and habits, which in turn points to the openness of Being itself. But it also reveals the absence of a shared anchor—an infinite void or fundamental nothingness—challenging philosophy's pretense to know the nature of our moral obligations and political responsibilities. Kierkegaard enacts the fear that follows from this challenge through an analysis of cases such as Abraham's sacrifice of his son, a case in which God's commandment is comprehensible, not as a universal law pertaining to all, but as an injunction addressed to Abraham in his singularity.

The tension between the ecstatic and the fearful is important to the way in which existentialism approaches its main themes: intentionality, intersubjectivity, meaning, and human freedom. One line of research—associated with theologians such as Karl Barth and Paul Tillich—interprets these themes from a theistic perspective according to which the affirmation of God, although itself an act of madness, is the proper answer to the meaninglessness of contemporary existence. Another line—perhaps better known—entails a turn to atheistic humanism. Sartre dramatizes this turn in his 1944 play *Huis Clos* (No Exit). At issue in this play is the way in which individuals take responsibility for their own lives. The play revolves around three strangers who confront the singularity of their deaths in a room that has no significance, no signs of some higher Being. The result is not only a sense of absurdity—one that reveals the inauthenticity of everyday life (whether lived in a bourgeoisie manner or not)—but also a need for turning this absurdity into a cause for engaging one's own life head on. We must transcend the contingency of our surroundings in order to become authentic beings. As Inez, one of the three main characters in the play, says, "You are—your life, and nothing else."

Although significant, it is important not to overstate the differences between the atheistic and theistic brands of existentialism. Both brands criticize the church's appropriation of God; and both brands emphasize living an authentic existence through an encounter with a transcendent of some sort. The political implications that impinge on existentialism's analysis of the human condition, then, are first and foremost related to the concepts of freedom and free will. Humans are free in the sense that (1) neither God nor any value or command binds their choices, (2) their concept of selfhood hinges on the intentional activity directed toward things in the world, and (3) reality proper is what follows from this kind of activity. While this may give the impression that existentialism is committed to an individualistic ideology, it is important not to mistake the affirmation of freedom (and free will) for a lack of interest in criticizing the liberal state. Because humans are free, and because they constitute reality through their own undertakings, they must also take active responsibility for society as a whole. The existentialist movement translates this responsibility into an often Marxist-inspired critique of male domination, technology, and capitalism.

SEE ALSO *Empiricism; Epistemology; Essentialism; Freedom; Phenomenology; Philosophy; Sartre, Jean-Paul; Supreme Being*

BIBLIOGRAPHY

Cooper, David E. 1990. *Existentialism: A Reconstruction.* Oxford: Blackwell.

Heidegger, Martin. 1927. *Being and Time.* Trans. John Macquarrie and Edward Robinson. Oxford: Blackwell, 1962.

Kierkegaard, Søren. 1843. *Fear and Trembling: Repetition.* Trans. Howard V. Hong and Edna H. Hong. Princeton, NJ: Princeton University Press, 1983.

Sartre, Jean-Paul. 1944. *No Exit.* In *No Exit, and Three Other Plays.* Trans. Stuart Gilbert. New York: Vintage, 1989.

Sartre, Jean-Paul. 1945. Existentialism and Humanism. Trans. Philip Mairet. In *Jean-Paul Sartre: Basic Writings,* ed. Stephen Priest. London and New York: Routledge, 2001.

Lars Tønder

EXIT, VOICE, AND LOYALTY

To extend the analysis of his fellow economists beyond their traditional focus on simple market exchanges, Albert O. Hirschman wrote *Exit, Voice, and Loyalty* (1970), a seminal work that examines how several different kinds of human behavior might be invoked when consumers confront a decline in firms, organizations, and states.

EVL MODEL

In Hirschman's exit, voice, and loyalty (EVL) model, consumers dissatisfied with a product in the marketplace, for example, might complain to the producer about declining quality (voice) or patiently wait for the product to improve (loyalty) instead of purchasing a rival good or service (exit). In politics, voters dissatisfied with their party's policies may vote for another (exit), work in party caucuses to change those policies (voice), or hope that the party platform will be revised (loyalty). And in an abusive interpersonal situation, one can leave (exit), complain (voice), or avoid confrontation in the hope that the storm will pass (loyalty). Indeed, Hirschman's analysis of the interrelations among various behaviors an individual might engage in when confronting declining quality in one's personal, political, economic, and social relationships was significant to all of the social sciences precisely because of its comprehensiveness.

If very different types of behaviors can effectively substitute for each other, one cannot study each independently without missing something vital. Voice behaviors like consumer complaints or writing letters to the city council, for example, cannot be understood without accounting for opportunities to exit through purchasing a substitute product or moving to another city. Hirschman further demonstrated that opportunities to exercise one type of behavior often influence—in sometimes very surprising ways—the effectiveness of other behaviors. The threat of exit, for example, may encourage declining firms, organizations, and states to be more or less attentive to voice depending on who is exiting, when the exiting occurs, and how it bears on the interests of those making decisions about their goods, services, or policies.

WEAKNESSES

Despite its sweeping and immediately recognized import, Hirschman's analysis is nonetheless incomplete. First, the EVL model does not give equal attention to the three types of behaviors; loyalty only makes an appearance two-thirds of the way through the analysis. In addition, loyalty is discussed almost exclusively as a brake on the exercise of exit and voice rather than as an independent mode of response to dissatisfaction. Second, exit, voice, and loyalty fail to encompass all of the possible behaviors that one might observe when consumers, voters, or family members confront a decline in the quality of their relationships. They may well do nothing. Indeed, Hirschman discussed how consumers might neither exit nor engage in voice behaviors when institutions do not provide producers with incentives to respond to consumer demand. However, he essentially treated such situations as pathologies rather than incorporating them into the model in a systematic manner, recognizing thereby that not responding to decline is potentially as interesting as exit, voice, or loyalty. Third, Hirschman did not develop a general model that communicated how consumers, voters, employees, or family members select among exit, voice, or loyalty behaviors.

CONTEMPORARY SCHOLARSHIP

In the early 1980s scholars addressed these weaknesses in extensions of Hirschman's EVL model. First, in their 1983

analysis, Caryl Rusbult and I. M. Zembrodt recast Hirschman's threefold typology as a two-dimensional space. The first distinguishes active and passive responses to dissatisfaction while the second distinguishes constructive and destructive responses. Thus, voice includes all active responses to dissatisfaction that are constructive with respect to the relationship giving rise to that dissatisfaction. In contrast, exit behaviors, while also active, are destructive to the relationship. Loyalty behaviors are passive, constructive responses to dissatisfaction. A fourth type of response not addressed by Hirschman except as pathological behavior is neglect; that is, passively responding to dissatisfaction by allowing the relationship to further deteriorate. In another significant extension of Hirschman's analysis, in 1981 Daniel Farrell and Rusbult developed a parsimonious, three-variable model explaining how individuals select among the responses to dissatisfaction. When one has many alternatives to a current job, a product or service, or a romantic partner, one is more likely to respond to dissatisfaction in an active manner through voice or exit rather than through the passive behaviors associated with loyalty or neglect. But when one is highly invested in and/or has had a high level of prior satisfaction with the relationship, one will more likely respond to dissatisfaction with constructive voice or loyalty behaviors and suppress negative behaviors characteristic of exit and neglect responses.

A number of social scientists continue to employ Hirschman's original threefold typology. By the mid-1980s, however, many others were employing its descendent, the exit, voice, loyalty, and neglect (EVLN) model. This extension of the original highlighted two dimensions defining four distinct responses to dissatisfaction, including the previously neglected category of neglect. Selection among the four responses was further hypothesized to be function of alternatives, prior satisfaction, and investments. The EVLN model was strongly supported in empirical work on private and public sector employment behaviors, romantic relationships, and political behavior in metropolitan settings. All of these studies examine a wide range of responses to dissatisfaction within a common theoretical framework linking what had been previously understood as disparate and distinct behaviors.

There have been fewer applications of either the original version of Hirschman's model or its EVLN extension in studies of traditional market economics, which was the main focus of *Exit, Voice, and Loyalty*. To some extent, this reflects some long recognized normative biases in the disciplines. In the same way that some political scientists might regard exiting a political jurisdiction as illegitimate to the point of constituting treason, some economists view voice, loyalty, or neglect as a failure on the part of consumers to exercise due diligence or as evidence of imprudence. But perhaps a more telling explanation, and one applicable to all social sciences, is that simultaneously accounting for exit, voice, loyalty, and neglect behaviors is very hard to do.

SEE ALSO *Economics; Political Science; Sociology*

BIBLIOGRAPHY

Farrell, Daniel, and Caryl E. Rusbult. 1981. Exchange Variables as Predictors of Job Satisfaction, Job Commitment, and Turnover: The Impact of Rewards, Costs, Alternatives, and Investments. *Organizational Behavior and Human Performance* 27: 78–95.

Hirschman, Albert O. 1970. *Exit, Voice, and Loyalty.* Cambridge, MA: Harvard University Press.

Lyons, William E., and David Lowery. 1989. Citizen Responses to Dissatisfaction in Urban Communities: A Partial Test of a General Model. *Journal of Politics* 51: 842–868.

Rusbult, Caryl E., and David Lowery. 1985. When Bureaucrats Get the Blues: Responses to Dissatisfaction among Federal Employees. *Journal of Applied Social Psychology* 15: 80–103.

Rusbult, Caryl E., and I. M. Zembrodt. 1983. Responses to Dissatisfaction in Romantic Involvements: A Multidimensional Scaling Analysis. *Journal of Experimental Social Psychology* 19: 274–293.

Rusbult, Caryl E., Daniel Farrell, G. Rogers, and A. G. Mainous III. 1988. Impact of Exchange Variables on Exit, Voice, Loyalty, and Neglect: An Integrative Model of Responses to Declining Job Satisfaction. *Academy of Management Journal* 31: 599–627.

Rusbult, Caryl E., Dennis J. Johnson, and G. D. Morrow. 1986. Determinants and Consequences of Exit, Voice, Loyalty, and Neglect: Responses to Dissatisfaction in Adult Romantic Involvements. *Human Relations* 39: 45–63.

Withy, Michael, and William H. Cooper. 1989. Predicting Exit, Voice, Loyalty, and Neglect. *Administrative Science Quarterly* 34: 521–539.

David Lowery

EXIT POLL

Exit polls are surveys based upon voter interviews immediately after they have finished voting. The exit polls play a significant part in media projecting election winners and their margin of victory. The polls are used mainly in major elections, usually concerning national or state candidates. Exit polls are part of the pervasive status of surveys and polls in American and other societies. Exit polls have been used in elections throughout the world, such as in 2005 in the Belarus and Ukraine and 2006 in Mexico. Media organizations purposely utilize exit polls to understand voters' choices and explain issue, partisan, and demographic differences in electoral outcomes. This information serves as a means of validating elections.

Exit polls are highly accurate because they remove main elements of potential survey research error problems by accounting for who actually votes and avoiding undecided voters. Problems for exit polls include a sample estimate of voter turnout, which may be incorrect for one or more candidates. Further, these polls do not consider absentee voting and other forms of early voting that do not require individuals to be at a polling place.

HOW CONDUCTED

An exit poll is conducted by selecting sample precincts in a state or other electoral area based upon historical voting data to judge outcomes of voting data. In each of the selected precincts, an interviewer requests a voluntary interview from a systematically selected voter; for example, every third or every tenth voter. Each voter completes a thirty- to forty-item questionnaire, which is placed in a box.

In each election cycle new questions are developed. The information is collected, tabulated, and transmitted to a central facility that tabulates a state or other electoral area total. In the 2004 U.S. presidential election nearly 150,000 people in nearly 1,500 precincts were interviewed in every state except Oregon. In 2004 the National Election Pool (NEP) also conducted a national sample of polling places to supplement exit poll data.

Prior to the 1990 U.S. midterm elections, each major network—ABC, CBS, NBC, CNN, and the Associated Press—conducted separate exit polls. For financial reasons, they created a consortium (also joined by Fox News) to conduct a single national exit poll, called News Election Service, and later called Voter News Service. After problems encountered with the 2000 presidential election, the 2004 presidential election exit poll was conducted through NEP by Edison Media Research/Mitofsky International. Exit polling results are delivered in three different times during election day, including mid-afternoon on that day. Multiple national exit polls can have different results based upon different sampling frames and different polling places. In other nations, major media organizations sponsor similar survey organizations to conduct exit polls. Media networks use exit poll data and actual vote returns from some exit poll sample precincts to project electoral victors. To project the outcome, exit poll findings must exceed the margin of sampling error in the sample design, generally plus or minus 4 percent at a 95 percent confidence level for state polls, and plus or minus 3 percent at the same confidence level for the national exit poll. Data within the sample design parameters is "too close to call."

PROBLEMS WITH U.S. PRESIDENTIAL ELECTIONS

High profile exit polls in U.S. presidential elections have encountered difficulties in analysis and reporting of information, especially in the 1980, 2000, and 2004 elections.

In 1980 television networks correctly predicted Ronald Reagan's victory over President Jimmy Carter prior to many election polls remaining open in the midwestern, mountain, and western states. Individuals argued that this projection diminished those individual's willingness to vote. In 1985 Congressional hearings—U.S. House Task Force on Elections—were held and resulted in network executives voluntarily promising to not release exit poll or election projections for a state prior to its poll closing time.

In 2000 the winner of Florida's twenty-five electoral votes would obtain the majority of national electoral votes and be the victor. On several occasions networks changed their exit poll projection for this state. First, they projected Democratic vice president Al Gore, then retracted their projection as actual vote return data arrived. At approximately 2:00 a.m. Eastern Standard Time (EST) they projected Florida for Republican George Bush, and about an hour later retracted it. Bush won Florida by 527 votes after a U.S. Supreme Court decision. The Florida vote was "too close to call" through exit polls, and individuals incorrectly reported their vote based upon the "butterfly ballot" or other difficulties, such as hanging chads.

In the 2004 Presidential election, there was confusion and controversy concerning reliance upon exit polls. As late as 9:15 p.m. EST, NEP indicated that Senator John Kerry was leading President Bush, 51 percent to 48 percent. The final outcome was President Bush 51 percent and Kerry 48 percent. It has not been clearly determined why the exit polls overstated the Kerry vote in several states.

SEE ALSO *Elections; Polling; Survey; Voting*

BIBLIOGRAPHY

Lavrakas, Paul J., and Michael W. Traugott. 2000. *Election Polls, The News Media and Democracy*. Washington DC: Congressional Quarterly Press.

Levy, Mark R. 1983. The Methodology and Performance of Election Day Polls. *Public Opinion Quarterly* 47 (1): 54–67.

Steven Puro

EXOGENOUS AND ENDOGENOUS VARIABLES

SEE *Variables, Predetermined.*

EXOTICISM

The term *exoticism* describes a cultural phenomenon that projects Western fantasies about profound cultural differences. It adopts a cultural perspective that is firmly entrenched in the conventions and belief systems of Western civilization and therefore constructs the East as the archetypical location of otherness.

Exoticism demonstrates itself in colorful spectacles of otherness purporting to be an unmediated expression of natural drives and instincts. Although exoticism is associated with notions of animality, it carefully distances itself from the violence and exploitation that characterize the related concept of barbarism.

Notions of the exotic are associated with the lush vegetation of the tropics, geographically positioned between the Tropics of Capricorn and Cancer. They conjure up ideas of a bountiful nature, fertility, and uninhibited sexuality. An abundance of colors, sounds, smells, and tactile experiences promise to gratify the senses within an economy that gives free rein to consumption, unrestrained by political responsibility and ethical commitment to the real actors of exotic fantasies: that is, it disregards the role of disadvantaged people, coming mainly from third-world nations, who make a meager living from appearing in the dramatized fantasies staged in tropical holiday resorts and nightclubs.

The exotic first emerged as a concept in Western history when European nations began to explore and appropriate far-flung parts of the world. It experienced its first boom during the age of Enlightenment, when the establishment of trade routes began to supply Europe with such vast quantities of exotic goods that the purchase of luxury goods, including china, silk, perfumes, and precious stones, became affordable by the increasingly wealthy middle classes. This period also engendered a taste for the rich costumes of the Orient, the main geographic location of Enlightenment fantasies about the exotic. The fashionable Lady Mary Wortley Montagu, for example, had her portrait painted in a Turkish costume; the dissemination of stereotypes about the supposedly effeminate Orientals allowed her to appropriate the male garment of the turban without this being viewed as an act of cross-dressing.

The attempt by the age of Enlightenment to study and describe the vast number of different peoples of this earth was thus soon reduced to a mere interest in costume and other extrinsic markers of otherness, which were eagerly displayed in the European homelands. The demand of the nineteenth century for information about non-European peoples gave rise to numerous cheap reproductions of ethnographic drawings. Such easily affordable, popular publications, in their turn, further reduced cultural otherness to a matter of costume, which, among other things, suggested that supposedly primitive natives of, for example, Australia could be forced to abjure their traditional identity merely by donning the clothes of a European gentleman. The fact that nineteenth-century photographs of indigenous people wearing the clothes of their colonial masters now strike us as more exotic than early photographs of nonwesternized, indigenous communities reminds us that exotic fantasies entail a contrast of, and hierarchy between, two different cultures, controlled by the Western point of view.

For the twenty-first century, the experience of the exotic frequently thrives on an imitation of a ritual presumed to be authentic, involving an act of mimicry whose comic potential is easily glazed over. Performances of corroborees and other cultural practices can therefore be staged for tourists while the traditional rituals are on the brink of extinction.

The exotic also notably unleashes the sexual desires of repressed Westerners. Prostitution and the exploitation of countless women, children, and some men are side effects of exoticism's tendency toward aesthetic abstraction and voyeuristic commodification of its participating actors.

Spaces set aside for expatriate consumption in international four- and five-star hotel chains (such as the Safari Bar in the Hyatt in Muscat, Oman) promise a sanitized encounter with a non-European subject that guarantees the absence of emotional involvement. Westerners, along with a westernized global elite, interact with one another against the background of scenery that refrains from challenging their privileges and supposed superiority.

Exoticism, as a cultural phenomenon, has mainly been examined via related critical concepts. Of special importance is Edward Said's description of Orientalism as a discursive construction of European fantasies. Said's study of Europe's most enduring exotic fantasies about the Middle East set the beginning for other postcolonial interrogations of romanticized projections of the cultural other by which the West continues to assert its superiority. Homi Bhabha and subsequent scholars of hybridity and the encounters between subaltern and dominant cultures, therefore, make every effort to draw attention to exoticism's parodic dimension in order to empower and render eloquent its latent subversion of oppressive and exploitative fantasies.

SEE ALSO *Cannibalism; Enlightenment; Gaze, Colonial; Gaze, The; Orientalism; Other, The; Prostitution; Sexuality; Stare, The; Stereotypes; Tourism; Travel and Travel Writing; White Supremacy*

BIBLIOGRAPHY

Bhabha, Homi. 2004 (1994). *The Location of Culture.* London and New York: Routledge.

Guha, Ranajit, ed. 1997. *A Subaltern Studies Reader: 1986–1995.* Minneapolis: University of Minnesota Press.

Huggan, Graham. 2001. *The Postcolonial Exotic: Marketing the Margins.* London: Routledge.

Kabbani, Rana. 1986. *Europe's Myths of Orient: Devise and Rule.* London: Macmillan.

Kiernan, Victor Gordon. 1972. *The Lords of Humankind: European Attitudes to the Outside World in the Imperial Age.* Harmondsworth, U.K.: Penguin.

Rousseau, George, and Roy Porter. 1990. *Exoticism in the Enlightenment.* Manchester, U.K.: Manchester University Press.

Said, Edward. 1978. *Orientalism: Western Conceptions of the Orient.* London: Routledge and Kegan Paul.

Young, Robert J. 1995. *Colonial Desire: Hybridity in Theory, Culture, and Race.* London and New York: Routledge.

Christa Knellwolf

EXPECTATIONS

Economics is concerned in large part with expectations. Consumers planning to smooth their spending over a lifetime form expectations about future income, prices, interest, and other factors in their decision-making processes. Producers spreading investment expenditures over future time periods form expectations of future costs and returns. Government policy makers aiming to stabilize the economy use monetary and fiscal policies to achieve their expected targets. In the global economy, gains from free trade occur because traders expect a country to produce at the lowest opportunity cost. Economists try to measure expectation, to analyze their effects on the economy, and to study how they are formed.

In a competitive economy, expectations are realized at the equilibrium state. A Keynesian view of expectation equilibrium is that planned savings should equal planned investments. One reason that expectations may not be correct in a competitive economy is that prices and output vary, creating problems for producers who incur costs now and are uncertain about future prices. One can analyze uncertain outcomes in order to assign a probability or likelihood to their occurrences. If uncertainty is too risky, one may choose to be risk averse, as in the case of oligopolistic firms that are unable to guess their rival's conduct. To understand and coordinate expectation, one can collect anticipation data on business plans, ask people about their expectation and attitude, or survey experts to learn about their consensus.

One forms expectations with the aid of logic, psychology, and probability. Cognitive psychologists, for instance, found that agents make future decisions based on the similarity of present evidence, playing down probabilities and even the quality of the evidence. An expected outcome may follow from conscious behavior or habits, which may be self-fulfilling, nonmaterial, and altruistic.

Agents may be content with little achievements, not necessarily looking for maximum outcomes.

An individual may be certain of his or her expectations. Certainty means one assigns a high probability or likelihood to the occurrence of the event. Besides high and low probability events, one finds some uncertain events to which one cannot possibly attach a probability. One distinguishes between measurable and unmeasurable uncertainty, assigning the term *risk* when uncertainty can be measured.

A workhorse in expectation analysis is the expected utility hypothesis (EUH). The EUH is a function that captures all of an individual's expectations about an outcome, assigns a numeric value for one's choices among alternatives, and allows one to maximize the expected outcome. But its results can be paradoxical. The St. Petersburg paradox, a "let's make a deal" situation, offers the player a fixed amount of money (say $20), or an uncertain outcome that pays one dollar if heads turn up when a fair coin is tossed N times. The outcome is 2^n, each with a probability of one half, so that the expected value of the game is infinite, the limit of $\sum_{n=1}^{\infty} (1/2^n)(2^n)$. The paradox is that no one is willing to pay a large sum to play the game. The probabilist Daniel Bernoulli (1700–1782) thought that the problem was that as a person wins more and more money in the game, one experiences diminishing returns for money. To capture diminishing utility, Bernoulli used a log utility function on the outcome, showing that the payoff becomes a small sum: $\sum_{n=1}^{\infty} (1/2^n)(\log 2^n) = \log 4$. The solution was not definitive in the sense that one can choose a utility sequence that would still yield an infinite payoff. What is needed is a bounded utility function.

From a microeconomic perspective, the economist Milton Friedman presented a lucid explanation of the utility concept that has telescoped further development. With a stream of income, I_i, and associated probabilities, P_i, the expected value is the sum of their products. Utility enters when one forms a function of income, $F(I)$, whose products with their respective probabilities give a special function, $G = \sum_{i=1}^{\infty} P_i F(I_i)$. In the special instance where income is expected with certainty, $P_i = 1$, both the G and F functions have the same value or utility. A plot of $F(I)$, against, income, I, highlights a concave or convex utility function, indicating risk aversion, and risk lover (plunger), respectively. A risk averse person prefers the expected value over the EUH outcome. A risk lover prefers the EUH to the expected value. If one eliminates scale and origin from the utility function by the restrictions $I = 0$, $F(I) = 0$, and $I = 1$, $F(I) = 1$ $F(I)I = 0$, then one can determine utility values for any amount of income. Without such restrictions, however, the utility function can take on a recurrent concave shape, explain-

ing why someone will not pay a large sum to play the St. Petersburg game.

From the macroeconomic perspective, one starts with the English economist John Maynard Keynes' equation where national income, $\varphi(N)$, equal to investment demand, D_2, plus consumption $\chi(N)$, could be solved for full employment, N. Given the state of employment, consumers, investors, and employers expect to consume, invest, and earn a prospective amount, respectively, which fluctuates with the state of long-term expectation. Keynes' concept of long-term expectation can be clothed in modern notations. Long-term expectation takes the form of a random variable, y, within a time frame of three months to a year, t, in a mass psychology "atmosphere", ω_{it}, given state of the news, Ω_{it}. Investors, i, calculate the average expectation, E, such as in a beauty contest where competitors must pick out the prettiest face among photographs that are published in a newspaper. In this competition, the average is an intersubjective representation, which may be expressed as $y_{it} = \lambda_i E(y_{it}|\Omega_{it}) + \omega_{it}$, and the competitor whose choice comes nearest to this average will win the competition.

Keynes' work created several research programs in expectations. John Hicks used a day-to-day model for up to a week to develop his elasticity of expectation hypothesis. Following Hicks in dating commodities, the Arrow-Debreu model of competitive equilibrium found current and expected prices that jointly clear supply and demand equations in present and future markets, and Jean-Michael Grandmonth formulated an intertemporal model, that extended the Arrow-Debreu model for sequences of time periods. On the other hand, G. L. S. Shackle steered expectation analysis away from a probability base. One makes several nonprobabilistic statements about the next period output, x, such as that it is impossible, possible, surprising if it would reach a specified high or low level, or very surprised it occurs. One can attach a corresponding number, y, to represent the degree of potential surprise those outcomes mean. One can further place a corresponding value on the surprise value when it reaches a maximum potential surprise, $\bar{y}$. The result is a function $y = f(x)$ that is bowl shaped, and centered at a neutral output level where $x = 0$. Further, one can assign numbers to the degree of surprise numbers to measure the degree of stimuli, $A(x, y(x))$, from the surprise function associated with the potential outcome.

Since the 1950s, economists have been using an adaptive expectation model to show how expectation is formed over time. The adaptive version follows the dictum that an individual learns from his or her mistakes. A rifleman calibrates his weapon by observing how far off his previous shot deviated from the target.

In macroeconomic forecasts, the adaptive model was employed to study the effect of expected prices and unemployment on present wages and inflation rates. In the Phillips Curve, the coefficient of the expected price variable was zero. A coefficient of the expected price variable equal to one would mean that expectations are fully adjusted into inflation and wage rates. For instance, if the expected rate of inflation, $\hat{\pi}$, is set by some proportion, γ, between the actual inflation, π, and the expected inflation, then one can use the equation: $\hat{\pi} - \hat{\pi}_{-1} = \gamma(\pi_{-1} - \hat{\pi}_{-1})$ $0 < \gamma < 1$ to represent the formation of expectations. Full adjustment means $\gamma = 1$, but empirically it was mostly less than unity, implying that the Phillips Curve was downward sloping.

The adaptive expectation model was integrated into the MPS model of the Federal Reserve Board, one of the first large-scale econometric models that were built in the 1960s. Expectation was captured in the form of lag structure both to parameters and error terms. The model, however, failed to capture drifts in the parameters of structural equations. The Rational Expectation Hypothesis (REH) has explained some of those problems and added other novelties to the formation and measurement of expectations.

The concept of REH is based on equilibrium analysis as opposed to Keynesian disequilibrium analysis. Under ideal conditions of competition, one expects economic agents to have perfect information or knowledge of the relevant market variables. Absent complete information, one settles for all the information that is available before making a forecast.

Robert Lucas is credited with making the REH practical. One incorporates information into REH models by replacing the expected variable with an equation or variable that measures the expectation. For instance, Thomas J. Sargent and Neil Wallace wrote equations for Aggregate Supply, IS, LM, and monetary policy. Some of the equations require that the expected price level prevailing at time t be set at time $t - 1$. In other words, one replaces the expression of the form $E(p_{it}|\Omega_{it})$ with values resulting from applying the mathematical expectation operator, E, on them, conditioned by the information one has at the time $t - 1$.

Faith in the RE hypothesis is still being determined. Edmund Phelps advocated dropping the equilibrium framework, for a more non-Walrasian framework in which economic agents are not price takers, which yields results more in line with Paul A. Samuelson's views that oppose the REH. Large-scale econometric models for the REH are still not within reach. To improve predictions, Finn Kydland and Edward Prescott have used time-consistent computational experiments in econometric models, subsequent to the REH revolution. These models allow policy makers such as the Federal Reserve Board, to have no concern about wrong models or wrong goals, or even histories and reputation, because they need only choose sequentially.

SEE ALSO *Adaptive Expectations; Beauty Contest Metaphor; Expectations, Implicit; Expectations, Rational; Expectations, Static; Expected Utility Theory; Friedman, Milton; Game Theory; Keynes, John Maynard; Lucas, Robert E., Jr.; Macroeconomics; Phillips Curve; Risk; Sargent, Thomas; Uncertainty; Utility, Von Neumann-Morgenstern*

BIBLIOGRAPHY

Bernoulli, Daniel. [1738] 1954. Exposition of a New Theory on the Measurement of Risk. Trans. L. Sommers. *Econometrica* 22: 23–36.

Borel, Emile. 1962. *Probabilities and Life.* Trans. Maurice Baudin. New York: Dover Publications.

Fisher, Irving. 1930. *The Theory of Interest.* New York: Macmillan.

Fisher, R. A. 1957. The Underworld of Probability. *Sankya* 18: 201–210.

Fisher, R. A. 1973. Uncertain Inference. In *Collected Papers of R. A. Fisher*, Vol. 3, ed. J. H. Bennett, 451–464. Adelaide: University of Adelaide.

Friedman, Milton. 1976. *Price Theory.* Chicago: Aldine Publishing.

Grandmonth, Jean-Michael. 1983. *Money and Value.* London: Cambridge University Press.

Hicks, John R. 1946. *Value and Capital.* Oxford: Clarendon Press.

Hicks, John R. 1984. *The Economics of John Hicks,* ed. Dieter Helm. Oxford: Basil Blackwell.

Katona, George. 1972. Theory of Expectations. In *Human Behavior in Economic Affairs*, eds. Burkhard Strumpel, James N. Morgan, and Ernest Zahan, 549–581. Amsterdam: Elsevier.

Keynes, John M. 1921. *A Treatise on Probability.* London: Macmillan.

Keynes, John M. 1937. The General Theory of Employment. *The Quarterly Journal of Economics* 51 (2): 209–223.

Knight, Frank H. 1971. *Risk, Uncertainty and Profit.* Chicago: University of Chicago Press.

Kydland, Finn E., and Edward C. Prescott. 1977. Rules Rather Than Discretion: The Inconsistency of Optimal Plans. *Journal of Political Economy* 85: 473–491.

Kydland, Finn E., and Edward C. Prescott. 1996. The Computational Experiment: An Econometric Tool. *The Journal of Economic Perspectives* 10 (1): 69–85.

Laffont, Jean-Jacques. 1989. *The Economics of Uncertainty and Information.* Trans. John P. Bonin and Helene Bonin. Cambridge, MA: MIT Press.

Lucas, Robert E., Jr. 1972. Econometric Testing of the Natural Rate Hypothesis. In *The Econometrics of Price Determination*

Conference, ed. Otto Eckstein. Washington, DC: BOG of the Federal Reserve System and SSRC.

Lucas, Robert E., Jr. 1972. Expectations and the Neutrality of Money. *Journal of Economic Theory* (4): 103–124.

Lucas, Robert E., Jr. 1975. Econometric Policy Evaluation: A Critique. In *The Phillips Curve and Labor Markets*, eds. Karl Brunner and Allan Meltzer. New York: Elsevier, 1976.

Lucas, Robert E., Jr., and Thomas J. Sargent. 1994. After Keynesian Macroeconomics. In *The Rational Expectation Revolution*, ed. Preston J. Miller, 5–30. Cambridge, MA: MIT Press.

Muth, John. 1961. Rational Expectation and the Theory of Price Movements. *Econometrica* (July): 315–335.

Papademos, Lucas, and Franco Modigliani. 1990. The Supply of Money and the Control of Nominal Income. In *Handbook of Monetary Economics*, Vol. 1, eds. B. M. Friedman and F. H. Hahn, 399–494. Amsterdam: North-Holland.

Pesaran, M. Hashem. 1987. *The Limits to Rational Expectation*. Oxford: Basil Blackwell, Inc.

Phelps, Edmund S. 2006. Prospective Shifts, Speculative Swings. In *Samuelsonian Economics and the Twenty-First Century*, eds. Michael Szenberg, Lall Ramrattan, and Aron A. Gottesman, 66–87. New York: Oxford University Press.

Popper, Karl. 1959. *The Logic of Scientific Discovery*. New York: Harper and Row Publishers.

Samuelson, Paul A., 1986. *The Collected Scientific Papers of Paul A. Samuelson*. Vol. 5. Ed. Kate Crowley. Cambridge, MA: MIT Press.

Sargent, Thomas J. 2002. Commentary: The Evolution of Economic Understanding and Postwar Stabilization Policy. In *Rethinking Stabilization Policy: A Symposium Sponsored by The Federal Reserve Bank of Kansas City*, 79–94. Kansas City, MO: Federal Reserve Bank of Kansas City.

Savage, Leonard J. 1972. *The Foundation of Statistics*. New York: Dover Publications.

Shackle, G. L. S. 1952. *Expectation in Economics*. Cambridge, U.K.: Cambridge University Press.

Shackle, G. L. S. 1961. *Decision Order and Time in Human Affairs*. Cambridge, U.K.: Cambridge University Press.

Shackle, G. L. S. 1970. *Expectation, Enterprise and Profit*. London: George Allen and Unwin Ltd.

Shackle, G. L. S. 1974. *Keynesian Kaleidics*. Chicago: Aldine Publishing Company.

Simon, Herbert A. 1976. From Substantive to Procedural Rationality. In *Method and Appraisal in Economics*, ed. Spiro Latsis, 129–148. Cambridge, U.K.: Cambridge University Press.

Tversky, A., and D. Kahnemann. 1974. Judgment under Uncertainty: Heuristics and Biases. *Science* 185: 1124–1132.

Young, Warren, and William Darity Jr. 2001. The Early History of Rational and Implicity Expectations. *History of Political Economy* 33 (4): 773–813.

Lall Ramrattan
Michael Szenberg

EXPECTATIONS, ADAPTIVE

SEE *Natural Rate of Unemployment.*

EXPECTATIONS, IMPLICIT

The concept of implicit expectations, which was pioneered in 1954–1955 by Edwin S. Mills, circumvents a problem encountered by economists who study the behavior of business enterprises: Although production and pricing decisions are made on the basis of expectations about future economic conditions, economic researchers must cope with a shortage of observations on actual sales anticipations. One research strategy is to work with explicit assumptions about the way expectations are formed. Thus, in 1953 Robert Ferber concluded on the basis of his examination of empirical evidence in the Railroad Shippers' Forecasts that expected sales are equal to actual sales of the same period of the preceding year adjusted for recent trend. In contrast, Mills did not attempt to model the process by which expectations are generated. His implicit expectations approach substitutes the actual realized sales—what sales turn out to be—for the unobserved expected sales under the assumption that the forecast error is random. That is to say,

$$E_t - X_t = \varepsilon_t,$$

where E_t is expected sales, X_t is what sales actually turn out to be, and ε_t is a random error with zero expected value (it averages out to zero). Mills used his implicit expectations concept in a number of theoretical and empirical articles, including a 1957 study in which he was able to estimate the magnitude of undesired inventories generated by sales forecast errors made by American corporations.

Mills's implicit expectations approach is closely related to John F. Muth's (1961) concept of rational expectations that Robert Lucas invoked in 1972 in spearheading a revolution in the field of macroeconomics. Muth, like Mills, assumed that forecast errors are random. This is an example of independent discovery, as often is encountered in scientific research (Merton 1973), but a rather subtle difference may distinguish the two concepts. Expectations are implicit if the random forecast error ε_t is distributed independently of E_t but rational if they are distributed independently of X_t. If a firm's sales anticipations are based on a random survey of customers about their expected demand, the error in forecasting total sales that results from sampling error will be distributed independently of what sales actually turn out to be; this means that the sample survey has generated an implicit forecast of sales. If instead a forecast is generated with data from prior years with a multiple regression of actual sales on observable variables, such as the unemployment rate, price, and sales in prior periods, the forecast will be rational because the errors of a correctly formulated regression forecast, as a mathematical necessity, are distributed independently of the prediction. Implicit forecasts can be converted into rational forecasts with the equation obtained from historical data by regressing the realization on the forecast.

In a paper published in 1985 Muth reported that his empirical investigations indicated that expectations are not rational: The forecast errors were correlated with the forecasts, and the variance of the forecasts was often larger than the variance of the variable that was being predicted. However, Muth found that the errors also were correlated with the actual realizations; that meant that they were not implicit expectations. He advanced as a synthesis an "errors in the variables" model that allowed the forecast error to be correlated with both the variable being forecast and the actual outcome but cautioned that this model was not fully in accord with the facts. Although Muth became skeptical about his own theory, it provides the foundation for macroeconomic studies of inflation and business cycle fluctuations.

SEE ALSO *Adaptive Expectations; Expectations; Expectations, Rational; Expectations, Static; Mills, Edwin; Rationality*

BIBLIOGRAPHY

Ferber, Robert. 1953. *The Railroad Shippers' Forecasts.* Urbana: University of Illinois Press.

Lucas, Robert. 1972. Expectations and the Neutrality of Money. *Journal of Economic Theory* 4 (2): 103–124.

Merton, Robert K. 1973. *The Sociology of Science: Theoretical and Empirical Investigations.* Chicago: University of Chicago Press.

Mills, Edwin S. 1954–1955. Expectations, Uncertainty and Inventory Fluctuations. *Review of Economic Studies* 22 (1): 15–22.

Mills, Edwin S. 1957. Expectations and Undesired Inventory. *Management Science* 4 (1): 105–109.

Mills, Edwin S. 1962. *Price Output and Inventory Policy: A Study of the Economics of the Firm and Industry.* New York: Wiley.

Muth, John F. 1961. Rational Expectations and the Theory of Price Movements. *Econometrica* 29 (3): 315–335.

Muth, John F. 1985. Properties of Some Short-run Business Forecasts. *Eastern Economic Journal* 11 (3): 200–210.

Young, Warren, and William A. Darity Jr. 2001. The Early History of Rational and Implicit Expectations. *History of Political Economy* 33 (4): 773–813.

Young, Warren, Robert Leeson, and William A. Darity Jr. 2004. *Economics, Economists, and Expectations: Microfoundations to Macroapplications.* London and New York: Routledge.

Michael C. Lovell

EXPECTATIONS, RATIONAL

A basic postulate of economics is that people "do the best with what they have" (Maddock and Carter 1982). Applied to the formation of expectations (or economic beliefs), the theory of rational expectations, first proposed by John Muth in 1961, assumes that agents acquire and process information rationally. Since the 1970s, this theory has been used to model phenomena as diverse as aggregate supply, exchange rates, consumption, and economic cycles. A number of important empirical predictions—about exchange rates (Frankel and Rose 1995) and the term structure of interest rates (Mankiw and Miron 1986), for example—employ rational expectations as a key assumption.

RATIONAL EXPECTATIONS: DEFINITIONS AND DEFENSES

Definitionally, a rational expectation is the best guess about an unknown variable, using all available information. Where the unknown variable is random (such as the exchange rate in k periods time represented in equations by (y_{t+k}) the rational expectation is the mean of the variable (i.e., the mathematical expectation $E(y_{t+k})$ equal to the integral of all possible values of y_{t+k}, weighted by their probabilities). The rational expectation is calculated using information up to the current period t, and so it is sometimes written as $E_t(y_{t+k})$ ($k > 0$). Obtaining the mathematical expectation within a model context requires knowing the full structure of the model. If information is costly to collect, then rational expectations cannot strictly be rational, as was recognized soon after rational expectations was proposed. In other words, assuming a positive marginal cost to information and a decreasing marginal benefit, the information collected will fall short of the information required to understand the full system.

The economics literature either ignores this problem for simplicity, or it acknowledges that expectations are formed on the basis of sample information. In the latter case, the rational expectation can be defined as an estimator of an unknown variable with desirable statistical properties, such as minimum forecast error (in the case of a random variable) or unbiasedness and efficiency (in the case of an unknown parameter). Alternatively, mirroring the use of estimators in classical inference, changes in beliefs about unknown parameters can be modeled by statistical hypothesis testing (Menzies and Zizzo 2005).

It is assumed that people do not make systematic errors when predicting the future, so the rational expectation of a random variable is the mean represented by $E_t(y_{t+k})$. In other words, departures from perfect foresight (that is, from $E_t(y_{t+k}) = y_{t+k}$) are a random process with a zero mean. Mathematically, rational expectations are modeled by making the outcome y_{t+k} equal to the rational expectation, plus a random error u_{t+k} representing ignorance, mistakes, and other influence only revealed in k periods time: $y_{t+k} = E_t(y_{t+k}) + u_{t+k}$.

As an example of rational expectations at work, if all agents hold rational expectations, if transactions costs are small, and if agents are unconcerned about risk, then the so-called efficient market hypothesis holds. If a security's price does not reflect all the information available about it, then someone can buy (or sell) the security to make a profit, thus driving the price toward the rational expectation. If all profit opportunities are eliminated, prices in financial markets fully reflect fundamentals (e.g., future interest rates, profits, or dividends).

Rational expectations have a number of advantages as a modeling tool. First, they are conceptually simple. Second, they prevent economic theorists from introducing ad hoc influences via arbitrary expectations mechanisms. Third, they create simple model solutions. Fourth, there is a close correspondence between the properties of random errors arising from the rational expectations (u above) and the random errors assumed in empirical work.

There are many ways of defending the notion that agents have rational expectations, based on *rationality* (rational agents should use all the available information in the most efficient way), *macro-aggregation* (rational expectations allow for mistakes, as long as they are not systematic mistakes), and *evolutionary dynamics* arguments (agents without rational expectations would be driven out of the market by more rational agents, who would be able to bankrupt them on the basis of their superior use of information). Even if these arguments are not accepted, however, mainstream economists could also claim that the parsimony and tractability of rational expectations justifies their use. While this is unlikely on its own to be sufficient to accept rational expectations as scientifically valid, it may be more palatable if one can claim that a lack of realism is an acceptable price when parsimony and tractability are matched by significant predictive power. The argument has also been made that it would not be safe to make policy on the basis of the assumption that policymakers have superior knowledge about how the economy works, and that macroeconomic models should therefore employ rational expectations (Sorensen and Whitta-Jacobsen 2005).

ARGUMENTS AGAINST RATIONAL EXPECTATIONS

There are a number of contrary views on rational expectations, however. First, rational expectations are rational only if collecting and processing information is costless in money and time, let alone cognitive effort. If agents are only boundedly rational, information collection and processing costs will be larger and will induce shortcuts in the use of information. Second, the theory of rational expectations assumes that agents not only hold a model of the economy, but that this model of the economy is correct. This is in stark contrast with the fact that disagreement exists within the economics profession on how the economy works. Further multiple models are normally used in practical policymaking. Interesting variations of rational expectations build on the assumption that agents do not know exactly how the economy works, so that they need to make hypotheses on models (or parameters of models) of how the economy works (Goldberg and Frydman 1996; Menzies and Zizzo 2005).

Third, there has been no general proof of the evolutionary dynamics argument. Indeed, there are models showing how less-than-rational agents may survive when mixed up with rational agents (e.g., noise trader models in finance; Shleifer 2000). Fourth, the usefulness argument is virtually unfalsifiable. This is because tests of rational expectations are also joint tests of the models they are embedded in, and because of the difficulty in identifying rational expectations relative to alternatives in regression analysis. Therefore, failures of rational expectations can be, and often are, blamed on other hypotheses (see, for example, Gerlach and Smets 1997 in relation to the term structure of interest rates), though the problem may ultimately lie in the model of expectation formation.

Fifth, in experimental settings, rational expectations predictions are not rejected as null hypotheses in some contexts, but the most common outcome is that individuals do not hold rational expectations. In addition, experimental research often finds either underutilization or overutilization of prior beliefs (Camerer 1995). These systematic empirical failures cannot be reconciled with the macro-aggregation argument.

Finally, if conservativeness in policymaking is considered desirable in the face of an uncertain economy, then it should be modeled explicitly (e.g., in the objective function), rather than by postulating an incorrect model of expectation formation. Doing otherwise may be counterproductive, and it may make it more difficult to provide an accurate account of the economy. Notwithstanding these points, however, the notion of rational expectations remains the mainstream conceptualization of expectations formation in economic modeling.

SEE ALSO *Efficient Market Hypothesis; Least Squares Regression*

BIBLIOGRAPHY

Camerer, Colin. 1995. Individual Decision Making. In *The Handbook of Experimental Economics*, eds. John H. Kagel and

Alvin E. Roth, 587–703. Princeton, NJ: Princeton University Press.

Evans, George, and Sepo Honkapohja. 2001. *Learning and Expectations in Macroeconomics*. Princeton, NJ: Princeton University Press.

Frankel, Jeffrey A., and Andrew K. Rose. 1995. Empirical Research on Nominal Exchange Rates. In *The Handbook of International Economics*, eds. Gene Grossman and Kenneth Rogoff, 1689–1729. Amsterdam: Elsevier.

Gerlach, Stefan, and Frank Smets. 1997. The Term Structure of Euro-Rates: Some Evidence in Support of the Expectations Hypothesis. *Journal of International Money and Finance* 16 (2): 305–321.

Goldberg, Michael D., and Roman Frydman. 1996. Imperfect Knowledge and Behavior in the Foreign Exchange Market. *Economic Journal* 106 (437): 869–893.

Maddock, Rodney, and Michael Carter. 1982. A Child's Guide to Rational Expectations. *Journal of Economic Literature* 20 (1): 39–51.

Mankiw, N. Gregory, and Jeffrey A. Miron. 1986. The Changing Behaviour of the Term Structure of Interest Rates. *Quarterly Journal of Economics* 101 (2): 211–228.

Menzies, Gordon D., and Daniel J. Zizzo. 2005. *Inferential Expectations*. Working Paper no. 12. Canberra: Australian National University, Centre for Applied Macroeconomics.

Muth, John F. 1961. Rational Expectations and the Theory of Price Movements. *Econometrica* 29 (3): 315–335.

Shleifer, Andrei. 2000. *Inefficient Markets: An Introduction to Behavioral Finance*. Oxford: Oxford University Press.

Sorensen, Peter Birch, and Hans Jorgen Whitta-Jacobsen. 2005. *Introducing Advanced Macroeconomics: Growth and Business Cycles*. London: McGraw-Hill.

Gordon Douglas Menzies
Daniel John Zizzo

EXPECTATIONS, STATIC

In economics, the concept of static expectations describes an assumption that economists make about the way people form their predictions regarding the future values of economic variables. Specifically, the static expectations assumption states that people expect the value of an economic variable next period to be equal to the current value of this variable.

The concept of static expectations has been widely used in the early economics literature, such as in the cobweb model of price determinations. In the cobweb model, the static expectations assumption states that sellers expect the price of a good next period to be the same as it is today and adjust their production accordingly. The early literature did not focus much on unexpected shocks.

The concept of static expectations and its more advanced variation, the concept of adaptive expectations, play an important role in the monetary economics, the branch of economics that addresses the design and the impact of monetary policy. This concept was formalized in 1968 simultaneously by Milton Friedman (1912–2006) in his article "The Role of Monetary Policy" and by Edmund Phelps (b. 1933) in his article "Money-Wage Dynamics and Labor Market Equilibrium." Because only unexpected inflation, or inflation rate in excess of the expected inflation rate, can increase the aggregate output of the economy, it is important for policymakers to know what inflation rate economic agents expect in the future. For economists this means that they have to make an assumption about how economic agents form their predictions of future inflation.

The most simple-minded assumption about expectations one can make is that of static, or naïve, expectations: Agents are assumed to expect the inflation rate next year to be the same as it was this year. Adaptive expectations assumption merely extrapolates the concept of static expectations—it suggests that economic agents expect the inflation rate to be equal to the weighted average of the inflation rate in the past few periods. Economists used the assumptions of static and adaptive expectations until the concept of rational expectations was developed.

The main criticism of the concept of static expectations is that it assumes that people ignore the information about possible shifts in policy variables. In case of monetary policy, if policymakers announce credibly that they will adopt an anti-inflationary stance, it would not be rational for economic agents to believe that the inflation rate will remain the same. Thus, rational expectations assumption incorporates all possible information available at the time the expectations are formulated, not just the past values of the variable being forecasted, as is the case with static or with adaptive expectations.

In modern economic theory most models that incorporate uncertainty about the future assume rational expectations, not static expectations. Nevertheless, some economic variables and many financial variables follow a specific stochastic process, called *martingale*, for which the best prediction of the future value is today's value. For these variables static expectations turn out to be rational expectations.

SEE ALSO *Expectations; Expectations, Implicit*

BIBLIOGRAPHY

Friedman, Milton. 1968. The Role of Monetary Policy. *American Economic Review* 58 (1): 1–17.

Phelps, Edmund. 1968. Money-Wage Dynamics and Labor Market Equilibrium. *Journal of Political Economy* 76 (4): 678–711.

Galina Hale

EXPECTATIONS, TEACHER

SEE *Teacher Expectations.*

EXPECTED UTILITY THEORY

Expected utility theory is a model that represents preference over risky objects, by weighted average of utility assigned to each possible outcome, where the weights are the probability of each outcome.

The primary motivation for introducing expected utility, instead of taking the expected value of outcomes, is to explain attitudes toward risk. Consider for example a lottery, which gives $100 and $0 with even chances, and a sure receipt of $50. Here typically one chooses the sure receipt, whereas the two alternatives yield the same expected return. Another example is the Saint Petersburg paradox. Consider a game of flipping a fair coin until one has a tail. When the number of flips obtained is k, one receives 2^k, which happens with probability $(1/2)^k$. The expected return of this game is $\sum_{k=1}^{\infty} 2^k (1/2)^k = \sum_{k=1}^{\infty} 1$, which is infinity. However, a typical decision maker is willing to pay only a finite amount for playing this game.

The theory resolves this problem by taking risk attitude into account. Here a risky object is a probability distribution over outcomes, denoted by p. Then the expected utility representation takes the form $U(p) = \sum u(x_k) p_k$, where p_k is the probability that outcome x_k is realized, and function u expresses the utility assigned to each outcome. Notice that $u(x)$ may not be x as it is, and the curvature of u explains the decision maker's risk attitude. When the graph of u is convex to the top, one has the formula $0.5u(100) + 0.5u(0) < u(50)$, which explains the first example (similarly for the second). When this is the case, the decision maker is said to be risk averse. Expected utility theory enables empirical analysis of choice under uncertainty such as financial decision, by quantifying the degree of curvature of u.

The theory originates from Daniel Bernoulli (1700–1782), an eighteenth-century mathematician, and was given an axiomatic foundation by John von Neumann and Oskar Morgenstern in the 1940s. They started from a preference ranking of probability distributions over outcomes, and provided the condition for its expected utility representability. The condition consists of three axioms: weak order, continuity, and independence. The most prominent axiom is independence: when the decision maker prefers distribution p to distribution q, then he or she prefers the distribution made by mixing p and any

another distribution r with proportion $\lambda: 1 - \lambda$, that is $\lambda p + (1 - \lambda)r$, to the distribution made by mixing q and r with the same proportion, that is $\lambda q + (1 - \lambda)r$. Here $\lambda p + (1 - \lambda)r$ refers to the distribution that assigns probability $\lambda p_k + (1 - \lambda)r_k$ on each outcome x_k respectively. Informally speaking, when p is preferred to q then having "p with probability λ and r with probability $1 - \lambda$" will be preferred to having "q with probability λ and r with probability $1 - \lambda$," since the difference lies only in p and q.

The theory is extended to subjective expected utility theory, where the probabilities are not given objectively, but the decision maker is to hold a subjective belief over relevant events.

Various criticisms to the expected utility theory motivate further developments, two of which are explained in this entry. The first criticism is that the independence axiom may be violated systematically, which is referred to as the Allais paradox. Consider for example a bet, which gives $120.00 with probability 0.9 and $0 with 0.1, and a sure receipt of $100.00. The typical choice here is to take the sure receipt. Now consider two bets, one gives $120.00 with probability 0.45 and $0 with 0.55, the other gives $100.00 with probability 0.5 and $0 with 0.5. Here the typical choice is to take the first bet. This violates independence since the second two bets are made by mixing the first two with the lottery that gives $0 for sure, with even proportion. One explanation of this is called certainty effect, that an outcome is overweighed when it is sure than when uncertain.

The second criticism is that risk attitudes may depend on status quo points, whereas the theory assumes that only the distributions over final outcomes matter. Suppose for example that the decision maker is given $1,000 initially and faces two alternatives, one gives $200 more and $0 (no change) with even chances, the other gives $100 more for sure. The typical choice here is to take the sure gain, which exhibits risk aversion. On the other hand, suppose one is given $1,200 initially and faces two alternatives, one yields a $200 loss and $0 with even chances, the other yields a $100 loss for sure. Now the typical choice is to take the risk, which exhibits risk loving, while the distributions over final outcomes are identical across the two comparisons.

These anomalies, together with other ones, motivate various models of nonexpected utility.

SEE ALSO *Expected Utility, Subjective*

BIBLIOGRAPHY

Machina, Mark. 1987. Choice under Uncertainty: Problems Solved and Unsolved. *Journal of Economic Perspectives* 1 (1): 121–154.

Takashi Hayashi

EXPERIMENT, SOCIAL

SEE *Social Experiment.*

EXPERIMENTAL ECONOMICS

SEE *Economics, Experimental.*

EXPERIMENTS

At the most basic level, social science is the process of developing and testing scientific explanations for various aspects of behavior and experience. Of the possible types of explanations, causal explanations are generally preferred in science because they specify *why* some phenomenon occurs rather than simply indicating *that* or *when* it occurred. This focus on causation allows scientists to predict and, in some cases, control phenomena. Other types of explanations, although important, are far less adept in this regard. A preference for causal explanations has led researchers to develop special procedures for testing putative cause-and-effect relationships, collectively known as *experimental methodology.*

RATIONALE AND STRUCTURE OF EXPERIMENTAL METHODOLOGY

Experimental methodology affords an inference of causality through a collection of specific procedures. First, the researcher creates two or more groups of research participants that are equivalent at the outset of the study. Second, the researcher introduces different levels (e.g., doses, versions, intensities) of an independent variable to each group of participants. An *independent variable* is the entity, experience, or situation, for example, that the researcher proposes as the "cause" in a cause-and-effect relationship. It is referred to as "independent" because the experimenter has independent control over the specific group of participants that gets one level or another, and as a "variable" because it has more than one level (e.g., more than one dose, version, intensity, etc.). After introducing a different level of the independent variable to each group of participants, the researcher then measures or records at least one *dependent variable*—that is, the behavior, experience, or event that the researcher proposes as the "effect" in a cause-and-effect relationship. It is referred to as "dependent" because its outcome depends upon the effects of the independent variable and as a "variable" because it has more than one value.

The logic of this arrangement and the ability to infer a causal relationship from an experiment are straightfor-

ward. If the groups of research participants were equivalent at the beginning of the study and the level of the independent variable was the only thing that differed systematically among the groups, then any difference found on the dependent variable must be attributed to the causal influence of the independent variable on the dependent variable. Beyond the logic of experimental methodology, a number of issues may arise when constructing experiments that complicate matters considerably.

Creating Equivalent Groups An important aspect of conducting an experiment is creating groups of participants that are equivalent prior to the introduction of the independent variable. There are two general strategies for accomplishing this equivalence—random assignment and blocking. *Random assignment* refers to the placement of each participant into one group or another on the basis of chance alone. This can be done by flipping a coin, consulting a random number table, or by using some other randomization technique to determine the specific group to which a participant is assigned. Random assignment has been called the "great equalizer" because any differences among participants prior to the introduction of the independent variable tend to be distributed equally across experimental groups.

The second strategy for creating equivalent groups is *blocking*, which refers to the practice of creating equivalent groups of participants by controlling for participants' characteristics that could potentially have a systematic effect on the dependent variable. Such control can be accomplished in a number of ways, but the two most common strategies are matching and statistical elimination. With *matching*, the researcher assesses participant characteristics that may influence the dependent variable, purposely creates pairs of participants that share those characteristics, and then assigns one member of the pair to one group and the other member to another group. With *statistical elimination*, the researcher measures participant characteristics that may influence the dependent variable, and uses statistical techniques to mathematically remove the effects of those characteristics from the dependent variable. Of the two techniques, matching is better suited to research designs with only two groups, whereas statistical elimination can be used in research designs with two or more groups.

Operational Definitions The independent and dependent variables are hypothetical constructs that carry with them conceptual definitions that researchers use to communicate information about the variables to other researchers. In order to conduct an experiment, however, the hypothetical construct must be made "real" by developing a strategy that will allow the independent variable to be manipulated and the dependent variable to be measured or recorded within the experimental context. The process of making hypothetical constructs real is called *operationalization*. To operationalize a hypothetical construct, a researcher must select or create a concrete, real-world manifestation of the construct and define it with enough precision so that other researchers can identify it within the context of the experiment and, should they so choose, use the same operationalizations in other research projects.

A researcher can select from a number of options in order to operationalize the independent variable. Among these options are manipulations of participants' *physiological states* (influencing the natural biological states of participants), *environmental context* (altering the situation or context in which participants are engaged), and *blocking* (dividing participants into groups or categories on the basis of certain characteristics such as age, gender, income, education level, etc.). Blocking is not a manipulation in the strict sense of the term, but naturally occurring differences among individuals can be used as a quasi-independent variable. Although many options for operationalizing independent variables are available, some may be more appropriate than others to the phenomenon at issue, and the final choice of operational definition is typically determined by the phenomenon in question, resources available to the researcher, and ethical considerations.

The researcher also has many options from which to choose when operationalizing the dependent variable. The research may measure the presence, frequency/intensity, or latency/duration of participants' thoughts, beliefs, attitudes, behaviors, or behavioral intentions. Again, although many operational definitions are available, the final choice is typically determined by the phenomenon in question, resources available to the researcher, and ethical considerations.

Replication The operational definitions used in an experiment are important not only for communicating how variables are manipulated and measured in the context of a study, but also for the purpose of replication. *Replication* refers to the ability of other researchers to repeat a study and produce results similar to those found in the original. There are two types of replication—direct and conceptual. *Direct replication* occurs when a researcher repeats an existing study exactly as it was conducted originally. *Conceptual replication* occurs when a researcher repeats an existing study using different operationalizations of the same independent and/or dependent variables, or other modifications of the original procedures. Both forms of replication are important, but conceptual replication provides stronger support for a hypothetical cause-and-effect relationship among variables because consistent results across many conceptual replications reduces the likelihood that the results are simply a consequence of a single operational definition.

Research Design The strategy used to create equivalent groups and the ability of the researcher to manipulate an independent variable restricts the type of research design that can be employed. Specifically, experimental methodology can be divided into two categories, true experiments and quasi experiments. *True experiments* are characterized by (1) random assignment and (2) manipulation of the independent variable. In contrast, *quasi experiments* possess only one of these characteristics, which in most cases is manipulation of the independent variable. Three distinct true experimental designs and at least ten quasi-experimental designs have been identified. These basic designs can be combined or modified to produce a large number of possible research designs that can be used to test a broad range of cause-and-effect explanations.

Research Setting In addition to design issues, researchers must also select a research setting. There are two settings for research—laboratory and field. A *laboratory setting* refers to research conducted in a dedicated scientific laboratory; a *field setting* refers to any location other than the laboratory. Field settings are typically less controlled than laboratory settings, but they make up for this deficit by affording researchers an opportunity to study phenomena in a context that is similar to, if not the same as, the environments in which the phenomena occur naturally.

Realism and Impact Another consideration when designing and conducting an experiment is realism. *Realism* is the extent to which an experiment stimulates or reflects various aspects of the phenomenon under investigation. There are two types of realism—mundane and experimental. *Mundane realism* is the extent to which a phenomenon is studied in an environment similar to the one in which it occurs naturally. In contrast, *experimental realism* is the extent to which real psychological processes occur within the context of the study, regardless of the artificiality of the experimental setting or procedures. As a general rule, researchers tend to maximize experimental realism even if doing so minimizes mundane realism, because the presence of extraneous variables that may accompany mundane realism reduces the capacity of researchers to derive a causal inference from the study. Although the distinction between mundane and experimental realism does map onto the distinction between laboratory and field settings, these issues are distinct and should be treated as such.

Related to the issue of realism is impact. *Impact* refers to the intensity of the process or phenomenon elicited in a study. High-impact studies typically involve situations designed to maximize the experience or expression of the phenomenon. Low-impact studies, which are sometimes called *judgment studies*, typically involve assessing or recording simulations of a process or phenomenon in an "as if" manner. Low-impact studies are typically less desirable than high-impact studies because participants asked to simulate a process may respond in a manner that is unrepresentative of how they would respond if the process or phenomenon in question were actually occurring. The choice of impact level is often determined by the phenomenon under investigation, resources available to the researcher, and ethical considerations.

Validity Of major concern to scientists is the validity of different research designs. In this connection, *validity* refers to the extent to which a design is free of confounds (i.e., flaws) that serve as alternative explanations for the proposed causal effects of the independent variable on the dependent variable. Confounds can be divided into two types—threats to internal validity and threats to external validity. *Internal validity* refers to the absence of alternative explanations for the causal relationship between the independent and dependent variables. *External validity* refers to the extent to which the results of an experiment can be generalized to other operationalizations of the independent or dependent variable, other populations, or other settings. Both types of validity are important, but researchers tend to focus on internal validity because a study with low internal validity is not interpretable. When research results are not interpretable, the generalizability of the results is irrelevant.

Eight threats to internal validity and four threats to external validity have been identified. The eight threats to internal validity are:

history (changes on the dependent variable due to events other than the independent variable),

maturation (changes on the dependent variable due to time-dependent changes in characteristics of the participants during a study),

testing (changes on the dependent variable due to the effects of measuring the dependent variable at an earlier point in time),

instrumentation (changes on the dependent variable due to changes in the calibration or accuracy of measurement instruments),

statistical regression (changes on the dependent variable due to the assignment of participants to different groups based on extreme characteristics or abilities),

selection (changes on the dependent variable due to differential selection of participants for possessing certain characteristics or abilities),

mortality (changes on the dependent variable due to differential loss of participants from different groups in a study), and

interactions between two or more threats to internal validity.

The four threats to external validity are: (1) interaction of testing and the independent variable (pretesting can alter participants' sensitivity or responsiveness to the independent variable, which can render responses from pretested participants unrepresentative of non-pretested participants); (2) interaction of selection and the independent variable (participants selected for a study because they possess certain characteristics may respond to different levels of the independent variable in a manner that is unrepresentative of participants who do not possess those characteristics); (3) reactive arrangement (the arrangement of the experimental context may produce effects that do not generalize to nonexperimental situations, particularly when participants' responses have been altered during a study because they know they are being observed); and (4) multiple-treatment interference (multiple levels of the independent variable applied to the same participant may produce interference among the different levels and produce effects that would not occur if each level were used independently).

ETHICS IN EXPERIMENTAL METHODS

Following a series of unethical studies in the first half of the twentieth century, the scientific community along with the Nuremberg war tribunal developed a code of ethics for scientific research. Succinctly, this code requires that research participants freely consent to participate, be fully informed of the purpose and potential risks associated with participation, and be afforded the right to discontinue participation for any reason at any time. Similarly, the researcher must strive to minimize risks to participants, protect them from harm insofar as possible, and be fully qualified to conduct the research with honesty and integrity. This code and other more stringent ethical principles developed by individual branches of social science are enforced by Internal Review Boards (IRBs). IRBs are institutional panels of experts and community volunteers that review the potential risks to participants of studies proposed by researchers. IRBs carefully examine the procedure and materials that are to be used in a study to ensure that the researcher is doing everything possible to protect participants from undue harm. Consequently, the goal of IRBs is to balance the benefits of acquiring scientific knowledge with protecting the rights of research participants.

One point of concern for IRBs is *informed consent*, which typically entails a document that outlines the rights of research participants as well as the potential risks and benefits associated with the study for which they have volunteered. It is necessary for participants to freely consent and fully understand these benefits and risks in order for a study to meet the ethical requirements set forth by the scientific community. However, informed consent is somewhat problematic in research that involves some form of deception. In such cases, it may be unclear whether enough information has been supplied at the outset for participants to fully understand the risks of participation. Similarly, informed consent is problematic when working with vulnerable populations such as young children or individuals with poor mental health who cannot understand or communicate informed consent, prisoners who may feel compelled to participate in research, individuals who do not speak the language in which the informed consent document is written, and people with poor physical health. Also, research on nonhuman animals poses problems with consent and raises additional ethical responsibilities. In such research, it is important to provide humane and ethical treatment, and to take steps to minimize discomfort, illness, stress, and privation.

The culmination of a study, and the resolution of a researcher's ethical obligations, is the *debriefing*—the full disclosure to participants by the researcher of the purpose and procedures of a study, including any deceptive elements. In addition to disclosure, another purpose of a debriefing is to assess and rectify any adverse effects that may have occurred during the study. Adverse effects include stress, pain, threats to self-esteem or identity, and the like. It is the researcher's responsibility to provide affected participants with appropriate remedies or treatment options, or to otherwise undo any harm done.

SEE ALSO *Ethics in Experimentation; Experiments, Human; Experiments, Shock; Regression; Scientific Method*

BIBLIOGRAPHY

Aronson, Eliot, Timothy D. Wilson, and Marylin B. Brewer. 1998. Experimentation in Social Psychology. In *The Handbook of Social Psychology*, 4th ed., ed. Daniel T. Gilbert, Susan T. Fiske, and Gardner Lindzey, 441–486. Boston: McGraw-Hill.

Campbell, Donald T., and Julian C. Stanley. 1966. *Experimental and Quasi-Experimental Designs for Research*. Boston: Houghton Mifflin.

Cook, Thomas D., and Donald T. Campbell. 1979. *Quasi-Experimentation: Design and Analysis Issues for Field Studies*. Chicago: Rand McNally.

E. L. Stocks
David A. Lishner

EXPERIMENTS, CONTROLLED

In the social sciences, a controlled experiment is any study in which at least one variable—a presumed cause—is manipulated, the units of observation (individuals, groups, or organizations) are randomly assigned to levels of the manipulated variable, and there is at least one control condition. Experiments can be contrasted with quasi-experiments, in which the putative cause is manipulated but there is either no randomization or no control condition, and with nonexperiments, in which there is no manipulation, randomization, or control condition. Although quasi- and nonexperimental studies are useful, and sometimes necessary, in social science research, the information they provide is of limited value when the goal of the research is to detect causal relations. Controlled experiments, by virtue of manipulation, randomization, and control conditions, are the social scientist's best option for detecting causal relations.

The power of controlled experiments lies in their capacity for achieving control and isolation of the causal variable in a presumed cause-effect relation. When variability in the presumed cause is controlled by the experimenter through manipulation, the only plausible direction of influence between the variables is from cause to effect. The context within which the putative cause varies also must be controlled. Control in this sense involves attending to other variables that covary with the presumed cause or are present in the research context that might contribute to variability in the outcome. Isolation concerns the potential co-occurrence of a causal variable and other variables. To the extent that the presumed cause is confounded with other variables, inferences about its influence will be ambiguous or even incorrect. Control over variability in the presumed cause and isolation of it from other potential causes are necessary for unequivocal inferences of causal influence.

Although random assignment to levels of the manipulated variables also figures into control over the putative cause, its primary role in causal inference is isolation. If the units of observation are randomly assigned to conditions then, apart from the manipulation, the conditions are presumed to be probabilistically equivalent. Their equivalence is only probabilistic because there is some likelihood that, apart from the manipulation, the conditions differ. This probability is accounted for in the construction of statistical tests allowing for apparent difference between levels of the putative cause to be attributed either to the manipulation or to nonequivalence. By convention, these tests ensure that an apparent difference attributable to nonequivalence is attributed to the manipulation no more than 5 percent of the time. Social scientists often report the precise probability, or *p*-value, of the statistical test comparing conditions in an experiment, with values less than .05 indicating statistical significance.

Although random assignment is essential for isolating a presumed cause from other causal influences, it does not rule out alternative explanations for differences on the presumed effect attributable to the manipulation itself. Strategically designed control conditions address this type of alternative explanation. The prototypical control condition is the placebo condition in experiments on the causal effects of medications. The goal of these experiments is to isolate the effects of active ingredients in the medication from other effects, such as those that accrue from simply receiving medication or attention from a physician. By comparing outcomes for individuals who take a medication with those for individuals who believe they are taking the medication but in fact receive none of the active ingredients, researchers can distinguish effects attributable to the active ingredients from the effects of receiving any medication or seeing a physician. Because a control condition of this sort keeps research participants "blind" to condition, it also rules out the possibility that participants' assumptions about the effects of the manipulation explain differences in the outcome.

Controlled experiments often include more than one causal variable, with each having two or more levels. In the typical experiment with multiple causal variables, the variables are "fully crossed" to create a factorial design. In factorial designs, units of observation are randomly assigned to all combinations of levels of the causal variables, with the total number of conditions equal to the product of the number of levels of the causal variables. Such designs often are referred to in terms of the number of levels of each causal variable. The simplest factorial design is the 2 x 2 ("two-by-two"), which comprises two causal variables, each with two levels. Such designs allow for the detection of causal effects of the individual variables as well as interaction effects, in which the causal effect of one of the variables varies across levels of the other.

Despite their appeal as a means of detecting causal relations, controlled experiments are not always appropriate in social science research. In some instances, particularly in the early stages of a program of research, social scientists are interested in simply capturing the natural co-occurrence of variables without concern for causality. Controlled experiments are unsuitable for such purposes. In other instances, social scientists are interested in causal relations but cannot, for practical or ethical reasons, design controlled experiments to study them. These limitations might preclude manipulation, random assignment, or the assignment of some individuals or groups to a control condition. For example, some characteristics of individuals, groups, and organizations either cannot be manipulated at all, or cannot be manipulated ethically in a manner that creates variability on the causal variable of interest. Furthermore, it is not always possible to randomly assign units of observation to condition, as, for instance, in the case of an intervention administered by teachers to students who are in a condition because they were assigned to that teacher's class according to school or district policy. Finally, in the case of studies of treatments that have the potential to save lives that otherwise could not be saved, it is unethical to withhold the treatment from research participants, thereby precluding inclusion of a no-treatment or placebo control condition. Thus, although controlled experiments are ideal for detecting causal relations, they are not always appropriate or feasible. Because of this, social scientists typically view controlled experiments as only one of numerous approaches to studying associations between variables.

SEE ALSO *Causality; Ethics in Experimentation; Experiments; Experiments, Human; Inference, Statistical; Random Samples; Social Science*

BIBLIOGRAPHY

Campbell, Donald T., and Julian C. Stanley. 1963. *Experimental and Quasi-Experimental Designs for Research*. Boston: Houghton Mifflin.

Haslam, S. Alexander, and Craig McGarty. 2000. Experimental Design and Causality in Social Psychological Research. In *The Sage Handbook of Methods in Social Psychology*, eds. Carol Sansone, Carolyn C. Morf, and A. T. Panter, 237–264. Thousand Oaks, CA: Sage Publications.

West, Stephen G., Jeremy C. Biesanz, and Steven C. Pitts. 2000. Causal Inference and Generalization in Field Settings: Experimental and Quasi-Experimental Designs. In *Handbook of Research Methods in Social and Personality Psychology*, eds. Harry T. Reis and Charles M. Judd, 40–84. Cambridge, U.K.: University Press.

Rick H. Hoyle

EXPERIMENTS, HUMAN

In the social sciences, human experimentation involves the study of human behavior under controlled conditions using scientific methods. The practice of using human beings as experimental subjects was borrowed from the medical sciences in the late nineteenth century by those who later were credited with helping to lay the foundation for modern psychology. Separately, William James (1842–1910) in the United States and Wilhelm Wundt (1832–1920) in Germany established the first experimental psychology laboratories in 1875. These pioneers conducted simple experiments involving human perception, memory, and cognition. Their success with the experimental approach revolutionized the study of human behavior and significantly influenced the development of all of the social sciences throughout the twentieth century. Today human experiments are widely accepted as an important research tool not only in psychology, but also in sociology, economics, and other specialized fields.

Experiments using human subjects can assume a wide variety of designs and employ simple to complex procedures. The most basic form of a human experiment involves two sets of subjects—a treatment group and a control group. Subjects in the treatment group are exposed to some form of stimulus (experience) that is under controlled manipulation by the experimenter. Subjects in the control group do not receive the stimulus, but are like the treatment group in all other respects. The resulting effect of the stimulus on the treatment group is then measured and compared to the control group. For example, a researcher interested in the effect of background noise on students' reading comprehension may design an experiment where students in a treatment group are asked to read a passage from a book while a radio is played nearby; meanwhile, students in a control group are asked to read the same passage, but in a noiseless environment. Both the treatment group and control group students then take a test on the assigned reading and the test results are quantitatively compared and contrasted. Researchers can manipulate various elements of an experiment to test a variety of hypotheses. In this example, the researcher could examine how the *type* of noise independently affects reading comprehension by alternating music with talk, or even white noise, while holding all of the other elements the same. Likewise, the effects of *age* or *gender* could be explored by selecting human subjects from differing populations. Thus, even a simply designed experiment can be a powerful research tool. Beginning with this basic approach, social scientists over the past century developed sophisticated techniques and procedures to study a vast array of human behavior. However, the widespread practice of human experimentation also caused social scientists to carefully examine their own motives and ethics.

ETHICAL CONSIDERATIONS

Just as the modern history of using human beings as experimental subjects in biomedical research is littered with controversy and scandal, the same is true in the social sciences. In the decades following World War II a number of human experiments made headline news due to the ethical questions that they raised. The most noteworthy of these include Stanley Milgram's "obedience to authority" study in 1963 and the Philip Zimbardo's "imprisonment" study in 1973.

In Milgram's study an experimenter instructed human subjects to administer increasingly severe electrical shocks to another, unseen person. Unknown to the subjects, the shocks were fictitious and the other person was collaborating with the experimenter. In response to the "shocks" the collaborator would scream, leading the subject to believe that the shocks were real. Milgram conducted the study to explore how people respond to authority figures when directed to perform harmful acts against other human beings. Likewise, Zimbardo too was interested in studying the human reaction to authority, but did so in a simulated prison context. Zimbardo assigned "guard" and "prisoner" roles to subjects and then proceeded to observe their behavior as subjects were instructed to undertake various activities common to life inside a U.S. prison. The experiment took place in a college laboratory especially redesigned, complete with cells, to simulate a prison environment. During the course of the experiment the confrontations between the guards and the prisoners became so intense that a prisoner rebellion ensued and a breakout was attempted. Given these events, concern for the physical and mental safety of the subjects caused the experiment to be terminated prior to its planned conclusion.

Although no one was seriously harmed in either study, the Milgram and Zimbardo experiments are often cited along with notorious cases in biomedical research, such as the decades-long "Tuskeegee syphilis study" in which, to serve as a control group, poor African Americans infected with syphilis were denied medical treatment; the fallout from this experiment led to regulatory oversight of human subjects research in the United States and in other nations. In 1974 the U.S. Congress passed the National Research Act, which established a National Commission for the Protection of Human Subjects of Biomedical and Behavioral Research. This body's 1979 "Belmont Report" (named after the conference center where the commission met) set forth the three basic ethical and moral principles that serve as the foundation for the regulatory rules that now govern all human experiments conducted at institutions receiving funds from the U.S. federal government. These three principles are respect, beneficence, and justice.

The principle of respect includes the tenet that experimental researchers should honor all human subjects' right to personal dignity, freedom of choice, and privacy. The beneficence principle stipulates that researchers conducting human experiments have a societal obligation to maximize the benefits and minimize the costs associated with their work. Finally, the principle of justice concerns the obligation of researchers to treat all human subjects with fairness.

The Belmont Report proposed that each of the three basic principles have equal moral weight and recognized that in some situations they may conflict with each other. Therefore, the commission recommended that experiments using human subjects should be objectively evaluated and judged based on their own merits relative to all three principles. This perspective is clearly reflected in the prevailing federal regulations that shape the way human experiments are conducted today.

REGULATORY ISSUES

The primary regulations that govern the practice of human experiments in the United States are included in the Federal Policy for the Protection of Human Subjects (*Code of Federal Regulations* Title 45–Part 46). This policy is often referred to as the "Common Rule" because it has been adopted by sixteen federal departments and agencies that conduct or financially support research using human subjects. The Common Rule is explicitly based on the Belmont Report's three ethical and moral principles.

Under the principle of respect, the Common Rule regulations require researchers to explicitly obtain each human subject's informed consent before proceeding with any experiment. All potential benefits and harms to the human subject must be clearly explained and each subject must have the option of quitting the experiment at any time. The regulations also require researchers to maintain the privacy of their human subjects by not divulging the names or any personally identifying information collected during the course of an experiment.

To uphold the principle of beneficence, the Common Rule regulations require researchers to ensure that all human experiments possess a favorable ratio of potential benefits to potential risks. Furthermore, researchers must demonstrate that they are capable of properly conducting human experiments and that they have procedures in place to handle the apparent risks.

Federal regulations derived from the principle of justice include the requirement that human subjects be selected in a manner such that the risks and benefits of participation are equitably shared across participants. The justice principle is also the foundation for a variety of rules that ensure that vulnerable populations are not exploited by researchers conducting human experiments. Thus, numerous regulations safeguard prisoners, children, the mentally impaired, and other special groups.

Enforcement of the Common Rule regulations is a decentralized process, and primary oversight is at the local level. The policy mandates the establishment of institutional review boards (IRBs, also known as internal review boards) at all institutions, including universities and research centers, that conduct human experiments and receive federal dollars. An IRB is composed of professional researchers and administrators who screen proposals for research involving human subjects. Researchers wishing to conduct human experiments, or any other research activity that includes the observation of human behavior or the collection of data from human beings, must receive approval from their institution's IRB before proceeding. Local IRBs are charged with enforcing the federal policies and protecting the rights of human subjects. Institutions have a powerful incentive to maintain a diligent IRB because the code allows for the withdrawal of all federal funding from institutions found in violation of the Common Rule.

The influence of the Common Rule and the institutionalization of local IRBs is a topic of debate among many American social scientists. Most agree that enforcement of the Common Rule does protect human subjects from overtly risky experimental practices, but some argue that the federal code stifles research activities that inherently carry low levels of risk. For example, researchers proposing to conduct a marketing survey or an oral history project must receive either approval or an exemption from their local IRB, even though the personal risk of participating in either of these practices is negligible. An IRB review requires paperwork and time commitments that may discourage some researchers from pursuing a project. Additionally, the decentralized approach of enforcing the Common Rule results in an uneven application of the regulations. Projects that receive approval from one local IRB may not be approved by another IRB, causing difficulties for research teams composed of members from different institutions. Even though these hurdles exist, the number of empirical research studies using human subjects, as recorded in the academic literature, continues to increase each year with little evidence to suggest that the regulations have significantly affected the quantity of research conducted.

BIBLIOGRAPHY

Friedman, Daniel, and Shyam Sunder. 1994. *Experimental Methods: A Primer for Economists.* New York: Cambridge University Press.

Levine, Robert J. 1988. *Ethics and Regulation of Clinical Research.* 2nd ed. New Haven, CT: Yale University Press.

Snodgrass, Joan G., Gail L. Berger, and Martin Haydon. 1985. *Human Experimental Psychology.* New York: Oxford University Press.

United States Department of Health, Education, and Welfare. 2005. Code of Federal Regulations. Title 45, Public Welfare. Part 46, Protection of Human Subjects. http://www.hhs.gov/ohrp/humansubjects/guidance/45cfr46.htm.

Zimbardo, Phillip G. 2006. Homepage of Professor Phillip G. Zimbardo. http://www.zimbardo.com/.

Paul W. Grimes

EXPERIMENTS, MONTE CARLO

SEE *Monte Carlo Experiments.*

EXPERIMENTS, NATURAL

SEE *Natural Experiments.*

EXPERIMENTS, PRISON

SEE *Zimbardo, Philip.*

EXPERIMENTS, SHOCK

The term *shock experiment* brings to mind ghastly images. Most of these experiments use animal participants and a level of shock that often is more startling than painful (like the shock we sometimes receive when exiting a car). Some shock experiments use human participants, but rather than shocking them, these experiments usually only lead people to believe they will receive a shock or will be delivering shocks to others. Even though these experiments carry a negative connotation, the conclusions drawn from some of them have had a significant impact on psychology and other disciplines. The three main areas in which shock experiments have been used are learning, emotion, and obedience.

LEARNING

Shock experiments are used to study learning (i.e., a change in behavior due to experience). Classical conditioning is a form of learning involving associations. Most humans and animals learn a behavior after being exposed to sequentially presented stimuli. For example, a researcher might expose a rat to a light and then deliver an electrical shock to its feet. Eventually, the rat will learn that the light is a signal for the shock; turning it on will cause the rat to behave in the same way it would if shocked. The rat has learned to associate shock with the light. Although this example is relevant, most shock experiments investigate the more complex aspects of learning.

EMOTION

Shock experiments are used to investigate emotions such as anger and moods such as depression. In a well-known set of experiments in the 1960s and 1970s, Martin Seligman (b. 1942) and colleagues used electrical shocks to study personal control and depression. In one experiment, Seligman delivered inescapable shocks to a group of dogs. Later, these dogs (and a control group of dogs not exposed to the inescapable shocks) were placed in a cage split in half by a barrier that could be jumped to reach the other side. When Seligman electrified one side of the floor, the dogs previously exposed to inescapable shocks were less likely than the control-group dogs to jump to the safe side of the cage. The dogs that failed to jump to safety had learned to be helpless and exhibited depressive-like symptoms.

This phenomenon was labeled *learned helplessness.* Experiments revealed that some humans also exhibit depressive-like symptoms when in uncontrollable situations (e.g., inescapable noise). The identification of learned helplessness was important in revealing the thought processes involved in depression. Researchers continue to study learned helplessness in humans and animals, and electrical shocks are routinely used in these experiments with animals (most often rats).

OBEDIENCE

Stanley Milgram (1933–1984) made shock experiments infamous in the 1960s, leading people to equate psychology with shocking people. Milgram was interested in the conditions that foster obedience and disobedience. Obedience is the carrying out of a command given by a person of authority. Milgram's interest in obedience was sparked partly by the Nazi atrocities, which spurred him to investigate to what extent ordinary people would harm an innocent person when ordered to.

Milgram studied 1,000 participants in several experiments. His basic experiment involved the use of a shock machine, an authority figure, and forty male participants who believed that the experiment was investigating punishment and memory. Participants were told that they would be required to deliver electrical shocks to a person in another room whenever he answered a question incorrectly, and they received sample shocks of 45 volts to convince them that the shock machine was real. The participant was told to increase the intensity of the shocks by 15 volts with each incorrect answer by flipping a switch on the machine, which had settings from 15 to 450 volts and ominous labels below the voltage readings (e.g., "slight shock," "moderate shock," "strong shock," "very strong shock"). Although the participants were convinced that they were delivering painful shocks, in fact, the person in the other room was a confederate (i.e., an accomplice) who did not actually receive shocks. The authority figure, a stern man in a lab coat, ordered the participants to shock the confederate whenever an incorrect answer was given. At several points, the confederate complained of pain and asked to be released, eventually shouting "My heart's starting to bother me now. Get me out of here, please. My heart's starting to bother me. I refuse to go on. Let me out."

Milgram was interested in determining the level at which participants would discontinue their obedience by refusing to deliver shocks. Of the participants in the experiment described here, 65 percent obeyed the order to deliver shocks up to 450 volts. These individuals obeyed even after the confederate stopped answering (presumably because he was incapacitated). This high level of obedience stunned Milgram and the world.

Milgram's experiments are classics in psychology. His findings are provocative because they revealed the capacity ordinary people have for obeying destructive orders. Milgram's use of deception, however, was considered unethical by many people. The participants believed they were inflicting harm, and many exhibited signs of extreme stress (e.g., trembling, sweating, biting of the lips, and stuttering). Critics contended that permanent harm was imposed on participants. Milgram countered critics by contacting many former participants; only 1 percent reported regret at having been in the experiment. Furthermore, a psychiatrist interviewed forty participants and found that none of them had suffered permanent harm.

The ethics of Milgram's experiments are debatable. Nonetheless, his and other controversial experiments (e.g., the Tuskegee study) prompted changes in research standards. In 1974 the National Research Act became law. This act, along with guidelines written by the American Psychological Association, required that human and animal research be reviewed by Institutional Review Boards (IRBs), which ensure that no undue harm is done to humans or animals, and that humans voluntarily consent to participate. Although deception is allowed, the deception permitted by IRBs does not typically involve physical harm, but rather the mental discomfort that comes from being deceived.

Although it is certainly doubtful that an IRB would approve an experiment such as Milgram's, shock experiments are routinely conducted on animals (and to a lesser extent on humans), but the level of shock typically used in these experiments is far from debilitating. In questioning the ethics of any experiment, one should consider the amount of pain inflicted and the knowledge to be gained before making definitive conclusions about the value of shock experiments.

SEE ALSO *Ethics in Experimentation; Experiments; Experiments, Human; Milgram, Stanley*

BIBLIOGRAPHY

Blass, Thomas. 2004. *The Man Who Shocked the World: The Life and Legacy of Stanley Milgram.* New York: Basic Books.

Milgram, Stanley. 1992. *The Individual in a Social World: Essays and Experiments.* 2nd ed. New York: McGraw-Hill.

Peterson, Christopher, Steven F. Maier, and Martin E. P. Seligman. 1993. *Learned Helplessness: A Theory of the Age of Personal Control.* New York: Oxford University Press.

Brian P. Meier

EXPLOITATION

In *Keywords* (1976), his foundational book on historical semantics, Raymond Williams includes discussion of the word *exploitation* because it illustrates the general problem of how important historical and social processes occur within language. On the one hand, *exploitation* is a key word in the English language because it is tightly bound up with the problems to which it refers; and on the other, it is an exemplar of what Williams calls "transfer"—that is, how new kinds of relationships and new ways of seeing relationships appear in languages, in this case by transferring a word from one semantic usage or historical context to another.

There are three broad senses in which exploitation is currently deployed. The first is as a modern form of industrial or commercial land use (or mineral extraction) derived probably from its Latin root meaning an "arrangement" or "explanation." This particular use came into English in the nineteenth century, often in regard to the commercial exploitation of the colonies, building upon the fourteenth- and fifteenth-century meanings of *exploit* as "successful progress" or "taking advantage." The meaning of *exploitation* as making use of resource opportunities for social advancement—the exploration of oil resources in Nigeria, for example—remains commonplace.

A second meaning is a generic sense of unjustness or oppression, referring to a potentially wide range of social relations across time and space (e.g., exploitation of men by women, workers by capitalists, slaves by slave owners, low castes by high castes, serfs by feudal overlords). The range of opinion as to what constitutes exploitation is substantial, ranging from the instrumental treatment of humans (Buchanan 1985)—a Kantian view—to coerced activity (Moore 1973) to psychological harm (Hill 1994). The analytical content is of less concern than its moral standing and the moral force of the reasoning (i.e., whether and how the state should prohibit exploitative transactions or refuse to enforce such agreements).

The third meaning, which is the focus of this entry, is explicitly analytical in the sense that it purports to provide a theoretical and conceptual ground on which the claim—A exploits B when A takes unfair advantage of B—can be assessed. In Old French, the feudal meaning of the word *exploitation*—a seizure of products from the land for which a tenant had failed to pay homage—provides a foretaste of its modern use in the mid-nineteenth century, as its reference is increasing the industrial capitalist system. In philosophical terms, one can say that social science seeks to understand the truth conditions under which such a claim can be made of a particular social setting. It is in this sense a term of social critique—exploitation refers to people, not resources—and it is very much rooted in classical political economy. Whether drawing from Adam Smith, David Ricardo, or Karl Marx, exploitation is inseparable from class structure and the operations of class-based power. Each of this trio has a moral core to his argument, but the forms of measurement differ radically among them. Although exploitation can also be accommodated within neoclassical economics or Weberian social theory, it is within the Marxist tradition that the analysis and theorization has received its fullest elaboration.

The notion of an unjust benefit from the labor of others that emerged by physiocratic thinking was formalized by Smith and Ricardo in the distinction between productive and unproductive labor and the question of the shares in the distribution of wealth. Neither Smith nor Ricardo was especially concerned with the moral class atlas of income distribution unless it concerned the landlord class. Conversely, the English anticapitalist and socialist writers of the 1830s (e.g., Thomas Hodgskin, Robert Owen) formulated the first Ricardo-inspired theory of exploitation that turned on the appropriation of wealth by the owners of capital and employers as an unjust deduction from the product of labor. In France, the Saint-Simonians and Pierre-Joseph Proudhon came to similar conclusions through an analysis of property ownership. Few of these public intellectuals agreed on the justness of the rewards due to property (rent, interest, profit), but they held in common the idea that, *contra* Simonde de Sismondi, exploitation was less a regrettable accident than central to the operations of the modern economic system.

From these tentative beginnings, the theorization of exploitation matured in the work of Marx and the notion of surplus appropriation and the labor theory of value. Marx's account identifies a fundamental contradiction at the heart of capitalism—a contradiction between two great classes (workers and owners of capital) that is fundamentally an exploitative relation shaped by the appropriation of surplus. Unlike feudalism, in which surplus appropriation is transparent (in the forms of taxes and levies made by landowners and lords backed by the power of the Church and Crown), surplus value is obscured in the capitalist labor process. Marx argued that labor is the only source of value, and value is the embodiment of a quantum of socially necessary labor. It is the difference between the sale of a worker's labor power and the amount of labor necessary to reproduce it that is the source of surplus value. The means by which capital extracts this surplus value under capitalism—through the working day, labor intensification, enhancing labor productivity—coupled to the changing relations between variable and constant capital determine, in Marx's view, the extent, degree, and forms of exploitation. In the first volume of *Capital* Marx identifies the origins of surplus value in the organization of production (the so-called "social relations of production"). In volume 2 Marx explains how exploitation affects the circulation of capital, and in volume 3 he traces the division of the total product of exploitation among its beneficiaries and the contradiction so created. In Marxist theory, two kinds of material interests—interests securing material welfare and interests enhancing economic power—are linked through exploitation (exploiters simultaneously obtain greater economic welfare and greater economic power by retaining control over the social allocation of surplus through investments). Members of a class, in short, hold a common set of interests and therefore have common interests with respect to the process of exploitation.

In the wake of Marx's work, the central debates over exploitation has turned on (1) whether the labor theory of value is a necessary condition for any truth claim about exploitation, (2) whether exploitation can be made congruent with complex forms of class differentiation associated with modern industrial society, and (3) whether there are non-Marxist accounts of exploitation. In neoclassical economics, for example, exploitation is a type of market failure due to the existence of monopoly or monopsony. In more developed versions of this organizational view, exploitation can be rooted in extramarket forces, for example free riding or asymmetric information (the so-called "principal agent problem"). There is a heterodox side to conventional marginalist approaches to economics—most readily seen in the work of Joan Robinson (1933) and the Cambridge school—in which exploitation is understood as wage payments less than the marginal product of labor (see also Brewer 1987).

More structural accounts of exploitation from a liberal vantage point are found in the ideas of Henry George (2006) and John Maynard Keynes (1936), for whom landowners or rentier classes (nonworking owners of financial wealth) produce not exploitation in the Marxist sense, but exploitation as waste and inefficiency due to "special interests."

In the Marxist tradition there has been in general an abandonment of the labor theory of value—away from the view of Jon Elster that "workers are exploited if they work longer hours than the number of hours employed in the goods they consume" (Elster 1986, p. 121)—toward John Roemer's notion that a group is exploited if it has "some conditionally feasible alternative under which its members would be better off" (Roemer 1986, p. 136). Perhaps the central figure in developing these arguments is Erik Olin Wright (1985, 1989), who developed a theory to account for the contradictory class location of the "middle classes"—that they are simultaneously exploiters and exploited. Building on the work of Roemer, Wright distinguishes four types of assets, the unequal control or ownership of which constitute four distinct forms of exploitation: labor power assets (feudal exploitation), capital assets (capitalist exploitation), organization assets (statist exploitation), and skill assets (socialist exploitation). While pure modes of production can be identified with single forms of exploitation, "actually existing capitalism" all consist of all four, opening up the possibility of the simultaneous operation of exploiter/exploitee relations (for example, managers are capitalistically exploited but organizational exploiters).

A long line of Marx-inspired theorizing has, of course, attempted to grasp exploitative relations between countries. This is the heart of theories of imperialism (Lenin 1916) as the coercive extraction of surplus through colonial states (Fanon 1967), through unequal exchange (Arrighi and Pearce 1972), or through the imperial operation of transnational banks and multilateral development institutions (the World Bank and the International Monetary Fund). The so-called "antiglobalization movement" (focusing especially on institutions such as the World Trade Organization) and "sweatshop movements" (focusing on transnational firms such as Nike) are contemporary exemplars of a politics of exploitation linking advanced capitalist state and transnational companies with the poverty and immiseration of the global south against a backdrop of neoliberalism and free trade (Harvey 2005; Starr 2005).

SEE ALSO *Bureaucracy; Class, Rentier; Colonialism; Economics, Neoclassical; Fanon, Frantz; Globalization, Social and Economic Aspects of; Imperialism; Inequality, Income; Keynes, John Maynard; Labor Theory of Value; Labor, Marginal Product of; Labor, Surplus: Marxist and Radical Economics; Landlords; Latifundia; Marginal Productivity; Marx, Karl; Marxism; Middle Class; Mode of Production; Poverty; Rate of Exploitation; Rate of Profit; Ricardo, David; Robinson, Joan; Slavery; Smith, Adam; Surplus; Surplus Value; Wages; World Trade Organization*

BIBLIOGRAPHY

Arrighi, Giovanni. 1972. *Unequal Exchange.* Trans. Brian Pearce. London: Monthly Review Press.

Brewer, John. 1987. Exploitation in the New Marxism of Collective Action. *Sociological Review* 35: 84–96.

Buchanan, Allen. 1985. *Ethics, Efficiency, and the Market.* Totowa, NJ: Rowman and Allanheld.

Elster, Jon, ed. 1986. *Karl Marx: A Reader.* London: Cambridge University Press.

Fanon, Frantz. 1967. *The Wretched of the Earth.* London: Penguin.

George, Henry. 2006. *Progress and Poverty.* London: Casimo.

Harvey, David. 2005. *A Brief History of Neoliberalism.* London: Clarendon.

Hill, John L. 1994. Exploitation. *Cornell Law Review* 79: 631–699.

Keynes, John Maynard. 1936. *The General Theory of Employment, Interest and Money.* London: Macmillan and Co.

Lenin, Vladimir. 1916. *Imperialism.* Moscow: Progress Publishers.

Marx, Karl. [1867–1894] 1992. *Capital.* Vols. 1–3. London: Penguin.

Moore, Barrington. 1973. *Reflections on the Causes of Human Misery.* Boston: Beacon Press.

Robinson, Joan. 1933. *The Economics of Imperfect Competition.* London: Macmillan.

Roemer, John. 1986. An Historical Materialist Alternative to Welfarism. In *Foundations of Social Choice Theory*, ed. Jon Elster and Aanund Hylland, 133–164. Cambridge, U.K.: Cambridge University Press.

Starr, A. 2005. *Global Revolt.* London: Zed Books.

Williams, Raymond. 1976. *Keywords.* New York: Oxford University Press.

Wright, Erik Olin. 1985. *Classes.* London: Verso.

Wright, Erik Olin, et al. 1989. *The Debate on Classes.* London: Verso.

Michael Watts

EXPLOITATION, RATE OF

SEE *Rate of Exploitation.*

EXPORT PENETRATION

In a world of increased international interdependence, the entry and capture of an increasing share of export markets (or expansion of export market share) plays an important role in a nation's industrial and overall economic growth. The expansion of export market share by a single product or a group of products is generally referred to in the literature as *export penetration*. The success or failure in export penetration depends on a host of domestic factors, such as production costs where the product is produced, and foreign factors, such as the degree of competition in foreign markets where the product is sold.

Export-oriented industries or countries can use their level of success in export penetration as a performance indicator. Researchers calculate export penetration ratio(s) to measure the degree of export penetration of industries or countries. In this way they can evaluate their export market performance over time and across industries and countries. Depending on the availability of data, export penetration ratios are measured in many ways. The most commonly used method measures the market share captured by the product(s) in the trading partner's import market. For example, if in a given year the value of U.S. agricultural exports to Canada is $100 billion (in U.S. dollars) and the value of Canada's total agricultural imports from all its trading partners is $200 billion, the export penetration ratio for U.S. agricultural exports to Canada is 0.5 (or 50%). This ratio indicates that U.S. agricultural exports to Canada accounted for half of the Canadian market for agricultural imports. Some researchers use other measures such as the proportion (or percentage) of the output exported as a measure of export penetration ratio. An increase in the ratio indicates a successful capture of a larger market share by the exporter, and hence indicates satisfactory market performance.

Export penetration has helped increase both internationalization of economic activity and international integration of economies that contribute to the process of globalization. Export promotion has become a popular development strategy among several developed and developing countries in the recent past. As a result, many countries have carried out economic liberalization and deregulation policies in support of export promotion. Export penetration is of vital importance for the growth of export-oriented industries and the success of these strategies. However, economic liberalization and deregulation policies in developed and developing countries have generated both positive and negative effects on export penetration. On the one hand, they have made export penetration easier by removing barriers to international trade. On the other hand, the removal of barriers has opened up markets for increased competition among exporters in external markets, making it difficult (or easy) for exporters to compete depending on their comparative advantages in international trade. Researchers have linked the level of productivity directly to the degree of export penetration.

SEE ALSO *Absolute and Comparative Advantage; Competition; Exchange Rates; Exports; Globalization, Social and Economic Aspects of; Import Penetration; Imports; Productivity; Trade; Trade Deficit; Trade Surplus; Trade, Bilateral*

BIBLIOGRAPHY

Eaton, Jonathan, Samuel Kortum, and Francis Kramarz. 2004. Dissecting Trade: Firms, Industries, and Export Destinations. *The American Economic Review* 94 (2): 150–154.

Hine, Robert C., and Peter W. Wright. 1998. Trade with Low Wage Economies: Employment and Productivity in UK Manufacturing. *Economic Journal* 108: 1500–1510.

Meredith, Lindsay N., and Dennis R. Maki. 1992. The United States Export and Foreign Direct Investment Linkage in Canadian Manufacturing Industries. *Journal of Business Research* 24 (1): 73–88.

Wimal Rankaduwa

EXPORT PROMOTION

Export promotion policies reflect the interest of national governments to stimulate exports. Subsidies, tax exceptions, and special credit lines are the main instruments used to promote exports. The regulatory aspects of export promotion changed significantly in the late twentieth century. In the past export promotion activities were not substantially regulated, but increasingly since the creation of the World Trade Organization (WTO) in 1995 some export promotion activities have been identified as trade-distorting practices. The WTO has devised rules that allow countries that have been affected by the export promotion practices of their trading partners to use the WTO's dispute-settlement procedure and in some cases retaliate.

Export promotion is sometimes seen as a complementary development strategy to import protection. While import protection usually allows infant industry to develop, export promotion allows access to external markets. Foreign demand is often required by the limited size of domestic markets and the need to achieve economies of scale, essential in many productive activities. In a 1984 article Paul Krugman argued that, under increasing returns to scale, import protection may act as a form of export promotion, because in this case protection would allow considerable gains in terms of productivity that would enhance the possibilities of exporting. However, in policy circles export promotion or export oriented industrialization (EOI) is seen more often as an alternative development strategy to import substitution industrialization (ISI).

There are two main interpretations about the advantages of export promotion. One has a laissez-faire bias, while the other emphasizes the role of state intervention in promoting exports. Conventional wisdom suggests that an emphasis on exports forces integration into world markets and a more efficient allocation of resources, because external markets impose discipline by eliminating uncompetitive firms. In other words, exports affect positively the supply side of the economy. This view, exposed by Ian Little, Tibor Scitovsky, and Maurice Scott in 1970 and by Bela Balassa in 1971, was influential within the World Bank and the International Monetary Fund (IMF), and it shaped the Structural Adjustment Programs (SAPs) of the 1980s and influenced the liberalization strategy of the Washington Consensus. The studies by Anne O. Krueger and Jagdish Bhagwati, both in 1978, and by Demetris Papageorgiou, Michael Michaely, and Armeane M. Choksi in 1991 suggested that ISI policies generally did not produce sustainable increases in income per capita and that export promotion policies were more appropriate for achieving that goal. Export promotion, in this view, is associated with liberalization and market reforms.

Defenders of outward orientation tended to argue that EOI was behind the successful experience of the Asian countries. The World Bank's 1993 report *The East Asian Miracle* supported the view that East Asian economies' successful export performance resulted from the implementation of market-friendly policies. Several authors have shown the limitations of the World Bank position. Ajit Singh, in his 1995 paper "The Causes of Fast Economic Growth in East Asia," argued that despite the strong export orientation, the East Asian economies were not fully integrated with the world economy and that ISI was an integral part of the East Asian strategy in the 1950s and the 1960s. The equalization of export orientation with free trade is also misleading. In her 2001 *The Rise of "the Rest,"* Alice H. Amsden argued that the state intervened heavily in the economy of successful least developed countries (LDCs). In the East Asian economies, protection, conditional on export promotion, allowed import-substituting infant industries to become internationally competitive export-oriented industries. More generally Francisco Rodríguez and Dani Rodrik, in an influential 2000 article published in the *National Bureau of Economic Research (NBER) Macroeconomics Annual*, showed that the evidence for a negative relationship between trade barriers and economic growth is weak at best.

The alternative view emphasizes the role of exports in expanding demand, in contrast with the conventional view that emphasizes supply effects associated with improved resource allocation. Higher demand provides an outlet for producers in economies with relatively limited domestic markets. The foreign trade multiplier, developed by Roy Harrod, indicates that net exports have a positive effect on the level of activity. Nicholas Kaldor argued that higher levels of exports lead to strengthening productivity, lowering unit costs, which would then positively impact exports. This positive effect of exports on productivity, known as the Verdoorn effect, reduced unit costs and led to further increases in export in a cumulative process of economic development formalized by Robert Dixon and Anthony Thirlwall in their 1975 paper. The notion of a circular and cumulative process of growth led by exports harks back to Adam Smith's vent for surplus principle.

The alternative view also differs from conventional wisdom in that it does not equate export promotion with free market policies. Raúl Prebisch, in a United Nations 1964 report, emphasized the importance of export promotion and access to the markets of developed countries to promote industrialization in LDCs. More importantly, to avoid recurrent balance of payments crises, LDCs should diversify their exports rather than rely on commodity exports. Prebisch argued that LDCs should replace traditional commodity exports with manufactures or semi-manufactures exports. Industrial policy would have a central role in promoting export diversification. State selective intervention, by providing support for research and development (R&D), imposing restrictions on licensing and royalties, and coordinating with and among private sector agents, is central to increase and diversify exports.

Several authors have also emphasized the limitations of the EOI strategy. Robert A. Blecker, in his 1999 essay "The Diminishing Returns to Export-Led Growth," noted that export-led growth is a strategy that cannot be pursued by all countries at the same time. Export promotion requires that at the other end there is an importer of last resort, in other words, a country with the international reserve currency and an incredible appetite for imports. Also the integration of China into the world economy and its relatively low labor costs suggest that countries with higher labor costs would find it increasingly difficult to pursue export oriented development strategies. The global imbalances that result from simultaneous export promotion efforts around the globe are a threat to the stability of the global economy.

SEE ALSO *Balance of Trade; Developing Countries; Economic Growth; Import Substitution; Industrialization; Infant Industry; International Monetary Fund; Mercantilism; Prebisch-Singer Hypothesis; Protectionism; Structural Adjustment; Surplus; Terms of Trade; Trade; Trade Deficit; Trade Surplus*

BIBLIOGRAPHY

Amsden, Alice H. 2001. *The Rise of "the Rest": Challenges to the West from Late-Industrializing Economies.* Oxford, U.K.: Oxford University Press.

Balassa, Bela. 1971. *The Structure of Protection in Developing Countries.* Baltimore, MD: Johns Hopkins Press.

Bhagwati, Jagdish. 1978. *Anatomy and Consequences of Exchange Control Regimes.* Foreign Trade Regimes and Economic Development series, vol. 11. Cambridge, MA: Ballinger.

Blecker, Robert A. 1999. The Diminishing Returns to Export-Led Growth. Occasional Paper, Council on Foreign Relations. http://www.cfr.org/publication/8709/diminishing_returns_to _exportled_growth_a_cfr_paper.html.

Dixon, Robert, and Anthony Thirlwall. 1975. A Model of Regional Growth-Rate Differences on Kaldorian Lines. *Oxford Economic Papers* 27 (2) (July): 201–214.

Krueger, Anne O. 1978. *Liberalization Attempts and Consequences.* Foreign Trade Regimes and Economic Development series, vol. 10. Cambridge, MA: Ballinger.

Krugman, Paul. 1984. Import Protection as Export Promotion: International Competition in the Presence of Oligopoly and Economies of Scale. In *Monopolistic Competition and International Trade*, ed. Henryk Kierzkowski, 180–193. New York: Oxford University Press.

Little, Ian, Tibor Scitovsky, and Maurice Scott. 1970. *Industry and Trade in Some Developing Countries: A Comparative Study.* New York: Oxford University Press.

Papageorgiou, Demetris, Michael Michaely, and Armeane M. Choksi, eds. 1991. *Lessons of Experience in the Developing World.* Vol. 7 of *Liberalizing Foreign Trade.* Cambridge, MA: Blackwell.

Prebisch, Raúl. 1964. *Towards a New Trade Policy for Development.* New York: United Nations.

Rodríguez, Francisco, and Dani Rodrik. 2000. Trade Policy and Economic Growth: A Skeptic's Guide to the Cross-National Evidence. In *NBER Macroeconomics Annual*, vol. 15, ed. Ben Bernanke and Kenneth Rogoff. Cambridge, MA: MIT Press.

Singh, Ajit. 1995. The Causes of Fast Economic Growth in East Asia. *UNCTAD Review*, 81–127.

Williamson, John. 1990. What Washington Means by Policy Reform. In *Latin American Adjustment: How Much Has Happened?* ed. John Williamson, 7–33. Washington, DC: Institute for International Economics.

World Bank, The. 1993. *The East Asian Miracle.* Policy Research Report, World Bank. New York: Oxford University Press.

Matías Vernengo

EXPORTS

Exports are goods and services produced within one country (or territory) and sold by economic agents (individuals or firms) of that country to economic agents of another country. Exports are an important part of international trade, the counterpart being imports, which allow countries to participate in the global economy by expanding their markets for goods and services.

Exports originated with the start of communication and have been present since prehistoric times. According to the historian Peter Watson, people begun bartering goods and services 150,000 years ago, as part of long-distance commerce. There is also evidence of exchange of obsidian and flint during the Stone Age, while materials used for making jewelry were exported to Egypt since 3,000 BCE. Long-range export routes first appeared in the third millennium BCE, when Sumerians in Mesopotamia traded with the Harappan civilization, and continued with the Phoenicians, who traveled across the Mediterranean Sea and established trade colonies. From the beginning of the Greek civilization until the fall of the Roman Empire in the fifth century, exports from the Far East to Europe flourished. However, the fall of the Roman Empire and the Dark Ages led to a disruption of the main export networks. Subsequently, noteworthy landmarks included the contribution of Vasco da Gama to the trade of spices and the dominance of Holland, Portugal, and Britain in the sixteenth, seventeenth, and eighteenth centuries, respectively. Exports continued to expand in the nineteenth and twentieth centuries, particularly after World War II with the creation of international institutions, and in the twenty-first century with the telecommunications revolution.

The reduction of barriers to international trade has been crucial for exports. With technology improvements—container ships, telecommunication networks, and the Internet—it is easy for producers in one country to reach consumers in another and to export their products quickly. Governments have also recognized the importance of free trade and have reduced export (and import) quotas and tariffs, including in the context of multilateral agreements (the European Union and the North American Free Trade Agreement). Moreover, the World Trade Organization was created to facilitate free trade by mandating mutual most favored nation trading status between all members. Finally, to help exporters find markets for their products, countries have set up export promotion agencies as an integral part of their export strategies.

The payments and receipts associated with exports take place in major international currencies (U.S. dollar, euro, and yen) and are recorded in the current account of the balance of payments. The latter is usually kept in terms of the international currency in which the country's majority of trade transactions are conducted. The current account balance is calculated as the difference between exports and imports of goods and services. When the value of receipts from external transactions exceeds (falls short of) the one of payments, the country runs a current account surplus (deficit). Several different models have been developed to study export developments and analyze the effects of export policies. The Ricardian model—

developed during the first quarter of the nineteenth century by economists David Ricardo, James Mill, and Robert Torrens—postulates that countries specialize in producing and exporting what they produce best. The Heckscher-Ohlin-Samuelson (H-O-S) model incorporates the neoclassical price mechanism and argues that the pattern of exports (and trade) is determined by differences in factor endowments (labor, capital, and know-how). It predicts that countries will export (or import) goods that make intensive use of locally abundant (or scarce) factors. Finally, the gravity model postulates that exports and imports are determined by the distance between countries and the interaction of the countries' economic sizes.

Macroeconomic policy could have significant influence on export developments, since the demand for a country's exports is a function of each good's price in foreign currency. Thus, macroeconomic policies that affect the exchange rate weigh on exports. For example, tight monetary and expansionary fiscal policy both lead to a higher real interest rate, which makes domestic assets attractive to foreign investors; as foreigners demand domestic assets, the real value of the domestic currency rises sharply. Because the domestic currency is strong, exports become more expensive and thus could fall sharply.

One measure to gauge the importance of exports is their ratio to gross domestic product, known as the index of openness. Countries with high value of the index are considered relatively open, while the opposite is the case for relatively closed economies. In line with globalization trends, the average (worldwide) index of openness increased from 30 percent in 1980–1990 to 40 percent in the beginning of the twenty-first century. The most open economies have values of the index over 100 percent: Hong Kong (190% in 2004), followed by Luxemburg (146%), and Malaysia (121%). On the other hand, relatively closed economies are characterized by low openness indexes: Burkina Faso (8.6%), Burundi (8.9%), and Rwanda (10.3%).

According to the World Trade Organization, in 2005 total exports reached $12.6 trillion, comprising $10.2 trillion of merchandise exports and $2.4 trillion exports of commercial services. Exports of goods and services each increased by an annual average of 10 percent over the 2000–2005 period. Europe dominates world exports, accounting for 43 percent of the total in 2005; Asia follows with 28 percent, and North America with 15 percent. At the individual country level, in 2005 the five largest exporters of merchandise goods were: Germany (9.3% of world exports), the United States (8.7%), China (7.3%), Japan (5.7%), and France (4.4%). The leading exporters of services were: the United States (14.7% of world exports), United Kingdom (7.8%), Germany (6.2%), France (4.8%), and Japan (4.5%).

Turning to the commodity composition, manufacturing exports have led overall growth, increasing by an average of 6.5 percent annually during 1990–2005 compared with 3.5 percent for agricultural products and 3.5 percent for fuels and mining products. In 2005 merchandise exports comprised: $7,312 billion manufacturing, $1,748 billion fuels and mining products, and $852 billion agricultural products. As for services, transportation accounted for $570 billion, travel for $685 billion, and other services for $1,160 billion.

Globalization trends and improvements in telecommunications will support strong export dynamics over the medium and long term. However, due attention needs to be paid to maximize the benefits for economic growth of all countries. In this connection, although recent efforts on trade liberalization are encouraging, some calls for protectionist policies raise concerns. There is no doubt that continued trade liberalization will create more opportunities and raise the potential for faster global growth.

SEE ALSO *Absolute and Comparative Advantage; Balance of Payments; Balance of Trade; Exchange Rates; Heckscher-Ohlin-Samuelson Model; Imports; Liberalization, Trade; Macroeconomics; Mill, James; Ricardo, David; Samuelson, Paul A.; Trade; Trade Deficit; Trade Surplus; World Trade Organization*

BIBLIOGRAPHY

Heckscher, Eli. [1919] 1949. The Effect of Foreign Trade on the Distribution of Income. In *Readings in the Theory of International Trade*, ed. American Economic Association. Philadelphia: Blakiston.

Ohlin, Bertil. 1933. *Interregional and International Trade.* Cambridge, MA: Harvard University Press.

Ricardo, David. 1821. *On the Principles of Political Economy and Taxation.* 3rd ed. London: John Murray.

Watson, Peter. 2005. *Ideas: A History of Thought and Invention from Fire to Feud.* New York: HarperCollins.

World Trade Organization. 2006. *International Trade Statistics.* Geneva: Author.

Costas Christou

EXPOSURE THERAPY

SEE *Psychotherapy.*

EXPROPRIATION

SEE *Confiscation.*

EXTERNALITY

The term *externality* originated in economics, but it is now widely used in the social sciences and the popular press. In economics it is defined as: (1) benefits or costs of an economic activity that spill over to a third party (e.g., pollution is a negative spillover, while a positive spillover would occur when neighborhood property values are enhanced by the restoration of a rundown house; (2) an incidental effect produced by economic activities, but that does not enter the cost or benefit decisions of either buyer or seller; (3) uncompensated benefits (costs) to others as a result of an action taken by an economic unit; (4) any cost or benefit generated by one agent in either production or consumption activities that also affects another agent in the economy.

The economist Ronald Coase (1960) suggests that externalities are reciprocal, and that it is a case of selective perception to say that A harms B rather than B harms A. Hence, the idea that pollution is a spillover and an incidental outcome seems misplaced. Take the production of steel for example. The recipe for steel includes iron ore, coke, labor, and blast furnaces. Also necessary is a place to put the waste, either on the land or in the atmosphere as a pollutant, as well as a warehouse to store the steel until it is to be used. One of these items is no more incidental than another, and any industrial engineer would know all the ingredients. Is the cost of the waste storage accounted for by the market? How is the cost of labor accounted for? The steel producer would not pay for labor if there were not a prohibition against slavery—that is, if people did not own their labor power. If a producer does not own a necessary ingredient to its production, it must be bought in the market. If it is already owned, the owner will consider its *opportunity cost*, or what it could be sold to others for. This is true of iron ore and labor as much as for a place to put the waste. An owner of the atmosphere, whether it be a steel company or the general public, may submit a bid to the company, and if the bid does not exceed its value in use for producing steel, the company will use it. This is how any resource input is accounted for.

Does the action to use an owned resource taken by the steel company produce an uncompensated cost (or benefit) for others? None could be expected if the resource is owned by the steel company. Thus, if the steel company uses its land for a blast furnace, farmers could not expect to be compensated for the land not being used for agriculture. If a farmer has a better use for the land, then a bid can be made for the resource. The issue then boils down to who owns the resource. To own is to deny opportunities to others who need the resource; to own is to coerce and visit uncompensated lost opportunities on non-owners; and to own is be the recipient of bids, not the payer of compensation to others. The ability of an owner to withhold what others need is the source of all income.

In a world of scarcity, any production or consumption activity affects another agent in the economy. The policy issue concerns who is the buyer and who is the seller of any contested economic opportunity. In the words of Coase, externalities are reciprocal. If A owns, it harms B, but if B owns, it harms A. Externalities are ubiquitous. They are the stuff of human interdependence. The term *externality* might be usefully replaced by *interdependence*, with nothing inherent in the term implying who should own or who should do without if they cannot make an attractive bid to the owner.

What about transaction costs? Given resource ownership, there may be buyers who are willing to meet the reservation price of seller-owners. Their potential bids may nevertheless be overcome by transaction costs and therefore rejected by the owners. The opportunity for a mutually beneficial trade may be lost. The most common example of transaction costs defeating a potential bid occurs in the case of high exclusion cost goods—those goods which if they exist for one person are available to all. This is sometimes called a "market failure," and the inefficiency is often used to justify public taxation (or regulation), perhaps to buy out owners now using the atmosphere as a place to put waste. Those opposed to a role for government in such goods argue that governments may also fail to do the right thing (if that can be agreed on).

New interconnections in the economy are constantly being brought to people's attention through new technology. No one worries whether a person has a particular opportunity to use or exchange an opportunity when that person does not have the ability to affect others. For example, no one worried about air rights before the Wright brothers. But then the issue arose as to who owned the air above the land. The interdependence between landowners and airlines became evident, and the question of ownership arose. Each wanted to be declared the owner, and to be entitled to compensation for any lost opportunity. The effect of each person's use on the other is not incidental. Who should compensate whom is the issue. There is nothing in nature or economics that dictates the outcome of this contest. Cost is not independent of rights when the willingness to pay and the willingness to sell differ. Nations gave ownership to the airlines, and the landowners could not enjoin their use. If this had not been the case, the airline industry would have followed a different growth path. Later, as noise became as issue, regulations set a maximum for noise near airports. These regulations in effect gave ownership of some aspects of the atmosphere to those living near airports. Public choice of ownership, whether implemented by taxes, fees, or liability rules, determines what kind of world we live in.

Externality just points to the interconnections in any economy that might be better understood by referring to the connections as interdependencies, without any presumed policy conclusion. The interdependencies are sorted out by formal and informal institutions serving as property rights (ownership) and determining use or exchange opportunities (who has to buy what from whom). Changing ownership can change what is efficient.

SEE ALSO *Overfishing; Tragedy of the Commons; Transaction Cost*

BIBLIOGRAPHY

Coase, Ronald H. 1960. The Problem of Social Cost. *Journal of Law and Economics* 3 (1): 1–44.

Samuels, Warren J. 1992. *Essays on the Economic Role of Government.* Vol. 1. New York: New York University Press.

Schmid, A. Allan. 2004. *Conflict and Cooperation: Institutional and Behavioral Economics.* Oxford: Blackwell.

A. Allan Schmid

F

FABIANISM

In January 1884, in London, about two dozen intellectuals created the Fabian Society. It has never had more than 80,000 members. Still, it has a universal significance in the history of social sciences that has been recognized even by its most outspoken critics.

The immediate antecedent of the creation of the society was a London visit of the New York philosopher Thomas Davidson. His twenty to thirty followers created the Fellowship of the New Life, which wanted to create a community of modest, unselfish people who with their way of life based on mutual love, tolerance, and wisdom would set an example for society. They hoped that the perfection of the individual would in turn lead to a perfection of the society. Some of the members, however, were also interested in direct political action. They created the Fabian Society, aimed at the gradual, democratic socialist transformation of British society. Being convinced of the inevitability of gradual change versus revolutionary turmoil, they adopted the name of the Roman general Fabius Cunctator (c. 280–203 BCE), who successfully delayed battles against the Carthagians in order to gain strength. In its 2004–2005 program the society defined itself as "Britain's leading left of centre think tank and political society committed to creating the political ideas and policy debates which can shape the future of progressive politics."

The founders and early members included some of the wittiest and brightest British minds of the time such as George Bernard Shaw, Beatrice and Sydney Webb, Edward Pease, Sydney Olivier, and Graham Wallas. The first Fabians were trying to pave the way toward the implementation of their ideas via the liberal and the conservative parties. In 1900 they participated in setting up the Labour Representation Committee, which was to become the Labour Party in 1906. They wanted to permeate society with their ideas; this aim was served by the publication of various small sized clearly worded tracts. Their first major publication, the *Fabian Essays in Socialism* of December 1889, gave them fame. In a year and a half the circulation reached 27,000, a number that previous socialist publications had never reached.

FABIAN POLITICAL VIEWS

The Fabians defined their political profile as socialist but clearly distanced themselves from Marxist socialism and socialists. They denied the necessity of a revolution for the transition from capitalism to socialism. The full realization of social and economic reforms (such as factory acts, housing acts, education acts) and legislation about the improvement of working conditions, together with a progressive taxation of capitalists' income, would—they argued—smoothly lead to socialism. As pointed out by G. D. H. Cole in his 1932 essay on Fabianism in the *Encyclopedia of the Social Sciences*: "The economic problem was … presented as a question of the socialisation of monopoly incomes through social ownership of the monopolies.… [There] was no fundamental difference between land and capital or in the incomes derived from them. Both were mainly the results of differential monopoly" (i.e., the extra profit due to variety of land qualities and the potentiality of industrial production). According to the Fabian argument, the social control and fair distribution of income could guarantee the greatest happiness for the greatest number of people. Fabians assumed that all classes of society could be convinced of the efficiency and utility of their reform proposals. Even after the shocking experiences of various forms of labor unrest they did not adopt any class point of view.

Fabians were keen on the scientific approach to practical political problems. The Webbs initiated such large-scale empirical social studies as *Life and Labour of the People in London* (by Charles Booth, 17 volumes, 1902–1903) or *The History of English Local Government* (9 volumes, 1906–1929).

It was also four Fabians—the two Webbs, Graham Wallas, and George Bernard Shaw—who decided to create the London School of Economics on August 4, 1894. They believed that the systematic scholarly investigations of the functioning of their society needed a new, independent institution that also offered evening classes to workers who wanted to understand the limits and possibilities of political action.

Their impact was not limited to Britain. Eduard Bernstein in Germany wrote the introduction to the German edition of the Webbs' *Industrial Democracy*. The same book was translated into Russian by Vladimir Lenin. What appealed to both Bernstein and Lenin was the Fabian call for the professional leadership of workers. Fabianism was echoed in Asia as well. Independent India's first prime minister, Jawaharlal Nehru, developed an economic policy along Fabian lines. The founder of Pakistan, its first governor Muhammad Ali Jinnah, was a devoted member of the Fabian Society in the early 1930s. The first prime minister of Singapore, Lee Kuan Yew, also admits to having been influenced by Fabianism during his formative years.

INFLUENCE OF FABIAN IDEAS

A great number of people learned of Fabian ideas of social criticism from George Bernard Shaw's plays, such as *Pygmalion*, *Mrs. Warren's Profession*, and *Major Barbara*. When presenting examples of shocking dishonesty and hypocrisy of capitalist exploiters in his works before World War I, with his sharp, witty style, Shaw called for reforms along Fabian lines. In and after 1917 Shaw celebrated the program of the Bolshevik revolution as the incarnation of his ideas. Together with some other Fabians, such as H. G. Wells or later in the early 1930s, the Webbs, he believed in the Soviet model of the forceful implementation of a society without exploitation. This led to a split among the Fabians, as during the interwar period the majority of the members of the society were highly critical of the Soviet agenda. The splits were further aggravated by the conflicts over the evaluation of British imperialism. The Fabian founders hoped that the empire could create resources for easing social tensions: The imperial

destiny would call for public expenditure to rear the imperial race. A number of second-generation Fabians were critical of British imperial policy.

Since 1918 when Sydney Webb drafted the Labour Party's first major policy statement (*New Social Order*), Fabian policy has been adopted by the Labour Party and the Society has been affiliated with the party. Leading figures of the party, such as Ramsay MacDonald, Clement Attlee, Tony Benn, Harold Wilson, and even Tony Blair and Gordon Brown have been members of the Society.

In the first decade of the twenty-first century the Fabian Society had about 7,000 members. The Society continues to be affiliated with the Labour Party and its main focus is on fighting inequality and child poverty.

An overall evaluation of the Fabian achievement must recognize that Fabians contributed to reshaping the British party landscape, made socialism an acceptable option in British politics, and have substantially shaped the development of empirical social sciences. In the history of political thought they are perhaps the last to follow the enlightened tradition of believing in the possibility of, and acting for, the reasonable reconstruction of government and society on what they perceive as a scientific basis.

SEE ALSO *Blair, Tony; Bolshevism; Class, Rentier; Communism; Imperialism; Income Distribution; Jinnah, Mohammed Ali; Labour Party (Britain); Lenin, Vladimir Ilitch; Monopoly; Nehru, Jawaharlal; Socialism; Syndicalism*

BIBLIOGRAPHY

Cole, G. D. H. 1935. Fabianism. In *Encyclopedia of the Social Sciences.* New York: Macmillan.

Cole, Margaret. 1961. *The Story of Fabian Socialism.* London: Heinemann; Stanford, CA: Stanford University Press, 1961.

Hobsbawm, Eric J. 1964. The Fabians Reconsidered. In *Labouring Men: Studies in the History of Labour,* ed. Eric Hobsbawm, 250–271. London: Weidenfeld and Nicolson; New York: Basic Books, 1965.

MacKenzie, Norman and Jeanne. 1977. *The First Fabians.* London: Weidenfeld and Nicolson; New York: Simon and Schuster.

McBriar, A. M. 1972. *Fabian Socialism and English Politics, 1884–1918.* Cambridge, U.K.: Cambridge University Press.

Wolfe, Willard. 1975. *From Radicalism to Socialism: Men and Ideas in the Formation of Fabian Socialist Doctrines, 1881–1889.* New Haven, CT, and London: Yale University Press.

Attila Pók

FACTOR ANALYSIS

Factor analysis is usually adopted in social scientific studies for the purposes of: (1) reducing the number of variables; and (2) detecting structure in the relationships between variables. The first is often referred to as *common factor analysis*, whereas the second is known as *component analysis* when both variables are operated as statistical techniques. While factor analysis expresses the underlying common factors for an entire group of variables, it also helps researchers differentiate these factors by grouping variables into different dimensions or factors, each of which is ideally uncorrelated with the others.

A major breakthrough in attitude measurement came with the development of factor analysis (1931) by psychologist L. L. Thurstone (1887–1955). Thurstone introduced *multiple-factors theory*, which identified seven distinct and primary mental abilities consisting of: verbal comprehension, word fluency, number facility, spatial visualization, associative memory, perceptual speed, and reasoning. This theory differed from the more general, less separated theories of intelligence that were prevalent at the time and was among the first to show that human beings can be intelligent in different areas. The concept of multiple factors slowly received validation from empirical studies and gradually replaced the unidimensional factor in social research.

In social science studies, researchers often face a large number of variables. Although it is a good idea for scientists to exhaust all the relevant variables in their research to provide thorough responses to research questions, such an approach makes a theory too complex to generalize to empirical applications. For example, a researcher may want to explain delinquent behaviors by exploring all relevant independent variables, such as illegal drug use, harsh parenting, school dropout, school failure, single-parent household, gang affiliation, parent-child bonding, smoking, alcohol use, and many other variables. With so many independent variables, it is difficult to provide a simplified model for a parsimonious explanation of delinquent behavior. A good theoretical explanation should achieve both consideration of completion and parsimony in its coverage of variables. Factor analysis reduces the number of variables to a smaller set of factors that facilitates our understanding of the social problem. It provides such functions to determine the "common factors" of these independent variables. Each of these common factors should be the best representative of certain independent variables, and every factor should be, theoretically, independent from the other factors. Researchers substitute these factors for the variables because the factors can explain a similar degree of variance on the dependent variable but are simpler in terms of the number of independent variables. In most cases, factors found in an analysis

may not provide a complete description of the relevant independent variables, but these factors should be the most important factors, the best way of summarizing a body of data.

Factor analysis may use either *correlations* or *covariances*. The covariance cov_{ab} between two variables, *a* and *b*, is their correlation times their two *standard deviations*: $cov_{ab} = r_{ab} s_a s_b$, where r_{ab} is their correlation and s_a and s_b are their standard deviations. Any variable's covariance with itself is its variance—the square of its standard deviation. A correlation matrix can be thought of as a matrix of variances and covariances of a set of variables that have already been adjusted to a standard deviation of 1. Since a correlation or covariance matrix can be translated to one another easily, in many statistical books, authors may use either a correlation or covariance matrix or both to illustrate how *factor scores* are obtained.

The central theorem of factor analysis, in mathematical terms, is that we can partition a covariance matrix *M* into a common portion *C* that is explained by a set of factors, and a unique portion *R* that is unexplained by those factors. In matrix language, $M = C + R$, which means that each entry in matrix *M* is the sum of the corresponding entries in matrices *C* and *R*. The explained *C* can be further broken down into component matrices *C1*, *C2*, *C3, …* and *Cx*, explained by individual factors. Each of these one-factor components *Cx* equals the "outer product" of a column of *factor loading*. A statistical program may rank several matrices *Cx* if it finds that there is more than one matrix with *eigenvalues* greater than 1. An eigenvalue is defined as the amount of variance explained by one more factor. Since a component analysis is adopted to summarize a set of data, it would not be meaningful to find another factor that explains less variance than is contained in one variable (eigenvalues of less than 1). Therefore, statistical programs often default this rule selecting factors.

Principal component analysis is commonly used in statistics for factor analysis and was introduced to achieve representation or summarization. It attempts to reduce *p* variables to a set of *m* linear functions of those variables that best describe and summarize the original *p*. Some conditions need to be satisfied to have a set of *m* factors for the purpose of factor analysis. First, the *m* factors must be mutually uncorrelated. Second, any set of *m* factors should include the functions of a smaller set. Third, the squared weights defining each linear function must sum to 1, denoting the total variance explained. By using all *p*, we get a perfect reconstruction of the original *X*-scores, while by using the first *m* (with the greatest eigenvalues), we get the best reconstruction possible for that value of *m* and the most simplified model for interpretation.

Statistical programs allow researchers to select how many factors will be chosen. Ideally, we want to identify a certain number of factors that would explain or represent all the relevant variables. However, the use of factor analysis is not just to find all the statistically "significant" factors; rather, those factors identified should be meaningful to the researchers and interpreted subjectively by them. If the factors generated are meaningless in terms of the compositions of variables, such a factor analysis is not useful. In general, researchers may use exploratory factor analysis to find statistically significant factors (eigenvalues > 1) if they do not have prior knowledge of what factors may be generated from a number of variables. Therefore, it is very common that two different researchers would have two sets of factors even though they used an identical dataset. It is not about who is right or wrong, but whether researchers can adopt a group of factors that lead to better interpretation of the data. If researchers have prior knowledge (e.g., theories) of those factors, they can limit the number of factors to be generated in statistical programs rather than allowing statistical programs to generate them. In other words, researchers determine if the proposed variables are grouped into factors as suggested by the theory.

Researchers may use the rotation of a *factor-loading* matrix to simplify structure in factor analysis. Consider a set of p multiple regressions from p observed variables, wherein each regression predicts one of the variables from all m factors. The *standardized coefficients* in this set of regressions form a $p \times m$ matrix called the factor-loading matrix. We may replace the original factors with a set of linear functions of those factors for the same predictions as before, but with a different factor-loading matrix. In practice, this rotated matrix is expected to be used with simpler structures to better serve researchers' subjective interpretations.

SEE ALSO *Covariance; Eigen-Values and Eigen-Vectors; Perron-Frobenius Theorem: Economic Applications; Methods, Quantitative; Models and Modeling; Regression Analysis; Statistics*

BIBLIOGRAPHY

Thurstone, L. L. 1931. Measurement of Social Attitudes. *Journal of Abnormal and Social Psychology* 26 (3): 249–269.

Cheng-Hsien Lin

FACTORIES

The word *factory* refers to a building that has the primary function of housing physical production activities, often referred to as *manufacturing*. Although the origins of the word lie in *manufactory*, implying *making by hand*, the term *factory* can also refer to fully automated production systems. Locating manual craft production within a single building allows it to be changed in a number of ways. Firstly, factories allow production to expand a *division of labor*, splitting a single task into its components. Secondly, factories allow automation of production processes by creating opportunities for *economies of scale*. Thirdly, factories allow greater management control over production, enabling the emergence of a new social system, the *factory system*. The geography of the world economy has been shaped by three profound revolutions through which the contemporary factory system has evolved.

THE PRECONDITIONS FOR THE RISE OF A FACTORY SYSTEM

The idea of the factory emerged as a growing demand for mass-produced goods stimulated the growth of manufacturing industry. International trade in Europe began to take off from the fourteenth century; in the course of the fifteenth and sixteenth centuries, the Dutch economy grew rapidly and the Netherlands became a world power due to Amsterdam's centrality to world trade. Trade provided a number of key preconditions for manufacturing's growth. The linking of farmers to large-scale markets rewarded land-rich farmers able to increase agricultural productivity, releasing surplus labor power. Trade allowed particular localities to specialize in nonagricultural production for international markets while generating competitive pressures on craft producers, who had hitherto operated in local markets protected by town charters and guild systems. At the same time land-poor peasants sought alternative livelihoods and began to undertake small-scale production of domestic goods, such as textiles and pottery. Although some production was undertaken independently, merchants began to control this trade and soon effectively allocated output, in what is known as a *putting-out* system. Trade brought putting-out systems into competition with other producers, stimulating the coordinators—the merchants—to invest in more effective production methods.

THE EARLY FACTORY SYSTEM

These various factors created a situation ripe for attempts at significant productivity improvements through changes in the organization of production. An initial cost-reduction strategy brought formerly dispersed and contracted producers together in a single location, where merchants could more easily coordinate production with sales; this system is known as *putting in*. Moreover *putting in* allowed production to be organized into a series of mechanical tasks undertaken at a much lower cost, which, notes Adam Smith in *The Wealth of Nations* (1776), allowed for innovation, notably the development of machinery to simplify and accelerate particular tasks.

Toward the end of the eighteenth century, Britain, which was protected by a patent system, underwent a huge mechanization of its craft industries. What can be regarded as the first modern factory was opened in 1769 by Richard Arkwright at Cromford, near Derby. This factory exploited a recently granted patent for a spinning frame, an invention that allowed one unskilled laborer to do the work formerly performed by twenty skilled weavers. Britain became the first world economy to harness external power sources through mechanization, thus providing the basis for the first factory revolution. The numbers of factories increased massively in this period, and the nature of British society evolved in response. On the basis of its improved productive capacity, Britain became a leading world power, supplanting the Netherlands.

In this period the negative features of the division of labor became most evident. The textiles industry experienced massive growth, creating rising demands for labor power. However, the demands for profits also drove the exploitation and immiscration of the labor force, and population pressures created by large-scale migration to industrialized regions led to a slum-based urbanization characterized by *working poverty*. Friedrich Engels cataloged the case of Manchester in great detail and at firsthand in *The Condition of the Working Class in England* (1845).

Factories provided a location in which workers had contact with others experiencing the same conditions as them, and this led to the realization that they could exercise power over capitalists through the collective withdrawal of their labor power. The early British factory system therefore drove the emergence of a politically mobilized and cohesive working class as well as the subsequent emergence of labor representation—namely, the trade union movement. Moreover through its impact on the thought of Engels and Karl Marx, the British factory system ultimately spawned the politics of communism.

THE SECOND FACTORY REVOLUTION: SCIENTIFIC MANUFACTURING

This first factory system depended on a particular contemporaneous British characteristic: a labor surplus resulting from workers having been driven out of agriculture by overseas competition and enclosure. This labor surplus drove down wage costs, which in turn encouraged minimal consideration for the human cost of production: child labor, long working days, and an absence of days off were all common features of the working environment. The labor surplus also reduced the incentive for ongoing investment in capital goods; it allowed for productivity to be raised by worsening employment conditions rather than through further mechanization.

However, this situation was specific to the British context. Other countries lacked a labor surplus; when Germany (after 1870) and the United States (during Reconstruction) began their own domestic industrialization, they faced a different calculus. An American labor power shortage and the ideological commitment of Kaiser Wilhelm to investing in the latest production techniques produced different factory arrangements in these newly industrializing economies. While British factories were limited in size by their surrounding communities and sunk investments into machinery and real estate, there were no such limits on the size of newly built American and German factories. Massive factories required massive investments and coordinated management, leading to the development of "trust" arrangements in America and Wilhelminian capitalism in Germany, in which profits were retained for future investment in large-scale mechanization.

This allowed a radical reconfiguration of the factory away from being the productive arm of a merchant capitalist to being a single element of a vertically integrated production process contained within a single firm. The potential for realizing further profits through resource efficiency achieved from more effectively managing vertical integration was recognized for the first time by Frederick Taylor in his 1911 opus *The Principles of Scientific Management*. Taylor's system was perfected by Henry Ford for the production of the Model T car, the first truly mass-produced automobile, by ensuring that the Ford Company controlled the entire manufacturing process, down to owning fields of cattle from which interior leather was derived. In this system conflict with workers was avoided by paying a high wage, famously five dollars a day; at the same time workers were required to eschew alcohol, gambling, and immorality, prohibitions enforced by company inspection officers. Despite the high wages, this system further reduced the worker to being merely the instrument of the capitalist, a dehumanization process brought to its ultimate conclusion by the scientific automation underpinning the (Jewish) Holocaust.

POST-FORDIST FLEXIBLE PRODUCTION

The Fordist organizational system became increasingly important in Europe during the post–World War II (1939–1945) reconstruction period, although with checks and balances to guard against the dehumanizing effects of capitalist control. Social peace was provided through agreements between corporations, states, and unions representing the interests of workers. In Europe and North

America a great number of large, vertically integrated corporations emerged and came to dominate their national markets.

Scientific management was also introduced in Asia during the postwar period, most notably in Japan, but its principles were based on voluntary teamwork rather than top-down managerial control, enabling individual employees to exercise creativity. This system, termed *Toyota-ism* by some, had a number of advantages over Fordism. Geared to continuous product, process, and technique improvement, it allowed firms to serve increasingly sophisticated consumer markets. The social coordination it required led to a third revolution in the factory system from large vertically integrated factories to the "just-in-time" (JIT) production process, in which networks of factories owned by related corporations deliver goods to each other as they are required in their customers' manufacturing processes. This innovation was complemented by novel developments in manufacturing, such as computer-controlled technologies allowing highly automated, flexible production systems with limited labor inputs.

Although the social contract underpinning JIT was not frequently adopted outside Asia, the competitive success of Japan in the 1980s encouraged many European and American corporations to reorient their production processes toward what has been called *lean manufacturing.* Falling labor costs in emerging economies alongside extreme specialization in the labor process has led many multinational companies to actively pursue separation of research, development, and design activities from manufacturing. This revolution of the factory system saw a change from the production line to more networked production organizations involving more extensive spatial and technical divisions of labor. Although individuals in the factory system exercised more creativity in tightly defined roles, the third revolution was characterized by increasing interdependence between corporate locations and a simultaneous separation of factories from their physical locations because of their involvement in global production networks, enabling increasing offshore manufacturing activities.

SEE ALSO *Automobile Industry; Clock Time; Division of Labor; Factory System; Labor; Management; Production; Productivity; Smith, Adam; Taylorism; Work; Work Day; Work Week*

BIBLIOGRAPHY

Black, Edwin. 2001. *IBM and the Holocaust: The Strategic Alliance between Nazi Germany and America's Most Powerful Corporation.* London: Little, Brown.

Engels, Friedrich. [1845] 1987. *The Condition of the Working Class in England,* ed. Victor Kiernan. Harmondsworth, U.K.: Penguin.

Landes, David S. 1997. *The Wealth and Poverty of Nations: Why Are Some So Rich and Others So Poor?* London: Little, Brown.

Smith, Adam. [1776] 1974. *The Wealth of Nations,* ed. Andrew S. Skinner. Harmondsworth, U.K.: Penguin.

Taylor, Frederick Winslow. [1911] 1989. *The Principles of Scientific Management.* Minneola, NY: Dover Books.

Paul Benneworth

FACTORY SYSTEM

The factory system is a mode of capitalist production that emerged in the late eighteenth century as a result of England's Industrial Revolution. Preindustrial England was largely organized around localized forms of production. Goods were produced on family-centered farms, and items such as yarn and other textiles were contracted for larger distribution or produced independently to be sold at a market. After technological innovations created the ability to produce textiles using waterpower, production became centralized in a single place: a factory owned in many cases by members of the former aristocratic class and staffed by workers who were paid a wage (see E. P. Thompson's 1963 book, *The Making of the English Working Class*). While this mode of production began with the cotton and textile industries, it was the development of the steam engine that fully established the shift from craftspeople and localized production into production under the factory system.

There are several interconnected factors beyond technological innovation that created the factory system in England in its particular moment in history. One was the development of banking institutions, which were able to channel investments into the establishment of factories, and which were also able to facilitate economic exchange. Similarly, landowners were able to take advantage of the banking industry's low interest rates to facilitate and finance the development of transit systems, created to move goods produced under this new system. At the same time, a rise in the British population not only increased demand for goods, but also created a large pool of laborers who would eventually work for a wage after the development of the factory system. Finally, social changes in Britain at the time both facilitated the training of upper-middle-class men who would administrate the factory system and also the development of British persons as free workers, as opposed to serfs, who could sell their labor power in exchange for a wage.

As such, the development of the factory system was central to the eventual entrenchment of capitalism on a world scale. It was this very shift in production and landownership, combined with the legal backing of free individuals who may enter into a state-sanctioned contractual relationship, that created what Karl Marx (1818–1883) would identify as the two classes in capitalist society: those who own the means of productions and those who own labor power, which they exchange for a wage in the marketplace. Although both workers and owners share the distinction of equality under the law, it was the old aristocrats who were able to develop the infrastructure and purchase the land to develop factories, and the old serfs who had nothing to sell and exchange but their capacity for labor. This system, whereby the owners of the factories could, through the labor process, transfer the value of the worker's productivity into the value of a commodity, established the efficient yet exploitative mode of capitalist production that is still with us today.

The factory system was not only the foundation for the development of capitalism; it also radically shifted many aspects of social organization and daily life. Agricultural families were largely disenfranchised by this process, and in many cases were required to move to industrial centers in order to survive. They were thrust into the system of wage labor, fundamentally changing relationships between men and women. Whereas in preindustrial societies, all members of the family were involved in production work, the advent of the factory system created a gendered division of labor for middle- and working-class families, whereby men went to work for a wage and women were relegated to household work. In poor and nonwhite families, women worked for a wage outside the home in both formal and informal settings. Men were nearly always wageworkers, while women were either relegated to unpaid work to support the work of the men in their families or themselves worked for wages as a means of survival.

The link of the wage system to factory production created not only a different work process and a gendered division of labor, but also a new form of work. Whereas work under preindustrial forms of organization was often exploitative, particularly under systems of slavery and feudalism, the development of the factory system as a defining feature of capitalism created *alienated* work for the first time. Work is said to be alienated when the worker is in a relationship of production whereby he or she has no autonomy or control over what he or she is producing, where the goods being produced belong exclusively to the owner of the factory, and whereby this process makes the worker alien to himself or herself and his or her community. Marx, in his book *Capital: A Critique of Political Economy* (1867) argued that workers are alienated to the same extent that they are subject to livelihood exclusively

through the wage labor market. This same process has created a social life whereby workers are more fundamentally tied to the workplace than to their homes in terms of livelihood and dependence. This process has also created levels of bureaucracy that divide labor into segmented, deskilled tasks.

There has been tremendous resistance to the organization of work and social life under the factory system of production. Historically, that resistance has resulted in the abolition of child labor, the creation of the eight-hour workday, and various other labor laws regulating the extent to which owners of the means of production may exploit their workers. Moral arguments about whose labor is fair to exploit, and under which conditions that labor power may be extracted, have resulted in change. Many of the first nations to develop the factory system are now seeing a decline in factory production, as its mode of efficiency under capitalism seeks ever-cheaper ways to produce goods outside the limits of environmental and labor laws. These same nations have seen a shift from factory production to a service economy. However, the fundamental form of factory production, and the inherent link to exploitative relationships under capitalism, is as yet unaltered.

SEE ALSO *Factories*

BIBLIOGRAPHY

Marx, Karl. [1867] 1906–1909. *Capital: A Critique of Political Economy*. Chicago: Kerr.

Thompson, E. P. 1963. *The Making of the English Working Class*. New York: Vintage.

Ward, J. T. 1970. *The Factory System*, Vol. 1: *Birth and Growth*. New York: Barnes & Noble.

Ward, J. T. 1970. *The Factory System*, Vol. 2: *The Factory System and Society*. New York: Barnes & Noble.

Meghan A. Burke
David G. Embrick

FAHRENHEIT 9/11

Fahrenheit 9/11 is a documentary-style film that explores both alleged causes and consequences of the terrorist attacks of September 11, 2001. The film is highly critical of Republican president George W. Bush and his administration, the U.S. Congress, and the mainstream media. It suggests that the Bush administration did not effectively pursue the perpetrators of the terrorist attacks because of close personal and financial ties to Saudi Arabia, and that Bush exploited the country's unity in the wake of the attacks to promote a predetermined agenda to invade

Iraq. Among other things, the film highlights the differential costs of the Iraq war for rich and poor Americans, and it addresses the extent to which U.S. corporations have profited from the war, juxtaposing this with images of insolvent American communities, where young men and women are heavily recruited to fight the war. *Fahrenheit 9/11* and its creator, Michael Moore, received lavish praise and harsh criticism, and both the film and filmmaker remain controversial subjects.

Michael Francis Moore, born April 23, 1954 in Michigan, is a filmmaker, author, and social commentator. Although most of his films are classified as documentaries, Moore's style deviates from the neutral, observational style that typifies this genre. He refers to his films as "op-ed pieces," and approaches his subject matter with a decidedly opinionated tone. He narrates his own films and employs humor, archival footage, movie clips, and sometimes strained, impromptu interviews to mock his adversaries and persuade audiences to adopt his liberal/left-wing perspective. Moore received an Academy Award for *Bowling for Columbine* (2002) and twice broke records for the highest-grossing documentary film (for *Bowling for Columbine* and *Fahrenheit 9/11*). His 2001 book *Stupid White Men* was a *New York Times* best-seller.

From a financial perspective, *Fahrenheit 9/11* was a huge success. It was the top-rated U.S. film on its opening weekend (despite a limited theater release) and eventually became the highest grossing documentary in history. It was also a critical success, earning Moore the prestigious Palme d'Or at the Cannes Film Festival. The political success of the film, however, is much less clear. A Pew Research Center poll suggested that Moore was "preaching to the choir." Seventy-six percent of those who reported seeing the film disapproved of President Bush, and those who stated that they did not plan to see it were much more likely to be politically conservative (47%) than liberal (13%).

Given Moore's confrontational style, it is not surprising that *Fahrenheit 9/11* was met with strong opposition from conservatives, including attempts to prevent cinemas from showing the film and to block advertising for it. Many conservatives have attacked the ideas presented in the film as well as the filmmaker's credibility. Perhaps more surprising was the opposition that Moore encountered from other liberals, such as *Boston Globe* columnist Ellen Goodman, journalism professor Robert Jensen, and former New York City mayor Ed Koch. Some observers have suggested that by provoking a backlash *Fahrenheit 9/11* may have actually helped conservatives in the 2004 elections, although such claims are difficult to evaluate given the available data. What is clear is that Michael Moore has brought ideologically explicit messages to commercially successful documentary filmmaking, thereby

inspiring other liberal documentaries including *The Yes Men* (2003) and *The Corporation* (2003), as well as numerous conservative parodies.

BIBLIOGRAPHY

Moore, Michael. 2004. *The Official* Fahrenheit 9/11 *Reader.* New York: Simon and Schuster.

Pew Research Center for the People and the Press. July 21, 2004. Democratic Party Image Improvement. http://people-press.org/reports/display.php3?ReportID=220.

Jaime L. Napier
John T. Jost

FAIR HOUSING ACT OF 1968

SEE *Integration.*

FAIRY TALES

SEE *Storytelling.*

FALKLAND ISLANDS WAR

The Falkland Islands conflict took place between April 2 and June 20, 1982, and is of interest as an episode of non-superpower military crisis and war. The dispute centered upon the sovereignty of the South Atlantic archipelago, with both Britain and Argentina claiming first discovery and possession. The competing claims were bolstered on the British side by the islanders' wish to remain a crown colony, and on the Argentinean side by the geographic proximity of the islands to the Argentinean mainland.

Prior to the conflict, successive British governments were prepared to reach a negotiated settlement of the sovereignty issue, but the islanders' protests as to their Britishness and their opposition to living under Argentinean rule made a resolution difficult. British policy had therefore assumed a status quo character, involving slow-moving negotiations with Argentina in order to avoid matters coming to a head and to keep the issue off the British domestic political agenda. Little attempt was made to effectively defend the islands. A token garrison on land was supplemented by the lightly armed patrol vessel, HMS *Endurance*, at sea.

Two developments disturbed the status quo and led to fighting. First, a military junta headed by General Leopoldo Galtieri (1926–2003) came to power in Argentina. The junta recognized that capturing the islands would represent a huge domestic political coup. Secondly, cuts in the British defense budget meant that the *Endurance* was publicly slated for withdrawal from Falklands duty, seemingly indicating that British commitment to the islands had waned even further.

Consequently, when an adventurous scrap-metal merchant, Constantino Davidoff, landed on the island of South Georgia and raised the Argentinean flag on March 19, the junta took note of the desultory British response and launched a full-scale invasion. To the junta's surprise, British Prime Minister Margaret Thatcher was not prepared to accept the fait accompli. A naval task force was quickly constituted to recapture the islands.

Given the 8,000-mile distance of the islands from the United Kingdom, the task force would take three weeks to reach its destination. The delay gave ample opportunity for diplomatic maneuvers, although the evidence is that Thatcher personally did not believe the matter could be resolved without the use of force. The United States, alarmed at the prospect of fighting between its European and Latin American allies, attempted to broker a compromise through the good offices of Secretary of State Alexander Haig. Haig, a protégé of Henry Kissinger, sought to repeat the latter's "shuttle diplomacy," but succeeded only in irritating Thatcher and misunderstanding the confusing signals emanating from the junta. His efforts came to naught.

When the fighting began it was episodic but fierce. The Argentinean air force, equipped with a limited number of French Super Etendard fighters and the dangerous Exocet missile, succeeded in sinking the British destroyer *Sheffield* on May 4, and HMS *Coventry* and the supply ship *Atlantic Conveyor* on May 25. The heaviest losses sustained by the British came on June 8, when the landing ships *Sir Galahad* and *Sir Tristram* were hit with the loss of two hundred men. However, the Argentineans failed in their primary mission of damaging the task force's two aircraft carriers, *Hermes* and *Invincible*, upon which the success of the British effort depended. The losses the Argentinean forces sustained in trying were heavy. The single costliest action was the sinking by the British submarine *Conqueror* of the Argentinean heavy cruiser *General Belgrano* on May 4, with the loss of over three hundred men. This episode would later become controversial, as it emerged that a peace plan, sponsored by the government of Peru, was in the process of consideration by the junta when the decision to sink the *Belgrano*, which was sailing away from the British fleet and outside of its declared "exclusion zone," was taken. Participants on the British side have always maintained that they were unaware of the plan and could not have accepted its terms in any case.

The fighting on land, beginning on May 21, pitted the British landing force against numerically superior but demoralized and poorly trained Argentinean defenders. The prospects for Argentinean military success had rested upon establishing superiority over the British naval force, and when this could not be achieved the Argentinean surrender, which came after several sharp engagements including the May 28 Battle of Goose Green, was inevitable.

In the years following the war, the British reinforced the islands through the so-called Fortress Falklands policy. Having failed to achieve the coup of recapturing the islands, the Argentinean junta fell shortly after the end of the conflict. The investment involved in the Fortress Falklands policy, including the influx of a sizable contingent of British troops, revitalized the islands' economy and, ironically, led to greater trade with the Argentinean mainland. Diplomatic relations between Argentina and the United Kingdom were restored in 1990, and in August 2001 Prime Minister Tony Blair became the first British leader to visit Argentina since the war.

SEE ALSO *Diplomacy; Thatcher, Margaret*

BIBLIOGRAPHY

Freedman, Lawrence. 2005. *The Official History of the Falklands Campaign.* London: Routledge.

Hastings, Max, and Simon Jenkins. 1983. *The Battle for the Falklands.* London: Norton.

Middlebrook, Martin. 1989. *The Fight for the "Malvinas": The Argentine Forces in the Falklands War.* New York: Penguin.

Stephen Dyson

FALSE CONSCIOUSNESS

The concept of "false consciousness" is derived from the Marxist theory of social class. The concept refers to the systematic misrepresentation of dominant social relations in the consciousness of subordinate classes. Marx himself did not use the phrase "false consciousness," but he paid extensive attention to the related concepts of ideology and commodity fetishism. Members of a subordinate class (e.g., workers, peasants, serfs) suffer from false consciousness in that their mental representations of the social relations around them systematically conceal or obscure the realities of subordination, exploitation, and domination those relations embody. Related concepts include mystification, ideology, and fetishism.

Marx offered an objective theory of class, based on an analysis of the objective features of the system of economic relations that form the social order. A person's social class is determined by his or her position within the system of property relations in a given economic society. People also have subjective characteristics, such as thoughts, mental frameworks, and identities. These mental constructs give a person a cognitive framework through which to understand his or her role in the world and the forces that govern his or her life. One's mental constructs, however, may not accurately reflect social reality. In a class-based society, there is an inherent conflict of material interests between privileged and subordinate groups. In such a society, Marx asserted, social mechanisms emerge that systematically create distortions, errors, and blind spots in the consciousness of the underclass. If these consciousness-shaping mechanisms did not exist, then the underclass, which is always a majority of the population, would quickly overthrow the system of their domination. So the institutions that shape the individual's thoughts, ideas, and frameworks develop in such a way as to generate false consciousness and ideology.

Marx's theory of ideology is presented in *The German Ideology* (1845), cowritten with Friedrich Engels. The term *ideology* refers to a system of ideas through which people understand their world. A central theoretical assertion in Marx's writings is the view that ideology and thought are dependent on the material circumstances in which a person lives. Material circumstances determine consciousness, rather than consciousness determining material reality: "The hand-mill gives you society with the feudal lord; the steam-mill society with the industrial capitalist" (Marx 1847). A system of ideology supports the advantage of the dominant class, according to Marxist theory. The concept of commodity fetishism is discussed in *Capital* (Marx 1867). Marx used this concept to refer to the pervasive and defining illusion that exists in a commodity society. A commodity is perceived solely in terms of its money equivalent (its price), rather than being understood as standing within a set of social relations of production. Thus, the labor of the operator of a shoe-sewing machine disappears, and only the money value of the shoes is visible. Marx believed that this is a socially important form of mystification. In other words, the market society obscures the relations of domination and exploitation on which it depends.

Twentieth-century Marxist thinkers have given more systematic attention to a Marxist theory of consciousness and ideology than Marx provided. Georg Lukács (1885–1971) was one of the first European philosophers to reflect seriously on Marx's philosophical ideas. Lukács introduced the concept of false consciousness into Marxist discourse (based on a brief reference by Engels) in relation to a dialectical theory of knowledge. A more sociological treatment of class consciousness was provided by Karl Mannheim (1893–1947) in his effort to formulate a "sociology of knowledge" in the 1930s. The sociology of knowledge attempts to provide a theoretical account of the relationship between knowledge systems and the social conditions within which they emerge; this provides a theoretical framework with which to understand the workings of a system of ideology. Mannheim supported the idea that the social position of the bourgeoisie and the proletariat deeply influence the forms of knowledge that they embody, and he argued that these forms of material bias lead to a systematic falsification of social reality.

Antonio Gramsci (1891–1937) significantly extended Marxist thinking about ideology and consciousness in the 1930s, giving ideology a more active role in politics and history than classical historical materialism. He argued that the proletariat has the ability to influence the terms of its consciousness, so that there is an extended struggle between the bourgeoisie and the proletariat over representations of the existing social reality. The bourgeoisie generally exercises "hegemony" over the terms of ideology through its control of the instruments of consciousness. The proletariat, however, can exert influence through its own cultural institutions. This perspective introduces a major change into the classical theory of ideology, in that it denies that the subordinate class is simply the passive tool of the dominant ideology. The French philosopher Louis Althusser (1918–1990) provided an influential perspective on the role of ideology in a class-based society in *Lenin and Philosophy* (1971). Generally characterized as offering a structuralist interpretation of Marxism, Althusser's writings on the role of ideology in the social system diverge from the interpretation offered in *The German Ideology*. Althusser took issue with the notion that ideology is a feature of consciousness. Instead, he referred to the set of institutions that produce and reproduce social states of knowledge as an "ideological state apparatus." He also disputed the assumption that there is an external social reality independent from ideology, believing instead that all features of reality are expressed in language and are inseparable from the features of consciousness singled out as "ideological."

SEE ALSO *Alienation; Factories; Ideology*

BIBLIOGRAPHY

Althusser, Louis. 1971. *Lenin and Philosophy, and Other Essays.* Trans. Ben Brewster. London: New Left Books.

Gramsci, Antonio. 1971. *Selections from the Prison Notebooks of Antonio Gramsci.* Ed. and trans. Q. Hoare and G. Nowell-Smith. London: Lawrence & Wishart.

Lukács, György. 1920. *History and Class Consciousness: Studies in Marxist Dialectics.* Trans. Rodney Livingstone. Cambridge, MA: MIT Press, 1971.

Mannheim, Karl. 1936. *Ideology and Utopia: An Introduction to the Sociology of Knowledge.* New York: Harcourt Brace.

Marx, Karl. 1847. *The Poverty of Philosophy.* Moscow: Progress Publishers, 1971.

Marx, Karl. 1867. *Capital.* Vol. 1. New York: Vintage. 1977.

Marx, Karl, and Friedrich Engels. 1845. *The German Ideology.* 3rd rev. ed. Moscow: Progress Publishers, 1970.

Daniel Little

FAMILIES, FEMALE-HEADED

SEE *Female-Headed Families.*

FAMILY

It is said that families have always existed and that people have always formed families. However, conceptions of *family* can vary considerably. Until the 1970s, it was believed that the *extended family* had been a social institution since medieval times throughout the Western world. This family form consists of a married couple and the parents of one of them plus the couple's children. However, Peter Laslett (1915–2001) and his Cambridge colleagues showed that although the extended family existed, it was not a social institution. This belief in the long history of the extended family can be understood to be a myth if one considers the high mortality rate during previous centuries, when many mothers and fathers died before their children became adults.

The term *nuclear family* refers to a family formed by a socially accepted marriage between a man and a woman who live together with their minor children. The anthropologist George Peter Murdock (1897–1985) coined the term in his book *Social Structure* (1949). Murdock assumed that almost all cultures have had this nucleus as their basic and preferred family form. Some cultures build upon the nuclear family, while others combine nuclear families. One type of nuclear family is an extended family that consists of at least three generations under the same roof. Another type of combined nuclear family is the polygamous family that, when polyandrous, consists of one woman married (socially) to at least two men. Polygyny is one man married (socially) to at least two women. Another variation would be group marriages consisting of at least two women married to at least two men, but this phenomenon has never been found anywhere as a social institution. Group marriages have certainly existed

but only for short periods of a decade or so, and they have never been a society's preferred living arrangement.

The issue of what can be considered a *social marriage* is complicated and unclear. As long as marriages have been known to exist in one form or another, they have mainly been the base upon which new generations grow up. Historically marriage seems also to have been the preferred arrangement for living together. A prerequisite for marriage has been that the couple should be able to afford a home, which means somewhere to live with a bed, a table, and necessary utensils. Situations in which couples have cohabited without marrying have also been common. In some cultures this arrangement, when lasting, is called *common-law marriage;* after some years, the two come to be counted as married (see Trost 1980).

The term *family formation* is still sometimes used as a synonym for marriage. The background is that over the centuries marriage has been linked to four normatively connected elements: holding a marriage ceremony, moving in together, having sex together, and bearing a child within about a year.

WHAT IS A FAMILY?

The term *family* is often presented in definite form, *the* family, a phrasing that indicates that there is only one kind of family. In Western culture at least, this might mean the nuclear family. However, this concept carries a kind of ideological code, which implies that the nuclear family is supposed to be the best and that the concept is reproduced over generations (see Smith 1993). The term *family* can also be connected to the entire range of relatives, especially close relatives.

Family can be considered from various levels. On a societal level, the law might define what a family is; this often means at least one parent and at least one minor child, where the parent is supposed to take care of the child. Another example is family responsibility, where an adult child is supposed to take care of elderly parents. Other persons can also be included—as in, for example, the Sami culture (previously known as Lapps) in Scandinavia, where many, but not all, relatives are counted as family members.

Another level on which family can be considered has to do with companies and other organizations. Some companies differentiate between who can be counted as family, depending upon the situation. For example, an employee may be granted an entire day of leave to attend a funeral for a close family member or relative, while the funeral of a more distant relative will not warrant any time off. Some organizations are considered "family friendly," which may mean that they offer various benefits or discounts to families. *Family* in such cases usually includes only the nuclear family or a simple variation of it.

If ordinary people are asked to name the members of their family, they will give a variety of answers, even when the person asked believes that the meaning of the term *family* is culturally determined. The number of family members can vary from none up to several hundred. Included as family members can be spouses, children, parents, uncles and aunts, grandparents, cousins, and so forth but also lovers, friends, and pets. Family members counted in this way can also include deceased persons. This way of looking at the meaning of family is dependent upon who is asked as well as the situation. For example, someone included in one person's family might not include that person as a member of his or her own family. There are no clear and objective boundaries of what constitutes family when it comes to the individual's definition of her or his family and who its members are.

If people are asked whom they consider to be included in possible constellations of families, they give a variety of answers. Some believe that a one-parent household is not a family, whereas others think it is a family. Some think that the parents have to be married, while others think that cohabiting couples can also be families. Some believe that same-gender couples cannot be counted as a family, while others have a different opinion. This variety of answers means that some individuals and some cultures are very inclusive when it comes to what to include as a family and some are very exclusive.

Sometimes the unit for the concept of family is limited to the *household*. That use occurs primarily in censuses and other demographic studies, but it also occurs among lay people. However, many households include members that no one else in the household would classify as members of their family. At the same time, there are many persons who fall outside the family when using household as equivalent to family. This was and still is the case in some parts of the world where households include servants and other employed persons (see Levin and Trost 1992).

FAMILY-RELATED MATTERS

There are a number of issues related to the term *family* and the concept of family. As mentioned above, marriage can be one of them. Poverty can cause couples to not marry, since societally it is costly to marry. In people's minds, one should have a home when marrying; informal norms in many cultures say that without a roof, a bed, and some kitchen utensils, one cannot marry. Social surroundings are also important, since people often normatively expect a marriage ceremony to be combined with a party for relatives and also for friends and neighbors. Therefore nonmarital cohabitation based on poverty has been common in many parts of the world and remains common in some (Rodman 1966).

A new type of nonmarital cohabitation has developed as a social institution in most of the Western world. With the liberalization that came after World War II (1939–1945), the normative structure of "family formation" was reduced. Now nonmarital cohabitation has made marriage less common, to the point of disappearing in some countries. This movement has made nonmarital cohabitation a social institution in many cultures; it is a kind of cohabitation that is not at all connected to poverty. In many countries, particularly the Scandinavian countries, all or almost all couples live together in a nonmarital cohabitation relationship for years before marrying. The trend toward more nonmarital cohabitation has decreased the number of marriages, and both brides and grooms are on average much older now than in the past.

Another change in the way couples live together is referred to as *living apart together* (LAT). Such relationships consist of a married or nonmarried couple, with or without children, who each have a home and who visit each other, perceive themselves to be an intimate couple, and are so perceived by those in their social surroundings. These relationships have always existed in the Western world among, for example, writers and other artists. The difference between these earlier relationships and those of the early twenty-first century lies in part in the number and in part by the fact that LAT relationships constitute a new social institution. For example, in Sweden about 5 percent of the adult population lives in an LAT relationship (Trost and Levin 2000).

Such relationships could not have developed as a social institution had not nonmarital cohabitation become a social institution with the dissolution of the normative structure of the four elements of traditional social structure listed above. Had not the normative connection disappeared between the acts of marrying, moving in together, having sexual intercourse together, and the expectation of a child within about a year, LAT relationships would not have been possible. The social institution of nonmarital cohabitation is thus a prerequisite for the existence of LAT relationships.

Another issue connected to family is changes in divorce laws and divorce practice. Divorce has for many centuries been a social institution permitted in many cultures but prohibited in others. In the Western world, where the changes have been obvious, claims for more liberal divorce laws came at the end of the nineteenth century as a result of rapidly decreasing mortality rates. With such decreases, the idea of lifelong marriages slowly became obsolete, and divorce laws changed slowly in a more liberal direction. (The number of remarriages in many countries is now the same as in the middle of the nineteenth century. Previously the high mortality rate widowed many married women and men; many of these widows and widowers remarried, while now most remarriages occur after one or both partners has divorced.)

During the nineteenth century the *total fertility rate* (TFR) was at a global level of above five (children per woman during her fertile lifespan). Partly as a result of improvements of contraceptive techniques and methods (better condoms and diaphragms, preventive pills, intrauterine devices) and propaganda, the TFR has decreased all over the world and even reached the low level of less than 1.5 (average number of children per woman) in many Western countries. These changes have caused few women to have more children than they want, but some will not have as many as they want. In the mid-twentieth century the average age of both parents at the birth of their children was much lower than now, which is one reason for the lower birthrates.

FAMILY FUNCTIONS

From a *functionalist* perspective, family has been seen as fulfilling a set of functions for the individual as well as for society. These functions, which have more and more come to be of historical interest, include the following.

The *reproductive* function means that women customarily give birth to children within a family union, and this makes society able to last in the long run. The early twenty-first century fertility rates in many less-developed countries will cause the population to increase, while in many developed countries the opposite will happen.

The *socialization* function refers to the upbringing of children into adulthood, a process that transfers habits and norms from one generation to another. Historically most socialization occurred within the family, but in the early twenty-first century much socialization is generated via school systems, mass media, and other sources.

The *protective* function gives the members of families protection against bad weather, keeps children in a safe environment, and leads family members to take care of the elderly and the sick. In most parts of the world this function has partly been taken over by society via social security and other social programs.

The *sexual* function means that sexual intercourse would occur within the marital union as part of family. In many parts of the world premarital and extramarital sex is taken care of through the use of prostitutes. Elsewhere the prohibition on premarital sex is no longer an issue with the liberalization of sex norms.

The *religious* function has to do with the exercise of religious activities, which are supposed to occur mainly within a family unit. In many parts of the world secularization has made this function less important.

The *leisure time* function is supposed to support family members during times when no work is needed. This function has in many parts of the world been subsumed by organizations outside the family.

Finally, the *emotional* or *primary group* function ideally takes care of the family members' emotional needs. The term *primary group* was coined by the American sociologist Charles Horton Cooley (1864–1929) in 1909. The idea is that in small groups, of which family is one, the members can feel safe and secure not only physically but also emotionally. Reality, however, can be the opposite, with physical as well as emotional abuse and cruelty sometimes occurring in primary groups. Furthermore family as a primary group depends highly upon the definition one has of family. As mentioned above, membership in a family can vary greatly when considered from an individual perspective. In any case, many studies show that when a disaster strikes, the most important aid givers are family members and other relatives, who tend to be more helpful toward one another than any organization can be. This occurs in part because organizational helpers can seldom give the same emotional support that close relatives can.

For society to work, social order is needed; otherwise chaos will occur, and society will fall apart. When these family functions are in accordance with social norms and when family members, however defined, follow the informal norms, social order will remain relatively stable, assuming no opposing changes occur.

SEE ALSO *Childlessness; Children; Cohabitation; Divorce and Separation; Family, Extended; Family, Nuclear; Family Functioning; Family Structure; Family Values; Fatherhood; Marriage; Motherhood; Parent-Child Relationships*

BIBLIOGRAPHY

Adams, Bert, and Jan Trost, eds. 2005. *Handbook of World Families.* Menlo Park, CA: Sage.

Cooley, Charles Horton. [1909] 1922. *Social Organisation.* New York: Scribner's.

Journal of Family Issues 14 (1) 1993.

Laslett, Peter, ed. 1972. *Household and Family in Past Time.* Cambridge, U.K.: Cambridge University Press.

Levin, Irene, and Jan Trost. 1992. Understanding the Concept of Family. *Family Relations* 41: 348–351.

Murdock, George Peter. 1949. *Social Structure.* New York: Free Press.

Rodman, Hyman. 1966. Illegitimacy in the Caribbean Social Structure: A Reconsideration. *American Sociological Review* 31: 673–683.

Smith, Dorothy. 1993. The Standard North American Family: SNAF as an Ideological Code. *Journal of Family Issues* 14: 50–67.

Trost, Jan. 1980. *Unmarried Cohabitation*. Västerås, Sweden: International Library.

Trost, Jan, and Irene Levin. 2000. *Särbo, ett par—Två Hushåll*. Lund, Sweden: Studentlitteratur.

Jan Trost

FAMILY, EXTENDED

Families are vitally important for patterning interpersonal behavior, roles, privileges, and obligations within society. These guidelines define how family relations are organized—how mates are selected; who marries whom; who lives together; who is the head of the family; which relatives are most important; and how children are to be reared and by whom. Throughout history, in most of the world, the extended family has been the most common household arrangement. Extended family refers to blood or kin connections that link successive generations through paternal or maternal lines of descent.

Definitions of the extended family incorporate other kin beyond the domestic group who do not belong to the nuclear family. When, for example, a married couple lives with the husband's parents, or a grandparent shares a household, the family changes from a nuclear to an extended one. In his 1995 article "Patterns of Kinship and Residence," Max E. Stanton offers clarity in defining an extended family as "an ongoing body with a geographical base and it transcends the lifetime of its members. The composition of the extended family with its nuclear families and independent single adults changes constantly, but the extended family itself continues with new leaders and new members as individuals depart or as the generations pass away" (p. 100).

An extended family can include a wide array of relationships. There can be genealogical connections between affinal relations (e.g., in-laws, adoptive or foster families, aunts/uncles), consanguineous relations (e.g., cousins, half-siblings), "fictive kin" (those perceived as extended family members, though they are not related by blood or law, e.g., godparents, best friends), or sundry other relations (e.g., stepparents or stepsiblings in blended/reconstituted families). To be succinct, Bernard Farber (2000) and Maria Schmeeckle and Susan Sprecher (2004) support a definition of extended family as a vertical extension of a core nuclear family to include a third (e.g., grandparents) or even fourth generation.

An extended family is composed of one or more of four variants. First, the compound family is formed through the combination of nuclear families or parts of them, such as a polygynous household consisting of one man, his three wives, and their respective children. A second variant is a joint family and includes the parental couple, all unmarried children, and married sons with their wives and children in the same household. The head of household, in which authority is vested, is usually the eldest male. Third, a stem family exists when unmarried children and one married sibling, along with spouse and children, reside in the parental household (i.e., stem family) to ensure the continuity, while the other siblings establish their own households upon marriage. Typically, the eldest son is responsible for caring for his parents until they die, at which time he inherits the estate. This inheritance rule is called primogeniture; whereas inheritance by the youngest son is referred to as ultimogeniture. Finally, the modified extended family is one in which children marry out or migrate from the parental household upon marriage, but engage in common activities with parents and other kin on a regular basis.

Colleen Leahy Johnson (1998), Riley and Riley (1993), and Judith Stacey (1990) observe that extended family occurs in various, voluntary, and malleable contexts, making membership changeable and somewhat ambiguous. It is composed of three interlocking nuclear families: family of origin, family of procreation, and family of affinal relations (e.g., in-laws). The family of origin (or family of orientation) is the group into which a person is born. Most early childhood experiences and learning occur here. By contrast, the family of procreation is a group created when adults adhere to a socially recognized bond, such as marriage, and raise children. The affinal family derives from social connections acquired through family of procreation. Most people retain stable, though changing, status in one or more extended families throughout their lives.

SEE ALSO *Family; Family, Nuclear; Family Structure; Kinship; Marriage*

BIBLIOGRAPHY

Farber, Bernard. 2000. Kinship Systems and Family Types. In *Encyclopedia of Sociology*, 2nd ed., Vol. 3, ed. Edgar F. Borgatta, 1501–1519. New York: Macmillan Reference USA.

Johnson, Colleen Leahy. 1988. *Ex familia: Grandparents, Parents, and Children Adjust to Divorce*. New Brunswick, NJ: Rutgers University Press.

Riley, M., and J. Riley. 1993. Connections: Kin and Cohort. In *The Changing Contract across Generations*, ed. V. Bengtson and W. Achenbaum, 169–189. New York: Aldine DeGruyter.

Schmeeckle, Maria, and Susan Sprecher. 2004. Extended Family and Social Networks. In *Handbook of Family Communication*, ed. Anita L. Vangelisti, 349–375. Mahwah, NJ: Erlbaum.

Stacey, Judith. 1990. *Brave New Families: Stories of Domestic Upheaval in Late Twentieth Century America*. New York: Basic Books.

Stanton, Max E. 1995. Patterns of Kinship and Residence. In *Families in Multicultural Perspective*, ed. Bron B. Ingoldsby and Suzanna Smith, 97–116. New York: Guilford.

James J. Ponzetti Jr.

FAMILY, NUCLEAR

When people speak of "family," they usually assume that what they mean is clear, yet the composition and structure of families around the world differ tremendously. Some equate family with a household, but this term is also ambiguous because it has been used to variously include all permanent members such as servants or to exclude unrelated relatives. Historically and cross-culturally, families are culturally determined interpretations of genetically and sexually grounded relationships. Further confusion, however, results for individuals involved in stable intimate relationships who consider themselves "family" but are either not willing (e.g., long term cohabiters), or unable (e.g., gay/lesbian relationships) to secure formal social recognition. Despite the complexities and challenges, however, two essential family structures have been posited; namely, nuclear family and extended family.

The basic family from which more complex forms arise is a nuclear family. At first glance, the definition of nuclear family appears to be straightforward. It is composed of parents and their children. A common, more nuanced definition specifies a nuclear family as two or more individuals affiliated by blood, marriage, or adoption. Regardless, a nuclear family is based on either consanguineous or blood relations, affinal relations (those related by marriage), or some combination thereof.

Genetic connections define consanguineous bonds (e.g., parent and child, or brother and sister), while relationships formed as a result of social convention (e.g., husband and wife, or in-laws) are affinally bonded. Affines also include all of a spouse's own genetic relations. Thus, a woman's brother is an affinal relation of her husband. Finally, the spouses of a person's own consanguinal relatives are his or her affines.

A nuclear family is usually, but not necessarily, coresidential. The affinal tie between husband and wife forms the core of a nuclear family. Although spouses may enjoy relative autonomy and mobility in a nuclear structure, the dynamism intrinsic to such an arrangement can threaten conjugal bonds. Yet Martine Segalen (1986) and Azubike Uzoka (1979) illustrate in their works that the notion of an isolated nuclear family fragmented from other kin is a myth. The myth is embedded within and receives recognition from kin or the social group, as Marvin Sussman notes in his 1959 article "The Isolated Nuclear Family: Fact or Fiction."

As comprehensive as definitions of family try to be, most focus on structural rather than functional aspects of the nuclear family. Whether a nuclear family is universal and necessary is debatable, as Arlene Skolnick (2003) and R. Smith (1968) have examined. Luis Lenero-Otero noted in his 1977 work *Beyond the Nuclear Family Model* that cross-cultural comparisons illuminate the ethnocentric problem of using structure as a basis for defining family. Thus, caution must be exercised in looking only at family structure—that is, the number of its members and their roles.

Families are ubiquitous in global society despite remarkable variability in form. The recognition of family heterogeneity is critical to understanding family from an international perspective. When a family includes other relatives beyond the nuclear core—consanguineous (e.g. grandparents) or affinal (e.g., aunts or uncles)—then an extended family exists.

SEE ALSO *Family; Family, Extended; Family Functioning; Family Structure; Kinship; Marriage*

BIBLIOGRAPHY

Lenero-Otero, Luis, ed. 1977. *Beyond the Nuclear Family Model: Cross-cultural Perspectives.* Beverly Hills, CA: Sage.

Segalen, Martine. 1986. *Historical Anthropology of the Family.* New York: Cambridge University Press.

Skolnick, Arlene. 2003. Nuclear Families. In *International Encyclopedia of Marriage and Family*, 2nd ed., ed. James J. Ponzetti, 1181–1183. New York: Macmillan Reference USA.

Smith, R. 1968. Family: Comparative Structure. In *International Encyclopedia of the Social Sciences*, ed. David L. Sills, 301–313. New York: Macmillan.

Sussman, Marvin B. 1959. The Isolated Nuclear Family: Fact or Fiction. *Social Problems* 6 (4): 333–340.

Uzoka, Azubike Felix. 1979. The Myth of the Nuclear Family: Historical Background and Clinical Implications. *American Psychologist* 34 (11): 1095–1106.

James J. Ponzetti Jr.

FAMILY FUNCTIONING

Recognizing the complicated mosaic of family patterns is important for fostering tolerance in light of global diversity. Yet, more attention is given to family structure than to the functions that families are expected to fulfill. Although what constitutes a family is cross-culturally variable, family functions are remarkably similar from culture to culture. Family life typically provides an environment for ensuring the vital needs of food and shelter, the generation and maintenance of wealth, and the provision of care and other nonmaterial resources. Family functions, regardless of family structure, elicit similar behaviors and practices worldwide (Georgas et al. 2001).

Societies around the world rely on the family to perform certain functions. The basic functions of the family are to: (1) regulate sexual access and activity; (2) provide an orderly context for procreation; (3) nurture and socialize children; (4) ensure economic stability; and (5) ascribe social status. Families further impart affection, care, and adaptive functions. In short, family is considered the supporter of coupling, the source of nurturance and the elemental education of children, the link to the market place, the place of remediation that takes the wayward back, and the hospice where infirm and dependent members seek solace.

Family functions are accomplished in a number of different ways. Typically, marriage or some variant is socially approved as the appropriate outlet for sexual behavior. Families teach and reiterate that certain persons and conditions are more apt for sexual intimacy and affection than others. For example, there are taboos against incest and at certain times against intercourse, such as during menstruation or pregnancy. The regulation of sexual behavior is concerned with more than coitus, and covers such behaviors as hugging, kissing, and touching, as well as attitudes and values. These attitudes and values influence family reactions and cultural prescriptions to such practices as premarital and extramarital relationships (Widmer et al. 1998).

Families are the most widely approved context for bearing and rearing children. Procreation within a family garners social approval for parenthood, and delineates legitimate progeny. Children born outside a conjugal family are often stigmatized. Socialization is perhaps the most important function because it teaches the rules and expectations for behavior both within the family as well as in the society outside. In this respect the family is a miniature social system, with parents as the chief promoters and enforcers of social order. The outcome of the socialization process within the family is critically important for the larger society, which is based on regulation and the shared willingness of citizens to conform to social norms. Typically, family provides the security and support best suited for teaching children life skills, cultural values, and social responsibility. It is doubtful whether children could develop into mentally, physically, and socially healthy human beings without family.

The provision and management of sufficient financial resources is an essential function in order to facilitate the efficacy of other family functions. Families influence the social placement and life chances of individuals. Children

generally assume the legal, religious, and political status of their family, whereas other roles are achieved through marriage, occupation, and education.

While some people prefer doing things alone, most need others who care for them, show affection, share joys and sorrows, and give support in times of need. Affection and emotional support are extremely important. A family can recognize changes and reorganize to adapt to its environment more rapidly than other groups. This adaptive function enables families to adjust to new demands and cope with change. Family life can exhibit openness to novel ways of living and thinking that have not developed in other spheres (Boulding 1981; Vincent 1966). While other institutions—religious, educational, political, and economic—may assist with these functions, the primary responsibility is relegated to family.

SEE ALSO *Children; Family; Family, Extended; Family, Nuclear; Family Structure; Family Values; Kinship; Marriage; Parent-Child Relationships; Parenting Styles; Sibling Relationships*

BIBLIOGRAPHY

Boulding, Elise. 1981. *The Place of the Family in Times of Social Transition.* Ottawa, ON: Vanier Institute of the Family.

Georgas, James, Kostas Mylonas, Tsabika Bafiti, et al. 2001. Functional Relationships in the Nuclear and Extended Family: A 16-Culture Study. *International Journal of Psychology* 36 (5): 289–300.

Vincent, Clark E. 1966. Familia Spongia: The Adaptive Function. *Journal of Marriage and the Family* 28 (1): 29–36.

Widmer, Eric, Judith Treas, and Robert Newcomb. 1998. Attitudes toward Nonmarital Sex in 24 Countries. *Journal of Sex Research* 35 (4): 349–358.

James J. Ponzetti Jr.

FAMILY PLANNING

Family planning is a term created in the mid-twentieth century to refer to the ability to control reproduction through access to contraception, abortion, and sterilization, in addition to access to information and education. Reproductive control allows a woman to determine when and whether she will have children. A woman's ability to control the birth and spacing of her children has a direct impact on her educational, economic, and social opportunities. A woman's enjoyment of heterosexual activity can be affected by the fear of becoming pregnant if she lacks information about, or access to, contraception and abortion.

Women have found ways to control their reproduction since the earliest days of recorded history. However, these methods have not always been safe or effective. By 1900, every method of contraception (chemical, barrier, and natural means) had been invented, except for the anovulant method (the contraceptive pill and related methods of hormone regulation developed in the mid-twentieth century). Access to contraception was limited by law or by technological inferiority. In the United States, contraception and abortion were available through midwives, with a variety of contraceptive methods also available in the open market and through the advice of friends and family. With industrialization, urbanization, and the advent of new reproductive technologies, there was a shift away from women's ability to control their reproductive lives. By 1900, every state had criminalized abortion in most circumstances. In 1873 Congress passed the Act of the Suppression of Trade in and Circulation of, Obscene Literature and Articles of Immoral Use. The Comstock Law, as it was known, was named for the U.S. Postal agent, Anthony Comstock (1844–1915), who lobbied for the bill's passage. The law criminalized, among other things, the distribution of information and materials related to contraception and abortion through the U.S. mail. Legal or not, women often found means of controlling their reproduction, utilizing methods which were sometimes ineffective, dangerous, or in some cases deadly.

In the first decades of the twentieth century, social activists such as Margaret Sanger (1879–1966) and some members of the medical profession initiated a campaign for legalized contraception. Sanger was born into a large working-class family. She attended nursing school and later served as an obstetrical nurse in the Lower East Side of New York City. From her experiences as a nurse and as a child among eleven in her family of origin (her mother died at a young age as a result of multiple pregnancies within a short span of years), Sanger recognized the connection between the inability to regulate fertility and families' economic struggles as well as women's health. Later in life, Sanger would recall stories of women who begged her for information on how to avoid having more children or who fell ill and in some cases died as a result of a botched, illegal abortion.

Sanger's efforts to find information on safe, legal, and effective means to regulate women's fertility merged easily with her socialist perspective. In her socialist-feminist periodical, *The Woman Rebel,* Sanger first coined the term *birth control* in 1914. In the same year, she authored and published a pamphlet on methods of contraception, *Family Limitation,* based on her research on techniques and technologies of contraception available around the world. With her international research in hand, Sanger opened the first birth control clinic in the United States in 1916. One year later, she began to publish the periodical *Birth Control Review.* For more than a decade, the *Birth Control Review* provided readers with news and informa-

tion on the fight for the legalization of contraception in the United States and overseas. In addition, Sanger traveled widely, organizing speaking tours and international conferences in an effort to coordinate the efforts of medical and social advocates for birth control. Thanks to the work of Sanger and others like her, by the mid-1930s various court rulings allowed contraception to be more widely available in the United States. Sanger's American Birth Control League (founded in 1921) merged with other advocacy groups to become the Planned Parenthood Federation of America in 1942.

Sanger's socialist roots in the birth control movement later evolved into a mainstream call for "planned parenthood"—the appropriate spacing of pregnancies to protect the health of mothers and children. The advent of the contraceptive pill in the United States in the 1960s led to a philosophical shift from birth control as a means of spacing pregnancies to a connection with the women's liberation movement—freeing women from a fear of pregnancy, allowing them to focus on their careers and shape their own destiny.

Sanger remains a controversial figure in American history. Because she founded Planned Parenthood, critics of abortion connect her work with the abortion services offered at Planned Parenthood clinics across the country. In vilifying its founder, they attempt to discredit her organization. However, Sanger repeatedly separated the provision of abortion from contraception. She believed that contraception was the best way to prevent abortion. A second controversy attached to Sanger is the assertion that she was racist. This is the result of her reliance on eugenics discourse in her speeches and articles in the 1920s and 1930s. Her support for the provision of contraception in the African American community and overseas (in China, for example) has fueled this argument. Eugenics, the science of selective breeding, has a long history. Before World War II (1939–1945), it was a term invoked by many in mainstream society, including politicians, physicians, and professors. Eugenicists often called for the use (sometimes compulsory) of birth control (sterilization or contraception) to create a more stable, wealthier society by eliminating society's weakest elements. While some in the eugenics movement focused on health concerns (mental and physical problems), others concentrated on moral concerns (alcoholism and criminal behavior). At its most extreme, racial prejudice led Caucasian middle- and upper-class eugenicists to blame the burgeoning African American and immigrant communities for the nation's problems. An examination of Sanger's perspective on eugenics reveals that her focus was on health and economic improvement (smaller families have a higher standard of living) and was not specifically connected with race.

Contraception was still illegal in many states in the mid-twentieth century until the U.S. Supreme Court, in *Griswold v. Connecticut*, overturned a Connecticut law banning contraceptive use in 1965. The Court ruling legalized contraceptive access for all married persons, based on the right to privacy. In 1972, in *Eisenstadt v. Baird*, the Court expanded the right to access to contraceptives to include unmarried people—again, based on the right to privacy. The same right was invoked in the *Roe v. Wade* decision in 1973, when the U.S. Supreme Court legalized abortion in the first two trimesters of a pregnancy.

Within years of the *Roe v. Wade* ruling, reproductive rights were again limited by law. Between 1996 and 2004, 335 new state laws were created to restrict access to abortion services. Access to abortion was limited by income (the prohibition on Medicaid funding for abortions) and age (parental consent laws instituted at the state level). Other obstacles to access were also created in many states, such as waiting periods mandated between the time of the consultation and the procedure. By 2004 just 13 percent of U.S. counties had an abortion provider. This was the result of both restrictive state legislative action and violence (and the threat of violence) against clinics and clinic personnel.

In 1999 the U.S. Food and Drug Administration approved emergency contraceptives (the "morning-after pill") for distribution with a prescription. Emergency contraception is a stronger dose of the standard contraceptive (anovulant) pill and is effective within seventy-two hours of unprotected intercourse. It prevents the implantation of a zygote (if there is one) on the uterine wall. As its name suggests, it is intended to prevent pregnancy if contraception fails or in the case of sexual assault. In 2006, following years of politically charged debate, the FDA approved emergency contraception for over-the-counter sales (without a prescription) for women over age eighteen.

A chemical abortifacient, RU-486 (named for the French pharmaceutical company Roussel-Uclaf, which patented it), was approved by the FDA in 2000. Women in Europe had used the drug since 1988. In U.S. tests, RU-486 was shown to be 92 percent effective in terminating pregnancies before the seventh week of gestation. The abortion pill was heralded as an alternative to surgical abortion, providing a more private experience—away from the clinics that are the focal point for abortion protesters.

Immediately following the *Roe v. Wade* decision, the religious and conservative right organized opposition to abortion. However, legislative lobbying and clinic protests against abortion have widened in scope to attacks on certain contraceptive methods. Those who believe life begins at conception see some methods—the contraceptive pill, the "morning-after pill," and intrauterine devices—as abortifacients because they act to prevent pregnancy after a zygote has been created. Physicians and pharmacists opposed to abortion may refuse to prescribe, or fill prescriptions for, these forms of contraception. Pro-choice forces, on the other hand, hope to prevent abortion through increased access to contraception and comprehensive sex education. Because abortion is a debate of absolutes, pro-life and pro-choice forces will continue to be engaged in this issue.

SEE ALSO *Abortion; Birth Control; Contraception; Eugenics; Family Structure; Fertility, Human; Population Control; Population Growth; Pro-Choice/ Pro-Life;* Roe v. Wade; *Supreme Court, U.S.*

BIBLIOGRAPHY

Chesler, Ellen. 1992. *Woman of Valor: Margaret Sanger and the Birth Control Movement in America.* New York: Simon & Schuster.

Feldt, Gloria, with Laura Fraser. 2004. *The War on Choice: The Right Wing Attack on Women's Rights and How to Fight Back.* New York: Bantam Books.

Gordon, Linda. 2002. *The Moral Property of Women: A History of Birth Control Politics in America,* 3rd ed. Urbana and Chicago: University of Illinois Press.

McCann, Carole R. 1994. *Birth Control Politics in the United States, 1916–1945.* Ithaca, NY: Cornell University Press.

Reagan, Leslie J. 1997. *When Abortion Was a Crime: Women, Medicine, and Law in the United States, 1867–1973.* Berkeley: University of California Press.

Sanger, Margaret. 1938. *Margaret Sanger: An Autobiography.* New York: Norton.

Julie L. Thomas

FAMILY RESEMBLANCE MODEL

SEE *Psychiatric Disorders.*

FAMILY STRUCTURE

Among the most significant social changes that have occurred in recent decades are profound transformations in the structure of the American family. Prior to the last third of the twentieth century, most Americans lived in a family consisting of a husband and wife and their biological children. Both divorce and nonmarital childbearing were relatively rare (Popenoe 1996). Consequently, during the 1950s, over 80 percent of American children under

Family structure changes 1970–2003

Characteristic	Year					
	1970	1980	1990	1995	2000	2003
Household by Type (Percent)	100.00	100.00	100.00	100.00	100.00	100.00
Family Households (TOTAL)	81.2	73.7	70.9	70.0	68.8	67.9
Married Couple (TOTAL)	70.6	60.8	56.1	54.4	52.8	51.5
Married Couple with Children	40.3	30.9	26.3	25.5	24.1	23.3
Married Couple without Children	30.3	29.9	29.8	28.9	28.7	28.2
Other Family Households (TOTAL)	10.6	12.9	14.8	15.6	16.0	16.4
Nonfamily Households (TOTAL)	18.8	26.2	29.2	29.9	31.2	32.0
Women Living Alone	11.5	14.0	14.9	14.7	14.8	15.2
Men Living Alone	5.6	8.6	9.7	10.2	10.7	11.2
Other Nonfamily Households	1.7	3.6	4.6	5.0	5.7	5.6
Median Age at First Marriage						
Men	23.2	24.7	26.1	26.9	26.8	27.1
Women	20.8	22.0	23.9	24.5	25.1	25.3

SOURCE: Fields 2004

Table 1

age eighteen were living with both biological parents, who were married to one another (Bumpass and Sweet 1989), and a large majority of adult men and women were married (Saluter and Lugaila 1998). Beginning in the 1960s, the structure of American families changed rapidly and dramatically (Wu and Wolfe 2001). The more prominent of these changes include much higher divorce rates (Cherlin 1992), more nonmarital births (Wu et al. 2001), the postponement of first marriage (Fields 2004), and an increase in nonmarital cohabitation (Bianchi and Casper 2000; Bumpass and Lu 2000). Understanding the factors leading to this dramatic transformation and the consequences of these changes is among the most significant issues faced by American society. In this entry, we explore recent data and research on family-structure issues and changes. Primary emphasis will be on the American family, but some international comparisons are provided.

FAMILY-STRUCTURE CHANGES SINCE 1970

For purposes of this entry, we use the definitions of *household* and *family* utilized by the U.S. Census Bureau. A *household* contains one or more people—everyone living in a *housing unit* makes up a household. There are two types of households: *family households* and *nonfamily households*. A family household has at least two members related by birth, marriage, or adoption. A family household is maintained by a married couple or by a man or women living with other relatives. A nonfamily household can be either a person living alone or a householder shar-

ing a housing unit with nonrelatives, such as borders or roommates.

The data in Table 1 shows some of the major family-structure changes that occurred from 1970 to 2003. Most apparent are significant declines in the proportion of family households, especially married-couple families, and a corresponding increase in other family households (generally single parent) and nonfamily households. In 1970, 81.2 percent of all households in the United States were family households, and 86.9 percent of the family households included a married couple. By 2003, only 67.9 percent of all households were family households, and 75.8 percent of the family households included a married couple.

Table 1 also shows a significant increase in the median age at first marriage. For men, this increase was from 23.2 in 1970 to 27.1 in 2003, while for women, the increase was from 20.8 in 1970 to 25.3 in 2003. Further indication of the postponement of first marriage is apparent in looking at different age cohorts (data not shown). Of the cohort of individuals born from 1940 to 1944, 70 percent of the men and 79 percent of the women had been married before their twenty-fifth birthday. In comparison, of the cohort of individuals born from 1965 to 1969, only 40.6 percent of the men and 54.8 percent of the women had been married before their twenty-fifth birthday (Kreider 2005).

Other critical family-structure changes not shown in Table 1 that have occurred since 1970 include a substantial increase in both the proportion of births that occur outside of marriage and the number of cohabitating couples. About one-third of all births in the United States now occur out of marriage (McLanahan et al. 2001), while there has been a sevenfold increase in the number of cohabitating couples (to 5.5 million) since 1970 (Casper and Cohen 2000). The majority of these unmarried-partner households had partners of the opposite sex (4.9 million), but about one in nine (594,000) had partners of the same sex. Of these same-sex unmarried-partner households, 301,000 had male partners and 293,000 had female partners (Simmons and O'Connell 2003).

Tables 2 through 4 present information on current measures of family structure for the United States. Table 2 presents data on the marital history of American adults. The increased divorce rate is apparent by comparing those individuals who were in the fifty to fifty-nine age cohort with those who were seventy or more in 2001. About 40 percent of all persons aged fifty to fifty-nine had been divorced at least once, and about 30 percent had been married two or more times. In comparison, for persons seventy years old and older, only about 18 percent had been divorced and about 20 percent had been married two or more times.

Marital history for people 15 years and over, by age and sex, 2001

Characteristic	Total 15 and Over	Age								
		15-19	20-24	25-29	30-34	35-39	40-49	50-59	60-69	70 or more
Men										
Never married	30.9	99.1	83.9	50.8	29.5	21.5	14.2	6.3	4.3	3.3
Married once	53.4	0.9	16.0	46.3	60.8	66.2	65.1	62.6	67.5	75.5
Married twice	12.5	–	0.1	2.8	8.7	10.9	17.1	23.2	21.3	16.5
Married 3 or more times	3.2	–	–	0.1	1.1	1.4	3.6	8.0	6.8	4.7
Ever divorced	21.0	0.1	1.0	7.5	15.4	22.9	29.5	40.8	30.9	18.6
Ever widowed	3.6	–	–	0.1	0.3	0.5	1.3	2.9	7.6	23.1
Women										
Never married	24.6	96.3	72.4	37.3	21.7	15.6	10.5	6.4	4.1	3.3
Married once	58.7	3.6	26.5	57.3	67.3	66.8	65.1	65.2	72.9	77.8
Married twice	13.6	0.1	1.1	5.1	10.0	15.7	19.8	22.1	17.4	15.5
Married 3 or more times	3.1	–	–	0.3	1.0	1.8	4.6	6.3	5.6	3.5
Ever divorced	23.1	0.2	2.6	11.9	18.6	28.1	35.4	38.9	28.4	17.7
Ever widowed	11.6	–	0.3	0.5	0.6	1.1	3.5	9.5	23.3	56.3

SOURCE: Kreider 2005

Table 2

Family and living arrangements and poverty status of Children from birth to 18, 2001–2002

Characteristic	Total Children[a]	Percent	Age			Percent in poverty[b]
			Under 6	6–11	12–18	
TOTAL	72,501	100.0	100.0	100.0	100.0	17.6
Two parent (TOTAL)	51,112	70.5	70.0	68.7	67.4	10.1
Both biological—married	44,363	61.2	–	–	–	–
Both biological—unmarried	1,845	2.5	–	–	–	27.4
Blended	4,904	6.8	–	–	–	–
Single parent (TOTAL)	18,472	25.5	26.9	27.5	27.6	–
Mother	16,297	22.5	22.0	23.4	22.9	36.4
Father	2,175	3.0	4.9	4.1	4.7	14.7
Neither parent	2,917	4.0	3.1	3.8	5.0	31.0

[a] SOURCE: Kreider and Fields 2005 (Based on 2001 data)
[b] SOURCE: Fields 2003 (Based on 2002 data)

Table 3

Family structure by race/ethnicity and poverty status, 2003

Characteristics	Race/Ethnicity[a]			Percent in poverty[b]
	Nonhispanic white	Black alone	Hispanic (any race)	
Family households (TOTAL)	66.3	66.3	80.2	10.0
Married couple	54.3	30.9	54.6	5.4
Other family	8.7	29.8	17.9	28.0
Female householder	3.3	5.6	7.7	13.5
Male householder				
Nonfamily households (TOTAL)	33.7	33.7	19.8	–
Female householder	18.9	18.5	9.0	–
Male householder	14.8	15.2	10.8	–

[a] SOURCE: Fields 2004
[b] SOURCE: DeNavas–Walt et al. 2004

Table 4

Table 3 presents data on the family and living arrangements of children. In 2001, 61.2 percent of children in the United States from birth to age eighteen were living with both biological parents, who were married to one another. Another 9 percent were living with cohabitating parents or in a blended family. About one-fourth of the children were living with a single parent (usually the mother), and 4 percent were not living with either of their parents.

Finally, Table 4 shows extensive differences in family structure by race and ethnicity. Most significantly, only 30.9 percent of black households in the United States consist of a married-couple family, a proportion much smaller than for either whites or Hispanics. Hispanics, in contrast, have a much higher proportion of family households and a much lower proportion of nonfamily households than whites or blacks.

Patterns of U.S. family-structure change show some similarities to changes occurring in other economically advanced societies, but there are important differences. For example, the percentage of births occurring out of marriage is greater in Scandinavia, the United Kingdom, and France than in the United States. However, these countries have lower child-poverty rates and fewer children living in single-parent households because most unwed mothers are in long-term cohabitating partnerships (Kiernan 2001). In less developed countries, family structures tend to be more traditional.

CAUSES OF FAMILY-STRUCTURE CHANGES IN THE UNITED STATES

Discussions of the causes of these major family structure transformations can be grouped into two categories. The first category includes significant cultural transformations in the United States, where norms and values regarding marriage, divorce, sexuality, and so on have changed extensively. Opinion polls during the 1950s indicated that most Americans considered divorce, sex outside of marriage, and remaining single while in adulthood as somewhat deviant. These same behaviors are much more acceptable today, and the stigma associated with an adult not being in a traditional married-couple family has mostly disappeared (Giele 2003; Hackstaff 2003).

The second category of factors affecting the American family structure includes economic changes, such as the increased employment of women and economic-restructuring processes that result in fewer men with jobs that pay enough to support a family. Women have entered the job force in increasing numbers since the 1960s, making American women much more economically independent. The result is that divorce and remaining single have become more attractive alternatives, especially when compared to an unfavorable marriage (Giele 2003).

Additionally, beginning in the 1970s, an economic-restructuring process in the United States and other advanced societies has resulted in a significant decline in the number of manufacturing jobs and a corresponding increase in the number of jobs in the service sector (Morris and Western 1999; Sassen 1990). This economic-structure transformation has family-structure implications for two major reasons. First, a majority of the employees in the declining manufacturing sector are male, while female employees predominate in the expanding service sector. Consequently, there are increased employment opportunities for females and reduced employment opportunities for males. Second, most of the manufacturing jobs that have been lost were middle-income, while the new service jobs vary extensively in quality. While some service jobs are high quality, many others are low-pay, low-skill, temporary, and seasonal (Albrecht 2004). In the past, even minimally skilled workers could often get a middle-income job in the manufacturing sector. This is no longer the case as workers who lack the skills to attain high-quality jobs are often forced to take low-quality jobs because many of the middle-income jobs no longer exist. The result is higher rates of unemployment and underemployment among males and shrinkage in the pool of male household heads financially able to support a family. Marriage thus becomes less attractive to women, the rate of unwed childbearing increases, and female-headed households proliferate (Albrecht et al. 2000; Wilson 1987, 1996).

CONSEQUENCES OF FAMILY-STRUCTURE CHANGES

In some sectors of society, the emergence of socially acceptable alternatives to the traditional family was met with euphoria because it was felt that the family had been an institution that generally suppressed women and limited individuality (Albrecht and Albrecht 2004). However, social science research is finding that many problems are emerging from changes in the American family (Haveman et al. 2001; Manning 2002; Waite and Gallagher 2000). A brief overview of the research on this topic indicates that men, women, and children in single-adult families all experience extensive disadvantages relative to their counterparts in married-couple families (Popenoe 1996). Of the long list of disadvantages, only a few will be highlighted here. Single-adult families experience much higher levels of poverty, especially for females, with all of its attendant problems (Albrecht et al. 2000; Corcoran et al. 1992; McLanahan 1985). Children who grow up with only one biological parent have significantly lower educational achievements. These young people are much less likely to graduate from high school and to attend and complete college (Amato and Keith 1991; Downey 1995; McLanahan and Sandefur 1994; Raley et al. 2005; Zill 1996). Girls from one-parent families are much more likely to become pregnant as teenagers than girls from married-couple families, while boys are much more likely to become delinquent (McLanahan and Sandefur 1994; Wells and Rankin 1991). These differences remain even when economic conditions are considered. The advantages of being part of a married-couple family are apparent for adults as well as children. In a variety of ways, both men and women are healthier, happier, and more economically prosperous when married (Lichter and Graefe 2001; Nock 1998; Haveman et al. 2001).

SEE ALSO *Family; Family, Extended; Family, Nuclear; Female-Headed Families*

BIBLIOGRAPHY

Albrecht, Don E. 2004. Amenities, Natural Resources, Economic Restructuring, and Socioeconomic Outcomes in Nonmetropolitan America. *Journal of the Community Development Society* 35 (2): 36–52.

Albrecht, Don E., and Carol Mulford Albrecht. 2004. Metro/Nonmetro Residence, Nonmarital Conception, and Conception Outcomes. *Rural Sociology* 69 (3): 430–452.

Albrecht, Don E., Carol Mulford Albrecht, and Stan L. Albrecht. 2000. Poverty in Nonmetropolitan America: Impacts of Industrial, Employment, and Family Structure Variables. *Rural Sociology* 65: 87–103.

Amato, Paul R., and Bruce Keith. 1991. Separation from a Parent During Childhood and Adult Socioeconomic Attainment. *Social Forces* 70 (1): 187–206.

Bianchi, Suzanne M., and Lynne M. Casper. 2000. American Families. *Population Bulletin* 55 (4). Washington, DC: Population Reference Bureau.

Bumpass, Larry L., and Hsien-Hen Lu. 2000. Trends in Cohabitation and Implications for Children's Family Contexts in the United States. *Population Studies* 54 (1): 29–41.

Bumpass, Larry L., and James Sweet. 1989. Children's Experience in Single-Parent Families: Implications of Cohabitation and Marital Transitions. *Family Planning Perspectives* 21 (6): 256–260.

Casper, Lynne M., and Philip N. Cohen. 2000. How Does POSSLQ Measure Up: Historical Estimates of Cohabitation. *Demography* 37: 237–245.

Cherlin, Andrew J. 1992. *Marriage, Divorce, Remarriage.* Rev. ed. Cambridge, MA: Harvard University Press.

Corcoran, Mary, Roger Gordon, Deborah Laren, and Gary Solon. 1992. The Association Between Men's Economic Status and Their Family and Community Origins. *Journal of Human Resources* 27: 575–601.

DeNavas-Walt, Carmen, Bernadette D. Proctor, and Robert J. Mills. 2004. *Income, Poverty, and Health Insurance Coverage in the United States: 2003.* U.S. Census Bureau, Current Population Reports, P60–226. Washington, DC: U.S. Government Printing Office. http://www.census.gov/prod/2004pubs/p60-226.pdf.

Downey, Douglas. 1995. Understanding Academic Achievement Among Children in Stephouseholds: The Role of Parental Resources, Sex of the Stepparent, and Sex of Child. *Social Forces* 73: 875–894.

Fields, Jason. 2003. *Children's Living Arrangements and Characteristics: March 2002.* U.S. Census Bureau, Current Population Reports, P20–547. Washington, DC: U.S. Government Printing Office. http://www.census.gov/prod/2003pubs/p20-547.pdf.

Fields, Jason. 2004. *America's Families and Living Arrangements: 2003.* U.S. Census Bureau, Current Population Reports, P20–553. Washington, DC: U.S. Government Printing Office. http://www.census.gov/prod/2004pubs/p20-553.pdf.

Giele, Janet Z. 2003. Decline of the Family: Conservative, Liberal, and Feminist Views. In *Family in Transition*, eds. Arlene S. Skolnick and Jerome H. Skolnick. 12th ed., 57–76. Boston: Allyn and Bacon.

Hackstaff, Karla B. 2003. Divorce Culture: A Quest for Relational Equality in Marriage. In *Family in Transition*, eds. Arlene S. Skolnick and Jerome H. Skolnick. 12th ed., 178–190. Boston: Allyn and Bacon.

Haveman, Robert, Barbara Wolfe, and Karen Pence. 2001. Intergenerational Effects of Nonmarital and Early Childbearing. In *Out of Wedlock: Causes and Consequences of Nonmarital Fertility*, eds. Lawrence Wu and Barbara Wolfe, 287–316. New York: Russell Sage Foundation.

Kiernan, Kathleen. 2001. European Perspectives on Nonmarital Childbearing. In *Out of Wedlock: Causes and Consequences of Nonmarital Fertility*, eds. Lawrence Wu and Barbara Wolfe, 77–108. New York: Russell Sage Foundation.

Kreider, Rose. 2005. *Number, Timing, and Duration of Marriages and Divorces: 2001*. U.S. Census Bureau, Current Population Reports, P70–97. Washington, DC: U.S. Government Printing Office. http://www.census.gov/prod/2005pubs/p70-97.pdf.

Kreider, Rose, and Jason Fields. 2005. *Living Arrangements of Children: 2001*. U.S. Census Bureau, Current Population Reports, P70–104. Washington, DC: U.S. Government Printing Office. http://www.census.gov/prod/2005pubs/p70-104.pdf.

Lichter, Daniel T., and Deborah Roempke Graefe. 2001. Finding a Mate? The Marital and Cohabitation Histories of Unwed Mothers. In *Out of Wedlock: Causes and Consequences of Nonmarital Fertility*, eds. Lawrence Wu and Barbara Wolfe. New York: Russell Sage Foundation.

Manning, Wendy D. 2002. The Implications of Cohabitation for Children's Well-Being. In *Just Living Together: Implications of Cohabitation on Families, Children, and Social Policy*, eds. Alan Booth and Anne C. Crouter, 121–152. Mahwah, NJ: Erlbaum.

McLanahan, Sara. 1985. Family Structure and the Reproduction of Poverty. *American Journal of Sociology* 56: 873–901.

McLanahan, Sara, Irwin Garfinkel, Nancy Reichman, and Julien Teitler. 2001. Unwed Parents or Fragile Families? Implications for Welfare and Child Support Policy. In *Out of Wedlock: Causes and Consequences of Nonmarital Fertility*, eds. Lawrence Wu and Barbara Wolfe. New York: Russell Sage Foundation.

McLanahan, Sara, and Gary Sandefur. 1994. *Growing Up with a Single Parent: What Hurts, What Helps*. Cambridge, MA: Harvard University Press.

Morris, Martina, and Bruce Western. 1999. Inequality in Earnings at the Close of the Twentieth Century. *Annual Review of Sociology* 25: 623–657.

Nock, Steven L. 1998. *Marriage in Men's Lives*. New York: Oxford University Press.

Popenoe, David. 1996. *Life Without Father: Compelling New Evidence that Fatherhood and Marriage are Indispensable for the Good of Children and Society*. New York: Martin Kessler.

Raley, R. Kelly, Michelle L. Frisco, and Elizabeth Wildsmith. 2005. Maternal Cohabitation and Educational Success. *Sociology of Education* 78: 144–164.

Saluter, Arlene F., and Terry A. Lugaila. 1998. *Marital Status and Living Arrangements: March 1996*. U.S. Census Bureau Current Population Reports P20–496. Washington, DC: U.S. Government Printing Office. http://www.census.gov/prod/3/98pubs/p20-496.pdf.

Sassen, Saskia. 1990. Economic Restructuring and the American City. *Annual Review of Sociology* 16: 465–490.

Simmons, Tavia, and Martin O'Connell. 2003. *Married-Couple and Unmarried-Partner Households: 2000*. U.S. Census Bureau, Census 2000 Special Reports CENSR-5. Washington, DC: U.S. Government Printing Office. http://www.census.gov/prod/2003pubs/censr-5.pdf.

Waite, Linda J., and Maggie Gallagher. 2000. *The Case for Marriage: Why Married People Are Happier, Healthier, and Better Off Financially*. New York: Doubleday.

Wells, L. Edward, and Joseph H. Rankin. 1991. Families and Delinquency: A Meta-Analysis of the Impact of Broken Homes. *Social Problems* 38: 71–93.

Wilson, William J. 1987. *The Truly Disadvantaged: The Inner City, the Underclass, and Public Policy*. Chicago: University of Chicago Press.

Wilson, William J. 1996. *When Work Disappears: The World of the New Urban Poor*. New York: Knopf.

Wu, Lawrence, Larry L. Bumpass, and Kelly Musick. 2001. Historical and Life Course Trajectories of Nonmarital Childbearing. In *Out of Wedlock: Causes and Consequences of Nonmarital Fertility*, eds. Lawrence Wu and Barbara Wolfe, 3–48. New York: Russell Sage Foundation.

Wu, Lawrence, and Barbara Wolfe, eds. 2001. *Out of Wedlock: Causes and Consequences of Nonmarital Fertility*. New York: Russell Sage Foundation.

Zill, Nicholas. 1996. Family Change and Student Achievement: What We Have Learned, What It Means for Schools. In *Family-School Links: How Do They Effect Educational Outcomes?* eds. Alan Booth and Judith F. Dunn, 139–174. Mahwah, NJ: Erlbaum.

Don E. Albrecht
Carol Mulford Albrecht

FAMILY SUPPORT ACT OF 1988

SEE *Fatherhood.*

FAMILY VALUES

Family values refers to those norms that emerge from our experiences within the family structure and that inform our understanding of that social construction we call the family. Just as family structures have changed over time and vary across cultures, so too have attitudes about the family, its relationship to society, and its relative value in the social order. These changes within the family and society often have occasioned fierce debate and have led to contested claims about the nature and definition of *fam-*

ily and those values that represent the many and varied forms of family life.

In the late-twentieth-century United States, political conservatives and liberals battled for culturally accepted definitions of the family and family values. According to sociologist James Davison Hunter, "the family is the most conspicuous field of conflict in the culture war" (1991, p. 176). This battle was an extension of a campaign by the Moral Majority, an organization formed in 1979 and composed of conservative, evangelical Christian activists. Among its stated tenets was opposition to feminism, gay rights, abortion, and pornography. The Moral Majority championed the patriarchal nuclear family as a biblical ideal and warned that the failure of the family would lead to the demise of American culture.

Family values as an ideological battleground came to prominence in U.S. political debate during the 1992 presidential campaign, when particular values were espoused by the "New Right," a movement that brought together religious and political conservatives who emphasized individual responsibility and the primacy of Christian moral values coupled with traditional gender roles. One powerful New Right group, Focus on the Family, claims, for example, that the church, the family, and the government are the three basic institutions ordained by God for the benefit of humanity. The traditional family as described by such conservatives presumes heterosexual marriage, patriarchal authority within the family, and the production and care of children. The term "family values" was adopted by the New Right and functions in public debate as shorthand for this conservative ideology of family. "Family values" proponents often carve out their position over and against social forces which they believe threaten the traditional family; they are antichoice (in regards to abortion), antigay, against sex education other than promotion of strict abstinence, against hate-crime legislation, against the separation of church and state, and against a host of other issues that they believe threaten the traditional family structure.

History tells us that rather than privileging the nuclear family, definitions of the family have changed with time and culture, as have the values attributed to family. In classical Greek culture, for example, the *paterfamilias* (the male head of a household) was responsible not only for his immediate family but also for his current slaves, former slaves who were now clients, hired laborers, and sometimes business associates or tenants. And even in the ancient world there were disagreements about the value of the family: The philosopher Aristotle thought that family life was an obligation one fulfilled for the good of society, whereas Plato argued in *The Republic* that private, individual families detracted from the social good.

Historian Stephanie Coontz notes in *The Social Origins of Private Life* (1988) that the model of the nuclear family idealized in contemporary conservative politics emerged in the United States after the Revolutionary War as a response to changing economic and political realities. The Industrial Revolution provided new sources of income, facilitating the growth of a middle class. The wives of this emergent class were expected to devote themselves to the domestic sphere; their most important political contribution was to raise patriotic children while men worked outside the home to support the family and society. This was, of course, a privileged ideal that was not realized in, for example, slave families. Even today, poor and working-class families continue to find it difficult to thrive outside of extended kinship networks that provide both financial and emotional support. With an increasingly diverse U.S. population, traditional "family values" fail to account for the variety of family structures that emerge from different ethnic and cultural backgrounds.

Despite conservative claims that traditional "family values" are divinely ordained and hold the key to the ideal society, recent social science research indicates that values are of secondary importance when it comes to social mobility as an indicator of success. In a longitudinal study Patrick L. Mason assessed the importance of family values and class status on interracial inequality and intergenerational mobility (1999). Mason found that although family values do have some effect on economic mobility from one generation to the next, class considerations (and the intersection of these with race) are more significant in predicting inequality. Put another way, although values may shape our perception of our place in society, material considerations have a greater influence on our ability to actually change that place.

Any contemporary attempt to define "family values" must take into account the multiple and varying forms in which family life takes place in diverse communities, including single-parent families, unmarried heterosexual couples with or without children, gay men and lesbians with or without children, and other nontraditional groupings who form "families of choice." The family is a cultural construction that has undergone multiple transformations throughout history without being destroyed. Despite "family values" rhetoric to the contrary, the family will survive future transformations, opening new horizons of human affiliation and identity.

SEE ALSO *Family; Family, Extended; Family, Nuclear; Religion*

BIBLIOGRAPHY

Abbott, Pamela, and Claire Wallace. 1992. *The Family and the New Right*. London: Pluto Press.

Coontz, Stephanie. 1988. *The Social Origins of Private Life: A History of American Families, 1600–1900.* New York: Verso Press.

Hunter, James Davison. 1991. *Culture Wars: The Struggle to Define America.* New York: Basic Books.

Marty, Martin E., and R. Scott Appleby, eds. 1993. *Fundamentalisms and Society: Reclaiming the Sciences, the Family, and Education.* Chicago: University of Chicago Press.

Mason, Patrick L. 1999. Family Environment and Intergenerational Well-Being: Some Preliminary Results. In *The State of Black America 1999.* Washington, DC: National Urban League.

Okin, Susan Moller. 1989. *Justice, Gender, and the Family.* New York: Basic Books.

Elizabeth A. Say

FAMILY WAGE

SEE *Gender and Development; Marriage.*

FAMINE

Drought is the proximate cause of most peacetime famines in peasant societies, but excessive rain can have the same effect. The best example of this is the Irish famine from 1845 to 1850. Three phrases guide analysis in this entry: peasant societies, proximate cause, and ultimate cause.

PEASANT SOCIETIES

The peasant concept of the good life is the minimum expenditure of physical labor. Minimum labor expenditures equate to subsistence labor norms in food production. In normal crop years, subsistence labor norms lead peasants to grow enough food to last until the next harvest on the assumption that every crop year will be normal. Peasants know that every crop year will not be normal, but they prefer the marginal food safety of normal crop years if they can minimize the labor of cultivation. A minimal expenditure of agricultural labor to grow subsistence amounts of food is known as the *subsistence compromise.* The practice of the subsistence compromise defines who are peasants.

The practice of the subsistence compromise is clearly seen in most photographs of peasant cultivation practices that reach the media. These photographs show women planting rice sprouts in ponded fields, or dibbling maize or sorghum seeds into poorly prepared ground, or hoeing a patch of maize or sorghum overgrown with weeds, or harvesting grain with a child strapped on their backs.

Where are the men for this sustained labor? The only labor that is gender specific to men is plowing and digging potatoes, yams, and cassava. Almost all of the rest of the labor of cultivation is done by women and children. This is why high birthrates are desirable in peasant societies. Children can do much of the agricultural labor that is gender specific to women.

PROXIMATE CAUSE

In order to live by subsistence labor norms, peasants willingly endure seasonal hunger in poor crop years and risk famines in consecutive poor crop years. Before the mid-twentieth century, there were few roads or vehicle tracks into peasant villages. Starving peasants fled their villages in search of food (as Irish peasants did) or watched their children starve so that some adults would survive. During the second half of the twentieth century, roads or vehicle tracks were built into most peasant villages. When there was severe hunger, food donations arrived from central governments (to prevent mass migrations to cities that governments could not control) or food was donated by nongovernmental agencies. Donated food was essential to prevent starvation because peasants produced few commodities to sell for money to purchase food.

ULTIMATE CAUSE

The marginal food safety of peasant households in normal crop years is due to deficient labor applied to cultivation. The subsistence compromise produces no food surplus for consumption in consecutive poor crop years, and peasants experience privation. The cumulative effect of consecutive poor crop years is famine conditions.

Subsistence Social Values This is an unfamiliar concept for most people in commercial cultures. They find it difficult to believe that cultivators voluntarily produce subsistence amounts of food when increased labor expenditures, especially by males, could produce abundant harvests.

Peasants use four strategies to minimize agricultural labor and, at the same time, produce sufficient food in normal crop years to last until the next harvest. They practice cultivation techniques requiring minimal labor expenditures; they control land use with some variety of communal tenure so that a village's arable land can be continually divided to accommodate additional households; they have many children to whom they can transfer labor at young ages; and they mitigate the worst effects of deficient harvests by sharing food among village households.

Analysis The welfare of peasant households does not depend on the acquisition of money. It depends on control of land use. When peasants control land use they can control labor expenditures and this means performing subsistence labor norms in cultivation. Peasant households can and do reject the earning of money incomes because earning money incomes requires continuous labor. As long as they control land use they have little interest in performing continuous wage labor (commercial labor norms). The reciprocal of subsistence labor norms is accepting privation in poor crop years.

Most economists do not recognize the distinction between subsistence labor norms (subsistence social values) and commercial labor norms (commercial social values). They assume that all persons want to earn money incomes and willingly perform commercial labor norms to acquire sufficient money to constitute an income. This is a false assumption. Economists make this assumption because they confuse monetization with commercial social values. Almost all peasant societies are monetized.

Peasants, however, want to acquire sufficient money to purchase a limited number of manufactured items. The most commonly purchased items are textiles, edged steel tools, steel cooking pots, plastic buckets, and sandals. After they have acquired enough money to purchase these items they cease laboring to produce additional products for market sale. Anthropologists call the money acquired to make these purchases a *target sum*.

Peasant households can subsist without the use of money as many do in the highlands of Papua, Indonesia, and Indian villages where the Hindu caste system operates. Households subsist without the use of money because the items they purchase can be made by resident artisans (pottery cooking pots, hand-loom textiles), as they were in the past. These items have a customary barter value, usually measured by handfuls or pots of grain.

It is, however, advantageous to purchase manufactured items because they have greater utility and durability. It is also advantageous to purchase them because the labor expended to produce products for market sale is less than that required to make artisan products, and much of this labor can be done by children. If households grow a small amount of food for sale, this is their exchange commodity. In poor crop years, however, it is eaten and no purchases are made of manufactured items. Households subsist without the use of money.

Most economists do not understand that money incomes do not exist in peasant villages. Economists, however, create them by assigning a money value to the harvest of peasants or to the number of hours of labor they assume were expended to grow a household's annual food supply. In reality, the food grown by peasants has no money value. If it were sold, peasant households would starve. Likewise, the labor that is expended to grow a sub-

sistence food supply has no market value because no money is received.

Economists create fictitious money incomes for peasant households in order to compare the welfare of peasant households with the welfare of households in commercial cultures. Fictitious incomes are created for peasant households by applying the techniques of financial analysis to subsistence cultures. Fictitious incomes created by economists make peasants poor in relation to the money incomes earned by households in commercial cultures. Peasant households, however, are not poor. They are subsistent. Sometimes economists use terms like *subsistence income*, *nonwage income*, *implicit income*, *leisure income*, or *income concept* to indicate that they know the incomes they have created are fictitious; however, they continue to compare real and fictitious incomes. The result is confusion.

The fictitious incomes created by economists cannot be used to compare the welfare of households in subsistence and commercial cultures because incomes in commercial cultures are real money. Real money incomes measure household welfare in commercial cultures because households require money to purchase their food, clothing, and housing needs. Financial analysis operates with reasonable efficiency in commercial cultures but has universally failed to measure household welfare when applied to subsistence cultures.

Creating fictitious incomes for peasant households creates huge distortions in policies recommended by economists to increase food production in peasant nations. The failure of economists to recognize the fundamental difference between subsistence and commercial labor norms has largely contributed to the continual failure of policies that economists recommend to initiate economic development. Economic development must begin with producing assured food surpluses in all crop years in order to feed full-time wage laborers living in cities. The failure of their policies is most obvious in sub-Saharan Africa and in many Latin American nations.

Increasing food production requires different policies from those recommended by economists. As the term *political economy* indicates, political policies precede economic policies. Unfortunately, most economists are poorly prepared to recommend political policies because their training is financial and they are indoctrinated to believe that money incomes are the universal way of measuring household welfare.

SUMMARY

The famines that occurred in the last twenty years of the twentieth century were due to war. Peacetime famines have been avoided by food gifts to households in affected peasant societies. Peacetime famine conditions will continue to recur in peasant societies until central governments enforce a change in land tenure from communal to freehold so that money taxes can be collected on agricultural land. In freehold tenure, households that practice the subsistence compromise and fail to pay money taxes can be evicted and forced to become supervised, paid agricultural laborers who can produce assured food surpluses.

SEE ALSO *Food Crisis; Peasantry; Subsistence Agriculture*

BIBLIOGRAPHY

Seavoy, Ronald E. 1986. *Famine in Peasant Societies*. Westport, CT: Greenwood Press.

Seavoy, Ronald E. 1989. *Famine in East Africa: Food Production and Food Policies*. Westport, CT: Greenwood Press.

Seavoy, Ronald E. 2000. *Subsistence and Economic Development*. Westport, CT: Praeger.

Ronald E. Seavoy

FANON, FRANTZ
1925–1961

A psychiatrist, a revolutionary, and a leading theorist of the Algerian national liberation struggle, Frantz Fanon was born on June 20, 1925, on the island of Martinique. He studied medicine in France and specialized in psychiatry. In 1953 Fanon began working as a psychiatrist at the Blida Psychiatric Hospital in Algiers, Algeria, where he supported the Algerian struggle against French colonialism. Fanon's dedication to this cause led to his expulsion from Algeria by the French authorities at the end of 1956. To continue his fight, Fanon moved to Tunis, Tunisia. In 1961 he fell ill with leukemia, and received treatment in the Soviet Union and later in Bethesda, Maryland, where he died on December 6, 1961.

Fanon played an instrumental role in the theorization of colonial desire, the dynamics of oppression, and the consequences of blackness. Among the sociohistorical and political issues that influenced his work and intellectual quest are the colonial history of Martinique, the manifestations of racism in France and in French colonial medicine, and the intricacies of the Algerian struggle. His work also shows, among other things, the influence of existentialist philosophy and the *négritude* movement. Fanon's thought, in turn, inspired a number of liberation movements and civil rights struggles.

Fanon's concerns are intimately linked to the history of Martinique, and more specifically to its experience of slavery and colonialism. Such concerns are reflected in his exploration of the power dynamics in the colonial world and the characteristics of two mutually constitutive "types": the colonizer and the colonized. Not only does Fanon probe the nature of these two categories in *The Wretched of the Earth* (*Les damnés de la terre*, 1961), but he also examines the elements and associations that contribute to, and result from, the establishment of this binary. In his analysis of the effects of colonialism on both colonizers and colonized, Fanon presents this institution as a system of exploitative oppression based on forms of psychological conditioning leading to the production of resentment and to the propagation of violence. This violence originates in the colonial movement and results from the colonizers' attempts to destroy "native social forms ... and systems of reference of ... [native] economy, the customs of dress and external life" (Fanon [1961] 1963, p. 40). This issue is important to note since many critics who claim that Fanon advocated the use of violence forget that violence is inherent to the colonizers' strategies of oppression.

Throughout his analysis of the psychology of the Negro in *Black Skin, White Masks* (*Peau noire, masques blancs*, 1952), Fanon insists on the necessity of perceiving blackness as a "lived experience," shaped not only by the gaze of whiteness but also by a state of alienation resulting from economic injustices and the "epidermalization" of the condition of inferiority (Fanon [1952] 1967, p. 11). In this book based on his observation of the condition of the Negro in the Antilles, Fanon also underlines the role that language plays in shaping the interactions within the black community on the one hand and between black people and their fellow white people on the other. Such a role is highlighted by Fanon's affirmation that "to speak is to exist absolutely for the other" (Fanon [1952] 1967, p. 17). In this context, language reflects and shapes the self through the transmission of a specific worldview. Advocating the need of black people to achieve liberation from their psychoexistential complex, *Black Skin, White Masks* also probes how gender interacts with "color" to produce specific power-based structures informing the interaction between women of color and white men, as well as men of color and white women.

Among Fanon's other significant contributions is the theorization of the role of the "native intellectual" in addressing the specific needs of struggles for justice in his or her country. Fanon also highlighted the role of the native intellectual in negotiating the problems pertaining to the conceptualization of national consciousness and resulting from the gap between the educated classes and the underprivileged masses. This negotiation is crucial in shaping ways of "acting back" and strategies of resistance described in *The Wretched of the Earth*.

Continuing his examination of the struggle against colonialism, Fanon analyzed the specific case of the Algerian liberation struggle, detailing its contexts and components in *A Dying Colonialism* (*L'An V de la révolution algérienne*, 1959). This book, which explores the conflict between old values, transitional identifications, and the new Algerian nationalism, details the elements contributing to the formation of an alternative sense of national identity in Algerian society. *A Dying Colonialism* examines such issues through the discussion of the shifting symbolism of the Algerian women's veil; the relationship between resistance to the radio and the Algerians' desire to preserve social stability and traditional sociability; and the trauma resulting from changes in traditional family structure and the forced separation of family members. In this book, Fanon also shows how medical knowledge functions as a tool of power; more specifically, he argues that medicine can be seen, in certain situations, as an extension of the colonizer's control over the colonized society.

An equal concern with unmasking the mechanisms and networks of power in its various forms and local as well as global dimensions permeates Fanon's *Toward the African Revolution* (*Pour la révolution africaine*, 1964). This book is a collection of essays, notes, and articles, most of which were published in *El Moudjahid* (roughly translated as "the militant"), the underground newspaper of the Algerian National Liberation Front. A number of these writings probe the connection between French strategies in the Algerian War and the international scene in the United States and Europe. These works also examine the interdependence of individual liberation, anticolonial struggles, and the birth of national consciousness; the Algerian revolution and other liberation struggles in Africa and the Caribbean; and the end of colonialism and the resulting racism among the proletariat in the colonizing countries.

Throughout his life and career, Fanon probed the complexity of the colonial encounter and its aftermath. To account for its multilayered nature, he drew on a number of disciplines, including medicine, sociology, psychiatry, and literature, in a humanistic gesture reflecting his uncompromising dedication to the cause of the oppressed.

SEE ALSO *Blackness; Caribbean, The; Colonialism; Empire; Imperialism; Liberation; Neocolonialism; Psychology; Racism; Slavery; Violence, Frantz Fanon on; Whiteness*

BIBLIOGRAPHY

PRIMARY WORKS

Fanon, Frantz. [1952] 1967 *Black Skin, White Masks*. Trans. Charles Lam Markmann. New York: Grove.

Fanon, Frantz. [1959] 1965. *A Dying Colonialism*. Trans. Haakon Chevalier. New York: Grove.

Fanon, Frantz. [1961] 1963. *The Wretched of the Earth*. Trans. Constance Farrington. New York: Grove.

Fanon, Frantz. [1964] 1967. *Toward the African Revolution: Political Essays*. Trans. Haakon Chevalier. New York: Grove.

SECONDARY WORKS

Alessandrini, Anthony C., ed. 1999. *Frantz Fanon: Critical Perspectives*. New York and London: Routledge.

Gates, Henry Louis, Jr. 1991. Critical Fanonism. *Critical Inquiry* 17: 457–470.

Gendzier, Irene L. 1973. *Frantz Fanon: A Critical Study*. New York: Pantheon.

Gibson, Nigel C., ed. 1999. *Rethinking Fanon: The Continuing Dialogue*. Amherst, NY: Humanity.

Gordon, Lewis R. 1995. *Fanon and the Crisis of European Man: An Essay on Philosophy and the Human Sciences*. New York and London: Routledge.

Gordon, Lewis R., ed. 1996. *Existence in Black: An Anthology of Black Existential Philosophy*. New York and London: Routledge.

Gordon, Lewis R., T. Denean Sharpley-Whiting, and Renée T. White, eds. 1996. *Fanon: A Critical Reader*. Oxford and Cambridge, MA: Blackwell.

Macey, David. 2000. *Frantz Fanon: A Biography*. London: Granta.

Sharpley-Whiting, T. Denean. 1998. *Frantz Fanon: Conflicts and Feminisms*. Lanham, MD: Rowman & Littlefield.

Sirène Harb

FARM QUOTA SYSTEM

SEE *Quota System, Farm.*

FARSIGHTEDNESS

Our religions, mythologies, and fables admonish us to overcome temptation, exercise self-discipline, and heed the future—consider Adam and Eve, Odysseus, and the Ant and the Grasshopper. Social scientists too offer helpful strategies for increasing willpower and avoiding indulgence (e.g., Ainslie 1975; Trope and Fishbach 2000; Wertenbroch 1998). The seemingly universal espousal of prudence and farsightedness as noble goals is reflected in the voluminous literature in the social sciences on self-control. This body of research is premised on the notion that people are shortsighted (myopic) and easily tempted by hedonic "sins," such as overbuying (oniomania), splurging on tasty but unhealthy food, and indulging in luxuries (see, e.g., Prelec and Herrnstein 1992; Thaler 1980).

An alternative research paradigm challenges the universality of myopia and proposes that people often suffer from a reverse self-control problem, namely excessive farsightedness ("hyperopia") and overcontrol (Kivetz and

Simonson 2002b; Kivetz and Keinan 2006; Keinan and Kivetz 2007). Such hyperopia leads people to deprive themselves of indulgence and instead overly focus on acting responsibly, delaying gratification, and doing "the right thing." Research on farsightedness examines the underlying processes (e.g., guilt, justification), the way people cope with hyperopia (e.g., by precommitting to indulgence), and the consequences of overcontrol (e.g., long-term regret).

Ran Kivetz and Yuhuang Zheng (2006) shed light on the antecedents of hyperopia by highlighting the role of justification and guilt in self-control decisions (see also Kivetz and Simonson 2002a). Building on prior analyses in the social sciences, they propose two complementary routes to justifying self-gratification: the first through hard work or excellent performance (an entitlement justification) and the second through the attainment of indulgence without depleting income or monetary resources. Consistent with the two routes to justification, it is demonstrated that (1) higher required effort enhances preference for indulgence rewards over more prudent necessities, but a reverse effect is observed when the interchangeability of effort and income is implied; (2) providing (bogus) excellence feedback on an effort task enhances choices of indulgence, unless the interchangeability of effort and income is suggested; and (3) sensitivity to effort and excellence (i.e., justification) cues is greater for individuals who experience stronger (chronic or manipulated) guilt.

EVIDENCE AND REMEDIES OF HYPEROPIA

Kivetz and Itamar Simonson (2002b) provide a more direct examination of the notion of excessive farsightedness and the strategies that people use to overcome this (reverse) self-control problem. They found that a large segment of people perceive themselves as having insufficient indulgence and seek ways to correct this imbalance in their lives. Such people force themselves to indulge in an attempt to avoid default forms of spending on utilitarian necessities and/or savings. In particular people who have difficulty choosing items that are perceived as indulgences or luxuries (e.g., a cruise) over necessities (e.g., saving for college education) and cash in everyday decisions use precommitments to future hedonic experiences. For example, a substantial segment of people choose hedonic luxury awards over cash of equal or greater value (the choices and incentives are real). People explain such choices based on the need to precommit to indulgence, to make sure that the award does not end up in the pool of money used for necessities.

Kivetz (2007) provides additional direct evidence for the concept of hyperopia (excessive farsightedness). It is shown that people select pleasurable vices when the con-sequences of their decisions are psychologically distal (e.g., temporally delayed, hypothetical, improbable, abstract, or self-irrelevant) but reverse their decisions when the consequences are psychologically proximal (e.g., temporally imminent, real, vivid, or self-relevant). These reversals are more pronounced among people with a chronic tendency to experience guilt.

CONSEQUENCES OF HYPEROPIA

Kivetz and Anat Keinan (2006) investigate the consequences of hyperopia for people's well-being and long-term feelings. The extant literature on self-control suggests that people not only yield to temptations they had originally planned to resist but also subsequently reverse their preferences and regret their myopic behaviors (e.g., Schelling 1992). Although yielding to temptation certainly can be harmful, Kivetz and Keinan argue that excessive farsightedness can also have negative long-term consequences. In particular they propose that with the passage of time, choices of virtue over vice (e.g., work over pleasure) increasingly evoke regret. Accordingly they demonstrate that increasing the temporal separation between the actual decision and its assessment enhances the regret (or anticipatory regret) of righteous choices. Building on research on self-control and on affect (e.g., Kivetz and Simonson 2002b; Kahneman 1995; Metcalfe and Mischel 1999), Kivetz and Keinan show that greater temporal perspective allows people to escape the influence of indulgence guilt and causes them to experience a wistful feeling of missing out on the pleasures of life.

A great deal of research in psychology, economics, marketing, and other social sciences has examined self-control and time inconsistency. Such research has relied on a myopic premise. Late-twentieth-century and early twenty-first-century research advances an alternative perspective, namely that of excessive farsightedness and overcontrol. By exploring what is essentially a reverse form of self-control, this research contributes to a fuller understanding of self-regulation as a dynamic and general process. Some key discoveries that are diametrically opposed to the myopic premise include:

the finding that people require special entitlement justifications (hard work, excellence) to indulge;

the finding that people are motivated to work harder for hedonic luxuries than cash equivalents but are willing to spend more money on the latter;

the finding that people perceive themselves as suffering from excessive farsightedness and consequently correct this imbalance in their lives by precommitting to future hedonic experiences;

the finding that people are more likely to precommit to indulgence and to select vice when the consequences of their decisions are psychologically distal (e.g., temporally delayed, hypothetical, or abstract);

the detrimental impact of excessive farsightedness on well-being in the long run; that is, righteous choices of virtue over vice give rise to increasing regret over time, and considering long-term regret motivates people to select indulgence and luxury; and

the fact that the preceding findings are more pronounced among people who experience stronger (chronic or manipulated) indulgence guilt.

SEE ALSO *Behavior, Self-Constrained; Saving Rate; Self-Control*

BIBLIOGRAPHY

Ainslie, George. 1975. Specious Reward: A Behavioral Theory of Impulsiveness and Impulse Control. *Psychology Bulletin* 82 (April): 463–496.

Kahneman, Daniel. 1995. Varieties of Counterfactual Thinking. In *What Might Have Been: The Social Psychology of Counterfactual Thinking*, ed. Neal J. Roese and James M. Olson, 375–396. Mahwah, NJ: Erlbaum.

Keinan, Anat, and Ran Kivetz. 2007. Remedying Hyperopia: The Effects of Self-Control Regret on Consumer Behavior. Working paper, Columbia University.

Kivetz, Ran. 2007. Hyperopia: A Theory of Reverse Self-Control. Working paper, Columbia University.

Kivetz, Ran, and Anat Keinan. 2006. Repenting Hyperopia: An Analysis of Self-Control Regrets. *Journal of Consumer Research* 33 (September): 273–282.

Kivetz, Ran, and Itamar Simonson. 2002a. Earning the Right to Indulge: Effort as a Determinant of Customer Preferences toward Frequency Program Rewards. *Journal of Marketing Research* 39 (2): 155–170.

Kivetz, Ran, and Itamar Simonson. 2002b. Self-Control for the Righteous: Toward a Theory of Pre-Commitment to Indulgence. *Journal of Consumer Research* 29 (2): 199–217.

Kivetz, Ran, and Yuhuang Zheng. 2006. Determinants of Justification and Self-Control. *Journal of Experimental Psychology* 135 (4): 572–587.

Metcalfe, Janet, and Walter Mischel. 1999. A Hot/Cool-System Analysis of Delay of Gratification: Dynamics of Willpower. *Psychological Review* 106 (1): 3–19.

Prelec, Drazen, and Richard J. Herrnstein. 1992. A Theory of Addiction. In *Choice over Time*, ed. George Loewenstein and Jon Elster. New York: Sage.

Schelling, Thomas C. 1992. Self-Command: A New Discipline. In *Choice over Time*, ed. George Loewenstein and Jon Elster, 167–176. New York: Sage.

Thaler, Richard. 1980. Toward a Positive Theory of Consumer Choice. *Journal of Economic Behavior and Organization* 1 (March): 39–60.

Trope, Yaacov, and Ayelet Fishbach. 2000. Counteractive Self-Control in Overcoming Temptation. *Journal of Personality and Social Psychology* 79: 493–506.

Wertenbroch, Klaus. 1998. Consumption Self-Control by Rationing Purchase Quantities of Virtue and Vice. *Marketing Science* 17 (4): 317–337.

Ran Kivetz

FASCISM

Fascism is a reactionary and revolutionary ideology that emerged across Europe after World War I. Fascism was partially developed in Italy and became fully developed in Germany as a reaction against the unrestrained liberal capitalism of the nineteenth and early twentieth centuries, which promoted individualism over communal organization. Fascism as an ideology is anti-Marxist in its militarization of culture, society, and the economy and its rejection of social reforms as a means to create community. As in communism, fascism emphasizes the primacy of the collective unit; however, fascists reject communism's internationalism and instead define the community as a racial group whose passionate, heroic sacrifice for the nation will fulfill its historical destiny.

Fascism also promotes the adulation of a dictatorial figure to act as a strong representative of the *Volk* (the "people") in this process. Fascists argue that true democracy exists only under these specific conditions, thereby creating a myth of *volkish* communal heroism that relies on militarism for its success. Since fascists think in terms of absolute enemies of the people, they view imperialistic war as an inevitability of the rise of fascism. The goals of war are twofold: first, to resolve "land hunger" by expanding the nation's access to land, natural resources, and labor of native populations and, second, to solve domestic economic and political crisis (usually due to economic depression that causes high unemployment and challenges to the new one-party state). They therefore stress the virtues of a warlike culture: authoritarianism, unity of methods and goals, discipline, and an abhorrence of political dissent. The creation of an active, warlike citizenry is what distinguishes fascist regimes from authoritarian or dictatorial ones.

CHARACTERISTICS OF FASCIST SOCIETIES

Fascists solidified their power by stripping citizens of their individual rights and subordinating them to the will of the collective. A single-party political system that used terror, a secret police, and a strong military established a dictatorship controlled by a new social elite representative of the party. The hierarchy differed from that of other social systems in that it was not defined in class terms, but rather in terms of service to the nation. Because of this distinction, fascist states introduced a new form of social mobility that appealed to many citizens. The fascist government also succeeded in co-opting the economic system into the national sphere. Capitalist economics continued in the preservation of private property, though high party officials ensured the alliance between industrial and agricultural sectors and the state. The exploitation of workers in the form of low wages and high production quotas created economic growth, thereby fulfilling the promises of fascist governments to solve the problems of high unemployment caused by economic depression. In these ways, fascists ensured the loyalty of worker, peasant, industrialist, and businessman.

The heavy use of propaganda was another hallmark of fascist politics through its creation of the myth of the volkish leader whose destiny was to resurrect the greatness of the Volk. Films, books, signs, leaflets, and artistic productions attempted to present fascism as a new form of spirituality by espousing the "eternal truths" of the state through the repetition of slogans and symbols. Organizations such as clubs and youth groups and public displays of nationalism (in the form of parades or rallies) attempted to destroy private and individual identities by exalting a communal one. Censorship stripped intellectuals of their creative freedom and demanded that they produce warrior-peasant art that reflected the racial superiority of the Volk. Additionally, state-sponsored architectural projects embraced themes of sacrifice and national greatness through the construction of its war monuments and government buildings. Because fascism proclaimed to be the mouthpiece of a lost moral system, psychological conversion of the masses was essential to its success.

HISTORICAL EXPLANATION FOR THE RISE OF FASCISM

The roots of fascism can be traced to the political climate of European society before the outbreak of World War I in 1914. At the turn of the twentieth century, the international tensions that would soon lead to war in Europe were already apparent. Most members of the rising bourgeoisie supported their European governments because they greatly benefited from successful nationalist industrial and colonial expansion in the late nineteenth century. The working classes, however, were not benefactors of industrial and colonial growth, and socialist politics were strong across Europe. The rise of minorities' middle classes—Slavs in the Habsburg Empire and Jews every-

where in Europe—also threatened traditional ethnic majorities. Nationalists at this point rejected their liberal roots and became more conservative as nationalism developed into an ideology that protected the rights of the ethnic community over those of the individual. Rightist parties at the turn of the century appealed mostly to the traditional middle and upper classes, those that stood to lose the most through the rise of workers' movements and new privileged ethnic groups. Persuading the working classes into rejecting the internationalist foundation of Marxist politics and accepting the nation as a protective body soon became the primary goal of rightist parties in the decades preceding the outbreak of World War I. This development led conservatives to define the nation in ethnic terms. The rise of nationalism as a condemnation of "others" allowed for the emergence of fascist politics across Europe in the 1920s and 1930s.

Fascism developed into mature political movements in European societies whose citizens experienced a recent, rapid, and intense possibility of social mobility as a result of concentrated industrial growth that threatened to destroy traditional hierarchy in the interwar period. Social anxiety over recent processes of modernity heightened when the United States stock market crashed in 1929 and the Great Depression paralyzed European economies. Fascism became a viable political response for millions of Europeans when their parliamentary systems failed to provide adequate economic relief in the 1930s. The success of fascist politics additionally depended upon the existence of a substantial volkish population, one whose identity could be interpreted as being representative of a greater national entity and used by fascist leaders as a symbol of past, organic national greatness. Therefore, the states that supported fascist politics on a national level in the 1920s and 1930s, mostly in Central and Eastern Europe, sustained substantial agricultural economies at that time. It is also notable that World War I left an unresolved national question, irredentist, colonial, or a high percentage of "outsiders" within national boundaries, in the countries that became fascist in the interwar period—Italy, Germany, Romania, Hungary, Austria, Croatia, and France. Fascist promises of a return to national greatness resonated with the masses who viewed their economic suffering as a social injustice. France is the exception to this pattern in that its fascist government—the Vichy regime—enjoyed very little popular support and was a puppet of the Nazis rather than a legitimate state. Fascism in all of its manifestations can be seen as one response to the social, economic, and political crisis that accompanied the process of modernity in Europe.

The emergence of Italian fascism deserves special attention because of Benito Mussolini's role in fascist ideological development. Mussolini, fascist dictator of Italy from 1922 to 1943, first used the term *fascism* in 1919 to describe this new political ideology of individual subordination to the ethnic community as a method of attaining national greatness. Mussolini developed this belief in the strength of the community as an active and politically prominent socialist during his youth. Like many socialists, Mussolini was critical of the politics and economics of European liberal capitalism. In Italy's case, the last quarter of the nineteenth century and the first decades of the twentieth century were years of grave economic crisis, primarily due to its ineffectiveness in industrializing and the weakness and inefficiency of its governments. Italy's lack of natural resources perpetuated a largely agricultural economy that was unable to support imperialist expansion, causing international embarrassment in a time when national greatness on the continent was largely defined by the building of empires abroad.

After World War I, Mussolini came to believe that socialist internationalism would only serve to subordinate Italy to more powerful European neighbors who had failed to reward his country adequately for its Allied support during the war and turned to rightist politics. In 1919, Mussolini founded the Fascist Party and defined fascism as a technique for gaining and solidifying power through the use of violent action. Fascism demanded first and foremost the cultivation of military discipline and a fighting spirit in every Italian citizen. Unlike Marxist theory, which believes in an end to the process of history through a democratically based revolution that establishes a communist state, Mussolini's fascism defined history as constant struggle through constant war. The necessity of action required the adulation of a leader who would manage his country's destiny through acts of war and violence. Complete confidence in the decisions of the leader, Il Duce, as Mussolini referred to himself, needed to be blindly obeyed in order for national goals to be met. Mussolini pointed to Italy's weakened economic state after the war as proof that such a leader was necessary for Italian recovery.

In 1922, Mussolini's fascist militia marched on Rome and he became the prime minister of Italy. Between 1922 and 1927, Mussolini concentrated on fascist state-building. The state and the Fascist Party became a single entity that oversaw the alignment of the legislative, executive, and judicial bodies with nationalist goals. Mussolini asked Italians to sacrifice their individual identities in order to establish Italy as the new leader of mankind. He further legitimized his dictatorship by pointing to the rise of fascist parties across Europe as evidence that parliamentarianism and liberal democracy were decadent political and social values and that fascism was indeed the new path of modernity.

What differentiated Italian fascism at this early stage from other young fascist movements across Europe was its rejection of anti-Semitic sentiment. This distinction is mostly due to the lack of a discernable Jewish population in Italy. Instead, Italian exposure to African populations during failed colonial ventures made Africans the targets of Italian racist nationalism during the interwar period. Mussolini integrated this race doctrine into the construction of his dictatorship but never fully developed it. Rather repulsed by the racist program of the National Socialists (Nazis) in Germany, Mussolini instead directed his energies toward imperialist expansion rather than cultivating an ethnically pure Italian state.

Anti-Semitism was the distinguishing feature of mature fascism developed by Adolf Hitler in Germany. Hitler's fusion of race doctrine—the belief in the natural inequality of human races and the superiority of the Teutonic race—with Mussolini's philosophy of power created a particularly virulent and highly destructive form of fascism. The anti-Semitic flavor of Imperial German society laid the foundations for the rise of racist nationalist politics in the interwar period. The increase of Jewish presence in trade, finance, politics, and journalism, particularly in Berlin, around the turn of the twentieth century fueled conspiracy theories about a Jewish "infiltration" of German society. Hitler's fascist National Socialist Party, begun in 1919 as the German Workers' Party, was an anti-Semitic, supra-nationalist political organization whose proclaimed goal was to protect the ethnic German community at all costs. The Nazis succeeded in earning millions of German votes in the late 1920s and early 1930s with its strong repudiation of the Versailles Treaty coupled with messages of moral and economic rebirth through the destruction of "Jewish" market competition, the annihilation of European Jewry, and territorial expansion. Hitler and the Nazi Party attempted to fulfill the promises of his propaganda through the creation of a totalitarian state in Germany. From 1933 to 1945, the Nazis exercised total control over the German population and conquered much of the European continent. The fascist period of German history was additionally responsible for the deaths of approximately six million Jews and three million Slavs, Roma, homosexuals, political dissidents, and other "undesirables" during the Holocaust.

INTERPRETATIONS OF FASCISM

It has been difficult for historians, political scientists, psychologists, and sociologists of fascism to agree on a single explanation for the rise of fascism in some countries but not in others. One leading interpretation supports the notion that fascism was an experience unique to certain countries, pointing to some kind of predestination of radical conservative nationalism. The second prominent interpretation is that fascism was a reaction to the failure of European liberalism to make good on its promises of promoting every individual's right to social mobility. This interpretation puts the rise of fascism in an international context of the struggles of European modernity.

SEE ALSO *Anti-Semitism; Capitalism; Censorship; Colonialism; Communalism; Great Depression; Hierarchy; Hitler, Adolf; Imperialism; Liberalism; Mussolini, Benito; Nationalism and Nationality; Nazism; Propaganda; Property; Racism; Right Wing*

BIBLIOGRAPHY

Brady, Robert A. 1971. *The Spirit and Structure of German Fascism.* New York: Citadel.

De Felice, Renzo. 1977. *Interpretations of Fascism.* Trans. Brenda Huff Everett. Cambridge, MA: Harvard University Press.

Falasca-Zamponi, Simonetta. 1997. *Fascist Spectacle: The Aesthetics of Power in Mussolini's Italy.* Berkeley: University of California Press.

Laqueur, Walter. 1996. *Fascism: Past, Present, Future.* New York: Oxford University Press.

Lubasz, Heinz, ed. 1973. *Fascism: Three Major Regimes.* New York: Wiley.

Paxton, Robert O. 2004. *The Anatomy of Fascism.* New York: Knopf.

Payne, Stanley G. 1995. *A History of Fascism, 1914–1945.* Madison: University of Wisconsin Press.

Smith, Denis Mack. 1982. *Mussolini.* New York: Knopf.

Tracey A. Pepper

FATHERHOOD

Issues of fatherhood have received considerable attention since the 1990s in academic, practice, and policy discussions as well as in the public domain. This focus on fatherhood, which subsequently came to address responsible fathering, reflects an assumption: that the meaning and enactment of responsible parenting are at the heart of social and cultural debates about the individual and combined roles of families and society in ensuring the health and well-being of children. Throughout the 1970s and 1980s most of the cultural debate about mothers highlighted the question: What, if anything, should mothers do outside the family? By the end of 1990s the debate about fathers had refocused the question to: What should fathers do inside the family (see Doherty, Kouneski, and Erickson 1998)? Several related questions were posed: What role should fathers play in the everyday lives of their children, that is, beyond the traditional breadwinner role? How much should they emulate the traditional nurturing activities of mothers, and how much should they represent a masculine sex-role model to their children? Advocacy organizations and those in the public domain

asked: Is fatherhood in a unique crisis? The discussion that follows provides an overview of the background and context of these questions, the resulting effort, and the current status of discussions in the field.

BACKGROUND AND CONTEXT OF THE ISSUES

Prior to the 1960s research and policy on family development were dominated by intact or nuclear family models. The role of fathers was framed within a decidedly Euro-American interpretation of family functioning in which fathers provided for the economic well-being of their children and mothers ensured their children's developmental progress (see Coltrane and Parke 1998; Gottman and Katz 1989; Parke 1996; Pruett and Pruett 1998). Much of family research through the 1970s also focused on the degree to which ethnically diverse families, particularly African American families, adhered to this model (see Coleman et al. 1966; Katz 1993; McDaniel 1994; Moynihan 1965, 1987). Not until the resurgence of interest in family studies in the 1990s did research or policy highlight the diversity of family functioning, interactions, and expectations embedded in the cultural and ethnic histories of families and communities in the United States (see Anderson 1990, 1999; McDaniel 1994; Zuberi 1998).

Much of the visibility of fatherhood can be traced to the passage of the 1988 Family Support Act, which called attention to the failure of many nonresidential, noncustodial parents, mostly fathers, to contribute to the financial support of their children. However, the act did not distinguish among different types of fathers and appeared to assume that all fathers shared a common experience in terms of their marital status at the birth of their children, employment and employability, ability to contribute financially, reasons for absence, and the quality of their relationship with their children, families, and communities. Divorced, middle-class, educated, nonresidential fathers were grouped alongside low-income, unemployed, poorly educated fathers. Issues of class, race, and cultural practices were relatively unexamined except in noting the disproportionate numbers of single, African American, low-income mothers raising their children as well as low-income fathers who neither had custody of their children (noncustodial) nor resided with them (nonresidential).

Despite its limitations, the act was effective in generating interest about nonresidential fathers and acknowledging the growing numbers of fathers who lived apart from their children. It also prompted researchers and practitioners to raise critical issues about the failure of policies in general to address the diversity of fathers and the disparities in their circumstances. The complexity of a changing society was evident in the struggles being experienced by large numbers of children and families.

However, it was clear that to understand the causes and effects of father absence, the field also needed to address the causes and effects of father presence, expanding the apparent urgency to examine all types of fathers, irrespective of their coresidence with their children and families, social class, race, and family ties. The discussions that ensued positioned, as a priority, the common problems of father absence; its effects on children, families, communities, and society; and the downward spiraling of two-parent families, father presence, and marriage. They pointed to the need to uncover and understand how men enact their roles as fathers, (re)negotiate gendered and social expectations, and (re)engage with their children and families over the short and long term.

RESPONSIBLE FATHERING

Since the mid-1990s researchers have distinguished various types of father involvement; however, the resulting literature defines and describes father-child *presence* with increased, though still inexact, precision. The use of the concept *responsible fathering* reflects a relatively recent shift among academics and professionals away from value-free language toward a more explicit value-advocacy approach (see Doherty et al. 1998; Gadsden 2002; Gadsden and Hall, 1996). *Responsible* suggests an *ought*, a set of desired norms for evaluating fathers' behavior. The term also conveys a moral meaning (right and wrong), since it suggests that some fathering could be judged *irresponsible* or *nonresponsible*. Michael Lamb and his colleagues (1985) offered the most influential scheme to organize the concept: (1) responsibility, the role that fathers take in ascertaining that their children are cared for and arranging for the availability of resources; (2) availability, fathers' potential for interaction by virtue of being present or being accessible to their children (whether or not direct interaction is occurring); and (3) engagement, fathers' direct interaction or contact with their children through caregiving and shared activities.

Several categorizing frameworks and measurement tools have been created since the mid-1990s, among them Vivian Gadsden and colleagues' (1999) *Fathering Indicators Framework* (National Center on Fathers and Families), Rob Palkovitz's (1997) list of 119 ways to be involved in parenting, Alan Hawkins and colleagues' (2002) *Inventory of Father Involvement*, and the Lewin Group's *Evaluability Assessment of Responsible Fatherhood Programs* (1997).

THE CURRENT STATUS

The study of fatherhood has progressed significantly as a field from the early 1990s to the early twenty-first century. In 1994 the National Center on Fathers and Families (NCOFF) was established at the University of Pennsylvania to create and implement a research agenda that took seriously the issues of practice, including a research database, the Fatherlit Research Database. The center and the resulting activities in the field demonstrated a consistent shift. For example, in fields such as developmental psychology, once characterized by a singular focus on mother–child relationships, the significance of the father in the daily routines of child support and nurturance was increasingly discussed. The implication of this work was that the role of fathers, and the family itself, was seen as contributing to the affective development of children; to the shaping of personality; and eventually to a sense of belonging, meaning, and socioemotional stability.

One might well ask, What has really changed in the field since the 1990s? Any review of data from the field reveals the measured but significant increase in focus and reach to multiple audiences. Through tracking of the FatherLit Database, NCOFF has systematically collected data on the number of refereed research articles and other research publications on fathers, including the creation of a journal, *Fathering*, in 2003. Although much of the discussion still dichotomizes the issues into father presence and absence and their effects, it also addresses specific questions such as fathers' relationships with their children, the effect of father presence on young children, the role of fathers in homes, and the effects of father engagement on mothers.

Outside the United States the focus on fatherhood has been equally compelling. However, a persistent problem centers on the degree to which and the way research, practice, and policy are constructed and implemented across cultural and national borders. As is true in the United States, questions about where and how to situate fatherhood and fathering are a critical focus of discussion. For example, should fathering be aligned with child wellbeing? Is it more appropriately studied as an issue of family development and family functioning? How should it be examined within economic and legal considerations? What is the role of fathers in children's lives?

In various parts of Africa (most notably South Africa) an increasing body of research and new programs have been initiated. Support for these efforts often began as grassroots initiatives but subsequently have been examined in relationship to family life, economic stressors, and the meaning of father presence and engagement. In *Baba: Men and Fatherhood in South Africa* (2006), edited by Linda Richter and Robert Morrell, chapters take up several of the concerns, questions, and problems that have been examined in the United States but with particular currency for explicating and understanding the cultural contexts in South Africa, such as migrancy, the experience of gold mine workers, Zulu-speaking men and fatherhood, and HIV/AIDS, to name a few (see also Madhaven et al. 2006 for a discussion of father presence in rural South Africa).

A. Bame Namenang (2000), in addressing related issues in Cameroon, similarly calls attention to the construction of father images, cultural practices, kin networks, and the ways fatherhood is situated within these larger familial and community contexts. Efforts throughout Europe, Australia, and the Caribbean reinforce the need to examine critically the cross-cultural and cross-national domains of fatherhood. Among the most well-known research is that of Margaret O'Brien (2004) in England, in which she takes up research and policy questions and the difficult intersections between programs and policies. Drawing upon work from large datasets in the United States, Alison Smith (2007) has used the European Community Household Panel to identify several trends throughout European countries, for example, cross-national differences in fathers' participation in child care, in employment and pay for fathers versus nonfathers, and in the amount of time spent working (see also Jaipaul Roopnarine and Janet Brown's [1997] work on Caribbean families).

At the same time programmatic efforts have increased and become better organized. A range of programs has emerged—from small, grassroots efforts to educational efforts to work affiliated with federally funded organizations. The National Practitioners Network for Fathers and Families; the National Fatherhood Initiative, which houses a federally funded clearinghouse; and the National Center on Fathering represent a few of these efforts, as does a group of experts representing different focuses—research, practice, and advocacy—and the National Fatherhood Leaders Group. Similar work is taking place throughout parts of Africa, Europe, Australia, and the Caribbean, much of it building upon practitioner efforts and cross-collaborations between the United States and groups abroad and supported by a range of foundations and governmental initiatives, including regional meetings in England, Jamaica, South Africa, and Australia. One example from England is Father Direct, the national information center that publishes guides and provides training, conferences, and briefings on fatherhood.

The interest in responsible fatherhood has both heightened and precipitated change. Work on fathers invariably points to the deleterious effects of father absence for children, families, communities, and society, including a focus on "fragile families" (see publications of the Center on Child Wellbeing at Princeton University; Garfinkel and McLanahan 2003; McLanahan 2006; McLanahan and Carlson 2004) and families experiencing hardship absent the supports necessary for optimal healthy development, with children thought to be espe-

cially at risk for poor academic achievement, juvenile delinquency and incarceration, victimization by violence and exploitation, and unmarried adolescent parenting (see also Shannon et al. 2002; Cabrera and Garcia-Coll 2004).

Finally, policy efforts have grown at all levels of government, though the question of "what constitutes a good father" persists (see Rosenberg and Wilcox 2006), as do issues related to father absence. For example, in a request for proposals from the U.S. Department of Health and Human Services (2006), the writers noted that in approximately 84 percent of cases where a parent is absent, that parent is the father and that if the trends continue, half of all children born in the early twenty-first century will live apart from one of their parents, usually their father, at some point before they turn eighteen. They also indicate that where families (whether intact or with a parent absent) are living in poverty, a significant factor is the father's lack of job skills. An estimated 19,400,000 children (27 percent) live apart from their biological fathers. Of children under age eighteen not living with their biological fathers, 40 percent had not seen their fathers even once in the last twelve months.

CLOSING THOUGHTS

It is no surprise that the field of fatherhood and the larger field of family studies grapple with an array of difficult questions and uncharted terrain. What is needed in this still growing field are deepened analyses that reflect the ways fathers, children, and families shape and revise their identities within families and respond to the social and cultural expectations of home and society. Several issues are still relatively unexamined, among them the diversity of fathers, both middle-income and low-income men and families; families of color and immigrant families; the cultural and social factors that influence fathering practices and community expectations; children of incarcerated fathers; the engagement of fathers and mothers as parents and in relationship to their children; the effects of racial stratification on fathers' engagement; preparation (through schooling and work) to assume the financial and emotional roles of fathering; issues of men's health; and social vulnerability. In order for change to occur, a conceptual framework is critical—one that reflects a deep understanding of the multifaceted issues and possibilities to effect change in all communities where there are fathers and children.

SEE ALSO *Child Development; Family; Family Structure; Masculinity; Men; Motherhood; Moynihan Report; Parent-Child Relationships; Public Policy; Role Theory; Unemployment*

BIBLIOGRAPHY

Anderson, Elijah. 1990. *Street Wise: Race, Class, and Change in an Urban Community*. Chicago: University of Chicago Press.

Anderson, Elijah. 1999. *The Code of the Street: Decency, Violence, and the Moral Life of the Inner City*. New York: Norton.

Cabrera, Natasha, and Cynthia Garcia-Coll. 2004. Latino Fathers: Uncharted Territory in Much Need of Exploration. In *The Role of the Father in Child Development*, 4th ed., ed. Michael E. Lamb, 98–120. Hoboken, NJ: Wiley.

Coleman, James S., Ernest Q. Campbell, Carol J. Hobson, et al. 1966. *Equality of Educational Opportunity*. Washington, DC: U.S. Department of Health, Education, and Welfare.

Coltrane, Scott, and Ross D. Parke. 1998. *Reinventing Fatherhood: Toward an Historical Understanding of Continuity and Change in Men's Family Lives*. Philadelphia: National Center on Fathers and Families, University of Pennsylvania.

Doherty, William J., Edward F. Kouneski, and Martha F. Erickson. 1998. Responsible Fathering: An Overview and Conceptual Framework. *Journal of Marriage and the Family* 60: 277–292.

Gadsden, Vivian L., and Marcia Hall. 1996. *Intergenerational Learning: A Review of the Literature*. Philadelphia: National Center on Fathers and Families, University of Pennsylvania.

Gadsden, Vivian L. 2002. Fathering Research and Policy. Keynote address. *National Family Research Consortium*. Lake Tahoe, CA.

Gadsden, Vivian L., Jay Fagan, Aisha Ray, and James E. Davis. 1999. *The Fathering Indicators Framework: A Tool for Qualitative and Quantitative Analysis*. Philadelphia: National Center on Fathers and Families, University of Pennsylvania.

Garfinkel, Irwin, and Sara McLanahan. 2003. Strengthening Fragile Families. In *One Percent for the Kids: New Policies, Brighter Futures for America's Children*, ed. Isabel Sawhill, 76–92. Washington, DC: Brookings Institution.

Gottman, John, and Lynn Katz. 1989. Effects of Marital Discord on Young Children's Peer Interaction and Health. *Developmental Psychology* 25: 373–381.

Hawkins, Alan, Kay Bradford, Rob Palkovitz, et al. 2002. The Inventory of Father Involvement: A Pilot Study of a New Measure of Father Involvement. *Journal of Men's Studies* 10: 183–196.

Katz, Michael. 1993. The Urban "Underclass" as a Metaphor of Social Transformation. In *The "Underclass" Debate: Views from History*, ed. Michael Katz, 3–23. Princeton, NJ: Princeton University Press.

Lamb, Michael, Joseph H. Pleck, Eric L. Charnov, and James A. Levine. 1985. Paternal Behavior in Humans. *American Zoologist* 25 (3): 883–894.

Lewin Group. 1997. *An Evaluability Assessment of Responsible Fatherhood Programs: Final Report*. Washington, DC: U.S. Department of Health and Human Services.

McDaniel, Antonio. 1994. Historical Racial Differences in the Residential Patterns of Children. *Journal of Family History* 19 (1): 57–77.

McLanahan, Sara. 2006. Fragile Families and the Marriage Agenda. In *Fragile Families and the Marriage Agenda*, ed. Lori Kowaleski-Jones and Nicholas Wolfinger, 1–21. New York: Springer Science.

McLanahan, Sara, and Marcia Carlson. 2004. Fathers in Fragile Families. In *Conceptualizing and Measuring Father Involvement*, ed. Randal Day and Michael E. Lamb, 241–271. Mahwah, NJ: Erlbaum.

Moynihan, Daniel Patrick. 1965. *The Negro Family: The Case for National Action*. Washington, DC: U.S. Department of Labor.

Moynihan, Daniel Patrick. 1987. *Family and Nation: The Godkin Lectures*. San Diego, CA: Harcourt Brace Jovanovich.

O'Brien, Margaret. 2004. Social Science and Public Policy Perspectives on Fatherhood in Europe. In *The Role of the Father in Child Development*, 4th ed., ed. Michael E. Lamb, 98–120. Hoboken, NJ: Wiley.

Palkovitz, Rob. 1997. Reconstructing "Involvement": Expanding Conceptualizations of Men's Caring in Contemporary Families. In *Generative Fathering: Beyond Deficit Perpsectives*, ed. Alan Hawkins and David Dollahite, 200–216. Thousand Oaks, CA: Sage.

Parke, Ross. 1996. *Fatherhood*. Cambridge, MA: Harvard University Press.

Pruett, Marsha Kline, and Kyle D. Pruett. 1998. Fathers, Divorce, and Their Children. *Child and Adolescent Psychiatric Clinics of North America* 7 (2): 389–407.

Richter, Linda, and Robert Morrell, eds. 2006. *Baba: Men and Fatherhood in South Africa*. Cape Town, South Africa: Human Sciences Research Council.

Roopnarine, Jaipaul, and Janet Brown. 1997. Caribbean Families: Diversity among Ethnic Groups. *Advances in Applied Developmental Psychology*, vol. 14. Greenwich, CT: Ablex.

Rosenberg, Jeffery, and W. Bradford Wilcox. 2006. *The Importance of Fathers in the Healthy Development of Children*. Child Abuse and Neglect User Manual Series. Washington, DC: U.S. Department of Health and Human Services.

Shannon, Jacqueline, Catherine Tamis-LeMonda, Kevin London, and Natasha Cabrera. 2002. Beyond Rough and Tumble: Low-Income Fathers' Interactions and Children's Cognitive Development at 24 Months. *Parenting: Science and Practice* 2 (2): 77–104.

Smith, Alison J. 2007. Working Fathers in Europe: Earning and Caring? Center for Research on Families and Relationships Research Briefing, 30.

U.S. Department of Health and Human Services. 2006. National Quality Improvement Center on Non-Resident Fathers. Requests for Proposals. http://www.acf.hhs.gov/grants/open/HHS-2006-ACF-ACYF-CO-0142.html.

Zuberi, Tukufu. 1998. *African American Men, Inequality, and Family Structure: A Research Note*. Philadelphia: National Center on Fathers and Families, University of Pennsylvania.

Vivian L. Gadsden

FEAGIN, JOSEPH
1938–

Joseph Feagin is a scholar, social justice advocate, professor, and leader in the field of urban sociology. Throughout his career, he has fought against the oppression of people of color within the United States. His passion for equity has essentially held a mirror to the country, reflecting the raw imagery of how the United States has historically oppressed people of color through social, economic, mental, and physical means. This reflection has at times caused those who view the issues of race conservatively to see Feagin's work as unbearable. For example, in his book *The Professors: The 101 Most Dangerous Academics in America* (2006), the conservative author David Horowitz included Feagin on his list of "threats." Horowitz claims that professors like Feagin "push" their liberal agenda onto college students, while at the same time stifling alternative viewpoints within the classroom. Regardless, many admirers of his work and efforts feel that he has spent a rich academic career attempting to answer the endless riddles of racial problems within the United States.

Joe Feagin was born in San Angelo, Texas, and he grew up in Houston during the Great Depression. After high school, he earned a degree in history, philosophy, and social ethics at Baylor University in 1960. He received a PhD in social ethics from Harvard University in 1966. He began his academic career as an assistant professor at the University of California at Riverside from 1966 to 1970. He went on to hold the positions of associate professor and full professor of sociology at the University of Texas, Austin (1970–1974 and 1974–1990, respectively). He has also been a scholar-in-residence at the U.S. Commission on Civil Rights (1974–1975) and a graduate professor at the University of Florida (1990–2004). In 2004 he was appointed the Ella C. McFadden Professor of Liberal Arts at Texas A&M University. Feagin has received countless honors and awards, including the Gustavus Myers Center Outstanding Human Rights Book Award in 1995 and 1996 and the Center for Healing of Racism Ally Award n 2006. He has twice been nominated for the Pulitzer Prize, and he served as the president of the American Sociological Association in 2000.

In his advocacy for social justice through the use of empirical and historical research and data, Feagin has explored the hatred that the white majority has toward people of color, especially blacks. He believes that this hatred is not only at the center of the foundation of the country, but that it is also the rationale for the current treatment of people of color. He has successfully correlated various problems that exist among people of color to the white racial frame that was first used successfully to disempower blacks through the means of social control. In fact, this white racial frame uses a manipulation of stereotypes of blacks and other people of color to galvanize the need for control over this population, who have historically been viewed as sexual and physical threats by white elites.

Feagin's prolific scholarship has spanned over forty-two years and yielded thought-provoking contributions in over 40 published books, 180 journal articles and monographs, and numerous consultations on issues of racism, discrimination, police brutality, gender racism, and other such experiences of people of color. Since 1989, with the help of other colleagues, he has completed field research studies involving approximately 600 black Americans in regard to social problems. In addition, in order to bring forth the voices of the marginalized within his work, he has been involved within dozens of field research studies that use diaries, focus groups, and in-depth interviews. But because the sample respondents used in various segments of his work are not selected from a sampling frame, the "snowball" sampling technique he and other qualitative researchers use cannot always ensure unbiased estimates. Thus, this technique has been called into question by some, particularly by pure quantitative researchers. Many researchers in the field, however, have adapted the technique because of its value in researching groups that are traditionally difficult for researchers to gain access to. Overall, Feagin has helped give a voice to the voiceless and marginalized populations within the United States.

SEE ALSO *Attitudes; Attitudes, Racial; Race; Racism; Sociology*

BIBLIOGRAPHY

Feagin, Joe R. 1982. *Social Problems: A Critical Power-Conflict Perspective.* Englewood Cliffs, NJ: Prentice-Hall.

Feagin, Joe R. 2000. *Racist America: Roots, Current Realities, and Future Reparations.* New York: Routledge.

Horowitz, David. 2006. *The Professors: The 101 Most Dangerous Academics in America.* Washington, DC: Regnery.

Terence D. Fitzgerald

FEAR
SEE *Psychosomatics.*

FECHNER, GUSTAV THEODORE
SEE *Mathematics in the Social Sciences.*

FEDERAL BUREAU OF INVESTIGATION
SEE *Hoover, J. Edgar.*

FEDERAL ELECTION ACT OF 1970
SEE *Campaigning.*

FEDERAL RESERVE SYSTEM, U.S.

Of all the central banks in the world, the Federal Reserve System ("the Fed") has one of the most unusual structures. The historic hostility of the American public to banks and centralized authority (which resulted in the demise in 1811 and 1832 of the first two experiments with central banking, the First and Second Bank of the United States) led the U.S. Congress to write an elaborate system of checks and balances into the Federal Reserve Act of 1913, which created the Federal Reserve System with its twelve regional Federal Reserve banks.

The writers of the Federal Reserve Act wanted to diffuse power along regional lines, between the private sector and the government, and among bankers, business people, and the public. This initial diffusion of power has resulted in the evolution of the Federal Reserve System to include the following entities: the Federal Reserve banks, the Board of Governors of the Federal Reserve System, the Federal Open Market Committee (FOMC), and around 2,800 member commercial banks.

FEDERAL RESERVE BANKS
Each of the twelve Federal Reserve districts has one main Federal Reserve bank, which may have branches in other cities in the district. The three largest Federal Reserve banks in terms of assets are those of New York, Chicago, and San Francisco—combined they hold more than 50 percent of the assets (discount loans, securities, and other holdings) of the Federal Reserve System. The New York bank, with around one-quarter of the assets, is the most important of the Federal Reserve banks because it conducts foreign-exchange interventions on behalf of the Federal Reserve System and the U.S. Treasury and also purchases and sells securities for the Federal Reserve System.

Each of the Federal Reserve banks is a quasi-public (part private, part government) institution owned by the private commercial banks in the district that are members of the Federal Reserve System. These member banks have purchased stock in their district Federal Reserve bank (a requirement of membership), and the dividends paid by that stock are limited by law to 6 percent annually. The member banks elect six directors for each district bank; three more are appointed by the Board of Governors. Together, these nine directors appoint the president of the bank (subject to the approval of the Board of Governors).

The directors of a district bank are classified into three categories: A, B, and C. The three A directors (elected by the member banks) are professional bankers, and the three B directors (also elected by the member banks) are prominent leaders from industry, labor, agriculture, or the consumer sector. The three C directors, who are appointed by the Board of Governors to represent the public interest, are not allowed to be officers, employees, or stockholders of banks. This design for choosing directors was intended by the framers of the Federal Reserve Act to ensure that the directors of each Federal Reserve bank would reflect all constituencies of the American public.

The twelve Federal Reserve banks perform the following functions:

- Clear checks;
- Issue new currency;
- Withdraw damaged currency from circulation;
- Administer and make discount loans to banks in their districts;
- Evaluate proposed mergers and applications for banks to expand their activities;
- Act as liaisons between the business community and the Federal Reserve System;
- Examine bank holding companies and state-chartered member banks;
- Collect data on local business conditions; and
- Use their staffs of professional economists to research topics related to the conduct of monetary policy.

The twelve Federal Reserve banks are involved in monetary policy in several ways. Their directors "establish" the discount rate (although the discount rate in each district is reviewed and determined by the Board of Governors) and decide which banks, member and nonmember alike, can obtain discount loans from the Federal Reserve bank. Their directors select one commercial banker from each bank's district to serve on the Federal Advisory Council, which consults with the Board of Governors and provides information that helps in the conduct of monetary policy. Five of the twelve bank presidents each have a vote in the Federal Open Market

Committee, which directs *open market operations* (the purchase and sale of government securities that affect both interest rates and the amount of reserves in the banking system). The president of the New York Fed always has a vote in the FOMC, another reason why it is the most important of the banks; the other four votes allocated to the district banks rotate annually among the remaining eleven presidents.

BOARD OF GOVERNORS OF THE FEDERAL RESERVE SYSTEM

At the head of the Federal Reserve System is the seven-member Board of Governors, headquartered in Washington, D.C. Each governor is appointed by the president of the United States and confirmed by the Senate. To limit the president's control over the Fed and insulate the Fed from other political pressures, the governors can serve one full nonrenewable fourteen-year term plus part of another term, with one governor's term expiring every other January. The governors (many are professional economists) must come from different Federal Reserve districts to prevent the interests of one region of the country from being over-represented. The chairman of the Board of Governors is chosen from among the seven governors and serves a four-year, renewable term. It is expected that once a new chairman is chosen, the old chairman resigns from the Board of Governors, even if there are many years left to his or her term as a governor. The chairman exercises enormous power because he is the spokesperson for the Fed and negotiates with Congress and the president of the United States. He also exercises control by setting the agenda of Board of Governors and FOMC meetings and by supervising the board's staff of professional economists and advisors.

The Board of Governors is actively involved in decisions concerning the conduct of monetary policy. All seven governors are members of the FOMC and vote on the conduct of open-market operations. Because there are only twelve voting members on this committee (seven governors and five presidents of the district banks), the board has the majority of the votes. The board also sets reserve requirements (within limits imposed by legislation) and effectively controls the discount rate by the "review and determination" process, whereby it approves or disapproves the discount rate "established" by the Federal Reserve banks. The chairman of the board advises the president of the United States on economic policy, testifies in Congress, and speaks for the Federal Reserve System to the media. The chairman and other governors may also represent the United States in negotiations with foreign governments on economic matters. The board has a staff of professional economists (larger than those of individual Federal Reserve banks) which provides economic analysis that the board uses in making its decisions.

Through legislation, the Board of Governors often has been given duties not directly related to the conduct of monetary policy. In the past, for example, the board set the maximum interest rates payable on certain types of deposits under Regulation Q. (After 1986, ceilings on time deposits were eliminated, but there is still a restriction on paying any interest on business demand deposits.) Under the Credit Control Act of 1969 (which expired in 1982) the board had the ability to regulate and control credit once the president of the United States approved. The Board of Governors also sets margin requirements—the fraction of the purchase price of securities that has to be paid for with cash rather than borrowed funds. It also sets the salary of the president and all officers of each Federal Reserve bank and reviews each bank's budget. Finally, the board has substantial bank regulatory functions: It approves bank mergers and applications for new activities, specifies the permissible activities of bank holding companies, and supervises the activities of foreign banks in the United States.

FEDERAL OPEN MARKET COMMITTEE (FOMC)

The FOMC usually meets eight times a year (about every six weeks) and makes decisions regarding the conduct of monetary policy, especially by setting the target for the policy interest rate and the federal funds rate (an overnight rate for loans between banking institutions). In addition, it also makes the decisions about reserve requirements and the discount rate (which play less of a prominent role in the conduct of monetary policy). The FOMC does not actually carry out securities purchases or sales. Instead, it issues directives to the trading desk at the Federal Reserve Bank of New York, where the manager for domestic open-market operations supervises a roomful of people who execute the purchases and sales of the government or agency securities. The manager communicates daily with the FOMC members and their staffs concerning the activities of the trading desk.

SEE ALSO *Central Banks; Greenspan, Alan; Policy, Monetary*

BIBLIOGRAPHY

Board of Governors of the Federal Reserve. 2006. About the Fed. http://www.federalreserve.gov/general.htm.

Mishkin, Frederic S. 2007. *The Economics of Money, Banking, and Financial Markets.* 8th ed. Boston: Addison-Wesley.

Frederic S. Mishkin

FEDERAL RESERVE SYSTEM, U.S.: ANALYSIS

A political compromise enabled Congress to find a majority to support the Federal Reserve Act of 1913. New York bankers wanted control vested in bankers, and favored a model based on the Bank of England. Rural and agricultural interests wanted political control to remain with the government. The compromise created twelve semiautonomous Reserve banks controlled by bankers, with a Reserve Board in Washington, D.C., appointed by the president with the consent of Congress. The compromise left open the question of degree of independence: Who would make the decisions, Reserve banks or the Board?

Policy decisions were in fact limited. The authors accepted the international gold standard as a monetary rule and the real bills doctrine as an operating procedure. That limited scope for discretion in decisions about the timing of discount rate changes.

Almost immediately, conflict over decisions began between the Board and the Reserve banks. The banks, led by Benjamin Strong of the New York Reserve bank, dominated decisions until Strong's death in 1928. Strong and his associates soon recognized that the real bills doctrine had a major flaw: It implied that a central bank could control the quantities of money and credit by controlling their quality. Specifically, they concluded that efforts to prevent speculative lending would not succeed. The Board adhered to the real bills doctrine and, until 1933, the gold standard. The result of this policy was to deepen the Great Depression. The Federal Reserve was inactive from 1933 to 1951, under the control of the Treasury. In 1935 Congress approved changes in the Federal Reserve Act that shifted control of decisions from the Reserve banks to the Board of Governors. Once the Federal Reserve resumed active policymaking in 1951, the Board began to change procedures to strengthen its control. At the time, it lacked a clear vision of its proper objectives and how to achieve them.

Congress passed two pieces of legislation at the end of World War II (1939–1945). The Employment Act (1946) made a vague commitment to economic stability. The Bretton Woods Agreement (1944) called for fixed but adjustable exchange rates. Monetary policy could achieve domestic stability or exchange rate stability, but not both. The Federal Reserve and many others interpreted the Employment Act as a commitment to "full employment," and although the Reserve never defined what that meant in practice, it gradually came to mean unemployment rates of about 4 to 5 percent. Federal Reserve Chairman William McChesney Martin Jr. stressed the importance of maintaining low inflation and a fixed exchange rate, but he did not develop procedures to achieve either.

One reason for this failure was the effort to coordinate monetary and fiscal policy actions. A popular belief at the time held that coordination would contribute to stability and prosperity; overlooked was the loss of Federal Reserve independence and the increased political influence on monetary policy actions. The administration of Lyndon Johnson wanted the Federal Reserve to coordinate by keeping interest rates from rising so they could finance their persistent budget deficits at lower cost. The Federal Reserve did just that. Also, when it became concerned enough to act against inflation by reducing money growth in 1966, homebuilding declined sharply. Political pressures increased.

Mistaken beliefs about the conduct of monetary policy added to the problem. Economists developed the Phillips curve, relating inflation and unemployment, and policy makers used this construct to reduce unemployment rates by increasing inflation. They discovered after the fact that the reduction in the unemployment rate did not persist, but inflation persisted. The Federal Reserve tried several times—in 1969, 1973, and 1976—to reduce inflation. When the unemployment rose to 7 percent or more, they abandoned the efforts.

Persistent and rising inflation brought an end to the Bretton Woods System of fixed exchange rates. European nations and Japan became willing to give up the fixed exchange rate system in order to free themselves from the effect of U.S. inflationary policies. By the end of the 1970s it was apparent to all that instead of trading off lower unemployment for higher inflation, U.S. policy resulted in higher inflation and higher unemployment. Public attitudes changed, and the change affected some congressional leaders. President Jimmy Carter appointed Paul Volcker as chairman of the Board of Governors of the Federal Reserve. Volcker made two lasting changes. First, he reestablished Federal Reserve independence of political control. This was a necessary step, but it required an acceptance of responsibility for policy outcomes that Chairmen Martin and Burns had been unwilling to make. Second, he accepted the temporary increase in unemployment needed to convince the public that he would not return to inflationary policy. High real interest rates and falling real balances produced a severe recession, with the unemployment rate reaching 10 percent.

But Volcker succeeded. The Federal Reserve and many others adopted and repeated a new mantra, very different from the Phillips curve, that low inflation was the best way to assure low unemployment. From the 1980s to 2005 the United States experienced the two longest peacetime expansions in its history, with inflation generally modest. Despite large budget deficits in the 1980s and after 2001, variability of output and inflation declined to low levels. The public remained confident that monetary policy would remain sufficiently independent to prevent a return to the instability of the 1970s, and that helped to build a political consensus and popular support for low inflation.

SEE ALSO *Central Banks; Federal Reserve System, U.S.; Full Employment; Inflation; Interest Rates; Macroeconomics; Phillips Curve; Policy, Monetary; Recession*

BIBLIOGRAPHY

Meltzer, Allan H. 2003. *A History of the Federal Reserve.* Chicago: University of Chicago Press.

Allan H. Meltzer

FEDERALISM

Federalism is one of the most fundamental principles of the American political system. Federalism can be defined as a principle of government in which political authority is divided between a national government and a collection of state (or regional) governments, acting side by side and sharing a large geographical space. The authority of the national government is exercised supremely over many areas of public policy. For example, the national government carries out the military and diplomatic functions of the country, as well as other important issues of national concern. The state or regional governments are semiautonomous and distinct entities that provide a convenient structure through which officials can administer policies of immediate and direct relevance to citizens. Some of the key services provided at the state level that most directly affect citizens are police and fire protection, criminal justice, and primary and secondary school education.

In a federal system, national and state governments are entities that operate as two mutually exclusive spheres of authority, although their functions often overlap and this can be a source of tension. One commentator on the structure of intergovernmental relations in the American system of government, James Bryce (1838–1922), noted that "the system is like a great factory wherein two sets of machinery are at work, their revolving wheels apparently intermixed, their bands crossing one another, yet each set doing its own work without touching or hampering the other" (Bryce 1916, vol. 1, p. 318). Under a system of federalism, both the federal and state governments have their own constitutions from which they derive the authority to act on behalf, and for the benefit, of the people.

In the United States, the national Constitution is the supreme law of the land. This implies, in part, that the state government must recognize and respect the national

Constitution, and that state governments must set up their state constitutions and enact their own laws in such a way that they avoid conflict with the national Constitution. Where such conflict emerges, it is generally understood that the state constitution must give way to the national Constitution. Because the national Constitution as interpreted by the Supreme Court supersedes state or regional constitutions in power and authority, state governments usually operate with less independence than they might like and with less independence than states in a confederacy or a league of nations.

Writing about the meaning of federalism, noted British authority K. C. Wheare (1907–1979) defined federalism as a "method of dividing powers so that the general and regional governments are each, within a sphere, coordinate and independent." He further noted "that each government should be limited to its own sphere and, within that sphere, should be independent of the other" (McClelland 2000, p. 297). Because federalism requires that the national and state governments should each "be limited to its own sphere," it becomes important for there to be a written constitution, which would define the boundaries of authority for each government. A written constitution is therefore one of the key characteristics of federalism. Without such a constitution, the national government can easily encroach upon or usurp the authority of the state governments, possibly leading to chaos.

FEDERALISM AS A HAPPY COMPROMISE

Federalism as practiced in the United States is what people around the world usually refer to when the word *federalism* is uttered or heard. It is based on one of the oldest written constitutions, the U.S. Constitution, which was ratified in 1787 after much eloquent and contentious debate over its content. The framers of the U.S. Constitution worked hard to establish a system of government they and their posterity could be proud of, a government that would "best secure the permanent liberty and happiness of their country" (Madison 1835, quoted in McClelland 2000, p. 293). The framers were not interested in setting up a central government, where political power would be concentrated in the hands of a national government, as was the case in prominent countries at that time, such as France and England. The framers were also not interested in continuing a confederate system because the Articles of Confederacy (the original governing charter of the United States) prevented the establishment of a strong and respected nation since the Articles created a natural inclination within the provinces to satisfy their own territorial interests rather than to secure the interest of the entire nation. The framers were, however, very much interested in a system that would reflect the wishes and preferences of the citizens, a system that would provide a high degree of independence and autonomy to the states while enhancing the international stature of the nation. Thus federalism as a theory of government was indeed an afterthought in that it emerged after the framers wrote and ratified the Constitution (McClelland 2000, p. 298).

Federalism is the product of a happy compromise in the formation of the nation and in its capacity to present a unified front when conducting foreign policy. That compromise was between Federalists such as George Washington (1732–1799) and John Adams (1735–1826), who wanted greater centralization of authority, and Anti-Federalists such as Thomas Jefferson (1743–1826), who favored placing power in the hands of ordinary individuals so that they can maximally manage their own affairs at the state and local levels.

The issue of individual states or regions protecting their own local territorial interests at the expense of national unity was not overcome with ratification of the Constitution, however. The Supreme Court under Chief Justice John Marshall (1755–1835) did much to establish and legitimate judicial review and to vigorously enforce the Constitution's contract clause toward a vision of centralizing power in order to nourish economic growth through free market capitalism. Had this vision been successfully maintained into the future, prolonged federal dominance over states would have been established sooner rather than later in the course of U.S. national development. But that vision collapsed under Chief Justice Roger Brook Taney (1777–1864). The Taney Court tolerated greater decentralization of the American political system (McCloskey 1994, chap. 4). The Court also wrongly and tragically tolerated slavery as a way of life in the South, as exemplified by its deplorable decision in *Dred Scott v. Sandford* (1857). Conflict over slavery (the placement of people, in this case black people, in bondage as the property of white owners) led to a secessionist push by southerners, culminating in a bloody civil war between armies from northern and southern states from 1861 to 1865. Federal dominance was more clearly established during the 1930s after President Franklin Delano Roosevelt (1882–1945) threatened to "pack" the Supreme Court with loyalists who would support and defend his New Deal policies, and the Court reversed its previous rejections of these policies.

Another characteristic of federalism is that the states provide plenty of opportunities to experiment with responses to public policy. As Justice Louis Brandeis (1856–1941) stated in his dissent in the 1932 case of *New State Ice Co. v. Liebmann*, "It is one of the happy incidents of the federal system that a single courageous state may, if its citizens choose, serve as a laboratory; and try novel social and economic experiments without risk to the rest of the country" (Ducat 2004, chap. 5). Those public policies that are chosen and implemented as a result of such experiments are afforded great legitimacy by the people who are most affected by them. But while this is a strong argument in favor of a federalist system, the crux of the argument in favor of federalism boils down to the expressed relationship between the application of governmental power and the preservation of individual freedom.

Under federalism, government power is decentralized and diffused among different levels and across different branches within the same level. Thus a third characteristic of federalism is that the diffusion of power afforded by such a system helps to preserve individual freedom and suppress tyranny, which is the systemic exploitation of the populace by a few self-serving individuals. Diffusion of power helps promote individual freedom because in smaller political units, individuals can participate more directly in a monolithic unitary government, and because individuals dissatisfied with conditions in one state can vote with their feet by moving to another state. But diffusion of power also suppresses tyranny, and it accomplishes this by minimizing the possibility that any one faction can gain enough access to government to push through any kind of policy that will exploit others without being detected. In addition, diffusion of power encourages coalition-building between individuals and groups operating at different levels of government in order to achieve public policy objectives.

But, generally speaking, there are some disadvantages to a federal system as well. Because federalism requires different institutions to approve a policy before it can be adopted, each decision point can unwittingly become a veto point that slows down the process of policymaking, or worse, prevents any action from being taken to resolve an important problem. Also, variation among states in their treatment of citizens, especially with respect to civil rights and liberties, can introduce a tension into the relationship between federalism and justice, which is thought to know no geographical boundaries.

SEE ALSO *Constitution, U.S.; Democracy*

BIBLIOGRAPHY

Bryce, James. 1916. *The American Commonwealth*. Vol. 1. New York: Macmillan.

Dred Scott v. Sandford, 60 U.S. (19 How) 393 (1857).

Ducat, Craig R. 2004. *Constitutional Interpretation*. 8th ed. Belmont, CA: Thomson-West.

Madison, James. [1835] 2000. Notes of the Debates in the Federal Convention. In *Liberty, Order, and Justice: An Introduction to the Constitutional Principles of American Government*, by James McClelland, 293. 3rd ed. Indianapolis, IN: Liberty Fund Press.

McClelland, James. 2000. *Liberty, Order, and Justice: An Introduction to the Constitutional Principles of American Government.* 3rd ed. Indianapolis, IN: Liberty Fund Press.

McCloskey, Robert G. 1994. *The American Supreme Court.* 2nd ed. Revised by Sanford Levinson. Chicago: University of Chicago Press.

New State Ice Co. v. Liebmann, 285 U.S. 262 (1932).

Isaac Unah

FEDERALIST PAPERS

SEE *Hamilton, Alexander; Madison, James.*

FEMALE-HEADED FAMILIES

Families are constructed from primary social relationships, either by circumstance or choice. Scholars and legal experts have defined families as collections of individuals who are related by birth, adoption, or marriage. The sociologist Talcott Parsons set forth a conception of the family as a unit including a breadwinner husband and a homemaker wife. The economist Gary Becker examined the social and economic exchanges that take place among partners, bringing both benefits and costs. Social science definitions of families have become more inclusive of people unrelated by legal marriage who are closely connected or intimately involved, have mutual responsibilities and common interests, and who care for each other. Popular understandings of family tend to focus on how people feel about each other (love) and what people do for each other (commitment). As definitions of families have changed, family configurations have shifted as well. Families are increasingly headed by women and in such cases are commonly referred to as *female*-headed, *women*-headed, or *mother*-headed families. The terms *lone* mother and *single* mother typically refer to the same family structure in different countries. Women raising children in any of these families may be divorced, separated, single, never married, or in a cohabiting relationship with a male or female partner or if married may be living apart from their partner.

WHY FAMILIES ARE CHANGING

The demographic shift away from the "nuclear" family model consisting of two married heterosexual parents living together with biological children represents a major change in social relationships. Most agree that families look quite different in the early twenty-first century than they did a generation ago. Yet some argue that there was never a single dominant family pattern in Western society. Marriage patterns in the United States have been largely based on the different cultural and economic conditions facing African American and white women (Cherlin 1992). Historical discrimination toward racial and ethnic groups and blocked economic opportunities have depressed marriage rates overall and have contributed to increases in female-headed families. Social historians find that the high marital stability of the mid-twentieth-century United States is best described as an anomaly when compared to earlier decades and to later periods (Coontz 1992, 1997; Stacey 1990). Unmarried cohabitation has become both more prevalent and socially acceptable in all social classes since the 1970s. In Scandinavian countries cohabitation has been a long-standing pattern. Couples live together before marriage, in place of marriage, and in between marriages. Demographers and sociologists point out that cohabitation is an increasingly common context for childbearing and child rearing (Wu and Wolfe 2001).

Separating out the causes and consequences of changes in family structure is a challenge. One of many possible explanations is that shifts in values and norms have affected gender roles and expectations for marriage. Women's sexual independence and the decline in the number of "marriageable" men—those who are employed and stable—is yet another explanation for the decline of marriage. Increases in women's full-time employment, wages, and sustained commitment to the labor force are other hypotheses. Women may be earning enough to be able to choose independence over marriages to men who either cannot contribute economically or are difficult spouses. In such situations, women and men's lives may be less "complementary" (see Burns and Scott 1994). Some also argue that welfare supplanted wives' reliance on husbands for financial support, although welfare policies vary widely by region, country, and historical period.

Poverty scholars see a strong cross-national connection between female-headed families and poverty. In North America and western Europe, there is an increasing trend toward single-parent families. Men and women are marrying later, are increasingly choosing to cohabit rather than marry, and are increasingly likely to divorce. Out-of-wedlock childbearing is also increasing and is especially high among young African Americans and lowest among Latina women (Cherlin 1992; Wong, Garfinkel, and McLanahan 1993). In Central and South America legal marriage is normative, but mothers may leave children in the care of relatives to find work elsewhere temporarily or permanently. Globally, impoverished mothers earn money through legal or illegal (and risky and dangerous) means to support themselves and their children. Barbara Ehrenreich and Arlie Russell Hochschild (2002) point to the sexual and economic exploitation of women around the world.

Sociological research reflects serious concern about the growing numbers of female-headed families. Numerous studies conceptualize single motherhood as a social problem, either because of the social stigma attached to it or because of the feminization of poverty. Worldwide the majority of families headed by women are poor. In the United States female-headed families are three times more likely to be poor than are those in two-parent families. While quantitative research shows that many female-headed families are "at risk," qualitative research focused on the meaning, arrangements, and flexibility of families headed by single women reveals that such arrangements can also bring greater stability compared to the existing alternatives.

COPING STRATEGIES AND FAMILY CHOICES

In the 1970s the anthropologist Carol Stack studied the kinship strategies of single women with children living in an urban housing project in the midwestern United States. She described a complex network of sharing and support among households. Similarly Kathryn Edin and Laura Lein (1997) found that poor single mothers rely on assistance from friends, relatives, and neighbors—both information and money to get through the month—whether they are working or receiving welfare payments.

Research has also explored how middle-class, single-mother families discuss their family circumstances, manage finances, and handle work and family responsibilities. Rosanna Hertz and Faith I. Ferguson (1997) found that the women they studied formed families without men for a number of different reasons, often related to childbearing—unexpected pregnancies, opportunities to adopt, anxiety about "biological clocks." Some single women—heterosexual and lesbian—choose to adopt or become pregnant through donor insemination. These women were not opposed to nuclear family arrangements; they were actively seeking out partners and commitment while not rejecting the possibility of bearing and raising children alone. Margaret K. Nelson (2005) has examined the "social economy" of single motherhood in rural communities. Her emphasis on the combined importance of social networks and financial resources is particularly instructive for understanding the complexity of single mothers' lives.

ECONOMIC CONSEQUENCES

The overall economic prognosis for single-mother families is bleak. Declining rates of marriage, increases in divorce, and the prevalence of out-of-wedlock childbearing means that a growing proportion of families with children are headed by a single parent for some period of time, and these households are much more likely to be poor. When fathers do not live with their children, they are much less likely to share in the financial costs of raising them. Single mothers bear most of the economic expenses and social responsibilities of child rearing. Low wages and high child-care costs contribute to the economic difficulties facing these households. Simply put, it costs more for single mothers to work, and many of the positions women hold do not pay enough to support their households or offer benefits that would help them or their children, like health care, vacations, or sick leave. Improving employment opportunities, strengthening the social welfare system, and increasing child support are all approaches that would contribute to the financial stability of female-headed families (McLanahan and Sandefur 1994; Edin and Lein 1997). The United Nations similarly points out that promoting gender equality and women's empowerment is essential if the position of female-headed families is to be improved.

Involving parents who do not live with their children in their children's lives may also be a way to ease the burdens experienced by one-parent families. Studies find that the overall workload at home of single mothers is much greater than that of married mothers. Single mothers spend more time on household tasks like cleaning and cooking as well as on the hands-on care of children. The work overload experienced by single mothers produces a great deal of stress and may affect parenting practices. It is unclear whether children receive more attention and supervision in two-parent or one-parent households. Nelson's 2005 study shows that rural single mothers sometimes have difficulty arranging for tasks typically performed by men, like landscaping and automobile repairs. Henny M. W. Bos, Frank van Balen, and C. Dymphna van den Boom (2004) find that lesbian-mother families are no more or less disadvantaged than are heterosexual families.

A number of studies have suggested that there is a "wage penalty" for motherhood that does not exist for fatherhood. Losing time from work to raise young children brings a decline in earnings in the United States and western Europe. In many cultures and countries caregiving is exclusively women's domain. The depressed education levels and limited work opportunities that result from this focus have negative economic repercussions for women. Michelle J. Budig and Paula England (2001) analyzed the characteristics of many different jobs—including female-dominated occupations—and found that wage penalties exist for all mothers. Divorced and married mothers experience higher child-related economic penalties than do never-married mothers, as do women with more than one child. However, the penalty for African American and Latina women with more than two children appears to be smaller than for others (Budig and England 2001). Some of the penalty, Budig and England maintain, is explained by work interruptions, changes to part-time status, lack of seniority, and relatively limited work experience. The wage penalty for women is found across jobs that otherwise have different characteristics. It is for future researchers to determine whether employer discrimination is entirely responsible or whether reduced productivity at work accounts for some of the wage differences. Much research also remains to be done on the relationship between the female-headed family and women and children's poverty levels and on the question of family stability

SEE ALSO *Family; Family Structure; Family Values; Pathology, Social; Poverty; Resiliency*

BIBLIOGRAPHY

Becker, Gary S. 1981. *A Treatise on the Family.* Cambridge, MA: Harvard University Press.

Bos, Henny M. W., Frank van Balen, and C. Dymphna van den Boom. 2004. Experience of Parenthood, Couple Relationships, Social Support, and Child-Rearing Goals in Planned Lesbian Mother Families. *Journal of Child Psychology and Psychiatry* 45 (4): 755–764.

Budig, Michelle J., and Paula England. 2001. The Wage Penalty for Motherhood. *American Sociological Review* 66 (2): 204–225.

Burns, Ailsa, and Cath Scott. 1994. *Mother-Headed Families and Why They Have Increased.* Hillsdale, NJ: Erlbaum Associates.

Cherlin, Andrew J. 1992. *Marriage, Divorce, Remarriage.* Rev. and enlarged ed. Cambridge, MA: Harvard University Press.

Coontz, Stephanie. 1992. *The Way We Never Were: American Families and the Nostalgia Trap.* New York: Basic Books.

Coontz, Stephanie. 1997. *The Way We Really Are: Coming to Terms with America's Changing Families.* New York: Basic Books.

Edin, Kathryn, and Laura Lein. 1997. Work, Welfare, and Single Mothers' Economic Survival Strategies. *American Sociological Review* 62 (2): 253–266.

Ehrenreich, Barbara, and Arlie Russell Hochschild, eds. 2002. *Global Woman: Nannies, Maids, and Sex Workers in the New Economy.* New York: Metropolitan Books.

Hertz, Rosanna, and Faith I. Ferguson. 1998. Only One Pair of Hands: Ways That Single Mothers Stretch Work and Family Resources. *Community, Work, and Family* 1 (1): 13–37.

Lichter, Daniel T., and Diane K. McLaughlin. 1995. Changing Economic Opportunities, Family Structure, and Poverty in Rural Areas. *Rural Sociology* 60 (4): 688–706.

Mazor, Aviva. 2004. Single Motherhood via Donor-Insemination (DI): Separation, Absence, and Family Creation. *Contemporary Family Therapy* 26 (2): 199–215.

McLanahan, Sara, and Gary Sandefur. 1994. *Growing Up with a Single Parent: What Hurts, What Helps.* Cambridge, MA: Harvard University Press.

Nelson, Margaret K. 2005. *The Social Economy of Single Motherhood: Raising Children in Rural America.* New York: Routledge.

Parsons, Talcott, and Robert F. Bales. 1955. *Family, Socialization, and Interaction Process.* Glencoe, IL: Free Press.

Stacey, Judith. 1990. *Brave New Families: Stories of Domestic Upheaval in Late Twentieth Century America.* New York: Basic Books.

Stack, Carol B. 1974. *All Our Kin: Strategies for Survival in a Black Community.* New York: Harper and Row.

Wong, Irene, Irwin Garfinkel, and Sara McLanahan. 1993. Single-Mother Families in Eight Countries: Economic Status and Social Policy. *Social Service Review* 67 (2): 177–197.

Wu, Lawrence L., and Barbara Wolfe, eds. 2001. *Out of Wedlock: Causes and Consequences of Nonmarital Fertility.* New York: Russell Sage Foundation.

Margaret Walsh

FEMININE MYSTIQUE
SEE *Friedan, Betty.*

FEMININITY

Femininity is commonly understood to refer to a collection of qualities or attributes associated with women in distinction from men, whose own qualities are signified by the antonym *masculinity*. Yet precisely what qualities qualify as feminine (or masculine) is subject to discussion and contention, as is whether such qualities should be considered innate essences or cultural norms. Passivity, submissiveness, and compassionate, caring, nurturing behavior toward others, especially infants, are widely considered feminine traits in comparison to masculine assertiveness and competitiveness. Their prevalence has lent credence to the belief that they are rooted in female biology and anatomy, whether by divine design or Darwinian natural selection. In the latter case, theory postulates higher rates of reproduction for passive women, who could most easily be sexually subdued, and higher survival rates for babies born to nurturing women. However, even the most widely shared so-called feminine traits are not universal, whether the comparison considers different cultures, different groups or individuals within a given society, or different periods of history. Since Margaret Mead's (1901–1978) groundbreaking anthropological study in 1936 first demonstrated cultural variability in behavior and temperament for both sexes, thus challenging previous presumptions about a universal feminine (or masculine) essential nature, much scholarly attention has been paid to how norms of gender may be socially and culturally constructed (Tarrant 2006).

Women come to participate in upholding standards culturally deemed feminine for behavior and appearance through mechanisms of socialization that are multiple and not always obvious. Enforcement is the most obvious. Over the last few millennia of known human history, broadly influential cultural systems, such as the religions Judaism, Christianity, Islam, and Hinduism and the Confucian code of conduct, have explicitly directed that women's primary social duty is to be obedient wives and devoted mothers. Legal and paralegal structures derived from such religious and moral traditions have enforced these directives using punishments ranging from mild to extreme in severity depending on specific social and historical circumstances. Under the Taliban regime in Afghanistan at the beginning of the twenty-first century, for example, punishment for noncompliance with brutally extreme restrictions on women's appearance and behavior included public flogging and execution. Compulsion, however, is not the only or even necessarily the most effective means for encouraging women to subscribe to femininity norms. Social rewards and personal satisfaction are also motivators. Piety is its own reward for a woman of any faith who believes she is behaving in accordance with divine will. Depending on how she interprets her faith, a contemporary Muslim woman may thus signal her femininity and her piety by choosing to wear the veil whether she lives under a theocratic or a secular political system. Her choice to veil may be reinforced by additional rewards, such as greater respect and personal autonomy accorded to her by her family and the local Muslim community (Hoodfar 2003).

Marriage, in most cultures, has been the principal reward for successful displays of femininity. Under economic conditions in which family well-being is heavily dependent on women's domestic production, wifely assets tend to reside primarily in a woman's skill in the feminine activities of domestic labor. When a wife's domestic productivity is not essential, whether due to class privilege or to postindustrial economic structures that shift production away from the home, her feminine assets come to be measured instead through her appearance and character. Patriarchal cultural conditions prevalent in most, but not all, societies determine ideal feminine appearance and character traits to be those that make a woman sexually attractive to a man, most suitable to represent his social status, and most trustworthy to mother his children. Thus physical beauty, both natural and artificial, balanced by character traits of sexual modesty, nurturing kindness, and a strong sense of duty to family have become widespread hallmarks of ideal femininity. But although women can derive personal satisfaction in meeting such measures, the accompanying price has often been problematic. Ironically, the sufferings of many upper-class women most palpably illustrate the point. Beauty norms that emerged

in stratified societies to simultaneously signal high social status sometimes entailed not just delicacy, refinement, and taste in adornment but actual physical fragility, frailty, even incapacity as symbols of the socioeconomic status of the husband, proving his wealth sufficient to support a wife whose physical labor was not necessary. The former practices of Chinese foot binding and European waist cinching illustrate the debilitating operations of such elite-class norms of feminine beauty. Although they were believed to enhance a woman's erotic appeal (while simultaneously symbolizing her sexual restraint), they also hobbled or otherwise constrained her physical capacity, not to mention causing her discomfort and pain.

Less self-evident forms of harm, whether through conformity to feminine ideals or through disqualification from femininity by social status, sexual orientation, or race, among other factors, as well as more nuanced sociological interpretations of incentives for feminine performances, are topics that have generated considerable theorizing across scholarly disciplines (Brownmiller 1984; Bartky 1990; Martin 1996; Skeggs 1998; Lee 2000; Burns-Ardolino 2003; Taylor 2003; Bathla 2004). The philosopher Simone de Beauvoir (1908–1986) is often quoted for her ideas about how the sense of self that conformity to ideals of femininity creates in women is a sense of self as "Other," existing only in secondary relation to the primary "Self," the fully human self that in patriarchal traditions can only be claimed by men.

Psychologists have explored how the expectation to nurture others has led legions of women to psychologically unhealthy degrees of self-sacrifice, labeled a "negative feminine trait" in the literature. Many scholars have written about how women effectively create themselves as objects, rather than subjects, in their pursuit of feminine beauty norms yet are bound not only to fail in this pursuit but also to be reminded of their failure incessantly and distracted repeatedly by promises for new ways to succeed. Pervasive modern mass media and capitalist commerce promulgate a beauty regime that harshly judges the femininity of women whose age, skin color, hair texture, physique type, or fashion sense do not match the dominant cultural ideal, then exploits feelings of inadequacy to sell beauty products and services from lipstick to skin lightener to liposuction and breast augmentation in order to turn a profit at their expense. This beauty regime thoroughly ensnares as well. Fashion is ever changing, but whatever the fashion, every detail of the body demands proper attention. Each minutiae of how a woman's body looks, feels, and smells, how it is clothed, coiffed, enhanced with makeup and other adornment, even how it speaks and moves or rests combines to express normative femininity successfully or not. Enormous ceaseless efforts of self-surveillance and self-discipline are required from an early age to produce the modern feminine body. A self-policing gendered identity also develops through this process. This form of feminine subjectivity is interpreted by some theorists as being more completely subjected to modern versions of patriarchal power than is possible under crude enforcement or injurious restraint which, albeit brutal techniques of control, are less thoroughly invasive of the whole being.

Critics of the physical, psychological, economic, and political harms resulting from socialization processes aimed at patriarchal ideals of femininity draw encouragement from the historic appearance of alternate ideals and socialization opportunities available to girls following the women's movements of the modern era. Competitive assertiveness, physical strength, and even muscularity are developed in the characters and bodies of girls and women who engage in amateur and professional sports, for example (Boyle 2005; Koca and Asci 2005; Kindlon 2006). Furthermore the representation of these athletes in mass media amplifies the scope of qualities that femininity is seen to signify culturally, stretching the meaning to incorporate qualities previously considered exclusively masculine (Carty 2005). Some critics of patriarchal femininity see reason to hope that social developments blurring traditional gender roles, such as women in sports, or politics, or the military, will help move common understanding of femininity beyond the still dominant, but demonstrably deleterious, dualistic framework in which femininity and masculinity are conceived as mutually exclusive opposites.

SEE ALSO *Determinism; Determinism, Biological; Essentialism; Feminism; Gender; Gender and Development; Gender, Alternatives to Binary; Marriage; Masculinity; Matriarchy; Motherhood; Natural Selection; Norms; Other, The; Patriarchy; Phenotype; Religion; Role Conflict; Self-Identity; Veil, in African American Culture; Veil, in Middle Eastern and North African Cultures; Women; Work and Women*

BIBLIOGRAPHY

Bartky, Sandra Lee. 1990. Foucault, Femininity, and the Modernization of Patriarchal Power. In *Femininity and Domination: Studies in the Phenomenology of Oppression*, 63–82. New York: Routledge.

Bathla, Sonia. 2004. Gender Construction in the Media: A Study of Two Indian Women Politicians. *Asian Journal of Women's Studies* 10 (3): 7–34.

Boyle, Lex. 2005. Flexing the Tensions of Female Muscularity: How Female Bodybuilders Negotiate Normative Femininity in Competitive Bodybuilding. *Women's Studies Quarterly* 33 (1–2): 134–149.

Brownmiller, Susan. 1984. *Femininity*. New York: Fawcett Columbine.

Burns-Ardolino, Wendy A. 2003. Reading Woman: Displacing the Foundations of Femininity. *Hypatia* 18 (3): 42–59.

Carty, Victoria. 2005. Textual Portrayals of Female Athletes: Liberation or Nuanced Forms of Patriarchy? *Frontiers* 26 (2): 132–155.

Hoodfar, Homa. 2003. More Than Clothing: Veiling as an Adaptive Strategy. In *The Muslim Veil in North America: Issues and Debates*, ed. Sajida Sultana Alvi, Homa Hoodfar, and Sheila McDonough, 3–40. Toronto: Women's Press.

Kindlon, Dan. 2006. *Alpha Girls: Understanding the New American Girl and How She Is Changing the World*. Emmaus, PA: Rodale.

Koca, Canan, and F. Hulya Asci. 2005. Gender Role Orientation in Turkish Female Athletes and Non-Athletes. *Women in Sport and Physical Activity Journal* 14 (1): 86–94.

Lee, Young-ja. 2000. Consumer Culture and Gender Identity in South Korea. *Asian Journal of Women's Studies* 6 (4): 11–38.

Martin, Biddy. 1996. Sexualities without Genders and Other Queer Utopias. In *Femininity Played Straight: The Significance of Being Lesbian*, 71–94. New York: Routledge.

Skeggs, Beverley. 1998. *Formations of Class and Gender: Becoming Respectable*. London: Sage.

Tarrant, Shira. 2006. *When Sex Became Gender*. New York: Routledge.

Taylor, Anthea. 2003. What's New about "the New Femininity"? Feminism, Femininity, and the Discourse of the New. *Hecate* 29 (2): 182–197.

Marymay Downing

FEMINISM

Feminism refers to social theories, economic ideologies, political movements, and moral philosophies aimed at bringing equality to women. Feminism has been identified with different groups and different issues over the course of its history. The first wave gave rise to liberal feminists, who fought for the right to vote, access to education, and marriage law reforms in the 1800s and early 1900s. The second wave witnessed the emergence of radical feminists, who protested for work and reproductive rights in the 1960s and 1970s. The numerous feminist groups concerned with all forms of oppression (e.g., racism, classism) evolved as the third wave in the 1990s.

ORIGINS OF FEMINISM

The desire for equality predates the existence of the term *feminism* or the movement it has come to represent. The term *feminism* comes from the French word *féminisme* and was popularized by Hubertine Auclert in 1882 when she organized the first women's suffragist society in France. However, prior to the advent of the word, there were publications that fell within the purview of feminism. One of the first, by the medieval French poet Christine de Pizan, was *Livre de la cité des dames* (1405; *The Book of the City of Ladies*, 1999), in which Pizan suggests that women should build their own cities, free of men, so as to avoid men's violence and oppression. Dealing more specifically with rights, John Locke's *Two Treatises of Government* (1690) argued that all individuals have indelible natural rights to life, liberty, and possessions, which no government can deny.

Locke's work inspired Mary Wollstonecraft's *Vindication of the Rights of Women* (1792), one of the first feminist manifestos. Wollstonecraft argued that women were human beings who should not be denied the same individual rights as men because of their sex. She advocated that women be viewed as equal to men under the law, with all the same rights and privileges, including the right to education, earnings, and property ownership. The rights of women were further advocated by John Stuart Mill in his treatise *The Subjection of Women* (1869). Mill contended that women should be granted the same rights and privileges as men under the law. In 1866, during his term as a member of Parliament for Westminster, Mill introduced a motion to enfranchise women on the grounds that taxpayers should have representation. The motion was defeated (196 to 73 votes), but the impetus for women's suffrage was not. The right to vote and the right to a proper education were two primary concerns that propelled the first of the three waves of the feminist movement.

THE FIRST WAVE OF FEMINISM

The period from the mid-nineteenth century to the early twentieth century saw tremendous activity for the women's movement. Key concerns included improvements in education, employment, and marriage laws. In much of North America and Europe, the right to higher education provided the movement's initial spark. In other nations, cultural and religious constrictions such as suttee (self-immolation by Hindu widows), purdah (isolation of women, shielding them from public view), child marriage, and foot binding provided the initial focus for reform. In England and the United States in the 1800s (dates vary by state), marital laws were reformed with the passage of married women's property acts, which enabled wives to own property, enter into contractual agreements, sue, and be sued. However, in many countries it became apparent that the right to vote was instrumental in obtaining other reforms, so voting became the focus of the movement.

In the United States the first women's rights convention was held in Seneca Falls, New York, in 1848. In 1869 Elizabeth Cady Stanton and Susan B. Anthony founded the National Woman Suffrage Association and demanded not just the right to vote but marital reform as well. The exclusion of male members and the request for marital reform, instead of focusing solely on the vote, was

frowned upon by some (e.g., Lucy Stone and Henry Blackwell), resulting in the creation of the American Women Suffrage Association. However, the two groups merged in 1890. Women in New Zealand were among the first to obtain the right to vote (1893), and other countries quickly followed. For example, women's suffrage was achieved in Australia in 1902, Finland in 1906, Denmark in 1915, Russia in 1917, Czechoslovakia, England, and Germany in 1918, the Netherlands and Sweden in 1919, and the United States in 1920.

In many countries, after winning the right to vote, women turned their attention to education and employment rights. Upon achieving greater educational and employment access, women entered both of these spheres in record numbers. However, this newfound freedom was quickly tempered by the Great Depression. Although the effects of the Depression were felt at different times in different countries, the 1930s saw immobilization in the feminist movement. During this period, women were discouraged from seeking employment because of the scarcity of jobs. This employment hiatus was quickly reversed with the start of World War II in 1939, as women were encouraged to fill voids in a number of professions previously closed to them (e.g., factory workers, pilots) because so many men were sent to battle. Women proved to be effectual workers, but they were nonetheless displaced by returning soldiers at the war's end.

The tumultuousness of the war years was followed by a period of relative calm, during which the movement waned. However, having tasted independence, career options, and good pay, women were no longer content to be housewives. The publication of Simone de Beauvoir's *Le deuxième sexe* in 1949 (*The Second Sex;* English trans., 1953) reminded women that there was still much work to be done. This period of tranquility soon ended in the 1960s with the start of the second wave of the feminist movement.

THE SECOND WAVE OF FEMINISM

The term *second wave* was coined by Martha Lear and refers to the feminist movement that began in the 1960s. The leading issues were demands for employment and reproductive rights. In the United States the second wave rose out of the civil rights and anti-Vietnam War movements. Even within these "pro-rights" organizations, women were relegated to second-class status. In an effort to gain a voice, two branches of the feminist movement emerged: the women's liberation movement (WLM) and the National Organization for Women (NOW). The WLM evolved out of the New Left and encompassed more loosely organized radical groups that formed following their exclusion from other New Left politics. They gained great notoriety in 1968, when they demonstrated against the Miss America pageant for its sexist objectification of women. NOW was a more structured, liberal group founded in 1966 by Betty Friedan, Aileen Hernandez, Pauli Murray, and others. Although NOW grew to become more inclusive, in 1968 Ti-Grace Atkinson left it and created her own group, the Feminists, to protest NOW's hierarchical structure. NOW also lost members because of its pro-choice stance; some conservative women, led by Elizabeth Boyer, left the organization and created the Women's Equity Action League. In spite of these early setbacks, NOW grew to become the largest women's organization in the United States and championed the equal rights amendment (ERA) as its primary cause. Despite approval by the U.S. House and Senate, the ERA was not ratified by the requisite thirty-eight states by the 1982 deadline.

This period was marked by a number of historic events, including the 1963 Commission on the Status of Women report that documented discrimination against women in all facets of life. The pervasiveness of discrimination was also the topic of Betty Friedan's best-selling book *The Feminine Mystique* (1963). These two documents invigorated the women's rights movement, and its activities were instrumental in bringing about changes. In 1963 Congress passed the Equal Pay Act, which prohibited unequal pay for equal work. In 1964 Congress passed Title VII of the Civil Rights Act, which prohibited employment discrimination on the basis of sex, race, color, religion, and national origin. Ironically, the inclusion of "sex" was actually a last-minute attempt to kill the bill, but it passed anyway. Prohibitions against sexual discrimination were further extended in 1972 with the passage of Title IX of the Education Amendment, which prohibited discrimination in educational settings. In 1973 the U.S. Supreme Court's decision in *Roe v. Wade* struck down state laws restricting a women's right to an abortion, thereby legalizing it in all fifty states.

In addition to employment and reproduction rights, concerns about pornography and sexuality more generally also came to the fore. However, there was little consensus on these issues, and this disagreement culminated in what is termed the *feminist sex wars*. The sex wars of the 1980s were between antipornography feminists (e.g., Catherine MacKinnon, Andrea Dworkin, and Robin Morgan), who argued that pornography degrades and promotes violence against women, and sex-positive feminists (e.g., Camille Paglia, Ellen Willis, and Gayle Rubin), who opposed limiting sexual expression. This conflict, along with the fact that many feminists felt that other sources of oppression, such as race and class, were being neglected, caused the already multipartite movement to become increasingly fractured, resulting in the birth of third-wave feminism.

THE THIRD WAVE OF FEMINISM

Third-wave feminism evolved out of the disillusionment of many feminists with the overemphasis on the experience of middle-class white women in the mainstream. Feminists of color (e.g., Gloria Anzaldúa, bell hooks, Chela Sandoval, Cherrie Moraga, Audre Lorde, and Maxine Hong Kingston) emphasized the significance of race, class, sexual orientation, and other socially structured forms of bias on women's lives (Kinser 2004). Critical race theorist and law professor Kimberlé W. Crenshaw introduced the term *intersectionalities* to highlight the multiplicative effect of these different sites of oppression. Counter to postfeminist contentions that feminism was obsolete as women had gained equality, third-wavers contended that there was still work to be done, specifically related to the "micropolitics" of gender oppression.

The term *third-wave feminist* was popularized by the 1992 *Ms.* magazine article titled "Becoming the Third Wave" by Rebecca Walker, who stated: "I am not a postfeminism feminist. I am the third wave" (Walker 1992, p. 40). In her article Walker describes her rage over the outcome of the Clarence Thomas hearings (in which Anita Hill testified that Thomas had sexually harassed her; Thomas was confirmed as a Supreme Court justice, while Hill was repudiated) and her subsequent commitment to feminism. Walker's article generated a large response from young women, who indicated that they have not given up the cause but are feminists in their own way. That is, they embrace a more pluralistic definition of feminism; they are concerned with the intersectionalities of oppression and the impact of globalism, technology, and other forces, and they operate on a more grassroots level (Kinser 2004). Although both second- and third-wave feminists are still at work, their divergent concerns spawned different groups, including black feminists, critical feminists, and global feminists.

TYPES OF FEMINISM

Although there are many types of feminism, the four most common are liberal, radical, Marxist, and socialist. What differentiates them is the degree to which they accept that the different social structures in power are responsible for oppression. Liberal feminism, considered the most mainstream, accepts that sex differences exist but contends that social, legal, and economic opportunities should be equal for men and women. Liberal feminists are concerned with individual rights and promoting change through legal and legislative means while still operating within the current patriarchal structure.

Radical feminism emerged from the ideals of the New Left and the women's liberation movement in the late 1960s. Radical feminists argue that men are the oppressors of women and that the patriarchal social structure must be replaced for women to gain equality. The term *radical feminism* is used to represent many divergent groups, including cultural feminism, lesbian feminism, and revolutionary feminism.

Marxist feminists believe that women's oppression stems largely from economic stratification brought about by the production methods inherent in capitalism. Accordingly, capitalism must be destroyed in order to emancipate women both as workers and as property within the marital sphere.

Drawing from both radical and Marxist ideologies, socialist feminists argue that both class and sexism are sources of women's oppression. They advocate the end of capitalist patriarchy to reduce all forms of exploitation, as they are also concerned with oppression resulting from race, age, religion, and the like. In contrast to liberal feminism's emphasis on individual rights, socialist feminists emphasize the social existence in the broader community.

IMPACT OF FEMINISM

In addition to voting, property, employment, and other rights, the women's movement has also promoted other changes. For instance, not only do women have the right to vote but a number of countries have had female political leaders, including Chile, Finland, Ireland, Israel, Liberia, and Switzerland. In addition access to education has brought about a large increase in the number of women students, such that women now outnumber men in many nations' schools. With regard to language, feminism has been influential in advancing the use of nonsexist terms (e.g., *humankind* in lieu of *mankind*). It has also had a tremendous impact on the institution of marriage, in terms not only of whether women marry but also whom they choose to marry (a man or a woman), as well as the distribution of familial labor within the marital union. Moreover following the lead of the nineteenth-century suffragist Lucy Stone, many women now maintain their maiden names after marriage. The movement has also influenced religion, with many liberal denominations now ordaining women. Feminist thinking has also influenced the social sciences. It is no longer acceptable to collect data solely on men and to apply the findings to women, because there are often important gender differences—for example, personality (Chodorow 1978). Further, feminist researchers advocate increased use of qualitative methods in which participants play a greater role in informing the definition and measurement of the phenomenon under study.

SEE ALSO *Critical Race Theory; Feminism, Second Wave; Friedan, Betty; Gender Gap; Inequality, Gender; Intersectionality; Marxism; National Organization for Women; Patriarchy; Reproductive Rights; Sexism; Sexual Harassment; Sexuality; Socialism; Steinem, Gloria; Suffrage, Women's; Womanism; Women; Women and Politics; Women's Liberation; Women's Movement; Women's Studies; Work and Women*

BIBLIOGRAPHY

Chodorow, Nancy. 1978. *The Reproduction of Mothering: Psychoanalysis and the Sociology of Gender.* Berkeley: University of California Press.

De Beauvoir, Simone. [1949] 1953. *The Second Sex.* Trans. H. M. Parshley. New York: Knopf.

De Pizan, Christine. [1405] 1999. *The Book of the City of Ladies.* Trans. Rosalind Brown-Grant. London and New York: Penguin.

Friedan, Betty. 1963. *The Feminine Mystique.* New York: Dell.

International Museum of Women. 2003. Chronology of Worldwide Woman Suffrage. http://www.imow.org/exhibits/suffrage/chronology_suffrage.pdf.

Kinser, Amber E. 2004. Negotiating Spaces for/through Third-Wave Feminism. *National Women's Studies Association Journal* 16 (3): 124–153.

Locke, John. [1690] 1992. *Two Treatises of Government.* New York: Classics of Liberty Library.

Mill, John Stuart. [1869] 2001. *The Subjection of Women,* ed. Edward Alexander. New Brunswick, NJ: Transaction.

President's Commission on the Status of Women. 1963. Report of the Committee on Education. Washington, DC: U.S. Government Printing Office.

Roe v. Wade. 1973. 410 U.S. 113.

Walker, Rebecca. 1992. Becoming the Third Wave. *Ms.,* January–February, 39–41.

Wollstonecraft, Mary. [1792] 1989. *Vindication of the Rights of Women.* Buffalo, NY: Prometheus.

Worldwide Guide to Women Leadership. 2007. Chronological List of Female Presidents. http://www.guide2womenleaders.com/Presidents-Chronological.htm.

Kim S. Ménard

FEMINISM, FIRST WAVE

SEE *Suffrage, Women's.*

FEMINISM, SECOND WAVE

Second Wave feminism applies to the women's movement that began at the end of 1963 and extended into the 1980s. First Wave feminism addressed employment, marriage laws, and education and later came to embrace the voting rights movement. Second Wave feminists went further to address the issues of equality of the sexes in the workplace, a woman's right to choose, feminine sexuality, and a furthering of political action to bring women's issues in a patriarchal society to light.

The starting point of the Second Wave is usually considered to be a 1963 report from the Committee on the Status of Women (CSW), which was begun by First Lady Eleanor Roosevelt and which she chaired until her death in 1962. The committee found that women were not being treated equally in the workplace and recommended mandatory fair hiring and pay, maternity leave for mothers, and affordable child care. Based on these recommendations, the Equal Pay Act was passed by Congress on June 10, 1963, making it illegal to pay women less for doing the same jobs as men.

Yet the women's movement at that time was relatively quiet. Most women were locked into traditional roles of wife, mother, nurse, teacher, secretary, and other "feminine" activities without the possibility of individual advancement or achievement. Then Betty Friedan, a New Jersey work-at-home journalist and mother, wrote *The Feminine Mystique* (1963) and her words sparked many more women into realizing that they wanted the freedom to control their own destinies. Friedan wrote about her own life and the frustrations that many other women were feeling about patriarchal attitudes regarding their roles. She equated American women with the inmates of Nazi concentration camps and evoked strong emotions in men and women, both pro and con. The book became a best seller, and the battle for equality of the sexes was reignited.

A major milestone in the women's movement was the passage of Title VII of the Civil Rights Act of 1964, which made gender and racial discrimination in the workplace illegal. At the same time, the Equal Employment Opportunity Commission (EEOC) was established to investigate complaints and impose penalties on those not acting in accordance with the law. Title VII meant that women no longer would have to resign themselves to working as nurses or secretaries because they could not get into medical school or become business executives, though the atmosphere was slow to change.

In 1966, at the Third National Conference of the Commission on the Status of Women, a new organization was formed. Friedan was furious over the government's failure to enforce Title VII, and she invited a few women from the conference to her hotel room. She wanted to discuss stronger options than merely passing a resolution to recommend enforcement, and the women at the meeting decided instead to form their own organization, dedicated to the attainment of full equality for women. Friedan

christened it the National Organization of Women (NOW) and the group drafted a statement of purpose.

In March 1969 New York journalist Gloria Steinem realized that the women's movement was not just for unhappy housewives when she attended a rally to "speak out" on abortion. It had been organized by the newly formed radical feminist group the Redstockings, and the meeting was standing room only. As women spoke about their own bad experiences, Steinem realized that she had felt the same anxieties over having had an abortion herself, and she identified with them. She immediately assumed responsibility in the cause of a woman's right to choose.

Steinem traveled around the country with a speaking partner, usually a woman of color, to address those who thought the movement was only for white middle-class women. The pair encouraged all women to understand their rights and to take part in the movement to demand them.

Where Friedan had been considered the founder of the Second Wave movement, Steinem was certainly its messenger. One of her early appearances was in testifying before a Senate subcommittee on the Equal Rights Amendment (ERA), and in 1971 Steinem used her journalistic connections to publish the first edition of *Ms.* magazine as a supplement to *New York Magazine*. In eight days, all 300,000 printed copies were sold. *Ms.* became the premiere forum for feminist issues and Steinem became a feminist icon.

Her testimony and that of other women helped put pressure on Congress to pass the ERA in 1972. The law was to be simple, as written by Alice Paul in 1923: "Equality of rights under the law shall not be denied or abridged by the United States or by any State on account of sex." Yet there was still a long battle, as the ERA had to be sent to all 50 states for ratification, and 38 would have to pass it before it would become law.

Legal wheels did not stop turning. Title XI of the Education Amendments banned sexual discrimination in schools, and the greatest victory was a result of the Supreme Court decision in the case of *Roe v. Wade* in 1973, making abortion in the first trimester of pregnancy legal. The first national convention of the National Women's Political Caucus was also held that year, as women became a force in national politics. Anne Armstrong, the first woman to hold a cabinet-level position, also became the first woman to make the keynote speech at the Republican National Convention.

The end of the Second Wave feminist movement is often seen as occurring sometime in the 1980s up to the 1990s when Third Wave feminism sprouted from an article written by Rebecca Walker, titled "Becoming the Third Wave," in *Ms.* in January 1992. The renewed emphasis of this movement is to expand definitions of gender and sexuality, race, and class. Many in this group are disappointed that the Second Wave did not fully achieve their ideals, and this was punctuated by the failure of the ERA to be ratified by the required 38 states, though ratification is still being pursued into the twenty-first century.

However, some view feminist advancement as the cause of many societal ills. The concept of women working outside the home has become a necessity for most families, leaving children to be raised by caregivers rather than parents. Many see the decline of the family in America as a result. The openness with which homosexuality and homosexual marriage is approached in today's society seems even more threatening to those with traditional values. However, most men and women working in the area of civil rights maintain that equality—regardless of race, creed, sexual orientation, or mental or physical ability—is a natural right. Feminist movements will undoubtedly continue in various forms until this ideal has been reached.

SEE ALSO *Feminism; Gender; Inequality, Political; Politics, Gay, Lesbian, Transgender, and Bisexual; Steinem, Gloria*

BIBLIOGRAPHY

Brownmiller, Susan. 1999. *In Our Time, Memoir of a Revolution.* New York: Dial.

Cohen, Marcia. 1988. *The Sisterhood: The True Story of the Women Who Changed the World.* New York: Simon and Schuster.

Dow, Bonnie J. 1996. *Prime-Time Feminism: Television, Media Culture, and the Women's Movement since 1970.* Philadelphia: University of Pennsylvania Press.

Friedan, Betty. 1963. *The Feminine Mystique.* New York: Norton.

Reed, Susan E. 2000. Sisterhood Was Powerful. *The American Prospect* July 17.

Simon, Rita J., and Gloria Danziger. 1991. *Women's Movements in America: Their Successes, Disappointments, and Aspirations.* New York: Praeger.

Steinem, Gloria. 1983. *Outrageous Acts and Everyday Rebellions.* New York: Holt, Rinehart, and Winston.

Walker, Rebecca. 1992. Becoming the Third Wave. *Ms.* 21: 86–87.

Patricia Cronin Marcello

FENNO, RICHARD F., JR.
1926–

The contributions of Richard F. Fenno Jr. to the political science world are many and varied. His work on Congress and the actions of legislators has pioneered fields of study in political science.

After studying at Amherst and Harvard, Fenno published his doctoral dissertation as his first book in 1959. An article on the House appropriations committee (1962) and a book, *The Power of the Purse: Appropriation Politics in Congress* (1966), soon followed. Although outdated by changes in Congress, Fenno's conceptualization of the power struggles, structures, and behavior of representatives have formed the basic vocabulary used in legislative studies.

In 1973 Fenno published *Congressmen in Committees*, which explores whether committees matter in Congress, and what role they play in fulfilling individual ambitions of congressmen. Fenno's next work, *Home Style: House Members in Their Districts* (1978), studies how representatives behave while at home in their districts. In *Home Style*, Fenno pioneered the "soaking and poking" method of social science research on politicians, in which the researcher follows the subject through the field, observing and documenting behavior. These works demonstrate the researcher's commitment to presenting politicians as necessary elements in the political world, whose actions are worth examination. This stance, which often separates Fenno from others in the field, has led to interesting discoveries about the nature of politicians and the political world. These works have also garnered criticism, as Fenno's research required him to develop friendships with his subjects, raising doubts about his level of objectivity. Other critics have charged that Fenno's observational studies are invalid, because his presence may affect the behavior of the representatives, and because those representatives that consent to be studied may not be an accurate sample of representatives as a whole. Furthermore, the very nature of participant-observer studies requires that only a small number of politicians is studied, thus decreasing the generalizability of any theory arising from the work. Fenno has responded to these criticisms by defending his work as purely exploratory in nature.

After *Home Style*, Fenno turned his eye to the Senate, publishing, among other works, *The Making of a Senator: Dan Quayle* (1988) and *Senators on the Campaign Trail: The Politics of Representation* (1996). In *Senators*, Fenno outlines representation in terms of "durable connections" or relationships that senators build with their constituents over time. Returning to the study of the House of Representatives, Fenno published *Congress at the Grassroots: Representational Change in the South, 1970–1998* (2000), which revisited areas explored in *Home Style*, and *Going Home: Black Representatives and Their Constituents* (2003).

Fenno has been president of the American Political Science Association, is a member of the National Academy of Sciences, and a fellow of the American Academy of Arts and Sciences. He is a distinguished professor and William R. Kenan professor of political science at the University of Rochester, where he has taught since 1957.

SEE ALSO *American Political Science Association; Representation*

BIBLIOGRAPHY

Kuklinski, James H. 1979. Representative-Constituency Linkages: A Review Article. *Legislative Studies Quarterly* 4 (1): 121–140.

Polsby, Nelson W. 1984. Contributions of President Richard F. Fenno Jr. *PS: Political Science and Politics* 17 (4): 778–781.

Mirya Rose Holman

FERGUSON, ADAM
SEE *Civil Society.*

FERTILE CRESCENT

The term *Fertile Crescent* refers to part of the ancient Near East that has been considered to be the principal center for the emergence of agriculture, villages, and cities, and hence the "cradle of civilization." The term was coined and popularized by James Henry Breasted (1865–1935), a scholar of ancient Egypt and director of the Oriental Institute at the University of Chicago, in his 1916 textbook for high school students, *Ancient Times: A History of the Early World.* As originally designated by Breasted, the Fertile Crescent is an arc or semicircle that included the relatively well-watered hilly areas of Palestine and Lebanon/western Syria (the Levant) on the west, stretching across northern Syria at the foot of the highland plateau of Anatolia, and then southward, east of the Tigris River to the foot of the Zagros Mountains in Iraq and Iran, ending in the alluvial plain created by the Tigris and Euphrates rivers southeast of contemporary Baghdad. As envisioned by Breasted, the Fertile Crescent's arc surrounded hostile desert and acted as a fertile shore against this "Desert Bay" (the Syrian Desert). The first "ancient civilizations" emerged from this region, including the Sumerians at the head of the Persian Gulf; the Akkadians, Babylonians, and Assyrians in Mesopotamia (Iraq) between the two great rivers; and, at a later period, the Phoenicians on the west. Many of the earliest settlements and cities of the ancient world are found within this arc. The Fertile Crescent is sometimes mentioned in conjunction with ancient Egypt, since it is one of the first civilizations as well. In popular usage, the Fertile Crescent sometimes even incorporates ancient Egypt of the Nile Valley, although scholars have never accepted this wider usage. Many works on the archaeology or the lands of the Bible have also used the term *Fertile Crescent* (e.g., Magnusson 1977).

Besides being designated as the cradle of civilization, the Fertile Crescent has been postulated as the key area for the earlier Neolithic Revolution, the beginnings of agriculture and farming on the more generously rain-fed outer margins of the arc. In fact, whereas Breasted formulated the term mainly for the beginnings of cities and "civilization," its usage for the region of the emergence of agriculture and villages has been much more common. Robert Braidwood's (1907–2003) excavations from 1948 to 1955 at Jarmo, a site in northeastern Iraq in the foothills of the Zagros Mountains, began to provide botanical evidence for the first plant domestication occurring in the "hilly flanks," and subsequent work has shown that the Fertile Crescent was indeed a focus for plant and animal domestication. Within this arc are found some of the earliest examples for the "founder crops" (Zohary 1996), such as the domesticated cereals of barley, emmer wheat, and einkorn wheat; the pulses of peas, chickpeas, lentils, and bitter vetch; and flax used as a fiber. Domesticated animals included goats, sheep, pigs, and cattle. The first evidence of cultivated crops begin to appear about 9000 BCE in the Levant, and by 6000 BCE villages, the farming of plants, and the use of domesticated animals were well established in many parts of the Fertile Crescent (and beyond in a few places). Horticulture began mainly in the Levant during the Chalcolithic period (5000–3500 BCE), which first focused on growing olives, figs, pomegranates, grapes, and dates (the latter perhaps first cultivated in other areas of the Near East). This core area for the Neolithic Revolution is somewhat larger than Breasted's original concept. The argument for the Fertile Crescent's central role has been popularized, for instance, by geographer and physiologist Jared Diamond in *Guns, Germs, and Steel* (1997), where he advocates the significance of the Mediterranean climate (wet winters, dry summers) and that most of the major plants and animals that were genetically and behaviorally predisposed to domestication were found basically together in parts of this arc. Diamond's rather generalized Fertile Crescent extends more northward onto the Anatolian Plateau and includes a tongue that stretches westward to incorporate the significant circa 6000 BCE site of Çatal Hüyük on the Konya Plain in central Anatolia.

The name *Fertile Crescent* has been criticized for not being a proper term or even a relevant concept. In William Hallo and William Simpson's 1998 edition of their textbook, *The Ancient Near East: A History*, they take the term to task, asserting that, in fact, the arc of the Fertile Crescent was not the area for the beginnings of agriculture (and the Neolithic Revolution), and that evidence now shows the origins to be also in highland areas, such as Anatolia, with greater rainfall and native vegetation. They (and others) also stress that many of the "civilizations" and cities that emerged in Mesopotamia could do so only after developing extensive irrigation systems (and hence these areas were not in a "fertile" region). On the other hand, different terms being proposed by some Near Eastern archaeologists also often refer to a semicircle for origins of agriculture and the emergence of cities, and actually cover a region similar to the Fertile Crescent, using such names as *Near Eastern nuclear arc* (Harlan 1977), *Zagrosian arc* (Maisels 1990), *Zagros-Kurdi-Taurus mountain arc* (Maisels 1990), or the *Near East arc* (Zohary and Hopf 1988). That many sites for early plant and animal domestication lie outside the Fertile Crescent may not necessarily entirely negate the importance of this core region for the beginnings of agriculture and farming, although further discoveries in Anatolia, Iran, and other areas (including India or China) may require significant reinterpretations or refinements in the future.

Following World War II (1939–1945), the use of the term *Fertile Crescent* became particularly popular in other fields besides ancient Near Eastern studies and archaeology. Some historians began to refer to the Arab countries (or previous mandates) of Syria, Iraq, and Lebanon as the Fertile Crescent. For example, in 1966 P. M. Holt published a political history entitled *Egypt and the Fertile Crescent: 1516–1922*, while the economist Charles Issawi (1916–2000), as one of his several books of translated documents, published *The Fertile Crescent, 1800–1914* (1988), in which all the chapters focus on either Iraq or Syria (with Lebanon sometimes included as part of the latter). H. G. Balfour-Paul, writing on "Fertile Crescent Unity Plans" (1996), discusses the various schemes to unite the Arabs of Iraq and Syria (and Lebanon) after World War I (1914–1918), yet the term *Fertile Crescent* was not used by the individuals and groups involved in these discussions; the use of *Fertile Crescent* for these unity plans is entirely artificially imposed.

At the beginning of the twenty-first century, historians, political scientists, and others who deal with the contemporary Arab world and Middle East seldom use the term *Fertile Crescent* for the countries of the Levant. Scholars of the ancient Near East also generally refrain from using the term. Yet, the Fertile Crescent, as a simple explanation for the origins of agriculture, villages, cities, and "civilization," is still used widely in the more popular literature, and with its long use by scholars in the past and its prominence in such works as *Guns, Germs, and Steel*, it is not a concept that will easily disappear from the literature or the imagination.

SEE ALSO *Agricultural Industry; Archaeology; Civilization; Material Culture*

BIBLIOGRAPHY

Balfour-Paul, H. G. 1996. Fertile Crescent Unity Plans. *Encyclopedia of the Modern Middle East*, eds. Reeva S. Simon, Philip Mattar, and Richard W. Bulliet, Vol. 2, 654–656. New York: Macmillan.

Braidwood, Robert J., and Bruce Howe. 1960. *Prehistoric Investigations in Iraqi Kurdistan*. Chicago: University of Chicago Press.

Breasted, James Henry. 1916. *Ancient Times: A History of the Early World*. Boston: Ginn.

Diamond, Jared. 1997. *Guns, Germs, and Steel: The Fates of Human Societies*. New York: Norton.

Hallo, William W., and William Kelly Simpson. 1998. *The Ancient Near East: A History*. 2nd ed. Fort Worth, TX: Harcourt Brace.

Harlan, Jack R. 1977. The Origins of Cereal Agriculture in the Old World. In *The Origins of Agriculture*, ed. Charles A. Reed, 357–383. The Hague, Netherlands: Mouton.

Holt, P. M. 1966. *Egypt and the Fertile Crescent, 1516–1922: A Political History*. Ithaca, NY: Cornell University Press.

Issawi, Charles. 1988. *The Fertile Crescent, 1800–1914: A Documentary Economic History*. New York: Oxford University Press.

Magnusson, Magnus. 1977. *BC: The Archaeology of the Bible Lands*. London: Bodley Head and British Broadcasting Corporation.

Maisels, Charles Keith. 1990. *The Emergence of Civilization: From Hunting and Gathering to Agriculture, Cities, and the State in the Near East*. London: Routledge.

Zohary, Daniel, 1996. The Mode of Domestication of the Founder Crops of Southwest Asian Agriculture. In *The Origins and Spread of Agriculture and Pastoralism in Eurasia*, ed. David R. Harris, 142–158. London: University College London Press.

Zohary, Daniel, and Maria Hopf. 1988. *Domestication of Plants in the Old World: The Origin and Spread of Cultivated Plants in West Asia, Europe, and the Nile Valley*. 3rd ed. Oxford: Clarendon.

Michael E. Bonine

FERTILITY, HUMAN

The term *fertility* refers to the actual production of children. It may be distinguished from *fecundity*, which is the capability to produce children. Demographers make this important distinction, but not all scientists do. Medical scientists, for instance, use the term fertility to refer to reproductive ability. Also, the meaning of the terms of fertility and fecundity are reversed among French-speaking and Spanish-speaking demographers. They too distinguish between the potential and actual production of children. But French-speaking demographers use the term *fertilité*, and Spanish-speaking demographers the term *fertilidad*, to refer to reproductive ability, and *fecundité* and *fecundidad*, respectively, to refer to actual reproductive performance.

One of the most popular and easily understood and interpreted methods for quantifying fertility is the crude birth rate (CBR), that is, the number of births in a population in a given year, per one thousand members of the population, expressed as follows:

$$CBR = \frac{\text{births in the year}}{\text{population at mid-year}} * 1,000$$

Using 2005 data for China (Population Reference Bureau 2005), the equation becomes:

$$CBR = \frac{15,637,000}{1,303,700,000} * 1,000 = 12$$

This means that in China in 2005, there were twelve babies born for every thousand persons in the population. Crude birth rates among the countries of the world in 2005 ranged from lows of nine in several countries, including Japan, Germany, Bulgaria, Poland, Italy, Hungary, and Greece, to highs of fifty-six in Niger and fifty in Liberia, Mali, Malawi, and Guinea-Bissau (Population Reference Bureau 2005). The range of crude birth rates is much greater than that for crude death rates, which in 2005 extended from a low of one in the United Arab Emirates to a high of twenty-eight in Botswana and Lesotho.

Lay persons employ the CBR more often than any other fertility measure, but it is not the most accurate of the measures. The CBR's denominator does not truly represent the population for which the possibility of giving birth is an issue because it includes males, prepuberty females, and postmenopausal females. Demographers refer to the population in the denominator as the "risk population." Because of this overly inclusive denominator, the CBR should be interpreted with caution.

Demographers use more refined fertility measures, including the general fertility rate (GFR), age-specific fertility rates (ASFR), the total fertility rate (TFR), the gross reproduction rate (GRR), and the net reproduction rate (NRR). The GFR, ASFR, and TFR are increasingly more accurate measures of the childbearing experiences of a population. The GRR and the NRR measure not fertility but reproduction, that is, the production of females (Rowland 2003).

Fecundity can be divided into five categories on the basis of the extent of fecundity impairment and the degree of certainty regarding this impairment. Badenhorst and Higgins (1962, p. 281) note that all couples may be clas-

sified as either *fecund* or *sub-fecund*; the latter may be subdivided into the following groups: *definitely sterile, probably sterile, semi-fecund*, and *fecundity indeterminate*. Badenhorst and Higgins define the *sub-fecund* groups as follows: *definitely sterile* couples are those "for whom conception is impossible because of certain physical or medical conditions, including an operation or other physical impairment or menopause"; *probably sterile* couples are those "for whom a birth is improbable on the basis of specific medical evidence"; *semi-fecund* couples are those who have married or cohabited for a relatively long time without using contraception but have not conceived; *fecundity indeterminate* couples are those who meet the criteria for semi-fecund couples, "except that the wife sometimes reported douching 'for cleanness only' soon after intercourse" (that is, a form of contraception is used). These couples are defined as *fecundity indeterminate* because they could be potentially fecund and some of them are observed to be fecund as well (Badenhorst and Higgins 1962). Demographic research has shown that the majority of sub-fecund couples are impaired according to one of the above definitions.

As for fertility, demographers have conducted extensive studies examining its trends and determinants. It has been found that during the past few decades, fertility in most countries of the world is in a declining pattern, and this is particularly the case in the more industrialized countries. Beginning in the 1990s, fertility below the replacement level of 2.1 children per woman (as measured using the total fertility rate) has emerged in many countries of the world (Kohler et al. 2002, Morgan 2003). Among the 205 countries worldwide (a country is defined here as a territory with at least 150,000 population), 73 had fertility rates at or below the replacement level in 2005. Following Billari (2004), we refer to fertility as being "low" when the TFR is below the replacement level of 2.1, as being "very low" when it is below 1.5, and as being "lowest low" when it is below 1.3. In 2005, eleven countries reported "lowest low" fertility, that is, a fertility rate below 1.3; these countries include South Korea, Taiwan, Poland, the Czech Republic, Slovakia, and Ukraine.

A number of theories have been proposed to explain the dynamics of fertility. Prominent explanations include proximate determinants theory (Bongaarts, 1994), demographic transition theory (Notestein 1945, Thompson 1929, Davis 1963, Hirschman 1994, Knodel and van de Walle 1979, Poston 2000), wealth flows theory (Caldwell 1976), human ecological theory (Browning and Poston 1980, Kasarda 1971, Poston and Frisbie 2005, London 1987, London and Hadden 1989), political economic theory (Greenhalgh 1990, Kertzer and Hogan 1989), and diffusion theory (Coale and Watkins 1986). Many of these theories use proximate determinants of fertility (proportion married, contraception use, induced abortion, and duration of fertility period) and other social, economic, ecological, political, and cultural factors to understand the dynamics of fertility change.

One limitation of the above fertility measures and theories is that they are usually derived from calculations and analyses only of females. The fertility of men and the determinants of male fertility are rarely examined and compared with those of females. Males are a neglected minority in fertility studies. Several reasons have been proposed to justify this exclusion. Some biological reasons are that the fecundity, and the childbearing years of women occur in a more sharply defined and narrower range (fifteen to forty-nine) than they do for men (fifteen to seventy-nine). In addition, "both the spacing and number of children are less subject to variation among women; a woman can have children only at intervals of 1 or 2 years, whereas a man can have hundreds" (Keyfitz 1977, p. 114). Some methodological justifications are that data on parental age at the birth of a child are more frequently collected on birth registration certificates for the mothers than for the fathers. When such data are obtained for mothers and fathers, there are a greater number of instances of unreported age data for fathers, and this is especially the situation for births occurring outside marriage. The sociological reasons include the fact that men have been regarded principally as breadwinners and "as typically uninvolved in fertility except to impregnate women and to stand in the way of their contraceptive use" (Greene and Biddlecom 2000, p. 83).

However, biological and demographic studies provide evidence that men are important to fertility outcomes and related behaviors. Considering mammalian species in general, Coleman indicates that "the male sex as a whole contributes an equivalent amount of genetic information to the next generation as the female, but the variance contributed by that of males to the next generation in many species—especially those which practice polygamy—is considerably greater than that of the female sex" (p. 33). That is, most females reproduce, some males do not reproduce, and other males have a large amount of offspring. In addition, biologists have found there are more childless males than childless females in many species (Coleman 2000).

Demographically, it has been shown that men have different patterns of fertility and fertility-related behavior. For men, age-specific fertility tends to start later, stops much later, and remains higher than that of women (Paget and Timaeus 1994). The total fertility rates (TFRs) for males and females also differ. Results show that in most industrialized countries male TFRs were historically higher than female TFRs. Over time this gap narrowed and eventually a crossover occurred between these rates.

This means that men and women who conformed to the sex- and age-specific fertility rates of an area at one point in time and had less than 2.2 children during their childbearing years were more likely to have similar than dissimilar fertility (Zhang 2007; Coleman 2000; also see Smith 1992, and Myers 1941).

The special importance of men is also seen in determinants of fertility and fertility-related behaviors such as cohabitation, marriage, and employment. Whereas the focus has been on women's fertility, in the United States it is men's fertility that is more likely to be influenced by marital and employment status. Being ever married and ever working significantly increases men's number of children ever born (CEB), whereas such factors do not have as strong of an impact on women, despite the frequent emphasis on the relevance of labor force participation for women's fertility (Zhang 2007). Research using various independent variables from several fertility paradigms—namely, human ecology, political economy, and wealth flows—to predict both male and female TFRs for the counties of Taiwan has shown that the variables have consistently performed better in predicting variation in female TFRs than in male TFRs (Zhang 2007).

Men also have different cohabitation and marriage patterns from women. In the United States, for birth cohorts born between 1958 and 1987, it has been shown that living alone, being foreign-born, and living in fragmented families increase the odds of cohabitation for women but not for men. Foreign-born men are more likely to marry than native-born men. But these factors do not have as significant an impact on women's marriage behavior. In Europe, researchers have conducted studies examining male and female transitions to adulthood in twenty-four countries using survey data for the 1980s and 1990s. They find that educational attainment's generally negative effect on fertility is stronger for women than for men. Also, unemployment leads to men's postponement of marriage, whereas it affects women in two distinct ways. It either accelerates or slows down women's timing of marriage. The effect of religion is stronger among women than men. Furthermore, being Catholic and attending church services affect men and women's parenthood timing in different ways in predominantly Catholic countries. Other relevant factors such as parental influence have been shown to have a different impact for males compared to females (Corijn and Klijzing 2001).

Historically, women have been tied to motherhood, and this association is deeply rooted in law and policy, in the ways that jobs are structured, and the ways that family relations are navigated. Many of the studies of fertility and parenthood undertaken by demographers have been shaped by this historical association as well (Riley 2005). Together with the biological and methodological factors stated above, this has resulted in the decreased attention given to males in fertility research. Yet, as mentioned earlier, biological and demographic analyses have shown that fertility and parenting are not simply female issues—they are issues involving both men and women. The study of fertility should not only focus on females. Critical demography has promoted bringing men into population studies (Horton 1999; Coleman 2000) and Greenhalgh (1990) and others have argued that it is necessary to incorporate gender studies into studies of demography in order to gain a more balanced picture of demographic issues. Together with lowest-low fertility, unbalanced sex ratios at birth, and the demography of gay males and lesbians, male fertility and men's influence on decisions about bearing and rearing children have become emerging issues of population study.

SEE ALSO *Demography; Gender; Population Growth*

BIBLIOGRAPHY

Badenhorst, L. T., and Edward Higgins. 1962. Fecundity of White Women in Johannesburg. *Population Studies* 15 (3): 279–290.

Billari, Francesco C. 2004. Choices, Opportunities, and Constraints of Partnership, Childbearing, and Parenting: The Patterns in the 1990s. Paper presented at the European Population Forum 2004: Population Challenges and Policy Responses.

Bongaarts, John. 1994. The Impact of the Proximate Determinants of Fertility: A Comment on Reinis. *Population Studies* 48 (1): 159–160.

Browning, Harley L., and Dudley L. Poston Jr. 1980. The Demographic Transition. In *Fertility Control: Biological and Social Aspects*, eds. Rochelle N. Shain and Carl J. Pauerstein, 197–203. New York: Harper & Row.

Caldwell, John C. 1976. Toward a Restatement of Demographic Transition Theory. *Population and Development Review* 2 (3–4): 321–366.

Coale, Ansley J., and Susan Cotts Watkins, eds. 1986. *The Decline of Fertility in Europe*. Princeton, NJ: Princeton University Press.

Coleman, David A. 2000. Male Fertility Trends in Industrial Countries: Theories in Search of Some Evidence. In *Fertility and the Male Life-Cycle in the Era of Fertility Decline*, eds. Caroline Bledsoe, Susana Lerner, and Jane I. Guyer, 29–60. Oxford and New York: Oxford University Press.

Corijn, Martine, and Erik Klijzing. 2001. *Transitions to Adulthood in Europe*. New York: Kluwer Academic Publishers.

Davis, Kingsley. 1963. The Theory of Change and Response in Modern Demographic History. *Population Index* 29 (4): 345–366.

Greene, Margaret E., and Ann E. Biddlecom. 2000. Absent and Problematic Men: Demographic Accounts of Male Reproductive Roles. *Population and Development Review* 26 (1): 81–115.

Greenhalgh, Susan. 1990. Toward a Political Economy of Fertility: Anthropological Contributions. *Population and Development Review* 16 (1): 85–106.

Hirschman, Charles. 1994. Why Fertility Changes. *Annual Review of Sociology* 20: 203–233.

Horton, Hayward Derrick. 1999. Critical Demography: The Paradigm of the Future? *Sociological Forum* 14 (3): 363–367.

Kasarda, John D. 1971. Economic Structure and Fertility: A Comparative Analysis. *Demography* 8 (3): 307–317.

Kertzer, David I., and Dennis P. Hogan. 1989. *Family, Political Economy, and Demographic Change: The Transformation of Life in Casalecchio, Italy, 1861–1921*. Madison: University of Wisconsin Press.

Keyfitz, Nathan. 1977. *Applied Mathematical Demography*. New York: John Wiley.

Knodel, John, and Etienne van de Walle. 1979. Lessons from the Past: Policy Implications of Historical Fertility Studies. *Population and Development Review* 5 (2): 217–245.

Kohler, Hans-Peter, Francesco C. Billari, and Jose Antonio Ortega. 2002. The Emergence of Lowest-Low Fertility in Europe during the 1990s. *Population and Development Review* 28 (4): 641–680.

London, Bruce. 1987. Ending Ecology's Ethnocentrism: Thai Replications and Extensions of Ecological Research. *Rural Sociology* 52 (4): 483–500.

London, Bruce, and Kenneth P. Hadden. 1989. The Spread of Education and Fertility Decline: A Thai Province Level Test of Caldwell's "Wealth Flows" Theory. *Rural Sociology* 54 (1): 17–36.

McKeown, Thomas. 1976. *The Modern Rise of Population*. New York: Academic Press.

Morgan, S. Philip. 2003. Is Low Fertility a Twenty-First-Century Demographic Crisis? *Demography* 40 (4): 589–603.

Myers, Robert J. 1941. The Validity and Significance of Male Net Reproduction Rates. *Journal of the American Statistical Association* 36 (2): 275–282.

Notestein, Frank W. 1945. Population: The Long View. In *Food for the World*, ed. Theodore W. Schultz, 36–57. Chicago: University of Chicago Press.

Paget, W. John, and Ian M. Timaeus. 1994. A Relational Gompertz Model of Male Fertility: Development and Assessment. *Population Studies* 48 (2): 333–340.

Population Reference Bureau. 2005. *2005 World Population Data Sheet*. Washington, DC: Population Reference Bureau.

Poston, Dudley L., Jr. 2000. Social and Economic Development and the Fertility Transition in Mainland China and Taiwan. *Population and Development Review* 26 (supplement): 40–60.

Poston, Dudley L., Jr., and W. Parker Frisbie. 2005. Ecological Demography. In *Handbook of Population*, eds. Dudley L. Poston Jr. and Michael Micklin, 601–624. New York: Springer.

Riley, Nancy E. 2005. Demography of Gender. In *Handbook of Population*, eds. Dudley L. Poston Jr. and Michael Micklin, 109–142. New York: Springer.

Rowland, Donald T. 2003. *Demographic Methods and Concepts*. New York: Oxford University Press.

Smith, David P. 1992. *Formal Demography*. New York: Plenum Press.

Thompson, Warren S. 1929. Population. *American Journal of Sociology* 34 (6): 959–975.

Zhang, Li. 2007. Bringing Men In: Analyses of Male and Female Fertility. Unpublished PhD diss., Texas A&M University.

Dudley L. Poston Jr.
Li Zhang
Heather K. M. Terrell

FERTILITY, LAND

The fertility of soil refers to its ability to function in the growing of crop plants. Soil fertility is frequently defined narrowly as the ability of the soil to provide nutrients that are essential for plant growth and the soil having a pH in the range needed for the specific crops grown (most plants do well in the pH range of 6 to 7). If soils are very acidic, below pH 5.5, many crop plants are harmed by the lack of nutrients as well as the presence of soluble aluminum, which can be toxic to plants. On the other hand, some crops such as cassava do well in the acidic and low-nutrient soils of the tropics. Most of the eighteen essential elements for plants come from the soil. Of the nutrients supplied by the soil, nitrogen, phosphorus, and potassium are the ones needed in the largest amounts and are frequently applied in commercial fertilizers. Other nutrients, such as calcium, sulfur, and magnesium, are needed in lesser amounts while the micronutrients, such as iron, manganese, copper, and zinc, are needed in very small amounts and are not as commonly deficient.

A broader view of soil fertility has recently developed that is sometimes referred to as soil health or soil quality. In this more comprehensive view, equal consideration is given to the physical and biological properties of soil that are important to plants, along with the chemical properties. For example, a soil may have excellent nutrient availability but be too wet or compact for crops to grow properly or might have high populations of plant disease organisms or parasitic nematodes. The chemical fertility of the soil is usually determined by laboratory analysis of a composite sample taken from a field. The tests normally included in routine soil analysis are for pH, available nutrients such as phosphorus, potassium, calcium, and magnesium, and lime requirements. Other tests commonly done are salinity and percent saturation with sodium (both in arid regions) and amount of organic matter. In determining the broader health of the soil, the degree of compaction, and root health are usually evaluated in the field, and some laboratories determine water-holding capacity and indicators of biological activity.

Topsoil, usually the top six inches or more, is the most fertile part of the soil. It contains higher amounts of organic matter and nutrients, has more biological activity, retains water more easily, and is usually better aerated than subsoil. Plentiful organic matter is the key to healthy, fertile soils because it has profound and positive effects on almost all soil properties—chemical, biological, and physical. It helps soils store water, resist compaction, make nutrients more available to plants, maintain a thriving and diverse populations of organisms, and so on.

When forests or grasslands are converted to agricultural use, these virgin soils are usually productive for a number of years, even without addition of fertilizers or amendments. The soils usually have good physical, chemical, and biological properties. This is the basis for tropical slash-and-burn agriculture, a twenty- to forty-year cycle in which the trees in a forest plot are first felled and burned. For a few short years, the nutrients stored in the soils and the positive effect of the ash on soils allow reasonable crop productivity. Much of the fertility of these soils is associated with organic matter or elements in the ash that are leached readily into the soil. Thus, in the traditional slash-and-burn system where no fertilizers or organic amendments are applied, after two or three years these soils are allowed to revert to forest.

DEGRADATION OF SOIL FERTILITY

Soil degradation is a worldwide phenomenon that has occurred in many places since the development of agriculture. Soils can be degraded in a number of ways, such as nutrient depletion, organic matter depletion, development of saline or sodic (excess sodium) soils, removal of topsoil by accelerated erosion, and compaction.

In ancient times, crop production decreased in parts of Mesopotamia (in the Tigris and Euphrates valleys), as salts accumulated from irrigation water were not washed out regularly. The hillside agriculture of Greece, Turkey, and the Middle East was first practiced without terraces. Removal of the original forests and repeated plowing and working of these soils left their exposed surfaces smooth or with aggregates that were easily broken under the impact of rainfall. Rainfall, not able to penetrate the soil at the rate it fell, caused runoff and soil erosion. As Homer put it in the *Iliad*, "Many a hillside do the torrents furrow deeply, and down to the dark sea they rush headlong from the mountains with a mighty roar, and the tilled fields of men are wasted" (cited in Hillel 1992, p. 103). The large area of denuded hillsides in the region, with large areas of exposed bedrock or boulders, testify to the magnitude of this problem, which many feel severely stressed these societies to the point of either decline or aggressive adventures to find extra sources of food in other countries.

On highly leached and geologically old landforms such as occur in much of Africa, the loss of soil's ability to provide adequate nutrition to crop plants can happen very rapidly—within two or three years following cutting down the trees and burning them. (In places where the cycle of crops to forest and back to crops is greatly reduced, soils are much decreased in their fertility.) On the other hand, on the deep fertile grassland soils that developed in humid temperate regions, it can take decades of cropping before added nutrients are needed to maintain plant growth. These soils, naturally high in organic matter and able to supply crops with large amounts of nitrogen for years, usually also have large supplies of other plant nutrients. In his classic book *Slavery and Capitalism* (1961), Eric Williams makes the case that in the southeastern United States and the Caribbean it was the institution of slavery that allowed the large-scale exploitation of the land for cash crops (cotton and sugarcane). If free laborers were brought for the purpose of working large estates, as was the case in Australia, they would have abandoned the estates and started their own small farms. These smaller farms, Williams argued, would have not have been so hard on the soil because they would have grown more varied crops and used crop rotation. While this argument makes sense, the soils of the Caribbean and southeastern United States are easily depleted of their nutrients and, when on sloping land, prone to erosion. Thus, small farms applying the practices of the time might also have led to soil degradation, but perhaps not as rapidly as under the institution of slavery.

Between the two extremes of highly leached tropical and subtropical soils and deep grassland soils of the temperate regions are many of the soils of Europe and the eastern United States. These are the regions where modern agriculture first developed and the more intensive nature of cropping required large quantities of external nutrients to maintain plant growth year after year. Modern agriculture developed in a symbiotic relationship with industrial capitalism, and through the break in nutrient cycling capitalism has added new dimensions to the issue of soil degradation. Part of the reason for the need for large quantities of external nutrients is that, with the development of cities and capitalist farmers who sold most or all of what they produced, large amounts of nutrients were being removed from farmland and transported to cities in the form of food products. As Karl Marx wrote in volume 1 of *Capital*:

> Capitalist production … disturbs the metabolic interaction between man and the earth, i.e. it prevents the return to the soil of its constituent elements consumed by man in the form of food and clothing; hence it hinders the operation of the eternal natural condition for the fertility of the soil.… All progress in capitalist agriculture is a progress in the art, not only of robbing the worker, but of robbing the soil; all progress in increasing the fertility of the soil for a given time is a progress towards ruining the more long-lasting sources of that fertility.… Capitalist production, therefore, only develops the techniques and degree of combination of the social process of production by simultaneously undermining the original sources of all wealth—the soil and the worker (1867, pp. 637–638).

USE OF AMENDMENTS TO ENHANCE SOIL FERTILITY

Although various animal manures and green manures were used for thousands of years to enhance the fertility of soils (and still are), in the nineteenth century the application of modern science to agriculture resulted in the knowledge that depletion of a few nutrients—nitrogen, phosphorus, and potassium—were likely to be limiting plant growth on many soils that had been farmed for years. The depleted, "worn-out" soils of Europe and the eastern United States created a strong demand for external nutrient sources. Bones, a source of phosphorus, were imported into Europe, and farmers even raided the graves of the Napoleonic battlefields to obtain them. In the 1840s phosphate became the first industrially produced fertilizer. But industrial production of nitrogen fertilizer would not happen until the after World War I (1914–1918), when the Haber-Bosch process for fixing nitrogen would begin to make this essential element more available. (And it was not until after World War II [1939–1945], when the munitions plants turned to making ammonium nitrate fertilizers, that the low price of nitrogen fertilizer greatly stimulated its use.) In the mid-1800s, in the absence of a ready supply of synthetically produced nitrogen, the use of guano from Peru, high in both nitrogen and phosphorus, came under British control. This caused the United States, in competition with European countries, to search abroad for sources of nutrients to help maintain soil fertility, referred to by the phrase "guano imperialism." During this period, from 1856 (after passage of the Guano Island Act) to the early 1900s, the United States seized close to 100 island sources of guano.

A second major change in the cycling of nutrients took place after World War II. In this period, low-cost nitrogen fertilizers allowed farmers to forgo planting legume forage crops that had been part of an integrated crop farming system that included complex rotations and raising animals as well as crops. Farmers, no longer needing legumes or animal manures to supply their grain crops with nitrogen, began to specialize in one or two crops such as wheat and corn (and later soybeans). Animals, especially poultry, beef cows, and hogs, started to be raised on large farms that frequently imported feeds, made from mainly corn and soybeans, from other regions. The growth of these large-scale industrial animal facilities was brought about by the location of meat-processing facilities by highly integrated corporations. Many farmers are now raising chickens and hogs under contract, with little control over the actual production process. This separation of a large number of animals from the land that grows their feed has resulted in the necessity for crop farmers to use large quantities of fertilizers (to make up for the nutrients exported in their crops), while at the same time nutrients accumulate on the animal farms and result in significant pollution of groundwater and surface waters.

ECOLOGICAL MANAGEMENT OF SOIL FERTILITY

Although commercial fertilizers still have their place in agriculture, the high cost of nitrogen fertilizer in terms of energy use (and, therefore, price) and the ecological harm caused by phosphate mining mean that in the future more emphasis needs to be placed on more efficient nutrient cycling, the reintegration of animals back into cropping systems, and the return to legumes and manures as major sources of nitrogen and other nutrients for nonleguminous crops. Most soils can be greatly improved by implementation of ecologically sound practices for building healthy soils. One of the best approaches to improving soil health is to use various means to build up soil organic matter levels—such as adding manures and composts or other local sources of organic materials, using cover crops routinely, rotating row crops with hay-type forages, and reducing tillage intensity.

SEE ALSO *Agricultural Industry; Boserup, Ester; Cultural Landscape; Development, Rural; Green Revolution; Productivity; Returns, Diminishing*

BIBLIOGRAPHY

Burnett, C. D. 2005. The Edges of Empire and the Limits of Sovereignty: American Guano Islands. *American Quarterly* 57(3): 779–803.

Foster, J. B., and F. Magdoff. 2000. Liebig, Marx and the Depletion of Soil Fertility: Relevance for Today's Agriculture. In *Hungry for Profit: The Agribusiness Threat to Farmers, Food, and the Environment*, eds. F. Magdoff, J. B. Foster, and F. H. Buttel, 43–60. New York: Monthly Review Press.

Hillel, D. 1992. *Out of the Earth: Civilization and the Life of the Soil.* Berkeley: University of California Press.

Hyams, E. 1976. *Soil and Civilization.* New York: Harper & Row.

Magdoff, F., and H. van Es. 2000. *Building Soils for Better Crops,* 2nd ed. Burlington, VT: Sustainable Agriculture Network (SAN).

Marx, K. [1867] 1976. *Capital: A Critique of Political Economy,* vol. 1. Trans. B. Fowkes. New York: Vintage.

Runnels, C. N. 1995. Environmental Degradation in Ancient Greece. *Scientific American* 272 (3): 96–99.

Williams, E. 1961. *Capitalism and Slavery.* New York: Russell and Russell.

Frederick Robin Magdoff

FESTINGER, LEON
1919–1989

Leon Festinger was a prominent American social psychologist. His work in social psychology focused on the impact of the social environment on the formation and change of attitudes, on processes of social comparison by which individuals evaluate their attitudes and abilities, and on the manner in which cognitive inconsistencies cause changes in attitudes and behaviors. He is best known for his work *A Theory of Cognitive Dissonance* (1957), which inspired a great deal of creative research and caused the term *cognitive dissonance* to become a part of public discourse.

Festinger was born on May 8, 1919, in Brooklyn, New York, and died on February 11, 1989. In 1939 he earned a bachelor of science degree in psychology at the City College of New York, where he became attracted to the work of psychologist Kurt Lewin (1890–1947). Festinger went to the University of Iowa to work with Lewin, and earned his PhD there in 1942. In 1945 Festinger joined Lewin in the Research Center for Group Dynamics at the Massachusetts Institute of Technology. When Lewin died unexpectedly in 1947, Festinger became director of the center and focused his attention fully on social psychology.

Festinger's main contributions to social psychology occurred over the next twenty years. There are three landmark publications, each of which inspired research by many investigators. The first was "Informal Social Communication," published in *Psychological Review* in 1950. This article showed how pressures toward uniformity of opinion in small, informal groups could lead to attitude change within the group. The second article, "A Theory of Social Comparison Processes," was published in *Human Relations* in 1954. In this publication, Festinger used a set of formal propositions to explain the antecedent conditions and the consequences of comparing one's own attitudes and abilities to those of others. In so doing, he showed how the pressures to uniformity, hypothesized in the earlier article, arose from the process of social comparison.

In *A Theory of Cognitive Dissonance*, Festinger's third landmark publication, he hypothesized that any two bits of knowledge held by an individual could have three relationships to one another: they could be *irrelevant* to one another, *consonant* if one follows from the other, or *dissonant* if the obverse of one follows from the other. Festinger hypothesized that cognitive dissonance is an aversive state and that an individual would be motivated to reduce dissonance. Dissonance could be reduced by changing attitudes, altering perceptions and evaluations, or changing one's own behavior. Because the theory was stated in such simple, general terms, it could be applied to a wide variety of situations. Festinger and his students were creative in finding applications for the theory and in devising incisive experiments to test their predictions. A number of these experiments are reported in Festinger's second book on dissonance theory, *Conflict, Decisions, and Dissonance* (1964).

Festinger's work on dissonance theory was the target of a number of critiques in the early 1960s. Critics attacked the structure of the theory as being too broad and not clearly defining the conditions under which dissonance would occur, as well as the complex experimental protocols employed by dissonance theory researchers. Over the ensuing decade, research replicating and extending earlier findings, as well as conceptual clarifications, notably by Elliot Aronson, effectively rebutted these critiques. As dissonance theory gained scientific acceptance, the term *cognitive dissonance* came to be used by columnists and other commentators to describe the psychological discomfort that follows the arrival of unwanted or unexpected information or events. This lay use of the term became popular, even though the conditions necessary for the occurrence of the state defined in the theory may not have been met in the situation to which the term was applied.

Subsequently, Festinger's research interests became focused on different issues. From 1963 to 1979 he studied human visual perception, making unique contributions to the research literature. He then turned his attention to early human history, producing a book, *The Human Legacy* (1983), in which he analyzed human problem solving and adaptation.

Leon Festinger left a legacy of enduring theoretical formulations, a distinctive style of experimentation in social psychology, and a large number of former students who have forged their own distinguished careers in social psychology.

SEE ALSO *Aronson, Elliot; Attitudes; Cognitive Dissonance; Lewin, Kurt; Social Comparison*

BIBLIOGRAPHY

Festinger, Leon. 1957. *A Theory of Cognitive Dissonance.* Evanston, IL: Row, Peterson.

Wicklund, Robert A., and Jack W. Brehm. 1976. *Perspectives on Cognitive Dissonance.* Hillsdale, NJ: Erlbaum.

Darwyn E. Linder

FETISHIZATION
SEE *Mystification.*

FEUDAL MODE OF PRODUCTION

The feudal mode of production appears in the theorization of successive socioeconomic formations provided by Karl Marx (1818–1883), where it precedes the capitalist mode of production. Marx developed the concept of the feudal mode of production, in particular, in the section on "Pre-capitalist Economic Formations" of the *Grundrisse* (1857–1858) and in chapter 47 of the first volume of *Capital* (1867). He was not, however, interested in providing an account of the main features of feudal society as much as he was in focusing on the distinctive characteristics of capitalism compared to previous modes of production. In analyzing the feudal mode of production and its decline, he also tried to pinpoint the main factors that historically explain the rise of capitalism. The original formulations provided by Marx, Friedrich Engels (1820–1895), and Vladimir I. Lenin (1870–1924) viewed the feudal mode of production as an essentially economic dynamic of subjugation and exploitation. Subsequently, three main problems have framed twentieth-century Marxist scholarly debates on the feudal mode of production: its relations with serfdom, its interactions with feudalism as a political and juridical concept, and the reasons for its collapse and the transition to capitalism.

THE FEUDAL MODE OF PRODUCTION IN THE ANALYSES OF MARX, ENGELS, AND LENIN

Marx's definition of the feudal mode of production rests largely on the concept of *feudal rent*, which characterizes both relations of production and ways to extract surplus from the direct producers. The feudal rent requires the existence of large agricultural productive units (manors, demesne) owned by a landlord who, through coercive means, is able to force peasants to pay a rent in the form of labor (corvée), produce, or monetary tributes. In exchange, peasants living in villages are allowed to possess small individual landholdings (strips, virgates) and to access forests and pastures as common land. Surplus extracted as feudal rent reveals a relation of personal subordination between the peasant and the landlord, which is confirmed by the fact that the landlord is the supreme political authority over the geographical unit (the fief) that contains the demesne, peasants' plots, and common land.

At the same time, the landlord is also a *vassal*, a personal subordinate of a higher-level noble or of the sovereign, who recognizes the landlord's feudal authority in exchange for military services. Traditional customs—a theme touched on in Engels's *Socialism: Utopian and Scientific* (1892)—play a decisive role in sustaining these webs of hierarchies, obligations, and subjection, which appear natural and immutable. Finally, for Marx and Engels, the feudal mode of production reflects a radical opposition between the countryside and the city, which remains economically marginal and undeveloped.

Engels's discussion of feudalism, especially in the *Origins of the Family, Private Property, and the State* (1884), balanced Marx's emphasis on economic causal relations with the significance of communal landownership as a source of peasant resistance to the landlord. Such themes also surfaced in debates on the feudal mode of production in revolutionary Russia. Nikolai Bukharin (1888–1938) and especially Lenin's *The Development of Capitalism in Russia* (1899) describe czarist Russia as a feudal society where the oppressed peasants constitute a serfdom that retains strong connections with communal forms of property. In Lenin, moreover, Russian feudalism is not a single mode of production but rather a "social formation" where other modes, including a rising capitalism, exist alongside feudal landholding under the authority of a strong, centralized absolutist state. As in other parts of eastern Europe, feudal landlords show for Lenin the tendency to evolve and become bourgeois agrarian *Junkers* who, in what Lenin calls the *Prussian road*, start hiring waged laborers to produce for the market.

LATER MARXIST DEBATES AND THE TRANSITION FROM FEUDALISM TO CAPITALISM

The issues raised by Lenin's discussion of feudalism—on the role of serfdom, political absolutism, and the modes of transition to capitalism—resonated in postwar Marxist debates. There, moreover, the geographical focus of the feudal mode of production was broadened beyond the European context as Marxist scholars identified feudal economic and political relations in the shogunate during the Tokugawa age in Japan (1600s to mid-1800s), in imperial Ethiopia (late 1800s to 1970s), and, more controversially, in prerevolutionary China.

A major object of debate concerned the relations between the feudal mode of production and feudalism intended as a broad political, juridical, and ideological construct. Non-Marxist historians (Marc Bloch, Otto Hintze, Robert Boutruche, Georges Duby) have advanced this latter perspective, which, however, also influences the thorough Marxist analysis proposed by Perry Anderson (1974). He sees the construction of the feudal mode of production in Europe, and its local specificities, not just as products of economic causality. They are also a reflec-

tion of different forms of "parcellization of sovereignty" and of shifting interactions between juridical concepts of private property in Roman law and village warrior aristocracy in the Germanic tradition. Conversely, he regards the rise of western European absolute monarchies in the 1500s and 1600s—when feudalism was also established in eastern Europe—as a sign of transformation in societies whose feudal economies are increasingly producing for international commodity markets.

Anderson's view markedly contrasts with that of Barry Hindess and Paul Hirst (1975), who argue that the political forms of feudalism are irrelevant to define the feudal mode of production, which was an economic formation based on a *tax-rent* surplus extraction that relied entirely on the aristocracy's control of the land. Consequently, for Hindess and Hirst, serfdom as a juridical condition is of secondary importance in conceptualizing the feudal mode of production. The concept, in fact, includes every rural society where landlords (not the state, as in the Asiatic mode of production) raise rent and taxes from peasants that are not waged laborers, as in capitalism, or slaves, as in antiquity.

Finally, from the 1950s to the 1970s, an important Marxist debate focused on the dynamics of the crisis of feudalism and its transition to capitalism. Economist Paul Sweezy (1910–2004) saw the feudal mode of production as an inefficient, unproductive, socioeconomic structure, which was ultimately destroyed by the growth of commodity markets and the rise of profit-oriented urban entrepreneurs. Robert Brenner opposed to this view an image of the feudal mode of production as a dynamic, differentiated, even market-oriented system, whose crisis is explained by changing forms of property and social relations. Therefore, in England, the state supported large landlords' "enclosures" and the expulsion of peasants in the context of the Industrial Revolution, while in France feudal landownership was undermined by the resilience of small independent peasant agriculture. Other Marxist historians, like Maurice Dobb (1900–1976) and Rodney Hilton (1916–2002), more directly emphasized the role of class struggles between landlords and peasants in explaining the crisis and collapse of the feudal mode of production.

BIBLIOGRAPHY

Anderson, Perry. 1974. *Passages from Antiquity to Feudalism.* London: New Left.

Banaji, Jairus. 1976. The Peasantry in the Feudal Mode of Production: Towards an Economic Model. *Journal of Peasant Studies* 3 (3): 299–320.

Gottlieb, Roger S. 1984. Feudalism and Historical Materialism: A Critique and a Synthesis. *Science and Society* 48 (1): 1–37.

Hindess, Barry, and Paul Hirst. 1975. *Pre-capitalist Modes of Production*. London: Routledge and Kegan Paul.

Holton, Robert J. 1985. *The Transition from Feudalism to Capitalism*. New York: St. Martin's Press.

Franco Barchiesi

FEUDALISM

The term *feudalism* is used to describe a variety of social, economic, and political obligations and relationships that were prevalent in medieval Europe, especially from the eleventh through thirteenth centuries, though the feudal system existed before and well after that period in several cases. For instance, serfdom was not abolished officially in czarist Russia until 1861. *Feudalism* also has been used to describe ancient or former social and political systems in Japan, China, India, the Middle East, and North Africa. The term is controversial and has been said to be overapplied or misapplied by historians and social scientists.

Feudalism was never a single monolithic system practiced by all societies in Europe. There was a great deal of variation across societies in the practice and rites of the feudal order in nations such as France, the German states, England, Spain, and Russia. Although feudalism in Japan, India, China, and Africa had a few common elements, those systems differed significantly from the European varieties. Nonetheless, the term *feudalism* has been applied most regularly and commonly to many medieval European systems of social, economic, and political organization.

THE ORIGINS OF FEUDALISM

Feudalism emerged as a form of social, economic, and political organization after the fall of the Roman Empire between 300 and 500 CE and especially after the death of the Holy Roman emperor Charlemagne in 814. The origins of feudalism are numerous and debated but tend to be identified as an intermixture of Germanic and Roman law as well as Catholic doctrine. However, its origins were as practical as they were legal or philosophical. Repeated invasions and attacks from the north and east had made the lands of the former Roman and Holy Roman empires insecure. New patterns of governance and security were required to protect crops, animals, and persons.

The feudal system was one of hierarchy in which nobles, who were sovereign over the most valuable commodity of that time—land—ruled over peasants (serfs) who were tied permanently to the land. The system was social in that it distinguished between classes: nobility and peasantry; economic in that it divided the major means of production—land for agriculture—among the elite nobil-

ity; and political in that it created a hierarchical power structure than ran from kings and other high nobles down to middle and lower nobles and finally to peasants, who had limited or no social, economic, and political power.

THE FEUDAL CONSTITUTION

The feudal system was based on what later would be called a contract, or constitution, encompassing the obligations and allegiances that bound king to lord. The feudal contract consisted of *homagium* and investitures, in which a tenant offered his fealty and a commitment of support by paying homage to a lord and the lord would grant the tenant an investiture, or title over the land, for a specific tenure in return for payments. Thus, it was a mutual relationship: The lord extended his protective services to his new vassal and his lands, and the tenant agreed to pay dues of wealth, food, arms, and military service to the lord.

The lowest rung on the feudal ladder was occupied by the peasantry. Before the tenth and eleventh centuries most farmers held tenancy of their own land through contracts with regional lords or nobles. However, as invasion and attack became more significant and the costs of security increased, lords began making higher demands of their tenants. This forced more tenants into direct servitude as serfs: peasants tied to the land and in service to the lord for an extended and perhaps permanent period. Although slavery generally had disappeared from medieval Europe, the economy was dominated by labor-intensive agricultural production, and peasants were needed to perform those tasks.

THE RISE AND FALL OF FEUDALISM

The feudal system expanded and became the dominant form of social, economic, and political organization in Europe because of both its success in providing security and stability and its promotion by the Catholic Church. The feudal order received strong support in the church and among the clergy, who saw its social and political hierarchy as a desirable form of governance and its economic organization as one of potential profit. The sovereignty and legitimacy of kings and nobles were tied closely to the Catholic Church, which thus was able to prosper by supporting and expanding the feudal order in Europe. The ascendancy of the church to great wealth and power coincided with the expansion of feudalism.

Feudalism began to decline in parts of western Europe by the fourteenth century as a result of pressure from a number of interrelated events. The Renaissance (starting in the late fourteenth century), the Reformation (beginning in 1517), and the Industrial Revolution (beginning in the mid-1700s) led to significant philosophical, social, economic, and political transformation across western Europe. The Reformation and the Thirty

Years' War (1618–1648) challenged and upended the Catholic Church's monopoly of spiritual and political authority, and the Industrial Revolution made the feudal agricultural order an anachronism. City-states and other feudal arrangements no longer were capable of providing social, economic, and political order and security in a more individualist and industrialized western Europe. The emergence of the modern state system based on nationality and the conceptions of popular and state sovereignty replaced that of the feudal state. The French Revolution of 1789 often is cited as supplying the death blow to the remnants of the ancient feudal regime. Although feudalism all but disappeared from western Europe between the fourteenth and eighteenth centuries, it survived in eastern Europe and Russia, which were affected far less by the progressive influences of the Renaissance, the Reformation, and the Industrial Revolution.

Feudalism has remained a topic of debate and study in the social sciences. In his early works, Karl Marx (Marx and Engels 2006) argued that feudalism, as a mode of production, was a necessary condition of societies on their way to capitalism and eventually communism. Some elements of feudal thought can be found in modern Catholic political doctrine and the principles of Christian democracy in many European societies and political parties. In addition, the feudal order has had long-standing social implications for class division, hierarchy, and identity in many European societies to the present day.

Beyond Europe, feudalism has been widely used to describe systems of elite-peasant socioeconomic and political arrangements in China, India, Japan, and especially Latin America. In the latter, *latifundia* relationships between landlords and peasants established during Spanish colonization survived the independence of the Latin American states. While resembling the European model imported from Spain, the feudalism of Latin America was also characterized by racial divisions between the white Spanish elite and the Indian or mixed-race peasantry, as well as imported African slaves. This, as well as other differences, have led to these systems being described as "semi-feudal" or "proto-feudal." In conclusion, while feudalism has primarily been used in the European context, there have been numerous comparable systems in Latin America, East Asia, South Asia, and elsewhere, where the concept of feudalism may be applicable.

SEE ALSO *Agricultural Industry; French Revolution; Hierarchy; Landlords; Latifundia; Marx, Karl; Mode of Production; Monarchy; Peasantry; Roman Catholic Church; Sovereignty; Stratification*

BIBLIOGRAPHY

Laclau, Ernesto. 1977. *Politics and Ideology in Marxist Theory: Capitalism, Fascism, Populism.* London: New Left Books.

Marx, Karl, and Friedrich Engels. 2006. *The Communist Manifesto*, ed. Garth Stedman Jones. New York: Penguin. (Orig. pub. 1848.)

Stephenson, Carl. 1942. *Mediaeval Feudalism.* Ithaca, NY: Cornell University Press.

Vinogradoff, Paul. 1924. Feudalism. In *Cambridge Medieval History*, Vol. 3. Cambridge, U.K.: Cambridge University Press.

Wiarda, Howard J. 1995. *Latin American Politics.* Belmont, CA: Wadsworth.

Paul S. Adams

FICTION

Fictions include a variety of things: face-saving untruths that no one believes; devices of convenience in law; and unreal postulates such as the supposed inner planet Vulcan. This entry will address a narrower field: discourse that aims to convey a narrative of events but which is not intended by its maker to be taken as true. Fiction in this sense may appear in any medium, sometimes in language and sometimes not, and in a variety of genres. Historically the most important genres seem to have been epic poetry, the comic and tragic forms of drama, and the novel, which has shown a generally increasing but not uniform tendency to naturalism over time. These genres have been transmuted by the vast and accelerating body of fictions in filmic and televisual media since the beginning of the twentieth century. Yet it is worth noting that nothing is known of most of the history of fictional narrative, since fiction may well be as old as language, and no story older than 5,000 years has survived. It is certainly hard to believe that fiction was absent from human society 30,000 years ago, given the impressive cultural, imaginative, and symbolic achievements of that period, visible in cave paintings and carved objects. Fiction may indeed be ten times older than that.

It is important to see that this definition of fiction is consistent with fiction having any number of purposes over and above the mere telling of a story, including didactic purposes. The definition requires only that the author should not present the events of the narrative as real; he or she may well intend to convince an audience of the truth of a certain ethical or political viewpoint that the narrative serves to suggest.

The idea of fiction generates a number of philosophical problems. One takes the form of puzzlement about why people are interested in fictional stories, given that they generally understand that events have not happened and characters do not exist. The answer is probably that the attraction of fiction is testimony to human delight in the exercise of imagination and the rich emotional responses that imagining certain events generates. This issue has recently been given an evolutionary formulation: Why, given the pressing need for true information about the world, should humans ever have developed an interest in misrepresentations, which do not tell them how to feed, clothe, or house themselves? Human mental evolution seems likely to have been driven partly by social forces, making it advantageous for people to be able to understand, cooperate with, and sometimes deceive one another. Fiction may have developed as a kind of training ground on which to exercise mind-reading powers: a social assault course where live ammunition is banned. However there is little empirical evidence to support this hypothesis. Alternatively a taste for fiction might be a useless by-product of mental capacities that evolved for other purposes.

A further puzzle, and one with important practical ramifications, concerns the relation of a fiction's *world* to the world of reality. Viewers or readers generally assume that a fiction will be set within a framework of truth, and are sensitive to any indication that the author is exploiting or has misplaced the boundary between this factual background and the events and characters created. The power of socially critical fiction, such as that of English novelist Charles Dickens (1812–1870) depends on this. Readers of espionage fiction will complain about minor mistakes in the description of technology; more seriously, others respond to fictions such as British writer Salman Rushdie's (b. 1947) *Satanic Verses* (1988) with violent protest. While such responses may be deplored, the general idea that that fiction has a capacity to generate and control powerful emotional response, which may then influence behavior and belief, is not implausible. And sensitivity in this area is also testimony to the finely tuned capacity of human beings to grasp an author's unarticulated intentions: One realizes that, while the story itself is fiction, there lies behind it a possibly multilayered set of intentions to persuade and perhaps to manipulate.

The status of fictional characters, who are often spoken of in familiar and even intimate terms, is an interesting facet of the analysis of fictions. Theorists have occasionally argued that fictional characters such as Sherlock Holmes exist in some way that, mysteriously, differs from the manner of existence of normal people. A better interpretation is that while what people think and say gives the impression that they are actually referring to fictional people as real, they in fact understand these characters to be make-believe. However creators of fiction do create entities subtly different from fictional people, namely the roles filled by fictional characters. These roles may be thought of as sets of characteristics that someone would have to possess if he were, for example, Sherlock Holmes (when in fact no one is). One can accept such

statements as "Dickens created some very memorable characters" as true, but understand the reference to characters really to be a reference to roles.

The definition proposed at the beginning of this entry might be regarded by some as intolerably restrictive: There is a tendency in early-twenty-first-century thinking, influenced by postmodern ideas, to identify representations of any kind with fiction, on the grounds that representations select, and so distort, reality. In defense of the approach here taken there is a very significant difference between a story that is, and that is honestly presented as being, *made up*, and one that purports, perhaps only partially and perhaps with significant elements of misrepresentation, to relate real events. Categories such as the documentary film certainly need a nuanced approach that recognizes they are not and cannot be mere reflections of the real, but it is not appropriate to lump them into a vastly inflated category of the fictional class.

SEE ALSO *Film Industry; Literature; Lying; Narratives; Postmodernism; Realism; Reality; Representation; Science Fiction*

BIBLIOGRAPHY

Byrne, Alex. 1993. Truth in Fiction: The Story Continued. *Australasian Journal of Philosophy* 71 (1): 24–35.

Currie, Gregory. 1990. *The Nature of Fiction*. Cambridge, U.K., and New York: Cambridge University Press.

Thomasson, Amie. 1999. *Fiction and Metaphysics*. Cambridge, U.K., and New York: Cambridge University Press.

Walton, Kendall L. 1990. *Mimesis as Make-Believe*. Cambridge, MA: Harvard University Press.

Greg Currie

FICTIVE KINSHIP

SEE *Kinship.*

FIELDS' INDEX OF ECONOMIC INEQUALITY

The task of devising proper measures of income inequality is inherently controversial. Individuals have different notions about inequality and cannot always agree on an equity-based ranking of income distributions. Despite theoretical disagreement on proper measurement, applied work frequently adopts measures such as the Gini coefficient. In a series of papers, Gary Fields questioned the use of conventional inequality measures and proposed an alternative measure.

Fields was specifically interested in measuring how inequality responds to income growth in a two-sector (dual) economy where each individual earns either a "low" or "high" income. Economic growth in this context consists in individuals transitioning from the low-income sector to the high-income sector.

Fields (1993) introduced the concepts of "elitism of the rich" and "isolation of the poor." "Elitism of the rich" captures the idea that when there are few rich people in an economy, these individuals enjoy an elite position that contributes to a high level of inequality in the economy. Conversely, when there are only a few poor individuals, then "isolation of the poor" contributes significantly to disparity.

Fields contended that for most individuals some combination of these two concepts is necessary to properly measure inequality. Consider a six-person dual economy starting at a point where five people are poor and one is rich and moving to a point where four are poor and two are rich. Fields would say that in this example, elitism of the rich has declined dramatically owing to the presence of a second rich individual. Isolation of the poor has increased in this case because the remaining poor are fewer in number. In this case Fields would argue that the drop in elitism overpowers the increase in isolation, thus reducing inequality. Continuing with this progression, one finds that economic growth generates a U-shaped inequality path on Fields' measure, in sharp contrast to the Gini coefficient, which produces an inverted-U for the same scenario.

Fields' controversial analysis has prompted a number of academic responses. Paolo Figini (1998) noted that Fields's measure fails the test for Lorenz consistency (i.e., it violates commonly accepted axioms) when one allows for intrasector income inequality. Fields restricted his analysis to the special case where income is identical for each member of the high-income and low-income sectors.

John Burger (2001) provided a response to Fields' (1987) contention that there is no intuition behind the traditional inverted-U shape generated by the Gini coefficient. Using Fields' example, Burger demonstrated that as a six-person dual economy moves from incomes of (1, 1, 1, 1, 1, 4) to (1, 1, 1, 1, 4, 4), the individual income shares change from (1/9, 1/9, 1/9, 1/9, 1/9, 4/9) to (1/12, 1/12, 1/12, 1/12, 1/3, 1/3). The result is a transfer of income *share* from the four poor and one rich person to the newly wealthy second rich individual. Burger argued that the reduction in income share of several poor individuals impacts inequality more than the reduction in income share of the one wealthy individual, thus resulting in increased income inequality. Continuing with this logic,

one finds that growth of the high-income sector generates an inequality path with an inverted-U shape. Burger concludes that the Gini coefficient and the resulting inverted-U shape are consistent with intuition based on income shares.

SEE ALSO *Gini Coefficient; Lewis, W. Arthur; Lorenz Curve*

BIBLIOGRAPHY

Burger, John D. 2001. U or Inverted-U? That Is the Question. *Review of Development Economics* 5 (1): 151–156.

Fields, Gary S. 1987. Measuring Inequality Change in an Economy with Income Growth. *Journal of Development Economics* 26: 357–374.

Fields, Gary S. 1993. Inequality in Dual Economy Models. *Economic Journal* 103: 1228–1235.

Figini, Paolo. 1998. On the Properties of the Fields' Index of Inequality. *Journal of Income Distribution* 8 (1): 131–141.

John D. Burger

FIELDWORK
SEE *Ethnography.*

FILIBUSTER

Filibustering is behavior intended to delay the legislative process for strategic gain. In modern politics, filibustering is most likely to occur in the U.S. Senate because senators may speak for as long as they wish. As a result, senators have made speeches lasting several hours in order to slow the progress of bills they oppose. The longest single speech in Senate history is Strom Thurmond's speech against the Civil Rights Act of 1957. Thurmond spoke for twenty-four hours and eighteen minutes.

Filibustering is not limited to long speeches, however, nor does it occur only in the U.S. Senate. Legislators also filibuster by making procedural motions to force unnecessary votes. Another popular tactic, known as a "disappearing quorum," occurs when legislators refuse to vote on a bill in the hope that less than a quorum (i.e. the minimum number of legislators who must participate for a legislature to make a decision) of legislators will participate in the vote. During the nineteenth century, members of the U.S. House filibustered often and enthusiastically, a tradition that was suppressed by drastic precedents and rule changes in the 1890s. In 2003 Democrats in the Texas legislature left the state to avoid participating in a vote on altering congressional district boundaries. Since the Texas

Constitution requires two-thirds of each chamber to constitute a quorum, the Texas Democrats were able to stall the redistricting plan for months. Finally, filibustering occurs in non-U.S. legislatures as well. For example, filibustering has occurred in Taiwan's Legislative Yuan during the final days of legislative sessions.

The Senate adopted a "cloture" rule to limit filibustering in 1917. Initially, the rule required a two-thirds majority to limit debate, and if cloture was approved each senator was limited to one additional hour of speaking. After several modifications between 1949 and 1986, the current version of the cloture rule allows a three-fifths majority to limit debate to a total of thirty hours for most issues, with a two-thirds majority necessary for rules changes. Additionally, senators have adopted rules and passed laws exempting a number of key issues, such as trade agreements and key budget legislation, from filibustering.

Despite these limits, filibustering has become increasingly common in the Senate. In the early twentieth century, filibusters were rare and typically occurred at the end of a legislative session. In addition, they were generally directed at budgetary or economic legislation. From the 1930s to the 1960s, filibusters were often used against civil rights legislation, but otherwise they were rare. But since about 1970, filibusters have become commonplace in the Senate. This change coincided with a tactical shift in Senate filibustering. While senators had historically been forced to physically occupy the chamber floor during a filibuster—as depicted in the 1939 film *Mr. Smith Goes to Washington*—during the 1960s and 1970s filibustering became less overt. Instead, senators typically *threaten* to filibuster as a strategic ploy, without ever actively filibustering on the Senate floor. Rather than waste the time of the chamber, Senate leaders typically avoid overt filibusters by compromising over the content of legislation and the terms of debate.

More recently, senators have disputed whether it is appropriate to filibuster judicial appointments. During President George W. Bush's first term, ten out of forty-four nominations for the federal appeals courts were blocked by Democratic senators. Senate Republicans responded by threatening to use the "constitutional" or "nuclear" option of revising Senate precedents to allow majority cloture on judicial nominations. This controversy was defused by a bipartisan agreement in May 2005 to only allow filibusters against judicial nominations in "extreme circumstances." The seven Republicans and seven Democrats who negotiated this agreement, who tended to be moderates within their party, were known as the "Gang of 14."

SEE ALSO *Congress, U.S.; Thurmond, Strom*

BIBLIOGRAPHY

Binder, Sarah A., and Steven S. Smith. 1997. *Politics or Principle? Filibustering in the U.S. Senate.* Washington, DC: Brookings Institution.

Burdette, Franklin L. 1940. *Filibustering in the Senate.* Princeton, NJ: Princeton University Press.

Dion, Douglas. 1997. *Turning the Legislative Thumbscrew: Minority Rights and Procedural Change in Legislative Politics.* Ann Arbor: University of Michigan Press.

Krehbiel, Keith. 1998. *Pivotal Politics: A Theory of U.S. Lawmaking.* Chicago: University of Chicago Press.

Gregory Koger

FILM INDUSTRY

Since the last years of the nineteenth century, filmmaking, distribution, and exhibition have been a major cultural activity around the world. The usual disciplines associated with the social sciences—including political science, geography, history, law, psychiatry, psychology, and sociology—have been used to study the influence of the film industry. But at its core, any film industry consists of economic institutions that seek to maximize profits. These corporations produce the first copy of a film, make copies in various forms for distribution, and then rent (as in theaters) or sell copies (as in home videos). There is a small film community independent of Hollywood in the United States, as well as large and small industries in nations around the world.

Yet, since the early 1920s Hollywood has dominated the world's film industry. In 1915 Adolph Zukor combined his production company (Famous Players Lasky) with Paramount distribution, and after World War II he began to acquire a chain of theaters, mostly in major U.S. cities, some outside the United States. Adroit competitors quickly followed: Loew's/MGM, Fox, Warner Bros., and the Radio-Keith-Orpheum (RKO). All owned production, worldwide distribution, and vast chains of theaters. The so-called Big Five permitted minor companies to survive, hoping the U.S. government would not sue them for antitrust violations, but in May 1948 the U.S. Supreme Court forced the production-distribution divisions to sell theater divisions.

From 1965 to 1975, led by agent-turned-mogul Lew Wassermann, the Hollywood industrial system reinvented itself as a series of media conglomerates. Today television production provides a steady base of revenues, and the cinema blockbuster—the first being Wasserman's *Jaws* in 1975—can pay off in billions. Other media business divisions synergize—meaning they cross-promote films with other products—as with Disney's theme parks. Although film revenues from cinema attendance plunged, Hollywood companies prospered by selling videos in the 1980s and DVDs since the late 1990s. By 2000, theatrical revenues in the United States had fallen to an average of only 15 percent of the profits of an average Hollywood film; the bulk came from revenues associated with watching films on TV (including VHS, DVD, via cable, satellite, and broadcast).

The Hollywood industry still dominates world film revenues while making fewer films than India or Hong Kong. The Hollywood firms of Disney, Fox, Paramount, Sony, Universal, and Warner Bros. represent an exceptional oligopoly; although these six corporations are competitors, they also cooperate on many things, including issuing ratings to inform viewers on the appropriateness of film content for children and keeping open international distribution by working closely with the U.S. Department of State. Indeed, the agency they have fashioned for cooperation—the Motion Picture Association of America—ranks as one of the top lobbyists in Washington, D.C.

By the late twentieth century, although still called a film industry, Hollywood knew it was in the television business. In the United States each of the major studios (except Sony) is allied with a major television network: Disney-ABC, News Corporation's Fox TV network, Viacom's [Paramount] CBS, Warner's CW, and General Electric's Universal-NBC. They thus make television stories and series for their networks on the same lots where they make feature films. Indeed, some films, called "made-for-TV films," premiere on television.

The "Hollywood" film industry has spanned the globe since the 1920s. Only Paramount has a Hollywood address, and it and its rivals distribute their films over the entire world, so although India and Hong Kong produce more movies, more Hollywood films are seen in more places than is any typical film from Asia. Indeed, all developed nations have film industries of their own, but all are limited in their globalization.

In addition, although Hollywood is the center of in-studio production and the final creative steps in film production, feature films are regularly shot away from Hollywood, on location. All states in the United States and most nations around the world are willing to subsidize production in their territories. For example, many Hollywood movies are filmed in Canada, which has fought to draw film production north of the United States. More often than not, a film set in New York City is really shot in Toronto or Vancouver, where it is cheaper to make. And although films are typically finally cut in studios in and around Los Angeles, the final decisions about which films will be made, which will be distributed, and in what forms they will be seen are made inside offices located in and around New York City.

Hollywood is also the most unionized industry in the United States today, because with a six-member oligopoly, unions face a common foe. Their members—from directors to the men and women who push sets and equipment—all are represented by guilds, or unions. Regularly, Hollywood's six members sign a basic agreement with each union, and occasionally a guild will go on strike. This most often happens with the Writer's Guild of America. These Hollywood-based unions are growing, bucking a trend of falling union membership in the United States.

Hollywood certainly has the most far reaching and profitable film industry in the world, but two other centers need to be singled out. India's film industry is mostly concentrated in Mumbai (formerly Bombay), and is commonly referred to as "Bollywood," an amalgamation of *Bombay* and *Hollywood*. The Indian film industry is multilingual and the largest in the world, producing more than 1,000 films per year as compared to Hollywood's 200. The industry is supported mainly by a vast film-going Indian public (the largest in the world in terms of annual ticket sales), and Indian films have been gaining increasing popularity in the rest of the world—particularly in countries with large numbers of expatriate Indians.

Hong Kong is a filmmaking hub for the Chinese-speaking world (including the worldwide diaspora) and East Asia in general. For decades it was the third-largest motion picture industry in the world (after India and Hollywood) and the second-largest exporter (after Hollywood), principally with kung-fu action films dubbed into English and other languages. Despite an industry crisis starting in the mid-1990s, and Hong Kong's return to Chinese sovereignty in July 1997, Hong Kong film has retained much of its distinctive identity and continues to play a prominent part on the world cinema stage. Unlike many other film industries, Hong Kong has enjoyed little to no direct government support, through either subsidies or import quotas. It has always been a thoroughly commercial cinema, concentrating on crowd-pleasing genres such as comedy and action, and heavily reliant on formulas, sequels, and remakes. As is typical of commercial cinemas, its heart is a highly developed star system, which in this case also features substantial overlap with the pop music industry.

The dominance of the industries in Hollywood, Bollywood, and Hong Kong has made it hard for the film industry to include independent filmmaking and documentaries. Yet these genres—truly independent filmmaking and filmed documentaries—turned to video in the late twentieth century; they were not shot on film, but on Beta video, then were premiered on TV networks, both privately owned and state-owned. Indeed, in most small nations of the world the few films made are subsidized by the government, and more and more often shot on video to lower costs. This is where the TV industry meets the film industry.

The much-anticipated coming of high-definition television (HDTV) at the beginning of the twenty-first century seemed to signal the end of the film industry. Yet, as HDTV standards develop, so does the quality of film. Thus, film remains easily the highest resolution of all "movie making." HDTV may "look like film," but engineers agree that the film image offers more information than any as yet developed or standardized high-definition image. As the twenty-first century began, if one wanted to see the highest definition, one still should attend a well-run cinema.

SEE ALSO Bamboozled; Birth of a Nation; *Entertainment Industry;* Gone with the Wind; Stepford Wives; Wizard of Oz

BIBLIOGRAPHY

Bordwell, David. 2000. *Planet Hong Kong.* Cambridge, MA: Harvard University Press.

Ganti, Tejaswini. 2004. *Bollywood.* New York: Routledge.

Gomery, Douglas. 1992. *Shared Pleasures: A History of Movie Presentation.* Madison: University of Wisconsin Press.

Gomery, Douglas. 2006. *The Hollywood Studio System: A History.* Berkeley: University of California Press.

Jackel, Anne. 2004. *European Film Industries.* London: British Film Industry.

Variety Web site. http://www.variety.com.

Douglas Gomery

FILTER THEORY
SEE *Marriage.*

FINAL SOLUTION
SEE *Holocaust, The.*

FINANCE

Finance refers to the study of the management of the assets of firms and households over time, given the calculated risks and expected returns. Also known as *financial economics*, it is one of the more recent fields in economics, with most of the key papers published after the middle of the twentieth century. The field of finance primarily includes: *portfolio theory*, which deals with how to achieve the maximum investment return for a given level of risk by diversifying between a risk-free asset and a portfolio of risky assets; *asset pricing*, which deals with the pricing of risky assets; and *corporate finance*, which explains corporate financial and investment decisions.

Modern finance started with the publication in 1952 of an article by Harry Markowitz (a 1990 Nobel laureate in economics) on portfolio selection. Markowitz introduced the notion of the mean-variance efficient portfolio, defined as the portfolio that provides either minimum variance for a given expected return, or maximum expected return for a given variance. Assuming a risk-averse investor, Markowitz proved that any other portfolio would not be optimal.

The next key contribution came more than a decade later in the area of asset pricing by William Sharpe (1964), John Lintner (1965), and Jan Mossin (1966) with the capital asset pricing model (CAPM). The model provides an equilibrium relationship between the risk of an asset and its expected return above the return of the risk-free asset. According to this relationship, the expected return of a risky asset in excess of the return of a risk-free asset, the so-called risk premium, is proportional to the risk premium of a portfolio holding the whole market and the extent to which the risky asset and the market move together, which is called the beta coefficient. The model implies that any other specific risk (nonmarket risk) can be diversified away and therefore does dot justify any risk premium. A decade later, Stephen Ross's (1976) arbitrage pricing theory (APT) proved that a similar relationship holds when one assumes no arbitrage opportunities (an arbitrage opportunity exists when a zero investment portfolio can yield a positive profit with certainty). The APT is less restrictive than the CAPM, since it only needs a few investors taking advantage of any existing arbitrage opportunities, eventually eliminating mispriced securities, while the CAPM assumes that all investors are mean-variance optimizers. Furthermore, the APT extends the CAPM by including other factors in addition to the market (multifactor models), such as macroeconomic variables.

Modern corporate finance theory, which studies a firm's financing decisions and its evaluation of investment projects based on expected returns, has been primarily built on two theorems: the Modigliani-Miller theorem of capital structure (1958) and the Modigliani-Miller dividend policy theorem (1961), which are also known as the MM theorems. The first theorem states that the financing decision of a firm between debt and equity does not affect its value, while the second states that the dividend policy of a firm also does affect its value. The MM theorems gave their two authors the Nobel Prize in Economics (in 1985 for Franco Modigliani and in 1990 for Merton Miller) and led to a huge literature to explain why the theorems may not hold. The practice of corporate finance is much broader. A typical corporate finance department in an investment bank deals primarily with initial public offerings (IPOs) and other underwriting services, as well as mergers and acquisitions.

The main financial assets include stocks (also called equity or shares) and fixed-income securities (also called bonds). Stocks are securities issued by private-owned firms to raise capital and are traded in the capital (or stock) markets (or exchanges). The investor's return is determined by the dividend paid by the issuing firm and the change in the stock price (capital gain or loss). The equity holders of the company are its residual claimants, meaning that in the case that the company goes bankrupt, their compensation equals whatever is left (if anything) after all debt holders have been paid. Fixed-income securities are issued either by private or state-owned firms or by governments (central and local) to raise debt and are claims on a stream of income over a predetermined period. Their interest rate (also called the coupon rate) determines the stream of income during the life of the bond, in addition to the payment of the face value at maturity. Although the investor's return is certain if the bond is held to maturity, and assuming the company does not go bankrupt, the return is uncertain if the investor decides to sell the bond before maturity, since the price of the bond fluctuates as the bond is traded in the market.

Since the mid-1970s, the study of more "exotic" financial instruments has gained popularity, and the trading of derivative securities has spread widely in the capital markets. Derivative securities (or contingent claims, or simply derivatives) are securities whose value depends on other securities. They include options, forward contracts, futures, swaps, and many other securities that give the right to its holder to buy, sell, or exchange the underlined security or securities under prespecified conditions. A call (put) option provides the option to its holder to buy (sell) a security by a prespecified date, at a prespecified price, called the exercise or strike price—the call (put) option will be exercised only if the market price is higher (lower) that the exercise price. A forward contract is an agreement to buy or sell a security at a prespecified date, at a prespecified price. A future contract is a forward contract that is traded in the market. In contrast to options, forward and future contracts are always exercised. Swaps are agreements to exchange cash flows during a prespecified period and based on a predetermined formula. The popularity of derivative securities increased rapidly in the years that followed the publication of the Black and Scholes option pricing formula (Black and Scholes 1973; Merton 1973), which gave Myron Scholes and Robert Merton the 1997 Nobel Prize in Economics—Fischer Black died two years before the award. The beauty of the formula is that it includes only known variables, as it depends on the

volatility of the price of the underlined stock rather than its expected return.

The main function of derivative securities is risk insurance (hedging), although derivatives are also used for speculation. To use some examples, a put option insures a stockholder from a fall in the stock price below the exercise price, a forward contract provides a fixed payment to a farmer for his or her future production regardless of weather conditions, and a swap agreement allows a firm to exchange a floating stream of revenue with a fixed stream in order to pay its fixed obligations. On the other hand, derivatives allow speculators to take large bets with relatively small initial capital, since instead of paying for the whole price of the underlined security they only have to pay the much lower price of the derivative. Speculators can take very large exposures using derivatives that can lead to huge gains or losses. Recent examples of such speculation going bad include the collapse of Britain's Barings Bank in 1995 from speculation from a single trader in its Singapore office, and the collapse of the U.S. hedge fund Long-Term Capital Management, which after an annual return of more than 40 percent in the 1994–1997 period, lost $4.6 billion in just four months in 1998 and had to be rescued by a package from leading U.S. investment and commercial banks orchestrated by the Federal Reserve (ironically, Scholes and Merton were on the board of the fund).

The trading of the financial instruments takes place in financial markets, while the financial transactions are performed by financial institutions and investors. The financial markets include the money market (trading of very short-term debt securities), the bond market, the stock market, and various derivative markets. A stock is first sold in a stock market through an IPO and is then traded in secondary markets. Some stocks are traded in informal exchanges, called over-the-counter markets (or OTC). The financial institutions can be separated into banks and nonbanks, although this distinction is not always clear and today's large and often multinational, or even global, financial conglomerates offer the whole range of financial services. The first includes primarily commercial banks, savings institutions, and credit unions, while the second includes investment banks, insurance companies, leasing companies, and investment funds.

Finance is linked with other fields in economics and is increasingly relevant for economic policy. Macroeconomists study finance to understand how capital markets affect the impact of economic policies on the economy. Effective monetary policy requires the knowledge of its potential impact on capital markets but also on the way capital markets allow the transmission of monetary policy itself. International economics includes the study of international finance (also called open-economy macroeconomics), which studies, among other issues, the interaction of international capital markets and the movement of capital across borders. The field of finance also uses concepts and tools from other fields to extend its understanding of capital markets and investment decisions. It uses microeconomic theory to explain the decisions of rational investors based on utility maximization, econometrics to study the behavior (trends and patterns) of financial variables, and mathematics to model the behavior of financial markets and of investors and to price financial assets.

It should be emphasized that finance is not what most noneconomists believe it is, which is the study of "how to make money." In such a case, all financial economists, quite smart people indeed, would have been rich. If anything, the field argues that markets are efficient and that one cannot consistently outperform the market—those who sometimes do are just lucky. There is a huge literature attempting to find evidence against the so-called efficient market hypothesis (EMH). Although some studies have discovered some patterns against the hypothesis, either there is no money to make once transaction costs are taken into account or the patterns disappear soon after being discovered as investors take advantage of them. The EMH suggests that in order to outperform the market one would need to have superior information from the other investors, which is impossible, except in the case of inside information. However, trading based on inside information, although not rare, is illegal in most countries.

The ongoing globalization process and the tremendous advances in information technology in recent decades are having a profound impact on the field of finance. Investors diversify by choosing from investment opportunities provided by a global market, firms can issue stocks at stock markets abroad, governments can sell their bonds to foreign investors, and speculators can bet against more or less any foreign currency they choose. The large size of international capital movements allows emerging markets to finance their development using foreign capital. However, when the investors' appetite for risk changes, either because of bad economic policies in the recipient countries or due to negative spillover effects from policies or shocks in other countries, the result can be a serious economic slowdown, or even a banking and a broader financial crisis, as shown by the crises in Mexico (1994), East Asia (1997–1998), Russia (1998), and Argentina (2001).

Optimists argue that the best is yet to come in the field of finance. Their belief is based on the argument that the use of advanced financial instruments and information technology has just started. Robert Shiller (2003) proposes a new financial order in which it will be possible to insure against more or less any nonfinancial risk.

Individuals will be able to insure against their uncertain income from the profession of their choice or against unexpected negative shocks to their economic well-being, countries will be able to sell debt with a repayment plan that depends on their economic growth, and different generations will be able to share the cost of social security. According to pure financial theory, one should be able to sell any kind of risk to someone willing to buy it for the right price and diversify it away. Indeed, this is increasingly seen in today's global financial markets.

SEE ALSO *Corporations; Equity Markets; Financial Instability Hypothesis; Financial Markets; Investment; Merton, Robert K.; Modigliani, Franco; Modigliani-Miller Theorem; Shocks; Stock Exchanges*

BIBLIOGRAPHY

Black, Fischer, and Myron Scholes. 1973. The Pricing of Options and Corporate Liabilities. *Journal of Political Economy* 81: 637–654.

Lintner, John. 1965. The Valuation of Risk Assets and the Selection of Risky Investments in Stock Portfolios and Capital Budgets. *Review of Economics and Statistics* 47: 13–37.

Markowitz, Harry M. 1952. Portfolio Selection. *Journal of Finance* 7 (1): 77–91.

Merton, Robert C. 1973. Theory of Rational Option Pricing. *Bell Journal of Economics and Management Science* 4: 141–183.

Miller, Merton H., and Franco Modigliani, 1961. Dividend Policy, Growth, and the Valuation of Shares. *Journal of Business* 34 (4): 411–433.

Modigliani, Franco, and Merton H. Miller. 1958. The Cost of Capital, Corporation Investment, and the Theory of Investment. *American Economic Review* 48: 261–297.

Mossin, Jan. 1966. Equilibrium in a Capital Asset Market. *Econometrica* 34: 768–783.

Ross, Stephen A. 1976. Return, Risk, and Arbitrage. In *Risk and Return in Finance*, ed. Irwin Friend and James Bicksler. Cambridge, MA: Ballinger.

Sharpe, William. 1964. Capital Asset Prices: A Theory of Market Equilibrium. *Journal of Finance* 19 (3): 425–442.

Shiller, Robert J. 2003. *The New Financial Order: Risk In the 21st Century*. Princeton, NJ: Princeton University Press.

Athanasios Vamvakidis

FINANCE, PUBLIC

Public finance is the study of the economic activities of governments. These activities are expressed mostly through budgets, so it is the taxes and expenditures that comprise those budgets that are the primary objects of fiscal theorizing. It should also be noted, however, that nearly anything that can be accomplished through a budget can also be accomplished through regulation. For instance, a government could simply require parents to send their children to approved schools; this would bypass the budget without eliminating government-directed schooling. Recognition that regulations can substitute for budgets calls into question the common use of budgetary magnitudes to measure the size of government within an economy.

TWO APPROACHES TO PUBLIC FINANCE

The history of fiscal scholarship reveals two distinct approaches to public finance, as set forth in chapter 1 of Richard Wagner's *Fiscal Sociology and the Theory of Public Finance* (2007). These contrasting approaches can be described as "systems design" and "social theorizing." In the second half of the twentieth century the most prominent expositors of these distinct approaches were Richard Musgrave and James Buchanan. Musgrave's *Theory of Public Finance* (1959) represents the modern-classic statement of public finance as an exercise in systems design. Buchanan's *Public Finance in Democratic Process* (1967) presents public finance as an element of social theorizing, and it set forth an orientation that subsequently blossomed into the field of study now known as public choice.

Systems design and social theorizing represent distinct orientations toward their subject matter. These orientations are not incompatible, but they do pose different analytical questions. The systems design orientation treats public finance as a practical discipline in the service of statecraft: The purpose of public finance is to supply guidance for the conduct of statecraft. Following Musgrave (1959), governments would act to correct market failures by providing public goods that would otherwise not be supplied through ordinary market transactions.

In contrast, public finance approached as an element of social theorizing seeks to provide understanding about the actual conduct of government within society. Following Buchanan (1967), governments are arenas of human interaction and are populated by the same types of people with the same types of interests and concerns as populate other arenas in society. If we start from the universal principle that people seek to replace circumstances they value less highly with circumstances they value more highly, public finance as social theorizing seeks to explore how this principle plays out within governments. Governments and markets are both treated as complex processes of human interaction, and the primary analytical challenge for this approach to public finance is to develop better understanding of the actual conduct of statecraft, as distinct from seeking to participate in statecraft.

ILLUSTRATING THE TWO APPROACHES

The systems design approach to public finance dichotomizes the world of goods into private goods and public goods, and assigns public goods to the domain of public finance. The central analytical question revolves around efficiency in the allocation of resources between public and private goods. It is commonly presumed that market arrangements operate well to organize the supply of private goods, but not of public goods. State action is thus conceptualized as providing what market-based organization cannot provide.

In contrast, the social theory orientation starts from recognition that the theoretical distinction between public and private goods does not provide a good frame of reference for understanding the world of practice. A person cannot take the theoretical distinction between public and private goods and apply it directly to the world of experience: Many public goods are provided through markets and governments provide many private goods. For instance, governments provide security services, but security is also organized through markets; educational services and recreational services are provided by governments as well as through markets; governments sometimes regulate product quality, but market arrangements likewise regulate product quality. This will be the same nearly everywhere one wanders throughout the world of goods.

For the social theory approach to public finance, the analytical focal point is the organization of human activity, not some notion of optimal resource allocation. After all, resources cannot allocate themselves. Only people can do this, and they do so within various societal configurations. The social theory approach seeks to locate fiscal activity as occurring on the same plane as market activity: Both types of activity reflect the same underlying economic principles of preference and cost, and fiscal theorizing seeks to explore how those simple principles generate complex patterns of societal organization through interactions among the members of society.

Vincent Ostrom's *The Intellectual Crisis in American Public Administration* (1973) is a splendid and seminal treatment of the distinction between the two approaches. Public finance has a presence throughout the world of goods, but in no case do state and market represent distinct domains of human activity. The domains are tightly intertwined, and in both complementary and competitive manners. If we ask whether water, airports, or anything else are better supplied by governments or through market-based commerce, we are asking a question that has little to do with understanding how societal processes actually operate.

Governments are typically involved at numerous places in the provision of water, airports, and numerous other activities. But so are market-based businesses. A reservoir might be owned by a city, whereas the facilities testing and purifying water are provided by market-based vendors. The city might send you a monthly bill for water, but the meter was produced by a market-based company, as was the paper on which the bill was printed.

The analytical challenge for a social theoretic approach to public finance, as illustrated by Wagner (2007), is to explain the emergence and evolution of observed patterns of social organization, recognizing that those patterns entail a mix of fiscal and market activity. The fiscal and the market denote two intertwined realms of organized activity within society, and both stem from the same source: the varied desires of the inhabitants of a society, as these are mediated through the various institutionalized relationships and modes of conduct that characterize that society.

SEE ALSO *Government; Policy, Fiscal; Taxes*

BIBLIOGRAPHY

Buchanan, James M. 1967. *Public Finance in Democratic Process.* Chapel Hill: University of North Carolina Press.

Musgrave, Richard A. 1959. *The Theory of Public Finance.* New York: McGraw-Hill.

Ostrom, Vincent. 1973. *The Intellectual Crisis in American Public Administration.* Tuscaloosa: University of Alabama Press.

Wagner, Richard E. 2007. *Fiscal Sociology and the Theory of Public Finance.* Cheltenham, U.K.: Edward Elgar.

Richard E. Wagner

FINANCIAL CRISES

SEE *Economic Crises.*

FINANCIAL INSTABILITY HYPOTHESIS

The American economist Hyman P. Minsky (1919–1996) set the realist criteria that, for a macroeconomic theory to be taken seriously, it had to make a depression "one of the possible states in which our type of capitalist economy can find itself" (1982, p. 5), and also explain why no such event had happened since the 1930s. Neoclassical theories failed that test, and Minsky devised the *financial instability hypothesis* (FIH) as an alternative. The hypothesis was based on an interpretation of chapter 12 of John Maynard Keynes's (1883–1946) *General Theory of Employment, Interest, and Money* (1936).

The FIH sees finance as both essential to the market economy and the source of debt-financed boom-bust cycles. This cyclical process has a secular consequence, as money borrowed during booms generates repayment obligations that have to be fulfilled during slumps. As a result, debt levels ratchet up over a sequence of cycles, culminating in a debt-deflation. This regularity of the nineteenth century has not occurred since the Great Depression of the 1930s because of the development of "big government" and Federal Reserve intervention.

Unlike most economic models, the FIH is grounded in historical time, with an uncertain future. It commences with the economy having just stabilized after a previous debt-induced crisis, and with investors and lenders that are consequently conservative in project valuation. As a result, given the stable economic conditions, most projects succeed. This surprises investors and financiers alike, leading both to revise their expectations upward. Stable economic times thus cause rising expectations—"stability is destabilizing," in one of Minsky's most apt aphorisms—and these expectations are shared. Information asymmetry, a popular neoclassical explanation for credit problems, is of little importance.

Rising expectations increase investment, the finance for which is forthcoming from equally optimistic banks, so that growing investment and endogenously expanding credit push the economy into a boom. Asset prices rise, causing them to diverge significantly from commodity prices. Expectations eventually become *euphoric*, setting the scene for the boom to unravel as the shift in expectations changes the economy's investment profile.

A *hedge* climate, where investments are expected to meet all repayment obligations out of cash flow, gives way to a *speculative* one, where principal must be rolled over. Ultimately, *Ponzi* finance becomes prominent: investments that can only succeed if the assets can be sold on a rising market.

The economy's fragility thus rises, and even a small knock can bring it down. Expectations collapse, investment ceases, endogenous credit creation ends, and the economy enters a slump. What happens next depends on the institutional structure of the economy. In a pure market economy with a high debt to output level or commodity price deflation, the economy will enter a depression. In a modern mixed economy, cash flow from countercyclical government spending enables firms to repay debts during a slump, while Reserve Bank lender-of-last-resort actions prevent runs on financial institutions. The cycle continues, and a prolonged slump is avoided.

Minsky's theory so suits the U.S. economic record that it sounds like a description, rather than a theory.

However, a theory it is, amenable to mathematical expression in differential equation models, and consonant with empirical findings on the U.S. trade cycle.

SEE ALSO *Business Cycles, Political; Business Cycles, Real; Business Cycles, Theories; Depression, Economic; Economic Crises; Economics, Neoclassical; Expectations; Long Waves; Lucas Critique; Panics; Ponzi Scheme; Recession; Say's Law; Shocks*

BIBLIOGRAPHY

Bellofiore, Riccardo, and Piero Ferri, eds. 2001. *Financial Keynesianism and Market Instability: The Economic Legacy of Hyman Minsky.* Vols. 1 and 2. Aldershot, U.K.: Edward Elgar.

Keen, Steve. 1995. Finance and Economic Breakdown: Modeling Minsky's Financial Instability Hypothesis. *Journal of Post Keynesian Economics* 17 (4): 607–635.

Minsky, Hyman P. 1982. *Can "It" Happen Again? Essays on Instability and Finance.* Armonk, NY: Sharpe.

Stephen Keen

FINANCIAL MARKETS

Financial markets are markets where financial transactions are conducted. Financial transactions generally refer to creation or transfer of financial assets, also known as financial instruments or securities. Financial transactions channel funds from investors who have an excess of available funds to issuers or borrowers who must borrow funds to finance their spending.

Since the early 1970s, financial markets in various countries have experienced significant development. As a result, world financial markets are larger, are highly integrated, and have a wide range of financial instruments available for investing and financing.

THE STRUCTURE OF FINANCIAL MARKETS

Financial markets comprise five key components: the debt market, the equity market, the foreign-exchange market, the mortgage market, and the derivative market. From the 1980s, each component market has been expanding in size, and an extensive array of new financial instruments have been initiated, especially in the mortgage market and the derivative market.

Debt instruments are traded in the debt market, also often referred to as the bond market. The debt market is important to economic activities because it provides an important channel for corporations and governments to finance their operations. Interactions between investors

and borrowers in the bond market determine interest rates. The size of the world bond market was estimated at around $37 trillion at the start of 2002 (all currency figures are in U.S. dollars). Bonds denominated in dollars currently represent roughly half the value of all outstanding bonds in the world.

Equity instruments are traded in the equity market, also known as the stock market. The stock market is the most widely followed financial market in the United States. It is important because fluctuations in stock prices effect investors' wealth and hence their saving and consumption behavior, as well as the amount of funds that can be raised by selling newly issued stocks to finance investment spending. The size of world developed equity markets expanded from $892 billion in 1974 to $25,276 billion at the end of 2001, with the U.S. market accounting for 57 percent of the world developed equity market in 2001.

Foreign-exchange markets are where currencies are converted so that funds can be moved from one country to another. Activities in the foreign-exchange market determine the foreign-exchange rate, the price of one currency in terms of another. The volume of foreign-exchange transactions worldwide averages over $1 trillion daily.

A mortgage is a long-term loan secured by a pledge of real estate. Mortgage-backed securities (also called securitized mortgages) are securities issued to sell mortgages directly to investors. The securities are secured by a large number of mortgages packaged into a mortgage pool. The most common type of mortgage-backed security is a mortgage pass-through, a security that promises to distribute to investors the cash flows from mortgage payments made by borrowers in the underlying mortgage pool. A 1980s innovation in the mortgage-backed security market has been the collateralized-mortgage obligation (CMO), a security created by redistributing the cash flows of the underlying mortgage pool into different bond classes. Mortgage-backed securities have been a very important development in financial markets in the 1980s and 1990s. The value of mortgage principal held in mortgage pools increased from $350 billion in 1984 to nearly $2,500 billion in 1999.

Financial derivatives are contracts that derive their values from the underlying financial assets. Derivative instruments include options contracts, futures contracts, forward contracts, swap agreements, and cap and floor agreements. These instruments allow market players to achieve financial goals and manage financial risks more efficiently. Since the introduction of financial derivatives in the 1970s, markets for them have been developing rapidly. In 2001 global exchange-traded futures and options contract volume reached 4.28 billion contracts, and the top three types of contracts—equity indices, interest rates, and individual equities—are all financial derivatives. Together they accounted for 88.7 percent of total contract volume.

CLASSIFICATION OF FINANCIAL MARKETS

Financial markets can be categorized in different several ways, revealing features of various market segments. One popular way to classify financial markets is by the maturity of the financial assets traded. The money market is a financial market in which only short-term debt instruments (original maturity of less than one year) are traded. The capital market is a market in which longer-term debt (original maturity of one year or greater) and equity instruments are traded. In general, money-market securities are more widely traded and tend to be more liquid.

Another way to classify financial markets is by whether the financial instruments are newly issued. A primary market is a financial market in which a borrower issues new securities in exchange for cash from investors. Once securities are sold by the original purchasers, they may be traded in the secondary market. Secondary markets can be organized in two ways. One is as an organized exchange, which brings buyers and sellers of securities together (via their representatives) in one central location to conduct trades. The other is as an over-the-counter (OTC) market, in which over-the-counter dealers located at different sites but connected with each other through computer networks undertake transactions to buy and sell securities "over the counter." Many common stocks are traded over the counter, although shares of the largest corporations are traded at organized stock exchanges, such as the New York Stock Exchange.

THE ROLE OF FINANCIAL MARKETS

By channeling funds from investors to issuers and borrowers, financial markets enhance production and allocation efficiencies in the overall economy. Financial markets also perform the important function of price discovery. The activities of buyers and sellers in a financial market determine the prices of the traded assets, which provide guidance on how funds in the economy should be allocated among financial assets.

Additionally, financial markets provide a mechanism for managing risks. Various financial assets traded in financial markets provide different payment patterns, and this redistributes and reallocates the risk associated with the future cash flows among issuers and investors.

Financial markets also offer liquidity by providing a mechanism for investors to sell or purchase financial assets. The presence of organized financial markets reduces the search and information costs of transactions, such as the money spent to advertise the desire to sell or purchase a financial asset. In an efficient market, the market price reflects the aggregate input of all market participants (Fabozzi and Modigliani 2003).

THE INTERNATIONALIZATION OF FINANCIAL MARKETS

The internationalization of financial markets has become an important trend. The significant growth of foreign financial markets has been driven mainly by deregulation of markets in financial centers worldwide and technological advances enabling more efficient communication, as well as market monitoring and analysis.

The internationalization of financial markets has also been prompted by numerous studies on the benefits of diversification that includes international stocks. Specifically, including securities from different countries in a portfolio may lower the portfolio's risk without reducing its expected return. The benefits of diversification arise from the fact that asset prices across international financial markets are not highly correlated.

The nature and extent of the internationalization of financial markets are well reflected by developments in international bond markets and world stock markets. Eurobonds are long-term debt securities sold outside the borrower's country to raise long-term capital in a currency other than that of the country where they are sold. Eurobonds are relatively new instruments in the international bond market, yet the volume of new issues of Eurobonds grew nearly four times from $167 billion in 1990 to $642 billion in 2001, and the market capitalization of Eurobonds stood at $7 trillion at the start of 2002. As for stock markets, while the U.S. stock market remains the largest in the world, foreign stock markets are becoming increasingly important. Japan and the United Kingdom have the largest markets outside of the United States. As of the end of 2001, the size of Japanese market was $2,528 billion, and that of British market was $2,275 billion. Stock markets in many developing economies, also known as emerging markets, picked up their pace of development in the 1980s. In 2001 the combined market value of emerging markets was around $2,400 billion, accounting for 8.7 percent of total world market capitalization that year.

Because financial markets are internationalized, issuers and investors in any country need not be limited to their domestic financial markets. The internationalization of financial markets is having a profound effect by leading the way to a more integrated world economy in which flows of goods and technology between countries are more commonplace (Mishkin and Eakins 2000).

SEE ALSO *Capital; Equity Markets; Hedging; Liquidity Premium*

BIBLIOGRAPHY

Chance, Don M., 2003. *Analysis of Derivatives for the CFA Program.* Charlottesville, VA: Association for Investment Management and Research.

Fabozzi, Frank, and Franco Modigliani. 2003. *Capital Markets: Institutions and Instruments.* Upper Saddle River, NJ: Prentice Hall.

Mishkin, Frederic S., and Stanley G. Eakins. 2000. *Financial Markets and Institutions.* Boston: Addison Wesley Longman.

Solnik, Bruno, and Dennis McLeavey. 2003. *International Investments.* Boston: Pearson Education.

Donald Lien
Mei Zhang

FIRM

In 1937, Ronald Coase, who would win a Nobel Prize in 1991, wrote a seminal paper titled "The Nature of the Firm." This paper is now traditionally considered to be the origin of the development of an economic theory of the firm. Coase argued that the firm was more than the purely technical vision of incorporating inputs and generating outputs, that it had a concrete existence in the business world, and that its internal modes of organization (especially the coordination of individuals by hierarchies) were different from simple market transactions (which are coordinated by prices). He encouraged economists to elaborate realistic hypotheses on what a firm is and what a firm does.

Today, the research agenda opened up by Coase (1937) is far from complete. More recent works on the economics of the firm show how difficult it is to fully grasp and qualify this subject. Thus, the economics of the firm is a combination of different subjects, and no single model or theory captures all elements of the puzzle.

MANAGERIAL FIRMS

The focus of economists on large managerial firms reflects the impact that this type of firm played in the early stages of the capitalist economist system (1900–1970s), when large, vertically integrated corporations were the dominant form of organization. Joseph Schumpeter (1942) qualified them as the major engines of production, while Alfred Chandler (1977) described the emergence of a "visible hand" era driven by these firms. These organizations represent an important field of investigation because they have significant power in the market, they are able to affect the social and economic environment, and they can elaborate complex strategies based on an appropriate organizational structure. Further, these firms have two distinctive features: (1) There is a separation between ownership and control, so the professional manager is able to define the objectives of the firm, and (2) There is a united, rather than a multidivisional, form of internal organization. These characteristics became one of the privileged fields of exploration of agency theory and the transaction costs approach, which were interpreted in terms of private information and opportunism. In the first case, the manager benefits from private information that the investor cannot access, leaving room for opportunistic behaviors. In the second case, the united organization of the firm favors the development of suboptimal levels of effort that only become observable when competition is introduced among the different divisions of the firm.

There is surprisingly little agreement on what the objectives of the firm are. William Baumol (1959), for example, supports the maximization of sales or the growth rate of sales as the main objective. Oliver Williamson (1964), however, advocates the maximization of the managers' discretionary power through opportunistic behaviors. Herbert Simon (1947) has criticized both alternatives, arguing that firms that have only a "limited rationality" due to the uncertainty of the environment will only pursue limited objectives, a process he calls "satisficing." In this perspective, the search for profit will not be made on the basis of achieving maximum profit. In fact, it is impossible to estimate maximum profit because knowledge is not perfect. The objective can only be to maintain a satisfying profit level in order to keep the firm afloat in an uncertain world.

ENTREPRENEURIAL FIRMS

The discovery that the capitalist system underwent a second period of transition during the latter half of the twentieth century, especially from the late 1970s (a period Richard Langlois [2003] labeled the "vanishing hand" era), marks the beginning of a specific focus by economists on a novel sort of firm. Small, vertically disintegrated firms have generally performed as well as large firms. This view is supported by the remarkable persistence of the skewed size distribution of firms in industrial dynamics (i.e., a large number of small firms and a small number of large firms), and by the extremely important contribution of small firms to global economic development (Geroski 1995; Audretsch 1995). In the late 1990s, the critical resource theory was developed by Rajuram Rajan and Luigi Zingales (1998) to explain the performance of knowledge-intensive companies in which an entrepreneur plays a central role in knowledge creation. The point of departure of the analysis is that the nature of the firm has effectively been changing. In the modern firm, the entrepreneur has a critical resource due to specific skills, talents, and ideas, which are the most important source of potential value creation for the firm. The effective value created by the firm is ultimately dependent on how the entrepreneur develops complementarities between his or her own specific resource and the resources of collaborators.

DECISION MAKING, OWNERSHIP, AND POWER

One of the important issues in the economics of the firm is related to who has the power to make decisions. The concept of ownership has traditionally been perceived of as the ownership of physical assets and power and authority have traditionally been based on this vision of ownership. Today, however, firms are also composed of a range of other resources, such as creative knowledge, ideas, and unique skills; professional control; and corporate reputation, which sometimes generate a higher value than physical assets.

Within small firms the founder/entrepreneur generally has the decision-making power, while in large firms the CEO and the board of directors make the major decisions. In small firms, however, the founder, who often has a technical skill, is often replaced, or at least assisted, by a professional manager or a venture capitalist, whose task is to transform this technical knowledge into a commercial opportunity. In large firms, the board of directors can be composed of shareholders, who may significantly influence the decision-making process.

These observations have stimulated a large number of analytical and empirical investigations. First, the respective tasks and scopes of experience of the entrepreneur, the manager, and the venture capitalist within small firms engendered a specific field of research. Different arrangements among the entrepreneur, the manager, and the venture capitalist can be envisaged, including a sharing of power where each contributes in a complementary manner to the development of the company, or exclusive power held by the fund provider in less risky businesses, where the entrepreneur or manager may have less incentive in terms of investment and effort (Blair 1995; Becht et al. 2005).

Second, the question of how large corporations should be owned and managed has been a recurrent theme. The emergence of the shareholder-value ideology has meant that corporate governance is often oriented toward the interests of investors. Uniformity in modes of governance, however, is now widely debated. The predominant thesis that there should be a unique and universal set of managerial rules neglects the diversity of national experiences and the heterogeneity of firms. Moreover, evidence and analytical results show that such a unique model tends to generate major failures and turbulences.

Thus, different types of rules have been proposed to govern firms that differ in size, type, industry of origins, and stages of development (Krafft and Ravix 2005; Lazonick and O'Sullivan 2002).

SEE ALSO *Business; Consumer; Cooperatives; Economics; Venture Capital*

BIBLIOGRAPHY

Audretsch, David. 1995. Innovation, Growth and Survival. *International Journal of Industrial Organization* 13 (4): 441–457.

Baumol, William. 1959. *Business Behavior, Value, and Growth.* New York: Macmillan.

Becht, Marco, Tim Jenkinson, and Colin Mayer. 2005. Corporate Governance: An Assessment. *Oxford Review of Economic Policy* 21 (2): 155–163.

Blair, Margaret. 1995. *Ownership and Control: Rethinking Corporate Governance for the Twenty-First Century.* Washington, DC: Brookings Institution Press.

Chandler, Alfred. 1977. *The Visible Hand: The Managerial Revolution in the American Business.* Cambridge, MA: Belknap Press.

Coase, Ronald. 1937. The Nature of the Firm. *Economica* 4 (16): 386–405.

Geroski, Paul. 1995. What Do We Know about Entry? *International Journal of Industrial Organization* 13 (4): 421–440.

Krafft, Jackie, and Jacques-Laurent Ravix. 2005. The Governance of Innovative Firms: An Evolutionary Perspective. *Economics of Innovation and New Technology* 14 (3): 125–147.

Langlois, Richard. 2003. The Vanishing Hand: The Changing Dynamics of Industrial Capitalism. *Industrial and Corporate Change* 12 (2): 351–385.

Lazonick, William, and Mary O'Sullivan. 2002. *Corporate Governance and Sustainable Prosperity.* New York: Palgrave.

Rajan, Rajuram, and Luigi Zingales. 1998. Power in a Theory of the Firm. *Quarterly Journal of Economics* 113 (2): 387–432.

Schumpeter, Joseph. 1942. *Capitalism, Socialism, and Democracy.* New York: Harper.

Simon, Herbert. 1947. *Administrative Behavior.* New York: Macmillan.

Williamson, Oliver. 1964. *The Economics of Discretionary Behavior, Managerial Objectives in a Theory of the Firm.* Englewood Cliffs, NJ: Prentice-Hall.

Jackie Krafft

FIRST-PAST-THE-POST

The "first-past-the-post" (FPTP) electoral system, or "plurality system," produces a one-party government as a result of nationwide elections in single electoral districts to form a national parliament. In existence since the twelfth century, FPTP is the oldest electoral system in political history. It can be found worldwide in thirteen countries, including the United Kingdom, the United States, Canada, India, Bangladesh, Jamaica, Malawi, Mongolia, Nepal, Pakistan, Papua New Guinea, Thailand, and Zambia. The ideal type of FPTP is the British electoral system, the so-called "Westminster model."

One important advantage of FPTP is its simplicity. First, FPTP divides the whole territory in single-member districts with candidate ballots. Within each constituency, voters cast a single ballot for one candidate rather than for a party. Another advantage of FPTP is constituency representation: Every voter knows the local member of parliament and has direct access to political representation, which is evenly distributed over the country. The candidate with the highest number of valid votes in a given district is elected. He or she is the "first past the post" in the race between candidates on election day in a specific constituency.

Candidates for a seat in the national parliament need neither a minimum threshold of votes nor an absolute majority within their constituency; instead, the candidate with the plurality of the vote wins the seat in question. He or she needs just one vote more than the candidate in second place in the FPTP race. One main disadvantage of FPTP is poor party system representation. For example, in the U.K. model, FPTP has the tendency to favor major parties such as Labour and Conservative and to weaken small parties such as the Liberal and Green parties.

Within the framework of the FPTP electoral system, the translation of votes at general elections to seats in Parliament and the formation of a national government are not based on the share of the national vote, but on the share of parliamentary seats. Since 1935, every British government has been formed on the basis of a minority of the vote, with less than 50 percent of electoral support. Hence, the FPTP electoral system has been described as a "plurality system," in contrast to a majority system; in fact, it is sometimes called a "single member plurality system" (SMP). The party with the highest number of winners of parliamentary seats forms a one-party government.

Another advantage of FPTP is the stability of the newly elected national government in particular, and of the political system in general, in contrast to coalition governments that might fall apart before the end of the parliamentary term. A further advantage is the speed of the political process: FPTP encourages a quick formation of a new government, avoiding lengthy interparty negotiations necessary to form a coalition government, and the single party in government with a clear majority of seats in parliament is able to decide and implement laws more quickly. A political system that uses FPTP as electoral law is normally stable, fast, and efficient, and displays a high degree of accountability for its actions and public policy.

SEE ALSO *Elections; Electoral Systems; Parliaments and Parliamentary Systems; Plurality; Voting Schemes*

BIBLIOGRAPHY

Farrell, David M. 2001. *Electoral Systems: A Comparative Introduction.* Basingstoke, U.K., and New York: Palgrave Macmillan.

Norris, Pippa. 2004. *Electoral Engineering: Voting Rules and Political Behavior.* Cambridge, U.K., and New York: Cambridge University Press.

Christian W. Haerpfer

FISCAL POLICY
SEE *Policy, Fiscal.*

FISHER, IRVING
1867–1947

Irving Fisher, the outstanding American neoclassical economist of the first half of the twentieth century, was born in Saugerties, New York, on February 27, 1867, and was living in New Haven, Connecticut, when he died on April 29, 1947. Fisher graduated with an A.B. in 1888 and a Ph.D. in economics and mathematics in 1891 from Yale University (from which his father, a Congregational clergyman, had also graduated). He taught at Yale until his retirement in 1937, initially in mathematics and then, from 1895, in political economy, and was promoted to full professor in 1898. A student of both the mathematical physicist Josiah Willard Gibbs and the political economist, sociologist, and social Darwinist William Graham Sumner, Fisher combined his interests in mathematics and economics in his dissertation and his first book, *Mathematical Investigations in the Theory of Value and Prices* (1892; Fisher 1997, vol. 1). This remarkable work made Fisher, along with John Bates Clark and Stuart Wood, a pioneer in introducing marginal utility and marginal product analysis into U.S. economics. Fisher's (re)discovery of both general equilibrium analysis and indifference curves (requiring only a preference ordering, not cardinally measurable utility) was an independent breakthrough because he did not read either Léon Walras or F. Y. Edgeworth until his thesis was almost finished. But modern opinion is consequently divided between Paul Samuelson's modest description of Fisher's thesis as the greatest doctoral dissertation by an American economist, and Robert Dorfman's belief that it should have been rejected for unnecessary reinvention of existing theory. The unique contribution of Fisher's thesis was his construction, in an age before electronic computers, of a hydraulic model simulating the determination of equilibrium prices and quantities (William Brainard and Herbert Scarf in Dimand and Geanakoplos 2005). In an article in 1896 Fisher used a simplified hydraulic model to analyze the bimetallic controversy in monetary economics (Fisher 1997, vol. 1).

Fisher's 1896 American Economic Association monograph *Appreciation and Interest* (Fisher 1997, vol. 1) attributed the difference between interest rates expressed in two standards (gold, silver, paper currencies, or commodities) to the expected rate of appreciation of one standard against the other. The Fisher equation, now expressed as equating nominal interest to the sum of real interest and expected inflation, formalized an insight briefly remarked upon by John Stuart Mill and Alfred Marshall. Fisher's monograph introduced uncovered interest parity for exchange rates and the expectations theory of the term structure of interest rates—that is, differences in interest rates for different lending periods reflect expected changes in the purchasing power of money. In *The Theory of Interest* (1930; Fisher 1997, vol. 9), Fisher tested his equation empirically by correlating nominal interest with a distributed lag of past price level changes (adaptive expectations), finding considerably less than perfect correlation.

Having shown in *Appreciation and Interest* that correctly anticipated inflation would affect only nominal interest, leaving real interest unaltered, Fisher and Harry G. Brown argued in *The Purchasing Power of Money* (1911; Fisher 1997, vol. 4) that, in the long run, a change in the quantity of money would change the price level in the same proportion, with no lasting effect on real variables. Fisher thus defended the quantity theory of money against both bimetallists who held that monetizing silver would have lasting real benefits and some of their hard-money opponents, notably J. Laurence Laughlin of the University of Chicago, who denied that changes in the quantity of money could explain observed changes in prices. While insisting on the long-run neutrality of money, Fisher viewed monetary shocks as the force driving short-run fluctuations in real output and unemployment: his 1926 *International Labour Review* article, "A Statistical Relation Between Unemployment and Price Changes," was reprinted in the *Journal of Political Economy* in 1973 as "Lost and Found: I Discovered the Phillips Curve—Irving Fisher" (also in Fisher 1997, vol. 8). Fisher's monetary theory of economic fluctuations depended on the slow adjustment of expected inflation, and hence of nominal interest, to monetary shocks.

If changes in the purchasing power of money were correctly perceived and expected, there would be no booms or depressions, so Fisher campaigned to educate the public against the "money illusion," which provided the title of his 1928 book (Fisher 1997, vol. 8). He also wished to neutralize price changes through indexation, and persuaded Rand Kardex to issue an indexed bond in 1925. Alternatively, fluctuations could be eliminated by avoiding changes in the purchasing power of money, so Fisher proposed a monetary policy rule (the compensated dollar) to peg the price level by varying the exchange rate (the dollar price of gold) to counteract any change in a price index. This monetary policy rule, eradication of money illusion, and statistical verification of the quantity theory of money and of the monetary theory of fluctuations all required an appropriate price index. When prices rise, a Laspeyres index with base-year quantity weights overestimates the price increase, which a Paasche index with current-year weights underestimates. In *The Making of Index Numbers* (1922; Fisher 1997, vol. 7) Fisher advocated, as an "ideal index" suitable for all purposes, the geometric mean of the Laspeyres and Paasche indexes, the formula that came closest to satisfying a list of seven criteria he proposed as desirable for an index number. (Ragnar Frisch and Subramanian Swamy later determined that no formula could satisfy all seven of Fisher's criteria.) In the 1990s several governments including the United States adopted Fisher's ideal index and issued some indexed bonds.

In *The Rate of Interest* (1907; Fisher 1997, vol. 3) and *The Theory of Interest*, Fisher systematized the neoclassical theory of how the equilibrium real rate of interest is determined by the interaction of impatience (time preference) and opportunity to invest (the expected rate of return over costs on new investments). The Fisher diagram, showing utility-maximizing consumption-smoothing over two periods, illustrated the Fisher separation theorem between the time-pattern of income and that of consumption: given perfect credit markets, consumption in any period depends only on the present discounted value of expected lifetime income, not on income in that period. Not only was this insight the basis for the later permanent-income and life-cycle theories of consumption and saving, but the Fisher diagram also proved useful in applications ranging from international trade to insurance (allocation across possible states of the world). Ironically, Fisher's 1907 numerical example of the possibility of multiple solutions for Böhm-Bawerk's average period of production prefigured criticisms of neoclassical capital and interest theory advanced in the Cambridge capital controversies of the 1960s (and Fisher's own concept of rate of return over costs was subject to the same possibility of multiple solutions).

From 1898 to 1904 Fisher battled successfully to recover from tuberculosis, which had killed his father. His heightened sensitivity to the value of health and longevity led him to advocate health insurance, a federal department of health, and prohibition of alcohol; to coauthor the best-seller *How To Live*; and to estimate the nation's human capital at five times the value of its physical capital. It also motivated Fisher's involvement with the dietary reforms proposed by Dr. Kellogg of Battle Creek and with the "race betterment" schemes of the eugenics movement, including support for the Immigration Restriction Act of 1924 (Fisher 1997, vol. 13). Fisher invented and patented a tent for tuberculosis patients.

Among Fisher's many subsequent inventions, the Index Visible (precursor of the rolodex) made him wealthy, temporarily, when it was absorbed by Rand Kardex. An enthusiastic "new economy" advocate of the permanence of the 1920s stock boom based on technological breakthroughs, Fisher had a net worth of ten million dollars before losing all of it, and more, in the Wall Street crash that began in October 1929. Fisher's memorable statement that month that "stock prices appear to have reached a permanently high plateau" continues to haunt his reputation with the general public. Among economists, however, after a period of eclipse by the rise of Keynesian macroeconomics, Fisher is now once again celebrated as America's outstanding scientific economist of the first half of the twentieth century, and perhaps of any time.

BIBLIOGRAPHY

Allen, Robert Loring. 1993. *Irving Fisher: A Biography*. Malden, MA, and Oxford: Blackwell.

Dimand, Robert W., and John Geanakoplos, eds. 2005. *Celebrating Irving Fisher: The Legacy of a Great Economist*. Malden, MA, and Oxford: Blackwell. Also published as *American Journal of Economics and Sociology* 64 (1): 1–456.

Fisher, Irving. 1997. *The Works of Irving Fisher*. 14 volumes. Ed. William J. Barber assisted by Robert W. Dimand and Kevin Foster, consulting ed. James Tobin. London: Pickering and Chatto.

Fisher, Irving Norton. 1956. *My Father Irving Fisher*. New York: Comet.

Loef, Hans-E., and Hans G. Monissen, eds. 1999. *The Economics of Irving Fisher*. Cheltenham, U.K., and Northampton, MA: Edward Elgar.

Robert W. Dimand

FISHING INDUSTRY

The modern fishing industry, with fleets of large capital-intensive vessels, can be traced back to the introduction of the trawler early in the twentieth century. Those ships enabled fishers to reach distant fishing grounds more quickly, stay out fishing longer, and catch more fish per trip. Subsequent growth in the number, size, and technological sophistication of trawlers steadily increased harvesting capacity and corresponding pressures on fish stocks. The introduction of "factory" trawlers in the early 1960s allowed even longer and more distant fishing trips and intensified fishing pressure on previously neglected fish stocks.

A little over 130 million metric tons of fish was harvested worldwide in 2003, almost 80 percent of which was for human consumption (United Nations Food and Agricultural Organization 2004). Reversing earlier trends, the output from ocean harvesting remained fairly constant in the early years of the twenty-first century, accounting for almost 60 percent of consumption. Around 7 percent of the harvest comes from inland waters, and the rest comes from aquaculture, most of which is conducted in fresh waters.

Developing countries provide around 70 percent of the total world supply of fish for human consumption, much of which is harvested using traditional small-scale and labor-intensive technologies. The top countries in 2002 were China, Peru, the United States, Indonesia, and Japan in that order, with China harvesting over twice the amount taken by Peru. One-third of global ocean harvesting occurs in the northwestern Pacific, roughly 20 percent in the southeastern Pacific, 16 percent in the northeastern Atlantic, and 15 percent in the western central Pacific. The major ocean stocks, which are harvested largely by factory fleets, are anchovies (a relatively low-value product), pollock, tuna, herring, and mackerel.

In contrast to the marine fishery, aquaculture production grew at an average annual rate of 6 percent per year after 2000, with China accounting for almost 70 percent of world aquaculture production in 2002, followed by India, Indonesia, Japan, and Bangladesh. The most important aquaculture species is carp, followed by various types of higher-value shellfish, such as oysters and clams.

Trade in fisheries products grew 45 percent from 1992 to 2002, and the value of fisheries exports reached $58.2 billion in 2002. Around 90 percent of this trade involves processed (frozen, salted, dried, and canned) fish products. China is the major exporter of fish, followed closely by Thailand and then the United States, Canada, Denmark, and Vietnam. Developed countries purchase over 80 percent of the total dollar value of traded fish products, with Japan accounting for 22 percent of world imports in 2002, followed by the United States (16%), Spain (6%), and France (5%).

DUAL ECONOMIC STRUCTURE

Although it is difficult to generalize about the structure of the fishing industry worldwide, the large-vessel fleet is aging and there has been a decline in the number of very large vessels being added to fleets (United Nations Food and Agricultural Organization 2004). Large factory vessels and distant-water fleets account for the majority of the harvest, but around 90 percent of all fishers, most of whom are in Asia, work on small vessels (International Labour Organization 2004). Although much of the small-scale fishing sector uses traditional technologies that limit harvesting to heavily fished near-shore waters, there is a growing group of small to midsize vessels with advanced technologies that can access more abundant offshore stocks that can be brought to market quickly enough to command premium prices for fresh fish.

COMMON PROPERTY ISSUES

The fishing industry represents a classic example of the common property problem. Unlike land-based agriculture, ocean fish stocks are a resource for which individuals traditionally do not hold property rights. There is a substantial literature documenting how, in the absence of ownership or regulation of fishing stocks, economic incentives motivate the owners of individual vessels to overfish the resource by harvesting as many fish as possible as quickly as possible (Anderson 1986).

Technological changes that have made harvesting more efficient, coupled with the growth of large-scale fleets and international fish markets, made this common property problem a global concern beginning in the mid-twentieth century. As fisheries stocks become depleted, the scarcity of fish drives up prices, and harvesting incentives become even stronger, threatening the sustainability of the resource. As a result, many of the world's fish stocks have been classified as having been fished beyond sustainable levels and concerns are being raised about the possible extinction of overfished species.

One response to depleted stocks has been to shift fishing efforts to previously underutilized species. However, experience has shown that those species soon become threatened and that the shifting species mix can have adverse effects on the ecosystem. A second outcome has been the rapid growth of aquaculture, much of which is conducted in areas where property rights can be established, but that has added to the growing concern about environmental pollution in marine and inland waters and its impact on the safety of fish products for human consumption.

REGULATION OF THE FISHING INDUSTRY

Economists have argued that regulation is the only long-term method to achieve the biological, economic, and environmental sustainability of the fishing industry. They also have advocated a form of regulation that relies heavily on markets and property rights to counter common

property problems. In practice, however, fisheries regulation has relied on indirect methods to reduce incentives for overfishing.

Initially, the most widely adopted policy was to reduce the access of large-scale foreign fishing fleets to continental fishing stocks to conserve the stocks for domestic fishers. Many coastal nations imposed limits on distant-water fleets in the 1970s by establishing Exclusive Economic Zones (EEZs) that extended territorial control over ocean resources up to 200 miles from their coastlines. The result in many cases, however, was that domestic fleets with increasingly sophisticated harvesting technologies took the place of foreign fishing vessels, and so the pressures on fish stocks continued to increase.

Thus, the focus of national regulatory policies shifted to fishing pressures within EEZs. The most common policy instruments have involved indirectly limiting harvesting activity through seasonal or permanent closures of fishing grounds, reducing fleet size by limiting entry and offering vessel buyouts, and raising the costs of fishing by constraining harvesting technologies, for example, limiting vessel size and power, increasing the minimum mesh size of nets, and reducing the number of days of fishing allowed. Those policies, however, often have proved costly to monitor and easy to evade, allowing overfishing to continue.

As a consequence, pressures have increased to restrict harvesting further. In the United States the 1996 and 2006 reauthorizations of federal fisheries management legislation were designed to force regulators to set allowable harvesting levels lower than the previous levels. The new levels are below what would be needed to ensure biological sustainability to take into account both the environmental and the economic costs of harvesting fish.

Although most management regulations continue to rely largely on indirect regulation of fishing effort, there has been increasing international interest in individual transferable quotas, one of the policies most often advocated by economists. The individual transferable quota policy involves allocating shares (quotas) of the allowable harvest that can be bought or sold. Ownership of a share gives a fisher a property right to a portion of the allowable harvest that essentially privatizes the resource and eliminates the incentive for fishers to compete for the same common stock of fish. Such market-based regulation can both reduce overfishing pressures and ensure the overall efficiency of the industry.

Regardless of the management methods adopted, there has been movement worldwide toward establishing stricter fisheries management controls that are intended to protect fish stocks more aggressively from the threat of extinction. As fish continue to play a major role in world trade and the food supply, most fisheries biologists and economists believe that continued vigilance is required to ensure that this resource remains available for future generations by using fishing methods that are economically sound and environmentally sustainable.

SEE ALSO *Developing Countries; Industry; Technological Progress, Economic Growth; Tragedy of the Commons*

BIBLIOGRAPHY

Anderson, Lee G. 1986. *The Economics of Fisheries Management*, rev. and enl. ed. Baltimore, MD: Johns Hopkins University Press.

International Labour Organization. 2004. *Conditions of Work in the Fishing Sector: A Comprehensive Standard (a Convention Supplemented by a Recommendation) on Work in the Fishing Sector*. International Labour Conference, 92nd Session. Geneva: International Labour Office.

United Nations Food and Agriculture Organization. 2004. *The State of the World Fisheries and Aquaculture*. Editorial Production and Design Group, Publishing Management Service. Rome: Food and Agricultural Organization.

United States Department of Commerce. 1999. *Our Living Oceans: Report on the Status of U.S. Living Marine Resources 1999*. Washington, DC: National Marine Fisheries Service.

David G. Terkla
Peter B. Doeringer

FISKE, D.W.
SEE *Campbell, Donald.*

FIXED COEFFICIENTS PRODUCTION FUNCTION

A production function associates the maximum level of output producible with given amounts of inputs. If the inputs must be combined in fixed proportions, like the ingredients of a recipe in a cookbook, the function is a fixed coefficients production function. It is also called a Leontief function, after its inventor, the economist and Nobel Prize winner, Wassily Leontif. Call centers require a one-to-one proportion between workers and telecommunication equipment. Denoting the input quantities by L and K, the isoquants are L-shaped (with the kink on the 45 degree line).

To introduce the formal definition, denote the quantities of inputs required per unit of some output by $a_1, \ldots, a_n$, where n is the number of inputs. These so-called input coefficients constitute the recipe or technique for the production of the output considered. Denote the available

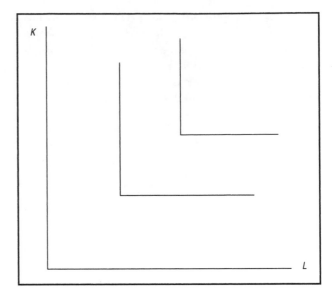

Figure 1

amounts of inputs by $x_1, \ldots, x_n$, respectively. Then the attainable level of output is given by $y = \min \{x_1/a_1, \ldots, x_n/a_n\}$. This is the defining formula of the fixed coefficients production function. The inputs for which the minimum value is assumed are called the bottlenecks.

The fixed coefficients production function is the cornerstone of input-output analysis, the quantitative economic tool developed in 1936 by Leontief, who traced the origin to Francois Quesnay's *Tableau Économique* of 1758. Scholars Heinz Kurz and Neri Salvadori described the roots of input-output analysis in detail in their 2000 work, and the theory is exposited in Thijs ten Raa's *Economics of Input-Output Analysis* (2005). The fixed coefficients function is popular, because only a single observation is needed to calculate it, making use of the input coefficients $a_i = x_i/y$. The connection between fixed coefficients and input-output analysis is as follows.

Since inputs are produced (such as electricity) or nonproduced (such as labor services), we may label them $1, \ldots, m, m+1, \ldots, n$, where the last $n - m$ inputs are the nonproduced or so-called factor inputs. Denote the input coefficients of output j by a_{ij}. The matrix of intermediate input coefficients is $A = (a_{ij})_{i,j = 1, \ldots, m}$ and the matrix of factor input coefficients is $B = (a_{ij})_{i = m+1, \ldots, n, j = 1, \ldots, m}$. The matrix of factor input coefficients gives the direct factor requirements of products. Post-multiplication of B with the so-called Leontief inverse, $(1 - A)^{-1} = 1 + A + A^2 + \ldots$, yields the matrix of total factor requirements or factor contents of products. The total requirements include the factor requirements of the produced inputs, BA, the factor requirements of the produced inputs of those inputs, BA^2, etcetera.

An important application is the Marxian theory of labor values, in which all commodities are produced, directly or indirectly, by labor. Then the factor input coefficients matrix B reduces to a row vector of direct labor coefficients and the total requirements becomes a row vector of labor contents, one for each product. Another application is energy economics. Here the direct coefficients measure the energy used per unit of output and the total coefficients measure the total amount of energy embodied in products. The inclusion of the indirect effects may cause reversals in the energy intensity of products, when the production of an output requires little energy, but much intermediate input of which the production is energy intensive. The inclination of politicians to subsidize goods of which the direct energy requirements are low may therefore be ill conceived.

Input coefficients tend to be fixed at the level of the firm. Indeed, managers know how many workers are needed to operate the machines. Input coefficients vary between firms though and, therefore, the fixed coefficients production function is less appropriate for industries or economies. For example, if the wage rate increases relative to the rate of interest, labor-intensive firms may shut down and capital-intensive firms may expand to full capacity. As a result, the economy will be more capital intensive. Though derived from micro fixed coefficients production functions, the macro production function will thus feature input substitutability, much like the Cobb-Douglas function. In fact, the latter can be derived mathematically if the production capacity across firms follows a Pareto distribution, which is defined by the same formula as the Cobb-Douglas function. Most applied general equilibrium models feature production functions with a mixture of fixed and variable coefficients, but even when all the production functions are of the fixed coefficients variety, the response to price shocks may be the same as in a model with variable coefficients production functions.

SEE ALSO *Input-Output Matrix; Leontief, Wassily; Production Function*

BIBLIOGRAPHY

Kurz, Heinz D., and Neri Salvadori. 2000. "Classical" Roots of Input-Output Analysis: A Short Account of Its Long Prehistory. *Economic Systems Research* 12 (2): 153–179.

Leontief, Wassily W. 1936. Quantitative Input and Output Relations in the Economic System of the United States. *The Review of Economics and Statistics* 18 (3): 105–125.

ten Raa, Thijs. 2005. *Economics of Input-Output Analysis.* Cambridge, U.K.: Cambridge University Press.

Thijs ten Raa

FIXED EFFECTS

SEE *Generalized Least Squares.*

FIXED EFFECTS REGRESSION

A fixed effects regression is an estimation technique employed in a panel data setting that allows one to control for time-invariant unobserved individual characteristics that can be correlated with the observed independent variables.

Let us assume we are interested in the causal relationship between a vector of observable random variables $x = (1, x_1, x_2, ..., x_K)'$ and a dependent random variable y where the true linear model is of the following form:

$$y_i = \beta' x_i + \mu_i + \varepsilon_i \text{ with } i = 1, ..., N$$

with μ being an unobserved random variable characterizing each unit of observation i and ε the stochastic error uncorrelated with x.

When μ is correlated with x we cannot consistently estimate the vector of parameters of interest β using Ordinary Least Squares because the standard assumption of no correlation between the error term and the regressors is violated. In a cross-sectional setting, typical strategies to solve this omitted variable problem are instrumental variables or the inclusion of proxies for μ. However, when the available data is longitudinal, that is, when it contains a cross-sectional as well as a time series dimension, it is possible to adopt alternative estimation methods known in the literature as "panel data" techniques.

Assuming we repeatedly observe N units for T periods of time, and that the unobservable variable μ is time invariant, we can write our model as:

$$y_{it} = \beta' x_{it} + \mu_i + \varepsilon_{it} \text{ with } i = 1, ..., N \text{ and } t = 1, ..., T$$

Depending on the correlation between the omitted variable μ and the regressors x, alternative estimation techniques are available to the researcher. A fixed effects regression allows for arbitrary correlation between μ and x, that is, $E(x_{jit}\mu_i) \neq 0$, whereas random effects regression techniques do not allow for such correlation, that is, the condition $E(x_{jit}\mu_i) = 0$ must be respected. This terminology is somehow misleading because in both cases the unobservable variable is to be considered random. However, the terminology is so widespread in the literature that it has been accepted as standard.

A fixed effects regression consists in subtracting the time mean from each variable in the model and then estimating the resulting transformed model by Ordinary Least Squares. This procedure, known as "within" transformation, allows one to drop the unobserved component and consistently estimate β. Analytically, the above model becomes

$$\tilde{y}_{it} = \beta' \tilde{x}_{it} + \tilde{\varepsilon}_{it}$$

where $\tilde{y}_{it} = y_{it} - \bar{y}_i$, with $\bar{y}_i = T^{-1}\Sigma_{t=1}^{T} y_{it}$ (and the same for x, μ, and ε). Because μ_i is fixed over time, we have $\mu_i - \bar{\mu}_i = 0$.

This procedure is numerically identical to including $N - 1$ dummies in the regression, suggesting intuitively that a fixed effects regression accounts for unobserved individual heterogeneity by means of individual specific intercepts. In other words, the slopes of the regression are common across units (the coefficients of x_1, x_2, …, x_K) whereas the intercept is allowed to vary.

One drawback of the fixed effects procedure is that the within transformation does not allow one to include time-invariant independent variables in the regression, because they get eliminated similarly to the fixed unobserved component. In addition, parameter estimates are likely to be imprecise if the time series dimension is limited.

Under classical assumptions, the fixed effects estimator is consistent (with $N \to \infty$ and T fixed) in the cases of both $E(x_{jit}\mu_i) = 0$ and $E(x_{jit}\mu_i) \neq 0$, where $j = 1$, …, K. It is efficient when all the explanatory variables are correlated with μ_i. However, it is less efficient than the random effect estimator when $E(x_{jit}\mu_i) = 0$.

The consistency property requires the strict exogeneity of x. However, this property is not satisfied when the estimated model includes a lagged dependent variable, as in $y_{it} = \alpha y_{it-1} + \beta' x_{it} + \mu_i + \varepsilon_{it}$.

This suggests the adoption of instrumental variables or Generalized Method of Moments techniques in order to obtain consistent estimates. However, a large time dimension T assures consistency even in the case of the dynamic specification above.

Sometimes the true model includes unobserved shocks common to all units i, but time-varying. In this case, the model includes an additional error component δ_t that can be controlled for by simply including time dummies in the equation.

A typical application of a fixed effects regression is in the context of wage equations. Let us assume that we are interested in assessing the impact of years of education in logs e on wages in logs w when the ability of individuals a is not observed. The true model is then

$$w_i = \beta_0 + \beta_1 e_i + v_i$$

where $v_i = a_i + \varepsilon_i$. Given that unobserved ability is likely to be correlated with education, then the composite stochastic error v is also correlated with the regressor and the estimate of β_1 will be biased. However, since innate ability does not change over time, if our data set is longitudinal we can use a fixed effect estimator to obtain a consistent estimate of β_1. Applying the within transformation

to the preceding equation we end up with $\tilde{w}_{it} = \beta_1 \tilde{e}_{it} + \tilde{\varepsilon}_{it}$ where we have eliminated the time invariant unobserved component a_i. Being $E(\tilde{e}_{it}\tilde{\varepsilon}_{it}) = 0$, the model now satisfies the classical assumptions and we can estimate it by Ordinary Least Squares.

SEE ALSO *Bayesian Econometrics; Random Effects Regression; Regression; Regression Analysis*

BIBLIOGRAPHY

Arellano, Manuel. 2003. *Panel Data Econometrics*. Oxford: Oxford University Press.

Baltagi, Badi H. 2001. *Econometric Analysis of Panel Data*. 2nd ed. New York: Wiley.

Wooldridge, Jeffrey M. 2001. *Econometric Analysis of Cross Section and Panel Data*. Cambridge, MA: MIT Press.

Luca Nunziata

FIXED EXCHANGE RATES

SEE *Exchange Rates.*

FLAGS

SEE *Symbols.*

FLEXIBILITY

The concept of flexibility generically indicates the capacity of adapting to changes in circumstances. In economics it is typically used to characterize price and quantity adjustments as responses to variations in market forces and organizational and regulatory patterns.

In a perfect competitive market with no transaction costs or attritions, any imbalance between supply and demand triggers an adjustment in prices that clears the market. However, in reality, prices are characterized by a certain degree of rigidity—that is, they do not fully or immediately adjust to changes in supply and demand. These rigidities are typically the result of market imperfections, asymmetric information, cognitive time lags, menu and transaction costs, or departure from a competitive framework. For example, macroeconomists make a distinction between the degree of price flexibility (or rigidity) in the short and the long run. The price of output is generally rigid in the short run because agents need time to adjust to changes in market conditions. As a consequence, an increase in money growth in the presence of rigid prices may have real effects on the economy. However, in the long run, prices are flexible and an increase in money growth translates into an identical increase in the rate of inflation, with no effects on unemployment and output.

Prices are characterized by different degrees of flexibility, even in the short run. For instance, stock prices adjust very quickly to changes in market conditions, whereas wages—that is, the price of labor—adjust much more slowly. Wage rigidity can be explained by the staggering of wage contracts, by the role of unions in the wage bargaining process, or by the firms' willingness to pay real wages above the equilibrium level in order to attract and maintain the best workers or to reduce shirking (efficiency wage theory).

Economists often use the notion of flexibility when describing labor markets in which firms are free to vary the amount of labor they use in production, for example through dismissals when they are hit by a negative shock. A broader definition of labor market flexibility involves the institutional features that may induce a deviation of labor market outcomes from the perfect competitive equilibrium. A flexible labor market is then characterized by minimal regulations in terms of dismissal costs (or employment protection legislation) and labor standards, limited unemployment benefits, no minimum wages, low taxation, and a marginal role for trade unions. But the dichotomous concept of flexibility (versus rigidity) applied to labor markets can be misleading. Indeed, it does not help in distinguishing the continuum of potential social models, each characterized by a certain degree of flexibility and/or rigidity in certain institutional dimensions.

Each labor market regulation may be rationalized on the basis of political economy considerations. It may also have desirable social and economic purposes. For example, a reasonable degree of employment protection may induce higher productivity if workers decide to invest more in firm-specific skills; a reasonable level of unemployment benefits contingent on effective job search may help smooth consumption patterns in the presence of negative idiosyncratic shocks and financial markets imperfections. However, if employment protection is too strict, firms may be reluctant to hire new workers during economic expansions because it would be more costly to dismiss them during contractions. The negative burden of the rigidity would then fall on new labor market entrants, who would find it harder to be hired in the first place (insider-outsider theory). A flexible labor market, in contrast, would adapt more easily to positive as well as negative shocks. This might result in a larger variance of employment along the business cycle, with ambiguous effects on average employment, but possibly a more efficient allocation of labor in the long run.

SEE ALSO *Barro-Grossman Model; Competition; Shocks; Sticky Prices; Transaction Cost*

BIBLIOGRAPHY

Blanchard, Olivier. 2005. *Macroeconomics*. 4th ed. Upper Saddle River, NJ: Prentice Hall.

Cahuc, Pierre, and André Zylberberg. 2004. *Labor Economics*. Cambridge, MA: MIT Press.

Luca Nunziata

FLOATING EXCHANGE RATES

SEE *Exchange Rates.*

FLOW

Embedded within and critical to the burgeoning field of positive psychology, the concept of flow represents an optimal state of consciousness, a positive psychological state. The American psychologist Mihaly Csikszentmihalyi (1990), who devised the concept of flow, describes how this experience helps promote creativity and psychosocial complexity. The study of flow began following interviews Csikszentmihalyi (1975) conducted with artists, mountain climbers, athletes, chess players, and surgeons, where a high level of consistency was found in descriptions of how things felt when their activity was going really well. Flow occurs when one is engaged in activities one enjoys and that extend one's capabilities.

Flow is an optimal state because it involves a fully focused mind. When in flow, nothing disturbs or detracts from this concentrated state. Neither external nor internal distractions take up mental space. This total focus on the task at hand is a defining feature of flow. It is one of the several dimensions comprising flow, as described below:

1. *Challenge-skill balance.* In flow, there is a perception of capability for the demands of the task one is engaged in. Described by Susan Jackson and Csikszentmihalyi (1999) as the *golden rule of flow*, this perceived balance between challenges and skills is the necessary precondition for flow to occur.

2. *Action-awareness merging.* When in flow, action follows action easily, sometimes providing a sense of automaticity of movements. This sense of oneness, or merging of the self with the activity, results from the total task focus of flow.

3. *Clear goals.* The person in flow knows clearly what it is he or she wants to do, and this clarity of purpose guides the person from moment to moment.

4. *Unambiguous feedback.* Flow provides clear feedback regarding task performance in relation to goal accomplishment. Immediate and clear feedback allows for adjustments to be made as required to ensure that one's performance matches one's goals.

5. *Concentration on the task at hand.* A defining feature of flow, a centered mind, provides the internal environment for the other flow dimensions.

6. *Sense of control.* When in flow, there is no worry about potential loss of control. This freedom from worry over control is a liberating state.

7. *Loss of self-consciousness.* In flow, there is freedom from self-consciousness. Instead of worrying about how one appears to other people, one is absorbed with processing information about the task at hand.

8. *Time transformation.* Often, but not always in flow, time drops from awareness. This results in perceptions of altered time. Generally, the sense is that time speeds up, akin to the adage that time flies when one is having fun.

9. *Autotelic experience.* The term *autotelic*, from the Greek words *auto* (self) and *telos* (goal), has been defined by Csikszentmihalyi as an experience that is intrinsically rewarding. This dimension is the end result of the other flow dimensions. Being in flow is an enjoyable experience, and once attained, the motivation is high to return to a flow state.

These flow dimensions work together synergistically to create an optimal psychological experience. In lay terms, flow can be described as enjoyment, and it provides highlights in one's experience of life. Enjoyment is distinguishable from pleasure according to Csikszentmihalyi (1990). While the latter is associated with satisfaction from having needs met, it is only enjoyment that leads to growth, since enjoyable experiences move one forward and in doing so, require investment of mental energy. There are also positive developmental implications of the flow model. Flow experiences lead to growth in competence and in psychological complexity, through the continually evolving process of matching challenges with skills in an activity. Flow is not an easy state to achieve, with the matching of challenges and skills not a straightforward process in many situations. Both external and internal obstacles can keep flow experiences from occurring. It may be by one's own choosing that negative psychological states are experienced, or the environment one is operating in may foster negative mindsets. While it may be possible to focus through the energy of negativity, flow

is a much more conducive state to clear and unfettered attention toward a task, and the enjoyment arising from flow experiences generates continuing motivation toward attainment of goals.

SEE ALSO *Optimism/Pessimism; Positive Psychology*

BIBLIOGRAPHY

Csikszentmihalyi, Mihaly. 1975. *Beyond Boredom and Anxiety.* San Francisco, CA: Jossey Bass.

Csikszentmihalyi, Mihaly. 1990. *Flow: The Psychology of Optimal Experience.* New York: Harper.

Jackson, Susan A., and Mihaly Csikszentmihalyi. 1999. *Flow in Sports: The Keys to Optimal Experiences and Performances.* Champaign, IL: Human Kinetics.

Susan A. Jackson

FLOWER INDUSTRY

Since the 1980s, there has been a consistent increase in the global demand for fresh cut flowers. While such flowers were previously purchased only by upper-income households, they have become a regular decorative feature in households with lower incomes. Although a variety of flowers are grown, roses are the main traded product, followed by carnations and chrysanthemums. The feminization of labor is deeply entrenched in the flower industry, which is characterized by high levels of young female employment. Women tend to occupy 60 to 90 percent of the jobs in the labor-intensive stages of flower production.

The commercialization of flowers began in Western Europe when the demand for tulips reached an all-time high in the middle of the seventeenth century. This triggered a massive speculation for tulips called *the Great Tulip Mania.* However, evolution of the flower industry into a global modern economic sector can be traced back to the 1970s. Prior to that, flower production was almost exclusively for consumption in the regions where it was produced. Production was also concentrated in the developed countries, and flowers were almost exclusively produced in the Netherlands, Japan, and the United States, which accounted for nearly 75 percent of production. While flowers produced in the United States and Japan were largely consumed locally, the Netherlands' production served the European regional market. By the 1980s, however, developing countries, particularly in Africa and Latin America, had began producing cut flowers for the global export market. The Netherlands, however, still remains the largest flower consumer, exporter, and producer globally. Virtually no fresh flowers were imported to the United States before 1960, but the U.S. demand is now increasingly being met by imports from Latin America. California is the largest flower producing state, accounting for about 66 percent of U.S. production.

At the beginning of the new millennium, total global acreage allocated to flower production was 200,000 hectares, with the three main producing countries being the Netherlands, United States, and Japan. Germany is the largest of the six importing countries, followed by the United States, the United Kingdom, France, the Netherlands, and Switzerland, which account for nearly 80 percent of global imports. The expansion of commercial production of flowers in developing countries has catapulted the African, Caribbean, and Pacific regions into the global market as key players.

The changing nature of product varieties, production techniques, markets, and retailing arrangements also characterize the flower industry as a highly dynamic sector. The traditional point of sale for flowers has historically been florist shops, but these retailers are increasingly losing their customers to supermarkets and discount stores. Simultaneously, the Netherlands' flower auctions, where the majority of flowers exported to and from Europe are traded, are being bypassed by supermarkets that buy large volumes of flowers directly from producers. With so many new sources of supply, intense competition has set in, leading to a downward spiraling of prices, particularly for roses. At the same time, the quality imperatives of the market have increased costs of production. Typically, costs of production tend to be pushed down to workers, most of whom work in precarious conditions—many are hired on a casual, low-paid basis, with no employment contracts and frequent exposure to pesticides.

The shift of flower production to the developing countries has increased worker exploitation and pesticide poisoning. In addition to the health hazards that the pesticides pose, the runoff of pesticides and fertilizers into streams and aquifers threatens already fragile water resources. As the industry becomes increasingly globalized, concerns are being raised about its social and environmental impacts. Having been the target of civil-society campaigns and media exposés for poor labor practices and environmentally damaging production processes, however, the industry appears poised to operate in a more socially and environmentally responsible manner. Flower producers now have to comply with a number of codes of conduct developed by their major market brokers, international organizations, and national industry associations.

SEE ALSO *Developing Countries; Great Tulip Mania, The; Imports*

BIBLIOGRAPHY

Dolan, C., M. Opondo, and S. Smith. 2003. *Gender, Rights, and Participation in the Kenya Cut Flower Industry.* Natural Resources Institute (NRI) Report No. 2768. Chatham, UK: NRI.

International Trade Center (ITC). 2001. *Product Profile: Cut Flowers and Foliage.* Third UN Conference on the Least Developed Countries, Business Sector Roundtable, Discussion Document. Brussels: ITC. http://www.intracen.org/bsrt/ppcutflowers.pdf.

Patrick L. Mason
Maggie Opondo

FLYNN EFFECT

The term *Flynn effect* refers to the worldwide phenomenon of markedly increasing mean performance on standardized IQ tests over time. Most current IQ tests are designed to have a population mean of 100 and a standard deviation of 15 at the time they are developed. The mean and standard deviation are set by administering the test to a large group of individuals designed to be representative of the population as a whole (a process referred to as "standardization" or "norming"). However, a growing body of evidence suggests that the mean population performance on IQ tests has improved markedly over the decades since they were first introduced in 1905. Over a period of several years after an IQ test is introduced, the test's mean of 100 becomes obsolete and IQ scores become elevated overall. Periodic renorming of IQ tests (typically at twelve- to twenty-five-year intervals) have helped mask the magnitude of this IQ increase. To compensate for improvements in performance over time and to ensure that the mean score is 100, individuals in the standardization group for a newer IQ test typically have to answer more (or harder) questions to obtain the same score on the new test as on an older test.

The degree and scope of the phenomenon of improved IQ test performance was not broadly known until James Flynn (b. 1934), a political scientist at the University of Otago in New Zealand, wrote two seminal articles on the topic that appeared in *Psychological Bulletin* in 1984 and 1987. Flynn reviewed dozens of studies in which groups were administered two or more IQ tests that were standardized at different times. Flynn noted that in these studies the groups' mean performance on a test with newer standardization samples was nearly always lower than their performance on a test with older standardization samples.

Flynn has estimated the size of the Flynn effect on the Wechsler and Stanford-Binet series of IQ tests (the most widely used IQ tests in the United States) as being at about 3 points per decade or about .3 points per year (Flynn 1984, 2006). This rate of improvement has been remarkably consistent across different time periods and tests within these series. However, the rate of improvement is not uniform across all varieties of IQ tests, or even on subtests within a particular IQ test. The largest gains (.5 points per year or more) have been found on Ravens Progressive Matrices, a nonverbal pattern recognition IQ test. Lowest gains (near 0 points per year) have been on Wechsler Verbal IQ subtests such as vocabulary, information, and arithmetic.

Because of the time and cost involved in administering standardized IQ tests, they are typically administered only to students who are being considered for special education or gifted and talented programs. The Flynn effect has been found to particularly affect the educational classifications of students who are being tested for eligibility for these services shortly before and after a revised IQ test comes out.

The impact of the Flynn effect on children being tested for mental retardation services in the early 1990s was quite substantial. The IQ criterion for mental retardation is typically an IQ of 70 or below, which is two standard deviations below the mean of 100 on current IQ tests (allowances for measurement error typically permit a score of up to 75). When the Wechsler Intelligence Scale for Children–Third Edition (WISC–III) supplanted the Wechsler Intelligence Scale for Children–Revised (WISC–R) in 1991, the test norms for the WISC–R were nineteen years old. Tomoe Kanaya, Matthew Scullin, and Stephen Ceci (2003) found that children in the mild mental retardation and borderline IQ ranges scored more than five points lower on the WISC–III than on the WISC–R, which is similar to what was found with children in the average range of intelligence. This five-point difference in scores more than doubled the number of children who were eligible for mental retardation services on the basis of their IQ scores. This is because about 2.27 percent of children would be expected to obtain an IQ score of 70 or below on the WISC–III at the time of its standardization, whereas the obsolete WISC–R was only capturing the bottom 0.87 percent of children by 1991. Scullin (2006) found that in forty-three states and in the United States as a whole, a long and steady decline in the percentage of schoolchildren receiving mental retardation services during the 1980s and early 1990s ended and indeed reversed around the time of the introduction of the WISC–III.

As the norms of an IQ test grow older, the Flynn effect increases the number of children eligible for learning disability services in areas in which the criterion for eligibility is a significant discrepancy between children's IQ scores and their performance on an achievement test. Higher IQ test scores relative to achievement result in an increased likelihood of finding a significant discrepancy. Similarly, more children become eligible for gifted and talented programs over time as it becomes easier to meet the criterion. Once a newly standardized test is introduced, these trends reverse themselves and it becomes harder to meet the IQ–achievement discrepancy criterion for learning disability and the IQ threshold for gifted and talented services.

As documented by Ulric Neisser (in *The Rising Curve*, 1998), the Flynn effect raises some important nature vs. nurture questions about the relative strength of genes and environment in determining intelligence, and about IQ as an estimate of intelligence. *The Rising Curve* was written in response to Richard Herrnstein and Charles Murray's best-selling book *The Bell Curve* (1994), in which the authors argued that intelligence is assessed well by IQ tests and that low IQ is related to a wide range of negative life outcomes, from criminality to risk for divorce. Herrnstein and Murray used behavioral genetics data to make a case for a strong genetic influence on IQ, including ethnic differences in mean IQ scores. Neisser counter-argued that IQ scores have been increasing at too rapid a rate to be explained by genetics alone, which suggests that there are strong environmental influences affecting IQ scores. Neisser's book noted that possible non-genetic explanations for the Flynn effect include increasing environmental complexity, new schooling techniques, and improvements in nutrition.

Just as there is no consensus about the origins of the Flynn effect, there is conflicting evidence about whether the Flynn effect is continuing unabated. In the United States, comparison study data for the Wechsler Adult Intelligence Scale–Third Edition (standardized in 1995) suggested that perhaps the rate of IQ increases in the United States was diminishing. Longitudinal data from IQ-test–like draft-board examinations of all draft-eligible males in some European countries also documented a leveling-off of IQ score gains during the 1990s. However, data from comparison studies for the Stanford-Binet Intelligence Scale–Fifth Edition and Wechsler Intelligence Scale for Children–Fourth Edition (both normed around 2001) suggest that the best estimate of the rate of IQ test improvement in the United States is currently still around .3 points per year (Flynn 2006).

SEE ALSO *Intelligence; IQ Controversy; Psychometrics; Scales*

BIBLIOGRAPHY

Flynn, James R. 1984. The Mean IQ of Americans: Massive Gains from 1932 to 1978. *Psychological Bulletin* 95 (1): 29–51.

Flynn, James R. 1987. Massive IQ Gains in 14 Nations: What Intelligence Tests Really Measure. *Psychological Bulletin* 101 (2): 171–191.

Flynn, James R. 2006. Tethering the Elephant: Capital Cases, IQ, and the Flynn Effect. *Psychology, Public Policy, and Law* 12 (2): 170–189.

Herrnstein, Richard J., and Charles Murray. 1994. *The Bell Curve: Intelligence and Class Structure in American Life.* New York: Free Press.

Kanaya, Tomoe, Matthew H. Scullin, and Stephen J. Ceci. 2003. The Flynn Effect and U.S. Policies: The Impact of Rising IQs on American Society via Mental Retardation Diagnoses. *American Psychologist* 58 (10): 778–790.

Neisser, Ulric, ed. 1998. *The Rising Curve: Long-Term Gains in IQ and Related Measures.* Washington, DC: American Psychological Association.

Scullin, Matthew H. 2006. Large State-Level Fluctuations in Mental Retardation Classifications Related to Introduction of Renormed Intelligence Test. *American Journal on Mental Retardation* 111 (5): 322–335.

Matthew H. Scullin

FOGEL, ROBERT
1926–

Robert Fogel is an economist and economic historian who has been a pioneer in the application of quantitative methods and economic theory to the measurement of long-term economic change. His work has stimulated and provoked historians, and he has argued for the value of mathematical and quantitative tools in the study of demographic, political, and social history as well as economic history.

Robert William Fogel was born in New York City on July 1, 1926. His parents were refugees from the Russian Revolution. After attending public school in New York, he began his undergraduate studies at Cornell University in electrical engineering. However, his awareness of the problems of unemployment in capitalist economies led him to switch his major to history with a minor in economics. He graduated in 1948, and in the early 1950s he worked as a Communist Party organizer.

In 1956 Fogel began graduate work in economic history at Columbia University, with a particular interest in the great Marxian questions concerning the nature of long-term economic change. He moved to Johns Hopkins University for doctoral research in order to pursue a quantitative approach to the study of economic growth under the direction of Simon Kuznets. He began his teaching career at Johns Hopkins as an instructor in 1958, before taking an appointment as assistant professor at the University of Rochester in 1960. In 1963 he moved to the University of Chicago, and between 1975 and 1981 he taught in Harvard's Economics Department. He was instrumental in the late 1970s in establishing the Development of the American Economy (DAE) program associated with the National Bureau of Economic Research. In 1981 he returned to the University of Chicago to become the Walgreen Professor of American Institutions and the director of the Center for Population Economics. Fogel's radical political activity as a young adult presents a striking contrast with the anti-Communist origins of the Walgreen chair. His occupancy of the chair can be interpreted as reflecting both his own movement toward the political center and the latitude the Walgreen family gave the University when the chair was offered to him. In 1993 he was awarded the Nobel Memorial Prize in Economic Sciences (shared with Douglass North) for the development of quantitative and theoretical tools for the study of economic history.

Fogel's early work focused on the determinants of American economic growth. His doctoral dissertation, and the subsequent book *Railroads and American Economic Growth: Essays in Econometric History* (1964), challenged the prevailing view that the railroad had a decisive influence on the growth of the American economy. He calculated how much higher the costs would have been to the U.S. economy in 1890 of providing the same level of transportation services with alternative modes of water and land transportation. Fogel's counterfactual methodology proposed a hypothetical canal system that would have been built in the absence of railroads. His estimated "social saving" of the railroad was less than 5 percent of 1890 U.S. gross national product. Fogel's findings spawned numerous challenges by other scholars. Fogel responded by arguing that, for the case of the United States, any plausible allowance for factors raised by critics (such as scale effects and problems of measuring freight rates on rail versus water traffic) would still imply a modest rather than indispensable contribution to economic growth. However, Fogel also acknowledged that for other economies—such as Mexico, with its more limited access to water transport—the impact of the railroad on growth may well have been substantially larger. His counterfactual methodology generated considerable controversy among historians, with some stating that it was fundamentally ahistorical and fictive. Fogel replied that an analytical and causal approach to economic history inevitably requires the posing of counterfactual questions.

Fogel's next major project was a collaborative effort with Stanley Engerman on the economics of U.S. slavery. In the two-volume *Time on the Cross* (1974), they came to the surprising conclusion that Southern slave plantations were more efficient than Northern free farms. Critics argued that this finding was due to inadequate allowance for differences in crop mix, land quality, scale, and economic aims. Fogel and Engerman maintained that their result held, even with due allowance for these other factors, and they attributed it to the extra work effort that could be coerced from slave gangs. They also argued that slave owners had incentives to protect the capital investments their slaves represented. They supported this conclusion with evidence that slaves tended to be well fed and housed, that they were in fact only relatively infrequently subjected to abusive physical punishment or the breakup of their families through sale, and that female slaves did not engage in unusually high rates of premarital sexual intercourse. Fogel has continued to defend these specific findings against an extensive body of scholarly criticism. However, he has conceded that an appropriate moral indictment of slavery requires going beyond a narrow quantitative economic framework. His later writings on slavery have used a more traditional narrative approach along with the examination of quantitative evidence. Moreover, Fogel employed a mix of quantitative and qualitative approaches to address moral issues in *The Fourth Great Reawakening and the Future of Egalitarianism* (2000).

Since the mid-1970s, Fogel has undertaken the use of large-scale databases, such as Union Army pension records, to study trends, determinants, and the consequences of improvements in nutrition, health, and mortality and morbidity rates. His work (with collaborators) employing evidence on human heights to measure trends in nutrition spawned the burgeoning field of anthropometrics. He has shown how poor nutrition and health in early childhood can have enduring consequences for health later in life.

The Royal Swedish Academy of Sciences awarded the Nobel Prize jointly to Fogel and North in 1993, recognizing that both scholars have shown how economic history can provide fundamental insights into processes of economic and institutional change. The academy noted that North's contributions have been primarily conceptual, while Fogel is an empiricist. North has been circumspect about prospects for human progress after making allowance for the contingencies of political processes and mistakes in human judgement. Fogel, however, is an unabashed optimist about the prospects for human material progress, though he acknowledges the ongoing presence of spiritual and ethical challenges. He has coined the term *technophysio evolution* to point to the interaction between technological and human physiological advances.

SEE ALSO *Cliometrics; Economics, Nobel Prize in; Railway Industry; Slavery; Transportation Industry*

BIBLIOGRAPHY

PRIMARY WORKS

Fogel, Robert. 1979. Notes on the Social Saving Controversy. *Journal of Economic History* 39 (1): 1–54.

Fogel, Robert. 1989. *Without Consent or Contract: The Rise and Fall of American Slavery.* New York: Norton.

Fogel, Robert. 2000. *The Fourth Great Awakening and the Future of Egalitarianism.* Chicago: University of Chicago Press.

Fogel, Robert. 2004. *The Escape from Hunger and Premature Death, 1700–2100: Europe, America, and the Third World.* Cambridge, U.K.: Cambridge University Press.

SECONDARY WORKS

Eichengreen, Barry. 1994. The Contributions of Robert W. Fogel to Economics and Economic History. *The Scandinavian Journal of Economics* 96 (2): 167–179.

Goldin, Claudia. 1995. Cliometrics and the Nobel. *Journal of Economic Perspectives* 9 (2): 191–208.

Mokyr, Joel. 2005. "Hockey-Stick Economics": A Review Essay of Robert Fogel, *The Escape from Hunger and Premature Death, 1700–2100. Technology and Culture* 46 (3): 613–617.

David Mitch

FOLKLORE

SEE *Ethnology and Folklore.*

FOOD

Food is a biological necessity. Like sex, it has implications for the perpetuation of the species, but unlike sex, it also has implications for the survival of each individual. Social anthropologists point out that food is further implicated in the social and cultural survival of human groups. Acquiring and eating food is thus extended into the realms of the economic, political, and psychological.

Human beings are omnivorous, capable of safely eating a particularly wide variety of plant and animal sources of nutrients—a characteristic that has enabled the worldwide distribution of the species. Major, very broad transitions in human modes of living can be traced. Some 10,000 years ago the protracted shift began from foraging—continually on the move, hunting and gathering—to farming—settling, domesticating plants, and tending livestock. Then there is the comparatively recent 500-year increase in the movement of both people and foodstuffs around the globe: for example, new people to the Americas, turkeys to Europe. Most recently is the approximately 200 years' industrialization of both food production—agriculture, preservation, and processing—and food consumption—wholesale and "ready-made" retail distribution—that has been coupled with and supported by the increasingly intense application of physical, chemical, and biological sciences. The role of food in this long history of human groups is shrewdly summarized by Raymond Firth, who observed that in industrial society, getting food occurs in breaks between work, whereas in nonindustrial society, getting food is the day's work (1973).

The contemporary supply and distribution of food worldwide is notoriously unequal and inequitable. Particular attention has been devoted to international policies for the relief of severe and devastating food shortages. A major theme of this work is to note serious disjunctions that have profound consequences for those whose plight is meant to be alleviated. On the one hand are the media images of famine conjured in more-developed countries, typically of children in profound distress—images that then get dovetailed with assumptions embedded in international agencies' debates on world food security as to the relief required. On the other hand are what Johan Pottier describes as the everyday realities food-insecure people face (1999). In *The Anthropology of Food* he includes a simple, but compelling example. Official agricultural programs had no space in their information-gathering exercises in Kenya for the testimony of an elderly woman farmer, reputed in her community to be the most knowledgeable about growing yams. The program was, "top down," informed by research scientists' knowledge, not local expertise.

Even desperately hungry people need "their own" food, because, despite being omnivores, people do not eat everything available that is nontoxic and nutritious. This observation is only partly explainable in biological terms. Human groups the world over are observed to be selective in what, culturally speaking, counts as food. Such social definitions of food vary from society to society and they change over time. Familiarly, horse meat is food in Belgium but not in the United States; dog is a delicacy in parts of China but not in France. And on their first introduction to England, tomatoes were regarded as attractive but poisonous, whereas potatoes were initially grown in Sweden only as a garden ornament.

The social definition of food extends to encompass whole cuisines—distinctive combinations of ingredients and modes of their transformation into dishes—and what has been called *culinary culture*, a shorthand term for the ensemble of attitudes and tastes (both literal and metaphorical) members of a social group bring to cooking and eating food they have selected. Certain cuisines and culinary cultures have a long and persistent history. The beginnings of a Japanese rice-based cuisine, for instance, can be dated from the introduction of wet-rice agriculture over 2,000 years ago. Rice features strongly in eighth-century myths seeking to establish a national identity distinguishing Japan from its neighbors. These stories entailed notions of abundance, a land of good rice harvests. Divine power was incorporated into every grain of rice, symbolizing not only the relation between deities and people, but

also of those among human beings themselves. Thus rice became central to commensality, the act of eating together, and thereby cemented and symbolized social relationships—and a meal without rice could not count as a meal.

The case of rice illustrates the manner in which some have stressed the prime significance of symbols in understanding culinary cultures. By contrast, others have argued that emphasizing the material and practical rather than the symbolic offers superior intellectual interpretations of the variability in social definitions of food. But in a study of the global reach of sugar over four centuries, Sidney Mintz presented a powerful case for a combined approach that recognizes the symbolic significance of a foodstuff while arguing that meaning thus attributed is a *consequence* of practical human activity (1985). That the meaning of sugar could change from medicine in late-medieval Europe to luxury (like a spice, available only to the exceptionally wealthy) in the early modern period, then to a commonplace necessity to the laboring classes of nineteenth-century Britain, occurred, Mintz argues, as a *result* of usage—and of supplier-induced demand.

The case of rice also introduces the idea of a proper meal—one that is culturally appropriately composed, prepared, and served on socially prescribed occasions—a version of which appears to be found in most human groups. A British version—the caricatured "meat and two vegetables"—continues to be readily detectable not only in Britain, but also in its erstwhile colonies in North America, southern Africa, and Australia. Scholars specializing in the study of late twentieth- and early twenty-first-century consumption have claimed, however, that allegiance to such "traditional" modes of eating are disappearing, as part of broader changes of postindustrial society. One element of such changes, they argue, is the proposal that social differentiation is diminishing: No longer are education, income, gender, or age systematically evident in preferred dishes, locales for eating (e.g., expensive restaurants or fast-food diners), or the household division of food-preparation tasks. Another is that the predominant mode of food provision in both household and public settings has become commercial rather than domestic: Coupled with an increase in the rate of eating away from home in cafés, restaurants, and diners is the use at home of ready-made complete meals rather than dishes prepared from raw ingredients. And a third element—finding frequent expression in popular and journalistic commentaries claiming that families no longer gather round the table to share a meal—is that institutional rhythms are subject to erosion. Substantiating these claims adequately is difficult, however, and determining the extent to which they apply remains incomplete.

What is clear, though, is that the twenty-first-century food supply is global, providing populations in more developed countries with year-round fresh produce from less developed countries and an apparently ever widening range of products on supermarket shelves, with consumer choice as a watchword. Critics point to the environmental as well as social costs, for example in the diversion of comparatively limited local supplies of water to agricultural production for export markets, or the additional carbon emissions of air freight. Trends such as this are paralleled by a strikingly rapid increase in rates of obesity in a growing number of countries. Some commentators are even predicting that a generation of children will suffer fatal diseases associated with obesity—for example, diabetes and heart disease—to such an extent that they may even predecease their parents. This kind of public concern looks set to supplant the food-safety scares that dominated the last two decades of the twentieth century, the most dramatic and most costly example of which was bovine spongiform encephalopathy (BSE), commonly called mad cow disease, responsible for an invariably fatal disease if eaten by human beings. Public health policies, especially those geared to limiting the rates of obesity, are not readily aligned with economic policies supporting industrialized food production and the associated provision of employment. This essential, but in its current incarnation highly contested, sphere of human existence represents a considerable intellectual challenge to the still comparatively small number of social scientists seeking to understand its myriad facets.

SEE ALSO *Food Crisis; Malnutrition*

BIBLIOGRAPHY

Firth, Raymond. 1973. Food Symbolism in a Pre-Industrial Society. In *Symbols, Public and Private*. London: Allen and Unwin.

Mennell, Stephen. 1985. *All Manners of Food: Eating and Taste in England and France from the Middle Ages to the Present*. Oxford: Blackwell.

Mintz, Sidney W. 1985. *Sweetness and Power: The Place of Sugar in Modern History*. New York: Viking Penguin.

Pottier, Johan. 1999. *Anthropology of Food: The Social Dynamics of Food Security*. Cambridge, U.K.: Cambridge University Press.

Warde, Alan. 1997. *Consumption, Food, and Taste: Cultural Antimonies and Commodity Culture*. London: Sage.

Anne Murcott

FOOD CRISIS

The understanding of the causes of food crises, in the history of the social sciences, has evolved, from those stressing "natural" or lawlike causes, to those emphasizing the social nature of such crises. When Thomas Malthus, the English cleric and economist, first wrote his *Essay on the Principle of Population* (1798), he understood the occurrence of food crises as the effect of lawlike processes, saying that food production grows "arithmetically," while population grows "geometrically." This Malthusian view of food crises as basically caused by insufficient production has in modern social science been replaced by an understanding stressing the social causation, both of the occurrence of food crises and of their causes. Seminal in this change of view is the economist Amartya Sen's *Poverty and Famines* (1981).

With the development of the division of labor, with food markets extending the local village-town nexus to national and global scale, the occurrence of famine and hunger in principle gets disconnected from the local production conditions and their annual fluctuations. Thus, Sen showed that the Bengal Famine in 1943 was not primarily caused by harvest failures in Bengal, but by wider economic, social, and political conditions pertaining to the colonial economy, the nature of Bengali society, and political conditions during World War II (1939–1945).

When Malthus wrote his *Essay*, British agriculture was undergoing a major transformation in farming systems, usually referred to as high farming, allowing a much larger nonagricultural population to be fed by a diminishing work force in agriculture. Although this development is reflected in later editions of the *Essay*, the transformation was not foreseen, nor adequately conceptualized by Malthus.

THE GREEN REVOLUTION

A similar mismatch between the development of food production systems and social scientists' understanding of them occurred during the Green Revolution. This term refers to the state-driven efforts from the late 1960s forward to increase national self-sufficiency in food grains in a number of Asian countries based on stepped-up investments in agricultural production and research in new crop technologies. For example, the economist Gunnar Myrdal published his *Asian Drama* in 1968. Typically for its time, the work was pessimistic about the future of an Asia with its high population growth rates. About a year earlier, the Green Revolution was launched, and over a generation, the threat of famine was almost entirely averted in the continent. While Myrdal was unable to foresee this development, younger generations of social scientists have emphasized and often exaggerated the negative distribution and environmental effects of the Green Revolution at the same time as its basic achievements of averting the threat of famine have been downplayed.

Never before and, as far as one can foresee, never again, have the challenges to the world food system been as great as during the second half of the twentieth century. During that period, global production of food grains grew at rates outstripping those of world population, thus defying Malthusian predictions. This is an obvious background to the shift in scholarly understanding of food crises, from stressing natural or lawlike tendencies to stressing the social dimension.

During the early years of the twenty-first century and despite record levels of world production of grain, approximately 15 percent of the world population was starving or suffering chronic undernutrition. This lack in food security affects the life chances of people, their longevity, and the chances of infants and mothers to survive childbirth. Also health conditions are affected and, in serious conditions of undernutrition, learning capabilities, thus impairing the overall life chances of the individual.

THE GEOGRAPHY OF HUNGER

In the early twenty-first century, the highest incidence of undernutrition (over 35%) was in sub-Saharan Africa, with somewhat lower rates (between 20 and 35%) in the Sahel region of Africa, in parts of South and Central America, and parts of South, Southeast, and Central Asia. In a country like India, widespread undernutrition coexisted with a huge surplus of grain in government stocks, emphasizing the social causation of hunger.

Since decolonization in the 1960s, food production in sub-Saharan Africa grew steadily, but did not keep pace with the growth of population. As a consequence, the dependence of the subcontinent on imported food likewise grew. Again, stressing the complicated causation of food crises, many scholars argued that the import of cheap grain damaged African food production systems. Surplus stocks were dumped on world markets by the United States and the European Union and contributed to the insufficient growth of domestic production and thus to the food crisis in Africa.

There is an easily traceable influence from the world community of social scientists on the definition of food crisis and thus on the general evolvement of agricultural policies. The support to the political project of a Green Revolution in the West, at the time, was inspired by a Malthusian view of the population-food nexus and by a fear, during the cold war, that widespread hunger would lead to the spread of communism in Asia. Not only the Malthusian assumption, but also the assumption that hunger breeds radicalism, has been largely discredited by social science. Victims of food crisis are seldom radical and more often meek, apathetic, and subservient.

FROM FOOD CRISIS TO FOOD SECURITY

In tandem with the shift of focus from production to distribution, and from food crisis to food security, the polit-

ical emphasis shifted both in national governments as well as in global organizations like the United Nations' Food and Agriculture Organization (FAO), its World Food Program (WFP), and the International Fund for Agricultural Development (IFAD). During the late 1990s, this shift in attention may have partly caused and at least legitimated the declining levels of aid going to the agricultural sector. In the early years of the twenty-first century this trend appeared to be broken, partly as a result of increased focus on world hunger in connection with the millennium shift, but perhaps partly due to a realization among policymakers and social scientists that the focus on issues of distribution should not be permitted to lead to the neglect of production. Without production there is obviously nothing to distribute.

SEE ALSO *Food; Malnutrition; Malthusian Trap*

BIBLIOGRAPHY

Djurfeldt, Göran, and Magnus Jirström. 2005. The Puzzle of the Policy Shift: The Early Green Revolution in India, Indonesia, and the Philippines. In *The African Food Crisis: Lessons from the Asian Green Revolution*, eds. Göran Djurfeldt, Hans Holmén, Magnus Jirström, and Rolf Larsson. London: CABI.

Dyson, Tim. 1996. *Population and Food: Global Trends and Future Prospects*. London: Routledge.

FAO Hunger Map. Food and Agriculture Organization of the United Nations. http://www.fao.org.

Malthus, Thomas Robert. 1798. *Essay on the Principle of Population, As It Affects the Future Improvement of Society with Remarks on the Speculation of Mr. Godwin, M. Condorcet, and Other Writers*. London: J. Johnson.

Myrdal, Gunnar. 1968. *Asian Drama: An Inquiry into the Poverty of Nations*. New York: Pantheon.

Sen, Amartya. 1981. *Poverty and Famines: An Essay on Entitlement and Deprivation*. Oxford: Clarendon Press.

Göran Djurfeldt

FOOD DIPLOMACY

Food has been a factor in diplomacy since the very inception of the institution of diplomacy and the modern nation-state in the seventeenth century. Throughout history states have competed (and at times fought) for control of and access to food and other natural resources, such as water and energy, because they are essential to human survival and inextricably tied to political and economic development. Food and "food security" have always been important concerns of governments, especially for developing countries that have chronic food problems, such as malnutrition, low agricultural productivity, instability of supply, and food scarcity. Food security is a complicated and increasingly difficult goal to achieve. Although world food output has significantly increased since the end of World War II, poverty, agricultural mismanagement, and population growth in many developing countries undermine prospects for solving the world's food problems. Indeed food insecurity in developing countries, particularly in Africa, appears to have worsened, highlighting the uneven availability of and access to food and the politicized nature of both food production and distribution and the food aid system.

In general the term *food diplomacy* refers to the use of a country's food resources to influence global food markets and to influence international political and economic relations beyond the food market. Using food resources to influence food markets involves goals associated with the functional and structural aspects of the world food economy and the international trade in food, such as increasing the efficiency of food production, meeting minimum levels of food consumption, stabilizing food prices, and managing the disposal and distribution of surpluses. It is this dimension of food diplomacy that deals most explicitly with questions of food security and the policy differences between the major "food exporters" (i.e., the United States, Canada, Australia, the European Union, and Argentina for wheat and coarse grains; China, Pakistan, Thailand, the United States, and Vietnam for rice) and food importers, particularly the poor "food-deficit" countries in the developing world. Using food resources to influence international relationships beyond international food markets involves other foreign policy goals, such as advancing geostrategic interests abroad, increasing economic cooperation or strengthening political relations with another country, and punishing or sanctioning adversaries. This dimension of food diplomacy is much more controversial because it can be at odds with international humanitarian principles and the goal of world food security.

As a practical matter, it is impossible to separate the two dimensions of food diplomacy. There are political and economic consequences of food transfers, as there are for other commodities, such as oil. Even food aid (e.g., the U.S. Food for Peace program) is politicized and is one of the more sensitive points in agricultural trade negotiations between the United States and the European Union in the World Trade Organization's Doha Round. While the number of instances in which food has been employed as a political instrument of a country's foreign policy is relatively small, there have been some prominent cases. During the cold war, for example, the United States cancelled 17 million tons of grain sales to the Soviet Union as a form of punishment for the Soviet invasion of Afghanistan and temporarily halted food shipments to Bangladesh because it had traded jute with Cuba. Food

has been a key element of efforts by the United States, China, Russia, Japan, and South Korea to convince North Korea to abandon its nuclear weapons program.

SEE ALSO *Agricultural Industry; Cold War; Diplomacy; European Union; Food; Foreign Policy; Human Rights; International Relations; Union of Soviet Socialist Republics; War; Weaponry, Nuclear; World Trade Organization*

BIBLIOGRAPHY

Barrett, Christopher B., and Daniel G. Maxwell. 2006. Towards a Global Food Aid Compact. *Food Policy* 31 (2): 105–118.

Nau, Henry R. 1978. The Diplomacy of World Food: Goals, Capabilities, Issues, and Arenas. *International Organization* 32 (3): 775–809.

Van Wyk, Jo-Ansie. 2001. Food for Thought? The Politics of Food, Resources, and Development in Africa. *New Zealand International Review* 26 (2): 14.

James P. Muldoon Jr.

FORCES OF PRODUCTION

Forces of production is a term used in political economy that refers to the physical means and techniques of production to which laborers add value and transform capital into products for sale. Forces of production include instruments of production and raw materials, as well as the productive faculties of producing agents manifested by strength, skill, and knowledge. G. A. Cohen (2000, p. 37) argues that instruments of production and raw materials *have* productive forces, whereas labor power *is* a productive force.

Distinction must be made between forces of production and the ways they are utilized. Karl Marx wrote: "Powder remains the same whether it is used to wound a man or to dress his wounds" ([1847] 1982, p. 185). It can be argued that in Marx's view, forces of production are the driving factor in historical development. A new mode of production evolves when there is a conflict between the emerging production forces and the existing social relations. Thus, at a certain stage of development, modern industry becomes incompatible with the social production relations of handicraft (Marx [1867] 1977).

The "correspondence" between forces of production and relations need not be interpreted only as symmetrical, but can be interpreted as implying a priority of one over the other. This is the case made by Cohen (2000), who argues that the distinction between relations of production and forces of production is a special case of Marx's opposition of social to material features of society.

Irrespective of the primacy of forces of production or of social relations, some have insisted that different modes of production may exist simultaneously, which implicitly questions the rigid correspondence of production forces to given social relations. In various ways, feminists have utilized the notion of feudal relations to describe serf-like relations within households in capitalist economies with regards to unpaid domestic work (Benston 1969; Fraad, Resnick, and Wolff 1994).

In Marx's formulation, people enter into historically and geographically specific social relations that correspond to a given stage in the development of the material forces of production. As Marx puts it, the hand-mill gives society with a feudal lord; the steam-mill—industrial capitalism (Marx [1847] 1982, p. 109). The pairing of forms of technology to forms of social relations implies certain inertia and warranted predictability of historical development, which Lary Hickman calls "future-technological stage determinism" (1990, pp. 142–144). Thorstein Veblen (1906) and most of his followers in the tradition of American institutionalism (evolutionary economics) critique this teleological notion of social change and the idea that there is a final known end to which production process converges.

A notion of forces of production that drive historical development in a teleological manner has ramifications with regards to our understanding of "progress" and "development." Marx argues: "The country that is more developed industrially only shows, to the less developed, the image of its own future" ([1867] 1977, p. 90). Hickman (1990, pp. 143–144) offers two readings of this statement. First these "iron laws" operate only as long as a society adopts specific forces of production, and this is not necessarily inevitable ("limited technological-stage determinism"). Thus, while there is pairing between forces of production and social forces, there is place for variation. Alternatively, a given society inevitably passes through a given technological stage ("unlimited technological-stage determinism"). Thus, there is a notion of an ideal that ought to be achieved if a society is to master "modern" forces of production and social relations. Such a notion of forces of production brings questions about the opposition between "traditional" and "modern" that is contested by postcolonial critique (Zein-Elabdin 2004).

SEE ALSO *Asiatic Mode of Production; Capitalist Mode of Production; Exchange Value; Feudal Mode of Production; Marx, Karl; Marxism; Power; Productivity; Slave Mode of Production; Social Relations; Value; Veblen, Thorstein*

BIBLIOGRAPHY

Benston, Margaret. 1969. The Political Economy of Women's Liberation. *Monthly Review* 21 (4): 13–27.

Cohen, G. A. 2000. *Karl Marx's Theory of History: A Defence.* Princeton, NJ: Princeton University Press.

Fraad, Harriet, Stephen Resnick, and Richard Wolff. 1994. *Bringing It All Back Home: Class, Gender, and Power in the Modern Household.* London and Boulder, CO: Pluto Press.

Hickman, Lary. 1990. *John Dewey's Pragmatic Technology.* Bloomington and Indianapolis: Indiana University Press.

Marx, Karl. [1847] 1982. *The Poverty of Philosophy.* New York: International Publishers.

Marx, Karl. [1859] 1999. *A Contribution to the Critique of Political Economy,* ed. Maurice Dobb. New York: International Publishers.

Marx, Karl. [1867] 1977. *Capital.* New York: Vintage Books.

Veblen, Thorstein. 1906. The Socialist Economics of Karl Marx and His Followers. *Quarterly Journal of Economics* 20.

Zein-Elabdin, Eiman. 2004. Articulating the Postcolonial (With Economics in Mind). In *Postcolonialism Meets Economics,* eds. Eiman Zein-Elabdin and S. Charuseela, 21–40. London and New York: Routledge.

Zdravka Todorova

FORD MOTOR COMPANY

The Ford Motor Company established a system of modern mass production, labor relations, and wage policies that made it one of the most influential corporations of the twentieth century.

While the Ford Motor Company is the enterprise most closely associated with its namesake, Henry Ford, its incorporation in 1903 marked Ford's third attempt to build an automobile company. Ford began his automotive career with the short-lived Detroit Automobile Company (1898–1900), which was followed by the Henry Ford Company (1901–1902).

Ford manufactured for both domestic and foreign markets. In its first year of operation, it contracted with an overseas distributor to sell cars in Canada and Europe. In 1905 a Canadian plant began producing Ford vehicles for the British Empire.

Ford, unlike its chief rival General Motors, did not adopt a multidivisional structure. Ford and Lincoln (later Lincoln-Mercury), purchased in 1922, remain the only divisions within the auto company. A similarly atavistic quality characterizes Ford's ownership and management. The Ford family has consistently played a dominant role in ownership or direct managerial control throughout the company's history. This structure of centralized control is at odds with the historical trajectory toward managerial capitalism typical of most large-scale twentieth-century American corporations.

Ford engineers did not invent the modern assembly line. The basic concept was adapted from the meatpacking industry, in which animals were transported along a system of overhead pulleys and systematically butchered. Over the years 1910 to 1914 the assembly line evolved from the system of conveyors and gravity slides on which the Model T car was assembled in tightly sequenced stages. Production at the Highland Park plant relied on work rhythms that matched the pace of machines. Rather than using general-purpose tools and machinery, Ford manufactured machines to achieve specific tasks. Individual parts were made to be interchangeable, in order to speed production and reduce the need for skilled craftsmen. Investment in expensive, specialized machinery allowed for the introduction of economies of scale whereby unit costs fall as output rises. Ford produced half a million cars in 1915 and two million cars and trucks in 1923. It diversified into shipbuilding during World War I and aircraft manufacture in 1926. In addition to Europe and the British Empire, the newly industrializing Soviet Union was an important market; by 1927 the majority of tractors in the Soviet Union were Ford-built Fordsons. That same year Ford announced plans to acquire a 3,900-square-mile tract of land in Brazil to use as a rubber plantation to be named Fordlandia.

Integrated mass production was taken even further with the construction of the sprawling Rouge River plant in Dearborn, Michigan, during the 1920s. The Rouge plant inspired the photographer Charles Sheeler, whose pictures of it appeared in the pages of *Vanity Fair* magazine, and the painter Diego Rivera, who included it in the *Detroit Industry* murals; both depicted the factory as an icon of modern capitalism.

Along with time studies, Ford used various other strategies to organize work to meet the efficiency standards of plant machinery. In this sense the Ford system represents a refinement and extension of F. W. Taylor's scientific management approach. The resulting work environment was fast-paced and continuous, and workers were hard-pressed to keep up. Turnover rates reached 370 percent in 1913. In 1914, to overcome workers' resistance to machine-paced industrial work, the company inaugurated a radical plan to double hourly wages to five dollars a day. The extra money took the form of profit-sharing. To qualify for the higher wage, workers needed to demonstrate proper behavior at work and at home. Ford Sociological Department investigators inquired about workers' drinking habits, marital strife, criminal records, church-going activities, and other evidence of moral character. In this way Ford Motor exerted social control over its employees off the job, as well as technical control of work efforts on the job.

Ford paid black workers the same wages as similarly qualified white workers. While blacks comprised between 10 and 20 percent of the workforce at Ford, they were overwhelmingly assigned the most dangerous, difficult, and unpleasant jobs, such as those in the foundry. Because their wages were far superior to those obtainable from any alternative sources of employment, black workers, especially young married men, were much less likely to quit these jobs and less willing to embrace unionization.

To expand sales, Ford needed to encourage new segments of the population to buy cars. Higher wages allowed workers to acquire mass-produced goods. The interdependence of mass production and mass consumption came to be characterized as *Fordism*. The Italian political theorist Antonio Gramsci used the term to describe the combination of social, technological, and political control over workers' lives. It has since been extended to cover all institutions (factories, unions, families, and the state) that help to regulate the accumulation of profit in advanced capitalist economies.

Workers at Ford Motor unionized in 1941, four years after the United Auto Workers gained recognition at General Motors and Chrysler. Unionization at Ford was preceded by a strike at the Rouge plant that resulted in Ford's recruitment of African American strikebreakers, thereby exacerbating racial divisions within the ranks of the working class at Ford. During this same year U.S. manufacturers, following directives from the government's Office of Production Management, shifted to wartime production. Ford announced plans to mass-produce bombers at a new plant in Willow Run, Michigan. The Rouge plant was turned over to the production of aircraft engines and jeeps.

After the death of Henry Ford in 1947 and, earlier, that of his son and heir apparent, Edsel, in 1943, Henry's grandson Henry II headed the company. He transformed the organization by bringing in modern management experts (nicknamed the "Whiz Kids") with little or no experience at Ford. Among these new Ford executives was Robert McNamara, who later served as secretary of defense in the Kennedy and Johnson administrations during the Vietnam War.

The U.S. automobile market after World War II was marked by both consolidation—leading to the dominance of the "Big Three" (GM, Ford, and Chrysler)—and the increasing presence of foreign models. In 1955 Toyota Motors built its first modern Japanese mass-production plant, modeled on Ford's Rouge factory. In 1957 foreign automobile imports to the United States exceeded exports for the first time in over half a century. Ford began to reassert control of its foreign subsidiaries in Canada and

Britain. In 1957 the European Common Market was formed. This spurred Ford to try to build cars for regional rather than national markets (Europe instead of Germany, for instance). In 1967 Ford of Europe was established and in the 1970s it introduced an ultra-subcompact car. From the 1980s through the mid-1990s Ford was the leading car company in Europe. Nevertheless, more aggressive plans to build a world car that would integrate North American and European markets failed to produce success.

As part of this strategy of global integration, Ford completed a series of acquisitions in the 1980s and 1990s that included producers from Japan (Mazda), Europe (Volvo), and Britain (Jaguar, Land Rover, and Aston Martin). Ford recovered from the OPEC oil crisis of the 1970s and the product quality problems of the 1980s by designing the best-selling Taurus along with the increasingly popular Explorer sport utility vehicle. By 1995 Ford's share of the U.S. automobile market stood at 25.6 percent. However, well into the first years of the twenty-first century the company continued to rely on sales of trucks and sport utility vehicles at a time when environmental concerns and dependence on foreign oil were emerging as major concerns for U.S. consumers. Ford CEO William Ford Jr. sought to reorient production toward environmentally friendly hybrid vehicles while continuing to offer traditional gas-powered cars. The Rouge plant was reengineered to incorporate green building technology. As Ford's share of the U.S. market fell below 20 percent during the 2000s, the company embarked on a strategy of planned shrinkage of facilities and workforce in the United States. This mirrored the trend toward shrinking market share and falling sales for each of the Big Three U.S. auto companies.

SEE ALSO *Automobile Industry*

BIBLIOGRAPHY

Bonin, Hubert, Yannick Lung, and Steven Tolliday, eds. 2003. *Ford, 1903–2003: The European History.* 2 vols. Paris: P.L.A.G.E.

Brinkley, Douglas G. 2003. *Wheels for the World: Henry Ford, His Company, and a Century of Progress.* New York: Penguin Books.

Edwards, Richard. 1979. *Contested Terrain: The Transformation of the Workplace in the Twentieth Century.* New York: Basic Books.

Foote, Christopher L., Warren C. Whatley, and Gavin Wright. 2003. Arbitraging a Discriminatory Labor Market: Black Workers at the Ford Motor Company, 1918–1947. *Journal of Labor Economics* 21 (3): 493–532.

Hounshell, David A. 1984. *From the American System to Mass Production, 1800–1932: The Development of Manufacturing Technology in the United States.* Baltimore, MD: Johns Hopkins University Press.

Meyer, Stephen, III. 1981. *The Five Dollar Day: Labor Management and Social Control in the Ford Motor Company, 1908–1921.* Albany: State University of New York Press.

Nevins, Allan, with Frank Ernest Hill. 1954–1962. *Ford.* Vol. 1: *The Times, The Man, The Company*; vol. 2: *Expansion and Challenge: 1915–1933*; vol. 3: *Decline and Rebirth: 1933–1962.* New York: Scribner's and Sons.

Wilkins, Mira, and Frank Ernest Hill. 1964. *American Business Abroad: Ford on Six Continents.* Detroit, MI: Wayne State University Press.

Bruce Pietrykowski

FORDHAM, SIGNITHIA

SEE *Acting White; Oppositionality.*

FOREIGN POLICY

Foreign policy, conceptualized most broadly and simply, is the totality of a state's external behavior toward other states and nonstate actors (e.g., international organizations and terrorist organizations). Foreign policy involves everything from the most consequential decisions about war and peace to more seemingly mundane issues of tariff levels on imports. Foreign policy encompasses long-term goals and objectives (e.g., the U.S. policy of containing the expansion of Soviet influence during the cold war) as well as discrete decisions and actions (e.g., the Soviet Union's decision to deploy nuclear weapons in Cuba in 1961).

In the social sciences, *foreign policy analysis* emerged in the 1960s as a subfield of international relations. Foreign policy analysis represented a conscious attempt to move beyond what were seen as predominantly descriptive, unsystematic, and atheoretical accounts of foreign policy often found in diplomatic histories and policy analyses in opinion journals. The goal was to study the determinants of foreign policy behavior in a more theoretically oriented and empirically rigorous manner. This rigor was reflected in greater attention to data gathering and analysis, the development and testing of theory, and a move away from single country studies to more comparative analyses designed to assess the relative importance of various determinants of foreign policy. In this sense, foreign policy analysis reflected the broader trend of behavioralism in political science and the social sciences more generally in the 1950s and 1960s.

One of the first manifestations of the move to greater rigor in foreign policy analysis was the development of frameworks to help organize both empirical research and theory development. The frameworks that eventually exerted the greatest impact on how scholars thought about foreign policy and conducted their research involved some version of what came to be known as the *levels of analysis*. The hope was that the use of such common frameworks would encourage scholars to think more systematically about the sources of foreign policy while making empirical research more cumulative.

LEVELS OF ANALYSIS

As with all social sciences, the study of foreign policy is ultimately about understanding human behavior, whether people are acting alone as individuals or in groups as social collectives. As Valerie Hudson notes, "Understanding how humans perceive and react to the world around them, and how humans shape and are shaped by the world around them, is central to the inquiry of all social scientists, including those in IR [i.e., international relations]" (Hudson 2005, p. 1). Though foreign policy analysis can be differentiated from other social sciences in terms of the actor and behavior in question, many of the basic insights for understanding any type of human behavior are relevant and have been adapted for the study of foreign policy.

Generally speaking, there are two types of explanations for the behavior of any social actor. We can loosely refer to these as *dispositional* and *situational*. Dispositional explanations portray an actor's behavior as the result of some feature or characteristic of the actor itself: An actor behaves in a certain way because something about the actor predisposed it to behave in a particular fashion. Situational explanations focus on external forces that shape an actor's behavior regardless of its unique characteristics: Something in the actor's environment led it to behave in a certain way. In all but the most extreme instances of course, social scientists recognize that any actor's behavior results from some combination of dispositional and situational forces. Thus the goal of most social scientific inquiry is to determine the relative importance of dispositional/internal and situational/external forces in shaping an actor's behavior.

Kenneth Waltz (1959) was among the first to introduce a similar scheme into international relations. Focusing on theories of war, not foreign policy per se, he drew a distinction between individual-, national-, and international-level explanations of state behavior. Numerous versions of the basic scheme incorporating further refinements and distinctions within the different levels have been developed and applied since its first appearance. The most influential of these was presented in 1966 by James Rosenau in his call for the development of "theories and pre-theories" of foreign policy.

Several levels of analysis highlighted by Rosenau are common to virtually all such frameworks. The *individual* or *idiosyncratic level* focuses on the decision makers themselves and draws heavily on research and theory from social and cognitive psychology. Research at this level has examined the impact of personality traits, beliefs/perceptions, and cognitive processes. The *societal level* deals with the impact of general national attributes, such as a state's economic system, regime type, level of development, public opinion, or political culture. The *governmental level* emphasizes the institutions and dynamics of decision-making processes, particularly bureaucratic competition and organizational dynamics. The *international level* stresses the general impact of the anarchic and competitive nature of an anarchic international system, a state's position in the overall distribution of power, and factors such as geography. Two things are apparent from the levels-of-analysis frameworks and determinants of foreign policy specified within each level: First, any explanation of a state's foreign policy will certainly incorporate elements from multiple, if not all, levels; second, the study of foreign policy is by its very nature multidisciplinary, drawing on insights from a wide array of social sciences. In this respect, once again, foreign policy is probably no different than most other social phenomena.

MODELS OF FOREIGN POLICY

Graham Allison (1969, 1971), in his seminal article and book on decision-making during the Cuban missile crisis, claimed that observers often analyze and explain foreign policy through the lens of a *rational actor model*. Either implicitly or explicitly, analysts portray states as unitary actors possessing a coherent set of ranked national goals and objectives. According to this model, states confronted with international circumstances that require action will craft, evaluate, select, and implement policy options that maximize these goals and objectives. This rational actor model is often applied in reverse to understand a state's foreign policy and determine what its goals and objectives might be. If a nation deploys a certain weapons system or decides to use force, for example, observers assume that this policy was chosen in order to maximize its goals and objectives. As Allison explains, "This paradigm leads analysts to rely on the following pattern of inference: if a nation performed a particular action, the nation must have ends toward which the action constituted an optimal means" (Allison 1969, p. 694). A rational actor model views foreign policy as an intellectual or analytical, as opposed to political, process. Though a rational model is often applied implicitly, some international relations adopt it explicitly, even though they realize that it is usually not an empirically accurate portrait of how foreign policy decisions are made. In their view, such unrealistic simplifications of reality are theoretically useful and necessary even if they are descriptively inaccurate. Allison, among others, argued that the routine application of the rational actor obscures a genuine understanding of foreign policy: The "black box" of the state needs to be opened and unrealistic assumptions abandoned or modified if we want to understand and explain state behavior. In fact one of the underlying goals of levels-of-analysis frameworks and their inclusion of domestic and individual variables is to direct attention to the internal workings of the state and decision-making processes.

With the goal of better understanding foreign policy, Allison presented two other models that offered better pictures of how foreign policy is actually made: the *bureaucratic politics model* and the *organizational process model*. In the bureaucratic model, the state is not seen as a unitary rational actor but rather as a collection of actors representing governmental organizations with different perspectives, goals, and objectives. There is no single, coherent, and ranked set of national goals and objectives. Policy is the result of a political process, not an analytical process. In this model, "the decisions and actions of governments are essentially intra-national political outcomes" (Allison 1969, p. 708). Decision makers are seen as reflecting the interests and perspectives of the government bureaucracies they represent, a tendency embodied in the cliché that where one stands (on any given issues) depends on where one sits (within the government). A state's behavior should be seen as reflecting the relative power of the players in the process, not as something designed to maximize a well-defined national interest. Under other circumstances, it might make more sense to understand foreign policy through the lens of an organizational process model. This model assumes that states are large organizations that seldom reevaluate policy from scratch and consider the full range of options when action is required. The crafting, evaluation, choice, and implementation of policy options are often determined by such factors as precedent and the standard operating procedures and routines usually found in any large organization.

Allison did not claim that the bureaucratic and organizational models were always more accurate than the rational actor model. Nor did he suggest a complete rejection of the rational actor model. In laying out the models and applying them to the Cuban missile crisis, Allison was attempting to make two points. First, there are some, perhaps many, circumstances in which foreign policy decisions may be the result of different decision-making processes and dynamics. Second, the alternative models are useful for highlighting and illustrating the real world constraints and forces that limit the applicability of rational models to understand foreign policy (or policy in any area for that matter).

EXPLAINING FOREIGN POLICY

One problem with levels-of-analysis frameworks is that they often result in a seemingly endless laundry list of variables that influence foreign policy. Those seeking to explain a state's behavior can easily become overwhelmed by the proliferation of determinants at each level. It is easy for the analyst to drown in a sea of details and determinants. Analysts need to find some way to include more without becoming overwhelmed. To deal with this problem, it is useful to emphasize that foreign policy can encompass everything from general policy orientations that persist over long periods to discrete decisions. There is a need for some precision about exactly what one wants to explain. If an analyst wants to explain why Great Britain pursued a policy of naval supremacy throughout most of the eighteenth and nineteenth centuries, this is very different from trying to explain a particular decision about the use of force. In thinking about the determinants of broad policy orientations such as Britain's policy of naval supremacy, it would make little sense to look to the personality traits of British prime ministers. Behaviors and policies pursued over long periods are more likely to be the result of similarly enduring determinants such as geography and culture. On the other hand, if one is trying to explain a specific decision, such as Britain's military response to the Argentinean seizure of the Falkland Islands in 1983, it might very well make sense to focus on leader traits (Prime Minister Margaret Thatcher in this case). Foreign policy analysis requires clarity not only in terms of the determinants of policy but also what is to be explained. In this way, one thinks about which determinants are likely to "match up" with the level of policy one is seeking to explain.

Similarly analysts sometimes worry about the proliferation of models. The critical point is to remember that there is no reason to assume that any one model is generally applicable. The description of various decision-making models merely highlights the fact that not all decisions are the result of the same process. The process itself is likely to vary with the nature and importance of the issue at hand, the amount of time decision makers have to act, and whether the problem is new or familiar. Critical issues of war and peace and the use of force, for example, are almost always decided at the highest levels, not within the confines of bureaucracies and organizations. As a result these decisions may more closely resemble the rational actor model. If the problem requiring a decision is novel or unfamiliar, there are unlikely to be preexisting, organizational, standard operation procedures that can be applied. If decision makers have little time to make a decision, they may be unable to craft and evaluate a wide range of new policy options and may thus choose to implement preexisting plans or routines. If the policy has important consequences for the allocation of resources, the influence of bureaucratic politics may be greater. Analysts need to think about the issues and conditions that are most conducive to different decision-making processes.

The development of levels-of-analysis frameworks and alternative decision-making models were both attempts to move analysts away from the tendency to view foreign policy as a rational and strategic response to external events. As Waltz, frequently criticized for treating states as unitary, rational actors, admits, "foreign-policy behavior can be explained only by a conjunction of external and internal conditions" (Waltz 1993, p. 79). In most political science departments, foreign policy is treated as a subfield of international relations. There are good reasons for this, given that the focus is on the external behavior of states. But one could make an equally compelling case that it should be viewed as a subfield of public policy, since there is no compelling reason to believe that foreign policy is free of all the same influences that shape policy in other areas. Foreign policy is, after all, foreign *policy*.

SEE ALSO *Alliances; Bureaucracy; Cold War; Cuban Missile Crisis; Decision-making; Deterrence; Deterrence, Mutual; Falkland Islands War; International Relations; Leadership; Neutral States; Non-alignment; Peace; Rationality; Strategic Behavior; Strategic Games; Thatcher, Margaret; Waltz, Kenneth; War*

BIBLIOGRAPHY

Allison, Graham. 1969. Conceptual Models and the Cuban Missile Crisis. *American Political Science Review* 63 (3): 689–718.

Allison, Graham. 1971. *The Essence of Decision: Explaining the Cuban Missile Crisis*. 2nd ed. Boston: Little, Brown, 1999.

Hudson, Valerie. 2005. Foreign Policy Analysis: Actor-Specific Theory and the Ground of International Relations. *Foreign Policy Analysis* 1 (1): 1–30.

Hudson, Valerie. 2006. *Foreign Policy Analysis: Classic and Contemporary Theory*. Lanham, MD: Rowman and Littlefield.

Ikenberry, G. John, ed. 2004. *American Foreign Policy: Theoretical Essays*. 5th ed. New York: Longman.

Neack, Laura, Jeanne A. K. Hey, and Patrick Haney, eds. 1995. *Foreign Policy Analysis: Continuity and Change in Its Second Generation*. Englewood Cliffs, NJ: Prentice Hall.

Rosenau, James. 1971. Pre-Theories and Theories of Foreign Policy (1966). In *The Scientific Study of Foreign Policy*, ed. James Rosenau, 95–151. New York: Free Press.

Waltz, Kenneth. 1959. *Man, the State, and War: A Theoretical Analysis*. New York: Columbia University Press.

Waltz, Kenneth. 1993. The Emerging Structure of International Politics. *International Security* 18 (2): 44–79.

Yetiv, Steve. 2004. *Explaining Foreign Policy: U.S. Decision-Making and the Persian Gulf War*. Baltimore, MD: Johns Hopkins University Press.

Keith Shimko

FORESIGHT, PERFECT

A term of everyday use, *foresight*, when qualified by *perfect*, is elevated to a concept of signal importance, certainly for modern economic theory with its proclivity to fixed points, but perhaps also for social sciences more generally. This entry attempts a brief overview.

In his analysis of investment decisions in chapter 12 of *The General Theory of Employment, Interest, and Money* (1936), John Maynard Keynes (1883–1946) draws attention partly to "existing facts, known more or less for certain" and partly to "future events, forecasted with more or less confidence" (Keynes 1936, p. 147).

> The state of long-term expectation does not solely depend on the most probable forecast that we can make. It also depends on the *confidence* with which we make this forecast—on how highly we rate the likelihood of our best forecast turning out quite wrong.... The *state of confidence* ... is a matter to which practical men always pay the closest and most anxious attention. (p. 148)

Keynes (p. 152) emphasizes that our projections into the future, as well as our assumption that the "existing market valuation, however arrived at, is uniquely *correct* in relation to our existing knowledge of the facts" are based on a convention whose essence lies in the assumption of stationarity.

> In practice we have tacitly agreed, as a rule, to fall back on what is, in truth, a convention. The conventional method of calculation will be compatible with a considerable measure of continuity and stability in our affairs, *so long as we can rely on the maintenance of the convention*. But it is not surprising that a convention, in an absolute view of things so arbitrary, should have its weak points. (p. 152)

These points are collected under four headings, but with the proviso that "philosophically speaking, [market evaluations] cannot be uniquely correct since our existing knowledge does not provide a sufficient basis for a calculated mathematical expectation" (p. 152).

Undoubtedly familiar with the writings of French mathematician and economist Antoine Augustin Cournot (1801–1877), Keynes does not formulate or work with the notions of *rational expectations equilibrium* or *self-fulfilling expectations*. (See Merton [1936, 1948] for his historical take on the idea encapsulated in these phrases.) In a Cournot-Nash equilibrium, each individual action, taken on the basis of a judgment about the facts of the situation, a judgment that not only takes the actions and judgments of others into account in ascertaining the facts of the situation as they find and judge it, but also allows their judgments, and consequent potential actions, to incorporate all that it itself takes into account, ends up by generating precisely the shape of the situation it initially took into account. In Keynes's *General Theory*, the word *foresight* is used nine times, *perfect* appears four times, and *imperfect* five times, but the two adjectives are never used to qualify the noun. Keynes refers to a correct state of expectation and correct foresight, the latter twice, but in as much a negative, possibly ironic, light as in a positive one. *Hindsight*, perfect or imperfect, is never employed to subdue and discipline history, as the assumption of perfect foresight is now sometimes used to discipline data and neutralize the future in theoretical thinking current in macroeconomics and associated with Brock (1972, 1974), Lucas, Lucas and Prescott (1971) and their followers. (For issues relating to *perception* and *individual observability*, see Chakrabarti and Khan, 1991.)

Nevertheless, Keynes's chapter 12 is impressive in how it draws on and anticipates the vernacular of modern game theory and finance. (For epistemological concerns stemming from Nash (1951), see Aumann and Brandenburger (1995) and Khan (1990, section 2.)) Referring to investment as a "battle of wits," and using metaphors for games that are played with "zest and enjoyment" even though the players know what they entail and their sorry end, Keynes introduces game-players and player-types: uninformed versus informed investors "as gulls among the public to feed the maws of the professionals" (Keynes 1936, p. 155), and speculators versus enterprisers. He emphasizes "animal spirits—a spontaneous urge to action rather than inaction [as opposed to an] outcome of a weighted average of quantitative benefits multiplied by quantitative probabilities" (p. 161), a maximization of von Neumann-Morgenstern expected utilities, and flatly denies that the "basis for making such calculations" exists. Anticipating David Lewis (1969) and Robert Aumann (1976), but stopping short of them and of infinite regress (see Parikh and Krasucki (1990) and their references to the work of Geanakoplos-Polemarchakis, Cave and Bacaharach), Keynes writes:

> We have reached the third degree where we devote our intelligences to anticipating what average opinion expects the average opinion to be. And there are some I believe who practice the fourth, fifth and higher degrees. (1936, p. 156)

Once the investment decision is reviewed as part of an anonymous multiplicity of decentralized decisions taken by producers and consumers, independent of each other except for their dependence on the price system, as in the Arrow-Debreu-McKenzie theory, the facts of the situation refer only to the price system. (Debreu (1959), Nikaido (1968), Arrow and Hahn (1971) and McKenzie (2002) represent the *loci classicus* of a theory to which many others have made fundamental contributions. See Khan (2004) for a reading of Debreu through the eyes of

Keynes and his Cambridge predecessors and successors, including Frank Hahn.) If however, there are facts that are not, perhaps cannot be, "priced out," and agents have differential informational access to these facts but not to each other, then the price system can be used by each to gauge the information and beliefs of the others, and to refine their decisions accordingly. (Hayek (1948) is now a classic reference on differential information.) Such a context is particularly amenable to attempts at equilibrium theorizing. James Jordan and Roy Radner refer to agents' individual models, endow these models with a measure of rationality, and introduce the 1982 *Journal of Economic Theory* symposium with these words:

> In a market for commodities whose future utility is uncertain, the equilibrium prices will reflect the information and beliefs that the traders bring to the market, as well as their tastes and endowments. The term rational expectations equilibrium is applied to a model of market equilibrium that takes account of this potential informational feedback. (Jordan and Radner 1982, p. 201)

A situation in which agents have identical information regarding an uncertain environment, Keynes's *convention* becomes the theoretical reality, and an equilibrium that features a "correct" *price-expectation function* can be formulated. Under the heading of a *perfect foresight approach*, Radner (1982) refers to this as Muth's (1961) idea of rational expectations, and distinguishes it from the one originally formulated, in 1967 and subsequently, to deal with differential information (see also Jordan and Radner 1982, para. 6, and Sent 1998).

Margaret Bray (1987) focuses on the perfect foresight hypothesis in what Radner describes as Muth's sense. In addition to following Radner in designating John Hicks (1939) as another precursor, Bray also discusses the early work of Nicholas Kaldor (1934). Her conclusion that "there is little to be gained in realism by exchanging the myth of complete markets for the fantasy of perfect foresight" (Bray 1987, p. 834) surely stands twenty years later; I leave it to the reader, and to a more detailed subsequent investigation, to determine how much the hypothesis has gained for the theory and for the understanding of competitive markets, themselves nothing if not intertemporal. (See Aumann (1998) and his references for issues centered on temporality.)

SEE ALSO *Arrow-Debreu Model; Beauty Contest Metaphor; Competition, Perfect; Expectations; Expectations, Implicit; Expectations, Rational; Game Theory; Hicks, John R.; Nash Equilibrium*

BIBLIOGRAPHY

Arrow, Kenneth J., and F. H. Hahn. 1971. *General Competitive Analysis*. San Francisco, CA: Holden-Day.

Aumann, Robert J. 1976. Agreeing to Disagree. *Annals of Statistics* 4: 1236–1239.

Aumann, Robert J. 1998. Common Priors: A Reply to Gul. *Econometrica* 66: 929–938.

Aumann, Robert J., and Adam Brandenburger. 1995. Epistemic Conditions for Nash Equilibrium. *Econometrica* 63: 1161–1180.

Bray, Margaret M. 1987. Perfect Foresight. In *The New Palgrave: A Dictionary of Economics*, ed. John Eatwell, Peter K. Newman, and Murray Milgate, 833–834. London: Macmillan.

Brock, William A. 1972. On Models of Expectations That Arise from Maximizing Behavior of Economic Agents over Time. *Journal of Economic Theory* 5: 348–376.

Brock, William A. 1974. Money and Growth: The Case of Long Run Perfect Foresight. *International Economic Review* 15: 750–777.

Chakrabarti, Subir K., and M. Ali Khan. 1991. Equilibria of Large Games with Imperfect Observability. In *Positive Operators, Reisz Spaces and Economics*, ed. C. D. Aliprantis, K. C. Border, and W. A. J. Luxemburg. New York: Springer Verlag.

Cournot, Antoine Augustin. 1838. *Recherches sur les principes mathématiques de la théorie des Richesses*. Paris: Librairie des Sciences Politiques et Sociales. English trans: 1897. *Researches into the Mathematical Principles of the Theory of Wealth*. Trans. Nathaniel T. Bacon. New York: Macmillan.

Debreu, Gerard. 1959. *The Theory of Value: An Axiomatic Analysis of Economic Equilibrium*. New York: Wiley.

Glahe, Fred R., ed. 1991. *Keynes's The General Theory of Employment, Interest, and Money: A Concordance*. Savage, MD: Rowman and Littlefield.

Hayek, Friedrich A. 1948. *Individualism and Economic Order*. Chicago: Chicago University Press.

Hicks, John R. 1939. *Value and Capital: An Inquiry into Some Fundamental Principles of Economic Theory*. Oxford: Clarendon.

Jordan, James, and Roy Radner. 1982. Rational Expectations in Microeconomic Models: An Overview. *Journal of Economic Theory* 26: 201–223.

Kaldor, Nicholas. 1934. A Classificatory Note on the Determinateness of Equilibrium. *Review of Economic Studies* 1: 122–136.

Keynes, John Maynard. 1936. *The General Theory of Employment, Interest, and Money*. New York: Harcourt, Brace.

Khan, M. Ali. 1990. On the Languages of Markets. *Pakistan Development Review* 30: 503–549.

Khan, M. Ali. 2004. Self-interest, Self-deception, and the Ethics of Commerce. *Journal of Business Ethics* 52: 189–206.

Lewis, David K. 1969. *Convention: A Philosophical Study*. Cambridge, MA: Harvard University Press.

Lucas, Robert E., Jr. 1972. Expectations and the Neutrality of Money. *Journal of Economic Theory* 5:103–124.

Lucas, Robert E., Jr., and Edward T. Prescott. 1971. Investment under Uncertainty. *Econometrica* 39: 659–681.

McKenzie, Lionel W. 2002. *Classical General Equilibrium Theory*. Cambridge, MA: MIT Press.

Merton, Robert K. 1936. The Unanticipated Consequences of Purposive Social Action. *American Sociological Review* 1: 894–904.

Merton, Robert K. 1948 [1968]. The Self-Fulfilling Prophecy. Reprinted in *Social Theory and Social Structure*. New York: Free Press.

Muth, John F. 1961. Rational Expectations and the Theory of Price Movements. *Econometrica* 29: 315–335.

Nash, John F., Jr. 1950. Equilibrium Points in N-person Games. *Proceedings of the National Academy of Sciences U.S.A.* 36: 48–49.

Nikaido, Hukukane. 1968. *Convex Structures and Economic Theory*. New York: Academic Press.

Parikh, Rohit, and Paul Krasucki. 1990. Communication, Consensus, and Knowledge. *Journal of Economic Theory* 52: 178–179.

Radner, Roy. 1967. Equilbre des marchés à terme et au comptant en cas d'incertitude. *Cahiers d'econométrie* 9: 30–47.

Radner, Roy. 1982. Equilibrium under Uncertainty. In *Handbook of Mathematical Economics*, ed. Kenneth J. Arrow and Michael D. Intriligator, Vol. 2, chap. 20. Amsterdam: North Holland.

Sent, Esther-Mirjam. 1998. *The Evolving Rationality of Rational Expectations*. Cambridge, U.K.: Cambridge University Press.

M. Ali Khan

FORMAN, JAMES
1928–2005

In his "Letter to My Sisters and Brothers," which opens his book *The Making of Black Revolutionaries*, James Forman writes, "We are not born revolutionary. Revolutionaries are forged through constant struggle and the study of revolutionary ideas and experiences." This statement captures a central aspect of the social and political thought of the civil rights leader. Throughout his life, Forman constantly emphasized the essential relationship between thought and action in the struggle for social and political change. In so doing, he left an indelible mark on the history of African American political thought and protest movements.

Born on October 4, 1928, in Chicago, Illinois, James Forman spent the first years of his life on his grandmother's farm in Benton County, Mississippi. At the age of six he went to live with his mother and stepfather in a four-room apartment on the South Side of Chicago. He attended grammar school at St. Anselm's Catholic School and then transferred to Betsy Ross Grammar School. During his grammar school years Forman sold the *Chicago Defender*, an influential African American newspaper that proved to be a catalyst in developing his political conscience. Graduating with honors from Englewood High School in 1947, James spent one semester at Wilson Junior College before volunteering for service in the United States Air Force. While stationed in California, he took classes at the University of Southern California. Upon returning to Chicago in 1954, Forman enrolled in Roosevelt University, where he took an active role in student politics. He graduated with honors in 1957 and, with the assistance of a professor, St. Clair Drake, began graduate school in the Government Department and the African Research and Studies Program at Boston University.

With the advent of a burgeoning civil rights movement, Forman decided to leave graduate school and take an active role in the struggle for racial justice. He covered the integration of the Little Rock public schools for the *Chicago Defender*, and while teaching at Paul Cornell Elementary School in Chicago, he took an active role in the protest struggles of African American sharecroppers in Tennessee. But it was through his work with the Student Nonviolent Coordinating Committee (SNCC)—as executive secretary and director of international affairs—that Forman was able to make a significant contribution to the civil rights revolution. Forman's organizational prowess, along with his deep commitment to forging effective ideological positions for SNCC, contributed to the organization's political effectiveness. Although he often disagreed with the strategies, tactics, and philosophies of other SNCC leaders, such as Bob Moses, as well as other civil rights organizations, Forman was a central figure in transforming SNCC into one of the "Big Five" civil rights organizations—the others being the Congress of Racial Equality (CORE), the National Association for the Advancement of Colored People (NAACP), the NAACP Legal Defense Fund (LDF), and the Southern Christian Leadership Conference (SCLC).

As SNCC experienced tremendous ideological tensions and fractures, Forman withdrew from active participation in the organization in 1968. He briefly affiliated with the League of Revolutionary Black Workers, a labor organization that worked with African American autoworkers in Michigan. In 1969, Forman formulated his "Black Manifesto" at the National Black Economic Development Conference. The Manifesto became widely known after he interrupted the May 4, 1969, service at New York's Riverside Church to read his formal call for reparations for African Americans. Over time, Forman's political thought evolved to more fully take into account thinkers and movements from the Third World. He also developed a more pointed critique of capitalist political

economy. Forman eventually earned his Master's degree in African and African American history from Cornell University and his PhD in political history from the Union of Experimental Colleges and Universities. In 1984, he published a revised version of his graduate school research as *Self-Determination and the African American People*. He continued to be active in a number of national and international political movements, including running an unsuccessful campaign in 1990 to become the "shadow" U.S. senator from Washington, D.C. (The two "shadow senators" are nonvoting representatives who lobby Congress on behalf of the District of Columbia.) James Forman died on January 10, 2005, after a battle with colon cancer.

SEE ALSO *Civil Rights Movement, U.S.; Student Nonviolent Coordinating Committee*

BIBLIOGRAPHY

Black Star Publishing, ed. 1970. *The Political Thought of James Forman*. Detroit, MI: Black Star Publishing.

Carson, Clayborne. 1981. *In Struggle: SNCC and the Black Awakening of the 1960s*. Cambridge, MA: Harvard University Press, 1995.

Forman, James. 1972. *The Making of Black Revolutionaries*. Seattle: University of Washington Press, 1997.

Corey D. B. Walker

FORMATION, RACIAL

Introduced in 1986 by Howard Winant and Michael Omi, the theory of *racial formation* has extensively influenced the field of racial and ethnic relations. Racial formation theory extends the general sociological principle of race being a socially constructed concept that is contested and undergoes changes over time. Primarily an analysis of how U.S. society has been re-racializing since the 1960s through a number of *racial projects*, the theory discusses the transformation of racial categories largely by efforts in the political arena and the ways in which racial meanings affect this process.

Omi and Winant define racial formation as "the sociohistorical process by which racial categories are created, inhabited, transformed, and destroyed" (1994, p. 55). They argue that this process of *racialization* is situated between structure and representation, whereby, at certain points in history, racial meaning is extended to a racial relationship, social practice, or group. Racial ideology is constructed and reconstructed from preexisting conceptual elements and emerges from the struggles of competing political projects and ideas seeking to articulate similar elements differently. Additionally, Omi and Winant argue that race is an organizing principle not just at the societal (macro) level, but also at the individual (micro) level, shaping the identities of individuals and affecting all areas of social life. However, they do give substantial emphasis in their analysis to the macro level, arguing that racial conflict occurs primarily at the level of the state. In their estimation, the process of racial formation takes place in two steps: through racial projects and the evolution of hegemony.

RACIAL PROJECTS

Omi and Winant (1994) argue that society is suffused with racial projects, which form the "heart" of the racial formation process. They define a racial project as "simultaneously an interpretation, representation, or explanation of racial dynamics, and an effort to reorganize and redistribute resources along particular racial lines" (1994, p. 56). Racial projects are the link between structure and ideology, in that they mediate between the discursive ways race is identified and signified on one hand, and the institutional forms in which it is routinized on the other. Racial projects give us new ways of reasoning about race, new plans for action, and often new language and discourse with which to talk about race and possibly even mask racist ideas.

Through historical analysis, Omi and Winant assert that the most successful racial projects since the 1960s (largely carried out by neoconservative members of the ruling class) have furthered the notion that liberal racial policies gone wrong are to blame for many of society's problems. For example, affirmative action programs created by whites to modestly address some extreme racial inequities have been effectively reframed as "reverse discrimination," harmful to white Americans' life chances, and even detrimental to beneficiaries of color on a psychological level. This racial project was one of several competing projects, but eventually prevailed in the political and social arenas.

CONTRIBUTION AND CRITICISM

The theory of racial formation had a major impact on the study of racial and ethnic relations and is incorporated into most critical race scholarship. Little prior theory, in addition to much current mainstream research, gives attention to the role of government in creating racial-ethnic groups and, instead, a great deal of scholarship attempts to subsume contemporary racial issues underneath matters of ethnicity, nationality, or class (e.g., Wilson 1980). However, while Omi and Winant's theory gives important insight into racial formation as a freestanding social process, critical race scholars give some noteworthy critique.

Some race theorists argue that Omi and Winant give ideological processes excessive emphasis, and little attention is devoted to how racial orders are structured (Bonilla-Silva 2001; Feagin 2006). Specifically, the racial formation theory does not aid understanding of the ways in which the ideological formation of race has been buttressed by extensive generation of wealth and assets for white Americans (Feagin 2006). Thus, Omi and Winant attend well to the symbolic and less well to the structural.

Similarly, because Omi and Winant do not present racial groups as collectivities who contest their positioning in the racial hierarchy, their analysis casts little light on why people fight over racial matters and either accept or challenge racial projects (Bonilla-Silva 2001). Omi and Winant also claim that the most recent rearticulation of the racial ideology has been carried out by certain rightwing members of the dominant class, but this analysis neglects a systemic understanding of the process (Bonilla-Silva 2001). Nevertheless, racial formation theory provides subsequent scholars with a solid reference point for the racial theories of the future.

SEE ALSO *Affirmative Action; Ethnic Conflict; Ethnic Fractionalization; Feagin, Joseph; Hierarchy; Inequality, Wealth; Poststructuralism; Race; Racial Classification; Racialization; Racism*

BIBLIOGRAPHY

Bonilla-Silva, Eduardo. 2001. *White Supremacy and Racism in the Post-Civil Rights Era.* Boulder, CO: Lynne Rienner.

Feagin, Joe R. 2006. *Systemic Racism: A Theory of Oppression.* New York: Routledge.

Omi, Michael, and Howard Winant. 1994. *Racial Formation in the United States: From the 1960s to the 1990s.* 2nd ed. New York: Routledge.

Wilson, William Julius. 1980. *The Declining Significance of Race: Blacks and Changing American Institutions.* 2nd ed. Chicago: University of Chicago Press.

Kristen Lavelle

FORMATION, SOCIAL

Social formation is a Marxist concept referring to the concrete, historical articulation between the capitalist mode of production, persisting precapitalist modes of production, and the institutional context of the economy. The theory of the capitalist mode of production—its elements, functioning at the enterprise level and the level of market relations among enterprises (e.g., processes of competition, concentration, and centralization), and its contradictions, tendencies, and laws of motion—can be found in

Karl Marx's *Capital* ([1867] 1967). The capitalist mode of production as such is an abstraction, accessible to research only through social formations; that is, through its concrete, historically specific manifestations in nation states, regions within nations (e.g., the South), or regions encompassing nations (e.g., the European Union). Though Marx (1818–1883) did not define this concept, its meaning and significance can be inferred from his work, particularly from this statement:

> The specific economic form, in which unpaid surplus-labor is pumped out of direct producers, determines the relationship of rulers and ruled … and, in turn, reacts upon it as a determining element. Upon this, however, is founded the entire foundation of the economic community which grows out of the production relations themselves, thereby simultaneously its specific political form. It is always the direct relationship between the owners of the conditions of production to the direct producers…. which reveals the innermost secret, the hidden basis of the entire social structure, and … the corresponding specific form of the state. This does not prevent the same economic basis—the same from the standpoint of its main conditions—due to innumerable different empirical circumstances, natural environment, racial relations, external historical influences, etc., from showing infinite variations and gradations in appearance, which can be ascertained only by analysis of the empirically given circumstances. (Marx [1867] 1967, vol. 3, pp. 791–792)

Marx postulates here a necessary, dialectical interrelation between relations of exploitation and political relations, between economic and social systems, a point previously made as follows: "The totality of these relations of production constitutes the economic structure of society, the real foundation, on which arises a legal and political superstructure and to which correspond definite forms of social consciousness" (Marx [1859] 1970, p. 20). The historical specificity of the relations of production is crucial for understanding the social formation in its universality (i.e., as a capitalist social formation) and in its particularity because, empirically, "the same economic basis" (i.e., the capitalist mode of production) will show "infinite variations" due to a social formation's unique characteristics among which, the presence and persistence of precapitalist modes of production are of key importance. This is why the study of social formations entails the investigation of the articulation of modes of production; that is, the specific ways in which the capitalist mode of production affects precapitalist modes of production, altering them, modifying them, and even destroying them (Wolpe 1980, p. 2).

RECENT INTERPRETATIONS

The relationship between the capitalist mode of production, social formations, and social change has been interpreted in determinist and dialectical ways. Literal, atheoretical readings of the work of Marx and Friedrich Engels (1820–1895) reduce their views to technological and economic determinism, a result produced also by sophisticated but undialectical readings (e.g., Cohen 1978) that ignore the dialectical nature of Marx's thought. Marxist concepts are essentially material and social; for example, a machine, in itself, is a physical object that becomes a means of production or a productive force when it enters the production process in the context of historically specific relations of production. Changes in the forces of production occur, it follows, always in the context of political struggles. Cohen, on the other hand, attributes to the productive forces a primary, determinant role in historical change, and he radically divides the social (e.g., relations of production) from the material or extrasocial (i.e., nature, humans, forces of production). Cohen's undialectical materialism and determinism has to rely, unavoidably, upon transhistorical sources of change: a universal tendency of the productive forces to develop and a "somewhat rational" human nature capable of coping with scarcity (Cohen 1978, pp. 132–160). From this standpoint, then, historical changes are the effect of changes in the forces of production, undialectically understood as mere technological change. Class struggles play no role in historical change for political actors are reduced to rationally adapting to the effects of changing circumstances.

A determinist understanding of Marx would lead social scientists to expect that the penetration of the capitalist mode of production in social formations where precapitalist modes of production are widespread would soon produce qualitative changes in their economic system (e.g., modification or destruction of the precapitalist modes of production) and their superstructure (e.g., culture, legal, and political institutions). Determinist perspectives, however, underestimate the resilience of the noneconomic characteristics of social formations and the extent to which production is a thoroughly social activity that requires social and cultural conditions of possibility that cannot be instituted by decree. Despite appearances, for example, the drastic economic changes introduced in Russia after 1917 and in Eastern Europe after World War II (1939–1945) were, to some extent, superficial, for those countries quickly reverted to capitalism. There are many complex economic and political reasons why revolutionary change did not produce deep and qualitative superstructural changes, but reliance on the determinant and automatic effects of changing the mode of production must have contributed in important ways.

The literature on social formations subject to the penetration of the capitalist mode of production through gradual, nonrevolutionary processes indicates that forms of articulation between the capitalist mode of production and precapitalist modes of production cannot be logically deduced from Marx's theory of the capitalist mode of production. The notion of articulation refers to "the relationship between the reproduction of the capitalist economy on the one hand and the reproduction of productive units organized according to pre-capitalist relations and forces of production on the other" (Wolpe 1980, p. 41). How these processes actually interact varies a great deal from one social formation to another, thus leading to the construction of conflicting perspectives about the nature of social formations: (1) Social formations lack a necessary structure; one mode of production may dominate or several modes of production may be articulated with or without one dominant mode; (2) A social formation's necessary structure may be formed by a dominant mode of production and its conditions of existence, which might include elements of precapitalist modes of production, or it may simply be the effect of the articulation of any number of modes and their respective conditions of existence; (3) Given a dominant mode (e.g., the capitalist mode of production) in any social formation, all other modes will be subordinate to its structures and processes so that they are reduced to mere "forms of existence" of the dominant mode (Wolpe 1980, p. 34).

These and other perspectives entail different implications depending on whether the mode of production is defined in a restricted sense, as a combination of relations and forces of production, or in an extended sense, encompassing linkages among enterprises as well as other economic and political/cultural elements constitutive of the mode of production and conducive to its reproduction over time (e.g., distribution, circulation, exchange, the state) (Wolpe 1980, p. 40; Marx [1859] 1970, pp. 188–199). Because modes of articulation are unique to specific social formations (e.g., in South Africa, racial ideology reproduced and sustained capitalist relations of production [Wolpe 1980, p. 317]; in Peru, agrarian reform contributed to the proletarianization of Indian communities [Bradby 1980, p. 120]), it could be erroneously concluded that social formation and articulation are useless concepts, for their use in research is unlikely to yield testable empirical generalizations.

These concepts are exceedingly important, for they contribute to the adjudication of an important issue in Marxist theory: the extent to which Marx is or is not an economic determinist. The historical and empirical variability in the conditions of reproduction of the capitalist mode of production that is documented through research in social formations and modes of articulation demonstrates the nondeterminist nature of Marx's theories.

While the structure, processes, contradictions, and tendencies of the capitalist mode of production remain the same, thus constituting the "innermost secret" of the economic and political structures in social formations where the capitalist mode of production is dominant, the historical conditions for the reproduction of the capitalist mode of production vary historically and cross-culturally in the terrain of social formations, where political struggles carried under a variety of banners (class, race, religion, and nationalism) shape the different and spacialized outcomes of capitalism's never-ending expansionary tendencies.

Dialectically considered, social formations are the unity between the universal (the capitalist mode of production) and the particular, the concrete conditions within which the capitalist mode of production operates. The concept of social formation, unlike the abstract non-Marxist concept of "society," opens up the possibility of a realistic and historical understanding of social reality, based not on inferences from transhistorical tendencies, functional prerequisites, or concepts of human nature, but upon the historical specificity of the social formations within which capitalism operates.

SEE ALSO *Marx, Karl*

BIBLIOGRAPHY

Bradby, Barbara. 1980. The Destruction of Natural Economy. In *The Articulation of Modes of Production: Essays from Economy and Society*, ed. Harold Wolpe, 93–127. London: Routledge & Kegan Paul.

Cohen, G. A. 1978. *Karl Marx's Theory of History: A Defence.* Princeton, NJ: Princeton University Press. Expanded ed., 2000.

Marx, Karl. [1859] 1970. *A Contribution to the Critique of Political Economy.* New York: International Publishers.

Marx, Karl. [1867] 1967. *Capital*. New York: International Publishers.

Wolpe, Harold, ed. 1980. *The Articulation of Modes of Production: Essays from Economy and Society.* London: Routledge & Kegan Paul.

Wolpe, Harold. 1980. Capitalism and Cheap Labor Power in South Africa: From Segregation to Apartheid. In *The Articulation of Modes of Production: Essays from Economy and Society*, ed. Harold Wolpe, 288–319. London: Routledge & Kegan Paul.

Martha E. Gimenez

FORMULAS

Although most social science research concerns characteristics of people, groups, organizations, and situations for which there is no inherent metric or measure, virtually all such research involves quantifying these characteristics. The data that result from this quantification are manipulated, analyzed, and interpreted using mathematical formulas. Formulas also are used by social scientists to describe or model behavior, particularly interpersonal behavior, using mathematical operations and principles. In some social science research literatures, such formulas are the principle means by which behavior is described and predicted.

William James, in his *Principles of Psychology* (1890), offered one of the earliest examples of a description of an aspect of human social experience in mathematical terms. James suggested that self-esteem is a function of the ratio of people's successes to their "pretensions":

$$\text{Self-Esteem} = \frac{successes}{pretensions}$$

In other words, a person's self-esteem depends on the degree to which they are meeting their own expectations. Inspired by James's work, psychologists a century later posited more complex formulas in which self-esteem is a measure of the sum of people's performances in various domains, weighted by the importance they ascribe to those domains.

An area of social science in which mathematical formulas have been particularly influential is interpersonal relations. Virtually all of these formulas derive in part from social exchange models of interpersonal behavior. The seminal social exchange account of interpersonal relations was proffered by J. Stacy Adams in 1963. Adams's specific concern was the degree to which individuals feel as if they are treated in a just and fair manner by their employers. According to Adams, perceptions of just and fair treatment stem from perceptions of equity, which can be modeled using the following formula:

$$\text{Equity} = \frac{inputs}{outputs}$$

Inputs are what the employee puts into the job (e.g., effort, loyalty), and outputs are what the employee gets in return (e.g., salary, job security). As this ratio departs from 1.0, particularly in the direction of inputs exceeding outputs, perceptions of fairness, as well as motivation, decline.

An important addition to this simple model is an accounting for the role of comparisons in such judgments. For instance, the equity ratio might be expanded to:

$$\text{Equity} = \frac{inputs_{own}}{outputs_{own}} - \frac{inputs_{other}}{outputs_{other}}$$

In this case, "other" could denote another person (e.g., a coworker) or another opportunity (e.g., a position with another employer). The addition of comparisons yields a model that can account for the fact that individuals sometimes remain in relationships despite inputs that exceed outputs, or that they leave relationships that are providing outputs in excess of inputs.

Other models inspired by the social exchange perspective use formulas as a basis for defining and predicting relationship outcomes. For instance, Caryl Rusbult's investment model defines relationship satisfaction using the following formula:

Satisfaction = (*rewards − costs*) − *comparison level*

This formula specifies that people experience satisfaction in relationships when the difference between rewards and costs in the relationship exceeds expectations. Satisfaction, defined in this way, is a term in the formula for defining commitment to the relationship:

Commitment = *satisfaction–alternatives* + *investments*

"Alternatives" corresponds to the perceived degree of satisfaction the individual could expect to experience in other relationships, and "investments" correspond to the accrued costs of staying in the relationship (e.g., opportunities not pursued in order to preserve the relationship). These formulas define relationship outcomes and suggest means by which they can be predicted and influenced, illustrating the strategic use of formulas in social science research.

Other theoretical models in the social sciences specify formulas for which specific values of terms are predicted. An instance of such a use of mathematical formulas is Bibb Latané's social impact theory. According to this theory, the influence of other people on an individual can be specified in terms of three factors: (1) *strength*, or how important the individuals are; (2) *immediacy*, or how close in space and time the individuals are; (3) *number*, or how many people there are. Social influence, or impact, is a product of these factors, so that:

Impact = *strength^i* × *immediacy^i* × *number^i*

For example, the model predicts that performance anxiety will increase as the number of individuals watching, their importance to the performer, and their proximity to the performer increases. An important feature of this model is the assumption that the influence of these factors is not linear (i.e., the exponents fall between 0 and 1). Take for instance, the number factor. The model specifies that, holding strength and immediacy constant, the addition of one more person in the situation has less influence if a large number of people are already present. Likewise, the addition of one more person in the situation has more influence if a small number of people are already present. Thus, associated with each factor is an exponent that describes in mathematical terms the relation between that factor and its impact.

Even in social science research for which concepts are not framed in mathematical terms, mathematical formulas are important, because the data generated by social science research is virtually always subjected to statistical analysis. The most prevalent use of formulas in this context is for the construction of test statistics. Test statistics, such as t, F, and χ^2, are used in hypothesis testing as a means of evaluating the likelihood that an observed pattern of results is attributable to chance. This likelihood is reflected in the p-values that accompany observed values of test statistics, with values lower than .05 indicating, by convention, statistical significance.

A related use of formulas is for the computation of effect sizes, which are means of indexing the practical, as opposed to statistical, significance of a research finding. A frequently used effect size, d, is attributable to the American psychological researcher Jacob Cohen. The formula for computing d is:

$$\frac{M_1 - M_2}{\sigma}.$$

Here, M_1 and M_2 are means on some outcome for two groups and σ is a standard deviation, either for one of the groups or for a "pooled" standard deviation. The resultant value is the difference between the two groups in standard deviation units, which is interpreted with reference to criteria for small, medium, and large effects, as described by Cohen. Other effect sizes can be generated using formulas specific to the statistical model used to analyze the data.

Mathematical reasoning is a routine activity in quantitative social science research. At the most fundamental level, mathematical formulas are, in some instances, used to define and predict variables. In all cases, mathematical formulas are used to construct test statistics required for hypothesis testing. Increasingly, these test statistics are accompanied by effect sizes, which make use of output from statistical analyses to construct indexes of practical significance. For these reasons, social scientists routinely use mathematical reasoning in their work.

SEE ALSO *Methods, Quantitative; Models and Modeling; Quantification; Social Science; Statistics; Statistics in the Social Sciences*

BIBLIOGRAPHY

Adams, J. Stacey. 1963. Toward an Understanding of Inequity. *Journal of Abnormal and Social Psychology* 67: 422–436.

Cohen, Jacob. 1988. *Statistical Power Analysis for the Behavioral Sciences.* 2nd ed. Mahwah, NJ: Erlbaum.

Kelley, Harold H., and John Thibaut. 1978. *Interpersonal Relations: A Theory of Interdependence.* New York: Wiley-Interscience.

Rusbult, Caryl E. 1980. Commitment and Satisfaction in Romantic Associations: A Test of the Investment Model. *Journal of Experimental Social Psychology* 16: 172–186.

Rick H. Hoyle

FORWARD AND FUTURES MARKETS

Futures markets and forward markets trade contracts that determine a current price for a commodity transaction designated to take place at a later date. Despite being fundamental to financial and commodity trading, there is some confusion over the precise definition of futures and forward contracts. While common usage sometimes defines *futures* and *forwards* as synonyms, a futures contract is a specialized form of forward contract that is standardized and traded on a futures exchange. As such, a technical distinction is required between futures markets and forwards markets. Some forward contracts, such as those traded on the London Metals Exchange, have many features of futures contracts. Other types of forward contracts are more complicated, such as the forward contracting provisions embedded in long-term oil delivery contracts. While it is tempting to claim that futures contracts represent an evolution of forward trading, much twenty-first-century progress in contract design has come in over-the-counter (OTC) trading, the primary venue for many types of forward contracting.

HISTORY OF FORWARD AND FUTURES CONTRACTS

The history of forward contracts can be traced back to ancient times. Due to the difficulties of transport and communication, trading based on samples was common and some form of forward contracting was essential. The contracting process usually involved only the producers and consumers of the goods being traded. During the sixteenth century, liquidity of forward markets was substantially increased by the emergence of the Antwerp bourse. By the mid-seventeenth century, forward markets had developed to where the Amsterdam bourse featured both forward and option contracts for commodities, such as wheat and herring, and for foreign stocks and shares. The beginning of trade in futures contracts is usually traced to mid-nineteenth-century Chicago, where the Board of Trade—founded in 1848—transacted the first "time contract" in 1851. The grain trade of that era typically involved merchants at various points along major waterways purchasing grain from farmers which was then held in storage, often from fall or winter into spring. In order to avoid the risk of price fluctuation and to satisfy bankers, merchants started going to Chicago to transact contracts for future, spring delivery of grain. The contracts set a price for delivery of a standardized grade at a later delivery date. While these early contracts were similar to modern futures contracts, some terms and conditions of these time contracts were specific to the original parties to the transaction, as with a forward contract.

THE FUTURES CONTRACT AND THE FUTURES EXCHANGE

A significant difference between futures and forward contracts arises because futures contracts are legally required to be traded on futures exchanges while forwards are usually created by individual parties operating in the decentralized OTC markets. Because a futures contract is transacted on an exchange, the traders originating the contract use the exchange clearinghouse as the counterparty to their trade. While both a short trader (seller) and long trader (buyer) are required to create a futures contract, both traders execute the trade with the clearinghouse as the direct counter-party. This allows a futures contract to be created without the problems associated with forward contracting, which typically depends on the creditworthiness of the counter-party. By design, futures contracts are readily transferable via the trading mechanisms provided by the exchange. Because forward contracts depend on the performance of the two original parties to the contract, these contracts are often difficult to transfer. One practical implication of this difference is that if a futures trader wants to close out a position, an equal number of offsetting contracts for that commodity month is transacted and the original position is cancelled. Forward contracts are usually offset by establishing another forward contract position with terms as close as possible to those in the original contract. Unless the forward contract provides a method for cash settlement at delivery, this will potentially involve two deliveries having to be matched in the cash market on the delivery date.

To facilitate exchange trading, futures contracts possess a number of key features, especially standardization and marking to market. The elements of standardization provided by the futures contract and by the rules and regulations of the exchange governing such contracts involve: the deliverable grade of the commodity; the quantity deliverable per contract; the range of quality within which delivery is permissible; the delivery months; and, the options associated with the specific grade and date of delivery that is permissible. Standardization is achieved by making each futures contract for a given commodity identical to all other contracts except for price and the delivery month. In addition to standardization, forwards and futures also differ in how changes in the value of the contract over time are handled. For futures, daily settlement, also known as marking to market, is required. In effect, a new futures contract is written at the start of every trading day with all gains or losses settled through a margin account at the end of trading for that day. This method of accounting requires the posting of a "good faith" initial margin deposit combined with an understanding that, if the value in the margin account falls below a maintenance margin amount, funds will be transferred into the account

to prevent the contract from being closed out. On the other hand, settlement on forward contracts usually occurs by delivery of the commodity at the maturity of the contract. Hence, futures contracts have cash flow implications during the life of the contract while forwards usually do not.

MODERN USAGE OF FORWARD AND FUTURES CONTRACTS

In modern markets, considerable variation is observed in the relative use of forward or futures contracting across commodity markets. For example, in currency markets, the large value and volume of many individual trades has the bulk of transactions for future delivery conducted in the currency forward market. Exchange traded currency futures contracts are an insignificant fraction of total trading volume in the global currency market. As trading in forwards is closely integrated with cash market transactions, direct trading in forward contracts is restricted to the significant spot market participants, effectively the largest banks and financial institutions. Because currency forward contracts do not have regular marking to market, restricted participation is needed to control default risk. As such, differences in the functioning of futures and forward markets impacts the specific method of contracting selected for conducting commodity transactions. For example, in contrast to forward trading, futures markets are designed to encourage participation by large and small speculative traders. The increased participation of speculators not directly involved in the spot market provides an important source of additional liquidity to futures markets not available in forward markets. In order to achieve this liquidity certain restrictions are imposed on trading, such as limits on position sizes and the imposition of filing requirements. By restricting participation to large players in the commodity market, many of the restrictions required for the functioning of futures markets are not present in forward markets.

SEE ALSO *Bubbles; Bull and Bear Markets; Contango; Discounted Present Value; Equity Markets; Expectations; Financial Instability Hypothesis; Financial Markets; Future Prices; Hedging; Interest Rates; Liquidity; Policy, Monetary; Selling Long and Selling Short; Selling Short; Speculation; Spot Market; Spreads; Yield Curve*

BIBLIOGRAPHY

Chance, Donald, and Robert Brooks. 2006. *An Introduction to Derivatives and Risk Management.* 7th ed. Cincinnati, OH: Southwestern.

Chicago Board of Trade. 2006. *The Chicago Board of Trade Handbook of Futures and Options.* New York: McGraw-Hill.

Poitras, Geoffrey. 2002. *Risk Management, Speculation and Derivative Securities*. New York: Academic Press.

Geoffrey Poitras

FOSSILS

SEE *Archaeology*.

FOUCAULT, MICHEL
1926–1984

Michel Foucault was a French philosopher who wrote widely on the history of thought. His influences include philosophers of science, such as his mentor Georges Canguilhem, but also Maurice Blanchot and Friedrich Nietzsche, from whom he derived his influential methodological notion of genealogy. Though Foucault's oeuvre treats seemingly disparate historical topics ranging from psychiatry to structuralism and on from sexuality to liberalism, a concern with the issues of knowledge and power as they constellate around the formation of subjectivities forms a constant, discernible thread.

Foucault's first major works are studies of psychiatry and mental illness. In *Madness and Civilization* (1961), Foucault examined how madness, the classical age inverse of reason, was systematized into the modern psychological category of mental illness. *The Birth of the Clinic* (1963) marks the beginning of Foucault's archaeological period, and examines the development of the perceptive apparatus of modern medicine. His attention to clinical confinement is demonstrative of his concern with dividing practices that progressively split certain individuals off from the social body.

The subsequent *Archaeology of Knowledge* (1969), Foucault's only methodological treatise, draws on the broad-sweep historiographical innovations of the Annales School to elaborate discursive formations as an analytical frame. In his archaeology of structuralism, *The Order of Things* (1966), Foucault historicized these discursive structures into distinct epistemes, which serve as the "condition of possibility" for knowledge. Tracing epistemic transformations in thought from the classical to the modern age, Foucault scrutinized the rise of man as the subject of the human sciences.

In his later work, Foucault shifted his approach to a process he called genealogy, which explicitly linked his analyses of knowledge to social structures of power. He argued against a purely repressive notion of power, elaborating instead on his oft-quoted maxim that "power is productive." In *Discipline and Punish* (1975), Foucault developed an explicit relationship between forms of knowledge of the body and the evolution of the modern prison system; disciplinary power, Foucault argued, arrays and organizes bodies into "analytical space," producing a logic that generalized itself from its application in concrete technologies such as the nineteenth-century Panopticon penitentiary to the level of society. In the first volume of his three-part *History of Sexuality* (1976), Foucault characterized disciplinary power as an anatomo-politics that operates on the level of the body, and juxtaposed it to its complement, bio-politics, which functions on the level of a population whose life forces it seeks to optimize. These populations, Foucault argued, are constituted in part via discourses about sexuality. In the second two volumes of his *History*, *The Use of Pleasure* (1984), and *The Care of the Self* (1984), Foucault turned to the processes of self-constitution in Greek and Roman sexual practices. The planned fourth and fifth volumes of the series remained unwritten upon Foucault's premature death at the age of fifty-eight.

Foucault's activism often related to the themes of his work. He advocated for penal reform and gay rights, and was associated with the anti-psychiatry movement. In his interviews and lectures, particularly those delivered at the Collège de France from the 1970s to 1984, Foucault reformulated many of the themes of his books into analyses applicable to the contemporary political situation. He responded to the ascendance of neoliberalism in the 1970s by refining his concept of bio-politics into that of governmentality, a governmental rationality operating in the realm of political economy.

Several scholars argued with Foucault over issues of historical accuracy, while others have contended that his attempts to transcend reason as the grounds of the subject's constitution remain methodologically fettered because they presuppose the existence of that self-same subject. Nevertheless, Foucault's many anglophone interpreters have ensured the profound methodological and theoretical impact of his work in many disciplines, including anthropology, gender studies, history, literature, postcolonial studies, and sociology.

SEE ALSO *Critical Theory; Habermas, Jürgen*

BIBLIOGRAPHY

PRIMARY WORKS

Foucault, Michel. [1961]. 1988. *Madness and Civilization: A History of Insanity in the Age of Reason*. Trans. Richard Howard. New York: Vintage.

Foucault, Michel. [1963] 1994. *The Birth of the Clinic: An Archaeology of Medical Perception*. Trans. A. M. Sheridan Smith. New York: Vintage.

Foucault, Michel. [1966] 1994. *The Order of Things: An Archaeology of the Human Sciences* New York: Vintage.

Foucault, Michel. [1969]. 1972. *The Archaeology of Knowledge.* Trans. A. M. Sheridan Smith. New York: Pantheon.

Foucault, Michel. [1975] 1995. *Discipline and Punish: The Birth of the Prison.* Trans. Alan Sheridan. New York: Vintage.

Foucault, Michel. [1976] 1990. *The History of Sexuality*, Vol. 1: *An Introduction.* Trans. Robert Hurley. New York: Vintage.

Foucault, Michel. [1984]. 1990. *The History of Sexuality*, Vol. 2: *The Use of Pleasure.* Trans. Robert Hurley. New York: Vintage.

Foucault, Michel. [1984]. 1988. *The History of Sexuality*, Vol. 3: *The Care of the Self.* Trans. Robert Hurley. New York: Vintage.

Foucault, Michel. 2003. *"Society Must Be Defended": Lectures at the Collège de France, 1975–1976.* Trans. David Macey. Ed. Arnold I. Davidson. New York: Picador.

SECONDARY WORKS

Derrida, Jacques. 1978. *Writing and Difference.* Trans. Alan Bass. Chicago: University of Chicago Press.

Faubion, James D. 2000. *Power: Essential Works of Foucault, 1954–1984.* New York: New Press.

Habermas, Jürgen. 1985. *The Philosophical Discourse of Modernity: Twelve Lectures.* Trans. Frederick Lawrence. Cambridge, MA: MIT Press.

Rabinow, Paul. 1984. *The Foucault Reader.* New York: Pantheon.

Steiner, George. 1971. The Mandarin of the Hour—Michel Foucault. *New York Times Book Review* 8: 23–31.

Stone, Lawrence. 1982. Madness. *New York Review of Books* 29 (20): 128–136.

Krista Hegburg

FOUNDATIONS, CHARITABLE

Charitable foundations are endowments that are devoted to the pursuit of public purposes. Foundations are typically set up to exist, in principle, in perpetuity—spending parts of their annual income on public purposes, while retaining the remainder to preserve and grow their endowment assets. On occasion, however, donors limit the life span of a charitable foundation, requiring the foundation to spend out all assets over a given number of years, as was the case with the Julian Rosenwald Fund (1917–1948) and more recently the Bradley Foundation, established in 1985. Foundations have existed in one form or another for many centuries, and some observers have pointed to the Library of Alexandria and Plato's Academy (bequeathed with income-producing lands to his nephew) as early examples in antiquity. Historically, foundations were closely linked to religious charity in the Judeo-Christian tradition, but similar concepts are found in other religious traditions as well, such as the *al-wakif* in Islam.

In the course of the twentieth century, however, much foundation activity has been linked to the concept of philanthropy. Literally "the love of humankind," philanthropy can be most poignantly defined as the use of resources to examine and address the causes of social ills or problems. As such, philanthropy contrasts with traditional charity, understood as the eleemosynary, ameliorative use of resources. Although many charitable trusts existed for various purposes in early American history, and the "foundations" of Benjamin Franklin (1706–1790), James Smithson (1765–1829), and George Peabody (1795–1869) were of great significance, the birth of the U.S. foundation sector, and with it the rise of the concept of philanthropy, is typically located around the beginning of the twentieth century.

In an influential series of articles published in the 1880s titled *Wealth*, the industrialist Andrew Carnegie (1835–1919) began to argue in favor of an obligation on the part of the rich to devote excess wealth to public purposes and to help provide opportunities for the less fortunate to better themselves. Over the following decades, the traditional focus of charitable trusts on providing relief and amelioration was gradually supplanted by a new orientation toward analyzing and addressing the causes of social problems rather than just addressing their effects. Using the emerging sciences to tackle the "root causes of social ills" set the ambitions and operations of the early twentieth-century foundations apart from earlier foundation activities in the United States and launched what historians Barry Karl and Stan Katz (1987) have termed the *modern philanthropic foundation.*

The earliest of these new foundations included the Russell Sage Foundation (1907), the Carnegie Corporation (1911), and the Rockefeller Foundation (1913), which popularized the foundation idea and provided a blueprint that other wealthy donors began to follow in the 1920s and 1930s. High marginal tax rates that originated during World War II (1939–1945) and continued into the postwar period, in combination with lax regulation, further propelled foundation growth in the 1940s and 1950s. By the 1960s, however, perceived economic misuses of foundations led to a political backlash culminating in the introduction of the new and relatively stringent regulation of foundations through the Tax Reform Act of 1969. This law instituted, among other provisions, a payout requirement for grant-making foundations that currently requires the annual payout in grants and other qualifying contributions to be the equivalent of 5 percent of the foundation's asset value. As such, the sum of foundation grants is closely tied to endowment value, and the run-up of the stock market in the 1990s—as well as the emergence of large-scale postindustrial philanthropists such as William Hewlett, David Packard, Bill Gates, Ted Turner, George Soros, and Warren Buffett—significantly increased the level of resources at the disposal of the foundation community at the beginning of the twenty-first century.

According to data provided by the New York–based Foundation Center, there were close to 68,000 grant-making foundations in the United States in 2005, holding aggregate total assets of close to $510 billion and spending $33.6 billion in grant and other expenditures. While the number of foundations had only doubled since the late 1980s (there were about 30,000 foundations in 1988), there was a dramatic acceleration of the financial means of the foundation sector in the space of only a few years. More specifically, total assets in nominal terms more than doubled between 1995 ($227 billion) and 2005, and grant dollars almost tripled between 1995 ($12.3 billion) and 2005. Despite this growth, funding patterns have remained stable: Education receives about 25 percent of all foundation support, followed by health with about 20 percent and human services with 15 percent. The other major funding areas are arts and culture and public affairs, with slightly more than 10 percent. The remainder is distributed between environmental causes, science, religion, and international affairs.

Although not insignificant, foundation resources remain overall rather limited. For example, the roughly $8 billion in annual educational spending by foundations equals no more than four times the 2005 operating budget of Harvard University or any large urban school district. As such, foundations are seldom the most appropriate vehicle to provide basic financing of educational ventures or scientific institutions or to serve as guarantors of sustainability over the long run. Rather, foundations have traditionally sought a different function. Faced with a scarcity of resources on the one hand, and flexibility and freedom from external constraints on the other, foundations are usually at their best when pursuing the development of new ideas and concepts. During the twentieth century, foundations had their greatest impact in fostering innovation and pioneering novel approaches and then moving on to different areas once the innovations took root.

This pioneering function of foundations is well reflected in the development of the social sciences in the twentieth century. The Russell Sage Foundation, founded in 1907 as the first of the great modern philanthropies with the mission to pursue "the improvement of social and living conditions in the United States," adopted early on a focus on a scientific understanding of the causes of poverty. This led to the development of the social work profession, and eventually turned the foundation into the mainstay of social science inquiry that it remains today. Similar to the Russell Sage Foundation, but with more of an economics focus, was the Twentieth Century Fund (now the Century Foundation) founded in 1919.

Other foundations focused on improving education, including the Julius Rosenwald Fund in the American South, but the larger foundations, particularly the Rockefeller and Carnegie philanthropies, soon devoted growing shares of their resources toward the development of the social sciences. These foundations were instrumental in helping to establish new independent institutions that would shape social science discourse for decades, including the National Bureau of Economic Research (1920), the Social Science Research Council (1923), and the Brookings Institution (1927). Beyond building an institutional infrastructure, foundations also sponsored a range of important research studies, such as Gunnar Myrdal's (1898–1987) seminal work on race in the 1940s, that gave prominence and helped validate emerging disciplines. All this work became crucial in consolidating the role of social science in the academy. After the Ford Foundation came to national prominence in 1949, fostering the social sciences was among its main programmatic objectives. Ford heavily supported social science development in European universities in the aftermath of World War II, and is widely credited with introducing area studies in the United States. Although federal funding has come to overshadow private foundation support for research, foundations have long shaped the development of the social sciences and remain important supporters of innovative work.

SEE ALSO *Philanthropy*

BIBLIOGRAPHY

Anheier, Helmut K., and Stefan Toepler, eds. 1999. *Private Funds, Public Purpose: Philanthropic Foundations in International Perspective.* New York: Kluwer Academic/Plenum.

Dowie, Mark. 2001. *American Foundations: An Investigative History.* Cambridge, MA: MIT Press.

Foundation Center. 2006. *Foundation Yearbook: Facts and Figures on Private and Community Foundations.* New York: Author.

Karl, Barry, and Stan Katz. 1987. Foundations and Ruling Class Elites. *Daedalus* 116: 1–40.

Lagemann, Ellen, ed. 1999. *Philanthropic Foundations: New Scholarship, New Possibilities.* Bloomington: Indiana University Press.

Nielsen, Waldemar. 1972. *The Big Foundations.* New York: Columbia University Press.

Prewitt, Kenneth, Mattei Doggone, Steven Heydemann, and Stefan Toepler. 2006. *The Legitimacy of Philanthropic Foundations: United States and European Perspectives.* New York: Russell Sage Foundation.

Weaver, Warren, ed. 1967. *U.S. Philanthropic Foundations: Their History, Structure, Management, and Record.* New York: Harper.

Stefan Toepler

FRAME OF REFERENCE

SEE *Sherif, Muzafer.*

FRAMES

SEE *Goffman, Erving; Performance.*

FRAMING

SEE *Rituals.*

FRANCHISE

The franchise, or the privilege or right to vote to elect public representatives or enact legislation, originated with the ancient Greek city-states of the fifth century BCE. As a political right, the franchise constitutes one of the core elements in modern citizenship, along with other political, civil, and social rights. In modern times the extension of franchise across European and North American nation-states marked the passage from a paternalistic form of government in the eighteenth century to the acceptance of the concept of citizenship, which is the foundation of democracy.

There has been wide variation across countries in the timing and regulation of the franchise. In most countries the franchise was extended gradually, as occurred in Great Britain, France, and the United States. In Finland, by contrast, it was extended all at once in the reform of 1906. The franchise may also be exercised at only certain levels of representation. In 1896, for example, women in Idaho were permitted to vote in school elections but not in state or federal elections, while women in Brazil were enfranchised in 1927 in the state of Rio Grande do Norte but not at the federal level. Since 2004 noncitizens in Belgium may vote in local elections only.

Where the franchise was extended gradually, voters entered the electorate in social groups. For instance, in Norway the franchise was extended to property holders in 1814, to manual workers and others in 1900, and to women in two stages in 1907 and 1913. Retractions of the franchise have also taken place. In France, for example, the franchise was granted to a large number of citizens in the late 1700s but was then severely contracted in 1815. Various qualifications have been used to regulate the franchise, including church membership, religious denomination, property ownership, taxpaying, literacy, a poll tax, residency, gender, and age. All such requirements have been aimed at disenfranchising different social groups at different times.

Franchise rules come about as a result of political conflict or as a by-product of conflicts over other issues. As E. E. Schattschneider points out in *The Semisovereign People* (1960), political conflicts that may produce franchise changes include political party competition, that is, from a conflict among governing elites for electoral advantage. In such cases extending the franchise to certain social groups may decide the outcome of elections to the advantage of the party or parties that appeal to the new voters. Franchise extensions may also be the product of conflict between governing elites and groups excluded from the electoral process, such as women or workers and their organizational representatives. Pressure from excluded groups may lead to franchise extensions by governing elites in an attempt to maintain the legitimacy of their governance (Freeman and Snidal 1982), especially when economic conditions or foreign policy objectives threaten the stability of the current political regime.

Conflicts over other issues, including economic conflict, may produce franchise changes as a by-product. For instance, international trade in nineteenth-century Europe and the United States, particularly the conflict between protectionists and free traders, is cited by Dietrich Rueschemeyer, Evelyne Huber Stephens, and John D. Stephens, the authors of *Capitalist Development and Democracy* (1992), as underlying the coalitions supporting or opposing franchise extensions. Opponents in the conflict devised franchise rules to change the balance of power in legislatures. Since about the mid-1900s democratic expectations have rendered the franchise a political right basic to democratic citizenship, so universal franchise with an age requirement has been generally granted automatically.

SEE ALSO *Citizenship; Democracy; Democracy, Representative and Participatory; Elections; Elite Theory; Free Trade; Protectionism; Schattschneider, E. E.; Suffrage, Women's; Voting; Voting Patterns*

BIBLIOGRAPHY

Freeman, John, and Duncan Snidal. 1982. Diffusion, Development and Democratization: Enfranchisement in Western Europe. *Canadian Journal of Political Science* 15 (2): 299–329.

Marshall, T. H., and Tom Bottomore. 1950. *Citizenship and Social Class, and Other Essays.* Cambridge, U.K.: Cambridge University Press.

Porter, Kirk H. 1918. *A History of Suffrage in the United States.* Chicago: University of Chicago Press.

Rueschemeyer, Dietrich, Evelyne Huber Stephens, and John D. Stephens. 1992. *Capitalist Development and Democracy.* Chicago: University of Chicago Press.

Schattschneider, E. E. 1960. *The Semisovereign People: A Realist's View of Democracy in America.* New York: Holt, Rinehart, and Winston.

Barbara Sgouraki Kinsey

FRANCO, FRANCISCO
1892–1975

The Spanish general and head of state Francisco Franco may have been the weakest of the fascist dictators to take over a European power during the troubled peace that followed World War I (1914–1918), but once in office, he survived the longest. To be sure, the *generalísimo* gained control of his country only after a bloody civil war that prefigured the weapons technology, indiscriminant destruction, and mass executions of the world war to come. Yet, Franco's survival instinct—for himself and for Spain—trumped whatever desire there was for vengeance or glory. During his sometimes violent forty-year reign as head of state, Franco nevertheless demonstrated sufficient tactical flexibility to keep his enemies divided and his country at peace.

Few incidents from Franco's early career set him apart as a revolutionary. In fact, his rapid ascent in the Spanish army came largely from his willingness and ability to quell dissent. After graduating from the Infantry Academy (Toledo) in 1910, Franco sought action and advancement fighting rebels from 1912 to 1916 in Spanish Morocco, where he was seriously wounded. He recovered in time to lead Spanish Foreign Legion (Legión Extranjera) troops against Abd el-Krim (c. 1882–1963) in the Rif War (1921–1926). Back in Spain—as a young officer in 1917 and later as a fast-rising general in 1934—Franco led army efforts to repress striking workers. Shortly after the latter disturbance in Asturias, the center-right government in Madrid selected Franco as chief of the general staff.

However, as Franco rose in rank, his career tracked with the vicissitudes of the fragile Second Republic. In February 1936, a popular front on the left won close national elections, and Franco soon found himself reassigned outside mainland Spain to the Canary Islands. As violence and political assassinations on the left and right escalated in the summer of 1936, several generals plotted a coup to save Spain from communist and anarchist influences in the government. Within forty-eight hours after the coup was declared on July 17, Franco rejoined his colonials and legionnaires in Morocco and became one of the leading figures in a conservative rebellion. By October 1936, Franco, invading from Morocco, captured the symbolic capital of Toledo. He was selected generalissimo of the Nationalist Army and shortly thereafter head of state for the new Spain.

Between July 1936 and April 1, 1939, the Spanish Civil War was hotly contested with neither side able to dominate militarily. Franco gradually pushed Republican forces into eastern Spain and managed to split them along a corridor to the Mediterranean in 1938, but the great cities of Madrid, Barcelona, and Valencia did not begin to fall until the end of January 1939. In the war, Franco stood out not so much for classic generalship but for his capacity to appreciate the mutual dependence of political and military strategy.

While his enemies suffered ideological divisions, Franco was able to unite Monarchists, Falange (Phalanx) elements, rural conservatives, and Catholics behind a single cause: keeping a united Spain out of the hands of leftist Republicans. He justified ruthless tactics, including siege warfare, aerial bombing of civilians, and summary execution, in the name of a holy crusade to save the state. He invited substantial foreign troops and equipment from Nazi Germany and Fascist Italy to crush democracy while preserving French and British neutrality. Even when they could not be subdued on the ground, Franco's enemies were outflanked politically.

Pragmatism for the purpose of maintaining stability continued under Franco's rule. Despite his pro-Axis leanings during World War II (1939–1945), Franco orchestrated a rapprochement with the United States, concluding economic and defense agreements with the Dwight D. Eisenhower (1890–1969) administration. Franco subsequently accepted innovations expanding tourism and joint production with foreign companies, which probably contributed to the Spanish Miracle, a long run of robust growth in the 1960s. Late in life, the dictator could not adjust to global waves of democracy and export-led expansion, both of which challenged conventions of state control, but his handpicked successor, Juan Carlos de Borbón y Borbón, would have more success after transitioning Spain back to constitutional monarchy.

The contrast between Franco's leading biographer in English, Paul Preston, and revisionist historians such as Pío Moa demonstrates how Franco's legacy depends on whether Nationalist tactics during and after the civil war are accepted as necessary evils. The generalissimo still rests with honors at the Valley of the Fallen, an enormous shroud of gray stone that covers twenty thousand dead on each side. It stands as a symbol of unbending unity, but it also underscores for both Republican and Nationalist descendants the consequences of abandoning peaceful compromise. Such wide recognition has, in turn, underwritten a democratic constitution that celebrated twenty-five years in 2003 and set the political conditions for transforming economic growth in Spain, which from 1986 routinely outpaced fellow members of the European Union.

SEE ALSO *Dictatorship; Spanish Civil War*

BIBLIOGRAPHY

Moa, Pío. 2003. *Los Mitos de la Guerra Civil.* Madrid: La Esfera de los Libros.

Preston, Paul. 1994. *Franco: A Biography.* New York: Basic Books.

Damon Coletta

Any comments or statements in this entry represent the views of the author only and not necessarily those of the U.S. government.

FRANK, ANDRE GUNDER
1929–2005

Andre Gunder Frank was born in Berlin on February 24, 1929. His parents first took refuge from the Nazis in Switzerland (1933), then later in the United States (1941). Frank obtained his undergraduate degree from Swarthmore (1950), and his PhD in economics from the University of Chicago (1957) under the supervision of Milton Friedman, whose neoclassical and monetarist development theory he would criticize throughout his academic life.

Initially a specialist in the economics of Soviet agriculture at Michigan State University (1957–1961), he soon left the United States for Latin America. While in Brazil, he influenced many economists, such as Theotonio dos Santos and Fernando Henrique Cardoso. After the coup d'état there in 1964, he went to Chile, where he joined the Center for Socioeconomic Studies at the University of Chile's School of Economics. It was in Chile that Frank met his wife, Marta Fuentes—with whom he coauthored numerous publications—and where he developed his first series of books on socioeconomic conditions in Latin America.

In studies such as *Capitalism and Underdevelopment in Latin America* (1967), Frank argued both against the

widely influential orthodox Marxist theory—which characterized Latin America as being in a semifeudal stage—and the Western-centric modernization theory, which considered the lack of development in the so-called "Third World" as a consequence of incomplete "modernization" and insufficient or backward capitalist institutions. Frank's thesis of "development of under-development" essentially argued that since its very origins, Latin America had been exploited as a periphery by major colonial powers within the context of capitalist development across the Atlantic. By the early 1970s, Frank had become one of the predominant intellectuals articulating *dependency theory*, which claimed that external influences (e.g., political, economic, and cultural) on national development policies could explain why the third world, and Latin America in particular, had been and remained subordinate to Western interests (see, for example, Frank's *World Accumulation, 1492–1789*, 1978).

Frank and others used the historical condition of dependency to explain why economic growth in the West does not translate into economic growth in the periphery: Even after colonies had gained nominal independence, colonial policies still linked the periphery to the world market by commodity chains, often through the export of single commodities with a low added value (raw materials). The metropolitan/satellite relationship between colonizer and colonized was an aspect of world-scale capitalist dynamics, not simply precapitalist imperialist history, and this relationship continues to impoverish the third world long after formal independence due to the existence of a local *lumpenbourgeoisie*, making it impossible for former colonies to catch up with the West. The latter then reinforces this neocolonization through its use of debt.

The military coup against President Allende's socialist government (1973) drove Frank out of Chile. After returning to his native Germany to work at the Max Planck Institute (1973–1978), Frank subsequently accepted a position as professor of Development Studies in Social Change at the University of East Anglia (1978–1983), and then became professor of Development Economics and Social Sciences at the University of Amsterdam (1983–1994). It was during this period that he became affiliated with the world-system school and coauthored several studies with Immanuel Wallerstein, Samir Amin, and others on the dynamics of social crisis and social movements in the world system.

From the 1990s onward Frank adopted a revisionist approach to world history, rejecting world-system theory as well as most mainstream historical and theoretical interpretations as profoundly Eurocentric. Drawing on his previous studies of long-term economic cycles, Frank analyzed a 5,000-year-old trading system and argued, most notably in his influential *ReOrient* (1998), that the world economy had been Asia-centered for thousands of years and was now moving back in that direction. In the last years of his life, Frank claimed that the recent rise of the West was a short-lived phenomenon due to a temporary decline of the East and that the analytical concept of capitalism had become meaningless.

When Frank died in Luxembourg on April 23, 2005, he had published over thirty-five books and hundreds of articles in dozens of languages. His contributions to the field of dependency theory and world-system theory influenced many in anthropology, sociology, political economy, and to a certain degree even liberation theology. His last interdisciplinary research agenda, cut short by his death, was an ambitious attempt to undermine Eurocentrism in both the field of history and in contemporary social theory. As much a social activist as an academic iconoclast, Frank was an intellectual who never quite received the recognition he deserved—yet his studies will continue to inspire many debates in the social sciences for decades to come.

SEE ALSO *Accumulation of Capital; Allende, Salvador; Central Intelligence Agency, U.S.; Chicago School; Colonialism; Dependency Theory; Friedman, Milton; Imperialism; Luxemburg, Rosa; Modernization; North and South, The (Global); North-South Models; Third World; World-System*

BIBLIOGRAPHY

Frank, A. G. 1967. *Capitalism and Underdevelopment in Latin America: Historical Studies of Chile and Brazil.* New York: Monthly Review Press.

Frank, A. G. 1971. *Sociology of Development and Underdevelopment of Sociology.* London: Pluto.

Frank, A. G. 1978. *World Accumulation, 1492–1789.* London: Macmillan.

Frank, A. G. 1998. *ReOrient: Global Economy in the Asian Age.* Berkeley: University of California Press.

Simon, Lawrence, and David Ruccio. 1986. A Methodological Analysis of Dependency Theory: Explanation in Andre Gunder Frank. *World Development* 14: 195–209.

So, Alvin. 1990. *Social Change and Development.* London: Sage.

Eric Mielants

FRANKFURT SCHOOL

The Frankfurt school refers to the members and associates of the Institut für Sozialforschung (Institute of Social Research) in Frankfurt am Main, Germany. The institute was established at the instigation of Felix Weil (1898–1975) as a privately endowed research foundation for the study of socialism within the University of Frankfurt in 1923. Prominent members of the institute included Max Horkheimer (1895–1973), Theodor W. Adorno (1903–1969), Herbert Marcuse (1898–1979), Leo Löwenthal (1900–1993), Friedrich Pollock (1894–1970), and Erich Fromm (1900–1980), and those associated with it included Walter Benjamin (1892–1940) and Siegfried Kracauer (1889–1966). During the period of the National Socialist (Nazi) regime in Germany, the institute, and its predominantly German-Jewish membership, was forced into exile, first in Geneva and subsequently in New York, where its members became affiliated with Columbia University. After World War II (1939–1945), the institute returned to Germany and reopened in Frankfurt in 1951, though some members, such as Marcuse and Löwenthal, chose to remain in the United States.

Between 1924 and 1930, the institute had close relations with the Moscow-based Marx-Engels Institute and was committed to the socioeconomic analysis of capitalism and such political issues as the crisis of the European labor movement. From 1931, under Horkheimer's directorship, the school began to develop a distinctive theoretical framework, known as *critical theory*, that underpinned the diverse research programs to follow. At the epistemological level, the members shared the idealist tradition of continental philosophy, following in particular Immanuel Kant (1724–1804) and G. W. F. Hegel (1770–1831). In his inaugural lecture, however, Horkheimer urged the employment of critical theory in order to overcome the fundamental divergence between philosophical thinking and empirical inquiry. In contrast to *traditional theory*, typified in the positivist understanding of science, critical theory seeks to grasp the totality of society through interdisciplinary research and to provide an uncompromising critique of ideology.

At the level of social theory, the Frankfurt school was inspired by Marxism, in particular Georg Lukács's (1885–1971) theory of reification, but the school was always highly critical of orthodox Soviet Marxism. The members of the institute rejected the simplistic doctrine of dialectical materialism, the mechanical application of a base-superstructure framework, and the role of the working class as the lone agent for social change. They strived instead to combine Marxist critique with Max Weber's (1864–1920) understanding of rationalization and Sigmund Freud's (1856–1939) psychoanalytic analysis of the individual.

Drawing upon this neo-Marxist perspective, the institute undertook research in three topical areas envisaged by Horkheimer and published them in their own journals, *Zeitschrift für Sozialforschung* (Journal of Social Research) from 1932 to 1939 and *Studies in Philosophy and Social Science* from 1939 to 1941. First, institute members searched for a comprehensive theory of contemporary postliberal capitalist society in terms of "state-capitalism." Second, drawing on Fromm and Wilhelm Reich's (1897–1957) social-psychological study of fascism and character, the institute investigated how individuals were integrated with so little resistance into a dominant system. This study became further developed in exile with the extensive research series Studies in Prejudice, which culminated in the collaborated work, *The Authoritarian Personality* (Adorno et al. 1950). Third, the institute saw the mass culture as central to a new configuration of the capitalist system, one that induced compliance with dominant social relations through culture and media, which Horkheimer and Adorno dubbed the *culture industry*.

Ultimately, the failure of the Weimar Republic, the emergence of totalitarian regimes in Europe, the Holocaust, and the self-destruction of Western "civilization" compelled the Frankfurt school to ask "why mankind, instead of entering into a truly human condition, is sinking into a new kind of barbarism" (Horkheimer and Adorno, [1947] 1997, p. xi). Horkheimer and Adorno found the answer lodged within a set of contradictions posed by an "instrumental reason" at the center of the Enlightenment project itself, providing a profoundly bleak and pessimistic diagnosis of modernity in the seminal collection of philosophical fragments, *Dialectic of Enlightenment* (1947).

After the institute's return to Frankfurt, Adorno served as director from 1958 until his sudden death in 1969. During this period, the institute continued to elaborate the systematic social theory, particularly through the positivism dispute. As shown in Horkheimer's *Eclipse of Reason* (1947) and Adorno's *Negative Dialectic* (1966), however, their pessimistic perspective became more pronounced. In a continuing turn from the empirical-analytical sciences, Adorno increasingly focused on aesthetics and, in particular, the philosophy of music. His *Aesthetic Theory* (1970), published posthumously, clearly illuminates how the utopian dimension of critical theory rests upon aesthetic motifs—a dimension that also preoccupied Marcuse. The equivocal relation of the institute to radical social movements during the 1960s came to an end in January 1969 when Adorno called the police to eject student protesters occupying the institute's Frankfurt premises. By contrast, in the United States, Marcuse's distinctive social theory of liberation, greatly influenced by Martin Heidegger (1889–1976) and Freud, appealed to the New Left throughout the 1960s and early 1970s.

There have been significant—yet often marginalized—contributions to the development of the Frankfurt school and critical theory made by intellectuals more loosely associated with the institute: Walter Benjamin's unique analysis of art and media; Franz Neumann (1900–1954) and Otto Kirchheimer's (1905–1965) profound inquiry of political forms of integration in advanced capitalism; and Kracauer's theory of film and propaganda. Jürgen Habermas, the most important representative of the second generation of the school, extensively criticized his predecessors' oversimplification of modernity and developed a different analysis of capitalist society that appreciates the normative dimension of rationality rooted in communicative interaction. The Frankfurt school has also been criticized for its overly negative view of mass culture and its overestimation of the autonomous character of high art. More recently, Axel Honneth, who became director of the institute in 2001, has elaborated critical theory with a new focus on the social theory of recognition.

SEE ALSO *Critical Theory; Fromm, Erich; Habermas, Jürgen; Marcuse, Herbert*

BIBLIOGRAPHY

Adorno, Theodor W., et al. 1959. *The Authoritarian Personality.* New York: Harper.

Adorno, Theodor W. [1966] 1973. *Negative Dialectics.* Trans. E. B. Ashton. New York: Seabury.

Benjamin, Walter. 1999. *The Arcades Project.* Ed. Rolf Tiedemann. Trans. Howard Eiland and Kevin McLaughlin. Cambridge, MA: Belknap.

Habermas, Jürgen. 1984–1987. *The Theory of Communicative Action.* 2 vols. Trans. Thomas McCarthy. Boston: Beacon.

Honneth, Axel. 1995. *The Struggle for Recognition: The Moral Grammar of Social Conflict.* Trans. Joel Anderson. Cambridge, MA: Polity.

Horkheimer, Max. 1947. *Eclipse of Reason.* New York: Oxford University Press.

Horkheimer, Max, and Theodor W. Adorno. [1947] 1997. *Dialectic of Enlightenment.* Trans. Edmund Jephcott. London, New York: Verso.

Jay, Martin. 1973. *The Dialectical Imagination: A History of the Frankfurt School and the Institute of Social Research, 1932–1950.* London: Heinemann.

Kirchheimer, Otto, and Georg Rusche. 1939. *Punishment and Social Structure.* New York: Columbia University Press.

Kracauer, Siegfried. 1947. *From Caligari to Hitler: A Psychological History of the German Film.* Princeton, NJ: Princeton University Press.

Löwenthal, Leo, and Norbert Guterman. 1970. *Prophets of Deceit: A Study of the Techniques of the American Agitator.* 2nd ed. Palo Alto, CA: Pacific Books.

Marcuse, Herbert. 1955. *Eros and Civilization: A Philosophical Inquiry into Freud.* Boston: Beacon.

Neumann, Franz. 1942. *Behemoth: The Structure and Practice of National Socialism.* London: Gollancz.

Wiggershaus, Rolf. 1994. *The Frankfurt School: Its History, Theories, and Political Significance.* Trans. Michael Robertson. Cambridge, MA: MIT Press.

Jae Ho Kang

FRANKLIN, BENJAMIN
1706–1790

Benjamin Franklin was not only one of the best-known founding fathers of the United States, he was a leading politician, diplomat, writer, publisher, librarian, and philosopher. He was also a scientist renowned for his experiments with electricity and lightning, as well as an inventor credited with inventing the lightning rod, the heat-efficient Franklin stove, bifocals, swim fins, and numerous useful gadgets. His famous scientific experiment with a kite in a thunderstorm proved the presence of electricity in lightning.

Born into the family of a Boston soap maker and having received almost no formal education, in 1723 Franklin ran away to Philadelphia where he made his fortune first as a printer and later as the publisher and editor of the widely read *Pennsylvania Gazette* newspaper. He wrote numerous editorials, opinion pieces (usually under aliases), essays, and pamphlets about politics, economics, science, ethics, and civic self-improvement. He attracted attention for his wit and commonsense philosophy, especially as reflected in his proverbs in *Poor Richard's Almanack*, a popular yearbook on science and technology, which he published between 1733 and 1757 under the pseudonym Richard Saunders.

In 1731 Franklin helped launch the Library Company, the first subscription library in the United States. Twelve years later he helped found the American Philosophical Society, the nation's first learned society (a society that exists to promote an academic discipline or group of disciplines). While serving as a Pennsylvania assemblyman, he helped establish a local academy in 1751 that became the present-day University of Pennsylvania. He was a member of the Continental Congress, which appointed him to serve as deputy postmaster-general in 1753. At the 1754 Congress of Commissioners from the several American colonies held in Albany, New York, Franklin, though a loyalist, proposed a plan for the union of all the colonies under one government for the purpose of common defense and other general purposes.

In 1757 Franklin became a diplomatic agent in London representing Pennsylvania, Georgia, New Jersey, and Massachusetts, but he returned home in 1775 because of the revolutionary unrest in America and the so-called "Hutchinson affair." Thomas Hutchinson (1711–1780) was the British-appointed governor of Massachusetts, who wrote to his friends in London to recommend curtailing the liberties of the American colonists. When Franklin obtained Governor Hutchinson's letters, he leaked them to the press, causing public uproar in America. The British government angrily denounced Franklin in public and in 1774 removed him from the office of deputy postmaster-general and agent for the colonies, resulting in his final break with Britain (which he otherwise deeply admired). He served as a member of the Committee of Five, which had been instructed by the Second Continental Congress to draw up a document declaring independence from Britain. He helped Thomas Jefferson and John Adams, two other members of the committee, to draft the Declaration of Independence, which Congress unanimously adopted in 1776.

During the War of Independence (1775–1783) Franklin was the most popular foreign diplomat in the court of Louis XVI (1754–1793) in Paris, signing the 1778 Treaty of Alliance, which secured a close military-political alliance with France as well as substantial French military and financial help that made American victory possible. In 1783 he signed the Treaty of Paris, a peace treaty ending the war with Britain. Franklin came home in 1785 to serve as the appointed president of the Commonwealth of Pennsylvania. He was a delegate to the federal Constitutional Convention and signed the Constitution in 1787. His last great public service was authoring a major abolitionist pamphlet in 1789. His autobiography, first published in 1791, is acclaimed today as the greatest autobiographical work produced in colonial America.

Franklin was the most illustrious American of his time. As a philosopher of the Enlightenment, an eighteenth-century philosophical movement that rejected traditional ideas held at the time, he cast off all religious dogma but saw order and harmony in the universe. Rationalism, materialism, and belief in progress and social evolution mark all his publications. Prior to the revolution he believed that progress could be achieved under an enlightened monarch—especially through the inspiration and guidance provided by his own teachings, maxims, and aphorisms. Later he abandoned his doubts about democratic politics, rejecting the British monarchy and aristocracy in favor of the egalitarian view that all men are equal. In order to achieve progress and social harmony, he advocated the cultivation of practical virtues such as temperance, frugality, resolve, industry, sincerity, moderation, chastity, humility, and cleanliness. After the revolution he argued against the rule of the wealthy, taxation without representation, and slavery. He championed universal male suffrage, which he believed would encourage loyalty and respect for the law, as well as a unicameral federal legislature (without a Senate), which could prevent the rich from dominating political life and provide for a united, more efficient government. Scholars have also suggested that Franklin's philosophy embodies the moral and political pragmatism of the American business class.

SEE ALSO *American Revolution; Constitution, U.S.; Democracy; Enlightenment; Jefferson, Thomas; Liberalism; Loyalists; Pragmatism*

BIBLIOGRAPHY

Amacher, Richard E. 1962. *Benjamin Franklin.* New York: Twayne.

Conn, Peter, ed. 2005. *The Autobiography of Benjamin Franklin.* Philadelphia: University of Pennsylvania Press.

Isaacson, Walter. 2003. *Benjamin Franklin: An American Life.* New York: Simon and Schuster.

Roop, Peter, and Connie Roop. 2000. *Benjamin Franklin.* New York: Scholastic.

Zall, Paul M., ed. 2000. *Franklin on Franklin.* Lexington: University Press of Kentucky.

Rossen Vassilev

FRAZIER, E. FRANKLIN
1894–1962

E. Franklin Frazier, one of the most prominent African American sociologists of the early twentieth century, studied at Howard University (BA 1916), Clark University (MA 1920), and the University of Chicago (PhD 1931). After completing his studies he spent most of his career at Howard University, where he became the chairperson of the Department of Sociology in 1934. He remained at Howard until his death. His central contribution to sociology was the formalizing of a research tradition on the African American family, which he first began to pursue seriously in his dissertation, "The Negro Family in Chicago." That study resulted in a book of the same title, published in 1932. Frazier expanded his contributions on the topic by publishing *The Negro Family in the United States* (1939) and *Negro Youth at the Crossways* (1940). He also contributed to the field of race relations and race theory more generally, perhaps best exemplified by his publications "Sociological Theory and Race Relations" (1947) and *Race and Culture Contacts in the Modern World* (1957).

Frazier's primary data sources were case histories and census statistics. Rather than employing micro-level analyses, however, he utilized this material to construct social organizational portraits of the African American family and, more generally, African American social life. As he conducted most of his research in the midst of the twentieth-century rural-to-urban migration of African Americans, Frazier's social organizational perspective allowed him to offer robust and penetrating commentaries about the means of mechanisms of their adjustment to the hyper-industrializing urban sphere—the manner by which African Americans adjusted to industrialized urban societies after leaving the largely rural South. In doing so, he emphasized the social organizational shortcomings of the African American community as it transferred to a mostly northern and urban milieu.

Frazier essentially regarded African American migration to the city as an adaptational challenge for the black American family, and he argued that a history of social disorganization in the South, followed by turbulent efforts at reorganization in the nonsouthern, urban sphere, encapsulated the situation of the black American family's confrontation with modern urban America. Frazier believed that the hardships of social and economic adjustment were the causal factors of crime, vice, illegitimacy, and delinquency. Because he asserted that social disorganization and pathology were a result of the African American community's adjustment to new geographic terrain, Frazier was regarded by many later readers of his work as a pioneering conservative voice on the cultural dimensions of African American life. In fact, Frazier's work has been regarded as the precursor to later works such as Daniel Patrick Moynihan's highly controversial 1960s-era study "The Negro Family: A Case for National Action," which argued that the pathology extant in lower-income African American families was largely due to the absence of an adult male figure.

Frazier was not a cultural theorist to the same extent as certain other scholars of African American life in the early twentieth century (e.g., Allison Davis, St. Claire Drake, W. E. B. Du Bois, and Zora Neale Hurston). However, his emphases in cultural analysis centered on what he perceived to be pathological and maladaptive dimensions of African American family and social life. His assertion that disorganization and pathology were prominent features of African American urban life was partly based on his embracing of the idea that African Americans did not retain any firm cultural roots in Africa. Thus, they were left without a rich, historically grounded cultural foundation in the United States, other than that produced in response to slavery. Accordingly, he regarded African Americans as consistently hampered by racism and social marginalization such that many developed cultural traits that were, if not fatalistic, at least certainly not conducive to social advancement in modern American society.

Quite early in his career, Frazier stressed the impossibility of African culture having endured the middle passage from Africa to slavery in the Western Hemisphere. He maintained this argument through investigations (albeit preliminary) of African American religious expression, social thoughts and ideologies, and social practices. Accordingly, he emphasized that the objective of formal education for black Americans should be to bind them to the American experience rather than aim to identify and proliferate some notion of cultural distinctiveness. Frazier's logic in arguing that black Americans were, foremost, products of the American experience was grounded in his consideration of the history of black Americans as a series of critical social shocks. The order of shocks was (1) the enslavement of blacks on the coast of Africa, (2) the middle passage, (3) the slave experience itself, and (4) a profound state of social disorganization following emancipation.

To Frazier, the product of this pattern of shock was a folk culture, largely exemplified by a southern-based, lower-income, black American constituency that was struggling to reconcile their awkward status in the American social landscape. In his doctoral dissertation and some early research, Frazier pointed out that the African American folk culture emanating from slavery and the postemancipation period was an expression of "surrender" to white America in terms of attitude and acceptance of life. He believed that this resulted in the black community's durable designation as a subaltern caste in American social structure.

Frazier's remedy for this condition was the cultivation of a form of race consciousness that could help fuel African Americans' motivation for social advancement. However, Frazier maintained that an appropriate race consciousness was not grounded in a shared cognizance of primordially derived cultural characteristics; instead, he argued that it should take the form of a sociopolitical orientation that could motivate a downtrodden constituency in American society to improve its social status. Hence, for Frazier the significance of fostering race consciousness was not what it did to reify any notion of a distinct African American culture, but rather its use as a basis for asserting the growth and proliferation of pragmatic strategies for social uplift.

Despite what may appear to be an extremely critical perspective on the social and psychological dynamics of African American life, Frazier maintained that the conditions affecting the African American community were structural in nature and not in any way derived from inherent racial traits. Accordingly, despite the problems that African Americans encountered in adjusting to the urban sphere, Frazier asserted that this migration created opportunities for the social and cultural renewal of black Americans (especially as the urban terrain encouraged black Americans to break with the fatalistic folk culture proliferating throughout their southern, more rural, social experience). He also believed that a more constructive and positive race consciousness would develop due to the narrowing of social distance between African Americans in the urban domain. Finally, Frazier also believed that urbanization would destroy any retention of mythical notions of blackness that had been cultivated throughout history.

Frazier's carefully nuanced approach to race consciousness was an indication of the nascent nationalist tendencies that underlay both his scholarship and his civic commitments. These tendencies emerged more directly in some of Frazier's later work, especially his classic *Black Bourgeoisie* (1957), in which he argued that the African American middle and upper classes were engaged in forms of socialization and consumption parallel to those pursued by the mainstream American middle and upper classes. While Frazier did ascribe to the idea that black Americans had to assimilate into the cultural and social fabric of mainstream American society, he also maintained that such assimilation had to take shape in a critical rather than a mimical fashion. By that he meant that black Americans should not simply adopt the full range of cultural and social practices engaged by white Americans, but instead selectively appropriate those that would reap some clear benefits for black Americans in garnering firm and secure status in mainstream culture. Although it was widely read, *Black Bourgeoisie* was a highly polemic and, in comparison to Frazier's other works, lightly researched commentary.

Because Franklin's methodological tools were specifically suited for macro-level analysis, he was not well equipped to consider the personal situation of the black American. His objectives, however, did not necessarily concern that perspective. He viewed the black community as a caste constituency in American society. Therefore, his research emphasis was on the black American community as a whole, not its individual members. Moreover, his agenda for social change did not consist of strategies for individual adjustment to mainstream social and cultural patterns in American society; instead, he attempted to articulate a vision of racial advancement that could evaluate the entire population of black Americans.

To a large extent, under the auspices of Frazier and others of his era (e.g., Charles S. Johnson, St. Claire Drake, Horace Cayton, and Allison Davis) black American social thought moved from polemically oriented, philosophically grounded defenses of the humanity of African Americans to more formal scientific investigations, analyses, and model constructions of the state of the black American condition in a rapidly modernizing American society. Frazier's assertions about African Americans' loss of African cultural traits helped him to view the black American condition in terms of future possibilities—the most immediate being its complete and permanent stake in American society. Frazier's commitment to this perspective was evident in both his scholarly pursuits and his political worldview.

SEE ALSO *Assimilation; Cox, Oliver C.; Drake, St. Clair; Park School, The; Sociology, Urban*

BIBLIOGRAPHY

Frazier, E. Franklin. 1932. *The Negro Family in Chicago.* Chicago: University of Chicago Press.

Frazier, E. Franklin. 1939. *The Negro Family in the United States.* Chicago: University of Chicago Press.

Frazier, E. Franklin. 1940. *Negro Youth at the Crossways: Their Personality Development in the Middle States.* Washington, D.C.: American Council on Education.

Frazier, E. Franklin. 1947. Sociological Theory and Race Relations. *American Sociological Review* (June 12): 265–271.

Frazier, E. Franklin. 1957. *Black Bourgeoisie.* New York: The Free Press.

Frazier, Franklin E. 1957. *Race and Culture Contacts in the Modern World.* Boston: Beacon Press.

Moynihan, Daniel Patrick. 1965. The Negro Family: A Case for National Action. Washington, D.C.: Department of Labor.

Alford A. Young Jr.

FREE ASSOCIATION
SEE *Psychoanalytic Theory.*

FREE LUNCH
SEE *Scarcity.*

FREE RIDER

The datum for any discussion on free riding and collective action is economist Mancur Olson's (1932–1998) *The Logic of Collective Action* (1965). Olson's thesis was a reaction to the pluralist view that when a political, social, or economic problem impinges significantly on the life of a citizen, he or she instinctively acts collectively on the basis of shared concern. Olson's counterargument was that: (1) mobilization was not a natural or spontaneous process; (2) not all potential groups would materialize; and (3) membership would be lower than pluralists envisaged. Olson proposed that large numbers of rational potential members of groups seeking collective (nonexcludable) goods free ride these organizations because any benefits gained will be freely available to them without incurring the costs of membership. Indeed, as Russell Hardin (2003) notes "free riding [in large groups] is often clearly in the interest of most and perhaps all members." Thus, for Olson, rational participators are special cases: they are either coerced to participate (e.g., compulsory membership as in trade union "closed shops") or they are attracted by selective incentives only available to members. In small groups, free riding can be assuaged by the imposition of sanctions while free riders remain group members, or by excluding free riders (Page et al. 2005). As Page et al. highlight,

"under favourable conditions, where the opportunities of entry and exit are symmetrically balanced, a process of voluntary association can mitigate the free-rider problem" (2005, p. 1032). Accordingly, "people are often observed to cooperate effectively in work groups, in local public goods provision, and in other settings" (Page et al 2005, p. 1050).

Many scholars have argued that Olson's work has been discredited (i.e., the collective action paradox has been negotiated) by several developments: (1) the advocacy explosion (that began in the mid-1960s) witnessed the emergence of large numbers of (public interest) groups that Olson said should not exist; (2) large numbers of citizens joined these organizations; and (3) numerous surveys demonstrate that members join for collective, not economically self-interested, ends. However, Olson's rebuttal to these critiques was pointed and persuasive. He argued that many of these groups offered selective incentives to stimulate membership and that membership—and political lobbying—were in fact the by-product (i.e., not the primary reason for membership). He also maintained that membership levels in these groups were suboptimal—these entities mobilized only a small fraction of the latent membership—and many potential members choose to free ride. Accordingly, some interests would be underresourced in comparison with the public support they reflected, and other interests would be easier to mobilize (e.g., business).

Olson and supporters such as Hardin also argue that surveys of joiners reveal little about the larger group of those who refuse to join. Olson accepted that (trivial) numbers of members would join (in addition to those seeking selective benefits), but he argued that the number joining for collective goods would be dwarfed by those failing to participate. He cited two examples in support of this argument. First, he argued that "tens of millions of Americans" believed the population should not grow, but only a "miniscule minority of 12,000" were members of the group Zero Population Growth (Olson 1979, p. 149). Secondly, he (conservatively) estimated that more than fifty million Americans valued "a wholesome environment, but in a typical year probably fewer than one in a hundred pays dues to any organization whose main activity is lobbying for a better environment" (Olson 1982, pp. 34–35). For Olson, all these nonmembers are free riders.

Finally, it is worth highlighting that in his arguments Olson makes the loose assumption that those who in some general way support a cause, and do not join, are free riding. Critics argue that such ubiquitous labeling of nonparticipation stretches the free-riding concept too far. It does not necessarily follow, for example, that those who share a concern about the environment with members of environmental groups also agree with the goals or strategies of environmental organizations, or believe that the groups' activities will produce desirable outcomes, or consider the groups to be efficient (see Jordan and Maloney [2006] for a fuller exposition of this argument). Nonparticipation can emerge from noneconomically rational reasons.

SEE ALSO *Collective Action; Tragedy of the Commons; Transaction Cost*

BIBLIOGRAPHY

Hardin, Russell. 2003. The Free Rider Problem. In *The Stanford Encyclopedia of Philosophy*, ed. Edward N. Zalta. Stanford, CA: Metaphysics Research Lab Center for the Study of Language and Information. http://plato.stanford.edu/entries/free-rider/.

Jordan, Grant, and William A. Maloney. 2006. "Letting George Do It": Accounting for Low Participation Rates? *Journal of Elections, Public Opinion, and Parties* 16 (2): 115–139.

Olson, Mancur. 1965. *The Logic of Collective Action: Public Goods and the Theory of Groups*. Cambridge, MA: Harvard University Press.

Olson, Mancur. 1979. Epilogue: Letter to Denton Morrison. *Research in Social Movements, Conflicts, and Change* 2: 149–150.

Olson, Mancur. 1982. *The Rise and Decline of Nations: Economic Growth, Stagflation, and Social Rigidities*. New Haven, CT: Yale University Press.

Page, Talbot, Louis Putterman, and Bulent Unel. 2005. Voluntary Association in Public Goods Experiments: Reciprocity, Mimicry, and Efficiency. *Economic Journal* 115: 1032–1053.

William A. Maloney

FREE TRADE

Free trade refers to the unregulated exchange of raw materials, commodities, and services among people and nations. One of the foundational propositions of economic theory since the seminal work of Adam Smith (1723–1790) is that free trade is ultimately superior to protectionism if the principal economic objective is the greatest possible quantity of aggregate wealth or national income, and, indeed, the greatest good for all people. This proposition has widely and regularly been subjected to theoretical and political critique, and, despite the contemporary resurgence in free trade economics, free trade remains far more a theoretical ideal than an actual mode of economic practice and organization.

Before Adam Smith published his exhaustive study, *The Wealth of Nations*, in 1776, the mercantilist argument for the protection of markets largely dominated economic literature and practice. The mercantilists composed their tracts during the seventeenth and eighteenth centuries, a period of tremendous colonial activity, trade growth, and, not coincidentally, nation-state formation. Mercantilists predictably celebrated foreign trade but also believed strongly in the need to protect national industries and markets. They supported a wide range of protectionist measures, including tariffs on imports and subsidies for exports.

While few, if any, of the central ideas in Smith's *Wealth of Nations* are original—many were asserted and developed by French physiocrats and British moral philosophers—he made a case for free trade that was and to a considerable degree remains incomparable in its rhetorical persuasiveness, thoroughness, and analytic precision.

Among Smith's contributions was the theoretical refutation of the mercantilist argument for the promotion of exports and discouragement of imports, especially manufactured imports. Smith argued that the *economy-wide* impact of trade policies and regulations had to be examined. For instance, high duties on imports that were produced more cheaply elsewhere tended to diminish domestic competition and promote expansion of an inefficient industry. For example, protecting the British textile industry from cheaper colonial imports would lead to more investment of labor and resources in a demonstrably inefficient sector of the economy. Without protections, resources could be allocated to industries that were more competitive on the world market and which would thus realize greater economic aggregate growth, also known as *static gains from trade*.

Full analyses of the economic benefits of the division of labor and the public benefits of private self-interest were among Smith's foremost contributions to free trade economics. The rewards from the division of labor are implicit in his argument for static gains: Nations that specialize in industries in which they are most competitive in unregulated conditions make the most efficient use of their labor and productive resources; thus both the specializing nations and the nations with which they trade will benefit. In the long term, these specialization-based static gains lead to dynamic gains; though dynamic gains are less clearly defined and more difficult to measure, they potentially accrue through the general economic impact of the more efficient use of resources.

The powerful case for free trade submitted by Smith was made into prescriptive economic doctrine by the next generation of economists, who further developed what came to be labeled *classical economics*. The most well-known figure is David Ricardo (1772–1823), who is generally credited with the theory of *comparative advantage*—in short, the idea that even nations that lacked *absolute advantage* (producing goods at the least possible cost) could still realize gains by concentrating on production of goods of the greatest market competitiveness relative to other goods. Though Ricardo's name is most frequently associated with this theory, scholars are now more prone to give credit to James Mill (1773–1836)—father of another great and influential economist, John Stuart Mill (1806–1873)—for developing the most comprehensive explanation of comparative advantage among the classical economists.

In response to a vigorous public debate regarding Britain's protectionist Corn Laws, Mill explained that protectionist tariffs led to an absolute economic loss. Taxes on imported corn led to increases in the price of corn in Britain, which in turn led to an increase in the cultivation of less-productive land, which in turn increased the value and rent costs of land, which finally led to necessary wage increases. Thus, in protecting an inefficient product, a widespread set of increased costs ensued, netting a general or absolute loss. Resources would have been far better and more naturally invested in sectors of the economy that did not need to be protected because they were already competitive, or, in other words, sectors in which national comparative advantage already existed.

The doctrine of comparative advantage did much to establish free trade as the ruling economic orthodoxy for several succeeding generations of economists and, until the arrival of the Great Depression and the British economist John Maynard Keynes (1883–1946), it ruled economic theory (if not quite practice) with little exception. Two exceptions that received the most vigorous debate were related to "infant industries" and national defense. The infant industries argument proposed that new industries deserved some form of government protection until they had the chance to establish themselves as competitors in the global market. While his assertion was vigorously disputed, the idea was effectively made practice (to no small success) by Alexander Hamilton (1755/57–1804) in the early years of American national economic development. Also, in times of national emergency (e.g., war), interference in the workings of the free market was widely accepted as advisable. How, for instance, was supplying your enemy with goods for war to be justified? While wars may well be fought in the interests of the free market, the conditions and implications of war merit exception.

Whatever the sideline debates among economists regarding the particular cases for suspending the rules of free trade, it took the work of Keynes to establish a rigorous and widely accepted critique of free trade doctrine. Keynes, with considerable theoretical sophistication, faced the facts of the catastrophic market failure that goes by the name of the Great Depression and demonstrated the need to pursue protectionist measures. His *General Theory of Employment, Interest, and Money* (1936) included arguments for government spending on public works and promoting public investment and consumption during periods of high unemployment. Keynes did not believe that free market conditions realized, or "settled" at, full employment and that unemployment was a principal indicator of economic inefficiency. Government interventions in the market, including protective tariffs and subsidies, were, he asserted, sometimes necessary to restore employment and general economic health.

Keynes was enormously influential, not least in the United States, where his theories informed Franklin D. Roosevelt's (1882–1945) massive government market intervention known as the New Deal. Toward the end of World War II (1939–1945), Keynes was a key figure at the meeting in Bretton Woods, New Hampshire, where two institutions were created that would come to dominate international economic relations in the later decades of the twentieth century: the International Monetary Fund (IMF) and the World Bank. However, these organizations, chartered under the banner of free trade principles, did not become important institutions of global economic management until after the cold war ended. Until the end of the cold war, the global free market was effectively compromised by the maneuverings of the superpowers as they intervened in the economic affairs of nations according to their particular national and ideological interests.

Since the cold war, the IMF and the World Bank, along with the World Trade Organization (WTO, established in 1995), have come to dominate the vigorous global articulation of free trade principles and practices. Throughout the cold war, developing nations were generally able to secure loans at very favorable terms, and banks were willing to lend freely under the assumption that bad loans would be covered by superpowers unwilling to see regimes fall to a competing ideology. When the cold war ended, the insecurity of these assumptions was revealed, and when bailouts were no longer forthcoming, debt crises struck developing nations hard. The World Bank and the IMF suddenly achieved a new relevance as they worked to negotiate debts no longer mediated by interested superpowers.

The terms demanded by the IMF and the World Bank for the renegotiations of loans were based firmly on free trade principles. These terms, which have been called *structural adjustments, austerity measures,* or *conditionalities,* have sparked spirited and sometimes violent debate. Nations, particularly the heavily indebted nations of Africa, Central and South America, and eastern Europe, in order to secure solvency loans, have been required to enact a host of free trade measures, including the devaluation of their currencies, removal of protective tariffs, reductions in public spending, and the privatization of key industries and services, including health care and education.

Those who dispute the effectiveness of these free trade conditions imposed on poorer countries argue that the "conditionalities" have never been fully practiced by the wealthy nations whose representatives dominate the IMF and World Bank. They point out that at no time during the critical years when the United States or Britain were developing their economies were their currencies devalued or key social support programs privatized. These critics can also point to the vivid and devastating consequences of reductions in public spending, particularly in the area of health care in Africa. For their part, the supporters of free trade doctrines can point to the indisputable economic growth of such major nations as India and China. In the early years of the twenty-first century, it was reliably estimated that one million people a month were being pulled out of poverty by China's embrace of the free market.

Though the neoliberal globalization of the free market increased rapidly after the fall of the Soviet Union and the opening of China to trade, the intellectual roots for the reemergence of free trade were established decades earlier in Europe and the United States. Important figures include the Austrian economist Friedrich von Hayek (1899–1992), who argued, in works such as *The Road to Serfdom* (1944), that any centralized control over social and economic matters would inevitably lead to totalitarianism. Even more influential was the University of Chicago economist Milton Friedman (1912–2006). Friedman was largely responsible for the shift in academic economics away from Keynesian ideas and toward monetarism, or the idea that money supply rather then employment should be the focus of economic policies. While Friedman's monetarist theories have proved of dubious value, his attacks on virtually all forms of government regulation or even involvement in social and economic life have been very influential indeed. Throughout the years of the Margaret Thatcher and Ronald Reagan (1911–2004) administrations in the 1980s, the deregulations advocated by Friedman and his followers were aggressively implemented, and they established the political basis for the free market orthodoxy that dominates national and international economic affairs even to this day.

In the first decade of the twenty-first century, the principles of free market globalization almost exclusively govern the economic practices of nations and the institutions that administer the world's economy, most notably the IMF, the World Bank, and the WTO. However, there are movements of national exception in countries such as Venezuela and Bolivia and activist assertions of dissent such as that expressed in the 1999 WTO protests in Seattle. A strong body of evidence now exists that the current free market orthodoxy has been implemented in ways that violate its core principles of economic freedom. This is especially evident in the removal of barriers to capital flows on the one hand but the increasing restrictions on the movement of labor on the other hand. Thus the North American Free Trade Agreement (NAFTA), negotiated among Mexico, Canada, and the United States and implemented in 1994, greatly increased the ability of goods and capital to move across borders even as the increasing militarization of the U.S.–Mexico border has made it more difficult for workers to pursue preferred employments. It remains to be seen if the current expansion of free trade ideas and practices will help or hinder the aspiration for the greatest common good that runs as a consistent theme in the writings of the movement's best thinkers.

SEE ALSO *Absolute and Comparative Advantage; Capital Controls; Cold War; Corn Laws; Customs Union; Economics, International; Friedman, Milton; Globalization, Social and Economic Aspects of; Great Depression; Industrialization; Infant Industry; International Monetary Fund; Keynes, John Maynard; Liberalization, Trade; Mercantilism; Mill, James; Mill, John Stuart; Monetarism; Neoliberalism; New Deal, The; North American Free Trade Agreement; Philosophy, Moral; Physiocracy; Protectionism; Quotas, Trade; Ricardo, David; Roosevelt, Franklin D.; Scottish Moralists; Smith, Adam; Tariffs; Trade; Washington Consensus; World Bank, The; World Trade Organization*

BIBLIOGRAPHY

Friedman, Milton. [1962] 2002. *Capitalism and Freedom.* Chicago: University of Chicago Press.

Keynes, John Maynard. [1936] 1997. *The General Theory of Employment, Interest, and Money.* Amherst, NY: Prometheus.

Polanyi, Karl. 1944 [2001]. *The Great Transformation: The Political and Economic Origins of Our Time.* Boston: Beacon.

Smith, Adam. [1776] 2000. *The Wealth of Nations.* New York: Modern Library.

Paul R. Krugman
Stephen A. Germic

FREE WILL

SEE *Existentialism.*

FREEDOM

Freedom, the capacity for self-directed thought and action, and the choice of one's own goals, is one of the central values of western thought. Often closely tied to questions of free will, freedom is also seen as central to questions of moral responsibility, personality, and identity, and to democratic political life. Rule by others, such as political domination as well as social oppression, through established forms of authority or psychological restrictions, are all opposed by forms of freedom. The idea of liberation from the limits of nature of entrenched authorities or despotic rulers is a central theme of both literature and politics.

Freedom does not have a simple or single essence. It has developed sometimes haltingly in the history of thought. For the ancients, freedom was not equated with worldly accomplishment or goal-directed action; it was primarily an inner state of being. The free person was one who rules his desires (freedom applied mostly to males) rather than being ruled by them. For Plato, freedom meant to be liberated from base desires. Rather than a life of self-chosen ends, however, the ancients saw the highest form of life as contemplation of the order of the universe. The free man was released from desires that impeded this goal.

The Greeks originated the political idea of self-rule (*koinonia*), but generally applied it only to a limited group of male, property-owning citizens. In Aristotle's political philosophy, freedom requires active participation by citizens in the life of the polis. This, too, is not a form of goal-directed action, but of acting in concert: The citizen alternates with others in holding office and engages in deliberation about laws and public affairs. Although there were examples of wider democracy in ancient Greece, political theorists such as Aristotle supported a limited republican form. Only propertied male heads of household had the requisite self-control over their own desires to be capable of self-rule, they believed; the rest were only fit to be ruled by others. The Stoics living under the Roman imperium reemphasized a purely inner freedom based on deliberate self-mastery. Still, the Stoics also had early notions of a cosmopolitan humanity in which all were naturally equal.

The roots of the modern notion of freedom can be traced back to the late Middle Ages. The rise of independent city-states in Italy and other parts of Europe was accompanied by a revival of ancient republicanism. These newer forms of republicanism were more disposed to give a role to the people and inclined to stress liberty. The later Middle Ages also provided some sources of the modern notion of individuation. The Renaissance that followed developed a modern idea of the self as a "work of art," and the development of individuality was the essence of freedom. In the seventeenth century there was a further elaboration of republican thought that stressed the relation of a free people to the new ideals of liberty.

LIBERAL THEORY

Modern philosophy rejected the idea that knowledge of the structure of the world could and must be achieved through individual human reason alone. Revealed religion or other idols had to be rejected. Although this philosophical ideal first justified only free scientific inquiry, it proved useful for politics as well. But the most influential notions of freedom in modernity are those associated with liberalism. Whereas the Aristotelian tradition saw humans as naturally political animals who realized their aims in community, the modern liberal view saw individuals as possessing natural liberty, prior to social relationships or attachments. Although this is certainly a fiction, it reflects the idea that the individual—not the social environment, the church, the state, or the family—is the source of social and political freedom. These forms of social and political freedom are now seen as a form of self-determination: the capacity to choose to decide upon and pursue one's own goals or plans of life. The individual is an active agent whose freedom is seen in accomplishments. Freedom is also the ability to act freely to achieve these goals. The republican emphasis on deliberating with others was replaced in the philosophies of Thomas Hobbes and John Locke by notions of self-interest. This conception was often linked to the new scientific consciousness, in which the individual was like all other things: a mechanism driven by material pursuit of interest, not by spiritual causality or teleology.

The liberal notion of freedom made a strong distinction between the public and the private that was quite different from what the ancients had conceived. Whereas Aristotle thought that freedom required public participation, liberals saw freedom first of all as applying to the private individual, who is free to act. Here freedom is the absence of constraint, or freedom *from* something. The idea of the social contract expressed the fact that legitimate political order is based on the freely given consent of the governed. This premise, emphasizing the equality and freedom of all, is the foundation of most modern democracies, where individuals are natural bearers of rights and freedoms that cannot be taken away by governments. In some respects, the liberal model of freedom as self-determination is restricted when combined with an economic model of human action, where the individual is a consumer rather than a creator, one who chooses between products on the market. As a maximizer of goods, the individual is primarily a possessive individual.

DEVELOPMENTAL THEORY

The theory of Jean-Jacques Rousseau was important in the development of a second conception of modern freedom. Rousseau held that the social contract (rejected by republican theories) was more than a contractual agreement—it created a general will that was the expression of a common moral will. In the romantic period this conception became what has been called a "developmental view of freedom." The Romantics rejected the Enlightenment view of man, which was overly rationalist and mechanistic, and sought a broader notion of human freedom that stressed aesthetic and relational qualities of freedom. In the developmental view, humans express their freedom through the development of all their human powers. Freedom is self-realization, or positive freedom. Karl Marx's notion of freedom embodied this view when he invoked the all-around development of capacities. Human action is not simply goal-directed, but includes many forms of human expression: artistic, expressive relations to others, and play, to name a few. Although this view draws on the Aristotelian tradition, it differs from it in its stress on individuality and its adoption of the modern view of the open-ended nature of capacities.

Developmental theories reject the atomism of liberal theory. They stress the interdependency of human activity. The development of freedom and capacities is not the result of individual initiative alone, but rather relies on a backdrop of prior social conditions: We are vulnerable, depending on a wide variety of conditions to develop and employ our human capacities.

Developmental theories have been central to radical democratic and socialist and social democratic conceptions of politics. Stressing the role of active citizen participation in politics, they agree with Aristotle that the fully realized individual has to be a participant in his or her own governance. Socialists extend this equal participation to models of economic production and reject liberal emphasis on private property. Socialized production, accordingly, is central to the development of selfhood and individuality.

For socialists and social democrats, political freedom rests on prior social freedoms, including a minimum of economic equality, retirement and unemployment benefits, health and safety, and other measures of human welfare. Conditions of complex human freedoms have become important not only for socialist states, but also for modern social democratic welfare states.

Critics of developmental views often have held that Rousseau's ideal of the general will have inherently totalitarian elements that are contrary to the liberal ideas of individual freedom. They also criticize the idea of inner powers unfolding in a natural manner. Others see expressive freedom as a socially pathological emphasis on pleasure or aesthetics for its own sake. The exclusive stress on aesthetic freedom reduces the influence of the work ethic and moral responsibility on human conduct.

COMMUNICATIVE FREEDOM

A third notion of freedom responds to recent concerns with cultural integrity, identity politics, and recent social movements, and new conflicts over the ability of participants to form their own unique relations to themselves and to social worlds. Influenced by the growing emphasis of language as central to philosophy and social science, ideas of communicative freedom have become an important element in contemporary debates. Communicative models stressing individual self-realization take place in a context of intersubjective community. Extending the liberal idea of free speech and expression, freedom involves the very capacity to communicate in language to formulate and express ideas in discussion, but it also is an element in the formation of the identity of individuals and groups. This capacity can be impeded by forms of authority and power that exclude us from discussion and deliberation, or distort our relations to ourselves and others. Deliberative models of democracy attempt to remedy some of the deficiencies of liberal and republican notions by stressing the centrality of discursive rationality.

In the mid-nineteenth century Alexis de Tocqueville raised an objection that has persisted to the present. Although de Tocqueville generally approved of new democracies, as represented by the young American state, he raised questions about the quality of democratic citizens as conformist and mediocre. Democracy may increase political freedom, but it also leads to impoverished personality. At the end of the century Friedrich Nietzsche provided a more aggressive critique of democracies. Opposing the abstract individual of liberal theory and the Protestantism underlying Immanuel Kant's notion of autonomy, Nietzsche argued that religion (namely Christianity) produced meek unfree subjects who feared authority and lacked the qualities needed for heroic struggle.

A third objection focuses on the distortions of democratic freedoms inherent in the concentration of power in mass democracies. Agreeing with developmental democrats such as John Stuart Mill and John Dewey that democratic citizenship requires an educated and informed public, critics argued that mass democracies are characterized by a manipulated mass culture. This mass culture is a product of the ownership and concentration of media in the hands of powerful economic and political interests that maintain their power positions, restricting political and social freedom, by controlling the production and reception of information. Access to the means to make sense of and deliberate about public issues remains a major concern for the health of democracies.

Max Weber's work on rationalization and bureaucracy raised another concern over the compatibility of large liberal democracies and freedom. Weber saw in social rationalization the increasing centrality of instrumental rationality. Bureaucratic authority became prominent in political regulation for reasons of efficiency or technical expertise, and it has come to displace not just deliberation and citizen participation but also the development of personality and social freedom. Bureaucracy itself further interprets the needs identified by developmentalists in an instrumental fashion, with resources of money or power rather than freedom or mutual understanding; citizens become subjugated clients and dependents.

In complex modern societies, democracies have grown in territory and population. The possibility of face-to-face democracy—the "town meeting" tradition with its stress on citizen participation—is difficult to maintain. Most modern democracies are representative, but the process of representing the varied subpublics of a democratic public can lead to conflicts. For critics, liberal and pluralist democracies are also thought to be dominated by interest groups and hence incapable of formulating a common good. Individual freedom does not lead to social or political freedom. This objection, which comes from all political outlooks, tends to see liberal democracy as a form driven by self- and group interests. For example, the conservative jurist Carl Schmitt thought that parliamentary systems were unworkable because of the conflict of interest groups, and contemporary communitarians see liberalism as lacking any orientation to a common good or moral core. This objection has some merit. Many proponents of the interest-group position devalued citizenship—already little more than voting. For some proponents, nonparticipation in even a minimum of democratic citizenship is seen as dysfunctional or unnecessary.

Conservative and communitarian objections, however, require a notion of sociocultural unity or homogeneity that is incompatible with the diversity of publics found in multicultural societies. These new challenges to liberal democratic society reflect a conflict between the claims of cultural integrity, which is not generally acknowledged in classical liberalism, and civil and political rights typical of liberal democratic notions of freedom. They also apply to newly important categories such as gender. Other conflicts between a developmental politics of distribution and the newer politics of resignation raise questions of the ways that liberal democracies reconcile the needs for solidarity, which are necessary for communicative freedom, with other freedoms producing a conflict between developmental politics of distribution and the newer politics of recognition. How do liberal democracies reconcile the need for solidarity, which is necessary for communicative freedom, with other freedoms? The renewal and reform of freedom in modern democratic societies rest with the healthy respect for and space for political protest and dissent. Freedom is not a fixed essence; instead, it has to be renewed and transformed in ever-changing social circumstances. Social movements have instituted new regimes, as in revolutions, but also have pressed claims for rights in established democracies, as in labor movements, movements for equal rights for women, racial minorities, and gays and lesbians, and even antiwar movements. The abil-

ity of a society to respond to dissent and protest is an important feature of a functioning democracy. In modern societies this often goes beyond mere tolerance to what postmodernists have called "openness to the other." Societies have to recognize that dissent takes place in the context of a broader solidarity: We have to be aware of and open to others who seem different, yet we must also accept the need for discussion that may or may not vindicate their claims.

Cultural movements can also be sources of freedom movements. These can often be generational conflicts, as in the Sturm und Drang movement in Germany in the romantic era, and the counterculture movement in the 1960s. Both of these challenged what they saw as repressive social and cultural practices well before they became forces for political change. It could also be argued that cultural resistance had a decisive if largely unacknowledged role in maintaining subterranean political resistance in Eastern Europe prior to the fall of Soviet Communism.

A deliberative model of democracy employing the insights of communicative freedom seems to propose a different model of democratic freedom. Political order is not constituted by a unified general will, but by a web of symbolic interactions in which solidarity and commonality is established through participation in social and political life, not in a reestablished common good. A healthy democracy requires a well functioning parliamentary or representational system, and significant civil rights and economic and social equality. But it also requires a substantial measure of private and public freedom, supported by extra-governmental publics who are able to discuss and actively challenge existing practices. It has to pay equal attention to the claims of solidarity and cultural integrity. It requires a greater interchange between the knowledge of experts and the judgment of citizens in the formation of policy and the formation of public policy. It also requires a truly democratic educational system open to all and a free system of media that promotes knowledge and discussion of significant issues.

Theories of freedom are associated with different institutional arrangements for the maximization of freedom. Theories of negative freedom have been linked most often to liberal political institutions such as constitutional governments with representative political institutions; elected representatives; free, fair, and frequent elections with a competitive party system; and an independent judiciary; along with extensive freedom of information and communications and a network of voluntary associations.

Developmental theorists argue that the institutional framework associated with negative freedom tends to negate the very conditions of freedom that it intends to facilitate. When combined with market economic institutions, liberal political institutions create large-scale inequalities of economic and social power that make the exercise of equal liberty impossible. Poverty, powerlessness, and forms of disrespect all combine to make the exercise of freedom difficult. A commitment to freedom requires maintaining a minimum satisfaction of human needs. In market societies, developmentalists have advocated extensive welfare measures to compensate for the effects of power. They contend that rather than restricting freedom, as classical and neoclassical liberals might think, extensive public support in fact enhances freedom, by providing a basis for equal employment to all. However, for developmentalists, such institutions have to include the promotion of civic equality as well. Developmentalists go beyond welfare-state reform to advocate replacing the private-property market system with social production, or radically democratizing areas of work education and communications.

Despite the triumphalism of neoclassical liberals in the post–cold war era, democracy has not increased. Only about half of the world's nations, consisting of less than half its population, can be considered democracies, and all of them do not meet all the criteria discussed above. The dissolution of the Soviet Empire has led to a rise in fundamentalist movements and ethnic conflicts that threaten to undermine democratic institutions in some newer states and to prevent their establishment in others. Some well established democracies have succeeded in accommodating ethnic diversity by forming "consociation democracies," but these require special conditions not achievable in all countries. Attempts to design constitutions or democratic institutions through planning or by "shock therapy" have not led to large-scale democratic movements in these countries—they have simply reinstituted the pathologies already present in advanced societies.

Pathologies of democratic freedom have sometimes resulted from restricted conceptions of representative institutions in the twentieth century. Examples include competitive elitism, which reduces democracy to a form of choosing leaders, and corporatist representation, which limits popular participation and substitutes consultations with large organized groups. Although contemporary democratic societies provide some room for competing groups, they are characterized by deepening asymmetries of power and wealth that limit the effective equal freedom of all. Actual capitalism, unlike the myth of self-equilibrating markets, requires concentration of economic and social power. The growth of corporations beyond nation-states is another important factor in the growth of poverty and income disparity. Many commentators question whether the nation-state and its conception of democratic freedom is a feasible model in light of the increasing global power of corporations. The nation-state, it is argued, no longer has the autonomy from the economic system to direct its own affairs and achieve its own goals.

In the developing world democratic freedom faces these obstacles and others. The subaltern economic status of developing nations has made them vulnerable to forced political and economic restructuring in order to obtain funds for development projects, and for the most part, attempts to create a civil society from above by local leaders or outside groups has led to limited democratization with a limited role for popular democratic initiatives.

SEE ALSO *Aristotle; Bureaucracy; Civil Liberties; Civil Rights; Constitutions; Cosmopolitanism; Democracy; Elitism; Hobbes, Thomas; Individualism; Kant, Immanuel; Liberalism; Liberation; Libertarianism; Liberty; Locke, John; Mill, John Stuart; Nietzsche, Friedrich; Participation, Political; Philosophy; Philosophy, Political; Plato; Political Culture; Political Science; Private Sector; Public Sector; Republicanism; Revolution; Rousseau, Jean-Jacques; Self-Determination; Social Movements; Tocqueville, Alexis de; Weber, Max*

BIBLIOGRAPHY

Arendt, Hannah. 1998. *The Human Condition.* 2nd ed. Chicago: University of Chicago Press.

Berlin, Isaiah. 1990. *Four Essays on Liberty.* New York: Oxford University Press.

Dahl, Robert. 2000. *On Democracy.* New Haven, CT: Yale University Press.

Fraser, Nancy, and Axel Honneth. 2003. *Redistribution or Recognition: A Political Philosophical Exchange.* London: Verso.

Habermas, Jürgen. 1974. *Theory and Practice.* Boston: Beacon Press.

Habermas, Jürgen. 1991. *The Structural Transformation the Public Sphere: An Inquiry into the Categories of Bourgeois Society.* Cambridge, MA: MIT Press.

Held, David. 2006. *Models of Democracy.* 3rd ed. London: Polity Press.

Macintyre, Alasdair. 1984. *After Virtue: A Study in Moral Theory.* Notre Dame, IN: University of Notre Dame Press.

MacPherson, C. B. 1964. *The Political Theory of Possessive Individualism: Hobbes to Locke.* Oxford: Oxford University Press.

Pettit, Phillip. 2000. *Republicanism: A Theory of Freedom and Government.* Oxford: Oxford University Press.

Skinner, Quentin. 1978. *The Foundations of Modern Political Thought.* Cambridge, U.K.: Cambridge University Press.

Taylor, Charles. 1975. *"Expressivism" in Hegel.* Cambridge, U.K.: Cambridge University Press.

Taylor, Charles, et al. 1994. *Multiculturalism.* Princeton, NJ: Princeton University Press.

Wolin, Sheldon. 2004. *Politics and Vision: Continuity and Innovation in Western Political Thought.* Expanded ed. Princeton, NJ: Princeton University Press.

Brian J. Caterino

FREEDOM OF INFORMATION ACT

Signed into law by President Lyndon B. Johnson in 1966, the U.S. Freedom of Information Act (FOIA) gives the public the right—within certain bounds—to be provided federal government records on request. The FOIA requires every department and agency in the executive branch (except for the president and the president's immediate advisors) to make duly requested government records "promptly available to any person." The law exempts several categories of government records from release, including records relating to classified defense and foreign policy matters, law enforcement records whose release would interfere with investigations and prosecutions, and records considered internal agency memoranda. The FOIA does not apply to Congress or the federal courts.

The key figure in the development and passage of the FOIA was Congressman John E. Moss, a California Democrat. As chair of the House Special Subcommittee on Government Information, Moss spent eleven years presiding over hearings and publishing reports that exhaustively documented the secrecy practices of the executive branch. Remarkably, his work drew little interest or support from members of the Washington press corps, who at that time were accustomed to a collegial, nonadversarial relationship with government officials. Thus, the bill's passage can be largely attributed to the diligent legislative maneuvering of Moss—as well as his party's control of both the presidency and Congress (by large majorities in the House and Senate) in 1966.

Controversy about the FOIA's implementation arose almost immediately after it became law, and the tenor of this debate has remained consistent over time. On the one hand, requestors of information have complained about delays in receipt of records, fees charged for duplication, and improper invoking of exemptions. On the other hand, agency staff and some elected officials have questioned the expenditure of significant resources required to comply with the law. All these concerns have shaped revisions and amendments to the FOIA, which has been significantly modified three times (in 1974, 1986, and 1996).

Records obtained under the FOIA are central to hundreds of news stories about the government that appear in the media each year. The FOIA thus plays an important role in efforts to keep government activity transparent and accountable. However, only a small proportion of FOIA requests are made by news organizations and legitimate researchers. A great number of requests are filed by commercial interests, who hope to repackage and sell the information obtained from their requests, or otherwise use it for business purposes. Access to government records has been dramatically altered by the diffusion of information technology. The vastly reduced cost of indexing, reproducing, and transmitting government records has made it easier for the public to locate and access government information—but it also makes it more conceivable that information of a sensitive or classified nature will fall into the wrong hands.

The FOIA has inspired the passage of similar legislation by U.S. state and local governments. Throughout the world, democracies both new and old adopted freedom of information (FOI) laws in the late twentieth century—many that consciously emulated the U.S. law. But FOI laws by themselves do not lead to greater government accountability. To have much effect, FOI laws require a media that is unhesitant to investigate government activity and is willing to use these laws as a tool to do so.

SEE ALSO *Secrecy; Transparency*

BIBLIOGRAPHY

Archibald, Sam. 1993. The Early Years of the Freedom of Information Act: 1955–1974. *PS: Political Science and Politics* 26 (4): 726–731.

Cain, Bruce E., Patrick Egan, and Sergio Fabbrini. 2003. Toward More Open Democracies: The Expansion of Freedom of Information Laws. In *Democracy Transformed? Expanding Political Opportunities in Advanced Industrial Democracies*, eds. Bruce E. Cain, Russell J. Dalton, Susan E. Scarrow. New York: Oxford University Press.

Patrick J. Egan

FREEDOM RIDERS

SEE *Student Nonviolent Coordinating Committee.*

FREEMAN, WALTER

SEE *Lobotomy.*

FREIRE, PAULO
1921–1997

Until his death from a heart attack on May 2, 1997, Paulo Freire devoted his life and work to a philosophy and practice of education committed to the empowerment and social transformation of communities marginalized by poverty, colonialism, and political repression. Freire worked extensively in Brazil, Chile, and West Africa, where he developed a method for teaching literacy to poor, working class, and indigenous people. The development of Freire's "pedagogy of the oppressed" cannot be viewed in isolation from his experience of life in Brazil during the first half of the twentieth century. Born in 1921 in Recife, a port town in the northeast province of Pernambuco, Paulo Reglus Neves Freire was raised in a middle class family that experienced severe poverty during the Great Depression. Poverty and hunger during Freire's youth caused several setbacks in his formal schooling, an experience that shaped the later development of his educational philosophy. Freire studied law at the University of Recife, but gave up his career as a lawyer after his first case to teach Portuguese in secondary schools (Gadotti 1994). Freire married Elza Maia Costa de Oliveria, a primary school teacher, in 1944. Throughout their marriage, Elza encouraged and inspired Freire to devote himself to his work in the field of adult education.

Northeast Brazil in the early 1960s was a region of acute social polarization and economic suffering. It was during this time that Freire began to elaborate a model of politically engaged pedagogy against the prevailing "culture of silence" under which the illiterate poor labored. He emphasized the dialectic relationship between theory and practice, which is expressed through three generative themes in his work: *concientization*, *dialogic learning*, and his critique of the *banking approach* to education. Underpinning these three generative themes is a student-centered system of learning that challenges how knowledge is constructed in the formal education system and in society at large. Freire's student-centered approach stands in stark contrast to conventional educational practice, which he referred to as the "banking approach" to education. He argued that conventional learning was the tool of the elite because it treated students as objects upon which knowledge is "deposited." Genuine learning, for Freire, could only be achieved through lived experience, critical reflection, and praxis (Aronowitz 1993, p. 9).

The idea that "experiences are lived and not transplanted" is a central tenet of Freire's philosophy (Gadotti 1994, p. 46). Concientization is the key process by which students develop a critical awareness of the world based on the concrete experience of their everyday lives. The development of critical awareness through concientization alters power relations between students and teachers, the colonized and the colonizer, thereby transforming objects of knowledge into historical subjects (Freire 1997). Freire proposed that a dialogical theory of action based on communication and cooperation was necessary not only for understanding the mediating role of historical, colonial, and class relations (concientization), but also for the active

work of changing them. Dialogic action challenges mediating social realities by posing them as problems that can be analyzed critically by those who have direct experience of them. Dialogue becomes a form of collective praxis directly concerned with unveiling inequitable conditions obscured by the ruling classes.

The success of Freire's method for teaching literacy to Brazil's impoverished citizens, coupled with his efforts to affect social and political change among the landless poor, led to his imprisonment after a reactionary military coup in 1964. He spent a total of seventy days in jail. After his imprisonment in Brazil, Freire was exiled to Chile, where he remained for five years before taking up posts at Harvard University and in Switzerland. He did not return to Brazil until 1980. Freire's most famous book is *Pedagogy of the Oppressed*, originally published in 1970. Other key works include *Cultural Action for Freedom* (1972), *Education: The Practice of Freedom* (1976), and *Pedagogy of the Heart* (1997). Thirty years on from his most influential work, the commitment to education as a pathway to liberation that Freire helped inspire remains a vibrant part of the social justice campaigns of grassroots activists, social policymakers, educators, and scholars (see McLaren 2000).

SEE ALSO *Education, USA; Ideology; Liberation; Liberation Movements; Pedagogy; Schooling; Tracking in Schools*

BIBLIOGRAPHY

PRIMARY WORKS

Freire, Paulo. 1970. *Cultural Action for Freedom*. Cambridge, MA: Harvard Educational Review.

Freire, Paulo. 1974. *Education: The Practice of Freedom*. London: Writers and Readers Publishing Co-operative.

Freire, Paulo. 1997. *Pedagogy of the Heart*. Trans. Donaldo Macedo and Alexandre Oliveira. New York: Continuum.

Freire, Paulo. 1997. *Pedagogy of the Oppressed*. Rev. ed. Trans. Myra Bergman Ramos. New York: Continuum. (Orig. pub. 1970).

SECONDARY WORKS

Aronowitz, Stanley. 1993. Paulo Freire's Radical Democratic Humanism. In *Paulo Freire: A Critical Encounter*, eds. Peter McLaren and Peter Leonard, 8–24. London: Routledge.

Gadotti, Moacir. 1994. *Reading Paulo Freire: His Life and Work*. Trans. John Milton. Albany: State University of New York Press.

McLaren, Peter. 2000. *Che Guevara, Paulo Freire, and the Pedagogy of Revolution*. Lanham, MD: Rowman and Littlefield.

Donna Houston

FRELIMO

SEE *Machel, Samora.*

FRENCH REVOLUTION

The French Revolution invented modern *revolution*—the idea that humans can transform the world according to a plan—and so has a central place in the study of the social sciences. It ushered in modernity by destroying the foundations of the "Old Regime"—absolutist politics, legal inequality, a "feudal" economy (characterized by guilds, manorialism, and even serfdom), an alliance of church and state, and created a vision for a new moral universe: that sovereignty resides in nations; that a constitution and the rule of law govern politics; that people are equal and enjoy inalienable rights; and that church and state should be separate. That vision is enshrined in the Declaration of the Rights of Man and Citizen of 1789, whose proclamation of "natural, imprescriptible, and inalienable" rights served as the model for the 1948 United Nations Universal Declaration of Human Rights.

Eighteenth-century France experienced overlapping tensions that erupted in revolution in 1789. First, the Enlightenment contributed to an environment in which revolution was possible by its insistence on reforming institutions to comply with standards of reason and utility. Furthermore, it coincided with the rise of public opinion, which undermined the absolutist notion that political decisions required no consultation or tolerated no opposition. Second, the French state faced bankruptcy because of a regressive and inefficient tax system as well as participation in the Seven Years War (1756–1763) and the War of American Independence (1775–1783). Third, France witnessed endemic political strife in the eighteenth century. Technically absolutist monarchs who ruled by divine right and who exercised sovereignty without the interference of representative institutions, French kings in reality met with opposition to their policies from the noble magistrates of the highest law courts (Parlements), who resisted fiscal reforms in the name of protecting traditional rights from arbitrary authority. Finally, while class conflict did not cause revolution, there existed stress zones in French society, as a growing population threatened many people with destitution and as talented commoners chafed at their exclusion from high offices in the church, state, and military. Economic problems intensified after bad weather doubled the price of bread in 1789.

These tensions reached a crisis point in the "prerevolution" from 1787 to 1789. To deal with impending fiscal insolvency, the government convened an Assembly of Notables in 1787 to propose a new tax levied on all land and the convocation of advisory provincial assemblies.

Repeated resistance to reform by the notables and Parlements forced Louis XVI (ruled 1774–1792) to convene the Estates-General, a representative body composed of clergy, nobles, and the Third Estate that had not met since 1614. The calling of the Estates-General in 1789 led to a debate over the leadership of reform, and France's struggle against royal despotism soon became a struggle against noble and clerical privilege. In this context, Emmanuel Sieyès's pamphlet "What Is the Third Estate?" galvanized patriot opinion by responding "Everything!" and by portraying the privileged groups as unproductive parasites on the body politic.

During a stalemate over whether the estates should vote by order or head, the Third Estate claimed on June 17 that it formed a National Assembly with the authority to write a constitution. This step transferred sovereignty from the king to the nation and constituted a legal revolution. The legal revolution was protected by a popular revolution on July 14 when the people of Paris stormed the Bastille fortress in search of weapons. Popular participation continued to radicalize the revolution. In the countryside, a peasant insurgency against manorial dues and church tithes prompted the National Assembly to decree the "abolition of feudalism" on August 4.

The revolution had three phases. The liberal phase found France under a constitutional monarchy during the National Assembly (1789–1791) and Legislative Assembly (1791–1792). After the destruction of absolutism and feudalism, legislation in this period guaranteed individual liberty, promoted secularism, and favored educated property owners. The aforementioned Declaration of Rights proclaimed freedom of thought, worship, and assembly as well as freedom from arbitrary arrest; it enshrined the principles of careers open to talent and equality before the law, and it hailed property as a sacred right (similarly, the National Assembly limited the vote to men with property). Other laws, enacted in conformity with reason, contributed to the "new regime." They offered full rights to Protestants and Jews, thereby divorcing religion from citizenship; they abolished guilds and internal tolls and opened trades to all people, thereby creating the conditions for economic individualism; they rationalized France's administration, creating departments in the place of provinces and giving them uniform and reformed institutions. Significantly, the National Assembly restructured the French Catholic Church, expropriating church lands, abolishing most monastic orders, and redrawing diocesan boundaries.

The revolution did not end despite the promulgation of the constitution of 1791. King Louis XVI had never reconciled himself to the revolution and as a devout Catholic was distressed after the pope condemned the restructuring of the church (known as the Civil

Constitution of the Clergy). Ultimately, the king attempted to flee France on June 20, 1791, but was stopped at Varennes. Radicalism constituted another problem for the assembly, for Parisian artisans and shopkeepers (called *sans-culottes*) resented their formal exclusion from politics in the Constitution and demanded legislation to deal with France's economic crisis and the revolution's enemies, particularly nobles and priests. After Varennes, radicals called increasingly for a republic. In addition, revolutionaries' fears of foreign nations and counterrevolutionary émigrés led to a declaration of war against Austria in April 1792. France's crusade against despotism began badly, and Louis XVI's veto of wartime measures appeared treasonous. On August 10, 1792, a revolutionary crowd attacked the royal palace. This "second revolution" overthrew the monarchy and resulted in the convocation of a democratically elected National Convention, which declared France a republic on September 22, 1792, and subsequently tried and executed the king.

The revolution's second, radical phase lasted from August 10, 1792, until the fall of Maximilien Robespierre (1758–1794) on July 27, 1794. The Convention's new declaration of rights and constitution in 1793 captured the regime's egalitarian social and political ideals and distinguished it from the liberal phase by proclaiming universal manhood suffrage, the right to education and subsistence, and the "common good" as the goal of society. The constitution, however, was never implemented amid the emergency situation resulting from civil war in the west (the Vendée), widespread revolts against the Convention, economic chaos, and foreign war against Austrian, Prussia, Britain, Holland, and Spain. Faced with imminent collapse in the summer of 1793, by spring 1794 the government had "saved" the revolution and organized military victories on all fronts.

The stunning change of events stemmed from the revolutionaries' three-pronged strategy under the leadership of Robespierre and the Committee of Public Safety. First, they established a planned economy, including price controls and nationalized workshops, for a total war effort. The planned economy largely provided bread for the poor and matériel for the army. Second, the government forced unity and limited political opposition through a Reign of Terror. Under the Terror, the Revolutionary Tribunal tried "enemies of the nation," some 40,000 of whom were executed—often by guillotine—or died in jail; another 300,000 people languished in prison under a vague "law of suspects." The unleashing of terrorism to silence political opponents imposed order at the cost of freedom. It raised complex moral issues about means and ends and has led to vigorous historical debate: Was the Terror an understandable response to the emergency, one that saved the revolution from a return of the Old Regime, or was it

a harbinger of totalitarianism that sacrificed individual life and liberty to an all-powerful state and the abstract goal of regenerating humankind? Finally, the revolutionary government harnessed the explosive force of nationalism. Unified by common institutions and a share of sovereign power, desirous of protecting the gains of revolution, and guided by a national mission to spread the gospel of freedom, patriotic French treated the revolutionary wars as a secular crusade. The combination of a planned economy, the Reign of Terror, and revolutionary nationalism allowed for a full-scale mobilization of resources that drove foreign armies from French soil at the Battle of Fleurus on June 26, 1794.

The revolution's third phase, the Thermidorian and Directory periods, commenced with the overthrow of Robespierre and the dismantling of the Terror on 9 Thermidor (July 27, 1794) and lasted until the coup d'état on November 9, 1799, that brought Napoléon Bonaparte (1769–1821) to power. A new constitution in 1795 rendered France a liberal republic under a five-man executive called the Directory. The reappearance of property qualifications for political office sought to guarantee the supremacy of the middle classes in politics and to avoid the anarchy that stemmed from popular participation. The seesaw politics of the Directory, which steered a middle course between left-wing radicalism and right-wing royalism, witnessed the annulment of electoral victories by royalists in 1797 and by radicals (Jacobins) in 1798 and undermined faith in the new constitution. Similarly, the regime won enemies with its attacks on Catholic worship while failing to rally educated and propertied elites in support of its policies. Initially, continued military victories by French armies (including those by Napoléon in Italy) buttressed the regime. But the reversal of military fortunes in 1799 and ten years of revolutionary upheaval prompted plotters to revise the constitution in a more authoritarian direction. In Napoléon, the plotters found their man as well as nearly continual warfare until 1815. "Citizens," he announced, "the Revolution is established on the principles with which it began. It is over."

The French Revolution is the quintessential revolution in modern history, its radicalism resting on a rejection of the French past and a vision of a new order based on universal rights and legal equality. The slogan "Liberty, Equality, Fraternity, or Death" embodies revolutionaries' vision for a new world and their commitment to die for the cause. Both aspects of the slogan influenced subsequent struggles for freedom throughout the world, but one might look at the French slave colony of Saint-Domingue for an example. On Saint-Domingue the outbreak of revolution received acclaim by the lower classes among the 30,000 whites, while planters opposed talk of liberty and equality and the destruction of privileges. Revolutionary ideals also quickly spread among the island's 30,000 free people of color (*affranchis*), who, despite owning property and indeed slaves, suffered racial discrimination. Free people of color demanded full civil and political rights after 1789, but the denial of these rights resulted in a rebellion of the *affranchis* that was brutally repressed. In 1791 Saint-Domingue's 450,000 slaves commenced the most successful slave revolt in history. Tensions among whites, mixed-race people, and slaves were exacerbated by British and Spanish actions to weaken their French rival, creating chaos on the island. The Convention's commitment to equality and desire to win the allegiance of rebels resulted in the abolition of slavery in 1794. A later attempt by Napoléon to reinstate bondage on Saint-Domingue failed despite the capture of the ex-slaves' skilled leader, Toussaint Louverture (c. 1743–1803), and the slave uprising culminated in the creation of an independent Haiti in 1804. Revolutionary principles of liberty and equality had led to national liberation and racial equality.

One also sees the revolution's significance in the fact that nineteenth-century ideologies traced their origins to the event. Conservatism rejected the radical change and emphasis on reason of the revolution, while liberalism reveled in the ideals of individual liberty and legal (but not social) equality of 1789. Nationalists treated the concept of national sovereignty as a call to awaken from their slumber in divided states or multiethnic empires. Democratic republicans celebrated the radical phase, finding in its democratic politics and concern for the poor a statement of egalitarianism and incipient social democracy. Socialists perceived in the *sans culotte* phenomenon the rumblings of a working-class movement, while communists considered the Russian Revolution of 1917 the fulfillment of the aborted proletarian revolution of 1792–1794.

For much of the twentieth century Marxist historians understood the revolution as the triumph of a capitalist bourgeoisie and considered it a bloc (in other words, the radical phase of 1792–1794 was necessary to protect the gains of 1789–1791). Revisionists destroyed this view, treating the revolution as the triumph of a new political culture instead of a new social class and whose main outcome was the realization of the absolutist dream of a strong centralized state rather than a complete break with the past. The revisionists' denial of social class as an important factor in the revolution opened the field to cultural studies and a focus on marginalized groups such as women and slaves. But the revisionist interpretation has failed to achieve consensus, and scholars continue to dispute the revolution's legacy. According to the neo-democratic view, the declaration of universal human rights, abolition of slavery, and pattern of modern democratic politics give the revolution a foundational place in the struggle for a better world. For revisionists, the violence of

the Terror, the destruction of revolutionary wars, the silencing of dissidents and Catholic worshipers, and the formation of a powerful centralized state render the revolution a source of twentieth-century political horrors ranging from nationalist wars to totalitarian regimes.

Students frequently puzzle over the significance of the revolution when, after all, the Bourbons were restored to the French throne after Napoléon's final exile in 1815. But the restoration never undid the major gains of the revolution, which included the destruction of absolutism, manorialism, legal inequality, and clerical privilege, as well as commitments to representative government, a constitution, and careers open to talent. Once the revolutionary genie announced the principles of national sovereignty, natural rights, freedom, and equality, history has shown that it could not be put back in the bottle.

SEE ALSO *Constitutionalism; Constitutions; Democracy; Jacobinism; Monarchy; Napoléon Bonaparte; Revolution*

BIBLIOGRAPHY

Bell, David. 2007. *The First Total War: Napoleon's Europe and the Birth of Warfare as We Know It.* New York: Houghton Mifflin.

Censer, Jack, and Lynn Hunt. 2001. *Liberty, Equality, Fraternity: Exploring the French Revolution.* University Park: Pennsylvania State University Press.

Doyle, William. 2002. *Oxford History of the French Revolution,* 2nd ed. Oxford, U.K.: Oxford University Press.

Dubois, Laurent. 2004. *Avengers of the New World: The Story of the Haitian Revolution.* Cambridge, MA: Harvard University Press.

Furet, François, and Mona Ozouf, eds. 1989. *A Critical Dictionary of the French Revolution.* Trans. Arthur Goldhammer. Cambridge, MA: Harvard University Press.

Palmer, R. R. 1969. *Twelve Who Ruled: The Year of the Terror in the French Revolution.* Princeton, NJ: Princeton University Press.

Tackett, Timothy. 1996. *Becoming a Revolutionary: The Deputies of the French National Assembly and the Emergence of a Revolutionary Culture (1789–1790).* Princeton, NJ: Princeton University Press.

Tocqueville, Alexis de. 1856. *The Old Regime and the French Revolution.* Trans. Stuart Gilbert. New York: Anchor, 1955.

Woloch, Isser. 1994. *The New Regime: Transformations of the French Civic Order, 1789–1820s.* New York: Norton.

Anthony Crubaugh

FREQUENCY DISTRIBUTIONS

Every day, people are confronted with large amounts of information. Occasionally, the amount of data may be so large that they cannot interpret it in a meaningful way. When this occurs, people often need to organize and summarize the data in such a way that it allows them to uncover patterns or relationships or to use it as tools for analysis and interpretation.

One way to organize large amounts of data is through frequency distributions. A frequency distribution is a summary of data that shows the frequency or number of times a particular observation occurs. To construct a frequency distribution, it is necessary to arrange the data into categories that "represent value ranges of the variables in question" (Fleming 2000, p. 15).

For example, imagine that you are responsible for creating a range of activities for a group of fifty people, and you want to organize the activities according to age. The following is a list of the ages of the individuals in the group:

4	15	20	18	4
22	36	7	24	11
27	33	13	7	17
18	30	25	9	23
11	16	14	5	31
31	36	22	15	24
13	11	22	9	11
28	21	8	14	18
34	13	17	16	7
23	29	5	16	20

The first step in constructing a frequency distribution is to arrange the data from the smallest to the largest value to determine, as in this case, the age range. Next, the different values need to be listed with the number of times a particular age appears—its frequency.

Arranging the data in this way provides people with a more organized way to understand any trends or patterns in the data. However, even after organizing the data based on the frequency distribution, it can still be very overwhelming. By using what researchers refer to as "interval scores" or "class intervals," frequency distributions become important tools to manage raw data (Hinkley 1982, p. 26). Interval scores or class intervals are intervals that include a range of values. There are several steps to establish class intervals. First, it is necessary to determine the number of non-overlapping classes. Classes need to be mutually exclusive, meaning that a value cannot belong to two different classes at the same time. According to convention, there should be between 5 and 15 classes.

The next step is to decide the width of each class. The size i will be the same for all classes, and it is calculated by subtracting the lowest score (4) from the highest score (36) and dividing it by the number of class intervals (e.g., 8). For the previous example, the approximate class width is 5. The larger the width of each class, the smaller the number of classes there will be.

List of values and their frequencies

Value	Frequency
4	1
5	2
7	3
8	1
9	2
11	4
13	3
14	2
15	2
16	3
17	2
18	3
20	2
21	2
22	3
23	2
24	2
25	1
27	1
28	1
29	1
30	1
31	2
33	1
34	1
36	2

Table 1.

Frequency distributions and cumulative frequencies

Class Interval	*f*	*Cumulative f*
1–5	3	3
6–10	6	9
11–15	11	20
16–20	10	30
21–25	9	39
26–30	4	43
31–35	4	47
36–40	2	49

Table 2. Frequency Distributions and Cumulative Frequencies

In addition, one needs to determine the limits of the frequency. The concept of exact limits of a score can be extended to frequency distributions by distinguishing between the exact limits of a given class interval and its score limits. The limits are determined so that each observation belongs to only one class. According to researcher Wiersma Hinkley, "the lower class limit identifies the smallest possible data value assigned to the class. The upper class limit identifies the largest possible data value assigned to the class. The exact limits are 0.5 units below and 0.5 units above the score limits of the class interval"

(1982, p. 27). Consider the age interval 11–15 in Table 2. The interval 11–15 represents the score limits, whereas the interval 10.5–15.5 represents the exact limits. The midpoint will always be the same regardless of what type of limits are used. The midpoint of the interval is defined as "the point on the scale of measurement that is halfway through the interval" (p. 28). There will be scenarios in which some class intervals are empty. When this occurs, researchers suggest that these intervals be eliminated by combining them.

In Table 2, a frequency distribution *f* table is presented as well as the cumulative frequencies *cumulative f*. The cumulative frequency is "the total number of scores in the class interval and all intervals below it" (Abrami 2001, p. 63).

In most cases, frequency distributions allow an individual to understand raw data in a more meaningful way. However, it is sometimes necessary to have a visual display of the data beyond numbers to recognize the patterns that otherwise would be difficult to identify. Graphs, when clearly presented, are two-dimensional representations of data that can help in this endeavor. Graphs typically consist of vertical and horizontal dimensions known as axes. By tradition, the horizontal axis is called the abscissa, or the x-axis, and represents the independent variable. The vertical axis is called ordinate, or y-axis, and represents the dependent variable. Histograms, bar graphs, and frequency polygons are graphs that are used to visually display frequency distributions.

HISTOGRAMS

Histograms are one of the most useful graphical representations of statistical data. Histograms display the frequency of an individual score or scores in class intervals by the length of its bars. The majority of histograms represent a single variable. The variable of interest is placed on the x-axis and the frequency distribution, relative frequency, or percent frequency distribution on the y-axis In histograms, the bars are shown touching one another representing their continuous nature. This means that the variables are interval- (e.g., height or weight) or ratio-scaled. Also, the height of each bar represents its frequency because the class intervals are equal (see Figure 1).

BAR CHARTS

Besides histograms, bar charts are used to visually display frequency distributions. However, contrary to histograms, the variable under study has a nominal and ordinal value, which is represented by the spaces between

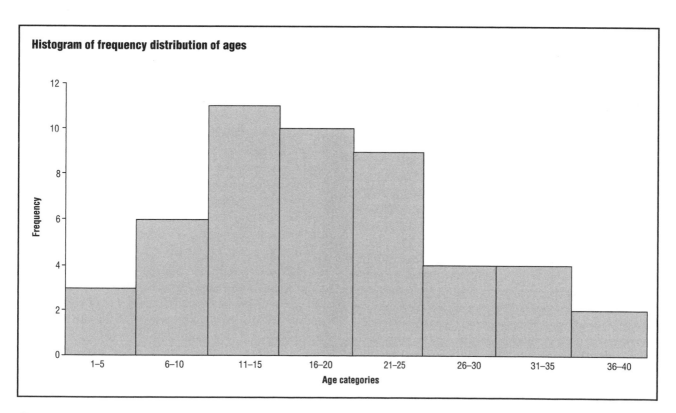

Figure 1.

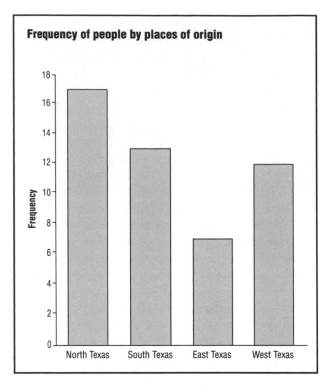

Frequency of people by places of origin

Figure 2.

each bar. In Figure 2, the specific variables (categories and frequencies) that are used for the classes on each axis are presented.

FREQUENCY POLYGON

Another way to display information is through frequency polygons, also known as frequency curves or line graphs. In this type of graph, the scores of the class interval are displayed by using the midpoint of each class interval. Once these points have been marked, they are connected with straight lines. Frequency polygons are useful when trying to compare two different frequencies in one graph or to highlight trends over time.

SEE ALSO *Methods, Quantitative*

BIBLIOGRAPHY

Abrami, Philip C., Paul Cholmsky, and Robert Gordon. 2001. *Statistical Analysis for the Social Sciences an Interactive Approach.* Boston: Allyn and Bacon.

Anderson, Sweeney William. 2000. Descriptive Statistics I: Tabular and Graphical Methods. In *Essentials of Statistics for Business and Economics.* Cincinnati, OH: South-Western College.

Christensen, Larry, and Charles M. Stoup. 1986. Frequency Distribution and Percentiles. Introduction to *Statistics for the*

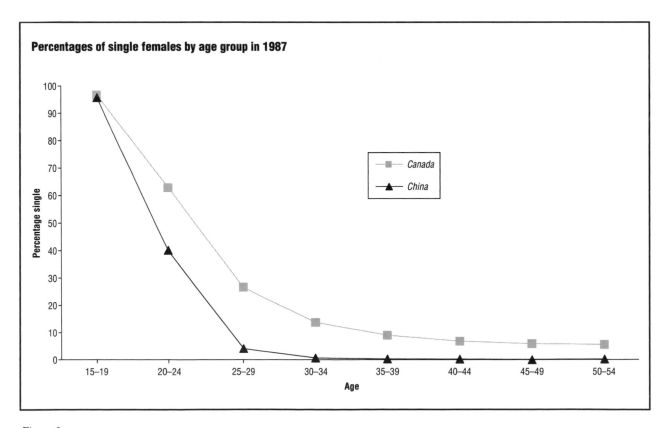

Percentages of single females by age group in 1987

Figure 3.

Social and Behavioral Sciences. Monterey, CA: Brooks/Cole Pub. Co.

Fleming, Michael C., and Joseph G. Nellis. 2000. Describing Data Tables, Charts, and Graphs. In *Principles of Applied Statistics,* 2nd ed., 13–50. New York: Thomson Learning.

Hays, William L. 1981. Frequency and Probability Distributions. In *Statistics,* 3rd ed. New York: Holt, Rinehart and Winston.

Hinkley, Wiersma Jurs. 1982. Frequency Statistics. In *Basic Behavioral Statistics.* Boston: Houghton Mifflin.

Wright, Daniel. 2002. Graphing Variables. In *First Steps in Statistics.* Thousand Oaks, CA: SAGE.

María Isabel Ayala

FREUDIAN SLIP

SEE *Psychoanalytic Theory.*

FREUD, SIGMUND
1856–1939

The founder of the intellectual discipline and psychotherapeutic method known as psychoanalysis, Sigmund Freud aimed to "throw light upon the unusual, abnormal, or pathological manifestations of the mind" by tracing them to the psychological forces that produced them (1936, p. 447). The odd manifestations he sought to illuminate ranged from the blatantly strange, such as neurotic symptoms, to deviations from strict rationality found in all people, such as those that occur in dreaming, mental lapses of waking life, such as slips of the tongue, or other special experiences, such as the feeling of "uncanniness." His inquiries also included ordinary experiences that defied straightforward explanation, such as the capacity of jokes to evoke laughter, and cultural trends that Freud believed exhibited properties of mental life he had identified in individual psychology, such as humans' susceptibility to religion.

The psychological forces to which Freud traced these phenomena led inevitably, in his view, to childhood. Childhood has the influence it does, Freud maintained, because it affords a unique mode of experience that, on account of its distinctness from later developments of the mind, both produces lasting impressions on people and renders these impressions inaccessible to later consciousness. The most dramatic and best-known consequence of this dynamic is the operation after infancy of unconscious mentation, or ideas and impulses of which people remain unaware that nonetheless influence their behavior. Since the publication in 1900 of *The Interpretation of Dreams,*

Freud's first major treatise on psychoanalysis, Freud's ideas have indelibly altered both popular thought and a wide array of professional disciplines.

THE BIRTH OF PSYCHOANALYSIS

Freud was born in Frieberg, Moravia (now the Czech Republic) on May 6, 1856, and his family moved to Vienna three years later. During the 1890s, as a young doctor collaborating with Viennese physician Josef Breuer, he began treating nervous disorders through the use of a "talking cure," as he and Breuer called it. The method initially consisted of patients under hypnosis recalling memories associated with their symptoms. This recall, accompanied by the affect connected with the memories, resulted in the elimination of symptoms. An early patient treated in this way, one Anna O., for example, who presented with paralyses and an inability to drink that lacked any organic base, regained her ability to drink when she recalled with disgust a scene from her childhood in which she had discovered her governess's dog drinking from a (human) cup.

On the basis of observations of this kind—reported with Breuer in *Studies on Hysteria* (1895)—Freud came to believe people are moved in part by mental forces unknown to them. The *unconscious,* as it came to be known, is composed mostly of thoughts and impressions people pushed from consciousness (or "repressed") when they were very young. The thoughts and impressions linger in the mind and, unable to discharge, remain on alert for opportunities for expression. When they reach expression, they usually appear in disguise, so as not to elicit fresh repressions. The resulting manifestations include psychopathological symptoms, dreams, lapses of (conscious) speech or action (which Freud called "parapraxes") such as slips of the tongue, and aspects of character, as well as a variety of ordinary individual and cultural experiences.

BASIC ASSUMPTIONS

Freud's is a general psychological theory that attempts to explain why people think, feel, see, and do as they do. A systematic theory, it contains an integrated body of concepts and propositions from which other concepts and propositions follow. It builds from a small group of first principles, described by Freud as essential constituents of human thought and action that admit of no further reduction and yet account for all conceivable instances of human behavior. Based upon observation and reflection over the course of the forty-plus years spanned by his psychoanalytic writings, Freud eventually changed his ideas about these principles.

Initially, Freud believed all human behavior conforms to what he called the pleasure (or pleasure-unpleasure) principle. According to the pleasure principle, people always strive to avoid pain and, where possible, attain pleasure. Even behavior that appears inconsistent with this principle, such as the nightmare, must in some way conform to it. Freud theorized in *The Interpretation of Dreams* (1900), for example, that nightmares serve to divert the dreamer from dangerous wishes whose fulfillment would produce frightening consequences. The fearsome content of the nightmare both embodies the dreamer's perception of danger—such that, on occasion, the dreamer might awaken and thereby terminate the dream—and serves to disguise the wish.

Freud originally conceived the state of pleasure as a reduction in excitation, or tension, on the model of the reflex. Our reflexes, such as the eye-blink or knee-jerk reflex, function to rid the body of stimuli. Thus, at bottom, according to this initial conception, the function of the nervous system is to keep the level of stimulation in the body as low as possible, and pleasure is the consequence of the reduction. As happened with the governing principle itself, Freud changed his view of the nature of pleasure over the course of his writings.

Freud believed that early in their development, in order to survive, humans would have to have formed a reality principle subordinate to the pleasure principle. Although the hallucinated satisfaction of one's needs, which would constitute the shortest path to their fulfillment, might produce pleasure in the short term, for example, it would lead to ultimate disappointment. Thus, Freud says in his "Formulations Regarding Two Principles in Mental Functioning" (1911), the mind had to "decide" to form a conception of circumstances in the real outer world, so as to be able to alter them and bring about real satisfaction.

Whereas the pleasure principle operates reflexively from birth, the reality principle develops over time in the individual, according to Freud, and likewise developed in the evolution of the species. The reality principle, in turn, would have prompted further developments of the mind, beyond reflexive, or direct wish-fulfilling, functioning. Attention would have given individuals the ability to search their environment for the results of their actions; memory would have given them a means of notating and storing the results; thought would have arisen as a kind of experimental action, allowing individuals to test the (real) consequences of their behavior.

Within the compass of the pleasure/reality principles, Freud distinguished instinct as the driving force of all action. Instinct, as he details in "Instincts and Their Vicissitudes" (1915), is a stimulus to the mind originating within the body that exerts a constant pressure, or "impetus" toward relief. Because instincts originate within the person and operate at a constant force, rather than originating externally and acting in a single impact, simple reflexive action, such as the withdrawal of the impacted portion of the body, has no effect against the impact. One needs instead to satisfy the instinct. When one's stomach grinds with hunger, for example, one cannot eliminate the pain by withdrawing one's stomach from any impinging force. One must eat or be fed. Because instincts require machinations more complicated than reflexive action to be discharged, Freud viewed them as important to the development of the nervous system beyond the primitive reflex.

Freud originally distinguished two classes of instincts, which he believed admit of no further reduction: the sexual instincts and the ego, or self-preservative, instincts. He defined *sexual* broadly, so that it includes, with respect to its physical quality, excitation to any portion of the body, including the skin, for example, as well as the oral, anal, and genital areas.

Psychologically, the sexual instincts subsume the entire field of erotic relations, including those relations "inhibited" in aim, such as friendships and parent-child relations, which entail positive and even excitatory feelings, but not, in the usual course of conscious life, an aim of genital satisfaction. In their most developed manifestation, the sexual instincts serve reproduction. The ego instincts, meanwhile, serve only the individual and have the individual's safety as their object. In claiming that all human behavior emanates from one or the other of these two classes of instincts, Freud meant that all human impulses and actions remain compatible with one or both fields, not that all human impulses and actions can be reduced to a sex or survival drive. One's labors on a mathematics problem reduce to a sex or survival drive no more than a sheet of paper reduces to the tree from which the paper was milled. Rather, according to Freud, all of our aspirations and behavior must be traceable in some way to the reflexive bundle from which we arose. The reflexive bundle, in turn, seeks, at bottom, to eliminate the tensions created by its needs, and thus to gain pleasure.

Approximately twenty years after he articulated the pleasure principle, Freud identified an apparent exception to the principle and suggested that a still more basic force operates in the mind. In *Beyond the Pleasure Principle* (1920) he argued that, in contrast with numerous other negative experiences that only appear to contradict the pleasure principle, the traumatic, and more specifically war, neuroses genuinely do so. These neuroses manifest in, among other symptoms, recurrent dreams in which dreamers return to the scene of previous near-death experiences and then awake in a terrible fright. For instance, soldiers returning from war relive attacks in the trenches, and survivors of train wrecks return to the wreck. Each then awakens in terror that no amount of repetition of the dream lessens.

Although Freud could detect no long- or short-term gain in the pattern, he conceded it could embody an attempt at a purpose. Extrapolating from his observation that traumatic neuroses tend to afflict those victims of trauma who did not incur a major injury, Freud surmised that, whereas direct physical insult tends to divert masses of energy to the site of the insult, victims who have escaped injury are left with rampant masses of energy released by the shock of the event. Wholly breached, the psychical system attempts to master the onslaught in retrospect, by generating anxiety that, had it been present during the traumatic event, would have reduced the shock of the event. But after the fact, the attempt serves no purpose. The system neither heals nor learns.

Freud extrapolated from these observations to the existence of a tendency more primordial than the pleasure principle and inherent in all organic life: the compulsion to repeat. The tendency can be witnessed, he believed, in behavior as primitive as the thumb sucking of human babies or the return of schools of fish to the site of previous spawning. In the psyche compromised by the war neuroses, the tendency manifests in a mechanical and almost diabolical repetition of a behavior, in total disregard of its impact upon the person.

From his extrapolation to the repetition compulsion, Freud made the admittedly speculative and far-fetched leap to the idea that all living things seek to return not only to previous states, but ultimately to their original state. Given that all living matter began as inorganic substance, all living things seek to return to an inorganic state; they seek to die.

Freud thus arrived at a new category of instinct, the death instinct, or "Thanatos," which he conceived as functioning in opposition to the life instincts, or "Eros." After equivocating briefly on the point, Freud subsumed under the life instincts the two classes of instinct he had originally delineated, the sexual and ego (self-preservative) instincts. Whereas the life instincts, especially as represented by the sexual instincts, seek to unify living matter and create more of it, the death instinct aims to dissolve it.

As Freud originally conceived it, the death instinct denotes the tendency of every living thing to drift toward a state of minimal, and ideally no, excitation. The death instinct of this formulation thus verges on the pleasure principle, according to which pleasure arises with a reduction in stimulation. Freud soon modified his view of the nature of pleasure, however, in a way that lessened this overlap. Although he continued to believe the nervous system functions, at bottom, to rid the organism of tension, and pleasure arises by this means, he acknowledged people's potential to derive pleasure from an increase in stimulation, as occurs in sexual foreplay, for example. Thenceforth, he distinguished between the Nirvāna prin-

ciple, which expresses organisms' tendency toward quiescence (and hence the death instinct), and the pleasure principle, which expresses the drive toward pleasure in all its forms, including excitatory ones, and which Freud attributed to the influence of the life instincts.

In the course of Freud's later works, the death instinct assumes an increasingly active aspect and becomes almost synonymous with aggression. As early as his discussion in *The Ego and the Id*, published three years after *Beyond the Pleasure Principle*, Freud reasoned that individual organisms live long enough to combine with one another, rather than die off, because the death instinct must be neutralized in some way by the life instincts. It is diverted outward over the musculature, he proposed, in the form of aggression, which is eventually directed against others. However, in the wanton destruction he observed in two world wars, Freud perceived an aggressiveness totally divorced from erotic aims, and hence a sign of the ascendance of something close to a culture of pure death instinct. He concluded the 1931 edition of *Civilization and Its Discontents* with the question of whether Eros would rise again and prevail over humanity.

CONSEQUENCES OF THE ASSUMPTIONS

Many of the remaining portions of Freud's theory follow from the foregoing primitives of mental life and particularly from the pleasure and reality principles, which Freud continued to believe dominate mental life even after he developed the scheme that incorporates the death instinct.

Meaning and Determinism One such result is the idea that all behavior, including the most apparently nonsensical, has a reason, or, as Freud says in his *Introductory Lectures on Psychoanalysis* (1917) with respect to psychopathological symptoms in particular, symptoms have a sense. Anna O.'s refusal to drink resulted from her (unconscious) disgust at her governess's dog, according to Breuer and Freud. Given that people who feel revolted by something normally find it difficult to eat or drink, Anna O.'s behavior followed coherently from its source. Unlike healthy people who refuse food or drink because they feel revolted, however, Anna O. was unaware of both her disgust and its source. Therein lay her pathology. In conceiving dreams as wish fulfillments and parapraxes as products of concealed motives, Freud again followed the assumption that all behavior has a source and a sense. He believed it possible, moreover, for unconsciously motivated behavior, such as dreams, to have not just one source or one meaning, but to be "overdetermined," having multiple sources and meanings. Thus, for instance, the leering monster in a nightmare might embody both a child's anger at a parent and the child's fear of recriminations from the parent.

Freud admitted that some apparently odd behavior arises without apparent motivation. However, he found the occurrence of such behavior improbable. Freud noted in *Five Lectures on Psychoanalysis* (1909) that although some aberrations, such as slips of the tongue, might occur when people operate under fatigue or other stresses, the mistakes cannot be caused by these limitations, because other similar mistakes occur when people are fully attentive (p. 29). Further, precisely because numerous associative pathways lie open and can cause a person accidentally to utter one word instead of another (in the case of slips of the tongue), one needs to explain why a given pathway is chosen on a given occasion.

Conscious and Unconscious The separation between conscious and unconscious mental processes arises, according to Freud, primarily through the operation of *repression*, a reflexive and hence infantile response driven by the pleasure principle, in which individuals withdraw consciousness from painful or frightening impulses in the manner in which one might withdraw one's hand from a hot stove. The pain can be caused either by the clash between impulse in itself and other motives the person may have, or by the individual's anticipation of the external consequences of acting upon the impulse. The repressed impulse, or idea, remains in unconscious memory, sustained by its struggle for expression and at the same time denied that end by the forces that originally led to its repression. In the final chapter of *Totem and Taboo* (1913), Freud postulates a second, smaller category of *inherited* unconscious ideas. This category includes the most primitive embodiments of the instincts and impulses that, based upon an analysis of modern emotion, he concluded must have been passed along by earlier generations. The latter impulses include guilt for the killing of the primal father and a portion of the hostility that led to the presumed deed.

Freud reserved the term *unconscious* for these two groups of ideas, repressed unconscious ideas created by individual experience and inherited unconscious ideas, both of which are unavailable to consciousness at the moment and inaccessible to consciousness in general (except with extraordinary effort of the sort embodied by psychoanalysis). As detailed in his 1915 essay "The Unconscious," Freud distinguished as "preconscious" a separate category of ideas not apprehended by consciousness that, like one's knowledge of one's street address, one can access easily if prompted. Consciousness, within this scheme, is but a characteristic that can attach to mental processes. Freud likened it to a sensory organ that, in this case, illuminates ideation in progress. He attributed to

language a primary role in allowing a mental process to become conscious.

Unconscious and conscious ideation exhibit different characteristics, Freud maintained, paralleling the divide between the pleasure principle, which dominates unconscious processes, and the reality principle, which operates only within conscious thought (for purposes of this discussion, preconscious thought is subsumed by conscious thought). Unconscious ideation observes primary process thought, wherein ideas are interconnected associatively one to the next, with no consideration for the whole. One idea may also replace another ("displacement") and several ideas may converge in a single embodiment ("condensation"). These methods produce dreams, symptoms, and other phenomena, such as jokes, to which Freud ascribed an unconscious contribution. Only conscious ideation incorporates secondary-process thought, which consists of the higher cognitive processes, such as judgment, reasoning, planned action, and the ordering of events in time.

It follows from the properties of the two types of thought that the unconscious admits of blatant contradiction. No feature of unconscious mentation can detect or feel troubled by incoherence. It also knows no denial. Thus, in one's unconscious, one can both love and despise one's mother, or both want freedom from one's parents and want to be constrained and even punished by them. In waking life, normally, one would have difficulty tolerating these ambivalences and would probably repress one pole of the conflict.

Id, Ego, and Superego Freud eventually decided that the division of mental qualities into conscious, preconscious, and unconscious did not entirely capture the dynamics of the mind. In particular, unconsciousness appears to attach to mental formations other than those produced by repression that, nonetheless, arise on the basis of experience. In addition to finding their repressed memories elusive, patients undergoing psychoanalysis resist discovering the memories. Other forces in their mind must act to keep the repressed material from consciousness, Freud inferred, and these forces, too, lie outside awareness. Freud labeled these opposing forces as "resistances."

He developed a new scheme, which he expounds in *The Ego and the Id* (1923), to capture this mental dynamic. He now designated as "id" the portion of the mind containing repressed and inherited unconscious impulses. He defined as "ego" people's efforts to avert danger, whether from internal (i.e., repressed) or external sources, and to maintain their bearings in the environment. The ego includes the resistances and thus has both a conscious and an unconscious portion. Freud designated a third entity, the "superego," which judges the ego. Although the superego resembles the ego in its judging role, it shares an unconscious and irrational element with the id, from which it derives.

According to Freud, the superego is the precipitate of the Oedipal complex. The Oedipal conflict, according to Freud, is a normal part of the development of every individual. All children desire more from their parents (or parent surrogates) early in life than the parents can give—at bottom, everyone wants total possession of them. Within this dynamic, children may form a preference for the parent of the opposite sex, although they yearn for both parents and experience the Oedipal conflict with respect to each. Thus, children harbor both love and hostility for each parent. Therefore, as Freud illustrates in *Totem and Taboo* (1913), ambivalence exists at the core of our emotional life. Eventually, children's desires are frustrated and, in the interest of survival, subjected to repression, with the conflicts embodied by them left unresolved.

The end of the Oedipal period, at around five years of age, prompts individuation from the parents, and consequently their loss. The loss, in turn, prompts children to internalize the parents, which preserves their relationship with them. The internalization is accompanied by an exaggeration of the parents' power, which results from children's earlier repression of their own hostile feelings toward the parents. Emanating now from the internalized parents, the hostile feelings are turned back upon the subject—the child—on whom they discharge more safely than they would have done if the child had unleashed the feelings against the real parents. In exchange, the now browbeaten ego suffers. The entire dynamic, according to Freud, explains much of both psychopathology and the psychology of healthy people.

The Concept of a Person Freud's view of the person is represented by his three schemes for describing the mind. From the perspective of the motivating forces of our action—the pleasure principle and its derivatives—people universally seek, on some level, to avoid pain. In the interest of long-term gain, they may modify their claim to comfort and pleasure in the short term, as Freud discusses in an exegesis on happiness in *Civilization and Its Discontents*. From the perspective of the division of the mind into conscious (including preconscious) and unconscious, people are ruled by forces both known and unknown to them, and they are thus capable of acts and thoughts both consistent and inconsistent with the traits and values they may (consciously) consider central to their identity. From the perspective of Freud's division of the mind into the dynamic entities of id, ego, and superego, both our behavior and our felt experience are colored by the deeply conflicting forces that confer our humanity upon us: our appetites and our drive for security and survival. In all three views, the person is a compilation of forces, defined by the interaction of dynamic parts. Freud did not distinguish more holistic entities such as the personality or the self.

The Concept of Illness The cause of (neurotic) illness, according to Freud, is unresolved and unconscious conflict, on account of which sufferers retreat into fantasy. Symptoms embody a fulfillment of the fantasies, distorted to escape recognition by the conscious mind. Healthy people struggle with the same conflicts as do neurotic people, and, like neurotic people, they form fantasies to improve upon a sometimes disappointing reality. However, whereas healthy people either find adaptive outlets for their fantasies or indulge them while otherwise going about their business, neurotics' repressed impulses overwhelm their capacity for normal function.

Beginning with his earliest cases, Freud maintained that neurosis is caused specifically by the conflict between sexual and ego drives. Patients' earliest sexual impulses lead to thoughts their self-protective inclinations regard as dangerous, and are thus subject to repression. Although Freud initially believed the forbidden thoughts traced back to actual experiences of seduction, he soon determined, as he noted in his 1909 "Rat Man" case history, that the impression or fantasy of such experiences can alone suffice to initiate pathogenic processes.

Therapy Psychoanalytic therapy presumes that, insofar as repressed complexes (conflicts) cause illness, the path to cure lies in the exposure of the repressed material to consciousness. Repressed complexes have the far-reaching effects they do because the cut-off ideas continue to strive for expression through an increasingly large web of associations. It follows, therefore, that one may recover the instigating ideas by undoing the web of associations. Thus, the "free association" of ideas forms the principal technique of therapy. Beginning with a symptom, dream, or passing thought, patients say whatever comes into their mind in connection with the symptom, and then whatever comes into their mind in connection with the new idea, and so on. Freud believed that all paths lead ultimately to the repressed complex or complexes, so that patients can start with any leading idea to begin to unravel the associative chain or chains.

As their associations veer progressively closer to the material under repression, patients find it increasingly difficult to pursue given lines of thought. Freud believed these experiences of "resistance" form an integral part of the therapeutic process. They provide a window on the forces that are keeping the repressed material hidden and, in becoming manifest, afford patients the means for defeating the forces and allowing the repressed ideas to reach consciousness, where they can be confronted. To defeat the resistances, patients need to express all associations that occur to them and combat the temptation to block them.

Because of the importance of uncovering and disarming the resistances to the achievement of a lasting cure, Freud abandoned the use of hypnosis in psychoanalysis. Although hypnosis might allow the freeing of repressed content in susceptible patients, in Freud's experience it led mostly to only short-term cures. Patients' resistances, still present, rose again and repressed the forbidden thoughts anew. Hypnosis carries the additional disadvantage that not everyone is susceptible to it, whereas the conscious talking cure via free association is open, in principle, to all.

Development The development of the mind, in Freud's conception, follows three broad pathways. The first, within sexual (or as Freud called it, libidinal) development, consists of a progression from *autoeroticism*, wherein individuals achieve satisfaction diversely from the stimulation of parts of their body, to *narcissism*, during which individuals, now having gained a unifying seat of experience in the form of the ego, take themselves as the love object, and finally to the phase of (external) *object love*. Having initially distinguished only autoeroticism and object love as phases in this development, Freud interpolated the phase of narcissism when he found himself otherwise unable to account for the so-called narcissistic disorders of adulthood, such as schizophrenia, in which the ego seems to lose its boundaries. Another development in sexuality encompasses changes in the focus of sexual sensitivity in people from the oral to the anal and, finally, to the genital areas, respectively.

The second trend in development progresses from impulsive toward reflective thought. It is embodied by the development of secondary-process thought, wherein impulses can be inhibited and action tested and planned, and by the gradual replacement of repression by judgment as a means of dispatching painful impressions. It is expressed by the reality principle.

A third trend proceeds from more transparent to more complexly derived, and thus more obscure, behavior. Whereas the dreams of small children often express the unfulfilled (conscious) wishes of the previous day, for example, adults' dreams contain bizarre and inscrutable ("manifest") imagery that must be painstakingly unpacked to uncover the instigating ("latent") dream thoughts. Whereas the motives of children's sense of humor are clear, adults, who may laugh from similar motives, do not know what they are laughing at. Trends of these kinds arise, Freud believed, from both the separation of conscious and unconscious thought, which makes repression possible, and from the natural "surmounting" (as Freud describes it in his 1919 essay "The Uncanny") of one developmental

stage by another. Regarding the latter process, when one stage succeeds another in development, both the mode of experience embodied by the earlier stage and the experiences accrued in it remain in the psyche. They continue to exert an influence there, though reshaped by the superimposition of later stages.

THE SCOPE OF FREUD'S WORK

After incorporating the three previously unlinked fields of dreams, neurotic symptoms, and parapraxes, Freud's theory came to encompass phenomena as diverse as art, creative writing, the appreciation of beauty, the comic, morality, religion, superstition, the fate of social movements such as communism, and people's disparagement of the transience of things. In these and other manifestations of human nature, Freud not only perceived the operation of unconscious thought, the contribution for which he is most widely known, but also speculated provocatively about the nature of phenomena that otherwise elude explanation. His commentary exposes the elusiveness.

Freud's account of the comic in *Jokes and Their Relation to the Unconscious* (1905), for instance, emphasizes the need for investigation to penetrate beyond the necessary and sufficient conditions of what makes something funny to the question of why laughing is what people do when an event meets these conditions. His brief remarks on beauty in *Civilization and Its Discontents* show the need for theory to reach beyond the delineation of the attributes of beautiful things to an account that explains the feeling that accompanies people's perception of beauty. In his extensive, though scattered, treatment of morality, he labors to account for the compulsiveness of morality and the feelings that accompany moral sensibility, such as moral righteousness and moral indignation, as well as the scope and nature of moral rules.

In his short essay "On Transience" (1916), Freud both awakens the reader to the possibility that one could appreciate things more, rather than less, on account of their transience (for instance, they could better appreciate the beauty of spring because it will disappear), and provides an explanation of the common tendency instead toward the disparagement of transience. With respect to communism, which he considers in a longer discussion of the problem of aggression in society in *Civilization and Its Discontents*, Freud, who reserved judgment on the economic claims of the system, suggested its psychological premises are untenable. He believed that when human aggression is deprived of one of its essential tools, namely material property, it will find other outlets. In all of these and in other areas, Freud opened lines of inquiry that remain interesting and novel. Because of its vast reach and systematic base, Freud's theory has profoundly influenced disciplines throughout the social sciences and humanities, as well as the arts. It has shaped the way human nature is viewed by scholar, practitioner, and layperson.

CRITICISM OF FREUD'S THEORY

Freud's theory has been challenged since its inception, initially for its stipulation of unconscious mentation altogether, and later for its claims regarding the nature and influence of unconscious thought. Many believe Freud overinterpreted behavior. Experimental psychologists such as J. Allan Hobson and Daniel Schacter, for instance, maintain that parapraxes and dreams, respectively, may arise from normal features of cognitive process and brain function, rather than from unconscious motives. Likewise, critics suggest neurotic symptoms may reflect relatively superficial adaptations to faulty wiring or chemical imbalance, rather than deep-seated conflict.

Adolf Grünbaum and other commentators have questioned Freud's characterization of psychoanalysis as a science on the grounds that the theory is not testable. For a theory to be testable, one needs to conceive limiting cases with respect to which the theory could be proved wrong, according to these authors. However, they continue, one cannot refute the claim that neurotic symptoms express repressed complexes or that dreams fulfill wishes (the dreams of traumatic neurosis, which Freud excepted, notwithstanding), because any given symptom might express a repressed complex and any given dream might fulfill a wish. One simply may not have uncovered the hidden material. It goes without saying that Freud's more speculative claims, such as his stipulation of a death instinct, are dismissed by critical and even supportive discourse altogether. Psychoanalysis, as a means of cure, has been variously assailed as ineffective, subject to suggestion by the analyst, and unnecessarily costly to patients. In its standard form it involves multiple sessions per week and a highly trained practitioner.

Theorists who followed Freud, including his own disciples, subsequently modified his theory and the practice of psychoanalysis. Some, such as Carl Jung, reconceived the nature of the unconscious, while others, such as Melanie Klein, replaced drives or instincts with interpersonal ("object") relations as the pivot of the psyche. Others, such as Alfred Adler, placed relatively greater emphasis than Freud did on the ego, while lessening the emphasis on the sexual drives. In Freud's wake, many varieties of talking therapy were created, some ultimately with little connection to the tenets of psychoanalysis, save the notion that people's ways of thinking about their lives, cultivated by their previous experience, may taint their happiness more than do the external events that befall them. Diverse therapies also share the belief that giving expression to one's concerns may both begin to lift the burden they impose and promote self-enlightenment.

Freud died on September 23, 1939, in England, where he lived for the last year of his life. The cause was mouth cancer, which had plagued him for many years. Since then, the controversies over the credibility of his theory and the promise of psychoanalytic treatment have continued. Regarding treatment, Freud established as an ideal the absence of suggestion, as Jonathan Lear notes. Conducted appropriately, psychoanalytic therapy has met with modest success. At the same time, no other type of therapy has proved universally effective. Regarding the credibility of the theory, Freud himself addressed many of the concerns raised by both his contemporary and subsequent critics. In numerous writings, for instance, he reviewed and rejected face-value accounts of the phenomena he addressed, and he made comparative assessments of the plausibility of competing psychoanalytic interpretations of behavior. In these exercises, he extrapolated to the predictions of competing claims and assessed their plausibility, given the data, as would befit any exercise in hypothesis-testing. He also stated, with respect to some claims, that he was following out the logic of an idea, rather than asserting testable claims. He claimed this, for instance, in the often-dismissed *Beyond the Pleasure Principle* (1920), regarding his ideas about the death instinct. Although it remains to be seen whether evidence and logic require hypotheses in the direction of Freud's tenets, it is difficult to identify alternative theories that address, let alone attempt to explain, the quintessentially human phenomena Freud took as his central object.

SEE ALSO *Jung, Carl; Memory in Psychology; Oedipus Complex; Psychoanalytic Theory; Psychology*

BIBLIOGRAPHY

PRIMARY WORKS

Freud, Sigmund. 1895. *Studies on Hysteria.* (With Josef Breuer.) Pelican Freud Library, Vol. 3. Trans. James and Alix Strachey. Harmondsworth, U.K.: Penguin, 1983.

Freud, Sigmund. 1900. *The Interpretation of Dreams.* Trans. James Strachey. New York: Avon, 1965.

Freud, Sigmund. 1905. *Jokes and Their Relation to the Unconscious.* Trans. James Strachey. New York: Norton, 1989.

Freud, Sigmund. 1910. *Five Lectures on Psychoanalysis.* Trans. James Strachey. New York: Norton, 1989.

Freud, Sigmund. 1911. Formulations Regarding Two Principles in Mental Functioning. In *Freud: General Psychological Theory*, ed. Philip Rieff, 21–28. Translation supervised by Joan Riviere. New York: Collier-Macmillan, 1963.

Freud, Sigmund. 1913. *Totem and Taboo.* Trans. James Strachey. New York: Norton, 1989.

Freud, Sigmund. 1914. On Narcissism: An Introduction. In *Freud: General Psychological Theory*, ed. Philip Reiff, 56–82. Translation supervised by Joan Riviere. New York: Collier-Macmillan, 1963.

Freud, Sigmund. 1915a. Instincts and Their Vicissitudes. In *Freud: General Psychological Theory*, ed. Philip Reiff, 83–103. Translation supervised by Joan Riviere. New York: Collier-Macmillan, 1963.

Freud, Sigmund. 1915b. Repression. In *Freud: General Psychological Theory*, ed. Philip Reiff. 104–115. Translation supervised by Joan Riviere. New York: Collier-Macmillan, 1963.

Freud, Sigmund. 1915c. The Unconscious. In *Freud: General Psychological Theory*, ed. Philip Reiff, 116–150. Translation supervised by Joan Riviere. New York: Collier-Macmillan, 1964.

Freud, Sigmund. 1917. *Introductory Lectures on Psychoanalysis*. Trans. James Strachey. New York: Norton, 1989.

Freud, Sigmund. 1919. The "Uncanny." In *Pelican Freud Library*. Vol. 14, *Art and Literature*, ed. Albert Dickson. Trans. James Strachey, 335–376. Harmondsworth, U.K.: Penguin, 1985.

Freud, Sigmund. 1920. *Beyond the Pleasure Principle*. Trans. James Strachey. New York: Norton, 1989.

Freud, Sigmund. 1923. *The Ego and the Id*. Trans. James Strachey. New York: Norton. 1989.

Freud, Sigmund. 1924. The Economic Problem of Masochism. In *Freud: General Psychological Theory*, ed. Philip Reiff, 190–201. Translation supervised by Joan Riviere. New York: Collier-Macmillan, 1963.

Freud, Sigmund. 1930. *Civilization and Its Discontents*. Trans. James Strachey. New York: Norton, 1989.

Freud, Sigmund. 1936. A Disturbance of Memory on the Acropolis: An Open Letter to Romain Rolland on the Occasion of His Seventieth Birthday. In *Pelican Freud Library*. Vol. 11, *On Metapsychology: The Theory of Psychoanalysis*, 443–456. Harmondsworth, U.K.: Penguin, 1984.

SECONDARY WORKS

Grünbaum, Adolf. 1984. *The Foundations of Psychoanalysis: A Philosophical Critique*. Berkeley: University of California Press.

Hobson, J. Allan. 1988. *The Dreaming Brain*. New York: Basic Books.

Laplanche, Jean, and J. B. Pontalis. 1967. *The Language of Psychoanalysis*. Trans. Donald Nicholson-Smith. New York: Norton, 1973.

Lear, Jonathan. 1999. *Open-Minded: Working Out the Logic of the Soul*. Cambridge, MA: Harvard University Press.

Schacter, Daniel L. 2001. *The Seven Sins of Memory: How the Mind Forgets and Remembers*. Boston: Houghton Mifflin.

Susan Sugarman

FRIEDAN, BETTY
1921–2006

Betty Friedan was a catalyst in the development of the women's movement in the United States in the 1960s. In 1963 her book *The Feminine Mystique* was published, and it provided a clarion call to women—especially suburban housewives—to move beyond their lives in the home and to actively pursue careers as well as social and political equality. Several decades later, the book had sold more than three million copies.

The daughter of a Russian immigrant who owned a successful jewelry store in Peoria, Illinois, and a mother who gave up a newspaper career to raise her children, Bettye (as she was named at birth) attended Smith College, graduating with honors in 1942. After earning her bachelor's degree, she dropped the "e" in her first name and attended the University of California, Berkeley, to pursue a graduate degree in psychology. She left the university in response to pressure from a boyfriend, eventually moving to New York, where she began writing for labor newspapers. She married Carl Friedan in 1947 (they divorced in 1969), and they moved to the suburbs of New York City, where she raised three children (Daniel, Emily, and Jonathan).

In preparation for her fifteenth college reunion, Friedan surveyed her classmates and discovered a vague but poignant dissatisfaction with their seemingly pleasant suburban lives. She extended her survey to alumna of other women's colleges and also interviewed numerous women; the results of her investigation provided the basis for *The Feminine Mystique*. The book galvanized women across the nation, particularly white women, and Friedan entered the national spotlight as an assertive spokeswoman. In 1966 she was one of the founders of the National Organization for Women (NOW), serving as its first president, a position she held until 1970. NOW provided women with a national platform to discuss their concerns, to advocate for political rights, and to engage in social and political activism. In 1969 Friedan was one of the founders of NARAL Pro-Choice America, an organization that advocates for abortion rights, and in 1971 she helped to found the National Women's Political Caucus.

Friedan authored six subsequent books, the last of which was a memoir. In her later books, she began to advocate for a broad movement for the working class, people of color, and gays and lesbians. She was a visiting professor at Columbia University, Temple University, and the University of Southern California. In the years just before her death, she worked with the Institute for Women and Work at Cornell University.

The Feminine Mystique remains a highly influential book, although much of its argument, focused on conditions in the 1960s, is now the source for more recent forms of feminism, and thus it is ironically both essential reading and dated. While her unflagging efforts on behalf of women focused attention on gender disparities, she achieved notoriety in the women's movement by calling lesbian feminists "the lavender menace" because they provided an easy target for critics who prophesied the demise of the family. Although *The Feminine Mystique* was focused on the conditions of suburban mothers, one of her cofounders of the National Women's Political Caucus, Fannie Lou Hamer (1917–1977), was a key African American activist in the long and bitter struggle for civil rights in Mississippi and political recognition in the national Democratic Party.

The first extensively organized effort for women's rights occurred in the 1800s and early 1900s when women fought for the right to vote. Betty Friedan was an architect of the second organized effort in the 1960s.

SEE ALSO *Feminism; Feminism, Second Wave; Suburbs; Women and Politics; Women's Liberation; Women's Movement*

BIBLIOGRAPHY

Friedan, Betty. 2000. *Life So Far*. New York: Simon & Schuster.

Hennessee, Judith Adler. 1999. *Betty Friedan: Her Life*. New York: Random House.

Horowitz, Daniel. 1998. *Betty Friedan and the Making of The Feminine Mystique: The American Left, The Cold War, and Modern Feminism*. Amherst: University of Massachusetts Press.

Philo A. Hutcheson

FRIEDMAN, MILTON
1912–2006

Milton Friedman is best known for his influential contributions to monetary macroeconomics and for his strong advocacy of the role of free markets in solving social problems. The son of poor Jewish immigrants in New York City, Friedman was educated under a scholarship at Rutgers University, where his main influences were Arthur F. Burns and Homer Jones. Upon graduation in 1932 with a joint major in economics and mathematics, he was offered a tuition scholarship in economics at the University of Chicago, where he was a student of Frank Knight and Jacob Viner, among others. After an academic year in Chicago, Friedman received a fellowship to move to Columbia University, where he was taught by Harold Hotelling and Wesley C. Mitchell. In his third year as a graduate student he returned to Chicago as research assistant to Henry Schultz. Apart from an academic year as visiting professor at the University of Wisconsin (1940–1941), between 1935 and 1945 Friedman worked in Washington, D.C., and New York for the National

Resources Institute (1935–1937), the National Bureau of Economic Research (NBER, 1937–1940), the Treasury Department (1941–1943), and the War Research Division of Columbia University (1943–1945). His Columbia doctoral dissertation was concluded at the NBER by 1940 as part of collaboration with Simon Kuznets on incomes from independent professional practice. However, its publication and Friedman's PhD were delayed until 1945 and 1946, respectively, because of a controversial result about the effect of monopoly powers on physicians' income. After a year as associate professor at the University of Minnesota, Friedman joined the faculty at the University of Chicago in 1946, replacing Viner as professor of economic theory. He became full professor in 1948, the same year he rejoined the NBER to carry out (together with Anna Schwartz) study of monetary factors in business cycles, a project that culminated with the Friedman-Schwartz 1982 volume *Monetary Trends in the United States and the United Kingdom*. Friedman continued to teach at Chicago until 1977, when he took up a position as senior research fellow at the Hoover Institution at Stanford University. In 1951 he received from the American Economic Association the John Bates Clark Medal, and in 1976 was awarded the Nobel Memorial Prize in economics.

CONSUMPTION AND UTILITY

Friedman's early contributions grew out of his statistical research of incomes and consumer expenditures carried out in the 1930s; these include the development in 1937 of a nonparametric significance test for ranked data, and the research that led to his 1945 book with Kuznets. That book introduced the concepts of permanent and transitory income, which would be the focal point of Friedman's 1957 econometric exercise in the *Theory of Consumption Function*. Friedman's hypothesis that permanent aggregate consumption is a function of permanent (in the sense of long-term expected) income was a solution to Kuznets's empirical findings that, contrary to prevailing Keynesian models at the time, the average propensity to consume does not decline with rising income. The permanent income hypothesis has had a profound impact on empirical work on the consumption function and other fields, despite its implicit treatment of lifetime as infinite, which makes it unsuitable to deal with optimization over the expected life of the economic agent. It was a crucial element of Friedman's overall attack on Keynesian economics because it implied (1) strong criticism of the so-called Keynes-Hansen secular stagnation thesis (which depends on the assumption of a rising saving-income ratio); (2) rejection of Keynesian unemployment equilibrium, on the basis of the introduction of wealth into the consumption function and by that of the positive effect of price reduction on consumers' expenditure; and (3) dismissal of the assumption that consumption is a stable function of current income, which undermined the stability of the Keynesian multiplier. Another important contribution by Friedman to the pure theory of statistics and decision-making was his 1948 essay (with Leonard Savage) on the implications of the von Neumann-Morgenstern cardinal utility function for risky choices, which influenced the development of portfolio selection theory. Friedman and Savage showed that choice under uncertainty could be represented by a process of maximizing expected utility, which allowed them to explain the simultaneous practice of gamble and insurance under some assumptions.

QUANTITY THEORY OF MONEY

Although monetary theory and policy had attracted Friedman's attention since his discussion of the inflationary gap at the Treasury Department in the early 1940s, it was only after the 1950s that money became the main topic of his research agenda, especially with the start of the Chicago Workshop on Money and Banking, set up by him in 1951. The first product of that workshop was the 1956 volume of *Studies in the Quantity Theory of Money*, edited by Friedman. The book opened with his "restatement" of the quantity theory as a proposition about the empirical stability of the demand for real money balances in relation to a few arguments, including income. Friedman's claim that his approach to money demand—as the outcome of the agents' portfolio decision about how to allocate their wealth among alternative assets—was in tune with the Chicago quantity theory tradition was challenged, however, by Don Patinkin and other commentators. In any event, Friedman's point that the velocity of circulation of money is determined mainly by changes in real income represented an alternative to the prevailing Keynesian income-expenditure mechanism based on the stability of the investment multiplier. It led to Friedman's proposition that substantial changes in prices or nominal incomes are the result of changes in the nominal supply of money. The empirical investigation of that claim was the object of Friedman and Schwartz's *Monetary History* (1963), the first of their books for the NBER. That book is the most important contribution to the "monetarist" approach to the business cycle, and it followed the NBER founder Wesley Mitchell's practice of extracting cycles and trends from detailed time series. It is also congruent with Friedman's emphasis on testing the empirical implications of theories, worked out in his influential 1953 essay on the methodology of positive economics. Friedman and Schwartz examined individual episodes in U.S. monetary history to establish the determining causal influence of changes in money stock on prices and economic activity.

In particular, they put forward an explanation of the Great Depression (1929–1933), alternative to the Keynesian one, as the consequence of inept policy responses by the Federal Reserve to the contraction in money supply brought about by bank failures and rising currency/deposit and reserve/deposit ratios.

NATURAL RATE OF UNEMPLOYMENT

Apart from the primacy of exogenous monetary impulses, another main element of Friedman's monetary economics is the stress on the role of expectations in the transmission of monetary changes to nominal and real variables. Although the theme of expectations already could be found in his writings in the 1950s and early 1960s, it was only after his 1967 seminal presidential address to the American Economic Association that the distinction between expected and unexpected values of variables became prominent. Friedman argued that the trade-off between inflation and unemployment measured by the traditional Phillips curve is a temporary phenomenon that disappears in the long run, once inflation becomes anticipated by economic agents (1968). Friedman coined the phrase *natural rate of unemployment* to express the notion that monetary authorities are only able to keep the current unemployment rate below its long-term equilibrium level if inflation is accelerating—the "natural rate" is the rate of unemployment (determined by real factors such as labor mobility, etc.) at which inflation is nonaccelerating and agents' expectations about the value of real variables (such as real wages) are fulfilled. In contrast with his other contributions to monetary economics, the natural rate of unemployment hypothesis was not subjected to empirical testing by Friedman, in part because his definition of the concept is not fully operational, as argued by Frank Hahn and others. As it happens, some key elements of Friedman's 1967 address could be found already in David Champernowne's 1936 critical reactions to J. M. Keynes's *General Theory*. The real wage rate that workers would demand if they forecast future prices correctly was called the *basic real wage* by Champernowne, and the corresponding unemployment level was termed the *basic unemployment rate*, just like Friedman's *natural rate*. According to Champernowne, the rate of price change will accelerate if actual unemployment differs from its "basic" value, which will bring it back to its long-run value through the effect of inflation (or deflation) acceleration on the setting of the interest rate by monetary authorities.

MONEY GROWTH RULE

The implications of Friedman's theoretical and empirical monetary studies for the operation of monetary policy were worked out in his 1959 *Program for Monetary*

Stability and in essays collected in 1969. One of his main empirical findings was that monetary changes affect output and prices with a long, variable, and unpredictable lag; this is behind his skepticism of the stabilizing role of discretionary monetary policy. Instead, Friedman argued—coherently with the Chicago tradition of Henry Simons and others—for a fixed rule to expand the money supply by a constant and known annual percentage. As Friedman was aware, such a rule could only be implemented with a system of flexible exchange rates, which had been advocated by him since the early 1950s on the grounds that flexible rates would lead to a more efficient process of adjustment of the balance of payments. At first, Friedman suggested that the rate of growth of money supply should aim at the stabilization of the price level (around 4%), but he later claimed that, from a purely economic-welfare perspective, the optimal money stock should grow at such a rate (around 2%) to bring about a rate of deflation equal to the rate of return of real capital. This would mean, in long-run equilibrium, that the private marginal cost of holding real cash balances (the nominal rate of interest) is the same as its social marginal cost (zero), a Pareto optimum situation. Whereas Friedman's notion of an optimum money supply was primarily of theoretical interest, his more general point—that the main feature of the money growth rule is not the growth rate itself but the adoption of some fixed rate that would produce some known and steady moderate inflation or deflation—has influenced central banks, especially in the monetarist experiments carried out between 1979 and 1982 in the United States and during Margaret Thatcher's premiership in the United Kingdom. Those experiments and their results were highly contended, however, as a result of the instability of the demand for money following financial deregulation and the weak link between money growth and inflation in the 1980s. Moreover, the publication of Friedman's last important work on money at about that time (Friedman and Schwartz 1982) raised strong criticism of their empirical analysis of the relation between money, income, and prices in the United Kingdom (Hendry and Ericsson 1991).

INFLUENCE AND CRITICAL REACTIONS

Despite the intense controversies that surrounded Friedman's monetary economics in the 1960s and 1970s—especially the criticism by James Tobin and others that he had not succeeded in specifying the mechanism of transmission from money to output and prices (Gordon 1974)—it is true that many of his propositions became by the end of the twentieth century part and parcel of macroeconomic theory and policy, even if they are not always explicitly associated with his name. These

include the notion that monetary policy should target nominal quantities (such as inflation) instead of output and employment, as well as the view that it is usually a more potent tool for economic stabilization than fiscal policy. It is worth noting that although Friedman's emphasis on the role of the market and limits to state intervention in the economy, plus his rejection of activist macroeconomic policies, are shared with "Austrian economics" (theories espoused by, for example, Friedrich von Hayek, Ludwig von Mises, and Murray Rothbard), his relationship with that group of economists has been difficult. Friedman's restatement of the quantity theory of money approach to monetary economics was partly motivated by his perception that, in contrast with the Chicago tradition of Simons, Viner, and others, Austrian economists (called "London School" by Friedman) are mistaken in their argument that depressions should not be avoided because they are the inevitable result of the prior boom. For their part, the Austrian economists have criticized Friedman's monetary economics for overlooking the role of intertemporal coordination failures and relative price changes in the business-cycle mechanism. They have also rejected Friedman's credential as the leader of free-market economics because, in their view, some of Friedman's proposals—such as the maintenance of government control over the money supply, state support of education by vouchers redeemable at private schools, guaranteed annual income through a negative income tax—indicate that he has intended to make the state more efficient, rather than just to remove it from the economic realm.

BIBLIOGRAPHY

PRIMARY WORKS

Friedman, Milton. 1937. The Use of Ranks to Avoid the Assumption of Normality Implicit in the Analysis of Variance. *Journal of the American Statistical Association* 32 (December): 675–201.

Friedman, Milton. 1953. *Essays in Positive Economics.* Chicago: University of Chicago Press.

Friedman, Milton. 1957. *A Theory of the Consumption Function.* Princeton, NJ: Princeton University Press for the National Bureau of Economic Research.

Friedman, Milton. 1959. *A Program for Monetary Stability.* New York: Fordham University Press.

Friedman, Milton. 1968. The Role of Monetary Policy. *American Economic Review* 58 (March): 1–17.

Friedman, Milton. 1969. *The Optimum Quantity of Money and Other Essays.* Chicago: Aldine.

Friedman, Milton, ed. 1956. *Studies in the Quantity Theory of Money.* Chicago: University of Chicago Press.

Friedman, Milton, and Rose Friedman. 1980. *Free to Choose.* New York: Harcourt Brace Jovanovich.

Friedman, Milton, and Simon Kuznets. 1945. *Income from Independent Professional Practice*. New York: National Bureau of Economic Research.

Friedman, Milton, and Leonard Savage. 1948. The Utility Analysis of Choices Involving Risk. *Journal of Political Economy* 56 (August): 279–304.

Friedman, Milton, and Anna J. Schwartz. 1963. *A Monetary History of the United States, 1867–1960*. Princeton, NJ: Princeton University Press for the National Bureau of Economic Research.

Friedman, Milton, and Anna J. Schwartz. 1982. *Monetary Trends in the United States and the United Kingdom*. Chicago: University of Chicago Press for the National Bureau of Economic Research.

SECONDARY WORKS

Bellante, Don, and Roger Garrison. 1988. Phillips Curves and Hayekian Triangles: Two Perspectives on Monetary Dynamics. *History of Political Economy* 20 (2): 207–234.

Boianovsky, Mauro. 2005. Some Cambridge Reactions to *The General Theory*: David Champernowne and Joan Robinson on Full Employment. *Cambridge Journal of Economics* 29 (1): 73–98.

Champernowne, David G. 1936. Unemployment, Basic and Monetary: The Classical Analysis and the Keynesian. *Review of Economic Studies* 3: 201–216.

De Long, Bradford. 2000. The Triumph of Monetarism? *Journal of Economic Perspectives* 14 (1): 83–94.

De Marchi, Neil, and Abraham Hirsch. 1990. *Milton Friedman: Economics in Theory and Practice*. Brighton, U.K.: Harvester Wheatsheaf.

Gordon, Robert, ed. 1974. *Milton Friedman's Monetary Framework: A Debate with His Critics*. Chicago: University of Chicago Press.

Hahn, Frank. 1971. Professor Friedman's Views on Money. *Economica* New Series 38 (February): 61–80.

Hammond, J. Daniel. 1996. *Theory and Measurement—Causality in Milton Friedman's Monetary Economics*. Cambridge, U.K.: Cambridge University Press.

Hendry, David F., and Neil Ericsson. 1991. An Econometric Analysis of the U.K. Money Demand in Monetary Trends in the United States and United Kingdom. *American Economic Review* 81 (March): 8–38.

Laidler, David. 2005. *Milton Friedman and the Evolution of Macroeconomics. Working Paper #2005-11*. London, Ontario: University of Western Ontario, Department of Economics, Economic Policy Research Institute.

Patinkin, Don. 1969. The Chicago Tradition, the Quantity Theory, and Friedman. *Journal of Money, Credit, and Banking* 63: 46–70.

Rothbard, Murray. 2002. Milton Friedman Unraveled. *Journal of Libertarian Studies* 16 (4): 37–54.

Silk, Leonard. 1976. Milton Friedman: Prophet of the Old-time Religion. In *The Economists*, 41–85. New York: Avon Books.

Thygesen, Niels. 1977. The Scientific Contributions of Milton Friedman. *Scandinavian Journal of Economics* 79 (1): 56–98.

Wood, John C., and Ronald N. Woods, eds. 1990. *Milton Friedman—Critical Assessments*. 4 vols. London and New York: Routledge.

Mauro Boianovsky

FRIENDSHIP

Friendships are enormously important in the lives of most people. Having good, mutually responsive friendships has been associated with better physical and mental health, higher self-esteem, and greater feelings of self-worth.

NATURE OF FRIENDSHIPS

What *are* friendships? Different researchers have emphasized features such as loyalty, trust, voluntary interdependence, proximity-seeking, and idiosyncratically thinking about and responding to one another. All these features are important, but most significant is the fact that friendships are normatively characterized by adherence to a communal norm. That is, friends are expected to be mutually responsive to one another's welfare by providing help, supporting one another's goal strivings, and including one another in enjoyable activities. Importantly, such responsiveness ought to be given voluntarily and it should occur on a noncontingent rather than a tit-for-tat basis. Indeed, research has demonstrated that observers are more likely to infer friendship when people give and accept noncomparable rather than comparable benefits, and when they split restaurant bills evenly rather than according to exactly who has ordered what.

Other relationships besides friendships also are normatively communal—romantic or spousal, parent-child, and sibling relationships. What, then, distinguishes friendships from these other relationships? We contend that friendships are communal relationships that also are nonexclusive, nonfamilial, and normatively nonsexual (although research indicates that some people engage in sexual contact with others whom they consider to be "just friends"). Friendships also are different in that there are no strong social prescriptions, legal obligations, or mutual investments holding them together. Interdependence theory therefore suggests that commitment in friendships is more voluntary than in other types of communal relationships, and that friendships may both form and fade with less fanfare than other communal relationships.

Whom do people choose as friends? Researchers have studied this topic extensively and have found several reliable predictors of friendship. For both children and adults, functional propinquity, or likelihood of mutual contact, is a basic and potent predictor of friendship choice. People simply have more opportunities to develop friendships with others whom they encounter regularly. According to the similarity-attraction principle, similarity is another powerful predictor of friendship. Indeed, research offers considerable support for the maxim, "birds of a feather flock together." People like others who are similar to them in terms of attitudes, values, race, and socioeconomic status. This may be because it is reinforcing to interact with others who agree with them, and because there is an increased likelihood of contact among those who are similar. Relevant to the former possibility, recent research has shown that people are especially likely to feel close to others with whom they share a negative attitude about another person. Relevant to the latter, research suggests that students in racially diverse schools are more likely to have cross-race friendships than those from more homogenous schools. One additional predictor of friendship is assumed reciprocity of liking. Both children and adults like others whom they think like them.

There is also some evidence for the maxim that "opposites attract." For example, self-evaluation maintenance theory suggests that people feel most comfortable with and find it easiest to be communally responsive to peers who excel in performance domains that are distinct from those domains about which they themselves care, and within which they themselves excel.

DIFFERENCES IN FRIENDSHIPS

Developmental research has emphasized the notion that friendship changes across the lifespan. Young children define friends as people with whom they spend time and engage in joint activities. For them, a primary goal of friendship is spending play time together. Older children begin to define friends based on interpersonally relevant traits and behaviors. To adolescents and adults, intimacy and self-disclosure are defining features of friendship, and a primary goal of friendship is meaningful conversation.

Researchers have long been interested in sex differences in friendship. Many have argued that female-female friendships are more intimate than male-male friendships. This was considered a truism for quite some time, and there is evidence to support this idea. Female friends talk with one another more than do male friends, and male friends perform joint activities with one another more than do female friends. Furthermore, when men do talk in their friendships, there is a greater tendency for their conversational topics to revolve around activities. Women, in contrast, tend to share feelings more directly and to talk more explicitly about their relationships. Several studies indicate that male-female friendships are more similar to female-female than male-male friendships, however. So, men might rely more on female than male friends for self-disclosure and intimacy. The idea that men's friendships

are less intimate is no longer uncontroversial, however. Several researchers have pointed out that the very definition of intimacy might be different for men and women. Others have raised the question of whether men are incapable of being more intimate, choose to be less intimate, or achieve intimacy through means other than self-disclosure. No matter whose relationships are most intimate, recent research has suggested that both men and women identify intimacy as a central component of friendship. Some research also suggests that women engage in joint activities and men self-disclose more than earlier evidence indicated. It may be the case that any differences between male and female friendships are matters of degree rather than qualitative differences.

As stated earlier, people are more likely to befriend members of their own racial and ethnic groups. Once friendships are formed between people from different racial or ethnic groups, there is a tendency for these friends to engage in fewer shared activities than same-race or same-ethnicity friends. The types of activities in which people engage are similar regardless of racial composition, however. Like sex differences, race differences in friendship may be more quantitative than qualitative.

Considering the importance of friendships for everyday life, one could argue that the topic is underrepresented in the social scientific literature. This is particularly true of the literature on adult relationships, which tends to emphasize romantic relationships. Research on children and adolescents, however, has placed a comparatively greater emphasis on friendships. Fortunately, the adult literature has begun to catch up in recent years. The future holds a number of exciting possibilities for research on friendship. In addition to continuing to elucidate basic friendship processes, researchers are increasingly investigating issues such as cross-cultural differences in friendships, the nature of long-distance friendships, and the nature of friendships formed in an online context or "e-friendships."

SEE ALSO *Men; Parent-Child Relationships; Romance; Sibling Relationships; Women*

BIBLIOGRAPHY

Fehr, Beverly. 1996. *Friendship Processes*. Thousand Oaks, CA: Sage.

Nardi, Peter M., ed. 1992. *Men's Friendships*. Thousand Oaks, CA: Sage.

O'Connor, Pat. 1992. *Friendships between Women: A Critical Review*. New York: Guilford.

Steven M. Graham
Margaret S. Clark

FRISCH, RAGNAR
1895–1973

The Norwegian economist Ragnar Frisch was a dominant force in the development of economics during the interwar period of the 1920s and 1930s. He pioneered the use of quantitative methods encompassing three fields of analysis: economic theory, mathematics, and statistics. Economists drew on these three areas to develop the specialized field of econometrics. Frisch continued to build this field of study after World War II (1939–1945) until his death in 1973. He was honored in 1969 with the Nobel Prize in Economics, which he received jointly with Jan Tinbergen (1903–1994) of the Netherlands, who was also a European pioneer in the field of econometrics.

Frisch's main contributions were in developing statistical and mathematical analysis of several branches of economics. He estimated production and demand relationships, theoretical mathematical models of economic cycles, and systems of international trade. Together with Joseph Schumpeter (1883–1950) of Harvard, Irving Fisher (1867–1947) of Yale, and many other leading scholars from Europe and the United States, Frisch influenced Alfred Cowles (1891–1984) to help finance the launching in 1930 of the Econometric Society and in 1933 of its journal, *Econometrica*, which was to become a leading scholarly publication. The Econometric Society remains a strong international force in many branches of economics.

Tinbergen's statistical models of the dynamic fluctuations of national or world economies constitute one path of econometric research that flourishes today, and Frisch's theoretical economic models, statistical archives, and estimation methods form a different path for understanding the working of economic systems. Frisch's model was, at an early stage, called an *ecocirc* system. It expanded a line of thinking that grew out of his celebrated article "Propagation Problems and Impulse Problems in Dynamic Economics" (1933), which shows how continuing external random shocks to an economy can propagate regular, maintained cycles that could otherwise fade away.

Students of Frisch became important in Norwegian and international organizations and institutions. Trygve Haavelmo (1911–1999), a favored student of Frisch, became a Nobel laureate in 1989. During the Great Depression, Frisch delivered radio addresses and published articles on economic policies to improve the Norwegian economy. His recommendations anticipated some of the proposals made by John Maynard Keynes (1883–1946) for the United Kingdom, the United States, and other European economies.

During World War II, Frisch was imprisoned in a German-controlled camp, Grini, where many intellectuals and senior Norwegian officials were held. Soon after his release, he visited the Cowles Commission at the University of Chicago, where Haavelmo and others were actively engaged in econometric analysis using many of Frisch's ideas. Frisch turned his attention in the postwar years not only to Norwegian and international economic systems, but also to economic development problems of comparatively poor countries. During this time he visited India, where he interacted with Indian economists and political leaders. Frisch continued to work on his ecocirc system, training Norwegian students and colleagues to deal with expanded subsystems for an enlarged master plan, but he did not complete his overall project—to build a complete economic accounting and planning system. In a larger framework, after World War II, he was inspired by the input-output analysis of Wassily Leontief (1906–1999), the social accounting systems of Richard Stone (1913–1991), and international trade matrices developed at the United Nations, where he consulted on applied economic analysis. Frisch also maintained a deep interest in bee populations and felt that the development of bees and their products was helpful in understanding the economic development of human populations. He was proud of their fine honey output as well.

BIBLIOGRAPHY

Arrow, Kenneth J. 1960. The Work of Ragnar Frisch, Econometrician. *Econometrica* 28: 175–192.

Frisch, Ragnar. 1933. Propagation Problems and Impulse Problems in Dynamic Economics. In *Economic Essays in Honor of Gustav Cassel*, 171–205. London: Allen and Unwin.

Frisch, Ragnar. 1947. On the Need for Forecasting a Multilateral Balance of Payments. *American Economic Review* 37 (September): 535–551.

Frisch, Ragnar, and Harald Holme. 1935. The Characteristic Solutions of a Mixed Difference and Differential Equation Occurring in Economic Dynamics. *Econometrica* 3 (2): 225–239.

Strom, Steinar, ed. 1998. *Econometrics and Economic Theory in the 20th Century*. For the 100th anniversary of the birth of Ragnar Frisch. Cambridge: Cambridge University Press.

Lawrence R. Klein

FROBENIUS-PERRON THEOREM

SEE *Eigen-Values and Eigen-Vectors, Perron-Frobenius Theorem.*

FROMM, ERICH
1900–1980

Born in Frankfurt, Germany, in 1900, Erich Fromm was affiliated with the Institute for Social Research, later known as the "Frankfurt school," from 1928 to 1938. Trained in psychoanalysis, Fromm combined Freudian psychology with Marxian social theory. In his early essays he indicates the common dialectical and materialist elements in Marx and Freud and applies his Marxian social psychology to interpret such phenomena as religion, the sadomasochistic roots of the authoritarian personality, and the dominant bourgeois character types.

Forced to flee from Nazi Germany in 1933, Fromm settled in the United States and lectured at the New School of Social Research, Columbia University, Yale University, and Bennington College. In the late 1930s Fromm broke with the Institute of Social Research, and with *Escape from Freedom* (1941) he began publishing a series of books that won him a large audience in the United States and eventually throughout the world.

Escape from Freedom argued that alienation from soil and community in the transition from feudalism to capitalism increased insecurity and fear. Documenting some of the strains and crises of individualism, Fromm attempted to explain how alienated individuals seek gratification and security from social orders such as fascism. Protestantism, with its emphasis on individual salvation and damnation, increased individuals' fears and made them susceptible, he argued, to manipulation by social forces. Moreover, capitalism, with its emphasis on individual gain and harsh market competition, which mediated success and failure, also contributed to feelings of insecurity. Migrations from country to towns and factories, central to industrial modernity, created a new urban civilization that increased individuals' feelings of rootlessness and alienation.

In the late 1930s Fromm broke with the Frankfurt school, in part over his interpretation of Freud and in part over personality conflicts with key members such as Theodor Adorno (1903–1969) and Herbert Marcuse (1898–1979). Henceforth, Fromm went his own way, often appearing as a prophet in the desert of American affluence and consumerism as he attacked the "marketing orientation," the bourgeois proclivity to privilege having over being, and indeed the entire American system of institutions and values.

His post–World War II books, *Man for Himself* (1947) and *The Sane Society* (1955), applied Fromm's Freudian-Marxian perspectives to sharp critiques of contemporary capitalism. Fromm popularized the neo-Marxian critiques of the media and consumer society, and promoted democratic socialist perspectives during an era when social repression made it difficult and dangerous to advocate radical positions. Although his social critique was similar in many ways to that of his former colleague Marcuse, the two thinkers engaged in sharp polemics from the mid-1950s into the 1970s. Marcuse began the polemic by attacking Fromm as a neo-Freudian revisionist (Marcuse 1955, p. 238), and Fromm retaliated by calling Marcuse a "nihilist" and "utopian" (Fromm 1970, p. 62). Marcuse claimed that Fromm's emphasis on the "productive character" simply reproduced the "productivism" intrinsic to capitalism, and that his celebration of the values of love, in books such as *The Art of Loving* (1957), and religion simply reproduced dominant idealist ideologies (Marcuse 1955, p. 258).

Fromm was a prolific writer up until his death in 1980, publishing a series of books promoting and developing Marxian and Freudian ideas. He was also politically active, helping to organize the National Committee for a Sane Nuclear Policy in 1957 and engaging in early "ban the bomb" campaigns, as well as participating in the U.S. antiwar movement of the 1960s. Fromm continued to argue for a humanistic and democratic socialist position, and claimed that such elements were intrinsic in Marxism. His many books and articles had some influence on the New Left and continue to be read and discussed today.

BIBLIOGRAPHY

PRIMARY WORKS

Fromm, Erich. 1941. *Escape from Freedom*. New York: Holt, Rinehart, and Winston.

Fromm, Erich. 1947. *Man for Himself*. New York: Holt, Rinehart, and Winston.

Fromm, Erich. 1955. *The Sane Society*. New York: Holt, Rinehart, and Winston.

Fromm, Erich. 1956. *The Art of Loving*. New York: Bantam Books.

Fromm, Erich. 1970. *The Crisis of Psychoanalysis*. Greenwich, CT: Fawcett Premier Books.

SECONDARY WORKS

Burston, Daniel. 1991. *The Legacy of Erich Fromm*. Cambridge, MA: Harvard University Press.

Funk, Rainer. 1982. *Erich Fromm: The Courage to Be Human*. New York: Continuum.

Marcuse, Herbert. 1955. *Eros and Civilization*. Boston: Beacon Press.

Douglas Kellner

F-STATISTIC

SEE *Test Statistics.*

F-TEST

SEE *Test Statistics.*

FULL CAPACITY

Full capacity refers to the potential output that could be produced with installed equipment within a specified period of time. Actual capacity output can vary within two limits: (1) an upper limit that refers to the engineering capacity—that is, the level of output that could be produced when the installed equipment is used to its maximum time of operation and maximum technical efficiency; and (2) a lower limit identified with the scrapping of plant and equipment—that is, the level of output that is no longer profitable to produce. By full (or normal) capacity at the microeconomic level, economists refer to the level of output that corresponds to minimum cost production, usually identified with the minimum point of a usual U-shaped average cost curve. Before this point, we have economies of scale that firms would be willing to take advantage of by expanding their output. Past this point, firms encounter diseconomies of scale that they would like to avoid by cutting down their level of production. The problem with this definition is that such a minimum point is hard to identify empirically. Furthermore, the average cost curves in manufacturing are usually characterized by constant returns to scale for fairly large variations in the output produced, and so full (normal) capacity is identified with the level of output past which the firm considers the installment of a new plant. Consequently, normal output is conceived differently in the various schools of economic thought.

Starting with the classical economists, full or normal capacity is identified with the level of output where the forces of demand and supply are equal and the production technique along with the distributive variables (i.e., the real wage and the rate of profit) are taken as givens. Hence, normal capacity is different from engineering capacity in the sense that it takes into account economic considerations. Consequently, normal or full capacity will equal a certain percentage of maximum engineering capacity simply because it does not pay to use the plant and equipment past this percentage point, even though engineering-wise such a use would be possible. It is important to point out that full capacity in classical economics is restricted to capital. The idea is that the purpose of production is the extraction of profits as an end in itself, so the primary concern of entrepreneurs is the full employment of their capital, while labor simply adjusts to the requirements of capital regardless of the level of unemployment. In short, full capacity may be accompanied by considerable unemployment of labor.

For neoclassical economists, full capacity is identified with both the full employment of capital and the full employment of labor. Full capacity is expected to prevail in the economy in the long run, and any deviations from full capacity are attributed to external economic shocks that may displace the actual output away from the full capacity output. However, neoclassical economics claims that if the price mechanism works freely it is expected that sooner rather than later the actual level of output will be restored back to its optimal level.

A characteristically different view was propounded by John Maynard Keynes (1883–1946), who argued that the unemployment of capital may coexist with the unemployment of labor, precisely because of the failure of the market system to generate effective demand sufficient to fully employ all the factors of production. Keynes further argued that once the economy finds itself in such a situation it stays there, since aggregate demand and aggregate supply are equal to each other. Output and therefore employment of both capital and labor can change through variations in aggregate demand induced by government intervention, and in this way the economy may reach a point that is consistent with the full capacity of both capital and labor. In the Keynesian perspective, prices do not play a role because of the assumption of constant returns to scale.

Modern macroeconomic approaches envisioned a novel concept of full capacity identified with the level of output at which there are no pressures for the acceleration or the deceleration of the inflation rate. Furthermore, the rate of capacity utilization defined as the ratio of actual output to the full capacity output has established, at least for the U.S. and Canadian economies, a benchmark capacity utilization rate that is consistent with a stable inflation rate. This concept came to be known with the acronym NAICU, that is, the nonaccelerating inflation capacity utilization rate, which is supposed to be more general than the currently more popular nonaccelerating inflation rate of unemployment known as the NAIRU, which is restricted to the employment of labor alone. Full capacity output is identified on the basis of survey measures for the U.S. and Canadian economies and is associated with a rate of capacity utilization approximately equal to 82 percent of potential output. The empirical evidence for the years before the mid-1990s has been supportive of this hypothesis for both the U.S. and the Canadian economies, but this hypothesis lost part of its explanatory force in the post-1990 years. These rather negative results raised doubts about the official measurement of potential output based on surveys, and encouraged research in the development of alternative measures of the full capacity output.

There are various methods for the estimation of potential output that can be distinguished between those based on economic theory and those that are not. Economic measures include those derived from the use of production or cost functions. More recently, there have been measures developed based on the use of econometric techniques such as the cointegration and the structural vector autoregressive models. Noneconomic measures include various statistical methods starting from peak-to-peak measures of capacity output to simple moving averages and sophisticated filtering techniques. Finally, among the atheoretic measures of capacity output, the approach based on surveys is the most popular and is conducted in many countries. The survey measures of capacity output of the U.S. Federal Reserve Board is the oldest one and is based on a nationwide survey where the managers of manufacturing firms are asked to identify "the maximum level of production that their establishment could reasonably expect to attain under normal and realistic operating conditions, fully utilizing the machinery and equipment in place." Despite the subjective content of the responses, surveys are used extensively in economic research and also for economic policy purposes.

Today there are many estimating methods of measurement of capacity output; nevertheless, full capacity output continues to be a slippery concept and, therefore, remains controversial within economic theory, attracting the attention of economists, who in spite of the recognition of its unquestionable theoretical significance and practical importance nevertheless are still far from reaching any agreement as to the adoption of a single estimating method.

SEE ALSO *Capital; Economics, Keynesian; Economics, Neoclassical; Full Employment; Keynes, John Maynard; Machinery*

BIBLIOGRAPHY

Artus, Jacques. 1977. Measures of Potential Output in Manufacturing for Eight Industrial Countries, 1955–1978. *International Monetary Fund Staff Papers* 24: 1–35.

Berndt, Ernst, and Dieter Hesse. 1986. Measuring and Assessing Capacity Utilization in the Manufacturing Sectors of Nine OECD Countries. *European Economic Review* 30: 961–989.

Tsoulfidis, Lefteris, and Theologos Dergiades. 2006. The Inflation-Capacity Utilization Conundrum: Evidence from the Canadian Economy. *Applied Econometrics and International Development* 6 (2).

Lefteris Tsoulfidis

FULL EMPLOYMENT

In a market economy, a resource is employed when engaged, in exchange for monetary payment, in the pro-

duction or sale of goods and services. Therefore *full employment* refers most broadly to employing all the available resources—the productive land, labor, and capital—on hand at a certain time and place. More often, however, full employment refers to the full utilization of *labor* inputs. The term *full employment* is closely connected to the concept of unemployment, and achieving a broad appreciation of these intertwined notions requires a historical look at both economic theory and public policy.

ECONOMIC THEORY

Macroeconomics, the study of national economic systems, is the realm of economics devoted to studying full employment and unemployment. Prior to the 1936 publication of John Maynard Keynes's *The General Theory of Employment, Interest, and Money* (written as a response to the mass unemployment of the Great Depression), macroeconomics did not exist apart from the broader discipline of economic theory.

When Keynes published *The General Theory*, most economists believed that market economies were self-adjusting systems that usually operated at full employment and would, on their own, return to full employment after a period of adjustment to external disturbances. Keynes disagreed. "The evidence indicates that full, or even approximately full, employment is of rare and short lived occurrence" (Keynes 1964, pp. 249–250). Thus *The General Theory* was offered to contrast Keynes's ideas about unemployment with the view of the period's conventional economists, which he called *classical* economic theory.

According to classical economics, there is no reason for the *involuntary* unemployment of workers. In this type of economics, wages adjust to equate workers' supply of labor and employers' demand for labor. The result is a state of "full employment," though this does not mean that all workers will be continuously employed. In fact classical economic theory allows for three forms of "voluntary" unemployment in a full-employment economy. (This discussion of full employment and unemployment in economic theory draws on Galbraith and Darity [1994]. Readers interested in a more detailed discussion of the theoretical perspectives discussed in the present essay should consult that volume; most macroeconomics texts offer similar analyses.)

In classical theory, unemployment can exist when a worker moves between jobs, refuses to accept work at the market wage rate, or is prevented from taking a job because of a social decision that keeps wages above their equilibrium level. The first situation describes what is called *frictional* unemployment and is considered "voluntary" because classical theory assumes that a job is available for that worker at the equilibrium wage rate. (To be more precise, the key wage of interest to classical economists is the "real" wage, which is the actual or "nominal" wage adjusted for paycheck purchasing power by taking into account the general level of prices.) The second situation is viewed as voluntary because the unemployed person could find work by lowering his or her "reservation" wage and accepting employment at a lower than desired level of pay. The third situation, which exists when a collective-bargaining agreement or minimum-wage law sets a wage above the market rate, is considered voluntary because society as a whole could remove the institutions that interfere with market forces.

In *The General Theory*, Keynes shifts attention from the labor market to the economy as a whole. Since Keynes argued that the total level of employment is a by-product of supply and demand for economic output as a whole, he focused on what determines the economy's equilibrium level of overall output. The key, he concluded, is total or "aggregate" spending by households, firms, and government (excluding considerations of international trade).

According to Keynes, the economy's equilibrium output is achieved when aggregate spending (called aggregate demand) absorbs the income earned (called national income). Since this can occur at any number of levels of income, aggregate demand is the crucial determinant of national output and employment. While classical economists focused on labor-market dynamics and assumed that the labor-market always yields employment equilibrium consistent with equilibrium in the overall economy, Keynes argued there is no reason to assume these equilibriums will be compatible. Thus Keynesian economics maintains that the economy could remain indefinitely at a total level of employment that is far below the full-employment level that labor-market considerations alone would generate. In Keynesian theory, there is *involuntary* unemployment whenever overall economic equilibrium generates a level of employment that falls below the labor market's market-clearing, "full-employment" level.

Here it is worth noting a difference regarding how full employment is described in "Keynesian economics" and in a portion of Keynes's *The General Theory*. In Keynesian economics, although there is no necessary connection between the equilibrium employment level generated by aggregate economic activity and the labor market's "full-employment" level, the labor market can at least be considered a conceptual benchmark, "telling us whether or not we are at full employment" (Galbraith and Darity 1994, p. 147). In a portion of *The General Theory*, however, there is no resort to full employment as this sort of conceptual notion (Keynes 1964, p. 26). Rather, full employment is a much more empirical construct: It exists when an increase in aggregate demand fails to result in more employment. James K. Galbraith and William Darity explain the latter view as follows: "If an expansion

of aggregate demand … leads to a higher level of employment, then involuntary unemployment prevailed prior to the expansion. If not, then the economy already was at full employment" (Galbraith and Darity 1994, p. 33).

Keynesian economics (and Keynes's *The General Theory*) suggests that closing the gap between actual and "full" employment involves boosting aggregate demand via fiscal or monetary policy. The problem, however, is that such macroeconomic policy alone often yields inflation, as economists recognized in the 1960s. At first Keynesians explained the "trade-off" between unemployment and inflation with reference to the Phillips curve, which plots inflation against unemployment for various moments in time and showed an inverse relationship between inflation and unemployment. This curve fit less neatly as an account of the 1970s, however, bolstering an emerging anti-Keynesian movement that eventually produced what is now called New Classical macroeconomics.

Edmund Phelps and Milton Friedman, whose work in the late 1960s suggested that there is no long-run trade-off between unemployment and inflation, offered an early challenge to Keynesian theory. The Phelps-Friedman analysis treats the long-run Phillips curve (again, inflation plotted against unemployment) as a vertical line rising upward from the "natural rate of unemployment." Moreover the "long run" here does not require a vast period of time. Rather, government efforts to boost aggregate demand will increase inflation without reducing unemployment *whenever workers correctly (observe or) expect an increase in prices and insist on an offsetting wage increase.*

The doctrine of the natural rate of unemployment is a strong argument against activist macroeconomic management in pursuit of greater employment. In fact the Phelps-Friedman theory indicates that the result of such activism would be higher *and accelerating* inflation. According to their theory, the main way to reduce unemployment is to raise the rate of labor productivity growth, but since productivity growth stalled during the 1970s, economists' estimates of the natural rate rose during that decade—from about 5.4 percent in the late 1960s to just over 7 percent in the late 1970s (Bennett 1997, p. 275).

The natural rate of unemployment (which in the early twenty-first century is often called the "non-accelerating inflation rate of unemployment") is widely believed to have fallen since the 1970s, but the precise rate is not really that important in New Classical macroeconomics. That is because New Classical theory restores the pre-Keynesian belief in an equilibrium alignment of the labor market and the overall economy. As a result of a notion called "rational expectations," New Classical economics assumes that most observed variations in the unemployment rate are simply changes in the natural rate; since the only exceptions are temporary and random employment fluctuations in response to surprise events (such as a hike in the price of oil), the economy is, in effect, *always* at full employment. New Classical theory restores the laissez-faire viewpoint that dominated pre-Keynesian economics.

Among the contemporary economic theorists who have attempted to revive portions of Keynes's macroeconomic policy insights are New Keynesians and Post-Keynesians. New Keynesians accept much of New Classical theory but introduce a number of reasons why wages—nominal wages in some cases and real wages in others—might nonetheless fail to adjust to ensure full employment. The result is a role for government to raise employment by removing wage rigidities or, at least temporarily, by increasing aggregate demand. While most New Keynesians explain unemployment in terms of sticky wages, some offer an explanation rooted in price inflexibility. See, for example, the discussion of New Keynesian economics in Galbraith and Darity's *Macroeconomics* (1994, pp. 315–319).

Post-Keynesians go further than New Keynesians and reject the notion that wage levels are a significant determinant of employment. Indeed, unlike most New Keynesians, they argue that efforts to make wages more flexible can actually worsen unemployment. Like Keynes, meanwhile, Post-Keynesians emphasize the role of aggregate demand, which they see as liable to sudden fluctuations as a result of volatility in the expectations governing investment. Post-Keynesian theory indicates that the state has an inescapable role to play in stabilizing the economy and maximizing employment by judiciously managing the level and composition of public spending (Pressman 2001, pp. 104–111).

PUBLIC POLICY

In response to the Great Depression, a number of economists in the United States and the United Kingdom offered policy-oriented volumes that presented strategies to achieve full employment. Among the most well known is William H. Beveridge's *Full Employment in a Free Society* (1945). Other early books on full employment include Mordecai Ezekiel, *Jobs for All through Industrial Expansion* (1939), and John H. G. Pierson, *Full Employment* (1941). Beveridge defined full employment as follows: "It means having always more vacant jobs than unemployed [workers]. It means that the jobs are at fair wages, of such a kind, and so located that the unemployed can reasonably be expected to take them; it means, by consequence, that the normal lag between losing one job and finding another will be very short" (Beveridge 1945, p. 18).

Beveridge gave the public sector responsibility for influencing and supplementing private activity so as to achieve and sustain full employment. He outlined a three-pronged policy attack on joblessness: There must be enough jobs; industry must be encouraged to locate facil-ities with an eye to matching job opportunities to labor force skills; and workers must be provided with job vacancy information, relocation assistance, and perhaps even training or job-placement assistance. An annual public budget with outlays in five categories was identified as the main government tool: (1) funds for roads, schools, and other public goods; (2) investments in rail transit systems and other government-owned industries; (3) loans and other incentives to promote private investment (coordinated by a national investment board); (4) subsidies that reduce prices for essential consumer goods; and (5) income-redistribution programs, such as social security, to ensure robust consumer spending.

In 1946 the U.S. Congress passed the Employment Act, proposed by legislators with a view similar to that of Beveridge. According to the legislation, "It is the continuing policy and responsibility of the Federal Government … to promote maximum employment, production and purchasing power." The Employment Act included provisions establishing the Council of Economic Advisers to the President and requiring an annual Economic Report of the President, designed to track trends in economic performance, review existing economic policies, and recommend policy changes that would better enable the government to achieve its objectives (Bailey 1950, pp. 227–232).

In policy circles, a distinction has long been drawn between three forms of unemployment: frictional, cyclical, and structural. As mentioned above, frictional unemployment exists when workers are between jobs. Cyclical unemployment exists when aggregate demand is insufficient to hire all who are actively searching for work. And structural unemployment exists when there is a skill or geographic mismatch between available workers and unfilled jobs. In the early 1960s the Council of Economic Advisers set an average annual unemployment rate of 4 percent as an "interim target," reflecting their belief that this level was consistent with tackling cyclical unemployment. These and other economic analysts also believed that unemployment could fall further by means of worker training and additional efforts to attack structural and frictional sources of joblessness (Galenson 1966; Gordon and Gordon 1966).

By the mid-1970s, however, the U.S. unemployment rate exceeded 7 percent, leading a frustrated Congress to revise the Employment Act through passage of the Full Employment and Balanced Growth Act in 1978. The new law provided stronger language by substituting "full employment" for "maximum employment" as the nation's employment objective and mandated a 4 percent unemployment rate as the country's primary economic goal. However, in the absence of a requirement that the public sector must serve as "employer of last resort" when citizens are unable to find work, the 1978 change proved to have little practical impact on economic policy and performance.

Behind the U.S. employment legislation of 1946 and 1978 was a policy debate that continues in the early twenty-first century—a debate over whether citizens should have a publicly guaranteed right to a job. Whether there should be a "right to work" has long received academic and public attention, but President Franklin D. Roosevelt brought the issue to the fore in his 1944 State of the Union Address. In that speech, Roosevelt stated that the nation must be guided by a "second Bill of Rights," including "the right to a useful and remunerative job" (Roosevelt 1944). (For a much earlier argument in favor of the right to employment, see John R. Commons [1899].)

A number of policymakers who worked on the 1946 and 1978 Employment Acts wanted to secure the right to employment by enabling the unemployed to turn to the federal government for some form of "public works" or "public service" employment. Since the Great Depression, such job opportunities have often been made available to the unemployed, usually on a rather limited basis, through various federal programs (such as the Works Progress Administration, created in 1935, and the Comprehensive Employment and Training Act of 1973). The current focus of U.S. employment policy, however, is on helping workers find training for private employment, and even that effort receives limited public funding. Public service employment and institutional mechanisms needed to establish government as the employer of last resort continue to receive attention from academics (Wray and Forstater 2004; Kaboub 2007), but these ideas have little backing from federal lawmakers.

SEE ALSO *Beveridge Curve; Business Cycles, Theories; Economics, Keynesian; Economics, New Classical; Economics, New Keynesian; Economics, Post Keynesian; Employment; Friedman, Milton; Full Capacity; Great Depression; Inflation; Involuntary Unemployment; Job Guarantee; Keynes, John Maynard; Monetarism; Natural Rate of Unemployment; Neutrality of Money; Phillips Curve; Unemployment; Unemployment Rate; Voluntary Unemployment*

BIBLIOGRAPHY

Bailey, Stephen Kemp. 1950. *Congress Makes a Law: The Story behind the Employment Act of 1946.* New York: Columbia University Press.

Bennett, Amanda. 1997. Inflation Calculus: Business and Academia Clash over Economic Concept of "Natural" Jobless Rate. *Journal of Socio-Economics* 26 (3): 271–276.

Beveridge, William H. 1945. *Full Employment in a Free Society.* New York: Norton.

Commons, John R. 1899. The Right to Work. *Arena* 21 (2): 131–142.

Ezekiel, Mordecai. 1939. *Jobs for All through Industrial Expansion.* New York: Knopf.

Galbraith, James K., and William Darity Jr. 1994. *Macroeconomics.* Boston: Houghton Mifflin.

Galenson, Walter. 1966. *A Primer on Employment and Wages.* New York: Random House.

Gordon, Robert A., and Margaret S. Gordon, eds. 1966. *Prosperity and Unemployment.* New York: Wiley.

Kaboub, Fadhel. 2007. Institutional Adjustment Planning for Full Employment. *Journal of Economic Issues* 41 (2): 495–502.

Keynes, John Maynard. 1964. *The General Theory of Employment, Interest, and Money.* New York: Harcourt Brace Jovanovich. (Orig. pub. 1936).

Pierson, John H. G. 1941. *Full Employment.* New Haven, CT: Yale University Press.

Pressman, Steven. 2001. The Role of the State and the State Budget. In *A New Guide to Post Keynesian Economics,* ed. Richard P. F. Holt and Steven Pressman, 102–113. London: Routledge.

Roosevelt, Franklin D. 1944. State of the Union Address. January 11. http://teachingamericanhistory.org/library/index.asp?documentprint=463.

Wray, L. Randall, and Mathew Forstater. 2004. Full Employment and Social Justice. In *The Institutionalist Tradition in Labor Economics,* ed. Dell P. Champlin and Janet T. Knoedler, 253–272. Armonk, NY: Sharpe.

Charles J. Whalen

FULLER, BUCKMINSTER
1895–1983

Richard Buckminster "Bucky" Fuller defined himself as a "random element," and he has been described variously as an American visionary, architect, mathematician, inventor, designer, philosopher, and a "poet of technology" (Cruikshank 1981). He was the son of Richard Buckminster Fuller (who died when he was 12 years old) and Caroline Wolcott Andrews. He grew up in Maine and attended Milton Academy in Massachusetts. Later he was expelled twice from Harvard University. In his youth, he worked as a mechanic in a textile mill and as a laborer in a meatpacking plant. In 1917 he married Anne Hewlitt. After serving in the navy during World War I, Fuller and his father-in-law, the architect James Monroe Hewlitt, developed a company that produced lightweight, weatherproof, fireproof structures, but the company was unsuccessful and by 1927 Fuller was 32, bankrupt, and jobless. Living in substandard housing in Chicago, Fuller's young daughter, Alexandra, died of a contagious disease. Fuller blamed himself, became suicidal, and contemplated jumping into Lake Michigan, but he was saved by an epiphany that he should devote himself fully to the betterment of all humanity. He spent a year without speaking as a discipline to focus his thoughts.

Fuller published *Shelter* magazine in the 1930s. He was science and technology consultant for *Fortune* magazine from 1938 until 1940, then lectured at numerous universities, including Harvard and the Massachusetts Institute of Technology, and in the late 1950s he became a professor at Southern Illinois University, where he and Anne lived in a geodesic dome. In 1972 he was named "World Fellow in Residence" to a consortium of universities in Philadelphia, including the University of Pennsylvania. He retained his connection with both Southern Illinois University and the University of Pennsylvania until his death.

Fuller is perhaps best known for his invention of the geodesic dome. The dome's design is based on "tensegrity" structures—tetrahedrons (triangular pyramids) and octahedrons (polyhedron with eight faces, resembling two pyramids attached at their bases). The geodesic dome is a perfect symbol to represent Fuller's life-long examination of nature's geometry. While Fuller was at Black Mountain College in 1948, using lightweight plastics he designed a small dome that became the first building that could sustain its own weight with no practical limits. Using his focus on nature, he had conceptualized that the natural analytic geometry of the universe is based on arrays of tetrahedra; independent research indicates that the strongest possible homogeneous truss is cyclically tetrahedral.

Fuller coined the word *Dymaxion* (from DYnamic MAXimum tensION) and used it when conceptualizing many of his works, including the Dymaxion map, which was the first map to depict the entire planet earth on a single flat surface without visible distortion of the relative shapes and sizes of the continents. Another feature of the map is that it can be reconfigured to put different regions at the center; this perspective supported his philosophy that people must consider the world's problems systemically rather than politically or regionally. His conceptualization of "spaceship earth" promoted the idea that the earth provides all that humans need in order to survive, but also that humans need to be wise stewards of these resources. He argued that we are all world citizens and that borders are arbitrary and typically unhelpful constructs. This philosophy led to the creation of his "world game," a simulation and series of workshops that Fuller designed using the Dymaxion map to teach players how best to use the earth's abundance.

Fuller devoted his life's work as to the optimal ways for humanity to survive successfully on earth. He coined the term *ephemeralization*, which refers to the tendency for contemporary technology to be replaced by much smaller, lighter, and more efficient technologies that offer multifunctionality. This was true to Fuller's basic philosophy of learning from nature and doing more with less and producing less waste. Fuller also introduced the concept of *synergetics*, which refers to holistic engineering structures in nature and the blending of complementary factors that result in a product greater than the sum of its parts.

Some of his other key concepts and inventions include:

- Dymaxion house (1928)
- Aerodynamic Dymaxion car (1933)
- Prefabricated compact bathroom cell (1937)
- Tensegrity structures (1949)
- Geodesic dome for Ford Motor Company (1953)
- Patent on octet truss (1961)

Fuller was nominated for several Nobel Prizes, and he received the Medal of Freedom (the highest national award given to a civilian) for his "contributions as a geometrician, educator, and architect-designer" and the Gold Medal award from the American Institute of Architects. He was awarded twenty-five U.S. patents and he received forty-seven honorary degrees. In 1991 *Science* magazine voted the Buckminsterfullerene the "molecule of the year." The Buckminsterfullerene molecule, which consists of 60 carbon atoms and very closely resembles a spherical version of Fuller's geodesic dome, was named in his honor.

BIBLIOGRAPHY

PRIMARY WORKS

Fuller, Richard Buckminster. [1938] 2000. *Nine Chains to the Moon.* New York: Doubleday.

Fuller, Richard Buckminster. [1963] 2000. *Operating Manual for Spaceship Earth.* Princeton, NJ: Princeton Architectural Press.

Fuller, Richard Buckminster. [1969] 1972. *Utopia or Oblivion: The Prospects for Humanity.* New York: Viking.

Fuller, Richard Buckminster. 1975. *Synergetics: Explorations in the Geometry of Thinking.* New York: Scribner.

Fuller, Richard Buckminster. 1981. *Critical Path.* New York: St. Martin's Griffin.

Fuller, Richard Buckminster. 1985. *Inventions: The Patented Works of R. Buckminster Fuller.* New York: St. Martin's Press.

SECONDARY WORKS

Applewhite, Edward J., ed. 1986. *Synergetics Dictionary: The Mind of Buckminster Fuller.* New York: Garland.

Baldwin, Jay. 1997. *BuckyWorks: Buckminster Fuller's Ideas for Today.* New York: JohnWiley and Sons.

Buckminster Fuller Institute Web site. 2005. http://www.bfi.org/

Cruikshank, Linda. 1981. Bucky Fuller: Poet of Technology. *Vacaville (CA) Reporter* (March 8).

Edmondson, Amy C. 1987. *A Fuller Explanation*. Basel, Switzerland: Birkhauser.

Fearnley, Christopher J. 2002. The R. Buckminster Fuller FAQ. http://www.cjfearnley.com/fuller-faq.html.

Kenner, Hugh. 1973. *Bucky: A Guided Tour of Buckminster Fuller*. New York: Morrow.

Krausse, Joachim, and Claude Lichtenstein, eds. 1999. *Your Private Sky, R. Buckminster Fuller: The Art of Design Science*. Baden, Switzerland: Lars Mueller Publishers.

Marks, Robert W. [1960] 1973. *The Dymaxion World of Buckminster Fuller*. New York: Anchor Press.

O'Connor, John J., and Edmund F. Robertson. 2003. Richard Buckminster Fuller. MacTutor History of Mathematics Archive. http://www-history.mcs.st-andrews.ac.uk/Mathematicians/Fuller.html.

Peck, Stacey. In Search of a Better World, They Put Their Faith in the Power of the Mind. March 15, 1981. http://www.salsburg.com/flyseye/flyseye.html.

Snyder, Robert. 1980. *Buckminster Fuller: An Autobiographical Monologue/Scenario*. New York: St. Martin's Press.

Ward, James, ed. 1984. *The Artifacts of R. Buckminster Fuller, A Comprehensive Collection of His Designs and Drawings in Four Volumes*. Vol. 1: *The Dymaxion Experiment, 1926–1943*; Vol. 2: *Dymaxion Deployment, 1927–1946*; Vol. 3: *The Geodesic Revolution, Part 1, 1947–1959*; Vol. 4: *The Geodesic Revolution, Part 2, 1960–1983*. New York: Taylor and Francis.

Chris E. Stout

FUNCTIONAL FORM

A mathematical model involves an explicit set of equations that describe the relationships among the variables contained in the model. It is important to know not only which variables to include in the model, but also the proper functional forms of the mathematical equations. In the natural sciences, the functional forms are often known from the laws of nature. If a = acceleration, t = time, and d = displacement, the laws of physics dictate the functional form $d = at^2/2$. The problem of selecting the proper functional form is particularly difficult in the social sciences because the laws of human behavior are not as precise as the laws of nature. Moreover, the social sciences are not like the laboratory sciences, which allow for repeated experiments with the aim of determining the precise mathematical relationships among the variables.

Consider the general functional form for the case of two independent variables x_1 and x_2: $y = f(x_1, x_2, \varepsilon)$, where y is the dependent variable, x_1 and x_2 are the independent variables, and ε is the error term representing the variation in y not explained by x_1 and x_2. Although a particular theory might specify the signs of the partial relationships

between y, x_1, and x_2, the form of the function $f()$ is typically unknown. The standard procedure is to posit a linear relationship and to estimate the coefficients a_0, a_1, and a_2 in the regression equation $y = a_0 + a_1x_1 + a_2x_2 + \varepsilon$.

The linear form can be viewed as a first-order approximation of the function $f()$. For many circumstances, such approximations can be quite useful. However, if the continued application of either independent variable has, say, diminishing effects on y, the linear approximation will be invalid when the change in x_1 or x_2 is large. Similarly, the linear approximation might be poor if the effect of x_1 on y depends on the level of the variable x_2.

A popular alternative to the standard linear model is to express some or all of the variables in logarithmic form. Consider (1):

$$(1) \qquad \ln(y) = a_0 + a_1\ln(x_1) + a_2\ln(x_2) + \varepsilon_1$$

This is equivalent to $y = c(x_1)^{a1}(x_2)^{a2}\varepsilon$, where $a_0 = \ln(c)$ and $\varepsilon_1 = \ln(\varepsilon)$

Notice that equation (1) is linear as a result of the logarithms, so the coefficients can be easily estimated using linear regression methods. Also, the coefficients have the straightforward interpretation that a_i ($i = 1, 2$) is the percentage change in y resulting from a 1 percent change in x_i.

Other popular specifications include those using powers of the variables and their products. In the two-variable case, a second-order approximation is (2):

$$(2) \qquad y = a_0 + a_1x_1 + a_2x_2$$
$$+ a_{11}x_1^2 + a_{22}x_2^2 + a_{12}x_1x_2 + \varepsilon$$

It is important to use the correct functional form to obtain unbiased and consistent coefficient estimates of the effects of the independent variables on the dependent variable y. One way to select the functional form is to use a general-to-specific methodology: Estimate a very general nonlinear form and, through hypothesis testing, determine whether it is possible to pare down the model to a more specific form. In equation (2), if a_{11}, a_{22}, and a_{12} are not significantly different from zero, it can be claimed that the linear form is more appropriate than the second-order approximation. When searching over many different functional forms, the usual t-tests and F-tests of statistical significance, as well as the usual measures of fit, such as R^2, are generally not appropriate, however. As one adds regressors and allows for more general functional forms, the fit of the regression to the data will necessarily improve. Moreover, since every sample has a few unusual observations, there is the danger that a general-specification search will lead to overfitting the data, in the sense of selecting an overly complicated functional form. Hence, in a specification search of the most appropriate functional form, most researchers use the specific-to-general methodology: Estimate a simple model, and perform a number of diagnostic checks to determine whether the model is adequate. Then estimate a more complicated specification only if there is some sort of diagnostic failure. Some diagnostic tests, such as Ramsey's (1969) RESET, attempt to determine whether the regression's error terms are truly random. Others, such as Brown, Durbin, and Evan's (1975) CUSUM test, attempt to determine whether the regression coefficients are constant over the entire sample. Nonrandom errors and/or nonconstant coefficients indicate that the functional form of the estimating equation is incorrect.

Another method that can be used to select the most appropriate functional form is out-of-sample forecasting (in which the researcher holds back a portion of the observations from the estimation process and estimates the alternative models over the shortened span of data). Forecasts from the alternative models are compared to the actual values of the data held back. The model with the smallest forecast errors is deemed the best.

SEE ALSO *Regression*

BIBLIOGRAPHY

Brown, R. L., J. Durbin, and J. M. Evans. 1975. Techniques for Testing the Constancy of Regression Relationships over Time. *Journal of the Royal Statistical Society*, Series B, 37: 149–192.

Ramsey, J. B. 1969. Tests for Specification Errors in Classical Least-Squares Regression Analysis. *Journal of the Royal Statistical Society*, Series B, 31: 350–371.

Walter Enders

FUNCTIONALISM

The term *functionalism* has been used in at least three different senses in the social sciences. In the philosophy of mind, functionalism is a view about the nature of mental states. In sociology and anthropology, functionalism is an approach to understanding social processes in terms of their contribution to the operation of a social system. In psychology, functionalism was an approach to mental phenomena that emphasized mental processes as opposed to static mental structures.

FUNCTIONALISM IN THE PHILOSOPHY OF MIND

Functionalism in the philosophy of mind was first systematically developed in the 1960s as a view about the nature

of mental states such as sensations, beliefs, desires, and emotions. It arose in response to questions about the relation between mind and body, in the context of a debate between opposed views known as *dualism* and *materialism*. Dualism was defended by the seventeenth-century philosopher René Descartes (1596–1650), who held that minds were nonphysical substances that were not located in space and indeed had no physical properties at all. A major difficulty for dualists has been to explain how mental states, if they have no physical properties, can cause or be caused by physical states of a person's body. Materialists, by contrast, have held that there are no nonphysical substances, and that mental states are nothing more than physical states.

The best-known materialist views in the 1950s were *behaviorism* and the *identity theory*. Behaviorism as a theory of the nature of mental states is sometimes called *logical behaviorism* to distinguish it from behaviorism as a methodological view in psychology. According to behaviorism, mental states were simply tendencies to behave in certain ways under certain circumstances. Behaviorists thus rejected not only dualism, but also the commonsense view that mental states are internal states that are causes of behavior. Identity theorists, on the other hand, held that mental states were identical with states of the central nervous system. The identity theory appeared to rule out by definition the possibility that mental states could be present in any being that did not have a human central nervous system.

Functionalism was intended to be a theory that was compatible with materialism, while avoiding the difficulties of behaviorism and the identity theory. It was motivated in part by the thought that the relation between mind and body is analogous to the relation between software and hardware in a computer. Computational states are defined, not in terms of specific hardware configurations, but in terms of their relations to inputs, outputs, and other computational states. Computational states are *multiply realizable*; that is, they can be realized or implemented by a wide range of different kinds of hardware. Functionalists held that a similar approach could be taken to mental states; that is, mental states could be defined as relations between perceptual inputs, behavioral outputs, and other functional states. For example, the beginnings of a functionalist analysis of pain might point out that it is a state that is produced by potentially harmful sensory inputs, leads to avoidance behaviors, and tends to produce such other mental states as a dislike for whatever caused the pain. According to the functionalist, it is relationships such as these, not a specific physical implementation, that are essential to pain.

Functionalism seems to avoid the difficulties of the other main approaches to the nature of mental states.

Because mental states, like computational states, must be implemented in a physical medium, functionalism seems to make it less mysterious than dualism how mental states can stand in causal relations with physical states of the body. Unlike behaviorism, functionalism is compatible with the view that mental states are internal causes of behavior. And unlike the identity theory, functionalism leaves open the possibility that beings very unlike humans could nevertheless have mental states.

Different versions of functionalism have been developed by different writers. The view described above most closely resembles the *machine functionalism* defended by Hilary Putnam in a number of papers reprinted in his *Mind, Language, and Reality* (1975). Somewhat different versions were defended by other writers; David Braddon-Mitchell and Frank Jackson offer a useful survey in their *Philosophy of Mind and Cognition* (1996), and a number of the original papers are reprinted in *Readings in the Philosophy of Psychology* (1980), edited by Ned Block.

The most serious difficulty for functionalism is the problem of accounting for conscious experiences, which philosophers call *qualia*. One thought experiment that illustrates the problem involves the apparent possibility of *inverted qualia*. It seems possible in principle that two people could be functionally identical even though their experiences were inverted, so that when one person saw something green, that person had an experience that felt to him or her the way an experience of something red felt to the other. If this is a real possibility, it follows that functionalism cannot be a complete account of the nature of all mental states, since if two people with identical functional properties could nevertheless have different qualia, then qualia cannot be functional states.

FUNCTIONALISM IN SOCIOLOGY AND ANTHROPOLOGY

In sociology, functionalism was a theoretical perspective that emphasized that the parts of a social system are interrelated in such a way that none of them can be fully understood except in terms of their effects on the others. The relationships between the parts of a social system constitute the structures of that system, and social structures, social processes, and other social phenomena are to be explained in terms of their functions, which are, for most theorists, their contributions to the continued stable existence of the system. The social systems to which functional analysis was applied ranged from units as small as the family to those as large as international organizations; the phenomena to which functions were imputed included social roles, social norms, devices for social control, and many others.

Functionalism originated in the late nineteenth century in the work of such thinkers as Herbert Spencer (1820–1903) and Émile Durkheim (1858–1917); it was developed in the early twentieth century as an approach to anthropology by A. R. Radcliffe-Brown (1881–1955) and Bronislaw Malinowski (1884–1942); and in the middle decades of the twentieth century, as elaborated by Talcott Parsons (1902–1979) and Robert Merton (1910–2003), it became the dominant perspective in American sociology.

Some functionalist writers were influenced by an analogy between societies and biological organisms, and their concept of social function was explicitly modeled on that of biological function. Radcliffe-Brown, for instance, in "Structure and Function in Primitive Society" (1935, reprinted in Coser and Rosenberg 1976), distinguishes between three sets of sociological problems: *social morphology*, which identifies social structures just as biological morphology identifies organic structures; *social physiology*, which identifies the functions of these structures; and *development*, which studies how new social structures arise, much as evolutionary theory explains the development of new kinds of organisms.

Functionalists have typically thought of the function of a social activity as its contribution to the needs of the society, especially to a social equilibrium, which tends to right itself if disturbed. Durkheim, in the first systematic development of a functionalist approach, distinguished between the cause of an activity such as the punishment of crime, on the one hand, and its function, on the other. The practice of punishment may initially be caused by an intention to deter crime or achieve justice, but its function, according to Durkheim, is to maintain our intense emotional disapproval of crime. Although a particular practice or activity may not initially be caused by a recognition of the function it will serve, Durkheim holds that its serving a useful function is nevertheless part of the explanation of the continued survival of that practice.

Malinowski, who introduced the term *functionalism* into anthropology, identified seven fundamental biological needs: metabolism, reproduction, bodily comforts, safety, movement, growth, and health, as well as *derived needs*, such as the need to produce goods and the need to regulate behavior. He held that the function of social processes was ultimately to satisfy these individual needs. Radcliffe-Brown rejected this view, going so far as to write that "as a consistent opponent of Malinowski's functionalism I may be called an anti-functionalist" ("Functionalism: A Protest" [1949], reprinted in Kuper 1977, p. 49). Although he regarded the concept of function as central to anthropology, in his view the function of social processes was not to satisfy individual needs, but rather to support or preserve social structures. Radcliffe-Brown's view is often called *structural functionalism* to distinguish it from Malinowski's.

The sociologists most closely associated with functionalism in the mid-twentieth century were Talcott Parsons and Robert Merton. (The terms *functionalism* and *structural functionalism* are both used to describe their work.) Parsons identified four functions that any social system needs in order to achieve and maintain equilibrium. These were: *adaptation*, or the acquisition and distribution of resources from the environment; *goal attainment*, which involves determining which goals of the system have priority and determining how to achieve them; *integration*, which involves coordinating relationships between various social actors to enable them to function smoothly together; and *latent pattern maintenance-tension management*, which involves transmitting values that will keep actors motivated to act in ways that are necessary for the continued functioning of the system.

Merton's contributions included his distinction between *manifest functions*, which are consequences that agents in the system recognize and intend to produce, and *latent functions*, which are not intended or recognized. Whereas Parsons had tended to emphasize manifest functions, Merton stressed that many important functions are latent. Merton also introduced the concept of *dysfunctions*, which are consequences of an activity that have negative effects on the stability of the system.

By the late 1970s, functionalism was no longer the dominant paradigm in sociology, in part because of the perceived conservatism of its emphasis on equilibrium, and its consequent lack of attention to social conflict and change, and in part because it was seen more as a set of abstract categories than as a testable empirical theory. In the 1980s and 1990s, there was some interest in a *neofunctionalist* sociology that attempted to preserve the insights of functionalism, especially as represented in Parsons's work, while addressing its perceived failings.

FUNCTIONALISM IN PSYCHOLOGY

In psychology, the term *functionalism* refers to an American school of psychology that was influential at the turn of the nineteenth century. Functionalism developed in response to the earlier structuralist view advanced by Wilhelm Wundt (1832–1920) and Edward B. Titchener (1867–1927). Structuralist psychology used an introspectionist methodology to attempt to identify basic elements of conscious experience into which more complex experiences, or structures, could be analyzed. Functionalism, by contrast, emphasized psychological processes rather than static psychological structures. Functionalism also stressed the role of the mind as a mediator between the environment and the needs of the organism; like the pragmatist philosophy that influenced it, functionalism held that

psychological processes should be understood in terms of their effects. The most influential contributors to this school were the pragmatist philosophers William James (1842–1910) and John Dewey (1859–1952), and the University of Chicago psychologist James Rowland Angell (1869–1949). Although functionalism influenced later approaches to psychology, as a distinct school it faded from view in the early decades of the twentieth century, as behaviorism rose to prominence.

SEE ALSO *Anthropology; Behaviorism; Durkheim, Émile; Identity; James, William; Malinowski, Bronislaw; Materialism; Merton, Robert K.; Parsons, Talcott; Philosophy; Pragmatism; Psychology; Radcliffe-Brown, A. R.; Sociology; Spencer, Herbert; Structuralism; Theory of Mind*

BIBLIOGRAPHY

Alexander, Jeffrey C. 1997. *Neofunctionalism and After*. Oxford: Blackwell.

Angell, James Rowland. 1907. The Province of Functional Psychology. *Psychological Review* 14: 61–91.

Block, Ned, ed. 1980. *Readings in Philosophy of Psychology*, Vol. 1. Cambridge, MA: Harvard University Press.

Braddon-Mitchell, David, and Frank Jackson. 1996. *Philosophy of Mind and Cognition*. Oxford: Blackwell.

Coser, Lewis A., and Bernard Rosenberg, eds. 1976. *Sociological Theory: A Book of Readings*. 4th ed. New York: Macmillan.

Kuper, Adam, ed. 1977. *The Social Anthropology of Radcliffe-Brown*. London: Routledge and Kegan Paul.

Levin, Janet. 2004. Functionalism. In *The Stanford Encyclopedia of Philosophy*, ed. Edward N. Zalta. http://plato.stanford.edu/entries/functionalism/.

Malinowski, Bronislaw. 1944. *A Scientific Theory of Culture and Other Essays*. Chapel Hill: University of North Carolina Press.

Putnam, Hilary. 1975. *Mind, Language, and Reality*. Cambridge, U.K.: Cambridge University Press.

Wallace, Ruth A., and Alison Wolf. 2005. *Contemporary Sociological Theory: Expanding the Classical Tradition*. 6th ed. Upper Saddle River, NJ: Prentice Hall.

Curtis Brown

FUNCTIONINGS

The concept of functionings was introduced by the Indian economist Amartya Sen in *Commodities and Capabilities* (1985), in the context of the "equality of what" debate. This debate involved scholars interested in the definition of social justice after the influential work of the American political philosopher John Rawls (1971). Rawls defined social justice in terms of equality of rights and of priority given to individuals who receive the smallest quantity of basic resources (which he called *primary goods*). This view represented a striking break with the utilitarian tradition focusing on individuals' subjective well-being and launched a debate about the quantity that should be equalized across individuals in a just society: welfare, resources, opportunities, and so on.

Sen criticized Rawls's choice of a resource metric for the definition of social justice on the grounds that different individuals may have different abilities to transform resources into achievements of various kinds. He called such achievements *functionings*, encompassing all achievements, not only actions (*doings*) but also states of the body and the mind (*beings*), that might be considered relevant. For instance, an individual's level of happiness is a functioning, as well as his marital status, his income, the kind of job he has, and how much he works. Sen, however, did not propose to define social justice as equality of some index of functionings across individuals, or as priority for those who have the smallest level of functionings. He argued that what is important, out of concern for freedom and responsibility, is not that people actually have good levels of functionings, but that they have access to such levels. The set of functioning levels that an individual is able to achieve is called a *capability*, or *capability set*, in his theory, and he favors a definition of social justice in terms of equality of capabilities (or priority for the worst off in terms of capabilities).

One difficulty with the concepts of functionings and capabilities as used in Sen's theory is that they are so large that one must find ways to determine how to weigh the importance of various functionings in the construction of a synthetic index. Whether individuals' personal preferences or expert opinion about prudential values should be relied upon in such an exercise is open to controversy. A list of important functionings has been proposed by Martha Nussbaum. There are also alternative theories of justice that combine the double concern for unequal abilities on the one hand and freedom and responsibility on the other hand in different ways, as in Richard Arneson's equality of opportunity for welfare (which singles out subjective welfare as the only ultimately relevant functioning) or Ronald Dworkin's equality of resources (which includes personal abilities in the definition of resources). Some authors (Elizabeth Anderson, John Baker, and Marc Fleurbaey) have argued that achievements (functionings) and not only opportunities (capabilities) are relevant for the evaluation of individual situations in terms of social justice.

The notion of functionings has been influential in empirical measurements of standards of living, most notably in the United Nations Development Program construction of a "human development index" that adds education and health data to income statistics for the comparison of countries. Many other applications are being pursued. A Human Development and Capabilities Association was created in 2004.

SEE ALSO *Needs; Needs, Basic; Sen, Amartya Kumar; Want Creation; Wants*

BIBLIOGRAPHY

Anderson, Elizabeth S. 1999. What is the Point of Equality? *Ethics* 109: 287–337.

Arneson, Richard J. 1989. Equality and Equal Opportunity for Welfare. *Philosophical Studies* 56: 77–93.

Baker, John, Kathleen Lynch, Sarah Cantillon, and Judy Walsh. 2004. *Equality: From Theory to Action*. Basingstoke, U.K.: Palgrave Macmillan.

Dworkin, Ronald. 2000. *Sovereign Virtue: The Theory and Practice of Equality*. Cambridge, MA: Harvard University Press.

Fleurbaey, Marc. 1995. Equal Opportunity or Equal Social Outcome? *Economics & Philosophy* 11: 25–55.

Nussbaum, Martha C., and Amartya K. Sen, eds. 1993. *The Quality of Life*. Oxford: Clarendon Press.

Rawls, John. 1971. *A Theory of Justice*. Cambridge, MA: Harvard University Press.

Sen, Amartya K. 1985. *Commodities and Capabilities*. Amsterdam: North-Holland.

Sen, Amartya K. 1992. *Inequality Reexamined*. Oxford: Clarendon Press.

Marc Fleurbaey

FUNDAMENTALISM

Fundamentalism originally referred to an American Protestant movement occurring at the turn of the twentieth century. It emerged from an interdenominational revivalist movement led by the evangelist preacher Dwight Moody (1837–1899). In the early part of the twentieth century, fundamentalism came to stand for opposition to certain trends in modern society, including the rise of liberal theology, science's challenge to religious beliefs, and increasing secularization of society in general.

In the early twenty-first century, scholars have referred to a worldwide fundamentalist movement that includes various faith traditions. This more recent use of the term *fundamentalism* shows its usefulness for capturing the form and functions of a great many religious groups and their agendas. As used by scholars, the term is meant to describe, not evaluate.

At the heart of fundamentalist movements, then, is their revolt against modernism and their call to return to the basic beliefs and practices of their original community and, most importantly, to the basic beliefs found in sacred texts such as the Bible and the Qur'an. Scholars' composite pictures of fundamentalist groups often represent them as energetic, sometimes aggressive, and, contrary to current stereotypes, only occasionally violent.

Fundamentalists feel that certain developments associated with modernism undermine religious identity and their own religious worldview. They believe these developments undermine the ability to lead a morally pure life and, in some cases, a life that prepares for the afterlife. Their concern is not with developments in technology and science per se but only with those developments that challenge their religious worldview and/or have moral implications—as when Darwinian evolutionary theory spawned social Darwinism with its counter-Christian ethic of survival of the fittest. As this example of social Darwinism indicates, fundamentalists' complaints about modernism are not altogether different from the complaints of many non-fundamentalists.

In North America, the term fundamentalism has often been used interchangeably with the term *evangelical*, although more so at the beginning of the fundamentalist movement than in the twenty-first century. Evangelical refers to the winning or saving of souls. To evangelize, then, means to lead others to becoming saved. North American fundamentalists are all about being saved and saving others: saved by believing in Jesus as the Lord and saved by accepting the Bible as the inerrant word of God.

For fundamentalists, being saved involves more than attending church or trying hard to lead a good life. Being saved, say the fundamentalists and evangelicals, entails no less than a total commitment to Christ and a total belief in the Bible. To be a North American, Protestant fundamentalist is, then, to embrace a biblical perspective that is clear, free from contradiction, and rejecting of alternative, non-fundamentalist worldviews. Being ecumenical is not, then, a part of the fundamentalist agenda. Therefore, North American Protestant fundamentalism, like other forms of fundamentalism around the world, runs counter to the dominant worldview in most societies today, a worldview that values pluralism and accepts there being multiple perspectives on what is true and valuable.

Nor is it a fundamentalist agenda to promote a separation of religion and state, a separation that has been central in North American and European democratic traditions. This is even more evident in Arab regions of the world where Islamic fundamentalism works to unite societies under Islamic law and under Islamic religious leadership.

Worldwide fundamentalism has been, then, both separatist and integrationist in spirit and political life. That is, while fundamentalists speak of the need to separate one's self from the unsaved and from this sinful or corrupt world they also speak of the need for humankind to become a single, religious community.

Fundamentalism is not simply about returning to a distant past or living in the present according to truths and prescriptions revealed in the distant past. It is also about working and waiting for an imagined future. In North American Christian fundamentalism, the imagined future is the Second Coming of Christ or *Parousia*, a time when sinners (non-believers) will be judged and the Kingdom of God will be established.

This theme of there being a cataclysmic future event or time when sinners will be judged and the righteous and true believers will prevail is not just a theme in North American Protestant Christian fundamentalism. It is also a theme in non-Christian, non-Western fundamentalist movements. All fundamentalist movements uphold the general theme that today's secular, pluralistic society will be replaced by a mono-religious society.

Non-fundamentalists often negatively stereotype fundamentalists. For example, fundamentalists are often pictured as being less educated on average, more authoritarian and dogmatic, anti-science, militant, and narrow-mindedly literal in their reading of sacred texts such as the Bible. However, the results of responsible research have shown each of these stereotypes to be distortions of the truth. In fact, fundamentalists make up a diverse group with respect to education, personality traits, and views about science and militancy. Furthermore, fundamentalists generally acknowledge the need to reflect and interpret when reading the sacred text. For fundamentalists, in general, discerning the revealed truth in the sacred text does not require taking each word, phrase, sentence, or portion literally.

Fundamentalism has and will continue to appeal to large segments of societies, especially in troubled times and in times of rapid transition. Its greatest appeal is in its offering clarity where there is doubt, order and continuity where there is disorder and discontinuity, and hope for being good and being saved where there is despair over being sinful and being lost. Fundamentalism appeals to a significant and diverse group for its providing a worldview and way of interpreting life that provides meaning, guidance, and personal satisfaction.

Despite these positive attributes, fundamentalism will likely continue to be rejected by the majority and for several reasons. First, its appeal to return to previous ways runs counter to the majority's desire to develop new ways that reflect new conditions in modern life. Second, its appeal to adopt an uncompromising perspective, one that does not value alternative faith traditions and alternative worldviews, runs counter to the majority's desire to value cultural and religious diversity so as to live harmoniously in a pluralistic society. Third, its appeal to believe in the inerrant, revealed truth of sacred texts runs counter to the philosophical and scientific ways of thinking that pervade modern academic and political institutions.

SEE ALSO *Christianity; Islam, Shia and Sunni*

BIBLIOGRAPHY

Hood, Ralph W., Peter C. Hill, and Paul Williamson. 2005. *The Psychology of Religious Fundamentalism.* New York: Guilford Press.

Marsden, George M. 1980. *Fundamentalism and American Culture: The Shaping of Twentieth Century Evangelicalism 1870–1925.* New York: Oxford University Press.

Marty, Martin E., and R. Scott Appleby, eds. 1991–1995. *The Fundamentalism Project.* 5 vols. Chicago: University of Chicago Press.

Williamson, W. P. 2002. Another Look at Fundamentalism: A New Model. *Psychology of Religion Newsletter: American Psychological Association* 36: 1–13.

W. George Scarlett

FUNDAMENTALISM, CHRISTIAN

Christian Fundamentalism is a twentieth-century development that originated in American Protestant circles. While most attention to the phenomenon still focuses on the United States, thanks to missionary endeavors, it is now represented around the Christian world.

While many casual observers often speak of fundamentalism as if it were the equivalent of Protestant conservatism, traditionalism, or orthodoxy, scholars point to significant differences. The word *fundamentalism* appears in no encyclopedias or dictionaries before the 1920s, a fact which signals that some new reality was on the scene, one that would evoke new terminology. Fundamentalism in its broadest sense is a defensive reaction against uncongenial and threatening forces that are often code-named *modernism.* The conservatisms that were already on the scene had developed gradually over the centuries. Modern fundamentalism appeared suddenly, when the perceived threats seemed unbearable.

The word first appeared in the name of an association in 1919 and a Baptist magazine in 1920. The editor, perceiving assaults on the faith as he knew it, complained that in the Baptist church most people wanted to be conservative, but no one would do battle for the Lord. He called for reaction—and *reaction* is the key word for understanding fundamentalism—by people who would "do battle for the Lord." The ensuing fundamentalist-modernist controversy led to some schisms in Baptist and Presbyterian denominations, and issued in a proliferation of Bible colleges, missionary societies, charitable agencies, and radio stations and programs that carried the message and work forward.

The main challenges in the 1920s were *evolution,* the teaching that human descent resulted from natural selection and, as the fundamentalists saw it, apart from the work of God or the story of the world's creation in the Bible. Another strand of thought that went into fundamentalist formation was a view that the world would end in a cataclysm, after which through one of a variety of scenarios, Jesus would return to rule for a millennium. Fundamentalists also favored the adjective *literal* as opposed to *symbolic* or *allegorical* when treating biblical miracles or teachings that Jesus was born of a virgin and was physically resurrected. The lynchpin of fundamentalism, however, came to be fiercely defended theories of biblical inerrancy, which held on a kind of philosophical ground that there were and could not have been any errors of historical, geographical, scientific, or any other sorts in the Bible.

Early fundamentalists faced scorn in the culture at large and were opposed by moderates in the Protestant denominations, yet they endured. In 1942 some of them organized as a national association, a move that was countered a year later by more moderate fundamentalists who came to call themselves *evangelical.* Evangelicalism, popularized by figures like Billy Graham, agreed with fundamentalism on most teachings, but evangelicals were culturally more moderate and they came to outnumber the hard-core fundamentalists.

As decades passed, moderate evangelicals came to prosper more than did fundamentalists. Fundamentalists tended to be separatist, reluctant to cooperate with even conservative Protestants who did not share every detail of their doctrines. Evangelicals moved more toward the cultural mainstream, and their leaders often shared platforms and programs with certain kinds of Catholics and mainline Protestants. Evangelicals and fundamentalists, who share so much by way of doctrine, have adopted quite different styles, and the separatism of fundamentalism has held it back in the competition for souls and influence.

For decades, fundamentalists professed to be and ordinarily were disengaged from politics, concentrating as they did on evangelizing, converting, and preparing believers for life in heaven. In the final third of the twentieth century, however, while some stayed back from the frays, most fundamentalists plunged eagerly into politics. The Supreme Court decisions that disallowed prayer in public schools in 1962 and 1963, followed by a decision that allowed for legalized abortion in 1973, galvanized fundamentalists. They did an about-face and developed sophisticated approaches to mass media, originally through radio but later using television and the Internet, and made political alliances with Republicans. In coalition with conservatives they came to have considerable power in electoral politics and in legislation.

Social scientists observe fundamentalists in various social circumstances and classes. Often typed as rural and lower-class in the early years, many of them became prosperous urbanites and suburbanites, and were known for erecting large churches and producing television programs, supporting colleges such as Jerry Falwell's Liberty University in Virginia, and favoring participation in the affluent society with a zest that would have appalled their grandparents. Christian rock music, Christian films and best-selling books, and Christian self-help programs took on the trappings of their worldly counterparts. In doing so, fundamentalists helped create a culture within the culture, a kind of Jesus-centered replica of their more secular counterparts.

Most fundamentalists inherited and fostered efforts to convert others, as their ancestors in less-threatened nineteenth-century evangelical Protestantism had done. Large numbers of them, particularly in the dominant Southern Baptist tradition, insisted on adult baptism after conversion, and brought a biblical concept of being "born again" into the cultural spotlight. There have been few pacifists among the fundamentalists, most of them being strong supporters of military ventures by the United States and expressing themselves as dedicated patriots. On such grounds, they were suspicious of cultural, social, and political moderates and liberals, and often lumped them together as the "other" who was "secular humanist." Fundamentalists tend to create psychic boundaries and spiritual distance from others, fearing that ecumenical or interreligious ventures would lead to a weakening of the faith that as militants they claim is the only valid form of approach to God.

SEE ALSO *Christianity; Jesus Christ; Religion*

BIBLIOGRAPHY

Ammerman, Nancy. 1987. *Bible Believers: Fundamentalists in the Modern World.* New Brunswick, NJ: Rutgers University Press.

Carpenter, Joel A. 1997. *Revive Us Again: The Reawakening of American Fundamentalism.* New York: Oxford University Press.

Marsden, George M. 2006. *Fundamentalism and American Culture.* 2nd ed. New York: Oxford University Press.

Martin E. Marty

FUNDAMENTALISM, ISLAMIC

The term *Islamic fundamentalists* commonly refers to groups who seek to promote the role of Islam in political, social, and economic life, and who contend the necessity of establishing an Islamic state based on Islamic *sharia* law. The term *Islamic extremists*, in contrast, refers to fundamentalist groups who operate outside the law and espouse violence to attain political power.

Islamic fundamentalist movements in the Middle East and North Africa claim to represent a periphery whose political recognition and economic interests have been excluded by incompetent, corrupt, and authoritarian pro-Western regimes. The sluggish performance of these states vis-à-vis the demands of civil society for greater political participation and socioeconomic equality has led many disenfranchised young people to support Islamic fundamentalist movements as a mode of protest. The limited ability of modern nation-states to overcome these domestic problems has become increasingly acute as a result of fiscal restrictions on their redistributive capacities in the era of globalization. In addition, Islamic fundamentalist movements view the globalization process as an imperialist plot to pollute their countries with Western businesses and consumption patterns, and to impose painful adjustment reforms arranged by international financial institutions. Moreover, these fundamentalist movements are often motivated by political grievances with what they consider to be inconsistent U.S. foreign policy toward the Islamic world.

Islamic fundamentalist movements often use populist rhetoric laced with anti-Western attitudes, and they rely on previously mobilized Islamic mission-oriented groups who have not benefited from open-door economic policies. Islamic fundamentalists perceive their relationship with the incompetent pro-Western regimes as a zero-sum game. In the majority of cases, these movements occupy part of the political space as important countermovements or sources of opposition to existing authoritarian (and mostly secularist) regimes, and as such they have enjoyed relative legitimacy. The tyrannical states, in turn, have responded with security crackdowns and tougher regimentation measures, and in so doing have pushed moderates toward more radical positions. The polarization between Islamic fundamentalist movements and their countries' incumbent regimes has been growing since the mid-1980s as the globalization process has deepened.

Historically, Muslim responses to the challenge of Western colonialism have affected the current tension between Islamic movements and the regimes under which they operate. The colonial era resulted in the incorporation of the countries of the Middle East and North Africa into the capitalist world system, and in the consolidation of internally bureaucratic and externally territorial states. The colonial legacy also contributed to the deficient nature of state building and capitalist development in the region. The most problematic legacy from the colonial era is overdeveloped states coupled with underdeveloped social structures. The state apparatus during the colonial period was not created by national bourgeoisie but by foreign colonial administrators who inflated the size of the bureaucratic machine, especially its military and security sectors, to serve the colonialists' own purposes and to confront any possible resistance. The rulers of the postcolonial states produced much the same type of effect via the creation of authoritarian systems with a lopsided size of state to society features but without a hegemonic and independent social class. Furthermore, under the forms of capitalism artificially established, the state role has been even more exaggerated in order to promote delayed capitalist development in the name of national interest. In such circumstances, social classes are excessively dependent on the state, and the absolute primacy of the state resulted in an embryonic class structure in these countries immediately after their independence.

Most governments in the Middle East and North Africa are characterized by a coercive security apparatus, a lack of legitimacy, and inefficient administration. They also tend to be nondemocratic, despite their differing or even contradictory ideological bases. When these states' attempts at capitalist development were undertaken by a small group of crony capitalists operating within a rigid bureaucracy, the military and security sectors resorted to raw coercion, and they repressed Islamic fundamentalist movements in order to preserve their invested interests. Although the state is supreme, the society is primordial and indeterminate in terms of its economic and political functions. The primacy of the state has in fact hindered the development of Islamic fundamentalist movements in the Middle East and North Africa, and most Islamist movements in the region have not developed organizational strength. They have, however, exhibited greater militancy toward the state and less coordination with civil society, which has resulted in greater repression by the state. Although exclusion and repression by the authoritarian states helped forge a sense of solidarity in Islamic society, the fundamentalist movements have exhibited a lack of centralized bargaining power at the national level. Islamist fundamentalist groups tend to push their own agendas regardless of the deleterious consequences for civil society as a whole, which has ultimately caused them to become more marginalized.

SEE ALSO *Jihad; Muslims; Nation of Islam; Secular, Secularism, Secularization; Taliban*

BIBLIOGRAPHY

Anderson, Lisa. 1987. The State in the Middle East and North Africa. *Comparative Politics* 20 (1): 1–18.

Ayubi, Nazih. 1995. *Over-Stating the Arab State: Politics and Society in the Middle East*. London: Tauris.

Diamond, Larry, Marc F. Plattner, and Daniel Brumberg, eds. 2003. *Islam and Democracy in the Middle East*. Baltimore, MD: Johns Hopkins University Press.

Esposito, John. 1999. *The Islamic Threat: Myth or Reality?* New York: Oxford University Press.

Henry, Clement M., and Robert Springborg. 2001. *Globalization and the Politics of Development in the Middle East*. Cambridge, U.K.: Cambridge University Press.

Mamdani, Mahmood. 2004. *Good Muslim, Bad Muslim: America, the Cold War, and the Roots of Terror*. New York: Pantheon.

Norton, Augustus Richard, ed. 1995–1996. *Civil Society in the Middle East*. 2 vols. Leiden, Netherlands: Brill.

Owen, Roger. 2004. *State, Power, and Politics in the Making of the Modern Middle East*. 3rd ed. London: Routledge.

Ji-Hyang Jang

FUNERALS

Polish anthropologist Bronislaw Malinowski once observed that when persons are actually "faced by death," they turn almost immediately instead "to the promise of life." In other words, "death and its denial—immortality"—coincide (1954, p. 47). In many ways funerals express these dualities and their contrasting, ambivalent feelings and realities. In effect, funerals commonly aim to turn death, which appears to represent an end, into its opposite, a transition to another kind of life. Moreover, they seek to reintegrate the group and especially those most bereaved following the sense of loss that death has eventuated.

The funeral is almost always a social occasion, a ceremony at which those with a relationship to the deceased or the bereaved are assembled in order to mark the change in status that death has occasioned. The function of the funeral is to dispose of the corpse and to recognize the sense of loss among the bereaved. It also seeks to demonstrate to all of the assembled that while a particular person has died, life itself and the group go on. Hence while the disposal of the cadaver, an essential feature of the funeral, expresses dread of the corpse and a desire to be rid of it and its impurities while also confirming the reality and finality of the death, almost everything else about the funeral asserts immortality and continuity: of the soul, the community, a relationship with the deceased, and faith in the future.

The public nature of the funeral as well as the common understanding that attendance at it trumps most other social obligations both reflect the fact that death is never just the concern of the immediately bereaved or only the affliction of those who have died. While ostensibly carried out for the dead person, the funeral rites in fact have important effects and benefits for the living, both as individuals and a group. These rites commonly entail practices that aim to confront death with repeated assertions of life and expressions and ceremonial displays that make the bereaved feel that they are not completely abandoned. Moreover, they aim to show that death may momentarily bring about chaos, but the funeral reinstates order. It does so with ritual.

At a funeral's successful conclusion, the dead body is disposed of and becomes separated from the person who inhabited it and the living are endowed with an enhanced sense of solidarity as they mourn and console one another back to life, while incorporating the deceased as part of a living memory. While this process is largely metaphorical in most funeral ceremonies, in some cases, the process is quite literal. Among the Melanesians of New Guinea, for example, parts of the dead person are ingested by some of the bereaved and later vomited. This practice allows the spirit of the deceased to remain within, and a sense of solidarity both among the mourners and between the mourners and the deceased to be established while the physical remains of the corpse are removed. The Catholic rite of communion, in which the body and spirit of Christ is ingested by those who recall him through the eating of consecrated bread and wine, may be understood as a reiteration of such funereal rites. All this shows that death ends a life but not a relationship.

Funerals may generally be divided into component parts. First comes the preparation of the corpse for disposal and its display. This may include washing, anointing or embalming, dressing, and even some forms of restoring the body. Often this is accompanied by a temporary public placement of the cadaver among the living, although always camouflaging its decay. This might, for example, include placing flowers or perfumes around the body. This use of flowers is as old as Neanderthal man, whose skeletons in the caves of Iraq were found covered with a layer of pollen, suggesting they were enclosed with flora.

In some cultures this public display may last several days—sometimes called "lying in state." In others, this is called "the viewing," and often the body is "improved" or adorned so that the repulsion of death does not overwhelm the living. Public placement includes placement of the body on a catafalque, sometimes in a casket, in shrouds, on a pyre, or some other visible site. In its origins, this public display of the corpse may have served as a means of making certain that the person was truly dead, as the certification of death was historically by no means always as accurate as it is today. The presence of the prepared corpse in public view thus provided both an opportunity to persuade everyone that the person was indeed

deceased while also in some way mitigating the dreadful vision of death and its reminder of universal mortality.

When bodies were placed in private homes, particularly in Victorian England, they were often put in the parlor, the room in which people gathered. This led to the parlor taking the name, "living room," as a way of offsetting the stigma and dread associated with the placement of corpses in it. In time, in North America, the placement of the corpse was moved from people's homes and parlors or living rooms to special sites that came to be called "funeral parlors" or "funeral homes." At times, funerals are carried on in places of worship, though in a number of religious traditions the corpse is considered defiling and hence not put in what are considered sacred places.

While a growing corps of professionals handle the preparation of the body, in some religious traditions volunteers from within the community of deceased or the bereaved carry this out. Thus, for example, among traditionally observant Jews, the preparations are carried out by the *Chevra Kaddisha* (holy fellowship) whose ritual washing, grooming, clothing, and preparation of the dead for burial are called *tahara* (purification).

The second part of the funeral consists of the rites and ceremonies of farewell. These include prayers, eulogies, and the marking of the mourners in some visible way. In some cultures, wailing or other forms of mourning are part of the funeral. But the possibilities of rites are as rich and varied as human culture. Thus, for example, among the Hmong of Vietnam, practices used during funeral ceremonies include: sacrificing a live chicken to place at the head of a deceased person in order that the soul of the chicken can lead the soul of the deceased person back to their ancestral home; burning gold paper money for the deceased to take on the journey home; and calling a shaman to communicate with the souls of the deceased to understand their wishes and communicate those wishes to family members. In general, the ceremonies of the funeral act to control the emotional damage that death may otherwise inflict by holding it within the framework of ritual behavior.

Part of the farewells consists of presenting the idea that death is really an alternative form of life, and the funeral initiates the transition from one form of life to another. In this sense, funerals may be seen as liminal or threshold rites, as described by Arnold van Gennep in his *Rites of Passage* (1960). For some groups, Jews for example, this period of transition should be short so as to hasten reintegration. For others, the farewell is extended so as to hold onto to the deceased a bit longer.

To assure the passage from death to a new life, the corpse must in some way be transformed. As Robert Hertz explained, "to make an object or living being pass from this world into the next, to free or create the soul, it must be destroyed," and then only as the "visible object vanishes," and becomes invisible, can it be "reconstructed in the beyond, transformed to a greater or less degree" (1960, p. 46). The removal or destruction of the dead body and the beginning of mourning marks the third and final part of the funeral. Among Hindus this is accomplished with the burning of the body and in India with floating it along the holy Ganges River. Among the Abrahamic faiths, this ends with the removal of the body for burial, although increasingly in modern society cremation is chosen as an option by many.

The transformation of the corpse is paralleled by a transformation of the bereaved into mourners. This is often marked either by activities they carry on at and after the funeral that publicly demonstrate their sense of loss. In some cases, the bereaved may tear their garments or hair, as if to reflect the tearing down of their own veneer of civility and social order that death itself has initiated. Of course by making this sort of rending ceremonial, funerary practices emotionally rein in the act and thereby assist the mourners in exercising self-control and limit the trauma of loss in public and to the collective life. The bereaved may be sequestered for a period of mourning that parallels the period of the deceased's journey to a new life. The conclusion of mourning marks the true end of the funeral, when the dead have reached their spiritual destination and the bereaved re-enter a full social life. Often this is marked with eating and drinking, activities associated with continuity and life.

SEE ALSO *Burial Grounds; Culture; Death and Dying; Heaven; Hell; Malinowski, Bronislaw; Religion; Rituals*

BIBLIOGRAPHY

Heilman, Samuel. 2001. *When a Jew Dies.* Berkeley: University of California Press.

Hertz, Robert. 1960. *A Contribution to the Study of the Collective Representation of Death.* Trans. Rodney and Claudia Needham. Glencoe, IL: Free Press.

Malinowski, Bronislaw. 1954. *Magic Science and Religion.* New York: Anchor.

Van Gennep, Arnold. 1960. *The Rites of Passage.* Trans. Monika Vizedom and Gabrielle Caffee. Chicago: University of Chicago Press.

Samuel C. Heilman

FUTURE PRICES

SEE *Forward and Futures Markets.*

FUTURE SHOCK

American author Alvin Toffler first used the term *future shock* in 1965 to refer to the psychological disorientation and physical stress experienced by individuals and societies when radical changes occur within short periods of time. In *Future Shock*, the 1970 book that popularized the term, Toffler argued that human beings have limited abilities to adapt to social and technological transformations. Thus, he argued, it was the rate of alteration in personal and social life, and not just the direction of change, that posed unique psychological challenges to contemporary human beings.

Toffler believed that future shock would become a common psychological and physical state in advanced industrialized nations due to the speed with which technologies were transforming all aspects of society. In 1970 he already saw what he perceived as symptoms of future shock. These included an increasing impermanence in everything from interpersonal relationships to the life of institutions, a rise in individual and collective mobility, an increase in social diversity, and an acceleration in the consumption of goods and novel experiences. Toffler believed that these changes might soon outstrip human abilities to cope with them. For that reason, he argued that societies must actively manage the technological and social changes under way.

Soon after the publication of *Future Shock*, the title concept became a staple of popular writing on technological change. In the scholarly literature, researchers deployed the term within the field of organizational theory to address the possible consequences of technological change in the workplace and the possibility that they could be effectively managed. Education scholars also invoked the concept as they studied how to prepare students for the rapid changes taking place in society. Though it remained popular in the organizational and educational literature, the concept of future shock never developed analytical purchase across the social sciences. As the Internet came on the scene in the mid-1990s, however, the term saw a brief resurgence. By the late 1990s, it was often used by political scientists studying Internet-based political processes and trying to forecast the effects of technological change in that arena.

Within the social sciences, many of the phenomena Toffler pointed to in 1970 have been subsumed under other analytical paradigms. Writing at about the same time as Toffler, sociologists Alain Touraine (1971) and Daniel Bell (1973) pointed to the rise of *postindustrial society.* In the mid-1990s, sociologist Manuel Castells argued that the *network society* has emerged. In the movement from postindustrial to network society, scholars have integrated many of Toffler's concerns with the consequences of technological change, but they have let go of the core features of future shock: the notion that the pace of change might outstrip human adaptability and the recommendation that change should be managed on that account.

SEE ALSO *Futurology*

BIBLIOGRAPHY

Bell, Daniel. 1973. *The Coming of Postindustrial Society: A Venture in Social Forecasting.* New York: Basic Books.

Castells, Manuel. 2000. *The Rise of the Network Society.* 2nd ed. Cambridge, MA: Blackwell.

Toffler, Alvin. 1965. The Future as a Way of Life. *Horizon* 7 (3): 108–115.

Toffler, Alvin. 1970. *Future Shock.* New York: Random House.

Touraine, Alain. 1971. *The Postindustrial Society: Tomorrow's Social History—Classes, Conflicts, and Culture in the Programmed Society.* Trans. Leonard F. X. Mayhew. New York: Random House.

Daniel Kreiss
Fred Turner

FUTURISM

SEE *Futurology.*

FUTUROLOGY

Futurology is the rigorous attempt to anticipate future developments, relying heavily upon social-science methods. Few futurologists actually try to forecast future conditions, but instead prefer to identify alternative possibilities and to critique naive forecasts that others may have proposed. Critical futurology has deep historical roots. For example, in 1872 Edward Jarvis addressed popular concerns that the United States was experiencing too much immigration through careful demographic analysis that showed the country was in little danger of becoming primarily foreign born.

In the 1960s a futurology craze gripped American intellectuals, many of whom wished to serve as advisors to the Kennedy-Johnson administration's New Frontier or Great Society and the competition with the Soviet Union cold war. The RAND corporation sponsored studies that combined the views of many experts into unified forecasts concerning a wide range of possible technological and social developments. Among the sequels were two visionary books, *The Year 2000* (1967), by Herman Kahn and Anthony J. Wiener, and *Towards the Year 2000* edited by Daniel Bell (1967).

In the 2000s conferences such as the annual meetings of the World Future Society offer diverse prospectives. Serious journals, such as *Futures* and *Futures Research Quarterly*, carry projections, scenarios, theory-based extrapolations, and expert judgments about the future.

A projection analyzes recent trends mathematically, then runs the trends forward in time to estimate particular variables, such as population, economic activity, or the diffusion of a new technology. In 1971 Jay Forrester used the simple computers of his day to model the interplay of economic and social variables on a global scale through systems dynamics projections. The approach was famously used in the 1972 Club of Rome report, *Limits to Growth*, predicting that the global economy would soon crash because of resource depletion, but in retrospect the numerous assumptions seem arbitrary, and the crash has not yet occurred. The report remains influential as a cautionary tale but not a prediction.

The point of a scenario is not to predict, but to clarify, presenting a coherent, internally consistent picture of a future possibility so that planners and scholars can think more clearly and creatively. The scenarios in the Kahn-Wiener and Bell books imagined the fall of the Soviet Union and the birth of the World Wide Web. In 2003 British astronomer Royal Sir Martin Rees examined realistic scenarios for many of the ways humankind could become extinct during this century.

A theory sketches the future implied by a particular set of formal ideas. Pitirim Sorokin argued that every great civilization follows a cycle from ideational culture based on a transcendent ideology such as a religion, to sensate culture that is secular, empirical, and destined for collapse, followed by a new ideational phase. While agreeing with Sorokin's general approach, Rodney Stark and William Bainbridge argued that civilization will not secularize in the long run, because religion responds with constant revival and innovation.

Scientific and technical expertise can identify the possible implications of discoveries. In 2000 the U.S. National Science Foundation considered the implications of nanotechnology for industry, medicine, environmental sustainability, space exploration, national security, and scientific understanding of nature. The finding that the societal impact would operate indirectly, led to an examination of the possible future convergence of nanotechnology with biotechnology, information technology, and new cognitive technologies.

Given that futurologists seldom attempt to predict precise outcomes, one may wonder how futurology differs from science fiction (SF), a genre of literature that often concerns speculations about the future and is sometimes praised for insight about the implications of science and technology. Sociological research suggests that SF has primarily four ideological dimensions: (1) "hard-science" stories favorable to technological innovation; (2) "new-wave" stories critical of technological development, emphasizing aesthetics and social science rather than natural science; (3) fantasy stories in which magic or the supernatural are more important than technology or science; and (4) the time dimension anchored in classical SF such as the century-old works of Jules Verne, H. G. Wells, and Edgar Rice Burroughs. Arguably, the first two of these dimensions might qualify as futurology, if the authors built upon a solid basis of knowledge in the natural or social sciences, using narrative fiction as a way of rendering their scenarios more vivid.

SEE ALSO *Technocracy; Technology*

BIBLIOGRAPHY

Bainbridge, William Sims. 1986. *Dimensions of Science Fiction.* Cambridge, MA: Harvard University Press.

Bell, Daniel, ed. 1967. *Towards the Year 2000.* Boston: Beacon Press.

Forrester, Jay W. 1971. *World Dynamics.* Cambridge, MA: Wright-Allen Press.

Helmer, Olaf, Bernice Brown, and Theodore Gordon. 1966. *Social Technology.* New York: Basic Books.

Jarvis, Edward. 1872. Immigration. *Atlantic Monthly* 29: 454–468.

Kahn, Herman, and Anthony J. Wiener. 1967. *The Year 2000.* New York: Macmillan.

Meadows, Donella H., Dennis L. Meadows, Jørgen Randers, and William W. Behrens III. 1972. *The Limits to Growth: A Report for the Club of Rome's Project on the Predicament of Mankind.* New York: Universe Books.

Rees, Martin. 2003. *Our Final Hour.* New York: Basic Books.

Roco, Mihail C., and William Sims Bainbridge, eds. 2001. *Societal Implications of Nanoscience and Nanotechnology.* Dordrecht, Netherlands: Kluwer.

Roco, Mihail C., and William Sims Bainbridge, eds. 2003. *Converging Technologies for Improving Human Performance.* Dordrecht, Netherlands: Kluwer.

Sorokin, Pitirim A. 1937. *Social and Cultural Dynamics.* New York: American Book Company.

Stark, Rodney, and William Sims Bainbridge. 1985. *The Future of Religion.* Berkeley: University of California Press.

Wagner, Cynthia G., ed. 2005. *Foresight, Innovation, and Strategy: Toward a Wiser Future.* Bethesda, MD: World Future Society.

William Sims Bainbridge

G

G7 COUNTRIES

In the 1970s, declining economies and a worldwide recession sparked a series of informal meetings among leaders of the world's major economies. In April 1973 the finance ministers of France, the United Kingdom, West Germany, and the United States met in Washington, D.C., to discuss ways to stabilize their economies and the failing international economic order. Two years later, in 1975, as the Western nations faced an oil crisis, trade deficits, unstable national currencies, the proliferation of weapons of mass destruction, threats of war, and chronic unemployment, the president of France requested a gathering of leaders from the industrialized nations. The meeting, intended to discuss ways to circumvent the bureaucratic conflict and economic nationalism hindering international economic cooperation, took place in Rambouillet, France, in November 1975. Present were the heads of government of France, Italy, Japan, the United Kingdom, the United States, and West Germany. The group became known as the Group of Six (G6). The following year, Britain, Canada, France, Germany, Italy, Japan, and the United States met as the Group of Seven, commonly referred to as the G7. The subsequent annual meetings of the G7 provided a forum in which leaders of the seven nations could discuss and coordinate actions on economic and commercial matters.

FROM THE G7 TO THE G8

The G7 became the G8 in 1998, when Russia was admitted formally to the group (it had been participating in summit meetings since 1994). Since 1998, G8 summits have extended their agendas beyond discussions of macroeconomic issues to include wider discussions of global economic concern, including microeconomic issues and regional security, transnational issues such as the environment, drug trafficking, and human rights. The G8 was criticized by emerging nations for forming an elite and undemocratic alliance in which policies were formulated by wealthy nations and then imposed upon the rest of the world. Developing nations protested that their interests were not addressed during the G8 meetings. These criticisms resulted in the formation of the Group of 20 (G20) in 1999. The G20 consists of finance ministers and central bank governors from nineteen industrialized and emerging market countries plus the European Union. The International Monetary Fund and the World Bank also participate in G20 meetings on an ex-officio basis. The G20 nations include the G8 plus Argentina, Australia, Brazil, China, India, Indonesia, Mexico, Russia, Saudi Arabia, South Africa, South Korea, and Turkey. The establishment of the G20 was intended to open up an informal dialogue on international financial affairs among a broader group of countries than the G8 alone.

Despite its noninclusive nature, defenders of the G8 contend it has promoted the global economic good. From this perspective, the G8 is responsible for stabilizing the international monetary system after the collapse of the limited gold standard. Some observers, including the former U.S. president Ronald Reagan, believe the G8 underwrote capitalism's victory in the cold war. The topic upon which the G8 has had the greatest influence is trade. During summit meetings leaders are able to collaborate on political and economic decisions. The influence of the G8 on multilateral trade negotiations resulted in the formation of the General Agreement on Tariffs and Trade 1994

(GATT 1994) and the creation of the World Trade Organization (WTO) in 1995. The G8's primary role is to expand the realm of capitalism, and one of the most enduring legacies of the G8 is the expansion and maintenance of mutual trust among the member nations. The G8's stated goal has shifted over time from a forum dealing essentially with macroeconomic issues to an annual meeting with a broad-based agenda that addresses a wide range of international economic, political, and social issues.

SEE ALSO *Developing Countries; European Union; G8 Countries; General Agreement on Tariffs and Trade; Recession; World Trade Organization*

BIBLIOGRAPHY

Baker, Andrew. 2006. *The Group of Seven: Finance Ministries, Central Banks, and Global Financial Governance.* New York: Routledge.

Barry, Tom. 2000. G8/G7 Global Governance. *Foreign Policy in Focus* 5 (23). http://www.fpif.org/briefs/vol5/v5n23g8g7.html.

Lorna Lueker Zukas

G8 COUNTRIES

The Group of Eight (G8) is an annual meeting of the leaders of the world's major industrial states. The purpose of the G8 is to have world leaders meet informally on economic and political issues facing their individual countries and the international community as a whole. Initially proposed by President Valéry Giscard d'Estaing of France and Chancellor Helmut Schmidt of Germany, the first summit, held at Rambouillet, France, in November 1975, included only six countries: France, the United States, Britain, Germany, Japan, and Italy. The impetus of the meeting was to discuss the oil crisis. In 1976 President Gerald R. Ford called for a second summit, which initiated the annual nature of the meetings and established it as an institution. When Canada joined the group in 1976 it became known as the G7.

From 1976 to 1990 the G7 met annually; sometimes on the eve of the summit it included fifteen developing countries as in the 1989 Paris summit. Russia became part of the post-summit discussions from 1991 to 1994. These meetings are sometimes referred to as the P8 or Political Eight. Russia had partial membership as it was excluded from financial and other economic discussions. Russia obtained full membership in 1998 and in doing so, the G8 was born. There is an additional member of both the G7 and G8: the European Union.

The chair and location of the G8 are selected in a rotating manner starting with France, the United States, the United Kingdom, Russia (as of 2006), Germany, Japan, Italy, and Canada. The position of chair is held for one full calendar year. The host country proposes the summit location and agenda and organizes preparatory meetings.

Despite the lack of formal structure, the G8 has had an effect on the world. A significant change to international organizations resulted from the 1995 Halifax, Canada, summit, where leaders agreed to amend the rules and procedures of the World Bank and the International Monetary Fund (IMF). The agenda for the summits change from year to year and focus on the most pressing economic and social issues. During the Okinawa, Japan, meeting in 2000 the G8 agreed to provide further funding to fight infectious disease. The meeting also focused on issues regarding information and communications technology. The 2001 Geneva, Switzerland, meeting created the Global Fund to fight infectious diseases such as AIDS, tuberculosis, and malaria.

Because of the cooperation and dialogue of the world's leaders accomplished through the G8, it has also attracted the attention of protestors. Probably the largest and most violent meeting was held in Genoa, Italy, in 2001, where an anti-capitalist protestor was shot and killed while hundreds of others were injured during a clash with police. In subsequent years the G8 has tried to open discussions with nongovernmental organizations and include other developing nations.

The G8 meeting hosted by Britain in Perthshire, Scotland, was interrupted by terrorist attacks on London's transit system on July 7, 2005. Tony Blair, the host of the meeting, left for a brief time to visit London while the other leaders remained to continue the discussion and agenda that was set. The issue of global terrorism has been on the agenda most years since 1978.

BIBLIOGRAPHY

G8 Information Centre. University of Toronto. http://www.g8.utoronto.ca/.

Lydia A. Miljan

GABRIEL (PROSSER)
1776–1800

The enslaved revolutionary known only as Gabriel was born near Richmond, Virginia, at Brookfield, the Henrico County plantation of Thomas Prosser. By Virginia standards, Brookfield was a large plantation, with a population of approximately fifty enslaved laborers. Unfortunately, the identity of Gabriel's parents is lost to history, but he had two older brothers, Martin and Solomon. Most likely, Gabriel's father was a blacksmith, the occupation chosen for Gabriel and Solomon; in Virginia, the offspring of skilled bondpersons frequently inherited their parent's profession.

Status as a craft artisan provided the young blacksmith with considerable standing in the slave community, as did his ability to read and write. In the 1780s, it was not yet illegal to teach Virginia slaves to be literate, and effective artisans needed the rudiments of literacy. According to tradition, his teacher was plantation mistress Ann Prosser. As Gabriel grew to be an unusually tall young man, even older slaves looked to him for leadership, a habit uncommon in African culture. By the mid-1790s, as he approached the age of twenty, Gabriel stood "six feet two or three inches high," and the muscles in his arms and chest betrayed nearly a decade in Brookfield's forge. A long and "bony face, well made," was marred by the loss of two front teeth and "two or three scars on his head" (Egerton 1993, p. 22). In later years, a racist legend arose which held that Gabriel wore his hair long in naïve imitation of Samson, in hopes that his locks would give him extraordinary strength. But contemporary descriptions say only that his hair was cut short and was as dark as his complexion. According to journalist James T. Callender, blacks and whites alike regarded him as "a fellow of courage and intellect above his rank in life" (p. 22).

During his years as an apprentice blacksmith, Gabriel married a young slave named Nanny. Little is known about her, including the identity of her owner. She does not appear in the few extant Brookfield records; most likely she lived on a nearby farm or tobacco plantation. But well into the twentieth century, area blacks believed that Nanny bore him children, who much later went under the surname of Randolph.

In the fall of 1798 Gabriel's old master died, and ownership of Brookfield passed to twenty-two-year-old Thomas Henry Prosser. An ambitious young man with a townhouse in Richmond and a lucrative auction business, Prosser maximized his profits by hiring out his surplus slaves. Even the most efficient planters could not find tasks enough to keep their enslaved artisans occupied year around, and many masters routinely hired out their craftsmen to neighboring farms and urban businesses. Despite all of the work to be done at Brookfield, Gabriel spent a considerable part of each month smithing in Richmond for artisans long on orders and short on labor. Although still a slave under Virginia law, Gabriel enjoyed a rough form of freedom. Indeed, his ties to the plantation became so tenuous that several historians have identified him as a free man.

Emboldened by this quasi liberty, in September 1799 Gabriel moved toward overt rebellion. Caught in the act of stealing a pig, a delicacy slaves used to supply their families with protein, Gabriel refused to endure the verbal abuse of its owner, a white neighbor. Instead, he wrestled his tormentor to the ground and bit off the better "part of his left Ear" (Egerton, p. 31). Under Virginia law, slaves were not tried as whites. They were prosecuted under a colonial statute of 1692 that created special segregated tribunals known as courts of oyer and terminer, composed of five justices of the peace. On October 7 Gabriel was formally charged with attacking a white man, a capital crime. Although found guilty, Gabriel escaped the gallows through an antiquated clause that since the Revolution had been denied to white defendants. Slaves yet possessed the right to "benefit of clergy" (p. 31), which allowed them to avoid hanging in exchange for being branded on the thumb with a small cross if they were able to recite a verse from the Bible.

Gabriel's branding and incarceration served as a brutal reminder that despite his literacy and special status, he remained a slave. By the early spring of 1800, his fury began to turn into a carefully considered plan to bring about his freedom, as well as the end of slavery in Virginia. As a literate man who moved among urban artisans, Gabriel surely knew that several states to the north had recently passed laws for gradual emancipation, and that New York had finally approved such a statute in 1799. As he explained it to his brothers Solomon and Martin, slaves and free blacks from Henrico County would gather at Brookfield on the evening of August 30 to march on Richmond. If Governor James Monroe and the town leaders agreed to Gabriel's demands for black liberty and an equitable distribution of the property, the slave general intended to "hoist a white flag" and drink a toast "with the merchants of the city" (Egerton, p. 51).

The uprising collapsed just before sunset on the appointed day, when a severe thunderstorm hit the Richmond area. The chaos of the storm convinced two Henrico slaves, Tom and Pharoah, that the revolt could not succeed. They informed their owner of the conspiracy, and he hurried word to Governor Monroe. As the state militia closed in, Gabriel escaped south by way of the swampy Chickahominy River. After hiding along the James River for nearly two weeks, Gabriel risked boarding the schooner *Mary*. Captain Richardson Taylor, a former overseer who had recently converted to Methodism, willingly spirited Gabriel downriver to Norfolk. There Gabriel was betrayed by a slave crewman, who had heard of Monroe's $300 reward for Gabriel's capture. Returned to Richmond under heavy guard, Gabriel was quickly tried and found guilty of "conspiracy and insurrection" (Egerton, p. 109). On October 10, 1800, the young revolutionary died with quiet composure at the town gallows near Fifteenth and Broad Streets. He was twenty-four. In 2002 the Richmond city council formally adopted a resolution proclaiming Gabriel to be "an American patriot and freedom fighter" (*Richmond Times-Dispatch*, October 11, 2002).

SEE ALSO *Freedom; Plantation; Slave Resistance; Slavery*

BIBLIOGRAPHY

Egerton, Douglas R. 1993. *Gabriel's Rebellion: The Virginia Slave Conspiracies of 1800 and 1802.* Chapel Hill: University of North Carolina Press.

Schwarz, Philip J. 1988. *Twice Condemned: Slaves and the Criminal Laws of Virginia, 1705–1865.* Baton Rouge: Louisiana State University Press.

Sidbury, James. 1997. *Ploughshares into Swords: Race, Rebellion, and Identity in Gabriel's Virginia, 1730–1810.* New York: Cambridge University Press.

Williams, Michael Paul. 2002. Views on Slave Revolt Leader Clash. *Richmond Times-Dispatch* (October 11): p. B3.

Douglas R. Egerton

GAIRY, ERIC

SEE *Grenadian Revolution.*

GALBRAITH, JOHN KENNETH
1908–2006

John Kenneth Galbraith was an institutional economist, Harvard professor, advisor to presidents, bureaucrat, ambassador to India, raconteur, caustic wit, and man of letters. His concepts of countervailing power, the affluent society, conventional wisdom, want creation, and the technostructure of the industrial state have become part of the modern vernacular and the battle for the controlling metaphors of economics and politics. Born on a farm in southern Ontario, Canada, he attended Ontario Agricultural College, graduating in 1931. His family and community background are detailed in his memoir, *The Scotch* (1964). A desire to understand the causes of the Great Depression led him to seek a PhD in agricultural economics at the University of California, Berkeley, graduating in 1934. The influence of Progressive Era economists such as Richard Ely (1854–1943), John R. Commons (1862–1945), and Thorstein Veblen (1857–1929) was in evidence and it created an atmos-

phere accepting of the New Deal initiatives of President Franklin D. Roosevelt (1882–1945).

Galbraith's first job involved research in agricultural economics under the tutelage of Harvard professor John D. Black (1883–1960), who was well connected in Washington, D.C. Before beginning, Galbraith served as a summer intern in the Agricultural Adjustment Administration. There he learned the role of power in the economy as he witnessed southern congressmen stopping the payment of agricultural subsidies to tenant farmers (mostly blacks). During World War II (1939–1945), Galbraith was placed in charge of price control and rationing in the Office of Price Administration. The political pressure from business was intense, charges of communism flew, and Galbraith was fired in 1943.

Galbraith's writing and analysis led to a stint at *Fortune* magazine from 1943 to 1948. During this time, he also participated in the Strategic Bombing Survey to assess the role of air power in winning the war. The survey concluded that strategic bombing played a minor role and that ground troops were essential in both Germany and Japan. Galbraith later objected to what he called "military Keynesianism"—stimulating the economy via military spending at the expense of social programs.

Upon his controversial return to Harvard, Galbraith wrote *American Capitalism* (1952), in which he argued that a decentralized private economy excelled in production and innovation. He further maintained that concentration and bigness were inevitable. Countervailing the power of buyers, unions, and government would be more effective in controlling the seller's power than traditional antitrust.

In his best-selling *Affluent Society* (1958), Galbraith observed that wealthy economies were no longer typified by scarcity. In fact, corporations maintained themselves by creating demand, rather than merely responding to it, as the "conventional wisdom" had it, producing what he called the "dependence effect." He observed a "social imbalance" between abundant private consumption goods and inadequate publicly provided goods, such as education, clean air and water, and transportation. His description of "the family which takes its mauve and cerise, air-conditioned, power steered, and power-braked car out for a tour passes through cities that are badly paved, made hideous by litter, blighted buildings, billboards and posts" (1958, pp. 199–200) has become legendary and still applies today.

The New Industrial State (1967) describes giant corporations that are run and planned by a hired bureaucratic technostructure rather than owners and that strive for survival and independence rather than profit maximization. Advertising, information management, and access to government are key assets. The economy cannot be understood without attention to the use of power in both politics and business. Robert M. Solow contested Galbraith's argument that giant corporations controlled the economy (1967). But, after subsequent decades of mergers, Galbraith's concerns seem warranted. Solow also objected to Galbraith's "revised sequence" of consumption (want creation rather than only prior want fulfillment) by asserting that advertising only serves to cancel other advertising. Galbraith's concerns drew the label of "sociologist" from Milton Friedman (1912–2006), and along with Galbraith's argument that public planning must balance the private planning of the corporate technostructure, the label of "socialist."

Galbraith questioned the monotheistic worship of gross domestic product as the test of a good society and wondered if the same energy (and the discipline of economics itself) might be better directed toward social harmony, aesthetic enjoyment, and leisure. Galbraith remained a social critic until his death in 2006.

SEE ALSO *Liberalism; Wage and Price Controls*

BIBLIOGRAPHY

PRIMARY WORKS

Galbraith, John Kenneth. 1952. *American Capitalism: The Concept of Countervailing Power.* Boston: Houghton Mifflin.

Galbraith, John Kenneth. 1958. *The Affluent Society.* Boston: Houghton Mifflin.

Galbraith, John Kenneth. 1964. *The Scotch.* Boston: Houghton Mifflin.

Galbraith, John Kenneth. 1967. *The New Industrial State.* Boston: Houghton Mifflin.

Galbraith, John Kenneth. 1983. *The Anatomy of Power.* Boston: Houghton Mifflin.

SECONDARY SOURCES

Parker, Richard. 2005. *John Kenneth Galbraith: His Life, His Politics, His Economics.* New York: Farrar, Straus, and Giroux.

Reisman, David. 1980. *Galbraith and Market Capitalism.* New York: New York University Press.

Sasson, Helen, ed. 1999. *Between Friends: Perspectives on John Kenneth Galbraith.* Boston: Houghton Mifflin.

Solow, Robert M. 1967. The New Industrial State or Son of Affluence. *The Public Interest* 9: 100–108.

A. Allan Schmid

GALLUP POLL

SEE *Pollsters.*

GALTON, FRANCIS
1822–1911

Cousin to Charles Darwin and a talented statistician, Sir Francis Galton had an influence on social science that was profound. His major contributions to mathematical statistics included the initial development of quantiles and linear regression techniques. Along with F. Y. Edgeworth and Karl Pearson, he developed general techniques of multiple regression and correlation analysis, statistical devices that serve as substitutes for experiments in social science. Galton had a major impact on economics, and with W. R. Greg, was instrumental in creating the "science" of eugenics.

Galton was born in Birmingham, England, on February 16, 1822, and died on January 17, 1911, in Haslemere. He spent two years (1836–1838) at King Edward's School in Birmingham, underwent a medical apprenticeship in Birmingham, then studied for a year (1839–1840) at the medical school of King's College, London, before entering Trinity College, Cambridge in 1840. Galton read mathematics at Trinity, from which he graduated without honors.

After inheriting a substantial fortune on the death of his father in 1844, Galton embarked on an African exploration. He published an account of his travels in 1853, and joined the council of the Royal Geographical Society. Galton was elected Fellow of the Royal Society in 1856, and served as Secretary of the British Association from 1863 to 1867.

Galton's focus on heredity was first manifested in the 1869 publication, *Hereditary Genius*, an attempt to marshal evidence in favor of the proposition that mental ability is inherited. In it, Galton, who presumed that mental ability is correlated with reputation in a given profession, examined the scores of two hundred candidates for the Mathematical Tripos at Cambridge as well as those of seventy-two candidates for civil service positions.

In 1883 Galton published *Inquiries into Human Faculty and Its Development*, in which he discussed the ideas now known as *eugenics*. Here, his argument began as an attack on the race-neutral accounts of ability in classical economics (Galton 1907, p. 207). Darwin's endorsement (Darwin 1871, pp. 138–139) gave warrant to Galton's eugenic ideas. Galton's claims for the importance of "race"—that is, characteristics preserved by inheritance in distinction to characteristics acquired by custom—was challenged in his time by the assertion that it was implausible that a child of Quaker parents raised in the North American woods by aboriginal people would show the "gentle altruistic nature of his progenitors" (Reid 1897, p. 945). This challenge would lead to twentieth-century studies of identical twins raised in separate environments.

Galton's study of eugenics illustrates his creativity as a researcher. He was, for example, ingenious in his use of composite photography to help identify inherited characteristics. "The individual faces [of criminals]," he wrote, "are villainous enough, but they are villainous in different ways, and when they are combined, the individual peculiarities disappear, and the common humanity of a low type is all that is left" (1907, p. 11). Because there is no reason to believe that criminality is inherited, Galton is partially correct in his deductions—that is, in his claim that there is no specifically criminal type. Of course, since Galton's time the idea that there is such a thing as a "low type" of humanity has been discounted. Similarly, the argument that ability is inherited by race has been questioned, notably by Tukufu Zuberi (2001), who argues that *race* is a concept devoid of biological meaning and is instead socially constructed.

Despite the fact that many of his conclusions about genetic differences are questioned, if not disproven, today, Galton's work reveals his integrity regarding test results—that is, his willingness to acknowledge cases where the data does not match his presuppositions. An example can be found in his attempt to use his system of fingerprint identification to establish a racial hierarchy, on the basis of his belief that a "higher" race would have less uniform fingerprints. Galton presupposed that the fingerprints of black people would be more uniform than those of white people, but confessed an inability to observe this in the data.

SEE ALSO *Darwin, Charles; Eugenics; Race; Racial Classification; Regression Analysis; Statistics*

BIBLIOGRAPHY

Darwin, Charles. [1871] 1989. *The Descent of Man, and Selection in Relation to Sex*. Vol. 21–22 of *The Works of Charles Darwin*, eds. Paul H. Barrett and R. B. Freeman. New York: New York University Press.

Galton, Francis. 1892. *Finger Prints*. London: Macmillan.

Galton, Francis. 1907. *Inquiries into Human Faculty and Its Development*. 2nd ed. London: J. M. Dent.

Peart, Sandra J., and David M. Levy. 2005. *The "Vanity of the Philosopher": From Equality to Hierarchy in Postclassical Economics*. Ann Arbor: University of Michigan Press.

Reid, G. Archdall. 1897. Characters, Congenital and Acquired II. *Science*, n.s., 6 (156): 933–948.

Stigler, Stephen M. 1986. *The History of Statistics: The Measurement of Uncertainty before 1900*. Cambridge, MA: Belknap Press.

Zuberi, Tukufu. 2001. *Thicker Than Blood: How Racial Statistics Lie*. Minneapolis: University of Minnesota Press.

Sandra Peart
David M. Levy

GAMBLING

Gambling and games of chance have been popular throughout history. The globalization of gambling has passed through a number of cycles. More so than in the past, gambling is viewed as a socially acceptable form of entertainment. While gambling activities can take many forms and vary across cultures and jurisdictions, most individuals gamble for enjoyment, for entertainment, to socialize, and to try their luck without experiencing many negative repercussions.

PATHOLOGICAL GAMBLING

Gambling can be viewed on a continuum, ranging from non-gambling to social gambling to pathological gambling. While most adults gamble without experiencing many adverse consequences, a small proportion of adults (0.4–3%) experience significant gambling-related problems, with an even larger proportion of adolescents (4–6%) reporting major gambling-related problems. The essential characteristic associated with pathological gambling is that it is a persistent and recurrent maladaptive gambling behavior that negatively disrupts personal, familial, social, economic, and vocational pursuits. Given the widespread proliferation and expansion of government-regulated and sponsored forms of gambling, gambling is quickly becoming a prominent social policy issue.

Pathological gambling, conceptualized as an impulse-control disorder, results in an individual's inability to stop his or her gambling in spite of multiple negative consequences. While a greater number of males experience pathological gambling compared to females (estimates are that a ratio of 3:1 exists), pathological gamblers frequently experience a preoccupation with gambling, the need to substantially increase the amount and frequency of their wagers, have great difficulty stopping or reducing their gambling, and become extremely irritable when trying to limit their gambling. These individuals often gamble to escape problems or relieve stress, return to gambling in order to recoup losses, frequently lie to family members, peers, and friends in order to conceal their gambling losses, and commit illegal behaviors (both within and outside the home) to finance their gambling. Pathological gamblers jeopardize familial, peer, and vocational relationships in order to continue gambling and help relieve financial difficulties resulting from their gambling behavior.

There is considerable discussion as to whether some forms of gambling may be more problematic than others. Some research suggests that machine gambling (e.g., slot machines, video poker machines, video lottery terminals) and Internet gambling may be more problematic to some individuals because of their relatively low cost and the frequency and speed of playing while simultaneously allowing the player to go into a disassociative state. Other research suggests that there are definite differential patterns of playing and preferences for different forms of gambling depending upon one's age, accessibility of venues, gender, and ethnic and cultural background.

An emerging body of literature suggests that certain familial factors (high rates of family gambling problems, substance abuse problems, spouse or partners with a gambling problem), biological factors (including brain chemistry and functioning, physiological indicators of arousal and the need for stimulation, genetic considerations), attentional problems, and a wide variety of physical health problems (including cardiovascular and gastrointestinal problems and chronic pain) are associated with pathological gambling disorders. Personality disorders related to impulsivity, sensation seeking, a high degree of risk-taking, antisocial personality disorders, oppositional defiant disorders, compulsivity, psychoticism, and neuroticism, and cognitive distortions (erroneous beliefs including an illusion that one can control the outcome of random events, a lack of recognition of the notion of independence of events, the belief in a system to "beat the odds") have similarly been linked to pathological gambling.

From a psychological perspective, pathological gamblers have been reported to exhibit high anxiety, depression and depressive symptomatology, suicidal ideation and suicide attempts, and a wide range of personality and mental health disorders. There is also a growing body of evidence to suggest that pathological gamblers have a variety of comorbid alcohol and substance abuse problems. While there is no personality profile of a pathological gambler per se, there are indications that an individual's psychological and mental state make certain individuals more susceptible to both gambling and the development of a gambling problem.

In spite of the large number of adverse behavioral traits associated with gambling, it is not unusual for individuals to fail to recognize their problems. They tend not to acknowledge their gambling problem and fail to seek help. Their perceived solution often rests on the "big win."

GAMBLING AMONG CHILDREN AND TEENS

Although problem gambling has been primarily thought of as an adult behavior, considerable research indicates that it remains a very popular activity among both children and adolescents. Whether one is gambling for money on personal games of skill, cards, dice, sporting events, or lottery tickets, a high percentage of children and adolescents worldwide have been found to engage in different forms of gambling.

Studies conducted since the 1990s suggest that gambling activities remain particularly attractive to today's youth and that its popularity is on the rise among both children and adolescents. Prevalence studies conducted in the United States, Canada, New Zealand, Europe, and Australia all confirm the rising prevalence rates of youth involvement in both legal and illegal forms of gambling. While approximately 80 percent of high school students report having gambled for money during the past year, 4 to 6 percent of adolescents exhibit serious gambling problems, with another 10 to 14 percent of adolescents remaining at-risk for developing a serious gambling problem.

Adolescent pathological gamblers, like their adult counterparts and independent of the negative consequences resulting from their excessive gambling, continue to chase their losses, exhibit a preoccupation with gambling, and have an impaired ability to stop gambling in spite of repeated attempts and their desire to do so. The growing body of research with adolescents suggests that gambling and problem gambling is more popular among males than females, adolescent prevalence rates of problem gamblers are higher than those reported by adults, and there is a rapid movement from social gambler to problem gambler. Adolescent problem gamblers report initiating gambling at an early age (approximately ten years of age) as compared with peers who report gambling but have few gambling-related problems. These adolescents are greater risk takers in general and on gambling tasks in particular, exhibit lower self-esteem, exhibit higher depressive symptomatology, remain at heightened risk for suicide ideation and suicide attempts, have poor general coping skills, and report a significant number of major traumatic life events (e.g., parental loss, divorce).

Individuals with gambling problems are also more likely to report school- or work-related problems. Personality traits reveal adolescent pathological gamblers are more excitable, extroverted, and anxious, tend to have difficulty conforming to societal norms, experience difficulties with self-discipline, exhibit more anxiety, exhibit higher levels of impulsivity, and remain at increased risk for the development of multiple addictions.

NEW FORMS OF GAMBLING

New forms of gambling continue to be developed. With more and more governments sanctioning and regulating a multitude of different forms of gambling, its accessibility has never been easier. Problem gambling is not associated with single-trial learning. Very few individuals become addicted to the lure of gambling after their first initiation. Pathological gambling remains a progressive disorder with certain identifiable risk factors developing over time accompanied by periods of euphoria and depression.

The gambling environment today is significantly different from that of past generations. Because of its widespread acceptability, its popularity, and the enormous revenues generated from gambling, the growth of the gaming industry continues. Gambling is viewed as significantly less harmful than other potentially addictive behaviors including substance abuse, alcohol abuse, and cigarette smoking.

New forms of gambling and games will continue to emerge. Efforts at developing effective empirically sound practices concerning prevention and treatment programs have yet to be realized. Given the widespread accessibility, social acceptance and new technologies bringing gambling into the home, there remains speculation that the prevalence of pathological gambling will likely increase.

BIBLIOGRAPHY

Abbott, Max, Rachel Volberg, Maria Bellringer, and Gerta Reith. 2004. *A Review of Research on Aspects of Problem Gambling.* Final Report. London: Responsibility for Gambling Trust.

American Psychiatric Association. 1992. *Diagnostic and Statistical Manual of Mental Disorders.* 4th ed. Washington, DC: Author.

Derevensky, Jeffrey, and Rina Gupta. 2004. Adolescents with Gambling Problems: A Review of Our Current Knowledge. *e-Gambling: The Electronic Journal of Gambling Issues* 10: 119–140.

Jacobs, Durand. 2004. Youth Gambling in North America: Long-Term Trends and Future Prospects. In *Gambling Problems in Youth: Theoretical and Applied Perspectives,* eds. Jeffrey Derevensky and Rina Gupta. New York: Kluwer Academic/Plenum Publishers.

Jeffrey L. Derevensky

GAME THEORY

Game theory is a branch of mathematics used to analyze competitive situations whose outcomes depend not only on one's own choices, and perhaps chance, but also on the choices made by other parties, or *players*. Because the outcome of a game is dependent on what *all* players do, each player tries to anticipate the choices of other players in order to determine his own best choice. How these interdependent strategic calculations are made is the subject of the theory. Game theory was created in practically one stroke with the publication of *Theory of Games and Economic Behavior* in 1944 by mathematician John von Neumann (1903–1957) and economist Oskar Morgenstern (1902–1977). This work was a monumental intellectual achievement and has given rise to hundreds of books and thousands of articles in a variety of disciplines.

The theory has several major divisions, the following being the most important:

Two-person versus n-person. The two-person theory deals with the optimal strategic choices of two players, whereas the *n*-person theory ($n > 2$) mostly concerns what coalitions, or subsets of players, will form and be stable, and what constitutes reasonable payments to their members.

Zero-sum versus nonzero-sum. The payoffs to all players sum to zero (or some other constant) at each outcome in zero-sum games but not in nonzero-sum games, wherein the sums are variable; zero-sum games are games of total conflict, in which what one player gains the others lose, whereas nonzero-sum games permit the players to gain or lose together.

Cooperative versus noncooperative. Cooperative games are those in which players can make binding and enforceable agreements, whereas noncooperative games may or may not allow for communication among the players but do assume that any agreement reached must be in equilibrium—that is, it is rational for a player not to violate it if other players do not, because the player would be worse off if he did.

Games can be described by several different forms, the three most important being:

1. *Extensive (game tree)*—indicates sequences of choices that players (and possibly chance, according to nature or some random device) can make, with payoffs defined at the end of each sequence of choices.

2. *Normal/strategic (payoff matrix)*—indicates strategies, or complete plans contingent on other players' choices, for each player, with payoffs defined at the intersection of each set of strategies in a matrix.

3. *Characteristic function*—indicates values that all possible coalitions (subsets) of players can ensure for their members, whatever the other players do.

These different game forms, or representations, give less and less detailed information about a game—with the sequences in form 1 dropped from form 2, and the strategies to implement particular outcomes in form 2 dropped from form 3—to highlight different aspects of a strategic situation.

Common to all areas of game theory is the assumption that players are rational: They have goals, can rank outcomes (or, more stringently, attach utilities, or values, to them), and choose better over worse outcomes. Complications arise from the fact that there is generally no dominant, or unconditionally best, strategy for a player because of the interdependency of player choices. (Games in which there is only one player are sometimes called *games against nature* and are the subject of *decision theory*.)

A game is sometimes defined as the sum-total of its rules. Common parlor games, like chess or poker, have well-specified rules and are generally zero-sum games, making cooperation with the other player(s) unprofitable. Poker differs from chess in being not only an *n*-person game (though two players can also play it) but also a game of *incomplete information*, because the players do not have full knowledge of each other's hands, which depend in part on chance.

The rules of most real-life games are equivocal; indeed, the "game" may be about the rules to be used (or abrogated). In economics, rules are generally better known and followed than in politics, which is why game theory has become the theoretical foundation of economics, especially microeconomics. But game-theoretic models also play a major role in other subfields of economics, including industrial organization, public economics, and international economics. Even in macroeconomics, in which fiscal and monetary policies are studied, questions about setting interest rates and determining the money supply have a strong strategic component, especially with respect to the timing of such actions. It is little wonder that economics, more than any of the other social sciences, uses game theory at all levels.

Game-theoretic modeling has made major headway in political science, including international relations, in the last generation. While international politics is considered to be quite anarchistic, there is certainly some constancy in the way conflicts develop and may, or may not, be resolved. Arms races, for instance, are almost always nonzero-sum games in which two nations can benefit if they reach some agreement on limiting weapons, but such agreements are often hard to verify or enforce and, consequently, may be unstable.

Since the demise of the superpower conflict around 1990, interest has shifted to whether a new "balance of power"—reminiscent of the political juggling acts of European countries in the nineteenth and early twentieth century—may emerge in different regions or even worldwide. For example, will China, as it becomes more and more a superpower in Asia, align itself with other major Asian countries, like India and Japan, or will it side more with Western powers to compete against its Asian rivals? Game theory offers tools for studying the stability of new alignments, including those that might develop on political-economy issues.

Consider, for example, the World Trade Organization (WTO), whose durability is now being tested by regional trading agreements that have sprung up among countries in the Americas, Europe, and Asia. The rationality of supporting the WTO, or joining a regional trading bloc, is very much a strategic question that can be illuminated by game theory. Game theory also provides insight into how the domestic politics of a country impinges on its foreign policy, and vice versa, which has led to a renewed interest in the interconnections between these two levels of politics.

Other applications of game theory in political science have been made to strategic voting in committees and elections, the formation and disintegration of parliamentary coalitions, and the distribution of power in weighted voting bodies. On the normative side, electoral reforms have been proposed to lessen the power of certain parties (e.g., the religious parties in Israel), based on game-theoretic analysis. Similarly, the voting weights of members of the European Union Council of Ministers, and its decision rules for taking action (e.g., simple majority or qualified majority), have been studied with an eye to making the body both representative of individual members' interests and capable of taking collective action.

As game-theoretic models have become more prominent in political science, they have, at the same time, created a good deal of controversy. Some critics charge that they abstract too much from strategic situations, reducing actors to hyperrational players or bloodless automatons that do not reflect the emotions or the social circumstances of people caught up in conflicts. Moreover, critics contend, game-theoretic models are difficult to test empirically, in part because they depend on counterfactuals that are never observed. That is, they assume that players take into account contingencies that are hard to reconstruct, much less model precisely.

But proponents of game theory counter that the theory brings rigor to the study of strategic choices that no other theory can match. Furthermore, they argue that actors *are*, by and large, rational—they choose better over worse means, even if the goals that they seek to advance are not always apparent.

When information is incomplete, so-called Bayesian calculations can be made that take account of this incompleteness. The different possible goals that players may have can also be analyzed and their consequences assessed.

Because such reconstruction is often difficult to do in real-life settings, laboratory experiments—in which conditions can be better controlled—are more and more frequently conducted. In fact, experiments that test theories of bargaining, voting, and other political-economic processes have become commonplace in economics and political science. Although they are less common in the other social sciences, social psychology has long used experiments to investigate the choices of subjects in games like prisoners' dilemma. This infamous game captures a situation in which two players have dominant strategies of not cooperating, as exemplified by an arms race or a price war. But doing so results in an outcome worse for both than had they cooperated. Because mutual cooperation is not a *Nash equilibrium*, however, each player has an incentive to defect from cooperation.

Equally vexing problems confront the players in another well-known game, chicken. Not only is cooperation unstable, but noncooperation leads to a disastrous outcome. It turns out that each player should defect if and only if the other player cooperates, but anticipating when an opponent will do so is no mean feat.

Since the invention of game theory in the mid-1940s, its development has been remarkable. Two Nobel prizes in economics were awarded to a total of five game theorists in 1994 and 2005 (including John Nash of the film *A Beautiful Mind* fame), but many other recipients of this prize have used game theory extensively. In addition, game-theoretic modeling has progressed rapidly in political science—and, to a lesser extent, in the other social sciences—as well as in a variety of other disciplines, including biology, business, and law.

SEE ALSO *Arms Control and Arms Race; Cold War; Deterrence, Mutual; Nash Equilibrium; Political Economy; Prisoner's Dilemma (Economics)*

BIBLIOGRAPHY

Aumann, Robert J., and Sergiu Hart, eds. 1992–2002. *Handbook of Game Theory with Economic Applications.* 3 vols. Amsterdam, NY: Elsevier.

Brams, Steven J. 1994. *Theory of Moves.* New York: Cambridge University Press.

Dixit, Avinash, and Susan Skeath. 2005. *Games of Strategy.* 2nd ed. New York: Norton.

Nasar, Sylvia. 1998. *A Beautiful Mind: A Biography of John Forbes Nash Jr., Winner of the Nobel Prize in Economics, 1994.* New York: Simon & Schuster.

Osborne, Martin J. 2004. *An Introduction to Game Theory.* New York: Oxford University Press.

von Neumann, John, and Oskar Morgenstern. 1953. *Theory of Games and Economic Behavior.* 3rd ed. Princeton, NJ: Princeton University Press.

Steven J. Brams

GANDHI, INDIRA
1917–1984

Indira Priyadarshini Gandhi (born November 19, 1917) was twice elected the prime minister of India and was the first woman to hold the position. Daughter of India's first prime minister, Pandit Jawaharlal Nehru (1889–1964), she was introduced to the vagaries of political instability early in life. As someone who participated in the anticolonial national movement in the 1930s and 1940s as a

youngster, and saw the carnage that accompanied the partitioning of British India into the independent nations India and Pakistan in 1947, Gandhi experienced firsthand the challenges and uncertainties experienced by a fledgling democracy. In this regard, her formative years introduced her to the political cultures that she would negotiate as one of independent India's most charismatic and controversial figures.

After attending educational institutions in Europe and India, she married an Indian National Congress (INC) activist named Feroze Gandhi (1912–1960) in 1942. Her sons, Rajiv and Sanjay, were born in 1944 and 1946 respectively. Following the deterioration of her marriage, she moved to Delhi to support her father as he prepared to contest India's first national election in 1951. The 1950s and early 1960s were a period of political education and preparation for Gandhi as she rose rapidly in the ranks of the INC, becoming a minister in the government formed by Lal Bahadur Shastri (1904–1966) soon after her father's death on May 24, 1964. In 1965, when war with Pakistan broke out, she emerged as a strong contender for the INC leadership with the backing of a cohort of INC leaders named the Syndicate. Warding off challenges from numerous constituencies within the party, and with the backing of the Syndicate, she became India's fifth prime minister.

From 1971 onward, Gandhi consolidated her dominance. In late 1971, civil war and the secessionist movement of East Pakistan led to the Indian Army's invasion of East Pakistan in the third Indo-Pakistan war since 1947. With the creation of the independent nation-state of Bangladesh in 1971, Gandhi's personality-centered political style became pronounced. Partly to underscore India's growing geopolitical stature in the cold war, she encouraged the development of India's nuclear program, which conducted a successful nuclear test in 1974. Even as India made economic gains in some areas, she undermined India's constitutionally mandated federalism when, unlike her father, she steadily undercut the authority of regional political leaders in order to consolidate power at the center. Her regime witnessed the arrival of a distinctively populist style of government, most apparent from her use of the slogan "Garibi Hatao" ("remove poverty"). While these changes bolstered her authority, they also made her the brunt of popular discontent, which became strident in the 1973–1974 period because of food shortages and inflation. Popular unrest and legal assaults on Gandhi's power precipitated, in June 1975, the declaration of a state of emergency by her government.

The only period of authoritarian rule in post-independence India and a phase denounced as one of the darkest of the postcolonial period, the state of emergency lasted from 1975 to 1977. Controversial constitutional amendments, censorship, and assaults on civil liberties were accompanied by the arrest of thousands of party workers, and perhaps most notoriously, the forced sterilization campaigns prompted by Gandhi's son Sanjay Gandhi (1946–1980). These policies raised severe discontent, but Prime Minister Gandhi misjudged the popular mood in 1977 and called parliamentary elections in which her party was comprehensively defeated.

The Janata Party government that came to power in 1977 under the prime ministership of Morarji Desai (1896–1995) did not survive for long, but the period after the state of emergency marked a decisive shift in Indian politics with the restoration of India's parliamentary democracy and the reversal of many of the authoritarian policies adopted by Gandhi. The INC itself split in the wake of the election debacle, and Gandhi sought to build a new political base for herself, one drawn largely from ethnic and religious minorities. Her reemergence as a political leader coincided with infighting in the Janata Party government, and in 1980 Gandhi was voted back to power as India's eighth prime minister.

Gandhi's second term in office was weighed down with problems in the Punjab, where the rise of Sikh militancy accompanied Sikh demands for an independent state. Matters escalated in mid-1984 with Operation Bluestar, when she ordered the Indian Army to storm the Golden Temple in Amritsar, one of the holiest Sikh shrines, to remove militants hiding in its premises. This act of desecration, accompanied by the excessive use of military force, has remained a source of enormous controversy. On October 31, 1984, Gandhi was gunned down by her Sikh bodyguards as she was walking out of her residence. The assassination triggered a pogrom against Sikhs in New Delhi and other northern Indian cities.

Gandhi's political career has left a deep imprint on Indian politics, not least through her descendants. Her son Rajiv Gandhi (1944–1991) became prime minister in 1984, and his widow Sonia Gandhi emerged during the late 1990s as the leader of the Congress Party. "Votebank" politics, with which Indira Gandhi is often identified, has remained an enduring facet of Indian political culture long after her death.

SEE ALSO *Anticolonial Movements; Authoritarianism; Civil Liberties; Cold War; Congress Party, India; Democracy; Federalism; Nehru, Jawaharlal; Partition; Pogroms; Populism; Poverty; Weaponry, Nuclear*

BIBLIOGRAPHY

Brass, Paul R. 1994. *The Politics of India since Independence.* 2nd ed. Cambridge, U.K.: Cambridge University Press.

Jayakar, Pupul. 1992. *Indira Gandhi: A Biography.* New Delhi: Viking.

Malhotra, Inder. 1991. *Indira Gandhi: A Personal and Political Biography.* Boston: Northeastern University Press.

Vivek Bhandari

GANDHI, MOHANDAS K.
1869–1948

Mohandas Karamchand Gandhi was born in Porbandar, Gujarat, India, on October 2, 1869, the youngest son in a family of four children. Due to his father's position as a local politician, the family was subject to transfer within the province, and the Gandhis moved to Rajkot when Gandhi was seven years old. He completed his primary and secondary studies there, and at age thirteen, in keeping with Indian custom at that time, was married (to Kasturba Kapadia).

As a young husband, Gandhi exhibited intense jealousy and sexual voracity. However, his sexual appetite would become the source of great guilt throughout his adult life. This began after his father fell ill and Gandhi became his constant bedside companion. One evening, a trusted uncle arrived to temporarily relieve Gandhi of his responsibility. Gandhi jumped at the chance to be with his wife, and during his absence, his father died. Gandhi never forgave himself, and the vow of celibacy (known as *Brachmacharya*) that he took later in life may have involved atonement for this event.

Gandhi left for college in Bhavnagar, about ninety miles from Rajkot, soon after his father's death, with the intention of replacing his father as provider for the extended family. Though he had always been an exemplary student, his college studies suffered because of his melancholy and his guilt intensified when he ultimately returned home defeated.

Not long after his return from Bhavnagar, a family advisor suggested that he travel to England to study law. Gandhi spent three years in England, and was "called to the Bar," or made an official barrister, in 1891. He then returned to India to begin a legal practice.

However, Gandhi was afraid to speak out in court. In fact, his first trial ended so badly that he refunded his client's money. He did have an aptitude for drawing up legal documents and briefs, however, and was offered a job with a Rajkot merchant who did business in South Africa. After much deliberation, Gandhi decided to accept the post in South Africa for one year.

In South Africa, Gandhi immediately encountered racial discrimination. Though also British subjects, Indians were not permitted first-class accommodations, always had to give way to British whites, and were treated very poorly in general. Gandhi objected to every indignity, but when his employer stepped in to solve the problem for him, Gandhi backed down and tried to ignore the insult; however, shortly before he was to return to India, the government sought to impose an annual £25 tax on indentured servants who had finished their tenure and continued to work in South Africa. The tax applied to each adult family member, and in many instances would have equaled almost as much as the family's earnings for a full year. It was an obvious ploy to reduce farming competition for white farmers. Gandhi was outraged and met with Indian businessmen to explain the situation. At their behest, Gandhi remained in South Africa to campaign against the tax.

In 1894 Gandhi founded the Natal National Congress, patterned after the National Congress of India, and soon after returned to India to drum up support. *The Green Pamphlet*, Gandhi's first political treatise on the plight of South African Indians, was widely distributed in India and roused greater support for the cause. After returning to South Africa in 1904, Gandhi bought and ran the *Indian Opinion* newspaper to spread the word among Indians living there. At the end of that same year, in order to run the paper more efficiently, Gandhi set up his first commune—the Phoenix Settlement—where he, his wife, and three of his four children lived. Harilal, his oldest son, had stayed in England to study.

Ultimately, the £25 Tax was reduced to a £3 tax, rather than being rescinded, by the South African Parliament, which only served to increase Indian resentment. A new battle arose over a government order to register all Asians, including longtime residents as well as new immigrants, and women and children. This order, commonly known as the "Black Act," also required fingerprinting. The entire community was outraged. This sparked Gandhi's first campaign based on *Satyagraha*, or political struggle through passive resistance and civil disobedience. Many were arrested for their failure to comply with the order, including Gandhi, who was imprisoned for the first time. Eventually, Gandhi reached an agreement with Cabinet Minister Jan Christen Smuts, whereby the amendment would be repealed once most of the Indian population had registered.

Even after a show of Indian compliance, the South African government reneged on the agreement and in 1908 the Indian community met to burn their registration certificates. Once again, many were arrested, including Gandhi, who was sentenced to prison. In 1913, when the Cape Supreme Court ruled that any marriage outside Christianity and/or not recorded by the Registrar of Marriages was invalid, Indian women became involved in the demonstrations.

To goad the British into revoking their harsh requirements, Gandhi organized a "Great March" of 2,000 Indians from Natal into the Transvaal. Indians were bound by law to present registration papers at the point of entry, though Europeans were not so restricted. The march was meant to overcrowd prisons and increase pressure on the government to repeal the law. This situation deteriorated into such harsh conditions for the Indians that even members of the British government began to support Gandhi's movement. Embarrassed, the South African government rescinded its order and the Satyagraha campaign in South Africa ended. Soon after, Gandhi returned to India for the rest of his life.

In 1915 Gandhi established the Satyagraha Ashram near Ahmedabad. At that time, Indian society was divided into a social hierarchy of four castes, with the Dalits or "untouchables" considered the lowest of the four. Those of higher castes were even bound not to touch them. Gandhi, who was adamant that all men were created equal and that the caste system should be abolished, was eager to admit an "untouchable" or Dalit family to his ashram. Despite such efforts, however, his continuing push to end the caste system had little result.

Gandhi practiced law in Bombay for a time, but was drawn into renewed Satyagraha for Indian social causes by people who had learned of his success in South Africa. At Champaran, he campaigned for the indigo workers and at Kheda, he pursued justice for factory workers who were being mistreated. When the British passed the *Rowlett Act* (1919), which gave them full authority to squelch "terrorist" demonstrations, Gandhi launched a series of marches and fasts known as *hartals* ("strikes").

Violence marred the *hartal* in Delhi and an outright massacre took place at Jallianwala Bagh, leading Gandhi to call a halt to the strikes. Many of Gandhi's followers were unhappy with this decision, which some saw as a sign of weakness. Muslims began to pull further away from the predominantly Hindu Indian population and to consider alternatives for themselves, such as an independent Pakistan. Gandhi could not sway them. Even his staunch supporters began to question his ability to lead the people.

But when the activist leader Bal Gangadhar Tilak died in 1920, Gandhi was called on to fill the void in the Home Rule movement, even as his health was failing. He called for a complete boycott of the legislature and proclaimed January 26, 1930, to be Purna Swaraj Day ("Total Independence Day").

On March 2 Gandhi wrote to the viceroy, Lord Irwin, warning him that he intended to lead followers on a civil disobedience march to protest the prohibition against collecting salt naturally. Actions contrary to this law were harshly dealt with, but when Gandhi had no reply to his ultimatum, the 200-mile march to the sea began on the morning of March 11. As the group traveled along, they stopped in villages and small towns, encouraging residents to burn all European cloth in their possession. Gandhi urged them to spin their own thread and to wear garments made only with Khadi, the homespun Indian material. When the throng reached the salt mines, Gandhi encouraged them to take up salt from the salt beds. Many people were assaulted by police and arrested. Gandhi was among those taken and imprisoned without trial.

In the ensuing months, more than 100,000 were arrested, and the upheaval continued until a pact aimed at ending the civil disobedience was made between Gandhi and Irwin. During the last four months of 1931, Gandhi attended a Round-Table Conference in London to discuss Indian issues with representatives of the British government. At the conference, the British offered to reserve a block of seats in a proposed bicameral legislature for Muslims, Sikhs, and Dalits. Gandhi was vehemently against this proposal because he thought that all Indians should be treated equally, and should not be divided into separate blocks. Though B. R. Ambedkar, the leading Dalit politician, tried to make Gandhi see that this was the Dalits' only chance of representation, Gandhi continued to oppose the proposal and began a "fast to the death" to stop it.

Gandhi would endure several fasts, more imprisonment, and the deaths of his wife and personal secretary before a final agreement—the Indian Independence Act of 1947—was reached, granting full independence to India. This agreement also called for the creation of an independent Pakistan, a provision that upset many Muslims. Not all Muslims lived in northern India, where Pakistan was formed, and many were displeased that relatives would be living in another country. They felt that Gandhi had failed them. While holding a prayer meeting at Birla House in Delhi on January 20, 1948, Gandhi was murdered by an angry Muslim.

Gandhi, know as the "Mahatma" or the "Great Soul," was at various times underestimated by the British and by Indian politicians. Though the latter had set him aside as an incompetent old man, they soon came to realize how much they needed him as a source of inspiration, because only Gandhi had been able to hold sway over the hearts and minds of the Indian people.

SEE ALSO *Caste; Civil Disobedience; Liberation Movements; Passive Resistance; Protest*

BIBLIOGRAPHY

PRIMARY WORKS

Gandhi, Mohandas K. [1927–1929] 1993. *An Autobiography: The Story of My Experiments with Truth.* Trans. Mahadev Desai. 2 vols. Boston: Beacon Press.

Gandhi, Mohandas K. *Collected Works of Mahatma Gandhi Online.* Vols. 1–98. http://www.gandhiserve.org/cwmg/cwmg.html.

SECONDARY WORKS

Arnold, David. 2001. *Gandhi: Profiles in Power.* London: Pearson Education.

Ashe, Geoffrey. 1968. *Gandhi: A Biography.* New York: Stein & Day, 1968. Reprint, New York: Cooper Square Press, 2000.

Gandhi, Arun, and Sunanda Gandhi. 1998. *The Forgotten Woman: The Untold Story of Kastur, Wife of Mahatma Gandhi.* Huntsville, AR: Ozark Mountain Publishers.

Shirer, William L. 1979. *Gandhi: A Memoir.* New York: Simon & Schuster.

Wolpert, Stanley. 2001. *Gandhi's Passion: The Life and Legacy of Mahatma Gandhi.* New York: Oxford University Press.

Patricia Cronin Marcello

GANDHI, RAJIV
SEE *Gandhi, Indira.*

GANDHI, SONIA
SEE *Gandhi, Indira.*

GANS, HERBERT J.
1927–

Herbert J. Gans was born in Cologne, Germany, in 1927. He escaped the worst of the Nazi Occupation, moving first to England in 1938 and then to the United States in 1940, becoming an American citizen in 1945. After graduating from the University of Chicago in 1950 with an MA in sociology and social science, Gans worked for three years with public and private agencies as a planner of two new towns. In 1953 he turned to academia, receiving his PhD from the University of Pennsylvania in 1957 and advancing to the position of associate professor of urban studies by 1964. Between 1964 and 1969, Gans worked as a research associate for the Institute for Urban Studies and Planning at the Massachusetts Institute of Technology. In 1971 he became a professor of sociology at Columbia University, and in 1985 he became the Robert S. Lynd Professor at Columbia. In 1989 he served as president of the American Sociological Association, and he received the association's Public Understanding of Sociology Award in 1999.

Gans's research and teaching activities have been largely concentrated in the area of urban sociology. Committed to the social-scientific method of participant observation, his first book, *The Urban Villagers* (1962), was a study of an Italian American neighborhood in Boston. Gans noted how economic terms such as *underclass* had evolved into judgments of moral value attached to the poor in society. From his analysis, Gans concluded that the various forms of social problems associated with poor neighborhoods were not a cultural characteristic of the people who lived there, but rather a direct result of the social and economic circumstances of their poverty. This was to be a recurrent theme in Gans's writings, emerging powerfully in a later work, *The War against the Poor* (1995), in which he analyzed the social, psychological, and political reasons that Americans continue to seek to indict millions of poor citizens as "undeserving."

The Levittowners (1967) focused specifically upon the origin and quality of suburban life, including its effects on human behavior. Gans then moved on to challenge the supposed universality of high cultural standards in *Popular Culture and High Culture* (1974). An outspoken advocate of cultural pluralism, Gans pointed out that the alleged convergence of high culture and popular culture could not be empirically sustained, because the lifestyle choices of middle-class and working-class social groups remained divergent. This concern with how various social groups make decisions informed his next publication, *Deciding What's News* (1979), in which he looked at the impact of news agendas on individual decision-making and the shaping of a nation's self-image. He returned to this theme in *Democracy and the News* (2003), arguing that a news media manipulated by private corporations threatens to undermine the basic foundations of American democracy by failing to properly inform its citizenry.

One of Gans's most influential concepts is "symbolic ethnicity," which refers to a nostalgic allegiance to an ethnic culture, typically of an immigrant generation, that can be felt without having to be frequently incorporated into everyday life practices. Symbolic ethnicity is thus about feeling ethnic, without necessarily being so.

A second influential idea is the "function of poverty," and Gans will be remembered for the controversy that this idea created. Gans argues that poverty satisfies a number of positive functions for many nonpoor groups in American society—such as carrying out the essential low-paid work that others will not undertake. Though he has controversially associated poverty with positive functions in this way, Gans maintains that recognizing this does not mean that poverty should, or must, continue to exist.

SEE ALSO *Democracy; Ethnic Enclave; Ethnicity; Functionalism; Journalism; Poverty; Suburban Sprawl; Suburbs; Urban Studies*

BIBLIOGRAPHY

Gans, Herbert J. 1962. *The Urban Villagers: Group and Class in the Life of Italian-Americans.* New York: Free Press.

Gans, Herbert J. 1995. *The War Against the Poor: The Underclass and Antipoverty Policy.* New York: Basic Books.

Mark Davis

GARDNER, HOWARD
SEE *Multiple Intelligences Theory; Talent.*

GARIFUNA

The population of people known as *Garifuna*, Black Carib, Charaib, and—as they refer to themselves in Belize, Central America—as *Garinagu*, is the product of ethnogenesis (a genetic and cultural mixture) resulting from the collision of the Atlantic slave trade, colonial settlement, and the region's aboriginal people. In the 1600s a cargo of slaves was shipwrecked off the coast of either Dominica and/or the Island of St. Vincent located in the Lesser Antilles of the Caribbean. These escapees found refuge among the aboriginal Carib Indians, and, over time, recruited others—mostly men—through raids of local plantations. This pattern of marronage produced a new group that populates Central America, specifically Honduras; Bluefield, Nicaragua; Livingston, Guatemala; and Belize. In 1974 William V. Davidson estimated the Garifuna population at 70,000 to 80,000 with the largest concentrations in the Honduras and Belize. In 1998 Mark Moberg placed the Garinagu population at 120,000. And in 2000, Pamela Conley estimated there were 200,000 people living in Honduras, with 15,000 and 6,000 residing in Belize and Guatemala respectively (Conley 2000). Smaller groups of a few thousand live in Nicaragua and the Windward Islands. Late-twentieth-century migration accounts for the presence of Garinagu in Brooklyn, Chicago, and Los Angeles.

The Garinagu's arrival to the coastal countries of Central America is a testimonial of group survival and what Moberg terms "their extraordinary adaptability" (1998, p. 1014). A hunter gatherer society, who were "fiercely independent" (1998, p. 1014), the British violently exiled them from the Island of St. Vincent in 1797 after intense military engagement that included the First Carib War (1772–1773) and the Second Carib War (1795–1796). Land disputes marred their relationship with the British, in stark contrast to their peaceful relationship with the French. At the end of the second war, the British, says anthropologist Joseph Palacio, "viciously extricated … [Garinagu] men, women, and children from their hideouts" (Palacio 2000, p. 4). Approximately 4,338 people, who were not among those decimated during the final altercation, were temporarily held on the desolate island of Baliceaux before being exiled to Roatan in Central America. From Roatan, which the British clearly intended as a place for their demise, the Garifuna with Spanish assistance migrated to Honduras. In 1832 a small group left the (Spanish) Honduras for Belize (formerly the British Honduras). What has emerged from this interaction of African and aboriginal Arawak/Carib Indians is an adaptive group with several unique cultural characteristics.

LANGUAGE

Garinagu speak the gendered language of Garifuna with different dialects for men and women, an aspect reflective of the social ecology of the Island of St. Vincent, whereby "Red" Caribs appropriated Arawak women as war prizes and intermarried with them—with women preserving their Arawak dialect. In the early twenty-first century the language retains this distinctive gender feature and reflects both African and aboriginal Arawak/Carib Indian influences. Garinagu are noted in the region for their "linguistic versatility," and are often fluent in multiple languages (Garifuna, Spanish, English [in Belize], and indigenous Maya languages). This multilingualism has translated itself into professional capital, with many becoming educators and teachers, especially in the rural (Maya) areas of Central America.

CULTURE

Palacio describes Garinagu as an anomaly because of the amalgamation of aboriginal cultural traits and African cultural survivals (2000, p. 2). Garifuna myth and folklore reveal strong aboriginal Indian components while diet reflects many West Indian Afro-American food ways. Historically reliant on a subsistence lifestyle, cassava carries symbolic significance as a diet staple, and as the food that enabled Garinagu to survive exile. Cassava is especially important to the *dügü* ceremony, a sacred religious ritual used to appease dead ancestors after a family experiences a difficult period; all relatives are required to attend the dügü, a communal event designed to reestablish spiritual, physical, and social equilibrium. Contemporary Garinagu religious practices reflect the syncretism of African ancestor worship and Roman Catholic beliefs.

GARINAGU TODAY

With the exception of Belize, Garinagu remain politically and economically marginalized in most of the countries where they reside. A reputation for resistance caused British colonial administrators to separate them from other colonized groups of Blacks—a divide and conquer strategy that in the twenty-first century translates into ethnic tensions between Garinagu and other African-descended populations; for example, in Belize, there is very little intermarriage between African-descended Creoles and Garinagu. The group's strong African phenotype caused some to question the validity of their claims of aboriginal ancestry. However, in 1992 they applied for membership within the Ottawa-based World Council for Indigenous Peoples and were accepted. Preservation of the Garinagu cultural heritage, especially language and the dügü ritual, as well as the struggle for land rights, continues to be a priority. The pervasiveness of the *punta*, however, throughout Central America, a dance derived from the dügü, attests to the ways in which even marginalized cultures have an impact on the larger societies.

SEE ALSO *African Diaspora; Discrimination; Indigenismo; Indigenous Rights*

BIBLIOGRAPHY

Conley, Pamela. March 2000. The Garifuna: A Changing Future. http://www.planeta.com/planeta/00/0003garifuna.html.

Gonzalez, Nancie L. (Solien). 1979. Garifuna Settlement in New York: A New Frontier. *International Migration Review* Spec. issue 13 (2): 255–263.

Interview with Joseph O. Palacio. April–May 2002. *The C.A.C. Review* (Newsletter of the Caribbean Amerindian Centrelink) 3 (3–4). http://www.centrelink.org/AprMay 2002.html.

McClaurin, Irma. 2000. *Women of Belize: Gender and Change in Central America*. Piscataway, NJ: Rutgers University Press.

Moberg, Mark. Winter 1992. Continuity under Colonial Rule: The Alcalde System and the Garifuna in Belize, 1858–1969. *Ethnohistory* 39 (1): 1–19.

Moberg, Mark. December 1998. Visual Anthropology: The Garifuna Journey. *American Anthropologists* 100 (4): 1014–1015.

Palacio, Joseph O. 2000. A Re-consideration of the Native American and African Roots of Garifuna Identity. Paper presented at the Professional Agricultural Workers Conference (PAWC), 58th Session, Tuskegee University, December 3–5. www.centrelink.org/palacio.html.

Palacio, Joseph O. 2001. Coastal Traditional Knowledge and Cultural Values—Their Significance to the Garifuna and Rest of the Caribbean Region. Paper presented at the Belize Country Conference, November 21–24.

Rust, Susie Post. 2001. The Garifuna: Weaving a Future from a Tangled Past. *National Geographic* 200 (3): 104.

Irma McClaurin

GARVEY, MARCUS
1887–1940

Marcus Garvey was the founder of the Universal Negro Improvement Association and African Communities League (UNIA). He was a prominent spokesman for the "back to Africa" movement within black nationalism, which urged people of African ancestry to return to the continent. He is revered as a prophet in Rastafarianism.

Garvey was born in Jamaica and traveled to London and the United States before World War I (1914–1918). He started the UNIA in Jamaica in 1914 as a fraternal organization calling for self-improvement for poor Jamaicans. As the movement took on a more political character in the 1920s, it gathered support from earlier movements for black liberation in the colony, such as the nineteenth-century ex-slaves reparations movement. Garvey corresponded with Booker T. Washington, who had called for black economic self-sufficiency in his Atlanta Address of 1895, and in the early days of his movement shared Washington's gradualist approach. When Garvey went to the United States in 1916, his hope was to emulate Booker T. Washington by starting a school in Jamaica to train poor blacks in practical subjects. Once in America, however, he established a branch of the UNIA there, and in the end it was in North America that the movement had its greatest membership and influence in the period after World War I.

The purpose of the UNIA as Garvey expounded it in the period between 1918 and 1922 was to unite blacks around the world and to work for independent economic improvement. He was not a black supremacist, but instead believed that the races would prosper best if they were separate and self-sufficient. Garvey gathered support from veterans of previous black campaigns, especially the movement for pensions for slaves that had been led by Callie House. Garvey provoked controversy when he lent support to President Harding's campaign against miscegenation and met with leaders of the Ku Klux Klan. His argument was that the races should remain separate, not so that one could dominate another, but so that each could work out its own destiny in keeping with its natural virtues. This is a position that more recent black nationalist groups including the Nation of Islam have also held.

In the 1920s Garveyism became a great international civic movement, whose supporters had an almost religious fervor about Garvey himself as well as his principles. Garvey hoped that blacks from the Americas could redeem Africa. He was opposed to colonialism and called on European powers, especially Britain, to leave Africa. He supported Ethiopian resistance to Italian aggression in 1935, but was harshly critical of Emperor Haile Selassie after Ethiopia's surrender in 1936 (a fact often overlooked by Rastafarians, for whom Selassie is a divine figure).

In order to put his philosophy of racial self-sufficiency and self-redemption into practice, Garvey founded a number of businesses. Most famous were the Black Star shipping line and the Negro Factories Corporation. Unfortunately, the realities of the business climate in the 1920s, colonial regulations in Africa, and American racial discrimination meant that his businesses were unsuccessful. After the failure of the Black Star Line, the American Department of Justice, spurred on by the new director of the FBI, J. Edgar Hoover, brought charges of fraud against Garvey. The charges hinged on a technicality—whether the Black Star Line had ever owned a ship depicted in the stock prospectus. It is still unclear to this day whether Garvey actually did anything wrong. Nonetheless, there had certainly been a lot of shaky financial deal-making in the company's history, and Garvey, if not guilty himself of participation, had at least overlooked some misdeeds. In any case, a black nationalist found it difficult to get a fair trial in 1920s America. Garvey was imprisoned for several years, before President Coolidge commuted his sentence. He was deported to Jamaica in 1927.

Garvey had a long dispute with black civil rights leader W. E. B. Du Bois. Du Bois argued in the early part of the twentieth century that American blacks should work to integrate public institutions and call upon the U.S. government to live up to the high standards of equal treatment under law enshrined in the Constitution. He was one of the founders of the National Association for the Advancement of Colored People (NAACP), which played a key role in the struggle for racial integration and civil rights for American blacks. Du Bois's position was, of course, diametrically opposed to Garvey's. To Garvey, racial integration was at best an illusion and at worst a snare to keep blacks subordinate to whites and away from their destiny in Africa. Their dispute took on an unfortunate personal tone, with Du Bois calling Garvey a "lunatic" and Garvey responding that Du Bois was a "white man's nigger" and a "mulatto monstrosity." Ironically, Du Bois later came to a position closer to that of Garvey than to his former integrationist stand, and himself emigrated to Africa, dying a Ghanaian citizen.

After his return to Jamaica, Garvey formed the People's Political Party (PPP), the first modern political party in Jamaica. Up to this time, Garvey had been reluctant to get involved in politics, seeing the political system as irredeemably white-dominated and participation a form of tokenism that could distract blacks from self-sufficient development. Garvey was elected twice to town council seats, but his views annoyed the colonial government and he was arrested. He finally left Jamaica in 1935 and spent the last five years of his life in London, continuing to work toward his vision of black self-sufficiency and African liberation, but with limited results.

Garvey's movement, although manifesting itself under a variety of different names and somewhat different ideological colors in its several homes, can be considered the first international African movement and perhaps the most dynamic force in the struggle for democracy, dignity, and human rights for black people of the first half of the twentieth century. Garvey deserves a place alongside better-known figures such as Martin Luther King Jr., Du Bois, Frederick Douglass, Sojourner Truth, and Toussaint Louverture as a hero in the struggle for black liberation in the Americas.

Garvey's remains were moved from London to Jamaica in 1964 and were buried in the national heroes' cemetery in Kingston. He is venerated today as a founding figure in Jamaica's struggle for national liberation.

Garvey's own religious practices were conventional—he was a Roman Catholic—and he never claimed any religious authority. However, the Rastafarian movement has adopted him as a major prophet, with many Rastas seeing him as the reincarnation of John the Baptist, Moses, or Elijah. Indeed, the modern Rastafarian movement sprang up after the collapse of the UNIA and the PPP and incorporated many members of those organizations. Garvey's project of returning blacks to Africa is a centerpiece of most Rastafarian theology. Of course, for Rastafarians, it is a religious duty to return Jah's people to the promised land, while for Garvey it was a practical necessity.

SEE ALSO *Black Nationalism; Du Bois, W. E. B.; Rastafari*

BIBLIOGRAPHY

Burning Spear. 2003. "Marcus Garvey." Audio CD. Palm Audio, 2003. Remastered version; original date of release 1975.

Garvey, Marcus. 1986. *Message to the People: The Course of African Philosophy.* Ed. Tony Martin. Dover, MA: Majority Press.

Hill, Robert A., ed. 1983–1995. *The Marcus Garvey and Universal Negro Improvement Association Papers.* Vols. 1–7, 9–10. Berkeley: University of California Press.

Hill, Robert A., ed. 1987. *Marcus Garvey, Life and Lessons: A Centennial Companion to the Marcus Garvey and Universal Negro Improvement Association Papers.* Berkeley: University of California Press.

Lewis, Rupert, and Patrick Bryan, eds. 1988. *Garvey: His Work and Impact.* Mona, Jamaica: Institute of Social and Economic Research, University of the West Indies.

Stewart R. King

GATES, WILLIAM

SEE *Microsoft.*

GAUSS, CARL FRIEDRICH

SEE *Distribution, Normal.*

GAUTREAUX RESIDENTIAL MOBILITY PROGRAM

The result of a 1976 Supreme Court decision, the Gautreaux program allowed low-income black public housing residents in Chicago to receive Section 8 housing certificates (vouchers) and move to private-sector apartments either in mostly white suburbs or the city. Between 1976 and 1998 over 7,000 families participated. The Gautreaux program presents an unusual opportunity to examine the outcomes associated with low-income families' moves to more advantaged neighborhoods with better labor markets and schools. Most research on neighborhood effects has focused on statistical analyses of the relationship between neighborhood attributes and many life outcomes. However, even after extensive statistical controls, one cannot be certain about the direction of causality or whether unmeasured factors might influence relationships. Housing mobility programs such as Gautreaux are one way to separate these effects.

Gautreaux participants circumvented the typical barriers to living in suburbs, not by their jobs, finances, or values, but by acceptance into the program and quasi-random assignment to the suburbs. The program provided housing subsidy vouchers, but not employment or transportation assistance. Unlike the usual case of working-class blacks living in working-class suburbs, Gautreaux permitted low-income blacks to live in middle-income white suburbs. Participants moved to more than 115 suburbs throughout the 6 counties surrounding Chicago. Suburbs with a population over 30 percent black were excluded. Few high-rent suburbs were excluded by funding limitations of Section 8 certificates.

Prior research on Gautreaux shows significant relationships between placement neighborhoods and subsequent employment and education. A study of children finds that, as young adults, suburb movers were more likely than city movers to graduate from high school, attend college, attend four-year colleges (versus two-year colleges), and (if they were not in college) to be employed and to have jobs with better pay and with benefits (Rosenbaum 1995). A study of 330 Gautreaux mothers finds that suburban movers had higher employment than city movers, but not higher earnings, and the employment difference was especially large for adults who were unemployed before the program (Rosenbaum 1995). Using administrative data to locate present addresses for 1,504 out of 1,507 movers, research finds that 65 percent of suburban families remained in the suburbs an average of fourteen years after placement. After premove individual and neighborhood attributes were controlled, program placement strongly predicted racial composition of current neighborhood (DeLuca and Rosenbaum 2003) and public aid receipt many years after moving (DeLuca and Rosenbaum 2003; Keels et al. 2005).

Because researchers had no input into implementation, families were not formally randomly assigned to conditions. However, placements approximate random assignment, because families were assigned to neighborhoods on a first-come, first-placed basis (according to reports of housing counselors and administrators in the 1980s). Few significant differences were evident with individual attributes, but premove neighborhood attributes show statistically significant differences (2 of 9 comparisons). This may indicate selection bias, although even random assignment programs find some substantial differences (Goering and Feins 2003, table 7.1). Other studies have examined multiple neighborhood level indicators, detailed preprogram neighborhood differences, and intergenerational effects (DeLuca 2006).

Based on Gautreaux, the Moving to Opportunity program (MTO) was an experiment with pre- and postmove data and random assignment of low-income families to three groups—one required to move to low-poverty areas, one with open-choice use of housing vouchers, or a control group given no vouchers. Like Gautreaux, MTO found large effects on mothers' and children's feelings of safety and other attitudes. MTO also found large effects on mothers' and daughters' health.

MTO had smaller effects on mothers' employment and children's education than Gautreaux. However, MTO measured outcomes in the late 1990s, during a strong labor market and strong welfare reform, so, although MTO found no difference between groups, it found an astounding 100 percent employment gain for the control group. One possible interpretation is that virtually everyone who could work was doing so, and residential moves had no additional effect for that reason.

Program attributes may explain other findings. While few MTO children attended schools with above-average achievement, nearly all Gautreaux children did. While families made short moves that allowed interaction with prior neighbors (only 16% of moves over 10 miles), Gautreaux's distant moves (90% over 10 miles; average 25 miles) prevented such interaction. While Gautreaux families moved to stronger labor markets, MTO treatment group moves were not necessarily to different labor markets.

The Gautreaux studies suggest the possibility that large changes of environment can have large impact. The MTO results do not contradict that lesson; few MTO moves entail distant moves to above-average schools or much better labor markets. However, MTO research provides strong evidence about modest changes of environment. While both studies indicate enormous effects of residential moves, the differences between the findings indicate the importance of being alert to design features of the program and to historical context influences.

SEE ALSO *Ethics in Experimentation; Experiments, Human; Moving to Opportunity; Social Experiment*

BIBLIOGRAPHY

DeLuca, Stefanie. 2006. The Continuing Relevance of the Gautreaux Program for Housing Mobility. In *Keeping the Promise: Preserving and Enhancing Housing Mobility in the Section 8 Housing Choice Voucher Program Conference Report of the Third National Conference on Housing Mobility*, eds. Philip Tegeler, Mary Cunningham, and Margery Austin Turner. Washington, DC: Urban Institute.

DeLuca, Stefanie, and James Rosenbaum. 2003. If Low-Income Blacks Are Given a Chance to Live in White Neighborhoods, Will They Stay? Examining Mobility Patterns with Quasi-Experimental Data. *Housing Policy Debate* 14, no. 3: 305–345.

Goering, John, and Judith D. Feins. 2003 *Choosing a Better Life?: Evaluating the Moving to Opportunity Social Experiment.* Washington, DC: Urban Institute Press

Keels, Micere, et al. 2005. Fifteen Years Later: Can Residential Mobility Programs Provide a Permanent Escape from Neighborhood Segregation, Crime, and Poverty? *Demography* 42, no. 1: 51–73.

Rosenbaum, James E. 1995. Housing Mobility Strategies for Changing the Geography of Opportunity. *Housing Policy Debate* 6, no. 1: 231–270.

James E. Rosenbaum
Stefanie DeLuca

GAYS

SEE *Politics, Gay, Lesbian, Transgender, and Bisexual; Sexual Orientation, Determinants of.*

GAZA STRIP

SEE *Intifada, The; Palestinians.*

GAZE, COLONIAL

Modern colonial rule relied not only on the military and economic power of conquering nations, but also on domination over forms of cultural representation. The period of Europe's political expansion, starting in the late fifteenth century, witnessed the development of significant new cultural technologies. From the printing press to photography, film, and sound recording, technical innovations enabled novel ways of documenting and disseminating knowledge about Europe's encounters with the non-Western world. Through newspapers, travelogues, popular magazines, and documentary films, European officials and travelers made images of distant colonial settings available to larger, more diverse metropolitan audiences. While such work rapidly expanded knowledge about hitherto remote regions, it was frequently riddled with stereotypes and assumptions that classified societies according to Eurocentric hierarchies. The power to represent colonized populations played an integral role in their subjugation, as narratives of backwardness and primitivity were essential elements in the justification of colonial rule.

Modern colonialism possessed a particularly ocular character, and based its ruling practices on the development of novel conventions for viewing and representing conquered lands. The earliest encounters of Europeans with Native Americans of the New World, for instance, produced an entirely new popular genre of eyewitness travel writing. In contrast to older speculative geographies, the credibility of such early ethnographic work derived from the firsthand nature of the accounts. Many were sensationalistic survival-adventure narratives that featured voyeuristic descriptions of primitive, foreign societies, with their colorful native costumes and spectacular rituals. Not coincidentally, this was also a period when modern techniques of observation and verification were reshaping claims to scientific authority in other fields. Breakthroughs in the study of optics and new scientific procedures for conducting experiments had emphasized the importance of visual evidence, and the accurate representation of observed phenomena. Valued for their observational insights, colonial travelogues often gained both scientific and commercial success. Many became best-selling publications and were reissued and translated into numerous different European languages.

Travelers' descriptions of colonial encounters helped European readers imagine the rest of the globe, and their place within it. By the early sixteenth century, images and descriptions of faraway places could be enjoyed, as vicarious journeys, directly from one's location in the metropole. Travelogues were frequently valued for their accompanying illustrations, as much as for the narrative descriptions of exotic cultures. For many sixteenth- and seventeenth-century readers, the New World was first made familiar through the engraved illustrations of the Dutch publisher, Theodor de Bry (1528–1598). While some of these representations, including his famous woodcut prints of ritual cannibalism in South America, might today be dismissed as sensationalistic distortions,

images of faraway people and places helped to structure the wider social imagination of the early modern European public. By representing the non-European "other" as a definable object of visual scrutiny, such work also helped Europeans establish a sense of cultural and scientific supremacy within an emerging global order. Such a planetary consciousness, as literary theorist Mary Louise Pratt (1992) has argued, helped direct and organize colonial expansion. Just as the iconic images of *National Geographic* helped define American political and social sensibilities in the middle of the twentieth century, early modern Europeans understood their role in the world through the production and consumptions of such images. It helped them imagine both the unity and the fault lines of a globe that was growing ever smaller through trade, discovery, and conquest.

By the eighteenth and nineteenth centuries, images of non-European societies had spilled over from the pages of print media into new forms of visual display. The Great Exhibitions, for instance, attempted to reproduce distant parts of the globe in painstaking detail. European audiences imagined that they were in fact walking through the bazaars and alleyways of Egypt or India, all for the price of an entrance ticket. Putting the world on display served not only to represent cultural differences, but also worked to define them and turn them into objects of modern consumption. Such displays, through world fairs, museums, and travel brochures, determined the way that the non-West was perceived by both casual visitors and colonial officials. The bird's-eye view employed in book illustrations, postcards, and travel guides was frequently reproduced in the work of official colonial cartographers. Such conventions for viewing and representing colonial people and places formed part of a formal repertoire, used by official cartographers and surveyors to demarcate boundaries, to catalog monuments, and to assist ethnologists and criminologists in categorizing racial types in the colonies. Documentary photography later replaced hand-drawn illustrations as a popular method of recording and classifying data on the architectural and social features of the colonies. Such documentation, in attempting to make the colonies legible to metropolitan observers, fixed and naturalized complicated social boundaries, and opened these up as sites of official intervention.

European practices for viewing and representing colonial realities often made social differences more rigid, and exacerbated racial and gender hierarchies. The colonial gaze played a singularly important role in defining gender relations by marking out colonial women as objects of particular interest, either as targets of official sympathy or casual lust. Harems, *zenanas*, and veiled women figured prominently in European accounts. Colonial officials also paid particular attention to social rituals associated with female oppression, such as *sati* (ritual suicide by Hindu widows), the wearing of the veil, and foot binding. While these practices were condemned, they remained subjects of fascination, and frequently found their way into travel accounts and novels set in colonial contexts.

Similarly, racial distinctions are also reproduced and enforced by the colonial gaze. Frantz Fanon (1925–1961), a psychologist and volunteer during the Algerian Revolution (1954–1962), in his semiautobiographical critical work *Black Skin, White Masks* (1952), writes about the psychical trauma of being identified as an object of the white gaze. Robbed of the possibility of being a full-fledged modern subject, a person of color is determined from the outside, as a thing, an object of scrutiny. The colonial gaze, determined by a set of technologies and conventions for viewing colonial realities, underwrote colonial power. It turned people into observed objects, and authorized the official discourses of European viewers, whose representations determined and fixed the status and stature of colonized subjects.

SEE ALSO *Colonialism; Fanon, Frantz; Gaze, Panoptic; Gaze, The; Media; Narratives; National Geographic; Other, The; Postcolonialism; Racism; Representation; Representation in Postcolonial Analysis; Stare, The; Tourism; Travel and Travel Writing*

BIBLIOGRAPHY

Fanon, Frantz. [1952] 1967. *Black Skin, White Masks.* Trans. Charles Lam Markmann. New York: Grove.

Lutz, Catherine A., and Jane L. Collins. 1993. *Reading National Geographic.* Chicago: University of Chicago Press.

Mitchell, Timothy. 1992. Orientalism and the Exhibitionary Order. In *Colonialism and Culture,* ed. Nicholas B. Dirks, 289–317. Ann Arbor: University of Michigan Press.

Pratt, Mary Louise. 1992. *Imperial Eyes: Travel Writing and Transculturation.* London: Routledge.

Said, Edward. 1978. *Orientalism.* New York: Pantheon.

Poornima Paidipaty

GAZE, PANOPTIC

The concepts of panopticon and panoptic gaze can be traced to the 1791 publication of Jeremy Bentham's *Panopticon; or, The Inspection House* (Bentham 1962, p. 37). Although he presented it primarily as a prison design, Bentham (1748–1832) believed the panoptic principle was "applicable to any sort of establishment, in which persons of any description are to be kept under inspection," including prisons, workhouses, manufactories, hospitals, and schools (vol. 4, p. 37). Bentham asserted that "gradual

adoption and diversified application" of this "simple idea in architecture" would have far-reaching benefits: "morals reformed, health preserved, industry invigorated, instruction diffused, public burdens lightened …" (vol. 4, p. 66).

The ideal panopticon consists of an observation tower within a large circular courtyard ringed by a cell-block several stories high but only one room deep. Each cell should be occupied by only one surveillant who is subject to constant observation from the tower; yet, the design of the panopticon simultaneously prevents communication between inmates. Ideally, the central tower is screened, so the inmates never know who (if anyone) is in the observatory at any particular time.

According to Michel Foucault's analysis of panopticism in *Discipline and Punish* (1979), this design has a number of effects. Because the observer is screened from the gaze of the inmates, the see/being-seen dyad is dissociated, inducing "in the inmates a state of consciousness and permanent visibility that assures the automatic functioning of power" (p. 201). Furthermore, the exercise of power is dispersed, depersonalized, and internalized by the inmates. Who, if anyone, actually occupies the tower is irrelevant to the functioning of the mechanism, so long as the inmates (or patients, students, workers, shoppers) behave as if they were under constant surveillance. "[In short], the inmates should be caught up in a power situation of which they are themselves the bearers" (p. 201). Although the panopticon in its pure and literal form was relatively rare, it was—and remains—an extremely pervasive "political technology that may and must be detached from any specific use" (p. 205).

Investigators in disparate social science fields have noted the importance of panoptic surveillance in both historic and contemporary contexts. For example, Thomas Jefferson was quite familiar with Bentham's work and utilized panoptic principles in the design of Monticello, his hilltop estate. He subsequently drew on French examples of panoptic institutions in his plan (never implemented) for a prison to be constructed in Richmond, Virginia (Epperson 2000; Upton 1990). Similarly, James Delle (1998) has analyzed the importance of the panoptic gaze in the spatial disciplining of enslaved plantation workers in Jamaica, and Mark Leone (1995) has discerned panoptic principles in city plans and public architecture in Annapolis and Baltimore, Maryland. According to urban geographer Edward Soja, "every city is to some degree a panopticon, a collection of surveillant nodes designed to impose and maintain a particular model of conduct and disciplined adherence on its inhabitants" (1996, p. 235). In contemporary Los Angeles the panoptic gaze is manifested architecturally in disciplinary institutions such as the Metropolitan Detention Center and electronically in closed-circuit surveillance cameras (Davis 1992; Soja 1996).

SEE ALSO *Foucault, Michel*

BIBLIOGRAPHY

Bentham, Jeremy. 1962. Panopticon; Or, The Inspection House. In *The Works of Jeremy Bentham, Published Under the Supervision of His Executor, John Bowring*, ed. J. Bowring. New York: Russell and Baker. Original edition, 1838–1842.

Davis, Mike. 1992. *City of Quartz: Excavating the Future in Los Angeles*. New York: Verso.

Delle, James A. 1998. *An Archaeology of Social Space: Analyzing Coffee Plantations in Jamaica's Blue Mountains*. New York: Plenum.

Epperson, Terrence W. 2000. Panoptic Plantations: The Garden Sights of Thomas Jefferson and George Mason. In *Lines That Divide: Historical Archaeologies of Race, Class, and Gender*, eds. James A. Delle, Stephen A. Mrozowski, and Robert Paynter. Knoxville: University of Tennessee Press.

Foucault, Michel. 1979. *Discipline and Punish: The Birth of the Prison*. Trans. Alan Sheridan. New York: Vintage Books.

Leone, Mark P. 1995. A Historical Archaeology of Capitalism. *American Anthropologist* 97 (2): 251–268.

Soja, Edward W. 1996. *Thirdspace: Journeys to Los Angeles and Other Real-and-Imagined Places*. Cambridge, MA: Blackwell.

Upton, Dell. 1990. Imagining the Early Virginia Landscape. In *Earth Patterns: Essays in Landscape Archaeology*, eds. William M. Kelso and Rachel Most. Charlottesville: University Press of Virginia.

Terrence W. Epperson

GAZE, THE

Until the nineteenth century, philosophical inquiry into the question of visuality mainly concerned matters of sense perception, the nature of imagination, and the truth-status of representations. A long tradition in western and many nonwestern philosophical discourses gives to vision a particular and relative significance as the medium of both apprehending the world and verifying the truth of predicative statements. Beginning in the seventeenth century, however, scientific inquiries into the mechanics of perception, and post-Cartesian investigations of the relationship between mind and body, led to a split in discourse about visuality. That split was oriented around the opposition between "seeing" and "being seen," and between the "eye" and the "gaze."

There have been a number of efforts to historicize this process, most notably by Michel Foucault, Jonathan Crary, and Martin Jay—the first in the realm of knowledge, the second in the realm of technology, the third in the domain of aesthetics. Despite their different disciplinary locations, these authors all undertake a twofold gesture. First, they trace the impact of optics and the development of associated technologies, noting that efforts to augment and extend the reach of vision (via the microscope, the telescope, and so forth) were associated with the idea that reality is limited to that which can be brought into the field of vision. Second, and simultaneously, they emphasize that these historical and technological developments made palpable the limits of the human eye as an organ for discerning reality.

Martin Heidegger had criticized the simultaneous valorization of technology and the limitation of human faculties to a practice of organizing the world for vision in his essay "The Age of the World Picture" (1952), but his philosophical intuition was not supported by historical research. In the writings of Michel Foucault, however, the historicization of vision is linked to an analysis of emerging forms of governance in the western polities.

Foucault identified a form of governmentality dominated by the logics of surveillance, which, he argues, were sustained by the discourses of institutionalized knowledge, from clinical medicine to geography, education, and psychology. In *Discipline and Punish* (1977), for example, Foucault states that penal architecture and social reform converged in the post-Enlightenment period around a new aim: the cultivation of a political subject who would internalize and anticipate the "gaze" of power. This new structure of subjectification, Foucault argues, was not only marked by a normative demand for self-discipline but was also associated with the depersonalization of power. As a result, power became a force no longer incarnated in the relatively sovereign body of the monarch, but one that was diffused through a vast capillary system of microinstitutions. Taken together, this system worked to generalize the sensation of being seen, precisely in the moment that overt spectacles of power lost their centrality; thus did a theater of power in which sovereignty showed itself as a local and even personal phenomenon give way to an unconscious and invisible dramaturgy that demanded the self-revelation of subjects. In many ways, Foucault's history of power's depersonalization resonates with Max Weber's conception of bureaucratization, but for Foucault the process was dependent on the relative privilege that vision enjoyed in the discourses of power and knowledge.

Foucault's writings entered a field in French philosophy that was equally concerned with the concept of "the gaze" (*le regard*). In the existentialist thought of Jean-Paul Sartre and the structural Marxism of Louis Althusser, the gaze features as a structure of negative identification. In strikingly analogous scenarios, these writers describe moments when a figure of power discovers the subject, often in some illicit act such as peeping through a keyhole or committing a crime. In Sartre's case, this moment of being discovered produces shame; in Althusser's case, it is followed by the subject's being "hailed" by the representative of power, a process that grants him (or her) a violent kind of recognition. Both cases express a sense of subjectification as that which takes place in and through the experience of being apprehended in the visual domain. Significantly, this "being seen" occurs from a point unseen by the subject.

This concept of the gaze is further developed in Jacques Lacan's famous seminar XI of 1964. However, Lacan revised this notion of the gaze as the condition of "being seen" by positing a prior state of "giving to be seen." Lacan's particular interventions responded to the writings of Maurice Merleau-Ponty, whom Lacan credits with the basic understanding that human subjects apprehend the world from the position of visceral materiality: as objects among other objects. According to Merleau-Ponty, what makes human beings exceptional is that they orient themselves to those other objects, and he calls this orientation *intentionality*. Moreover, in Merleau-Ponty's analysis, intentionality is organized by the perception of form, and by the imagination of an all-seeing being behind the myriad objects that constitute the world.

Lacan insists that this all-seer is merely metaphoric, the name of a principle by which the visible is actually dependent on a structure that places the subject under the gaze of an "other." But this gaze of the other is also a metaphor in Lacan's writing, or rather it designates the process by which the subject covers over the fact of the gaze's invisibility with an image of a seer's eye. This misrecognition is necessary, argues Lacan, if the subject is to feel attracted to or aroused by desire. Here, desire designates a lack in the subject, and this sensation of lack is what compels the subject toward intimate social relationships, but also, as later thinkers such as Judith Butler have reminded us, toward normative forms of identification. This normative dimension of the gaze is not lost on Lacan, and he notes that, in patriarchal contexts, this "giving to be seen" is realized and demanded most especially of women.

Frantz Fanon had, in fact, already discerned the unequal distribution of the effects of the gaze in his reading of the experience of being looked at as a "negro." Fanon emphasizes the nonreciprocity of looks in colonial milieux, noting that only racially dominant subjects can appropriate the power that is located in the gaze, whereas black subjects must constantly give themselves to be seen in a process that renders them vulnerable to catastrophic psychic injury. Although this appropriation is itself born of a misrecognition or conflation of eye with gaze, it is nonetheless one that is withheld from black subjects under colonial conditions, according to Fanon.

It is often assumed that Lacan's theory of the gaze represents the apogee of a tradition that renders the question of the subject a matter only of ontology. By contrast, Foucault's reading of the gaze is said to represent an absolute historicization of the concept, and a repudiation of ontological arguments. To be sure, Foucault's historicist critique of psychoanalysis encouraged the reading of their approaches to the question as mutually exclusive. It is important to recognize that Lacan himself undertook his analysis of the gaze with an explicit invocation of the Cartesian turn in philosophy and with a nod to the representational histories that precede and follow upon it in the plastic arts. It therefore may be more helpful to understand these two thinkers, and the approaches that they inaugurated, as symptoms and diagnoses of a persisting moment lived in thrall of vision's hegemony. Foucault approaches the question of the gaze from the point of view of what he calls "human multiplicities," whereas Lacan treats the subject who, precisely, possesses a "point of view" rather than a gaze.

It is nonetheless notable that this development of theories about the gaze occurred in the space between World War I and the conclusion of the space race toward the end of the 1960s. In other words, the problematization of the gaze occurred in the moment that European modernity seemed to be in ruins thanks to the experience of aerial warfare (in which oversight had made total destruction possible), and, simultaneously, on the brink of a new kind of total visibility made possible by space travel, satellite imaging, and the first experience of earth as apprehended from elsewhere. In France, where most of this work was generated, the exposure of rationalism's apotheosis in the death camps of World War II was followed by the revelation that Soviet socialism had become a totalized penal society, and together these spurred a massive rethinking of both sovereignty and subjectivity. It is in this nexus that the question of the gaze itself becomes visible.

SEE ALSO *Gaze, Colonial*

BIBLIOGRAPHY

Althusser, Louis. 1971. Ideology and the Ideological State Apparatus. In *Lenin and Philosophy and Other Essays*, trans. Ben Brewster. New York: Monthly Review Press.

Butler, Judith. 1993. *Bodies That Matter: On the Discursive Limits of "Sex"*. New York: Routledge.

Crary, Jonathan. 1990. *Techniques of the Observer: On Vision and Modernity in the Nineteenth Century*. Cambridge, MA: MIT Press.

Fanon, Frantz. 1967. *Black Skin, White Masks*. [Peau noire, masques blancs]. Trans. Charles Lam Markmann. London: Pluto.

Foucault, Michel. 1977. *Discipline and Punish: The Birth of the Prison* [Surveillir et punir]. Trans. Alan Sheridan. New York: Vintage.

Foucault, Michel. 1980. The Eye of Power [L'oeil du pouvoir]. In *Power/Knowledge: Selected Interviews, 1927–1977*, ed. and trans. Colin Gordon, 146–165. New York: Pantheon.

Heidegger, Martin. [1952] 1977. The Age of the World Picture [Die Zeit des Weltbildes]. In *The Question Concerning Technology and Other Essays*, trans. William Lovitt, 115–154. New York: Harper.

Jay, Martin. 1993. *Downcast Eyes: The Denigration of Vision in Twentieth Century Thought.* Berkeley: University of California Press.

Lacan, Jacques. 1977. *Four Fundamental Concepts of Psychoanalysis* [Les Quatre Concepts fondamentaux de la psychoanalyse]. Ed. Jacques-Alain Miller, trans. Alan Sheridan. New York and London: Penguin.

Merleau-Ponty, Maurice. 1968. *The Visible and the Invisible* [Le visible et l'invisible]. Ed. Claude Lefort, trans. Alphonso Lingis. Evanston, IL: Northwestern University Press.

Rosalind C. Morris

GEARING RATIO

SEE *Leverage.*

GEERTZ, CLIFFORD
1926–2006

The American cultural anthropologist Clifford Geertz was known for contending that culture is the enacted and public creation of meaning and that therefore ethnographic inquiry requires interpretation. Drawing on extensive fieldwork in Indonesia and Morocco, Geertz's theory of "interpretive anthropology" was articulated in his 1973 collection, *The Interpretation of Cultures*, in which he stated, "The concept of culture I espouse … is essentially a semiotic one. Believing, with Max Weber, that man is an animal suspended in webs of significance he himself has spun, I take culture to be those webs, and the analysis of it to be therefore not an experimental science in search of law but an interpretive one in search of meaning" (p. 5).

This search, Geertz noted thirty years later, involved "ferreting out the singularities of other peoples' ways of life.…" (2000, p. xi). Geertz emphasized the particularistic nature of cultural experience, highlighting the explanatory priority of symbols and attending to "local knowledge." While sharing the American anthropologist Franz Boas's goal of viewing cultures within their specific contexts, Geertz specifically focused on the cultural creation of symbolic meaning.

Geertz pursued graduate studies in the 1950s in Harvard University's interdisciplinary Department of Social Relations and conducted ethnographic research in Java, receiving his Ph.D. in 1956. After a postdoctorate stint at the Center for Advanced Study in the Behavioral Sciences (1958–1959) and a year teaching at the University of California at Berkeley (1959–1960), Geertz joined the University of Chicago where he taught for a decade (1960–1970) and participated in the Committee for Comparative Studies of New Nations. In 1970 he joined the Institute for Advanced Study at Princeton, retiring as professor emeritus in 2000. A fellow of the National Academy of Sciences, the American Academy of Arts and Sciences, and other academic societies, Geertz penned *Works and Lives: The Anthropologist as Author* (1988) for which he was named the 1989 winner of the National Book Critics Circle Award for literary criticism.

Geertz's writings chart a progressive concern with ethnographic interpretation that built on his fieldwork in Java (1952–1954, 1986), Bali (1957–1958), and Morocco (1965–1966, 1985–1986). His early monographs—*The Religion of Java* (1960), *Agricultural Involution: The Process of Ecological Change in Indonesia* (1963), *Peddlers and Princes: Social Change and Economic Modernization in an Indonesian Town* (1963), and *The Social History of an Indonesian Town* (1965)—variously considered the historical, political, religious, and environmental variables that shaped the cultural contours of an evolving Indonesia.

Geertz's thinking about interpretive ethnography was foreshadowed in the final chapter of *The Social History of an Indonesian Town* in which he outlined, following Harold Garfinkel, "the document approach." In this approach, a specific ethnographic case is analyzed such that "the ineradicable specificity of actual events and the elusive generality of meaningful form render one another intelligible" (p. 154).

Having documented the event, it is the anthropologist's task to decipher and expose its meanings: This requires interpretation. In *The Interpretation of Cultures*, Geertz argued that the ethographer "must contrive to somehow first to grasp and then to render" the multiple conceptual structures that account for the meanings of cultural acts (p. 10). "An acted, public document" culture is "written not in conventionalized graphs of sound but in transient examples of shaped behavior" (p. 10). The anthropologist's goals are to sort through "the structures of signification" that make such behaviors meaning-full, to decipher those connections in an ethnographic text, and to thus enlarge the consultable record of human experience.

Several objections can be raised to Geertz's theory of interpretive anthropology. First, Geertz's position is idealist, contending that culturally mediated concepts shape human behavior rather than, for example, the material conditions of existence. Second, the interpretive approach leads to several problems of method and validation. For example, how is one to think about the "structures of signification"? Are some structures more central and durable than others, and in what contexts are they deployed? Explicitly focused on the microcosm, how can an interpretive approach address broader connections of history, economy, and power? Third, interpretive approaches are designed "not to generalize across cases but to generalize within them" (Geertz 1973, p. 26), thus precluding cross-cultural comparative studies. Finally, as Geertz acknowledged, interpretive accounts "escape systematic modes of assessment"; how can any interpretation be proven false? (p. 24).

Geertz's interpretive anthropology departed from the paradigm of anthropology as a science in search of law-like generalizations about humanity. From the 1970s to the present, the unbridgeable differences between interpretive versus scientific theoretical positions have crystallized into deep divisions within American anthropology.

SEE ALSO *Anthropology, U.S.; Weber, Max*

BIBLIOGRAPHY

PRIMARY WORKS

Geertz, Clifford. 1960. *The Religion of Java.* New York: The Free Press.

Geertz, Clifford. 1963. *Agricultural Involution: The Process of Ecological Change in Indonesia.* Berkeley: University of California Press.

Geertz, Clifford. 1963. *Peddlers and Princes: Social Change and Economic Modernization in Two Indonesian Towns.* Chicago: University of Chicago Press.

Geertz, Clifford. 1965. *The Social History of an Indonesian Town.* Cambridge, MA: MIT Press.

Geertz, Clifford. 1973. *The Interpretation of Cultures.* New York: Basic Books.

Geertz, Clifford. 1983. *Local Knowledge: Further Essays in Interpretive Anthropology.* New York: Basic Books.

Geertz, Clifford. 1988. *Works and Lives: The Anthropologist as Author.* Stanford, CA: Stanford University Press.

Geertz, Clifford. 1995. *After the Fact: Two Countries, Four Decades, One Anthropologist.* Cambridge, MA: Harvard University Press.

Geertz, Clifford. 2000. *Available Light: Anthropological Reflections on Philosophical Topics.* Princeton, NJ: Princeton University Press.

SECONDARY WORKS

Harris, Marvin. 1979. *Cultural Materialism: The Struggle for a Science of Culture.* New York: Random House.

Harris, Marvin. 1999. *Theories of Culture in Postmodern Times.* Walnut Creek, CA: Altamira Press.

Wolf, Eric. 1999. *Envisioning Power: Ideologies of Dominance and Crisis.* Berkeley: University of California Press.

Jerry D. Moore

GEMEINSCHAFT AND GESELLSCHAFT

In *Gemeinschaft und Gesellschaft* (community and society) by Ferdinand Toennies (1855–1936), the former refers to "all intimate, private, and exclusive living together," whereas the latter is "public life—it is the world itself" (1955, pp. 37–38). The book contains an elaborate architecture of classifications covering the whole of social reality, from kinship to the modern metropolis. One of the most striking features of this is the way Toennies based his social forms on types of the human will: *Wesenwille* and *Kürwille*, the will that directs thought (natural will) and the will that is subject to it (rational will). The relevance is evident, of calculation of means and ends to articulated purposes, to exchange relations of the *Gesellschaft* type. So, too, is the "natural" basis of the *Wesenwille* in drives, instincts, and emotions. *Wesenwille* is seen predominantly in *Gemeinschaft* forms.

The outward forms of the *Gemeinschaft* are the house, the village, and the country town, its general form the people (*Volk*). *Gesellschaft* is to be found in the larger cities. Its general form is the nation-state. Toennies stressed that his concepts were "types," not classifications of the concrete. Reality always showed a mixture of elements. Nonetheless, Toennies also implied at one stage an evolutionary scheme in which *Gesellschaft* is seen as a temporary phase, *Gemeinschaft* returning on a higher level in an international socialist order of the future. Each type showed gradations of natural will and rational will—for example, in *Gemeinschaft*, kin, neighbor, and friend relations—so that natural will does not equate to emotion, drives, and instinct. Toennies's point was that whereas the first is real and natural, the second is "ideal and artificial," just as *Gemeinschaft* is real and organic life, the essence of community, and *Gesellschaft* is ideal and mechanical structure, the concept of society. *Gemeinschaft* is an original unity of will, *Gesellschaft* its individualized forms. Disintegration is built into *Gesellschaft*. It is checked by convention, agreement, politics, and public debate.

Robert Redfield (1857–1958) in his folk-urban typology (or continuum) spelled out *Gemeinschaft* and *Gesellschaft* in a more direct and usable way than Toennies, enriching and supporting it with current ethnographic evidence (1930). Howard Becker (b. 1928) in his sacred and secular societal types broke down *Gemeinschaft* and *Gesellschaft* into a set of subtypes, again with a view to making them more empirically flexible, and again enriching the basic pairing from evidence not available to Toennies. Robert E. Park (1864–1940) and the Chicago school took the role of place or locality as being central to *Gemeinschaft* and *Gesellschaft*. It was so for Toennies. This was because *Gemeinschaft*-type relations require enduring physical proximity as their condition. They used the the-

INTERNATIONAL ENCYCLOPEDIA OF THE SOCIAL SCIENCES, 2ND EDITION

ory of ecology, suggesting that all living organisms are shaped in their relations by the physical environment, to study the city as a series of concentric areas or zones, each having their characteristic associational and cultural forms, and succession being visible as groups moved out of a zone and others moved in to replace them. *Gemeinschaft* and *Gesellschaft* can, finally, be treated as types of social relationship. Toennies was used this way by Max Weber (1865–1920), and Talcott Parsons (1902–1979) also read him for clues about the possible orientations of social action. Hermann Schmalenbach (1885–1950) added the important category "communion."

Toennies has fallen into the background since the 1930s. For example, the importance of community as place rather than as social relations was challenged by Herbert Gans in his studies of community ties in suburbia, particulary in *The Levittowners* (1967). Nevertheless, Toennies's place in the canon is secure: *Gemeinschaft* and *Gesellschaft* are basic categories. They may be approached on the level of our own experience.

In a *Gesellschaft* everything is clearly spelled out, so that everyone has clearly defined rights. If anyone asks us to go beyond our duties then they must give a reason, demonstrating why this extra demand is part of our "job description." Only when this is demonstrated are we obligated to take on something further. In a *Gemeinschaft* the opposite is the case. We feel we cannot say "no" to virtually any demand. Indeed, it would not occur to us to assess the demand as a demand. This kind of calculation does not enter the picture. Here the burden of proof is on us to say why we should not respond positively, and if we feel we cannot, there will be a great deal of inner struggle. In a "full" *Gemeinschaft* this inner struggle does not occur at all, and we unreflectingly meet our obligation. Here, then, people make demands that are "total." As today with a close family member, we are bound to them "come what may," "for better or worse," because the love involved is unconditional. No matter what the other person has done, irrespective of whether we feel drawn to them on a personal level—one might not feel "close," or that the parties like and understand one another—the obligation is there. The other person does not have to have earned our trust and affection for the aid and assistance to be forthcoming. Here we have no escape from our duty, for example as a parent or as a child.

In a *Gesellschaft* it is the performance of a contractual obligation that matters. Whether it is done willingly or grudgingly, with affection or calculatingly, makes no difference. All that matters is that the contract is fulfilled to the letter, for example that the goods are delivered. In a *Gemeinschaft how* things are done *is* of interest. It matters, for example, that food is served in the family setting with love (though the food may be burned); it is the care that

goes into the act that is at least as important as the act itself. It matters that the gift is carefully wrapped, showing that the giver has taken trouble.

These considerations show that Toennies's original distinction has lost none of its relevance over the years. The problem of what makes us human, under what conditions people and their culture can thrive, and what in our culture threatens, as anomie, the mass society or latterly, "disembedding" and globalization, the nurturing, solidarity-generating, direct, sustained and deep contact between human beings, is a continuing one. It is both a public issue and a sociological question.

SEE ALSO *Sociology*

BIBLIOGRAPHY

Becker, Howard. 1950. *Through Values to Social Interpretation.* Durham, NC: Duke University Press.

Bell, Colin, and Howard Newby. 1971. *Community Studies.* London: George Allen and Unwin.

Cahnman, Werner J., and Rudolf Heberle, eds. 1971. *Ferdinand Toennies. On Sociology: Pure, Applied, and Empirical.* Chicago: University of Chicago Press.

Gans, Herbert. 1967. *The Levittowners.* New York: Pantheon.

Redfield, Robert. 1930. *Tepotzlan, A Mexican Village.* Chicago: University of Chicago Press.

Toennies, Ferdinand. [1887] 1955. *Community and Association (Gemeinschaft und gesellschaft).* Trans. Charles P. Loomis. London: Routledge and Kegan Paul.

Ian Varcoe

GENDER

In *The Second Sex* (first published in 1949), the French feminist Simone de Beauvoir led the way in distinguishing biological anatomy and chemistry from socialized gendered expectations: "One is not born but rather becomes a woman" (de Beauvoir 1953, p. 249). For de Beauvoir, being a female did not constitute being a woman. Rather, one's biological makeup is subscribed with a social-cultural shaping of one's gendered characteristics; for women this is the development of appropriate feminine behaviors. Though the term is highly contested and laden with political implications, at its most basic level *gender* is used to describe socially constructed characteristics of masculinity and femininity, whereas *sex* is used to describe one's biological makeup (chromosomes, hormones, and reproductive/sexual anatomy).

THE SECOND-WAVE FEMINIST MOVEMENT

The distinction between sex and gender was an essential element for many issues addressed during the second-wave feminist movement (1960–1995). Though immensely diverse, many feminist schools of thought did agree that characteristics associated with femininity in the United States created norms and roles that oppressed women by limiting their access to public space and economic opportunities. Discussions of gender during the second-wave feminist movement often attempted to overturn what the scholar Harold Garfinkel described as the "natural attitude" towards gender (1967, p. 122)—the common belief that the gender dichotomy is a natural distinction between the two sexes. This assumption, according to activists, perpetuated inequality for women. In understanding the creation of the natural attitude, many feminists turned to the structure of the family and women's connection to childbearing. Woman's biological ability to give birth, combined with industrial changes, had led to social expectations of woman as nurturer, domestic caretaker, and other roles traditionally associated with the private sphere. Dichotomously, man's inability to give birth and his larger physical makeup had led to social expectations to fulfill the role of protector, provider, and roles traditionally associated with the public sphere.

For feminists, these gendered characteristics, complicated by an array of other factors, had perpetuated a division of labor that empowered men and disempowered women. Men's more active and dominant roles created an unequal relationship between the sexes that gave rise to an oppressive ideology both within the home and, more broadly, within institutionalized sexism. Overall, the most prominent goal of the second-wave feminist movement was to bring about a sense of gender equality. Concerns such as motherhood, beauty regimes, and domestic upkeep were seen as essential components of a public discussion about expectations of femininity that focused on issues of equal access to the workplace, equal pay for equal work, and an overall attempt to allow women to have control over their lives and their bodies. Theories on how to deal with this hierarchal division of labor were vastly varied. For example, Marxist feminists saw the capitalistic economic structure as inherently patriarchal. Thus, attempts at more equal power relations between men and women were reliant upon a restructuring of the economic system. Conversely, more conservative feminists, who constituted the liberal feminist school of thought, looked more closely at ways to reform the current system to allow for more women within the public sphere. These various feminist schools reflect the differences in conceptualization and approach to the concept of gender. Some feminists worked relentlessly to prove that both men and women could be rational, active members of public space, challenging the preconceived notion that masculine gendered characteristics are inherent to men. Others fought to revalorize qualities of femininity, attempting to recognize the power of women's roles as well as the usefulness of feminine approaches in public space. What united many of the perspectives was a desire to engage in a larger public discussion about issues of masculinity and femininity and how they influence the daily lives of women and men.

GENDER AND ELITISM: WHOSE "PERSONAL IS POLITICAL"?

Since the beginning of the second-wave movement, the meaning of the term *gender* has been disputed. Despite some public understanding of the second wave's fight for gender equality for women, the movement was fractured, with discontentment from many sides. For example, although Betty Friedan's *The Feminine Mystique* (1963) was commended for its attack on women's limited role as domestic caretaker, her analysis was criticized for its elitism. Although Friedan called attention to the oppression rooted in gendered expectations and roles, her white, heterosexual, middle-class perspectives were specific to a single group of women. Such criticisms called into question the stability of the category *woman*. Do all women share a similar experience? Questions of race, class, and sexual orientation brought forth recognition that gender expectations and gender identity were not the same for all women, nor were they the same for all men.

Though cross-cultural comparisons were used to draw attention to the socialization of gender roles and expectations, many second-wave feminists still failed to recognize the cultural differences within their own communities. As gender expectations and what it means to be a woman were debated, critics began to question the assumption that all women shared the same experiences. In her 1981 book *Ain't I a Woman*, the literary scholar bell hooks discussed the racism that circulated and continues to circulate in feminist literature. She identified the struggle for black women to find a space of visibility within a movement embedded in racism. Her analysis, and those of other critics, draws attention to both the racial and economic advantage embedded in the positions of many noted feminists of the second wave. Theorizing about "women" when in actuality only discussing the experiences of white women exemplified this privileged perspective. Core issues such as beauty and domestic expectations were far removed from racially oppressed women whose economic and social positions typically demanded out-of-home labor. As hooks pointed out, the racism within the women's movement coupled with the sexism in the civil rights movement left little to no space for a public debate about the experiences and oppression of black women.

Compounding the criticisms of racial and economic privilege were the objections voiced by members of the lesbian feminist school of thought, who pointed out the homophobia inherent in the women's movement. The notion of a shared sisterhood of all women provoked anger from those women who felt their experiences differed and their perspectives were silenced. Often, core discussions of gender focused on social expectations of men and women as they function in heterosexual relationships. Lesbian feminists pointed out the institutionalization of heterosexuality and the unwillingness of many heterosexual feminists to challenge this unequal power dynamic.

Overall, there was a sense from critics that discussions of power within the second-wave feminist movement were oversimplified. Many feminists failed to recognize that they could be both oppressed and oppressor, thus ignoring the intersections of race, class, and sexual orientation in a society that privileges white, male, middle- or upper-class status, and heterosexuality.

COMPLICATING AND DESTABILIZING GENDER

As gender became a more common topic of discussion in both academic institutions and activist forums, its unstable and complex nature was a frequent part of debate. Attempting to move past the charges of elitism and oversimplification, scholars such as Joan Scott defended the usefulness of gender as an analytic category. Scott maintained that gender is not constant, but rather constantly shifting and changing as it operates in multiple fields (1986). She argued that discussions and studies utilizing gender as an analytic category must be carefully understood based on context and history. Her analysis defended its usefulness while simultaneously complicating the power dynamics that intersect with gender construction.

Similarly, the gender scholar Judith Butler significantly contributed to the complication of a theoretical understanding of gender. Her *Gender Trouble* (1990) is foundational in pointing out the intricate connection between gender and sexuality. Butler drew attention to the policing of heterosexuality through gender norms, arguing that a core component of the current gender system, which calls women to be highly feminine and men to be highly masculine, is as much about upholding heterosexuality as it is about policing public space. Additionally, Butler is noted for her theory of gender performativity, which holds that gender is maintained through performative acts that naturalize and create an appearance of an internal essence. Her position can be understood as an extreme social constructionist stand that sees both sexuality and gender as constitutive of our practices, policies, language, and overall daily norms.

Both Scott and Butler echo the reflective position taken by many gender scholars in the last decades of the twentieth century. The desire to complicate gender and illuminate its instability is found in works that addressed the realization that *gender* cannot be equated with *woman*. Masculinity studies became much more common, and indeed expected when addressing issues of gender, and gender literature and courses more frequently recognized the gendered nature of every individual. Most gender literature focused on femininity and oppression; however, a look towards masculinity revealed the limiting role placed upon many men who are primarily defined by success in the public realm. Expectations of aggression, detachment, and control are problematic for both men and women. The antisexist male activist Jackson Katz has since 1993 created high school and college-based educational programs, which include videos and lectures that focus on the construction of masculinity in the United States and the violence inherent in many male-gendered norms. The aim is to liberate not only women but also men from limited roles and expectations; recognizing that all individuals are gendered allows for a more complete understanding of how the patriarchal system is maintained. Privy to earlier criticisms, scholars studying masculinity are acutely aware of the vast differences in norms and expectations across racial and class divides.

Many gender scholars have called for an understanding of gender that moves beyond basic binary discussions of masculinity and femininity to a greater understanding of transgendered issues and the fluidity of gendered identities. The twenty-first century has brought more frequent discussions and practices that illustrate at least a partial public understanding of "gender bending." Public populations are often not familiar with the work of Butler who calls for disruptions of gender expectations. However, cross dressing, transexuality, and overall gendered norm violations are infiltrated in media and other mainstream elements of United States culture. Thus, the public is both exposed and often partially aware of transgendered or gender bending practices. Overall, gender has come to be understood as unstable, allowing for resistance, reinforcement, or recreation of gender identity and expectations in a multitude of ways.

For women who identify with the third wave of feminism, this unstable and complex view of gender is central. Though there still is dispute over whether or not a new wave has indeed emerged, many young women active in gender discussions claim a third wave of feminism whose focus is on creating a solidarity that recognizes difference. In its discussion of difference, coalitions, and popular culture, this third wave, thought to have begun in the mid-1990s, both veered away from and built upon the second-wave movement. Although "third wavers" are as diverse in their positions as the feminists who preceded them, there is a general sense that the movement needs to be privy to difference and to build coalitions with other activist movements, because many gendered issues entail struggle against racism, homophobia, class privilege, and imperialism simultaneously. Additionally, although earlier movements criticized popular culture and many of the feminine-gendered expectations, some third wavers distinguish their understanding of gender by claiming power in their sexuality and femininity, seeking ways to co-opt patriarchal ideologies for their own empowerment. This is exemplified in debates over wearing high heels and makeup and embracing one's feminine sexuality. Some third wavers argue that the pop star Madonna does not represent female oppression, but rather sexual agency. This position strays from the second wave's desire to free women (typically and critically, mostly white women) from such beauty expectations.

GLOBALIZING GENDER

Twenty-first-century feminism is as diversified as ever, but earlier charges of elitism, both national and international, have produced feminist schools of thought that seek to better understand gendered issues on a global scale. Many postcolonial feminist scholars seek ways to create a feminist solidarity that addresses global concerns while recognizing racial, economic, regional, national, and religious differences. A leader in academic discussions about transnational gender issues is feminist postcolonial theorist Chandra Talpade Mohanty. In *Feminism without Borders: Decolonizing Theory, Practicing Solidarity* (2003) she provides a summary of her feminist position, which argues for economic stability worldwide for all individuals. Her vision is antiracist and anticapitalist and seeks to create democratic participation through a more complex and reflective solidarity.

Also illustrating a global commitment to gender equity are the many transnational feminist networks such as the Women's Environment and Development Organization, which "advocates for women's equality in global policy. It seeks to empower women as decision makers to achieve economic, social, and gender justice, a healthy, peaceful planet, and human rights for all" (2004). This desire to address issues of gender globally comes with a great deal of cultural reflexivity and international collaboration. Global scholars and transnational feminist networks seek to acknowledge and manage issues of difference that arise in multicultural coalitions. Despite these challenges, twenty-first-century gender scholars and activists find it increasingly difficult to ignore globalization and the fact that worldwide gender inequity involves a multiplicity of economic, environmental, ethnic, and many other postcolonial factors.

Although gender research has followed numerous threads, the intellectual compass seems to be pointing toward a focus on global issues. This recent direction is frequently freighted with a complicated theory of power and difference that requires a highly reflective researcher who can represent such issues without colonizing the voices of those they study. Despite shifts in the focus of gender research, the twentieth and twenty-first centuries have proven the importance and longevity of gender as an essential topic of political and social discussion.

SEE ALSO *Feminism; Gender, Alternatives to Binary; Gender Gap; Gender Studies; Glass Ceiling; Inequality, Gender; Patriarchy; Sexuality; Transgender*

BIBLIOGRAPHY

Beauvoir, Simone de. [1949] 1953. *The Second Sex*. Trans. H. M. Parshley. New York: Knopf.

Butler, Judith. 1990. *Gender Trouble: Feminism and the Subversion of Identity*. New York: Routledge.

Connell, Robert W. 2002. *Gender*. Malden, MA: Blackwell Publishers.

Friedan, Betty. 1963. *The Feminine Mystique*. New York: Dell.

Garfinkel, Harold. 1967. *Studies in Ethnomethodology*. Englewood Cliffs, NJ: Prentice-Hall.

hooks, bell. 1981. *Ain't I a Woman: Black Women and Feminism*. Boston: South End Press.

Mohanty, Chandra Talpade. 2003. *Feminism without Borders: Decolonizing Theory, Practicing Solidarity*. Durham, NC: Duke University Press.

Scott, Joan W. 1986. Gender: A Useful Category for Historical Analysis. *American Historical Review* 91 (December): 1053–1075.

Tong, Rosemarie. 1998. *Feminist Thought*. 2nd ed. Boulder, CO: Westview Press.

Whelehan, Imelda. 1995. *Modern Feminist Thought: From the Second Wave to "Post-Feminism"*. New York: New York University Press.

Women's Environment and Development Organization. 2004. About Us. http://www.wedo.org/aboutus.aspx.

Wood, Julia T. 2005. *Gendered Lives: Communication, Gender, and Culture*. 6th ed. Belmont, CA: Wadsworth.

Erin Foley-Reynolds

GENDER, ALTERNATIVES TO BINARY

It is widely taken for granted, especially in Europe and the Americas, that gender is binary: that male and female are sharply different in feelings, anatomy, and behavior, and all people ought to fit neatly into one of these two categories. Certain realities contradict this assumption, including homosexual orientation, intersex (hermaphrodite) anatomy, and transvestite behavior, and they can appear in every society. A small number of nonwestern societies accommodate alternative genders, including the *hijras* of India, the Native American Half-Man–Half-Woman, and the Navajo *nadle*. From these and other cases, social scientists infer that there can be creative ways for people to be legitimate members of society without necessarily fitting squarely into only-male or only-female categories.

In the case of the *hijras*, teenage boys in India expect to become husbands and fathers, but a few realize that, because they are homosexual or intersex, they will not fulfill traditional male roles. These ones find that some cities harbor a group called the *hijras* who adopt female names, dress, and speech, and who relate to each other as sisters, and as daughters to their leaders. Their place in society is based on the belief that, even if homosexuals and intersex males will not marry women or have children, they still possess male procreative energy that they can transfer by blessing bridegrooms at weddings and baby boys at birth. By giving up normative male identity to become *hijras*, they are thought of as former males who help other males become better men. The *hijras* also constitute a separate caste, made distinct from other castes by their own rituals, taboos, myths, and patron goddess.

A "true" *hijra* eventually undergoes an emasculation ritual to remove the male genitalia. Ideally, they earn livings from the blessing rituals, but many have to supplement that income through prostitution. Others marry male lovers. Sex between a man and a *hijra* is not thought of as homosexual; it is heterosexual in the sense that a *hijra* is not a man, and not a woman either, but a third gender.

During the nineteenth century, Native American societies expected boys to become warriors, but at puberty a small number displayed a female-oriented vision of one's future that permitted them to enter into the status of the Half-Man–Half-Woman. Society valued them as mediators because it was thought that they were especially able to see both sides of a question. They also served as chaperones during courtship, and were believed to possess special magical energy that supported blessings and healing. Sometimes a Half-Man–Half-Woman became an additional wife in a polygamous marriage. As with the *hijras*, a sexual relationship between a man and a Half-Man–Half-Woman was considered to be heterosexual.

The Navajo *nadle* moved between quasi-male and quasi-female identities. The *nadle* began life as an intersex, which eliminated options such as becoming a father, hunter, or warrior. But *nadles* were believed to have a spe-cial ability to manage wealth, and it was a blessing to have a *nadle* in the family. The *nadle* was more woman than man: She practiced women's activities such as cooking, had the legal status and sex life of a woman, and was usually (but not always) addressed as a woman. In other circumstances the *nadle* could be manlike, as in presiding over rituals or managing wealth. The *nadle* was appreciated as a wise mediator for the same reasons the Half-Man–Half-Woman was.

Some Navajo transvestites, also called *nadle*, could dress as either male or female, depending on the activity, and could have sex with either men or women. The transvestite had more freedom than the intersex *nadle* to move between male and female roles. Many other Native American societies had gender statuses that enabled a limited number of people to alternate gender roles, but this flexibility became very rare as Native American life was assimilated into the dominant western culture of the United States. The same kind of cultural assimilation also brought an end to other societies' gender alternatives, including the Thai *kathoey* and the Philippine *bakla*.

Alternative gender models are not whimsical lifestyle options. The pressures that steer people into these roles are approximately as powerful as those that require other people in the same societies to conform to male or female models. In most cases, the people who enter these statuses remain in them for the rest of their lives. Very few people in these societies have these statuses, partly because very few are inclined toward them, and partly because these societies have ways to discourage large-scale deviations from normative binary gender.

The alternative models challenge the assumption that binary gender is inevitable. The anatomy of male, female, and intersex can be universal, but gender—the cultural interpretation of sexuality—is highly variable. Yet it is difficult to use an alternative model as a formula for changing the ways westerners experience gender, because each alternative form is intimately situated within a matrix of local beliefs, statuses, and values, and they are not easily adapted from one society to another. Another reason is because reform in the western world is concerned with legal rights. Following in the footsteps of feminist reform, it identifies a portfolio of well-established rights that heterosexuals have (to marry, for example, or to raise children) and then extends those rights to gays, lesbians, bisexuals, intersexes, and transgendered people. This is not an experiment in creating new categories, but rather universal access to existing rights. For those two reasons, nonwestern alternatives to binary gender are unlikely to lead to western versions of *hijras* or *nadles*.

Still, one cannot ignore certain provocative questions that arise in light of these alternative models. If western societies become more tolerant of gay and lesbian people, along with practices such as same-sex unions, how will gay or lesbian roles coexist with binary gender roles? If some gay men are normatively male in everything except their sex lives, are they not ironically reinforcing the tenets of binary gender, even as conservatives accuse them of subverting it? Aren't female impersonators such as Danny LaRue, Holly Woodlawn, The Lady Chablis and RuPaul reinforcing binary gender by distilling an essence of feminine looks and personalities?

Fiction presents some imaginative insights. Ursula LeGuin's science-fiction novel *The Left Hand of Darkness* (1969) describes a planet where humans are "hermaphroditic neuters" who periodically morph into male or female forms to mate with the opposite form. Each can become male or female, father or mother, then revert back to neutral anatomy. Earthlings are considered perverts because they are stabilized in male or female form, which is taken to mean that they are always sexually aroused. Jeffrey Eugenides's *Middlesex* (2002) is the story of a teenage girl who abruptly learns that she is genetically male, and that puberty has been changing her body from girl to man. At the point in the story where this girl/man becomes a medical curiosity, there is a twenty-seven-page presentation on the anatomy and psychology of the intersex condition, as well as facetious accounts of gender-socialization theories and sociobiology as a backlash against them: "Men and women, tired of being the same, want to be different again" (p. 478).

Alternatives to binary gender reveal that there is much more to gender than just sexuality, and that there is more than one way for a society to understand gender. In the words of Cal, the girl who develops into a man in *Middlesex*, "My family found that, contrary to popular opinion, gender was not all that important" (p. 250).

SEE ALSO *Gender; Sexuality; Transgender*

BIBLIOGRAPHY

Eugenides, Jeffrey. 2002. *Middlesex.* New York: Farrar, Straus, and Giroux.

Herdt, Gilbert, ed. 1994. *Third Sex/Third Gender: Beyond Sexual Dimorphism in Culture and History.* New York: Zone Books.

Hill, W. W. 1935. The Status of the Hermaphrodite and Transvestite in Navaho Culture. *American Anthropologist* 37: 273–279.

Jacobs, Sue-Ellen, Wesley Thomas, and Sabine Lang, eds. 1997. *Two-Spirit People: Native American Gender Identity, Sexuality, and Spirituality.* Urbana: University of Illinois Press.

LeGuin, Ursula. 1969. *The Left Hand of Darkness.* New York: Ace Books.

Nanda, Serena. 1999. *Neither Man Nor Woman: The Hijras of India.* 2nd ed. Belmont, CA: Wadsworth.

Nanda, Serena. 2000. *Gender Diversity: Crosscultural Variations.* Prospect Heights, IL: Waveland.

Williams, Walter L. 1992. *The Spirit and the Flesh: Sexual Diversity in American Indian Culture.* Boston: Beacon.

Chris Toumey

GENDER AND DEVELOPMENT

Gender and development is an interdisciplinary field focusing on the social relations between women and men in developing and transitional economies. The field has grown rapidly since the 1970s and includes "innovations in research, analysis, and political strategies brought about by diversely located researchers and activists," as well as a set of practices and discourses that are institutionalized within multilateral organizations (such as United Nations agencies and the World Bank) and national governments (Cornwall et al. 2004, p. 2). Many fine collections have been compiled on gender and development (see Cornwall et al. 2007; Jacquette and Summerfield 2006; Benería and Bisnath 2001; Jackson and Pearson 1998; and Visvanathan et al. 1997). There are also several excellent summaries tracing the intellectual and political evolution of this field from the 1970s to the 1990s (see Elson 1999; Bakker 1999).

This entry will concentrate on gender issues in the context of development theories and policies since the late 1990s, focusing on five related but distinct issues that are debated in the literature: gender and poverty, women's empowerment, paid employment and unpaid work, gender and the macroeconomic policy environment, and institutional issues and gender mainstreaming. For the large and growing literature on other topics in gender and development, see: Mark Pitt and Shahidur Khandker (1998), Linda Mayoux (1999), and Naila Kabeer (2001a) on microfinance; UNESCO (2004) and Michael Kevane (2004) on education; Harriet Presser and Gita Sen (2000) on population; Gita Sen, Asha George, and Piroska Ostlin (2002) on health; UNFPA (2005) on the feminization of AIDS; and Claudia Garcia-Moreno et al. (2005) and Sunita Kishor and Kiersten Johnson (2004) on violence against women.

DEFINING GENDER AND DEVELOPMENT

The literature on gender and development originated in opposition to views common in the 1970s and 1980s that women were excluded from the development process and needed to be incorporated into mainstream policies, institutions, and programs. Early gender and development theorists critiqued the prevailing development paradigm that promoted market-led development and structural adjustment and stabilization packages as a response to debt and balance-of-payments problems, as well as the view that women should be integrated into a process that benefits a few and impoverishes many (Benería and Sen 1982). In contrast to the earlier "women in development" literature, gender and development theorists had an explicit objective of social transformation, both of the ultimate aims and practices of development and of the relations between men and women (Jackson and Pearson 1998).

The feminist academics and activists who chose the language of gender used it in a particular way. Gender is a social construct that refers to the relations between women and men and reflects hierarchies among them, based not only on their biology, but also on their age, life-cycle position, ethnicity, race, income and wealth, and other features (Barker 1999). Gender relations change over time and vary across societies, but in all societies, they structure the division of labor and distribution of work, income, wealth, education, productive inputs, publicly provided goods, and the like.

Kate Young (1997) outlines six issues that characterize approaches used by gender and development scholars. (1) The focus is not on women per se but on gender relations, that is, relations between women and men in a variety of settings interlocked with other social relationships such as income, race, caste, and ethnicity. (2) Women are viewed as active agents, although they may not have perfect knowledge or understanding of the roots of discrimination and subordination. (3) The perspective is holistic, and focuses on the reproductive aspects of social and economic life (caring for dependents), as well as the gendered social relations of production and distribution of goods and services. (4) Development is viewed as a set of complex processes involving economic, political, and cultural transformation over time and space that should aim to produce improvements in capabilities, freedoms, and living standards for individuals and societies. (5) Achieving gender equality and women's empowerment requires multiple approaches and strategies that will necessarily differ by circumstances. (6) The role of organization and collective action by women is central to the achievement of gender equality and women's empowerment.

THE DEVELOPMENT CONTEXT: 1990–2007

Examining the field of gender and development since the 1990s requires an understanding of the global political economy at the turn of the century. Although globalization had accelerated, the patterns were uneven (Stiglitz 2002). Some countries, such as China and India, were growing rapidly while others, such as Ecuador and Bolivia, were growing only slowly. Many countries, espe-

cially those in sub-Saharan Africa, were experiencing negative growth (Birdsall 2006; Wade 2004). Although there is debate over whether global poverty has increased or decreased since the 1990s, analysts agree that a billion-plus people were living on less than $1 per day in 2000 (Reddy and Minoiu 2006; Chen and Ravallion 2004; UN Millennium Project 2005). The widening of income inequality both within and between countries, a series of environmental crises from loss of species to global warming, growing religious fundamentalism, and violence and conflict also posed major development challenges (Milanovic 2006 and 2005; Melnick et al. 2005).

The concern over poverty, inequality, and differential economic growth led world leaders from 189 countries in 2000 to adopt the Millennium Development Goals (MDGs), a set of eight goals with related time-bound targets to reduce extreme poverty and its correlates by 2015 (UN Millennium Project 2005; Thorbecke and Nissanke 2006). The MDGs have become the global development policy paradigm for the early part of the twenty-first century and one of the key entry points for advocates of gender and development. Although many development economists and activists agree on the importance of reducing absolute poverty and improving human capabilities, they disagree about whether the MDGs can be achieved in the current era of globalization, and whether growth can be made to be pro-poor.

GENDER AND POVERTY

Reducing gender inequality and empowering women is the third Millennium Development Goal. In setting this goal, governments recognized the contributions that women make to economic development and the costs to societies of the multiple disadvantages that women face in nearly every country (Grown et al. 2005). As noted in the World Bank's *Engendering Development*:

> In no region of the developing world are women equal to men in legal, social, and economic rights. Gender gaps are widespread in access to and control of resources, in economic opportunities, in power, and political voice. Women and girls bear the largest and most direct costs of these inequalities—but the costs cut more broadly across society, ultimately harming everyone. For these reasons, gender equality is a core development issue—a development objective in its own right. (World Bank 2001, p. 1)

Beginning in the 1990s, the concept of poverty broadened beyond a focus on shortfalls in income or consumption to lack of capabilities (e.g., education and health), lack of voice, lack of opportunities, and lack of dignity. When these broader criteria are factored in, females appear to be more vulnerable than males to the risk of poverty and vulnerability, although data limitations make it difficult to quantify the relative proportion of female poverty (Quisumbing et al. 2001). They also experience poverty differently than men (Razavi 1999; Jackson 1998). Because of their responsibilities for social reproduction, as well as gender inequalities in ownership of assets and access to employment and productive resources, women find it harder than men to transform their capabilities into steady income streams that would allow them to escape poverty (Deere and Doss 2006; Cagatay 1998).

Early work on gender and poverty focused on female-headed households, identifying them as the poorest of the poor (Chant 2003, p. 11). In a meta-analysis of sixty-one empirical studies, Mayra Buvinic and Geeta Rao Gupta (1997) found that in thirty-eight studies, female-headed households were overrepresented among the poor. More recent work has debunked the notion equating female headship and poverty, noting the wide economic diversity of female-headed households in countries around the world and the heterogeneity of intrahousehold sharing rules, which may disadvantage females in male-headed households more than females in female-headed households (Chant 2003).

Since poverty encompasses many dimensions other than earned income, including lack of public provision of goods and services, access to common property resources, and voice in political processes and decision-making, poverty reduction strategies need to be multidimensional. Within the context of the MDGs, Caren Grown and colleagues (2005) recommend seven strategic priorities to achieve gender equality in the context of poverty reduction, including strengthening opportunities for postprimary education for girls, guaranteeing sexual and reproductive health and rights, investing in infrastructure to reduce women's and girls' time burdens, securing women's and girls' property and inheritance rights, eliminating gender inequality in employment by decreasing women's reliance on informal employment and closing gender gaps in earnings, and significantly reducing violence against girls and women.

Although the broader focus on the gender dimensions of poverty is welcome, Cecile Jackson (1998) cautions against seeing gender and development as a variant of poverty problems; poverty is not entirely responsible for the subordination of women, and even antipoverty strategies may not be sufficient on their own to improve the position of women.

WOMEN'S EMPOWERMENT

The concept of women's empowerment features prominently in the gender and development literature, and many development interventions not only aim to increase income and assets but also to empower women. The World Bank's sourcebook on *Empowerment and Poverty Reduction* (Narayan 2002) defines *empowerment* as the expansion of freedom of choice and action. Feminist scholars point out that women's empowerment encompasses unique additional elements. Women are not just one group among several disempowered subsets of society, but are spread throughout all categories of disadvantage, including race, caste, ethnicity, and class. Second, the household and interfamilial relations are a central locus of women's disempowerment in a way that is not true for other disadvantaged groups (Malhotra et al. 2002). At the same time, empowerment requires systemic transformation in household relations, social norms, and market and government institutions (Kabeer 2001b).

PAID EMPLOYMENT AND UNPAID WORK

Access to employment and income are a critical component of poverty reduction and women's empowerment. Women's participation in paid employment has increased everywhere since 1990, but there is still a large gap between female-male activity rates in most regions. Most analysts attribute the increase to opportunities provided by globalization and structural changes, including commercialization of agriculture, industrialization, and the replacement of unpaid provision of services by women in families and communities by the paid provision of services by women employed in both the public sector and private firms (Standing 1999). Controlling for long-term economic development, Cagatay and Ozler (1995) find that structural adjustment policies and export-oriented growth lead to a feminization of the labor force

As the International Labor Organization (ILO 2007) points out, indicators of paid employment (such as labor force participation rates or the female share of paid nonagricultural employment) show little about the likelihood of being employed or having decent work. In almost all regions, the female unemployment rate is higher than the male rate, occupations are sex-segregated, and gender gaps persist in earnings. Women predominate in informal employment—jobs that lack formal contracts, security, benefits, or social protection (ILO 2002). The average earnings from informal employment are too low, in the absence of other sources of income or social protection policies, to raise households out of poverty (Chen et al. 2005). And the conditions of informal employment perpetuate the financial dependency of women wage earners on male relatives and partners because they do not earn enough in informal employment to support themselves and any children they may have (Chen et al. 2006).

Time-use data are necessary for calculating the total amount of work, paid and unpaid, that women and men perform. Although progress has been made in collecting time-use statistics, data are limited and trend data are lacking (UNDESA 2006). Yet available evidence suggests that women and girls spend more time on unpaid work than men and boys, and when both paid and unpaid work is taken into account, women and girls have a longer working day than men and boys. Jacques Charmes (2006), for instance, finds that females in Benin spent 7.5 hours a day in paid employment compared to 5 hours a day for men in 1998, yet females spent almost 3.5 hours per day on unpaid work, while men spent just over 1 hour. Moreover, a number of studies suggest that women's performance of overlapping activities has intensified with globalization (Floro 1995).

GENDER, MACROECONOMIC POLICIES, AND THE ENABLING ENVIRONMENT FOR POLICY REDUCTION

The development economics literature is divided about the policies that promote growth that is pro-poor, with some arguing for greater liberalization of trade and financial capital markets and others arguing for greater control over markets and attention to policies that create domestic demand for goods and services. Most of the gender and development literature takes a skeptical position toward the view that gender equality can be achieved in a context of export-led growth (Benería 2003; Elson 2002).

In this vein, Stephanie Seguino and Caren Grown (2006) propose shifting economies from profit-led, export-oriented growth to wage-led, full-employment growth. This entails state-level industrial and agricultural development strategies to promote both articulation with the domestic economy and an export product mix that permits rising female wages without a (large) negative effect on exports, as well as policies that stabilize the economy, including limits on physical capital mobility (inward and outward foreign direct investment) and capital controls that act as speed bumps, reducing financial volatility. Elissa Braunstein (2006) notes a number of other policies specifically targeted to foreign direct investment and gender equity simultaneously, including restrictions on entry of foreign direct investment in key strategic industries, support to domestically owned firms for technological and human capital upgrading with priority for women workers, and the enforcement of core labor standards.

DEVELOPMENT INSTITUTIONS AND GENDER MAINSTREAMING

The goal of gender and development—gender equality and women's empowerment—is now institutionalized in policy and organizational mandates. At the Fourth World Conference on Women in 1995, the international community endorsed gender mainstreaming as a key institu-

tional response for promoting gender equality and empowering women. In 1997 the UN Economic and Social Council defined gender mainstreaming as:

> the process of assessing the implications for women and men of any planned action, including legislation, policies or programs, in all areas and at all levels. It is a strategy for making women's as well as men's concerns and experiences an integral dimension of the design, implementation, monitoring and evaluation of policies and programs in all political, economic and societal spheres so that women and men benefit equally and inequality is not perpetuated. The ultimate goal is to achieve gender equality. (UN ECOSOC 1997)

This definition makes clear that gender mainstreaming is a means toward the achievement of gender equality and women's empowerment. It is both a technical and political process requiring shifts in organizational culture and ways of thinking and in the structures and resource allocations of organizations (Oxaal and Baden 1997). As currently understood, gender mainstreaming encompasses all aspects of planning, implementing, and monitoring any social, political, or economic action.

Feminist scholars have pointed out a number of problems with the way that gender mainstreaming has been operationalized in development institutions. Some claim that "doing gender" has reduced a fundamentally political process aimed at social transformation into a technical process reliant on tools, checklists, and training (Mukhopadhyay 2004). Other critiques focus on the gap between governmental policy commitments and actual implementation (Verloo 2001). Within multilateral and bilateral development organizations, the process of gender mainstreaming has stopped short of operations—of the very dimension that impacts development on the ground and can show results in terms of development effectiveness (Hannan 2004; Moser and Moser 2005).

Others point out that gender mainstreaming has not been pursued fully or systematically enough to support definitive conclusions about its success or failure (Woodford-Berger 2004). In most cases, the process is incomplete or not properly implemented. Since it is likely that mainstreaming will continue to be the dominant strategy for incorporating gender equality issues in development policy institutions, more work will be necessary to understand the conditions under which it can successfully achieve its objectives.

CONCLUSION

There are many development challenges to be tackled in the early decades of the twenty-first century. The field of gender and development has much to offer for developing both new analytic paradigms and new institutional practices.

SEE ALSO *Development Economics; Economic Growth; Female-Headed Families; Feminism; Gender; Hierarchy; Inequality, Gender; Poverty; Work and Women*

BIBLIOGRAPHY

Bakker, Isabella. 1999. Development Policies. In *The Elgar Companion to Feminist Economics*, ed. Janice Peterson and Margaret Lewis, 83–95. Cheltenham, U.K.: Elgar.

Barker, Drue. 1999 Gender. In *The Elgar Companion to Feminist Economics*, ed. Janice Peterson and Margaret Lewis, 390–395. Cheltenham, U.K.: Elgar.

Benería, Lourdes. 2003. *Gender, Development, and Globalization: Economics as if All People Mattered*. London: Routledge.

Benería, Lourdes, and Savitri Bisnath, eds. 2001. *Gender and Development: Theoretical, Empirical, and Practical Approaches*. 2 vols. Cheltenham, U.K.: Elgar.

Benería, Lourdes, and Gita Sen. 1982. Class and Gender Inequalities and Women's Role in Economic Development: Theoretical and Practical Implications. *Feminist Studies* 8 (1): 157–176.

Birdsall, Nancy. 2006. Stormy Days on an Open Field: Asymmetries in the Global Economy. UN University Research Paper No. 2006/31. Helsinki: UNU-WIDER.

Braunstein, Elissa. 2006. Foreign Direct Investment, Development, and Gender Equity: A Review of Research and Policy. UNRISD Occasional Paper No. 12. Geneva: UNRISD.

Buvinic, Mayra, and Geeta Rao Gupta. 1997. Female-Headed Households and Female-Maintained Families: Are They Worth Targeting to Reduce Poverty in Developing Countries? *Economic Development and Cultural Change* 45 (2): 259–280.

Cagatay, Nilufer. 1998. Gender and Poverty. Social Development and Poverty Elimination Division Working Paper 5. New York: UNDP.

Chant, Sylvia. 2003. The "Engendering" of Poverty Analysis in Developing Regions: Progress Since the United Nations Decade for Women, and Priorities for the Future. Gender Institute New Working Paper Series No. 11. London: London School of Economics.

Charmes, Jacques. 2006. A Review of Empirical Evidence on Time Use in Africa from UN-Sponsored Surveys. In *Gender, Time Use, and Poverty in Sub-Saharan Africa*, ed. C. Mark Blackden and Quentin Wodon, 39–72. Washington DC: World Bank.

Chen, Martha, Joann Vanek, and James Heintz. 2006. Informality, Gender, and Poverty: A Global Picture. *Economic and Political Weekly* 41 (21): 2131–2139.

Chen, Martha, Joann Vanek, Francie Lund, et al. 2005. *The Progress of the World's Women 2005: Women, Work, and Poverty*. New York: UNIFEM.

Chen, Shaohua, and Martin Ravallion. 2004. How Have the World's Poorest Fared Since the Early 1980s? *World Bank Research Observer* 19 (2): 141–170.

Cornwall, Andrea, Elizabeth Harrison, and Ann Whitehead. 2004. Introduction: Repositioning Feminisms in Gender and Development. *IDS Bulletin* 35 (4): 1–10.

Cornwall, Andrea, Elizabeth Harrison, and Ann Whitehead, eds. 2007. *Feminisms in Development: Contradictions, Contestations, and Challenges*. London: Zed.

Deere, Carmen Diana, and Cheryl Doss. 2006. The Gender Asset Gap: What Do We Know and Why Does It Matter? *Feminist Economics* 12 (1–2): 1–50.

Elson, Diane. 1999. Theories of Development. In *The Elgar Companion to Feminist Economics*, ed. Janice Peterson and Margaret Lewis, 95–105. Cheltenham, U.K.: Elgar.

Elson, Diane. 2002. Gender Justice, Human Rights, and Neo-liberal Economic Policies. In *Gender Justice, Development, and Rights*, ed. Maxine Molyneux and Shahra Razavi, 79–115. New York: Oxford University Press.

Floro, Maria. 1995. Economic Restructuring, Gender, and the Allocation of Time. *World Development* 23 (11): 1913–1929.

Garcia-Moreno, Claudia, Henrica A. F. M. Jansen, Mary Ellsberg, et al. 2005. *WHO Multi-country Study on Women's Health and Domestic Violence against Women*. Geneva: WHO.

Grown, Caren, Geeta Rao Gupta, and Aslihan Kes. 2005. *Taking Action: Achieving Gender Equality and Empowering Women*. London: Earthscan.

Hannan, Caroline. 2004. Gender Mainstreaming: A Key Strategy for Promoting Gender Equality at National Level. *UN-ESCAP High-level Intergovernmental Meeting to Review Regional Implementation of the Beijing Platform for Action and its Regional and Global Outcomes*. Bangkok, Thailand, September 7–10.

International Labor Organization (ILO). 2002. *Women and Men in the Informal Economy: A Statistical Picture*. Geneva: Author.

International Labor Organization. 2007. *Global Employment Trends for Women*. Geneva: Author.

Jackson, Cecile. 1998. Rescuing Gender from the Poverty Trap. In *Feminist Visions of Development: Gender Analysis and Policy*, ed. Cecile Jackson and Ruth Pearson, 39–64. London: Routledge.

Jackson, Cecile, and Ruth Pearson, eds. 1998. *Feminist Visions of Development: Gender Analysis and Policy*. London: Routledge.

Jacquette, Jane S., and Gale Summerfield, eds. 2006. *Women and Gender Equity in Development: Theory and Practice*. Durham, NC: Duke University Press.

Kabeer, Naila. 2001a. Conflicts Over Credit: Re-evaluating the Empowerment Potential of Loans to Women in Bangladesh. *World Development* 29 (1): 63–84.

Kabeer, Naila. 2001b. Reflections on the Measurement of Women's Empowerment. In *Discussing Women's Empowerment-Theory and Practice*, 17–57. Stockholm: Novum Grafiska AB.

Kevane, Michael. 2004. *Women and Development in Africa: How Gender Works*. Boulder, CO: Lynne Rienner.

Kishor, Sunita, and Kiersten Johnson. 2004. *Profiling Domestic Violence: A Multi-country Study*. Calverton, MD: ORC Macro.

Malhotra, Anju, Sydney Schuler, and Carol Boender. 2002. Measuring Women's Empowerment as a Variable in International Development. Background Paper prepared for the World Bank Workshop on Poverty and Gender: New Perspectives, June 28, 2002. Washington, DC: World Bank.

Mayoux, Linda. 1999. Questioning Virtuous Spirals: Micro-Finance and Women's Empowerment in Africa. *Journal of International Development* 11 (7): 957–984.

Melnick, Don, Jeffrey McNeely, Yolanda Kakabadse Navarro, et al. 2005. Environment and Human Well-Being: A Practical Strategy. UN Millennium Project Task Force on Environmental Sustainability. London: Earthscan.

Milanovic, Branko. 2005. *Worlds Apart: Measuring International and Global Inequality*. Princeton, NJ: Princeton University Press.

Milanovic, Branko. 2006. Global Income Inequality: What It Is and Why It Matters. World Bank Policy Research Paper 3865. Washington, DC: World Bank.

Moser, Caroline, and Annalise Moser. 2005. Gender Mainstreaming Since Beijing: A Review of Successes and Limitations in International Institutions. *Gender and Development* 13 (2): 11–22.

Mukhopadhyay, Maitrayee. 2004. Mainstreaming Gender or "Streaming" Gender Away: Feminists Marooned in the Development Business. *IDS Bulletin* 35 (4): 95 103.

Narayan, Deepa. 2002. *Empowerment and Poverty Reduction: A Sourcebook*. Washington, DC: World Bank.

Oxaal, Zoe, and Sally Baden. 1997. Gender and Empowerment: Definitions, Approaches, and Implications for Policy. BRIDGE Development and Gender Report 40. Brighton, U.K.: Institute of Development Studies.

Pitt, Mark, and Shahidur Khandker. 1998. The Impact of Group-Based Credit Programs on Poor Households in Bangladesh: Does the Gender of Participants Matter? *Journal of Political Economy* 106 (5): 958–996.

Presser, Harriet B., and Gita Sen. 2000. *Women's Empowerment and Demographic Processes: Moving Beyond Cairo*. Oxford and New York: Oxford University Press.

Quisumbing, Agnes, Lawrence Haddad, and Christine Peña. 2001. Are Women Overrepresented Among Poor? An Analysis of Poverty in Ten Developing Countries. FCND Discussion Paper No. 115. Washington, DC: International Food Policy Research Institute.

Razavi, Shahra. 1999. Gendered Poverty and Well-Being: Introduction. *Development and Change* 30: 409–433.

Reddy, Sanjay, and Camelia Minoiu. 2006. Real Income Stagnation of Countries, 1960–2001. Working Paper No. 2006/03. Institute for Social and Economic Research and Policy. New York: Columbia University.

Seguino, Stephanie, and Caren Grown. 2006. Gender Equity and Globalization: Macroeconomic Policy for Developing Countries. *Journal of International Development* 18: 1–24.

Sen, Gita, Asha George, and Piroska Ostlin, eds. 2002. *Engendering International Health: The Challenge of Equity*. Cambridge, MA: MIT Press.

Standing, Guy. 1999. Global Feminization Revisited. *World Development* 27 (7): 583–602.

Stiglitz, Joseph. 2002. *Globalization and Its Discontents*. New York: Norton.

Thorbecke, Erik, and Machiko Nissanke. 2006. Introduction: The Impact of Globalization on the World's Poor. *World Development* 34 (8): 1333–1337.

UN ECOSOC. 1997. Mainstreaming the Gender Perspective into all Policies and Programmes in the United Nations System. New York: Author.

UNESCO. 2004. *Education for All Global Monitoring Report 2003/4*. Paris: Author.

UNDESA. 2006. *The World's Women 2005: Progress in Statistics*. New York: Author.

UNFPA. 2005. *State of the World Population*. New York: Author.

UN Millennium Project. 2005. *Investing in Development: A Practical Plan to Achieve the Millennium Development Goals*. London: Earthscan.

Verloo, Mieke. 2001. Another Velvet Revolution? Gender Mainstreaming and the Politics of Implementation. IWM Working Paper No. 5/2001. Vienna: Institut für die Wissenschaften vom Menschen/Institute for Human Sciences.

Visvanathan, Nalini, Lynn Duggan, Laurie Nisonoff, and Nan Wiegersma, eds. 1997. *The Women, Gender, and Development Reader*. London: Zed.

Wade, Robert Hunter. 2004. Is Globalization Reducing Poverty and Inequality? *World Development* 32 (4): 567–589.

Woodford-Berger, Prudence. 2004. Gender Mainstreaming: What Is It (About) and Should We Continue Doing It? *IDS Bulletin* 35 (4): 65–72.

World Bank. 2001. *Engendering Development: Through Gender Equality in Rights, Resources, and Voice*. New York: Oxford University Press.

Young, Kate. 1997. Gender and Development. In *The Women, Gender, and Development Reader*, ed. Nalini Visvanathan, Lynn Duggan, Laurie Nisonoff, and Nan Wiegersma, 51–54. London: Zed.

Caren Grown

GENDER EMPOWERMENT MEASURE

SEE *Women and Politics.*

GENDER GAP

Gender gap refers to systematic differences in the outcome of men and women on a variety of issues ranging from economic participation and opportunity, political empowerment, and educational attainment to health and well-being. Unlike sex stereotypes that ascribe social roles to men and women based on a traditional distribution of labor within a particular society and thereby reinforce stereotypes, gender gap measures difference in the outcome to gain a better understanding of how these differences can be narrowed. Closing the gender gap is constitutive of achieving gender equality, which can be defined as "a stage of human social development at which the rights, responsibilities and opportunities of individuals will not be determined by the fact of being born male or female, in other words, a stage where both men and women realize their full potential" (Lopez-Claros and Zahidi 2005, p. 1).

State policies are an important factor in shaping gender relations and, in certain respects, state actions are constitutive of gender. Countries vary significantly in their efforts to close the gender gap through "women-friendly" policies—social policies that seek to mediate social inequalities, particularly those flowing from women's disproportionate responsibilities in caregiving. A 2006 study by the World Economic Forum (WEF) examined fifty-eight countries and their efforts in closing the gender gap. The Nordic countries, particularly Sweden, Norway, and Iceland, had the lowest gender gap. These states are characterized by liberal societies, protection of minorities, and a comprehensive welfare state that actively promotes gender equality through women-friendly policies. The United States was ranked seventeenth. The United States ranks poorly on the specific dimensions of economic opportunity and health and well-being, compromised by meager maternity leave, the lack of maternity leave benefits, and limited government-provided childcare. The overall rating is low, given that many scholars and policymakers consider the antidiscrimination and sexual violence legislation in the United States to be the strongest in the world. Countries with the largest gender gap were four of the seven predominantly Muslim countries, namely Jordan, Pakistan, Egypt, and Turkey. Sweden, in spite of being the country with the lowest gender gap, encounters occupational segregation with women working predominantly in the public sector. Thus no country has yet achieved full gender equality, making gender gap a global phenomenon.

Since 1990 the United Nations Development Program (UNDP) has published an annual report that examines human development based on four indices: the Human Development Index (HDI), the Gender-Related Development Index (GDI), the Gender-Empowerment Measure (GEM), and the Human Poverty Index (HPI). Based on these indices 174 countries are ranked. For the evaluation of gender gaps the GDI and the GEM are important measures. The GDI is composed of an average of three indices that measure gender differences in terms of life expectancy at birth, gross enrollment and literacy rates, and earned income. The GEM is an average of three other variables that reflect the importance of women in society, specifically the participation of women in employment, the male to female ratio among administration, managers and professional and technical workers, and the female to male Gross Domestic Product (GDP) per capita ratio calculated from female and male share of earned income. While the GDI assesses the status of women in society the GEM points to the relative empowerment of women and men in the political and economic spheres.

Based on the GDI and GEM countries are ranked annually, thereby making it possible to evaluate their progress in closing gender gaps as well as the relative status of countries vis-à-vis each other on gender equality. While the indices are important tools for measuring the results of gender discrimination they do not address the underlying causes. Thus, although indices represent an important first step in comparing and monitoring the progress of countries toward closing the gender gap they are not sufficient to actually reduce gender discrimination. To promote policy change these indices need to be accompanied by, for instance, broader strategies for change that address the underlying causes of gender discrimination and best practice examples that enable governments and activists to learn from each other about how to close gender gaps.

GENDER GAPS IN ECONOMY, POLITICS, EDUCATION, AND HEALTH

Economic participation, or a high employment rate of both men and women, is important for lowering household poverty, enabling women to establish and maintain an independent household, and supporting an inclusive society. Access to employment alone is not sufficient to achieve gender equality. Equality within employment requires a closing of the gender pay gap, meaning that women are paid the same as men for the same work or work of equivalent value, and establishing economic opportunities to reduce horizontal and vertical segregation. Horizontal segregation means women and men are concentrated in different sectors and professions, with women working in areas with less opportunity for professional development and low pay. States can promote the opening of a wider range of occupations to women through equal opportunity legislation and affirmative action programs as well as antidiscrimination and sexual harassment legislation. Vertical segregation refers to the blocking of higher positions for women or limited opportunities for women to advance to managerial professions (the proverbial "glass ceiling"). To promote women's upward mobility the state can establish, for instance, social services that provide caregiving for dependents, limit working time, and promote a "work-life balance." (International Labor Organization 2003.)

Political empowerment of women is concerned with equitable representation of women in decision-making structures and their ability to influence the policymaking process. While most countries have de jure equality in political participation, actual participation varies by country. A 2005 United Nations report found that "women still hold only 16 per cent of parliamentary seats world-wide (only Rwanda and the Nordic countries have come close to parity) … by the end of 2004, 81 countries had adopted some form of affirmative action, such as party quotas or reserving seats for women in parliament to ensure their political participation" (United Nations 2005, p. 16).

Education has gender gaps in a number of areas, such as literacy rates and years of schooling (primary, secondary, and tertiary education). While the gender gap in primary and secondary school attendance has narrowed over the past thirty years, the gap is still wide in tertiary education, particularly computer science and mathematics.

Finally, gender gaps can be found in health and well-being. The focus is particularly on access to nutrition, health care, reproductive facilities, and overall security in terms of safety and integrity of a person. A 2005 OECD study pointed to the relationship between birth rates and attitudes toward equality. Countries with "more traditional family structures in modern economies face chronically low birth rates, whereas the birth rate trend is positive and the demographic structure more balanced in countries where gender equality in the workplace is more developed. For these countries, that points to fewer problems with ageing, as well as higher labour activity and a more robust economy" (Mörtvik and Spånt 2005).

Gender gap and gender equality are two sides of the same coin. In order to achieve gender equality gender gaps have to be closed. Looking at gender gaps and monitoring their development can serve as a valuable tool for policy-makers and activists to integrate gender equality in economic models for sustainable growth and development and create conditions for inclusive societies.

SEE ALSO *Gender; Glass Ceiling; Inequality, Political*

BIBLIOGRAPHY

Borchorst, Anette. 1994. The Scandinavian Welfare States—Patriarchal, Gender-Neutral, or Woman-Friendly? *International Journal of Contemporary Sociology* 1 (8): 3–21.

Connell, R. W. 1987. *Gender and Power*. Stanford, CA: Stanford University Press.

Hernes, Helga. 1987. *Welfare State and Woman Power: Essays in State Feminism*. Oslo Norwegian University Press.

International Labor Organization. 2003 Global Report. *Time for Equality at Work*. Geneva: International Labor Office.

Jütting, Johannes, and Christian Morrison. 2005. Changing Social Institutions to Improve the Status of Women in Developing Countries. *OECD Policy Brief* 27.

Lopez-Claros, Augusto, and Saadia Zahidi. 2005. *Women's Empowerment: Measuring the Global Gender Gap*. Geneva: World Economic Forum.

Mörtvik, Roger, and Roland Spånt. 2005. Does Gender Equality Spur Growth? *OECD Observer* 250 (October).

http://www.oecdobserver.org/news/fullstory.php/aid/1664/Does_gender_equality_spur_growth_.html.

O'Connor, Julia S., Ann Shola Orloff, and Sheila Shaver. 1999. *States, Markets, Families*. Cambridge, U.K.: Cambridge University Press.

OECD. 2002. *Employment Outlook 2002: Surveying the Job Horizon*. Paris: Author.

OECD. 2004. *Education at a Glance 2004*. Paris: Author.

United Nations. 2005. *The Millennium Development Goal Report 2005*. New York: Author.

Zippel, Kathrin. 2006. *The Politics of Sexual Harassment: A Comparative Study of the United States, the European Union, and Germany*. Cambridge, U.K.: Cambridge University Press.

Nicole Richardt

GENDER STUDIES

Interdisciplinary gender studies started with the opening call of the new feminist or women's liberation movement in the United States—Betty Friedan's 1963 *The Feminine Mystique*, the sociological critique of Freud's view of women's natural inferiority.

This movement inspired research, mainly sociological and anthropological but also economical, historical, and psychological. During its first two decades the terms *sex roles* and *sexual stratification* were current, until the terms *gender*, *gender roles*, and *gender relations* gained circulation and replaced them. This research shared a conviction and a goal. The conviction is that equal status of women and men is possible today, all the forms and causes of women's inferior status in different societies and in different historical periods notwithstanding. The goal of this research is openly declared: to discover the ways and means to facilitate the achievement of gender equality.

The basic questions/problems/analyses of gender research are the following:

The formal political equality achieved by the old, "classical" women's movement did not result in de facto equal opportunity and participation of women. Why?

The status of American (and other Western) women declined after World War II. Why?

Marx and Engels postulated inevitable stages of development from primitive communism with no private property, no family, and no gender inequality, through stages of different class societies toward socialist revolution leading to communism, where private property (the means of production), the nuclear family, and gender inequality will all disappear. They were in error. Where did they go wrong?

Were/are there any societies where women are equal? What were/are their characteristics? What is the relative importance of economic conditions and religious beliefs for the status of women?

What is the actual and the possible impact of recent innovations on the likelihood of achieving equality for women? In particular, research centers on improved means for birth control, on the electronic and computer revolutions in the economy, and, more generally, on the decline in the importance of physical strength for most kinds of work that traditionally gave men an advantage in occupational work.

Can there be solidarity between women of different social classes and "races"? In particular, researchers differed on the possibility of cooperation between white, educated "middle-class" women and "women of color" belonging to the "working classes."

How serious is the "sex-typing" of occupations? How unequal is the distribution of men and women over the range of occupations and their position in the hierarchies of economic and academic organizations, public service, and the professions? How does the income of employed or self-employed women compare to that of men?

How do the attitudes to work of women and men compare? In particular, research centered on the so-called instrumental attitude toward work as compared to interest in its content and quality, as well as interest in advancement at work.

What are the characteristics and the impact of "genderized" education of boys and girls in families, schools, and religious organizations compared to the impact of their own life experiences?

Does the fact that most babies are nurtured by their mothers during the first year of their life necessarily cause a stronger tendency toward and capacity for attachment in females and a stronger tendency toward and capacity for autonomy in males?

What are the achievements and chances of achieving reforms and real changes in the current inferior status of women and their segregation, preached and maintained by leaders of various religious communities?

Has there been a qualitative impact from the entry of women into local, national, and international politics and into councils, parliaments, governments, the diplomatic corps, the army, the judiciary, and law enforcement?

What was the impact of women's massive entry into the labor market and their demand for equality on the incidence, age, and frequency of marriage and divorce and on the birth rate? How has family law changed? What importance has the availability or absence of civil marriage and divorce and of the recognition of cohabitation (as well as the recognition of same-sex unions) for the status of women?

What custody policies have been tried, and how can their degree of fairness—to mothers as well as to fathers and children—be assessed? How can the degree of practicality of solutions of "shared custody" be assessed? The same goes for policies encouraging equal parenting and their effectiveness as well as for the quantity and quality of men's participation in child care and housework.

What have we learned about fighting violence against women, about the effectiveness of safe houses for battered women, and about police action against violent husbands and other partners and their reeducation? What is the experience of public action against clan murder of women in the name of "family honor"? What is the experience of public action against "bride-price murders"? What success have we had in eliminating the mutilation of girls ("female circumcision")? How successful is the fight against rape? The same goes for the fight against the sexual abuse of children—especially girls.

Does pornography encourage sexual violence and should it be banned, or does it relieve violent sexual urges? Is prostitution mainly "sex work" or "sexual slavery"?

Should women establish separate organizations (such as trade unions or political parties) and institutions (such as health services, banks, or "women's studies" university departments) to gain appropriate services and attention? What are the achievements and defects of such separate organizations and institutions?

What is the impact, actual and potential, of women's international nongovernmental organizations on the United Nations and through them on pressuring the member states to raise their standards of women's participation in politics and the economy?

Since the 1990s some "postmodernist" or "postfeminist" literature discourages the struggle for global gender equality. The writers deny the possibility of a common rationality of women and men, as well as that of common interests and even of a common rationality of different groups of women—those who belong to different classes and races, to Western or Eastern societies, as well as of women with different sexual orientations. They rule out the possibility of gender studies advancing knowledge of the causes and circumstances of and the possible remedies to the ubiquitous sociopolitical problem of gender inequality. Fortunately, the ongoing gender studies are too robust and successful to be obliterated by this unserious trend. The results of these studies, moderate as they may be, are very encouraging.

SEE ALSO *Crowding Hypothesis; Discrimination, Wage, by Gender; Fatherhood; Femininity; Feminism; Feminism, Second Wave; Gender Gap; Gender,*

Alternatives to Binary; Inequality, Gender; Masculinity; Motherhood; Prostitution; Reproductive Rights; Sexual Orientation, Social and Economic Consequences; Work and Women

BIBLIOGRAPHY

Agassi, Judith Buber. 1982. *Comparing the Work Attitudes of Women and Men*. Lexington, MA: Lexington Books.

Agassi, Judith Buber. 1989. Theories of Gender Equality: Lessons from the Israeli Kibbutz. *Gender and Society* 3 (2): 160–186.

Bernard, Jessie. 1971. The Paradox of the Happy Marriage. In *Women in Sexist Society*, ed. Vivian Gornick and Barbara Moran, 148–152. New York: Free Press.

Ferree, Myra Marx, Judith Lorber, and Beth Hess, eds. 1999. *Revisioning Gender*. Thousand Oaks, CA: Sage.

Friedan, Betty. 1963. *The Feminine Mystique*. New York: Norton.

Hepburn, Stephanie, and Rita J. Simon. 2006. *Women's Roles and Statuses the World Over*. Lanham, MD: Lexington Books.

Lorber, Judith. 1994. *Paradoxes of Gender*. New Haven, CT: Yale University Press.

Rosaldo, Michelle Zimbalist, and Louise Lamphere, eds. 1974. *Women, Culture, and Society: A Theoretical Overview*. Stanford, CA: Stanford University Press.

Rossi, Alice S. 1964. Equality between the Sexes: An Immodest Proposal. *Daedalus* 93: 607–652.

Schlegel, Alice, ed. 1977. *Sexual Stratification: A Cross-Cultural View*. New York: Columbia University Press.

Judith Buber Agassi

GENDERS, MULTIPLE

SEE *Gender, Alternatives to Binary.*

GENDER-TYPING OF JOBS

SEE *Crowding Hypothesis; Discrimination, Wage, by Gender.*

GENERAL AGREEMENT ON TARIFFS AND TRADE

The General Agreement on Tariffs and Trade (GATT) is the predecessor to the World Trade Organization (WTO). From 1947 to 1994, the GATT provided the world's main institutional framework for multilateral trade negotiations. It was created in Geneva in 1947 to remedy the protectionism and economic discrimination that arose during the interwar period and that arguably deepened the Great Depression. It was thus designed to facilitate nondiscriminatory trade liberalization among the world's major trading partners.

GATT members reduce trade barriers through periodic negotiating rounds, each of which produces an agreement that must be ratified by all members before it takes effect. Although these negotiations typically take place in small groups, the resulting concessions are extended to all members through the *most-favored-nation* rule, which grants each member the same treatment as the most-favored trading partner. The most-favored-nation rule ensures that any liberalization achieved during GATT rounds is nondiscriminatory. Eight rounds have been concluded as of 2006: Geneva (1947), Annecy (1949), Torquay (1951), Geneva (1956), Dillon (1960–1961), Kennedy (1964–1967), Tokyo (1973–1979), and Uruguay (1986–1994). A ninth, Doha, began in 2001. These rounds have reduced global tariffs on manufactured goods from nearly 40 percent in 1947 to under 4 percent in 2006. These tariff reductions are considered one of the foremost achievements of the GATT system.

Since its founding, the GATT has evolved in important ways. First, its membership has grown from twenty-three countries in 1947 to 149 in 2006. The GATT system has thus become global in scope. Second, the range of policies covered by GATT strictures has expanded over time. While early rounds focused on tariffs, later ones addressed nontariff barriers such as subsidies, voluntary export restraints, and antidumping duties. The Uruguay Round went further still, tackling policies such as technical barriers to trade, sanitary and phytosanitary standards, trade-related intellectual property rights, and trade-related investment measures. Third, the range of economic sectors covered by GATT rules has also grown over time. Whereas early GATT rounds focused on manufactures, the Uruguay Round produced agreements to liberalize trade in traditionally protected sectors such as agriculture, textiles and clothing, and services. Fourth, in 1995 the GATT was subsumed into the newly created WTO. The GATT continues to govern trade in goods but is now part of the broader WTO framework that also addresses new issues such as trade in services and the enforcement of intellectual property rights. Finally, the Uruguay Round also strengthened GATT dispute-settlement procedures, establishing stricter timetables for settling disputes and making it more difficult for losing parties to block unfavorable rulings from dispute-settlement panels. Notably, however, the Uruguay Round did not create any new enforcement mechanisms: Although panels can authorize retaliatory sanctions from complainant states, panels have no power to enforce their own decisions. WTO panel decisions, like GATT decisions, must thus be enforced by trade sanctions from member states.

The GATT system has both supporters and critics. Its supporters contend that it is crucial to achieving the benefits of free trade, such as lower prices for consumers and export opportunities for producers. Supporters also note that GATT rules against trade discrimination make it more difficult for governments to use trade preferences and sanctions as diplomatic tools. Critics, however, claim that the GATT system is deficient in several ways. Some critics, particularly from developing countries, feel that the GATT has not gone far enough in liberalizing trade in agriculture and textiles. Others feel that the GATT has gone too far in constraining national policymaking autonomy. For example, WTO panels have ruled against the European Union's ban on hormone-treated beef, stating that scientific evidence does not justify such a ban. Critics contend that such decisions about health, safety, and the environment should be left to national governments. Similarly, some have criticized the WTO's rules on intellectual property rights, which could prevent developing countries from obtaining cheap, generic pharmaceuticals. Finally, some contend that the GATT process is undemocratic because agreements are negotiated by unelected officials.

In light of this controversy, it is worth noting that the GATT is not a supranational policymaking body but rather an institutional forum within which governments negotiate agreements via a consensus decision-making process. Hence, while GATT agreements do constrain policies, no member is constrained without its consent. Moreover, because GATT agreements must be ratified by national governments, the GATT process remains under the control of elected representatives. The GATT is thus not qualitatively different from many other international agreements, all of which constrain national policies. For this reason, the controversy surrounding the GATT probably has less to do with procedural concerns than with disagreements about the substantive content of GATT rules. Finally, it is worth noting that empirical studies have found little evidence that the GATT affects either trade or trade policies. Such research suggests that both supporters and critics of the GATT may have overstated its true importance.

SEE ALSO *Uruguay Round; World Trade Organization*

BIBLIOGRAPHY

Hoekman, Bernard M., and Michel M. Kostecki. 1995. *The Political Economy of the World Trading System: From GATT to WTO.* New York: Oxford University Press.

Jackson, John H. 1997. *The World Trading System: Law and Policy of International Economic Relations.* 2nd ed. Cambridge, MA: MIT Press.

Rose, Andrew K. 2004. Do We Really Know That the WTO Increases Trade? *American Economic Review* 94 (1): 98–114.

Daniel Y. Kono

GENERAL ELECTRIC

General Electric is one of the largest corporations in the United States. Formed in 1892 from the merger of two U.S. electrical manufacturing companies, Edison General Electric Company and Thomson-Houston Electric Company, by 2006 General Electric had become a $163 billion corporation. General Electric today is a multinational diversified company operating in more than 100 countries in sectors as diverse as aviation and nuclear power, industrial and domestic electrical appliances, personal and industrial finance, and media and entertainment. Despite the level of diversification, its traditional electrical manufacturing activities linked to aviation and energy contributed almost 30 percent of sales in 2006 (General Electric 2006). General Electric continues to be one of the world's largest producers of jet engines, supplying Boeing and Lockheed Martin, among others.

General Electric's rise to dominance derived from the company's ability to restrict market competition through cartelization in the newly expanding consumer markets of the Second Industrial Revolution, and its ability to gain access to large, secure government markets, especially those linked to electricity generation and military equipment. General Electric was at the forefront of the development of international cartels before World War II, instigating market sharing and price-fixing through the creation of "rings" regulated by the International Electrical Association (Barjot 1995). Despite challenges by U.S. antitrust authorities after World War II, international cooperation and market sharing continued (Mirow and Maurer 1982). In the area of military technology, General Electric developed extensive capabilities as a result of high U.S. government defense expenditure during the cold war, and it continues to benefit from the rises in defense expenditure by every government since Ronald Reagan's; in 2005 its defense contracts amounted to $2.2 billion.

Large protected markets provided the backdrop for diversification into the financial and media sectors. Thus, in the areas of media and entertainment General Electric succeeded in creating large organizations capable of developing market power in entertainment and communication sectors, most notably in 2004 with the creation of NBC Universal, which combined NBC and Vivendi Universal to create a $43 billion media empire (CorpWatch 2006).

General Electric, along with other U.S. manufacturing multinationals, has utilized outsourcing and the establishment of maquila production systems along the U.S.–Mexican border as a mechanism for cost reduction. The company's diversification into distribution and logistics through its Trailer Fleet Services division has been used to service U.S. companies in the linking of the maquila production centers to U.S. markets. The resultant low-wage and poor labor conditions within the maquila system of production and redundancies and reductions in living standards for U.S. workers has led to extensive criticism of the company from labor unions.

SEE ALSO *Antitrust; Cold War; Corporate Social Responsibility; Corporate Strategies; Corporations; Defense, National; Maquiladoras; Military-Industrial Complex; Unions*

BIBLIOGRAPHY

Barjot, Dominique. 1995. *International Cartels Revisited, 1880–1980.* Caen, France: Éditions-Diffusion du Lys.

CorpWatch. 2006. General Electric. http://www.corpwatch.org/article.php?list=type&type=16.

General Electric. 2006. Invest and Deliver: GE Annual Report 2006. http://www.ge.com/ar2006/?c_id=ar06IR.

Global Exchange. 2006. Sweatfree Campaigns. http://www.globalexchange.org/campaigns/sweatshops.

Mirow, Kurt Rudolf, and Harry Maurer. 1982. *Webs of Power: International Cartels and the World Economy.* Boston: Houghton Mifflin.

Carlo Morelli

GENERAL EQUILIBRIUM

General equilibrium theory deals with the existence of efficient competitive prices in an individual private enterprise economy. This discussion of general equilibrium theory (GET) is divided into four parts: (1) the context and history of GET, (2) comments on the appropriate mathematization and method of proof, (3) the problems with the parsimonious modeling and solution concept used, and (4) what lies beyond the theory.

CONTEXT AND HISTORY

The French economist Léon Walras (1834–1910) was the first to attempt a mathematization of the conditions necessary and sufficient to determine the prices of all goods and services produced and consumed by firms and individuals in a closed economy. He distinguished between services and durable production goods, and he developed the theory of competitive exchange, noting the possibility

of multiple solutions to the existence of competitive prices. In particular he did not prove rigorously the existence of an efficient price system, but he did recognize that this would require the simultaneous solution to the set of equations he had utilized to describe the overall system of production and consumption. In writing down his production conditions, he utilized simple fixed coefficients for the structure of production.

Walras sketched the roles of both a rate of interest and a currency in his system, but these were not fully developed. These features, unlike his integration of production and consumption into a consistent whole, may be regarded as more or less undeveloped when compared with the market structure for the production and consumptions of goods and services. Although Walras discussed the important role of government, he left it out as being beyond the more strictly economic problems he was addressing.

The full modeling of an exchange and production economy presented a challenge. The construction of a formal closed mathematical model of the economy called for Draconian simplification, and it was thus a major achievement in abstraction. As is often the case, even in the purest of mathematical economics, the distinction between the verbal treatment and the mathematization offered is often considerable. Words permit a richness of discourse at the cost of precision, while mathematics offers precision and logical tightness at the cost of qualification, nuance, and the recognition of complexity. Mathematics thus facilitates the analysis at the cost of minimizing concern with context.

The work of Walras was accepted relatively slowly. The mathematical problems surrounding the solution of the simultaneous equation structure of the general equilibrium model were posed in a modern mathematical context by Abraham Wald, who considered production with inputs in fixed proportion, and with a single output. He also, however, assumed the existence of demand functions rather than deriving them from utility maximization.

THE MODEL AND PROOF

The key papers presenting the first rigorous proofs of GET were written by Kenneth Arrow and Gerard Debreu (1954) and Lionel McKenzie (1959). The sketch here primarily follows the treatment presented in Debreu's *Theory of Value* (1959).

An economy is considered initially with l commodities (goods or services), m utility maximizing agents, and n profit maximizing multi-product firms. The economy exists over a specific finite period of time sectioned into T time periods. The existence of money is not considered. It is as though there exists some vast smoothly functioning central clearinghouse that balances all accounts at the end of the trading period after which the economy ceases. A commodity or service is characterized not merely by its physical aspects, but by both a time of availability and a location, providing a considerable simplification of the model structure. It is as though all trade takes place in a single time period, with a vast array of futures markets available that make further trade unnecessary.

All real persons or individuals are assumed to have well-defined preferences that can be represented by utility functions. It is further assumed that individual preferences are such that more goods are always of value.

Production is described by a convex production set, in which each individual producer selects a set of inputs to maximize the profits obtained from the sale of its outputs. In the process of production, free disposal is assumed. The profits are distributed to individuals who hold shares in the firms. It is proved (under reasonably plausible conditions on the utility functions and production sets) that a set of prices exist (not necessarily unique) such that supply equals demand in every market and that the resultant imputation of goods and services is efficient or Pareto optimal, meaning that there is no way that any individual can improve utility without another individual obtaining less utility. The method of proof is highly technical; it utilized fixed-point theory (Kakutani 1941), which has been of considerable use in both subsequent developments in general equilibrium theory and in the application of the theory of games in economics.

PROBLEMS WITH THE ASSUMPTIONS AND DEVELOPMENTS IN *GET*

Since the development of the original models, there have been many modifications of the original stringent assumptions. In particular, the original models deal with a finite sector of time, but in the real world there is a past and a future. There is thus a question as to how one can extend the general equilibrium analysis to infinite horizon models. Furthermore, given an infinite horizon model, an overlapping generations structure to the population appears to be more appropriate than viewing individuals as living forever. The seminal work of Maurice Allais (1946) and Paul Samuelson (1958) opened up a literature extending the investigation of competitive markets (see Geanakoplos 1987 for an extensive summary).

When dealing with a high level of abstraction, the linkage between the assumption and the underlying reality must be considered, for there are empirical exceptions to virtually every assumption made. But, on the whole, the question to be considered is whether the rigor, when confronted with the reality, provides a good enough fit to cast light on the function of a significant part of the economy. The considerable developments in the computation

of applied general equilibrium models suggests that it does. The computational methods are based on the work of Herbert Scarf.

A basic assumption in the original proofs is that individual consumers and firms are "price takers." In other words, they are so small that their actions have no influence on market prices. But, as presented, the proofs were based on there being a finite number of agents. This affects the stated basic assumption of price taking. The Debreu proof does not depend on whether there is one agent or a million in any market. If this finite number is taken into account, then the actions of individual agents may influence price. A precise proof is needed to show the conditions under which the individual influence can be ignored. Robert Aumann (1964), using technical results from the mathematics of measure theory, provided a solution reflecting the lack of power of an individual small agent. The strategic market game (SMG) model of Lloyd Shapley and Martin Shubik (1977) provided the basis for non-cooperative game models of a closed economy, while Pradeep Dubey and Shubik (1978) showed the basic inefficiency of the noncooperative equilibria. However, the equilibria approach a competitive price as the number of agents in the economy increases. The noncooperative game models and the general equilibrium models are mathematically distinct, but for a continuum of agents the solutions may coincide.

The original models avoided problems with uncertainty through an ingenious but unsatisfactory enlargement of the number of goods, including a myriad of markets with contingent goods. This is currently being avoided in the development of general equilibrium with incomplete (GEI) markets.

The SMG models of the economy are more institutional than those of GET. They require an explicit specification of the price formation mechanism in the markets and a description of what happens to the traders under all circumstances. The mathematical model is so complete that it could be played as an experimental game, and the role of money and markets appears naturally and explicitly as a way of simplifying trading activity. The game-theoretic formulation has permitted the handling of three important items left out by GET: the influence of oligopolistic markets (i.e., markets with powerful players whose individual action influences price), the role of possible default, and the role of different levels of information.

At a high level of abstraction, there is an important link between work in cooperative game theory and GET. There are two cooperative game theory solutions called the core and value that can be related to the competitive equilibrium. These solutions stress group power and individual equity. The core characterizes outcomes that cannot be effectively challenged by group behavior, while the value reflects the expected marginal productivity of an individual over all groups he or she could join. It can be shown that in an economy with many individuals the price system has the properties of both the core and the value.

WHAT LIES BEYOND?

One of the major concerns in economic theory is the reconciliation between general equilibrium microeconomic theory and macroeconomics. It has been suggested that a natural extension beyond basic general equilibrium will incorporate both the financial structure and government. The next series of basic micro-macro models will have a continuum of private agents plus government as a large player. Beyond this, the addition of taxation and public goods to the basic micro-macro models of the economy will be difficult but rewarding. Game-theoretic methods that permit the blending of price taking and oligopolistic elements, and that take into account nonsymmetries in information, are currently being developed in the study of macroeconomic control.

SEE ALSO *Arrow, Kenneth J.; Arrow-Debreu Model; Debreu, Gerard; Economic Model; Economics; Equilibrium in Economics; Game Theory; Macroeconomics; Market Economy; Microeconomics; Stability in Economics*

BIBLIOGRAPHY

Allais, Maurice. 1946 *Economie et Interet.* Imprimerie National: Paris.

Aumann, Robert. J. 1964. Markets with a Continuum of Traders. *Econometrica* 32: 39–50.

Arrow, Kenneth J. and Gerard Debreu. 1954. Existence of Equilibrium for a Competitive Economy. *Econometrica* 22: 265–290.

Debreu, Gerard. 1959. *Theory of Value, an Axiomatic Analysis of Economic Equilibrium.* New York: Wiley.

Dubey, Pradeep, and Martin Shubik. 1978. The Noncooperative Equilibria of a Closed Trading Economy with Market Supply and Bidding Strategies. *Journal of Economic Theory* 17 (1): 1–20.

Geanakoplos, John D. 1987. The Overlapping Generations Model of General Equilibrium. In *The New Palgrave: A Dictionary of Economics*, ed. J. Eatwell, M. Millgate and P. Newman, 767–779. London: Macmillan.

Kakutani, Shizuo. 1941. A Generalization of Brouwer's Fixed Point Theorem. *Duke Mathematical Journal* 8 (3): 437–459.

McKenzie, Lionel W. 1959. On the Existence of General Equilibrium for a Competitive Market. *Econometrica* 27: 54–71.

Samuelson, Paul. 1958. Aspects of Public Expenditure Theory. *Review of Economics and Statistics* 40: 335–338.

Shapley, Lloyd S., and Martin Shubik. 1977. Trade Using One Commodity as a Means of Payment. *Journal of Political Economy* 85 (5): 937–968.

Walras, Léon. *Eléments d'économie politique pure.* 4th ed. Lausanne: L. Corbaz.

Martin Shubik

GENERAL MOTORS

In 2006 Detroit-headquartered auto giant General Motors (GM) was the world's largest automaker and ranked number three on the *Fortune* 500 list of America's largest corporations. The company has been a major player in U.S. labor history, and its vast worldwide expansion has had, and continues to have, many social consequences.

In 1897 Ransom E. Olds (1864–1950) formed the Olds Motor Vehicle Company and created several different automobile models powered by electricity and gasoline. After a fire in its factory, the company was forced to change its marketing and development strategy, which had previously focused on the wealthy, and instead moved to create a mass market for its vehicles, making them competitively priced with horses and buggies. This strategy was effective, and by 1904 the company had sold more than 12,500 vehicles.

Meanwhile, the owner of Buick was developing a complex network of suppliers to lower its costs, and incorporated with its holdings as General Motors. From 1908 to 1910 Oldsmobile, Cadillac, and several other smaller companies joined forces with the new company to create a larger, more powerful automaker. The incorporation included many more suppliers and an expansion to trucks and airplanes, and in the first half of the twentieth century, GM grew rapidly. The company also benefited from many defense contracts during World War I (1914–1918) and World War II (1939–1945).

GM's massive growth led to a need for large numbers of workers to assemble parts and automobiles. To improve their working conditions and increase their pay, workers throughout GM began to unionize in 1935 under the AFL-CIO. Later, a split in this organization led to the development of what would become one of the largest and most powerful unions in U.S. history: the United Auto Workers (UAW). The UAW was one of the first unions in the United States to include black workers.

Shortly after its formation, the UAW demanded contracts for GM autoworkers, but was denied negotiations with the automaker. On December 29, 1936, GM was informed that its largest stamping plant, in Flint, Michigan, was going to strike, and the company quickly made plans to move the machinery from the facility. In order to keep GM from removing the machinery, the workers staged a sit-down strike. Police attacked the strikers with tear gas, but workers remained at the plant for forty-four days until GM signed a document recognizing the UAW as the official representative of its workers for bargaining purposes. This was a significant event in U.S. labor history, as a large corporation conceded to the demands of a union.

The unionization of autoworkers at GM helped the American middle class grow rapidly in the 1950s. Despite their blue-collar jobs, workers had salaries and benefits that allowed them the luxuries of middle-class life. Many scholars believe this change in status allowed embourgeoisement to take place; that is, working-class laborers gained middle-class values and lifestyles because of their increased wages and class position, and their support for radical political movements declined (Abercrombie et al. 2000).

GM has been criticized for corporate practices that are ecologically unsound or that violate human rights. Throughout the 1990s, there was much concern about GM's use of factories in the developing world (especially Mexico) for cheap and less-restricted labor. According to a 1998 Human Rights Watch report, the directors of GM-run *maquiladoras* (foreign-owned plants that are operated by multinational corporations) in Mexico were repeatedly accused by their workers of unfair work termination and sex discrimination, especially pregnancy-related discrimination. Female employees complained that they were forced to undergo pregnancy tests before gaining employment, and some said they were even made to show their sanitary napkins to prove that they were not pregnant to retain employment. Other concerns have been raised over GM's relationship with the environment. For example, its Hummer brand has been repeatedly cited as one of the worse violators in the consumer truck market because of its high emissions and a fuel economy of less than ten miles per gallon. A 2006 documentary, *Who Killed the Electric Car*, attacks GM for the systematic dismantling of its electric-car program and for what the filmmakers imply was a conspiracy between GM and the oil industry.

SEE ALSO *Automobile Industry; Corporations*

BIBLIOGRAPHY

Abercrombie, Nicholas, Stephen Hill, and Bryan S. Turner, eds. 2000. *The Penguin Dictionary of Sociology*. 4th ed. New York: Penguin.

Bailey, L. Scott, ed. 1983. *General Motors: The First 75 Years of Transportation Products*. Princeton, NJ: Automobile Quarterly.

Jefferson, LaShawn, and Phoebe McKinney. 1998. A Job or Your Rights: Continued Sex Discrimination in Mexico's Maquiladora Sector. Human Rights Watch report 10 (1) December. http://www.hrw.org/reports98/women2/.

Paine, Chris, dir. 2006. *Who Killed the Electric Car*. Plinyminor and Electric Entertainment.

Remembering the Flint Sit-Down Strike, 1936–1937. HistoricalVoices.org presented by Michigan State University. http://www.historicalvoices.org/flint/.

Weisman, Jonathan. 2004. No Guzzle, No Glory: History Says Gas Spike Won't Smother SUV Love. *The Washington Post*, June 13: F01.

Elizabeth Alexander
David G. Embrick

GENERALIZED AUTOREGRESSIVE CONDITIONAL HETEROSKEDASTICITY (GARCH) MODEL

SEE *Autoregressive Models*.

GENERALIZED LEAST SQUARES

Generalized least squares (GLS) is a method for fitting coefficients of explanatory variables that help to predict the outcomes of a dependent random variable. As its name suggests, GLS includes *ordinary least squares* (OLS) as a special case. GLS is also called "Aitken's estimator," after A. C. Aitken (1935). The principal motivation for generalizing OLS is the presence of covariance among the observations of the dependent variable or of different variances across these observations, conditional on the explanatory variables. Both phenomena lead to problems with statistical inference procedures commonly used with OLS. Most critically, the standard methods for estimating sampling variances and testing hypotheses become biased. In addition, the OLS-fitted coefficients are inaccurate relative to the GLS-fitted coefficients.

In its simplest form, the linear model of statistics postulates the existence of a linear conditional expectation for a scalar, dependent random variable y given a set of nonrandom scalar explanatory variables $\{x_1, \ldots, x_K\}$:

$$E[y] = \beta_1 x_1 + \ldots + \beta_K x_K$$

where the β_k, $k = 1, \ldots, K$, are constant parameters for all values of the x_k. Interest focuses on estimating the β_k given a sample of N observations of y, denoted here by $y_1, \ldots, y_N$, and corresponding observations of the x_k, denoted $x_{1k}, \ldots, x_{Nk}$ for each explanatory variable indexed by k. Using matrix notation, the linear conditional expectations for the sample are

$$E[\mathbf{y}] = \mathbf{X}\beta,$$

where $\mathbf{y} = [y_1, \ldots, y_N]'$ is an $N \times 1$ column vector, $\mathbf{X} = [x_{nk};$ $n = 1, \ldots, N, k = 1, \ldots, K]$ is a $N \times K$ matrix, and $\boldsymbol{\beta} = [\beta_1, \ldots, \beta_K]'$ is a $K \times 1$ column vector. It is generally assumed that the explanatory variables in $\mathbf{X}$ are not linearly dependent so that $N \geq K$ and there is no $\alpha \in \mathbb{R}^K$, $\boldsymbol{\alpha} \neq \mathbf{0}$, such that $X\alpha = \mathbf{0}$.

In addition, the linear model assumes that the variances of the y_n are equal to a common, finite positive constant σ^2 and that the covariances among the y_n are equal to zero. In matrix notation, these assumptions assign to $\mathbf{y}$ a scalar variance-covariance matrix:

$$\mathrm{Var}[\mathbf{y}] = \sigma^2 \cdot \mathbf{I} = \begin{bmatrix} \sigma^2 & 0 & \cdots & 0 \\ 0 & \sigma^2 & \ddots & 0 \\ \vdots & \ddots & \ddots & \vdots \\ 0 & 0 & 0 & \sigma^2 \end{bmatrix}$$

where $\mathbf{I}$ denotes an $N \times N$ identity matrix. The fundamental difference between such a linear model and one leading to generalized least squares is that the latter permits an unrestricted variance-covariance matrix, often denoted by

$$\mathrm{Var}[\mathbf{y}] = \boldsymbol{\Sigma}$$

where $\boldsymbol{\Sigma} = [\sigma_{mn}; m, n = 1, \ldots, N]$ is an $N \times N$ positive semidefinite matrix. In this extension of the linear model, the variances along the diagonal of $\boldsymbol{\Sigma}$ may vary across observations, and the covariances in the off-diagonal positions of $\boldsymbol{\Sigma}$ may be nonzero and may also vary across pairs of observations. In this essay, $\boldsymbol{\Sigma}$ is also assumed to be nonsingular.

Many authors refer to the generalized model as the linear model with *nonspherical errors*. This term derives, in part, from viewing $\mathbf{y}$ as the sum of $\mathbf{X}\boldsymbol{\beta}$ and an additional, unobserved variable that is an error term. Rather than making assumptions about the observable $\mathbf{y}$ and $\mathbf{X}$ as above, these writers make equivalent assumptions about the unobserved error term. The term *nonspherical* refers to the type of variance-covariance matrix possessed by the error term. Multivariate distributions with scalar variance-covariance matrices are often called *spherical*. This term can be traced to interpreting the set

$$\{\mathbf{u} \in \mathbb{R}^N \mid \mathbf{u}'(\sigma^2 \cdot \mathbf{I})^{-1}\mathbf{u} = 1\}$$

as an N-dimensional sphere (or spheroid) with radius σ. In the nonscalar case, the set

$$\{\mathbf{u} \in \mathbb{R}^N \mid \mathbf{u}'\boldsymbol{\Sigma}^{-1}\mathbf{u} = 1\}$$

is an N-dimensional ellipsoid and distributions with nonscalar variance-covariance matrices are called *nonspherical*. Hence, a linear regression accompanied by a nonscalar variance-covariance matrix may be called the case with nonspherical errors.

EXAMPLES

Leading examples motivating nonscalar variance-covariance matrices include *heteroskedasticity* and *first-order autoregressive serial correlation*. Under heteroskedasticity, the variances σ_{nn} differ across observations $n = 1, \ldots, N$ but the covariances σ_{mn}, $m \neq n$, all equal zero. This occurs, for example, in the conditional distribution of individual income given years of schooling where high levels of schooling correspond to relatively high levels of the conditional variance of income. This heteroskedasticity is explained in part by the narrower range of job opportunities faced by people with low levels of schooling compared to those with high levels.

Serial correlation arises in time-series data where the observations are ordered sequentially by the time period of each observation; y_n is observed in the nth time period. First-order autoregressive (AR(1)) serial correlation occurs when deviations from means (also called *errors*) satisfy the linear model

$$\mathrm{E}[y_n - x'_n\beta \mid y_1, \ldots, y_{n-1}] = \rho(y_{n-1} - x'_{n-1}\beta), n > 1,$$
$|\rho| < 1,$

while maintaining the assumption that the marginal variance of y_n equals a constant σ^2. Nonzero covariances of the form

$$\mathrm{Cov}[y_{n-s}, y_n] = \rho^s\sigma^2, \qquad (1)$$
$$s = 0, 1, 2, \ldots, n-1, n > 1,$$

are implied by the recursion

$$\mathrm{Cov}[y_{n-s}, y_n] = \rho\,\mathrm{Cov}[y_{n-s}, y_{n-1}]. \qquad (2)$$

A times series of monthly unemployment rates exhibits such autoregressive serial correlation, reflecting unobserved social, economic, and political influences that change relatively slowly as months pass.

A second leading example of serial correlation occurs in *panel data* models, designed for datasets with two sampling dimensions, typically one cross-sectional and the other time-series. Repetitive testing of a cross-section of subjects in a laboratory gives this structure as do repeated surveys of a cross-section of households. Panel data models are usually expressed in an *error components* form:

$$y_{nt} = \mathbf{x}'_{nt}\boldsymbol{\beta} + \alpha_n + \varepsilon_{nt}$$

where α_n and ε_{nt} are unobserved error terms with $\mathrm{E}[\alpha_n] = \mathrm{E}[\varepsilon_{nt}] = 0$ and $\mathrm{Var}[\alpha_n] = \sigma_\alpha^2$, $\mathrm{Var}[\varepsilon_{nt}] = \sigma_\varepsilon^2$, and $\mathrm{Cov}[\alpha_n, \varepsilon_{mt}] = 0$, $\mathrm{Cov}[\varepsilon_{nt}, \varepsilon_{js}] = 0$ for all $m, n, j = 1, \ldots, N, t, s = 1, \ldots, T$, and $n \neq j, s \neq t$. The α_n are individual effects that recur for all observations of a particular individual and they induce serial correlation:

$$\mathrm{Cov}[y_{nt}, y_{ms}] = \sigma_\alpha^2$$

for $m = n$ and $t \neq s$. Unlike the AR(1) case, this covariance does not diminish as the time between observations increases. Instead, all of the observations for an individual are equally correlated.

Correlation also occurs in cross-sectional data. In the seemingly unrelated regressions (SUR) setting, there are several dependent variables and corresponding mean functions:

$$E[y_{ng}] = \mathbf{x}'_{ng}\boldsymbol{\beta}_g, \; g = 1, \ldots, G.$$

Such dependent variables are typically related as different characteristics of a single experiment or observational unit. For example, the y_{ng} might be test scores for substantively different tests written by the same individual. Even after accounting for observable differences among the tests and test takers with $\mathbf{x}_{ng}$, covariance among the test scores may reflect the influence of unobserved personal abilities that affect all of the tests taken by a particular person. Alternatively, the y_{ng} could be total income in countries during the same time period so that neighboring states possess similar underlying characteristics or face similar environments that induce covariance among their incomes.

STATISTICAL ISSUES

The general linear model motivates two principal issues with statistical inferences about $\boldsymbol{\beta}$ in the simpler linear model. First, hypothesis tests and estimators of sampling variances and confidence intervals developed under the linear model are biased when $\boldsymbol{\Sigma}$ is not scalar. Second, the OLS estimator for $\boldsymbol{\beta}$ generally will not be the minimum-variance linear unbiased estimator. The OLS estimator

$$\hat{\beta}_{\mathrm{OLS}} = \arg\min_{\mathbf{b} \in \mathbb{R}^K} (\mathbf{y} - \mathbf{Xb})'(\mathbf{y} - \mathbf{Xb})$$
$$= (\mathbf{X}'\mathbf{X})^{-1}\mathbf{X}'\mathbf{y}$$

is a linear (in $\mathbf{y}$) and unbiased estimator when $\boldsymbol{\Sigma}$ is not scalar. However, its sampling variance is

$$\mathrm{Var}[\hat{\beta}_{\mathrm{OLS}}] = (\mathbf{X}'\mathbf{X})^{-1}\mathbf{X}'\boldsymbol{\Sigma}\mathbf{X}(\mathbf{X}'\mathbf{X})^{-1} \quad (3)$$

which is generally not proportional to $(\mathbf{X}'\mathbf{X})^{-1}$, an outcome implied by the simple linear model. When $\boldsymbol{\Sigma}$ is nonsingular, the GLS estimator

$$\hat{\beta}_{\mathrm{GLS}} = \arg\min_{\mathbf{b} \in \mathbb{R}^K} (\mathbf{y} - \mathbf{Xb})'\boldsymbol{\Sigma}^{-1}(\mathbf{y} - \mathbf{Xb})$$
$$= (\mathbf{X}'\boldsymbol{\Sigma}^{-1}\mathbf{X})^{-1}\mathbf{X}'\boldsymbol{\Sigma}^{-1}\mathbf{y}$$

is the minimum-variance linear and unbiased estimator. Its variance-covariance matrix is

$$\mathrm{Var}[\hat{\beta}_{\mathrm{GLS}}] = (\mathbf{X}'\boldsymbol{\Sigma}^{-1}\mathbf{X})^{-1}.$$

GLS can be understood as OLS applied to a linear model transformed to satisfy the scalar variance-covari-

ance restriction. For every $\boldsymbol{\Sigma}$, one can always find a matrix $\mathbf{A}$ such that $\boldsymbol{\Sigma} = \mathbf{AA}'$. We will give some examples shortly. Given such an $\mathbf{A}$, it follows that

$$\mathrm{Var}[\mathbf{A}^{-1}\mathbf{y}] = \mathbf{A}^{-1}\mathrm{Var}[\mathbf{y}]\mathbf{A}^{-1'} = \mathbf{A}^{-1}\boldsymbol{\Sigma}\mathbf{A}^{-1'} = \mathbf{I}$$

or, in words, that $\tilde{\mathbf{y}} = \mathbf{A}^{-1}\mathbf{y}$ has a scalar variance-covariance matrix. At the same time,

$$E[\mathbf{A}^{-1}\mathbf{y}] = \mathbf{A}^{-1}E[\mathbf{y}] = \mathbf{A}^{-1}\mathbf{X}\boldsymbol{\beta}$$

so that the expectation of the transformed $\mathbf{y}$ has corresponding transformed explanatory variables $\tilde{\mathbf{X}} = \mathbf{A}^{-1}\mathbf{X}$. Applying OLS to estimate $\boldsymbol{\beta}$ with the transformed variables yields the GLS estimator:

$$\begin{aligned}
(\tilde{\mathbf{X}}'\tilde{\mathbf{X}})^{-1}\tilde{\mathbf{X}}'\tilde{\mathbf{y}} &= ((\mathbf{A}^{-1}\mathbf{X})'\mathbf{A}^{-1}\mathbf{X})^{-1}(\mathbf{A}^{-1}\mathbf{X})'\mathbf{A}^{-1}\mathbf{y} \\
&= (\mathbf{X}'(\mathbf{A}^{-1})'\mathbf{A}^{-1}\mathbf{X})^{-1}\mathbf{X}'(\mathbf{A}^{-1})'\mathbf{A}^{-1}\mathbf{y} \\
&= (\mathbf{X}'\boldsymbol{\Sigma}^{-1}\mathbf{X})^{-1}\mathbf{X}'\boldsymbol{\Sigma}^{-1}\mathbf{y}
\end{aligned}$$

because $\boldsymbol{\Sigma}^{-1} = (\mathbf{A}^{-1})'\mathbf{A}^{-1}$. In a similar fashion, one sees that the OLS criterion function is transformed into the GLS criterion function:

$$(\tilde{\mathbf{y}} - \tilde{\mathbf{X}}\mathbf{b})'(\tilde{\mathbf{y}} - \tilde{\mathbf{X}}\mathbf{b}) = (\mathbf{y} - \mathbf{Xb})'\boldsymbol{\Sigma}^{-1}(\mathbf{y} - \mathbf{Xb}).$$

Heteroskedasticity produces a simple example. To produce observations with equal variances, each data point is divided by the standard deviation

$$\sigma_n = \sqrt{\mathrm{Var}[y_n]}:$$

$$\mathrm{Var}\left[\frac{y_n}{\sigma_n}\right] = \frac{1}{\sigma_n^2}\mathrm{Var}[y_n] = \frac{1}{\sigma_n^2}\sigma_n^2 = 1.$$

This corresponds to choosing $\mathbf{A}^{-1}$ equal to a diagonal matrix with the reciprocals of these standard deviations arrayed along its diagonal. The estimation criterion function is

$$\sum_{n=1}^{N}\frac{(y_n - x'_n\mathbf{b})^2}{\sigma_n^2}$$

which is a *weighted* sum of squared residuals. For this reason, in this special case GLS is often called *weighted least squares* (WLS). WLS puts most weight on the observations with the smallest variances, showing how GLS improves upon OLS, which puts equal weight on all observations. Those n for which σ_n is relatively small tend to be closest to the mean of y_n and, hence, more informative about $\boldsymbol{\beta}$.

Faced with AR(1) serial correlation in a time series, the appropriate choice of A transforms each data point (except the first) into differences:

$$\tilde{y}_n = y_n - \rho y_{n-1},$$
$$\tilde{x}_{nk} = x_{nk} - \rho x_{n-1,k}, \; k = 1, \ldots, K.$$

This transformed $\bar{y}_n$ display zero covariances:

$$\text{Cov}[y_{n-s} - \rho y_{n-s-1}, y_n - \rho y_{n-1}]$$

$$= \text{Cov}[y_{n-s}, y_n] - \rho \text{Cov}[y_{n-s}, y_{n-1}]$$

$$- \rho \text{Cov}[y_{n-s}, y_n] + \rho^2 \text{Cov}[y_{n-s-1}, y_{n-1}]$$

$$= \rho \text{Cov}[y_{n-s}, y_{n-1}] - \rho \text{Cov}[y_{n-s}, y_{n-1}]$$

$$- \rho^2 \text{Cov}[y_{n-s-1}, y_{n-1}] + \rho^2 \text{Cov}[y_{n-s-1}, y_{n-1}]$$

$$= 0$$

using (2) for the first and third terms on the right-hand side. This transformation uncovers the new or additional information available in each observation, whereas OLS treats highly correlated observations the same way as uncorrelated observations, giving the former relatively too much weight in that estimator.

The panel data model has a simple GLS transformation as well:

$$\tilde{y}_{nt} = y_{nt} - (1 - \omega)\bar{y}_n,$$
$$\tilde{x}_{ntk} = x_{ntk} - (1 - \omega)\bar{x}_{nk}, \quad k = 1, \ldots, K$$

where $\bar{y}_n$ and $\bar{x}_{nk}$ are the individual averages over time $\sum_{n=1}^{N} y_{nt}/T$ and $\sum_{n=1}^{N} x_{ntk}/T$, respectively, and

$$\omega = \frac{\sigma_\epsilon}{\sqrt{T\sigma_\alpha^2 + \sigma_\epsilon^2}}.$$

If there is no serial correlation, then $\sigma_\alpha = 0$ and $\tilde{y}_{nt} = y_{nt}$. Conversely, the greater σ_α is, the more important the individual average $\bar{y}_n$ becomes. Like the AR(1) case, a weighted difference removes the covariance among the original y_{nt}. In this case, however, a common time-series sample average appears in every difference, reflecting the equal covariance structure.

Note that the GLS estimator is an instrumental variables (IV) estimator,

$$\hat{\beta}_{IV} = (Z'X)^{-1}Z'y,$$

for an $N \times K$ matrix Z of instrumental variables such that $Z'X$ is invertible. For GLS, $Z = \Sigma^{-1}X$. Researchers use instrumental variables estimators to overcome omission of explanatory variables in models of the form

$$y = x'\beta + \varepsilon$$

where ε is an unobserved term. Even though $E[\varepsilon] = 0$, correlation between the explanatory variables in x and ε biases $\hat{\beta}_{OLS}$ and the IV estimator is employed to overcome this bias by using instrumental variables, the variables in Z, that are uncorrelated with ε yet correlated with the explanatory variables. In some cases of the linear model, the GLS estimator provides such instrumental variables. If, for example, x_n includes the lagged value of y_n in a

time-series application, then residual serial correlation usually invalidates the OLS estimator while GLS still produces an estimator for β.

In the panel data setting, particular concern about the behavior of the unobserved individual effect α_n has led researchers to compare the GLS estimator with another IV estimator. The concern is that the expected value of α_n may vary with some of the observed explanatory variables in x_{nt}. Various observable characteristics of individuals or households are typically correlated so that one would expect the unobserved characteristics captured in α_n to be correlated with the observed characteristics in x_{nt} as well. In this situation, the OLS- and GLS-fitted coefficients are not estimators for β because these fitted coefficients pick up the influence of the α_n omitted as explanatory variables. An IV estimator of β that is robust to such correlation is the so-called *fixed effects* estimator. This estimator is often described as the OLS fit of $y_{nt} - \bar{y}_n$ to the explanatory variables $x_{ntk} - \bar{x}_{nk}$, $k = 1, \ldots, K$, but an equivalent IV estimator uses the instrumental variables $z_{ntk} = x_{ntk} - \bar{x}_{nk}$. In the special case when $\omega = 0$, the fixed effects and GLS estimators are equal. The GLS estimator is often called the *random effects* estimator in this context, and the difference between the fixed-effects and random-effects estimators is often used as a diagnostic test for the reliability of GLS estimation (Hausman 1978).

The OLS and GLS estimators are equal for a general Σ if the GLS instrument matrix $\Sigma^{-1}X$ produces the same set of fitted values as the explanatory variable matrix X. Formally, $\hat{\beta}_{OLS} = \hat{\beta}_{GLS}$ if and only if every vector $X\alpha$, $\alpha \in \mathbb{R}^K$, equals $\Sigma^{-1}X\gamma$ for some $\gamma \in \mathbb{R}^K$, and vice versa. A practical situation in which this occurs approximately is when AR(1) serial correlation is accompanied by explanatory variables that are powers of n or trigonometric functions of n. Another example arises when all covariances are equal (and not necessarily zero) and the regression function includes an intercept (or constant term), as it usually does. A third example is the case of SUR where the explanatory variables are identical for all equations, so that $x_{ng} = x_n$, $g = 1, \ldots, G$.

FEASIBLE METHODS

Feasible inference for β in the general linear model typically must overcome that Σ is unknown. There are two popular strategies: (1) to specify Σ as a function of a few parameters that can be replaced with estimators, and (2) to use *heteroskedasticity-consistent* variance estimators.

The AR(1) serial correlation model illustrates the first approach. A natural estimator for the autocorrelation parameter ρ is the fitted OLS coefficient $\hat{\rho}$ for predicting the OLS-fitted residual $y_n - x'_n \hat{\beta}_{OLS}$ with the single explanatory variable $y_{n-1} - \mathbf{x}'_{n-1}\hat{\boldsymbol{\beta}}_{\mathrm{OLS}}$, the lagged OLS-fitted residual:

$$\hat{\rho} = \frac{\sum_{n=2}^{N} \left(y_{n-1} - \mathbf{x}'_{n-1}\hat{\beta}_{\mathrm{OLS}} \right)\left(y_n - \mathbf{x}'_n\hat{\beta}_{\mathrm{OLS}} \right)}{\sum_{n=2}^{N} \left(y_{n-1} - \mathbf{x}'_{n-1}\hat{\beta}_{\mathrm{OLS}} \right)^2}.$$

Under certain conditions, this $\hat{\rho}$ can replace ρ in $\boldsymbol{\Sigma}(\rho)$ to estimate the variance-covariance matrix of $\hat{\boldsymbol{\beta}}_{\mathrm{OLS}}$, as in

$$(\mathbf{X}'\mathbf{X})^{-1}\mathbf{X}'\hat{\boldsymbol{\Sigma}}\mathbf{X}(\mathbf{X}'\mathbf{X})^{-1}$$

where $\hat{\boldsymbol{\Sigma}} = \boldsymbol{\Sigma}(\hat{\rho})$, or to compute the feasible GLS (FGLS) estimator

$$\hat{\boldsymbol{\beta}}_{\mathrm{FGLS}} = (\mathbf{X}'\hat{\boldsymbol{\Sigma}}^{-1}\mathbf{X})^{-1}\mathbf{X}'\hat{\boldsymbol{\Sigma}}^{-1}\mathbf{y}.$$

Similarly, one estimates the variance-covariance matrix of $\hat{\boldsymbol{\beta}}_{\mathrm{FGLS}}$ with $(\mathbf{X}'\hat{\boldsymbol{\Sigma}}^{-1}\mathbf{X})^{-1}$. In large samples, the differences between the feasible and infeasible versions are negligible. In small samples, many researchers use an estimator that requires iterative calculations to find a $\hat{\rho}$ and $\hat{\boldsymbol{\beta}}$ that are mutually consistent: The fitted residuals produced by $\hat{\boldsymbol{\beta}}$ yield $\hat{\rho}$ and the variance-covariance matrix produced by $\hat{\rho}$ yields $\hat{\boldsymbol{\beta}}$ as the fitted FGLS coefficients. Maximum likelihood estimators, based on an additional assumption that the y_n possess a joint multivariate normal distribution, are leading examples of such estimators.

We will use the pure heteroskedasticity case to illustrate heteroskedasticity-consistent variance estimators. The unknown term in the $\mathrm{Var}[\hat{\boldsymbol{\beta}}_{\mathrm{OLS}}]$ (shown in (3)) can be written as a sample average:

$$\frac{1}{N} \cdot (\mathbf{X}'\boldsymbol{\Sigma}\mathbf{X}) = \sum_{n=1}^{N} \frac{1}{N} \sigma_n^2 \cdot \mathbf{x}_n\mathbf{x}'_n$$

where $\sigma_n^2 = \sigma_{nn}$, the nth diagonal element of $\boldsymbol{\Sigma}$. In a heteroskedasticity-consistent variance estimator this average is replaced by

$$\sum_{n=1}^{N} \frac{1}{N} \left(y_n - \mathbf{x}'_n\beta_{\mathrm{OLS}} \right)^2 \cdot \mathbf{x}_n\mathbf{x}'_n$$

so that the unknown variances σ_n^2 are replaced by the squared OLS fitted residuals. Such estimators do not require a parametric model for $\boldsymbol{\Sigma}$ and, hence, are more widely applicable. Their justification rests, in part, on

$$\mathrm{E}[(y_n - \mathbf{x}'_n\beta)^2] = \sigma_n^2$$

so that one can show that

$$\sum_{n=1}^{N} \frac{1}{N} \left(y_n - \mathbf{x}'_n\beta \right)^2 \cdot \mathbf{x}_n\mathbf{x}'_n$$

is a valid estimator for $\frac{1}{N} \cdot \mathbf{X}'\boldsymbol{\Sigma}\mathbf{X}$. The feasible heteroskedasticity-consistent variance estimator replaces the unknown $\boldsymbol{\beta}$ with its estimator $\hat{\boldsymbol{\beta}}_{\mathrm{OLS}}$. This variance-covariance estimator is often called the "Eicker-White estimator," for Friedjielm Eicker and Halbert White.

The heteroskedasticity-consistent variance estimator does not yield a direct counterpart to $\hat{\boldsymbol{\beta}}_{\mathrm{FGLS}}$. Nevertheless, estimators that dominate OLS are available. The transformed linear model

$$\mathrm{E}[\mathbf{Z}'\mathbf{y}] = \mathbf{Z}'\mathbf{X}\boldsymbol{\beta}$$

has a corresponding variance-covariance matrix

$$\mathrm{Var}[\mathbf{Z}'\mathbf{y}] = \mathbf{Z}'\boldsymbol{\Sigma}\mathbf{Z}$$

which has a heteroskedasticity-consistent counterpart

$$\hat{\boldsymbol{\Omega}} = \sum_{n=1}^{N} \frac{1}{N} \left(y_n - \mathbf{x}'_n\hat{\beta}_{\mathrm{OLS}} \right)^2 \cdot \mathbf{z}_n\mathbf{z}'_n$$

and the FGLS analogue

$$\hat{\beta}_{\mathrm{C}} = \left((\mathbf{Z}'\mathbf{X})' \hat{\boldsymbol{\Omega}}^{-1}\mathbf{Z}'\mathbf{X} \right)^{-1} (\mathbf{Z}'\mathbf{X})' \hat{\boldsymbol{\Omega}}^{-1}\mathbf{Z}'\mathbf{y}$$
$$= \left(\mathbf{X}'\mathbf{Z}\hat{\boldsymbol{\Omega}}^{-1}\mathbf{Z}'\mathbf{X} \right)^{-1} \mathbf{X}'\mathbf{Z}\hat{\boldsymbol{\Omega}}^{-1}\mathbf{Z}'\mathbf{y}.$$

This estimator reduces to OLS if $\mathbf{Z} = \mathbf{X}$ and produces superior estimators to the extent that $\boldsymbol{\Sigma}^{1/2}\mathbf{Z}$ provides a better linear predictor of $\boldsymbol{\Sigma}^{-1/2}\mathbf{X}$ than $\boldsymbol{\Sigma}^{1/2}\mathbf{X}$ does.

The heteroskedasticity-consistent variance estimator has been extended to cover time-series cases with nonzero covariances as well. For example, if only first-order covariances are nonzero then

$$\frac{1}{N} \cdot \mathbf{X}'\boldsymbol{\Sigma}\mathbf{X} = \sum_{n=1}^{N} \frac{1}{N} \sigma_n^2 \cdot \mathbf{x}_n\mathbf{x}'_n$$
$$+ \sum_{n=2}^{N} \frac{1}{N} \sigma_{n,n-1}\left(\mathbf{x}_n\mathbf{x}'_{n-1} + \mathbf{x}_{n-1}\mathbf{x}'_n \right)$$

because $\sigma_{n,n-j} = 0$ for $j > 1$. This term in the OLS variance-covariance matrix can be estimated by

$$\hat{\mathbf{V}}_{\mathrm{HAC}} = \sum_{n=1}^{N} \frac{1}{N} \left(y_n - \mathbf{x}'_n\hat{\beta}_{\mathrm{OLS}} \right)^2 \mathbf{x}_n\mathbf{x}'_n$$
$$+ \sum_{n=2}^{N} \frac{1}{N} \left(y_n - \mathbf{x}'_n\hat{\beta}_{\mathrm{OLS}} \right)$$
$$\left(y_{n-1} - \mathbf{x}'_{n-1}\hat{\beta}_{\mathrm{OLS}} \right)\left(\mathbf{x}_n\mathbf{x}'_{n-1} + \mathbf{x}_{n-1}\mathbf{x}'_n \right),$$

a heteroskedasticity and autocorrelation consistent (HAC) variance-covariance matrix estimator. This works because the second average behaves much like the first in that

$$\mathrm{E}[(y_n - \mathbf{x}'_n\beta)(y_{n-1} - \mathbf{x}'_{n-1}\beta)] = \sigma_{n,n-1}$$

so that one can show that

$$\sum_{n=1}^{N} \frac{1}{N} \left(y_n - \mathbf{x}'_n\beta \right)\left(y_{n-1} - \mathbf{x}'_{n-1}\beta \right)$$
$$\cdot \left(\mathbf{x}_n\mathbf{x}'_{n-1} + \mathbf{x}_{n-1}\mathbf{x}'_n \right)$$

is an estimator for the second term.

One can extend the HAC approach to cover *m*-dependence in which only *m*th-order covariances are nonzero for a finite *m*. However, in practice *m* should be small relative to the number of observations *N*. To illustrate the difficulties with large *m*, consider setting $m = N - 1$ so that all of the covariances in Σ are replaced by a product of OLS-fitted residuals. Then this approach yields the estimator

$$\frac{1}{N} \cdot \mathbf{X}' \left(\mathbf{y} - \mathbf{X} \hat{\beta}_{\text{OLS}} \right)' \left(\mathbf{y} - \mathbf{X}' \hat{\beta}_{\text{OLS}} \right) \mathbf{X}$$
$$= \frac{1}{N} \cdot \mathbf{X}' \left(\mathbf{y} - \mathbf{X} \hat{\beta}_{\text{OLS}} \right) \left(\mathbf{X}' \left(\mathbf{y} - \mathbf{X}' \hat{\beta}_{\text{OLS}} \right) \right)'$$

which is the outerproduct of the $K \times 1$ column vector $\mathbf{X}'(\mathbf{y} - \mathbf{X} \hat{\beta}_{\text{OLS}})$. It follows that this matrix has a rank of one, contradicting the property that $\mathbf{X}'\Sigma\mathbf{X}$ has a rank of *K*. Nevertheless, the heteroskedasticity-consistent variance-covariance estimator has been generalized to cover situations where all of the covariances may be nonzero. The Newey-West estimator is a popular choice:

$$\hat{\Omega}_0 + \sum_{j=1}^{m} w(j, m) \cdot \left(\hat{\Omega}_j + \hat{\Omega}_j' \right)$$

where

$$\hat{\Omega}_j = \sum_{n=j+1}^{N} \left(y_n - \mathbf{x}_n' \beta \right) \left(y_{n-j} - \mathbf{x}_{n-j}' \beta \right) \cdot \mathbf{x}_n \mathbf{x}_{n-j}'$$

and

$$w(j, m) = 1 - \frac{j}{m+1}.$$

The supporting approximate distribution theory requires *m* to depend on the sample size *N* and methods for choosing *m* are available.

Often statistical inference for β based upon estimation of Σ or $\mathbf{X}'\Sigma\mathbf{X}$ can treat these terms as equal to the objects that they estimate. For example, the statistical distribution theory typically shows that

$$Q = (\mathbf{R}\hat{\beta}_{\text{GLS}} - \mathbf{R}\beta)'(\mathbf{R}(\mathbf{X}'\Sigma^{-1}\mathbf{X})^{-1}\mathbf{R}')^{-1}(\mathbf{R}\hat{\beta}_{\text{GLS}} - \mathbf{R}\beta)$$

is approximately (or exactly) distributed as a chi-squared random variable. This pivotal statistic yields a hypothesis test or confidence interval for $\mathbf{R}\beta$. In large samples,

$$\hat{Q} = (\mathbf{R}\hat{\beta}_{\text{FGLS}} - \mathbf{R}\beta)'(\mathbf{R}(\mathbf{X}'\hat{\Sigma}^{-1}\mathbf{X})^{-1}\mathbf{R}')^{-1}(\mathbf{R}\hat{\beta}_{\text{FGLS}} - \mathbf{R}\beta)$$

may be treated as an equivalent statistic. Researchers have shown that bootstrap methods, appropriately applied, can provide better probability approximations in situations with small sample sizes.

SEE ALSO *Autoregressive Models; Bootstrap Method; Covariance; Heteroskedasticity; Least Squares, Ordinary; Least Squares, Two-Stage; Residuals; Serial Correlation; Specification; Variance*

BIBLIOGRAPHY

Aitken, A. C. 1935. On Least Squares and Linear Combination of Observations. *Proceedings of the Royal Society of Edinburgh* 55: 42–48.

Cragg, John G. 1983. More Efficient Estimation in the Presence of Heteroscedasticity of Unknown Form. *Econometrica* 51 (3): 751–764.

Eicker, Friedjielm. 1967. Limit Theorems for Regressions with Unequal and Dependent Errors. In *Fifth Berkeley Symposium on Mathematical Statistics and Probability*, Vol. 1, ed. Lucien Le Cam and Jerzy Neyman, 59–82. Berkeley: University of California Press.

Hausman, Jerry A. 1978. Specification Tests in Econometrics. *Econometrica* 46 (6): 1251–1272.

Newey, Whitney K., and Kenneth D. West. 1987. A Simple, Positive Semi-definite, Heteroskedasticity and Autocorrelation Consistent Covariance Matrix. *Econometrica* 55 (3): 703–708.

White, Halbert. 1980. A Heteroskedasticity-Consistent Covariance Matrix Estimator and a Direct Test for Heteroskedasticity. *Econometrica* 48 (4): 817–838.

Paul A. Ruud

GENERALIZED METHOD OF MOMENTS

SEE *Method of Moments.*

GENERATION X

Throughout U.S. history, social commentators and historians have labeled each succeeding generation in an attempt to capture the defining characteristics of its members as well as to contextualize the generation within the spirit of the times. *Generation X* is the label used to define the more than 79 million people born roughly between 1961 and 1981. Although both social scientists and marketers employ this tag, the U.S. mainstream media gets credit for skyrocketing this label into our popular culture lexicon, particularly throughout the 1990s.

The term, however, was coined decades earlier in a 1964 pop sociology study conducted by two British journalists, Charles Hamblett and Jane Deverson, who used the term to describe their subjects—British teens—whom they interviewed on matters of sex, money, parents, and politics. In 1976 Generation X, a British punk band featuring Billy Idol, hit the London scene. The term eventually worked its way—via the media—into American popular vernacular after the release of Douglas Coupland's 1991 novel *Generation X: Tales for an Accelerated Culture*, a bleak social commentary by three twenty-somethings who "drop out" from their corporate-world careers to take on no-future "McJobs" that provide little pay, benefits, or dignity. Immediately, Gen Xers—subsequently referred to as "slackers"—were officially characterized as lazy, laconic, and unfocused; however, many took issue with this assessment, describing themselves as diverse, independent, and individualistic.

The members of Generation X are arguably natural products of the intellectual atmosphere in which they grew up, for they are the first generation to be raised in the age of postmodernism—a widespread cultural development of the last quarter of the twentieth century. This paradigm shift marked a generational difference between Generation X and their baby boomer parents. Understanding the transition from modern to postmodern culture is necessary to understanding Gen Xers. Whereas modernism values a single worldview rooted in objective science, postmodernism values multiple worldviews based on subjective experiences and contingencies. Information and knowledge are gathered in a linear fashion by modernists, but Gen Xers seek out information from fragmented and nonlinear sources, such as hypertext, visuals, and audio sampling. Whereas the modernists revere classical art and literature, postmodernists broaden their frame of reference to include pop-culture productions such as music videos and animation. Institutions such as government, education, corporations, and media, which are seen as authoritative by modernists, are viewed with a critical eye by members of Generation X.

The civil unrest of the late 1960s and early1970s, followed by the overconsumption of the 1980s, provided the background to the 1990s—a decade laden with social problems. Violent crime, environmental degradation, widespread homelessness, spikes in both teen pregnancies and suicides, corrupt politics, and the AIDS epidemic, coupled with fundamental changes in the family unit caused by rising divorces rates and dual-working parents, were the realities in which Generation X came of age. Many Xers resented the baby boomers for leaving them to repair or endure a society seemingly gone mad.

Despite the initially dismissive media portrayals and self-proclaimed cynicism about the condition of the world in which they came of age, most members of Generation X—who have reached adulthood—have learned to cope. They, like all preceding generations, are striving to attain or maintain the American Dream, albeit in different ways from the methods of their predecessors.

SEE ALSO *Baby Boomers*

BIBLIOGRAPHY

Coupland, Douglas. 1991. *Generation X: Tales for an Accelerated Culture*. New York: St. Martin's Press.

Hamblett, Charles, and Jane Deverson. 1964. *Generation X*. London: Tandem Press.

Howe, Neil, and Bill Strauss. 1993. *13th Gen: Abort, Retry, Ignore, Fail?* New York: Vintage Press.

Judy L. Isaksen

GENEROSITY/SELFISHNESS

Researchers at the National Institute of Neurological Disorders and Stroke, working on a new collaborative project with the National Institute on Mental Health and the National Institute on Aging (*Cognitive and Emotional Health Project: The Healthy Brain*) have discovered that there is a physiological basis for the warm glow that seems often to accompany altruistic giving. Nineteen subjects were each given $128 and told to donate it anonymously to any of a number of socially controversial causes, ranging from support for abortion rights to opposition to the death penalty. Subjects could accept or reject each charity, some of which would require more of their $128 pots than others. Functional magnetic resonance imaging (fMRI) revealed that making a donation activated the donors' brain reward centers, the mesolimbic pathways responsible for the dopamine-mediated euphoria associated with sex, money, food, and drugs (Moll et al. 2006).

We should not be surprised to learn that people feel good when they do good. Group selection theory in evolution shows that groups that are strong in internal altruism have a selective advantage over other groups (Sober and Wilson 1998). Thus, it makes evolutionary sense that helping behavior within groups would be connected with stimulating feelings of well-being. On the genetic level, it appears that altruism is associated with the dopamine D4 receptor (Bachner-Melman et al. 2005).

The psychological benefits of helping others may have been demonstrated first in the early 1980s. "Well-being" is characterized by feeling hopeful, happy, and good about oneself, as well as energetic and connected to others. In an early study that compared retirees over age 65 who volunteered with those who did not, volunteers scored significantly higher in life satisfaction and will to live, and had fewer symptoms of depression, anxiety, and somatization (Hunter and Lin 1981). More recent studies confirm an association between altruistic activities and well-being and life satisfaction in older adults (Dulin and Hill 2003; Liang et al. 2001; Morrow-Howell et al. 2003). Midlarsky (1991) found five benefits to older adults who engage in altruistic behavior: enhanced social integration;

distraction from the agent's own problems; enhanced meaningfulness; increased perception of self-efficacy and competence; and improved mood and/or more physically active lifestyle. Midlarsky and Kahana (1994) associated adult altruism—that is, voluntary behavior that is "motivated by concern for the welfare of the other, rather than by anticipation of rewards" (p. 11)—with improved morale and self-esteem, positive affect, and well-being. The mental health benefits of giving in the form of volunteerism—a wider form of giving than charitable donation—include fewer depressive symptoms (Musick and Wilson 2003) and greater happiness and well-being (Krueger et al. 2001).

In his book *The Happiness Hypothesis* (2006), Jonathan Haidt, a social psychologist at the University of Virginia, discusses great ancient ideas about human flourishing—that is, what makes for a happy and meaningful human life. Haidt explains how the human system of attachment has evolved and how important it is to our successful development, emphasizing Émile Durkheim's idea that the ties, bonds, and obligations of our lives are actually mentally and physically good for us. Helping others provides more benefits than receiving help, and strong social relationships increase immunity, speed healing, and reduce the risks of depression. It makes sense that volunteering appears to be most beneficial to the elderly—both because of the increased social isolation of this life stage, and because giving back fits particularly well into the end-of-life story (Haidt 2006).

In a literature review on the relationship between volunteering and psychological health, "Doing Well by Doing Good: Benefits for the Benefactor" (2003), Jane Piliavin narrows the review by including only studies of community service, defined as "taking actions, carried out within an institutional framework, that potentially provide some service to one or more other people or to the community at large" (p. 227). The studies are organized by the life-cycle stage of the participants (e.g., youth, adult, and elderly), reflecting the belief that volunteering plays different roles, and therefore has different effects, depending on the age of the volunteer. Most studies have focused on the youth stage, when the first opportunities to volunteer arise, and the elderly stage, when volunteering may replace important family and work roles as a source of identity and self-esteem. After reviewing numerous studies of adolescents and college students, Piliavin concludes that there is "considerable evidence that community service has positive impacts on youth" (p. 235). The studies have shown decreased delinquency and other problem behaviors, as well as positive impacts on social values and academic achievements. Studies on service learning—"academic experiences in which students engage both in social action and in reflection on their experiences in performing that action" (p. 236)—have

revealed positive effects on self-esteem, confidence, and self-efficacy, particularly for at-risk students. The comparatively vast literature on volunteering in elderly populations has perhaps contributed the most to the idea that doing good is good for you. Piliavin reviewed studies investigating impacts on mental health, morbidity, and mortality and concluded that "there appears to be a strong and consistent effect, such that the more an elderly person volunteers, the higher is his or her life satisfaction ... similarly, some volunteering enhances physical health and even can stave off death" (p. 241).

SEE ALSO *Altruism; Cooperation; Dopamine; Evolutionary Psychology; Happiness; Hope; Neuroscience*

BIBLIOGRAPHY

Bachner-Melman, Rachel, I. Gritsenko, L. Nemanov, et al. 2005. Dopaminergic Polymorphisms Associated with Self-Report Measures of Human Altruism: A Fresh Phenotype for the Dopamine D4 Receptor. *Molecular Psychiatry* 10: 333–335.

Dulin, P., and R. Hill. 2003. Relationships between Altruistic Activity and Positive and Negative Affect among Low-Income Older Adult Service Providers. *Aging and Mental Health* 7 (4): 294–299.

Haidt, Jonathan. 2006. *The Happiness Hypothesis: Finding Modern Truth in Ancient Wisdom.* New York: Basic Books.

Hunter, Kathleen I., and Margaret W. Linn. 1980–1981. Psychosocial Differences between Elderly Volunteers and Non-Volunteers. *International Journal of Aging and Human Development* 12 (3): 205–213.

Liang, Jersey, Neal M. Krause, and Joan M. Bennett. 2001. Social Exchange and Well-Being: Is Giving Better Than Receiving? *Psychology and Aging* 16 (3): 511–523.

Midlarsky, Elizabeth. 1991. Helping as Coping. *Prosocial Behavior: Review of Personality and Social Psychology* 12: 238–264.

Midlarsky, Elizabeth, and Eva Kahana. 1994. *Altruism in Later Life.* Thousand Oaks, CA: Sage.

Moll, Jorge, Frank Krueger, Roland Zahn, et al. 2006. Human Fronto-Mesolimbic Networks Guide Decisions about Charitable Donation. *Proceedings of the National Academy of Sciences* 103 (42): 15623–15628.

Morrow-Howell, Nancy, Jim Hinterlong, Philip A. Rozario, and Fengyan Tang. 2003. Effects of Volunteering on the Well-Being of Older Adults. *Journal of Gerontology: Social Sciences* 58B (3): S137–145.

Piliavin, Jane Allyn. 2003. Doing Well by Doing Good: Benefits for the Benefactor. In *Flourishing: Positive Psychology and the Life Well-Lived,* eds. Corey L. M. Keyes and Jonathan Haidt, 227–247. Washington, DC: American Psychological Association.

Post, Stephen G., ed. 2007. *Altruism and Health: Empirical Perspectives.* New York: Oxford University Press.

Sober, Elliott, and David Sloan Wilson. 1998. *Unto Others: The Evolution of Unselfish Behavior*. Cambridge, MA: Harvard University Press.

Stephen G. Post

GENETIC TESTING

The term *genetic testing* refers to the molecular analysis of DNA for genetic markers associated with particular genetic conditions, to tests for enzymes or proteins related to gene function, and to chromosomal analysis. Social science studies of genetic testing practices and their social and cultural implications involve, for example, considerations of community, family, kinship, and health and address issues such as informed consent, intellectual property rights, and privacy. Critical assessments of screening and testing practices and of the interpretations of genetic information illuminate the normative effects and premises, past and present, that occur both in institutional settings and in everyday life and are reflected in policy.

PRENATAL DIAGNOSTIC TESTING

One of the earliest and most enduring areas of social science research on genetic testing concerns the social implications of *prenatal diagnostic testing* (PND). PND involves genetic testing during pregnancy for genetic conditions and chromosomal anomalies in the developing fetus using practices such as *chorionic villus sampling* (testing placental blood cells) and *amniocentesis* (testing fetal cells from amniotic fluid). Studies of prenatal diagnostic testing have illustrated the influence it has on experiences of pregnancy, conceptualizations of disability, mediations of genetic information, and knowledge and performances of parental and civil responsibility. Barbara Katz Rothman's *The Tentative Pregnancy: How Amniocentesis Changes the Experience of Motherhood* (1986) was among the first studies following the introduction of amniocentesis (at that time done between sixteen and twenty weeks) to illustrate the complexity of women's experiences of mediating the possibility of undergoing the test, abortion, and/or results indicating a possible disability during the first four to five months of pregnancy. By the late 1990s, amniocentesis had become a routine testing possibility during pregnancy, concurrent with the emergence of an understanding of the fetus as patient (Casper 1998). Published in 1999, Rayna Rapp's book *Testing Women, Testing the Fetus* speaks to the duality of women and fetuses as the subjects of prenatal testing. Employing a multi-sited approach, including research with lab technicians, genetic counselors, and pregnant women, Rapp explores the meanings of amniocentesis within this shifting context. Critical

decisions stemming from the availability of PND involve the interpretation of genetic information and embodied experience by medical practitioners, genetic counselors, lab technicians, and prospective parents.

In 1989 the first child born as a result of the application of *preimplantation genetic diagnosis* (PGD), involving the molecular analysis of one or two cells taken from an embryo created by in vitro fertilization prior to transferring the embryo to a woman's uterus, was reported. In most cases, PGD involves tests for specific genetic mutations, which are offered on the basis of an understanding that one or both potential parents (or egg or sperm donor) is a carrier of a genetically inheritable condition or has a prior history of having a child with a genetic condition. In common parlance and media coverage, children born following PGD have been called *designer babies*, a term referring to the growing potential to influence the genetic make-up of one's child and reflecting concerns over the procedure's implications for social perceptions of normalcy and disability. Aneuploidy screening, generally testing embryos for chromosomal anomalies rather than for specific genetic mutations, is referred to as *preimplantation genetic screening* (PGS), rather than PGD.

In 2000 Adam Nash became the first child reported to be born as a result of the use of PGD not only for the purpose of selecting out embryos with a particular genetic marker, but also for selecting in embryos whose HLA tissue type directly matches that of an already existing sibling, rendering the child-to-be a compatible stem cell donor. In the media, such children have been referred to as *savior siblings*, invoking associations with sacrifice as well as life-saving. The use of PGD, or PID as it is sometimes called, is banned in many countries (for example, Germany) and restricted to use in relation to particular genetic conditions in others (for example, the United Kingdom).

Preimplantation genetic diagnosis is also applied to test embryos for late-onset disorders and genetic susceptibility to particular conditions, including Huntington's disease, breast cancer, and hereditary colon cancer. Debates in this area highlight the perceptions and cultural management of "genetic risk status" in relation to disorders with variable degrees of *penetrance* (or the degree to which the genetic mutation corresponds to the manifestation of the condition) and for which preventative measures or treatment may be available. For example, the genetic mutation associated with Huntington's disease is highly penetrant, corresponding to an expected certainty of developing the disease over the course of a lifetime. In contrast, the mutations on the BRCA 1 and BRCA 2 genes, associated with hereditary forms of breast cancer (accounting for 5 to 10 percent of breast cancer cases), have a penetrance level of approximately 80 percent. This means that not everyone who carries the BRCA 1 and BRCA 2 gene mutations will develop breast cancer in their lifetime and that the likelihood of developing this form of breast cancer increases with age.

PREDICTIVE GENETIC TESTING

The term *predictive genetic testing* (PGT) refers to testing that occurs prior to the appearance of symptoms. It is used in situations where there is a known history of a perceived genetic condition among genetically related individuals. While issues involving the individual are often the focus of studies of genetic testing—for example, the autonomy of the individual to make an informed decision regarding a test and follow-up actions or the specificity and uniqueness of an individual's "genetic code"—social science research on PGT provides critical data and insight into the construction and experience of hereditary risk and the familial and social context of genetic testing. In the case of testing for genetically inherited mutations, testing may require the prior or parallel testing of a family member and the communication of their potential genetic risk status. Results of genetic tests for one family member may implicate the "risk" status of other genetically related family members, who may or may not choose to undergo genetic testing.

The Human Genome Project, which ran from 1991 to 2003, resulted in the identification of increasing numbers of specific genes and genetic mutations implicated in genetic conditions, as well as the function of enzymes and proteins. There is increasing emphasis placed on the use of predictive genetic testing among a broader population with no prior awareness or familial history of specific genetic conditions. This form of predictive testing is proposed with respect to the implementation of preventative measures and personalized medicine. Routine genetic screening, for example of newborns for cystic fibrosis, raises additional questions regarding the disclosure and use of information about the gene carrier status of individuals, as well as about potential implications for individuals who did not consent to genetic testing. While in many cultural contexts, predictive testing of children is advised against, research demonstrates that testing occurs and, in the name of preventative medicine, is promoted. The availability of genetic tests and their use on a broader scale raises concerns regarding genetic discrimination, specifically in the areas of health insurance and employment.

The field of *pharmacogenomics* (sometimes referred to as *personalized medicine*) focuses on the development of medical and preventative care tailored to an individual's genetic makeup. In 2005 the U.S. Food and Drug Agency approved the use of BiDil, a post-heart-attack drug treatment marketed by NitroMed, for black individuals following a clinical trial exclusively involving self-identifying black patients. Because women of Ashkenazi Jewish descent are seen to have a significantly higher percentage of mutations at particular points along the BRCA 1 and BRCA 2 genes, in some jurisdictions they may be given access to breast cancer gene testing without the involvement of another living family member with breast cancer, which is often otherwise required. This relationship between genetic testing and ethnic identification has manifested differently in Europe, where in 2005 Myriad Genetics won the right to a patent on a particular mutation associated with the Ashkenazi Jewish population, requiring physicians to ask breast cancer gene test candidates whether they are of Ashkenazi Jewish descent. While variations in the manifestation, management, and recognition of various conditions have been recognized in comparative and cross-cultural studies of health, reducing these variations to genetic difference runs the risk of reifying and geneticizing concepts such as race and ethnicity and obscuring social determinants of health.

The turn toward *genomics*, the study of the interaction between genes and the environment, has resulted in the implementation of *biobanks*, or population genetic databases, as genetic research resource centers. Members of communities and nation-states are requested to donate blood (DNA) samples for research purposes. When genetic testing is conducted within the framework and for the purpose of health care, there is a normative expectation that individuals are aware of the tests being carried out and also of how resulting genetic information will be managed. Studies of biobanking reveal, however, that research participants (those who donated DNA samples) do not have a clear idea of what will be done with the sample or the information derived from it and are not aware of whom it could be distributed to or for how long it will be retained (see Hoeyer 2003). Children are also being included as participants in larger genomic studies, enrolled at birth via the donation of umbilical cord blood by consenting parents.

The advent of genetic testing in the form of PND, PGD, predictive testing, and population-based genetic research is captured by the phrase *new genetics*, within which is embedded a distinction from eugenics and other previous uses and abuses of genetics. Whereas eugenics is depicted as the imposition on individuals of decisions made by states or other authorities, the new genetics is associated with choice, information, knowledge, autonomy, and responsibility. Social science research and analysis of the new genetics is needed in order to address, for example, how concepts of normalcy are mobilized in new ways, how new forms of genetic information may lead to present and future discrimination, and how concepts such as reproductive choice and civil responsibility are experienced in the context of increasing emphasis on the significance of genetic information, genetic health, and genetic research.

SEE ALSO *Bioethics; Eugenics; Genomics*

BIBLIOGRAPHY

Casper, Monica. 1998. *The Making of the Unborn Patient. A Social Anatomy of Fetal Surgery.* New Brunswick, NJ: Rutgers University Press.

Cox, Susan M., and William H. McKellin. 1999. "There's This Thing in Our Family": Predictive Testing and the Social Construction of Risk for Huntington Disease. *Sociology of Health and Illness* 21 (5): 622–646.

Hoeyer, Klaus. 2003. "Science Is Really Needed—That's All I Know": Informed Consent and the Non-Verbal Practices of Collecting Blood for Genetic Research in Northern Sweden. *New Genetics and Society* 22 (3): 229–244.

Koch, Lene. 2004. The Meaning of Eugenics: Reflections on the Government of Genetic Knowledge in the Past and the Present. *Science in Context* 17 (3): 315–331.

Rapp, Rayna. 1999. *Testing Women, Testing the Fetus: The Social Impact of Amniocentesis in America.* New York: Routledge.

Rothman, Barbara Katz. 1986. *The Tentative Pregnancy: How Amniocentesis Changes the Experience of Motherhood.* New York: Viking.

Jacquelyne Marie Luce

GENEVA CONVENTION

SEE *War Crimes.*

GENOCIDE

Genocide is one of the foundational moral, legal, and political concepts of modern society. While the terrible suffering named by the term is not new, the meaning of genocide is intimately bound to the creation of the modern human rights movement in the wake of World War II (1939–1945) and the subsequent evolution and expansion of new mechanisms of global governance.

Genocide is a term of profound moral, legal, and political significance. On moral terms, genocide references extreme inhumanity, naming a boundary where the central tenets of civilized behavior are called into question by the most reprehensible acts of political violence. Legally, genocide is understood as a crime whose severity demands immediate and total condemnation. As the special rapporteur to the UN Economic and Social Council Commission on Human Rights stated, "Genocide is the ultimate crime and the gravest violation of human rights it is possible to commit" (1985, part I, para. A14).

Politically, the term helped establish the foundations of modern human rights discourse and practice. The United Nations began discussing genocide in its first year of operation (1946), and the Convention for the Prevention and Punishment of the Crime of Genocide (Genocide Convention), entered into force in 1951, was the first legally binding international human rights convention. In these interconnected ways, genocide represents a major element of an evolving human rights consciousness as well as a growing global commitment to protecting people from harm and preventing the worst excesses of the exercise of power.

Throughout human history, there are records of massacres and violence directed toward the destruction of entire peoples. References of mass violence that might be termed *genocide* can be found in the Bible, the works of the ancient Greeks and Romans, the religious-military campaigns of the Middle Ages, and the mass killing of indigenous peoples in the Americas, Africa, and elsewhere associated with "discovery" and colonization. The modern discussion of the concept is often associated with Turkish atrocities against the Armenians (1915–1923), when as many as 1.5 million may have been killed. However, it was the Nazi atrocities of the Holocaust that led to the evocation of genocide as a distinct crime, in which over 6 million Jews were exterminated in a systematic and calculated manner, along with Roma, Slavs, and other groups viewed to be dangerous or undesirable.

The word *genocide* was invented in 1943 by Polish jurist Raphael Lemkin (1900–1959). Lemkin also wrote *Military Government in Europe*, which was a preliminary version of his more fully developed publication *Axis Rule in Occupied Europe* (1944). In 1943 Lemkin was appointed consultant to the U.S. Board of Economic Warfare and Foreign Economic Administration and later became a special adviser on foreign affairs to the War Department, largely because of his expertise in international law.

The term is based on the Greek word *genos*, referring to race or tribe, and the Latin term *cide*, meaning murder. Lemkin created the term to refer to a new crime committed against group victims and involving, "a coordinated plan of different actions aiming at the destruction of essential foundations of the life of national groups, with the aim of annihilating the groups themselves" (1944).

Lemkin invented the term because he believed that the Nazi's planned eradication of various groups represented an irreparable harm to global society, as well as a special challenge to existing conceptions of criminal law, which tended to focus on crimes committed against individuals.

The text of the UN Genocide Convention was completed in 1948, and in 1951 the Convention became a legally binding document. By mid-2006, 138 nations had accepted the Convention as legally binding. The Genocide Convention declares genocide a crime under international law whether committed during war or peacetime. It requires all the nations that accept the document to take measures to prevent and punish acts of genocide committed within their jurisdiction and to enact appropriate domestic legislation to criminalize genocide. The treaty also criminalizes attempts to commit genocide, conspiracy or incitement to commit genocide, as well as complicity in the commission of the crime. Nations that sign the Genocide Convention agree to try individuals suspected of having committed genocide in domestic courts or in an appropriate international tribunal (which did not exist at the time the Convention was written, but is now present in the form of the International Criminal Court). The prohibition on genocide is now so widely accepted that it has become a part of international customary law so that it is understood to be binding on all states, regardless of whether or not they have ratified the Genocide Convention.

The legal definition of *genocide* is found in Article II of the Convention. This definition is widely accepted and has been reinforced by its repetition in relevant domestic legislation and in the statutes of the International Criminal Tribunal for Yugoslavia (ICTY), the International Criminal Tribunal for Rwanda (ICTR), and the International Criminal Court (ICC). Article II defines the crime as follows:

> In the present Convention, genocide means any of the following acts committed with intent to destroy, in whole or in part, a national, ethnical, racial or religious group, as such:
>
> (a) Killing members of the group;
>
> (b) Causing serious bodily or mental harm to members of the group;
>
> (c) Deliberately inflicting on the group conditions of life calculated to bring about its physical destruction in whole or in part;
>
> (d) Imposing measures intended to prevent births within the group;
>
> (e) Forcibly transferring children of the group to another group. (OHCHR [1948] 1951)

In this way, genocide is composed of three key elements: acts, intent, and victim group. The five enumerated acts are distinct in nature, yet unified as strategies that can either destroy an existing group (killing, causing serious harm, creating destructive conditions) or ruin the possibility of the group's continued existence (preventing reproduction and forcibly removing children). The issue of intent is complex, but is generally understood to limit

claims of genocide to those cases where political violence is purposefully directed, either as an officially stated policy to destroy a group or as expressed through an analysis of repressive strategies. The idea of a victim group defines genocide as a unique crime in which individuals are targeted for repression because of their membership in either a national, ethnic, racial, or religious group.

Each element of the legal definition of genocide raises complex questions, many of which run counter to dominant moral and social understandings of the term. That is, genocide is widely understood to be a crime involving mass murder and the idea of destroying "in whole or in part" suggests some numerical threshold. So, while it would trivialize the moral power of the concept to include cases of hate crimes or small-scale racial killing, the Genocide Convention allows a case of genocide to involve few casualties, as with the forced transfer of children. Similarly, the popular understanding of the crime assumes that the mass killing of hundreds of thousands would constitute genocide, yet the Convention's definition only covers acts committed against one or more of the four protected groups and may not, for example, cover the brutal destruction of political opponents (as in the Khmer Rouge's killing of 1.7 million in Cambodia in the 1970s). Equally complex is the question of whether group status is a function of perpetrators' understandings of targeted victims (so that the Nazi's vision of Jewish identity would define the group) or whether the concept seeks to protect a group defined by some inherent, objective, or actual identity, a problem heightened where different groups appear highly similar (as with Rwandan Hutus and Tutsis, who speak the same language, practice the same religions, and commonly intermarried).

In order to address these issues, scholars have expanded the interpretation of the crime to cover many instances of mass violence, or created new terms such as *autogenocide* to deal with mass murder where perpetrators and victims are of the same group, or *democide* to refer to mass killing based on any justification. While these efforts play an important role in evolving understandings of the crime, the Genocide Convention's definition remains the central understanding of the concept.

Despite the widespread acceptance of genocide as a crime, there were few twentieth-century attempts to prosecute individuals. In fact, it was not until 1998 that the first international prosecution and conviction for genocide took place in the Jean-Paul Akayesu case at the ICTR. This historic decision was followed by a number of additional cases in the same court (Jean Kambanda, etc.), as well as other important cases at the ICTY (Milan Kovasevic, Radislav Krstic, Dusko Tadic, etc.), allowing for the evolution of a new jurisprudence of genocide. The decisions of these ad hoc tribunals represented an important expansion of the international legal commitment to prosecuting genocide. This commitment was further supported by the creation of the ICC in 2002, which provides a permanent body for prosecuting cases of genocide and other severe atrocities. Also in 1998, a Spanish judge brought genocide charges against former Chilean dictator General Augusto Pinochet in a domestic court for crimes committed in South America. This ushered in a new era of using the concept of universal jurisdiction as a means of prosecuting individuals accused of genocide in national courts in countries distinct from where the violations occurred.

The Genocide Convention was also created to prevent genocide, ideally by stopping potential genocides before they occur, or by taking action against severe violations before they reach a genocidal intensity. Yet, since the mid-twentieth century, the world has witnessed many atrocities often described as genocide. These include Cambodia (1975–1979), Rwanda (1994), and mass political violence in the former Yugoslavia (1992–1995) that brought the world a new, nonlegal term, *ethnic cleansing*. In addition, there have been formal claims of genocide associated with atrocities throughout Latin America in the 1970s and 1980s, especially the Guatemalan military regime's attacks on indigenous people. And, there have been claims of genocide against the former Soviet Union for military actions in Afghanistan and elsewhere, as well as state policies such as the use of famine to kill seven to fifteen million Ukrainians. In Africa, there have been numerous genocide claims, most recently in the Sudan.

The case of Rwanda is especially chilling in that an estimated 800,000 people, generally Tutsis, were killed with machetes and small arms by a Hutu-dominated regime in 1994. Before the killing began, UN peacekeepers warned of an upcoming genocide and estimated that an international force of around five thousand could have prevented the violence. During the hundred-day killing, the international community refused to acknowledge that genocide was taking place, in part to avoid the legal responsibility to act. Later, most nations recognized these killings as an example of genocide, but by then the murderous regime had been removed from power by a Rwandan rebel army.

In many respects, genocide defines the twentieth century, representing a harsh warning of the destructive capacity of modernity as well as the open promise of the benefits of international cooperation. Genocide is one of the central, foundational ideas within human rights discourse, which represents the first universal structuring discourse of an emerging global order. Genocide was defined formally through global commitment toward its punishment and prevention. In this sense, the term is almost iconic in its representation of the complexity of modernity, defining both the worst and best of human society, a word that names acts of unforgivable brutality while offering the promise of a world where such acts cannot be tolerated and can only exist within the imaginary, banished from the real through concerted, coordinated, international action.

SEE ALSO *Ethnic Conflict; Ethnic Fractionalization; Ethnocentrism; Racism; Tribalism*

BIBLIOGRAPHY

Andreopoulos, George, ed. 1994. *Genocide: Conceptual and Historical Dimensions.* Philadelphia: University of Pennsylvania Press.

Chalk, Frank, and Kurt Jonassohn. 1900. *The History and Sociology of Genocide: Analyses and Case Studies.* New Haven, CT: Yale University Press.

Charny, Israel W. 1982. *How Can We Commit the Unthinkable? Genocide, the Human Cancer.* Boulder, CO: Westview.

Fein, Helen. [1990] 1993. *Genocide: A Sociological Perspective.* London: Sage.

Horowitz, Irving Louis. 2002. *Taking Lives: Genocide and State Power.* 5th ed. New Brunswick, NJ: Transaction.

Kuper, Leo. 1981. *Genocide: Its Political Use in the Twentieth Century.* New Haven, CT: Yale University Press.

Lemkin, Raphael. 1944. *Axis Rule in Occupied Europe: Laws of Occupation, Analysis of Government, Proposals for Redress.* Washington, DC: Carnegie Endowment of International Peace.

Rummel, R. J. 1994. *Death by Government: Genocide and Mass Murder since 1900.* New Brunswick, NJ: Transaction.

Schabas, William A. 2000. *Genocide in International Law: The Crimes of Crimes.* Cambridge, U.K.: Cambridge University Press.

Staub, Ervin. 1989. *The Roots of Evil: The Origins of Genocide and Other Group Violence.* Cambridge, U.K.: Cambridge University Press.

United Nations Economic and Social Council Commission on Human Rights, Sub-Commission on Prevention of Discrimination and Protection of Minorities. 1985. Revised and Updated Report on the Question of the Prevention and Punishment of the Crime of Genocide, prepared by Benjamin Whitaker. Thirty-eighth Session, Item 4 of the Provisional Agenda, E/CN.4/Sub.2/1985/6. 2 July. http://www.preventgenocide.org/prevent/UNdocs/whitaker/.

United Nations Office of the High Commissioner for Human Rights (OHCHR). 1948/1951. Convention on the Prevention and Punishment of the Crime of Genocide. http://www.ohchr.org/english/law/genocide.htm.

Daniel Rothenberg

GENOMICS

The term *genomics* was coined in 1987 by Victor A. McKusick and Frank H. Ruddle as the title for a new journal of that name. McKusick and Ruddle derived it from *genome*, a concept that had been circulating in biology since the early 1920s. The roots of *genome* are the Greek *genos* (class, kind, race) and the suffix *-ome* (as used in rhizome and chromosome.). *Genome* is defined as the entire sequence of DNA found in the nucleus of every cell.

In the 1980s and 1990s, *genomics* primarily referred to large-scale projects to map the genes and sequence the DNA of organisms. As it turned out, a bacteriophage called phi-x174 was the first organism whose complete DNA sequence was revealed. The sequencing of its 5,375 nucleotides was accomplished in 1977 by Frederick Sanger and his colleagues at the University of Cambridge. In the ensuing two decades, a series of further viral genome-sequencing projects were undertaken. In July 1995 Robert David Fleischmann reported the completion of the sequencing of the first genome of a nonviral organism (*H. influenzae*).

Encouraged by the chancellor of the University of California, Santa Cruz, Robert Sinsheimer, and the U.S. Office of Health and Environmental Research, biologists began in the mid-1980s to evaluate the possibility of mapping the genes and sequencing the DNA of the human genome. As part of its mission to assess the health effects of radiation, the U.S. Department of Energy established in 1987 three human genome research centers at Los Alamos, New Mexico; Livermore, California; and the Lawrence Berkeley National Laboratory in Berkeley, California. The initiative to first map and then sequence the complete human genome was formally launched in 1990 as a joint program of the Department of Energy and the National Institutes of Health. In France, the Centre d'Étude du Polymorphisme Humain conducted a successful gene-mapping project funded by the Muscular Dystrophy Association. In the United Kingdom, the Wellcome Trust supported human genome research. Germany and Japan soon joined the international efforts in what was called a "race" to map the genes and sequence the 3.1 billion base pairs of the human genome.

In the wake of a successful initial mapping of the human genome, the Human Genome Organization decided by the mid-1990s to decode the DNA of model organisms before sequencing the human genome. In 1997 the complete DNA sequence of the yeast genome was published; a year later the ninety-seven million base pairs of the worm *C. elegans* followed; in early 2000 an advanced draft of the genome of the fruit fly *Drosophila* was announced.

Using different approaches, the Human Genome Sequencing Consortium and a team led by Craig Venter at Celera Genomics separately published in February 2001 their preliminary findings, estimating the number of genes in the human genome at 30,000 to 40,000. A later reanalysis reduced the number to approximately 20,000

to 25,000. The completion of the project in April 2003 has led to the identification of millions of sites on the genome where individuals differ.

The challenges in completing gene-mapping and DNA-sequencing projects were primarily technical, organizational, and financial rather than scientific. The problem scientists face today is how to use genomic information to gain biological understanding. Accordingly, genomics has increasingly given way to postgenomic studies focusing on the functions of genes and the complex interactions between cells, systems of cells, multicellular organisms, populations of organisms, and their environment. The three terms *functional genomics* (the study of genetic function), *proteomics* (the study of the proteins expressed by a genome), and *transcriptomics* (the study of RNA transcripts) indicate that the epistemic status of the genome has shifted from an object of analysis to a tool of research. In the emerging world of postgenomics, sequences are used as giant reference tools.

The social relevance of genomics lies primarily in the agricultural and biomedical utilization of genetic information. Knowledge gained from genetic and genomic research has enabled biomedicine to envision the organism at a molecular scale. New diagnostic tests based on a molecular understanding of life reveal susceptibility to a broadening range of diseases. The concept of genetic risk factors has led to a redrawing of the line between the normal and the pathological. Additionally, various patient groups have formed around specific diseases, inflecting new styles of collective thought, action, and passion that entail a redefinition of both the biological and the social. As a consequence, a new moral landscape has emerged that contrasts with the ethical discourse of the public sphere.

The challenge of contemporary molecular biology is to proceed from the generation of genomic information to the assessment of hypothetical propositions in experimental settings. For social scientists, it will be of paramount importance to continue observing and analyzing the unexpected emergence of objects and the unpredictable reconfiguration of forms as they assemble into an ever-shifting understanding of life.

BIBLIOGRAPHY

Brent, Roger. 2000. Genomic Biology. *Cell* 100: 169–183.

Cook-Deegan, Robert. 1995. *The Gene Wars: Science, Politics, and the Human Genome.* New York: Norton.

Kevles, Daniel J., and Leroy Hood, eds. 1992. *The Code of Codes: Scientific and Social Issues in the Human Genome Project.* Cambridge, MA: Harvard University Press.

Rabinow, Paul. 1999. *French DNA: Trouble in Purgatory.* Chicago: University of Chicago Press.

Carlo Caduff

GENTILITY

For over five centuries, English-speaking societies have given the terms *genteel* and *gentility* a series of definitions and connotations. To varying degrees in different historical contexts, believers in gentility have made honorable family roots, refined manners, and tasteful elegance signs that distinguish those in the genteel ranks from decadent aristocrats, showy upstarts, vulgar tradesmen, and ordinary hardworking people. Individuals have maintained their elite status through an artful pretense that masks both their true feelings and the effort they exert to make their genteel appearance seem "natural." Throughout the centuries, there has been a tendency for many who were looked down on as "provincial," "frontier," "colonial," "nouveau riche," or simply "common" to seek upward mobility and new privileges by emulating their "betters," often with the guidance of prescriptive literature. Even in periods when gentility no longer required upper-class ancestors, it has never lived comfortably with egalitarian democracy.

THE ROOTS OF GENTILITY

Etymologists have traced the roots of the word *gentility* to Latin, then to French, and finally to *gentilete* in Middle English. In the thirteenth century, English speakers used the word *gentle* to describe the landed gentry, and by the sixteenth century, gentle had evolved into *genteel*. During the Renaissance, some Europeans merged the new humanistic respect for learning with the medieval admiration of military glory to create a new class of gentleman who were neither nobles nor common folk. They displayed their status, in part, through their right to "bear arms," meaning the right to display both a sword and a coat of arms.

In the eighteenth century, English and American pamphlets used *genteel,* in the sense of "being appropriate for gentlemen," as a modifier in their titles for a wide variety of terms and activities, including "genteel places of amusement," "genteel toasts, sentiments, and hobnobs," "genteel feats of action," "genteel designs for parsonages and farm houses," and "genteel ingenious conversation." By the time of the American Revolution, anyone in the broader class of gentlemen—wealthy merchants and planters, court and government officials, some members of the clergy, and other professionals—needed to live by the genteel code, while those in the lower classes could be shunned if they tried to pass themselves off as true gentlemen. Some twentieth-century historians, such as Howard Mumford Jones, Louis B. Wright, and Thomas Wertenbaker, have depicted gentility in eighteenth-century America as a positive force, while others, including Carl and Jessica Bridenbaugh, Jack P. Greene, and Kenneth Lockridge, have asserted that it was an obstacle to the development of a more authentically American culture.

GENTILITY, INDUSTRY, AND COLONIALISM

As gentility continued to evolve in the nineteenth century, definitions for *gentleman* in the *Encyclopaedia Britannica* changed from "one, who without any title, bears a coat of arms, or whose ancestors have been freemen" in 1815 to "all above the rank of yeoman" with "that self-respect and intellectual refinement which manifest themselves in unrestrained yet delicate manners" in 1856. In 1891, America's *Century Dictionary* added the possibility that gentlemen might be "fastidious," demonstrating excessive "pride in refinement and family position." These variations on the basic theme sometimes reflected political tensions, as when the genteel supporters of John Quincy Adams shuddered at the news of rough supporters of Jacksonian democracy celebrating in the White House after the inauguration of their hero, Andrew Jackson. In the decades before the U.S. Civil War, southern planters developed an image of genteel slaveownership characterized by benevolent paternalism, partly as a counter to abolitionist challenges to their moral character.

As industrial capitalism allowed men who had made quick fortunes to gain more power than established gentlemen, a group of authors, including Ralph Waldo Emerson, James Russell Lowell, Oliver Wendell Holmes, Henry Adams, Henry James, and Charles Eliot Norton, sought to cultivate an elite esthetic sense of culture. George Santayana labeled their writings the "genteel tradition." In the twentieth century, Van Wyck Brooks and Vernon Parrington were among the scholars who criticized the genteel tradition for having inhibited realism in American literature and having been indifferent to the needs of ordinary people.

The spread of colonialism stimulated an imperialistic gentility to distinguish colonial authorities from the "less civilized" natives. British consular officials, for example, dressed in formal dinner attire while dining by a tent in an African jungle. Some individuals from the colonized societies emulated such behavior to gain favors from officials. Virginia tobacco planters, for example, built homes according to the standards of the English gentry, and educated natives of India learned to play cricket. Those with dark skin could not, however, expect to gain total approval from their rulers. White supremacists took it for granted that the basic nature of "people of color" was too dishonorable for them to be capable of refined taste and manners. This made those categorized in this demeaning fashion even more determined to display genteel qualities whenever they could afford to do so. Nevertheless, in the Jim Crow South, white southerners were extremely hostile to public genteel behavior by African Americans. Some black families decided not to paint their homes, lest the local white community discover that they possessed a refined parlor, complete with a piano.

GENTILITY AND THE RISE OF THE MIDDLE CLASS

Even though gentility can never be truly democratic, the rise of the middle classes in the nineteenth century led to an increase in individuals seeking a genteel identity. While those who were born into elite status claimed to notice a marked difference between a person who was "acting like" a lady or gentleman and someone who actually was one, the popularity of advice books indicates that not everyone agreed with such rigid exclusivity. Emily Thornwell, for example, published an especially popular manual in 1856 titled *The Lady's Guide to Perfect Gentility, in Manners, Dress, and Conversation, in the Family, in Company, at the Piano Forte, the Table, in the Street, and in Gentlemen's Society*. While explaining what forks to use when, these etiquette advisers also encouraged their readers to buy everything needed to furnish a genteel home, creating what the historian Richard Bushman has labeled "vernacular gentility." After World War I, according to the historian Stow Persons, distinguishing between gentlemen and common men was no longer socially useful.

GENTILITY, GENDER, AND WORK

Whether in the sixteenth century or the twentieth, certain assumptions have been standard elements of gentility. A firm opposition to any ambiguity in gender roles has led to the dismissal of anyone whose behavior was not up to the standards of genteel femininity and masculinity. In the nineteenth century, some men focused on countering assumptions that refined style might be effeminate by calling for a more "manly" gentry. Courtship rituals reflected an idealization of the medieval code of chivalry, which gave demure belles the most public power they would have in their lives, as they charmed suitors before choosing one to be their husband.

A genteel work ethic has encouraged gentlemen to focus almost exclusively on elite leisure activities, whether studying Greek classics or betting on horse races, rather than on practical survival strategies and tactics. In the fourteenth century, John Ball, the leader of a peasants' revolt against privileges for elites who did no work, summarized this assumption in a couplet referring to the story of Adam and Even in Genesis that lived on as a nursery rhyme: "When Adam delved and Eve span, / Who was then the Gentleman?" (Bartlett, 871). A prejudice against "tradesmen" lasted into the twentieth century on the European continent and inspired a number of New England businessmen in the nineteenth century to seek to become "gentleman farmers" once their fortunes were secure. For much of the twentieth century, upper-class male college students were proud of earning a "gentleman's C."

The genteel work ethic for ladies has required socializing frequently enough to assure their families' elite connections while also avoiding the company of anyone without the proper genteel credentials. Women made time for visiting by engaging in a genteel domesticity that involved overseeing servants rather than undertaking any menial chores themselves. Elite mothers trained their children in genteel behavior, including the art of polite conversation, but servants did much of the childcare. For ladies, ornamental sewing and occasional baking, as well as singing to entertain guests, needed to be obviously optional amateur activities that would showcase a lady's "accomplishments" for the pleasure of others.

When gentlemen who refused to pay attention to business matters lost some of their family's fortune, they could depend on their peers to ascribe their genteel poverty to historical victimization rather than to individual failings. Nevertheless, those without much financial wealth sought to heighten the value of the cultural capital of genteel behavior relative to economic capital, and to avoid social contact with anyone whose "new wealth" made their social status questionable (unless they were quietly seeking a "blood and money marriage" for one of their children). "Shabby gentility" first became a popular topic in English fiction in the eighteenth century. In his novel *The Old Curiosity Shop* (1840-1841), Charles Dickens described "poor streets where faded gentility essayed … to make its last feeble stand" (Dickens, 115).

In recent decades, the status of celebrity has overtaken that of gentility, allowing rock stars to be knighted by the Queen of England for their contributions to the British economy. But the terms *genteel* and *gentility* are not obsolete. At least one American fraternity still instructs its members that each should, "through his gentility," seek to follow the ideals of chivalry, including good manners and respect for women. From another perspective, the newspaper columnist Frank Fitzpatrick, on July 14, 2006, published an article condemning the owners of the Philadelphia Phillies baseball team for their inability to understand the anger of the "real Phillies fans" because their anachronistic "genteel worldview" still considered sports to be "an aristocratic club." Whether future generations will be equally contemptuous of the concept of gentility, or develop a new version to suit their particular social ambitions, remains to be seen.

SEE ALSO *Distinctions, Social and Cultural; Elites; Hierarchy; Middle Class; Mobility; Norms; Upward Mobility*

BIBLIOGRAPHY

Bartlett, John, ed. 1919. *Familiar Quotations*, 10th ed. Boston: Little, Brown, and Co.

Bushman, Richard L. 1992. *The Refinement of America: Persons, Houses, Cities.* New York: Alfred A. Knopf.

Dawidoff, Robert. 1993. *The Genteel Tradition and the Sacred Rage: High Culture vs. Democracy in Adams, James, and Santayana.* Chapel Hill: University of North Carolina Press.

Dickens, Charles. 1841. *The Old Curiosity Shop.* London: Cleave.

Fitzpatrick, Frank. 2006. A Harsh Reality for Phils' Gentility. *Philadelphia Inquirer* (July 14): NA.

Kasson, John F. 1990. *Rudeness and Civility: Manners in Nineteenth-Century Urban America.* New York: Hill and Wang.

Persons, Stow. 1973. *The Decline of American Gentility.* New York: Columbia University Press.

Rozbicki, Michal J. 1998. *The Complete Colonial Gentleman: Cultural Legitimacy in Plantation America.* Charlottesville: University Press of Virginia.

Shields, David S. 1997. *Civil Tongues and Polite Letters in British America.* Chapel Hill: University of North Carolina Press.

Thornwell, Emily. 1856. *The Lady's Guide to Perfect Gentility, in Manners, Dress, and Conversation, in the Family, in Company, at the Piano Forte, the Table, in the Street, and in Gentlemen's Society.* New York: Derby & Jackson.

Tomisch, John. 1971. *A Genteel Endeavor: American Culture and Politics in the Gilded Age.* Stanford, CA: Stanford University Press.

Cita Cook

GENTRIFICATION

Gentrification marks the revival of urban areas by a set of interrelated demographic, economic, and spatial changes: new investment in housing, an influx of highly educated, culturally aware residents and consumers, and the shift from an industrial to a service economy with jobs in the center city for professionals and artists. First observed in London during the 1950s but gradually spreading through North American, Australian, and European cities, the movement of middle-class households into old working-class neighborhoods took most observers by surprise because it contradicts the much greater flow of people and capital outward to new suburbs and the presumed decline of urban life. But gentrifiers reject the social class and ethnic homogeneity of most suburban housing developments. They are attracted to the social diversity of city life, the aesthetic qualities of old buildings, and the cultural vitality of the streets. The low cost of housing in centrally located but derelict and often crime-ridden neighborhoods also appeals to them. Although they take a

risk by investing in and moving to these areas, they benefit from the cultural amenities they help to develop and from steadily rising property values.

Because gentrification raises housing prices and brings a different sort of commercial culture to older neighborhoods, gentrifiers are nearly always suspected of displacing low-income residents. In many cities where high-level business services and high-tech sectors have expanded and redevelopment plans focus on the downtown, rising rents and sale prices do increase the housing burden for a large part of the urban population. Higher rents also threaten the cheap stores and local services that cater to low-income residents; landlords prefer to end their leases and replace them with boutiques, cafés, and bars that will draw middle-class customers. The types of services these consumers want—and the atmosphere they prefer—are often seen as alien by their poorer, older, and less educated neighbors and tend to make these earlier residents feel culturally as well as economically displaced. But precise data on displacement are difficult to find, and some local residents may choose to move either to a cheaper location in the same area or to a different place entirely. Older home owners in particular may take the opportunity to move away if their children do not want to live in their house and they can make a large profit by selling it.

City governments and the media downplay displacement in order to encourage new investment and develop attractions for tourists and residents. Along with new residents, they describe the existing area as a "wilderness" and the gentrifiers as "pioneers." These metaphors thinly veil a continuous pressure to upgrade the city by replacing low-income groups, who often depend on public services, with more affluent taxpayers and to replace low-rent, low-status manufacturers with residential tenants. Because gentrification in the form of loft living became widespread during the 1970s due to the residential conversion of manufacturing space, it is difficult to say whether gentrifiers contribute to or simply follow industrial dislocations and factory shutdowns. By the same token, gentrifiers often move into neighborhoods that have already lost residents because of property owners' disinvestment and abandonment as well as a decline in public services.

The media actively promote the sense of style that gentrification evokes. While loft living is associated with open spaces, high ceilings, and stark modern decor and the rehabilitation of town houses with small rooms and original, Victorian architectural detail, each suggests a cultural transformation of the inner city from physical dilapidation and social disadvantage to an attractive consumers' zone. Because of new residents' higher salaries, dual income households, and cultural capital, gentrified areas of the city soon sprout ambitious restaurants, art galleries, performance spaces, and unusual designer boutiques. The high degree of self-employment among gentrifiers who work in cultural fields provides them with both a daytime and a nighttime clientele. Moreover new shops and cafés are featured in going-out guides and style magazines, bringing more visitors from other areas of the city as well as from suburbs and overseas. In this way the lifestyle elements of gentrification repair damage to the city's image from post–World War II disinvestment and the flight of many middle-class residents. Together with housing prices, gentrifiers' cultural tastes act as agents of change, reducing the number of working-class, middle-income, and "minority" neighborhoods.

Although gentrification is viewed as a market-based alternative to state-sponsored urban renewal, it cannot succeed without active state intervention. Local government condones years of disinvestment and capital flight from older areas, creating a "rent gap" between the profit to be gained at current housing prices and the likely profit from reinvestment in the future. Zoning laws prohibit the expansion of manufacturing, encourage historic preservation, and create special cultural districts. Vigilant policing makes gentrified neighborhoods safer. In some cases elected officials, business leaders, and old social elites plan the gentrification of a center city neighborhood to stall further decline of property values.

If it raises a neighborhood's profile, gentrification may lead to rezoning for new construction, and successive waves of gentrification replace middle-class home buyers with even richer residents. Over time the character of these neighborhoods changes, although not enough to eliminate social inequality in the city as a whole.

SEE ALSO *Ghetto; Poverty; Racism; Urban Renewal*

BIBLIOGRAPHY

Freeman, Lance. 2006. *There Goes the 'Hood: Views of Gentrification from the Ground Up.* Philadelphia: Temple University Press.

Smith, Neil, and Peter Williams, eds. 1986. *Gentrification of the City.* Boston: Allen and Unwin.

Zukin, Sharon. 1989. *Loft Living: Culture and Capital in Urban Change.* 2nd ed. New Brunswick, NJ: Rutgers University Press.

Sharon Zukin

GEOGRAPHY

Geography is the study of the field of knowledge relating to the temporal and spatial dimensions of the processes that shape the Earth's surface. Implicit within geography as a discipline is an emphasis on ways that diverse systems interact over time, producing particular landscapes in particular places. Geography is distinct from other disciplines (such as spatial economics and geology) in that it emphasizes the dual dimensions of time and space as causal, and because it highlights the importance of feedback between these different dimensions. A landscape can be understood as a place-specific configuration of interacting systems (at any scale), whose features influence the geographical processes operating in that particular case (this interaction produces feedback). The term *landscape* is often used to describe systems in which natural processes predominate, while *place* is used to describe systems dominated by human processes, though this distinction is not absolute. Indeed, in human geography the term *landscape* is used by many to describe anthropogenic systems, giving the effect that the phenomenon is distinct from the humans inhabiting it.

There are several ways of subdividing the discipline of geography. A common distinction is often made between physical geography as an environmental science and human geography as a social science. Human geography can further be divided according to the topic of study, creating subfields such as urban, political, economic, social, historical or cultural geography. More abstract dividing lines can also be drawn on the basis of methodologies, so that a distinction can be made between quantitative approaches, which have much in common with orthodox economics and cartography, and qualitative approaches, which can be similar to sociology, planning anthropology, and political science. Since the quantitative revolution of the 1960s, geographers have also distinguished themselves according to their epistemological perspectives on the nature of reality and the possibility of individuals adequately understanding and describing that reality.

THE EMERGENCE OF THE DISCIPLINE OF GEOGRAPHY

Geography as a discipline emerged in Germany in the eighteenth century in the context of attempts associated with Alexander von Humboldt at the University of Berlin to systematically harness the benefits that universities provided to society by creating applied disciplines linked to social needs. The ancient civilizations were interested in geographical topics such as cartography and cultural geography in the context of operating their military and trading empires. These proto-geographical ways of thinking were primarily concerned with describing the form of the earth, often in an attempt to better control a particular activity rather than produce pure knowledge of geographical systems. It is important to note that these applied uses of geography have created a continual stream of wealthy patrons willing to fund exploration to producing spatial knowledges, which have often served those patrons' own power interests.

According to Richard Hartshorne's *The Nature of Geography*, geography as a discipline emerged from a growing body of practical studies after 1500, but it was from 1750 onward that serious attempts were made to establish the two preconditions for a discipline, namely a distinctive subject area and a rigorous analytic methodology. The renowned philosopher Immanuel Kant (1724–1804) saw a close and necessary connection between understanding the nature of the world, and developing a more general (abstract) philosophical method. Hartshorne relates that Kant's physical geography course became a staple of his philosophy curriculum, being repeated forty-eight times from 1756 to 1796 at the University of Köningsberg (now Kaliningrad). Kant developed the idea of *Länderkunde*, of studying particular distinctive regions in detail to understand their emergence. This approach was extended throughout the early nineteenth century by other early geographers, such as Von Humboldt and Carl Ritter, who viewed the human and physical elements of places as inseparable elements of a unitary whole (*die Ganzheit*), of a region or landscape. Humboldt, in particular, tried to ensure that the focus of study was on classes of places (classified, perhaps by climate, geology, social form) rather than classes of objects (such as species).

Humboldt's efforts to create a science of geography were ultimately responsible for a postmortem split between *systematic* geographers, studying physical processes and landforms, and *regional* geographers, studying societies in particular climatic and geological regions. This cleavage deepened in the course of the nineteenth century, as geographers sought to specialize and establish themselves in the many new and growing universities. However, this tension was never fully resolved, and as geography began to institutionalize, the newly formed learned societies reflected both halves of the discipline: systematic (physical) geography and regional (human) geography.

GEOGRAPHY FROM 1900 ONWARD

The story of geography since 1900 is one of an established discipline advancing rapidly, driven by and responding to the huge social and physical changes accompanying the rise of industrial society, alongside increasing technological opportunities for new forms of research and knowledge production. During the twentieth century, a number of currents of thinking emerged that were driven by ideological considerations. Environmental determinism, for example, provided an intellectual underpinning for the imperialistic "Race for Africa" in the late nineteenth century by arguing that climatic considerations meant that

African civilizations were incapable of developing stable social institutions. Likewise, desire for *Lebensraum* (living space) of the National Socialists in Germany drew on geopolitical thinking that originated with the English geographer Halford Mackinder's concept of geopolitics to rationalize these ideological desires within the school of *Geopolitik*. The collapse of both underpinning ideologies carried a collateral cost for their parent disciplines as a whole. It was this tendency for supposedly neutral geographical analyses to favor particular powerful groups that was the stimulus behind the radical turn in human geography that emerged in the 1970s.

In parallel with these changes, two important geographical movements emerged to reshape the discipline in the period from 1900 to 1970. The first of these was the systematization of regional (human) geography, which attempted to move beyond ideographic descriptions of societal phenomenon in particular places to more analytic expressions of places in terms of underlying processes. However, it is important to stress that national geographies remained highly distinctive at this time, and these new regional geographies reflected these national distinctions. British regional geography, particularly in the works of Henry Daysh, H. C. Darby, and Hilda Ormsby reflected national traditions of empiricism and pragmatism while emphasizing the importance of historical development. French writers, led by Paul Vidal de la Blache, produced the *Annales* school, named after its journal, which developed notions of "environmental possibilism," in which social configurations (*genres de vie*) were influenced both by physical environment and social and political decisions. German writers, notably Walter Christaller and Alfred Weber, used mathematical modeling to understand the spatial allocation of human activity such as settlements and industry. This represented a more analytic attempt to understand human activity. Although these diverse national approaches differed in the extent to which they emphasized theory over practical observation, they clearly all represented an attempt to systematize the production of geographical knowledge.

This consensus emphasizing systematization enabled the second great geographical movement of the twentieth century, the quantitative revolution. Early systematic approaches, inspired by the natural sciences, suggested that everything in nature was knowable, given sufficient data and analytic capacity. The increasing "scientization" of society in general, and the rise of computer power after 1947 in particular, seemed to bring this dream of total geographical knowledge within reach. The basis for quantitative geography lay in creating mathematical spatial models to account for the distribution and evolution of particular phenomenon over space. The quantitative revolution became associated in the United States with the Regional Science movement, pioneered by Walter Isard, then a professor at University of Pennsylvania, and his supporters. By infusing geography with mathematical and statistical tools, Regional Science superficially avoided the charges of selectivity and ideological determination that afflicted more ideographic geographical approaches. In part, the popularity of these quantitative approaches derived from the apparent certainty of knowledge thereby produced, which gave policymakers a robust evidence base for making decisions about land use and economic planning.

However, quantitative approaches often suffered from failing to adequately capture the independent variables, the factors responsible for causing particular phenomena. Quantitative practitioners were making assumptions and using convenient proxy variables rather than capturing complex social and cultural phenomena. The increasing urban segregation and deprivation in the 1960s and 1970s in western Europe and America provided a direct challenge to quantitative geography's capacity to explain away the emergence of ghettos, dereliction, and, frequently, rioting. Faced with the inability to measure causal variables, a number of geographers instead began to form theories to try to understand how large-scale "social structures" created micro- and meso-scale problems.

Arguably the most celebrated of these geographers is David Harvey, whose empiricist manifesto *Explanation in Geography* (1969) was supplanted by a Marxian commitment to understanding spatial process in terms of class struggle, beginning with his 1973 treatise *Social Justice and the City*. Harvey exemplified a "radical geography" in which class theory allowed hidden power relationships to be exposed and unexpected causalities to be identified. This radical approach fitted neatly with, and has since become associated with, a more general postmodern or relativistic turn in the social sciences. Harvey's neo-Marxian writings reached what many regard as an apex of a theoretical research project with the publication of *The Limits to Capital* in 1982. This volume set out a sweeping vision for an ever-deepening form of capitalism that would eventually penetrate into every corner of the world, and it has proven to be an important foundation for radical critiques of globalization and neoliberalism.

Radical geography subsequently proceeded through a number of further "turns," which have critiqued their predecessors in an attempt to better understand what drives the development of human societies. The cultural turn emphasized the importance of noneconomic interaction and transactions; the institutional turn noted the importance of durable organizations and social norms; and the relational turn highlighted the fact that people are influenced by what is close to them, and that proximity is not just physical but can be organizational, cultural, or

virtual in nature. These turns were all led by movements comprising both established geographers who recanted or redacted their established positions and emerging geographers who became a new generation of intellectual leaders for geography. The cultural turn was signaled in 1989 by the parallel publications of David Harvey's *The Condition of Postmodernity* and Edward Soja's *Postmodern Geographies*. Both books asked fundamental questions about the economic focus of much Marxian geography, and they laid the foundations for more reflexive understandings of economic activity. These "turns" have been contested by other geographers, who have expressed concerns that the intellectual efforts involved in reflexivity have detached them from geographers' central task of understanding real places and spaces.

At the same time, quantitative approaches have continued to develop. Geographical information systems (GISs) are massive computer databases into which huge quantities of locational data is entered, allowing the performance of additional "fieldwork" capable of identifying regularities that are not immediately obvious. Although they are academic tools, much of the investment in them came from customers seeking to make sense of unknown and uncertain environments, notably the military and oil exploration companies. The continual investments these tools produce have generated a wide range of applications, and GISs are now commonplace across the spatial sciences beyond geography.

Quantitative geographers have also used novel mathematical techniques and increasing computing power to address "traditional" geographical problems of understanding how spatial distribution and irregularities in distribution cause geographical processes to behave in different ways in different places. These approaches are exemplified by the geographically weighted regression (GWR) technique. There has also been an increasing dialogue between physical and human geographers trying to deal with the complex environmental problems that have emerged with the increasing industrialization of society. This neatly emphasizes the ongoing indivisibility of the "natural" and the "anthropogenic" elements of geographical systems, as well as the mutual understanding necessary to understand the development of spatial systems.

SEE ALSO *Cities; Cultural Landscape; Determinism, Environmental; Kant, Immanuel; Metropolis; Peasantry; Planning; Regions; Regions, Metropolitan; Segregation, Residential; Spatial Theory; Suburbs; Topography; Urbanization*

BIBLIOGRAPHY

Hartshorne, Richard. 1939. *The Nature of Geography: A Critical Survey of Current Thought in the Light of the Past.* Lancaster, PA: Association of American Geographers.

Harvey, David. 1969. *Explanation in Geography*. London: Edward Arnold.

Harvey, David. 1973. *Social Justice and the City*. London: Edward Arnold.

Isard, Walter. 1956. *Location and Space Economy*. New York: John Wiley.

Scott, Alan. 2000. Economic Geography: The Great Half-Century. In *The Oxford Handbook of Economic Geography*, eds. Gordon Clark, Maryann Feldman, and Meric Gertler, 18–44. Oxford: Oxford University Press.

Paul Benneworth

GERIATRICS

SEE *Gerontology.*

GERM WARFARE

SEE *Bioterrorism.*

GERONTOLOGY

The scientific study of the biological, psychological, and sociological phenomena associated with age and aging, gerontology had its origins in the study of longevity from Francis Bacon (1561–1626) onward. While Jean-Martin Charcot (1825–1893) had explored the relationship between old age and illness, the term *gerontology* was introduced by Élie Metchnikoff (1845–1916), who developed theories of aging based on his work in medicine and biology. Social science perspectives on aging did not emerge until later, when the economic consequences of aging were recognized. Professional associations were created to support research on aging, such as the Gerontological Society of America (1945) and the International Association of Gerontology (1948). In the 1930s the Josiah Macey Jr. Foundation in New York, under the directorship of Ludwig Kast, ran a series of conferences on aging exploring the relationship between degenerative disease and aging. The Foundation encouraged E. V. Cowdry, professor of cytology at Washington University, to organize a book that would explore not only the biomedical aspects of aging but also the psychological, sociological, and environmental aspects. These activities resulted in the Club for Research on Aging, which promoted the study of aging as an aspect of public health. Major figures in the development of the social and psychological study of aging included, in the United States, Matilda White Riley (1911–2004), and in the United

Kingdom, Peter Laslett (1915–2001). Riley and her colleagues developed the "aging and society paradigm" in her *Aging and Society* (1968–1972), which examines the interaction between a cohort flow of population and social change, and explains age as an aspect of the social structure. Laslett, the author of *The World We Have Lost* (1965), challenged many conventional, but dubious assumptions in demography and gerontology, such as the idea that the nuclear family is a modern development. He was a founder of the influential Cambridge Group for the History of Population and Social Structure, which pioneered the methodology of using local records in the historical study of population.

Gerontology has become an increasingly important discipline as the governments of the developed world face up to the problem of aging populations. The causes of population aging are either a rising life expectancy or declining fertility, or both. Increasing longevity raises the average age of the population; a decline in fertility increases the average age of the population by changing the balance between the young and old. In the modern world, declining fertility—in precise terms the actual number of live births per thousand women of reproductive age—is the most significant cause of population aging. In terms of the world population, in the year 2000 approximately 30 percent were under the age of fourteen years, but this is expected to fall to around 20 percent by 2050. In the developed world, the median age of the population rose from 29 in 1950 to 37.3 in 2000, and it is predicted to rise to 45.5 by 2050. For the world as a whole, the figure was 23.9 in 1950, 26.8 in 2000, and is predicted to be 37.8 for 2050. One of the fastest-aging populations is modern Japan; in 1950 there were 9.3 people under the age of 20 for every person over 65 in Japan, but by 2002 this ratio was anticipated to be 0.59 people under 20 for every person over 65 years. Worldwide, there are important regional variations. If we define an aging population as one in which at least 10 percent are over 60, then most of sub-Saharan Africa will only see the development of aging populations after 2040, but North Africa will have them before 2030. Most of the Latin American and Caribbean countries will have aging populations after 2010. Many Asian countries, such as China, Singapore, and South Korea, already do.

The United States and Northern Europe face an acute problem of rapid aging. In the United States, the proportion of the population over sixty-five years of age is expected to increase from 12.4 percent in 2000 to 19.6 percent in 2030. In absolute terms, this means an increase from 35 million over sixty-five in 2000 to 71 million in 2030. In Europe the number of people over sixty-five years will increase from 15.5 percent in 2000 to 24.3 percent in 2030.

The aging of the world population is an aspect of an ongoing demographic transition—a switch from high fertility and high mortality rates to low fertility and delayed mortality. This transition also produces an epidemiological transition—a switch from infectious diseases in childhood and acute illness, to chronic disease and degenerative illness. The principal causes of death in the developed world are cardiovascular disease, cancer, respiratory disease, and injuries.

These demographic changes have major implications for health care, the labor force, welfare, insurance, and pensions. In the United States 80 percent of people over sixty-five years have at least one chronic disease and 50 percent have two. Diabetes now affects one in five Americans. The incidence of Alzheimer's disease in the United States doubles every five years after the age of sixty-five. The economic consequences of an aging population are various and significant. There will be major increases in health care, nursing care, and retirement home costs. As the ratio of working to retired persons increases, there will be a decline in taxation and an erosion of funds for public expenditure. There is already a significant pension crisis in the United States and the United Kingdom, where the combination of compulsory retirement and increasing life expectancy means that people do not have sufficient savings for old age. The problem is a major policy issue because labor force participation of people over sixty-five years has declined by more than 40 percent worldwide. In the United States, the growth rate of the working-age population is projected to decline from its current level of 1 percent per year to half a percent by 2030.

Life expectancy has increased significantly in the developed world. More people are surviving into old age, and once they achieve old age, they tend to live longer. Over the next half century, global life expectancy at age 60 will increase from 18.8 years in 2000–2005 to 22.2 years in 2045–2050, from 15.3 to 18.2 years at age 65, and from 7.2 to 8.8 years at age 80. In over thirty countries female life expectancy at birth already exceeds 80 years. Can life expectancy increase indefinitely?

Contemporary gerontology as a field of research is changing rapidly under the impact of advances in the biological sciences. In conventional gerontology, living a long life had meant in practical terms living a full life, according to some agreed upon set of cultural and social criteria, and achieving the average expectation of longevity according to gender and social class. More recently however, there has been considerable speculation as to whether medical science can reverse the aging process. Between the 1960s and 1980s, biologists such as Leonard Hayflick (1982) argued that normal cells had what was known as a *replicative senescence*, that is, normal tissues can only

divide a finite number of times before entering a stage of inevitable quiescence. Cells were observed in vitro in a process of natural senescence, but eventually experiments in vivo established an important and far-reaching distinction between normal and pathological cells in terms of their cellular division. It was paradoxical that pathological cells appeared to have no such necessary limitation on replication, and therefore a process of *immortalization* was the defining feature of a pathological cell line. Biologists concluded that finite division at the cellular level meant that the aging of whole organisms was an inevitable process. These scientific findings supported the view, shared by most religious traditions, that human life had a predetermined limit, and that it was only through pathological developments that some cells might outsurvive the otherwise inescapable senescence of cellular life. Aging was regarded as both natural and normal.

This traditional conception of aging was eventually overthrown by the discovery that human embryonic cells were capable of continuous division in laboratory conditions, where they showed no sign of any inevitable "replicative crisis" or natural limitation. Certain nonpathological cells (or stem cells) were capable of indefinite division, and these new developments in the conceptualization of cellular life have consequently challenged existing scientific assumptions about the distinctions between the normal and the pathological. Stem-cell research is beginning to redefine the human body in terms of renewable tissue, and suggests that the limits of biological growth are not immutable or inflexible. The human body has a surplus of stem cells capable of survival beyond the death of the organism. With these developments in micro-bio-gerontology, the capacity of regenerative medicine to expand the limits of life becomes a plausible prospect of medicine, creating new economic opportunities in the application of life sciences.

The controversies that surround modern gerontology are primarily to do with population aging, resource allocation, and equality. First, can prolongevity be increased almost indefinitely? Secondly, will significant increases in life expectancy severely increase the inequality in the distribution of resources worldwide? Finally, can intergenerational justice be maintained?

In contemporary debates about the legitimacy of the life-extension project, faith-oriented beliefs and moral justifications are prominent. It is clearly the aspiration of furthering biomedical science that is the most common supporting argument in the literature. In general, scientific curiosity and potential health-enhancing discoveries are cited as justifications for life-extension research. The ethical principle of beneficence is also included, because the research, it is argued, can help to decelerate the aging process and diminish the onset of chronic illness. Such a view emerges from a conception of aging as a condition to be cured (that is, as a disease), and it assumes that health and life extension will necessarily evolve together. In these debates on life extension, Gregory Stock, director of the program on Medicine, Technology, and Society at University of California, Los Angeles (UCLA) School of Public Health, argues that we should not accept the natural life span as a fixed state of affairs, because prolonged health is a general good. Because the technological advancements in anti-aging intend to provide more youthfulness to aging people, he contends that life extension is valuable both to individuals and for societies. Similar sentiments are reflected in the *posthumanist* perspective, which strongly advocates the overcoming of biological limitations through technological progress. One public figure promoting life extension in England is the editor in chief of *Rejuvenation Research*, Aubrey de Grey at the University of Cambridge, who has vigorously supported the life-extension project.

The arguments against life extension are that, given a scarcity of resources, it will greatly contribute to the depletion of natural resources and significantly increase environmental degradation. It will increase inequality between the Southern Hemisphere and the affluent Northern Hemisphere. It will have an adverse effect on intergenerational justice by further concentrating wealth in the hands of the elderly rich. Finally, it raises important issues about the psychological and spiritual distress that the elderly but disabled cohort of survivors would confront. The prospect of "living forever" would only be tolerable if medical science could guarantee a reasonable level of mobility and well-being (such as freedom from chronic disease). There would also be the prospect of intergenerational conflict, for example in the form of ageism.

The term *ageism* was first employed by Robert N. Butler, then director of the American Institute of Aging, in 1968. Referring to negative stereotypes of elderly individuals that classify them as senile, dependent, or conservative in their attitudes, ageism has become an important political issue. Against the background of the rapid aging of populations, *new ageism* refers to intergenerational conflicts of interests where the elderly are criticized for being parasitic on society, that is for being "takers" rather than "givers." Some aspects of ageism can be overcome by making more accurate information about aging available, especially to young people. Another change would be to remove a fixed or compulsory retirement age, thereby allowing fit and able elderly to continue in employment. These strategies will come up against the fact that, given high unemployment, housing shortages, and other scarcities, there will be an inevitable conflict of interests between age groups. There are few convincing social policies to resolve the pension crisis, the impact on health care, and the erosion of the tax base that are outcomes of population aging.

This pessimistic conclusion can be challenged by arguing that technological improvements will continue to increase the productivity of those who remain at work, and that flexible retirement regulations will allow people to remain employed on a voluntary basis past sixty-five. We cannot assume that the values and attitudes of old people in the past will be characteristic of future generations. The postwar Baby Boomers who are now close to retirement are socially and culturally very different from their parents and grandparents. The social character of aging and the cultures of the elderly will continue to change and evolve over time, thereby making pessimistic extrapolations from past generations unreliable, and often prejudicial.

SEE ALSO *Baby Boomers; Demographic Transition; Demography; Maturation; Welfare State*

BIBLIOGRAPHY

Cowdry, E. V., ed. 1939. *Problems of Ageing: Biological and Medical Aspects.* Baltimore, MD: Williams and Wilkins.

De Grey, Aubrey. 2003. The Foreseeability of Real Anti-Aging Medicine: Focusing the Debate. *Experimental Gerontology* 38 (9): 927–934.

De Grey, Aubrey. 2004. Welcome to Rejuvenation Research. *Rejuvenation Research* 7 (1): 1–2.

Hayflick, Leonard. 1982. Biological Aspects of Aging. In *Biological and Social Aspects of Mortality and the Length of Life*, ed. Samuel H. Preston, 223–258. Liege, Belgium: Ordina.

Laslett, Peter. 2005. *The World We Have Lost.* 4th rev. ed. London: Routledge. (Orig. pub. in 1965.)

Riley, Matilda White, Marilyn E. Johnson, and Anne Foner, eds. 1968–1972. *Aging and Society: A Sociology of Age Stratification.* 3 vols. New York: Russell Sage Foundation.

Shostak, Stanley. 2002. *Becoming Immortal: Combining Cloning and Stem-Cell Therapy.* Albany: State University of New York Press.

Bryan S. Turner

GERRYMANDERING

The term *gerrymander* typically refers to the creation of electoral districts that have bizarre shapes in order to condition the outcome of an election. In "Considering the Gerrymander" (1977), Leroy C. Hardy recounts that the term *gerrymander* was coined after the Jeffersonian-controlled legislature of Massachusetts drew contorted senatorial districts in order to ensure the defeat of Federalist candidates in 1812. One particular district located north of Boston was so contorted that it was said to look like the mythical salamander. Since this all took place during Elbridge Gerry's (1744–1814) term as governor, the district was christened a "Gerrymander," and the term has stuck ever since.

Bizarre district shape is but one manifestation of the real evil of gerrymandering: the conscious attempt by someone to organize voters in a manner will result in the over- or underrepresentation of a particular group or political party. This can be accomplished using very unremarkable district boundaries. In addition, an electoral system can be gerrymandered by other means, such as unfairly altering the rules by which votes are counted and translated into electoral seats or changing the laws governing the qualification of candidates and political parties to appear on ballots.

Gerrymandering takes on benign as well as evil forms. Perhaps the most egregious example of modern gerrymandering in the United States took place in Alabama in 1958. The black population of the city of Tuskegee was about to become a majority of the electorate. White residents petitioned the state legislature to redraw the boundaries of the city to remove the black voters. The state legislature obliged and transformed the city's border from a simple square to what the Supreme Court of the United States described in *Gomillion v. Lightfoot* (1960) as an "uncouth" twenty-three-sided figure. The Supreme Court declared that this transformation of Tuskegee amounted to a denial of the black residents' right to vote.

In 1965 the U.S. Congress passed the Voting Rights Act. When it was amended in 1982, it was read by the Justice Department and the Supreme Court (in *Thornburg v. Gingles*, 1983) to require states to create legislative and congressional districts with voting majorities comprised of minority voters ("majority-minority districts") wherever possible.

With this decision the Supreme Court essentially endorsed a congressional mandate to gerrymander legislative and congressional districts to help minority voters. While the Voting Rights Act was thus regarded as a benevolent attempt to rectify a heinous history of disenfranchisement of minority voters, it nonetheless endorsed a policy of officially mandated manipulation of the electoral system.

Beginning in 1993 with the decision in *Shaw v. Reno*, the Supreme Court retreated from its holding in *Gingles*. In so doing, it placed restrictions on the extent to which the federal government could require states to gerrymander districts on behalf of minority voters. While congressionally mandated gerrymandering was clearly benign in its intent, it was nonetheless a clear perversion of the electoral system.

Gerrymandering is unavoidable because it is impossible to draw electoral district lines or change electoral laws without having a clearly favorable or unfavorable impact on someone. Gerrymandering occurs throughout the world and in many different circumstances. Drawing on examples from the United Kingdom and Ireland, Richard Katz (1998) notes that in countries that use other electoral systems (such as proportional representation systems with multimember electoral districts), the size of districts can be manipulated so that particular parties end up wasting their votes and electing fewer candidates than they would in a district of a different size.

In addition, an electoral system can be gerrymandered by making it harder for minor parties or independent candidates to challenge the established political powers. In Canada, for example, the Supreme Court has heard challenges to laws restricting the access of small political parties to government funds (*Figueroa v. Canada*, 2003), restricting campaign spending (*Harper v. Canada*, 2004), and allowing for great population discrepancies among voting districts (*Reference re Provincial Electoral Boundaries [Sask.]*, 1991). The first two cases embodied claims that laws unfairly favored incumbent political powers by making it harder for minor political actors to garner enough influence to challenge the government. This not only discriminated against minor parties, it also rendered political competition less robust and the electoral system correspondingly unfair. In the Saskatchewan case, challengers claimed that population disparities among electoral districts unfairly favored rural interests at the expense of urban voters.

In conclusion, the term *gerrymander* has transformed since the mid-twentieth century from a reference to bizarrely shaped electoral districts to a broader term addressing myriad ways in which an electoral system can be rendered less competitive in hopes of achieving partisan gain. As a result, around the world, the trend is to place the authority to make changes to the electoral system in the hands of nonpartisan commissions or agencies.

SEE ALSO *Campaigning; Elections*

BIBLIOGRAPHY

Figueroa v. Canada, [2003] 1 S.C.R. 912.

Gomillion v. Lightfoot, 364 U.S. 339 (1960).

Hardy, Leroy C. 1977. Considering the Gerrymander. *Pepperdine Law Review* 4: 243–283.

Harper v. Canada, [2004] 1 S.C.R. 827.

Katz, Richard S. 1998. Malapportionment and Gerrymandering in Other Countries and Alternative Electoral Systems. In *Voting Rights and Redistricting in the United States*, ed. Mark E. Rush, 245–260. Westport, CT: Greenwood.

Reference re Provincial Electoral Boundaries (Sask.), [1991] 2 S.C.R. 158.

Shaw v. Reno, 509 U.S. 630 (1993).

Thornburg v. Gingles, 478 U.S. 30 (1986).

Mark Rush

GESTALT PSYCHOLOGY

Gestalt theory, a major school of psychology during the first half of the twentieth century, was an influential counterpoint to the other mostly atomistic psychological systems of the time: structuralism, functionalism, and behaviorism. While its controversies with these other systems during the "age of schools" in psychology have receded into history, its major tenets once again became salient toward the end of the twentieth century in such fields as social psychology, cognition, personality psychology, and visual neuroscience.

Gestalt psychology proposed a radical revision of the atomistic view that had prevailed for centuries in Western science and social science. Natural wholes, according to the Gestalt view, are not simply the sum total of their constituent parts. Rather, characteristics of the whole determine the nature of its parts, prescribing the place, role, and function of each part in the unified whole. The Gestalt principle of *Prägnanz*, furthermore, asserts that the organization of any whole will be as "good" (i.e., balanced, simple, integrated) as the prevailing conditions allow. This insistence on holistic processes applies equally to all integrated wholes, from physical systems such as electrical fields, magnetic fields, and soap films to psychological systems such as cognitive processes, the organization of perception, personality, and social phenomena.

The Gestalt movement is generally viewed (Ash 1995; King and Wertheimer 2005) as having been launched by a series of experiments by Max Wertheimer (1880–1943) on apparent movement published in 1912, although clear indications of a Gestalt perspective were already evident in two earlier publications of Wertheimer on musical structures (1910) and on aboriginal thinking about numerical issues (1912). Two of Wertheimer's colleagues who served as observers in these experiments, Wolfgang Köhler (1887–1967) and Kurt Koffka (1886–1941), became his collaborators during the next decades in promulgating the new Gestalt approach (Köhler 1929; Koffka 1935). A typical experiment in Wertheimer's series involved, for example, exposure of a short vertical line in the visual field, followed after a brief interval by exposure of a second similar vertical line a short distance away from where the first one had been exposed. If the time and distance relations are appropriate, observers see a single line moving from one location to the other. The experience is indistinguishable from watching an actual short vertical line move from one location to the other; in both cases, the perception of motion is immediate and compelling. The prevailing alternate theoretical orientations, maintaining that percepts always correspond with their correlated physical stimuli, could not explain the perceived motion when the actual stimuli are two stationary lines successively exposed. The whole, the experience of motion as a Gestalt, cannot be derived from a combination of the "component sensations" of the two stationary stimuli.

The Gestalt school became prominent in European and American psychology. Its principles of perceptual organization have been summarized in almost every introductory psychology textbook; Wertheimer's book *Productive Thinking* (1945) challenged the computer models of the late twentieth century to try to account for the ubiquitous cognitive processes of insight and understanding.

SEE ALSO *Gestalt Therapy*

BIBLIOGRAPHY

Ash, Mitchell G. 1995. *Gestalt Psychology in German Culture, 1890–1967: Holism and the Quest for Objectivity*. Cambridge, U.K.: Cambridge University Press.

King, D. Brett, and Michael Wertheimer. 2005. *Max Wertheimer and Gestalt Theory*. New Brunswick, NJ: Transaction.

Koffka, Kurt. 1935. *Principles of Gestalt Psychology*. New York: Harcourt, Brace.

Köhler, Wolfgang. 1929. *Gestalt Psychology*. New York: Liveright.

Wertheimer, Max. 1910. Musik der Wedda [Music of the Veddas]. *Sammelbände der internationalen Musikgesellschaft* 11: 300–309.

Wertheimer, Max. 1912. Experimentelle Studien über das Sehen von Bewegung [Experimental studies of the seeing of motion]. *Zeitschrift für Psychologie* 61: 161–265.

Wertheimer, Max. 1912. Über das Denken der Naturvölker, I. Zahlen und Zahlgebilde [On the thinking of aboriginal people, I: Numbers and number structures]. *Zeitschrift für Psychologie* 60: 321–378.

Wertheimer, Max. 1945, 1959, 1971, 1982. *Productive Thinking*. New York: Harper; University of Chicago Press.

Michael Wertheimer

GESTALT THERAPY

Gestalt therapy is a therapeutic approach in psychology that helped foster the humanistic theories of the 1950s and 1960s and that was, in turn, influenced by them. In Gestalt philosophy, the patient is seen as having better insight into himself or herself than the therapist does. Thus, the therapist guides the person on a self-directed path to awareness and refrains from interpreting the patient's behaviors. Awareness comprises recognition of one's responsibility for choices, self-knowledge, and ability to solve problems.

Its originators, Frederick S. (Fritz) Perls (1893–1970) and Laura Perls (born Lore Posner, 1905–1990), were born in Germany and studied psychology there. They fled Germany during the Nazi regime, moving to South Africa and then to New York City. They were both initially influenced by Sigmund Freud's psychoanalytic approaches and by Wilhelm Reich's Orgonomic psychotherapy. Their later ideas on Gestalt therapy broke with the psychoanalytic tradition, moving toward existentialism and, ultimately, humanism.

In New York City the Perls founded the Gestalt Therapy Institute in 1952. Their novel technique in therapy was to face the patient, in contrast to the typical Freudian technique of sitting behind a reclining person. The face-to-face positioning permitted the therapist to direct the patient's attention to movements, gestures, and postures so the patient could strive to gain a fuller awareness of his or her immediate behaviors and environment. Another well-known approach introduced in Gestalt therapy is the so-called "empty chair technique," in which a person sits across from and talks to an empty chair, envisioning a significant person (or object) associated with psychological tensions.

By using these techniques, the Perls believed, the patient would be able to gain insight into how thoughts and behaviors are used to deflect attention from important psychological issues and would learn to recognize the presence of issues from the past that affect current behavior. The aim was for the patient to experience feelings, not to gain insight into the reasons for them, as psychoanalysts favored.

In the evolution of their therapy, Laura and Fritz Perls differed in some of their approaches. Laura emphasized more direct, physical contact and movement than Fritz did, and the contact favored by Fritz Perls was more symbolic than physical.

Gestalt therapy took its name from the school of academic psychology called Gestalt psychology. Perls asserted that Gestalt psychology had influenced the development of his ideas, but the Gestaltists claimed that there was no connection between the two. Later scholars suggested a common substrate linking the academic Gestalt psychology of Max Wertheimer (1880–1943), Wolfgang Köhler (1887–1967), and Kurt Koffka (1886–1941) and the Gestalt therapy of the Perls and their collaborators Ralph Hefferline (1910–1974) and Paul Goodman (1911–1972). This commonality involved appreciation of the whole rather than a reductionistic approach to understanding psychological phenomena and behavior.

Gestalt therapy took form in the 1950s and 1960s, when humanism first flourished. The optimistic theory promulgated by the Perls was quite compatible with the ideas of other humanistically oriented psychologists such as Carl Rogers (1902–1987). Its influence has waned since the 1980s, although current therapies have been influenced by the humanistic and optimistic outlook of the theory and by some of the interactive techniques developed by the Perls and their followers.

BIBLIOGRAPHY

Levitsky, Abraham, and Frederick S. Perls. 1982. The Rules and Games of Gestalt Therapy. In *The Essential Psychotherapies: Theory and Practice by the Masters*, eds. Daniel Goleman and Kathleen Riordan Speeth, 143–154. New York: New American Library.

Perls, Frederick S., Ralph F. Hefferline, and Paul Goodman. 1951. *Gestalt Therapy: Excitement and Growth in the Human Personality*. New York: Dell.

Reisman, John M. 1991. *A History of Clinical Psychology*. 2nd ed. New York: Hemisphere Publishing.

Bernard C. Beins

GHETTO

Social scientists have long studied the effects of economic, political, and social inequality on lives, attitudes, and behavior. Central issues in this research include how and why societies tend to treat certain groups negatively, how such groups respond to such conditions, and whether and how society should address the historic and contemporary social problems that result. The history of ghettos provides an exemplar of the effects and implications of differential treatment of minority groups in society.

The term *ghetto* has been historically used to describe legally sanctioned segregated areas occupied by ethnic minorities. Although some writers contend that the first ghettos were created to segregate Jews during the Roman Empire between the first and fourth century CE, the term is most commonly used to describe segregated Jewish sections in Italy, Germany, and Portugal in the 1200s. The translation of the term *ghetto* originally referred to the Venice Ghetto in the 1300s and areas of town that were originally iron foundries or *gettos* before being converted to secluded Jewish sections. The term is also translated "gated" to characterize residentially isolated neighborhoods that existed in Venice and parts of northern Italy until as late as the 1600s. Other derivatives of the term refer to a small neighborhood (Italian, *borghetto*) or a "bill of divorce" (Hebrew, *get*). As suggested by these translations, it was illegal for non-Jews to live in ghettos and Jews were prohibited from leaving. To impose these sanctions, the gates of this section of the town were locked at night.

Roman ghettos were created in the mid-1500s via a decree by Pope Paul IV (1476–1559) and lasted until the Papal States were overthrown by Italy in 1870. Roman ghettos were used to separate Jews from Christians, but also enabled the Jewish community to maintain its religious and cultural practices and avoid assimilation. Other Jewish ghettos were located in Prague, Frankfurt, and Mainz. Although legal restrictions were no longer imposed in Europe during the 1800s, many ghettos continued to exist based on cultural or religious dictates. Most European ghettos were destroyed in the nineteenth century following the French Revolution. However, the rise of Adolf Hitler (1889–1945) in Nazi Germany in the twentieth century saw the return of Jewish ghettos in eastern European cities. Other international ghettos include the predominately black area of Soweto in Johannesburg, South Africa; KwaMashu in Durban, South Africa; and ghettos in the United States in South Central Los Angeles, sections of Chicago, and rust-belt cities such as Flint, Michigan.

GHETTOS IN THE UNITED STATES

Ghettos in the United States are generally defined as poor inner-city areas where a disproportionate percentage of ethnic minorities reside. Although African Americans are generally associated with ghettos, Hispanics and whites also live in them. Ghetto neighborhoods are also defined as census tracts where 40 percent or more of residents, regardless of their race or ethnicity, are poor. The latter definition is widely used for comparative purposes in quantitative urban sociological research. Although ghetto residents tend to be ethnic minorities, it is important to note that neighborhoods where a large number of ethnic minorities reside are not necessarily ghettos. For example, prior to deindustrialization, many African Americans were segregated in northern communities such as Chicago's Bronzeville. Although the area was predominately African American, it was also the place of residence for relatively affluent African American families and businesses. Furthermore, economically stable ethnic enclaves such as Chinatowns and Germantowns exist in many cities across the United States.

The distinguishing factor that generally constitutes a ghetto is the prevalence of poverty. Ghettos are also often distinguished from other racially or ethnically homogeneous communities (for example, a predominately white or black suburban area) because of the inability of many residents to relocate from ghettos—even if they desire to do so. Poverty among many U.S. ghetto residents makes it difficult to out-migrate. The involuntary nature of ghetto areas often reflects constrained residential choices

less evident in non-ghetto locales. Thus, as compared to historic ghettos that were formed due to direct or indirect racial or ethnic coercion and isolation, contemporary U.S. ghettos generally reflect class-based formation and the resulting isolation.

U.S. ghettos developed as a result of dramatic postindustrial economic, political, and social changes. Several urban migrations during the early and mid-twentieth century resulted in the exodus of many African Americans to such northern states as Illinois, New York, Michigan, and Pennsylvania in search of employment and to escape segregation and discrimination in the rural South. During the same period, persons of Hispanic descent migrated from Puerto Rico, Mexico, and Central and South America to New York, Miami, and Chicago for similar reasons. Cities provided industrious, less-educated persons with manufacturing jobs to earn a family wage.

After World War II (1939–1945), globalization and deindustrialization resulted in significant international and national economic restructuring. The United States responded to increased international economic competition by spurring technological advances and relocating industrial enterprises abroad and to the suburbs to increase profits. Increased efficiency and fewer manufacturing positions unduly affected residents in northern cities—especially ethnic minorities. From about 1967 to 1987, cities such as New York, Chicago, and Detroit lost more than 50 percent of their manufacturing jobs. By the late 1900s, many persons who had been gainfully employed in northern industrial cites became unemployed or underemployed or were forced to work in service occupations for substantially lower wages and reduced benefits.

The dramatic decline in manufacturing jobs affected a disproportionate percentage of African Americans and Hispanics. The out-migration of manufacturing firms coupled with an exodus of middle-class families and other businesses from cities to suburbs and abroad left many inner cities economically devastated. Economic restructuring coupled with the effects of poorly underserviced infrastructures, inadequate housing to accommodate a growing urban populace, group conflict and competition over limited jobs and space, the inability for many residents to compete for new technology-based jobs, and tensions between the public and private sectors led to the formation and growth of U.S. ghettos. Furthermore, housing discrimination in the form of redlining by lending institutions, discriminatory practices by realtors, and the development of large housing projects resulted in densely populated urban locales of primarily poor ethnic minorities. Economic challenges were exacerbated by the effects of historic and contemporary classism, segregation, and racism. The cumulative effects of these systemic forces contributed to the existence and prevalence of concentrated urban poverty in many U.S. ghettos.

CONDITIONS IN GHETTOS

Ghettos were historically developed to physically isolate a group with clearly identifiable physical features and cultural markers. Contemporary U.S. ghettos have had similar effects on many African American and Hispanic residents. Whether the result of legal sanctions or due to societal norms and values, physical isolation in ghettos usually results in social, political, and economic isolation. Such separation also directly or indirectly conveys superior status and privilege on majority group members and, by default, inferior status and privilege on the segregated group.

Although the Venice Ghetto was actually a relatively wealthy section of town where moneylenders and merchants resided, overall, conditions in ghettos were and continue to be negative. Jews could maintain their cultural and religious practices, but a segregated existence meant political and social isolation from the larger society. Because Jews could not purchase land outside the ghetto, population increases resulted in overcrowded conditions and infrastructure problems characterized by narrow streets and tall houses. Jews were allowed to organize and maintain their own political system within the ghetto. However, they often needed official passes to travel outside the ghetto walls.

The Warsaw Ghetto of Nazi Germany housed almost 400,000 Jews and was the largest and possibly most notorious ghetto. These ghettos were walled off, and Jews were shot if they attempted to escape. Other horrific conditions included extreme overcrowding, limited food supplies rationed by the Nazis, poor sanitation, starvation, and disease. Jews who survived these circumstances were forced to contend with the ever-present threat of death or deportation to concentration camps. In 1942 systematic efforts were implemented to deport Jews from ghettos around Europe to eastern ghettos or to concentration camps such as Treblinka in Poland. Historians suggest that various direct and indirect ghetto uprisings broke out, but the majority of residents in the ghettos of Nazi Germany were killed.

Contemporary ghettos are generally characterized by neighborhood and household poverty, social isolation, segregation, discrimination, overcrowding, increased crime, neighborhood disinvestment, and political disempowerment. Ghetto residents are more likely to live in substandard housing, frequent understaffed hospitals and healthcare providers, and have limited access to gainful employment. Businesses such as grocery stores, banks, retailers, and other institutions needed to complete the daily round are also limited and often overpriced or underserviced as compared to their suburban counter-

parts. Children who reside in ghetto areas tend to attend ill-equipped schools and must often learn at an early age to negotiate potentially crime-ridden neighborhoods. Research also suggests that the life chances of many ghetto residents are constrained largely because their place of residence isolates them from important resources needed to locate gainful employment, establish informational networks, and interact consistently in the larger society. Political disenfranchisement in ghettos is usually a result of isolation by predominately white state-run governments from predominately ethnic minority residents in ghetto spaces. Although studies show that most ghetto residents subscribe to mainstream values and goals, limited opportunities and resources often constrain their chances to realize them.

Urban renewal efforts are underway in many inner-city ghettos—with varied results. In some instances, renewal has resulted in refurbished neighborhoods, increased tax bases, and strengthened infrastructures. Supporters of urban renewal efforts point to the in-migration of young professionals as an important factor in revitalizing ghettos. However, detractors suggest that gentrification benefits persons who in-migrate and are able to use their greater discretionary income to take advantage of depressed housing markets at the expense of existing, poor ethnic minorities who are often forced out of their homes because they cannot afford to live in the newly renovated, higher-taxed neighborhoods.

Research is inconclusive regarding exactly how to characterize experiences in contemporary ghettos. The prevailing economic, political, and social disenfranchisement does not suggest a positive portrait of life. However, studies attest to the adaptive, resilient nature of many residents that belie the harsh reality of their experiences. A comprehensive discourse on the effects and implications of ghetto life and needed interventions should consider the challenges associated with ghetto living, the strengths of persons who live in ghettos, and the role the larger society should play to improve ghetto conditions.

SEE ALSO *Cities; Neighborhoods; Shtetl*

BIBLIOGRAPHY

Barnes, Sandra L. 2002. Achievement or Ascription Ideology? An Analysis of Attitudes about Future Success for Residents in Poor Urban Neighborhoods. *Sociological Focus* 35 (2): 207–225.

Barnes, Sandra L. 2005. *The Cost of Being Poor: A Comparative Study of Life in Poor Urban Neighborhoods in Gary, Indiana.* Albany: State University of New York Press.

Billingsley, Andrew. 1992. *Climbing Jacob's Ladder: The Enduring Legacy of African-American Families.* New York: Touchstone.

Chadwick, Owen. 1998. *A History of the Popes, 1830–1914.* New York: Oxford University Press.

Einwohner, Rachel. 2003. Opportunity, Honor, and Action in the Warsaw Ghetto Uprising of 1943. *American Journal of Sociology* 3: 650–675.

Massey, Douglas S., and Nancy A. Denton. 1993. *American Apartheid: Segregation and the Making of the Underclass.* Cambridge, MA: Harvard University Press.

Wilson, William Julius. 1996. *When Work Disappears: The World of the New Urban Poor.* New York: Knopf.

Sandra L. Barnes

GIBSON, WILLIAM

SEE *Matrix, The.*

GIDDENS, ANTHONY
1938–

Anthony Giddens was educated as a sociologist at Hull University and the London School of Economics (LSE). He held a lectureship at Leicester University before being appointed lecturer and subsequently professor of sociology in the University of Cambridge. In 1996 he left Cambridge to become director of the LSE.

Giddens was certain at the end of the 1970s that nineteenth-century thought, on certain themes of which sociology had tended to remain focused, was an inadequate basis on which to proceed. In particular, Talcott Parsons's (1902–1979) theory of the mid-twentieth century, supposedly resolving the main questions associated with these themes, had degenerated into an objectivistic, teleological framework in which the original "action" element had been lost, whilst his "interpretivist" opponents, while dealing with action and interaction, were unable to conceptualize "structure" in a satisfactory way. For Giddens, readdressing these issues in *The Constitution of Society* (1984), agency and structure are not merely mutually implicated in the sense that "structure" involves agents acting and acting is inconceivable apart from "conditions" and unintended consequences, they are the same. They merge in "practice." Structure is virtual. It exists only in doing, moment by moment. This virtual "rules and resources" is "instantiated" and simultaneously reproduced in the action it "recursively" permits, as actors draw upon it to act, their concrete actions making up "social systems." For critics of this, such as Margaret Archer (1990) and Nicos Mouzelis, there are certain important advantages to be gained from retaining the *dualism* of structure and agency, and not conflating them, and this need not mean returning to a sterile opposition between objectivism on the one hand and subjectivism on the other: Agency and structure should be seen as interrelated, but also as different kinds of things.

This is only the most fundamental of the arguments critical of Giddens's work in all its aspects.

"Reflexivity" is at the core of Giddens's structuration theory, appearing in the shape of the self-monitoring actor, taken over and adapted from radical subjectivism. Agents' knowledge of the mechanism of system reproduction, used by them to control this reproduction, influences substantially the causal feedback loops effecting system reproduction. In *The Consequences of Modernity* (1990) this reflexivity moves into a more prominent position in Giddens's thinking than it had previously held; he sees it as being at the heart of what he began to call "late" or "radicalized" modernity. For it was reflexivity, both of the actor and of the social institution, that was becoming stepped up as tradition retreated more than in the "modern" past in the face of social relations that were increasingly "stretched" globally and lifted out of communal and face-to-face settings. ("Distanciation" or "stretching" of social relations in both time and space to form ever more extensive social systems was central to structuration theory.) In this phase of his development Giddens returned to the sociological analysis of modernity, the point from which he professed to have started out, resuming the interpretation of modern society that had been begun with the critique of historical materialism in *A Contemporary Critique of Historical Materialism*, vol. 1 (1981), and continued with his analysis of the nation-state in *The Nation-State and Violence* (1985). The latest phase has seen Giddens turning to politics.

Giddens became convinced in the 1990s that the ideological positions of the "first" modernity had become frozen and increasingly out of touch with the current detraditionalized, increasingly globalized social reality of the emerging "late" or "reflexive" modernity. The Left had become conservative in their clinging to the welfare state (the product of a now passed, post-war class compromise or social settlement) whereas neoliberal celebrants of the market were caught in the growing contradiction of advocating the advance of forces that undermined moral coherence, which they as conservatives also espoused. Giddens urged in *Beyond Left and Right* (1994) a "Third Way" between Left and Right. This was, for some, an imprecise set of recommendations attached to a vague idea. But Giddens did specify the need for negotiation in personal life and for a politics outside of the old structures: a "life politics" and a "generative politics," as he called them, by means of which people could seize hold of their own lives, taking advantage of the opportunities created by globalization and the retreat of the nation-state, recasting themselves in a social environment located always at some point between "trust" (security) and "risk" (perceived danger). Basic trust is for Giddens an essential part of personality development, but now more than ever it must be "worked for" in intimate relationships; it can no longer be as taken for granted as it once was, and, moreover, extensive locality-transcending social relations simultaneously require and place in jeopardy, through its very integralness, trust—the opposite of which is risk. Giddens's analysis of reflexive modernization was the key to the Third Way in ways spelled out in detail in *The Third Way* (1998)—for example, reflexivity in personal relations could form the basis for democratic renewal from the grassroots "upwards," and reaching beyond the nation-state, and was central to the "life politics" that Giddens saw taking shape around him in a radicalized modernity, where the global and the local interpenetrate, and with new social movements displacing the old institutionalized parties and historic ideologies of an earlier industrial period.

Giddens's action recommendations are locatable in his four institutional orders of modernity (industrialism, capitalism, administration-surveillance, and the military), but their principles could also be related, at least schematically, to the "rules" (signification and legitimation) and allocative and authoritative "resources" (domination) of his 1984 structuration schema. His influence on sociologists worldwide has been enormous, as is attested by the number of citations of his numerous works both scholarly and popular, the latter affecting parties and governments of a Third Way complexion. It is a measure of their author's distinction that the issues they raise continue to be debated around the world.

BIBLIOGRAPHY

Archer, Margaret S. 1990. Human Agency and Social Structure: A Critique of Giddens. In *Anthony Giddens: Consensus and Controversy*, eds. Jon Clarke, Celia Modgil, and Sohan Modgil, 73–85. Basingstoke, U.K.: Falmer Press.

Giddens, Anthony. 1984. *The Constitution of Society: Outline of the Theory of Structuration*. Cambridge, U.K.: Polity Press.

Giddens, Anthony. 1990. *The Consequences of Modernity*. Cambridge, U.K.: Polity Press.

Giddens, Anthony. 1994. *Beyond Left and Right: The Future of Radical Politics*. Cambridge, U.K.: Polity Press.

Ian Varcoe

GIFT TAX

SEE *In Vivo Transfers.*

GIFTED AND TALENTED

The history of gifted education is filled with controversy and concerns regarding how best to define and assess giftedness, and also how best to serve those who are deemed to be in need of gifted education programs and services. Gifted education programs in public schools have also received national attention as a result of the low percentage of culturally and linguistically diverse students identified as gifted and served in these programs.

IDENTIFYING GIFTED STUDENTS

Federal-level initiatives provide guidance for local and state gifted program policies and practice. The 1993 National Excellence Report provided a foundation upon which advocates of gifted education can be proactive in defining giftedness and identifying and serving gifted students. According to the report:

> Children and youth with outstanding talent perform or show the potential for performing at remarkably high levels of accomplishment when compared with others of their age, experience, or environment. These children and youth exhibit high performance capability in intellectual, creative, and/or artistic areas, possess an unusual leadership capacity, or excel in specific academic fields. They require services or activities not ordinarily provided by the schools. Outstanding talents are present in children and youth from all cultural groups, across all economic strata, and in all areas of human endeavor. (USDE 1993, p. 27)

This definition may be the most culturally sensitive federal definition to date, with its focus on talent, potential, and comparisons of students of the same age who come from similar backgrounds and experiences. It also boldly states that giftedness exists in all groups, and that no group should have a monopoly on being identified and served.

In addition to developing this new definition of *gifted*, the Jacob K. Javits Gifted and Talented Students Education Program, enacted in 1988, supports demonstration grants, a national research center, and national leadership activities designed to focus attention on the needs of students with demonstrated or potential talent. It is now clear that conventional views of giftedness and traditional ways of identifying giftedness (e.g., using single IQ scores or standardized achievement tests) often create barriers for culturally and linguistically diverse and low-income students to gain access to gifted programs. Thus, the Javits Program is also important because priority funding is given to efforts to serve gifted and talented students who are economically disadvantaged, speak limited English, or have disabilities.

GIFTED PROGRAMS AND RACISM

Gifted education has encountered much criticism due to a legacy of racial inequality in the United States that has

Trends in the representation of minority students in gifted education programs from 1978 to 1992

Student population	1978	1980	1982	1984	1992
Hispanic American	6.8	9.0	8.6	13.2	13.7
	5.15	5.4	4.0	7.2	7.9
	(u = 25%)	(u = 40%)	(u = 53%)	(u = 45%)	(u = 42%)
American Indian	.8	.7	.5	.8	1.0
	.3	.3	.3	.3	.5
	(u = 62%)	(u = 57%)	(u = 40%)	(u = 62%)	(u = 50%)
Asian American	1.4	2.2	2.6	3.7	4.0
	3.4	4.4	4.7	6.8	7.0
	(o = 59%)	(o = 50%)	(o = 45%)	(o = 46%)	(o = 43%)
African American	15.7	20.1	25.8	24.5	21.1
	10.3	11.1	11.0	12.9	12.0
	(u = 33%)	(u = 45%)	(u = 57%)	(u = 47%)	(u = 41%)

Notes: Percentages are rounded; top number indicates percentage of student population and middle number represents percentage of gifted education. "o" indicates overrepresentation; "u" indicates underrepresentation. Percentage of underrepresentation was calculated using the following formula: 1− (percentage of gifted education program divided by percentage of school district). Source for 1978 to 1984 data: Chinn & Hughes (1987). Source for 1992 data; OCR Elementary and Secondary School Civil Rights Compliance Report (1992).

SOURCE: From "The underrepresentation of minority students in gifted education: Problems and promises in recruitment and retention" by Donna Y. Ford, 1998, *The Journal of Special Education*, 32, p. 7. Copyright date by PRO-ED, Inc. Reprinted with permission.

Table 1

often been tantamount to de facto segregation. Throughout its history, gifted education has not been truly desegregated. Rather, Hispanic American, American Indian, and African American students remain underrepresented by large percentages (see Table 1).

This historical problem is rooted in the deficit views of culturally diverse groups, as well as in the overreliance on intelligence tests as the single or primary means of selection. For example, in the early 1900s, many researchers who examined intelligence among students held the belief that culturally diverse children, particularly African American children, were innately inferior to white children (see Figure 1). In addition, many scholars maintained that poor children, regardless of race, were also intellectually inferior to white students from middle- and upper-income families. While scholars vehemently refuted the biased views that resulted from the use (or abuse) of intelligence tests, intelligence quotient (IQ) scores on standardized tests were used to reinforce and distort beliefs about the intellectual capacity of white children, and to perpetuate their superiority and worth within society.

The emergence of gifted education coincided with the end of the "separate but equal" doctrine, which was validated by the U.S. Supreme Court in *Plessy v. Ferguson* in 1856. This decision made it legal for white and black children to be educated in separate schools. As a result, white children generally went to schools of higher quality than black and other culturally diverse children. White children were believed to be innately higher in their capacity for academic achievement and educational attainment. They were also perceived to be smarter, more motivated, and more creative, and therefore more deserving of instructional services and facilities than black children, who, "by nature," required less access to or need for quality educational opportunity or instruction. Genes were considered to be the main determinant of destiny, while the environment—including education—was deemed to be of little significance for blacks (see Herrnstein and Murray 1994).

Today, some scholars continue to criticize gifted education because it is viewed as serving a racist or elitist

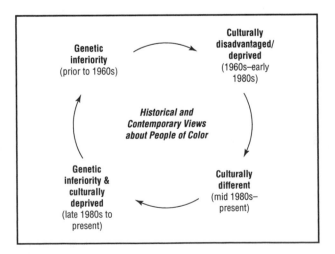

Figure 1

agenda seeped in educational politics (see Sapon-Shevin 1993; Wells and Serna 1996). More than any other educational program in public schools, gifted education faces the ongoing struggle to desegregate its programs. As of 2002, for example, black students were underrepresented by 60 percent in gifted programs nationally. Essentially, segregation, as it existed almost two centuries ago, seems to still be evident in gifted education.

Essentially, while the *Brown v. Board of Education* court decision in 1954 ended legalized segregation in public schools, the politics of education made way for a new form of segregation through gifted education. Cloaked behind the guise of valiant goals—such as meeting the needs of talented youth and preparing the next generation to be competitive in global markets—gifted education programs have primarily provided services to white students from middle- and upper-income families. Indeed, the concept of the "gifted child" remains synonymous with white middle-class children in the minds of too many public school educators and parents. In many ways, the advent of gifted education pleased white parents who were angry at the social and political changes occurring in the educational landscape that mandated schools to integrate, and not only were white parents infuriated by their children being forced to learn with "inferior" and "disadvantaged" black children, they also opposed white children being educated by black teachers.

Gifted education is based on the general premise that students with a high level of intellectual ability, or who excel in specific academic areas, need special instructional services to achieve their full potential. In essence, special instructional services (e.g., accelerated classes, enrichment programs, advanced academic experiences) for students with outstanding talent are essential to meet the gifted student's needs, just as special education services (e.g., remedial reading or tutoring) are essential for meeting the needs of students with learning disabilities. However, because of the historical racial inequity in programs for gifted students, gifted education still lacks essential support because it is seen as a modern form of promoting separate and unequal education. For example, the field of gifted education is plagued by the reality that standardized IQ testing, which was the primary tool that researchers used to perpetuate the inferiority of blacks and the superiority of whites, is still the primary method by which black and other diverse students are kept out of gifted programs.

Why do some want to keep gifted education segregated? Gifted students often receive the best instructional resources, the most effective or qualified teachers, and the lowest student-teacher ratios, all of which are critical to a quality education. Therefore, some parents may not want their children to remain in general education; they may aggressively push to have their children in gifted pro-grams, even if they do not meet criteria. Further, some administrators may resist admitting more diverse students into gifted education classes if parents and community members are resistant to diversifying gifted (and advanced placement) classes, as has been found in several court cases investigated by the Office for Civil Rights.

To address the historical inequality in the representation of ethnic minorities in gifted education, the National Association for Gifted Children (NAGC) is being proactive by building upon the legacy of Dr. Mary M. Frasier, an early pioneer for underrepresented groups in gifted education. The primary purpose of NAGC's Mary Frasier Teacher Scholarship Fund for Diverse Talent Development is to increase culturally and linguistically diverse students' access to talent development opportunities through teacher training and support related to equity and excellence in gifted education. In addition, several scholars continue their efforts to eliminate identification criteria that adversely affect the representation of diverse students in gifted education.

SEE ALSO *Education, Unequal; Education, USA; Tracking in Schools*

BIBLIOGRAPHY

Du Bois, W. E. B. 1903. *The Souls of Black Folks*. New York: The New American Library, 1982.

Ford, Donna Y. 1995. Desegregating Gifted Education: A Need Unmet. *Journal of Negro Education* 64 (1): 52–62.

Ford, Donna Y. 2004. *Intelligence Testing and Cultural Diversity: Concerns, Cautions, and Considerations*. Storrs, CT: National Research Center on the Gifted and Talented, University of Connecticut.

Ford, Donna Y. 2005. Ten Strategies for Increasing Diversity in Gifted Education. *Gifted Education Press Quarterly* 19 (4): 2–4.

Ford, Donna Y. and Tarek C. Grantham. 2003. Providing Access for Gifted Culturally Diverse Students: From Deficit Thinking to Dynamic Thinking. *Theory into Practice* 42 (3): 217–225.

Ford, Donna Y., and Gilman W. Whiting. 2006. Under-Representation of Diverse Students in Gifted Education: Recommendations for Nondiscriminatory Assessment (Part 1). *Gifted Education Press Quarterly* 20 (2): 2–6.

Frasier, Mary M., Jaime H. Garcia, and A. Harry Passow. 1995. *A Review of Assessment Issues in Gifted Education and their Implications for Identifying Gifted Minority Students*. Storrs, CT: National Research Center on the Gifted and Talented, University of Connecticut.

Gould, Stephen J. 1981. *The Mismeasure of Man*. New York: W.W. Norton.

Herrnstein, Richard, and Charles Murray. 1994. *The Bell Curve*. New York: Free Press.

Renzulli, Joseph. S., ed. 2004. *Essential Readings in Gifted Education. Vol. 2, Identification of Students for Gifted and*

Talented Programs. Washington, DC: National Association for Gifted Children.

Sapon-Shevin, Mara. 1993. Gifted Education and the Protection of Privilege: Breaking the Silence, Opening the Discourse. In *Beyond Silenced Voices: Class, Race, and Gender in the United States Schools*, edited by Lois Weis and Michelle Fine. Albany: State University of New York Press.

Shuey, Audrey M. 1966. *The Testing of Negro Intelligence*. 2nd ed. New York: Social Science Press.

United States Department of Education. 1993. *A National Excellence Report: A Case for Developing America's Talent*. Washington, DC.

Wells, Amy Stuart, and Irene Serna. 1996. The Politics of Culture: Understanding Local Political Resistance to Detracking in Racially Mixed Schools. *Harvard Educational Review* 66 (1): 93–118.

Donna Y. Ford
Tarek Grantham

GIFTEDNESS
SEE *Talent*.

GILDED AGE

Mark Twain and Charles Dudley Warner's *The Gilded Age* (1873), a satire of Americans' rush for material gain and political corruption in the years immediately following the Civil War, provided succeeding generations with a ready frame of reference for this period. Many historians' examinations of this era emphasized the political parties' keen competition and how the ruthless, if innovative, industrialists that Matthew Josephson dubbed "the robber barons" used a complaisant federal government to build vast fortunes from the United States's abundant natural resources. For several generations the Gilded Age (1866–1900) received far less attention from students of history than other eras in American history. But in recent years historians have argued that, together with the decades known as the Progressive Era (roughly 1900–1919), it represents a central chapter in the history of the United States. Examining aspects of American life beyond the robber barons and party politics, these accounts have shown how in these years Americans built a modern nation and grappled with its consequences.

The Gilded Age marked a major watershed in the history of American race relations. Historians have shown how in the period between the Civil War and the turn of the twentieth century white Americans decisively rejected the Civil War and Reconstruction's seeming promise of racial equality, and subjected African Americans, Chinese Americans, and other racial minorities to new systems of segregation, discrimination, and domination, as well as elaborate cultural rationales for their development.

In an industrial economy marked by severe depressions, a growing number of wage laborers found themselves seemingly consigned to lives of bitter toil with little hope for advancement. Many responded by struggling to build trade unions to represent their interests in dealings with employers, but faced judges and other public officials eager to promote business interests as representing the common good. In this context, employers and workers engaged in a series of violent clashes. These episodes led many intellectuals and members of the well-to-do and middle classes to perceive a fundamental crisis in American public life, a sentiment that informed both government officials' vigorous repression of strike activities and the rise of movements seeking reform through legislation and voluntary action.

An urban-industrial society characterized by increased wage labor and salaried professional work also manifested major changes in gender relations. Earlier in the nineteenth century many women had identified themselves as occupants of a "separate sphere" quite removed from public life and characterized by child-rearing and moral insight. But in the Gilded Age, growing numbers of women used their imputed status as moral arbiters to assert themselves in public life, even if they could not vote. While some continued to seek the ballot, others constructed reform organizations such as the Women's Christian Temperance Union to influence individual behavior and public policy through persuasion.

A new synthesis of scholarship on the Gilded Age has identified this period's nation-building dynamic as a multifaceted process of "incorporation." In addition to establishing effective control over many of their wage workers, managers of many large corporations also used their size and scope to establish significant advantages over their suppliers and customers in the marketplace. Government officials systematically removed Native Americans from the American West's more attractive locales to a set of reservations in this period. American officials extended this geographic dynamic of incorporation by making the Hawaiian Islands a territory and assuming Spanish colonial possessions, most notably the Philippines, after a one-sided conflict in 1898. In one sense these activities represented a nation-state exerting control over captured territories. But white Americans' development of elaborate theories for the subjugation of members of other races also represented a cultural process of incorporation. Many historians have concluded that these activities represented a desperate attempt to lend some semblance of hierarchy to a modernizing, democratic society increasingly breaking down more familiar sources of order, ranging from simple geographic isolation to differences in education and literacy to slavery itself. Where many earlier scholars of the period described political corruption largely redeemed by the Progressive Era's reforms, the emerging synthesis has elaborated an alternative view of American national development, highlighting pervasive patterns of exclusion and injustice only partly mitigated by federal regulations and the mass social movements of the mid- to late twentieth century. A significant number of scholars continue to examine the dynamics of political corruption and reform, as well as other aspects of political, economic, and intellectual history. But in the early years of the twenty-first century this new synthesis has placed the Gilded Age firmly at the center of American historical discourse.

SEE ALSO *Beard, Charles and Mary; Cross of Gold; Industrialization; Nast, Thomas; Populism*

BIBLIOGRAPHY

Edwards, Rebecca. 2006. *New Spirits: Americans in the Gilded Age, 1865–1905.* New York: Oxford University Press.

Josephson, Matthew. 1934. *The Robber Barons: The Great American Capitalists, 1861–1901.* New York: Harcourt, Brace.

Trachtenberg, Alan. 1982. *The Incorporation of America: Society and Culture in the Gilded Age.* New York: Hill and Wang

Drew E. VandeCreek

GILLIGAN, CAROL
1936–

Carol Friedman Gilligan was born November 28, 1936, in New York City. Her book *In a Different Voice* ushered in an era of research and theory about gender differences that valued the voices of girls and women.

Gilligan grew up in New York City. She went on to do her undergraduate work at Swarthmore College, where she majored in English and history, graduating summa cum laude in 1958. She earned a master's degree in clinical psychology from Radcliffe College in 1960 and a PhD in social psychology from Harvard in 1964. She began teaching at Harvard with the psychologist Erik Erikson in 1967 and continued teaching at Harvard's School of Education, receiving tenure as a full professor in 1986. During her early years at the School of Education she co-taught a course with Lawrence Kohlberg, whom she considered a friend (although many biographies wrongly describe her as his student). As a teacher in the 1980s at the School of Education, she taught courses on the psychology of moral development and adolescence and was known for lectures

integrating literature, mythology, biography, and history. In 1997 Gilligan was appointed to a newly endowed professorship at the Harvard Graduate School of Education, the Patricia Albjerg Graham Chair in Gender Studies, Harvard University's first position in gender studies. In 2002, shortly after the announcement of a 12.5 million dollar grant to the School of Education from Jane Fonda, who stated she was inspired by Carol Gilligan's work, Gilligan joined the faculty of New York University as a full-time professor in the schools of education and law.

In *In a Different Voice: Psychological Theory and Women's Development* (1982), Gilligan identified a kind of moral reasoning that was based on an ethic of care rather than an ethic of justice. Although the ethic of care has been identified as women's moral voice, the "different voice" Gilligan describes is "characterized not by gender but theme. Its association with women is an empirical observation, and it is primarily through women's voice that I trace its development" (p. 2). The voices of women and girls, she claimed, had been neglected by those who studied morality, such as Piaget and Freud. She pointed out first that these men and others based their theories of human development on a male model of separation and individuation, often studying, observing, or speaking only to boys and men and later describing as an afterthought how girls and women did not fit the norm. In this groundbreaking book, Gilligan criticized the work of Lawrence Kohlberg (whose theory was based on a study that included only adolescent boys), because women, in his six stages of moral development, seemed unable to advance beyond Stage 3, also known as the "good boy/nice girl stage." Kohlberg's research showed more men than women advancing to stages in which they preferred to use a morality that was based on contracts, individual rights, justice, and even what he called a universal morality; females were more likely to remain in adulthood in the so-named "conventional" morality stages. Through several studies that included interviews discussing Kohlberg's moral dilemmas as well as what Gilligan called "real-life" dilemmas, she showed girls and women to be responding not only to issues of justice, but issues of care. Although the point was not elaborated in *In a Different Voice*, she later argued that women's association with stage 3 was not structural, but a function of patriarchy. She then further developed the cultural/social side of her argument and the element of resistance so key to her work with girls. Over time Gilligan's work has been inaccurately described as suggesting that women are more caring than men. Rather, she argues that women are more likely to make moral decisions based on issues of care, inclusion, and personal connection, rather than on a more abstract and distant notion of justice.

The methodological shortcomings in others' works that Gilligan critiqued in *In a Different Voice* were the impetus for new research methods used and developed in Gilligan's later work and in the work of her students. In this work she and those influenced by her continued to fault researchers for using a male perspective as a starting point. She also encouraged the increasing use of open-ended interviews focused on self in relation to a range of issues, an approach that had largely been dismissed as producing suspect "self-report" data. In addition, her work valued qualitative, thematic analysis. The "Listener's Guide," written with Lyn Mikel Brown, describes a voice-sensitive method attuned to a psyche in active dialogue with the sociopolitical realities of everyday life.

Following her publication of *In a Different Voice*, Gilligan herself continued to pursue qualitative research exploring the relational world of girls, resulting in *Meeting at the Crossroads* (1992), coauthored with Brown, and *Between Voice and Silence: Women and Girls, Race and Relationship* (1996), coauthored with students Jill McLean Taylor and Amy M. Sullivan. She has helped guide the work of former students, such as Janie Victoria Ward (*The Skin We're In*, 2000), Dana Jack (*Silencing the Self*, 1991, and *Behind the Mask*, 1999), Deborah Tolman (*Dilemmas of Desire*, 2003), Niobe Way (*Everyday Courage*, 1998), and Lyn Mikel Brown (*Raising Their Voices*, 1998, and *Girlfighting*, 2005). Her work has also been influential in feminist discourse theory, law, medicine, and philosophy. Gilligan was a founder of the Harvard Project on Women's Psychology and Girls' Development, and of Strengthening Healthy Resistance and Courage in Girls, a prevention project that also was expanded to include boys and men as her interests shifted to examine the plight of boys in Western society.

Gilligan's 2002 book *The Birth of Pleasure* summarizes themes of love and caring that were suggested in earlier work. Using the Cupid and Psyche myth as the quintessential Western love story, she discusses familiar themes of the objectification of women, the pitting of woman against woman in patriarchy, men's fear of the intimacy they long for, and "dissociation"—or the process by which women learn to forget or cover over what they know to be true and by which men learn to replace feelings of vulnerability and tenderness with masks of masculinity.

In 1992 Gilligan, the recipient of numerous awards, was given the prestigious Grawemeyer Award in Education. This is given to honor achievements in areas not recognized by the Nobel prizes. She was also named one of *Time Magazine*'s twenty-five most influential people in 1996. In 1997 she received the Heinz Award for knowledge of the human condition and for her challenges to previously held assumptions in the field of human development.

SEE ALSO *Kohlberg, Lawrence*

BIBLIOGRAPHY

Gilligan, Carol. 1982. *In a Different Voice: Psychological Theory and Women's Development*. Cambridge, MA: Harvard University Press.

Sharon Lamb

GINI COEFFICIENT

The Gini coefficient is the most popular measure of inequality in use today. The measurement is named for its developer, Corrado Gini (1884–1965), and is based on the Lorenz curve (Sen 1997; Xu 2004). Although the Gini was traditionally used to measure income as a measure of welfare, it is now often used to measure other variables such as expenditures, wealth, and even health.

The clearest way to portray the Gini coefficient is diagrammatically. Take a population of ten individuals, as shown in Table 1. If you sort the population from poorest to richest and graph the cumulative share of income against population, what you get is a Lorenz curve, as depicted by the curve in Figure 1. If every individual in the society had equal income, the graph would be the diagonal. But in any society, the poorest will have a share less than their proportion in the population, so the Lorenz curve will always be below the diagonal. The Gini coefficient is measured as the ratio of the area between the diagonal and the Lorenz curve (X) and the area under the

Individual	Share of Population	Individual Income	Cumulative Share of Income
1	0	0	0
2	10	2	2
3	20	3	5
4	30	4	9
5	40	6	15
6	50	8	23
7	60	9	32
8	70	11	43
9	80	15	58
10	90	17	75
	100	25	100
Total Income		100	

Table 1

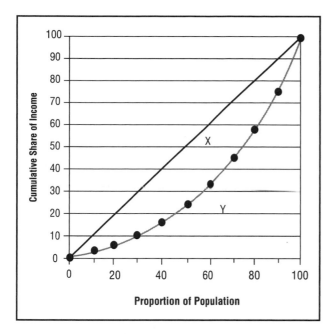

Figure 1

the population. The Gini coefficient is, thus, a measure of the overall inequality in the population (Sen 1997).

In Table 2 and Figure 2, in addition to the original distribution used above (labeled as *B*), we add two other distributions (*A* and *C*). As income inequality increases, the Lorenz curve moves farther away from the diagonal (see distribution *C*), and the opposite occurs as inequality decreases (see distribution *A*). In a society where income is equally shared, the area *X* = 0 because the Lorenz curve would coincide with the diagonal and the Gini coefficient would equal 0. In contrast, if all income is held by the richest individual in society, then *Y* = 0 and the ratio would equal 1. The Gini coefficient thus always lies between 0 and 1. The most common convention nowadays is to multiply the ratio by 100 and then report the Gini coefficient as a number between 0 and 100. One of the great strengths of the Gini is that any redistribution of income from a poorer person to a richer person results in an increase of the coefficient, and thus it captures distribution across the entire population rather than just at the mean.

Despite its popularity, the Gini suffers from the fact that there is no intuitive meaning to any particular magnitude of the coefficent. Nor does any specific magnitude represent a unique distribution. A Gini of 30, for example, can represent two different distributions, and there is no objective way to differentiate the distributions. This occurs because Lorenz curves may cross. It follows from this that determining distributions that are highly unequal versus those that are not is more an empirical question.

diagonal (*X* + *Y*). The formula for the coefficient can be stated as

$$G = (1/2n^2\mu)\Sigma_{i=1}^{n}\Sigma_{j=1}^{n}|y_i - y_j|$$

where *n* is the population, μ is the mean of incomes, *y* is income, and *i* and *j* are individuals in the population. This is effectively a sum of all pair-wise income inequalities in

Individual	Share of Population	Individual Income			Cumulative Share of Income		
		A	*B*	*C*	*A*	*B*	*C*
1	0	0	0	0	0	0	0
2	10	1	2	4	1	2	4
3	20	3	3	5	3	5	9
4	30	4	4	6	5	9	15
5	40	6	6	7	10	15	22
6	50	8	8	10	15	23	32
7	60	9	9	11	21	32	43
8	70	11	11	12	28	43	55
9	80	15	15	13	38	58	68
10	90	17	17	15	53	75	83
	100	47	25	17	100	100	100
Total Income		100	100	100			

Table 2

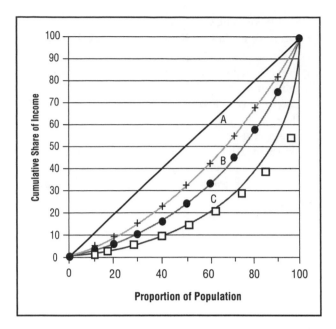

Figure 2

In order to give the reader some sense of what levels of inequality different sizes of Gini represent, Table 3 illustrates the average Gini coeffecients and the average level of income accruing to each quintile of the population for thirty-eight countries, from a dataset compiled by Klaus Deininger and Lyn Squire (1996). The thirty-eight countries were picked because they had a measurement of Gini that Deininger and Squire considered reliable and comparable across countries between 1990 and 1995, as well as information on the quintile distributions of income, which gives us more information on the underlying distribution. If we divide the countries evenly into three groups we find that the group with lowest inequality has Ginis that range from 22 to 30, the middle group from 31 to 34, and the most unequal group from 35 to 62. Because this last group has such high variation we divide the group into two at 45.

Although these observations do not encompass the whole range of measured distributions, they do provide us with some more information. On average, developing countries, particularly in Africa and Latin America, dominate the group of highly unequal countries, whereas the group of low inequality is dominated by European countries, particularly those that formerly belonged to the socialist bloc. For countries with low inequality, the richest 20 percent of the population earned less than 40 percent of national income, whereas for those with high inequality the richest earned over 47 percent, averaging close to 60 percent. In contrast, for the poorest 20 percent in the low-inequality countries earned between 7 and 11 percent of national income, whereas in the highly unequal countries they only earned between 2 and 4 percent of national income.

Since the late 1980s a number of strides have been made in estimating the Gini from functional forms including the diagrammatic methods discussed above, as well as in decomposing it so that one can estimate the impact of different components of income on inequality. For a good summary of this literature, see Xu (2004).

	Gini	Quintile 1	Quintile 1	Quintile 1	Quintile 1	Quintile 1	Number of Observations
Low Inequality	27	0.09	0.14	0.18	0.23	0.36	13
Range for Variable	21-30	0.07-0.11	0.13-0.15	0.17-0.20	0.21-0.25	0.33-0.39	
Average Inequality	33	0.07	0.12	0.17	0.24	0.40	13
Range for Variable	31-34	0.05-0.08	0.11-0.13	0.16-0.19	0.21-0.25	0.37-0.42	
Moderately High Inequality	39	0.05	0.11	0.16	0.24	0.44	7
Range for Variable	35-45	0.05-0.07	0.10-0.12	0.14-0.17	0.21-0.26	0.40-0.49	
High Inequality	54	0.03	0.07	0.12	0.20	0.57	6
Range for Variable	45-62	0.02-0.04	0.05-0.09	0.09-0.18	0.18-0.24	0.47-0.65	

Table 3

SEE ALSO *Development Economics; Inequality, Income; Inequality, Political; Kuznets Hypothesis; Lorenz Curve; Poverty, Indices of*

BIBLIOGRAPHY

Anand, Sudhir. 1983. *Inequality and Poverty in Malaysia: Measurement and Decomposition.* New York: Oxford University Press.

Deaton, Angus. 1997. *The Analysis of Household Surveys.* Baltimore, MD: Johns Hopkins University Press.

Deininger, Klaus, and Lyn Squire. 1996. A New Data Set Measuring Income Inequality. *World Bank Economic Review* 10: 565–591.

Sen, Amartya K. 1973. *On Economic Inequality.* Oxford: Clarendon.

Sen, Amartya K. 1997. *On Economic Inequality.* Expanded ed. with a substantial annexe by James E. Foster and Amartya Sen. Oxford: Clarendon.

Xu, Kuan. 2004. How Has the Literature on Gini's Index Evolved in the Past 80 Years? Department of Economics Working Papers, Dalhousie University. http://economics.dal.ca/RePEc/dal/wparch/howgini.pdf.

Mwangi wa Gīthīnji

GINZBERG, ELI
1911–2002

Eli Ginzberg was born in New York City, the son of prominent rabbi Louis Ginzberg and the former Adele Katzenstein. He was the great-great-grandnephew on his father's side of the "Vilna Gaon," an eighteenth-century rabbi, Talmud scholar, kabbalist, and mathematician. The Vilna Gaon had studied Euclid, caused one of his students to translate Euclid into Hebrew, and was the author of "A Ram in Three Parts," a mathematical analysis of Genesis 15:9. His followers initiated the modern Zionist movement. The family thus belonged to the intellectual, political, and financial elite of the Jewish community.

Ginzberg earned the AB, AM, and PhD from Columbia University in 1931, 1932, and 1935, respectively. Wesley Clair Mitchell and E. R. A. Seligman were his principal mentors, and his graduate schoolmates included Abram L. Harris Jr., Joseph Dorfman, and Robert Dorfman.

Ginzberg's career may perhaps be best categorized as that of an entrepreneurial statesman of economic ideas in academia and government. Upon receiving the doctorate, he joined the economics faculty of Columbia Graduate Business School, remaining until his 1979 retirement. There, Ginzberg uniquely focused his research and teaching on labor, health, and race policy issues in economics.

He taught three courses or seminars per semester for more than thirty-three years. He also was given occasional responsibilities in the Graduate Department of Economics, College of General Studies, Barnard College, College of Physicians and Surgeons, and the School of Public Health. In 1938, he and Mitchell offered a seminar titled Economic Change and Economic Theory in the economics department. In the School of Public Health he taught Political Economy of Health Care.

During World War II, Ginzberg served the United Jewish Appeal and many agencies in the federal government, including the White House and the surgeon-general's office. At the Five-Power Conference on Reparations for Non-Repatriable Victims of Germany in June 1946, he served as a U.S. delegate. He was awarded the medal for Exceptional Civilian Service from the War Department in 1946. As a consultant to the U.S. Army from 1946 to 1955, he played a role in the army's desegregation.

Back at Columbia Business School in 1950, Ginzberg was appointed director of the Eisenhower Center for the Conservation of Human Resources, a position he held until 1979. He was promoted to full professor in 1952.

He was involved with the establishment of the National Institutes of Mental Health (NIMH), being appointed a member of the National Mental Health Advisory Board in 1959. NIMH funded the nation's first community-based advocacy planning institute in Brooklyn in 1968, a project that employed black Columbia and Yale graduate students in economics and a White House Fellow. He was involved with the establishment of Medicare and Medicaid in 1965.

Ginzberg published at least 179 books and hundreds of articles, which may be categorized into six major themes: (1) history of economic thought, 2) labor economics, (3) industrial organization, (4) race and economics, (5) autobiography and biography, and (6) health economics.

His writings in the history of economic thought included "Studies in the Economics of the Bible" in the *Jewish Quarterly Review* (1932), the first systematic treatment of biblical economics since Adam Smith; his dissertation, "Adam Smith and the Founding of Market Economics" (1934); *The House of Adam Smith* (1964); *The House of Adam Smith Revisited* (1977); "Economics at Columbia: Recollections of the Early 1930s" (1990); and "Wesley Clair Mitchell" (1997).

In labor economics, Ginzberg's most important contributions were a theory of occupational choice and a general theory of the development and use of human resources. Most of his publications in this area addressed federal labor policy issues. He also served on the National Advisory Committee on Manpower Development and Training from 1962 to 1982.

Ginzberg's works in industrial organization contain his most important theoretical contributions. He developed the concept of a pluralistic economy including private, public, and nonprofit sectors, thus adding an explicit third sector to the private and public sectors of the mixed capitalist-socialist economy. The concept of the coequal third sector was the most striking view of the structure of a modern economy since Marx. It spawned a still growing international literature on the economics of nonprofit organizations (including most notably hospitals and universities) as a macrosector. Many interesting implications for welfare economics flooded the literature, led by Burton A. Weisbrod of the University of Wisconsin. Weisbrod argued that these organizations were substitutes for markets that had "failed," so they assumed the functions of the market. Others argued that participants in such organizations did not seek to optimize objective functions but only "satificed." Despite the empirical reality and growing significance of this sector, however, and the novelty of explanations for its existence, this literature may nevertheless be considered simply a more highly theoretical form of the utopian socialist literature of the early nineteenth century. In 1985 appeared the most interesting of all Ginzberg's works, *Beyond Human Scale: The Large Corporation at Risk*, with George Vojta. It showed the similarity of economic relations among micro-units of a macro-unit among such large-scale, complex organizations as corporations, the military, the Catholic Church, universities, and hospitals. The authors uniquely use the example of not-for-profit institutions whose pricing structures are "hidden," that is, utilize "transfer prices." Although explicit recognition of such prices dated to the 1890s and their naming to the 1950s, this was the first analysis of their implication for nongovernmental nonprofit organizations.

Ginzberg published more on the economics of race than any other nonblack economist of his time. Many of these publications addressed public policy as it affected racial issues.

Ginzberg published six biographies or autobiographies, including one on his father and one about a man from his father's hometown, Emanuel Piore, whose wife, Nora Kahn Piore, was a professor of public health economics with Ginzberg at the Columbia School of Public Health.

Ginzberg wrote more about heath economic policy than any other subject. Among his many associates in medical and health economics were Michael M. Davis, Walton H. Hamilton, George H. H. Soule, Hugh Smythe, Roscoe G. Leland, Algie M. Simons, Frank G. Dickinson, Nora Kahn Piore, Eveline M. Burns, and Michael Grossman. He opposed the Clinton heath plan of the early 1990s, largely because he thought the president was politically inept in its pursuit.

In 1983, Ginzberg's separate focus on labor and the nonprofit sector were joined by the *Monthly Labor Review* in an article containing statistics on the size of the labor force in that sector. This article subsequently was cited by twenty-eight publications.

Because his books and articles generally represented policy and empirical analyses rather than the high mathematical economics favored by most economic journals beginning in the 1950s, he was involved in no professional polemics, and his critics were so few as to be unidentifiable.

SEE ALSO *Capitalism, Black; Desegregation; Economics; Economics, Labor; Entrepreneurship; Harris, Abram L., Jr.; Health Economics; Industry; Jews; Medicaid; Medicare; Mitchell, Wesley Clair; Public Health; Public Policy; Race; Smith, Adam; Welfare; Work*

BIBLIOGRAPHY

Berg, Ivar E., ed. 1972. *Human Resources and Economic Welfare: Essays in Honor of Eli Ginzberg*. New York: Columbia University.

Berkowitz, Edward. 1998. History of Health Services Research Project: Interview with Eli Ginzberg. New York City, March 2. U.S. National Library of Medicine, National Institutes of Health. http://www.nlm.nih.gov/hmd/nichsr/ginzberg.html.

Ginzberg, Eli. 1966. *Keeper of the Law*. Philadelphia: Jewish Publication Society of America.

Ginzberg, Eli. 1989. *My Brother's Keeper: Personal Memoirs of a Public Life*. New Brunswick, NJ: Transaction.

Ginzberg, Eli. 1993. *The Eye of Illusion*. New Brunswick, NJ: Transaction.

Ginzberg, Eli. 1997. *New Deal Days, 1933–1934*. New Brunswick, NJ: Transaction.

Ginzberg, Eli. 1997. The Long View: When Teaching Came Second. *21stC: The World of Research at Columbia University* 2.2 (winter). http://www.columbia.edu/cu/21stC/issue-2.2/ginzberg.html.

Ginzberg, Eli. 2002. *The Economist as a Public Intellectual*. Ed. Irving Louis Horowitz. New Brunswick, NJ: Transaction.

Piore, Emanuel R. 1990. *Science and Academic Life in Transition*. Ed. Eli Ginzberg. New Brunswick, NJ: Transaction.

Rutherford, Malcolm. 2004. Institutional Economics at Columbia University. *History of Political Economy* 36 (1): 31–78.

Julian Ellison

GLASNOST

Glasnost is the Russian word for publicity, openness, the state of being public. It refers to a policy of openness in private and public discussions about social, economic, and cultural issues that was initiated by Mikhail Gorbachev after his ascension to the leadership of the Union of Soviet Socialistic Republics (USSR) in 1985. Gorbachev tried to use open public discussions about the state of the country to generate grassroots political support for his policy of economic restructuring (perestroika) and to outmaneuver his political opponents within the Communist Party. It could be argued that Gorbachev envisioned glasnost as a sort of compensation for the temporary economic hardship that his perestroika program of reforms unavoidably involved.

As a result of the glasnost policy, many sensitive historical issues, such as the brutality of the regime of Joseph Stalin (1879–1953), were acknowledged and the Soviet Union's "official" history was rewritten. The policy also brought to public attention the economic stagnation in the country and permitted open criticism of government policies. It was one of the main aims of Gorbachev's glasnost policy to make the state and its entrenched elites accountable to the public by revealing the real economic situation and by allowing the Soviet people to express their wishes. Glasnost destroyed the myth that everyone was happy under the Soviet Union and praised the country's leadership, but the policy exposed many more fundamental problems than Gorbachev had expected.

It is generally believed that Gorbachev had planned to use the Leninist ideology to thoroughly reform the Soviet Union without destroying it. Nikita Khrushchev (1894–1971), an earlier Soviet leader, tried to reform the USSR using soft methods but was not successful, so Gorbachev may have thought that a policy like glasnost was his only chance to push the necessary economic reforms through. However, freedom of expression unleashed forces that Gorbachev could not control: The media started to aggressively criticize long-denied problems, especially the country's poor quality of life; revelations about the horrors of the Stalin era undermined Soviet political elites; and Moscow's grip on the Soviet republics weakened and nationalistic feelings revived. The rapid rise of nationalism and calls for independence in such places as Azerbaijan, Estonia, Georgia, Lithuania, Latvia, and Ukraine were important consequences of glasnost, which allowed and to some degree encouraged people to think about their sovereignty and independence. Thus, glasnost contributed to the eventual demise of the Soviet Union.

Glasnost achieved Gorbachev's aim of giving people freedom of expression, which before then had been strictly prohibited in the Soviet Union, but undermined his other aims and resulted in the collapse of the Soviet Union in 1991. Although Russia remains a relatively poor country, its citizens now have more freedom than at any other time in Russian and Soviet history. Glasnost also resulted in a renaissance in Soviet cultural and artistic life and in a revival of religion. Previously banned writers became widely read by the general public and new writers and artists emerged. *Glasnost* has also become one of the few Russian words commonly used in English, which shows the extent of its international influence.

SEE ALSO *Brezhnev, Leonid; Cold War; Communism; Gorbachev, Mikhail; Gulags; Iron Curtain; Khrushchev, Nikita; Stalin, Joseph; Union of Soviet Socialist Republics*

BIBLIOGRAPHY

Brown, Archie, Michael Kaser, and Gerald S. Smith, eds. 1994. *The Cambridge Encyclopedia of Russia and the Former Soviet Union.* 2nd ed. Cambridge, U.K.: Cambridge University Press.

Gilbert, Martin. 2002. *The Routledge Atlas of Russian History.* 3rd ed. London: Routledge.

Gorbachev, Mikhail. 1996. *Memoirs.* New York: Doubleday.

Gorbachev, Mikhail. 2000. *On My Country and the World.* Trans. George Shriver. New York: Columbia University Press.

Hewett, Ed A., and Victor H. Winston, eds. 1991. *Milestones in Glasnost and Perestroika.* Washington, DC: Brookings Institution.

Tarasulo, Isaac J., ed. 1992. *Perils of Perestroika: Viewpoints from the Soviet Press, 1989–1991.* Wilmington, DE: Scholarly Resources.

Pavel Erochkine

GLASS CEILING

The expression *glass ceiling* has been used to describe artificial barriers based on attitudinal or organizational bias that prevent qualified individuals from advancing to positions of power offering higher salaries and more responsibility and authority. Research has shown that, compared to men and whites, women and racial minorities in professional occupations are concentrated in lower- and middle-level positions and are underrepresented in upper managerial ranks. Positive steps have been taken to promote equality of opportunity, ranging from affirmative action legislation to greater diversity in hiring and promotions on the part of employers. Yet, despite these widely publicized efforts, women and minorities still do not enjoy the same advancement opportunities as men and whites. The continued existence of a glass ceiling can be attributed to an interplay of cultural and structural factors.

There are a number of explanations for the existence of a glass ceiling. The concept of *homosocial reproduction* suggests that when there is imperfect information on the potential of a candidate, employers or managers generally prefer to hire or promote someone who looks and thinks like them. (The questionable assumption underlying this argument is that people with similar gender, racial, or educational backgrounds tend to think and act alike.) This puts women and minorities are at a competitive disadvantage, because the majority of decisions regarding hiring and promotion are still made by men/whites.

There is much evidence to suggest that "who you know" (network ties) is as important as "what you know" (education, skills) in moving up the organizational hierarchy. Due to their comparatively recent entry into the labor market, women and minorities still have difficulty in setting up and expanding professional connections. Not being able to tap into the "old boy" network is detrimental to their career progress. To crack the glass ceiling, female and minority workers have had to build up their reputation and gain access to resources through relationships with people with status and authority inside and outside their organization, be they acquaintances, mentors, sponsors, or colleagues. Additionally, female and minority workers are especially vulnerable when they are present in only token numbers. Limited representation increases the pressure on them to perform, heightens their differences from the dominant group, and constrains their roles within the organization. This situation will inevitably improve as the presence of women and minorities increases over time.

Much evidence suggests that a range of discriminatory attitudes make women and minorities less likely to get as far as their male/white counterparts with similar backgrounds. Employers may be reluctant to groom women or racial minorities for leadership positions, owing to stereotypes they hold about members of certain groups as well as their concern about potential bias on the part of customers and male/white workers. Employers tend to view women as less dependable and less career-oriented, because of women's marriage and family responsibilities. Because of their marginal status in society, women and minorities may have difficulty in commanding respect or obedience from male/white subordinates or in exercising authority in negotiations or confrontations. Furthermore, management and administration have traditionally been considered masculine activities. The *queuing* theory postulates that discrimination results in a gender/race hierarchy in hiring and promotions. Employers tend to prefer male and white workers to female and minority workers. As a result, men/whites tend to monopolize the most desirable jobs, such as management positions, while women and minorities are relegated to low-paying or less-prestigious positions such as staff or technical work.

The existence of the glass ceiling can result in several outcomes for women and minorities:

1. Title inflation: For window-dressing purposes, firms may promote women and minorities at a relatively high rate to high-profile positions as tokens or glorified managers without conferring any real or additional authority upon them.

2. Job segregation by sex/race: To preserve the existing power structure in an organization and society, employers may place women and minorities in positions or departments that only allow them to supervise female or minority subordinates (e.g., affirmative action or human resource departments).

3. Career changes: The glass ceiling that limits how many women and minorities move up the organizational hierarchy may be a powerful incentive for them to contemplate alternative routes to improved occupational status, such as self-employment or setting up a business where they will be their own boss.

Compounding the cultural and structural factors already discussed, declining opportunities in middle and upper management resulting from corporate downsizing may have intensified competition between and discrimination against women and minorities.

SEE ALSO *Gender; Gender Gap; Inequality, Gender*

BIBLIOGRAPHY

Collins, Sharon M. 1997. *Black Corporate Executives: The Making and Breaking of a Black Middle Class.* Philadelphia: Temple University Press.

Cox, Taylor. 1993. *Cultural Diversity in Organizations: Theory, Research, and Practice.* San Francisco: Berrett-Koehler.

DiTomaso, Nancy, and Steven A. Smith. 1996. Race and Ethnic Minorities and White Women in Management: Changes and Challenges. In *Women and Minorities in American Professions*, eds. Joyce Tang and Earl Smith, 87–109. Albany: State University of New York Press.

Granovetter, Mark. 1995. *Getting a Job: A Study of Contacts and Careers.* 2nd ed. Chicago: University of Chicago Press.

Jacobs, Jerry A. 1992. Women's Entry into Management: Trends in Earnings, Authority, Values, and Attitudes among Salaried Managers. *Administrative Science Quarterly* 37 (2): 282–301.

Osterman, Paul, ed. 1996. *Broken Ladders: Managerial Careers in the New Economy.* New York: Oxford University Press.

Rosenbaum, James E. 1984. *Career Mobility in a Corporate Hierarchy.* New York: Academic Press.

Tang, Joyce. 1997. The Glass Ceiling in Science and Engineering. *Journal of Socio-Economics* 26 (4): 383–406.

U.S. Department of Labor. 1991. *A Report on the Glass Ceiling Initiative.* Washington, DC: Bureau of the Census.

Joyce Tang

GLAZER, NATHAN
1924–

Formerly professor of Education and Social Structure and now professor emeritus in the Graduate School of Education, Harvard University, Nathan Glazer (1924–) is also the coeditor of *The Public Interest*, assistant editor of *Commentary*, and contributing editor to *The New Republic*. He has been an influential and at times controversial figure in American public life due to his analyses of immigration, affirmative action, race relations, and multiculturalism. Closely associated with New York intellectuals such as Daniel Bell, Glazer was a student follower of Leon Trotsky (1879–1940), the Russian revolutionary. With the economic recovery that followed the Great Depression (1929–1932), Glazer, like many Jewish intellectuals, came to see capitalist America as a successful liberal democracy in which each successive wave of immigrants had been eventually incorporated into society and had benefited from growing economic prosperity. Glazer assumed that Americanization was an unproblematic process, but that optimism has been challenged by the fact that black progress appears to have come to an end in the 1970s. His critics have argued that the ethnic integration he described occurred because immigrants took on the mantle of whiteness in a society where anti-black racism was endemic.

Glazer collaborated with David Riesman on *The Lonely Crowd* (1950), and his first academic publication, *The Social Basis of American Communism*, appeared in 1961. However, Glazer first attracted academic attention through his publications on race and ethnicity, such as *American Judaism* (1957) and his collaborations with Daniel Moynihan (1927–2003), *Beyond the Melting Pot* (1963) and *Ethnicity: Theory and Practice* (1975). Various articles on these topics appeared as *Ethnic Dilemmas, 1964–1982* (1983).

An early critic of Great Society programs, Glazer has emerged as an influential figure in American politics, opposing affirmative-action programs in support of black Americans. In *Affirmative Discrimination* (1975)—a collection of essays dating back to the early 1970s—Glazer claimed that the apparent failure of black Americans to achieve assimilation and social mobility in an affluent American society was the result of fragmented families, declining inner-city schools, and disorganized communities. Glazer concluded that the main problem in the United States was not systematic racism, but employment discrimination against blacks. In *Beyond the Melting Pot*, Glazer and Moynihan argued that it is because black Americans have suffered profoundly from the effects of slavery that they have not experienced the upward social mobility enjoyed by many ethnic minorities. Repairing this deep-seated historical problem of black Americans

was beyond the capacity of social policies. Glazer has therefore been one of the main proponents of the black dysfunctionality hypothesis that has been embraced by Daniel Moynihan, Edward Banfield, and Richard Herrnstein, and his arguments against affirmative action policies were significant in the growth of neoconservatism in American public life. Critics such as Stephen Steinberg (see Steinberg's *Turning Back: The Retreat from Racial Justice in American Thought and Policy*, 1995) have argued that Glazer's policy prescriptions amount to blaming the victim.

Glazer has also been influential in the movement against liberal policies in multicultural school curricula. In *We Are All Multiculturalists Now* (1997) and *Sovereignty under Challenge* (2002) he claims that a multicultural education compromises historical truth and erodes national unity through the "Balkanization" of the American republic. Glazer himself rejects the neoconservative label and has been critical of small groups whose veto power keeps controversial subjects out of the school curricula, thereby, in his estimation, creating a bland, unreal America.

SEE ALSO *Education, Unequal; Moynihan, Daniel Patrick*

BIBLIOGRAPHY
Steinberg, Stephen. 1995. *Turning Back: The Retreat from Racial Justice in American Thought and Policy*. Boston: Beacon.

Bryan S. Turner

GLOBAL WARMING

Understanding the causes of and responses to global warming requires interdisciplinary cooperation between social and natural scientists. The theory behind global warming has been understood by climatologists since at least the 1980s, but only in the new millennium, with an apparent tipping point in 2005, has the mounting empirical evidence convinced most doubters, politicians, and the general public as well as growing sections of business that global warming caused by human action is occurring.

DEFINITION OF GLOBAL WARMING

Global warming is understood to result from an overall, long-term increase in the retention of the sun's heat around Earth due to blanketing by "greenhouse gases," especially CO_2 and methane. Emissions of CO_2 have been rising at a speed unprecedented in human history, due to accelerating fossil fuel burning that began in the Industrial Revolution.

The effects of the resulting "climate change" are uneven and can even produce localized cooling (if warm currents change direction). The climate change may also initiate positive feedback in which the initial impact is further enhanced by its own effects, for example if melting ice reduces the reflective properties of white surfaces (the "albedo" effect) or if melting tundra releases frozen methane, leading to further warming. Debate continues about which manifestations are due to long-term climate change and which to normal climate variability.

SPEEDING UP THE PROCESS

Global warming involves an unprecedented speeding up of the rate of change in natural processes, which now converges with the (previously much faster) rate of change in human societies, leading to a crisis of adaptation. Most authoritative scientific bodies predict that on present trends a point of no return could come within ten years, and that the world needs to cut emissions by 50 percent by mid twenty-first century.

It was natural scientists who first discovered and raised global warming as a political problem. This makes many of the global warming concerns unique. "Science becomes the author of issues that dominate the political agenda and become the sources of political conflict" (Stehr 2001, p. 85). Perhaps for this reason, many social scientists, particularly sociologists, wary of trusting the truth claims of natural science but knowing themselves lacking the expertise to judge their validity, have avoided saying much about global warming and its possible consequences. Even sociologists such as Ulrich Beck and Anthony Giddens, who see "risk" as a key attribute of advanced modernity, have said little about climate change.

For practical purposes, it can no longer be assumed that nature is a stable, well understood, background constant and thus social scientists do not need direct knowledge about its changes. Any discussion of likely social, economic, and political futures will have to heed what natural scientists say about the likely impacts of climate change.

GROWING EVIDENCE OF GLOBAL WARMING

While originally eccentric, global warming was placed firmly on the agenda in 1985, at a conference in Austria of eighty-nine climate researchers participating as individuals from twenty-three countries. The researchers forecast substantial warming, unambiguously attributable to human activities.

Since that conference the researchers' position has guided targeted empirical research, leading to supporting (and increasingly dire) evidence, resolving anomalies and winning near unanimous peer endorsement. Skeptics have been confounded and reduced to a handful, some discredited by revelations of dubious funding from fossil fuel industries.

Just before the end of the twentieth century, American researchers released ice-thickness data, gathered by nuclear submarines. The data showed that over the previous forty years the ice depth in all regions of the Arctic Ocean had declined by approximately 40 percent.

Five yearly aerial photographs show the ice cover on the Arctic Ocean at a record low, with a loss of 50 cubic kilometers annually and glacier retreat doubling to 12 kilometers a year. In September 2005 the National Aeronautics and Space Administration (NASA) doubled its estimates of the volume of melted fresh water flowing into the North Atlantic, reducing salinity and thus potentially threatening the conveyor that drives the Gulf Stream. Temperate mussels have been found in Arctic waters, and news broadcasts in 2005 and 2006 have repeatedly shown scenes of Inuit and polar bears (recently listed as endangered) cut off from their hunting grounds as the ice bridges melt.

In 2001 the Intergovernmental Panel on Climate Change (IPCC), the United Nation's scientific panel on climate change, had predicted that Antarctica would not contribute significantly to sea level rise this century. The massive west Antarctic ice sheet was assumed to be stable. However, in June 2005 a British Antarctic survey reported measurements of the glaciers on this ice sheet shrinking. In October 2005 glaciologists reported that the edges of the Antarctic ice sheets were crumbling at an unprecedented rate and, in one area, glaciers were discharging ice three times faster than a decade earlier.

In 2005 an eight-year European study drilling Antarctic ice cores to measure the past composition of the atmosphere reported that CO_2 levels were at least 30 percent higher than at any time in the last 65,000 years. The speed of the rise in CO_2 was unprecedented, from 280 parts per million (ppm) before the Industrial Revolution to 388 ppm in 2006. Early in 2007 the Norwegian Polar Institute reported acceleration to a new level of 390 ppm. In January 2006 a British Antarctic survey, analyzing CO_2 in crevasse ice in the Antarctic Peninsula, found levels of CO_2 higher than at any time in the previous 800,000 years.

In April 2005 a NASA Goddard Institute oceanic study reported that the earth was holding on to more solar energy than it was emitting into space. The Institute's director said: "This energy imbalance is the 'smoking gun' that we have been looking for" (Columbia 2005).

The second IPCC report in 1996 had predicted a maximum temperature rise of 3.5 degrees Fahrenheit by the end of the twenty-first century. The third report, in 2001, predicted a maximum rise of 5.8 degrees Fahrenheit by the end of the twenty-first century. In October 2006 Austrian glaciologists reported in *Geophysical Research Letters* (Kaser et al.) that almost all the world's glaciers had been shrinking since the 1940s, and the shrinking rate had increased since 2001. None of the glaciers (contrary to skeptics) was growing. Melting glaciers could pose threats to the water supply of major South American cities and is already manifest in the appearance of many new lakes in Bhutan.

In January 2007 global average land and sea temperatures were the highest ever recorded for this month; in February 2007 the IPCC Fourth Report, expressing greater certainty and worse fears than the previous one, made headlines around the world. In 1995 few scientists believed the effects of global warming were already manifest, but by 2005 few scientists doubted it and in 2007 few politicians were willing to appear skeptical.

Although rising temperatures; melting tundra, ice and glaciers; droughts; extreme storms; stressed coral reefs; changing geographical range of plants, animals, and diseases; and sinking atolls may conceivably all be results of many temporary climate variations, their cumulative impact is hard to refute.

ANOMALIES AND REFUTATIONS

The science of global warming has progressed through tackling anomalies cited by skeptics. Critics of global warming made attempts to discredit the methodology of climatologist Michael Mann's famous "Hockey stick" graph (first published in *Nature* in 1998). Mann's graph showed average global temperatures over the last 1,000 years, with little variation for the first 900 and a sharp rise in the last century. After more than a dozen replication studies, some using different statistical techniques and different combinations of proxy records (indirect measures of past temperatures such as ice cores or tree rings), Mann's results were vindicated. A report in 2006 by the U.S. National Academy of Sciences, National Research Council, supported much of Mann's image of global warming history. "There is sufficient evidence from the tree rings, boreholes, retreating glaciers and other 'proxies' of past surface temperatures to say with a high level of confidence that the last few decades of the twentieth century were warmer than any comparable period for the last 400 years." For periods before 1600, the 2006 report found there was not enough reliable data to be sure but the committee found the "Mann team's conclusion that warming in the last few decades of the twentieth century was unprecedented over the last 1,000 years to be plausible" (National Academy of Science press release 2006).

Measurements from satellites and balloons in the lower troposphere have until recently indicated cooling, which contradicted measurements from the surface and the upper troposphere. In August 2005 a publication in *Science*

of the findings of three independent studies described their measurements as "nails in the coffin" of the skeptics' case. These showed that faulty data, which failed to allow for satellite drift, lay behind the apparent anomaly.

Another anomaly was that observed temperature rises were in fact less than the modelling of CO_2 impacts predicted. This is now explained by evidence on the temporary masking properties of aerosols, from rising pollution and a cyclical upward swing of volcanic eruptions since 1960.

Critics of global warming have been disarmed and discredited. Media investigations and social research have increasingly highlighted the industry funding of skeptics and their think tanks, and the political pressures on government scientists to keep silent. Estimates of the catastrophic costs of action on emissions have also been contradicted most dramatically by the British Stern Report in October 2006. Many companies have been abandoning the skeptical business coalitions. The Australian Business Round Table on Climate Change estimated in 2005 that the cost to gross domestic product of strong early action would be minimal and would create jobs.

SCIENTIFIC CONSENSUS

In May 2001 sixteen of the world's national academies of science issued a statement, confirming that the IPCC should be seen as the world's most reliable source of scientific information on climate change, endorsing its conclusions and stating that doubts about the conclusions were not justified.

In July 2005 the heads of eleven influential national science academies (from Brazil, Canada, China, France, Germany, India, Italy, Japan, Russia, the United Kingdom, and the United States) wrote to the G8 leaders warning that global climate change was "a clear and increasing threat" and that they must act immediately. They outlined strong and long-term evidence "from direct measurements of rising surface air temperatures and subsurface ocean temperatures and from phenomena such as increases in average global sea levels, retreating glaciers and changes to many physical and biological systems" (Joint Science Academies Statement 2005).

There are many unknowns regarding global warming, particularly those dependent on human choices; yet the consequences for society of either inadequate action or of any effective responses (through reduced consumption or enforced and subsidized technological change) will be huge. It is, for example, unlikely that the practices and values of free markets, individualism, diversity, and choice will not be significantly modified either by economic and political breakdowns or alternatively by the radical measures needed to preempt them.

INADEQUATE ACTION AND NEEDED TRANSFORMATIONS

Kyoto targets are at best a useful first step. However, even these targets, which seek to peg back emissions to 1990 levels by 2010, are unlikely to be met. World CO_2 emissions in 2004 continued to rise in all regions of the world, by another 4.5 percent, to a level 26 percent higher than in 1990. A rise of over 2 degrees is considered inevitable if CO_2 concentrations pass 400 ppm. At current growing emission rates, the concentration would reach 700 ppm by the end of the twenty-first century. The continuing industrialization of China, recently joined by India, points to the possibility of even faster rises than these projections indicate.

If unpredictable, amplifying feedback loops are triggered, improbable catastrophes become more likely. The Gulf Stream flow could be halted, freezing Britain and Northern Europe. Droughts could wipe out the agriculture of Africa and Australia, as well as Asia, where millions depend on Himalayan melt water and monsoon rains. If the ice caps melt completely over the next centuries, seas could rise by 7 meters, devastating all coastal cities. Will the human response to widespread ecological disasters give rise to solidarity and collective action, such as the aid that came after the 2004 Asian Tsunami or to social breakdowns, as seen in New Orleans after 2005's Hurricane Katrina and in the Rwandan genocide?

Social and technical changes with the scale and speed required are not unprecedented. The displacement of horsepower by automobiles, for example, was meteoric. Production of vehicles in the United States increased from 8,000 in 1900 to nearly a million by 1912. Substantial regulation or differential taxation and subsidies would be indispensable to overcome short term profit motives and free riding dilemmas (where some evade their share of the cost of collective goods from which they benefit). Gains in auto efficiency in the 1980s, for example, were rapidly reversed by a new fashion for sport utility vehicles.

The debates that have emerged in the early twenty-first century have been related to responses, with different winners and losers, costs, benefits, dangers, and time scales for each response. Advocates of reduced energy consumption or increased efficiency, or energy generation by solar, wind, tidal, hydro, biomass, geothermal, nuclear, or clean coal and geo-sequestration, argue often cacophonously. Yet it seems probable that all these options are needed.

It will be essential for social and natural scientists to learn to cooperate in understanding and preempting the potentially catastrophic collision of nature and society. In order to accomplish this, market mechanisms; technological innovation; international, national, and local regulations; and cultural change will all be needed. Agents of change include governments, nongovernmental organizations, and public opinion, but the most likely front-runner might be sectors of capital seeking profit by retooling the energy and transport systems, while able to mobilize political enforcement.

SEE ALSO *Disaster Management; Greenhouse Effects; Science*

BIBLIOGRAPHY

Columbia University Earth Institute. 2005. Press release 28, April. http://www.earthinstitute.columbia.edu/news/2005/story04-28-05.html.

Cooper, Richard N., and Richard Layard. 2002. *What the Future Holds: Insights from Social Science.* Cambridge MA: MIT Press.

Diamond, Jared. 2005. *Collapse: How Societies Choose to Fail or Survive.* Camberwell, U.K.: Penguin, Allen Lane.

Dunlap, Riley H., Frederick H. Buttel, Peter H. Dickens, and August Gijswijt, eds. 2002, *Sociological Theory and the Environment: Classical Foundations, Contemporary Insights,* Lanham, MD: Rowman and Littlefield.

Flannery, Tim. 2006. *The Weather Makers.* Berkeley, CA: Grove Atlantic.

Kaser, G., et al. Mass Balance of Glaciers and Ice Caps: Consensus Estimates for 1961-2004. *Geophysical Research Letters,* Vol. 33. 2006.

Legget, Jeremy. 2000. *The Carbon War: Global Warming and the End of the Oil Era.* New York: Routledge.

Leggett, Jeremy. 2005. *Half Gone: Oil, Gas, Hot Air and the Global Energy Crisis.* London: Portobello.

Monbiot, George. 2006. *Heat: How to Stop the Planet Burning.* London: Allen Lane.

National Academy of Sciences. 2006. Press release 22, June. http://www8.nationalacademies.org/onpinews/newsitem.aspx?RecordID=11676.

Stehr, Nico. 2001. Economy and Ecology in an Era of Knowledge-Base Economies. *Current Sociology* 49(1) January: 67–90.

Zillman, John W. 2005. Uncertainty in the Science of Climate Change. In *Uncertainty and Climate Change: The Challenge for Policy,* Policy Paper 3. Canberra: Academy of the Social Sciences in Australia. http://www.assa.edu.au/publications/op/op22005.pdf.

Constance Lever-Tracy

GLOBALIZATION, ANTHROPOLOGICAL ASPECTS OF

In popular and scholarly discourse, the term *globalization* is widely used to put a name to the shape of the contemporary world. In the realms of advertising, policy making, politics, academia, and everyday talk, *globalization* refers to the sense that we are now living in a deeply and increasingly interconnected, mobile, and sped up world that is unprecedented, fueled by technological innovations and geopolitical and economic transformations. As a way to name our contemporary moment, the term *globalization* entered popular media and advertising in the early 1990s (Tsing 2000). After the fall of the Berlin Wall in 1989 and the breakup of the Soviet Union, enthusiasm accelerated for increasing international trade, deregulating national economies, privatizing the state, structurally adjusting developing-world economies, and increasing the transnationalization of corporations. *Globalization* was the new term that signaled this triumph of the capitalist market. As social science became increasingly focused on globalization, theories of globalization emphasized the transformations in labor, capital, state, and technology that have created a heightened sense of global interconnection or what has been called by the geographer David Harvey "time-space compression" (Harvey 1989).

As globalization has become a dominant narrative of our times, it also has become so for the discipline of anthropology, where it is both a specific object of methodological and theoretical reflection and one of the dominant horizons for a wide variety of scholarship. It became an increasingly central preoccupation at a time when the discipline was in crisis, both methodologically and theoretically. Anthropological attempts to grapple with globalization were crucial for reworking the anthropological concept of culture and for reconfiguring ethnographic methodology. In so doing, the anthropology of globalization has expanded and nuanced dominant theories of globalization while raising questions about its effects, scope, and reach.

Dominant theories of globalization are, more often than not, macrosociological, emphasizing large-scale perspectives on economic, political, and cultural transformations that are understood to either fuel or be the effects of globalization. One of the key contributions of the anthropology of globalization has been to emphasize the interconnection between what is called the "local" and the "global," emphasizing the interplay between large-scale global transformations and the realities of long-standing social and cultural worlds. An attention to this interplay has led to a focus on mapping and naming the large-scale shifts in culture and political economy that constitute globalization—something that characterizes much literature on globalization across the social sciences—but also a focus on people's everyday lived experiences and their transformations under conditions of globalization.

While the local-global framework of analysis shifted the macro, horizontal view of dominant theories of globalization, it also contributed to rethinking the conventional scales of ethnographic analysis. By the late 1980s the highly localized, isolated, and holistic frameworks that characterized ethnographic methodology, which is often divorced from attention to larger power structures and cultural interactions, had come under scrutiny. Whereas the anthropology of globalization emphasized the local in the face of assertions about the dominance and power of large-scale global processes, within the discipline itself contextualizing the local within the global was a key way anthropology began to shift its own frameworks for understanding the productions of culture and meaning within the contemporary world. This has led to new ways of thinking about ethnography beyond a focus on the purely place-based, local context, ones that emphasize multisited ethnography, ethnography across social scales, and ethnographies of networks, among others.

The framework of the local-global goes along with a central focus on the cultural dimensions of globalization. Dominant theories of globalization understand it as a primarily economic and political process. If these theories do pay attention to the cultural dimensions of globalization, it is often to argue that economic and political transformations that underlie globalization lead to cultural homogenization, often understood as "Americanization." This thesis is often rendered in terms of the cultural consequences of dominant U.S. commodity exports such as McDonald's and U.S. television programs. The anthropology of globalization, in particular the work of Arjun Appadurai, has argued that globalization is not a monolithic U.S. export but rather a "disjunctive," heterogeneous process with multiple centers of influence and interaction (Appadurai 1996). Further, culture is not simply derivative of economy and politics. The emphasis on people's experiences, lived realities, and what Appadurai calls the "social imaginary" has led to an emphasis on notions of agency and resistance in the face of large-scale global processes and transformations, ones that create cultural worlds that overlap but are not simply derivative of dominant capital and labor "flows." This has led to an emphasis on heterogeneous, multiple, and varied cultural responses to globalization, ones that emphasize the production of meaning within localized contexts.

An emphasis on the cultural dimensions of globalization has complicated theories of globalization focused on economy and politics, but it also has been central to transforming the anthropological concept of culture. The critique of ethnography in the late 1980s went hand in hand with a rethinking of the culture concept, which was also understood to be overly holistic, consensual, isolated, and divorced from power. Examining the productions of culture within a global framework that emphasizes everyday life as it interacts with the increasing importance of mass media and migration, among other factors, has challenged the ways anthropology has assumed the isomorphism between place and culture. The anthropology of globalization has paid significant attention to the deterritorialization of culture, which has led to a more mobile and dynamic sense of cultural production.

Anthropological scholarship on globalization is vast and varied. Ethnographies of labor, work, and capital have examined inequality and opportunity within free-trade zones and under new conditions of migration, focusing on issues of gender, generation, and class. A significant body of work has explored the experiences of migrants, particularly on identity formation and nationalism within various diasporic and transnational communities. Another important area of research has explored the impact of new consumer and commodity regimes, and significant attention has been paid to the effects and experiences of new media and other technologies on various axes of identity formation, including gender, youth, class, and nation. Increasing attention is also being paid to the effects of globalization on social movements, politics, and community organizing. Finally, significant work has examined the role of the state and transformations in nation-state formation in the context of globalization.

Although the conceptualization of "local-global" has been instrumental in challenging overly homogenizing and macrosociological views of globalization, it sometimes has produced an overly romanticized and simplistic view of the local as a space of resistance and authenticity. The anthropology of globalization continues to produce dynamic work that refines and complicates our sense of what constitutes the local, with attention to the intersection between history and culture at multiple scales that include the local, regional, and national as they crisscross each other in and through transnational interactions. A key challenge for the anthropology of globalization is in maintaining its assumption of the global as the space of homogeneity while arguing against this homogeneity through locating particularity and difference within the realm of the local. Contemporary work in the anthropology of globalization is complicating our sense of what constitutes the global, emphasizing the productions of locality within global capitalism and demonstrating the ways the global itself is not some abstract set of large-scale social processes; instead, it has its own particularities that can be tracked and named (Tsing 2000). Finally, anthropology continues to debate and explore what has been called the "abjection" of globalization (Ferguson 2002). The question of whether globalization is a good or a bad thing, particularly for the world's poor, has been a subject of popular and political struggles that has fueled a worldwide antiglobalization movement. Anthropology has emphasized both the cultural resilience and creativity of local populations under conditions of globalization while recognizing new conditions and structures of exploitation and vulnerability. Although some argue that there is no singular notion of globalization that can be termed "good" or "bad"—only an altered terrain of struggle and hope in different arenas—others seek to track, in multiple ways, structures of expanding opportunity or greater exploitation under conditions of globalization.

SEE ALSO *Americanism; Culture; Cyberspace; Empire; Geography; Internet; Neoliberalism; Sociology, Macro-; State, The; Technological Progress, Economic Growth; Technological Progress, Skill Bias; Telecommunications Industry*

BIBLIOGRAPHY

Appadurai, Arjun. 1996. *Modernity at Large: The Cultural Dimensions of Globalization.* Minneapolis: University of Minnesota Press.

Ferguson, James. 2002. Of Mimicry and Membership: Africans and the "New World Society." *Cultural Anthropology* 17 (4): 551–569.

Harvey, David. 1989. *The Condition of Postmodernity.* Cambridge, MA: Blackwell.

Tsing, Anna. 2000. The Global Situation. *Cultural Anthropology* 15 (3): 327–360.

Ritty Lukose

GLOBALIZATION, SOCIAL AND ECONOMIC ASPECTS OF

Since the 1970s and 1980s, the increasing intensity of international economic exchange, the rising prominence and influence of international organizations, the diffusion of cultural products across national boundaries, the spanning of social ties across international borders, and global environmental problems have all placed globalization prominently on the agenda of social science. The definition of *globalization* remains contested, but globalization can be conceptualized as a multidimensional process of international network formation. (Globalization could also be understood as an ideology, but this would more accurately be termed *globalism*.) The network metaphor clarifies the concept of globalization by highlighting both the *nodes* (e.g., people, organizations, and states) and the *relations* (e.g., trade, investment, organization membership, consumption, and migration) that are central to the globalization process. Thinking about globalization as multidimensional network formation is also a useful heuristic for understanding the established facts and unresolved debates surrounding the phenomenon. Moreover, it helps differentiate the multiple levels of analysis inherent in the process: globalization involves local, regional, national, international, and world levels of social life.

Below, this entry employs the network heuristic to discuss the central issues in the social science of globalization. The discussion begins by exploring relatively settled terrain: the multiple dimensions of globalization. From there, the entry moves to rockier ground: the questions of whether globalization is really new, how extensive it is, and precisely what effects it has.

FIVE DIMENSIONS OF GLOBALIZATION

Cross-national connections are created in the economic, political, cultural, social, and environmental domains. Although these dimensions necessarily overlap, it is analytically useful to distinguish them. Economic globalization results when corporations go multinational, either by selling their products in other countries, buying corporations located in foreign countries, or opening branch offices or subsidiaries outside their home country. Multinational corporate expansion, and the consumption of foreign-sourced goods and services, aggregate into exports, imports, and investment relations among national economies. Political globalization, or the formation of international connections among elected officials, bureaucrats, judges, social movement activists, and states, has also generated intense interest. Political globalization results in part through the formation of intergovernmental organizations (IGOs) like the United Nations and the World Trade Organization, and international nongovernmental organizations (INGOs) like the International Committee of the Red Cross. For instance, Anne-Marie Slaughter (2004) shows how political officials, especially regulators and judges, weave a web of global governance and "world order" through international ties formed by these organizations.

In the cultural field, the major world religions, media conglomerates, multinational corporations, and international tourism transmit and translate meaning (embedded in faith traditions, ideas, products, and practices) and symbols across international boundaries. The development of the international communication infrastructure (radio, satellites, intercontinental telecommunication cables) and the rapid expansion of communication technologies (Internet, cell phones, television) foster this process. Closely related is social globalization, or transnational connections formed by mobile individuals as they create social relationships. For instance, the density of international ties across countries grows as migrants maintain connections to their origin countries (e.g., through remitting money back home) while building new relationships in their destination countries (e.g., through work, community, and family).

Many identify the environment as a fifth dimension of globalization. If nations are the nodes in international networks, then environmental problems create connections by crossing borders: global warming, ozone depletion, and acid rain have all been defined by social movement activists and scientists as international problems that require international solutions. Indeed, environmental problems illustrate how the various dimensions of globalization sometimes reinforce one another: social movement activists bind together through international social movement organizations (social globalization) to spread awareness of environmental problems (cultural globalization) caused in part by multinational corporations (economic globalization), and urge the adoption of international agreements like the 1997 Kyoto Protocol on greenhouse gas emissions (political globalization).

WHEN AND WHERE IS GLOBALIZATION?

While the example of the Kyoto Protocol illustrates how the dimensions of globalization can cohere, intense international debate over the protocol raises questions about the pace and periodization of globalization, and, more fundamentally, about how "global" globalization is. Indeed, debate over the timing and extent of globalization animates much research. For instance, world-systems theorists such as Immanuel Wallerstein and Christopher Chase-Dunn trace the millennia-long evolution of international economic and political systems, and world-society theorists such as John Meyer and John Boli view social and cultural globalization through a long historical lens that looks back over a century. Social scientists have not reached consensus on when globalization in its various forms began, but there is an emerging consensus that the world has experienced a renewed and possibly distinct economic globalization since the mid-1970s (i.e., after the oil crises and the collapse of the Bretton Woods system of fixed exchange rates in 1973). Only during this period did the level of international trade surpass its previous peak in the early twentieth century. Thus, economic globalization may follow waves, with crests of integration followed by troughs of separation.

In the political dimension, there is also evidence that globalization substantially intensified in the latter half of the twentieth century. With the establishment of the United Nations and related IGOs (including the International Monetary Fund, World Bank Group, International Labour Organization, and World Health Organization), a global governance framework emerged. It has fostered the creation of thousands of intergovernmental and nongovernmental organizations that generate a network of international association (Boli and Thomas 1999). Key nodes in this network include regional organizations like the European Union (EU) that liberalize trade and create common policies among nations within negotiated geographical boundaries. The EU has progressed furthest toward the creation of a regional market and government, as it has allowed the free movement of people across borders, eliminated barriers to trade, created a supranational court, and established supranational policies. The EU, established as the European Economic Community in 1957, may have inspired regional integration efforts in other parts of the world, including Southeast Asia—the Association of Southeast Asian Nations (ASEAN, 1967); South America—Mercado Común del Sur (Southern Common Market or Mercosur, 1991); North America—the North American Free Trade Agreement (NAFTA, 1994); Central America—the Central American Common Market (CACM, 1960); and Africa—the Organization of African Unity (OAU, 1963). These organizations may transform world politics by changing how states interact and by generating new layers of policy and politics.

The accelerating economic liberalization and polity construction within geographical regions fuels the debate over where globalization actually happens (indeed, a large literature addresses whether regional integration creates "stepping-stones" or "stumbling blocks" to a fully integrated global system). Here again, the network heuristic helps. Some images of globalization depict a world where national nodes worldwide are increasingly interconnected without regard to place, while others allow for a more fragmented and uneven network where some nodes are linked much more densely than others. These contrasting images manifest in research that has shown, for instance, that Western Europe is much more densely intertwined in both the economic and political dimensions than nations in other world regions.

WHAT DOES GLOBALIZATION DO?

Setting aside controversies of period and place, social scientists blame or credit globalization for a panoply of social ills and goods, from economic inequality to economic growth, from political domination to democratization, from the decline of national sovereignty to the renaissance of the state, from social engagement to xenophobia, and from cultural homogenization to ethnic conflict. Meanwhile, others see a feeble globalization. Here, this entry reviews some of the key arguments for what globalization does.

Globalization, advanced partly by IGOs like the World Trade Organization and the International Monetary Fund that compel economic liberalization, has been the subject of vigorous debate about growing income gaps between rich and poor. The argument is that, in the name of international competitiveness, government revenue and

expenditures are cut, and industries are deregulated and privatized. Globalization is also blamed for lowering the wages of less-skilled workers by shifting manufacturing jobs to lower-wage countries, and by enlarging the pool of low-wage labor through immigration. In turn, in low-wage countries of the "Global South," globalization is blamed for proliferating sweatshops owned by multinational corporations, producing an underclass of nonunionized labor, and generating an exploitive transnational capitalist and entrepreneurial class. Moving from individuals to countries, globalization arguably benefits rich countries at the expense of poor countries, by further concentrating wealth in rich countries as profits are repatriated from the Global South to the Global North. On the other hand, much of the literature has been skeptical of the criticisms that have been leveled at globalization. Just to take one example of the potentially salutary effects of globalization, it has been argued that globalization actually reduces disparities among rich and poor countries in their overall levels of economic development, by spreading industrialization to poor countries.

Social scientists also disagree intensely over whether globalization brings about political convergence among states. There is evidence that states adopt increasingly similar policies in areas such as education, welfare, the environment, human rights, and population as they interact more with international organizations. International organizations, it is argued, create and diffuse policy models (or "scripts") to states, and states adopt these models, in part, to appear as legitimate members of a world society. This process may reflect the spread of modern, Western culture (e.g., individualism, universalism, rationalism, science, and progress) around the globe. These claims remain controversial, and some argue that international organizations serve national interests and as such have strictly limited independent influence. It is a major challenge to contemporary social science to bring some resolution to the varied, contradictory, and multivalent picture of globalization that has emerged.

SEE ALSO *International Nongovernmental Organizations (INGOs); Internet; Transfer Pricing; Transnationalism; World Trade Organization*

BIBLIOGRAPHY

Alderson, Arthur S., and Francois Nielsen. 2002. Globalization and the Great U-Turn: Income Inequality Trends in 16 OECD Countries. *American Journal of Sociology* 107: 1244–1299.

Boli, John, and George M. Thomas, eds. 1999. *Constructing World Culture: International Nongovernmental Organizations Since 1875.* Stanford, CA: Stanford University Press.

Boswell, Terry, and Christopher Chase-Dunn. 1999. *The Spiral of Capitalism and Socialism: Toward Global Democracy.* Boulder, CO: Lynne Rienner.

Brady, David, Jason Beckfield, and Martin Seeleib-Kaiser. 2005. Economic Globalization and the Welfare State in Affluent Democracies, 1975–2001. *American Sociological Review* 70: 921–948.

Chase-Dunn, Christopher, Yukio Kawano, and Benjamin D. Brewer. 2000. Trade Globalization Since 1795: Waves of Integration in the World System. *American Sociological Review* 65: 77–95.

Firebaugh, Glenn. 2003. *The New Geography of Global Income Inequality.* Cambridge, MA: Harvard University Press.

Guillén, Mauro F. 2001. Is Globalization Civilizing, Destructive, or Feeble? A Critique of Five Key Debates in the Social Science Literature. *Annual Review of Sociology* 27: 235–260.

Held, David, Anthony McGrew, David Goldblatt, and Jonathan Perraton. 1999. *Global Transformations: Politics, Economics, and Culture.* Stanford, CA: Stanford University Press.

Meyer, John W., John Boli, George Thomas, and Francisco Ramirez. 1997. World Society and the Nation-State. *American Journal of Sociology* 103: 144–181.

Slaughter, Anne-Marie. 2004. *A New World Order.* Princeton, NJ: Princeton University Press.

Jason Beckfield
David Brady

GOBINEAU, COMTE DE
1814–1882

Discredited today and largely ignored by his compatriots during his lifetime, Comte Joseph Arthur de Gobineau was nonetheless a key contributor to nineteenth-century race theories. Born in Ville-d'Avray, France, in 1814, he argued that racial difference was not only key to understanding the problems of history, but that it was the precondition of history. Comte de Gobineau posited two broad categories based on the shape of people's heads: *Aryan* or *dolichocephalic* populations, and *Alpine* or *brachycephalic* people. But it was his theory of racial mixing and degeneracy that won him admirers and detractors.

In the *Essai sur l'inégalité des races humaines* (Essay on the Inequality of the Human Races, 1853–1855), Gobineau claims the existence of three original, distinct human races: white, black, and yellow. Of these, white people, or Aryans, occupied the highest rank in a hierarchy of three. However, the "fusion" of these original races in history had, Gobineau argues, resulted in degeneracy and would eventually account for the decline of all civilization. The *Essai* and other writings, such as *La fleur d'or* (The Golden Flower) which was published posthumously in Germany in 1918 and in France in 1923, are thus

infused with apocalyptic inferences: despite notable exceptions of "golden" flowering, all human societies face decline, not because of corruption or the abandonment of religious ideals, or even because of bad government. In themselves, these factors—"poisonous blossoms"—cannot undermine a nation unless its people had already degenerated through mixing. The "*degenerate* man properly so called" is racially different from "the heroes of the great ages" who, for example, were to be found in the Roman Empire prior to its greatest successes. Despite his French nationality, Gobineau's Martinican Creole mother took him to Germany and had him educated in the gymnasium system, where he acquired his admiration for things Germanic. He came to believe that the Germanic race was heir to Roman purity, and he dedicated his *Essai* to George V (1819–1878), king of Hanover.

Gobineau's work built on the earlier racial typologies of the French naturalist Baron George de Cuvier (1769–1832), but it incorporated new developments in biology, archeology, and the emerging sciences of ethnology and physiology. It was also inflected by his royalism and Orientalism, the latter inspired by his years as a diplomat in Persia (1855–1858, 1862–1863).

Although a protégé of Alexis de Tocqueville (1805–1859), through whom he received his first diplomatic postings in Persia, Gobineau eschewed Enlightenment notions of intellectual equality or fraternity across different races. Tocqueville labeled Gobineau's views false and pernicious. In turn, Gobineau claimed that intellectual fraternity across races was the deluded product of miscegenation. This was the risk of imperialism. According to Gobineau, a "principle of death" emerges when a stronger people assumes ownership over conquered lands. Although growing into nationhood, such societies faced the danger of "mixing" their blood. Despite producing an initial strength, these newly mixed people would lack the power of their ancestors. Segregation was thus natural and manifested itself in a "spirit of isolation" that persists in peoples despite their mixed origins. In his broad-sweeping claims, he praises Arabs, Persians, Jews, Farsis, and Turks for being "repulsed" by the prospect of "crossing" blood.

Gobineau's elevation of a blond, blue-eyed Aryanism as the racial ideal found acceptance in Imperial Germany, attracting the admiration of Richard Wagner (1813–1883), Ludwig Schemann (1852–1938), and Chancellor Bernhard von Bulow (1849–1929). With von Bulow's support, Schemann founded the Gobineau Society in 1894. Members included Swiss jurist Johann Kaspar Bluntschli (1808–1881) and British-born political philosopher and proponent of the theory of a German master race, Houston Swiss Chamberlain (1855–1927). Under the sway of Gobineau's writings, Chamberlain argued for social practices that reflected the inequality of the races. Chamberlain, however, adjusted Gobineau's theory of degeneracy and predicted instead a growing "Aryan" strength. Gobineau's influence upon German National Socialism would eventually be incorporated, along with a racialized reading of Charles Darwin (1809–1882), into the pro-Nordic writings of Ludwig Woltmann (1871–1907). In the United States, Gobineau's *Essai* was translated by Swiss immigrant Henry Hotz, with an appendix by the proslavery physician and polygenist, Josiah Nott (1804–1873). Gobineau was not pleased with the American translation of his *Essai sur l'iné-galité des races humaines*, which he thought too selective. Where the original edition ran to over one thousand pages, the American translation was cut down to less than four hundred pages.

What Chamberlain, supporter Robert Knox, and others failed to acknowledge was Gobineau's insistence that the Aryan ideal had been overtaken by history. They also overlooked Gobineau's less than flattering condemnation of white Americans as "an assortment of the most degenerate races of olden-day Europe," as well as his resistance to American treatment of slaves and Native Americans, and his argument that racial mixing, and specifically black blood, had produced artistic mastery.

Within fifty years of his death, a systematic challenge to and rejection of Gobineau's work had emerged in the writings of Léopold Senghor (1906–2001), Aimé Césaire, and Léon Damas (1912–1978). Their formulation of the *negritude* movement in Paris in the 1930s to 1940s owed much to Senghor's opposition to Gobineau's pronouncements upon race mixing. Senghor's rethinking of Gobineau's work led to his influential theory of cultural *métissage*, an alternative energized multiplicity that incorporated an African past into a hybridized present in the Americas and Caribbean. Among the African diasporic writers influenced by *negritude* was Martinican essayist Suzanne Roussy Césaire (1915–1966). Her call to "cannibalize" and incorporate white Western culture into African diasporic culture reflected the strong cultural backlash against Gobineau's purist agenda.

SEE ALSO *Anthropology, Biological; Racism; Tocqueville, Alexis de*

BIBLIOGRAPHY

PRIMARY WORKS

Gobineau, Comte de, Arthur. 1856. *The Moral and Intellectual Diversity of Races, with Particular Reference to their Respective Influence in the Civil and Political History of Mankind*, ed. Henry Hotz. Philadelphia: Lippincott.

Gobineau, Comte de, Arthur. 1869. *Histoire des Perses*. Paris: Plon.

Gobineau, Comte de, Arthur. [1876] 1935. *Nouvelles Asiatiques*. Paris: Librairie academique Perrin.

Gobineau, Comte de, Arthur. [1915] 1999. *The Inequality of Human Races*. Trans. Adrian Collins. New York: Fertig.

Gobineau, Comte de, Arthur. 1924. *The Golden Flower*. Trans. Ben Ray Redman. New York: Putnam.

Gobineau, Comte de, Arthur. 1925. *Five Oriental Tales*. New York: Viking.

Gobineau, Comte de, Arthur. 1970. *Selected Political Writings*, ed. Michael D. Biddiss. New York: Harper.

Gobineau, Comte de, Arthur. 1988. *"Mademoiselle Irnois" and Other Stories*. Trans. and eds. Annette Smith and David Smith. Berkeley: University of California Press.

SECONDARY WORKS

Banton, Michael. 1998. *Racial Theories*. 2nd ed. Cambridge, U.K.: Cambridge University Press.

Bernasconi, Robert, ed. 2003. *Race and Racism in Continental Philosophy*. Bloomington: Indiana University Press.

Biddiss, Michael. 1970. *Father of Racist Ideology: The Social and Political Thought of Count Gobineau*. New York: Weybright and Talley.

Biddiss, Michael, ed. 1970. *Gobineau: Selected Political Writings*. London: Cape.

Blumenbach, Johan Friedrich. 2000. On the Natural Variety of Mankind. In *The Idea of Race*, eds. Robert Bernasconi and Tommy C. Lott. 27–37. Indianapolis, IN: Hackett.

Césaire, Suzanne Roussy. 1942. Misère d'une poèsie: John Antoine-Nau. *Tropiques* 4: 49–50. Reprinted in *Tropiques: Collection complete, 1941–1945*. 1978. Paris: Jean-Michel Place.

Césaire, Suzanne Roussy. 1943. Le surréalisme et nous. *Tropiques* 8–9.

Césaire, Suzanne Roussy. 1945. Le grand camou age. *Tropiques* 13–14.

Clinton, David. 2003. *Tocqueville, Lieber, and Bagehot: Liberalism Confronts the World*. New York: Palgrave Macmillan.

Gobineau, C. Serpeille de, ed. 1933. *Correspondence entre le Comte de Gobineau et le Comte de Prokesch-Osten, 1854–1876*. Paris: Plon.

Mitchell, Harvey. 2002. *America after Tocqueville: Democracy against Difference*. Cambridge, U.K.: Cambridge University Press.

Solomos, John, and Les Back, eds. 1999. *Theories of Race and Racism: A Reader*. London: Routledge.

Tocqueville, Alexis de. 1959. *The European Revolution and Correspondence with Gobineau*. Trans. and ed. John Lukacs. Garden City, NY: Doubleday.

Yvette Christiansë

GOD

SEE *Supreme Being*.

GÖDEL, KURT
SEE *Logic, Symbolic.*

GODWIN, WILLIAM
SEE *Anarchism.*

GOFFMAN, ERVING
1922–1983

Perhaps the most colorful of American sociologists, Erving Goffman, born in Alberta, Canada, led the turn to the micro-sociology of everyday life. He received a PhD in 1953 from the University of Chicago. Goffman's program began as a development of the work of the French sociologist Émile Durkheim, which set out to uncover the moral order that makes society possible. Where his predecessors, the British social anthropologists, analyzed religious rituals in tribal societies, Goffman examined the secular rituals of modern social interaction. He believed that such rituals construct the modern self, which he studied by examining the conditions in which it is threatened or blatantly manipulated. Goffman analyzed abnormal situations and institutions, including mental hospitals, confidence games, gambling, spying, and embarrassment in social encounters, to reveal the social conditions upholding conventional realities.

In *The Presentation of Self in Everyday Life* (1959), Goffman analyzed social life as a theater, divided into frontstage regions, where official definitions of reality are presented, and backstage regions, where dirty work is hidden and performances are prepared. Privileged occupations and social classes dominate frontstages and present idealized images of selves and institutions, whereas subordinated persons do much of their work backstage and are dominated by frontstage performers.

In *Asylums* (1961) and *Stigma* (1963), Goffman analyzed the extreme backstages of society, such as the schizophrenic wards of mental hospitals. Proposing the concept of "total institutions" for places where all aspects of life are subject to all-encompassing authority that allows no private backstages for the individual, Goffman argued that patients and other inmates engage in resistance through bizarre behavior aimed at supporting a sense of self beyond institutional controls. Thus, the official social processing of persons as deviant tends to promote still further deviance.

Mental illness, in Goffman's view, is not a characteristic of the individual so much as a social enactment, a spiral of violations of the ritual proprieties of everyday life. In *Behavior in Public Places* (1963) and *Relations in Public* (1971), Goffman made use of the violations exhibited by mental patients, as well as close ethnographic studies of pedestrian traffic and sociable gatherings, to develop a taxonomy of social situations and their tacit requirements and constraints. Unfocused interaction among persons in each others' physical presence involves tacit monitoring and signals indicating a respect for personal space. Focused interaction carries implications of memberships in groups, however small or temporary, and involves devices for entry and exit into the focus of attention, as well as for guarding boundaries of intimacy and warding off offenses that violate respect for the relationship. In "On Face-Work" (1955) and "The Nature of Deference and Demeanor" (1956), and in *Interaction Ritual* (1967), Goffman applied the theories of Durkheim and Alfred Radcliffe-Brown to the polite ceremonies of greetings, departures, and conversation. The everyday situation is constructed out of efforts at ritual enactment, and the modern individual self is elevated into a Durkheimian sacred object—much as the tribal gods were situationally re-created by the worship of them—through deference given in everyday rituals. There is therefore no essential self, but only an ongoing social construction.

Although Goffman did not contextualize his observations historically, his work casts light on the prestigeful pattern of the self in the late twentieth century. Goffman introduced the concept of "role-distance" (in *Encounters*, 1961), in which the actor claims superior sophistication by displaying signs of detachment from the demands of the social role. Games and entertainment, which take up an increasing portion of "postmodernity," were seen by Goffman as producing a sense of "fun" and excitement by requiring the actor to display engrossment in an activity bracketed from ordinary mundane reality, while also courting risks that allow a display of "coolness."

The ritualism of everyday encounters allows some actors to manipulate situations, engage in face-work contests to subtly embarrass others, or deceive them for criminal, business, or political purposes. These analyses have led some theorists to conclude that Goffman viewed the world as a Machiavellian contest of false reality-constructions. But Goffman argued that the social order is basically accommodative, and that situations involve ritual constraints that must be largely respected if any social reality is to be constructed at all. In *Strategic Interaction* (1969), he analyzed espionage and other self-interested manipulations of impressions, concluding that such behavior is limited by the inherent difficulties of sustaining complex deception. Social conflict and domination are possible only when placed upon the background of ritual solidarity enacted in most social encounters.

Goffman's later works, *Frame Analysis* (1974) and *Forms of Talk* (1981), take up the social construction of multiple social realities. Goffman adopted a moderate position, holding that complex social frames or definitions of reality are built up hierarchically, by bracketing or transforming activity at more basic levels of bodily action, human ecology, and social rituals. Highly laminated social meanings emerge situationally. For example, individuals (1) may make ironic backstage comments (2) during a rehearsal (3) for a commemoration of (4) a historical event, but if a fire breaks out during the rehearsal, all four levels are collapsed to the lowest level of framing, the fire. Language itself is built up through a hierarchy of framing devices. Talk is a move in the interaction ritual through which social membership is negotiated. It is built upon prior enactments and constrained by the framing or stage-work necessary to sustain or transform the current situational definition. Social reality, self, and language are all emergent phenomena, built out of the ritual constraints of the interaction order. Goffman died in 1983 in Philadelphia, Pennsylvania.

SEE ALSO *Behavior, Self-Constrained; Ethnography; Role Theory; Self-Concept; Self-Presentation; Stigma; Subject/Self*

BIBLIOGRAPHY

Burns, Tom. 1992. *Erving Goffman.* London: Routledge.

Collins, Randall. 2004. *Interaction Ritual Chains.* Princeton: Princeton University Press.

Goffman, Erving. 1959. *The Presentation of Self in Everyday Life.* Garden City, NY: Doubleday.

Goffman, Erving. 1967. *Interaction Ritual: Essays in Face-to-Face Behavior.* Chicago: Aldine.

Trevino, A. Javier, ed. 2003. *Goffman's Legacy.* New York: Rowman and Littlefield.

Winkin, Yves. 1988. *Erving Goffman: Les Moments et leurs homes.* Paris: Minuit.

Randall Collins

GOING NATIVE

The phenomenon of *going native* is one of the less commonly known outgrowths of European colonialism. It emerged as a result of the meeting of European and indigenous cultures and drew its strength from the perceived differences between those cultures. The term refers to the desire of non-aboriginals to identify with and immerse themselves in native culture.

In North America, cultural conversions of this type have taken a variety of forms. During the sixteenth and seventeenth centuries, Europeans intent on survival in an unfamiliar terrain were wise to adopt aspects of aboriginal lifestyles in matters ranging from food and clothing to language and transportation. During military conflicts, colonialists taken captive by aboriginal groups frequently recovered from their initial terror and were quite happily absorbed into native societies, following long-standing practice within aboriginal communities.

As an era of exploration gave way to one of permanent white settlement and aboriginal marginalization between the late-eighteenth and early-nineteenth centuries, incidents of going native took different and, generally, more limited forms. Most commonly, the desire to go native now manifested as an interest in "playing Indian." Those who played Indian did not seek the permanent adoption of a new culture, but rather borrowed elements of native cultures to serve specific social, cultural, and sometimes political ends. For instance, during the American Revolutionary War of the 1770s, colonials borrowed aboriginal imagery (and sometimes dress) to help identify themselves with the aboriginal spirit of independence and to fashion a national identity distinct from that of their European cousins. Into the nineteenth century, members of fraternal orders adopted aboriginal dress for their initiation rituals, and native metaphors and imagery for the nationalist literature they crafted. By the early twentieth century, playing Indian was deemed especially appropriate for children. As Boy Scouts, Girl Guides, and summer campers, children were invited to emulate aboriginal lifestyles during afternoons of woodcraft, evenings of Indian council ring, and weeklong canoe trips.

By the twentieth century, only a few took their interest in playing Indian beyond the realm of leisure-time pursuits. Anthropologists, for one, occasionally lost themselves, wittingly or otherwise, in the indigenous cultures they studied. More sensationally, a few rare individuals consciously adopted new identities, attempting, frequently with success, to pass themselves off as aboriginal to white society. Naturalist and early conservationist Grey Owl and journalist and war hero Buffalo Child Long Lance were just two who reinvented themselves as Indians, gaining significant public attention in the 1930s.

As a rule, those who played Indian after the mid-nineteenth century had more limited understandings of the indigenous cultures they sought to embrace than those who went native in earlier centuries. Typically, aboriginal people were understood in simplistic and frequently inaccurate ways. Above all, to white society, native peoples symbolized innocence, connection to nature, and immersion in the simple life that white society had left behind. Those troubled by the pace and direction of modern cultural change found in this invented Indian a comforting symbol of simpler days. Even into the late twentieth century, the desire for this comfort shaped aspects of the counterculture of the 1960s and the New Age spirituality of the 1980s.

These modern forms of going native, then, had less to do with understanding or honoring native cultures and more to do with filling the social, cultural, and psychic needs of white society. By playing Indian, white North Americans, whether as revolutionaries, as members of fraternal orders, or as campers, distanced themselves from, and also eased their guilt about, the realities of colonial conquest. At the same time, they bolstered their own sense of national identity and attempted to redeem the racial category of whiteness.

Similar incidents of going native have occurred elsewhere around the world as colonialists interacted with indigenous peoples of other regions, including North Africa, the South Pacific, and the Near and Middle East. While the two cultures interacting may have differed, the fundamental dynamic was similar to the process found in North America. Members of dominant and usually colonizing cultures frequently became enamored with indigenous "others" and desirous of immersing themselves in their indigenous cultures. Ultimately, these colonial intruders moved from the belief that originally justified colonization—namely, that indigenous cultures were inferior—to one that romanticized those same cultures as providing the exotic and intense experience their own societies discouraged.

SEE ALSO *Anthropology; Travel and Travel Writing*

BIBLIOGRAPHY

Axtell, James. 1975. The White Indians of North America. *William and Mary Quarterly* 32: 55–88.

Deloria, Philip J. 1998. *Playing Indian.* New Haven, CT, and London: Yale University Press.

Sharon Wall

GOLD

Gold is a precious metal. Its several qualities have made it valuable throughout history. It is an attractive color (yellow), bright, malleable, and workable in various forms. It is also long-lasting and tough. All these properties have made it the metal of choice for decoration and art objects. Gold has also been the standard of wealth for seven thousand years, dating from the time of the ancient civilizations of Egypt and Mesopotamia. More recently, gold has become the standard of currencies.

Gold is found across a wide range of the earth's landscape, but its accumulation in large quantities dates from the era of European explorations that began in the middle of the fifteenth century. Ventures to the New World opened new chapters in the history of gold. The first of these new stages was the Spanish conquest of the Americas with the accompanying destruction of the Aztec and Incan civilizations. Within a generation, these expeditions of plunder had produced an outpouring of gold from the New World that astonished the Old and led to endless expeditions of discovery and conquest, all in search of the legendary golden city known as El Dorado. Over the seventeenth and eighteenth centuries, the gold flowing out of the South American mines continued to dominate world production. As the nineteenth century unfolded, Russia became the leading producer. By 1847 Russia was the source of about three-fifths of the gold mined annually in the world.

The second great era of gold production was associated with major discoveries in California and Australia in the middle of the nineteenth century. In addition to the large quantities of gold harvested, these discoveries led to a new departure in the history of gold. Heretofore, gold discoveries and the gold mined from them had been a monopoly of the state. California and Australia represented a dramatic change in the sense that these mid-nineteenth century bonanzas belonged to any individual who could stake a claim. In this fashion, the gold passed directly into the hands of private citizens (or noncitizens, as was frequently the case). California's gold production moved rapidly from $10 million in 1849 to $80 million in 1851, thereafter settling at about $40 million annually. California almost immediately produced half the world's supply. Within the first five years, California produced as much gold as the Roman Empire had taken from the mines in northern Spain in half a century. The yields in Australia were almost as great. The Australian gold rush, like that of California, had a short life. After a dozen years, gold mining became industrialized. Still, the returns were remarkable. In the quarter century from 1850 to 1875, more gold was produced than in all the years since 1492, almost all of it in California and Australia.

The gold discoveries and the availability of these riches to anyone led to a remarkable rise in the numbers of miners. In California, the numbers rose from perhaps 5,000 in 1848 to 125,000 in 1851. This harvesting of gold on such a scale changed California from an isolated pastoral community into the most cosmopolitan place in the world. By 1852 its population had passed 250,000 people. California now became a pioneer in new patterns of rapid and intense migration associated with mining. These would include the astonishing rise of towns (and sometimes cities), the recruitment and use of labor forces, and shifts in capital and labor to remote areas all over the world. Such phenomena appeared first in California and Australia. The arrival of overseas Chinese, Irish, and other northern European immigrants in the gold fields created a diverse population and led to later racial strife. In both Australia and the mining camps of the American West, the Chinese were a particular target. Everywhere, whatever the racial and ethnic composition, mining camps were intensely male. Only gradually did the emerging towns come to include women and children.

At the same time, the techniques used to harvest the gold changed in decisive ways. Mining in California began with picks, pans, and shovels, as individuals and small companies washed gold from mountain streams. Within a few short years, gold mining had progressed to damming (then mining dry river beds), to hydraulic mining (using water streams to wash away hills), and to underground mining. What had begun as the work of individual miners had within a dozen years become an extension of industrial techniques, with wage laborers deep underground, complex processing machinery and plants above ground, and a stock market that enabled absentee investors to speculate.

These bonanzas of the 1850s enormously increased the world's supply of gold. The gold reserves in the Bank of England almost doubled between 1848 and 1852; the gold inventory of the Bank of France increased seven times. Thus, the impact of the Californian and Australian gold rushes was quickly reflected in the gold reserves of Britain, France, and other powerful European nations. Great wealth also accrued to individuals and companies of various sizes. This increase led to extended debate within financial circles about the role of gold in the currencies of individual nations and the significance of gold as a worldwide standard.

The third great increase in the world's supply was associated with gold discoveries in Alaska at the close of the nineteenth century and in South Africa at the opening of the twentieth century. The Alaskan strikes began as a reprise of the Californian dream of riches for individuals and small groups, then rapidly shifted to production by well-financed companies with the latest equipment, all within the context of a climate that severely limited the mining season. In South Africa, the gold discoveries laid the basis of some of the more remarkable mineral fortunes in the world. They also established a labor system in which thousands of black Africans labored deep in the mines for the benefit of a few white-owned South African companies. The increase in gold production in these years was notably aided by a new chemical process, the use of cyanide to recover gold from low-grade ores.

The flooding of gold into Europe at the opening of the sixteenth century and in the middle of the nineteenth century raised continuing questions about national currencies. Over the course of the nineteenth century, most major Western nations went on the gold standard; that is

to say, their national currency acquired a fixed relation to gold and was supposedly freely convertible into gold at that price. England was the first to adopt the gold standard, in 1821. France, Germany, Spain, and the United States followed in the 1870s. The gold standard spread across Europe, but ended with the outbreak of war in 1914. It was reinstituted in 1928. As national economies grew, nations without sufficient gold reserves (the majority of nations) supplemented their currency reserves with U.S. dollars or British pounds, thought to be the most stable of the world's currencies. With the onset of the Great Depression, the gold standard collapsed again. Although it was restored after the war, the dominance of the U.S currency (the dollar) and dwindling gold reserves led to the gold standard's abandonment in 1971.

SEE ALSO *Gold Industry*

BIBLIOGRAPHY

Green, Timothy. 1973. *The World of Gold Today.* Rev. ed. New York: Walker & Company.

Hawtrey, R. G. 1948. *The Gold Standard in Theory and Practice.* 5th ed. London: Longmans.

Jastrom, Roy W. 1977. *The Gold Constant: The English and American Experience, 1560–1976.* New York: John Wiley & Sons.

Kettell, Brian. 1982. *Gold.* Cambridge, MA: Ballinger Press.

Rohrbough, Malcolm. 1997. *Days of Gold: The California Gold Rush and the American Nation.* Berkeley: University of California Press.

Vilar, Pierre. 1976. *A History of Gold and Money, 1450–1920.* Trans. Judith White. London: Atlantic Highlands Press.

Malcolm Rohrbough

GOLD, GOD, AND GLORY

Historians use a standard shorthand, "Gold, God, and Glory," to describe the motives generating the overseas exploration, expansion, and conquests that allowed various European countries to rise to world power between 1400 and 1750. "Gold" refers to the search for material gain through acquiring and selling Asian spices, African slaves, American metals, and other resources. As merchants gained influence in late-medieval western Europe, they convinced their governments to establish a direct connection to the lucrative Asian trade, leading to the first European voyages of discovery in the 1400s. "God" refers to the militant crusading and missionary traditions of Christianity, characterized in part by rivalry with Islam and hatred of non-Christian religions. "Glory" alludes to the competition between monarchies. Some kings sought to establish their claims to newly contacted territories so as to strengthen their position in European politics and increase their power at the expense of the landowning nobility. They also embraced the ideology of mercantilism, which held that governments and large private companies should cooperate to increase the state's wealth by increasing the reserves of precious metals. Motivated by these three aims, several western European peoples gained control or influence over widening segments of the globe during the Early Modern Era. By 1914 Europeans dominated much of the world politically and economically.

The Spanish and Portuguese were pioneers in the new era of overseas expeditions because they had a favorable geographic location facing the Atlantic and North Africa, a maritime tradition of deep sea fishing, an aggressive Christian crusading tradition, and possession of the best ships and navigation techniques in Europe by the 1400s. They were also motivated by the desire to circumnavigate the Venetian domination of Afro-Asian trade into Europe. Combining Chinese and Arab technologies with local inventions, the Portuguese, Spanish, and other Europeans built better ships to sail the rough Atlantic and learned how to mount weapons on ships, increasing their advantage at sea. The Spanish and Portuguese, using artillery, naval cannon, and muskets, could now conquer or control large territories in the Americas, Africa, and Asia, whose people lacked guns. The English were building the most maneuverable ships and the best iron cannon by the late 1500s. By the 1700s European land and sea weapons greatly outclassed those of once militarily powerful China, India, Persia, and Ottoman Turkey.

The intense competition between major European powers led to increased exploration, the building of trade networks, and a scramble for colonies—subject territories where Europeans ruled and directly controlled economic production and trade. In the later 1400s the Portuguese began direct encounters with the peoples of coastal West and Central Africa. By 1500 Portuguese explorers had opened a new era of exploration by entering the Indian Ocean, reaching East Africa, and then sailing to India. Soon, they seized several key Asian ports. Meanwhile Spanish fleets led by a Genoese mariner, Christopher Columbus, discovered that a huge landmass to the west, soon to be named America, lay between Europe and East Asia. Columbus had hoped to find the sea route to the silk- and spice-rich lands of China and Southeast Asia, and to introduce Christianity into these distant realms. Both the Portuguese and Spanish promised the pope to evangelize and colonize the "heathen" peoples they encountered.

By the later 1500s the Spanish had explored large regions of the Americas and conquered many of its peo-

ples, including the great Inca and Aztec empires, and the Portuguese had established footholds in Brazil. Diseases brought from the Eastern Hemisphere, especially smallpox, killed off some 90 percent of the American population in the 1500s and 1600s, facilitating colonization. The only practical sea route to Asia via the Americas was finally discovered in 1520, by a Spanish expedition across the Pacific led by Ferdinand Magellan. After sponsoring their own explorations of the Americas, England, France, and Holland also colonized eastern North America and some Caribbean islands, and, like the Portuguese and Spanish, sent emigrants and Christian missionaries to what they called "the New World."

Various European states established colonies or outposts in several African regions and carried increasing numbers of enslaved Africans to the Americas to work on plantations growing cash crops, such as sugar, cotton, and coffee, for European consumption. In the sixteenth and seventeenth centuries the Dutch colonized parts of Indonesia, including Java and the Spice islands, and the Spanish conquered and Christianized the Philippines. The English and French became active in Asia in the 1600s. American minerals supported a great expansion of the European economy and allowed Europeans to buy into the rich Asian trade, especially of goods from China. These conquests and economic activities enabled the transfer of vast resources to Europe, especially silver, gold, sugar, coffee, and spices.

Thanks to exploration and conquest resulting from the quest for "Gold, God, and Glory," Europeans gradually brought various peoples into their economic and political sphere, laying the foundations for Western global dominance. Undergoing a profound economic, intellectual, and political transition, western Europeans left many of their medieval beliefs and institutions behind, and between 1750 and 1914 introduced even more profound changes in the world, including capitalism, industrialization, and the building of great Western empires in Asia and Africa.

SEE ALSO *Gold; Missionaries; Slave Trade*

BIBLIOGRAPHY

Abernethy, David B. 2002. *The Dynamics of Global Dominance: European Overseas Empires, 1415–1980.* New Haven, CT: Yale University Press.

Boorstin, Daniel J. 1983. *The Discoverers.* New York: Vintage.

Marks, Robert B. 2007. *The Origins of the Modern World.* 2nd ed. Lanham, MD: Rowman and Littlefield.

Craig A. Lockard

GOLD INDUSTRY

The world gold industry is a truly unique industry. It consists of miners, refiners, traders, and hoarders. Understanding the uniqueness of the industry begins with knowing that physical gold is virtually indestructible. That is, it does not rust, corrode, or otherwise break down like other metals. The upshot of this physical quality is that every ounce of gold ever mined in the approximately seven thousand years that humans have sought gold is still around.

Identifiable aboveground gold stocks at the end of 2003 were estimated at 150,500 metric tons or 4.8 billion ounces. A majority of these stocks, 63 percent, are held in the form of fabricated products, primarily jewelry, and 35 percent is held in the form of bullion, which is gold refined to 99.99 percent (24 carat) purity. The largest part of the 52,600 tons of bullion stocks, or 29,200 tons, is held by Western central banks. The balance of bullion stocks is held by private individuals (Klapwijk et al. 2004, p. 54). A cubic foot of gold weighs approximately one-half a (short) ton (Mohide 1981); accordingly, world identifiable aboveground stocks, if brought together, would form a cube approximately 70 feet per side. It is an indication of how scarce gold is that the entire world's supply could be stored in a modestly sized building.

Annual mine production from 1994 to 2003 ranged between 2,300 and 2,600 metric tons (74 to 84 million ounces). Because of the large aboveground stocks, annual mine supply only increases total supply by about 1.7 percent. The largest-producing countries during this period were South Africa, the United States, and Australia. The mine production of these countries declined slightly in the latter years of this period as a result of declining ore grades, higher production costs, and low gold prices. However, their production decline was compensated by rising production out of Latin America and Asia, most notably China and Indonesia.

Gold is mined at thousands of locations on all continents except Antarctica. *Placer* mining involves sifting and washing sands and gravels to isolate visible gold. *Lode* or *hardrock* mining involves crushing rock or soils containing gold and chemically processing the material to extract the gold. The chemical process used prior to the twentieth century was *amalgamation*, which involves applying mercury to the ore. The gold adheres to the mercury and can then be separated by boiling off the mercury. The amalgamation process is not only inefficient, recovering only about one-half to two-thirds of the gold, but it also does serious environmental damage if the mercury is not contained. Mercury is poisonous and does not break down in the environment. Numerous sites around the world where amalgamation is or was used remain seriously contaminated with mercury.

In the late nineteenth century, a more efficient method of processing lode ore was developed using a dilute cyanide solution to dissolve gold from crushed ore. Cyanide is also poisonous but is easier to contain and will break down in the environment over time. Recovery rates for the cyanide process range from around 70 percent for heap-leach processing (rinsing roughly crushed ore on large plastic-lined pads) to 95 percent for milling more finely ground ore in containment vessels. Depending upon the price, these higher recovery rates allow for economic recovery of gold from ores with as little as 0.01 ounces per ton of material processed—gold so fine that it can only be seen under a microscope.

Gold is mined by both "formal" and "informal" sectors. The formal sector involves sometimes large, publicly traded companies operating under the scrutiny of government environmental, financial, and other regulators. The formal sector accounts for the vast majority of world gold production. The five largest producers are Newmont Mining (United States), AngloGold (South Africa), Barrick Gold (Canada), Gold Fields Limited (South Africa), and Placer Dome (Canada). There are, however, thousands of other companies in the formal sector that explore for, mine, and trade in mining properties.

Perhaps the most controversial aspect of the gold industry is the environmental impact of gold mining and processing. Environmental regulation of the mining industry typically involves a permit process in which operators develop and get government approval of a mine and reclamation plan. These plans specify how an operator will extract and process ore, how they will store waste materials, and how they will reclaim disturbed areas. Presumably, government approval is only provided if these plans are in compliance with environmental regulations, but problematic issues include whether these regulations are adequate, whether government oversight and enforcement are adequate, and the fact that, despite the best-laid plans, accidents happen.

The informal mining sector consists of many thousands of individuals who mine gold without formal property rights or mining claims, and without the oversight of government regulators. Perhaps the most famous of the informal or "artisanal" miners are the *garimpeiros* of Brazil, but significant artisanal mining takes place in many other lesser-developed countries. There were an estimated eleven to thirteen million artisanal miners worldwide in 1999 (Viega and Hinton 2002). Artisanal mining involves both placer and lode mining and generally uses amalgamation for processing. The use of mercury in artisanal mining results in significant public health and environmental problems.

Artisanal miners typically sell their gold in local markets, where it is manufactured into jewelry. Operators in the formal sector produce an intermediate product called *doré* whose gold content will depend upon the metallic composition of the ore. Gold frequently occurs with other metals, such as silver, arsenic, and copper, so the doré must be sent to a refinery, where it will be melted down and the metals separated. Refineries on every continent except Antarctica produce various refined products ranging from bullion bars, which are 24 carat in purity, to lower-carat alloys (18, 14, 10 carat, etc.) used in fabricating jewelry, electronics, dental fillings, and other items. These lower-carat products (as well as some 24-carat items) are sold for fabrication in the form of wire, beads, sheets, powder, and so on. By far the largest fabrication use of gold is jewelry. In 2003 jewelry fabrication accounted for 61 percent of total demand for gold, a total of 2,533 tons out of 4,142 tons sold on organized exchanges (Klapwijk et al. 2004, p. 7).

Labor market conditions in the gold industry vary greatly around the world. In South Africa and other less-developed countries, large mines can employ tens of thousands of laborers working deep underground, sometimes as much as 8,000 feet below the surface, under what most would consider harsh conditions. In contrast, in the United States most gold production comes from open-pit operations where working conditions are much better and far less dangerous. U.S. mine workers are required to undergo safety training before they are employed and periodic refresher courses thereafter, and state and federal governments conduct routine safety inspections. In general, hardrock mining is far safer than coal mining because the latter involves cutting into a combustible material, which results in explosions.

The degree of unionization of mine workforces also varies greatly around the world. South Africa's mine workers are unionized, while in the United States most hardrock mine workers are not unionized. However, some categories of tradespeople who work at U.S. gold mines under contract, such as electricians, pipe fitters, and masons, tend to be unionized.

Labor market conditions in the informal sector are far worse than in the formal sector, primarily because of the widespread use of mercury amalgamation. Artisanal mining is generally unregulated and the use of mercury poses a significant health risk to the miners, to others, and to the environment.

Refiners also play an important role in the functioning of bullion markets by guaranteeing the purity of gold used in transactions. For historic reasons, the world bullion trade primarily involves countries in the Middle East and the Indian subcontinent as importers and European refiners as exporters through the London market. The demand side of the Asian bullion market is historically rooted in a variety of causes, some cultural, such as the giving of dowries in Muslim and Hindu cultures. But other factors, such as the historic political and financial instability of the region, play a role. In these cultures, bullion continues to play the traditional role of a store of wealth and a medium of exchange.

In Western cultures, the bullion trade arose from the historic monetary uses of gold. Most countries minted gold coin, which served as a medium of exchange. However, as fractional reserve banking gained acceptance in the nineteenth century, the use of bullion coin in trade diminished in favor of paper money issued by private banks that held bullion and bullion coin in reserve to back the paper money. At the same time, Western governments started issuing *fiat money*—paper legal tender backed by a fixed quantity of bullion—and maintained bullion reserves, creating the *gold standard* for domestic and international financial transactions. This system proved to be unstable, was modified several times during the twentieth century, and was essentially ended when the United States went off the gold standard in 1971 by refusing to redeem dollars with gold. In 2006 the U.S. central bank held approximately 8,600 tons of gold bullion at various locations but primarily at Fort Knox, Kentucky, and engaged in little if any bullion trading.

In spite of these U.S. actions, European central banks maintained various quantities of bullion stocks for traditional foreign exchange stabilization purposes and continued to be active traders in bullion markets. With the creation of the single European currency in 2000, a significant portion of these bullion stocks was transferred to the newly created European Central Bank, which uses bullion in a similar manner as the individual national banks did when they managed currencies. This changing role of gold in the monetary system has led most European banks to liquidate significant portions of their holdings, primarily shifting bullion stocks into private ownership in Asia.

Even with these significant changes in the gold market, it still works in a traditional and somewhat secretive way. The world price is set twice daily by a committee in London representing major bullion banks, including the Bank of England. In the morning the committee makes its *a.m. fix*, setting a price at which the banks are willing to buy or sell any quantity of gold. The process is repeated in the afternoon to determine the *p.m. fix*. Many contracts use the p.m. fix as the basis for transactions involving both doré and refined products. Prices in various local markets around the world will not vary significantly from the London price because gold bullion can be loaded on an airplane and shipped to or from London for a few pennies on the ounce. Gold is also traded actively in options and futures markets around the world, where a gold market is open twenty-two hours out of the twenty-four-hour day.

SEE ALSO *Colonialism; Gold; Gold, God, and Glory; Imperialism; Industry; Mining Industry; Money; Reserves, Foreign*

BIBLIOGRAPHY

Klapwijk, Philip, et al. 2004. *Gold.* London: Gold Fields Mineral Services.

Mohide, Thomas Patrick. 1981. *Gold.* Toronto, Ont.: Ministry of Natural Resources.

Viega, Marcello, and Jennifer Hinton. 2002. Abandoned Artisanal Gold Mines in the Brazilian Amazon: A Legacy of Mercury Pollution. *Natural Resources Forum* 26 (1): 13–24.

John L. Dobra

GOLD STANDARD

Gold has been a medium of exchange for a very long time. Although until the late nineteenth century gold had to compete with silver as the preferred standard unit of account in international financial transactions, gold has been used to measure wealth since antiquity. In the sixteenth and seventeenth centuries, following the discovery of rich gold mines in the Americas, the prevailing economic theory, mercantilism, recommended the pursuit of restrictive trade policies designed to discourage the importation of foreign goods and to encourage the exportation of domestic goods so as to increase the stock of precious metals, and of gold in particular, in the treasuries of the most important European kingdoms. But the gold standard refers to a more recent and specific phase in monetary history—a phase that is now past, and probably irrevocably so. Most contemporary economics textbooks pay only scant attention to it (Kimball 2005). A few economists, however, still advocate a return to the practices that defined the gold standard for reasons that are discussed further below.

Under the gold standard, as it began to take shape in the 1870s, currencies were backed by gold exclusively. Within a country, paper money could be redeemed for a guaranteed amount of gold and, internationally, fixed exchange rates determined the quantities of gold that central banks could use to clear international balance of payment accounts. In practice, however, this strict principle allowed for a limited degree of flexibility allowing the central banks of the countries that adhered to the gold standard regime to engage in a variety of manipulations (e.g., convertibility was severely limited in many of the less powerful countries). Great Britain was almost continually on a gold standard from the 1750s until 1913, with the exception of about two decades (1798 to 1821) when the

Napoleonic wars and their aftermath forced the Bank of England to issue nonconvertible paper currency. Most of the other powers, however, including the United States, based their currencies on both gold and silver until the 1870s. (In fact, the word for silver in French also means money.) But by the 1870s because the price of silver had become too unstable, most European powers and the United States chose to hold only gold in their bank reserves, and to officially establish the convertibility of their currencies in gold only. By the 1890s a process of gold standardization had occurred: Most countries were by then part of an international financial regime based on a fixed exchange rate for gold.

The transition to the gold standard was not entirely smooth. There were political interests that opposed it. In the United States, for example, farmers in the Midwest continued to support a return to bimetallism for about two decades after the United States (unofficially) adopted the gold standard in 1879, in part because they felt that the rules of the gold standard made it more difficult for them to obtain credit and made them more dependent on what they perceived as the whims of the "eastern banks," impersonated as the wicked Witch of the East in L. Frank Baum's fairy tale *The Wizard of Oz.* In fact, the United States did not legally switch to the gold standard until 1900 (Littlefield 1964).

BEFORE WORLD WAR I

The pre–World War I gold standard worked very efficiently as a means to maintain price stability. Gold, and to a lesser extent British pounds, flowed between countries to compensate for trade surpluses and deficits. In theory, the system functioned automatically: If the real exchange rate for a given currency was above the nominal exchange rate in gold, exports suffered and imports increased, creating a balance of payments deficit; external creditors asked to be paid in gold and the resulting outflow of gold had the effect of lowering domestic prices, thereby stimulating exports and discouraging imports and eventually bringing down the real exchange rate nearer to, or even below, the nominal rate, and the pendulum swung in the other direction. The monetary authorities were expected to take appropriate measures to facilitate this process: raising the bank rate, which, in turn, led to rising interest rates, in order to decrease investments and reinforce the deflationary effect of an outflow of gold, while at the same time ensuring that the outflow of gold would not continue indefinitely, or lowering it to reinforce the inflationary effects of an inflow of gold, but also thereby preparing the ground for a reduction in that inflow. That these measures often had a deflationary effect was of little concern at a time when governments were not held responsible for unemployment. The effectiveness of the system was reinforced by the fact that investors, often anticipating the measures that monetary authorities were about to adopt, moved their funds from country to country, thereby bringing about the equilibrium that these measures would have reestablished and diminishing at the same time the need for such measures.

Already in the years immediately preceding World War I there were signs of tension in the system. The outbreak of the war led to its collapse. The interwar years were much more troubled as far as the international monetary system is concerned. Although most nations that had suspended convertibility into gold reinstituted it in the 1920s, it never functioned as well as it had before the war and by 1937 it had been abandoned by all countries. (Germany had done so in 1931, Britain in 1933, and the United States in 1933; France and Japan held on until 1936.) There is no complete agreement on the question of whether the demise of the gold standard was brought about by the Great Depression or whether the gold standard was itself a major cause of the severity of the depression. The latter thesis points to the fact that the United States and France, two countries with trade surpluses, together held more than half of the gold while also pursuing deflationary policies, which led to a contraction of the money supplies in much of the rest of the world that made it impossible to initiate expansionary programs in timely fashion to deal with the onset of the depression (Bordo 1993; Eichengreen 1992). But what is certain is that at the end of World War II, the gold standard was widely regarded as having been a failure.

THE BRETTON WOODS AGREEMENT

The participants in the 1944 conference held in Bretton Woods, New Hampshire, were seeking to establish an international system that would retain the stability and predictability of the pre–World War I gold standard but would not cause the rigidities that many then suspected had significantly contributed to the worsening of the worldwide 1930s depression. The agreement they adopted resulted in a system that was still, at least indirectly, based on gold, although by this time only the U.S. dollar was directly convertible into gold, and only among central banks. However, all signatories to the Bretton Woods Agreement were committed to maintain something approximating fixed rates of exchange in relation to the dollar, but with enough flexibility to allow them to manage their economies so as to produce full employment. Hence dollars rather than gold became the main components of the reserves of most central banks. The heyday of that system from the mid-1950s to the mid-1960s coincided with—and to an extent that is difficult to measure, helped to bring about—a period of exceptional economic growth (especially in western Europe and Japan) and expanding international trade. But it also placed severe constraints on the United States. By 1971 the United States had definitely ceased to guarantee the convertibility of the dollar. Since that date gold has been demonetized, even though the central banks of many countries continue to hold more or less significant stocks of gold. Floating rates are now the rule, with the exception of some countries that have more or less permanently pegged their currencies to a stronger one or others, such as the euro zone, that have established a monetary union.

A return to something like the gold standard has been advocated by some economists, notably those associated with the school of thought known as Austrian economics, so named because it can trace its roots to the writings of prominent Austrian economists such as Carl Menger. Adherents of Austrian economics have very little confidence in the ability of governments and central banks to effectively guide the course of economic events. It is, therefore, the self-regulating nature of the old gold standard that leads them to advocate revisiting this concept. They usually recommend the creation of a system in which the central banks would be forced to "play by the rules," if necessary by privatizing these banks. Although this would certainly offer strong guarantees against inflation, the need for such a system appears less compelling in the early twenty-first century than it did in the 1970s and 1980s, when inflation was much more of threat than it has been since then. There is very little political support in the world for such a reform.

SEE ALSO *Balance of Payments; Central Banks; Currency; Exchange Rates; Gold; Gold Industry; Inflation; Interest Rates; Mercantilism; Mining Industry; World War I; World War II*

BIBLIOGRAPHY

Bordo, Michael D. 1993. The Bretton Woods International Monetary System: A Historical Overview. In *A Retrospective on the Bretton Woods System*, ed. Michael D. Bordo and Barry Eichengreen. Chicago: University of Chicago Press.

Eichengreen, Barry. 1992. *Golden Fetters: The Gold Standard and the Great Depression, 1919–1939*. New York: Oxford University Press.

Kimball, James. 2005. The Gold Standard in Contemporary Economic Principle Textbooks: A Survey. *Quarterly Journal of Austrian Economics* 8 (3): 59–80.

Littlefield, Henry M. 1964. *The Wizard of Oz*: Parable of Populism. *American Quarterly* 16 (1): 47–58.

Laurent Dobuzinskis

GOLDEN RULE IN GROWTH MODELS

The Nobel laureate Robert M. Solow (b. 1924) famously argued that a steady state growth will involve a higher savings and a higher capital-to-labor ratio to achieve a higher per capita income. Higher per capita income, however, does not automatically imply higher per capita consumption. Therefore this is a typical case of optimization in which we have to find the level of capital-to-labor ratio that provides at the same time the maximum possible per capita consumption. This problem was posed initially by Edmond Phelps (1961), and the solution provided was called the *golden rule of accumulation (growth)*. According to this rule, an economy reaches the optimum growth rate at the point where each generation saves and invests at the level that it wishes the previous generation would have invested. That is, each generation saves (on behalf of future generations, as it were) that fraction of income that it would have liked past generations to have saved, subject to the constraint that all generations past and present are to save the same fraction of income. This condition requires that the rate of profit (interest) equals the rate of growth of an economy.

Let us define the per capita consumption (c) as the difference between the per capita income ($f(k)$) and the per capita savings/investment ($sf(k)$), that is: $c = f(k) - sf(k)$. Equilibrium is attained at the point where the per capita saving (investment) is equal to the amount needed to keep the increasing labor force (n) with the same capital equipment (growth rate of capital labor ratio equals zero). Formally, $sf(k) = nk$. If we now revise the previous equation accordingly, we have $c = f(k) - nk$. Because we are not interested in any level of consumption, but rather the maximum possible, we get the first derivative of the above equation and we set it equal to zero: $dc/dk = f'(k) - n = 0$ and $f'(k) = n$. Thus the marginal product of capital (read rate of profit) equals the growth rate of the economy, because at the steady state growth rate, the growth rate of output equals the growth rate of labor force.

It is clear that public policy and private propensities can be designed to achieve this golden rule. That is, for example, even though a relatively low capital-poor economy will pursue optimum growth by steadily increasing its capital-to-labor ratio, it may accomplish this by saving relatively more in the future than in the present. However, major concerns about the existence of the golden rule of growth have been raised that refer mainly to the conditions for its existence. Some economists suggest that the rule exists only in neoclassical models in which capital and labor are continuously substitutable, there is no technical progress, unlimited influence on subsequent generations' choices is present, proper population policies exist, and so on. Phelps showed that the golden rule "always exists in the neoclassical and Harrod-Domar models if the labor force increases at a constant rate, the depreciation rate is constant, technical progress, if any, is purely labor-augmenting, labor augmentation occurs at a constant rate, and positive labor is required for positive output" (Phelps 1965, p. 812). Otherwise, the growth paths are dynamically inefficient and the golden growth rate of accumulation is unattainable.

SEE ALSO *Economic Growth; Neoclassical Growth Model; Optimal Growth; Solow, Robert M.*

BIBLIOGRAPHY

Phelps, Edmond. 1961. The Golden Rule of Accumulation: A Fable for Growthmen. *American Economic Review* 51 (4): 638–643.

Phelps, Edmond. 1965. Second Essay on the Golden Rule of Accumulation. *American Economic Review* 55 (4): 793–814.

Persefoni Tsaliki

GOLLIWOGS

SEE *Blackface.*

GONE WITH THE WIND

Margaret Mitchell, a descendant of the southern aristocracy of Atlanta, Georgia, and a former writer for the *Atlanta Journal*, was author of the 1,037-page Pulitzer Prize–winning novel *Gone with the Wind*. The novel represented a culmination of her family's southern history, Atlanta's local history, and the South's reconstruction in the aftermath of the Civil War.

SUMMARY

Depicted through the gaze of the novel's protagonist, *Gone with the Wind* features Scarlett O'Hara, one of the most popular southern belles in Clayton County, Georgia. Scarlett is a woman with a determined spirit and uncompromising sensibility, willing to do whatever is necessary to survive and to maintain her home, the Tara plantation. In the turbulence of the Civil War, Scarlett's love life is entangled when Melanie Hamilton marries the object of Scarlett's desire, Ashley Wilkes. Disillusioned, Scarlett marries Melanie's brother, Charles, but their marriage is short-lived due to his untimely death as a Confederate soldier. As the war continues, Melanie and Scarlett find themselves caring for wounded soldiers. Attacked by Yankee forces, both women are compelled to flee, Melanie with her newborn baby and Scarlett with her surrogate family—her black servant, Prissy—an escape assisted by Rhett Butler, a blockade runner and outcast.

At Tara, Scarlett discovers that her mother died, and the plantation, with only a few faithful slaves, was nearly destroyed. In dire straits for money, Scarlett returns to Atlanta to secure funds from Rhett. Again, in an effort to save the plantation, she marries, this time her sister's fiancé. Exhibiting independence and entrepreneurship, Scarlett purchases and operates a lumber mill; this results in her becoming the victim of an attack and in her husband's death.

Although still maintaining her affection for Ashley, Scarlett reunites with Rhett and is provided with an enormous estate and luxuries. She has Rhett's child, a daughter (her third child, as she had two children in prior marriages), but the daughter is accidentally killed, devastating both Rhett and Scarlett. As the novel ends, Melanie, facing death, entrusts Scarlett with the care of Ashley, but now Scarlett recognizes that her real love is for Rhett. By this time, however, Rhett has lost his affection and respect for Scarlett, demonstrated by his dramatic exit at the novel's end.

In addition to winning the Pulitzer Prize and becoming a Book of the Month selection, *Gone with the Wind* sold over one million copies in its first year of publication. Its popularity as a literary work has been debated by a number of critics who attribute Mitchell's success to her ability to infuse characters with captivating attributes; or to her ability to reconstruct southern history in an emotional and meaningful way from the perspective of a victim who is also a survivor; or to her ability to convey hope and optimism in the face of despair and defeat; or to its interdisciplinary appeal as a literary work to those interested in the military, in geography, anthropology, psychology, sociology, and in other fields.

Mitchell's novel provided a response to the mythical view of the Lost Cause fueled by the defeat of the South in the aftermath of the Civil War and represented by the loss of wealth and power, as Atlanta was reduced to ruins. Despite the wealth formerly achieved from the South's plantation economy and idealized by its glamorized past, Mitchell's work responded to the Lost Cause myth through the assertiveness and aggressiveness of her protagonist, Scarlett—a character who symbolized that the South could emerge from its past degradation and despair.

In 1936, producer David O. Selznick purchased the screen rights to the novel for some $50,000—at that time one of the largest sums ever paid for a screenplay. The film's production was complicated by changes in the director and scriptwriters, searches for appropriate actors, and other problems. Rhett Butler, played by Clark Gable, was reluctant to accept the role, although he was the public's

popular choice. Scarlett O'Hara, played by British actress Vivien Leigh, won the role despite consideration of a number of widely known American actresses such as Katharine Hepburn and Bette Davis. The film cost some $4.25 million and ran well over 3 hours and 40 minutes. Appearing in the novel but not in the film were Scarlett's first two children, Rhett's blockade activities and his relationship with Belle Watling, and the Ku Klux Klan.

COMPARISON OF *GONE WITH THE WIND* AND *BIRTH OF A NATION*

Gone with the Wind was widely compared with the film *Birth of a Nation* (1915), based on Thomas Dixon's novel *The Clansman* and produced by D. W. Griffith. Both films were Civil War epics, both were massive productions, both attempted to capitalize on historical facts, and both were regarded as controversial because of their racialized representations. These two films were also similar in sharing a common respect for the dramatization of American history by foregrounding the importance of romance and family. *Birth of a Nation* was nearly an attempt to embrace and resuscitate the past, while *Gone with the Wind* acknowledged the past from which it was fleeing and utilized this past as a means to reconstruct a new future and a new identity.

Both films endured censorship difficulties, with *Birth of a Nation* facing numerous censor boards prior to its exhibition because of its racial politics. *Gone with the Wind* challenged the Production Code's profanity restrictions with Butler's famous line, "Frankly, my dear, I don't give a damn." *Birth of a Nation* spawned riots in some northern cities and invited protests. *Gone with the Wind,* in comparison, elicited protests even prior to its completion and raised the ire of black newspapers.

FILM'S RECEPTION

Carlton Moss, an African American dramatist, submitted a letter to Selznick in 1940 that appeared in the *Daily Worker*. The letter outlined the racial insults committed by *Gone with the Wind* and suggested that it fabricated the myths that blacks were not concerned with freedom and that they lacked the innate ability to govern themselves. These views were echoed by members of the black press. The *New York Amsterdam News* described *Gone with the Wind* as the "pus oozing from beneath the scab of a badly healed wound." The *Chicago Defender* charged that the film glorified slavery and depicted the black male as a "grotesque and ravishing beast." The *Crisis* expressed its objections to the film's racial epithets. These offenses were further compounded when black actress Hattie McDaniel was not invited to attend *Gone with the Wind*'s Atlanta premiere in December 1939. In spite of such derision, McDaniel received an Academy Award as best supporting actress for her role as "Mammy," becoming the first African American to receive this award.

The mainstream press was much more enamored with the film. The *New York Times* claimed that while the picture may not have been the greatest motion picture ever made, it was "the greatest motion mural … seen and the most ambitious film-making venture in Hollywood's history." Other critics noted that the film was extremely well cast and acted with "costuming … above reproach; the interior sets are first rate; [and] much of the Technicolor photography is beautiful." The film's overwhelming reception, coupled with its movie attendance records, was further testament to its appeal and popularity. When *Gone with the Wind* premiered, some 55 million people reported that they intended to see it. Over one million people traveled to Atlanta for the film's premier, which was accompanied by parades and celebrations. Added to these accolades, the film won ten Academy Awards, including an award for best picture.

FILM IMPACT AND SUBSEQUENT WORKS

Gone with the Wind was a powerful force in garnering sympathy for the South in the postbellum period. One critic suggested that even northerners stood to be influenced by this southern mythology to the extent that though the North and South were once divided, northerners were now willing to join southern forces and "whistle Dixie." The film's impact continues to evolve with subsequent releases. The impact of both the novel and the film is further apparent when the Mitchell estate commissioned Alexandra Ripley to write a sequel to *Gone with the Wind*, titled *Scarlett* and published in 1991. This novel was also transformed into a 1994 television miniseries, but it met with much less success. *Variety* stated that "viewers' best hope, however, is to try to forget that classic book and film, and approach Scarlett for what it is: an eight-hour bodice-ripper."

Interest in the novel was reignited when Alice Randall published *The Wind Done Gone* in 2000, described as a parody of *Gone with the Wind*. Randall's work challenges the views propagated by *Gone with the Wind* by creating characters antithetical to those in the previous work. *The Wind Done Gone* provoked controversy, with many critics claiming that Randall infringed on the copyright of the 1936 novel. In a legal dispute to prevent the publication of Randall's work, the court found it to be distinctly different from *Gone with the Wind* in that it explored the intersection of race and sex and defied the myth of black savagery and primitivism.

Both the novel and the film continue to surface in contemporary discussions and debates, with the film becoming a part of Hollywood legend and the novel becoming an integral part of the American literary canon. *Gone with the Wind* has solidified its place in American history and cinema—capturing and marking historical moments that deserve to be returned to again and again.

SEE ALSO *Birth of a Nation; Confederate States of America; Ku Klux Klan; Plantation; Politics, Southern; Racism; Reconstruction Era (U.S.); Slavery; South, The (USA); U.S. Civil War*

BIBLIOGRAPHY

BOOKS

Farr, Finis. 1965. *Margaret Mitchell of Atlanta*. New York: Morrow.

Hanson, Elizabeth I. 1990. *Margaret Mitchell*. Boston: Twayne.

Harwell, Richard, ed. 1983. Gone with the Wind *as Book and Film*. Columbia: University of South Carolina Press.

Mitchell, Margaret. 1936. *Gone with the Wind*. New York: Macmillan.

Pyron, Darden Asbury. 1983. *Recasting:* Gone with the Wind *in American Culture*. Miami: University Presses of Florida.

Ripley, Alexandra. 1991. *Scarlett: The Sequel to Margaret Mitchell's* Gone with the Wind. New York: Warner Books.

Young, Elizabeth. 1999. *Disarming the Nation: Women's Writing and the American Civil War*. Chicago: University of Chicago Press.

CHAPTERS AND BOOK ARTICLES

Dunagan, Clyde Kelly. 1990. *Gone with the Wind*. In *International Dictionary of Films and Filmmakers-1 Films*, 2nd ed., ed. Nicholas Thomas and James Vinson, 350–352. Chicago and London: St. James Press.

JOURNAL ARTICLES

Burks, Ruth Elizabeth. 2004. *Gone with the Wind*: Black and White in Technicolor. *Quarterly Review of Film and Video* 21: 53–73.

Leff, Leonard J. 1984. David Selznick's *Gone with the Wind*: "The Negro Problem." *Georgia Review* 38 (1): 146–164.

Pyron, Darden Asbury. 1986. *Gone with the Wind* and the Southern Cultural Awakening. *Virginia Quarterly Review* 62 (4): 565–587.

Reddick, L. D. 1937. Review of *Gone with the Wind*, by Margaret Mitchell. *Journal of Negro History* 22 (3): 363–366.

Stevens, John D. 1973. The Black Reaction to *Gone with the Wind*. *Journal of Popular Film* 2 (4): 366–371.

Charlene Regester

GOOD SAMARITAN

SEE *Sympathy.*

GOODS, NONTRADED

While international trade involves the international shipment of an incredibly diverse range of goods and services—from cars, furniture, and insurance to umbrella knobs, pedestal actuators, holiday ornaments, and tax preparation services—not all products and services are internationally traded. Those products or services that are not exported are called *nontraded goods.*

There are two reasons that goods are not traded. The first reason is obvious: it is impossible to ship certain products from one country to another. A haircut is the prototypical example of a nontraded good. This service cannot be ordered for international shipment; the customer must travel to another country to visit a foreign barber, or the barber must travel to cut the customer's hair in the customer's country.

The second category of nontraded goods involves products that could be transported internationally but remain nontraded because the economic benefits of international trade are offset by the costs of trade. For example, while cement can be exported, it is generally unprofitable to do so because of the high transportation costs of moving such a heavy and bulky product. Thus, some products will be traded between countries that are close to each other and have low trade costs, while the same products will not be traded between countries that have high trade costs due to their distance from each other. In addition to transportation costs, other barriers to trade—such as tariffs or quotas, the inability to ship a product in a timely manner, or the inability to ship a product before it spoils, also cause a number of products to remain nontraded.

Nontraded goods may become traded goods when the original impediments to international trade decline sufficiently to make international trade profitable. In addition, advances in technology reduce the range of products that are nontraded. For example, since optimal patient care requires physicians to rapidly diagnosis an illness or assess the severity of an injury, the reading of X-rays was originally performed by local radiologists in the patient's and doctor's country of residence. As a result, the need for immediate assessment and evaluation of X-ray results caused diagnostic services to be internationally nontraded. However, radiological services became tradable when improvements in communications technologies made it possible for X-ray technicians to quickly send electronic images of X-ray results to radiologists in other countries for immediate analysis.

The prevalence of nontraded goods has implications for national economies. First, as formerly nontraded goods become tradable, a wider range of a country's production is organized according to international comparative advantage. A trading country reaps economic benefits from the efficiency improvements that are made possible by this change. In addition, fundamental differences in the nature of traded and nontraded goods have implications for cross-country differences in economic outcomes. According to the hypothesis known as the Balassa-Samuelson effect, the higher rates of productivity growth in traded goods can help explain the cross-country observation that prices are higher in high-income countries than they are in low-income countries.

SEE ALSO *Balance of Trade; Trade*

BIBLIOGRAPHY

Balassa, Bela. 1964. The Purchasing-Power Doctrine: A Reappraisal. *Journal of Political Economy* 72 (6): 584–596.

Samuelson, Paul A. 1964. Theoretical Notes on Trade Problems. *Review of Economics and Statistics* 46 (2): 145–154.

Deborah L. Swenson

GOODWILL

Goodwill is the value placed on the expectation that the clients or customers of an established company will continue to patronize it out of habit or confidence in the conduct of its business. In practice it is simply the amount by which the price of a going concern exceeds the sum of fair values of all of its other net assets. In other words, it is the amount of money that may be paid to the owners of a business over and above the costs of merely buying the assets that the company uses.

The origin of the term lies in developments in accounting that accompanied the rise of the capital market in the second half of the nineteenth century. The easing of the establishment of joint stock companies during this period facilitated the purchase of many retail businesses, whose previous owners were paid for referring their previous customers to the business under new management or ownership. Goodwill came to be used to pay the existing owners of a company's equity a price for their stock inflated above the value of any actual underlying assets by the more active capital markets of the late nineteenth century. The American political economist Thorstein Veblen regarded goodwill as reflecting competitive advantages, which a company may have and which may not be incorporated in the cost of assets. In the course of mergers and acquisitions, the value of a company's stock comes to reflect its increasingly monopolistic market position. However, John Hobson and Alfred Marshall expressed a more common view in the first decades of the twentieth century that goodwill was used to exaggerate a company's business prospects leading to the overcapitalization of that company. In this way financiers and company promoters profited at the expense of the investing public. Despite the relevance of these views, there was little discussion of them amid the inflated capital markets of the late twentieth century and early twenty-first century.

Goodwill purchased in the course of buying a company has wider implications because the cost of it is treated as a business expense. In the United States and Canada this expense is amortized against company earnings over a period of up to forty years. Because, after a company has been purchased, these amortization payments are purely bookkeeping transactions, it has been argued that the recording of these payments in the income and expenditure statement of a company makes that statement less clearly a reflection of actual business income and expenditure. In the United Kingdom an accounting standard in force since 1984 recommends that goodwill should "normally" be written off immediately after acquisition against the owners' equity or reserves. However, such immediate write-off can lead to extreme shifts in the "leverage" or gearing of a company (the ratio of its debt to equity). It is not unknown for such a write-off to result in negative owners' equity. Even before that arises, the sudden fall in the value of owners' equity may cause difficulty where a company has loan agreements that stipulate a maximum permissible leverage ratio. Such shifts in the value of owners' equity also affect the vulnerability of a company to takeover or even to reporting, as the London Stock Exchange obliges its companies to do, where the payment for a company represents 15 percent or more of the acquiring company's equity.

Because business expenses reduce the tax liability of companies, the accounting treatment of goodwill—that is, whether and how it is amortized—may have significant tax implications for a company. Among service companies with limited scope for capital investments that may be set against tax over a period of years, goodwill may be an important factor in the tax planning of a company.

The significance of goodwill in corporate finance has been inflated by the proliferation of mergers and takeovers in active capital markets. The emergence of such markets in Europe and other parts of the world extends the geographical area where goodwill has fiscal and accounting importance.

SEE ALSO *Bull and Bear Markets; Capital; Equity Markets; Financial Markets; Stock Exchanges; Veblen, Thorstein*

BIBLIOGRAPHY

Daniell, Alfred. 1894–1899. Goodwill. In *Dictionary of Political Economy*, ed. Robert Harry Inglis Palgrave. London: Macmillan.

Financial Accounting Standards Board. 2001. Goodwill and Other Intangible Assets. Statement no. 142. Norwalk, CT.

Hughes, H. P. 1982. *Goodwill in Accounting: A History of the Issues and Problems*. Atlanta: College of Business Administration, Georgia State University.

Veblen, Thorstein. 1904. *The Theory of Business Enterprise*. New York: Scribner.

Jan Toporowski

GORBACHEV, MIKHAIL
1931–

Mikhail Gorbachev, leader of the Soviet Union from 1985 until that country's demise in 1991, has gone down in history for peacefully dismantling the seventy-year-old repressive Communist system and for initiating the cold war's nonviolent end after four decades of international tension. For this, he received the Nobel Peace Prize in 1990 and is regarded by many, particularly outside Russia, as one of the twentieth century's greatest leaders. Inside Russia, Gorbachev is more often blamed for the collapse of the Soviet Union, a breakup most Russians regret. Whether Gorbachev should be held directly responsible for that collapse is contested by many scholars who cite complex reasons for that country's disintegration.

Born into a peasant family, Gorbachev grew up in the important agricultural region of Stavropol, in southern Russia. Highly intelligent and winning awards for both academic achievement and agricultural work, Gorbachev was accepted to the prestigious law faculty of Moscow State University in 1950. There, Gorbachev met educated, urban students from the U.S.S.R. and Eastern Europe, one of whom, the Czech intellectual Zdeněk Mlynář (1930–1997)—later a prominent 1968 Prague Spring reformer—became Gorbachev's lifelong friend.

Returning to Stavropol in 1955, Gorbachev advanced to the top of the regional party hierarchy, and by 1978, he reached Moscow as the secretary of the central committee of the Communist Party of the Soviet Union (CPSU) in charge of agriculture. By 1980 this young, energetic agricultural expert was elected as full member of the fourteen-strong Soviet *Politburo* (the highest Soviet decision-making body, stocked with octogenarians). Once the CPSU general secretary Leonid Brezhnev died in November 1982, Yuri Andropov emerged victorious from the leadership struggle, only to die fifteen months later and be replaced by the ailing Konstantin Chernenko, who survived for only thirteen months. Gorbachev became general secretary, and thus Soviet leader, in March 1985.

With skillful use of his new powers, Gorbachev pushed aside the old guard and reassigned top posts to like-minded anti-Stalinists such as Eduard Shevardnadze (b. 1928) and radical reformers, notably Aleksandr Yakovlev (1923–2005). He then embarked on diplomatic campaigns abroad that, over five years, grew into a foreign policy revolution featuring massive, asymmetrical cuts in Soviet weapons arsenals, acceptance of the peaceful liberation of Eastern Europe, and finally, a radical push to join Europe as a democracy.

At home, Gorbachev managed—despite incessant opposition—to introduce increasingly important political reforms, dubbed *perestroika* (political and economic restructuring) and *glasnost* (openness in media and society). Though always predisposed toward reform, Gorbachev did not stress democratization until 1987, when his powers had grown strong enough and his own views consolidated. In 1988 he established competitive elections and a genuine legislative body. He worked to implement checks and balances, a law-governed state, political and religious freedoms, and genuine federalism. Radical economic reform proved far harder, because liberalizing prices risked social upheaval. The economy stagnated as the command economy unraveled, while market institutions remained unborn. The combination of political freedoms, high expectations, and economic decline exacerbated tensions between the fifteen republics and the Soviet state. Striving to keep the U.S.S.R. together, Gorbachev embarked on a new federal framework; but politics at home undercut him. An attempted coup in August 1991 left him critically weakened. In December Boris Yeltsin (1931–2007), president of the Russian Republic, dealt the final blow to Gorbachev—and to the U.S.S.R.—by withdrawing Russia from the Soviet Union. Gorbachev resigned, leaving a great legacy. He brought freedom to Russia and played the most decisive part in ending the cold war.

SEE ALSO *Cold War; Democracy; Democratization; Economies, Transitional; Glasnost; Russian Federation; Union of Soviet Socialist Republics; Yeltsin, Boris*

BIBLIOGRAPHY

Brown, Archie. 1996. *The Gorbachev Factor.* Oxford: Oxford University Press.

English, Robert. 2000. *Russia and the Idea of the West.* New York: Columbia University Press.

Mlynář, Zdeněk, and Mikhail Gorbachev. 2002. *Conversations with Gorbachev.* Trans. George Shriver. New York: Columbia University Press.

Julie M. Newton

GORDON, MILTON
SEE *Assimilation.*

GOSNELL, HAROLD
1896–1997

Harold F. Gosnell played a major role in the development of the scientific approach to political research. He was among the first political scientists to utilize randomized field experiments, correlation, regression, and factor analysis, which he skillfully blended with archival research, participant observation, elite interviewing, and ethnography to produce seminal studies of elections, voting behavior, party politics, political machines, and African American politics.

Harold Gosnell grew up in Rochester, New York, and received a bachelor's degree from the Univeristy of Rochester in 1918. He matriculated as a graduate student at the University of Chicago, where, under the tutelage of Charles Merriam, he received a PhD in 1922. Gosnell immediately joined the political science faculty at the University of Chicago, where he was part of the nucleus of the Chicago School of Political Science, which endeavored to construct a science of politics on the model of the natural sciences.

Gosnell was deeply concerned with the functioning of elections and the factors that led citizens to participate in them or not. His *Non-Voting: Causes and Methods of Control* (1924), authored with Merriam, examined a random sample of 6,000 nonvoters in the Chicago mayoral election of 1923. It identified the principal causes of nonvoting as non-registration, disbelief in women's voting, disgust or indifference, and physical impairments or difficulties. Merriam and Gosnell argued that efficient party organization and simplification of registration laws would enhance citizen participation in elections. In *Getting Out the Vote* (1927) Gosnell conducted randomized field experiments in the Chicago elections of 1924 and 1925 to determine whether nonpartisan notices could stimulate citizen registration and voting. He found that a nonpartisan appeals could boost registration by about 9 percent but mattered less where party organizations were strong and education levels high; they had a greater marginal effect on women, African Americans, and the less educated.

A fascination with party organizations, especially political machines, permeated almost all of Gosnell's work, starting with the first of his twelve books, *Boss Platt and His New York Machine* (1924), which traced the rise and fall of machine politics in New York. In *Negro Politicians* (1935) he documented changes in Chicago politics brought about by the northward migration of African

Americans, their loyalty to and role in the Republican Party, and the first signs of shifting loyalties to the Democrats after the initiation of the New Deal. He detailed the centrality of black churches and the black press (especially the *Chicago Defender*) in mobilizing opinion and sustaining organization in the community. Gosnell generalized his arguments on party organization in *Machine Politics: Chicago Model* (1937). He demonstrated the success of ward bosses and precinct captains in insulating the parties from broader trends in national politics brought about by the Great Depression. Gosnell saw ballot simplification, proportional representation, civil service laws, and other reforms as ways to wean democracy from the imperatives of patronage and graft.

Gosnell left Chicago in 1941 for Washington, D.C., where he held positions in several federal agencies and then served as professor of political science at Howard University from 1962 to 1970. The American Political Science Association recognizes his achievements by awarding each year the Harold F. Gosnell Prize of Excellence for the best work of political methodology presented at a political science conference.

SEE ALSO *American Political Science Association; Chicago Defender; Democratic Party, U.S.; Elections; New Deal, The; Political Science; Politics, Black; Politics, Urban; Random Samples; Republican Party; Sampling; Science; Statistics; Survey; Voting*

BIBLIOGRAPHY

Hansen, John Mark. 1997. In Memoriam: Harold F. Gosnell. *PS: Political Science and Politics* 30 (3): 582–587.

Heaney, Michael T., and John Mark Hansen. 2006. Building the Chicago School. *American Political Science Review* 100 (4): 589–596.

Michael T. Heaney

GOSPEL, GLORY AND GOLD

SEE *Gold, God, and Glory.*

GOSPELS

SEE *Christianity.*

GOSSIP

SEE *Rumors.*

GOULD, STEPHEN JAY
1941–2002

Stephen Jay Gould was a paleontologist, evolutionary biologist, essayist, and public intellectual. He lived a rich life achieving heights of academic success as a professor at Harvard University as well as attaining public recognition as an erudite, literate scientific essayist. Gould's importance stems from his distinctive and important contributions as an evolutionary biologist and paleontologist, as well as his participation in public debates bringing his humanist and scientific commitments to bear on important social and scientific issues.

As a biologist Gould is best known for the theory of "punctuated equilibria" which he formulated jointly with the American paleontologist Niles Eldredge. The fossil record is an imprint of the past providing researchers with extensive evidence not only for the fact of evolution but a detailed map of the branching pathways connecting the diversity of life. The evolutionary paths emanating from different life forms can be traced through the chronological ordering of this fossil record. In standard Darwinian explanation the pace of evolutionary change is assumed to be slow. Accordingly, small incremental changes are accumulated to amount eventually to the grand differences that scientists associate with distinct species. The fossil record, however, does not show continuous change between life forms; rather there seem to be gaps. These discontinuities in the record could reflect scientists' incomplete knowledge or simply gaps in the fossil record itself. Gould and Eldredge attempted to explain the "gaps" in the fossil record by questioning the assumptions made about the pace of evolutionary change. They argued that for long periods species enjoy stability, giving way to rapid and drastic change over short periods of time. Thus, the so-called gaps in the fossil record actually reflect a fact about the pace of evolutionary change rather than representing missing evidence.

Gould viewed evolutionary biology as a historical science. To him evolution was not a deterministic unfolding of events but a process highly contingent on the vicissitudes of circumstance. His views brought him into conflict with some of his peers who tried to veer evolutionary biology toward a more mechanical paradigm in which the evolutionary process was reduced to natural selection operating at the genetic level. Perhaps his most visible sparring partner in this debate was Richard Dawkins, who had presented arguably the strongest version of the mechanical paradigm. Dawkins envisioned organisms as "lumbering robots" carrying out instructions encoded in the organism's DNA. Dawkins departed from orthodox Darwinism in placing the gene as opposed to the organism as the unit of selection. Gould's opposition to this view found expression in a number of interesting ways.

First, he argued that natural selection, while an important and perhaps even dominant motor of evolution, was not the only driving force. He derided the panselectionism of his opponents as a "panglossian paradigm" in which every feature of the organism was furnished with an adaptationist "Just So" story—a reference to Rudyard Kipling's humorous children's stories, particularly the ones about the origin of features of animals. Gould considered a multiplicity of mechanisms as important in evolution. These mechanisms included random reproductive success of some features due to the dynamics of finite populations, as well as structurally inevitable correlates of selected features where these correlates provide no reproductive advantage.

Second, Gould opposed reduction of evolution to the level of genes. He accepted as a fact that genes are responsible for the heritability of traits, but argued that selection occurs at the level of the organism per the Darwinian paradigm. Evolution to Gould could not be understood unless one allowed for different hierarchical levels of study; this hierarchy included the genetic level, the organism, and the species—each one important for a different set of evolutionary questions.

Third, Gould argued that the reduction of the organism to its genotype led ineluctably to a whole set of mistaken ideas which he collectively termed *biological determinism*. Biological determinism, as expressed in the ideas of sociobiology and evolutionary psychology, is the belief that complex behavior of organisms can be understood as following from the organism's genetic make up, and are thus permanent features of the organism. As an example, a determinist might argue that a person's genes determine her or his level of intelligence.

Gould went on to understand the questions that biological determinists tried to answer as historically conditioned. He saw in the determinist program a program that justified the stratification of our present-day society along gender, racial, and economic lines by providing these social realities a biological justification.

Gould's scientific interests intersected significantly with his social commitments. He participated in public debates arguing against creationism and the genetic basis for behavioral differences between racial, gender, and class groupings. He wrote prolifically for the lay public on science, history, and society and achieved a considerable amount of fame and influence as a writer of popular science.

SEE ALSO *Darwin, Charles; Punctuated Equilibrium*

BIBLIOGRAPHY

PRIMARY WORKS

Gould, Stephen Jay. 1992. *The Panda's Thumb: More Reflections in Natural History*. New York: Norton.

Gould, Stephen Jay. 1996. *The Mismeasure of Man*. New York: Norton.

Ansar Fayyazuddin

GOULDNER, ALVIN

SEE *Managerial Class; New Class, The; Reciprocity, Norm of.*

GOVERNMENT

Government is as old as human beings themselves. All human societies are governed by rulers, no matter what their titles and characteristics may be. On the theoretical level, government is intrinsic to human societies. Nevertheless, at a more tangible level, nothing about government is static. Structures and functions of governing are constantly in change.

The word *government* has a Greek origin, *kyvernites*, which means "governor," or "rudder." Government is a body or organization that has the power to make and enforce laws and regulations for a certain territory. *Government* refers to the act of governing, meaning exercising authority over a community or a country. It is a system by which a political unit is governed. The two central features of government are the ability to make collective, binding decisions and the capacity to enforce them. Thus, the core functions of modern government are to make law (legislation), to implement law (execution), and to interpret law (adjudication). On the national level, the basic duty of any government is to ensure a country's survival. Survival involves two basic tasks: defending independence against external threats, and maintaining internal security and preventing civil war or secession. In parliamentary systems, the political executive alone is referred to as "the government."

Each efficient government should have an authority, or a "legitimate power." Power is the ability to influence the behavior of others, whereas authority is the right to exercise that power and to get the people's obedience by using various means, including direct physical coercion, threats, exile, banishment, and so on. Such an authority should be legitimate, that is, as Max Weber noted, the use of force by a government should be recognized as legitimate and justified by both the powerful and the powerless. Legitimacy is considered a basic condition for governing, and without a minimal amount of legitimacy, a government will deadlock or collapse.

Government differs from other social or private organizations in many ways, as noted by Austin Ranney (1996). It has legitimate monopoly of vast force (the army, the police, etc.), and can use coercion to enforce its rules and to punish rule breakers. Furthermore, government has inclusive and authoritative powers; that is, whereas rules made by nongovernmental organizations apply only to the members of those organizations and often conflict with those set by other organizations, governmental rules apply to all members of the country and usually are considered to be binding upon all members of a society. In any conflict between the decisions of government and the decisions of nongovernmental organizations, government decisions should prevail. Additionally, while membership in most organizations other than government is voluntary, citizenship is largely involuntary; most people become subject to governmental rules and decisions without any intentional choice.

FORMS OF GOVERNMENT

There are several ways to classify governments. One traditional classification is based on who holds political power: one man or woman (autocratic government), a few (oligarchic government), or a majority (democratic government).

An autocratic government is a government in which one individual holds all power, as is the case in absolute monarchies and dictatorships. One feature of most hereditary monarchies is that the monarch usually rules as head of state for life. In absolute monarchies, monarchs hold substantial power over every aspect of the country. Contemporary examples of such a form of government include Brunei, Bhutan, and Saudi Arabia. In other hereditary monarchies, real authority is held by military rulers, as was the case in Japan during the eighteenth and nineteenth centuries. Under the fascists Benito Mussolini (1883–1945) in Italy and Francisco Franco (1892–1975) in Spain, the two countries were officially monarchies. Some current monarchies are established by tradition, thus the monarch has little real authority. Examples of such a form of government include democratic constitutional monarchies in the United Kingdom, Canada, New Zealand, and Spain.

Dictatorships are usually regarded as synonymous with other forms of autocratic governments, such as totalitarianism and authoritarianism, though each of these forms has a different meaning. *Dictatorship* refers to absolute, repressive rule by one leader who is unrestricted by any law or constitution. Many dictators tend to suppress any opinion that disagrees with their own, and often use military and security forces, propaganda, and arbitrary detention to enforce their will. Such dictatorships survive because of the fear of the dictator. Some dictators create single-party regimes, without democratic elections or with rigged ones, in an attempt to acquire popular legitimacy.

Totalitarian government is a term employed by political scientists to describe modern regimes in which a regime regulates nearly all aspects of public and private behavior. Totalitarian rulers mobilize entire populations in support of the state and a political ideology. Such rulers do not tolerate political activities by individuals or groups such as labor unions and political parties. They maintain themselves in power by means of widespread use of terror tactics, secret police, a one-party system, propaganda, and restriction of freedoms and free discussion. Examples of such regimes include the Soviet Union and the Nazi regime of the 1930s and 1940s.

Authoritarianism is a form of government in which rulers are not appointed via free and fair elections. Authoritarian leaders tend to enforce strong and oppressive acts against those in their domain of influence. Examples of such regimes include the People's Republic of China and Cuba.

In contrast, an oligarchic government is a government where political power is held by a small group of individuals such as aristocrats (the upper class) or plutocrats (the wealthy). Another example of an oligarchic rule, one based on race, was in South Africa under the apartheid system, where the white minority held power. Some theorists such as Gaetano Mosca, Vilfredo Pareto, and Robert Michels argue that in a capitalist society, political and economic power is held by a few members of the capitalist class that seek to maintain the capitalist system at the expense of other classes. In his book *Political Parties* (1968), Michels mentions the "iron law of oligarchy," arguing that all forms of organizations, including the political system, will eventually develop into an oligarchy.

A democratic government is one in which the majority of the people hold political power. Democracy could be direct (all citizens exercise power, as was the case with Athenian democracy) or indirect (where power is exercised by elected representatives, as is the case with contemporary representative democracies in the West). The core characteristic of a democratic government, in the contemporary usage, is "the rule of law." This means that a democratic system is a constitutional government in which the law is supreme, and all citizens and classes are equal before the law. According to the nineteenth-century British jurist Albert Venn Dicey, the objective of this principle, the rule of law, was to substitute "a government of laws" for a "government of men." The rule of law is not a new value: The Romans provided the foundations of the rule of law and limited government in the West, and in fact the rule of law in Arabic-Islamic civilization antedated the Western principle. There is more than a century between the emergence of this principle in the Islamic state in the seventh and eighth centuries and its recent manifestation in the thought of seventeenth- and eighteenth-century liberal thinkers and, later, in the democratic systems in western Europe and North America.

A democratic government is also a government in which all citizens, rather than one autocratic leader or a few people, have the right and opportunity to participate in the decision-making process. In a democratic system, the people are the ultimate source of authority, and the authority of the majority is limited by law (a written or unwritten constitution) as well as institutional means (such as separated and shared powers, checks and balances, and leadership succession through frequent and fairly conducted elections) so that the rights of individuals and minorities are protected. This form of government exists in western Europe, North America, Australia, New Zealand, Japan, and other regions and countries.

STRUCTURE AND FUNCTIONS OF MODERN DEMOCRATIC GOVERNMENT

The constitutions of modern democratic governments are the main mechanisms by which the principles of constitutional democracy can be enacted into specific institutions and procedures. On the practical level, modern democratic governments can be classified according to the basis of the institutional organization of the political executive body and the relationship between executive and legislative bodies into parliamentary, presidential, and semipresidential systems.

The executive power is composed of two organs in parliamentary governments. First is the head of the state, who is often a monarch or a president. Second, the government, which includes the head of government (called the prime minister, or chancellor) and the council of ministers, or the cabinet. The head of state is an inherited or elected figurehead with minor and ceremonial duties. He or she may have reserve authority (either by convention or by constitutional rule) that is usable in a crisis. Such authority, however, is usually exercised upon the advice and endorsement of the prime minister. The prime minister and the ministers of the cabinet are usually members of the parliament. The leader of the leading party (or group of parties) in the parliament is often appointed to be the prime minister. The government depends on the support of the parliament. Either the entire cabinet or single members can be removed by the parliament through a vote of no confidence. In turn, the executive body can dissolve the parliament and call for new elections. Thus, there is no clear-cut separation between the executive and legislative powers. The origins of this system go back to the British political system. The system also exists in many other democratic countries such as Spain, Japan, Sweden, Canada, and Australia.

In a presidential government, the executive organ, the president, is elected independent of the legislative institution. The president is both head of state and head of government, and there is sharp separation between the executive president and the legislature. Thus, the president is not a member, nor can he or she propose bills. Most importantly, the president cannot be removed by a vote of no confidence or any other political procedures. The president is elected for office for a fixed term and heads most of the agencies charged with executive functions such as enforcing and administering acts of the legislature. The president appoints a group of assistants (known as a cabinet) as heads of the executive departments and supervisors of the administrative agencies. This system of governing originated in the United States. Other countries with presidential systems include Indonesia, the Philippines, Mexico, and most countries in South America.

A semipresidential government is a system that has a cabinet and a president who both have substantial executive duties. This system differs from the parliamentary government because it has an elected president who is assigned substantial duties. Moreover, a semipresidential government differs from the presidential one in that it has a prime minister and a cabinet who are dependent on the support of the legislature. As in the parliamentary government, the cabinet, or a single minister, can be removed by a vote of no confidence in the parliament, and the president can dissolve the legislative assembly. France, Finland, Portugal, Romania, Taiwan, and Ukraine have semipresidential systems.

LEVELS OF GOVERNMENT

Modern states may be also classified according to the distribution of power at different levels of government into two main systems: unitary and federal. A unitary state is a state where the ultimate authority lies exclusively with a central government that controls central and local affairs. In such a system, local and regional authorities may make and implement policies, but they must have the permission of the central government. This form of government has emerged in former monarchies and empires such as France, Britain, and Japan. It also exists in countries with no ethnic divisions, such as the Scandinavian states, Egypt, and Turkey. The other form is a federal state, where political power is constitutionally shared between a federal government and local governments of constituent states or provinces. The function of the federal government is to handle foreign affairs, defense relations, and some internal functions such as monetary affairs. The local governments of the provinces or states usually handle education and law enforcement. The existence and functions of the provinces or states may be changed only by amending the constitution, a process that protects them from the federal power.

SEE ALSO *Administrative Law; Authoritarianism; Authority; Autocracy; Citizenship; Civil Society; Corporatism; Democracy; Dictatorship; Due Process; Fascism; Franco, Francisco; Judicial Review; Judiciary; Michels, Robert; Military Regimes; Monarchy; Mussolini, Benito; Oligarchy; Oligarchy, Iron Law of; Pareto, Vilfredo; Public Administration; Republicanism; Rule of Law; State, The; Totalitarianism*

BIBLIOGRAPHY

Alexander, Larry, ed. 1998. *Constitutionalism.* Cambridge, U.K.: Cambridge University Press.

Almond, Gabriel A., and Bingham Powell. 1966. *Comparative Politics: A Developmental Approach.* Boston: Little, Brown.

Almond, Gabriel A., G. Bingham Powell Jr., Kaare Strøm, et al. 2003. *Comparative Politics Today: A World View.* 7th ed. New York: Longman.

Arblaster, Anthony. 1994. *Democracy.* 2nd ed. Minneapolis: University of Minnesota Press.

Beer, Samuel H. 1973. *Patterns of Government: The Major Political Systems of Europe.* 3rd ed. New York: Random House.

Blondel, Jean. 1997. *Comparative Government: An Introduction.* 2nd ed. New York: Prentice-Hall.

Broszat, Martin. 1981. *The Hitler State: The Foundation and Development of the Internal Structure of the Third Reich.* London: Longman.

Buchanan, James M., and Gordon Tullock. 1965. *The Calculus of Consent: Logical Foundations of Constitutional Democracy.* Ann Arbor: University of Michigan Press.

Christiano, Thomas. 1996. *The Rule of the Many: Fundamental Issues in Democratic Theory.* Boulder, CO: Westview.

Christiano, Thomas. 2004. The Authority of Democracy. *Journal of Political Philosophy* 12 (3): 266–290.

Dahl, Robert. 1959. *A Preface to Democratic Theory.* Chicago: University of Chicago Press.

Dahl, Robert. 1998. *On Democracy.* New Haven, CT: Yale University Press.

Dicey, Albert Venn. 1967. *Introduction to the Study of the Law of the Constitution.* London: Macmillan.

Downs, Anthony. 1957. *An Economic Theory of Democracy.* New York: Harper and Row.

Elazar, Daniel J., and John Kincaid, eds. 2000. *The Covenant Connection: From Federal Theology to Modern Federalism.* Lanham, MD: Lexington Books.

Finer, Samuel Edward. 1970. *Comparative Government.* New York: Basic Books.

Finer, Samuel Edward. 1999. *The History of Government from the Earliest Times.* Oxford, U.K., and New York: Oxford University Press.

Gallagher, Michael, Michael Laver, and Peter Mair. 2000. *Representative Government in Modern Europe.* New York: McGraw-Hill.

Galston, William A. 2005. *The Practice of Liberal Pluralism.* Cambridge, U.K.: Cambridge University Press.

Goodwin, Albert, ed. 1953. *The European Nobility in the Eighteenth Century.* 2nd ed. London: Adam and Charles Black.

Greenberg, Douglas, Stanley N. Katz, Melanie Beth Oliviero, and Steven C. Wheatley. 1993. *Constitutionalism and Democracy: Transitions in the Contemporary World.* New York: Oxford University Press.

Griffiths, Ann L., ed. 2002. *Handbook of Federal Countries.* Montreal: McGill–Queen's University Press.

Hague, Rod, and Martin Harrop. 2004. *Political Science: A Comparative Introduction.* New York: Palgrave Macmillan.

Hamilton, Alexander, James Madison, and John Jay. [1787–1788] 1961. *The Federalist.* Ed. Jacob E. Cooke. Middletown, CT: Wesleyan University Press.

Held, David. 1997. *Models of Democracy.* 2nd ed. Palo Alto, CA: Stanford University Press.

Horowitz, Donald L. 1999. Comparing Democratic Systems. *Journal of Democracy* 1 (4): 73–79.

Jacobsohn, Gary Jeffrey, and Susan Dunn, eds. 1996. *Diversity and Citizenship: Rediscovering American Nationhood.* Lanham, MD: Rowman and Littlefield.

Kincaid, John, and G. Alan Tarr, eds. 2005. *Constitutional Origins, Structure, and Change in Federal Countries.* Montreal: McGill–Queen's University Press.

Lijphart, Arend, ed. 1992. *Parliamentary versus Presidential Government.* Oxford, U.K.: Oxford University Press.

Lijphart, Arend. 1999. *Patterns of Democracy: Government Forms and Performance in Thirty-Six Countries.* New Haven, CT, and London: Yale University Press.

Linz, Juan J. 1990. The Perils of Presidentialism. *Journal of Democracy* 1 (Winter): 51–69.

Linz, Juan J. 1994. Presidential or Parliamentary Democracy: Does It Make a Difference? In *The Failure of Presidential Democracy, Comparative Perspectives*, ed. Juan J. Linz and Arturo Valenzuela, 3–87. Baltimore, MD: Johns Hopkins University Press.

McCormick, John. 2004. *Comparative Politics in Transition.* 4th ed. Belmont, CA: Wadsworth.

Michels, Robert. 1968. *Political Parties: A Sociological Study of the Oligarchical Tendencies of Modern Democracy.* Trans. Eden Paul and Cedar Paul. New York: Free Press.

Ranney, Austin. 1996. *Governing: An Introduction to Political Science.* 7th ed. Upper Saddle River, NJ: Prentice Hall.

Rawls, John. 1996. *Political Liberalism.* Rev. ed. New York: Columbia University Press.

Riesenberg, Peter. 1992. *Citizenship in the Western Tradition.* Chapel Hill: University of North Carolina Press.

Riker, William. 1964. *Federalism: Origin, Operation, Significance.* Boston: Little, Brown.

Rosenbaum, Alan S., ed. 1988. *Constitutionalism: The Philosophical Dimension.* New York: Greenwood.

Sachedina, Abdulaziz. 2001. *The Islamic Roots of Democratic Pluralism.* Oxford, U.K.: Oxford University Press.

Schapiro, Leonard. 1956. *The Origin of the Communist Autocracy: Political Opposition in the Soviet State, First Phase 1917–1922.* 2nd ed. London: G. Bell.

Schumpeter, Joseph. 1950. *Capitalism, Socialism, and Democracy.* New York: Harper and Row.

Watts, Ronald L. 1999. *Comparing Federal Systems.* 2nd ed. Kingston, Canada: Institute of Intergovernmental Relations, Queen's University.

Abdel-Fattah Mady

GOVERNMENT, COALITION

A coalition government exists when two or more political parties formally agree to share executive responsibility and cabinet posts. Proportional representation systems common among parliamentary democracies often produce election results in which no single party wins an absolute majority of seats in a legislature. Such situations yield incentives for parties to build alliances in order to form a new government; absent the emergence of a coalition, the country is left either with leadership that does not command majority support or with the necessity of calling new elections. In political systems that encourage government by coalition, votes do not directly determine the composition of a new government; rather, they only determine which political parties will sit in parliament. Once that initial issue is settled, elected representatives and party leaders negotiate from among a potentially huge number of party combinations and permutations in search of a winning majority. Postelection coalition building can take days, weeks, and even months to complete, with the result being capture by one party of the premiership and distribution across coalition members of important posts such as foreign affairs, finance, justice, and the like. Coalition government stands as an alternative model to majoritarian governance, the latter being characterized by winner-take-all "first-past-the-post" electoral systems that favor clear distinctions between winners and losers.

Coalition government is the subject of a voluminous literature within the political science discipline. As a system of governance, the multiparty coalition is studied most frequently in European democracies whose electoral rules provide for even a modicum of proportionality. Italy's penchant for short-lived postwar coalition governments is notorious, as is Belgium's complex process of managing a delicate linguistic divide through coalitions. The reluctance of postwar German electorates to grant power exclusively to a single party has meant that coalition government—sometimes matching the country's two largest parties in the same "grand coalition"—has been the norm there. Beyond Europe, coalition government is a standard expectation of democratic process in such countries as Israel, India, and Japan.

Advocates of coalition government tout the model's ability to forge compromise and cooperation, and they point to greater inclusiveness as an additional virtue. Political parties in coalitional systems are competitive, but the prospect of governing with one's competitors after an election can moderate campaign rhetoric. Granting new or untested parties a share of executive power as junior coalition partners may likewise moderate political extremism. According to supporters of this institutional approach to democratic governance, policies emerging from multiparty coalition governments should have a better chance of societal acceptance and successful implementation because they are the products of compromise rather than the imposition of political will by a lone dominant party.

Detractors claim that coalition governments are prone to weakness and instability, and because they can blur lines of accountability their democratic credentials are sometimes called into question. Opponents also object to the possibility of governments that are little more than "coalitions of losers," marked by parties and adversaries whose electoral scores have just dropped precipitously but who nonetheless join forces to cling to power and forestall their mutual demise.

SEE ALSO *Elections; First-past-the-post; Government; Parliaments and Parliamentary Systems; Plurality; Winner-Take-All Society*

BIBLIOGRAPHY

Dodd, Lawrence C. 1976. *Coalitions in Parliamentary Government.* Princeton, NJ: Princeton University Press.

Downs, William M. 1998. *Coalition Government, Subnational Style: Multiparty Politics in Europe's Regional Parliaments.* Columbus: Ohio State University Press.

Mershon, Carol. 2002. *Costs of Coalition.* Stanford, CA: Stanford University Press.

Müller, Wolfgang C. and Kaare Strøm, eds. 2000. *Coalition Governments in Western Europe.* Oxford and New York: Oxford University Press.

William M. Downs

GOVERNMENT, FEDERAL

The member states of confederations establish federal governments to concentrate power in a central authority while maintaining the independence of their own governments. Traditionally, the member states of confederations have established federal governments as a means of combining their military and economic resources in response to regional threats and rivalries at the same time as they faced deep-seated ethnic, linguistic, or religious barriers to further national integration. The precise institutional structure that most skillfully juggled those two different sets of demands was difficult to define in theory, much less establish in practice. Centripetal forces within a federal system could produce political conflict among the member states just as easily as centrifugal forces could. Tudor England and the Holy Roman Empire exemplified those two tendencies.

The United States presents a somewhat unique case because at the time the federal government was established its member states were not divided along deep-seated ethnic, linguistic, or religious lines, nor had they enjoyed an independent existence before the establishment of the confederation. The framers of the U.S. Constitution generally agreed on the need to create a stronger federal government than had existed under the Articles of Confederation, but they differed on how much to strengthen it. Surprisingly, convention debates over specific powers were rare, except when they engaged existing interstate cleavages. In particular, the convention debate over a federal commerce power, including the power to regulate the slave trade, was heated because it engaged a number of interstate cleavages, between northern and southern states, between upper-South and lower-South states, between New England and mid-Atlantic states, and between commercial and agrarian states. However, in general the sense of the convention was to strengthen the federal government so that it was structured less like traditional federal governments and more like the national governments of the western European powers, which the delegates viewed as the future military and commercial rivals to their newly independent nation. At the same time, they sought to retain the state governments as viable parts of a new federal system of government, if for no other reason than that the Constitution would not otherwise have been ratified.

HISTORICAL DEVELOPMENTS

After the formation of this new type of "half federal, half national" system in the United States, some federal systems have been patterned more on this new, U.S. model (Australia) and some have been patterned more on the traditional, confederal model (Nigeria). Other federal systems represent a hybrid of the two models (Germany) or are clearly transitional in character (Russia). The confederal model has tended to be the least stable, though the original reasons for adopting such a model probably explain its instability more than any flaws in the model

itself. The interaction between cultural and institutional causes of political instability was apparent in the case of the former Yugoslavia. As the twenty-first century began, there were twenty-five federal nations in the world, ranging in size from India to St. Kitts and Nevis, with a total of approximately 40 percent of the world's population.

In debating how much to strengthen the federal government, the framers of the U.S. Constitution weighed three separate standards of comparison: prior federal governments, including their own; the western European national governments; and the member-state governments. Similarly, social scientists debate how much the federal government has strengthened its administrative, fiscal, and coercive capacities over the last two centuries relative to each of those three standards of comparison. Generally, they conclude that the federal government has strengthened its capacities, dramatically, as measured against its own earlier permutations, the western European national governments, and the member-state governments. Revisionists then present the "glass half-full" case. They argue that the nineteenth-century federal government was not as weak as supposed, pointing to such developments as the Federalists' establishment of a highly elastic fiscal-military, military-fiscal state during the 1790s, the bureaucratization of the post and land offices during the 1820s and 1830s, and the exponential expansion of military pensioners over the course of the whole century.

RECENT RESEARCH AND CONTEMPORARY PROBLEMS

One interesting area of recent research examines the ways that indigenous and slave populations affected, both negatively and positively, the development of the federal government. Another area of research explores the ways that governing authority has constantly shifted back and forth across the relatively porous constitutional boundaries between the federal and state governments to create and re-create Morton Grodzins's (1966) "marble cake" system. A third area of research involves comparative studies of federal systems. The best of these studies not only distinguish federal systems in terms of their different constitutional, legal, and institutional structures but also analyze the fit between those structures and the underlying political culture.

Beginning in the last two decades of the twentieth century Americans have witnessed a reinvigorated debate among their political elites, especially Supreme Court justices, over the constitutional boundaries of their federal system. The significance of this debate, however, pales before the debates over the viability of federal systems as solutions to the deep-seated ethnic, linguistic, and religious divisions in the developing nations of the world as many of these nations continue to struggle with the artificial national boundaries that were imposed on them by their European colonizers. Power sharing between various ethnic, linguistic, and religious groups has become the rhetoric of success in nations as diverse as Iraq and the Sudan. Still, even the process of adopting a mutually acceptable constitution has proven extremely difficult. The federal solution remains available as a way of attempting to translate the rhetoric of power sharing into reality, but it is hardly sufficient as a solution to the multiple challenges these nations face.

SEE ALSO *Federalism; Government; State, The*

BIBLIOGRAPHY

Elazar, Daniel J., comp. and ed. 1994. *Federal Systems of the World: A Handbook of Federal, Confederal, and Autonomy Arrangements*, 2nd ed. Harlow, U.K.: Longman Current Affairs.

Farrand, Max, ed. 1937 [1911]. *The Records of the Federal Convention of 1787*, 4 vols. New Haven, CT: Yale University Press.

Grodzins, Morton. 1966. *The American System: A New View of Government in the United States*. Ed. Daniel J. Elazar. Chicago: Rand McNally.

Hamilton, Alexander, James Madison, and John Jay. 1961. *The Federalist Papers*. Ed. Clinton Rossiter. New York: New American Library.

Kincaid, John, and G. Alan Tarr, eds. 2005. *A Global Dialogue on Federalism*, Vol. 1: *Constitutional Origins, Structure, and Change in Federal Countries*. Montreal, Canada: McGill-Queen's University Press.

David F. Ericson

GOVERNMENT, UNITARY

The term *unitary government* refers to a constitutional arrangement by which ultimate political authority is held by the central government of a state. In this system sovereignty is vested in the central government alone.

A unitary state does not necessarily imply that only one level of government exists. In fact, unitary states often have multiple levels of government, and in those states political authority is divided across different territorial levels. Japan is an example of a unitary state. It has a central government and below that forty-seven prefectures and over three thousand municipal governments. France is another example of a state with a unitary government. What makes a state unitary is that the central government has ultimate power over the other geographic levels of government and determines what those governments do,

how much money they may spend, the location of their boundaries, and whether they exist. In unitary states, therefore, local or regional governments exist alongside central governments, but their financial and political autonomy and even their right to exist are determined by the central government.

The United Kingdom traditionally has been a unitary state with power heavily centralized in London. In that system local governments exist but are created and controlled by central government statute. An example of that control occurred in 1986 when the Conservative government passed legislation to abolish the metropolitan level of government in many major cities, including London. Since 1997, under a Labour government, there has been a devolution of political power in the United Kingdom. Part of the process has been the establishment of a Scottish parliament and a Welsh assembly with independent authority over a range of policy decisions in those territories. Constitutionally, however, the United Kingdom remains a unitary state. The devolved administrations in Scotland and Wales were created by acts of Parliament and in theory could be abolished in the same fashion.

Unitary systems stand in direct contrast to federal political systems. A federal system is one in which two or more levels of government exist but those governmental levels have a constitutionally guaranteed right to exist and constitutionally guaranteed powers. Unlike a unitary system, neither level of government can be abolished or reformed without the consent of the other. In the United States, for example, the federal government cannot abolish California or reform its borders without the consent of California. Other examples of federal states are Australia, Canada, India, and Brazil.

Arguments in favor of a unitary system include the fact that it allows for consistency of policymaking and service delivery across the whole state, in contrast to the differences that frequently are found in federal states. This has the potential to create a strong sense of national identity within a state.

SEE ALSO *Conservative Party (Britain); Federalism; Government; Government, Federal; Labour Party (Britain); Nationalism and Nationality; Sovereignty; State, The*

BIBLIOGRAPHY

Dickerson, Mark O., and Thomas Flanagan. 2006. *An Introduction to Government and Politics: A Conceptual Approach*. 7th ed. Toronto: Nelson Canada.

Wheare, K. C. 1964. *Federal Government*. 4th ed. New York: Oxford University Press.

John B. Sutcliffe

GOVERNMENT, WORLD

The concept of *world government* refers to the institutional organization and administration of global affairs, including issues of peace and security, economics, the environment, and the potential constitution of a comprehensive international system of law and justice. In today's international system, the United Nations (UN) most closely approximates the idea of an institutionalized world government. However, to the extent that the UN system does indeed represent a world government, it differs from state or domestic governments in that it possesses no centralized authority with the power to enforce its rule. Generally speaking, domestic governments have a clear vertical or hierarchical structure of authority, with clear rules delineating who has the final say concerning executive decision-making, legislation, jurisprudence, and law enforcement. The international system does not operate under such a clear chain of command. To reflect this distinction the term "global governance" is often used in place of the concept of world government.

An alternative tradition also exists that understands world government in darker, more ambiguous terms. From this perspective, the concept of world government evokes the specter of global domination by a single national power, faceless bureaucracy, or conspiratorial group controlling world affairs from behind closed doors. Nationalists and libertarians see the potential evolution of a world government as a potentially totalitarian threat to liberty and national identity. And for centuries, conspiracy theorists have claimed secret societies such as the "Illuminati" or Freemasons are the true powers that orchestrate global politics. Today, some fear that private-sector networks of the international political and business elite—such as the Trilateral Commission or the World Economic Forum—pull the strings of the global economy, representing a pseudo world government beyond the reach of public accountability.

THE UNITED NATIONS AS WORLD GOVERNMENT

While the UN is structured like a typical domestic government with executive, legislative, and judicial branches, it does not function like one. For example, the General Assembly of the UN is not the primary legislative body of international law. Rather, international law has two recognized foundations independent of the UN system: interstate treaties and long-standing customs—and as a result, in comparison to domestic governments, lawmaking at the level of world government is decentralized. Treaties are the most common way in which international rules are made. They involve the mutual agreement by two or more states to regulate behavior according to predetermined limits. The Geneva Conventions represent a series of such treaties. Customary laws, on the other hand—for example, the recognized freedom of the high seas—develop over time as a consequence of accepted long-standing conduct in international relations. Whereas treaty-based laws only regulate signatories, customary laws are held to be universal. To be effective, however, most international rules must be incorporated into domestic law by domestic legislators—thus the common requirement that national legislative bodies ratify international treaties. In the United States this is the responsibility of the Senate.

Considered as a form of world government, the UN also has very little independent enforcement power beyond threats of force issued by the Security Council. As a result, the authority of the UN depends upon either the willful compliance of member states or the force of a few dominant military and economic powers. For example, the International Court of Justice, representing the primary judicial institution of the UN system—and otherwise known as the World Court—was established to settle legal disputes between member states, and to issue advisory opinions if requested by other UN organs, such as the Security Council or the General Assembly. The statute of the International Court of Justice is part of the UN Charter, yet the enforcement of its decisions is generally dependent upon member-states' willingness to comply. No state may be sued before the Court without accepting its jurisdiction over the particular case beforehand. Thus the more powerful a state, the more difficult it is to enforce decisions against it. The record of the United States is particularly poor in this regard. In 1986 the Court ruled against it in a case regarding the mining of Nicaraguan waters. The United States refused to recognize the process, and Nicaragua was powerless to appeal.

THE DEVELOPMENT OF INTERNATIONAL LAW

In fact, rather than referring to the international system as a present-day world government, it is more common to refer to international law as representing only the potential roots of a possible future world government. The modern rise of international law can be traced back to the Peace of Westphalia of 1648, which ended the Thirty Years' War in part by recognizing the right of territorial sovereignty in interstate affairs. What came to be known as the Westphalian order is defined by two principles: state territoriality—the international recognition of well-defined borders—and the right to nonintervention in domestic affairs. The Westphalian order placed the independent nation-state at the center of the international system at the expense of larger supranational authorities such as the Holy Roman Empire or the Roman Catholic Church. Nonetheless, international law constituted only a minimal system of coexistence, and military force remained the primary mechanism for the settlement of conflict. The early nineteenth century witnessed the formation of the Concert of Europe—a balance of power arrangement with the goal of establishing security on the continent in the wake of the Napoleonic wars. Yet it was not until the end of World War I (1914–1918) and the founding of the League of Nations that the first systemic international organization was formed with the purpose of avoiding war altogether. And it was not until the close of World War II (1939–1945) that the formation of the United Nations, and the establishment of the International Military Tribunal for the Punishment of War Criminals, made aggressive war an internationally recognized crime.

After World War II, international law entered a new stage represented by the ban on the use of force and the elevation of human rights to the status of international law through the Universal Declaration of Human Rights. Historically, the subjects of international law had always been groups or collective actors, principally states. But with the rise of human rights and war crimes legislation more and more international law came to refer directly to the individual person, independent of particular group membership. With this development some understand international law to be following a trajectory that points away from the statist Westphalian model of international relations toward a universalist, cosmopolitan model of world government.

Most international law, however, remained state- or group-based well into the start of the twenty-first century. Many late-twentieth century developments do, however, point toward the coexistence of an alternative cosmopolitan model. For example, the International Criminal Court (ICC) points toward the development of an international system of justice in which individuals could claim to be citizens of the world subject to a single law executed by a single world government. Thus one might imagine a future world government as taking form around such a notion of universal citizenship. The ICC was founded in 1998 to prosecute perpetrators of the most heinous crimes recognized by the entire international community, including "genocide" and "crimes against humanity." However, important obstacles to its success remain: Not all countries immediately recognized its authority, subsequently undermining its claim to universality; most important, the United States disputed its mandate, claimed special exemption from its jurisdiction, and pressured other countries—especially its aid recipients—to do the same. Similarly, other trends suggest that the decentralized structure of the international system could just as easily develop away from the consolidation of a coherent world government. For example, in the early years of the twenty-first century, international regulation was increasingly the product of private-public partnerships, resulting in a plu-

ralization of rule-making structures rather than their institutional concentration.

SEE ALSO *League of Nations; United Nations*

BIBLIOGRAPHY

Cassese, Antonio. 2005. *International Law*. 2nd ed. Oxford: Oxford University Press.

Held, David. 1995. *Democracy and the Global Order: From the Modern State to Cosmopolitan Governance*. Stanford, CA: Stanford University Press.

Held, David, and Anthony McGrew, eds. 2002. *Governing Globalization: Power, Authority, and Global Governance*. Oxford: Polity Press.

Slaughter, Anne-Marie. 2004. *A New World Order*. Princeton, NJ: Princeton University Press.

Adam Lupel

GOVERNMENTALITY

The term *governmentality* was coined by the French philosopher and historian Michel Foucault (1926–1984). Foucault's *gouvernementalité* was derived from the French word *gouvernemental* meaning "concerning government." Foucault introduced the notion in his lectures of 1978 and 1979 at the Collège de France as a guiding principle in his "genealogy of the modern state" (Foucault 2004a, 2004b) illustrating his working hypothesis on the reciprocal constitution of technologies of power and political rationalities. Also, Foucault uses the notion of government in a sense geared strongly to the older meaning of the term, stressing the close link between forms of power and processes of subjectification. He demonstrates that in addition to the management by the state or the administration, *government* in the past also signified problems of self-control, guidance for the family, management of the household, or directing the soul. For this reason, Foucault defines government as "the conduct of conduct" and thus as a term that ranges from "governing the self" to "governing others" (Foucault 1982, pp. 220–221).

Foucault's lectures trace the genealogy of governmentality from classical Greek and Roman days via the notion of state reason and the science of the police in early modernity through to liberal and neoliberal forms of government. While Foucault's analytics of government remained more a fragmentary sketch than an elaborated theory, it has nevertheless inspired many studies in the social sciences and historical investigations. Especially in Great Britain, Australia, Canada, and the United States, scholars have sought to refine and extend Foucault's work for a critical analysis of political technologies and governmental rationalities in contemporary societies.

These "studies of governmentality" have focused on the shift from the Keynesian welfare state toward the so-called free market policies in Western democracies and the rise of neoliberal political programs. The concept of governmentality offers two important theoretical advantages for this line of investigation. First, power relations are not restricted to the government of the state but include all forms of directing and guiding individuals and collectives in civil society and in the economic sphere. According to this theoretical perspective, the differences between state and society, politics and economy, the private and the public sphere do not function as universal foundations or essential borderlines, but as elements and effects of technologies of government that could be studied and critically assessed (see Foucault 1991, p. 103). Secondly, the liberal polarity of subjectivity and power ceases to be plausible. From the perspective of governmentality, government refers to a continuum, which extends from political government right through to forms of self-regulation. This theoretical stance allows for a more complex analysis of neoliberal forms of government that feature not only direct intervention by political authorities and empowered state agencies, but also develop indirect techniques for guiding and controlling individuals.

SEE ALSO *Economics, Keynesian; Foucault, Michel; Government; Liberalism; Welfare State*

BIBLIOGRAPHY

Dean, Mitchell. 1999. *Governmentality: Power and Rule in Modern Society*. Thousand Oaks, CA: Sage.

Foucault, Michel. 1982. The Subject and the Power. In *Michel Foucault: Beyond Structuralism and Hermeneutics*, by Hubert Dreyfus and Paul Rabinow, 208–226. Chicago: University of Chicago Press.

Foucault, Michel. 1991. Governmentality. In *The Foucault Effect: Studies in Governmentality*, eds. Graham Burchell, Colin Gordon, and Peter Miller, 87–104. Chicago: University of Chicago Press.

Foucault, Michel. 2004a. *Sécurité, territoire, population: Cours au Collège de France, 1977–1978*. Paris: Gallimard/Seuil.

Foucault, Michel. 2004b. *Naissance de la biopolitique: Cours au Collège de France, 1978–1979*. Paris: Gallimard/Seuil.

Lemke, Thomas. 1997. *Eine Kritik der politischen Vernunft: Foucaults Analyse der modernen Gouvernementalität*. Hamburg/Berlin: Argument.

Thomas Lemke

GRAMEEN BANK

The genesis of Grameen Bank (GB) can be traced back to 1974, when Mohammed Yunus, a professor in Chittagong University, loaned the equivalent of $27 to forty-two indebted residents of Jobra, a village in Bangladesh. Witnessing the grinding poverty and famine conditions, Yunus and his students conducted surveys and discovered the critical significance of credit for breaking out of the proverbial poverty trap. The distinctive feature of these loans was the absence of any collateral. The success of the experiment was almost immediate and led to the formal establishment of the GB on October 2, 1983, as a semiprivate institution to help alleviate poverty in rural Bangladesh. The word *Grameen* comes from the Bengali word *gram*, meaning "village." The 2006 Nobel Peace Prize was awarded to Yunus and the GB, and today the bank is among the most famous nongovernmental organizations (NGOs) in the world.

Mohammed Yunus was born on June 28, 1940, in the port city of Chittagong, Bangladesh. His father was a goldsmith and his upbringing was comfortable. He was a successful entrepreneur starting a new family business, which he gave up when he received a Fulbright grant in 1965 to study economics at Vanderbilt University. After completing his PhD he taught briefly at Middle Tennessee State University (MTSU). The 1971 civil war and birth of the newly independent Bangladesh convinced him to return home. He first joined the planning commission in Dhaka, but soon returned to academia as the head of the economics program at Chittagong University. From this campus, he studied the economic lives of the poor and came up with the idea of the GB.

Yunus realized that the skilled poor could substantially raise their incomes and standard of living if they could bypass the middleman or the village moneylender, so he focused on how to make institutional credit available to the poor. Established banks had no interest in poor borrowers because the transaction cost of dealing with low-income customers in villages was high, and lending to them would violate the cardinal rule of banking—to lend only against valuable assets, or "collateral." In his Nobel lecture, Yunus recalled, "I was shocked to discover a woman in the village borrowing less than a dollar from the moneylender on the condition that he would have the exclusive right to buy all she produces at the price he decides. This, to me, was a way of recruiting slave labor" (Yunus 2006).

Gradually, through trial and error and with the help of a dedicated group of students, Yunus developed the concept of a new type of banker who would visit poor rural customers in their homes and workplaces. The small loans are given only to the very poor—mostly women—who are disciplined and ambitious, with ideas for small (micro-) businesses, and successful in joining a team of four. After training, the team member with the best business model receives a micro loan, with the first installment to be paid the following week. Only when the first borrower has substantially returned her loan can the other team members have their projects financed. The average loan is roughly $200 at 16 percent annually. Given the weekly returns, the effective annual interest rates are in the range of 20 to 30 percent, which may sound high, but they are significantly below the rates charged by village moneylenders, which are often around 120 percent annually. The bank offers additional products for its members—home loans, compulsory savings, disaster funds, life insurance, loans to beggars, and so on. The housing loan program has helped construct 640,000 new sturdy homes for its customers. In 1995 the bank stopped accepting donor funds, and today the bank is entirely self-financed and self-sustaining. According to internal studies, 58 percent of its clients have crossed the poverty line.

The Grameen Bank was created by a special presidential proclamation, which makes it a unique institution. At first, the ownership split between government and members was 60:40, but this was later changed to 25:75 in favor of the members or borrowers. The bank has given over $5.7 billion in micro loans since its inception to more than 7 million clients across 73,000 villages in Bangladesh (and with an average of five members in a Bangladeshi household, this amounts to a potential impact on 35 million citizens). A significant percentage of the members (97%) are women, and the loan repayment rate is an impressive 98 percent. As of 2007, the bank has 2,226 branches all over the country. The model with some variations has spread across the world, and can be found in communities in Europe, Latin America, and North America. According to one estimate, today more than 60 million poor worldwide have access to microfinance. The Grameen Bank is a shining instance of the success of idealistic ventures in the struggle against poverty.

SEE ALSO *Development; Development Economics; Loans; Microfinance; Nobel Peace Prize; Nongovernmental Organizations (NGOs); Poverty; Transaction Cost*

BIBLIOGRAPHY

Bornstein, David. 1996. *The Price of a Dream: The Story of Grameen Bank and the Idea That Is Helping the Poor to Change Their Lives.* New York: Simon and Schuster.

Yunus, Mohammad. 2006. Nobel Lecture. Nobel Foundation Web site. http://nobelpeaceprize.org/eng_lec_2006b.html.

Yunus, Mohammad, with Alan Jolis. 1998. *Banker to the Poor: The Autobiography of Mohammad Yunus, Founder of the Grameen Bank.* London: Aurum Press.

Salim Rashid
Munir Quddus

GRAMSCI, ANTONIO
1891–1937

Antonio Gramsci counts among the most influential thinkers of the Left in the twentieth century. Born to a family of modest means in Caligari, Sardinia, Italy, Gramsci's early life was characterized by poverty, and for most of his life he suffered from poor health, which was worsened by his long imprisonment in fascist Italy. He died in 1937 after more than ten years in prison.

LIFE

In addition to poverty and work to support his family, Gramsci's early years in Sardinia introduced him to socialist politics, as well as to the writings of prominent Italian thinkers of his time, including Gaetano Salvemini (1873–1957), Benedetto Croce (1866–1952), Giuseppe Prezzolini (1882–1982), and Pilade Cecchi, in addition to becoming introduced to the writings of Karl Marx (1818–1883). The beginnings of Gramsci's entry into the larger spheres of Italian political and intellectual life can roughly be dated to the years 1911 and 1912, when after obtaining a scholarship to attend the University of Turin, he immersed himself in the study of linguistics, philosophy, and literature, and also met a number of individuals who were to exercise a profound impact on his life, notably the leaders of the future Italian Communist Party (PCI), Palmiro Togliatti (1893–1964) and Angelo Tasca (1892–1960), as well as such intellectuals as Matteo Bartoli (1873–1946) and Umberto Cosmo (1868–1944).

His early academic promise notwithstanding, Gramsci dedicated much of his time after 1915 to journalism, becoming one of the most effective public voices of the Italian Socialist Party, from whose split the PCI was born with Gramsci's active participation in 1921. In those years he wrote regular columns for the Turin edition of the newspaper *Avanti!* (Forward!), and in 1919 he cofounded *L'Ordine Nuovo* (The New Order), which became an influential review. During those years Gramsci was constantly active in workers' militant organizing, and devoted much time to the factory council movement, in addition to giving talks to workers' study groups on historical revolutionary experiences, including the French Revolution and the Paris Commune, as well as on literature and Marxist philosophy.

Following the split that produced the PCI in 1921, Gramsci lived for over a year in Moscow (1922–1923) as an Italian delegate to the Communist International (Comintern), returning to Italy after his election to the Chamber of Deputies in 1924 gave him temporary immunity from arrest. During that period he also became the general secretary of the PCI. His writings at that point show concern about the main issues of the moment, including the rise of Joseph Stalin (1879–1953) in the Soviet Union and the elimination of the opposition in the Comintern, as well as the "southern question" in Italy—namely the less developed status of southern Italy, its status as a colonial periphery of the north, and the need of the communist party for a distinct strategy to mobilize the agrarian population—and the relationship between workers and intellectuals.

THOUGHT

The bulk of Gramsci's intellectual output, however, is contained in his *Prison Notebooks*, a large compendium of essays, commentaries, and letters written during his internment, which began to be published in piecemeal fashion by the PCI after World War II (1939–1945). It is these writings that reveal Gramsci's distinctive contribution to social theory and Left analysis, even though they are colored by a certain cryptic style designed to maneuver around issues sensitive to prison censors. The most significant innovations in these writings include Gramsci's thesis on hegemony, the role of intellectuals, and the status of the peasantry in Left analysis.

The notion of hegemony, in particular, was developed by Gramsci as a way to account for a deficiency in the revolutionary character of the working class, as well as to amend the economic determinism that had plagued Marxist analysis. In some ways, "hegemony" was Gramsci's way of elaborating the actual working out of Marx's famous dictum, "the ideas of the ruling class are always the ruling ideas." In Gramsci's formulation, hegemony accounts for how domination is exercised apart from coercion and force. The dominated classes or groups have their own reasons for accepting the ideas of a ruling class or elite, and such reasons are the ground for the spontaneous consent given to a dominant ideology by classes that are dominated by it.

This concept has obvious affinities to other terms used in the social sciences, such as unquestioned "common sense." However, contrary to appearances, hegemony, even if taken as "common sense," is not stable. It is liable to break down as the subordinated groups develop alternative ways of seeing the world, and as crises within established systems create room for precisely the emergence of alternative hegemonies. The key to this kind of transformation consists thus of cultural and political work in society, rather than simply revolutionary action. This is precisely what Gramsci meant by "war of position" (the long, patient work in civil society oriented to combating established hegemony), to be distinguished from "war of maneuver" (the revolutionary takeover in a society where domination is not complemented by hegemonic sway over society at large).

It was such an orientation toward questions of culture, consciousness, and active agency that also highlighted for Gramsci the role of intellectuals. He saw that intellectuals are crucial in articulating and disseminating the outlooks of the classes for which they speak, in a way that goes beyond the simple expression of economic interests. For the working class, an intellectual who fulfilled that role was not confined in Gramsci's thought to a stratum of educated, revolutionary elite. Rather, the "organic intellectual" could also be a lay person whose expression of the specific ideology of his class originates out of his actual working life. This conception arises out of Gramsci's argument that all individuals are intellectual in the sense of having and using an intellect, though not all are intellectuals in terms of their formal social role.

Finally, unlike many intellectuals on the left who ignored the peasantry while highlighting the role of the working class, Gramsci emphasized the need to address the "southern question," especially in countries like Italy (and Russia) where the peasantry comprised a large proportion of the population. His cryptic references to the "subaltern" encapsulate this orientation, and suggest the need for the party to assimilate the work of the organic intellectuals of segments of the population that it had ignored.

These various dimensions of Gramsci's outlook have insured him great influence over twentieth-century thought. Those looking for sources of inspiration in Marxist thought beyond economic determinism have turned to his work, as have media scholars who were interested in exploring how certain ideas disseminate more broadly than others.

SEE ALSO *Hegemony; Marxism; Socialism*

BIBLIOGRAPHY

Crehan, Kate. 2002. *Gramsci, Culture, and Anthropology.* Berkeley: University of California Press.

Finocchiaro, Maurice A. 1988. *Gramsci and the History of Dialectical Thought.* Cambridge, U.K.: Cambridge University Press.

Simon, Roger. 1991. *Gramsci's Political Thought: An Introduction,* rev. ed. London: Lawrence and Wishart.

Mohammed A. Bamyeh

GRAND THEFT AUTO

SEE *Video games.*

GRANGER CAUSALITY
SEE *Causality.*

GRANGER-SIMS TEST
SEE *Causality.*

GRANT, ULYSSES S.
1822–1885

Born as Hiram Ulysses Grant on April 27, 1822, at Point Pleasant, Ohio, the son of Jesse Root and Hannah Simpson Grant, Grant grew up in nearby Georgetown. In 1839 he entered the U.S. Military Academy at West Point, graduating in the middle of his class in 1843; it was at this time that he became Ulysses S. Grant, a result of a West Point clerical error. During the Mexican-American War (1846–1848), he saw action in several battles, despite the fact that he served as quartermaster and commissary officer for his regiment. Marrying Julia Dent in 1848, he found peacetime military service frustrating professionally and personally, and resigned his commission as captain in 1854. Over the next seven years, Grant struggled to provide for his family, which eventually included four children. A combination of bad luck, uncertain health, and the impact of the economic panic of 1857 left him impoverished before he took a position at his father's general store in Galena, Illinois, in 1860. With the outbreak of the Civil War (1861–1865) the following year, he offered his services, eventually securing a colonel's commission; before long he found himself a brigadier general, courtesy of the influence of his hometown congressman.

In 1861 Grant led U.S. forces southward into Kentucky and Missouri, securing Paducah in September. The following year, forces under his command, aided by a gunboat flotilla, captured Fort Henry (February 6, 1862) and Fort Donelson (February 16, 1862), along with some twelve thousand Confederate soldiers. Two months later, he fended off a Confederate attack at Shiloh, Tennessee (April 6–7, 1862), although the high losses he suffered and his lack of preparedness brought him under heavy criticism.

Late in the fall of 1862, after fending off several Confederate efforts to retake western Tennessee, Grant began planning to capture Vicksburg, Mississippi, the major remaining Confederate stronghold along the Mississippi River. After several abortive efforts, he took the city on July 4, 1863, following a campaign of marching and fighting that kept superior enemy forces off balance. The victory secured his hold on an important command: In November he scored another triumph at Chattanooga, Tennessee, a victory that paved the way for President Abraham Lincoln (1809–1865) to elevate him to overall command of the armies of the United States in 1864. In less than fourteen months from assuming command, Grant devised the grand strategy and coordinated the campaigns that led to the collapse of the Confederacy. He took charge of the forces opposing the Confederacy's leading general, Robert E. Lee (1807–1870), and in some six weeks of bloody campaigning forced Lee back to defend the Confederate capital at Richmond, Virginia. Holding Lee in check while other Union armies triumphed (as did Lincoln in his reelection bid), Grant pushed Lee out of Richmond at the beginning of April, tracked him down, and forced him to surrender what remained of his army on April 9, 1865.

Immediately after the war, Grant urged reconciliation between North and South, but he quickly came to oppose white supremacist violence and to support recognizing black civil and eventually political rights. His popularity as a war hero made him an ideal presidential candidate for the Republican Party in 1868: His triumph came in the first election in which black Americans voted in large numbers, enough to secure Grant's majority in the popular vote. Having run for the presidency in the belief that only he could stave off a Democratic resurgence and preserve the fruits of military victory, Grant unsuccessfully attempted to balance sectional reconciliation with federal protection of black equality before the law.

During Grant's first term, the former Confederate states completed their return to civil government, while the ratification of the Fifteenth Amendment appeared to safeguard black voting. His efforts to subdue terrorist groups such as the Ku Klux Klan enjoyed initial success, although eventually a combination of white supremacist persistence, eroding public support, adverse court decisions, and inadequate institutional foundations led to the recapture of the former Confederate states by the Democratic Party. Although Grant oversaw the establishment of a stable deflationary monetary policy and a peaceful settlement of outstanding issues with Great Britain, his efforts to build a political base through patronage to help him pass his agenda, especially the attempted annexation of the Dominican Republic, only spurred greater opposition within his own party. Eventually, these opponents formed the short-lived Liberal Republican movement, which unsuccessfully tried to thwart Grant's bid for reelection in 1872.

The onset of economic depression and the revelation of corruption within the administration marred Grant's second term, as did the collapse of his peace policy toward Native Americans. Leaving office in 1877 after playing a critical role in resolving the disputed election of 1876, Grant took a trip around the world, returning to fail in a bid for the 1880 Republican presidential nomination. Moving to Wall Street, Grant tried his hand at business once more, only to be impoverished when he became the victim of a swindler. Soon thereafter, he learned he had throat cancer. In order to provide for his family, Grant commenced writing his autobiography, completing the manuscript, widely praised as a masterpiece, only days before his death at Mount MacGregor, New York, on July 23, 1885. He was buried in New York City; in 1897 his remains were reinterred in a massive tomb overlooking the Hudson River.

As a general, Grant displayed a doggedness and aggressiveness that sometimes overshadowed his ability to plan and conduct major campaigns and coordinate his forces, skills not evident in his predecessors in high command. Critics claim that he was a blundering bloody butcher, but the indictment does not stand up under examination. He also displayed a shrewd willingness to cooperate with his civil superiors and came to embrace both emancipation and the waging of hard war as keys to victory. As such, he has been cited as a model for military leadership and business management, something of an irony given his failures in business. Assessments of his presidency as a flat failure have given way to a more balanced view that takes into account the difficult problems Grant faced and gives him due credit for his successes and for exhibiting some political skill.

SEE ALSO *Ku Klux Klan; Lee, Robert E.; Lincoln, Abraham; Mexican-American War; Native Americans; Presidency, The; Reconstruction Era (U.S.); Republican Party; Slavery; Terrorism; U.S. Civil War*

BIBLIOGRAPHY

Bunting, Josiah, III. 2004. *Ulysses S. Grant.* New York: Times Books.

Simon, John Y., et al., eds. 1967–2005. *The Papers of Ulysses S. Grant.* Carbondale: Southern Illinois University Press.

Simpson, Brooks D. 2000. *Ulysses S. Grant: Triumph Over Adversity.* Boston: Houghton Mifflin.

Brooks D. Simpson

GRATZ V. BOLLINGER

SEE *Grutter Decision.*

GRAUNT, JOHN
1620–1674

John Graunt is recognized as the father of demography for his systematic yet critical use of population data to inves-

tigate demographic processes. He originated a number of demographic techniques and demonstrated a healthy skepticism of his own data.

Graunt was born in England in 1620. He was the son of a draper and, after completing his apprenticeship, he inherited his father's business. Graunt acquired some degree of wealth and prestige and rose through the ranks of civil service, although he was not among the educated class of his day.

As a pastime, Graunt studied the Bills of Mortality—birth and death registers published weekly and annually in the *London Times* throughout the seventeenth century. Birth data was collected from christenings; mortality data was collected by older women, called *searchers*, who were paid to inquire about cause of death from family and physicians. Graunt's *Natural and Political Observations on the Bills of Mortality*, which appeared around 1662, explored many demographic questions. His empirical investigation revealed that females tended to have a longer lifespan than males, that London was growing through internal migration from the country, and that the population of London was actually much smaller (around 460,000 people) than commonly asserted (estimates ranged up to seven million).

Graunt also formulated a number of methods that continue to be used by demographers today. He expressed the number of male births relative to female births as a ratio, creating what has come to be known as the *sex ratio at birth*. He estimated a *doubling time* for the growth of the city of London. In addition, Graunt observed that mortality varies by age. This insight led him to develop the first *life table*—a table that follows a virtual population of one hundred people through the age-specific mortality rates of the actual population. Edmund Halley (1656–1742) later perfected the life table and gave it its actuarial application.

One of Graunt's most important methodological contributions was a skepticism of his own data. Graunt was concerned with unavailable data, poorly defined categories, misspecification of the cause of death, and underreporting. He discussed at length the possibility of searchers being inaccurate, bribed, or drunk at the time of inquiry.

Graunt's work also made the critical contribution of substantive interpretation. Previously, the Royal Statistical Society's official goal was merely to gather data, not to interpret it. The Society claimed that "threshing out" the implications of data should be left to the court (i.e., politicians), a position that protected the Society from appearing partisan, but discouraged demographic research.

Late in life, Graunt converted to Catholicism. In the politically and religiously charged atmosphere of England at the time, his conversion had tragic consequences. He was forced to resign from his positions in civil service. The Great Fire of London in 1666 destroyed his home—a setback from which he never recovered. He lived out his last years with the financial help of his friend William Petty (1623–1687). Graunt died in 1674 in such poverty that the Draper Society awarded his widow £4 annually for her upkeep.

BIBLIOGRAPHY

Sutherland, Ian. 1963. John Graunt: A Tercentenary Tribute. *Journal of the Royal Statistical Society* 126 (4): 537–556.

Warren Waren

GRAVITATION

SEE *Long Period Analysis;* Tâtonnement.

GRE TEST, THE

SEE *Standardized Tests.*

GREAT CONTRACTION

SEE *Great Depression.*

GREAT CRASH

SEE *Great Depression; Wall Street.*

GREAT DEPRESSION

Between 1929 and 1933 the world economy collapsed. In country after country, although not in all, prices fell, output shrank, and unemployment soared. In the United States the rate of unemployment reached 25 percent of the labor force, in the United Kingdom 16 percent, and in Germany a staggering 30 percent. These rates are only roughly comparable across countries and with twenty-first century unemployment rates because of different definitions of unemployment and methods of collection; nevertheless, they show the extremity of the crisis. The recovery, moreover, was slow and in some countries incomplete. In 1938 the rate of unemployment was still at double-digit levels in the United States and the United Kingdom, although thanks to rearmament it was considerably lower

in Germany. A number of previous depressions were extremely painful, but none was as deep or lasted as long. There were many recessions that came after, but none could begin to compare in terms of prolonged industrial stagnation and high unemployment. The consequences stemming from the Great Depression for economies and polities throughout the world were profound. The early appearance of depression in the United States and the crucial role of the United States in world trade make it important to consider the U.S. case in some detail.

THE GREAT DEPRESSION IN THE UNITED STATES

There had been severe depression in the United States before the 1930s. The most similar occurred in the 1890s. Indeed, the sequence of events in the 1890s foreshadowed what was to happen in the 1930s in some detail. Prices of stocks began to decline in January 1893, and a crash came in May and June after the failure of several well-regarded firms. The market continued to decline, and at its low point in 1896 had lost 30 percent of its value. The decline in the stock market was associated with a sharp contraction in economic activity. A banking panic intensified the contraction. There seem to have been two sources for the panic. First, fears that the United States would leave the gold standard prompted by the growing strength of the free silver movement led to withdrawals of gold from New York. In addition, a wave of bank failures in the South and West produced by low agricultural prices also undermined confidence in the banking system. Runs on banks spread throughout the country and the crisis ended with a general restriction of the conversion of bank notes and deposits into gold. The money supply fell, the economy slowed, bank and business failures multiplied, and unemployment rose. Although a recovery began in June 1894, the recovery was slow and uneven. By 1897 one-third of the railroad mileage in the United States was in receivership. It took until 1898 for the stock market to match its 1893 peak, and for annual real gross domestic product (GDP) per capita to match its 1892 level.

During the early 1930s events unfolded in a similar fashion. There were few signs in 1929, however, that a Great Depression was on the horizon. There had been a severe contraction in 1920–1921, but the economy had recovered quickly. There were minor contractions in 1923–1924 and 1926–1927, and the agricultural sector had struggled during the 1920s, but overall the economy prospered after the 1920–1921 recession. In 1929 unemployment in the United States was just 3.2 percent of the labor force; in many ways it was a vintage year.

The stock market boomed in the late 1920s and reached a peak in 1929; prices rose nearly 2.5 times between 1927 and its peak in 1929. Economic historians have long debated whether there was a bubble in the market in the late 1920s, meaning that prices of shares had risen more rapidly than "fundamentals." Research conducted in 1993 by Peter Rappoport and Eugene White and other late-twentieth-century views have strengthened the case for a bubble. They have shown that many well-informed investors doubted the long-run viability of prevailing prices. There were undoubtedly, however, many other investors who believed that the economy had entered a so-called New Age, as was said at the time, in which scientific and technical research would produce rising real incomes, rising profits, and an eventual end to poverty.

The crash of the stock market in the fall of 1929 was partly a reflection of the state of the economy—a recession was already under way—but the crash also intensified the slowdown by undermining confidence in the economic future. The major impact of the crash, as shown by Christina Romer in her 1990 work, was to slow the sale of consumer durables. The crash may also have influenced markets around the world by forcing investors to reassess their optimistic view of the future. In any case, the stock markets in most other industrial countries after having risen in the 1920s also fell to very low levels in the first half of the 1930s. The U.S. market lost two-thirds of its value by 1933, the German market (which had peaked before the American market) lost one half, and the British market, which did somewhat better, lost one-fifth.

The collapse of the American banking system then intensified the contraction. There were repeated waves of bank failures between 1930 and 1933 produced by the economic contraction, by the decline in prices, especially in the agricultural sector, and perhaps by a contagion of fear. As people withdrew their cash from banks to protect their wealth, and as banks increased their reserves to prepare for runs, the stock of money shrank. The collapse of the American banking system reflected a number of unique circumstances. First, laws that prevented banks based in one state from establishing branches in other states, and sometimes from establishing additional branches within a state, had created a system characterized by thousands of small independent banks. In contrast, most other countries had systems dominated by a few large banks with branches. In Canada where the system consisted of a small number of banks with head offices in Toronto or Montreal and branches throughout the country there were no bank failures. In addition, the young and inexperienced Federal Reserve System (it was established in 1913) proved incapable of taking the bold actions needed to end the crisis.

Many explanations have been put forward for the failure of the Federal Reserve to stem the tide of bank runs and closures. Milton Friedman and Anna J. Schwartz in their classic *Monetary History of the United States* (1963) stressed an internal political conflict between the Federal Reserve Board in Washington and the New York Federal Reserve Bank that paralyzed the system. A 2003 study by Allan Meltzer stresses adherence to economic doctrines that led the Federal Reserve to misinterpret the fall in nominal interest rates during the contraction. The Treasury bill rate fell from about 5 percent in May 1929 to .10 percent in September 1933. The Federal Reserve viewed low rates as proof that it had made liquidity abundant and that there was little more it could do to combat the depression. The bank failures, which were concentrated among smaller banks in rural areas, or in some cases larger banks that had engaged in questionable activities, the Federal Reserve regarded as a benign process that would result in a stronger banking system. From 1930 to 1933 about 9,000 banks in the United States suspended operation and the money supply fell by one-third.

During the interregnum between the election of President Franklin Roosevelt in November 1932 and his taking office in March 1933 the banking system underwent further turmoil. In state after state governors proclaimed "bank holidays" that prohibited or limited withdrawals from banks and brought the banking and economic system to a standstill. The purpose of the holidays was to protect the banks from panicky withdrawals, but the result was to disrupt commerce and increase fears that the system was collapsing. By the time Roosevelt took office virtually all of the banks in the United States were closed and perhaps one-quarter of the labor force was unemployed. Roosevelt addressed the situation boldly. Part of his response was to rally the spirits of the nation. In his famous first inaugural address he told the people that "the only thing we have to fear is fear itself." His address also promised work for the unemployed and reforms of the banking system. The administration soon followed through. Public works programs, which focused on conservation in national parks and building infrastructure, were created to hire the unemployed. In the peak year of 1936 approximately 7 percent of the labor force was working in emergency relief programs.

The banking crisis was addressed in several ways. Banks were inspected and only "sound" banks were allowed to reopen. The process of inspection and phased reopening was largely cosmetic, but it appears to have calmed fears about the safety of the system. Deposit insurance was also instituted. In 1963 Milton Friedman and Ann Jacobson Schwartz argued that deposit insurance was important in ending the banking crisis and preventing a new eruption of bank failures by removing the fears that produced bank runs. Once depositors were insured by a federal agency they had no reason to withdraw their funds in cash when there was a rumor that the bank was in trouble. The number of bank failures in the United States dropped drastically after the introduction of deposit insurance.

The recovery that began in 1933, although not without setbacks, was vigorous and prolonged. By the middle of 1937 industrial production was close to the 1929 average. Still, there was considerable concern about the pace of recovery and the level of the economy. After all, with normal economic growth the levels of industrial production and real output would have been above their 1929 levels in 1937. Unemployment, moreover, remained stubbornly high. With a few more years of continued growth the economy might well have recovered fully. However, another recession, the "recession within the depression," hit the economy in 1937. By the trough in 1938 industrial production had fallen almost 60 percent and unemployment had risen once more. Mistakes in both fiscal and monetary policy contributed to the severity of the contraction, although the amounts contributed are disputed. The new Social Security system financed by a tax on wages was instituted in 1935, and the taxes were now put in place. The Federal Reserve, moreover, chose at this time to double the required reserve ratios of the banks. The main purpose of the increase was to prevent the reserves from being a factor in the future, to tie them down. The banks, however, were now accustomed to having a large margin of reserves above the required level and they appear to have cut their lending in order to rebuild this margin. The economic expansion that began in the summer of 1938, however, would last throughout the war and pull the economy completely out of the depression. Indeed, even before the United States entered the war as an active participant at the end of 1941, fiscal and monetary stimuli had done much to cure the depression.

THE DEPRESSION WIDENS

Most market-oriented countries, especially those that adhered to the gold standard, were affected by the Great Depression. One reason was the downward spiral of world trade. The economic decline in the United States hit hard at firms throughout the world that produced for the American market. As the depression spread from country to country, imports declined further.

The gold standard, to which most industrial countries adhered, provided another channel for the transmission of the Great Depression. The reputation of the gold standard had reached unchallenged heights during the period of expanding world trade before World War I. Most countries, with the exception of the United States, had abandoned the gold standard during the war to be free to print money to finance wartime expenditures. After the war, the gold standard had been reconstructed, but in a way that left it fragile. Most countries decided not to deflate their price levels back to prewar levels. Hence

the nominal value of world trade relative to the amount of gold in reserve was much higher after the war than before. Under the gold standard orthodoxy of the day central banks were supposed to place maintenance of the gold standard above other priorities. If a country was losing gold because its exports had fallen faster than its imports, the central bank was supposed to raise interest rates to protect its gold reserve, even if this policy exacerbated the economic contraction. Countries that gained gold might have lowered their rates, but they were reluctant to do so because lower rates would put their gold reserves at risk.

The global transmission of information and opinion provided a third, hard to measure, but potentially important channel. The severe slide on the U.S. stock market and other stock markets focused attention throughout the rest of the world on factors that might produce a decline in local markets. Waves of bank failures in the United States and central Europe forced depositors throughout the rest of the world to raise questions about the safety of their own funds. Panic, in other words, did not respect international borders.

Although these transmission channels assured that the whole world was affected in some degree by the depression, the experience varied markedly from country to country, as even a few examples will illustrate. In Britain output fell from 1929 to 1932, but the fall was less than 6 percent. The recovery, moreover, seems to have started sooner in Britain than in the United States and the growth of output from 1932 to 1937 was extremely rapid. Unemployment, however, soared in 1929 to 1931 and remained stubbornly high for the remainder of the decade. Although Britain was becoming less dependent on exports, exports were still about 15 percent of national product. The fall in exports produced by the economic decline in the United States and other countries, therefore, probably explains a good deal of the decline in economic activity in Britain. In September 1931 Britain devalued the pound and left the gold standard. The recovery in Britain began soon after. Export growth produced by a cheaper pound does not seem to have played a prominent part in the recovery, but a more expansionary monetary policy permitted by leaving gold does seem to have played a role. On the whole it may be said that the British economy displayed surprising resiliency in the face of the loss of its export markets.

Germany, on the other hand, suffered one of the most catastrophic declines. A severe banking crisis hit Germany in July 1931, punctuated by the failure of the Darmstädter-und Nationalbank on July 13. The German crisis may have been provoked by the failure of the Credit Anstalt bank in Austria in May 1931 and the subsequent run on the Austrian shilling, although economists have debated these factors. Germany soon closed its banks in an effort to stem the runs, and abandoned the gold standard. Germany, however, did not use the monetary freedom won by abandoning the commitment to gold to introduce expansionary policies. Between June 1930 and June 1933 the stock of money in Germany fell by nearly 40 percent. Prices and industrial production fell, and unemployment soared. Under the Nazis government spending, much of it for rearmament, and monetary expansion produced an extended economic boom that restored industrial production and full employment.

The experience of Japan where the depression was unusually mild has stimulated considerable interest. Unemployment rose mildly by Western standards between 1929 and 1933 and fell to 3.8 percent by 1938. Other indicators, such as the stock market, also rose between 1933 and 1938. Many observers have attributed this performance to the actions of Finance Minister Korekiyo Takahashi. In 1931 Takahashi introduced a stimulus package that included a major devaluation of the yen, interest rate cuts, and increases in government spending. The latter element of his package has led some observers to refer to Takahashi as a "Keynesian before Keynes." Late twentieth-century research has challenged the notion that Takahashi was able to break completely free of the economic orthodoxies of the day, but the strong performance of the Japanese economy remains an important signpost for scholars attempting to understand the factors that determined the course of events in the 1930s.

THEORIES

The factors previously stressed, the collapse of the banking system in the early 1930s, and the policy mistakes by the Federal Reserve and other central banks are of most relevance to what has come to be called the monetarist interpretation of the Great Depression. Some economists writing in the 1930s, such as Jacob Viner and Laughlin Currie, developed this view, concluding that much of the trouble could have been avoided if the Federal Reserve and other central banks had acted wisely.

In the aftermath of the publication of John Maynard Keynes' *General Theory* (1936), however, an alternative interpretation held sway. The Keynesians argued that the breakdown of the banking system, although disturbing, was mainly a consequence of the collapse of aggregate demand. The behavior of the Federal Reserve was at most a secondary problem. The Keynesians blamed the fall in aggregate demand on the failure of one or more categories of autonomous spending. At first, attention focused on investment; later attention shifted to consumption. The answer to the Great Depression was public works financed, if necessary, by borrowing. The New Deal in the United States had spent a great deal of money and run up highly controversial deficits; 1956 calculations by E. Cary

Brown, however, showed that a number of factors, including cuts in spending at the state and local level, had offset the effects of New Deal spending. Fiscal policy had failed to return the economy to full employment, according to Brown, "not because it did not work, but because it was not tried" (1956, pp. 863–866).

Friedman and Schwartz's *Monetary History*, which provided an extraordinarily detailed account of the effects of monetary policies during the 1930s and put the Great Depression into the broader context of American monetary history, returned the collapse of the banking system to center stage. Their interpretation was challenged in turn by Peter Temin in *Did Monetary Forces Cause the Great Depression* (1976) who defended the Keynesian interpretation. Subsequent work, however, continued to emphasize the banking crisis. The 1983 research of Ben Bernanke, who later became chair of the U.S. Federal Reserve, was particularly influential. Bernanke argued that the banking and financial crises had disrupted the ability of the banking system to act as an efficient financial intermediary. Even sound businesses found it hard to borrow when their customary lender had closed its doors and the assets they could offer as collateral to another lender had lost value. The Bernanke thesis not only explained why the contraction was severe, but also why it took so long for the economy to recover: It took time for financial markets to rebuild the relationships that had been sundered in the early 1930s.

Research that took a more global view of the Great Depression, such as Peter Temin's 1989 work, reinforced the case for viewing monetary forces as decisive. Barry Eichengreen's *Golden Fetters* (1992), one of the most influential statements of this view, stressed the role of the gold standard in transmitting the Depression and inhibiting recovery. Countries faced with balance of trade deficits because of declining exports should have maintained their stocks of money and aimed for internal price stability. Instead they often adopted contractionary policies aimed at stemming the outflow of gold. Those countries that abandoned the gold standard and undertook expansionary monetary policies recovered more rapidly than those who clung to gold. The examples provided by countries, such as Japan, which avoided trouble because they had never been on gold or quickly abandoned it were particularly telling.

In the twenty-first century economists have turned to formal models, such as dynamic computable general equilibrium models, to address macroeconomic questions, and have used these models to formulate and test ideas about the Great Depression. The 2002 and 2005 work of Harold Cole and Lee Ohanian has received considerable attention in both academic and mainstream circles. It is too early to say, however, whether this work will serve to reinforce traditional interpretations of the Great Depression reached by other methods or produce entirely new interpretations. It is not too soon to predict, however, that the Great Depression will continue to attract the interest of scholars attempting to understand basic macroeconomic processes.

One cannot say for certain that another Great Depression is impossible, but important lessons have been learned and important changes made in the financial system that make a repetition highly unlikely. For example, it seems improbable that any modern central bank would allow a massive collapse of the banking system and deflation to proceed unabated as happened in a number of countries in the early 1930s.

SEE ALSO *Aggregate Demand; Banking; Bull and Bear Markets; Business Cycles, Real; Central Banks; Depression, Economic; Economic Crises; Economics, Keynesian; Federal Reserve System, U.S.; Finance; Financial Markets; Fisher, Irving; Friedman, Milton; Gold Standard; Interest Rates; Investment; Keynes, John Maynard; Kindleberger, Charles Poor; Long Waves; Monetarism; Policy, Fiscal; Policy, Monetary; Recession; Stagnation; Unemployment*

BIBLIOGRAPHY

Bernanke, Ben S. 1983. Nonmonetary Effects of the Financial Crisis in the Propagation of the Great Depression. *American Economic Review* 73 (3): 257–276.

Bernanke, Ben S. 1995. The Macroeconomics of the Great Depression: A Comparative Approach. *Journal of Money, Credit and Banking* 27 (1): 1–28.

Brown, E. Cary. 1956. Fiscal Policy in the Thirties: A Reappraisal. *American Economic Review* 46 (5): 857–879.

Cole, Harold L., and Lee E. Ohanian. 2002. The U.S. and U.K. Great Depressions through the Lens of Neoclassical Growth Theory. *American Economic Review* 92 (2): 28–32.

Cole, Harold L., Lee E. Ohanian, and Ron Leung. 2005. *Deflation and the International Great Depression: A Productivity Puzzle*. Minneapolis, MN: Federal Reserve Bank of Minneapolis.

Eichengreen, Barry J. 1992. *Golden Fetters: The Gold Standard and the Great Depression, 1919–1939*. New York: Oxford University Press.

Friedman, Milton, and Anna Jacobson Schwartz. 1963. *A Monetary History of the United States, 1867–1960*. Princeton, NJ: Princeton University Press.

James, Harold. 1984. The Causes of the German Banking Crisis of 1931. *Economic History Review* 37 (1): 68–87.

Kindleberger, Charles Poor. 1973. *The World in Depression, 1929–1939*. Berkeley: University of California Press.

Meltzer, Allan H. 2003. *A History of the Federal Reserve*. Chicago: University of Chicago Press.

Rappoport, Peter, and Eugene N. White. 1993. Was There a Bubble in the 1929 Stock Market? *Journal of Economic History* 53 (3): 549–574.

Romer, Christina D. 1990. The Great Crash and the Onset of the Great Depression. *Quarterly Journal of Economics* 105 (3): 597–624.

Romer, Christina D. 1993. The Nation in Depression. *Journal of Economic Perspectives* 7 (2): 19–39.

Sicsic, Pierre. 1992. Was the Franc Poincaré Deliberately Undervalued? *Explorations in Economic History* 29: 69–92.

Temin, Peter. 1976. *Did Monetary Forces Cause the Great Depression?* New York: Norton.

Temin, Peter. 1989. *Lessons from the Great Depression*. Cambridge, MA: MIT Press.

Temin, Peter. 1993. Transmission of the Great Depression. *Journal of Economic Perspectives* 7 (2): 87–102.

Hugh Rockoff

GREAT MIGRATION

SEE *African Americans; Migration; Segregation, Residential.*

GREAT SOCIETY, THE

The term *Great Society*, which refers to the set of domestic programs initiated by Lyndon B. Johnson, who became the U.S. president after the assassination of John F. Kennedy in 1963, was coined by Johnson's speechwriter Richard N. Goodwin early in 1964. In an address during commencement exercises at the University of Michigan at Ann Arbor on May 22, Johnson used the term publicly for the first time. The new chief executive, eager to map out his own legislative agenda, challenged the American people to build a society "where progress is the servant of our needs," a society "where old values and new visions are buried under unbridled growth," a society that "rests on abundance and liberty for all," a society that "demands an end to poverty and racial injustice." Johnson identified the three places to begin the building of the Great Society—in the cities, in the countryside, and in the classrooms. He catalogued the social ills that needed to be corrected—urban decay, inadequate housing, poor transportation, environmental pollution, overburdened seashores, disappearing green fields, a poorly educated adult population, overcrowded classrooms, outdated curricula, unqualified teachers, and inadequate college funding. The far-thinking president envisioned a society where people are more concerned with the "quality of their goals" than the "quantity of their goods," a glorious America where the meaning of people's lives matches the marvelous products of their labor (*Public Papers of the Presidents of the United States*, pp. 704–707).

Johnson, who came to Washington during the 1930s, modeled his domestic initiatives on Franklin D. Roosevelt's New Deal, the policies implemented to combat the effects of the Great Depression. At the same time, the concept of the Great Society was meant to continue the legislative program begun by President Kennedy, called the New Frontier, and its implementation followed the same path.

The 1960s legislation, in contrast to the New Deal of the 1930s, was begun in a period of economic prosperity. After Johnson's Ann Arbor speech, fourteen separate task forces comprised of government experts and university scholars were assembled to study all major aspects of American society. One task force addressed foreign affairs, and the rest tackled domestic policies concerning agriculture, economic recession, civil rights, education, economic efficiency, health, income maintenance, intergovernmental cooperation, natural resources, environmental pollution, preservation of natural beauty, transportation, and urban problems. During the 1964 presidential campaign, however, the proposed Great Society agenda, other than civil rights, was not widely discussed. Johnson's popular vote majority of 61 percent, combined with the Democrats' winning enough seats to control two-thirds of the House and Senate, set the stage for the subsequent passage of bills submitted to both chambers. Lingering public and congressional sympathy for the slain president's program undoubtedly helped as well.

In late 1964 Johnson reviewed the task force reports submitted to the White House, and a number of recommendations were briefly mentioned in his State of the Union address on January 7, 1965. The president, now elected in his own right, confidently talked about the "beginning of the road to the Great Society" and summit meetings ahead with foreign heads of state, "where freedom from the wants of the body can help fulfill the needs of the spirit." He sought opportunity for all, a just nation that would provide hospital care for the elderly under social security, eliminate poverty in the midst of plenty, assure civil and voting rights for blacks, and provide to immigrants the promise of America based on the work they could do and not where they were born. In 1965 eighty-seven bills were submitted to Congress by the new administration, eighty-four of which were signed by Johnson. With this legislation, in addition to the Civil Rights Act passed in 1964, the core of the Great Society was created.

LEGISLATIVE ACTIONS

It was in the areas of civil rights and economic assistance that the Great Society was most effective. The Civil Rights Act (1964) made employment discrimination and segregation in public accommodations—on the basis of race, color, religion, sex, or national origin—illegal. This legislation was followed by the Voting Rights Act (1965), which guaranteed minority voter registration and voting by restricting the use of literacy tests and poll taxes. The Immigration and Nationality Services Act (1965) did away with the national origin quotas put in place in 1924; this law opened the door to waves of Asian and Latin American immigrants, a pattern still apparent in the early twenty-first century. The 1968 Civil Rights Act outlawed discrimination in housing and granted constitutional protections to Native Americans living on reservations. Johnson's so-called War on Poverty had its roots in the Economic Opportunity Act (1964), which established an Office of Economic Opportunity (OEO) to manage a variety of "community action" programs. The OEO was never meant to deal with poverty by raising welfare payments or guaranteeing wages, but to help the poor help themselves through education, job training, and community development. The Job Corps, Project Head Start, the Model Cities Program, the Neighborhood Youth Corps, Upward Bound, and VISTA were the most important new programs designed to assist poor people.

The Great Society also spawned well-known legislation in the areas of education and healthcare. The Elementary and Secondary Education Act (1965) provided significant federal aid to public education, and secured Head Start, originally a summer program, as a permanent component. Since education was a state and local matter, the federal government previously had refrained from assisting public schools for fear of violating the principle of "separation of powers." The Higher Education Act (1965) raised federal aid to public and private universities, granted scholarships and low-interest loans to students, and set up a National Teachers Corps. The Bilingual Education Act (1968) helped local school districts address the English-language needs of minority children. Medicare and Medicaid, today the bedrock of the U.S. healthcare system, had their origins in the Social Security Act of 1965. Initially bitterly opposed by the American Medical Association, these publicly funded programs that covered hospital costs and doctors' fees have been indispensable to older Americans, welfare recipients, and low-income families.

Legislative actions in the areas of culture, transportation, consumer protection, and the environment are likewise the direct result of President Johnson's vision for a better America. The National Foundation on the Arts and Humanities Act (1965) created two separate federal agencies for the funding of artistic and humanistic pursuits to counterbalance the emphasis given to scientific endeavors. The Urban Mass Transportation Act (1964) provided hundreds of millions of dollars in matching funds to cities for public and private rail projects, and the Highway Safety Act (1966) was enacted to protect motorists from unsafe roads and vehicles. American consumers benefited from a number of laws such as the Child Safety Act (1966), the Flammable Fabrics Act (1967), the Wholesale Meat Act (1967), and the Truth-in-Lending Act (1968).

More than any of the other sets of laws associated with the Great Society, the civil rights legislation of the 1960s stirred public controversy, which has continued for four decades. Johnson issued in 1965, and later expanded in 1967, Executive Order 11246, which required federal contractors to "take affirmative action" to ensure that people are hired and treated during employment without regard to their race, color, religion, sex, or national origin. By 1972 this presidential mandate, together with the legal ban on discrimination, led to federal pressure on employers (and then schools and housing providers) to take positive steps to correct past wrongs by giving "preferential treatment" to minorities and women. Before long, quotas were introduced, setting "goals" for protected classes of Americans and "timetables" for achieving them. White males responded with cries of "reverse discrimination": Complaints before the Equal Employment Opportunity Commission, state human rights agencies, and federal and state courts numbered in the hundreds of thousands. A few cases reached the Supreme Court

In a series of split and often very close decisions on both sides of the affirmative action debate, the Supreme Court itself added to the controversy. In *Regents of the University of California v. Bakke* in 1978, the Court in a five-to-four decision prohibited a California medical school from using a quota—reserving a specific number of places—for minorities in admissions. A year later, however, in *United Steelworkers of America v. Weber*, the same court ruled that it was okay for the steelworkers union to select only minorities for a special training program. Two cases two years apart, both involving firefighters, are also contradictory. In 1984, in *Firefighters Local Union No. 1784 v. Stotts*, it was decided that seniority was more important than race, that the City of Memphis could lay off recently hired minorities first in staff reductions. However, in *International Association of Firefighters v. City of Cleveland* (1986), the municipality was permitted to promote minorities over more senior whites. Three recent cases, two concerning the same educational institution, have further confused the issue of affirmative action with decisions that alternately sustained and reversed earlier rulings. In *Texas v. Hopwood* (1996) the high court let stand a lower court decision that race could not be used in college admissions. In *Gratz v. Bollinger* (2003), in a six-to-three decision the University of Michigan's strict formula awarding advantage based on race for admissions was struck down, but in the very same year, in *Grutter v.*

Bollinger, by five to four the University of Michigan Law School was permitted to use race as a factor in admissions.

FUNDING PROBLEMS

Funding the Great Society initiatives became difficult beginning in 1968 because of the burden of the Vietnam War, Johnson's reluctance to ask Congress for a tax increase, and the goal of reaching a balanced budget. Many of the programs had no political constituencies, that is, they did not originate from outside lobbying and thus lacked the support necessary for continued financing. Johnson's decision to withdraw from the 1968 presidential race further weakened his advocacy of government intervention on the side of racial justice and economic equality. Under the Republican administration of President Richard M. Nixon, in 1969 the OEO was dismantled and its poverty programs transferred to other federal agencies. Democrat Jimmy Carter's one-term presidency, bogged down with the twin problems of inflation and recession, did little to restore the earlier funding for social causes. Carter offered no new initiatives along the lines of Johnson's program, focusing instead on international affairs.

In the 1980s Ronald Reagan's strong conservative views on the role of government and federal spending, combined with a Republican Congress's disinclination to continue social programs, led to draconian cuts for the Great Society. The huge increase in appropriations for the military during this period further tolled the bell for the two-decades-old set of domestic programs. The administration of George H. W. Bush (1989–1993) essentially held fast to the new conservative agenda in Washington. By the time Bill Clinton took the oath of office in 1993 the Democrats had accepted the hard fact that most of the Great Society goals had not been, nor could they ever be, accomplished, and they did not push for new social legislation. Clinton's failure to get approval for a national health insurance program but success at passing a welfare reform bill only served to scale back the accomplishments of earlier Democratic presidents. Welfare reform now meant that time limits were imposed on the benefits received, able-bodied adult recipients were required to perform public service work, and more rigorous eligibility requirements were imposed, changes all contrary to Johnson's original goals for a better America. Under the administration of George W. Bush, which began in 2001, the Republican Congress did not kill all previous social programs, and it kept up some funding, but Bush's efforts toward the global war on terror and his initiation of the war in Iraq devoured budget surpluses and rendered impossible any meaningful attempt to reinvigorate Great Society spending, just as the war in Southeast Asia had almost four decades earlier.

THE GREAT SOCIETY REVISITED

The Great Society has always been closely identified with Democratic political agendas and the cold war liberalism of the 1960s. It was premised on Johnson's "guns and butter" approach, the idea that the United States can wage wars against communism in far-off places and, at the same time, still provide sufficient funding for domestic social programs. Critics of the Great Society were from the start skeptical of the federal government's ability to bring about the promised social change, and they are credited with paving the way for the conservative backlash of later decades. In the post-Vietnam era, liberal thinking gave way as Americans lost confidence in the effectiveness of military interventions. The cold war liberal Democratic presidents (Truman, Kennedy, Johnson) freely used military might to solve international problems (as in Korea, Cuba, the Dominican Republic, and Vietnam), but later Democratic presidents (Carter, Clinton) were reluctant to use force and turned to diplomacy instead (as in Panama, the Middle East, and the Balkans).

The War on Poverty, perhaps the most ambitious feature of the Kennedy-Johnson proposals, was also the most controversial and it has left a mixed legacy. Billions were spent on dozens of programs, but the poverty rate was just modestly reduced in the late 1960s, only to rise again in the 1970s and 1980s due to changing economic and social conditions. The leftist critique of the Great Society claimed that throwing money at problems will not solve underlying social problems without fundamental changes in the structure of the economy and the reduction of inequality in America. Nevertheless, Johnson's "other war" permanently expanded the U.S. welfare system, gave the federal government important new responsibilities, and provided a "safety net" of programs and benefits that poor people rely on today.

Despite reductions in programs and funding, much of what comprised the Great Society has aided the middle class, not just the poor, and is still with us in some form. Medicare and Medicaid, frequently criticized as wasteful and inefficient, have grown considerably and now enjoy wide political backing. Despite welfare reform, with its "workfare" provisions, the poor have not been thrown out on the street, and public assistance to the non-poor has actually increased. Federal funds for public and higher education are appreciably greater since the Great Society days, probably because they have been supported by both Democrats and Republicans over the years. Importantly, funding for transportation and the environment has continued, and funds earmarked for the arts, humanities, and public broadcasting have survived in the face of many attempts to eliminate them.

All of the civil rights laws, amended many times and continually challenged in the courts, remain on the books, but the Supreme Court, much altered with conservative justices appointed by Republican administrations, has weakened attempts at affirmative action in education, housing, and the workplace. In the face of the recent *Gratz* and *Grutter* decisions, the reconstituted court may now have an anti-affirmative action majority. The 2004 election, however, may have demonstrated that cold war liberalism is not dead. Senator John Edwards, campaigning for the Democratic nomination on a platform of old Great Society ideas and promises, did well in the primaries. The selection of Edwards as the running mate of John Kerry, a more moderate politician and well-known early critic of the Vietnam War, was perhaps a final accession to Johnson's outmoded programs.

Well into the first decade of the twenty-first century, it is apparent that the ideals first proposed by President Kennedy, expanded by President Johnson, and enacted into law by a Congress bent on building a better America, are not forgotten. Perhaps Edward M. Kennedy, in his 1980 speech before the Democratic National Convention, summed it up best. He had just pulled out of the race for his party's nomination, ostensibly ruling out any further attempt to reclaim his martyred brother's presidency. The senator from Massachusetts, in a patent reference to the liberalism of the New Frontier, poignantly expressed the sense of the Great Society for future generations when he exclaimed: "… the work goes on, the cause endures, the hope still lives, and the dream shall never die."

SEE ALSO *Desegregation; Head Start; Johnson, Lyndon B.; War on Poverty*

BIBLIOGRAPHY

Andrew, John A. 1998. *Lyndon Johnson and the Great Society.* Chicago: I.R. Dee.

Beckwith, Francis J., and Todd E. Jones, eds. 1997. *Affirmative Action: Social Justice or Reverse Discrimination?* Amherst, NY: Prometheus Books.

Bergmann, Barbara R. 1996. *In Defense of Affirmative Action.* New York: Basic Books.

Cohen, Carl, and James P. Sterba. 2003. *Affirmative Action and Racial Preference.* New York: Oxford University Press.

Helsing, Jeffrey W. 2000. *Johnson's War/Johnson's Great Society: The Guns and Butter Trap.* Westport, CT: Praeger Greenwood.

Jordan, Barbara C., and Elspeth D. Rostow, eds. 1986. *The Great Society: A Twenty-Year Critique.* Austin, TX: Lyndon B. Johnson School of Public Affairs.

Public Papers of the Presidents of the United States: Lyndon B. Johnson, 1963-64. 1965. Vol. 1, entry 357, 704–707. Washington, DC: Government Printing Office.

Unger, Irwin. 1996. *The Best of Intentions: The Triumphs and Failures of the Great Society under Kennedy, Johnson, and Nixon.* New York: Doubleday.

Raymond M. Weinstein

GREAT TULIP MANIA, THE

The Great Tulip Mania refers to the spectacular rise and fall in the price of tulip bulbs between the end of 1634 and February of 1637 in what is now the Netherlands. The episode is less significant as an event of great historical importance than as a paradigm of a speculative mania ending in a panic, and it produced a term, *tulipomania*, that often is used as a metaphor for economic bubbles.

References to the Tulip Mania in economics and finance cite Charles MacKay's 1852 account, though, as with the event itself, the value of this account lies more in its portrayal of the emotions and irrational action that typify frenzied speculation than in its veracity as historical record. Such references typically motivate discussions of the dynamic instability in heterogeneous capital goods models and discussions of speculative bubbles in financial markets.

Nicholaas Posthumus (1929) provided English-language readers with the first serious documentation of historical details and an interpretation of the event based on excerpts from contemporaneous pamphlets and notary transcripts. Centered in the tulip-growing region of the municipality of Haarlem, the mania was the result of a speculation in tulips that spread from professional tulip growers and experts to those who had no previous connection to bulb growing, first the wealthy and then the lower-middle and working classes.

As much as historians are able to discern from surviving records, evidence suggests that there was heightened speculation in the trading of contracts on rare, and later common, tulip bulbs. At its peak, the event saw the rarer bulbs commanding prices that exceeded the estimated average annual per capita income by a considerable margin. Yet, whether the prices were "excessive" in relation to the fundamental, nonspeculative elements governing the demand for and supply of the bulbs is as debatable as the possibility that the subsequent crash in the market for tulip bulbs caused any economic crisis. What is apparent is that institutionally, the episode is an early experience with futures and options contracts, although this emerged only after the fact when a group of professional traders, attempting to calm the market, permitted holders of futures contracts the right to decline to buy in exchange for a small fraction of the previously agreed-upon price.

Researchers have examined the records of the seventeenth-century tulip market for evidence of a speculative bubble with prices rising in excess of that which might have been warranted by fundamentals. Peter Garber's 1989 study, for example, suggests that the bulb speculation did not lead to obvious excesses, at least for much of the 1634 to 1637 "mania." As with most attempts to debate the efficiency of a given market wherein prices reflect fundamentals rather than irrational speculative influences, conflicting interpretations typically revolve around the interpretation of econometric signals. There will always exist scope for considerable debate, however, because a speculative bubble in the market price of tulips—or any other object of speculation—is indistinguishable in the data from time-varying expected returns and disappointed but otherwise well-grounded expectations of optimistic outcomes.

SEE ALSO *Economic Crises; Manias; Panic*

BIBLIOGRAPHY

Garber, Peter M. 1989. Tulipmania. *Journal of Political Economy* 97 (3): 535–560. Reprinted in 1996 *Stock Market Crashes and Speculative Manias*, ed. Eugene N. White, 36–61. Cheltenham, U.K.: Elgar.

MacKay, Charles. [1852] 1980. *Memoirs of Extraordinary Popular Delusions and the Madness of Crowds*, Vol. 1, 2nd ed. London and New York: Harmony Books.

Posthumus, Nicholaas W. 1929. The Tulip Mania in Holland in the Years 1636 and 1637. *Journal of Economic and Business History* 1 (3): 434–466. Reprinted in 1996 *Stock Market Crashes and Speculative Manias*, ed. Eugene N. White, 3–35. Cheltenham, U.K.: Elgar.

Brenda Spotton Visano

GREAT WAR

SEE *World War I.*

GREEK ORTHODOX CHURCH

The Greek Orthodox Church refers to any number of Eastern Orthodox Church groups whose heritage derives predominantly from Greek language and culture. These churches are organized around three Greek-speaking patriarchs (exalted bishops who historically have co-administered the Orthodox churches): the Ecumenical Patriarch, who resides in Constantinople (Istanbul) and has jurisdiction over present-day Turkey and all Christian areas beyond those territories that have been explicitly designated to another jurisdiciton; the Patriarch of Jerusalem who presides primarily over Palestine; and the Greek Patriarch of Alexandria, who is responsible for Egypt and all of Africa. For historical reasons, three separate relational patterns have emerged between these Greek Patriarchs and their daughter churches:

1. *Eparchy.* Some Greek Orthodox Churches are Patriarchal eparchies, ecclesiastical provinces that are directly under the auspices of one of the three Greek-speaking Patriarchs. These include the large emigrant churches formed in the West such as the Greek Orthodox Archdiocese of North and South America (formed in 1922, with about 1.5 million members) and the Greek Orthodox Archdiocese of Australia (formed in 1924, with about 400,000 members). The leaders of these churches are usually given the title Eparch, Metropolitan, or Archbishop and are selected by the Holy Synod of the Ecumenical Patriarch with advice of a local synod of bishops.

2. *Autonomous.* Autonomous churches operate with full administrative independence but have leaders who are chosen or affirmed by a Patriarch. Autonomous Greek Orthodox Churches include the small but important Church of Sinai, which is limited to the famous Monastery of Saint Catharine and several dependencies.

3. *Autocephaly.* As self-governing churches, autocephalous churches have hierarchies independent of the Patriarch and operate with complete independence. While maintaining ecclesiastical and theological communion with the Patriarchs, these autocephalous Greek Orthodox Churches are responsible for all church matters affecting the life and administration of the church with the exception of doctrinal and canonical positions. Historically, these churches often emerged as a result of nationalistic movements and are closely identified with the national ethos of the people. The largest Greek Orthodox autocephalous churches are the Church of Greece (formed in 1833, with about 8 million members) and the ancient Church of Cyprus (formed in 431, with about 1 million members).

All of the Greek Orthodox Churches trace their origins to the earliest Christian movements, which were primarily composed of Greek-speaking Christians in the Eastern Roman Empire. While Rome remained an important religious center from Christianity's inception, most of the growth and theological development during the first four centuries of Christianity occurred in the Greek-speaking East. The unity of the Eastern Christians was repeatedly challenged, leading to a major schism in 451 that resulted in the formation of a Coptic Christian Church in Egypt. Because of cultural, political, and theological differences, a gradual estrangement emerged between the remaining Greek-speaking Christians of the East and the predominantly Latin-speaking Christians of the West. This led to the "Great Schism" of 1054, which became entrenched after the Fourth Crusade, during which western Christians sacked the eastern capital of Constantinople. After the fall of Constantinople to Islamic forces in 1453, the theological and liturgical center of Eastern Christianity shifted to Russia until the twentieth century. The Greek churches continue to be out of communion with the Roman Catholic Church, despite repeated attempts for reunification.

Greek Orthodoxy stresses two foundations for the church's beliefs: the Bible, which is believed to be inspired by God, and Holy Traditions that have been passed down through the church. The primary dogmas of the church, including the nature of the Trinity, the person of Jesus, the role of the Virgin Mary, and the veneration of icons, were defined in seven "Ecumenical" councils that the Greek churches share with the Roman Catholic Church. Compared to Western theology, Greek Orthodoxy tends to emphasize a direct mystical encounter with God gained through ascetic and liturgical practices rather than emphasizing discursive reasoning as in the West. The ultimate goal is described as deification of the human person through sanctification by Christ. The sacraments, called mysteries in the East, are seen as transformative vehicles that guide the human person toward deification.

Greek churches are led by celibate bishops who stand in apostolic succession to the original apostles. Local churches are led by priests and deacons who are usually married and always men. Historically, there was no official number of sacraments, though baptism and the Eucharist service are universally recognized as the central pillars of the Greek Christian life. One of the most distinctive aspects of Greek Orthodox worship is the use of icons—paintings of saints, the Virgin Mary, and Jesus—that are seen as "windows into heaven." The most important holiday is Easter, called Pascha (Passover) in Greek churches, which is understood as Jesus' resurrection destroying "death by death," thus offering everlasting life to those who believe.

SEE ALSO *Christianity; Coptic Christian Church; Jesus Christ; Religion; Roman Catholic Church*

BIBLIOGRAPHY

Behr, John. 2001–. *The Formation of Christian Theology.* 2 vols. Crestwood, NY: St. Vladimir's Orthodox Theological Press.

Ware, Timothy. 1993. *The Orthodox Church,* 2nd ed. London: Penguin.

Stephen R. Lloyd-Moffett

GREEN BOOK, THE (LIBYA)

The Green Book is the Libyan leader Muammar al Qadhafi's codification of his philosophy on how to resolve political, economic, and social problems in society. It is set out in three parts: *The Solution of the Problem of Democracy: The Authority of the People* (1975), *The Solution of the Economic Problem: Socialism* (1977), and *The Social Basis of the Third Universal Theory* (1978).

The driving force behind *The Green Book* was Qadhafi's resolve to nurture and consolidate the revolution set in motion by his ascent to power in 1969. By the time it attained independence on December 24, 1951, Libya was a poor and underdeveloped country. The discovery of oil in 1955 generated significant wealth but no corresponding benefits to the impoverished majority of Libyans because the monarchic government's unchecked corruption, fiscal malfeasance, and nepotistic inclinations encouraged brazen exploitation by some Western powers and their proxies. It was against this backdrop of corrupt administration and international exploitation and popular disillusionment and discontent that Qadhafi emerged. Armed with a vision to unify the Arab world (in the mold of his hero, Egypt's Abdel Gamel Nasser) and the grudges of anticolonialism, Qadhafi led a small group of his fellow military officers known as the Unionist Free Officers and toppled King Idris in a bloodless coup on September 1, 1969, marking the end of the monarchy.

On his ascent to power, Qadhafi embarked on changing Libya from a conservative postcolonial state to a modern progressive one. He launched a "cultural revolution" in 1973 to inspire a major transformation of society through changes in roles, attitudes, perceptions, and behaviors. In *The Green Book* he explicated the philosophy of the revolution as a national guide to the complete eradication of the old order and its replacement with a new order governed by the ideals of liberty, unity, and socialism.

The main thrust of Qadhafi's philosophy is the removal of all vestiges of foreign influence and ideologies and the establishment of a new society based on the basic principles of Islam and homegrown socialism. He condemns parliamentary democracies and their components in preference to socialism and progressive Islam, rejects capitalism and communism as false ideologies, and develops his "third universal theory" in which he envisions the dismantling of the traditional apparatus of government and the establishment of a form of direct democracy through institutionalized use of popular congresses and committees at the local, regional, and national levels to guarantee mass participation in the nation's decision-making process. This form of government has been in place since March 2, 1977, when Qadhafi declared Libya a *jamahiriya* (government of the masses), although critics see a stiflingly rigid structure that provides no mechanism for a democratic change of government. At any rate, Qadhafi believes that adherence to the basic fundamentals of Islam in line with the third universal theory will enable Libyans to lead Muslims everywhere toward economic development and political change. However, Qadhafi's unorthodox approach to Islam and his elevation of *The Green Book* as a guide to the emancipation of the human race has brought him into conflict with Muslims in Libya and beyond. Although *The Green Book* professes universality in its scope and purpose, the peculiar circumstances of the Libyan people and the Islamic Arab heritage underlie its general framework.

SEE ALSO *Islam, Shia and Sunni; Muslims; Nasser, Gamal Abdel; Pan-Arabism; Qadhafi, Muammar al; Socialism, Islamic*

BIBLIOGRAPHY

Ayoub, Mahmoud. 1987. *Islam and the Third Universal Theory: The Religious Thought of Mu'ammar al Qadhdhafi.* London: Kegan Paul International.

Greavette, Gordon. 2005. Great Aspirations: The Fall and Rise of Muammar Qaddafi. http://www.cda-cdai.ca/symposia/2005/Greavette,.pdf.

Hajja, Samir R. 1980. The Jamahiriya Experiment in Libya: Qadhafi and Rousseau. *Journal of Modern African Studies* 18 (2): 181–200.

Charles Ebere

GREEN REVOLUTION

Green Revolution is the term applied to the introduction of "modern" crop varieties in developing countries beginning in 1964–1965. The Green Revolution was introduced at different rates in different countries. It was produced by more than five hundred National Agricultural Research Systems (NARS) in developing countries and supported by eight International Agricultural Research Centers (IARCs) located in developing countries. IARCs produced roughly 35 percent of Green Revolution Modern Varieties (GRMVs), which included highly productive lines of rice and wheat. NARS produced 60 percent of

GRMVs. Private sector breeders in developing countries produced 5 percent of GRMVs. Developed countries did not produce GRMVs for developing countries.

Twelve countries with populations in 2000 of one million or more did not have a significant Green Revolution (these countries had less than 2 percent GRMV adoption in 2000). Nine of these countries were in sub-Saharan Africa. An additional eighteen countries had less than 10 percent GRMV adoption in 2000 (eleven of these were also in sub-Saharan Africa). Another eighteen countries had less than 20 percent GRMV adoption in 2000 (twelve of these were in sub-Saharan Africa). Forty-five countries had significant Green Revolutions.

The forty-eight countries with low levels of GRMV adoption had low levels of crop value per hectare because crop yields were low. They used very little fertilizer and had low rates of productivity growth. The UNIDO index of industrial competitiveness for these forty-eight countries was low. Most of these countries were small. By contrast, the countries with significant Green Revolutions were larger countries (including India and China).

In 1960 birth rates were similar for all developing countries. By 2000, birth rates in the successful Green Revolution countries had declined to roughly half of the birth rates of 1960. For the unsuccessful countries, birth rates declined by only 15 percent. Food consumption per capita (as measured by calories consumed per capita) increased by 10 percent for the unsuccessful Green Revolution countries and by 25 percent for the successful Green Revolution countries. The unsuccessful countries increased food consumption because the "real" prices of food grains in world markets declined. In 2000 the real prices of food grains in world markets were 40 percent of their 1960 levels. Child mortality rates improved for all countries because of better diets.

The Green Revolution was criticized by two groups. In the 1980s it was criticized because farmers adopting GRMVs used more fertilizer. The first two GRMV crops were wheat and rice, and indeed fertilizer use did increase for these crops. It was also widely perceived in the 1980s that GRMVs were adopted only in "favorable" production environments. The second round of critics, who appeared at the end of the 1980s, emphasized environmental factors and increased use of chemicals.

The Green Revolution is continuing as new generations of GRMVs are being developed, and overall GRMV production is increasing, not declining. For example, by the 1990s two IARCs, ICRISAT in India and ICARDA in Syria, had begun developing GRMVs for unfavorable semi-arid and dryland conditions. The Green Revolution is seen today as having had a major impact in spite of its "uneven" delivery.

SEE ALSO *Food Crisis*

BIBLIOGRAPHY

Ehrlich, Paul R. 1968. *The Population Bomb*. New York: Ballantine.

Evenson, Robert E., and Douglas Gollin, eds. 2003. *Crop Variety Improvement and Its Effect on Productivity: The Impact of International Agricultural Research*. Wallingford, U.K., and Cambridge, MA: CABI Publishers.

Evenson, Robert E., and Yoav Kislev. 1975. *Agricultural Research and Productivity*. New Haven, CT: Yale University Press.

Griliches, Zvi. 1957. Hybrid Corn: An Exploration in the Economics of Technological Change. PhD diss., University of Chicago.

Wilson, Edward O. 1992. *The Diversity of Life*. Cambridge, MA: Belknap.

Robert E. Evenson

GREENHOUSE EFFECTS

The natural greenhouse effect was first described by Joseph Fourier (1768–1830) in 1827. Solar energy reaches the earth in the entire spectrum. The earth reemits this energy as infrared radiation. Greenhouse gases in the atmosphere, such as water vapor and carbon dioxide, absorb outgoing infrared radiation and reemit it in any direction. As a result the earth holds more energy than it would have without the presence of greenhouse gases. The natural greenhouse effect raises the global annual surface air temperature by some 90 degrees Fahrenheit (30 degrees Celsius) and therefore enables life as we know it.

The enhanced or anthropogenic greenhouse effect was first described by Svante August Arrhenius (1859–1927) in 1896. Deforestation and coal burning release carbon dioxide, which accumulates in the atmosphere. As a result the greenhouse effect is strengthened, and temperatures rise.

The enhanced greenhouse effect was long a curiosity in the natural sciences. In the 1970s the first climatologists were more worried about global cooling—as the next ice age was overdue and temperatures were falling, probably because of sulphur emissions (now reduced because of concerns over acid rain). Global warming returned to the scientific agenda in the early 1980s and got on the political agenda a decade later.

The enhanced greenhouse effect is clouded by large uncertainties caused by imperfect data, limited computing power, and the vast complexity of the earth system. There is virtual agreement, however, that temperatures will rise, and more so at the poles, during winter and at night. Rainfall patterns will change and may well intensify—leading to droughts in some places and in some seasons and floods in others. Storms may become more frequent and intense, but the evidence for this is weak where this matters most, namely in the tropics. Rising temperatures will cause sea levels to rise, mostly through expansion of seawater but perhaps also through ice melt.

The uncertainty about how the climate would respond to greenhouse gas concentrations is compounded by the uncertainty about future emissions, which depend on the number of people, their economic activities, and the types of energy they will use. High future emissions would put the earth into a state it has not been in for millions of years, perhaps with strongly nonlinear consequences.

Impacts of climate change are many. Less heating would be needed in winter, but more cooling would be needed in summer. Heat-related diseases would increase, but cold-related ones would decrease. Tropical diseases may spread or intensify. Lands would drown unless costly dikes are built. Crops would benefit from the higher carbon dioxide concentration but may be hurt by drought. Tourists would seek different holiday destinations. Urban infrastructure, particularly for water discharge, would need to be redesigned. Vegetation patterns would change, probably at the expense of many specialized plants and animals. Aggregate estimates suggest that the initial warming may be positive but that greater warming would bring net damages. Poorer countries would suffer greater damages.

Carbon dioxide is the main anthropogenic greenhouse gas, followed by methane and nitrous oxide. Carbon dioxide is emitted by the burning of fossil fuels and by deforestation. Methane comes from agriculture, waste, and fossil fuel production; nitrous oxide come from agriculture and industry. Chlorofluorocarbons (CFCs) are greenhouse gases too, but they have been phased out to protect the ozone layer. Their replacements, hydrofluorocarbons (HFCs), are even stronger greenhouse gases.

Greenhouse gases can be reduced by slowing or even reversing economic growth. This was shown to be particularly effective when the Soviet Union collapsed, but it is also responsible for the limited emissions growth in western Europe and Japan. Alternatively energy efficiency can be improved, alternative fuels can be used, or emissions can be captured and stored (biologically or geologically). Substantial emission reduction can be achieved with proven technologies. The costs would be small if policies are implemented gradually and implementation allows for flexibility.

Because greenhouse gases stay in the atmosphere for decades and longer, it does not matter where they are emitted. International coordination is needed for an effective solution. The oceans respond only slowly to changes in greenhouse gas concentrations. Energy infrastructure lasts for decades. As a result both the climate change problem and its solutions span many electoral cycles. Climate policy is therefore weak. The United Nations Framework on Climate Change is universally accepted, but it establishes obligations only to report emissions and to negotiate. Its first implementation, the Kyoto Protocol, sets targets for a limited number of countries only; of these, some have abandoned the treaty, while others are likely to meet their targets by coincidence rather than design.

Climate change has become a cultural phenomenon too. The press and television devote considerable attention to climate science and policy. Major motion pictures are devoted to the topic, and climate change regularly features in advertisements for a wide range of products, sometimes without an obvious connection.

SEE ALSO *Change, Technological; Deforestation; Economic Growth; Energy; Energy Industry; Energy Sector; Global Warming; Pollution, Air; Resource Economics; Resources; United Nations*

BIBLIOGRAPHY

World Meteorological Organization and United Nations Environment Programme. The Intergovernmental Panel on Climate Change. http://www.ipcc.ch/. Produces regular and authoritative assessment reports.

Richard S. J. Tol

GREENSPAN, ALAN
1926–

Alan Greenspan spent much of his career at the highest levels of government economics. He served as a top advisor to presidents Ford and Nixon, but is most widely known for his long tenure as chairman of the Federal Reserve, a position he held from 1987 to 2006.

For much of that period, Greenspan was arguably the most influential economist in the world. His early reputation as chairman of the Fed was boosted by his able handling of the 1987 stock market crash, wherein he quickly provided the economy with the liquidity needed to offset the market's falloff. Beginning in the mid-1990s, Greenspan was among the first to recognize the importance of productivity's acceleration. Given this increase in the growth of output per hour, Greenspan believed that the economy's "speed limit"—the rate of growth consistent with stable inflation—had increased. During the latter 1990s, the unemployment rate fell well below the comfort level of most economists, yet inflation decelerated, and broadly shared real wage gains were handily paid for out of rising productivity growth.

Greenspan was widely viewed as favoring conservative economic policy, a view reinforced by his early association with the libertarian, antiregulatory philosophy of the writer Ayn Rand. And while he exhibited throughout his career a strong preference for market-driven outcomes and a diminished role for government, his approach to monetary policy was largely pragmatic and data-driven. Though he avoided true "inflation-targeting"—explicitly stating the range of price growth acceptable to the Fed, a practice he viewed as too restrictive—he focused closely on measures of inflation and resource utilization, urging the Federal Open Market Committee (the group of Fed governors that set interest-rate policy) to adjust rates based on the relationships between these variables.

Though generally highly regarded by the economics and policy community, Greenspan has had his critics. Throughout his term at the Fed, he was sometimes viewed as elevating inflationary concerns above the goal of full employment, despite the Fed's mandate to maintain balance in its simultaneous pursuit of stable prices and low unemployment. Most recently, some have maintained that Greenspan played a decisive role in the swing from fiscal surplus to fiscal deficits. Based on what turned out to be a highly optimistic forecast of government revenues, Greenspan endorsed large tax cuts proposed by the Bush administration. Though the chairperson of the Fed is a political appointee, it is rare for the Fed chief to play such an overtly political role in a policy matter before the Congress. Furthermore, his endorsement was instrumental in the passage of these cuts, which ultimately played an integral role in the move from federal budget surpluses in the latter 1990s to deficits in the 2000s.

The most common criticism of Greenspan, however, is that he presided over damaging investment bubbles that could have been avoided by more aggressive Fed policy. Two major speculative bubbles emerged over Greenspan's tenure: the information technology (IT) bubble of the latter 1990s and the housing bubble of the 2000s. Speculation in IT firms, some of which had little more than a sketchy business plan, was rampant in the 1990s, while at the same time, many firms overinvested in IT-related goods and personnel. When it became clear that returns on these investments could not be sustained, a large sell-off of stocks and IT-related assets ensued. Shortly thereafter—in March 2001—the economy entered an investment-driven recession.

More recently, speculative bubbles formed in housing markets as prices were steeply bid up, particularly in highly populated areas of the country. Though Greenspan observed the sharp rise in home values, he again refrained from criticizing the development of what some observers recognized as a housing bubble. In fact, critics argue that Greenspan and the Fed further inflated the bubble by sharply lowering interest rates in response to the recession of 2001. Moreover, many homeowners took advantage of the rising value of their home equity, and boosted their consumption with cash borrowed against their homes. As this bubble began to burst in the mid-2000s, home prices fell steeply, slowing the economy and hurting key economic sectors, such as construction and real estate.

In both cases, Greenspan and the Fed did nothing to intervene as speculative bubbles formed. During the formation of the IT-bubble in 1996, Greenspan popularized the oft-repeated term "irrational exuberance," suggesting speculation was inflating asset values. Thereafter, however, he refrained from either critical scrutiny of the stock market's run-up, or more concrete policies, such as raising the Fed's margin requirements (i.e., limiting the amount that investors could borrow to purchase stocks "on margin").

Prior to retiring from the Fed, Greenspan defended his lack of action in these cases by claiming the Fed has neither the ability to recognize bubbles, nor the tools to deflate them. Especially given the fact that Greenspan himself clearly recognized the irrational nature of the stock market's climb in the latter 1990s, the first part of this defense seems weak. Whether the Fed could have intervened is another question. Reflecting on the IT bubble, Greenspan reasonably argued that "it was far from obvious [that the bubble] could be pre-empted short of the central bank inducing a substantial contraction in economic activity, the very outcome we were seeking to avoid" (Greenspan 2002).

These criticisms aside, Greenspan will likely be remembered in a positive light, as an excellent crisis manager and an able central banker who presided over two of the longest economic expansions in the country's history. True, his conservative political ideology inappropriately broke through on occasion, and he might have led the Fed to do more to push back against speculative bubbles that formed on his watch. Nonetheless, his economic insights and data-driven approach to monetary policy remain the model for central bankers today. In fact, when nominated by President George W. Bush to succeed Greenspan, current Fed chief Ben Bernanke paid a high compliment to the retiring chairman: "[I]f I am confirmed to this position, my first priority will be to maintain continuity with the policies and policy strategies established during the Greenspan years" (The White House 2005).

SEE ALSO *Bubbles; Bull and Bear Markets; Central Banks; Depression, Economic; Economic Crises; Federal Reserve System, U.S.; Financial Instability Hypothesis; Financial Markets; Interest Rates; Internet Bubble; Macroeconomics; Policy, Monetary; Recession; Speculation; Stock Exchanges*

BIBLIOGRAPHY

Galbraith, James K. 2006. *Unbearable Cost: Bush, Greenspan, and the Economics of Empire.* Basingstoke, U.K.: Palgrave Macmillan.

Greenspan, Alan. 2002. Economic Volatility. Remarks by Chairman Alan Greenspan at a Symposium Sponsored by the Federal Reserve Bank of Kansas City, Jackson Hole, Wyoming, August 30. http://www.federalreserve.gov/boarddocs/speeches/2002/2002 0830/.

Jones, David M. 2002. *Unlocking the Secrets of the Fed: How Monetary Policy Affects the Economy and Your Wealth-Creation Potential.* Hoboken, NJ: Wiley.

The White House. 2005. President Appoints Dr. Ben Bernanke for Chairman of the Federal Reserve. October 24. http://www.whitehouse.gov/news/releases/2005/10/2005102 4-2.html.

Tuccille, Jerome. 2002. *Alan Shrugged: The Life and Times of Alan Greenspan, the World's Most Powerful Banker.* Hoboken, NJ: Wiley.

Woodward, Bob. 2001. *Maestro: Greenspan's Fed and the American Boom.* New York: Simon & Schuster.

Jared Bernstein

GRENADIAN REVOLUTION

Residents on the 121-square-mile tri-island nation of Grenada, Carriacou, and Petit Martinique (population 110,000) awoke on the morning of March 13, 1979, to radio reports that the elected government of Prime Minister Eric Gairy had been replaced in a relatively bloodless coup by the New Jewel Movement (NJM). The NJM set up the People's Revolutionary Government (PRG) with the avowed task of transforming Grenada's society and political culture and creating a socialist state.

REVOLUTIONARY ORIGINS

Seeds of this revolution had been sown during the previous twelve years of Gairy's rule, during which he had alienated many Grenadians through his increasing use of legal and extralegal means to silence his critics. Chief among these techniques was his seizure of the lands and property of his political opponents, intimidation of civil servants, the establishment of a system in which decision-making depended on the Gairy-dominated Cabinet, and the establishment of an extralegal paramilitary body that inflicted bloody beatings on his political opponents.

The emergence and rise of the NJM must be seen within the context of several international movements of the late 1950s and 1960s that had a great impact on the Caribbean. The Cuban Revolution, successful independence struggles in Africa, the growth of Rastafarianism, and the U.S. civil rights movement were all inspirational in the English-speaking Caribbean. By the 1970s, the flourishing of new ideas shaped by these international developments had produced a generation of young people who openly questioned the appropriateness of the inherited British political system. Guyanese-born university lecturer Walter Rodney had also shown the relevance of Black Power to the cultural and political situation in the Caribbean.

In Grenada, Maurice Bishop was among this new generation of Caribbean activists. On returning home from England, where he had studied law and had been politically active, Bishop teamed up with another London-trained lawyer, Kendrick Radix, to form an urban-based study group, the Movement for the Assemblies of the People (MAP). At the same time, Unison Whiteman founded another group to promote rural development, the Joint Endeavour for Welfare, Education, and Liberation (JEWEL). In March 1973 these groups merged into the NJM, which advocated agricultural and educational reform, preventive medicine campaigns, social planning, the nationalization of banks, the phasing out of foreign-owned insurance companies, an end to party politics, and the institution of People's Assemblies as the mechanism to ensure participatory democracy and the permanent involvement of the working people in decision-making. Their model was Tanzania's Ujaama system.

The NJM flourished during a period of pervasive clientelism, political conservatism, and corruption on the part of Grenada's two main political parties. As its influence grew and the number of its sympathizers and followers increased, the NJM was increasingly attacked by Gairy who sought to silence its supporters. As the NJM made increasing inroads into the trade union leadership, Gairy passed laws in early 1978 prohibiting strikes and introducing compulsory arbitration to settle disputes where "essential" services were affected.

Partly because of the terror he had unleashed on his political opponents, particularly NJM members, Gairy's political base was being systematically eroded. A history of dubious electoral practices, including alleged use of rigged electoral lists, caused the NJM to despair of effecting governmental change at the polls despite the fact that by 1978 some of their members had won election to the legislature. By then, most Grenadians were apparently fed up with Gairy's misrule. Thus, when the NJM seized power in 1979, few Grenadians complained.

THE REVOLUTIONARY MOVEMENT

Once in office, the PRG consolidated its power by forming a government that included members of the mercantile community and persons of middle class background. This temporarily allayed the fears of individuals concerned that the country would soon be turned into a Cuban-style socialist state. Though they suspended the 1974 constitution, the PRG retained the office of governor general in an obvious attempt to gain the support of the politically conservative Grenadian and British Caribbean peoples. As prime minister, Bishop signed into effect laws that were passed by the Parliament, of which he was a part, in the name of the PRG.

While pledging to observe fundamental rights and freedoms of Grenadians, the PRG also declared its determination to eradicate all vestiges of Gairyism and to protect the revolution. It established a People's Revolutionary Army (PRA), whose members had the same powers of arrest and search that members of the local police force enjoyed. By using preventive detention without bail, the PRG could detain indefinitely persons suspected of activities aimed at undermining the revolution or deemed prejudicial to public safety or public order. This proved to be a sore point for Grenadians who had expected the PRG to respect their human and civil rights. Although the government had pledged a Consultative Assembly where Grenadians would participate in shaping a new constitution, by 1980 PRG members were openly asserting that elections and a return to parliamentary government were no longer priorities.

The revolution did have positive effects on Grenada, however. The awakening of national spirit on an unprecedented level was evident in the widespread use of voluntary labor for community development. Educational and medical improvements stemmed from the generous assistance provided by Cuban doctors and teachers. Farmer cooperatives expanded agricultural output. Marketing boards regularized the availability of these goods locally and in neighboring Caribbean countries. Agribusiness initiatives transformed surplus fruits into canned nectars and juices. A spice-grinding project brought to the marketplace a range of locally produced and ground packaged spices. The Livestock Production and Genetic Centre set out to enhance the island's livestock industry to remove the need for importing meats. Government promoted "new tourism" aimed at attracting visitors from Latin America, Africa, and the United States. The centerpiece of this tourism initiative was the construction of an international airport to accommodate large jet aircrafts.

Financing these ambitious programs was challenging. The PRG initially sought support from moderate foreign-owned banks operating locally. Later it purchased one of them and enhanced the capitalization of the government-owned Grenada Development Bank. But these resources remained inadequate, forcing the PRG to increase its requests for aid from Cuba and the Soviet Union. Cuba

provided technical expertise, heavy equipment, and skilled labor for the construction of the airport. Syria, Libya, Iraq, and Algeria provided more than US$19 million, while Venezuela donated much-needed diesel fuel.

This reliance on aid from leftist countries irked the United States, which, increasingly concerned about the leftward drift of the revolution, feared that Grenada would become a proxy for the Soviets. President Ronald Reagan openly declared that the new airport was for military rather than economic purposes. PRG fears that the United States would destabilize its experiment in socialism forced the revolutionaries to boost the country's military preparedness through a series of secret agreements with Eastern European countries. According to these agreements, Grenada would receive counterintelligence equipment, agent training, and arms and other military materiel. Local preparedness was enhanced through participation in the army, militia, and other neighborhood bodies geared to protecting the revolution at home.

The greatest threat to the revolution eventually came not from the United States or local counterrevolutionaries, but from the revolutionaries' own actions. Long-suspected though rarely publicly articulated ideological differences within the NJM leadership came to light in October 1983. Minutes from Central Committee meetings reflect a sharp divide centering on leadership issues and the direction the revolution should follow. It appears that revolutionary élan was receding partly because the revolutionaries had allowed their rhetoric to exceed the possibilities the situation allowed. An awareness of the revolution's failure to achieve its full potential led to serious self-reflection and evaluation of both the leadership and the governmental structure. In addition, personal differences contributed mightily to the internal crisis that the PRG experienced in the autumn of 1983. Bishop's detractors accused him of being inefficient and middle class, and of lacking political leadership skills and sufficient ideological coherence. After much debate over three days, the party proposed the institution of a joint leadership structure, with power to be shared by Bishop and Bernard Coard. Bishop initially accepted this proposal. Two days later, he left for a visit to Hungary and Czechoslovakia.

On his return via Cuba on October 8, Bishop told Central Committee members that he was no longer willing to go along with the power-sharing proposal the party had approved. Committee members then sought to impose this agreement without the support of Bishop. In response, Bishop, who was for many the personification of the revolution, set out to turn the people against Coard by spreading a rumor that Coard was conspiring to kill him. Confronted at a Central Committee meeting with his security guard's testimony about this plot, Bishop remained silent. Convinced of his guilt, the Central Committee placed him under house arrest.

Bishop's house arrest failed to neutralize him; instead, it roused the people. After days of unrest, Unison Whiteman and George Louison, two of Bishop's faithful supporters, began organizing protestors for a rescue attempt. By this time, all the ministers, except Bishop, Selwyn Strachan, and Hudson Austin, had resigned their portfolio. Government was in disarray. On October 19, 1983, Whiteman and a group of Bishop loyalists freed Bishop. Bishop then led a crowd to Fort Rupert, the head-quarters of the Grenadian armed forces, with the apparent goal of using the military to reassert his authority. Accounts of what transpired differ. Speaking for the PRA, General Hudson Austin later claimed that Bishop's group disarmed the soldiers guarding the fort and declared their intention to eliminate the entire Central Committee—the senior members of the party—and to smash the revolutionary armed forces. Thus, Austin declared, relief soldiers were sent to reestablish control of Fort Rupert. Bishop and his group fired on the soldiers, prompting them to retaliate. In the crossfire, Bishop, a number of his colleagues, and an unknown number of cit-izens were killed in what many regard as an execution. The bodies of Bishop and the ministers were reportedly burned beyond recognition and then secretly buried. Some suggest that U.S. forces removed the charred remains from the island.

The killing of these ministers created a leadership vacuum that the PRA under Austin initially sought to fill. Because the army lacked popular support, it declared a twenty-four-hour curfew to both maintain order and impose its will on the people. Fearful of governance by the group that had killed their popular prime minister, Grenadians panicked. At the request of Governor General Sir Paul Scoon, who invoked the doctrine of necessity embedded in the 1974 constitution and assumed plenipo-tentiary powers, forces from the United States and the Caribbean staged a military intervention that quickly eliminated remaining pockets of resistance from the PRA and Cuban sympathizers. Grenadians viewed the foreign troops as liberators rather than as invaders.

In an attempt to restore a state of political normalcy, Sir Paul appointed a broad-based advisory council to form an interim government that would help in the country's administration. Among its most memorable achievements was paving the way for the elections that took place in December 1984.

By then, Coard and those suspected of involvement in the killings at Fort Rupert had been detained. They were tried and found guilty of murder, but their death sentences were later commuted to life imprisonment by the governor general. A successful appeal to the Privy Council resulted in a 2007 ruling that they should be resentenced because of the unconstitutionality of the orig-inal sentences.

SEE ALSO *Anticolonial Movements; Black Power; Caribbean, The; Castro, Fidel; Civil Rights Movement, U.S.; Colonialism; Cuban Revolution; Haitian Revolution; Human Rights; Left and Right; Left Wing; Reagan, Ronald; Revolution; Rodney, Walter; Social Movements; Socialism; Terror; Tourism*

BIBLIOGRAPHY

Heine, Jorge, ed. 1990. *A Revolution Aborted: The Lessons of Grenada.* Pittsburgh, PA: University of Pittsburgh Press.

Lewis, Gordon K. 1987. *Grenada: The Jewel Despoiled.* London and Baltimore, MD: Johns Hopkins University Press.

Mandle, Jay R. 1985. *Big Revolution, Small Country: The Rise and Fall of the Grenada Revolution.* Lanham, MD: North-South Publishing Company.

O'Shaughnessy, Hugh. 1984. *Grenada: Revolution, Invasion, and Aftermath.* London: Sphere Books.

Payne, Anthony, Paul Sutton, and Tony Thorndike. 1984. *Grenada: Revolution and Invasion.* New York: St. Martin's Press.

Scoon, Paul. 2003. *Survival for Service: My Experiences as Governor General.* Oxford: Macmillan Caribbean.

Valenta, Jiri, and Herbert J. Ellison, eds. 1986. *Grenada and Soviet/Cuban Policy: Internal Crisis and U.S./OECS Intervention.* Boulder, CO, and London: Westview Press.

Edward L. Cox

GRIEF AND LOSS
SEE *Death and Dying.*

GROSS DOMESTIC PRODUCT

As a measure of the aggregate level of economic activity, gross domestic product (GDP) is the main indicator used to monitor the state of an economy. GDP growth, com-monly referred to as economic growth, is thus of great interest to policymakers for the conduct of fiscal and monetary policy. It is also widely used to measure produc-tivity of an economy.

GDP is defined as the value-added of all goods and services produced in a given period of time within a coun-try. The measurement of GDP can be approached from three angles: value added by industry, final expenditures, and factor incomes.

- Value added created by industry (output less inputs purchased from other producers);

- Expenditures by consumers, businesses on investment goods, government on goods and services, and foreigners for exports (minus expenditures by domestic residents on imports); and

- Incomes generated in production, operating surplus generated by business and compensation of employees.

GDP is usually expressed in terms of current prices in national currency units, or in real terms (real GDP) after removing the effects of price change to reflect the volume of production in the economy. For international comparisons, GDP is also expressed in a common currency such as U.S. dollars using purchasing power parity exchange rates.

Up to the 1980s, the term gross national product (GNP) was more commonly used than GDP. The former, more correctly called gross national income (GNI), includes incomes of residents of a country earned abroad and excludes incomes from domestic production sent abroad. In contrast, GDP includes only domestically produced incomes. GNI in combination with GDP are often expressed in per capita terms and used as measures of living standards of the nation.

National income accounting (the methodologies to measure GNI and GDP) originated in the 1930s and 1940s with the work of Simon Kuznets in the United States and Richard Stone in the United Kingdom. A detailed history of national accounting is found in Andre Vanoli's work *A History of National Accounting* (2005). Since the 1950s, the United Nations, working with other international organizations such as the International Monetary Fund, World Bank, and Organization for Economic Cooperation and Development, has coordinated the development of international standards for the national accounts. The current international standard was last issued in 1993. These standards evolve over time with the world economies, and a new edition of the standard will be released in 2008. The International Association for Research in Income and Wealth was founded in 1947 for the advancement of knowledge related to national accounting. The publications of this Association, including the journal *Review of Income and Wealth*, document the evolution of the field.

GDP is not a measure of economic welfare. It does not incorporate into its official estimates environmental degradation and resources depletion, nor the value of leisure. Neither does it take into account the influence on income inequality and economic insecurity on well-being.

BIBLIOGRAPHY

United Nations. 1993. System of National Accounts. http://unstats.un.org/unsd/sna1993/toctop.asp.

Vanoli, Andre. 2005. *A History of National Accounting*. Amsterdam: IOS Press.

Andrew Sharpe

GROSS NATIONAL INCOME

Gross national income (GNI), also known as gross national product (GNP), is an estimate of the value of goods and services produced in an economy. In other words, it is an estimate of the size of an economy. This measure is highly important, having economic, political, and societal implications.

The GNI is defined as the total value of final goods and services produced within a country's borders in a year, thus the country's gross domestic product (GDP), minus its net foreign assets. The net foreign assets are composed of the income received from assets owned by nationals in other countries minus similar payments made to foreigners who own assets in the national economy. For instance, if a Japanese-owned company operates in the United States and sends some of its profits back to Japan, then the Japanese GNI is enhanced. However, the repatriation of profit from a U.S. company operating in Japan increases the U.S. GNI but does not affect the Japanese GNI. Hence, unlike GDP, the GNI counts income produced according to who owns the factors of production rather than where it is earned. The conversion from GNI to GDP can easily be done by subtracting the income received from domestically owned goods and services that have been supplied to the production abroad of foreign goods and services. However, the conversion from GDP to GNI requires that one add to GNI the income payments to foreigners for the use of their goods and services supplied to the domestic economy. Thus:

GNI = GDP + Net Foreign Assets

where Net Foreign assets = Foreign Assets – Foreign Liabilities.

The measure of GNI is of great policy significance. GNI, consisting of a basic measure of national income accounting, has been regarded since World War II as an important indicator of the status of the economy. For instance, in the United States the economy is considered to be in recession if GNI decreases during two consecutive quarters. Moreover GNI, as a measure of economic health, is used for the purpose of cross-country comparisons. For example, one defines the importance of an economy according to the level of its GNI or according to each country's contribution to the world's income production. In addition GNI per person is often used as a measure of people's welfare. Thus countries with high GNI often score high on other measures of welfare.

As previously mentioned, GNI is a function of the GDP. The latter is more common as a measurement of the size of an economy. In some cases the difference between the two measures is negligible. For instance, in the United States the difference between GDP and GNI is only about 1 percent and can be ignored. However, in some countries where net foreign assets' role is significant, GNI is considered to be the most representative quantitative measure of economic activity. This is the case, for example, in Ireland, where in 2000 GDP was 15 percent higher than GNI. In any case, GNI has important policy implications, both at a national level and at an international level (for example, it defines a country's status in an international organization).

SEE ALSO *Gross Domestic Product; National Income Accounts*

BIBLIOGRAPHY

Dornbusch, Rudiger, Stanley Fischer, and Richard Startz. 2004. *Macroeconomics.* Boston: McGraw-Hill/Irwin.

Heilbroner, Robert L., and Lester C. Thurow. 1986. *Economics Explained.* New York: Simon and Schuster.

Eleni Simintzi

GROSS NATIONAL PRODUCT

SEE *Gross Domestic Product.*

GROUPS

A *group* is a collection of individuals with some degree of interdependence and some element of common or shared identity. Most often, membership in a group involves face-to-face interaction with other members, although such interaction is not a necessary component of a group. (For example, Internet "groups," which do not involve face-to-face interaction, are becoming increasingly important in the twenty-first century.) Scholarly interest in groups began with sociology's birth. German sociologist Ferdinand Tönnies (1855–1936) made an early contribution when he developed the influential concepts of *Gemeinschaft* and *Gesellschaft* to depict two different types of groups related to different kinds of economic and social structures. *Gesellschaft* refers to instrumentally-based groups or communities in which social relations are formal and little consensus exists. *Gemeinschaft* refers to small communities in which social interactions are based on friendship or kinship.

The importance of groups and community were also a focus of the French sociologist Émile Durkheim's (1858–1917) writings. For example, in *The Elementary Forms of Religious Life* (1915), Durkheim discussed the significance of religion for one's sense of belonging. Religion might take different forms in different societies, but all religions stress the importance of social control and cohesion of the group. In this way, the rituals associated with religion serve as visible evidence of the power of the community as they are enacted in a group and for the group.

The American social psychologists Charles H. Cooley (1864–1929) and George H. Mead (1863–1931) both frequently addressed the central importance of groups, especially small groups, and made important contributions to the construction of a framework for understanding symbolic interaction. Cooley, for example, developed the idea of primary groups, that is, groups that are important in intimate interaction. Mead's theoretical conceptualizations in *Mind, Self, and Society* (1934), including the centrality of groups and the importance of role-taking, were influential in the development of the field of group dynamics.

The German sociologist Georg Simmel (1858–1918) detailed many concepts and perspectives that have preoccupied group theorists since the early twentieth century. His discussion of conflict and exchange framed issues in terms of a dynamic. Simmel argued that exchange was pervasive and that what might at first appear to be purely individual acts are actually influenced by others. To use one of his examples, a teacher teaches, but this involves an exchange with students in part because the teacher considers the students as an audience. People are not isolated agents, acting on their own; rather they act in response to groups.

The study of groups and their structure is sometimes termed *group dynamics* or *group processes*. While there are many areas of study within group dynamics, some of the most important are group identity, status, cooperation and competition, exchange, justice, and legitimation.

GROUP IDENTITY

The intensity of identity as a group member varies according to the members' common fate. If membership within a particular group seems to predict important outcomes, group identity may be strong. For example, minorities are likely to feel a strong identity as minority group members because it is evident that their categorization both comes from and creates common experiences.

Collectivities can have elements of common fate, but members may not have group identification and as a result are not usually considered groups. For example, Karl Marx (1818–1883) clearly delineated class interests based upon the means of production; membership in a class was fundamental to life chances. The bourgeoisie controlled the means of production, while the proletariat did not. However, at times, members of those groups may not conceive of themselves as sharing commonalities; in fact, as Marx argued, although members of the proletariat had powerful class interests uniting them, they often lacked the critical recognition of membership in this group. This lack of recognition served the purposes of the bourgeoisie and was an important means of control and power.

Group identity can also be created solely through common experiences, even where no categorization preceded the experience. Experiences such as surviving a hurricane or cancer, for example, can create a powerful group identity among the survivors. Research, especially in the social identity tradition, also indicates that, under some conditions, the slightest form of categorization can function as a type of group identity—strong enough to create in-group favoritism. Research in the area of social identity theory, which developed within European social psychology, emphasizes how individual cognition and group identities are related.

STATUS

Status is usually defined as a position in a social network. Importantly, status involves *status beliefs*, beliefs about the social worth of the individuals who occupy positions within a network such that a person who occupies one position is "better than" a person who occupies another position (Sewell 1992). Early status studies examined the concept of leadership and different forms of group rules that corresponded to different political processes (such as democratic rules versus autocratic rules). In the 1950s, attention turned more to the internal dynamics of groups. The social psychologist Robert Bales (1916–2004) and his associates developed *interaction process analysis* (IPA), a categorization technique that, in different forms, shaped much of group analysis. In particular, these researchers were interested in how the behavior of one group member conditioned the behavior of others. This idea that status was relative to the group was a central insight and formed the impetus for thinking about characteristics once viewed as fixed (such as sex or ethnicity) as varying in intensity and salience depending upon context.

One of the most developed research programs in the analysis of status is *expectations state theory*. The theory has several subsets; one of these is *status characteristics theory*, which concerns how status generates and then sustains inequality of power and prestige within groups. It is posited that this process, called the *burden of proof process*, is so strong that unless some event or some information intervenes, it organizes interaction consistent with prior evaluations of the status characteristics. In other words, the cultural stereotyping associated with status characteristics are reproduced in different settings and within different groups. Dissolving status hierarchies is difficult because there are layers of group interactions that support and uphold the status quo. However, under some conditions, hierarchies can be dissolved; particularly noteworthy are a series of applied studies in school settings (Cohen 1993).

LEGITIMATION AND JUSTICE

Related to issues of status are issues of legitimation, the process through which a principle or set of rules is adhered to even in the absence of incentives. There have been studies of differing sources and processes of legitimation, and particularly promising is research concerning how the granting of power within groups is affected by and reinforced by *referential belief structures*, or socially validated beliefs at the cultural level that are imported into the local setting.

Other research has addressed how conflict between different sources of legitimation might affect interactions and the establishment or disruption of norms and routines. There is a large literature that aims to answer how individuals make assessments of justice based on their own and others' benefits. The sociological contribution to justice is the extension of the justice concept beyond the specific individual. Referential belief structures, for example, serve as an external comparison by which to judge the fairness of local settings.

EXCHANGE

The social aspects of exchanges are central to the study of groups. Some of the early sociological formulations were patterned after economic models, while others were patterned after behavioral psychology. Sociologist Richard Emerson (d. 1982), relying on behavioral models as a foundation, developed a conceptual framework that viewed the exchange, rather than individual actors, as the unit of analysis. This formulation took the power-dependency relationship among actors or groups as the determining factor in dictating interaction. For a given relationship, the more powerful the actor (whether that actor is an individual or a group), the less dependent the actor. According to Emerson, this power dependency leads to a continual "balancing," so that the actor who has the most power uses it (because it is to that actor's advantage to do so), but such use of power leads to some loss of power. This shift in power leads to balancing or sets of strategies by which actors try to retain their power. Theories developed after this initial formulation sometimes refuted the idea that power was lost. This seems to be especially true in settings in which the social network provides some actors with particularly advantageous positions.

Work on coercive power indicates that in small groups (and perhaps in large groups as well), coercive power (in the sense of punishing others) is a risky strategy because it can decrease the possibilities of future exchanges. Of course, the risk to the coercer is related to the alternatives present for the coerced. Relatedly, the *conflict spiral*, a theory about bargaining processes, predicts that unequal power, even without punishment, can produce negative emotion.

COOPERATION AND COMPETITION

One of the longest traditions in the study of groups is the investigation of cooperation and competition. The form and type of incentives that encourage or discourage competition have been extensively examined. These incentives might be material rewards, such as money, or social rewards, such as honor or friendship. Even when the incentives are structured so that all might be better off cooperating, cooperation does not always obtain. This is because even in simple settings, coordination can be problematic.

Social dilemmas, settings in which individual and group incentives conflict in some way, are prominent research areas because they are pervasive in many different aspects of life. Such dilemmas range from the small and intimate (e.g., how to maintain a clean house), to the large and relatively anonymous (e.g., how to maintain biodiversity). Many solutions to social dilemmas involve changing the incentives and thereby changing the structure. These might involve punishments for not cooperating or rewards for cooperating.

Other solutions have focused upon social factors arising from group interaction. Two powerful such factors are group identity and trust. If, for example, one actor trusts another to cooperate and then acts on this basis, the dilemma can sometimes be solved. Group identity, as mentioned, can arise from cooperation. Once born, group identity can also lead to cooperation.

SEE ALSO *Collective Action; Competition; Cooperation; Durkheim, Emile; Ethnicity;* Gemeinschaft and Gesellschaft*; Group; Groupthink; Identity; Marx, Karl; Mead, George Herbert; Nationalism and Nationality; Race; Social Exchange Theory; Social Identification; Sociology*

BIBLIOGRAPHY

Berger, Joseph, Morris Zelditch Jr., Bo Anderson, and Bernard P. Cohen. 1972. Structural Aspects of Distributive Justice: A Status Value Formulation. In *Sociological Theories in Progress*, vol. 2, eds. Joseph Berger, Morris Zelditch Jr., and Bo Anderson, 119–146. Boston: Houghton Mifflin.

Cohen, Elizabeth. 1993. From Theory to Practice: The Development of an Applied Research Program. In *Theoretical Research Programs: Studies in the Growth of Theory*, eds. Joseph Berger and Morris Zelditch Jr., 385–415. Stanford, CA: Stanford University Press.

Durkheim, Émile. [1915] 1965. *The Elementary Forms of Religious Life*. New York: Free Press.

Lovaglia, Michael J., Elizabeth A. Mannix, Charles D. Samuelson, et al. 2005. Conflict, Power, and Status in Groups. In *Theories of Small Groups: Interdisciplinary Perspectives*, eds. Marshall Scott Poole and Andrea B. Hollingshead, 139–184. Thousand Oaks, CA.: Sage.

Mead, George Herbert. 1934. *Mind, Self, and Society: From the Standpoint of a Social Behaviorist*. Chicago: University of Chicago Press.

Molm, Linda D., Nobuyuki Takahashi, and Gretchen Peterson. 2000. Risk and Trust in Social Exchange: An Experimental Test of a Classical Proposition. *American Journal of Sociology* 105: 1396–1427.

Sewell, William H., Jr. 1992. A Theory of Structure: Duality, Agency, and Transformation. *American Journal of Sociology* 98 (1): 1–29

Simmel, Georg. [1907] 1971. *On Individuality and Social Forms: Selected Writings*. Ed. Donald N. Levine. Chicago: University of Chicago Press.

Jane Sell

GROUPS, NONCOMPETING

SEE *Noncompeting Groups.*

GROUPTHINK

Irving Janis (1972, 1982) originated the term groupthink to describe a set of definitive beliefs and behaviors found in decision-making groups when their motivation to maintain internal consensus overrides their rational appraisal of information. The model was developed from qualitative case studies of the flawed decision processes that preceded U.S. government fiascoes like the failure to protect Pearl Harbor against Japanese invasion in 1941, the Bay of Pigs invasion of Cuba during the Kennedy Administration, and the burglary of the Watergate complex during the Nixon Administration. The attractiveness of the model rests largely on its explicit attention to seven antecedent conditions and eight associated patterns of in-group cognition and action that can influence the quality of solutions to business and organizational problems. The principal antecedent condition of groupthink is extreme in-group cohesiveness. Other antecedent conditions linked to in-group cohesion include insulation of the group from outside information and critics, directive leadership, a lack of group norms prescribing methodical problem-solving procedures, homogeneous attitudes or values among members, high stress due to external competition or threat, and a temporary loss of self-esteem produced by recent failure or the complexities of the task at hand. According to the groupthink model, these contextual antecedents lead to specific psychological symptoms shared by decision-makers that result in a detrimental tendency to seek premature concurrence. The symptoms show up as an illusion shared by group members that they are invulnerable to bad outcomes, an unquestioned belief in the moral superiority of the in-group, an inclination to collectively rationalize support for the group's decisions, stereotyping of out-group members as weak and wrong, self-censorship through the withholding of dissenting opinions, a perception that other in-group members are unanimous, direct pressure on dissenters to conform, and the emergence of "mindguards" whose role is to protect the group's preferred position from counterargument. Janis expected this constellation of biased reactions to cause critical flaws in the procedures group members adopt to solve important dilemmas.

The specific errors of group process that are thought to be caused by groupthink include the incomplete review of decision alternatives, inadequate consideration of how proposed actions fit group objectives, failure to examine the negative risks of proceeding with proposed actions, insufficient search for and review of available information, failure to reexamine previously rejected alternatives, and failure to develop backup contingency plans. Researchers generally agree that these procedural shortcomings can reduce decision quality (Baron 2005). However, empirical studies that directly test the effects of Janis's antecedent conditions on the other components of the groupthink model reveal the risks inherent in developing general propositions from narrative case studies.

SUPPORT FOR THE THEORY

Statements made by NASA officials and consulting engineers at Morton Thiokol just prior to the disastrous 1986 decision to launch the Challenger shuttlecraft were content analyzed in one of a handful of quantitative case studies that show some support for a negative association between specific symptoms of poorly functioning groups (e.g., self-censorship and directive leadership) and decision-making (Esser, 1998). However, these studies also fail to verify essential causes of bad decisions that are specific to the groupthink model. Empirical justification for retaining group cohesion as a key variable in groupthink

is especially elusive. Controlled studies designed to experimentally test the effects of group cohesion on groupthink symptoms and outcomes show results that are inconsistent and sometimes contrary to the theory's primary predictions (McCauley 1998). One reason is that while Janis defined group cohesion as a high degree of attraction or esprit de corps between group members, premature concurrence can also be attributed to a fear of rejection by in-group members or a fear of losing status, especially when self-censorship and directive leadership are involved. In sum, critics argue that groupthink theory is based on a selective sample of cases. Retrospective case studies are an inadequate means of establishing necessary conditions and sound explanations for behavior.

Despite the vagaries of interpreting tests of the groupthink model, there is little doubt that research in this area has revealed a number of reasons why groups may fail to achieve optimal decisions. Pressure to conform to a seemingly popular group decision can follow from *pluralistic ignorance*, which is a false assumption by individuals that other in-group members are unanimous in their beliefs or knowledge. Likewise, *false uniqueness* is the sense that one is without support for dissenting from what is apparently the group's position. When group members are able to discuss their preferred decisions, *group polarization* can foster confidence that the popular group decision is correct even if all relevant information has not been considered. Finally, extreme group positions may indicate *ethnocentrism*, which reduces consideration of alternative positions, particularly those that would lead to relationships with out-group members.

SEE ALSO *Solidarity*

BIBLIOGRAPHY

Baron, Robert S. 2005. So Right It's Wrong: Groupthink and the Ubiquitous Nature of Polarized Group Decision Making. In *Advances in Experimental Social Psychology* 37, ed. Mark P. Zanna, 219–253. San Diego, CA: Elsevier Academic Press.

Esser, James K. 1998. Alive and Well after Twenty-Five Years: A Review of Groupthink Research. *Organizational Behavior and Human Decision Processes* 73 (2–3): 116–141.

Janis, Irving L. 1982. *Groupthink: Psychological Studies of Policy Decisions and Fiascoes.* 2nd rev. ed. Boston: Houghton-Mifflin. Originally published as *Victims of Groupthink: A Psychological Study of Foreign-Policy Decisions and Fiascoes.* (Boston: Houghton-Mifflin, 1972).

McCauley, Clark. 1998. Group Dynamics in Janis's Theory of Groupthink: Backward and Forward. *Organizational Behavior and Human Decision Processes* 73 (2–3): 142–162.

Rolf Holtz

GROWTH ACCOUNTING

Growth accounting describes the growth in the total product (output) of an economy or industry by decomposing it into its underlying determinants. This idea is very closely related to productivity growth (or technical change), typically defined as the amount of output growth not accounted for by its identifiable determinants, a residual often called a "measure of our ignorance" (Abramovitz 1962).

The economic building block underlying growth accounting is the production function $Y = f(X,t)$, where Y is output (total production of goods and services), X is a vector (group) of inputs used for production, and t is a time counter. For example, the production function written as $Y = f(K,L,M,t)$ says that the amount of output produced during a particular time period (say, a year) depends on the amount of physical capital (K, such as equipment and buildings) used, labor (L) employed, and primary and intermediate materials (M) purchased.

Based on this production function, and assuming that it represents all factors contributing to production, observed output growth over time can be attributed to (accounted for by) four causes—changes in each of the three inputs ($j = K,L,M$) and the passage of time (t, proxying technical change). Formally, this is written as the total derivative $dY/dt = \Sigma_j \, \partial Y/\partial X_j \, dX_j/dt + \partial Y/\partial t$. Because, mathematically, d refers to the full observed change in a variable and ∂ to a change "holding all else fixed," this equation says that the full output change observed in the data is accounted for by the contribution of each input to output (marginal product of input j, $\partial Y/\partial X_j$) multiplied by the input change observed in the data, plus the remaining time trend (residual).

Usually this expression is written in proportional terms by taking the derivative in logarithmic form, as $d\ln Y/dt = \Sigma_j \, \partial \ln Y/\partial \ln X_j \cdot d\ln X_j/dt + \partial \ln Y/\partial t$, so each term becomes a percentage change. To then measure productivity growth or technical change (the percentage of output growth not accounted for by changes in input use), this expression is inverted to read $\partial \ln Y/\partial t = d\ln Y/dt - \Sigma_j \, \partial \ln Y/\partial \ln X_j \cdot d\ln X_j/dt$, so the left-hand side of the expression, productivity growth, captures growth in output not accounted for by the measured inputs.

Two primary implementation issues immediately arise for measuring these expressions. First, $d\ln Y/dt$ and $d\ln X_j/dt$ are simply data; assuming one has valid measures of real (not nominal) output and inputs, these are just the percentage changes in these measures between two time periods. However, $\partial \ln Y/\partial \ln X_j$ is defined as the change in output from *only* changing X_j, which is not evident from actual data. Second, many other potentially measurable factors that contribute to output growth should not just be lumped into a residual, because that seriously limits its interpretability. For example, research and development (R&D) may be a specific cause of greater production from given input levels, which if distinguished separately would facilitate interpreting or explaining the "drivers" accounting for output growth. Further, even for standard factors of production, their measured changes may not reflect quality variations (say, education of laborers), which one would want to recognize to explain output growth patterns.

The first issue is typically dealt with by the theoretical assumption that firms maximize profits, which implies that inputs are paid the value of their marginal products (for example, a manager is willing to pay a worker up to the amount of money his labor generates). More formally, this means the input revenue share $S_j = p_j X_j / p_y Y$ (where p_j and p_y are the prices of X_j and Y, so $p_j X_j$ is the total amount of money paid to input j and $p_y Y$ is the total value of output) can be substituted for $\partial \ln Y/\partial \ln X_j$. The output growth expression then becomes $d\ln Y/dt = \Sigma_j S_j \, d\ln X_j/dt + \partial \ln Y/\partial t$. Although this substitution is based on restrictive assumptions such as full equilibrium and perfectly competitive markets, it means all the components of the growth accounting expression are measurable directly from data on output and input levels and prices (in contrast to econometric estimation).

The second issue is somewhat more difficult to deal with, because even if factors such as R&D are included in the production function, there is no measurable "value" or "weight" for their productive contribution, such as the share paid to an input (S_j). That is, if the production function is written as $Y = f(X,R,t)$ (where $R = $ R&D), the growth accounting expression becomes $d\ln Y/dt = \Sigma_j S_j \, d\ln X_j/dt + \partial \ln Y/\partial \ln R \cdot d\ln R/dt + \partial \ln Y/\partial t$. This equation states that the percentage total output growth observed in the data is explained by the cost share of each of the j inputs multiplied by its percentage change, the marginal contribution to production of R&D multiplied by its percentage change, and the passage of time (trend). However, there is no measurable weight to substitute for $\partial \ln Y/\partial \ln R$ without econometrically estimating the production function. Similarly, there is no clear way to separately identify changes in the quality or characteristics of the j inputs.

Early research in the growth accounting literature initially adjusted measures of capital and labor inputs by measures of quality or composition changes to put them in "effective" units. For example, Dale Jorgenson and Zvi Griliches (1967) "explained" the large productivity growth residual found by Robert Solow (1957) by direct adjustments of capital measures. The typically ad hoc nature of such adjustments, however, caused disputes among researchers about appropriate adjustment methodologies.

Additional issues arose from the more detailed growth accounting models of researchers such as Edward Denison (1979, 1985) and John Kendrick (1979), who included many additional potential growth drivers such as R&D, scale economies, capital obsolescence, and allocation, environmental, and "irregular" factors (such as weather). The multitude of factors that may affect output growth are, however, virtually impossible to measure and weight reliably and consistently for the growth accounting measure. Methodological problems emerging from the limited theoretical and empirical bases of many of the adjustments thus raised serious questions about their validity.

Due to these measurement and consistency issues, detailed growth accounting models have rarely been implemented recently, although this literature has provided the methodological foundation for growth accounting–based productivity or technical change measures. The focus of such studies has been identifying as carefully as possible the various inputs one can measure and find cost share weights for, so the components of the measure can be calculated without econometric estimation.

SEE ALSO *Change, Technological; Solow Residual, The; Solow, Robert M.*

BIBLIOGRAPHY

Abramovitz, Moses. 1962. Economic Growth in the United States. *American Economics Review* 52: 762–782.

Denison, Edward F. 1979. *Accounting for Slower Economic Growth.* Washington, DC: The Brookings Institution.

Denison, Edward F. 1985. *Trends in American Economic Growth, 1929–1982.* Washington, DC: The Brookings Institution.

Jorgenson, Dale W., and Zvi Griliches. 1967. The Explanation of Productivity Change. *Review of Economic Studies* 34 (3): 249–282.

Kendrick, John W. 1979. Productivity Trends and the Recent Slowdown. In *Contemporary Economic Problems*, ed. William Fellner, 17–69. Washington, DC: American Enterprise Institute.

Solow, Robert M. 1957. Technical Change and the Aggregate Production Function. *Review of Economics and Statistics* 39 (5): 312–320.

Catherine J. Morrison Paul

GROWTH CURVE ANALYSIS

Growth curve analysis, or trajectory analysis, is a specialized set of techniques for modeling change over time. The time frame might be seconds in a psychophysiology study, or years or even decades in a longitudinal panel study.

Growth curve analysis is a data reduction technique: it is used to summarize longitudinal data into a smooth curve defined by relatively few parameters for descriptive purposes or further inquiry. It is especially useful in developmental psychology research, measuring intraindividual change over childhood years or life course, but it can also be used to measure change at group levels in sociology or demography. Discussion in this entry will be in terms of intraindividual change, for ease of communication, but the principles apply to other levels of change.

Before the advent of growth curve analysis, longitudinal analysis usually focused on timepoint-to-timepoint relations, or even cross-sectional relations involving different cohorts of participants (and often still does, of course, depending on the nature of the data collection and research question). With only two timepoints of data collection, longitudinal analysis is largely limited to correlation or regression (either predicting an outcome from earlier variables, including the earlier score on the outcome, or predicting a change score). If the researcher has data from at least three measurement occasions, growth-curve analysis becomes a useful tool.

The core idea of growth curve analysis in longitudinal data is that the researcher can estimate a best-fit line or curve to each individual's responses over time. In subsequent analysis steps, the parameters defining those curves can be analyzed. To take an example of the simplest case, consider reading-competency tests administered at ages six, seven, and eight. With three measurement occasions, growth curve analysis involves estimating a best-fit line (and a residual or error component). The line for each respondent is characterized by an intercept or overall level and slope or linear change over time. In this example, the intercept would typically be set at age six, with the slope representing the rate of change through age eight, as shown in Figure 1 and discussed further below. The means of these intercepts and slopes represent a sample-average trajectory, and the variances of those parameters across individuals represent the variability in the growth curve (line). The individual variation in growth curves can then be predicted from respondent-level variables (e.g., gender, socioeconomic status, treatment condition). If the data collection includes at least four measurement occasions, more complex growth curves can be estimated—for example, with a relation with a quadratic component of time (time squared) in order to model curvature, or acceleration.

ESTIMATION TECHNIQUES

There are two primary analysis techniques for growth curve analysis: *multilevel modeling* (MLM) and *structural equation modeling* (SEM). Multilevel models, also known as *hierarchical linear models, mixed models*, and other terms, are based on the disaggregation of the model into

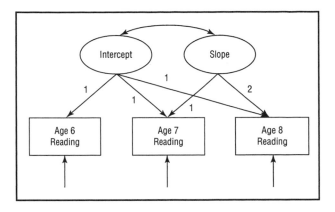

Figure 1

multiple levels of explanation. For growth-curve analysis, this typically involves a within-person level and a between-person level. The outcome is measured at a within-person level, across multiple occasions. The outcome is directly predicted by an intercept and a time variable or variables. It can also be predicted by time-varying covariates (e.g., teacher qualification) that the investigator wishes to separate from the growth curve. The regression coefficients associated with some or all of these variables are, in turn, predicted by variables at the between-person level. In the example above, there is a person-level equation for each child—a best-fit regression line fitted to the three points. The intercept and slope of this line vary between children. This variance can be predicted by child gender or other between-person predictors.

Structural equation models are used in the specific case of growth-curve models known as *latent trajectory analysis*. In this instance, the growth parameters (intercept, slope, etc.) are modeled as latent variables that have the individual measurement occasions as indicators. The loadings of the indicators on the growth variables are typically fixed as functions of time, as shown in Figure 1. Reading ability at age six is a function only of the intercept (the value of the intercept for that child multiplied by the loading of 1). Age-seven reading scores reflect the intercept (again multiplied by 1) plus the slope multiplied by 1; at age eight the slope value is multiplied by 2. Thus the slope is the estimated rate of improvement from one year to the next. Finally, as in multilevel models, the latent growth variables can be predicted by other variables in the model.

It is possible to estimate the same models in SEM (modeling means and intercepts, in addition to variances and covariances) as in MLM. In the most common applications, the only differences are in the handling of the occasion-specific residuals, and those differences can be resolved. MLM has the advantage that certain statistics are commonly output that can be useful, such as the apportionment of variance between the two levels. It is also pos-

sible to create elaborate nesting structures (e.g., occasion within person, person within classroom, classroom within school, etc.). SEM approaches have the advantage of greater flexibility in the modeling approach. For example, it is possible to model the slopes as dependent on the intercepts, and it is relatively simple to incorporate a second or even third growth process in the same model. Also, characteristic of SEM, the indicators of the growth curve can themselves be latent variables, measured by observed indicators taken over time.

In either approach, it is not necessary that all respondents have the same occasions of measurement. As the key variables are the growth parameters, it is not critical that the growth parameters be estimated for different respondents in exactly the same way—if a child's reading is measured at age 7.5, the slope value would merely have a loading (multiplier) of 1.5 to characterize the time elapsed since the intercept. As a consequence, even in a fixed-occasion design, the methods easily accommodate missing data collection points, insofar as the missingness is at random (MAR). The consequence of fewer measurement points for an individual is simply that that individual's data contribute less to the solution of the model.

EXTENSIONS

Much can be done on the basis of a growth curve analysis. For example, more sophisticated models of change can be estimated, especially in the SEM latent growth framework. The growth curve, while a longitudinal model, is essentially a time-invariant estimate of a respondent's change over time—the curve parameters are constant. Typically, of course, there will be deviations from that curve, because it is, by necessity, a simplification of the data (three data points can rarely be exactly defined by two parameters). One way to model that deviation is by the autoregressive latent trajectory (ALT) presented by Kenneth Bollen and Patrick Curran (2003). In this model, the time-invariant elements of change (intercept and slope) are modeled by the growth curve, while time-specific deviations from the curve (the extent and direction in which measured values differ from predicted values) are predicted in an autoregressive model, where each timepoint is linearly predicted by previous points, so that deviations propagate through time.

Hypotheses about the interrelations over time between two variables are common in developmental research. Historically, these have been typically studied in an autoregressive cross-lagged path analysis model (i.e., a model in which each variable at each timepoint is affected by the previous measurements of both the same variable and the other variable). This can be extended with growth curve analysis to a bivariate ALT, where the relations among the growth parameters of each process are modeled according to hypothesis, and the time-specific change in one variable is influenced by the other variable as well.

APPLICATIONS

Two major applications of growth curve analysis beyond the descriptive aspects discussed so far are in analysis of intervention effects and in estimation of predictive models. Continuing the example, in a growth curve in an intervention study to improve reading ability, it is possible to estimate a curve with one intercept and two slopes (or higher-order curves), in which the value of the second slope is constrained to zero for each child in the control condition, and is added to the model for children in the treatment condition beginning with the timepoint after initiation of the intervention. In this case, the first slope represents the baseline growth, and the second slope represents the deviation from the baseline trajectory induced by the intervention.

A second interesting application is the development of predictive models. If the growth curve is well established in observed data, it is possible to project the curve beyond the observed data and make reasonable predictions of future events. Of course, this includes the risk common to any regression model in which prediction is extended beyond the observed range of predictors, but applied with caution, it can be a highly useful tool.

BIBLIOGRAPHY

Bollen, Kenneth A., and Patrick J. Curran. 2003. Autoregressive Latent Trajectory (ALT) Models: A Synthesis of Two Traditions. *Sociological Methods and Research* 32: 336–383.

Raudenbush, Stephen W., and Anthony S. Bryk. 2002. *Hierarchical Linear Models: Applications and Data Analysis Methods.* 2nd ed. Thousand Oaks, CA: Sage.

Singer, Judith D., and John B. Willett. 2003. *Applied Longitudinal Data Analysis: Modeling Change and Event Occurrence.* New York: Oxford University Press.

Willett, John B., and Aline G. Sayer. 1994. Using Covariance Structure Analysis to Detect Correlates and Predictors of Change. *Psychological Bulletin* 116: 363–381.

Patrick S. Malone

GRUTTER DECISION

Grutter v. Bollinger (2003) was an attempt by the U.S. Supreme Court to define the acceptable boundaries of university affirmative action programs. While setting limits on the design of such programs, *Grutter*, along with *Gratz v. Bollinger* (decided the same day), upheld the practice generally and answered some existing questions about allowable techniques.

Prior to these cases, affirmative action law followed *California v. Bakke* (1978). *Bakke*, however, confused college admissions officers because six separate opinions were produced, none of which garnered a majority of the Court's nine votes. Many legal commentators supported Justice Lewis F. Powell's (1907–1998) opinion as the precedent around which programs should be formed. His opinion upheld diversity in educational institutions—but not correction of past harms—as an acceptable public goal, while limiting the options available to achieve diversity. In particular, *Bakke* has been interpreted to mean that racial quotas are unconstitutional. However, due to the overlapping opinions, universities and federal circuit courts were unclear about which practices remained acceptable. Some states, therefore, were forced to abandon affirmative action completely, while others encountered a more permissive environment.

Arising in this context, *Grutter* and *Gratz* involved the University of Michigan Law School and undergraduate admissions offices, respectively. *Grutter* left the Law School admissions practice intact, while *Gratz* found the undergraduate process flawed. Together, the cases upheld affirmative action, while imposing limits on its implementation.

Constitutional jurisprudence has applied "strict scrutiny" analysis for state-sponsored activities that treat "suspect classes" (i.e., groups who tend to experience discrimination) differently. Strict scrutiny first requires that the policy in question be used to forward some compelling state interest. *Grutter* affirmed diversity as a worthwhile goal of state-funded educational institutions. Second, to survive strict scrutiny, a policy must be narrowly tailored to meet that interest. Quota systems, therefore, remained unconstitutional, and universities were required to make a good-faith effort towards race-neutral policies to further their goals. At Michigan Law School, "plus factors" granted to underrepresented minorities were deemed sufficiently narrow to avoid racial discrimination. This format was accepted as a means of making admissions decisions about individuals rather than seeing them merely as representatives of their racial group. The undergraduate admissions program was invalidated because of the weighting it gave simply for group membership. Justice Sandra Day O'Connor also expressed hope "that 25 years from now, the use of racial preferences will no longer be necessary to further" the interest of diversity.

Future jurisprudence, particularly in light of Justice O'Connor's retirement in 2006, may revisit the issue and alter the *Grutter* approach. For the time being, in response to *Grutter*, some state universities have resurrected affirmative action programs that were locally banned after

Bakke. In order to comply with *Grutter* and *Gratz*, others have dropped point-based systems in favor of more individualized application review. Michigan, for instance, has moved to a system based on essays about the applicant's diverse experiences. Although such changes are popular, they require additional admissions staff and financial resources.

Some legal confusion persists, leading risk-averse universities to question whether other diversity efforts, such as minority scholarships, may be at risk. In addition to compliance efforts, *Grutter* has had other political consequences. Most notably, opponents have introduced ballot initiatives to block affirmative action programs. Nonetheless, *Grutter* affirmed the constitutionality of racial preferences in university admissions, significantly reducing previous uncertainty.

SEE ALSO *Affirmative Action; Supreme Court, U.S.*

BIBLIOGRAPHY

U.S. Supreme Court. 1978. *Regents of the University of California v. Bakke*, 438 U.S. 265.
http://supreme.justia.com/us/438/265/case.html.

U.S. Supreme Court. 2003. *Gratz v. Bollinger*, 539 U.S. 244.
http://www.supremecourtus.gov/opinions/02pdf/02-516.pdf.

U.S. Supreme Court. 2003. *Grutter v. Bollinger*, 539 U.S. 306.
http://www.supremecourtus.gov/opinions/02pdf/02-241.pdf.

Mark Axelrod

GUANTÁNAMO BAY

Guantánamo Bay, Cuba, has played a critical role in U.S. foreign policy since the nineteenth century. The U.S. Naval Station there is the oldest American base outside of the continental United States, and the only U.S. base located in a country with which the United States does not have diplomatic relations. Known alternately as GITMO, the 45-square-mile base is located at Cuba's southeastern tip and is approximately four hundred miles from Miami, Florida. In 2006 GITMO was home to approximately 8,500 U.S. service personnel (and their dependents) whose mission includes providing logistical support to the U.S. Navy and Coast Guard, maintaining migrant operations, and hosting the Detainee Mission of the "War on Terror" under the direction of the Joint Task Force Guantánamo.

American presence began when the United States invaded Guantánamo Bay and established a marine base during the Spanish-American War. Cuban independence fighters worked with American forces to expel Spain. At the end of the war in August 1898, the United States con-trolled Cuba. The 1901 Platt Amendment, adopted by the U.S. Congress and incorporated into Cuba's constitution, defined U.S. involvement in Cuba's affairs. Until such time as Cuba had an independent government, the United States would intervene to preserve Cuban independence or to maintain "a government adequate for the protection of life, property, and individual liberty." The amendment also ceded Guantánamo to the United States.

After Cuba's independence in 1903, the Cuban-American Treaty stipulated that the United States would lease Guantánamo Bay as a coaling and naval station. The lease gave the United States "complete jurisdiction and control" of the territory while recognizing "the continuance of the ultimate sovereignty of the Republic of Cuba." Guantánamo Bay's unique status was born. The Platt Amendment was annulled in 1934, and the Permanent Treaty codified the leasing arrangement, specifying that the United States would pay an annual sum of approximately $4,085. Since the Revolution of 1959, the Cuban government has accepted only one payment for the lease of Guantánamo, in the first year after the Cuban Revolution. By its own terms, the lease can be abrogated only by mutual agreement. The Cuban government maintains that the base constitutes an unlawful military occupation resulting from an agreement forcefully imposed on Cuba.

In 1964 Cuban president Fidel Castro cut water and supplies to the base hoping to compel U.S. withdrawal. Instead, the base became self-sufficient for its own water and energy. American personnel have been evacuated temporarily from Guantánamo on two occasions: during the Cuban Missile Crisis in 1962 and in 1994, as the population exceeded 40,000 when the base became a holding facility for Haitian and Cuban migrants seeking refuge in the United States. The base continues to serve as an ongoing migrant processing facility, capable of accommodating 40 people, or 10,000 in an emergency.

After September 11, 2001, the base's mission expanded to include the Detainee Mission of the War on Terror. Beginning in 2002, more than 600 prisoners from approximately thirty countries were brought by the United States to Guantánamo from Afghanistan. The detainees were suspected of having ties to either the Taliban or Al Qaeda, and they were held indefinitely, without charges, without counsel, and without access to American courts. The detainees' legal status and treatment have been a matter of grave international concern. In 2007 approximately 385 detainees remained imprisoned in Guantánamo.

The U.S. government first posited that the detainees were not subject to the jurisdiction of U.S. courts because Guantánamo was not part of the sovereign territory of the United States. Second, the government consistently held that the detainees in Guantánamo were "enemy combatants" and thus beyond the protections provided to Prisoners of War under the Geneva Conventions.

In summer 2004 the Supreme Court held in *Rasul v. Bush* that the United States exercises "complete jurisdiction and control" over Guantánamo under the 1903 treaty, even though Guantánamo is under the "ultimate sovereignty" of Cuba. Hence, the detainees had the right to be heard in U.S. courts. As a result, the U.S. government instituted military tribunals to determine whether the detainees were enemy combatants. These tribunals lacked fundamental constitutional protections guaranteed in U.S. courts.

In 2006 the Supreme Court heard the case of Salim Ahmed Hamdan, Osama bin Laden's former driver, who had been detained at Guantánamo since 2002. In *Hamdan v. Rumsfeld*, the Supreme Court found, by a vote of 5-3, that the president overstepped his powers by authorizing these military tribunals, which lacked essential legal and constitutional safeguards. Additionally, the Court held that the tribunals violated the Geneva Conventions, rejecting the Bush administration's argument that the Conventions did not apply to the detainees at Guantánamo. However, the Court did not require Congress to apply the Geneva Convention to the war on terror.

Late in 2006, the U.S. Congress passed the Military Commissions Act, eliminating the right of *habeas corpus* for enemy combatants, allowing the admission of coerced evidence, and giving the president the power to define who is an enemy combatant. The Act does, however, give detainees fair notice of the charges against them, counsel paid for by the American government, and considerable discovery of the prosecution's case against them. In March 2007, the military tribunals in Guantánamo recommenced with high profile cases resulting in a number of guilty pleas. At the same time, skepticism from left-wing politicians regarding the proceedings grew with increasing calls for the closing of the Gitmo detention center.

Most notably, Robert Gates, who replaced Donald Rumsfeld as secretary of defense in 2007, reportedly called for the closing of the detention center because of concern that the prosecution of war on terror was burdened by the proceedings and their perception by foreign nations. The U.S. Supreme Court may be compelled to address the constitutionality of the Military Commissions Act.

SEE ALSO *Al-Qaeda; Castro, Fidel; Cuban Missile Crisis; Imprisonment; Interrogation; Iraq-U.S. War; Military*

BIBLIOGRAPHY

Guantánamo Bay. GITMO. http://www.globalsecurity.org/military/facility/guantanamo-bay.htm.

The Illegal United States Naval Base in Guantánamo. Official Cuban Foreign Ministry Website.

http://www.cubaminrex.cu/CDH/60cdh/Guantanamo/English/Historical%20Background.htm.

Lease of Coaling or Naval Stations Agreement Between the United States and Cuba (1903). 2004. In *Guantánamo: What the World Should Know*, eds. Michael Ratner and Ellen Ray, 94–96. White River Junction, VT: Chelsea Green Publishing.

Shanker, Thom and David E. Sanger. 2007. New to Job, Gates Argued for Closing Guantánamo. *New York Times*, March 22.

Mary M. McKenzie

GUERRILLA WARFARE

Guerrilla warfare relies on hit-and-run tactics by highly mobile, lightly to moderately armed units that feature deception, speed, and flexibility. Usually conducted by indigenous antigovernment forces, not the regular armed forces of a state, its characteristic attacks include ambushes, raids, sabotage, and blocking of enemy lines of communication. Examples of guerrilla warfare, such as in Iraq and Afghanistan since 2003, increasingly feature the use of road mines and suicide attacks. Guerrilla warfare is classically considered a weapon of the weak to fight a much stronger enemy, such as the state, an occupier, or a colonial power, and is directed not so much at defeating the enemy's regular forces on the battlefield as at eroding the enemy's will and capacity to sustain its control.

The first documented record of this kind of irregular warfare occurs on a Hittite parchment from fifteenth century BCE. Since then it has been used among others by the Gauls against Julius Caesar's (100–44 BCE) Roman army, the Incas against the Spanish conquerors, and the Apache Indians in the U.S. Southwest. Guerrilla warfare became especially prominent during the twentieth century and may be increasingly seen in the twenty-first century, reflecting the great asymmetry in the physical capabilities of the military establishments of modern industrialized states and those of anti-state and revolutionary movements.

Secure bases, internal or external sanctuaries, and good intelligence are important ingredients for the success of guerrilla warfare, as is popular support for the insurgency. It is vital for the success of the guerrillas that the larger population of the area being contested, at minimum, acquiesce to guerrilla activity. In fact, winning the hearts and minds of the people is frequently the goal of both the guerrillas and the anti-guerrilla forces. When guerrillas are able to secure the support of the larger population and are hidden or protected by it, anti-guerrilla forces find it difficult to distinguish between friends, foes, and neutrals and easily slip into punishing the entire population to deter it from supporting the guerrillas. In a famous case in South Vietnam, a U.S. officer seeking to deprive the Viet Cong of its sanctuary ordered an entire village to be burned, commenting that "we had to destroy the village to save it."

The success of Mao Zedong's "people's war" has served as a model for modern guerrilla warfare for many other guerrilla leaders and counterinsurgency theorists. Mao transformed guerrilla warfare from operations that involved only irregular military tactics to warfare that also featured social, psychological, economic, and—crucially—political components. Mao envisioned insurgency as a protracted social and political revolution, where guerrilla warfare was the means to survive in the initial phases of the struggle before a regular conventional army could be fielded and used to defeat the government.

The process would take place in three phases. The goal of the first phase, strategic defensive, was to expand the communist party organization and establish the infrastructure necessary for further development of the revolution. Party workers were to generate public support and infiltrate the state's political apparatus. The first period was understood to be a long one, with only a limited resort to force to intimidate the population and create a climate of dissent, civil disobedience, and economic unrest. Once sufficient support, or at minimum acquiescence, among the population was achieved, the second phase, strategic stalemate or strategic equilibrium, was to be launched. In this phase the expansion of terrorism into guerrilla warfare would take place and revolutionary administration—more capable than that of the government—would be established. Finally, in the third phase, strategic offensive, the balance would have clearly swung in the direction of the revolutionary movement and regular units would be introduced and engage in near conventional warfare while the incidence of guerrilla warfare would decrease. The marked feature of Mao's concept was the emphasis on political and psychological elements as the key to victory, not simply military factors. Mao's principles have been applied in many guerrilla struggles since, and not only by communist rebels, including in Malaya (1948–1960), the Philippines (1946–1954), Algeria (1954–1962), Angola (1962–1974), Rhodesia (1972–1980), Oman (1965–1975), and Peru (1980–1994).

The *foco* theory of insurgency and revolutionary warfare developed as an alternative rural guerrilla approach, inspired by the success of a relatively small number of revolutionaries toppling the Batista regime in Cuba in 1959 and hoping to compress the protracted struggle envisioned by Mao into a swift victory. Among its most prominent theorists were Ernesto "Che" Guevara (1928–1967) and Jules Régis Debray (1940–). In contrast to Mao, who stressed the importance of political structures and in fact the dominance of the political, Guevara and Debray argued that the guerrillas themselves were a fusion of the military and the political authority. Instead of a protracted struggle, they argued that a minimum level of discontent with the government could be translated into conditions favorable to revolution. By military action alone, an elite group could provide the focus, or *foco*, for the revolution. Inspired by the actions of the elite, progressively greater and greater number of sympathizers, alienated by the corruption and brutality of the state, would attach themselves to the revolutionaries and rebel, thus provoking an even more brutal reaction on the part of the government and alienating even more people. Although *foco* was applied in Colombia, Bolivia, Peru, Guatemala, and Ecuador throughout the 1960s and 1980s, it proved a manifest failure.

The dismal success record of the *foco* guerrilla theory contributed to the development of urban guerrilla warfare. Carlos Marighela (1911–1969) was among its most influential theorists. Like Guevara and Debray, Marighela rejected the need for a prolonged preparation for revolution. However, instead of the countryside, Marighela situated the center of the revolution back to the cities. The urban guerrillas would be a small band of highly dedicated individuals, who through the use of terror, such as parcel bombs and ambushes, would provoke the authorities into overreaction, thus alienating the population and creating the revolutionary situation. Actions were to be spectacular and aimed at not just the government but also foreign multinationals, with the intention of weakening the economy. In practice, urban guerrilla warfare becomes rather difficult to distinguish from terrorism. The urban guerrilla approach has been applied, for example, by Michael Collins (1890–1922) during the Irish Republican Army struggle against the British in the 1920s, in the latter phases of the Sendero Luminoso (Shining Path) insurgency in Peru in the early 1990s, in Iraq since 2003, and may likely be a prominent feature of twenty-first-century conflicts.

SEE ALSO *American Revolution; Vietnam War*

BIBLIOGRAPHY

Debray, Régis. 1970. *Strategy for Revolution*. Ed. Robin Blackburn. New York: Monthly Review Press.

Debray, Régis. 1975. *Che's Guerrilla War*. Trans. Rosemary Sheed. Harmondsworth, U.K.: Penguin.

Griffith, Samuel B., ed. 1978. *Mao Tse-tung on Guerrilla War*. New York: Anchor Press.

Guevara, Ernesto. 1969. *Guerrilla Warfare*. Harmondsworth, U.K.: Penguin.

Marighela, Carlos. 1971. *For the Liberation of Brazil*. Trans. John Butt and Rosemary Sheed. Harmondsworth, U.K.: Penguin.

O'Neill, Bard E. 2005. *Insurgency and Terrorism: From Revolution to Apocalypse*. Washington, DC: Potomac Books.

Zedong, Mao. 1963. *Selected Military Writings*. Beijing: Foreign Language Press.

Vanda Felbab-Brown

GUILLOTINE

SEE *French Revolution*.

GUILT

SEE *Farsightedness*.

GULAGS

The term *gulag* refers primarily to the system of forced labor camps existing in the Soviet Union from the 1920s until the mid-1950s, although it is also used in a more generic sense to refer to later labor camps in the Soviet Union and to similar institutions elsewhere. *Gulag* is an acronym from the Russian phrase *Glavnoe upravlenie lagerei* ("main administration of camps"). The gulag played a key role during the dictatorship of Joseph Stalin as both a source of labor for the Soviet Union's industrialization drive, and a means of removing from society those deemed undesirable by the Soviet state.

The gulag incarcerated around twenty million people in total between the late 1920s and the early 1950s. The number of inmates in the gulag was a matter of fierce scholarly debate during the cold war, but with the opening up of Russian archives beginning in the early 1990s, a broad consensus has been reached, although precise figures remain a matter of dispute, depending on which categories of imprisonment are counted as part of the gulag. Twenty million represents the total number of individuals in the gulag during the Stalin era; the highest gulag population at any given time was just over two and half million, in 1952.

A Soviet Politburo decision of June 1929, "On the Use of the Labor of Convicted Criminals," marked the beginning of the widespread use of forced labor to contribute to the national economy, and coincided with Stalin's drive for rapid industrialization of his largely rural country. The growing gulag camp network provided a means of forcing the millions of people thrown off the land during the collectivization of agriculture to be used in the cause of industrialization, chiefly plant and infrastructure construction and the development of remote areas rich in raw materials. Soviet economic plans included targets for gulag production, and the prisoner population grew inexorably, interrupted only by World War II, to its peak in the early 1950s. Judicial procedures were cursory and entirely subject to the Communist Party, dominated by Stalin.

Living conditions for gulag prisoners undermined the view that they were a valuable labor resource. Rations were poor and used as a reward for meeting output targets. In some periods, particularly around World War II, starvation and disease were rife.

Following Stalin's death in 1953, his successor Nikita Khrushchev authorized the rapid winding down of the mass gulag system. At first celebrated as enlightened, "corrective labor" by the Soviet authorities in propagandistic films and books, the gulag system was shrouded in a veil of official secrecy from the late 1930s until the Khrushchev years. In 1962 the publication of Aleksandr Solzhenitsyn's *A Day in the Life of Ivan Denisovich* caused a sensation and marked the height of the relative cultural thaw of that time. A decade later, with the more conservative Leonid Brezhnev in power, Solzhenitsyn's *Gulag Archipelago* (1973) had to be published abroad. Solzhenitsyn (b. 1918) was awarded the Nobel Prize for Literature in 1970; in 1974 he was deported from the Soviet Union and stripped of his citizenship. In the post-Soviet era, the fate of gulag prisoners has been written about widely in Russia and abroad; memorials have been raised, though there is still no single central memorial, and independent groups, often made up of survivors and the relatives of victims, have sought to keep the memory of the gulag alive.

SEE ALSO *Colonialism; Concentration Camps; Imprisonment; Khrushchev, Nikita; Prison Psychology; Prisons; Solzhenitsyn, Aleksandr; Stalin, Joseph; Union of Soviet Socialist Republics*

BIBLIOGRAPHY

Applebaum, Anne. 2003. *Gulag: A History*. New York: Doubleday.

Solzhenitsyn, Aleksandr. [1962] 1974. *A Day in the Life of Ivan Denisovich*. New York: Signet.

Solzhenitsyn, Aleksandr. [1973] 2002. *The Gulag Archipelago*. Trans. Thomas P. Whitney and Harry Willetts, abr. Edward E. Ericson Jr. New York: Harper Perennial Classics.

Edwin Bacon

GULF STATES

The six nations that formed the Gulf Cooperation Council (GCC) in 1981—Saudi Arabia, Kuwait, Bahrain, Qatar, the United Arab Emirates, and Oman—are all oil-producing monarchies. Until a few decades ago, they were among the poorest countries in the world. Since the discovery of oil and particularly the oil price revolution of the early 1970s, the six have been able to carry out massive programs of socioeconomic development that have dramatically increased the per capita income of their citizens, resulted in a huge immigration of foreign workers, strengthened the control of ruling families over the states, and thrust the members into the international spotlight. Saudi Arabia is by far the largest of the group with a population estimated at 27 million. The other five range in size between 700,000 and 3 million.

Saudi Arabia has emerged as a major actor in Middle Eastern affairs. It has provided aid to and supported various Arab governments, even those with which it is at ideological odds. It has valued its "special relationship" with the United States and has supported U.S. policy aims in various parts of the world, despite fundamental differences over U.S. policy regarding Israel. The smaller five states have also sought to follow a neutral path in regional differences, although they were all alarmed by the Iranian revolution of 1979 and supported Iraq in its 1980–1988 war against Iran. But Iraq also proved to be an aggressor when Saddam Hussein's troops invaded Kuwait in 1990, requiring a U.S.-led international coalition to dislodge him. The GCC states also opened up their military facilities to provide assistance to the U.S.-led coalition attacking Iraq in 2003, although many of their citizens disagreed with the action.

A principal impetus for the creation of the GCC was to assure the security of its members in a volatile region. A small joint force was established near the Iraqi/Kuwaiti border and the six states have engaged in numerous joint exercises. However, the GCC members continue to depend heavily on Western assistance and their national armed forces have not been coordinated either in terms of equipment (purchased from a wide variety of countries) or doctrine and training.

But there were other legitimate purposes for the formation of the GCC as well, in which the GCC has succeeded relatively better than in security. Politically, the GCC has seen considerable coordination between the individual states, and many issues are thrashed out in advance of the six rulers' annual summit. The majority of differences between members have been settled, although some remain. A GCC headquarters and secretariat has been established in Riyadh and the position of secretary-general is rotated between the members.

In the economic sphere, the body has succeeded in standardizing weights and measures, creating a common tariff, assuring the free movement of (indigenous) labor and capital throughout the GCC, and taking steps toward a common currency. The members also have created cultural organizations to exchange information and ideas in such areas as education, professional disciplines, and the arts.

SEE ALSO *Alliances; Customs Union; Developing Countries; Development; Development Economics; Economic Growth; Organization of Petroleum Exporting Countries (OPEC); Petroleum Industry*

BIBLIOGRAPHY

Aarts, Paul, and Gerd Nonneman, eds. 2005. *Saudi Arabia in the Balance: Political Economy, Society, Foreign Affairs.* London: Hurst & Company.

Alkim, Hassan Hamdan al-. 1994. *The GCC States in an Unstable World: Foreign-Policy Dilemmas of Small States.* London: Al Saqi Books.

Crystal, Jill. 1990. *Oil and Politics in the Gulf: Rulers and Merchants in Kuwait and Qatar.* Cambridge, U.K.: Cambridge University Press.

Dresch, Paul, and James Piscatori, eds. 2005. *Monarchies and Nations: Globalisation and Identity in the Arab States of the Gulf.* London: I. B. Tauris.

Gause, F. Gregory, III. 1994. *Oil Monarchies: Domestic and Security Challenges in the Arab Gulf States.* New York: Council on Foreign Relations Press.

Naqeeb, Khaldoun Hasan al-. 1990. *Society and State in the Gulf and Arab Peninsula: A Different Perspective.* Trans. L. M. Kenny. London and New York: Routledge; Beirut: Center for Arab Unity Studies.

Potter, Lawrence G., and Gary G. Sick, eds. 2002. *Security in the Persian Gulf: Origins, Obstacles, and the Search for Consensus.* New York: Palgrave.

Said Zahlan, Rosemarie. 1998. *The Making of the Modern Gulf States: Kuwait, Bahrain, Qatar, the United Arab Emirates, and Oman.* Rev. ed. Reading, U.K.: Ithaca Press.

J. E. Peterson

GULF WAR OF 1991

The invasion of Kuwait by neighboring Iraq on August 2, 1990, triggered the first major international crisis of the post–Cold War era. The United States had uneasily supported Iraq during its eight-year war against Iran (1980–1988), a conflict known in the region as the First Gulf War, but Iraqi president Saddam Hussein misinterpreted certain diplomatic signals about whether the Unites States would acquiesce over this latest military action. Kuwait had also sided with Iraq against Iran, but

Kuwait and Iraq had fallen out over war debts, border disputes, and competing oil prices. When Iraq invaded in 1990, Kuwaiti defenses were quickly overrun and its government fled into exile. Because Iraq now threatened the Saudi Arabian oilfields, the United States spent the next six months assembling an international coalition of thirty-four nations, including regional Arab and Muslim states. The United States also secured ten United Nations resolutions to isolate Iraq and prepare for "all necessary means" to expel Iraq from Kuwait by force if it did not withdraw voluntarily. On the night of January 16 to 17, 1991, the U.S.-led "coalition of the willing" launched massive air strikes against Iraq's command-and-control infrastructure and its antiaircraft defenses. This conflict began under the title Operation Desert Storm.

For the next five weeks, coalition aircraft and missiles degraded the occupying Iraqi army's capacity to resist a land-war offensive. Iraq tried to expand the conflict and split the Arab members from the coalition by firing Scud missiles at Israel. The Iraqi air force fled to Iran after the loss of thirty-eight of its planes, giving the coalition air superiority for the rest of the war. Iraq released crude oil into Persian Gulf waters and even, briefly, occupied the Saudi coastal town of Khafji. Coalition "strategic" bombing missions were largely confined to Iraqi military forces and targets, while a new generation of "smart" missiles hit their military targets with unprecedented accuracy. Some "collateral damage" did occur, when some missiles missed their intended targets, causing unintentional damage and casualties and also causing intense media debate in the new age of real-time reporting around the clock by the Cable News Network (CNN). The two most controversial incidents were the bombings of an alleged baby-milk plant and the Al Firdos installation in Baghdad. The coalition insisted the baby-milk plant was really a chemical weapons facility and the Al Firdos installation was a command and control facility rather than a civilian bomb shelter as the Iraqis maintained. Around 400 civilians were killed on the occasion of the latter. The presence of journalists from coalition countries in the enemy capital while Iraq was under fire was unprecedented and made the propaganda war more complex.

The ground war began on February 24 and lasted barely a week, with Iraqi commanders agreeing to a "cessation of hostilities" at Safwan air base in southern Iraq on March 3. Although Saddam Hussein had promised "the mother of all battles," the Gulf War was one of the most one-sided conflicts in military history. An unknown number of Iraqi soldiers and civilians died (estimates vary from 25,000 to 200,000) and almost 70,000 Iraqi soldiers surrendered to the coalition, which suffered fewer than 350 dead, the majority of them Americans. Television images of bombed-out Iraqi convoys fleeing Kuwait may have had an impact on the decision to end the war.

In the long term, the war had disastrous consequences: It marked the arrival of Western military forces into the Muslim holy land of Mecca, which prompted the Saudi-born terrorist Osama bin Laden to turn against the United States, which had sponsored him during the Soviet invasion of Afghanistan.

SEE ALSO *Bush, George H. W.; Diplomacy; Hussein, Saddam; Multilateralism; United Nations*

BIBLIOGRAPHY

Atkinson, Rick. 1993. *Crusade: The Untold Story of the Persian Gulf War.* Boston: Houghton Mifflin.

Freedman, Lawrence, and Efraim Karsh. 1993. *The Gulf Conflict, 1990–1991: Diplomacy and War in the New World Order.* Princeton, NJ: Princeton University Press.

Philip M. Taylor

GUNDER FRANK, ANDRE
SEE *Frank, Andre Gunder.*

GUNS AND BUTTER
SEE *Trade-offs.*

GUOMINGDANG
SEE *Chinese Revolution.*

GUTTMAN, LOUIS
SEE *Guttman Scale; Likert Scale.*

GUTTMAN SCALE

Guttman scaling is a method of scale construction developed by Louis Guttman (1916–1987) in the 1940s. Widely used in the measurement of attitudes and public opinion, the goal of Guttman scaling is to establish unidimensional measurement instruments. A typical Guttman scale includes a series of items or statements tapping progressively higher levels of a single attribute. For instance, a scale designed to measure attitudes toward immigrants might ask people to indicate whether or not they would be accepting of immigrants as (a) citizens in the country, (b) coworkers in the same company, (c) neighbors, (d) close friends, and (e) close relatives by marriage. A tolerant individual would probably endorse each one of these statements in the scale. A less tolerant individual might be willing to accept immigrants as citizens in the country but not as neighbors or close family members. Thus, knowing that a person is not willing to accept immigrants as neighbors allows us to infer that this person probably would not want immigrants as close friends either; accepting them as family members would be even less likely for this person. By knowing the last statement endorsed by a respondent, one can easily reproduce his or her pattern of responding to the rest of the statements. In a perfect Guttman scale, the pattern of responding across the scale can be reproduced without any errors.

When the issue is relatively concrete, such as the amount of smoking, or when the construct is hierarchical in nature, such as social distance, Guttman scales work quite well; however, when it comes to measuring relatively more abstract attributes such as attitudes toward immigrants or marriage, it is not always easy to construct such highly reproducible scales.

As in all methods of scale construction, the first step in Guttman scaling is to generate a large set of items representing the construct. Then, a group of judges (80–100) evaluates each of the statements. Depending on the nature of the construct, the evaluations might be to indicate whether or not they agree with each statement, or to indicate whether the statement reflects the absence or presence of the phenomenon. For instance, if the construct in question is attitudes toward gun control, the judges will try to determine whether each item in the scale (e.g., "future manufacture of handguns should be banned") is in favor of or against gun control. In the next step, the responses of each judge are tabulated. In this table, the columns represent items in the scale, and the rows represent each judge. Once all the entries are laid out, the table is sorted so that judges who agree with more statements are listed at the top and those agreeing with fewer are at the bottom; then the number of affirmative responses are summed to create a total score for each judge. If the set of items were to form a cumulative scale, then it should be possible to reproduce the responses of each judge from his or her total score. Errors in reproduction indicate deviation from the optimum form, and suggest a call for revision of the scale, which can be done by changing or dropping existing items or even adding new items. The scale is revised until it becomes possible to reproduce over 90 percent of the responses from the total score. At this point, some statistical analyses can be conducted to examine deviations from a perfectly cumulative scale. These statistics can also be used to estimate a scale score for each item, just as in Thurstone scaling; ultimately, these scale scores are used in the calculation of a respondent's final score. A final set of items emerges after several revisions. Once the final set of items is established, the order of the items is mixed again to derive the final form of the scale to be shared with actual respondents.

The primary area of application has been in attitudes and public opinion—Guttman constructed a number of attitude scales during World War II using these procedures. Currently, however, as a method of constructing attitude scales, Guttman scaling is almost never used. Investigators prefer to use simpler methods of scale construction such as Likert scaling and the semantic differential technique.

SEE ALSO *Attitudes; Likert Scale; Psychology; Psychometrics; Public Opinion; Scales*

BIBLIOGRAPHY

Eagly, Alice H., and Shelly Chaiken. 1993. *The Psychology of Attitudes.* Orlando, FL: Harcourt Brace Jovanovich.

Edwards, Allen L. 1957. *Techniques of Attitude Scale Construction.* New York: Appleton-Century-Crofts.

Guttman, Louis. 1950. The Basis for Scalogram Analysis. In *Measurement and Prediction*, ed. Samuel A. Stouffer, Louis Guttman, Edward A. Suchman, et al., 60–90. Princeton, NJ: Princeton University Press.

G. Tarcan Kumkale

GYPSIES

SEE *Roma, The.*

H

HABERMAS, JÜRGEN
1929–

Jürgen Habermas is a philosopher and a prominent public intellectual in Germany. He is considered the leading representative of the second generation of the Frankfurt School, whose Critical Theory he has sought to reinvigorate in his sustained reflections on social theory. Habermas, however, diverges from his predecessors in his analysis of the emancipatory promise of the Enlightenment, whose political legacy, he maintains, remains unrealized. Drawing on the philosophy of Immanuel Kant, one of the foundational theoreticians of modernity, Habermas perceives a sublated potential in modernity. He posits the realm of communication as a counterweight to the Frankfurt School's disillusionment with a modernity corrupted by the destructive ascendancy of instrumental reason.

In his first book, *The Structural Transformation of the Public Sphere* (1962), Habermas demarcates theoretical concerns with public discourse and reason that would animate much of his later writings. This sociological and historical work examines the emergent bourgeois public sphere in Western Europe in the eighteenth century, tracing its origins as a "sphere of private people come together as a public" (1989, p. 27) and the concomitant transformations in modes of communication that it fostered as the new public deployed reason against the contemporary absolutist political order. As he chronicled the subsequent decline of the public sphere, Geoff Eley notes, Habermas was also criticizing the straitened confines of West Germany's authoritarian postwar political culture of the 1950s and 1960s (Eley 2002, p. 292). Many scholars have engaged Habermas's thesis, extending his analysis to other settings while also arguing for greater attention to the exclusionary mechanisms that hinder participation in the public sphere (Calhoun 1992, Gilroy 1993, Landes 1988).

Habermas's *Knowledge and Human Interests* (1968) is a critique of positivism elaborated through a comparison of social theory and psychoanalysis. *Knowledge and Human Interests* represents an early iteration of Habermas's theory of communication, and prefigures the linguistic turn of his magnum opus, *The Theory of Communicative Action* (1981). Here Habermas argues that the sphere of the everyday, or the *life-world*, has been progressively "colonized" by instrumental reason. Habermas asserts that the counterbalance to this process must be found in an intersubjective reciprocity arising in the sphere of language, arguing for a distinct *communicative rationality* in which language coordinates action among subjects as it socializes them. Habermas's writings on political theory, such as *Legitimation Crisis* (1973), *Between Facts and Norms* (1992), or *The Inclusion of the Other* (1996), anchor a theory of *discursive democracy* in his analyses of communicative practice in the public sphere. Critics counter that Habermas's theory of discourse is totalizing, wrongly assuming that all actors ultimately seek consensus as the outcome of their communicative interventions in the world (Lyotard 1979).

In *The Philosophical Discourse of Modernity* (1985), Habermas turns to the debates about postmodernism, criticizing Theodor Adorno's negative dialectics, Michel Foucault's genealogy, and Jacques Derrida's deconstruction for providing insufficient grounds for breaking free from the totalizing reason their practitioners' critique. He holds that the predicament of the transcendental subject that "philosophies of consciousness" pose can only be surpassed in the realm of intersubjectivity.

Habermas has often participated in the public sphere he analyzes in his scholarly writings. He was a leading spokesman for the student movement of the 1960s, and in the 1980s, he intervened in the Historians' Debate against the attempts of revisionist West German historians to lay the Nazi past to rest. More recently, Habermas has weighed in on issues of European identity and integration.

SEE ALSO *Critical Theory; Foucault, Michel*

BIBLIOGRAPHY

PRIMARY WORKS

Habermas, Jürgen. 1962. *The Structural Transformation of the Public Sphere: An Inquiry into a Category of Bourgeois Society.* Trans. Thomas Burger and Frederick Lawrence. Cambridge, MA: MIT Press, 1989.

Habermas, Jürgen. 1968. *Knowledge and Human Interests.* Trans. Jeremy J. Shapiro. Boston: Beacon Press, 1971.

Habermas, Jürgen. 1973. *Legitimation Crisis.* Trans. Thomas McCarthy. Boston: Beacon Press, 1975.

Habermas, Jürgen. 1981. *The Theory of Communicative Action.* 2 vols. Trans. Thomas McCarthy. Boston: Beacon Press, 1984.

Habermas, Jürgen. 1985. *The Philosophical Discourse of Modernity: Twelve Lectures.* Trans. Frederick G. Lawrence. Cambridge, MA: MIT Press, 1987.

Habermas, Jürgen. 1992. *Between Facts and Norms: Contributions to a Discourse Theory of Law and Democracy.* Trans. William Rehg. Cambridge, MA: MIT Press, 1996.

Habermas, Jürgen. 1996. *The Inclusion of the Other: Studies in Political Theory.* Ed. Ciaran Cronin and Pablo De Greiff. Cambridge, MA: MIT Press, 1998.

SECONDARY WORKS

Calhoun, Craig, ed. 1992. *Habermas and the Public Sphere.* Cambridge, MA: MIT Press.

Eley, Geoff. 2002. "Politics, Culture, and the Public Sphere: Toward a Postmodern Conception." *positions: east asia cultures critique* 10 (1): 219–236.

Gilroy, Paul. 1993. *The Black Atlantic: Modernity and Double Consciousness.* Cambridge, MA: Harvard University Press.

Holub, Robert C. 1991. *Jürgen Habermas: Critic in the Public Sphere.* New York: Routledge.

Landes, Joan B. 1988. *Women and the Public Sphere in the Age of the French Revolution.* Ithaca, NY: Cornell University Press.

Lyotard, Jean-François. 1984 (1979). *The Postmodern Condition: A Report on Knowledge.* Trans. Geoff Bennington and Brian Massumi. Minneapolis: University of Minnesota Press.

Krista Hegburg

HABITS

The term *habit* receives broad and varied usage across branches of the social sciences. According to essentially all definitions, habits are learned, recurrent patterns of behavior that are enacted with minimal reliance on conscious resources or effort. They typically are tied to an environment or another action that historically has co-occurred with the habit and thereby has come to serve as a stimulus, or cue, for its automatic performance. When *habit* is defined in purely behavioral terms (e.g., as an action performed almost daily and consistently in response to a specific environment), research suggests that around 45 percent of people's daily life can be deemed *habitual* (Wood, Quinn, and Kashy 2002).

Disciplines differ substantially, though, over the subset of behavior to which the term is applied. In general, psychological usage focuses on relatively simple, low-level behaviors, including those that benefit the individual (e.g., typing, coffee making, seat belt wearing, and condom use) and those that exact costs (e.g., nail biting, smoking, drug use, and overeating). Within sociology and related disciplines, the term is often applied more broadly to describe any stable pattern of action that is spontaneously reproduced via humans' preconscious engagement in the world around them. This broader application can encompass habits of social, linguistic, economic, political, religious, or moral conduct, and may involve the performance of even complex forms of action.

A BRIEF HISTORY OF HABITS

Contemporary conceptions of habit draw from multiple historical traditions, including pragmatism, behaviorism, and phenomenology. Early psychological use of the term can be traced most strongly to the pragmatist and behaviorist schools. For pragmatists, such as William James and John Dewey (1859–1952), habits were acquired reflexes that emerged due to the inherent plasticity of the nervous tissue. As a behavioral sequence is repeatedly enacted, the brain matter underlying the action was thought to become ever more predisposed to reproduce the sequence. Physiologically, this process was thought to be sustained through the development of reflex paths (or "reflex arcs") in the nervous system that linked a sensory cue with a (typically) muscular response. Once established, the habitual response could then be initiated by the sensory cue alone (i.e., without recourse to an idea, will, or volition) and would run off to completion in a ballistic fashion (i.e., each action in the sequence would prompt performance of the next). For William James, this inherent tendency towards the habitual constituted "the enormous fly-wheel of society" ([1890] 1981, p. 121), explaining myriad forms of routine action, from habits of speech, gesture, and movement to habits of character and even the inertia of social classes.

Behaviorists also viewed habits as learned, stimulus-cued responses, but largely rejected psychological mediators as irrelevant to the explanation and prediction of behavior. Especially for radical behaviorists such as John Watson (1878–1958) and B. F. Skinner (1904–1990), habits were under the direct control of environmental stimuli, and this control was better understood by examining objectively specifiable schedules of reinforcement (e.g., patterns of reward) than by examining mental processes. This stimulus-response model of habit was expanded, albeit unsuccessfully, by Skinner to encompass even verbal behavior.

In contrast to the behaviorists, phenomenologists such as Maurice Merleau-Ponty (1908–1961) and Alfred Schütz (1899–1959) focused on the role habits play in providing a preconscious, taken-for-granted framework that guides people's interactions with the world around them. Habits, in this sense, reflect a set of action possibilities that present to consciousness as natural and given (e.g., a chair appears to lend itself to sitting), but are actually the product of the individual's social and embodied action history. Some phenomenologists (especially Schütz) emphasized the role of social experience in the development of this prereflective framework of habit, and his work went on to influence both ethnomethodologists such as Harold Garfinkel (b. 1917) and social constructivists such as Peter Berger (b. 1929) and Thomas Luckmann (b. 1927). The phenomenologists' emphasis on the embodied dimension of habit (especially Merleau-Ponty's) also resonates with Pierre Bourdieu's articulation of *habitus* as a set of bodily dispositions that strategically but unconsciously reproduce past action sequences in a contextually tuned manner.

Despite these broad and differentiated applications, the habit construct lost popularity around the mid-twentieth century due to its close identification with the behaviorist research agenda and its apparent neglect of people's capacity to plan, deliberate, and reflect upon their actions. As a powerful counterpoint, many social scientists rallied around the idea that human behavior is fundamentally purposive, reflective, and under the control of goals, attitudes, intentions, and conscious rules. Rational choice theorists epitomized this view, and indeed their premise that people act to maximize outcomes in accordance with personal preferences remains a dominant theoretical paradigm in contemporary economics, political science, game theory, and some social theory. Within psychology, the value of the habit construct was also challenged by Martin Fishbein and Icek Ajzen's influential "theory of reasoned action" (1975), which stipulates that performance of behavior is determined directly by intentions (which, in

turn, are said to be influenced by one's attitudes and perceived norms). By portraying the human actor as a relatively rational, goal-driven entity whose actions are determined by their intended effects, these perspectives left little room for habit as an explanatory mechanism, and the term entered a state of relative hibernation until the 1980s.

CONTEMPORARY RESEARCH INTO HABIT

Fueled by advances in cognitive science and a zeitgeist more skeptical of wholly rationalist, reflective views of human action, contemporary social science has returned to the active study of habit. One catalyst has been evidence that people draw on relatively independent (but interacting) psychological systems in the control of action. These systems are variously termed *procedural v. declarative, implicit v. explicit, automatic v. controlled,* or *nonconscious v. conscious.* Habits tend to be associated with the first term in each dichotomy, whereas novel, deliberative actions tend to be associated with the second term. The independent nature of these behavioral control systems is compellingly evident when brain damage affects one, but leaves the other intact (Knowlton, Mangels, and Squire 1996). Patients with Parkinson's disease, for example, are able consciously to remember a complex sequence of cues, but cannot incorporate these cues into routinized habits. Conversely, patients with amnesia will not be able to remember the cues, and yet will successfully acquire habitual responses to them. Such research suggests that habits are grounded in psychological systems that are distinct from those used to guide more deliberative, reflective behavior.

A similar conclusion flows from behavior prediction studies, which identify the psychological states and environmental factors that are associated with performance of a given behavior (Wood, Quinn, and Kashy 2002). Such studies suggest that nonhabits and habits exhibit distinct predictors. Consistent with rationalist perspectives, the performance of novel or newly acquired behaviors (e.g., sticking to a new gym routine) is best predicted by the presence of favorable attitudes and intentions (e.g., a strong positive attitude or intention toward fitness). When a behavior has been repeated sufficiently to become habitual, however, attitudes and intentions become less determinative of continued performance. Instead, habitual behaviors are predicted by the mere presence of contextual cues (e.g., people, places, other actions, time of day) that co-occurred with the behavior in the past. Thus, whereas novel actions are guided largely by people's plans, desires, goals, and intentions, habits are guided largely by the context provided by preceding actions and the external social and physical environment.

Due to their highly automated, contextually cued nature habits are not readily inhibited or overcome by methods that are effective at controlling more deliberative forms of action (e.g., public information campaigns that alter people's beliefs or attitudes). Instead, habits may be more responsive to techniques that mitigate or redirect their underlying automatic associations. These techniques include stimulus control (avoiding environmental cues that trigger habits) and counter-conditioning (identifying environmental cues and substituting desired behaviors). That said, habits are notoriously difficult to overcome, and relapse is the modal outcome following many attempts at habit change (e.g., diet change, smoking cessation).

FUTURE DIRECTIONS

Contrary to both strict rationalist and strict behaviorist positions, contemporary social science acknowledges that the human actor can be driven by reflective, goal-directed mechanisms on some occasions and reflexive, habitual mechanisms on others. As discussed, these forms of behavior are subserved by relatively independent psychological systems and neural substrates. That said, research is beginning to address important interactions between the conscious, deliberative dimension of behavior and the nonconscious, habitual dimension. Notably, some sociologists argue that habits are integral to free will and agency insofar as they provide a framework of action possibilities that can be imaginatively reconfigured to meet a person's current goals and circumstances (see, for example, Emirbayer and Mische 1998). Furthermore, recent work in psychology suggests that habits can be motivated by a very general sense of reward, without necessarily being directed by specific goals (see Neal, Wood, and Quinn 2006). These approaches move away from the earlier sharp distinctions between habitual and deliberative action, and toward a view of human behavior as involving a dynamic interplay of goal-directed, intentional, reflective processes along with automated context-cued habits.

SEE ALSO *Habitus*

BIBLIOGRAPHY

Emirbayer, Mustafa, and Ann Mische. 1998. What Is Agency? *American Journal of Sociology* 103 (4): 962–1023.

Fishbein, Martin, and Icek Ajzen. 1975. *Belief, Attitude, Intention, and Behavior: An Introduction to Theory and Research.* Reading, MA: Addison-Wesley.

James, William. [1890] 1981. *The Principles of Psychology.* Cambridge, MA: Harvard University Press.

Knowlton, Barbara, Jennifer Mangels, and Larry Squire. 1996. A Neostriatal Habit Learning System in Humans. *Science* 273: 1399–1402.

Neal, David, Wendy Wood, and Jeff Quinn. 2006. Habits: A Repeat Performance. *Current Directions in Psychological Science* 15 (4): 198–202.

Wood, Wendy, Jeff Quinn, and Deborah Kashy. 2002. Habits in Everyday Life: Thought, Emotion, and Action. *Journal of Personality and Social Psychology* 83: 1281–1297.

David T. Neal

HABITUS

Habitus is a term used by the French sociologist Pierre Bourdieu (1930–2002) to describe a social property of individuals that orients human behavior without strictly determining it. While habitus encompasses a sense of practical expertise, it is not a conscious expertise; rather, it may be seen as common sense. It is constituted of dispositions that are inculcated, structured, durable, generative, and transposable (see Thompson 1991, p. 12). Habitus is a state of the body and of being, a repository of ingrained dispositions that thus seem natural. Bourdieu calls this the *bodily hexis*, where "the body is the site of incorporated history" (Thompson 1991, p. 13; see also Bourdieu 1984, pp. 437, 466–468). Thus, habitus is purposeful without being questionable; it is transmitted but not actively taught.

Bourdieu presents habitus as a conceptual framework in which there are varying degrees of explicitness of, and competition among, norms. Under this framework, there are three ways that people experience the norms of their social existence. They do so through (1) a set of materially predisposed practices that express a belief about the way the world works and that reproduce that worldview. These predisposed practices tend to produce *doxa*, situations in which "the natural and social world appears as self-evident" (Bourdieu 1994, p. 160; 1976, p. 118); this is habitus, the unquestioned order of things. People also experience the norms of their social existence through (2) the contrasting situation of orthodoxy, in which "social classifications become the object and instrument of … struggle" and in which the arbitrariness of the current system becomes evident, and through (3) heterodoxy—a situation of more or less equally "competing possibilities" (1994, pp. 164–165). Bourdieu emphasizes the "complicitous silence" of community members in the continuous reproduction of the "collective rhythms," or habitus, of the community (1994, p. 182).

A tension then exists between the formalized codes that dictate practices and "the generating and unifying principle of practices … constituted by a whole system of predispositions inculcated by the material circumstances of life and by family upbringing" (Bourdieu 1976, p.

118). The habitus is "the end product of structures which practices tend to reproduce in such a way that the individuals involved are bound to reproduce them, either by consciously reinventing or by subconsciously imitating already proven strategies as the accepted, most respectable, or even simplest course to follow. [They] … come to be seen as inherent in the nature of things" (1976, p. 118).

Thus, with this concept Bourdieu seeks to demystify the very concept of "natural" and to emphasize the creation of "a second nature" (1991, p. 123). For example, every day we don clothing. While we may think about what to wear, we do not think about whether we will wear something. The conventions of style in dress themselves are nearly as inculcated as dressing. Only within the field of fashion are these styles and meanings routinely discussed explicitly. There are those who challenge the professional fashionista's (or the everyday women's magazine reader's) habitus of style, while punks are known for their ironic appropriation of military uniforms and their practice of making ugliness into beauty (see LeBlanc 1999). Andrew Martinez (Berkeley's "Naked Guy" from the early 1990s) engaged in a practice of public nudity that sought to challenge the basic habitus of getting dressed at all (see Seligman 1992; Jacobssex 1992; and Jones 2006).

CRITICAL INTERPRETATIONS

Habitus is a process, at once deeply embedded and simultaneously available for analysis; it is often discursively ephemeral, and yet easily accessed and employed. At points in his work, Bourdieu suggests that habitus is quite active, an activity of power of at least some savvy agents:

> The work of inculcation through which the lasting imposition of the arbitrary limit is achieved can seek to naturalize the decisive breaks that constitute an arbitrary cultural limit—those expressed in fundamental oppositions like masculine/feminine, etc.—in the form of a *sense of limits*, which inclines some people to maintain their rank and distance and others to know their place and be happy with what they are, to be what they have to be, thus depriving them of the very sense of deprivation (Bourdieu 1991, p. 123).

For Bourdieu, if one does not understand that what one thinks is natural is actually accreted practice, and practice inculcated from a particular social position, one can never engage in true social change (see Brubaker 1993, p. 217). At the same time, he emphasizes that habitus is subconscious—it is embedded bodily. The question of when habitus does become concerted effort, analysis, or argument (that is, when does the situation of either orthodoxy or heterodoxy arise?) is often inadequately dealt with (see Calhoun 1993, pp. 80–82).

Though habitus is conceived of as deeply embodied and self-evidently nondiscursive, there is a sense that habitus competes across fields—that people can, indeed often must, acquire a particular habitus that they then must apply in particular situations (Calhoun 1993, pp. 77–80). Because Bourdieu uses habitus to deal with the cultural arbitrariness of language and discourse itself (see especially Bourdieu 1991), it is something of a paradox that he asserts its nondiscursive character.

The field of law is a particularly problematic arena when one is considering the place of habitus in social processes. "Predispositions" and the process of naturalization are important in the legal system, but habitus does not easily explain the existence of laws, especially in frontier situations of transition, where there are formative struggles over what the laws should be. This is especially significant in the legal process, where it is explicit that language and discourse are key. Indeed, while social actors may be "subconsciously imitating" and "consciously reinventing" social structures, a struggle is involved. Thus, actors are not necessarily "bound to reproduce" the prevailing images and structures of their community. Formal law has a role to play beyond that of everyday activities and reasoning, although these play a part in forming law. In other words, as Mindie Lazarus-Black argues, "common sense understanding, or … *habitus*, 'is generated not only out of small scale networks of practice but also out of the legitimation project of the state.' One function of [this] project is to define the people under its control (creating the external boundaries of the system) and to differentiate between them (creating internal boundaries within the system)" (1994, p. 6).

In terms of the symbolic power of language, there is a sense that actors in public fields such as law are playing to doxa, with a highly crafted and explicit discourse—the sound bites and metaphors of color blindness and racially neutral language, for example, which expose that race is a habit within a system that also acknowledges a doxa of democracy (see Gatson 1999; Bonilla-Silva 2003, pp. 49, 104, 125).

Thus, instead of suggesting that analyzing formal law is useless by stating that it is "unnecessary to make explicit or … invoke or impose any rules," one should perhaps rather attempt to examine situations in which the struggle to invoke certain rules over others is very explicit (Bourdieu 1976, p. 141). Calhoun argues that Bourdieu's "sociology does not offer much purchase on the transformation of social systems.… His accounts of the general system of social and cultural organization always render it as essentially conservative … imply[ing] dynamism … at the level of the strategic actor.… [Habitus] is at its best as a theory of reproduction, and at its weakest as a theory of transformation" (Calhoun 1993, pp. 70, 72). But that weakness is perhaps telling, signaling the inertia of systems, and the need for everyday sociology in the citizenry. For each of us, the habitus is cycle and process. There is a simultaneity of habitus—doxa, orthodoxy, and heterodoxy may be clearly delineated when they are used to describe a macrolevel history of a particular field. As to the everyday, and at points of conflict, the cycle of habitus may be far more difficult to tease apart.

SEE ALSO *Bourdieu, Pierre; Cultural Capital; Habits; Social Capital*

BIBLIOGRAPHY

Bonilla-Silva, Eduardo. 2003. *Racism without Racists: Color-Blind Racism and the Persistence of Racial Inequality in the United States.* Lanham, MD: Rowman and Littlefield.

Bourdieu, Pierre. 1976. Marriage Strategies as Strategies of Social Reproduction. In *Family and Society: Selections from the Annales, Économies, Sociétés, Civilisations,* eds. Robert Forster and Orest Ranum; trans. Elborg Forster and Patricia M. Ranum, 117–144. Baltimore, MD: Johns Hopkins University Press, 1976.

Bourdieu, Pierre. 1984. *Distinction: A Social Critique of the Judgement of Taste.* Trans. Richard Nice. Cambridge, MA: Harvard University Press.

Bourdieu, Pierre. 1991. *Language and Symbolic Power.* Trans. Gino Raymond and Matthew Adamson. Cambridge, U.K.: Harvard University Press.

Bourdieu, Pierre. 1994. Structures, Habitus, Power: Basis for a Theory for Symbolic Power. In *Culture/Power/History: A Reader in Contemporary Social Theory,* eds. Nicholas B. Dirks, Geoff Eley, and Sherry B. Ortner, 155–199. Princeton, NJ: Princeton University Press.

Bourdieu, Pierre. 2000. *Pascalian Meditations.* Trans. Richard Nice. Stanford, CA: Stanford University Press.

Brubaker, Rogers. 1993. Social Theory as Habitus. In *Bourdieu: Critical Perspectives,* eds. Craig Calhoun, Edward LiPuma, and Moishe Postone, 212–234. Chicago: University of Chicago Press.

Calhoun, Craig. 1993. Habitus, Field, and Capital: The Question of Historical Specificity. In *Bourdieu: Critical Perspectives,* eds. Craig Calhoun, Edward LiPuma, and Moishe Postone, 61–88. Chicago: University of Chicago Press.

Cohn, Bernard S., and Nicholas B. Kirks. 1988. Beyond the Fringe: The Nation State, Colonialism, and the Technologies of Power. *Journal of Historical Sociology* 1 (2): 224–229.

Gatson, Sarah N. 1999. Farmers, Fanatics, Politicians, and Slaves: Racial Citizenship in U.S. Communities, 1840–1900. PhD diss., Northwestern University, Evanston, IL.

Jacobssex, Joanne. 1992. Our Social Conventions Need to Be Obeyed, Even by the Naked Guy. *Atlanta Journal and Constitution,* p. A22.

Jones, Carolyn. 2006. Champion of Nudity Found Dead in Jail Cell. *San Francisco Chronicle,* May 21: B1.

Lazarus-Black, Mindie. 1994. *Legitimate Acts and Illegal Encounters: Law and Society in Antigua and Barbuda.* Washington, DC: Smithsonian Institution Press.

LeBlanc, Lauraine. 1999. *Pretty in Punk: Girls' Gender Resistance in a Boys' Subculture.* New Brunswick, NJ: Rutgers University Press.

Seligman, Katherine. 1992. The Bareable Lightness of Being: What to Do about the Naked Guy? *The Ottawa Citizen,* A5.

Thompson, John B. 1991. Introduction. In *Language and Symbolic Power,* trans. Gino Raymond and Matthew Adamson, 1–31. Cambridge, MA: Harvard University Press.

Sarah N. Gatson

HACKING, IAN
SEE *Probability Theory.*

HAGUE CONVENTION
SEE *War Crimes.*

HAITIAN DIASPORA
SEE *Trouillot, Michel-Rolph; Diaspora.*

HAITIAN REVOLUTION

The Haitian Revolution (1790–1804) brought political independence to Haiti, the second nation in the Americas to free itself from colonial rule. It also brought freedom to some 450,000 Afro-Caribbean slaves and served as a potent symbol of liberty to millions of their fellows who remained enslaved throughout the Americas. Other independence movements in the Americas at the time, like the American Revolution (1775–1783) or the independence struggles in Spanish America, pitted colonial elites against metropolitan governments and offered little possibility for immediate change in society. The Haitian Revolution, on the other hand, was a true social revolution, which led to remarkable changes in the lives of ordinary people on the island and the colony's role in the world economy.

THE COLONIAL BACKGROUND

Haiti, known as Saint-Domingue before the revolution, was the richest colony in the Americas in 1789. Almost half a million slaves toiled on its sugar, coffee, indigo, and cotton plantations. More than thirty thousand new

African slaves arrived each year, both to replace the many who died of overwork or disease and also to fuel the rapid economic expansion that the colony experienced in the 1780s. Between a third and a half of all slaves on the island were born in Africa. While the slaves had been evangelized and educated by Jesuit missionaries in the early days of the colony, the Jesuits were expelled from Haiti in 1767. After that, the slaves were left to their own resources, and had developed their own culture, complete with a language, *kweyol*, and a religion, *vaudou*, both strongly influenced by African models. The slaves were owned and supervised by a population of around fifty thousand free persons, about half of whom were Afro-Caribbean free coloreds. The largest plantations on the island were owned by whites, many of whom were absentee landlords living in France. There was a growing class of poorer whites who hoped to become planters. Alongside the poor whites, there were free coloreds, some of whom owned plantations while others competed with the lower-class whites for plantation management or craft jobs.

Saint-Domingue's free people, both whites and blacks, despised French mercantilist economic regulations and dealt with smugglers whenever they could. They undermined the colonial government in other ways as well, rebelling against increased military obligations in the 1760s, for example. There is considerable evidence that the wealthier inhabitants of Saint-Domingue were developing an "American" identity in much the same way that wealthy North Americans had done in the period before the American Revolution and that wealthy Spanish Americans did in the 1800s before the independence struggles there.

But Saint-Domingue society was sharply divided on racial and class lines. Racial distinctions between whites and free coloreds were always significant and became even more marked after the 1760s. Some scholars have suggested that this was a calculated "divide and conquer" strategy by the colonial government to drive a wedge between wealthy white and free colored inhabitants. In any case, the racially divided masters of the colony were vastly outnumbered by their slaves. The need to be eternally vigilant against slave uprisings, and the need for French troops to provide the final element of security, made it less likely that wealthy colonists would think of independence in Saint-Domingue—or that poor people could make common cause across the divide of race and status.

THE OUTBREAK OF THE REVOLUTION

But revolution did come. At first, it came as an echo of the revolution going on in France. Both white and free col-

ored planters appealed to the French revolutionary assemblies in 1789. But the French legislatures avoided the questions of slavery and civil rights for free people of color for two years. During this time, political struggles broke out in the colony between white planters and less-wealthy whites. Each side appealed to free colored allies, and the slaves watched everything that was going on.

Two wealthy free colored men, Vincent Ogé (c. 1750–1791) and Jean-Baptiste Chavannes (c. 1748–1791), rose up in rebellion in 1790, calling for civil rights for free coloreds. Their movement was quickly crushed and they were executed, but the first shots had been fired. Free coloreds continued to fight their own struggle throughout the larger revolution that followed, and indeed went on to play an important role in post-independence Haitian society.

REVOLUTION FROM BELOW

The slaves did not need French political philosophers or wealthy free colored planters to tell them that they ought to be free. There had been slave uprisings and other acts of resistance on the island since the first Africans arrived, brought by the Spanish, in the sixteenth century. But rebellions were always crushed by the superior military force of the colonial government. Even the maroons, or runaway slaves, who had hidden in the mountains and lived as free peasants in the early days of the colony were pretty much eradicated by the 1780s, as plantations spread throughout the island. But when the masters fought among themselves, the slaves saw their opportunity.

Slaves with leadership positions, such as coachmen, foremen of work gangs, technical specialists, and hunters, together with *vaudou* practitioners and some free people of color organized a great uprising among the slaves of the northern plain. This area was the most heavily populated and richest area of the colony. The slaves rose up the fourth week of August 1791, burning hundreds of plantations and killing or driving out the masters. The early leaders of the rebellion were slaves, such as Boukman, the organizer of a famous *vaudou* ceremony at Bois Cayman that may have been the signal for the uprising. But the ultimate leader of the slave army was Toussaint Louverture (c. 1743–1803), a pre-revolutionary free black planter and slave owner.

Toussaint's soldiers fought from 1791 until 1799 against a dizzying variety of enemies: French revolutionary governors, French royalists, English and Spanish invaders, and free colored leaders. In the midst of this struggle, in 1793, the French revolutionary commissioner Léger-Félicité Sonthonax (1763–1813) proclaimed the end of slavery in the colony and Toussaint's forces became officially part of the French army.

But by 1801 the government back in France was beginning to reconsider the abolition of slavery. Napoléon Bonaparte (1769–1821) was first consul. He needed the wealth of Saint-Domingue and he distrusted freedom. Toussaint had succeeded in taking military control of the island but not at restoring sugar production. The slaves were not interested in working on plantations, even for wages. They wanted to own their own farms. As the man-power behind Toussaint's military triumphs, they were in a good position to insist. And anyway, Toussaint had written a new constitution for the island in which he proclaimed his loyalty to France but declared himself governor-general for life. For all these reasons, Napoléon decided to reconquer the island and restore slavery. He sent an army under his brother-in-law Charles Leclerc (1772–1802) in 1801.

THE FINAL STRUGGLE

Toussaint and some of his soldiers put up a stiff resistance, but ultimately the French troops, fresh from victories across Europe, triumphed. Toussaint himself was arrested and imprisoned in France, where he died in 1803. But disease began to take a toll on the French forces. At the same time, those Haitian soldiers who had surrendered when the French came began to realize that slavery was going to be restored. Toussaint's officers rose up in a new rebellion and fought a terrible struggle. More than a year of heavy fighting, marked by many massacres on both sides, resulted in the final defeat of the French forces at Vertières on November 18, 1803. The new commander of the Haitian forces, Jean-Jacques Dessalines (c. 1758–1806), tore the white out of the French flag, expelled or massacred the remaining white inhabitants, and declared Haitian independence on January 1, 1804. The cost of freedom will never be known, but the population of Haiti fell by at least 125,000 between 1789 and 1804.

AFTERMATH AND WIDER IMPLICATIONS

Haiti became independent in 1804, but no nation recognized it until the 1820s. Simón Bolívar (1783–1830) took refuge in Haiti during his struggle against Spain, but even the newly independent nations of the Americas did not want to have anything to do with a nation of freed slaves. Haiti was too potent an example to the blacks in the rest of the hemisphere. Haiti's leaders were demonized in French and American propaganda of the time and since, and Haiti was and to some extent still is held up as an example of how black people cannot rule themselves and need supervision. But black people were not so easily fooled. Haiti became a rallying cry for black liberation movements from Denmark Vesey's (c. 1767–1822)

planned uprising in South Carolina in 1822 to Ahmed Sékou Touré's (1922–1984) call for the independence of the Republic of Guinea in Africa in 1957.

Haiti ceased to be a major producer of sugar or coffee after 1804, as most Haitians left the plantations and became peasants. Isolated from the world, Haiti preserved many elements of African culture, including a vibrant spiritual and artistic tradition. The pre-revolutionary free coloreds, many of them of mixed race, and the leaders of the military struggle became an urban commercial ruling class who lorded it over the mostly black peasants and affected a very European culture.

SEE ALSO *Cuban Revolution; Grenadian Revolution*

BIBLIOGRAPHY

Bell, Madison Smartt. 1995. *All Souls' Rising.* New York: Pantheon.

Bell, Madison Smartt. 2000. *Master of the Crossroads.* New York: Pantheon.

Bell, Madison Smartt. 2004. *The Stone that the Builder Refused.* New York: Pantheon.

Dubois, Laurent. 2004. *Avengers of the New World: The Story of the Haitian Revolution.* Cambridge, MA: Belknap.

Fick, Carolyn. 1990. *The Making of Haiti: The Saint-Domingue Revolution from Below.* Knoxville: University of Tennessee Press.

Garrigus, John. 2006. *Before Haiti: Race and Citizenship in French Saint-Domingue.* New York: Palgrave MacMillan.

Geggus, David P. 2002 *Haitian Revolutionary Studies.* Bloomington: Indiana University Press.

James, C. L. R. 1963. *The Black Jacobins: Toussaint L'Ouverture and the San Domingo Revolution.* 2nd rev. ed. New York: Vintage.

Stewart R. King

HALL, STUART
1932–

Stuart Hall, a black Jamaican born in 1932, was schooled—in the English manner—for a future as a member of the colonial elite. As he recounted on many occasions subsequently, he quickly discovered that he was living in two worlds simultaneously: as a black native of the Caribbean and on the other in the imaginative world of the colonizers, well attuned to the finest nuances in the history and the literature of the English. This discrepant sense of his place in the colonial world was at first puzzling and painful, but he learned over many years to make it his own. What once had been a burden came, through an intellectual journey of impressive imaginative power, to become a resource and indeed a lifeline. This migrant's-eye view of the center from the margins informed every aspect of Hall's intellectual life. It underwrote, if only implicitly, the emergence in Great Britain of cultural studies, with which Hall himself became so closely identified. Later in life, this view explicitly defined his intellectual project.

Hall's early experience as a colonial subject produced a political radicalism that remained with him through his life. In 1951 he arrived in Britain as a student at Oxford University. He experienced England not only in its idealized manifestations, but also in its raw everydayness, in which the dispositions of racial exclusion loomed large. Later in the 1950s he was drawn to the emergent New Left, alongside the slightly older generation of Raymond Williams (1921–1988) and Edward Palmer Thompson (1924–1993). Crucial to the political critique that came from this moment was the realization that culture was not only the preserve of the educated elite, but that it was also properly the inheritance of all. To later generations this may sound a truism, but at the time it served to shift the study of culture away from a restricted meaning, in which culture represented only the most elevated, to a broader, more anthropological reading of the cultural dimensions of the everyday, in which the relations of a society are embedded in their symbolic conditions of existence. It served, too, to highlight the connections between political power and culture. From this point on, the characteristic tenor of Hall's interventions was to highlight his belief that the seemingly arcane practice of politics was in fact rooted in and fought out on the terrain of culture itself. More specifically, any politics of value needed to situate itself within the field of popular life, for it was there that political energies were generated and political causes won and lost.

Many of these ideas came together in the *Universities and Left Review*, with which Hall was associated, and then in its more famous successor, the *New Left Review*, which Hall edited for the first year of its existence, from 1960.

In 1964 Hall moved to the Centre for Contemporary Cultural Studies based at the University of Birmingham under the leadership of Richard Hoggart (b. 1918). Here he was given the space to develop conceptually the ideas that he—and those around him—had pursued in more practical form in early works such as his study *The Popular Arts* (1964), written with Paddy Whannel. Hall became the presiding figure in the emergence of cultural studies in the United Kingdom. His migrant perspective was an essential element in his reading of the culture of the British, and from this position the erstwhile colonial subject could offer his own anthropology of the erstwhile colonizer. The passions and excitement of early cultural studies ran deep. A vast range of previously excluded or derided cultural forms burst into view: popular music, advertising, women's magazines, youth fashion, movies, and television. All were taken as serious subjects for critical analysis and, collectively, as the site where (through many displacements) politics in its expanded sense occurred.

A decisive theoretical influence for Hall was the work of the Italian Marxist Antonio Gramsci (1891–1937). Gramsci's insistence on the place of culture as a constituent element in political struggle offered an analytical framework that served Hall well. The field of cultural studies, in its early incarnations, sought to unravel the many determinations by which political power was exercised. From this period in the 1960s, Hall collaborated with others to produce a mesmerizing stream of work, interpreting the emergent cultures of the time. His readings of youth subcultures and of the media comprehensively recast the field of the social sciences.

As this work evolved it met much resistance, not least because it was perceived as overly theoretical and as prone to an abstract formalism. Hall himself was certainly influenced by the work of the great structuralist theorists of culture—Ferdinand de Saussure (1857–1913), Claude Lévi-Strauss (b. 1908), Roland Barthes (1915–1980), and later Louis Althusser (1918–1990)—and was persuaded of the need to pitch his arguments, when the occasion demanded, at a high level of abstraction. But he also possessed a sharp sense of the movements of historical time. His analytical interpretations began from the chaos of the concrete realities of the everyday, and—although they often involved some theoretical detour—always returned to the concrete. Here especially the influence of Gramsci was profound. Often Hall described his own intellectual practice as one devoted to explaining the shifts and turns in the movement of political conjunctures.

This bid to bend formal structural analysis into a practice more alive to the movements of historical forces and cultural relations generated two classic essays in the early 1970s: his famous rumination on the workings of the mass media, "Encoding and Decoding in the Media Discourse" (1973), which set the conceptual frame of the emerging discipline of media studies for the next 30 years, and his more philosophically inspired (if modestly titled) "Marx's Notes on Method" (1974) in which, in explicating Marx, he outlined the basis of his own commitment to "theorising" the concrete.

It was during this period, too, that Hall and his colleagues embarked upon a comprehensive account of the drift in Britain toward a more authoritarian politics. Crucial to this analysis was his insistence that race—the management of the black population who, like him, had come to settle in Great Britain after the end of World War II (1939–1945), and of their sons and daughters—was a central, defining feature of an increasingly conservative political reflex, in which recourse to authority dominated. His jointly authored volume, *Policing the Crisis* (1978), represented a landmark text, which in a bravura intellectual act brought into a single analytical frame the workings of high politics in Westminster with the emergent street politics of the new racialized ghettos.

Beginning in the late 1970s, Hall reworked and refined these early insights into a succession of inspirational articles that plotted the makings of Thatcherism, a term Hall employed even before Margaret Thatcher became prime minister in May 1979. Hall argued that Thatcherism represented a new form of authoritarian populism that marked a decisive shift to the right in British politics.

The drama of these writings was driven by a clear sense of political urgency created by the success of the Thatcherite project. At the same time, Hall also delivered broadsides to the political left, insisting that its characteristic inability to modernize or to think in terms of the future rather than the past was contributing to the confidence of the right. Many on the left took exception. At this point, too, Hall—having earlier been condemned for his formalism—found himself under attack for being too historical and not formal enough. His critics believed that the concepts that animated his discussion—authoritarian populism, crisis of hegemony, war of position, and so on (all derived from Gramsci)—were too inconsistent to be of use to social scientists. Hall's response was simply to insist on the necessity of conjunctural analysis. Less contentious, however, was Hall's early prediction that, whatever the fate of Thatcher herself, Thatcherism as a broader political project would define what was politically possible for many years to come, in which respect he provided a prescient perspective on the subsequent years of the New Labour government.

Race was still a major part of Hall's intellectual concern, and beginning in the 1970s it became ever more prominent in his theorizations. From his study of race—of blackness—he became ever more preoccupied with questions of identity and subjectivity, especially of those on the racialized margins of the former colonizing nations.

An important interlocutor for Hall at this time was his student, Paul Gilroy, the author of *There Ain't No Black in the Union Jack* (1987), which delivered a devastating critique of the racial encodings of the English nation. Gilroy learned much from Hall, though there remain significant political and intellectual differences between them, particularly in relation to their respective interpretations of the idea of black Britishness.

In 1997 Hall retired from his appointment as professor of sociology at the United Kingdom's Open University, a position he had held since 1979. As his formal academic career came to an end, Hall moved into a new intellectual field: that of the visual arts. He believed it was here, among young black artists in the United Kingdom, that questions of race and identity were being addressed most fruitfully. As he came to discover, the artists he was interested in were, as he would say, "doing the theory for you."

SEE ALSO *Critical Theory; Cultural Studies; Culture; Foucault, Michel; Gramsci, Antonio; Habermas, Jürgen; Immigration; Left and Right; Marginalization; Popular Culture; Race; Racialization; Radicalism; Thompson, Edward P.; Visual Arts*

BIBLIOGRAPHY

Gilroy, Paul. 1987. *There Ain't No Black in the Union Jack: The Cultural Politics of Race and Nation.* London: Hutchinson.

Hall, Stuart. 1973. Encoding and Decoding in the Media Discourse. Stencilled paper No. 7, Birmingham, U.K.: Centre for Contemporary Cultural Studies, University of Birmingham.

Hall, Stuart. [1974] 2003. Marx's Notes on Method: A "Reading" of the "1857 Introduction." *Cultural Studies* 17 (2): 113–149.

Hall, Stuart. 1988. *The Hard Road to Renewal: Thatcherism and the Crisis of the Left.* London: Verso.

Hall, Stuart. 1992. New Ethnicities. In *"Race," Culture, and Difference*, eds. James Donald and Ali Rattansi, 252–259. London: Sage Publications.

Hall, Stuart, and Paddy Whannel. 1964. *The Popular Arts.* London: Hutchinson.

Hall, Stuart, and Tony Jefferson, eds. 1976. *Resistance through Rituals: Youth Subcultures in Post-war Britain.* London: Hutchinson.

Hall, Stuart, Chas Critcher, Tony Jefferson, et al. 1978. *Policing the Crisis: Mugging, the State, and Law and Order.* London: Macmillan.

David Morley
Bill Schwarz

HALLUCINOGENS

The term *hallucinogen* refers to a variety of substances capable of inducing profound altered states of consciousness. Also known as *phantastica, psychedelics, entheogens,* and *psychointegrators,* these substances have a long history of use in societies throughout the world.

The "major" hallucinogens are LSD, mescaline, psilocybin (found in "magic mushrooms"), and the tryptamine derivatives (found in ayahuasca). These substances alter sensory perception and produce changes in a person's body image and awareness of space and time, but they do not cloud consciousness and have little impact upon memory. Persons typically remain fully aware of the effects as they are occurring and retain vivid memories afterwards. Although the chemical structures of these substances vary and their mechanisms of action are not yet fully understood, dopamine, serotonin, and norepinephrine receptor sites have been implicated in their activity. While *Cannabis* ("marijuana") is sometimes included in this list, its effects and mechanism of action are distinct and involve other receptor sites.

The "minor" hallucinogens include anticholinergic substances (atropine and scopolamine) that block acetylcholine receptors. These produce relatively mild perceptual and cognitive changes, but they do cloud consciousness and impact memory, so that individuals may be unable to recall their experiences. The "psychedelic anesthetics" (ketamine and phencyclidine or PCP) affect NMDA receptors and induce profound dissociative effects.

The use of hallucinogens in traditional cultural settings has been extensively documented. These substances induce a hypersuggestible state that makes those who ingest them receptive to the messages received during initiation into adulthood and in religious rituals. Because the experiences are explained before they are induced, the effects are understood within a culturally defined and socially sanctioned framework that reassures the initiates and provides emphatic evidence of the "correctness" of the foundational premises of their society's worldview.

Although traditional societies have been using hallucinogens for culturally constructive purposes for millennia, scientific interest in hallucinogens is comparatively recent. In the late 1800s, anthropological studies led to the recognition of the visionary effects of the peyote cactus. Subsequent research led to the isolation (1896) and synthesis (1919) of mescaline, the primary hallucinogenic component of peyote. Mescaline was thus the first hallucinogen to become available as a pharmaceutical preparation. The fantastic descriptions of the effects produced by mescaline attracted the attention of both scientists and artists, a pattern that would be repeated with other hallucinogens.

In 1938, Albert Hofmann, a Swiss chemist working at Sandoz Laboratories, first synthesized LSD (lysergic acid diethylamide) during his research into potential analgesics. During subsequent research in 1943, Hofmann accidentally ingested a miniscule amount of the drug (through the skin) and soon noticed marked perceptual changes and other effects. He then undertook a self-experiment using what he thought was an extremely small dose (250 micrograms) and experienced even more profound effects. Hofmann was later asked to identify the active

constituents (psilocybin and psilocin) in samples of "magic mushrooms" (*Psilocybe* spp.) collected in Mexico. Uncertain of their usefulness and desiring to determine if there was a market for these substances, Sandoz made LSD (under the name Delysid) and psilocybin (known as Indocybin) available for psychiatric, therapeutic, and experimental research.

During the 1950s and early 1960s, considerable scientific research was conducted into hallucinogens. In clinical settings, these substances showed promise in treating chronic alcoholism, psychological trauma, pain, and obsessive-compulsive disorders. The U.S. and British governments also investigated the potential of hallucinogens as agents of chemical and psychological warfare. In the 1950s and 1960s, the CIA, in a project known as MKULTRA, gave scopolamine, mescaline, LSD, psilocybin, and other agents to numerous individuals, often without their knowledge. The unpredictability of the effects and the suicide of several subjects led to the termination of this work.

As knowledge about the visionary effects and therapeutic potential of the hallucinogens became more widespread, numerous artists, writers, and scientists had "psychedelic" experiences that profoundly affected their work. One of the first was Aldous Huxley (1894-1963), whose experiences with mescaline led him to write *The Doors of Perception* (1954) and *Heaven and Hell* (1956), two essays that introduced hallucinogens to the public. Another influential figure was the Harvard psychologist Timothy Leary (1920–1996), who first encountered psilocybin mushrooms during a trip to Mexico in 1960. Leary subsequently obtained a large quantity of psilocybin from Sandoz and began to offer it to other Harvard faculty and graduate students. With his team, he also administered psilocybin to violent criminals, with promising results.

Leary and others also investigated the effects of hallucinogens upon artists, musicians, and other creative individuals. As the circle of people who had had an experience with a hallucinogen expanded, increasing numbers of individuals became interested in these substances. Eventually, "acid tests," "be-ins," and other events provided the opportunity for thousands of people to simultaneously experience the effects of a hallucinogen. For many, the inner worlds revealed by these substances offered a stark contrast to consumerism, the push to conform, and the war in Vietnam. "Psychedelic" music, art, and poetry gave expression to these experiences, challenged conventional morality and authority, and led to the emergence of a "counterculture" that maintained that peace, love, and "flower power" could change human consciousness and alter the political landscape. In the late 1960s, governments reacted by enacting laws prohibiting the use, possession, manufacture, and distribution of most hallucinogens. While this did curtail some illicit use, it also put a stop to legitimate research.

Scientific research with human subjects resumed in the 1990s. In pilot studies, hallucinogens have been administered to terminal patients to help them confront their impending death, and they have been used to treat victims of post-traumatic stress disorder and sufferers of cluster headaches. The ancient tradition of hallucinogen use within a religious context is continued in the Native American Church, which uses peyote, and by several Brazilian churches (including the Santo Daime and União de Vegetal [UDV]) that use ayahuasca. These religious movements have achieved great success in helping their members overcome addictions to alcohol and other drugs, and they are legally allowed to use specific hallucinogens as "sacraments."

In 1999, U.S. Customs agents seized a shipment of ayahuasca that had been shipped to the United States for use by an American chapter of União de Vegetal. The government claimed that the mixture contained substances banned by U.S. and international law. However, a 2006 U.S. Supreme Court decision unanimously affirmed that the government had not demonstrated a compelling interest in prohibiting the UDV from using ayahuacsa in their religious services, thereby allowing them to use it legally in the United States.

Increased recognition that hallucinogens can be used for constructive purposes has led to renewed calls to review and, where appropriate, reduce the legal restrictions on these substances. In the United States, mescaline, LSD, psilocybin, psilocin, and even *Cannabis* are currently categorized as Schedule I substances, which are defined as having a high potential for abuse, a lack of acceptable safety when used under medical supervision, and a lack of currently accepted medical use. Similar restrictions exist internationally. However, these legal classifications are not consistent and are rarely adjusted as new scientific findings and patterns of illegal use become known. In many jurisdictions, drug classification often reflects political and social trends rather than scientific data. For example, in the United States the major hallucinogens are listed in Schedule I along with heroin, a substance that is available to physicians and patients in Europe. In contrast, methamphetamine, one of the most addictive and personally destructive drugs known, is classified as a Schedule II drug with a currently acceptable medical use. Moreover, many experts consider alcohol and tobacco to have a much greater potential for both personal and social harm than any of the hallucinogens (including *Cannabis*).

The 2003 National Survey on Drug Use & Health estimated that 34,363,000 Americans (14.5% of the population) had used a hallucinogen (excluding *Cannabis*) at least once in their lives. The same survey estimated that 96,611,000 persons (40.6%) had used *Cannabis* at least once. Worldwide, the United Nations Office on Drugs and Crime (UNODC) reported in 2006 that approximately 162,400,000 people used *Cannabis* in 2005 (3.9% of the total world population between the ages of 15 and 64). The UNODC did not report on the prevalence of LSD, peyote, or mescaline use.

In contrast to heroin and methamphetamine and the legal drugs ethyl alcohol and nicotine, hallucinogens (including *Cannabis*) are not physically addictive, and such substances as LSD, mescaline, and psilocybin even exhibit cross-tolerance with one another, meaning that daily dosages quickly lose their effectiveness. Both the traditional patterns of use and the increasing scientific evidence that many of the major hallucinogens can be useful in treating various disorders and in personal growth, and that *Cannabis* is an effective remedy for glaucoma, pain, the side effects of chemotherapy, and for many other purposes, demonstrates that a rethinking of drug laws in general, and the potential roles of hallucinogens in particular, is long overdue.

SEE ALSO *Drugs of Abuse; Leary, Timothy; Native Americans; Psychotropic Drugs*

BIBLIOGRAPHY

Julien, Robert M. 2005. *A Primer of Drug Action*. 10th ed. New York: Worth Publishers.

Nutt, David, Leslie A. King, William Saulsbury, and Colin Blakemore. 2007. Development of a Rational Scale to Assess the Harm of Drugs of Potential Misuse. *The Lancet*. Vol. 369, March 24, 2006, pp. 1047–1053.

Rätsch, Christian. 2005. *The Encyclopedia of Psychoactive Plants*. Trans. John R. Baker. Rochester, VT: Park Street Press.

Stevens, Jay. 1987. *Storming Heaven: LSD and the American Dream*. New York: Atlantic Monthly Press.

United Nations Office on Drugs and Crime. 2006. *World Drug Report*. New York: United Nations. http://www.unodc.org/unodc/world_drug_report.html.

U.S. Substance Abuse and Mental Health Services Administration (SAMHSA). 2003. *National Survey on Drug Use & Health*. Washington, DC: SAMHSA. http://www.drugabusestatistics.samhsa.gov/.

Winkleman, Michael J., and Thomas B. Roberts, eds. 2007. *Psychedelic Medicine: New Evidence for Hallucinogenic Substances as Treatments*. Westport, CT: Praeger.

John R. Baker

HAMAS
SEE *Intifada, The.*

HAMILTON, ALEXANDER
1755–1804

When Alexander Hamilton was born on the small Caribbean island of Nevis, probably in 1755, he seemed destined for obscurity. His parents never married. When Hamilton was ten his father abandoned Hamilton and his mother and brother, and his mother died two years later. Strong natural abilities and the patronage of well-to-do citizens made possible Hamilton's escape. He was sent to North America to receive a college education, which was cut short by the American Revolution. Hamilton took up arms on the American side. His abilities came to the attention of George Washington (1732–1799), who brought him into his personal staff. This began one of the most consequential partnerships in American history. Hamilton was always the junior partner, but the vigor of his character and intellect were critical for Washington's success.

After the Revolution, Hamilton took up law as a profession and became active in local, state, and national politics. He served as member to the Continental Congress, agitated for a constitutional convention, and participated in the 1787 Constitutional Convention in Philadelphia. It was after the convention that Hamilton's primary contributions to the new Republic began. Hamilton organized the writing of *The Federalist Papers* and contributed a little more than half the essays. He contributed mightily in the very difficult struggle to get the Constitution ratified in the critical state of New York. Washington, as the United States' first president, appointed Hamilton his first secretary of the treasury, a role in which Hamilton distinguished himself as an original economic thinker and a model civil servant. He established the Treasury Department, dealt decisively with the nation's financial crisis, put in place a financial system that remains in the early twenty-first century, and sketched out a plan and justification for the encouragement of manufactures. As treasury secretary, Hamilton also made a substantial contribution to the debates regarding the scope of the executive power and the proper way to interpret the Constitution.

Much was of enduring significance in Hamilton's political and economic thought. Hamilton believed the task facing Americans was to show that, despite its historical record of failure, republican government was compatible with liberty and the public interest. In a speech at the Constitutional Convention on June 18, 1787, Hamilton advocated the inclusion of institutions, "as far … as republican principles will admit," that would lend energy and stability to the republican form, which he defined as an equality of political rights—that is, a system without any hereditary political privileges (Hamilton 2001). At the Constitutional Convention, Hamilton proposed an elected president and senate to serve during good behavior. His suggestions about the presidency led to a charge of monarchism that followed him for the rest of his life. Although Hamilton favored a lower house that was democratic, he believed that republicanism's best chance for success lay in establishing institutions that could check the popular spirit and pursue a steady course of administration.

The Constitution of course did not meet Hamilton's expectations, but he threw his prodigious energies into the fight for its ratification. During this debate and while serving as secretary of the treasury, Hamilton elaborated an argument for energetic government in general and energy in the executive in particular. Hamilton may have been the first to employ the term *energy* in a political sense, using it to mean activity, vigor, and decisiveness in government. Energy is, he reasoned, more likely to arise when power is placed in one set or a very few sets of hands. Hamilton argued for a prompt and generally strict execution of the law. He considered it his job as treasury secretary to provide guidance for the legislative branch in its deliberations on economic matters. More generally, Hamilton provided the classic argument for a broad construction of the executive power under the Constitution. During the controversy over Washington's declaration of neutrality between revolutionary France and its enemies, Hamilton argued that Article II granted the president the executive power as a whole, including what the English philosopher and economist John Locke (1632–1704) had termed the "federative power" over foreign affairs, subject to the exceptions explicitly spelled out in the Constitution. Hamilton's position was consistent with his overall view that the Constitution should be construed liberally, or broadly, so that it might meet not just today's needs but "the probable exigencies of ages," as he put it in essay No. 34 of *The Federalist Papers* (Hamilton 2001, p. 311).

Joseph A. Schumpeter described Hamilton's reports as treasury secretary as " 'applied economics' at its best" (Schumpeter 1954, p. 199). The reports contain both sophisticated economic theorizing and an extraordinary attention to the details of administration. To correct the nation's financial crisis, Hamilton proposed a funding system that dedicated revenues to meeting the nation's debts, new taxes, an assumption of the state debts accumulated during the American Revolution, and the establishment of an independently operated national bank that would be both the government's banker and a facilitator of economic development. Believing that a capital shortage was the nation's deepest economic problem, Hamilton attempted to modernize the financial system of the public and private sectors. He also proposed a plan to encourage manufacturing by providing government support for essential defense industries and for infant industries. In general, Hamilton supported free trade at home and abroad, but he was willing to make exceptions to compensate for the restrictions on trade established by other governments and to overcome the force of habit that attached Americans to agricultural employments. In this regard, Hamilton departed from the free-market prescriptions of the Scottish economist Adam Smith (1723–1790). In addition, unlike Thomas Jefferson (1743–1826) and James Madison (1751–1836), Hamilton did not see anything degrading or corrupting in manufacturing.

Hamilton struggled to find a political role for himself after he resigned from the Treasury in January 1795. His chief achievements of the period were the drafting of Washington's Farewell Address and his argument in the Croswell case. In the 1804 Croswell case Hamilton argued before the New York Supreme Court that truth ought to be a defense in libel cases. Croswell had published claims that while he was vice president, Jefferson had paid for attacks on the characters of Washington and John Adams. Hamilton lost the case, but his position soon became the law in New York and in many other states. Other ventures did not go as well. His interference with the cabinet of the second U.S. president, John Adams (1735–1826), earned him Adams's intense hatred. His affair while treasury secretary with Maria Reynolds became the new Republic's first great sex scandal when it was revealed in 1797. When recalled to serve as second in command of the army during the "quasi-war," the significant but undeclared naval war with France (1798–1800), his ambitions for the army led to suspicions that he harbored imperial ambitions for himself.

Hamilton's remarkable life came to an end in his duel with Aaron Burr (1756–1836) in 1804. Hamilton had been working to thwart Burr's political ambitions for more than a decade, but his work to defeat Burr's gubernatorial hopes that year was probably the last straw. The challenge to a duel was an affair of honor that Hamilton could not, as a man of the world, decline. Hamilton seems to have decided to throw away his shot, but Burr shot to kill, taking the life of one of the most consequential men of the founding generation.

SEE ALSO *American Revolution; Burr, Aaron; Caribbean, The; Central Banks; Constitution, U.S.; Federalism; Law; Liberty; Public Interest; Republicanism; Washington, George*

BIBLIOGRAPHY

Chernow, Ron. 2004. *Alexander Hamilton.* New York: Penguin.

Freeman, Joanne B. 2001. *Affairs of Honor: National Politics in the New Republic.* New Haven, CT: Yale University Press.

Hamilton, Alexander. 2001 *Hamilton: Writings,* ed. Joanne Freeman. New York: Library of America.

Knott, Stephen F. 2002. *Alexander Hamilton and the Persistence of Myth.* Lawrence: University Press of Kansas.

McDonald, Forrest. 1979. *Alexander Hamilton: A Biography.* New York: Norton.

Schumpeter, Joseph A. 1954. *History of Economic Analysis.* New York: Oxford University Press.

Walling, Karl-Friedrich. 1999. *Republican Empire: Alexander Hamilton on War and Free Government.* Lawrence: University Press of Kansas.

Peter McNamara

HAMILTON, WILLIAM D.

SEE *Hamilton's Rule; Kinship, Evolutionary Theory of.*

HAMILTON'S RULE

The dominant paradigm in economics holds that individuals in society seek to maximize their own self-interest. As Adam Smith observed, however, even selfish individuals have something in their nature that makes them altruistic. The British evolutionary biologist William D. Hamilton (1936–2000) attempted to give this altruism a biological basis. Hamilton expressed a rule for the evolution of social behavior as $rb - c > 0$, where r is a measure of genetic relatedness between an actor and a recipient, b is benefits to a recipient, and c is the cost to the actor of altruistic behavior.

The degree of genetic relatedness among kin follows a declining progression—from mother and child, to mother and nephew or niece, and so on. The implication of the progression is that closely related kin have a higher measure of genetic relatedness. Indeed, the probability that two relatives possess the same rare gene is high, because of a phenomenon known as *kin selection.* According to Hamilton, one's willingness to sacrifice for others—whether individuals, a group, or society—can be measured by the degree of kinship involved.

Hamilton's rule has been used to study altruism, aggression, and selfishness in social interaction. Genes that have survived through Darwinian competition can be deemed selfish and are responsible for the selfish behavior in individuals known as individual selection. In Darwin's view of natural selection, the fittest survive. However, individuals evolve to act for the good of the species or society, through a process known as group selection. The argument for group selection is that a person who sacrifices for a group is more likely to survive than one who sacrifices for selfish benefits.

Individual and group selections can be profitably analyzed using the tools of game theory. If a woman is able to select the sex of a child, she will choose the sex that will maximize the welfare of her grandchildren. Gaming enters the process because the outcome of her decision will depend on the sex ratio in the population, which is a consequence of what other females selected as the sex of their child. Building on Hamilton's and others' works, John Maynard Smith has derived an *evolutionary stable strategy* (ESS) for such games. An ESS can be achieved by each woman tossing a coin to make her selection, yielding a 50:50 chance of selecting a male or a female. With today's technology, a person can know the sex of a child before birth, but if abortion or other changes relating to wars, customs, and politics occur, then no ESS is guaranteed.

Some applications of Hamilton's rule to economics have been successful. In a 2005 study, Samuel Bowles and Dori Posel examined migrant workers who remit income to their families. If a migrant with wage w transfers an amount, t, to his or her family with pre-remittance income, y, then the marginal cost to the migrant is $1/(w-t)$, and the marginal benefit to the recipient is $r/(y+t/n)$. Optimal transfer occurs when the marginal benefit equals the marginal cost.

Some aspects of the Hamilton rule appear anomalous. Hamilton assumes that parents invest equally in male and female children, whereas economists usually think of parents as investing up to the point where equality of marginal benefits and costs occurs—and thus generally investing more in male children. More generally, the idea that genetic selection guides economic behavior seems somewhat problematic: Genetic changes are slow, whereas changes in prices, advertising, and R&D have an immediate effect.

SEE ALSO *Aggression; Darwin, Charles; Evolutionary Games; Game Theory; Kinship, Evolutionary Theory of; Maximization*

BIBLIOGRAPHY

Axelrod, Robert, and William D. Hamilton. 1981. The Evolution of Cooperation. *Science* n.s., 211 (4489): 1390–1396.

Bowles, Samuel, and Dori Posel. 2005. Genetic Relatedness Predicts South African Migrant Workers' Remittances to Their Families. *Nature* 434 (7031): 380–383.

Dawkins, Richard. 1989. *The Selfish Gene*. Oxford and New York: Oxford University Press.

Day, Troy, and Peter D. Taylor. 1997. Hamilton's Rule Meets the Hamiltonian: Kin Selection on Dynamic Characters. *Proceedings: Biological Sciences* 264 (1382): 639–644.

Hamilton, William D. 1964. Altruism and Related Phenomena, Mainly in the Social Insects. *Annual Review of Ecology and Systematics* 3: 193–232.

Hamilton, William D. 1964. The Genetical Theory of Social Behavior, I, II. *Journal of Theoretical Biology* 7 (1): 1–52.

Lessard, Sabin. 2001. William D. Hamilton: A Tribute. *Theoretical Population Biology* 59 (1): 7–9.

Matessi, Carlo, and Samuel Karlin. 1984. On the Evolution of Altruism by Kin Selection. *Proceedings of the National Academy of Sciences U.S.A.* 81 (6): 1754–1758.

Samuelson, Paul A. 1985. Modes of Thought in Economics and Biology. *American Economic Review* 75 (2): 166–172.

Smith, Adam, 1976. *The Theory of Moral Sentiments*, eds. D. D. Raphael and A. L. Macfie. Oxford: Clarendon Press.

Smith, John Maynard. 1993. *The Theory of Evolution*. Canto Edition. Cambridge, U.K.: Cambridge University Press.

Lall Ramrattan
Michael Szenberg

HAMMURABI, CODE OF
SEE *Retaliation.*

HAPPINESS

The economics of happiness is an approach to assessing welfare that combines the techniques typically used by economists with those more commonly used by psychologists.

While psychologists have long used surveys of reported well-being to study happiness, economists only recently ventured into this arena. Early economists and philosophers, ranging from Aristotle (384–322 BCE) to Adam Smith (1723–1790), Jeremy Bentham (1748–1832), and John Stuart Mill (1806–1873), incorporated the pursuit of happiness in their work. Yet, as economics grew more rigorous and quantitative, more parsimonious definitions of *welfare* took hold. Utility was taken to depend only on income as mediated by individual choices or preferences within a rational individual's budget constraint.

The study of happiness or subjective well-being is part of a more general move in economics that challenges these narrow assumptions. The introduction of bounded rationality and the establishment of behavioral economics opened new lines of research. *Happiness economics*—which represents one new direction—relies on more expansive notions of utility and welfare, including interdependent utility functions, procedural utility, and the interaction between rational and nonrational influences.

Richard Easterlin was the first modern economist to revisit the concept of happiness, beginning in the early 1970s. More generalized interest took hold in the late 1990s (see, among others, Easterlin 1974, 2003; Blanchflower and Oswald 2004; Clark and Oswald 1994;

Frey and Stutzer 2002a; Graham and Pettinato 2002; and Layard 2005).

The approach does not purport to replace income-based measures of welfare but instead to complement them with broader measures. These measures are based on the results of large-scale surveys, across countries and over time, of hundreds of thousands of individuals. The surveys provide information about the importance of a range of factors that affect well-being, including income but also others, such as health, marital and employment status, and civic trust.

The approach, which relies on expressed preferences rather than on revealed choices, is particularly well suited to answering questions in areas where a revealed-preferences approach provides limited information. Indeed, it often uncovers discrepancies between expressed and revealed preferences. Revealed preferences cannot fully gauge the welfare effects of particular policies or institutional arrangements that individuals are powerless to change. Examples of these include the welfare effects of inequality, environmental degradation, and macroeconomic policies. Amartya Sen's (1995) capabilities-based approach to poverty, for example, highlights the lack of capacity of the poor to make choices or to take certain actions. Another area where a choice approach is limited is the welfare effects of addictive behaviors such as smoking and drug abuse.

Happiness surveys are based on questions in which the individual is asked, "Generally speaking, how happy are you with your life?" or "How satisfied are you with your life?" with possible answers on a four- to seven-point scale. The answers to happiness and life satisfaction questions correlate closely—ranging between .56 and .50 (Blanchflower and Oswald 2004; Graham and Pettinato 2002).

This approach presents several methodological challenges (Bertrand and Mullainathan 2001; Frey and Stutzer 2002b). To minimize order bias, happiness questions must be placed at the beginning of surveys. As with all economic measurements, the answer of any specific individual may be biased by idiosyncratic, unobserved events. Bias in answers to happiness surveys can also result from unobserved personality traits and correlated measurement errors (which can be corrected via individual fixed effects if and when panel data are available).

Despite the potential pitfalls, cross sections of large samples across countries and over time find remarkably consistent patterns in the determinants of happiness. Many errors are uncorrelated with the observed variables, and do not systematically bias the results. Psychologists also find validation in the way that people answer these surveys based in physiological measures of happiness, such as the number of "genuine"—Duchenne—smiles (Diener and Seligman 2004).

Microeconometric happiness equations have the standard form: $W_{it} = \alpha + \beta x_{it} + \varepsilon_{it}$, where W is the reported well-being of individual i at time t, and X is a vector of known variables including sociodemographic and socioeconomic characteristics. Unobserved characteristics and measurement errors are captured in the error term. Because the answers to happiness surveys are ordinal rather than cardinal, they are best analyzed via ordered logit or probit equations. These regressions typically yield lower R-squares than economists are used to, reflecting the extent to which emotions and other components of true well-being are driving the results, as opposed to the variables that we are able to measure, such as income, education, and marital and employment status.

The availability of panel data in some instances, as well as advances in econometric techniques, are increasingly allowing for sounder analysis (van Praag and Ferrer-i-Carbonell 2004). The coefficients produced from ordered probit or logistic regressions are remarkably similar to those from OLS regressions based on the same equations. While it is impossible to measure the precise effects of independent variables on true well-being, happiness researchers have used the OLS coefficients as a basis for assigning relative weights to them. They can estimate how much income a typical individual in the United States or Britain would need to produce the same change in stated happiness that comes from the well-being loss resulting from, for example, divorce ($100,000) or job loss ($60,000) (Blanchflower and Oswald 2004).

THE EASTERLIN PARADOX

In his original study, Richard Easterlin revealed a paradox that sparked interest in the topic but is as yet unresolved. While most happiness studies find that *within* countries wealthier people are, on average, happier than poor ones, studies across countries and over time find very little, if any, relationship between increases in per capita income and average happiness levels. On average, wealthier countries (as a group) are happier than poor ones (as a group); happiness seems to rise with income up to a point, but not beyond it. Yet even among the less happy, poorer countries, there is not a clear relationship between average income and average happiness levels, suggesting that many other factors—including cultural traits—are at play (see Figure 1).

Within countries, income matters to happiness (Oswald 1997; Diener et al. 2003). Deprivation and abject poverty in particular are very bad for happiness. Yet after basic needs are met, other factors such as rising aspirations, relative income differences, and the security of gains become increasingly important in addition to

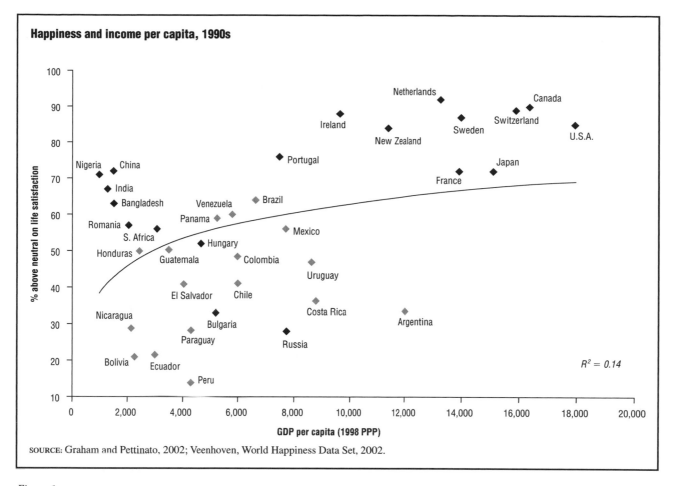

Happiness and income per capita, 1990s

SOURCE: Graham and Pettinato, 2002; Veenhoven, World Happiness Data Set, 2002.

Figure 1

income. James Duesenberry (1949) noted the impact of changing aspirations on income satisfaction and its potential effects on consumption and savings rates. A number of happiness studies have since confirmed the effects of rising aspirations, and their potential role in driving excessive consumption and other perverse economic behaviors (Frank 1999).

A common interpretation of the Easterlin paradox is that humans are on a "hedonic treadmill": aspirations increase along with income and, after basic needs are met, relative levels of income matter to well-being. Psychologists' "set point" theory of happiness, in which every individual is presumed to have a happiness level that he or she goes back to over time, even after major events such as winning the lottery or getting divorced (Easterlin 2003), provides a complementary interpretation.

Individuals are remarkably adaptable and in the end can get used to most things, and in particular to income gains (Kahneman et al. 1999). Easterlin argues that individuals adapt more in the pecuniary arena than in the nonpecuniary arena. Yet, because most policy is based on

pecuniary factors, measures of well-being underestimate the effects of non-income factors, such as health, family, and stable employment.

There is no consensus about which interpretation is most accurate. Yet numerous studies demonstrate that happiness levels can change significantly in response to a variety of factors. Even under the rubric of set point theory, happiness levels can fall significantly in the aftermath of events like illness or unemployment. Even if levels eventually adapt upward to a longer-term equilibrium, mitigating or preventing the unhappiness and disruption that individuals experience for months, or even years, in the interim certainly seems a worthwhile objective for policy.

SELECTED APPLICATIONS OF HAPPINESS ECONOMICS

Happiness research has been applied to a range of issues. These include the relationship between income and happiness, the relationship between inequality and poverty, the effects of macropolicies on individual welfare, and the effects of public policies aimed at controlling addictive substances.

Some studies have attempted to separate the effects of income from those of other endogenous factors, such as satisfaction in the workplace. Studies of unexpected lottery gains find that these isolated gains have positive effects on happiness, although it is not clear that they are of a lasting nature (Gardner and Oswald 2001). Other studies have explored the reverse direction of causality, and find that people with higher happiness levels tend to perform better in the labor market and to earn more income (Diener et al. 2003; Graham, Eggers, and Sukhtankar 2004).

A related question is how income inequality affects individual welfare. Most studies of OECD (Organization for Economic Cooperation and Development) countries find that inequality has modest or insignificant effects on happiness. The mixed results may reflect the fact that inequality can be a signal of future opportunity and mobility as much as it can be a sign of injustice (Alesina et al. 2004). In contrast, recent research on Latin America finds that inequality is negative for the well-being of the poor and positive for the rich. In a region with high inequality and weak public institutions and labor markets, inequality signals persistent disadvantage or advantage rather than future opportunity (Graham and Felton 2005).

Happiness surveys also facilitate the measurement of the effects of non-income components of inequality, such as race, gender, and status, all of which seem to be highly significant (Graham and Felton 2005). Relative social standing, meanwhile, has significant effects on health outcomes (Marmot 2004).

Happiness research can deepen our understanding of poverty. The set point theory suggests that a destitute peasant can be very happy. While this contradicts a standard finding in the literature—namely, that poor people are less happy than wealthier people within countries—it is suggestive of the role that low expectations play in explaining persistent poverty in some cases.

Perceptions of poverty vary. People who are high up the income ladder can identify themselves as poor, while many of those who are below the objective poverty line do not, because of different expectations (Rojas 2004). In addition, the well-being of those who have escaped poverty is often undermined by insecurity, and their reported well-being is often lower than that of the poor (Graham and Pettinato 2002).

Most studies find that inflation and unemployment have negative effects on happiness. The effects of unemployment are stronger than those of inflation, and hold above and beyond those of forgone income (Di Tella et al. 2001). The standard "misery index," which assigns equal weight to inflation and unemployment, may be underestimating the effects of the latter (Frey and Stutzer 2002b).

Political arrangements also matter. Both trust and freedom have positive effects on happiness (Helliwell 2003; Layard 2005). Research based on voting across cantons in Switzerland finds that there are positive effects from *participating* in direct democracy (Frey and Stutzer 2002b). Research in Latin America finds a strong positive correlation between happiness and preference for democracy (Graham and Sukhtankar 2004).

Happiness surveys can also be utilized to gauge the welfare effects of various public policies. How does a tax on addictive substances, such as tobacco and alcohol, for example, affect well-being? A recent study on cigarette taxes suggests that the negative financial effects may be outweighed by positive self-control effects (Gruber and Mullainathan 2002).

POLICY IMPLICATIONS

Richard Layard (2005) makes a bold statement about the potential of happiness research to improve people's lives directly via changes in public policy. He highlights the extent to which people's happiness is affected by status—resulting in a rat race approach to work and to income gains, which in the end reduces well-being. He also notes the strong positive role of security in the workplace and in the home, and of the quality of social relationships and trust. He identifies direct implications for fiscal and labor market policy—in the form of taxation on excessive income gains and via reevaluating the merits of performance-based pay.

While not all agree with Layard's specific recommendations, there is nascent consensus that happiness surveys can serve as an important complementary tool for public policy. Scholars such as Ed Diener and Martin Seligman (2004) and Daniel Kahneman and his colleagues (2004) advocate the creation of national well-being accounts to complement income accounts.

Still, a sound note of caution is necessary in directly applying the findings of happiness research to policy, both because of the potential biases in survey data and because of the difficulties associated with analyzing this kind of data in the absence of controls for unobservable personality traits. In addition, happiness surveys at times yield anomalous results that provide novel insights into human psychology—such as adaptation and coping during economic crises—but do not translate into viable policy recommendations. One example is the finding that unemployed respondents are happier (or less unhappy) in contexts with higher unemployment rates. The positive effect that reduced stigma has on the well-being of the unemployed outweighs the negative effects of a lower probability of future employment (Clark and Oswald

1994; Stutzer and Lalive 2004; and Eggers et al. 2006). One interpretation of these results for policy—raising unemployment rates—would obviously be a mistake. At the same time, the research suggests a new focus on the effects of stigma on the welfare of the unemployed. Happiness economics also opens a field of research questions that still need to be addressed, including the implications of well-being findings for national indicators and economic growth patterns; the effects of happiness on behavior such as work effort, consumption, and investment; and the effects on political behavior.

BIBLIOGRAPHY

Alesina, Alberto, Rafael Di Tella, and Robert MacCulloch. 2004. Inequality and Happiness: Are Europeans and Americans Different? *Journal of Public Economics* 88: 2009–2042.

Bertrand, Marianne, and Sendhil Mullainathan. 2001. Do People Mean What They Say? Implications for Subjective Survey Data. *American Economic Review* 91: 67–72.

Blanchflower, David, and Andrew Oswald. 2004. Well-Being over Time in Britain and the USA. *Journal of Public Economics* 88: 1359–1387.

Clark, Andrew, and Andrew Oswald. 1994. Unhappiness and Unemployment. *Economic Journal* 104: 648–659.

Diener, Ed, and Martin Seligman. 2004. Beyond Money: Toward an Economy of Well-Being. *Psychological Science in the Public Interest* 5 (1): 1–31.

Diener, Ed, et al. 2003. The Relationship between Income and Subjective Well-Being: Relative or Absolute? *Social Indicators Research* 28: 195–223.

Di Tella, Rafael, Robert MacCulloch, and Andrew J. Oswald. 2001. Preferences over Inflation and Unemployment: Evidence from Surveys of Happiness. *American Economic Review* 91: 335–341.

Duesenberry, James. 1949. *Income, Saving, and the Theory of Consumer Behavior*. Cambridge, MA: Harvard University Press.

Easterlin, Richard. 1974. Does Economic Growth Improve the Human Lot? Some Empirical Evidence. In *Nations and Households in Economic Growth: Essays in Honor of Moses Abramovitz*, eds. Paul David and Melvin Reder. New York: Academic Press.

Easterlin, Richard. 2003. Explaining Happiness. *Proceedings of the National Academy of Sciences* 100 (19): 11176–11183.

Eggers, Andrew, Clifford Gaddy, and Carol Graham. 2006. Well-Being and Unemployment in Russia in the 1990's: Can Society's Suffering Be Individuals' Solace? *Journal of Socioeconomics* 35 (2): 209–242.

Frank, Robert. 1999. *Luxury Fever: Money and Happiness in an Era of Excess*. Princeton, NJ: Princeton University Press.

Frey, Bruno, and Alois Stutzer. 2002a. *Happiness and Economics: How the Economy and Institutions Affect Well-Being*. Princeton, NJ: Princeton University Press.

Frey, Bruno, and Alois Stutzer. 2002b. What Can Economists Learn from Happiness Research? *Journal of Economic Literature* 40: 401–435.

Gardner, Jonathan, and Andrew Oswald. 2001. Does Money Buy Happiness? Some Evidence from Windfalls. Mimeo. Coventry, U.K.: University of Warwick.

Graham, Carol, Andrew Eggers, and Sandip Sukhtankar. 2004. Does Happiness Pay? An Exploration Based on Panel Data from Russia. *Journal of Economic Behavior and Organization* 55: 319–342.

Graham, Carol, and Andrew Felton. 2005. *Does Inequality Matter to Individual Welfare: An Initial Exploration Based on Happiness Surveys from Latin America*. Center on Social and Economic Dynamics Working Papers Series No. 38. Washington, DC: Brookings Institution. http://www.brook.edu/es/dynamics/papers/csed_wp38.htm.

Graham, Carol, and Sandip Sukhtankar. 2004. Does Economic Crisis Reduce Support for Markets and Democracy in Latin America? Some Evidence from Surveys of Public Opinion and Well-Being. *Journal of Latin American Studies* 36: 349–377.

Graham, Carol, and Stefano Pettinato. 2002. *Happiness and Hardship: Opportunity and Insecurity in New Market Economies*. Washington, DC: Brookings Institution Press.

Gruber, Jonathan, and Sendhil Mullainathan. 2002. Do Cigarette Taxes Make Smokers Happier? Working Paper No. 8872. Cambridge, MA: NBER.

Helliwell, John. 2003. Well-Being and Social Capital: Does Suicide Pose a Puzzle? Unpublished manuscript. Vancouver: University of British Columbia.

Kahneman, Daniel, Ed Diener, and Norbert Schwarz. 1999. *Well-Being: The Foundations of Hedonic Psychology*. New York: Russell Sage Foundation.

Kahneman, Daniel, et al. 2004. Toward National Well-Being Accounts. *AEA Papers and Proceedings* 94: 429–434.

Layard, Richard. 2005. *Happiness: Lessons from a New Science*. New York: Penguin.

Marmot, Michael. 2004. *The Status Syndrome: How Social Standing Affects Our Health and Longevity*. London: Bloomsbury.

Oswald, Andrew. 1997. Happiness and Economic Performance. *Economic Journal* 107: 1815–1831.

Rojas, Mariano. 2004. *Well-Being and the Complexity of Poverty*. Research Paper No. 2004/29. Helsinki: World Institute for Development Research.

Sen, Amartya. 1995. Rationality and Social Choice. *American Economic Review* 85: 1–24.

Stutzer, Alois, and Rafael Lalive. 2004. The Role of Social Work Norms in Job Searching and Subjective Well-Being. *Journal of the European Economic Association* 2: 696–719.

van Praag, Bernard, and Ada Ferrer-i-Carbonell. 2004. *Happiness Quantified: A Satisfaction Calculus Approach*. Oxford: Oxford University Press.

Veenhoven, Ruut. World Database of Happiness: Continuous Register of Scientific Research on Subjective Appreciation of Life. http://www2.eur.nl/fsw/research/happiness/index.htm.

Carol Graham

HARASSMENT

Harassment, which exists in many forms with different names, is most basically offensive behavior directed at a person, place, or entity. Most frequently, the target or victim of harassment defines or names the particular form of offensive behavior. Among the more common types of harassment are racial profiling, bullying, sexual harassment, hate crimes, and hazing. Regardless of the demographic or other characteristic of the victim, the goal of the harassment is to intimidate, exert power, or impose control over a victim.

The distinction between harassment and other forms of aggressive communication that are legal is based on societal and community standards. In societies that devalue free speech and open communication—in particular, disagreement with the government or other official personnel—harassment is often very broadly defined as written or verbal communications that are not sanctioned by an official governing body or that express open disagreement with the government.

In contrast, in societies where free speech is encouraged, harassment is typically defined as speech or communication that does not meet normal standards of accuracy or appropriateness, and is directed at a target who perceives the communication as disturbing, disruptive of occupational, educational, or interpersonal functioning, or injurious to reputation, position, or authority. That is to say, when brief and not overly frequent communications express concerns that validly correspond to errors or issues, then harassment is typically not present. Conversely, the greater the duration and frequency of communications and the smaller the validity of the claim, the greater is the likelihood that harassment is present.

These relatively complex definitions highlight the difficulty of identifying what meets the legal definition of harassment. For example, a communication that is perceived as harassment by its receiver may not have been sent for that purpose. Similarly, lengthy, frequent, but accurate communications directed at a person, place, or entity (as with political criticism) may or may not rise to the legal threshold of harassment. Nonetheless, despite these conceptual difficulties, the essential definition of harassment remains valid: It is an unwelcomed and unwanted verbal or nonverbal communication that produces an adverse consequence or negatively affects the emotional, cognitive, or behavioral functioning of one or more victims.

Sexual harassment in the workplace is a form of unwelcomed communication familiar to many individuals in the United States. Victims are frequently expected to accept harassment without complaint in exchange for promotions, raises, or continued employment. The Equal Employment Opportunity Commission defines sexual harassment as unwelcome sexual advances, requests for sexual favors, and other verbal or physical conduct of a sexual nature that explicitly or implicitly affects an individual's employment, unreasonably interferes with an individual's work performance, or creates an intimidating, hostile, or offensive work environment. Victimization by workplace harassment has been correlated with greater inefficiency, lowered productivity, and higher rates of absences.

Racial harassment is also a common form of unwelcome and harmful communication. Victims of ethnic or racial harassment, a specific form of racism, can experience negative health outcomes, including high blood pressure, elevated hostility, and frequent somatic complaints. Researchers have found that individuals experiencing racial or ethnic harassment are twice as likely to be daily tobacco users than those with no reported harassment experiences (Bennett et al 2005). Adjusting for age, harassed individuals are 70 percent more likely to report daily tobacco use in the past thirty days. It is beginning to be recognized that racial and ethnic harassment may be an important factor in explaining tobacco use among young African Americans. Those who perceive greater racial/ethnic harassment may also be at greater risk for affective disturbance and pathological cardiovascular reactivity (Bennett et al 2003; Merritt et al 2006). Continuous harassment can lead to persisting complications, including excessive self-blame, lowered mood, reexperience of the unwelcomed event, and generally increased anxiety.

Some forms of harassment are more socially acceptable than others. Because sexual harassment and hate crimes are illegal, there is an implied social agreement that these behaviors are wrong. In other instances, such as harassment of the obese, guidelines for acceptable behavior are much less clear and the prevalence of unwelcomed communications, both subtle and overt, is thought to be high.

Less recognized forms of harassment are also present. For example, a recent content analysis of prime-time television found that depictions of explicit and implicit sexual harassment of women are frequent (Grauerholz and King 1997). Incidents involving quid-pro-quo harassment were numerous. More than 80 percent of television shows in prime time contained at least one incident of sexual harassment not labeled as such.

Recently, behavioral scientists have begun to examine the effectiveness of training programs used to enhance the listening and helping skills of sexual harassment contact persons in the workplace (see Blaxall, Parsonson, and Robertson 1993). The majority of these studies have found that teaching designated and appropriate individuals in the workplace to respond appropriately to complaints of harassment, to recognize harassment's warning signs, and to respond empathetically to victims and firmly but fairly to perpetrators can help decrease sexual harassment and reduce its long-term consequences. Despite these encouraging indications, the most important mechanisms for the management of harassment inside and outside of the workplace appear to be laws, rules, regulations, and education.

SEE ALSO *Aggression; Communication; Discrimination; Hypertension; Post-Traumatic Stress; Power; Racism; Sexism; Sexual Harassment; Smoking; Trauma; Violence*

BIBLIOGRAPHY

Bennett, Gary G., Marcellus M. Merritt, Christopher L. Edwards, and John J. Sollers III. 2003. Perceived Racism and Affective Responses to Ambiguous Interpersonal Interactions among African American Men. *American Behavioral Scientist* 47 (7): 963–976.

Bennett, Gary G., Kathleen Yaus Wolin, Elwood L. Robinson, Sherrye Fowler, and Christopher L. Edwards. 2005. Perceived Racial/Ethnic Harassment and Tobacco Use among African American Young Adults. *American Journal of Public Health* 95 (2): 238–240.

Blaxall, Michelle C., Barry S. Parsonson, and Neville R. Robertson. 1993. The Development and Evaluation of a Sexual Harassment Contact Person Training Package. *Behavior Modification* 17 (2): 148–163.

Grauerholz, Elizabeth, and Amy King. 1997. Prime Time Sexual Harassment. *Violence Against Women* 3 (2): 129–148.

Merritt, Marcellus M., Gary G. Bennett, Redford B. Williams, et al. 2006. Perceived Racism and Cardiovascular Reactivity and Recovery to Personally-Relevant Stress. *Health Psychology* 25 (3): 364–369.

Priebe, S., K. Bolze, and H. Rudolf. 1994. Persisting Psychological Disorders following Harassment Because of an Application to Leave the GDR. *Fortschritte der Neurologie-Psychiatrie* 62 (11): 433–437.

Christopher L. Edwards
Andrea Reeves

HARD-CORE UNEMPLOYED

The term *hard-core unemployed* was popularized in the late 1960s to refer to persons facing multiple barriers that appeared to block them from active, consistent participation in the job market. The term has largely fallen out of favor, though the concept—now termed *structural unemployed*—still has utility in today's policy debates, particularly regarding economic disadvantages related to race.

HISTORY

Policymakers, economists, and historians have long been interested in the problem of chronic joblessness. Much of this interest has corresponded to periods of market failures, like the Great Depression of the 1930s, when huge swaths of working-age persons were unable to find gainful work due to the collapse in aggregate demand.

However, policymakers, civil-rights leaders, and social critics noted a different, though related, phenomenon beginning in the 1960s. Significant numbers of persons were experiencing chronic unemployment even in economic "good times," that is, periods of solid overall growth and low national unemployment. Moreover, there was a set of identifiable characteristics among these jobless persons.

First, they were generally disconnected from the labor market. Though some worked intermittently, they experienced long spells of joblessness that lasted anywhere from six months to numerous years. Second, they tended to have lower levels of education, at most a high-school diploma. Third, they were disproportionately, though by no means exclusively, minority. Fourth, in part due to their lack of employment, they were often poor or near-poor urban residents, and typically received some form of government assistance. Finally, some members of this group were alleged to have physical or mental handicaps; more recently, a criminal history has also been associated with long-term joblessness.

In his fifth State of the Union address (1968), President Lyndon Johnson (1908–1973) used the term *hard-core unemployed*, referring to approximately 500,000 Americans with these characteristics. Johnson also dubbed them the "last in line … the hardest to reach."

THEORIES AND EXPLANATIONS FOR THE EXISTENCE OF STRUCTURAL UNEMPLOYMENT

There are three somewhat competing theories for the existence of chronic unemployment: these theories are based on productivity/skills mismatch and cultural explanations.

The first theory maintains that some persons, though willing to sell their labor at the going wage, simply lack the productivity to justify even the lowest wage on offer. Employers thus have no motivation to hire such persons, since their contribution to the firm's output will be less than their pay, making them a net cost to the employer. As discussed below, policymakers motivated by this reasoning created tax credits to lower the labor cost to the employers associated with such hires.

The second theory stresses structural barriers: forces beyond the control of the individual that preclude him or her from active participation in the job market. These barriers include racism; exclusion from opportunities available to the majority, such as a decent education; and economic changes that have reduced job opportunities to non-college-educated workers and those in particular geographical areas. In this explanation, the chronically unemployed have the necessary skills and attitudes to maintain a lasting connection to the job market. But forces outside their control, such as employers' aversion to hiring minorities or the disappearance of jobs for which they are qualified, leave them without work for extended periods.

The third theory stresses personal shortcomings having more to do with attitudes, habits, and personal preferences than with skill limitations. The argument here is that the chronically unemployed have failed to internalize the dominant work ethic common among the majority. The result is that they devalue work in the paid job market, preferring outside sources of support, such as government assistance or the black market.

Of course, these theories overlap, and subsequent research has revealed that no single theory suitably explains the phenomenon. Relative to the other two theories, attitudinal explanations have less salience, as events and research have revealed that skill enhancement, policy interventions, and periods of strong labor demand have at times proven to diminish long-term joblessness among disadvantaged workers. That said, the problem is still very much with us.

POLICY DEVELOPMENTS AND THEIR IMPACT ON OUR UNDERSTANDING OF THE PROBLEM

The explanations discussed above, particularly the first two, led to various policy interventions designed to break the cycle of chronic joblessness in the United States. Presidents since Johnson have introduced and extended policy sets of training initiatives and tax credits to raise the skills of the hard-core unemployed and to lower their labor costs to employers (under such a credit, the government will pay some portion of the wage of workers who meet certain criteria).

Most of these programs remain in place today. The Targeted Jobs Tax Credit introduced in 1978, an employer-side credit of the type just noted, became the Work Opportunity Tax Credit in 1996. Numerous training programs for the least advantaged also remain in place under the rubric of the 1998 Workforce Investment Act. The welfare reform legislation of the mid-1990s also extended some of these programs.

The evidence of their effectiveness is mixed. The research on employer-side tax credits shows that while these programs sometimes have their intended effect, they are just as often used as an unnecessary windfall to employers who would have hired the same workers in the absence of the subsidy. Worker training programs also have a checkered history in terms of their effectiveness in offsetting the skill mismatch, but more recent, localized initiatives have shown greater success.

To some extent, the full employment period of the latter 1990s proved to be a potent antidote to structural unemployment, suggesting that depressed labor demand has been one factor responsible for chronic joblessness. During this period, the employment rates of many populations that had formerly been left behind grew sharply. Public policy interventions, including a higher minimum wage, an expanded Earned Income Tax Credit (an employee-side wage subsidy for low-wage workers in low-income families), and a set of work supports associated with welfare reform (e.g., subsidized child care or health care for working families), also played a role.

But the pull of the strong labor market, characterized by the lowest overall unemployment rates in three decades, was likely the dominant force in play in these years, and the employment rates (the share of the population at work) increased significantly for many, though not all, disadvantaged groups. Even some of the most disconnected groups benefited. For example, young African American males without a high-school diploma experienced a gain in employment rates from 32 percent in 1995 to 38 percent in 2005. Of course, even with this six point gain, such a low rate of employment is indicative of the problem of structural unemployment, but the positive trend is still notable evidence of the importance of very tight job markets.

CONCLUSION

Though the term *hard-core unemployed* is rarely used in contemporary discussions, compelling evidence reveals that certain groups of persons still face high barriers between them and the employment opportunities they need to raise their living standards. Unemployment rates for African Americans are consistently twice that of whites; the employment rates of young workers with less education, particularly minorities, remain far below overall averages.

Even in 2000, when national unemployment was 4 percent, the employment rate for young, African-American, male, high-school dropouts was 38 percent, far below the national average of 64 percent. Other research has shown that over 70 percent of young men with these characteristics were jobless or incarcerated in the mid-2000s.

Numerous explanations for this damaging phenomenon have been articulated and explored by researchers and policymakers. The findings generally show that these workers face both skill deficits that hurt their employment prospects and a set of structural barriers, including weak labor demand, discrimination, and the absence of sustainable jobs where they live. Public policy and positive macroeconomic trends have been shown to make a helpful difference in the lives of these workers, but steep barriers remain in place.

For example, as economic inequality has grown and public budgets have become ever more strained, investments in public education have often lagged, particularly in disadvantaged areas where they are needed most. Rising inequality and poverty rates that are less responsive to economic growth have also meant that too many poor and near-poor families are unable to provide the necessary opportunities and advantages for young children, and these early disadvantages have lasting, negative consequences. Correcting these inequities, in tandem with pursuing policies to chip away at the deficits and barriers facing the structurally unemployed will help to diminish their numbers and connect them to the growing economy.

SEE ALSO *Discouraged Workers; Employment; Full Employment; Inequality, Racial; Labor Force Participation; Lumpenproletariat; Unemployment*

BIBLIOGRAPHY

Bernstein, Jared, and Dean Baker. 2003. *The Benefits of Full Employment: When Markets Work for People.* Washington, DC: Economic Policy Institute.

Edelman, Peter, Harry J. Holzer, and Paul Offner. 2006. *Reconnecting Disadvantaged Young Men.* Washington, DC: Urban Institute Press.

Johnson, Lyndon Baines. 1968. Annual Message to the Congress on the State of the Union. January 17. Lyndon Baines Johnson Library and Museum. http://www.lbjlib.utexas.edu/johnson/archives.hom/speeches.hom/680117.asp.

Kaplan, Roy H., and Curt Tausky. 1974. The Meaning of Work Among the Hard Core Unemployed. *The Pacific Sociological Review* 17 (2): 185–198.

Mincy, Ronald B., ed. 2006. *Black Males Left Behind.* Washington, DC: Urban Institute Press.

Wilson, William Julius. 1987. *The Truly Disadvantaged: The Inner City, the Underclass, and Public Policy.* Chicago: University of Chicago Press.

Wilson, William Julius. 1996. *When Work Disappears: The World of the New Urban Poor.* New York: Knopf.

Jared Bernstein
James Lin

HARIJANS
SEE *Dalits.*

HARLEM

"In the history of New York," begins James Weldon Johnson's authoritative 1930s history *Black Manhattan*, "the significance of the name Harlem has changed from Dutch to Irish to Jewish to Negro" (p. 3). Though Johnson's historical vantage was the dawn of the twentieth century, his observation is an ideal start for locating a fluid, rather than fixed, meaning for Harlem. His words pinpoint for his contemporaries, as well as later generations, three aspects of Harlem—its meaning, its transitions, and its multiethnicity—suggesting that it be infinitely defined in a shifting matrix of politics, economy, and culture.

Nieuw Harlem, as it was named by early Dutch settlers, was a farming community in the mid-1600s. Through the seventeenth and eighteenth centuries, Harlem belonged to the descendants of Dutch, French, and English settlers who oversaw its transition from an isolated, poor, and rural village to an upper- and upper-middle-class residential suburb. By the 1840s and 1850s, as the land's productivity declined, many estate owners sold off or abandoned their properties. Irish immigrants arrived in Harlem as squatters, establishing shantytowns as well as a territorial claim to street and neighborhood boundaries.

With the elevated train pushing farther north between 1878 and 1881, fashionable brownstones and exclusive apartments were built to house a genteel class. By the 1890s Harlem's brownstone aristocracy lived alongside Irish and Italian immigrants who populated low-lying spaces, marshland, and peripheral areas filled with tenement housing. German immigrants, including German Jews, joined the wealthy native American and European immigrant population. Economic success in the late 1890s also pulled upwardly mobile Eastern European Jews out of the Lower East Side as they, too, became Harlemites. Harlem was even home to a "little Russia."

In spite of its well-known reputation as the cultural capital of black America, Harlem had few black residents until a wave of white flight produced a remarkable transition at the beginning of the twentieth century. The "great subway proposition" to extend a streetcar line to Manhattan's upper reaches spurred wild real-estate speculation in Harlem. A bust came in 1905, however, as speculators faced an uncertain completion date for the subway. To save themselves from financial ruin, landlords were willing to rent properties to blacks. As middlemen, black real estate agents such as Philip A. Payton Jr., founder of the Afro American Realty Company, John E. Nail, and Henry C. Parker steered clients to Harlem. Whites at first resisted, though in the end, established (white) tenants and white realtors were unsuccessful against what they called a "negro invasion." As Jervis Anderson, a cultural historian of the Harlem Renaissance era, noted: "As the community became predominantly black, the very word 'Harlem' seemed to lose its old meaning" (1981, p. 60).

From about 1905, then, the formation of black Harlem was located at the spatial intersection of race relations and the demographic transformation of urbanizing America. The community, which covers 3,829 acres, is surrounded on all sides by the East, Harlem, and Hudson Rivers; its official boundaries run south to north from 96th Street to 178th Street in upper Manhattan. From the start of the twentieth century, however, Harlem has existed beyond geography.

From a period that roughly spans 1919 to 1929, the cultural movement defining the neighborhood's heyday took place: the Harlem Renaissance. Black artists and intellectuals participated jointly in the creation of a new urban collective identity. As a center of urban black America, it was home to churches, hospitals, and other important social institutions that served a segregated community in Jim Crow America. The black "city within a city" exerted a magnetic pull as Harlem loomed large as a "symbol of liberty" and a "promised land." As "queen of the blackbelts," Harlem was a mecca for black activists, intellectuals, painters, and musicians. Its prominent writers included Langston Hughes, Claude McKay, Nella Larsen, and Zora Neale Hurston. Harlem was a stage, too, for important political spokespersons such as W. E. B. Du Bois and Marcus Garvey, who used Harlem as a platform from which to challenge racist America.

Those were the years, wrote Langston Hughes, when "Harlem was in vogue" (Hughes 1986, p. 227). For white downtowners a variety of Harlem's clubs offered a glimpse and a thrill beyond the color line. Establishments such as Connie's Inn, the Nest, Small's Paradise, the Capitol, the Cotton Club, the Green Cat, the Sugar Cane Club, Happy Rhones, the Hoofers Club, and the Little Savoy staged music and dance numbers and, skirting the ban of prohibition, offered booze to white "slummers" and curiosity seekers. Ironically, some of the clubs had a Jim Crow policy that allowed black performers but excluded blacks as customers.

No consensus holds about the precise end of the Harlem Renaissance. The 1929 American stock market crash and the onset of the Great Depression, coupled with the end of Prohibition in 1933, loosely mark a transition to post-Renaissance Harlem. By the time of the 1935 Harlem Riot the luster was off. In a 1948 essay titled "Harlem Is Nowhere," Ralph Ellison equated Harlem with madness, and argued that for "over four hundred thousand Americans ... overcrowded and exploited politically and economically, Harlem is the scene and symbol of the Negro's perpetual alienation in the land of his birth" (p. 296). From the 1930s to the 1960s, Harlem's declining social conditions gave the neighborhood a sensationalist and decidedly negative reputation.

In the late 1960s and early 1970s urban renewal turned up on Harlem's doorstep promising a turnaround. Within the community these slum clearance policies were derisively tagged "Negro removal." This time Harlem's transition became a struggle over whether redevelopment and reinvestment could coexist alongside preservation of its black cultural heritage. When 1980s noises of gentrification sounded through postindustrial urban America, they could be heard knocking at Harlem's door. With the establishment of the Upper Manhattan Empowerment Zone in the mid-1990s, an era of public and private investment was initiated in Harlem to offset years of decline and disinvestment. By 2000 Starbucks had arrived in Harlem, touching off complicated questions about who belongs in Harlem and to whom Harlem belongs. As far back as 1930, James Weldon Johnson had presciently asked: "Will the Negroes of Harlem be able to hold it?" (p. 158). At the dawn of the twenty-first century, gentrification offers a window into the past, present, and unknown future definition(s) of Harlem.

BIBLIOGRAPHY

Anderson, Jervis. 1981. *This Was Harlem: A Cultural Portrait, 1900–1950.* New York: Farrar, Straus and Giroux.

Ellison, Ralph. [1948] 1995. Harlem Is Nowhere. In *Shadow and Act.* New York: Vintage.

Hughes, Langston. [1940] 1986. *The Big Sea: An Autobiography.* New York: Thunder's Mouth Press.

Johnson, James Weldon. 1930. *Black Manhattan.* New York: Da Capo Press.

Osofsky, Gilbert. 1971. *Harlem: The Making of a Ghetto.* 2nd ed. New York: Harper Torchbooks.

Taylor, Monique. 2002. *Harlem: Between Heaven and Hell.* Minneapolis: University of Minnesota Press.

Monique M. Taylor

HARLEM RENAISSANCE

The Harlem Renaissance (c. 1918–1935) was a blossoming of African American creative arts associated with the larger New Negro movement, a multifaceted phenomenon that helped set the directions African American writers and artists would pursue throughout the twentieth century. The social foundations of the movement included the Great Migration of African Americans from rural to urban spaces and from South to North, dramatically rising levels of literacy, and the development of national organizations dedicated to pressing African American civil rights (the NAACP), "uplifting" the race and opening up socioeconomic opportunities (the National Urban League), and developing race pride, including Pan-African sensibilities and programs (the United Negro Improvement Association and the Pan-African conferences). Black exiles and expatriates from the Caribbean and Africa crossed paths in metropoles like New York and Paris following World War I (1914–1918) and had an invigorating influence on each other that gave the broader "Negro renaissance" (as it was then known) a profoundly important international cast.

The term *Harlem Renaissance*, which became popular in later years, particularly after the term *Negro* lost currency, derives from the fact that Harlem served as a symbolic capital of the cultural awakening, a dynamic crucible of cultural cross-fertilization, and a highly popular nightlife destination. Harlem was a relatively new black neighborhood becoming virtually a black city just north of Central Park, and it attracted a remarkable concentration of intellect and talent. More "liberal" in matters of race than most American cities (although, of course, racism was rampant), New York had an extraordinarily diverse and decentered black social world in which no one group could monopolize cultural authority, making it a particularly fertile place for cultural experimentation. Moreover, being situated in New York—the publishing capital of the Western Hemisphere, one of the world's great ports, and the financial as well as cultural capital of the United States—put Harlem in a strategic position for developing black arts and sending them out to the world. Few of the well-known black writers or artists were born in Harlem, but almost all of them passed through it, were inspired by it, or achieved their reputations in part because of what happened there.

The Harlem Renaissance took place at a time when European and white American writers and artists were particularly interested in African American artistic production, in part because of their interest in the "primitive." Modernist primitivism was a multifaceted phenomenon partly inspired by Freudian psychology, but it tended to extol so-called "primitive" peoples as enjoying a more direct and authentic relationship to the natural world and to simple human feeling than so-called "over-civilized" whites. They therefore were presumed by some to hold the key to the renovation of the arts. Early in the twentieth century, European avant-garde artists including Pablo Picasso (1881–1974) had been inspired in part by African masks to break from earlier representational styles toward abstraction in painting and sculpture. The prestige of these revolutionary experiments caused African American intellectuals to look on African artistic traditions with new appreciation and to imagine new forms of self-representation, a desire reinforced by rising interest in black history. Black History Week, now Black History Month, was first celebrated in 1928 at the instigation of the historian Carter G. Woodson (1875–1950).

The interest in black heritage coincided with a general interest, among American intellectuals and artists generally, in defining an "American" culture distinct from that of Europe and characterized by ethnic pluralism as well as a democratic ethos. Thus the concept of cultural pluralism inspired notions of the United States as the first "transnational" nation, in which diverse heritages should develop side-by-side in harmony rather than be "melted" together or ranked on a scale of evolving "civilization." W. E. B. Du Bois (1868–1963), the dominant black intellectual of the day, had already advocated something like this position in his famous book, *The Souls of Black Folk* (1903), a defining text of the New Negro movement because of its profound effect on an entire generation that formed the core of the Harlem Renaissance.

According to Du Bois and his colleague at the NAACP, James Weldon Johnson (1871–1938), the only uniquely "American" expressive traditions in the United States had been developed by African Americans because they, more than any other group, had been forced to remake themselves in the New World, while whites continued to look to Europe, or sacrificed artistic values to commercial ones. The very oppression that African Americans had suffered had made them the prophets and artistic vanguard of "American" culture. This judgment was reinforced by the immense popularity of African American music, especially jazz, worldwide. The popularity of jazz among whites was shaped in part by interest in the "primitive and exotic" and helped spark a "Negro Vogue" in cities like New York and Paris in the mid to late 1920s. Simultaneously, European dramatists extolled the body language of African American dance and stage humor (descended from blackface minstrelsy, America's most popular and original form of theatrical comedy). The most well-known white man to bring attention to the "Harlem" Renaissance was undoubtedly Carl Van Vechten (1880–1964), whose music criticism extolled jazz and blues and whose provocatively titled novel *Nigger Heaven* (1926) helped spread the Negro Vogue, serving virtually as a tourist guide to Harlem and capitalizing on the supposed "exotic" aspects of black urban life, even while focusing, primarily, on the frustrations of black urban professionals and aspiring writers. Vilified by many but defended by the likes of Langston Hughes (1902–1967), James Weldon Johnson, and Nella Larsen (1893–1963), Van Vechten became a key contact for several black artists and authors because of his interracial parties and publishing connections.

In addition to primitivism, the tendencies to press for "authentic" American art forms, and to find them in black America, led black writers to "the folk" at a time when American anthropologists led by Franz Boas (1858–1942) were revolutionizing their discipline with arguments against the racist paradigms of the past. The "folk"—people of the rural South particularly, but also the new migrants to northern cities—were presumed to carry the seeds of black artistic development with relative autonomy from "white" traditions. Thus James Weldon Johnson, in *God's Trombones* (1927), set traditional African American sermons in free-verse poetic forms modeled on the techniques of black preachers. Jean Toomer (1894–1967) was inspired by southern folk songs and jazz to lyrical modifications of prose form. Most famously, Langston Hughes turned to the blues for a poetic form derived from and answering to the desires, needs, and aesthetic sensibilities of the black working class. Sterling Brown (1901–1989) followed Hughes in a similar spirit with ballads and other poetic forms, attempting to catch the spirit of the folk heritage without merely imitating "folk" performance.

The Jamaican-born author and radical socialist Claude McKay (1889–1948) produced "proletarian" novels extolling the primitive authenticity and vitality of the black working class in *Home to Harlem* (1928) and *Banjo* (1929), a Pan-Africanist novel set in Marseilles, France. More influentially, Zora Neale Hurston (1891–1960)—an anthropologist and folklorist partly trained by Franz Boas—developed a new language and approach to narrative fiction inspired by black "folk" expressive traditions, most famously and successfully in her novel *Their Eyes Were Watching God* (1937).

In a completely different register, Nella Larsen explored the psychology of urban sophisticates in her novels *Quicksand* (1928) and *Passing* (1929), analyzing the psychological intricacies of race consciousness, and exposing the massive pressures to subordinate women's sexuality to the rules of "race" and class. The daughter of a white immigrant from Denmark and a black West Indian cook, Larsen knew intimately the price that color-line culture exacted of those who transgressed its most fundamental rules, and her fiction remains unequaled for the originality and incisiveness with which it exposes the contradictions of identities founded on the assertion of absolute difference between "black" and "white." Hers was a unique achievement at a time when de facto and de jure segregation were becoming ever more entrenched features of American society.

By the mid-1930s, the optimism of the "renaissance" was wearing thin as the Great Depression clamped down and Marxist orientations (never absent from the renaissance) gained dominance. Black writers—above all,

Langston Hughes, who had emerged as one of the stars of the "renaissance" and began working in numerous genres—began defining their new directions in contrast to the renaissance of the 1920s, describing the work of the earlier decade as too "racialist" in orientation (as opposed to Marxist and class-conscious) and as too dependent on wealthy white "patrons." The characterization was reductive, as most such attempts at generational self-definition tend to be. Today it is clear that the Harlem Renaissance marked a turning point in black cultural history and helped establish the authority of black artists over the representation of black culture and experience, while creating a semiautonomous aesthetic field in the realm of "high culture" that has continuously expanded.

SEE ALSO *Du Bois, W. E. B.; Hurston, Zora Neale; Pan-Africanism*

BIBLIOGRAPHY

Edwards, Brent Hayes. 2003. *The Practice of Diaspora: Literature, Translation, and the Rise of Black Internationalism.* Cambridge, MA: Harvard University Press.

Huggins, Nathan Irvin. 1971. *Harlem Renaissance.* New York and Oxford: Oxford University Press.

Hutchinson, George. 1995. *The Harlem Renaissance in Black and White.* Cambridge, MA: Harvard University Press.

Lewis, David Levering. 1981. *When Harlem Was in Vogue.* New York: Random House.

George Hutchinson

HARRIS, ABRAM L., JR.
1899–1963

Abram Lincoln Harris Jr., an African American scholar and activist, was born in 1899 in Richmond, Virginia, and finished his undergraduate work in 1922 at Virginia State University, a historically black college in Petersburg, Virginia, near his hometown. He completed an MA in economics at the University of Pittsburgh in 1924, and received his PhD in political economy at Columbia University in 1930. Harris served as a faculty member and chair of the Department of Economics at Howard University, the capstone of black higher education, in Washington, D.C., from 1927 to 1945 and subsequently served on the faculty of the University of Chicago until his death in 1963.

Harris was the first African American PhD in economics who pursued a rigorous academic career, publishing fifty works, including two seminal books and important essays in leading economics journals, such as the *Journal of Political Economy* and the *American*

Economic Review. He also wrote extensively for public intellectual and activist journals, including *Opportunity,* the *Crisis,* the *Nation,* and the *New Republic.* His early scholarly books and articles focused on the economic conditions of African Americans and the best strategy to ameliorate these conditions. These studies reflected a decidedly activist and Marxian inclination. His later work retreated from concrete strategies of social reform and focused instead on the doctrines of economic reform in the writings of Karl Marx (1818–1883), Thorstein Veblen (1857–1929), and John Stuart Mill (1806–1873).

During his early professional years in the 1930s, Harris played a pivotal role in the critical and contentious debate over the best strategy for black progress in the United States. He decried the strategy of "black capitalism" as unrealistic (Harris 1936) and advocated instead the formation of a national multiracial working-class party to bring about social reform (Spero and Harris 1931). Leading the "Young Turks" of the Second Amenia Conference in 1933, and with W. E. B. Du Bois (1868–1963) looking on with general favor, he proposed that the U.S. African American leadership change course from its focus on civil rights (i.e., legal and political reform organized around individual cases) and undertake instead a more radical, class-based, mass approach to social reform. The following year, at the request of the NAACP's board chair Joel Spingarn (1875–1939), Harris assembled the Committee on the Future Plan and Program of the NAACP, which proposed a breathtaking reform of the organization that, if implemented, would have transformed it into a politically active workers' university with local chapters serving as branch campuses. This reform would have immersed the NAACP in labor advocacy and education, laying the intellectual basis for black-white labor action on immediate issues, including pensions, unemployment insurance, child and female labor, lynching, public discrimination, and Jim Crow (Holloway 2002, pp. 93–100).

The radical Abram Harris of the 1930s rejected interracial conciliation of the Booker T. Washington (1856–1915) variety, the civil libertarianism of Walter White (1893–1955), and the militant race-consciousness of Marcus Garvey (1887–1940). He opposed the more nuanced version of race consciousness advanced by Du Bois, who argued (Du Bois 1940, chap. 7) for a period of self-segregation by African Americans, during which time they would form consumer and producer collectives to create a strong social foundation that would allow them to ultimately unify with white workers (currently blinded by racial prejudice) in establishing a socialist United States. Du Bois advocated this position as early as May 1933 in his address to the Conference on the Economic Status of the Negro sponsored by the Rosenwald Fund (Lewis 2000, p. 311). Harris rejected this strategy while fully recognizing the extraordinary challenge of bridging the racial chasm in the labor movement (Spero and Harris 1931).

Harris left Howard University and joined the faculty at the University of Chicago in 1945, a transition that marked (but did not initiate) a dramatic change in his worldview and intellectual focus. Leaving behind both his sympathy for Marx and his focus on social reform to achieve black progress, he adopted the moderate socialism of John Stuart Mill. Mill's philosophy accepts the individualist assumptions about human nature and society, assumptions that Harris had earlier skewered in defending the class perspective of Marx (Harris 1935). His rejection of Marxian tenets (Harris 1950) coincided with his withdrawal from engagement in the struggle for black progress. Enhancing human capital through better education and a stronger home life, he came to believe, would allow his black brethren to succeed in the marketplace. This point of view largely accepts the false promise that the market will, in a competitive process, reward firms that recognize talent regardless of race; the problem of racial inequity thus has a labor supply-side solution (Harris 1964). The solution to the race problem lay in improving black character and skills, a familiar theme sounded by today's conservatives who oppose positive legal and economic action that might compensate for the legacy of slavery, sharecropping, Jim Crow laws and practices, and contemporary racial discrimination.

At Chicago, Harris remained close to his lifelong friend Frank Knight (1885–1972), the renowned conservative economist, and even found common ground with archconservative Milton Friedman (1912–2006) (Broder 2006; Darity 1989). Students at the University of Chicago considered Harris one of their best teachers, and he won the Quantrell Prize for Excellence in Undergraduate Teaching in 1961. Chicago posthumously honored Harris's contributions to undergraduate education by naming a series of scholarship awards in his honor in 1976. Harris's work remains seminal in the debate on the strategic way forward for black progress, ironically occupying important positions on dramatically opposite sides of the debate.

SEE ALSO *Capitalism; Du Bois, W. E. B.; Human Capital; Inequality, Racial; Marxism; National Association for the Advancement of Colored People (NAACP); Politics, Black; Socialism*

BIBLIOGRAPHY

PRIMARY WORKS

Harris, Abram L. 1935. The Marxian Right to the Whole Product. In *Economic Essays in Honor of Wesley Clair Mitchell.* New York: Columbia University Press. Reprinted in Harris 1989, 236–301.

Harris, Abram L. 1936. *The Negro as Capitalist: A Study of Banking and Business among American Negroes.* Philadelphia: American Academy of Political and Social Science.

Harris, Abram L. 1950. Utopian Elements in Marx's Thought. *Ethics* 60 (2): 79–99. Reprinted in Harris 1989, 302–329.

Harris, Abram L. 1964. Education and the Economic Status of Negroes. In *100 Years of Emancipation*, ed. Robert A. Goldwin, 129–157. Chicago: Rand McNally. Reprinted in Harris 1989, 100–123.

Harris, Abram L. 1989. *Race, Radicalism, and Reform: Selected Papers.* Ed. William Darity Jr. New Brunswick, NJ: Transaction.

Spero, Sterling D., and Abram L. Harris. 1931. *The Black Worker: The Negro and the Labor Movement.* New York: Columbia University Press.

SECONDARY WORKS

Broder, David S. 2006. Free Thinking to the End. *Washington Post*, November 23.

Darity, William, Jr. 1989. Introduction: The Odyssey of Abram Harris from Howard to Chicago. In *Race, Radicalism, and Reform: Selected Papers*, by Abram L. Harris, ed. William Darity Jr., 1–34. New Brunswick, NJ: Transaction.

Du Bois, W. E. B. 1940. *Dusk of Dawn: An Essay toward an Autobiography of a Race Concept.* New York: Harcourt.

Holloway, Jonathan S. 2002. *Confronting the Veil: Abram Harris Jr., E. Franklin Frazier, and Ralph Bunche, 1919–1941.* Chapel Hill: University of North Carolina Press.

Lewis, David Levering. 2000. *W. E. B. Du Bois: The Fight for Equality and the American Century, 1919–1963.* New York: Holt.

Rodney D. Green
Marie-José Kouassi

HARRIS, JUDITH RICH

SEE *Peer Effects.*

HARRIS-TODARO MODEL

In the 1960s the government of newly independent Kenya faced a difficult situation: Unemployment in Nairobi and other major cities was high and apparently rising. To cope with this problem, Tripartite Agreements were reached in which private-sector and public-sector employers agreed to increase employment in exchange for unions agreeing to hold wages at their current levels. The larger number of jobs was expected to reduce unemployment. However, in the event, urban unemployment appeared to have *increased* following the Tripartite Agreements rather than decreased, as far as anyone could tell.

In light of these events, John Harris and Michael Todaro formulated the Harris-Todaro model to explain the puzzle. At the core of the Harris-Todaro model were the following features. First, real wages (adjusted for cost-of-living differences) are higher in urban formal-sector jobs than in rural traditional-sector jobs. Second, to be hired for a formal-sector job, one has to be physically present in the urban areas where the formal-sector jobs are located. Third, and as a consequence of the first two features, more workers search for formal-sector jobs than are hired, employers hire some of the job seekers but not all of them, and those not hired end up unemployed. Fourth, for equality to be maintained between the expected wage associated with searching for an urban job and the expected wage associated with taking up a lower-paying rural job, the equilibrium arising in such a setting is characterized by urban unemployment. And fifth, any temporary difference in the expected wages between one sector and another is eroded as workers migrate from the low-expected-wage labor market to the high-expected-wage labor market.

The Harris-Todaro model produced two powerful policy results. The first concerns the policy of formal-sector job creation to employ the unemployed (who, in the Harris-Todaro model, are all in urban areas, because that is where the formal-sector jobs are assumed to be located). Such a policy, they concluded, would increase the formal-sector labor force by more than the number of new jobs created, thereby raising the number of urban unemployed. Thus, the solution to urban unemployment is *not* to create urban employment.

The second policy option that Harris and Todaro considered was a policy of rural development. If such a program could increase the rural traditional-sector wage, unemployment would then fall. Thus, in the Harris-Todaro model, the solution to urban unemployment is rural development.

Soon after the model was published, the government of Kenya followed the Harris-Todaro precepts by putting into place an integrated program of rural development. The result was that unemployment in Kenya fell.

Harris and Todaro's fundamental contribution was building a model that fit the stylized facts of the labor market they were analyzing and that was based on sound micro foundations. The fact that the model remains part of the economist's intellectual toolkit today is a tribute to its basic insight and enduring analytic power.

The original model has been both simplified for some purposes and expanded for others by later contributors, including Stiglitz, Bell, Khan, Anand and Joshi, Bourguignon, Corden and Findlay, and others (Fields

2005). Harris and Todaro formulated general processes for determining prices of the products produced by the two sectors and also for determining a rural-sector wage that varies inversely with the number of people in the rural sector. A simplified version of the Harris-Todaro model was developed in which product prices and rural-sector wages are taken as constant. Numerous additional analytic and policy results were derived in the simplified Harris-Todaro model. At the same time, some of the assumptions of the Harris-Todaro model were judged to be too restrictive, and so the model was generalized in the years that followed to nest their specific formulation within a broader framework. The initial Harris-Todaro model has been extended to allow for on-the-job search from a rural agriculture setting, the existence of an urban informal sector, preferential hiring of the better-educated, employment fixity, duality of production conditions and earnings levels within the rural sector, capital mobility, endogenous urban wage setting, risk aversion, and a system of demand for goods, among other factors.

As an early multisector labor-market model, the Harris-Todaro model set forth a principal alternative framework for policy analysis. It showed how employment and wage levels in one labor market reflect supply, demand, and institutional conditions not only in that labor market but also in other labor markets.

In terms of pro-poor economic growth, the Harris-Todaro model and other multisector-labor-market models can help policy makers avoid two mistakes. One is to assume that development efforts should be channeled to the sectors where the poor are. The other is to assume that efforts should always be focused on getting the poor out of the sectors in which they now are. Careful cost-benefit analysis based on well-specified labor-market models is required to decide among such alternatives.

SEE ALSO *Development Economics; Distortions; Dual Economy; Migration*

BIBLIOGRAPHY

Fields, Gary S. 2005. A Guide to Multisector Labor Market Models. Social Protection Discussion Paper Number 0505. Washington, DC: World Bank.

Harris, John, and Michael Todaro. 1970. Migration, Unemployment, and Development: A Two-Sector Analysis. *American Economic Review* 60: 126–142.

Gary S. Fields

HART-CELLAR ACT

SEE *Immigrants, Black.*

HARTZ, LOUIS
1918–1986

Louis Hartz, the distinguished American political philosopher and intellectual historian, was to some degree a one-book celebrity scholar. His notable *The Liberal Tradition in America*, published in 1955, offered an original and influential interpretation of the American liberal paradigm that has remained at the center of debates over liberalism ever since. It was this book alone that defined Hartz's career.

Hartz was born in 1918 in Youngstown, Ohio, to Russian immigrant parents, and grew up in Omaha. He spent most of his professional life at Harvard University. Hartz graduated from Harvard College in 1940 (supported in part by a scholarship from the *Omaha World-Herald*, as well as by a job waiting tables), and earned his PhD from Harvard in 1946. Ten years later he was a professor in Harvard's Department of Government and the celebrated author of *The Liberal Tradition*. His Harvard lectures on eighteenth and nineteenth century European thought, and on American political theory and historiography, were notable and influential.

Hartz's doctoral dissertation on the political and economic doctrines behind constitutional and political thinking in Pennsylvania after the Revolution was published as *Economic Policy and Democratic Thought: Pennsylvania, 1776–1860*, and helped set the agenda for his thinking about American liberalism. His later work included a volume he edited called *The Founding of New Societies* (1964) and his lectures on European thought, edited by Paul Roazen and published in 1990 as *The Necessity of Choice: Nineteenth Century European Political Theory*. The collection of essays published in *The Founding of New Societies* used the American founding experience as a comparative template to examine other new constitutions in Canada, Australia, and elsewhere. It also served to highlight Hartz's own view of American liberalism as a unique manifestation rooted in a special history.

The core work in Hartz's lifelong study of liberalism in its American and European settings, however, was *The Liberal Tradition in America: An Interpretation of American Political Thought since the Revolution* ([1955] 1991); everything he taught and wrote revolved around its arguments. The book won both the Woodrow Wilson Prize in 1956 and the Lippincott Prize (for a significant work still in print fifteen years after its publication) several decades later. Samuel Beer's summary of the book's thesis—"America's democratic capitalism was so powerful that it excluded any ideas of socialism or Toryism"—only touched the surface of Hartz's argument, which focused on what Hartz understood to be America's defining narrative as a centrist society dominated by Locke's liberal consensualism. Locke might have appeared as a revolutionary figure and Enlightenment leader to France in the eighteenth century, as that country was deeply bound by feudalism. But in America, where landed property and feudal jurisdictions had never taken hold, Locke was a benign model of liberal consensus politics.

An historian as well as a theorist, Hartz embedded his argument about America's putative centrist tendencies in the story of an exceptionalist country that, lacking a feudal past, was immune to socialist revolutionary appeals. In Hartz's pithy words, "one of the central characteristics of a nonfeudal society is that it lacks a genuine revolutionary tradition, the tradition which in Europe has been linked with the Puritan and French revolutions.... And this being the case, it also lacks a tradition of reaction: lacking Robespierre it lacks Maistre, lacking Sydney it lacks Charles II" (1991, p. 5). No feudalism, no socialism; no traditionalism, no radicalism, and hence no reaction against radicalism. The result in the United States was a nation that never strayed too far from the center. Those individuals who did stray, whether Southern "feudalists" or modern socialists, exhibited in Hartz's view a similar "fecklessness."

Hartz used his analysis of liberalism in America to examine liberalism and revolution around the world. He worried less about the tyranny of the majority—a "puppy dog forever tethered to a lion's leash"—than about whether people born equal could "ever understand peoples elsewhere that have to become so" (1991, p. 309). There is evidence enough today that they cannot.

Hartz became ill in the early 1970s and resigned from Harvard. His last years were tragic. He withdrew from family and friends and traveled the world with a kind of despondent urgency, stopping in London, Zurich, and New Delhi, and eventually reaching Turkey, where he died in 1986. A few years before his death he assembled extended but wildly uneven notes for a work to be called "A Synthesis of World History" (later privately printed as a typescript by Humanities Press in Zurich). This sprawling essay, an opus of Spenglerian ambitions, concludes with a turgid and frightening chapter on a Manichean "last battle" between Jihadists and pluralists. It envisioned an "explosion of fear" associated with a "drive for a single absolute" on the part of radical Islam and related movements, against which forces of diversity would be compelled to do battle—or witness the eclipse of civilization. Seen by many at the time as an expression of Hartz's psychological problems, this final unfinished work today seems to exhibit a kind of perverse prescience, and reminds us that even after he had ceased to function as a scholar and teacher, Hartz continued to evince an ingenious mind informed by a brilliant if perfervid imagination. It was Hartz's pedagogical and intellectual imagina-

tion that may explain why the author of a single great book written over a half century ago can continue to excite philosophers and historians into the new millennium.

SEE ALSO *Civilizations, Clash of; Democracy; Egalitarianism; Fundamentalism; Jihad; Liberalism; Tocqueville, Alexis de*

BIBLIOGRAPHY

Diggins, John Patrick. 1984. *The Lost Soul of American Politics: Virtue, Self-interest, and the Foundations of Liberalism.* New York: Basic Books.

Hartz, Louis. 1948. *Economic Policy and Democratic Thought: Pennsylvania, 1776–1860.* Cambridge, MA: Harvard University Press.

Hartz, Louis, ed. 1964. *The Founding of New Societies: Studies in the History of the United States, Latin America, South Africa, Canada, and Australia.* New York: Harcourt, Brace, & World.

Hartz, Louis. 1990. *The Necessity of Choice: Nineteenth-Century European Political Theory,* ed. Paul Roazen. New Brunswick, NJ: Transaction Publishers.

Hartz, Louis. 1991. *The Liberal Tradition in America: An Interpretation of American Political Thought since the Revolution.* 2nd ed. San Diego, CA: Harcourt Brace Jovanovich. First edition originally published in 1955 (New York: Harcourt Brace).

Masur, Louis P., ed. 1999. *The Challenge of American History.* Baltimore, MD: Johns Hopkins University Press.

Benjamin R. Barber

HARVEY, DAVID

SEE *Geography.*

HATE CRIMES

Although crimes against individuals based on their race, religion, ethnicity, and sexual orientation have a long and ignoble history throughout the world, the term *hate crime* was first popularized in the United States. In 1985 three members of the U.S. House of Representatives introduced legislation requiring the U.S. government to collect and publish statistical information on the growing number of bias-motivated crimes committed throughout the country. Enacted in April 1990, the Hate Crimes Statistics Act requires the U.S. Department of Justice to acquire and publish data from local law enforcement agencies on crimes that "manifest prejudice based on race, religion, sexual orientation or ethnicity." The coverage was expanded to include disability in 1997. According to the

Federal Bureau of Investigation (FBI), "a hate crime, also known as a bias crime, is a criminal offense committed against a person, property, or society which is motivated, in whole or in part, by the offender's bias against a race, religion, disability, sexual orientation, or ethnicity/national origin."

The first FBI hate crimes report was published in 1993 and covered the calendar year 1991. Although this report, *Hate Crime Statistics*, is the official U.S. government tabulation of these crimes, some ethnic and other advocacy groups—including the National Asian Pacific American Legal Consortium and the National Coalition of Anti-Violence Programs, a gay rights organization—conduct their own annual audits of hate crimes. These groups claim that the FBI statistics underreport the number of hate crimes because victims are often afraid to contact law enforcement officials, fearing either stigmatization or the jeopardizing of their status as recent immigrants.

Prior to the passage of national hate crimes reporting legislation, the Anti-Defamation League (ADL)—the preeminent Jewish civil rights organization in the United States—drafted model hate crimes legislation in the early 1980s to punish criminal actions aimed at racial and other minority groups, including Jews. As of 2006, forty-six states and the District of Columbia have enacted legislation similar to the ADL model. These laws cover a wide variety of criminal activities, including vandalism directed at religious institutions and bias-motivated violence against individuals. Many states have enacted "penalty enhancement" statutes for hate crimes.

Some late twentieth-century bias-motivated crimes have received national attention. When a Hasidic Jewish driver accidentally ran over a seven-year-old African American boy in a Brooklyn, New York, neighborhood in 1991, an anti-Jewish riot ensued and local black youths murdered Yankel Rosenbaum, a visiting Australian scholar. On October 6, 1998, Matthew Shepard, a gay college student in Laramie, Wyoming, was savagely beaten because of his sexual orientation and later died. Earlier that year, James Byrd Jr., a forty-nine-year-old African American man was chained to a pickup truck in Jasper, Texas, and dragged to his death. His attackers were members of a white supremacist group.

Why should a hate crime be treated differently than any other criminal activity directed at individuals or property? What is the legal justification for enhancing the punishment for these crimes? These questions have persisted since the passage of the earliest hate crimes legislation and continue to provoke vigorous debate among legal scholars, legislators, and law enforcement officials. In his scholarly legal and philosophical defense of hate crime statutes, *Punishing Hate*, law professor Frederick M. Lawrence noted that:

> Bias crimes spread fear and intimidation beyond the immediate victims to those who share only racial characteristics with the victims. Members of the target group suffer injuries similar to those felt by the direct victim of the actual crime.... Bias crimes, therefore, cause a greater harm to a society's collective living standard than do parallel crimes ... and thus warrant enhanced criminal punishment. (Lawrence 1999, p. 63)

Legal scholars James B. Jacobs and Kimberly Potter, however, suggest that hate crime laws are unnecessary and create new crime categories that "may exacerbate rather than ameliorate social schisms and conflict" (1998, p. 144). Despite the continuing intellectual debate about the merits of hate crime statutes, the constitutional basis for these laws has been affirmed in the 1993 Supreme Court decision *Wisconsin v. Mitchell.* In addition, some state courts have upheld the legality of these laws.

Outside the United States, some European countries have enacted laws to criminalize hate crimes. The Vienna Declaration and Programme of Action, adopted in 1993 by the United Nations World Conference on Human Rights, calls on governments around the world to adopt measures "to counter intolerance and related violence based on religion or belief" and other practices directed against different minority groups. In 2005 Human Rights First—formerly the Lawyers Committee for Human Rights—conducted a study of the fifty-five members of the OSCE (Organization for Security and Cooperation in Europe) and found that nineteen of the fifty-five OSCE member states had enacted legislation declaring that racist motivation in crimes is to be "considered an aggravating circumstance in sentencing" (McClintock 2005, p. vii). Only five surveyed OSCE countries had hate crime statutes for bias-motivated crimes based on sexual orientation. Most third world countries do not have hate crimes legislation comparable to the West; some Muslim countries, in fact, prosecute homosexual behavior and there is occasional government-sanctioned or citizen-sponsored violence directed at gay men and lesbians.

BIBLIOGRAPHY

Altschiller, Donald. 2005. *Hate Crimes: A Reference Handbook.* 2nd ed. Santa Barbara, CA: ABC-CLIO.

Federal Bureau of Investigation. Hate Crime Statistics. 1995–2005. http://www.fbi.gov/hq/cid/civilrights/hate.htm.

Gerstenfeld, Phyllis B. 2004. *Hate Crimes: Causes, Controls, and Controversies.* Thousand Oaks, CA: Sage.

Jacobs, James B., and Kimberly Potter. 1998. *Hate Crimes: Criminal Law and Identity Politics.* New York: Oxford University Press.

Lawrence, Frederick M. 1999. *Punishing Hate: Bias Crimes under American Law.* Cambridge, MA: Harvard University Press.

McClintock, Michael. 2005. *Everyday Fears: A Survey of Violent Hate Crimes in Europe and North America.* Washington, DC: Human Rights First.

United National High Commissioner for Human Rights: World Conference on Human Rights in Vienna on 25 June 1993. Vienna Declaration and Programme of Action. http://www.ohchr.org/english/law/vienna.htm.

Donald Altschiller

HAUSMAN TESTS

Hausman tests (Hausman 1978) are tests for econometric model misspecification based on a comparison of two different estimators of the model parameters. The estimators compared should have the properties that (1) under the null hypothesis of correct model specification both estimators are consistent for the "true parameters" of the model (those corresponding to the data generating process), whereas (2) under misspecification (the alternative hypothesis) the estimators should have differing probability limits. The former property ensures that the size of the test can be controlled asymptotically, and the latter property gives the test its power. Heuristically, the key idea is that when the model is correctly specified, the compared estimators will be close to one another, but when the model is misspecified, the compared estimators will be far apart.

A Hausman statistic is constructed as a function of the difference between the two estimators. The sampling distribution of the Hausman statistic determines how big a difference is too big to be compatible with the null hypothesis of correct specification. One performs a Hausman test by comparing the Hausman statistic to a critical value obtained from its sampling distribution, and rejecting the null hypothesis of correct specification if the Hausman statistic exceeds its critical value. The large sample distribution of the Hausman statistic is straightforward to derive; a high-level analysis appears below. This distribution simplifies usefully when one of the compared estimators is efficient under the null, as originally proposed by Jerry Hausman (1978).

Two examples originally considered by Hausman help illustrate the ideas. First, consider estimating the coefficients of a single equation, say the first, of a system of linear simultaneous equations. Provided (among other things) that the system of equations is correctly specified, it is a standard result that both the two-stage least squares (2SLS) and the three-stage least squares (3SLS) estimators of the parameters of this equation are consistent. Further, under standard assumptions, the 3SLS estimator is asymptotically efficient; in particular, it is efficient relative

to the 2SLS estimator. The difference between 2SLS and 3SLS will tend to be small in this situation. On the other hand, if one of the equations of the system is misspecified, then 3SLS is generally an inconsistent estimator for the parameters of every equation of the system. If the first equation is not misspecified, then 2SLS remains consistent. The difference between 2SLS and 3SLS may be large in this situation. Thus, by comparing the 2SLS and 3SLS estimators for one or more equations of a system of linear simultaneous equations, one can gain insight into the question of whether some equations of that system may be misspecified.

Another example treated by Hausman involves comparison of two different estimators for the parameters of a panel data regression model. Specifically, it is well known that both the "random effects" and the "fixed effects" panel estimators are consistent under the assumption that the model is correctly specified and that (among other things) the regressors are independent of the "individual-specific effects" (the "random effects" assumption). In this case, the random effects estimator is also asymptotically efficient. The difference between the random effects and the fixed effects estimators will thus tend to be small. On the other hand, if the random effects assumption fails but the model is otherwise correctly specified, then the fixed effects estimator remains consistent, but the random effects estimator is inconsistent. The difference between the random effects and the fixed effects estimators may therefore be large. A comparison of the random and fixed effects estimators can thus shed light on the correctness of the random effects assumption.

The first application of this approach appears to be that of James Durbin (1954), who proposed a test for "errors in variables" in a linear regression, based on a comparison of ordinary least squares (OLS) and instrumental variables (IV) estimators. Under correct specification (no errors in variables), OLS is consistent and efficient, whereas IV is consistent but inefficient. Under misspecification, OLS is inconsistent but IV remains consistent. De-Min Wu (1973) also considered tests based on a comparison of OLS and IV estimators, describing applications to linear simultaneous equations (OLS vs. 2SLS) and dynamic panel models. Alice Nakamura and Masao Nakamura (1981) discuss the relations among the test statistics of Durbin (1954), Wu (1973), and Hausman (1978).

Although Hausman's initial motivation and examples concerned linear models and the orthogonality assumptions (e.g., independence) that are typically central to identification in econometric models, he particularly emphasizes the generality and unifying nature of the estimator comparison approach. Hausman's formal results apply not just to linear models, but to maximum likelihood methods generally. As Halbert White (1994, chap.

10.3) discusses, Hausman's approach further extends to quasi-maximum likelihood methods. This leads to useful specification tests based on two estimators such that (1) under partially correct specification both are consistent, but neither is necessarily efficient; and (2) under misspecification neither is necessarily consistent—it suffices merely that the estimators have differing probability limits.

Hausman's unifying approach extends even more broadly. As a straightforward illustration, we give a result establishing the large-sample properties of the Hausman statistic based on a comparison of two asymptotically linear estimators. A wide variety of econometric estimators, including quasi-maximum likelihood, method of moments, and empirical likelihood estimators are asymptotically linear.

ASSUMPTION A.1 (ASYMPTOTIC LINEARITY)

Suppose each of two estimators, say $\hat{\theta}_{1n}$ and $\hat{\theta}_{2n}$, is a random $q \times 1$ vector such that for finite $q \times 1$ nonstochastic vectors θ_j^*, $\hat{\theta}_{jn} \xrightarrow{p} \theta_j^*$, $j = 1, 2$. Suppose further that for each $j = 1, 2$ there exists a $q \times q$ nonstochastic matrix H_j^*, finite and nonsingular, and a random $q \times 1$ vector $s_{jn}^* = O_p(n^{-1/2})$ such that

$$\sqrt{n}(\hat{\theta}_{jn} - \theta_j^*) = H_j^{*-1} \sqrt{n} \, s_{jn}^* + o_p(1).$$

All limits here are taken as the sample size n tends to infinity. Our next assumption ensures the joint asymptotic normality of $\sqrt{n} \, s_{1n}^*$ and $\sqrt{n} \, s_{2n}^*$.

ASSUMPTION A.2 (JOINT ASYMPTOTIC NORMALITY)

For s_{jn}^* as in Assumption A.1, $j = 1, 2$, suppose that

$$\sqrt{n}(s_{1n}^{*\prime}, s_{2n}^{*\prime})' \xrightarrow{d} N(0, J^*),$$

where J^* is a finite $2q \times 2q$ nonstochastic matrix having $q \times q$ diagonal blocks J_{11}^*, J_{22}^* and $q \times q$ off-diagonal blocks $J_{12}^*, J_{21}^* = J_{12}^{*\prime}$.

Hausman statistics are based on the difference $\sqrt{n}(\hat{\theta}_{1n} - \hat{\theta}_{2n})$. If Assumptions A.1 and A.2 hold and if, as can usually be arranged, the assumption of correct model specification ensures that $\theta_1^* = \theta_2^*$, then it follows straightforwardly that

$$\sqrt{n}(\hat{\theta}_{1n} - \hat{\theta}_{2n}) \xrightarrow{d} N(0, V^*),$$

where

$$V^* \equiv H_1^{*-1} J_{11}^* H_1^{*-1\prime} - H_1^{*-1} J_{12}^* H_2^{*-1\prime} - H_2^{*-1} J_{21}^* H_1^{*-1\prime} + H_2^{*-1} J_{22}^* H_2^{*-1\prime}.$$

Under mild conditions, it is typically straightforward to obtain a covariance matrix estimator consistent for V^*.

Let $\hat{V}_n$ be such an estimator. If V^* is nonsingular, then an asymptotic chi-squared statistic is delivered by the analog of the Wald statistic,

$$n(\hat{\theta}_{1n} - \hat{\theta}_{2n})' \, \hat{V}_n^{-1}(\hat{\theta}_{1n} - \hat{\theta}_{2n}).$$

Nevertheless, a common occurrence in applications is that V^* fails to be nonsingular, due to the singularity of J^*. A straightforward remedy for this is to consider a subvector of $\sqrt{n}(\hat{\theta}_{1n} - \hat{\theta}_{2n})$ or, more generally, a linear combination $\sqrt{n} \, S(\hat{\theta}_{1n} - \hat{\theta}_{2n})$, where S is a known finite nonstochastic $k \times q$ matrix, $k \leq q$, such that $S V^* S'$ is nonsingular. A Hausman statistic can then be computed as the quadratic form

$$H_n \equiv n(\hat{\theta}_{1n} - \hat{\theta}_{2n})' \, S' \, [S \hat{V}_n S']^{-1} S(\hat{\theta}_{1n} - \hat{\theta}_{2n}).$$

In testing partially correct specification, S can also play a useful role by selecting or combining only those coefficients consistently estimated under partially correct specification.

We can now formally state the large-sample properties of this Hausman statistic.

PROPOSITION 1

Suppose Assumptions A.1 and A.2 hold and that S is a known finite nonstochastic $k \times q$ matrix of full row rank. (i) If the model is correctly specified, and if correct model specification implies that $S(\theta_1^* - \theta_2^*) = 0$ and $\hat{V}_n \xrightarrow{p} V^*$, where $S V^* S'$ is nonsingular, then $H_n \xrightarrow{d} \chi_k^2$. (ii) If the model is misspecified, and if model misspecification implies that $S(\theta_1^* - \theta_2^*) \neq 0$ and $\hat{V}_n \xrightarrow{p} W^*$, where W^* is a finite, nonstochastic $q \times q$ matrix such that $S W^* S'$ is nonsingular, then for any sequence $\{c_n\}$, $c_n = o(n^{-1})$, $P[H_n > c_n] \to 1$.

The respective proofs of (i) and (ii) follow those of Theorems 8.6 and 8.16 of White (1994).

Part (i) establishes that under the null hypothesis of correct specification, the Hausman statistic is distributed asymptotically as chi-squared with k degrees of freedom (χ_k^2), delivering convenient asymptotic critical values. Part (ii) describes the behavior of the Hausman statistic under the global alternative of model misspecification. This establishes the consistency of the test (power approaching one) for sequences of critical values going to infinity with n (but more slowly than n), thus driving the probability of Type I error to zero.

An important caveat for part (ii) is the necessity of the requirement that misspecification entails $S(\theta_1^* - \theta_2^*) \neq 0$. As Alberto Holly (1982) has pointed out, this can fail for particular types of misspecification in combination with particular choices of compared estimators. The

Hausman statistic just given is thus not guaranteed to yield a test consistent against arbitrary model misspecification. Nevertheless, a clever modification of the Hausman statistic proposed by Herman Bierens (1988) gives a variant of the Hausman test that does have this consistency property (see also Bierens 1990).

As mentioned above, the asymptotic distribution simplifies usefully when one of the compared estimators is efficient under correct specification. Specifically, the asymptotic covariance matrix of the estimator difference simplifies to the difference of the asymptotic covariance matrices. With asymptotic linearity, this arises because typically when one of the compared estimators (say $\hat{\theta}_{2n}$) is asymptotically efficient, then $J_{22}^* = H_2^*$ and $J_{12}^* = H_1^*$ (see Bates and White 1993). Substitution into the expression for V^* above then gives the more convenient expression

$$V^* \equiv H_1^{*-1} J_{11}^* H_1^{*-1'} - H_2^{*-1}.$$

The first term is the asymptotic covariance matrix of $\hat{\theta}_{1n}$; the second term is that of $\hat{\theta}_{2n}$. A direct benefit of this expression is that it suggests simpler forms for the covariance estimator $\hat{V}_n$.

The specific form given above for the Hausman statistic is only one of several possible forms. Hausman describes a convenient version for linear regression applications that involves testing whether certain transformations of the original regressors have zero coefficients. Russell Davidson and James MacKinnon (1993) discuss further convenient versions of the Hausman test based on "double-length" regressions. Applying the results of White (1994, chap. 9) yields further variants of the Hausman statistic that have convenient computation properties.

The focus here has been on parametric versions of the Hausman test. The unifying principle of estimator comparison for specification testing also extends to comparing parametric and nonparametric estimators and to comparing nonparametric estimators. White and Yongmiao Hong (1999) give some relevant theory and examples for these cases.

SEE ALSO *Fixed Effects Regression; Random Effects Regression; Specification Error*

BIBLIOGRAPHY

Bates, Charles, and Halbert White. 1993. Determination of Estimators with Minimum Asymptotic Covariance Matrices. *Econometric Theory* 9: 633–648.

Bierens, Herman. 1988. A Consistent Hausman-Type Model Specification Test. Vrije Universiteit Faculteit der Economische Wetenschappen Research Memorandum 1987–2 (rev.).

Bierens, Herman. 1990. A Consistent Conditional Moment Test of Functional Form. *Econometrica* 58: 1443–1458.

Davidson, Russell, and James MacKinnon. 1993. *Estimation and Inference in Econometrics*. New York: Oxford University Press.

Durbin, James. 1954. Errors in Variables. *Review of the International Statistical Institute* 22: 23–32.

Hausman, Jerry. 1978. Specification Tests in Econometrics. *Econometrica* 46: 1251–1272.

Holly, Alberto. 1982. A Remark on Hausman's Specification Test. *Econometrica* 50: 749–759.

Nakamura, Alice, and Masao Nakamura. 1981. On the Relationships among Several Specification Error Tests Presented by Durbin, Wu, and Hausman. *Econometrica* 49: 1582–1588.

White, Halbert. 1994. *Estimation, Inference, and Specification Analysis*. New York: Cambridge University Press.

White, Halbert, and Yongmiao Hong. 1999. M-Testing Using Finite and Infinite Dimensional Parameter Estimators. In *Cointegration, Causality, and Forecasting: A Festschrift in Honor of Clive W. J. Granger*, eds. Robert Engle and Halbert White, 326–345. Oxford: Oxford University Press.

Wu, De-Min. 1973. Alternative Tests of Independence Between Stochastic Regressors and Disturbances. *Econometrica* 41: 733–750.

Jerry A. Hausman
Halbert White

HAYEK, FRIEDRICH AUGUST VON
1899–1992

F. A. Hayek, as he is known throughout the English-speaking world, is generally considered to be the leading twentieth-century representative of classical, nineteenth-century liberalism and the foremost scourge of socialism. Hayek was a corecipient, with Gunnar Myrdal (1898–1987), of the Nobel Prize in Economic Science in 1974, awarded "for their pioneering work in the theory of money and economic fluctuations and for their penetrating analysis of the interdependence of economic, social and institutional phenomena" (Nobel Foundation).

Hayek was born in Vienna on May 8, 1899, into a family of academic distinction on both parental sides. Having served in the Austrian army as an artillery officer on the Piave front during the latter stages of World War I (1914–1918), he entered the University of Vienna and earned doctorates in both law (1921) and political science (1923). In 1927 he became director of the newly established Austrian Institute for Business Cycle Research. In January 1931 Hayek delivered a series of lectures at the London School of Economics and Political Science, subsequently published as *Prices and Production*. As a result of these lectures, he was appointed Tooke Professor of

Economic Science and Statistics in the University of London later that year. In 1950 he joined the interdisciplinary Committee on Social Thought at the University of Chicago as professor of social and moral sciences. He returned to Europe in 1962 as professor of economic policy at the University of Freiburg, Germany. In 1969 he accepted a visiting professorship at the University of Salzburg in his native Austria. Hayek died in Freiburg on March 23, 1992.

Hayek was a strong believer in the supreme power of ideas. In 1947 he convened a group of like-minded scholars dedicated to classical liberalism to a meeting in Vevey, Switzerland, and thus the Mont Pelerin Society was born. From the mid-1970s Hayek was a pivotal figure in the renaissance of Austrian economics in the United States, and his ideas have exerted increasing political influence through think tanks such as the Institute of Economic Affairs in London and the Washington-based Cato Institute.

Hayek has made lasting contributions not only to economics but also to legal philosophy, theoretical psychology, social anthropology, political philosophy, the methodology of the social sciences, and the history of ideas. The polymathic range, far from suggesting a lack of focus, is indicative of a magnificent architectonic unity to his work. Steeped in the teachings of the Austrian school of economics derived from Carl Menger (1840–1921), Friedrich von Wieser (1851–1926), and Eugen Böhm von Bawerk (1851–1914), his early work on economic theory focused on marrying monetary theory, trade-cycle theory, and the theory of capital. His policy recommendation of "waiting it out" during the years of the Great Depression brought him into immediate conflict with Keynesian notions of underinvestment and underconsumption. As Sir John Hicks (1904–1989) pointed out in a retrospective assessment, Hayek's model of the maladjusted time structure of production triggered by low interest rates is not so much a theory of fluctuation as a theory of growth. In this sense, Hayek's theory of overinvestment was much more applicable to the situation of the long-lasting Japanese recession of the 1980s and 1990s or to the predicament in the United States in the late 1990s when interest rates were held too low relative to higher expected returns on capital, encouraging excessive investment, reduced savings, and the biggest stock-market bubble in U.S. history. Given Hayek's objections to the possibility of measuring the money supply and of distinguishing sharply between money and other financial assets, it is full of irony to find him frequently dubbed "the father of monetarism."

It was also during his London years that Hayek, elaborating on an argument of his mentor, Ludwig von Mises (1881–1973), attended to the issue of rational economic calculation in planning under centralist socialism. His misgivings about the latter as a viable economic system were closely linked to his views on how knowledge is generated and disseminated in markets and paved the way for his notion of *competition as a discovery procedure* in a world where tastes and production techniques are frequently changing and knowledge about these matters is dispersed. Market transactions draw on the scattered—among market participants—bits of practical, local knowledge, facilitating increasingly complex layers of specialization of labor without relying on any directing agency. The role of market prices, however imperfect as signals they may be, is to enable their users to adapt to events and circumstances about whose existence they may not have any clue whatsoever. The interactions of market participants using their own specific knowledge for their own projects generate a *spontaneous order*. The essential point about such a regular pattern of activities is that (1) it is emphatically not the result of design, neither by a single nor by a group mind, and that (2) its complexity puts insuperable limitations on control and prediction of the overall behavior of the system. In this sense, Hayek's view of the workings of an economy is much more akin to biology than to mechanics.

Following in the footsteps of Scottish Enlightenment philosophers such as David Hume (1711–1776), Adam Smith (1723–1790), and Adam Ferguson (1723–1816), Hayek extended the notion of a spontaneously generated order to the evolution of social institutions such as law, language, and morals. The recognition of complex orders, and the nature of rules conducive to their formation and preservation, was the central enigma fueling Hayek's intellectual ambition. It took him almost fifty years to grasp its full significance and to put it as succinctly as possible. This was a remote, painstaking academic pursuit constituting Hayek's legacy as a scholar. But at the same time, he was a preacher possessed by an urge to save the world from collectivism.

SEE ALSO *Austrian Economics; Great Depression; Hume, David; Individualism; Keynes, John Maynard; Laissez Faire; Libertarianism; Liberty; Markets; Mises, Ludwig Edler von; Mont Pelerin Society; Scottish Moralists; Sraffa, Piero*

BIBLIOGRAPHY

PRIMARY WORKS

Hayek, F. A. 1935. *Prices and Production.* 2nd ed. London: Routledge.

Hayek, F. A. 1948. *Individualism and Economic Order.* Chicago: University of Chicago Press.

Hayek, F. A. 1960. *The Constitution of Liberty.* Chicago: University of Chicago Press.

Hayek, F. A. 1992. *The Collected Works of F. A. Hayek,* ed. Bruce Caldwell. Chicago: University of Chicago Press.

Hayek, F. A. 1994. *Hayek on Hayek: An Autobiographical Dialogue*, eds. Stephen Kresge and Leif Wenar. London: Routledge.

SECONDARY WORKS

Brittan, Samuel. 2005. Hayek's Contribution. In *Against the Flow: Reflections of an Individualist*, 300–315. London: Atlantic.

Caldwell, Bruce. 2004. *Hayek's Challenge: An Intellectual Biography of F. A. Hayek*. Chicago: University of Chicago Press.

Hicks, John. 1967. The Hayek Story. In *Critical Essays in Monetary Theory*, 203–215. Oxford: Clarendon.

Kukathas, Chandran. 1990. *Hayek and Modern Liberalism*. Oxford: Clarendon Press.

Machlup, Fritz, ed. 1976. *Essays on Hayek*. New York: New York University Press.

Nobel Foundation. 1974. Press Release: Sveriges Riksbank Prize in Economic Sciences in Memory of Alfred Nobel. http://nobelprize.org/nobel_prizes/economics/laureates/1974/press.html.

Stephan Boehm

HAYMARKET SQUARE RIOT

The Haymarket Square riot was a bloody confrontation between Chicago police and protesting workers. The state repression that followed in its wake left a permanent mark on U.S. and international politics. On May 4, 1886, a group of workers met in Haymarket Square in Chicago to protest an earlier police attack on workers that had left six people dead. The city had recently been the center of a bitter nationwide fight concerning the right of workers to an eight-hour workday.

Approximately three thousand workers turned out for the Haymarket protest. The mayor of Chicago, Carter Harrison (1825–1893), attended the meeting and informed police officials that the audience and the speakers were peaceful. The mayor and most of the workers left by 10:20 p.m., when a light rain set in. Only 500 workers remained when 180 Chicago policemen arrived to disband the meeting. A police official who had been in political conflict with the mayor ordered the immediate evacuation of the public square.

Just after the evacuation command was shouted, a dynamite bomb was thrown into the midst of the police. Whether the bomb was thrown by an agent provocateur or a worker has never been determined. The police responded with indiscriminate gunfire, killing both police officers and workers in the square. By morning almost all of the deaths in Haymarket Square had been blamed on labor leaders. This was the story reported by major newspapers, both locally and nationally, and it was the conclusion immediately reached by law enforcement officials.

Although there was no evidence linking them to the crime, eight prominent labor leaders and anarchists were arrested and tried for murder. The judge instructed the jury that evidence linking them to the deaths in Haymarket Square was not necessary for conviction. After a blatantly biased trial, seven of the men were found guilty and sentenced to death. Four men—Albert Parsons, August Spies, George Engel, and Adolph Fischer—were hanged on November 11, 1887, a date commemorated long after as Black Friday. The dominant media of the time portrayed the trial, the verdict, and the executions as triumphs of law and order.

The impact of the Haymarket Square riot, both on the labor movement and on American politics, was long-lasting. In the short term the Haymarket incident, after interpretation by the media, sparked America's first red scare. Locally Chicago police banned public meetings and attacked labor leaders, anarchists, and socialists. The fact that four men had been executed for the public expression of controversial ideas had a negative effect on all of these groups. Nationally there was wider coordinated repression of such groups. Haymarket was blamed for destroying the Knights of Labor, then America's largest and most inclusive labor union.

In the long run, however, the impact in the United States and internationally was more positive. The Haymarket narrative dramatized what came to be called "the Chicago idea," which was that large labor unions could take concerted action to change economic, social, and political conditions. In addition the incident directly inspired the careers of future labor leaders, such as Bill Haywood (1869–1928) and Emma Goldman (1869–1940). The execution of the men, who became known as "the martyrs of Chicago," not only inspired labor leaders globally but also led to the designation of May 1 as an international labor holiday. In short, the Haymarket massacre resonated long afterward as an enduring symbol of the heroic age of the labor movement.

SEE ALSO *Anarchism; Labor; Law and Order; Marxism; Riots; Socialism; Unions*

BIBLIOGRAPHY

Avrich, Paul. 1984. *The Haymarket Tragedy*. Princeton, NJ: Princeton University Press.

Green, James. 2006. *Death in the Haymarket: A Story of Chicago, the First Labor Movement, and the Bombing That Divided Gilded Age America*. New York: Pantheon.

Richard Bradley

HAZARD FUNCTION

SEE *Duration Models; Probability Distributions.*

HAZARDOUS WASTE

SEE *Toxic Waste.*

HAZING

SEE *Rites of Passage.*

HEAD START

Head Start began as an eight-week summer demonstration program in 1965, a small part of a larger antipoverty effort of the Lyndon B. Johnson (1908–1973) administration. The program was created to promote school readiness by enhancing the cognitive and social development of low-income children through provision, to such children and their families, of health, educational, nutritional, social, and other services that are determined, based on family needs assessment, to be necessary. Low-income children are those who come from families whose annual income falls below official poverty thresholds, although up to 10 percent of Head Start participants in local groups are allowed to come from families who do not meet the low-income criterion. Head Start is one of the few antipoverty measures that has enjoyed continued bipartisan political support in the U.S. Congress, and by 1975 what became known as the National Head Start Association was formally organized as an advocacy group for the program. Head Start operates full-day (six hours per day for four or five days per week year round) in about 50 percent of its local programs, with many service options. Although Head Start has served families with children three years of age and under in some programs since 1967, in 1995 the Early Head Start program awarded the first formal grants for birth-to-age-three services.

By the early 2000s Head Start had served about nineteen million children since its inception. In 1968 Head Start began funding a program that eventually was called *Sesame Street*, a Carnegie Corporation preschool television show. During its 2004 fiscal year Head Start enrolled nearly 906,000 children. Of these, 52 percent were four-year-olds, another 34 percent were three-year-olds, and another 9 percent were under three years of age; 31.2 percent were Hispanic, 31.1 percent were black, and 26.9 percent were white; and 12.7 percent had physical or mental disabilities. The average cost per child was $7,222, for a total cost of nearly $6.1 billion.

Although Head Start is a federal program, it is administered through the states and operated by local public and private for-profit and not-for-profit agencies. Hence, there is a great diversity of programs across the country and within states, thereby making difficult efforts to evaluate how well Head Start "works" in the nation as a whole. A national reporting system was created only in 2002, and the U.S. Department of Health and Human Services issued its first Head Start impact report in 2005. Data based on that reporting system indicate that Head Start children achieve a 38 percent gain in letter recognition and improved prewriting skills, but they still lag behind their more advanced peers at entry into kindergarten and such gains are likely to dissipate over time. One regional study reported in 2000 by Sherri Oden and others found that girls who attended Head Start in Florida in 1970 to 1971 were significantly more likely to graduate high school or earn a GED (95% versus 81%) and significantly less likely to be arrested at age twenty-two (5% versus 15%) than were girls in the non–Head Start comparison group.

Two studies by Janet Currie and Duncan Thomas relied on national-level data to examine the effects of Head Start participants. Their 1995 study showed that Head Start was associated with significant gains in test scores among both whites and African Americans, but that African Americans quickly lost those gains. Head Start also reduced the probability that whites would repeat a grade, but no such effect was found for African Americans. In their 2000 study, Currie and Thomas again reported that test scores "faded out" more quickly for black children than for white children, but they also showed that black children who attended Head Start were more likely to attend schools of worse quality than other black children. No such pattern was found for white children. These results suggested that the "fade out" effects for black Head Start children may be due to the inferior schools they attend.

A long-term study based on national-level survey data reported by Richard Caputo in 2003 indicated that Head Start children had the lowest income to poverty ratios between 1985 and 1998 (2.6 versus 3.3 for nonpreschoolers and 3.8 for other preschoolers). In regard to economic mobility between 1985 and 1998, both Head Starters and other preschoolers had statistically similar and greater upward mobility (0.67 and 0.51 deciles respectively) than did nonpreschoolers (0.16 deciles). These findings, however, should be interpreted cautiously given the lack of experimental controls. More rigorous studies with random assignment into experimental and control groups are necessary to provide more definitive knowledge about both the short-term and long-term effects of Head Start.

SEE ALSO *Education, USA; Great Society, The*

BIBLIOGRAPHY

Bennett, W. Steven, and Jason T. Hustedt. 2005. Head Start's Lasting Benefits. *Infants & Young Children* 18 (1): 16–24.

Caputo, Richard K. 2003. Head Start, Other Pre-school Programs, & Life Success in a Youth Cohort. *Journal of Sociology and Social Welfare* 30 (2): 105–126.

Caputo, Richard K. 2004. The Impact of Intergenerational Head Start Participation on Success Measures among Adolescent Children. *Journal of Economic and Family Issues* 25 (2): 199–223.

Currie, Janet, and Duncan Thomas. 1995. Does Head Start Make a Difference? *American Economic Review* 85 (3): 341–364.

Currie, Janet, and Duncan Thomas. 2000. School Quality and the Longer-Term Effects of Head Start. *Journal of Human Resources* 35 (4): 755–774.

Oden, Sherri, Lawrence J. Schweinhart, David P. Weikart, et al. 2000. *Into Adulthood: A Study of the Effects of Head Start.* Ypsilanti, MI: High/Scope Press.

U.S. Department of Health and Human Services. 2004. *Biennial Report to Congress: The Status of Children in Head Start Programs.* Arlington, VA: National Head Start Training and Technical Assistance Resource Center.

U.S. Department of Health and Human Services. 2005. *Head Start Impact Study: First Year Findings, Executive Summary.* Washington, DC: Author. http://www.acf.hhs.gov/programs/opre/hs/impact_study/.

Zigler, Edward, and Susan Muenchow. 1992. *Head Start: The Inside Story of America's Most Successful Educational Experiment.* New York: Basic Books.

Richard K. Caputo

HEAD START EXPERIMENTS

With growing concern about the number of children living in poverty in the United States, the Head Start program was initiated in 1965 as Project Head Start, one component in the "war on poverty." Originally conceived as an eight-week summer pilot program implemented in nearly 2,500 communities across the country, the first trial served 500,000 four- and five-year-old children. From this initial beginning, Head Start programs quickly expanded to nine-month and even full-year programs, either half-day or full-day. As of 2006, the Head Start program served about 900,000 three- and four-year-old children nationally in nearly 19,000 centers for a total annual cost of $6.8 billion. Over time, the reach of the program has been substantial: Between 1965 and 2006, Head Start has enrolled more than twenty-four million children.

CHALLENGES OF PROGRAM EVALUATION

By providing a comprehensive set of education, health, and social services, Head Start aimed to counteract the detrimental influences of poverty and prepare children academically and socially for school entry. From its inception, there has been an interest in understanding whether Head Start indeed achieves this objective. However, a comparison of outcomes for children who participated in Head Start with those who did not would not measure the true effect of Head Start if program participants are systematically different from nonparticipants. For example, Head Start participants are on average from poorer families and they may come from families whose parents are more motivated to see their children succeed. These selectivity factors could confound efforts to measure the true effects of Head Start participation.

Ideally, we want to measure the effects of Head Start on children's outcomes compared to what those outcomes would have been for the same children in the absence of the program. Since it is not possible to observe the same children both participating and not participating in the program, researchers turn to experimental and quasi-experimental methods to assess program effects. Well-designed and implemented randomized control trials—with study participants randomly assigned to participate in the program or remain in the control group—remain the gold standard among social science evaluation methods. Potential selectivity bias is eliminated because program participation is determined at random. A second-best alternative is the use of quasi-experimental methods using data on participants and nonparticipants where statistical methods are employed to minimize any selectivity bias.

The history of Head Start evaluations reveals many of the challenges associated with conducting systematic scientific evaluations of large-scale social programs. First, while a randomized control trial is the gold standard, implementation of such experiments may not be compatible with the objectives of delivering social services. For example, such experiments require resources that could alternatively be used for program delivery, and it is often considered unethical to withhold program services for a control group. Second, while much of the initial focus of Head Start supporters was on the potential short-term gains in IQ, other evidence indicated that the benefits of Head Start may be both broader and longer-lasting. In the context of experimental evaluations, this requires careful measurement of multiple outcomes and the ability to conduct a longitudinal evaluation that follows treatment and control-group children years or even decades into the future. Finally, Head Start is not one uniform national program. Rather, there is tremendous variation across program sites in the nature and delivery of program services. This variation means that evaluations of selected Head Start programs may not represent the effects on average for the country as a whole.

EARLY EVALUATION EFFORTS

Until the 1998 congressional reauthorization of Head Start, there was no nationally representative evaluation of the program using a randomized experimental design. Early evaluation efforts sometimes used experimental designs to study local area programs, or quasi-experimental designs to study larger, national samples of children who participated in Head Start and comparison children who did not. Results from this early body of research were potentially compromised by small sample sizes, high rates of attrition, nonrepresentative samples, and the selectivity of program participation. Such potential biases were also present in the seventy-six studies that were the focus of a meta-analysis of the literature known as the Head Start Evaluation, Synthesis, and Utilization Project (McKey et al. 1985).

Despite these limitations, the conclusion that emerged from this meta-analysis in the mid-1980s and the literature that preceded it was that Head Start could generate immediate cognitive benefits (e.g., higher IQ scores or achievement scores) for participating children, but those benefits did not persist after the first few years of elementary school as the gap between Head Start and non-Head Start children narrowed. There was some evidence that Head Start participants showed other improved outcomes over nonparticipants, such as lower rates of grade repetition and special education use, as well as physical health benefits. Similar findings had also been demonstrated for smaller-scale demonstration programs that offer one or two years of high-quality preschool education, although the magnitude of the effects for these smaller-scale and more resource-intensive programs were often larger than those measured for Head Start participants. More recent syntheses of this literature suggest that while the fade-out (relative to nonparticipants) of IQ gains from participation in Head Start or other high-quality early intervention programs may be real, the fade-out of achievement test scores may result from flaws in evaluation designs and follow-up procedures. This explanation can help reconcile the apparent achievement fade-out with the longer-lasting effects measured for such educational outcomes as grade repetition and special education use.

LATER EVALUATION EFFORTS

In the absence of large-scale experimental studies, researchers in the 1990s turned to nationally representative survey samples to estimate the short- and long-term benefits of participating in Head Start. Using rigorous quasi-experimental methods, these studies demonstrated that Head Start had favorable and more sustained effects on test scores and other school outcomes for white children, but the initial cognitive benefits for black children faded with time. For both white and black children, Head Start participation led to higher immunization rates but had no effect on nutritional status. Analysis of longer-term data also showed favorable effects of Head Start on high school completion, college attendance, and criminal activity, but again the benefits differed by race and ethnicity.

In the 1998 reauthorization of Head Start, Congress mandated a national study to measure the effects of Head Start on school readiness, broadly defined to include cognitive development, general knowledge, approaches to learning, social and emotional development, health status, and access to health care. The study also aims to evaluate the effects on parental practices that influence school readiness and the conditions under which the program is most effective and for which children. The evaluation underway randomly assigned about five thousand newly entering three- and four-year-old children applying for Head Start in nearly four hundred randomly selected Head Start centers to either participate in Head Start or be in a non-Head Start group (with access to non-Head Start programs in the community as selected by the parents). Findings from the first-year follow-up released in 2005 showed small to moderate gains for Head Start children in most of the domains listed above for entering three-year-olds, while fewer effects were found for the four-year-olds. The children in the study will continue to be followed through first grade, and possibly beyond, with an effort to identify overall program impacts as well as how the effects of Head Start vary with program characteristics or for different types of children.

Other demonstration projects implemented in the 1990s assessed other aspects of the Head Start program. One such evaluation—the National Head Start/Public School Early Childhood Transition Demonstration Study implemented from 1991 to 1998—was designed to test the effects of providing comprehensive transition supports (e.g., social services to strengthen families and links to school, services to increase parent involvement, and promotion of developmentally appropriate activities in the classroom curriculum) for Head Start children and their families, schools, and communities in kindergarten through third grade. The study design randomly assigned more than 450 schools in thirty-one sites to the treatment or control conditions, with more than eight thousand former Head Start children studied. While inferences that could be drawn about the effects of the transition supports were limited by the site-to-site variation in the treatment conditions and similar activities implemented in control schools, the study documented consistently large gains among former Head Start children (both treatment and control children) in reading and math achievement in these early grades, as well as substantial parent involvement in school and home activities.

BIBLIOGRAPHY

Barnett, W. Steven. 1995. Long-Term Effects of Early Childhood Programs on Cognitive and School Outcomes. *The Future of Children* 5: 25–50.

Currie, Janet, and Duncan Thomas. 1995. Does Head Start Make a Difference? *American Economic Review* 85 (3): 235–262.

Garces, Eliana, Duncan Thomas, and Janet Currie. 2002. Longer-Term Effects of Head Start. *American Economic Review* 92 (4): 999–1012.

McKey, Ruth Hubbell, Larry Condelli, Harriet Ganson, et al. 1985. *The Impact of Head Start on Children, Families, and Communities: Final Report of the Head Start Evaluation, Synthesis, and Utilization Project.* Washington, DC: U.S. Department of Health and Human Services.

Ramey, Sharon L., Craig T. Ramey, Martha M. Phillips, et al. 2000. *Head Start Children's Entry into Public School: A Report on the National Head Start/Public School Early Childhood Transition Demonstration Study.* Washington, DC: U.S. Department of Health and Human Services.

U.S. Department of Health and Human Services, Administration for Children and Families. 2005. *Head Start Impact Study: First Year Findings.* Washington, DC: Author.

Zigler, Edward F., and Susan Muenchow. 1992. *Head Start: The Inside Story of America's Most Successful Educational Experiment.* New York: Basic Books.

Zigler, Edward, and Sally J. Styfco, eds. 2004. *The Head Start Debates.* Baltimore, MD: Brookes.

Lynn A. Karoly

HEALTH ECONOMICS

An enormous expansion in the scope and effectiveness of medical care services to diagnose and treat diseases began in the 1930s with the scientific research and development techniques that produced the first antibiotics. Those advances have been followed by continual changes in the organization of the institutions that constitute the supply and demand sides of the medical service industry, continual changes in pricing and payment mechanisms, and continual growth in the amount of nations' resources that are allocated to medical services.

Theses changes have been universal among countries, even in the presence of substantial heterogeneity in institutional and market structures for health care delivery and financing. The United Kingdom and the United States are examples of nations with very different structures. In 1946 the United Kingdom established universal, government-funded medical insurance, and hospital and medical specialists' services are produced by the government. In the United States, medical insurance is not universal; government expenditure is substantial, but provides coverage for only selected populations; physician practices are privately owned and organized on a for-profit basis; and most hospitals are privately owned but organized as nonprofit-based corporations. Yet, between 1960 and 2004, total health care expenditure as a share of gross domestic profit doubled in the United Kingdom and tripled in the United States (Organisation for Economic Co-operation and Development 2007).

Health economics applies the tools of microeconomics to individual and societal decisions regarding the allocation and distribution of resources to the production of health and health care services. Kenneth Arrow's 1963 article "Uncertainty and the Welfare Economics of Medical Care" established health economics as a field by making the case that virtually all of the special features of the medical care industry stem from the prevalence of risk and uncertainty, arguing that "the failure of the market to insure against uncertainties has created many social institutions in which the usual assumptions of the market are to some extent contradicted" (Arrow 1963, p. 946).

Demand- and supply-side analysis is the primary theoretical tool in health economics. On the demand side, health is characterized as a stock of human capital (Schultz 1961; Becker 1962) that produces both direct utility and investment services—capacity to function—over the life cycle. With aging it depreciates naturally and is increasingly subject to shocks from diseases. Replacement health cannot be purchased—it must be produced by combining personal resources such as time and health-affecting behaviors with purchased health or medical care services (Grossman 1972). On the supply side, purchased health care services are regulated by government and produced in hospitals, physicians' offices, and clinics, and long-term care facilities by physicians, nurses, and other medical care providers using pharmaceutical and other diagnostic and treatment technologies.

The role of third-party payors—predominately employers and governments—constitutes a distinguishing feature of health economics. Given third-party payors, consumers often are not aware of the full range of alternative health care services and do not directly face, or even know, the resource cost—the full price—of their health care. Most consumers are enrolled in managed care type plans that have contracts with providers. Those contracts influence providers' treatment decisions by specifying which services are covered and what the payment mechanism is between the plan and medical services provider; the consumer does not see the plan-provider contract.

Health economics draws on tools used in several other fields to address this configuration of health and health care institutional characteristics: from public finance, the major government role; from labor economics, the major employer role; from industrial organization, restricted entry and nonprofit organizational form; and from econometrics, quantitative answers to policy-related questions. Variations of cost-effectiveness analysis are more frequently used by health economists in nations such as the United Kingdom, where government-financed third-party coverage is complete.

Much growth in the field of health economics is policy oriented. This can be attributed to the fact that governments are major third-party payors and face the fiscal implications of the costs associated with the expansion in the scope of medical care services. Thus, the research has focused on societal decisions regarding the efficient (cost-containing) allocation of resources to the production of health care services. Research concerning the distributional component of enhancing social welfare (Arrow 1963) has received much less attention in health economics. This has implications for policy because there is substantial evidence of nonrandom heterogeneity in health stock and health outcomes among demographic groups. Racial and ethnic health disparities continue to persist whether health care coverage is universal and provided by government, as in the United Kingdom (Townsend and Davidson 1982), or provided through fragmented systems of imperfect markets that include private and government third parties, as in the United States (U.S. Department of Health and Human Services 2000).

Viewed as human capital, investment in the health of the most vulnerable members of society may be a powerful tool for promoting growth. Public investment in programs that eliminate acquired immunodeficiency syndrome (HIV/AIDS) enhances social welfare and facilitates economic growth in developing African countries. Programs that increase breast-feeding enhance the health of infants and thereby generate positive long-term returns. But John Akin and colleagues reported that in Sri Lanka, highly educated mothers from families in the highest income or asset categories were among the least likely to breast-feed (Akin, Bilsborrow, Guilkey et al. 1981); thus the social rate of return from investment in health may be particularly high for developing countries, but the eco-

nomic and policy issues are complex. Additional health economics studies can help clarify these issues.

SEE ALSO *Arrow, Kenneth J.; Developing Countries; Development Economics; Disease; Health in Developing Countries; Microeconomics; Modernization; Public Health; Risk; Sanitation; Uncertainty*

BIBLIOGRAPHY

Akin, John, Richard Bilsborrow, David Guilkey, et al. 1981. The Determinants of Breast-Feeding in Sri Lanka. *Demography* 18 (3): 287–307.

Arrow, Kenneth J. 1963. Uncertainty and the Welfare Economics of Medical Care. *American Economic Review* 53 (5): 941–973.

Becker, Gary S. 1962. Investment in Human Capital: A Theoretical Analysis. *Journal of Political Economy* 70 (5, pt. 2): 9–49.

Grossman, Michael. 1972. On the Concept of Health Capital and the Demand for Health. *Journal of Political Economy* 80 (2): 223–255.

Law, Sylvia A. 1974. *Blue Cross What Went Wrong?* New Haven, CT: Yale University Press.

Schultz, Theodore W. 1961. Investment in Human Capital. *American Economic Review* 51 (1): 1–17.

Townsend, Peter, and Nick Davidson, eds. 1982. *Inequalities in Health: The Black Report*. New York: Penguin Books.

U.S. Department of Health and Human Services. 2000. *Healthy People 2010*. 2 vols. 2nd ed. Washington, DC: U.S. Government Printing Office. http://www.healthypeople.gov/publications/.

Alvin E. Headen Jr.

HEALTH IN DEVELOPING COUNTRIES

The most commonly accepted definition of *health* was proposed by the World Health Organization (WHO) in its 1948 constitution: "Health is a state of complete physical, social, and mental well-being and not merely the absence of disease or infirmity." Some academics argue that this definition is utopian, and they propose a more narrow definition that considers health to be "the absence of illness" (Alban and Christiansen 1995).

Health is regarded by the WHO as a fundamental human right. The preamble of the WHO constitution states that "the enjoyment of the highest attainable standard of health is one of the fundamental rights of every human being." However, people do not enjoy the same standard of health in all parts of the world. Many factors influence health status and a country's ability to provide quality health services for its people. Researchers on health in developing countries try to make sense of these factors and to understand their complex links in "low- and middle-income countries in which most people have a lower standard of living with access to fewer goods and services" (World Bank 2003).

Research on health in developing countries can include the study of clinical and epidemiological aspects of diseases, such as variations in disease frequency in different populations; the natural processes of biology and their relation to disease; the environmental and social determinants of health; and the development, implementation, and evaluation of health policy, which can include, among other things, how health systems should be organized.

The range of disciplines and professionals represented in the study of health in developing countries is very broad. This group can include epidemiologists, sociologists, physiologists, economists, mathematicians, historians, health policy analysts, nurses, doctors, and pharmacists. In recent years, there has been a move toward establishing research partnerships of interdisciplinary teams from both developed and developing countries in an effort to find solutions to the health challenges facing developing countries in the new millennium. The spectrum of diseases studied is wide, and there are major research groups working on topics that include reproductive health, undernutrition, and infectious disease (e.g., tuberculosis, malaria, diarrheal diseases, HIV/AIDS); noncommunicable disease and injury (e.g., diabetes, mental disorders, interpersonal violence); risk factors (e.g., water supply, sanitation, and hygiene); and the consequences of disease and injury (e.g., learning and developmental disabilities).

The global community acknowledges the need to tackle health-related conditions in order to support aspirations toward development of people living in developing countries. An example of this includes the United Nations Millennium Declaration (2000), signed by 189 countries, which includes eight Millennium Development Goals, three of which are related to health: reducing child mortality; improving maternal health; and combating HIV/AIDS, malaria, and other diseases (Travis et al. 2001). The following sections explore how some of these goals are being addressed.

HIV/AIDS poses a serious health, social, and economic threat worldwide, and both rapid action and drastic initiatives are needed to care for adults and children living with and affected by HIV/AIDS, as well as to prevent further infections from occurring. By 2004 AIDS had killed more than twenty million people, and an esti-

mated thirty-four to forty-six million people were living with HIV/AIDS (WHO 2004). The solutions proposed by most experts include implementing a comprehensive HIV/AIDS strategy that links prevention, treatment, care, and support for people living with the virus. Providing effective antiretroviral treatment and new care strategies to strengthen existing prevention programs can result in the improvement of health, the reduction of HIV/AIDS stigma, and the rebuilding of social capital while restoring economic growth (WHO 2004).

According to the WHO's *World Health Report 2003*, around 530,000 women die each year in pregnancy or childbirth, and 10.6 million children die every year before they reach the age of five. In many countries, universal access to health care for women and children is not assured. Women and children are often excluded from health-care services, which reinforces inequity in health delivery and increases barriers to progress. The WHO report also states that mortality could be reduced through a wider use of key interventions and a continuum of care for mother and child. Some cost-effective interventions include: expanding immunization coverage; treating diarrhea; preventing the transmission of and mortality from malaria; ensuring the widespread distribution of key micronutrients; improving prenatal and delivery care; and expanding the use of measures aimed at preventing mother-to-child transmission of HIV (Jamison et al. 2006). The most pressing task for reducing child mortality, improving maternal health, and treating and preventing HIV/AIDS consists of putting in place the health-care workforce needed to implement these interventions.

The effectiveness of health systems varies dramatically around the globe, even among countries with similar levels of income and health expenditure. In 2000 the WHO carried out the first analysis assessing the performance of health systems worldwide. The report emphasized that failures in health systems had a more severe impact on the poor. According to the report, out-of-pocket payments for health care exacerbate poverty. In light of this finding, governments should pursue policies that expand insurance and prepayment schemes as a way of reducing excessive out-of-pocket expenses for health care (WHO 2000; van Doorslaer et al. 2006).

International involvement in health care remains common in developing countries, largely because the provision of health care is expensive and few countries can afford universal coverage. International involvement includes the work of multilateral organizations such as the United Nations, bilateral or government-to-government organizations, and the global civil society. In addition, a wide range of global partnerships to finance the fight against major diseases in developing and middle-income countries have flourished since the mid-1990s.

Organizations participating in such partnerships include the Global Fund to Fight AIDS, Tuberculosis, and Malaria; the Bill and Melinda Gates Foundation; and the World Bank Multi-country HIV/AIDS Program. It is still too early to assess or predict the effects of these initiatives on health systems. The funds of such initiatives must be managed with caution, and they face daunting problems associated with coordinating their efforts within countries (Brugha 2004; Coovadia and Hadingham 2005).

In general, two approaches to delivering health interventions are prevalent. These approaches date back to a debate that started when the Alma-Ata Declaration was adopted at the International Conference on Primary Health Care in Alma-Ata (Almaty), Kazakhstan, in 1978. At that time, the debate centered on two distinctive views on primary health care (PHC) intervention. The first approach, referred to as *selective PHC*, focuses on diseases with the highest prevalence and morbidity, the highest risk of mortality, and the greatest possibility of control in terms of cost and effectiveness of the intervention (Walsh and Warren 1979). The second approach, named *comprehensive PHC*, considers health to be more than the absence of disease, and defines health in the holistic sense. Comprehensive PHC considers equity, multisectoral approaches, and community involvement as critical components of any health intervention (Rifkin and Walt 1986).

The debate between advocates of these two approaches has not completely faded, but it has been obscured by the fact that many governments and global health partnerships have implemented the selective PHC approach to tackle HIV/AIDS, as well as tuberculosis and malaria. However, the WHO's *World Health Report 2003* stressed that the principles of the Alma-Ata Declaration remain valid, and should be reinterpreted in light of dramatic changes in the health field since 1978.

Health systems in developing countries need to be strengthened in view of the global health challenges facing them, including the health-care workforce crisis, a lack of financial resources, and poorly organized and financed health systems (WHO 2005). *The World Health Report 2003* indicates that despite many reforms, inadequate progress has been made in building health systems that promote collective improvement in health. Solutions could include offering more training for local officials, strengthening health-care infrastructure through restructuring, and developing accountability mechanisms and a larger role for civil society. However, experts agree that context-specific strategies and responses are essential, and goals and priorities should be established and tailored to each country's context (Sepúlveda 2006). Finally, there is a need for greater research on epidemiology and health systems to improve the efficiency and reduce the costs of available interventions, as well as biomedical research to develop new tools for dealing with emerging health problems (Sepúlveda 2006).

SEE ALSO *AIDS/HIV in Developing Countries, Impact of; Developing Countries; Development, Rural; Disease; Ethno-epidemiological Methodology; Health Economics; Human Rights; Public Health; Sanitation; Toilets; World Health Organization*

BIBLIOGRAPHY

Alban, Anita, and Terkel Christiansen. 1995. *The Nordic Lights: New Initiatives in Health Care Systems.* Odense, Denmark: Odense University Press.

Brugha, Ruairí. 2004. The Global Fund: Managing Great Expectations. *Lancet* 364: 95–100.

Coovadia, Hoosen, and Jacqui Hadingham. 2005. HIV/AIDS: Global Trends, Global Funds, and Delivery Bottlenecks. *Globalization and Health* 1 (13). http://www.globalizationandhealth.com/content/1/1/13.

Jamison, Dean, Joel Breman, Anthony R. Measham, et al. 2006. *Disease Control Priorities in Developing Countries.* 2nd ed. Washington, DC: World Bank; New York: Oxford University Press.

Rifkin, Susan, and Gill Walt. 1986. Why Health Improves: Defining the Issues Concerning "Comprehensive Primary Health Care" and "Selective Primary Health Care." *Social Science and Medicine* 23 (6): 559–566.

Sepúlveda, Jaime. 2006. Foreword. In *Disease Control Priorities in Developing Countries*, eds. Dean Jamison et al. 2nd ed. Washington, DC: World Bank; New York: Oxford University Press: xiii-xv.

Travis, Phyllida, Sara Bennett, Andy Haines, et al. 2001. Overcoming Health-systems Constraints to Achieve the Millennium Development Goals. *Lancet* 364: 900–906.

United Nations. 2000. United Nations Millennium Declaration. http://www.un.org/millennium/declaration/ares552e.htm.

van Doorslaer, Eddy, Owen O'Donnell, Ravi P. Rannan-Eliya, et al. 2006. Effect of Payments for Health Care on Poverty Estimates in 11 Countries in Asia: An Analysis of Household Survey Data. *Lancet* 368 (9544): 1357–1364.

Walsh, Julia A., and Kenneth S. Warren. 1979. Selective Primary Health Care: An Interim Strategy for Disease Control in Developing Countries. *New England Journal of Medicine* 301: 967–974.

World Bank: Development Education Program. 2003. Glossary: Developing country. http://www.worldbank.org/depweb/english/modules/glossary.html.

World Health Organization. 1948. Constitution of the World Health Organization. http://www.yale.edu/lawweb/avalon/decade/decad051.htm.

World Health Organization. 2000. *The World Health Report 2000—Health Systems: Improving Performance.* Geneva: Author. http://www.who.int/whr/2000/en/.

World Health Organization. 2003. *The World Health Report 2003—Shaping the Future*. Geneva: Author. http://www.who.int/whr/2003/en/.

World Health Organization. 2004. *The World Health Report 2004—Changing History*. Geneva: Author. http://www.who.int/whr/2004/en/.

World Health Organization. 2005. *The World Health Report 2005—Make Every Mother and Child Count*. Geneva: Author. http://www.who.int/whr/2005/en/.

Helena Legido-Quigley

HEARSAY

In legal cases where the primary witness is a child, the courts face a dilemma: They must attempt to prosecute alleged criminals while also protecting child eyewitnesses. One way that the courts have attempted to deal with this dilemma has been to have a hearsay witness testify in place of the child eyewitness. In the U.S. legal system, *hearsay* is defined as "a statement, other than one made by the declarant while testifying at the trial or hearing, offered in evidence to prove the truth of the matter asserted" (Federal Rules of Evidence 801[c]). (The *declarant* is the witness of the original event).

Hearsay statements have not traditionally been allowed in the courts for several reasons. Not only is the veracity of hearsay testimony questionable, but hearsay testimony may also violate the defendant's Sixth and Fourteenth Amendment rights to due process and to confront the accuser. However, there are still twenty-nine exceptions to the hearsay rule under the Federal Rules of Evidence, allowing hearsay testimony to be admissible in numerous instances.

The majority of these exceptions to the hearsay rule (twenty-three) are made when the declarant is available to testify. For these exceptions, the statement made by the declarant is seen as so reliable by the courts that the declarant does not have to testify. For example, these statements may relate to official written documents, or a statement may have been made for the purpose of medical treatment and therefore may be admissible under the *medical diagnosis or treatment* exception (Federal Rules of Evidence 803[4]). There are also several exceptions to the hearsay rule that are made only when the declarant is unavailable to testify. For example, if the declarant is not available to testify, then under the *statement against interest* exception (Federal Rules of Evidence 804[3]), a declarant's prior statement may be admissible if it is self-incriminating. However, these statements are viewed by the courts as less reliable than the statements that are admissible when the declarant is present.

To accommodate cases where the declarant is a child who was allegedly abused, most states have special exceptions to the hearsay rule. The goal of such exceptions is to protect the child from the trauma of in-court testimony, while still providing the courts with a means of pursuing legal cases involving child victims. However, there are many problems with the use of hearsay testimony, including the inability of the prosecution to cross-examine the eyewitness and the fact that the declarant would not be under oath while making the original statement. Also, the jury will not be able to use the demeanor of the child as an aid in determining his or her accuracy. Finally, when a hearsay witness testifies in place of a child eyewitness or victim, there is the possibility that the hearsay witness either misunderstood the child or is fabricating the child's statements, allowing further potential distortions in the declarant's original statements.

Research evaluating the accuracy of hearsay testimony suggests that information is indeed lost when hearsay is used in place of the child's testimony. Research indicates that while the interviewers of children tend to give complete and accurate reports of the gist of their interviews, this is not the case when interviewers are asked to report the types and content of the questions they asked children. Interviewers tend to report less than 50 percent of their own utterances made during the interview and 20 percent or less of the types of questions they asked the children. Interviewers consistently report more free-recall prompts and fewer suggestive or leading prompts than were actually used, making the interview of the child appear to be more spontaneous than it really was. Therefore, jurors who are exposed to the testimony of a hearsay witness are likely to think that the child's statements were more spontaneous than they were in reality, possibly leading jurors to be overly confident in the accuracy of the disclosure.

Although research demonstrates that hearsay witnesses leave out a substantial amount of information about how the child's statement was elicited, jurors' reactions to hearsay testimony do not suggest that jurors are sensitive to this lack of information. For example, mock jurors exposed to typical gist hearsay testimony tend to think that children were interviewed in a less suggestive manner than jurors exposed to the actual interview. Therefore, jurors who were only exposed to hearsay testimony did not seem to understand how the interview of the child was really conducted. Also, in research involving child sexual abuse cases, adult hearsay witnesses are generally seen as more accurate, confident, consistent, truthful, in possession of better memory abilities, and less suggestible than child witnesses. And not surprisingly, hearsay testimony tends to be at least as effective as the child's testimony in producing pro-prosecution ratings and more effective than having no witness testify.

Specific characteristics of an individual trial are also likely to influence trial results in cases involving hearsay testimony. For example, the exception under which hearsay is admitted, the child's or the hearsay witness's appearance of credibility, the nature of the abuse, the use of multiple hearsay witnesses, and the child's demeanor when testifying are all likely to affect trial results. However, these case characteristics have yet to be explored through research.

SEE ALSO *Psychology*

BIBLIOGRAPHY

Buck, Julie A., Amye R. Warren, and John C. Brigham. 2004. When Does Quality Count? Perceptions of Hearsay Testimony about Child Sexual Abuse Interviews. *Law and Human Behavior* 28 (6): 599–621.

Federal Rules of Evidence. 2005. Washington, DC: U.S. Government Printing Office. http://judiciary.house.gov/media/pdfs/printers/109th/evid2005.pdf.

Lamb, Michael E., et al. 2000. Accuracy of Investigators' Verbatim Notes of Their Forensic Interviews with Alleged Child Abuse Victims. *Law and Human Behavior* 24 (6): 699–708.

McGough, Lucy S. 1994. *Child Witnesses: Fragile Voices in the American Legal System.* New Haven, CT: Yale University Press.

Ross, David, Amye R. Warren, and Lucy S. McGough, eds. 1999. Forward: Hearsay Testimony in Trials Involving Child Witnesses. *Psychology, Public Policy, and Law* 5 (2): 251–254.

Warren, Amye R., and Cara E. Woodall. 1999. The Reliability of Hearsay Testimony: How Well Do Interviewers Recall Their Interviews with Children? *Psychology, Public Policy, and Law* 5 (2): 355–371.

Warren, Amye R., et al. 2002. The Believability of Children and Their Interviewer's Hearsay Testimony: When Less is More. *Journal of Applied Psychology* 87 (5): 846–857.

Julie A. Buck

HEAVEN

Heaven is one of the most common names for a positive location or situation for humans in the afterlife. Different religions use different names for such an otherworldly circumstance, but few fail to minister to the human impulse and need to imagine and realize some sort of continuation or transformation of life after physical death. Until recent times life expectancy was very brief. People had to see their parents die young and, healthcare being what it was, they often saw their children die as well. In the face of this sense of loss, it was only natural that human yearning for meaning and reward focused on some sort of heaven. Participants in various faith communities (i.e., "religions") have often borrowed details of heaven envisioned by other faith communities.

At other times, visionaries within one religious tradition might reject the heaven in other traditions, as they vied for supremacy. These competing visions of heaven were both natural and useful; natural because human life took on more value with the promise that it would be extended or transformed, and useful because claims about heaven attracted new adherents and could not be disproved by rival claims. Seers, prophets, revealers, and authors of holy books could claim to have come from or visited other realms, but in normal human experience people did not have neighbors or fellow worshipers who had returned to earth or come back from the dead to report on the place that was their reward and destiny. The absence of certifiable signs did not mean the end of heaven; if anything, it stimulated imaginations. Heaven came to be a major aspect of revelation in most holy books.

Ideas of heaven that can be traced to ancient Egyptian and Mesopotamian civilizations have been highly influential on Western conceptions of the afterlife. These cultures did not leave written descriptions of heaven, but their conceptions of the afterlife can be deduced from temples, tombs, and monuments. Egyptian heaven, judging from representations in art adorning pyramids and tombs, was an attractive stage or place for pharaohs and other exalted humans, who needed sustenance and comfort and were served by slaves in the life to come. In Mesopotamia, evidence suggests, people believed that heaven was "above," and references to a vertical dimension are present in many depictions of ritual found in tombs. "Heaven" was less often found on the horizontal level, though some paradises were pictured as bountiful and blessed utopias established here on earth. "Heaven" was still less frequently "below," and what lay there was usually a shadowy nether existence or a place of eternal misery. Even in the modern world, believers in many faiths picture a literal place "up there"; all but instinctively, people look up or point up to locate heaven.

Among the Semitic peoples, who were most influential in the development of Judaism, Christianity, and Islam, the dominant concepts of the afterlife originated in Israel and in the Hebrew Scriptures. It surprises many whose faith derives from Hebrew scriptures that no very vivid heaven is promised or pictured in them. The abode of the dead was Sheol, a largely featureless and limited place. In later Judaism, as a reaction to captivity, military defeats, and other disasters, many in Israel did begin to make apocalyptic predictions. Many of these predictions were of coming catastrophes, but some foresaw the arrival of the Creator, the God of Israel, and a coming heaven on earth. In this environment, Jesus of Nazareth could take for granted contemporary pictures of heaven, fostered mainly by the party of the Pharisees, just as he could point to another school, the Sadducees, as being deficient because they did not believe in an afterlife.

The New Testament offers many promises and pictures of paradise or heaven, the reward of those who properly follow Christ, or the gift to those who believe in him. For Christians, Paradise meant being in the presence of God, along with angelic beings and other "saints," amid pleasures revealed in parables or vividly described in the visionary biblical books. During Christianity's first three centuries, many Christians endured persecution, which proved a great stimulus to the paradisiacal imagination. When Christianity began to prosper and become established, Christian images of heaven and its promises took on triumphal and lavish elements.

In the modern world, in the face of new understandings of the physical universe, heaven as a place "above" survived only metaphorically and was regarded by many as an obsolete concept. At the same time, opinion polls continually found clear majorities believing in some sort of heaven. As people became aware of cultures other than their own, they also learned of the vision of heaven in other religions. Muslims and Christians, especially when in conflict, came to be aware of each other's promises. In the Qur'an, poetic language and lavish promises of paradise inspired Muslims to devotion, but also often inspired *jihad* ("holy cause") and even martyrdom. Anti-Muslim propagandists publicized and exaggerated some references in the Qur'an to virgins who would be at the command of martyrs in heaven.

Buddhism teaches the concept of *Nirvana*, a means by which or a place where one is removed from the travails and suffering of this world, though Buddhists do not equate Nirvana with heaven. Hindus in their many texts and religious expressions have imagined many benign and blissful versions of an afterlife, including a kind of heaven, Swarga loka, where one remains only temporarily. In Hinduism, revealed and foreseen heavens tended to be paired, as they are in other faiths, with prescriptions on how to live in order to attain them.

For all the belief in heaven, it must be said that often it has become recessive in religious teaching. Karl Marx thought of religion as the opium of the people, offering a haven in a heartless world and what critics colloquially dismissed as "pie in the sky by and by." Many of the faithful professed that they were not believers in God in order to get such rewards, but for intrinsic reasons. If the belief in heaven as a reward survives, it must be said that for many this belief is casual, minimal, not a primary motivating force. At the same time, as funeral liturgies and sermons in some religions, notably Christianity, suggest,

preaching about an angel-filled heaven of bliss serves as a comfort to millions who mourn a departed loved one.

SEE ALSO *Hell; Religion*

BIBLIOGRAPHY

Emerson, Jan S., and Hugh Feiss, eds. 2000. *Imagining Heaven in the Middle Ages*. New York: Garland.

Kueng, Hans. 1984. *Eternal Life? Life after Death as a Medical, Philosophical, and Theological Problem*, trans. Edward Quinn. Garden City, New York: Doubleday.

McDannell, Colleen, and Bernhard Lang. 1988. *Heaven: A History*. New Haven, CT: Yale University Press.

Wright, J. Edward. 2000. *The Early History of Heaven*. New York: Oxford University Press.

Zaleski, Carol. 1996. *The Life of the World to Come: Near-Death Experience and Christian Hope: The Albert Cardinal Meyer Lectures*. New York: Oxford University Press.

Martin E. Marty

HECKIT

SEE *Tobit.*

HECKMAN SELECTION CORRECTION PROCEDURE

The Heckman selection correction procedure, introduced by American economist James J. Heckman, is a statistical solution to a form of sample selection bias. Sample selection bias can emerge when a population parameter of interest is estimated with a sample obtained from that population by other than random means. Such sampling yields a distorted empirical representation of the population of interest with which to estimate such parameters (Heckman 1990), possibly leading to biased estimates of them. Heckman (1979) was specifically concerned with this possibility in a certain regression context.

Suppose that we are interested in estimating the population regression model

$$y = \beta_0 + \beta_1 \cdot x_1 + \beta_2 \cdot x_2 + \varepsilon_1.$$

With a truly random sample from the population of interest, it should be straightforward to estimate β_0, β_1, and β_2 via ordinary least squares. Suppose, however, that we observe y only if the units of observation in that random sample make some decision. For instance, we might observe y only if

$$v^* = \gamma_0 + \gamma_1 \cdot x_1 + \gamma_2 \cdot x_2 + \varepsilon_2 > 0$$

or

$$\varepsilon_2 > -\gamma_0 - \gamma_1 \cdot x_1 - \gamma_2 \cdot x_2$$

This allows us to characterize the sample selection bias that might emerge from attempting to estimate the regression with only the subsample for whom we observe y.

We wish to evaluate the population expectation

$$E(y) = E(\beta_0 + \beta_1 \cdot x_1 + \beta_2 \cdot x_2 + \varepsilon_1)$$
$$= \beta_0 + \beta_1 \cdot x_1 + \beta_2 \cdot x_2 + E(\varepsilon_1)$$
$$= \beta_0 + \beta_1 \cdot x_1 + \beta_2 \cdot x_2$$

However, if we observe y only when $v^* > 0$, available data allows us to evaluate only the expectation

$$E(y) = (\beta_0 + \beta_1 \cdot x_1 + \beta_2 \cdot x_2 + E(\varepsilon_1 \mid v^* > 0)$$
$$= \beta_0 + \beta_1 \cdot x_1 + \beta_2 \cdot x_2 + E(\sigma_1 \mid \varepsilon_2 > -\gamma_0 - \gamma_1 \cdot x_1 - \gamma_2 \cdot x_2)$$

In this setting, it will generally not be possible to separately identify β_0, β_1, and β_2. To see this more clearly, assume that

$$E(\varepsilon_1 \mid \varepsilon_2 > -\gamma_0 - \gamma_1 \cdot x_1 - \gamma_2 \cdot x_2) \neq 0$$

and consider a linear approximation of $E(\varepsilon_1 \mid \varepsilon_2 > -\gamma_0 -\gamma_1 \cdot x_1 -\gamma_2 \cdot x_2)$,

$$\bar{\omega}_0 + \bar{\omega}_1 \cdot x_1 + \bar{\omega}_2 \cdot x_2 + \zeta$$

where $E(\zeta) = 0$. Then, the overall expectation that can be gleaned from available data would be

$$E(y) = \beta_0 + \beta_1 \cdot x_1 + \beta_2 \cdot x_2 + E(\varepsilon_1 \mid v^* > 0)$$
$$= \beta_0 + \beta_1 \cdot x_1 + \beta_2 \cdot x_2 + E(\varepsilon_1 \mid \varepsilon_2 > -\gamma_0 - \gamma_1 \cdot x_1 - \gamma_2 \cdot x_2)$$
$$= \beta_0 + \beta_1 \cdot x_1 + \beta_2 \cdot x_2 + \bar{\omega}_0 + \bar{\omega}_1 \cdot x_1 + \bar{\omega}_2 \cdot x_2$$
$$\neq \beta_0 + \beta_1 \cdot x_1 + \beta_2 \cdot x_2$$

Thus, in general, one would not be able to recover valid estimates of β_0, β_1, and β_2 with the subsample for which we observe y. The only exception is when

$$E(\varepsilon_1 \mid \varepsilon_2 > -\gamma_0 - \gamma_1 \cdot x_1 - \gamma_2 \cdot x_2)$$
$$= E(\varepsilon_1) = 0$$

In other words, if ε_1 and ε_2 are independent, sample selection bias disappears.

The Heckman selection correction procedure can recover unbiased estimates of β_0, β_1, and β_2 with available data (i.e., where x_1 and x_2 are observed for the full random sample from the population of interest and y is observed only for the subsample for which $v^* > 0$). The departure point for this technique is to recognize that the sample selection bias problem really stems from a type of specification error. With the subsample for which y is observed we estimate

$$E(y) = \beta_0 + \beta_1 \cdot x_1 + \beta_2 \cdot x_2 + E(\varepsilon_1 \mid v^* > 0)$$
$$= \beta_0 + \beta_1 \cdot x_1 + \beta_2 \cdot x_2 + E(\varepsilon_1 \mid \varepsilon_2 > -\gamma_0 - \gamma_1 \cdot x_1 - \gamma_2 \cdot x_2)$$

The problem, from the standpoint of recovering unbiased estimates of β_0, β_1, and β_2, is that we do not observe $E(\varepsilon_1 \mid \varepsilon_2 > \gamma_0 -\gamma_1 \cdot x_1 -\gamma_2 \cdot x_2)$ (which is a function of x_1 and x_2) and hence cannot separately identify β_0, β_1, and β_2 from it. However, if one could form an estimate of $E(\varepsilon_1 \mid \varepsilon_2 > \gamma_0 -\gamma_1 \cdot x_1 -\gamma_2 \cdot x_2)$ and regress y on x_1, x_2, and that estimate, it would be possible to identify separately β_0, β_1, and β_2.

To form an estimate of

$$E(\varepsilon_1 \mid \varepsilon_2 > -\gamma_0 - \gamma_1 \cdot x_1 - \gamma_2 \cdot x_2)$$

the Heckman procedure begins by assuming that ε_1 and ε_2 follow a bivariate normal distribution with correlation ρ. Then, using well-known properties of the bivariate normal distribution, we have

$$E(\varepsilon_1 \mid \varepsilon_2 > -\gamma_0 - \gamma_1 \cdot x_1 - \gamma_2 \cdot x_2)$$
$$= \rho \cdot \sigma_{\varepsilon_1} \cdot \frac{\phi(-\gamma_0 - \gamma_1 \cdot x_1 - \gamma_2 \cdot x_2)}{1 - \Phi(-\gamma_0 - \gamma_1 \cdot x_1 - \gamma_2 \cdot x_2)} = \rho \cdot \sigma_{\varepsilon_1} \cdot \lambda(-\gamma_0 - \gamma_1 \cdot x_1 - \gamma_2 \cdot$$

where $\psi(\cdot)$ and $\Phi(\cdot)$ are the normal density and cumulative density functions, respectively, $\lambda(\cdot)$ is referred to as the *inverse Mill's ratio*. An estimate of it can be formed from the fitted model emerging from estimation of a probit regression of a dummy variable indicating whether y is observed on x_1 and x_2. Once that estimate of $\lambda(\cdot)$ has been formed, a second-stage regression of y on x_1, x_2, and that estimate recovers unbiased estimates of β_0, β_1, and β_2. The two steps are: (1) Estimate the probit model under which the binary status of y (i.e., missing/not missing) is a function of x_1 and x_2. From the fitted model, form an estimate of the inverse Mill's ratio ($\hat{\lambda}$) for each observation in the subsample for which y is observed. (2) Regress y on x_1, x_2, and $\hat{\lambda}$ with the subsample for which y is observed. Owing to heteroskedasticity concerns it is common practice actually to estimate the equation of interest via a procedure such as weighted least squares.

The estimated coefficient on $\hat{\lambda}$ in the second-stage regression is an estimate of $\rho \cdot \sigma_{\varepsilon1}$. A test of its significance is thus in practice a test for correlation between ε_1 and ε_2. Since ε_1 and ε_2 are assumed to follow a bivariate normal distribution, this is tantamount to testing whether they are independent. There is a full-information maximum-likelihood version of this model, but this "two-step" procedure has been more widely utilized in applied work.

A few caveats are in order. First, in the decade following its introduction, it became increasingly clear that the model often performs poorly without some source of identification beyond the assumption of joint-normality of the errors ε_1 and ε_2. Technically, it should be identified by the nonlinearity of the inverse Mill's ratio (which arises naturally from the assumption of joint normality). The underlying reason for the poor performance evident in some applications is that the inverse Mill's ratio is nearly linear over much of its range, introducing potentially severe multicollinearity between x_1 and x_2 and the inverse Mill's ratio during the second-stage regression. The best remedy for this problem is to introduce an instrument z to the first-stage probit estimations that provides some source of variation in the inverse Mill's ratio unrelated to that provided by x_1 and x_2.

Second, there have been growing warnings about misapplication of the model (an excellent example of such a critique is presented by William Dow and Edward Norton [2003]). The basic concern has been with the popularity of the Heckman procedure in applications where a continuous dependent variable y is characterized by significant mass at zero (with the first-stage probit component used to explain whether $y = 0$ or $y > 0$ and the second-stage linear regression component applied to the subsample for which $y > 0$). However, the Heckman procedure is appropriate only in cases where the zeroes emerge from the censoring of some true value for y. In cases where the zeroes are valid values for y, and as such represent a legitimate corner solution for that variable, some other tool (such as the two-part model) might be more appropriate.

Even in the face of variation in common first and second stage regressors sufficient to exploit non-linearity in the inverse Mill's ratio (which might obviate the need for first-stage identifying instruments), the model still relies on an assumed joint normality of errors to achieve identification by non-linearity. If the error terms are not in fact jointly normally distributed, the parameter estimates provided by the Heckman selection correction procedure might be biased (and, depending on the precise nature of the problem at hand, the degree of bias might exceed that which would result from simply ignoring the censoring and estimating the equation of interest over only those for whom the outcome y is observed). A variety of alternatives to the assumption of joint normality have been proposed in response to this. In principle, one tack would be to rely on different parametric joint distributional assumptions. However, since most of the readily obvious alternatives would likely involve no less heroic an assumption than joint-normality, the focus has instead shifted to more semiparametric approaches that rely less on explicit assumptions regarding the joint distribution of the error terms.

SEE ALSO *Regression; Selection Bias*

BIBLIOGRAPHY

Dow, William H., and Edward C. Norton. 2003. Choosing Between and Interpreting the Heckit and Two-Part Models for Corner Solutions. *Health Services and Outcomes Research Methodology* 4 (1): 5–18.

Heckman, James J. 1979. Sample Selection Bias as a Specification Error. *Econometrica* 47 (1): 153–161.

Heckman, James J. 1990. Selection Bias and Self-selection. In *The New Palgrave: Econometrics*, eds. John Eatwell, Murray Milgate, and Peter Newman, 201–224. New York: Norton.

Peter M. Lance

HECKSCHER-OHLIN-SAMUELSON MODEL

The Heckscher-Ohlin-Samuelson model attempts to explain the composition of trade between countries and the implications of trade for income distribution within the countries. The seminal work was presented in a 1919 Swedish paper (English translation, 1950) by Eli F. Heckscher (1879–1952) and a 1933 book by his student Bertil Ohlin (1899–1979). In later articles (especially 1949 and 1953–1954), Paul A. Samuelson added substantial rigor to the analysis and expanded the original Heckscher-Ohlin model. The analysis has been subjected to countless empirical tests to determine its applicability to actual trading patterns.

Building upon the earlier classical (David Ricardo [1772–1823]) comparative advantage trade model, the Heckscher-Ohlin-Samuelson model (hereafter H-O-S) goes behind comparative advantage to ask, "What determines comparative advantage in the first place?" The H-O-S answer is found by utilizing Heckscher's observations that (1) countries differ in their relative endowments of the factors of production, and (2) production processes for different goods employ different relative intensities of the factors. Suppose a situation with only two factors of production (e.g., labor and capital, where "capital" refers to plant and equipment used to produce output), two goods (e.g., clothing and automobiles), and two countries (e.g., A and B). If labor is more abundant (in greater supply) relative to capital in country A than in country B, then, other things being equal, labor will be relatively cheaper in A than in B. That is, the wage rate in A (wA) divided by the return to capital in A (rA) will be less than the ratio of the corresponding values in B [(wB/rB)]. If clothing production is specified to use more labor relative to capital than automobile production, then, because labor is cheaper in A than in B, country A will be able to produce clothing at a relatively lower cost than country B. By parallel reasoning, with abundant capital in B and capital-intensive automobile production, autos will be relatively cheaper in B than in A. Hence, the trade pattern is that A exports clothing to B, and B exports automobiles to A. This is the *Heckscher-Ohlin theorem:* a country exports goods that are produced relatively intensively by the country's relatively abundant factor of production, and imports goods that are produced relatively intensively by the country's relatively scarce factor of production. The formal analysis contains many underlying assumptions, but this trade pattern conclusion is straightforward and accords with common sense.

Besides predicting trade patterns theoretically, H-O-S also yields implications of trade for factor prices and income distribution in the countries. As trade begins in the above example, there will be greater relative demand for A's abundant factor (labor) in order to produce the new clothing exports; there will be less relative demand for the scarce factor (capital) due to the reduced need for domestic auto production because of the auto imports. These changes mean that wA will rise and rA will fall, so (wA/rA) rises. At the same time, wB will fall and rB will rise [so (wB/rB) falls] as country B demands relatively more capital to produce auto exports and relatively less labor to produce clothing. These factor price changes continue until an equilibrium is reached where there is no further upward or downward pressure on any factor return. Before trade, (wA/rA) < (wB/rB) but, with trade, the rise in (wA/rA) and the fall in (wB/rB) cause these ratios to converge. In equilibrium, (wA/rA) = (wB/rB). Given the assumptions of the model, not only relative factor prices but also absolute factor prices across countries are equalized, meaning that wA = wB and rA = rB. If equality is not reached, trade continues to expand until it is. This powerful implication of trade for factor prices is known as the *factor-price equalization theorem*. While such equalization clearly does not happen in practice, it is the convergence or the tendency toward equalization that is important.

Even more powerful in H-O-S is the extension of the factor-price analysis to the result known as the *Stolper-Samuelson theorem*—a country's scarce factor of production loses real income from trade (and gains from restrictions on trade) and the country's abundant factor of production gains from trade (and loses from trade restrictions). These outcomes occur because of the changing demands stated above. Hence, trade policy becomes intertwined with politics—in country A in our example, labor favors trade because labor's real income thereby increases, while owners of capital lose and would oppose trade.

Finally, a fourth major theorem that arises from H-O-S is the *Rybczynski theorem*. This theorem states that an increase in the supply of a factor of production in a country (say, labor) leads to an increase in output of the good that uses that factor intensively (clothing) and to a decrease in production of the other good (autos). Thus, H-O-S has a growth dimension with implications for future output and future trade patterns.

Empirical testing of H-O-S has centered around examining whether actual trade patterns correspond to the model's predicted patterns. An early test (1953) by Wassily Leontief (1906–1999) surprised economists because the results suggested that the relatively capital-abundant United States was exporting labor-intensive goods and importing capital-intensive goods. This "paradox" led to much later testing that included a greater number of factors (e.g., by dividing labor into different skill categories) and different testing techniques. Some studies, such as those by Daniel Trefler (1995) for thirty-three countries and nine factors and by Harry P. Bowen, Edward E. Leamer, and Leo Sveikauskas (1987) for twenty-seven countries and twelve factors, found limited verification of the predicted patterns. When adjustments are made in the literature for elements outside the model, results get better for H-O-S, but much trade still goes "unexplained."

Another aspect of H-O-S that has been empirically investigated concerns the Stolper-Samuelson theorem, in that economists have sought to determine whether, particularly in the United States, relatively unskilled labor (a scarce factor in the United States) has lost real income because of increased trade. This research, done in the context of the observed increased inequality in income distribution in the late twentieth century, is generally regarded as having found some small effect in the expected direction but also as having found that the growing inequality was due more importantly to the nature of technological change. Empirical work as well as other considerations regarding H-O-S have led to a recognition that the theoretical model, while widely employed, can be criticized for lack of attention to "real-world" characteristics such as differing production functions across countries, economies of scale, and product differentiation.

SEE ALSO *Absolute and Comparative Advantage; Rybczynski Theorem; Stolper-Samuelson Theorem; Tariffs*

BIBLIOGRAPHY

Bowen, Harry P., Edward E. Leamer, and Leo Sveikauskas. 1987. Multicountry, Multifactor Tests of the Factor Abundance Theory. *American Economic Review* 77 (5): 791–809.

Heckscher, Eli F. 1950. The Effect of Foreign Trade on the Distribution of Income. In *Readings in the Theory of International Trade*, eds. Howard S. Ellis and Lloyd A. Metzler for the American Economic Association, 272–300. Homewood, IL: Irwin. Slightly abridged version translated from *Ekonomisk Tidskrift* (1919).

Leontief, Wassily. 1953. Domestic Production and Foreign Trade: The American Capital Position Re-examined. *Proceedings of the American Philosophical Society* 97 (4): 332–349.

Ohlin, Bertil. 1933. *Interregional and International Trade.* Cambridge, MA: Harvard University Press.

Samuelson, Paul A. 1949. International Factor-Price Equalisation Once Again. *Economic Journal* 59 (234): 181–197.

Samuelson, Paul A. 1953–1954. Prices of Goods and Factors in General Equilibrium. *Review of Economic Studies* 21 (1): 1–20.

Stolper, Wolfgang F., and Paul A. Samuelson. 1941–1942. Protection and Real Wages. *Review of Economic Studies* 9 (1): 58–73.

Trefler, Daniel. 1995. The Case of the Missing Trade and Other Mysteries. *American Economic Review* 85 (5): 1029–1046.

Dennis R. Appleyard

HEDGING

Hedging is the process of using derivative financial instruments to reduce the price risks that either arise in the course of normal business operations or are associated with investments. Hedging is one of the most important functions of financial markets. Traders performing hedging transactions are hedgers. Hedgers are often investors, producers, or major users of a given commodity who have preexisting risks associated with the price fluctuation of the specific investment or commodity.

There are many ways that hedging can be carried out through derivative instruments—that is, financial instruments that derive their values from the underlying assets, such as futures contracts, forward contracts, options, and swap agreements. For example, a futures contract allows the holder to carry out a transaction in the future at a price determined in the present. The value of the contract therefore depends upon the asset or commodity underlying the transaction. Hedging with futures contracts is fairly straightforward. Hedgers can hedge by either buying or selling futures contracts as a temporary substitute for a transaction to be made in the spot market. As long as spot and futures prices move together, any loss realized on one market (whether spot or futures) will be offset by a profit on the other market. Using options for hedging purposes is more complicated as it requires an analytical determination of the appropriate number of options contracts to buy or sell.

As an example of hedging with futures contracts, consider a corn farmer who anticipates selling certain bushels of corn three months from now and is concerned that the price of corn might fall in the next three months. The farmer may sell corn futures contracts for hedging. If corn prices in both spot and futures markets fall, the loss on the spot market will be offset by the profit on the futures market. Another example is related to a food-processing com-pany that plans to purchase corn and is concerned that the price of corn might rise. The company can buy corn futures contracts for hedging. If the corn price rises, a loss on the spot market is met with a profit on the futures market, resulting in a reduced price risk.

A hedge is perfect if the gain (or loss) on the futures market matches perfectly with the loss (or gain) on the spot market. In practice, hedging may not be perfect because the difference between the spot price and the futures price (that is, the basis) may not converge to zero at the time the futures position is closed. Hedging effectiveness measures the extent to which the price risk is reduced through hedging. A hedge ratio is the number of derivative contracts transacted to reduce the price risk of a given position in the underlying asset. Hedging strategies are formed to choose the suitable derivative contracts and the amount of such contracts to be used. Traditional views hold that the optimal hedging strategy is one that maximizes the expected utility or minimizes the variance of the value of the hedged portfolio. Recent developments explore alternative approaches. For example, it is argued that a one-sided measure for hedging, such as the downside risk, is more accurate.

With the internationalization of financial markets, currency derivative instruments have increasingly been used to hedge currency risks in an international portfolio, which usually contains multiple risks. Optimal coordinated hedging strategies, which consider the effects of correlation among multiple risk factors in a portfolio, can be applied to hedge multiple risks and to achieve optimal hedging effectiveness.

The recognition of hedging as a purpose of derivatives transactions is important. Accounting rules treat the changes in the fair value of derivatives differently depending on the purpose for which the derivatives positions are entered. New derivatives that have been developed recently are intended to reduce quantity or revenue risks, which may complicate the appropriate accounting treatment.

SEE ALSO *Discounted Present Value; Financial Markets; Forward and Futures Markets; Stock Options*

BIBLIOGRAPHY

Chance, Don M. 2003. *Analysis of Derivatives for the CFA Program.* Charlottesville, VA: Association for Investment Management and Research.

Fabozzi, Frank J., and Franco Modigliani. 2003. *Capital Markets: Institutions and Instruments.* 3rd ed. Upper Saddle River, NJ: Prentice Hall.

Financial Accounting Standards Board of the Financial Accounting Foundation. 1998. *Accounting for Derivative Instruments and Hedging Activities.* Stamford, CT: FASB.

Glen, Jack, and Philippe Jorion. 1993. Currency Hedging for International Portfolios. *Journal of Finance* 48 (5): 1865–1886.

Kolb, Robert W. 2000. *Futures, Options, and Swaps.* 3rd ed. Malden, MA: Blackwell Publishers.

Lien, Donald, and Y. K. Tse. 2002. Some Recent Development in Futures Hedging. *Journal of Economic Surveys* 16 (3): 357–396.

Donald Lien
Mei Zhang

HEDONIC PRICES

Hedonic prices reflect the value of differences in the quality of goods. Hedonic price models provide a useful way of comparing the prices of heterogeneous goods of differing quality so long as consumers are not themselves using prices to judge quality (consumers are assumed in these models to compare the quality of goods independently of their prices). In hedonic models, goods are seen as being produced with different characteristics, and the quality of these goods reflects differences in the mixture of these characteristics. In making a purchase, consumers consider both the quantity of the good that they purchase and the quality of the good. The quality of the good is reflected in the price consumers are willing to pay. This tradeoff between quality and quantity is central both to models of hedonic prices and to household production theory.

In hedonic pricing models, both the characteristics and the prices are known. Differences in the prices of heterogeneous goods are viewed as reflecting quality differences resulting from different characteristics. For example, in a 1928 study, Frederick V. Waugh viewed the perceived quality of asparagus as being determined by the greenness of the asparagus and the size of the stalk. Greenness was held to be positively related to perceived quality, while stock size was held to be negatively related to perceived quality.

The price of other heterogeneous goods can be, and has been, similarly modeled as a function of a vector of characteristics of that good. Examples include automobiles, houses, and computers. To model the price of a particular version of a heterogeneous good, let P_i be its price, let C_i be a vector of m characteristics and let e_i be a stochastic error term. If there are n different versions of the good, the price of each version might be written as:

$$P_i = \beta_0 + \beta_1 C_{1i} + \beta_2 C_{2i} + \ldots + \beta_m C_{mi} + e_i$$

A hedonic price index can then be created as the characteristics and prices of the good change through time.

Hedonic price models have been applied to the construction of price indexes of goods such as automobiles, houses, and computers, for which the characteristics (quality) of the good have been changing over time. They have also been applied to estimates of the quality of life in different locations. The quality of regional amenities is assumed to be capitalized into housing prices and what is commonly thought of as the cost of living. Larry Sjaastad, in a 1962 article, argued that the only way that families can purchase the amenities that a location offers is to migrate to that location. Hence, housing prices are, in essence, the hedonic prices of those amenities. In 1979 Sherwin Rosen developed a hedonic method for measuring the quality of life within a region, based on the assumption that differences in regional amenities are capitalized by lower wage rates and higher housing costs for an amenity-rich region. A hedonic index of regional quality can then be estimated as a function of the characteristics of the location.

The hedonic model of regional quality is an extension of a model in public economics created by Charles M. Tiebout in 1956. Tiebout was concerned about the allocation of local public goods, and he developed a model based on the competition between locations for new residents. Cities attract residents by providing local public goods, and consumers are held to be aware of the public goods and the taxes of different regions, and they then move to the region that has the profile of public goods that maximizes their individual utility. Taxes are simply the prices of these public goods. Hedonic migration models extend Tiebout's model by including amenities provided by nature and the private sector alongside publicly provided amenities in determining the quality of life in various locations. Tiebout's model can also be made more general by including housing costs in determining the migration decision.

SEE ALSO *Migration; Neighborhoods; Price Indices; Public Goods; Quality Controls; Regions; Taxes*

BIBLIOGRAPHY

Becker, Gary S. 1965. A Theory of the Allocation of Time. *Economic Journal* 75 (299): 493–517.

Chow, Gregory C. 1967. Technological Change and the Demand for Computers. *American Economic Review* 57 (5): 1117–1130.

Griliches, Zvi. 1971. Introduction: Hedonic Price Indexes Revisited. In *Price Indexes and Quality Change: Studies in New Methods of Measurement*, ed. Zvi Griliches. Cambridge, MA: Harvard University Press.

Houthakker, Hendrik S. 1952. Compensated Changes in Quantities and Qualities Consumed. *Review of Economic Studies* 19 (3): 155–161.

Rosen, Sherwin. 1979. Wage-Based Indexes of Urban Quality of Life. In *Current Issues in Urban Economics*, eds. Peter Mieszkowski and Mahlon Straszhein, 74–108. Baltimore, MD: Johns Hopkins Press.

Sjaastad, Larry A. 1962. The Costs and Returns of Human Migration. *Journal of Political Economy* Supplement 70 (October), 80–93.

Theil, Henri. 1952. Qualities, Prices, and Budget Inquiries. *Review of Economic Studies* 19 (3) (1952): 129–147.

Tiebout, Charles M. 1956. A Pure Theory of Local Expenditures. *Journal of Political Economy* 64 (5): 416–424.

Waugh, Frederick V. 1928. Quality Factors Influencing Vegetable Prices. *Journal of Farm Economics* 10 (2): 185–196.

Michael P. Shields

HEDONISM

SEE *Farsightedness.*

HEGEL, GEORG WILHELM FRIEDRICH
1770–1831

Hegel is a difficult thinker. The complexity of the arguments of his major works—the *Phenomenology of Spirit* (1807), the *Science of Logic* (1812–1816), the *Philosophy of Right* (1821), and the lectures on aesthetics and world history, which are, perhaps, the least inaccessible—defies capsule summarization. Yet a characterization of the major concerns that *connect* Hegel's writings can be essayed readily enough.

The recent florescence of interest in Hegel among English-language philosophers is a development no one predicted forty years ago. Yet there are good reasons why it has taken place. First and foremost, Hegel (unlike his contemporary Immanuel Kant) emphasized the historically located character of our thinking. Nothing exists out of history; once nature and religion wane as validations, only history is left. The *Philosophy of Right* characterizes philosophy as "its own time apprehended in thought." The facts of history, which add up to a process, are the raw material to which the philosopher gives form and meaning. Reason is dynamic, kinetic; its content unfolds over time. History, which Hegel painted in broad strokes, is a rational process of development; progress in freedom and progress in thought are linked.

Although Hegel, secondly, is a precursor of Karl Marx (1818–1883) and Marxism, he believed that philosophy has no business "giving instruction to what the world ought to be"; over and above the still-vexed issue of Marx's "materialism" versus Hegel's "idealism," Hegel, for his part, emphasized philosophy's retrospective dimension, not its prospective implications. Philosophy is *Nach-denken* ("thinking after the fact to be thought about"). It interprets the present in light of the past. "The owl of Minerva," as Hegel famously put it in the *Philosophy of Right*, "spreads its wings only with the falling of the dusk." We may advance views only when the time is ripe. It makes sense to see Hegel not only as a post-Enlightenment and post-Kantian thinker, but also as a post–(French) Revolutionary one. He at first welcomed the Revolution, only to recoil from the Terror—deficient principle run riot and eventuating in disaster. Hegel had had no love for the ancien régime, but he was infuriated by the revolutionaries' failure to replace it with anything more substantial or enduring.

But what makes Hegel post-Kantian? After all, his *idée maîtresse*—that we are free only when we act in accordance with our reason—is eminently Kantian. What separates Hegel from Kant is what he does with this conviction. Kant's notions of freedom and morality derive from a categorical imperative figurable by pure reason. This to Hegel—who did not believe in "pure" reason—was formal and skeletal. It lacked the substance that "ethical life" (the customs and mores that situate us in a particular time and place) alone can provide. "Ethical life" is an *historical* category, not an abstractly rational one; "abstract," meaning partial, unsubstantiated, fragmentary—the part standing for the whole as in a synecdoche—is always used pejoratively by Hegel. The battle lines are arrayed from book to book: Particularity, subjectivism, and disruption are on the negative side of the ledger, whereas substance, connectedness, coherence, and unity rest on the positive side. Hegel was relentlessly opposed to every source of disconnection he could identify. Then as now, there was no shortage of contenders: The atomistic individualism that threatened in the early nineteenth century to dominate the German as it had the British economy was but one of them.

Hegel's ledger (with these two sides counterposed) has a political, not to say utopian implication that was not to be lost, either immediately on the Young (left) Hegelians or later among twentieth-century critical theorists. This is that if history, rationality, and "ethical life" could be harmonized, the result would be an ethical community in which we could fulfill our own potentialities as we contribute to the well-being of the whole to which it is ours to belong. *This* ideal, not Kant's arbitrary distinction between noumena and phenomena, is the true legacy of the Enlightenment. Kant had mapped out a no-man's-land by declaring certain issues unknowable. Hegel, by contrast, held that nothing is beyond the scope of human thought—despite (or because of) the false starts, falterings, stumblings, and blind alleys almost gleefully detailed, serially, throughout the *Phenomenology of Spirit*.

Hegel's notion of *Geist*, renderable either as "spirit" or "mind," has seemed amorphous, threatening, or both to English-language commentators, some of whom suppose that *Geist* (along with its corollary, "the cunning of reason") signifies a superhuman *demiurgos* pulling the strings of "its" human puppets. This is not what Hegel meant. *Geist* is both how a community understands itself, gives itself form and content, and the way the individual knows him- or herself through the community of which he or she is a constitutive part. Either way, it forms identity. Hegel distinguishes "objective" from "absolute" spirit. The former, the subject matter of the *Philosophy of Right*, is the institutional framework for the latter, which finds expression in our "spiritual" pursuits: art, religion, and (most importantly) philosophy. "Objective spirit" is anything but its own justification; there is nothing ultimate about it. "Absolute spirit" in its ultimate form, philosophy, can *account for* "objective spirit," its precondition. "Objective" cannot account for "absolute" spirit in anything like the same way.

Hegelianism, as John Toews makes clear, enjoyed some philosophical and even some institutional purchase in Germany, though the latter in particular petered out during the 1840s. Hegelianism remained strong enough to provoke Søren Kierkegaard (1813–1855) through several important books: In Britain, however, where it was introduced (after a fashion) by James Hutchison Stirling's *The Secret of Hegel* (1865), its adoption by Idealists (T. H. Green, F. H. Bradley, Bernard Bosanquet, J. T. E. McTaggart) served mainly to buttress the Idealists' *positions déjà prises* (preconceptions); Hegel influenced Pragmatism in the United States via Josiah Royce and John Dewey; in Italy he influenced Benedetto Croce and Giovanni Gentile. Hegelianism was particularly influential in France: On Hippolyte Taine and Ernest Renan in the nineteenth century, and on Alexandre Kojève (whose lectures in the 1930s attracted the interest of Jean Hyppolite and Jean-Paul Sartre, among many others) in the twentieth.

SEE ALSO *Frankfurt School; Idealism; Marx, Karl; Marxism; Teleology*

BIBLIOGRAPHY

PRIMARY WORKS

Hegel, Georg Wilhelm Friedrich. [1807] 1977. *Phenomenology of Spirit*. Trans. A. V. Miller. Oxford: Oxford University Press.

Hegel, Georg Wilhelm Friedrich. [1812–1816] 1969. *Science of Logic*. Trans. A. V. Miller. London: Allen and Unwin.

Hegel, Georg Wilhelm Friedrich. [1821] 1967. *Philosophy of Right*. Trans. T. M. Knox. Oxford: Oxford University Press.

Hegel, Georg Wilhelm Friedrich. [1830] 1956. *Lectures on the Philosophy of World History*. Trans. J. Sibree. New York: Dover.

SECONDARY WORKS

Avineri, Shlomo. 1973. *Hegel's Theory of the Modern State*. Cambridge, U.K.: Cambridge University Press.

Harris, H. S. 1972. *Hegel's Development*. Oxford: Oxford University Press.

Inwood, Michael. 1992. *A Hegel Dictionary*. Oxford: Oxford University Press.

Inwood, Michael, ed. 1985. *Hegel* Oxford: Oxford University Press.

Marcuse, Herbert. 1963. *Reason and Revolution: Hegel and the Rise of Social Theory*. New York: Humanities Press.

Shklar, Judith N. 1976. *Freedom and Independence: A Study of the Political Ideas of Hegel's "Phenomenology of Mind."* Cambridge, U.K.: Cambridge University Press.

Stirling, James Hutchison. [1865] 1971. *The Secret of Hegel: Being the Hegelian System in Origin, Principle, Form, and Matter*. Dubuque, IA: William C. Brown.

Taylor, Charles. 1979. *Hegel*. Cambridge, U.K.: Cambridge University Press.

Toews, John Edward. 1985. *Hegelianism*. Cambridge, U.K.: Cambridge University Press.

Thomas, Paul. 1985. Hegelian Roots. In *Karl Marx and the Anarchists*, 212–255. London and Boston: Routledge and Kegan Paul.

Thomas, Paul. 2004. Property's Properties: From Hegel to Locke. *Representations* 84: 30–43.

Paul Thomas

HEGELIANS

In the opening years of the twenty-first century, the enormous influence of Georg Wilhelm Friedrich Hegel (1770–1831) within the social sciences shows no sign of lessening. This influence is strongest and most obvious in historiography, political theory, and sociology, a discipline that is difficult to imagine in the absence of Hegel. Modern philosophy of religion is similarly inconceivable without Hegel. Hegel's analysis, in *The Philosophy of Right*, of capitalist "civil society" and the poverty it inevitably generates is one of the most important early instances of social (as opposed to political) theory, and it decisively shaped Marx's critique of alienated labor and the history of class struggle, as well as the Frankfurt school's analysis of the "Dialectic of Enlightenment" in the 1940s. Through Alexander Kojève's lectures in 1930s Paris, Hegelian themes were absorbed by Jean-Paul Sartre, Jacques Lacan, and Maurice Merleau-Ponty, and they were passed on in their contributions to existentialism, psychoanalysis, and phenomenology, respectively. Another set of Hegelian concerns was crucial to the "communitarian" critique of Rawlsian liberalism in the 1970s and the "politics of recognition" of Charles Taylor, Axel Honneth, and Nancy Fraser in the 1990s. Even as a bogey to be challenged, Hegel has been crucial. For example, Bertrand Russell and G. E. Moore gave birth to Anglo-American analytic philosophy in rebelling against the Hegelian orthodoxy of late nineteenth-century Britain, and much contemporary post-structuralism and post-modernism continues to take Hegel as its great adversary.

Hegel has played an important role in such varied settings in part because of the extraordinary breadth and depth of his work, and in part because of the immense difficulty this poses for the interpreter. While still alive and lecturing at the University of Berlin, he replaced Immanuel Kant, Johann Fichte, and his former schoolmate Friedrich von Schelling as the dominant philosophical figure of his age in Germany. Even then, the meaning of Hegel's teaching was hotly contested, and Hegel quipped that none of his students understood him—with the exception of one, who misunderstood him. "Old," or "Right," Hegelians emphasized the commitment to the status quo in Hegel's infamous claim that "What is rational is actual (*wirklich*), and what is actual is rational," while "Young," or "Left," Hegelians emphasized the commitment to reason (*Vernunft*).

As with later battles over Hegel, each side in this contest advanced a partial, and hence misleading, account of the matter. Though it still largely determines the popular judgment of Hegel, the Right Hegelian interpretation is most obviously lacking, for Hegel himself took care to distinguish actuality from the "superficial outer rind" of the merely existent; he asked, sarcastically, "Who is not clever enough to see much in his environment that is not in fact as it ought to be?" To argue that the real is rational is in part to define the real as something more than the merely existent, as non-Hegelians do when they castigate a poor teacher for not being a "real" teacher. Just as not all teachers are real teachers in this sense, so not all states are real states for Hegel. In particular, the Prussian and Nazi states, for which he has been wrongly blamed, fail to meet the rational standards of the real in modern times, standards that in Hegel's own account include a constitutional monarch, trials by jury, parliamentary government, freedom of conscience and of the press, and the other prerequisites of individual autonomy.

In all his writings, Hegel struggled to find a way to relate the individual to the greater community that escapes the alienation and "positivity" of an externally imposed law backed only by custom and the threat of force. His initial attempts in this regard center on *love, life,* and some form of *Volksreligion* as modes of experience that attain this moment of community without the sacrifice of individuality. In his mature political philosophy, Hegel used the less religious term *freedom* to characterize the state of being at home in another (*Beisichselbstsein in einem Anderen*) in which one is neither opposed by an alien, hostile world nor engulfed in an unmediated totality that is equally inhospitable to the claims of individual fulfillment. Hegel argues that this is attainable only in a modern polity that the individual can recognize as the precondition and expression of its own freedom.

If the Left Hegelians properly appreciated this, Marx (the most famous of them) nonetheless advanced his own profound misunderstandings of Hegel, misunderstandings that persist to this day. The most significant of these concerns his interpretation of Hegel's understanding of the dialectic that shapes both history and reason. Marx has passed on to millions a bowdlerization of Hegel developed by Heinrich Chalybäus, according to which the dialectic can be easily broken down to a cookie-cutter triad of thesis, antithesis, and synthesis. But these were never used as terms of art by Hegel himself, who described "this monotonous formalism" as "a lifeless schema."

For Hegel, the dialectic is a means of conceiving of both history and reason as processes centering upon *negation*. In the case of the former, this reflects the goals of Hegel's theodicy, his attempt to demonstrate that, appearances notwithstanding, the bloody history of the West has a rational structure and outcome. In the case of the latter, it is an attempt to overcome the aporias of Kant's theoretical and practical philosophy, and to give an account of subjectivity that neither rests upon an incoherent conception of a thing-in-itself nor sacrifices human autonomy to heteronomous forces. Only by means of a dialectical philosophy in which what *is* contains its own negation can Hegel argue, as he does in the *Philosophy of Right*, that an understanding of the moral and political structures required by the free will can be generated from out of that will itself. Here, as elsewhere, negation takes the form of *sublation*, an awkward term used to translate Hegel's *Aufhebung*, the simultaneous destruction and preservation—at a higher, more rational (and hence real) level— of what is. If Hegel's account of this process is hardly without problems, it remains one of the most important attempts to develop a conception of reason that does not stand aloof from history and society, but rather engages with the details of their unfolding.

SEE ALSO *Hegel, Georg Wilhelm Friedrich; Idealism; Left and Right; Liberation Movements; Marx, Karl; Philosophy; Philosophy, Political; Poverty; Rationality; Resistance; Social Science*

BIBLIOGRAPHY

Franco, Paul. 1999. *Hegel's Philosophy of Freedom*. New Haven, CT: Yale University Press.

Hegel, G. W. F. [1820] 1991. *Elements of the Philosophy of Right*, ed. A. W. Wood. Cambridge, U.K.: Cambridge University Press.

Pinkard, Terry. 2000. *Hegel: A Biography*. Cambridge, U.K.: Cambridge University Press.

Schnädelbach, Herbert. 2000. *Hegels praktische Philosophie: Ein Kommentar der Texte in der Reihenfolge ihrer Entstehung*. Frankfurt am Main, Germany: Suhrkamp.

Stewart, Jon. 1996. *The Hegel Myths and Legends*. Evanston, IL: Northwestern University Press.

Andrew Norris

HEGEMONY

The concept of *hegemony* has been central and most developed in the work of Antonio Gramsci, the leading Italian Marxist intellectual who spent the last eleven years of his life in Benito Mussolini's prisons between 1927 and 1935. Gramsci defined hegemony as a condition under which a group establishes its supremacy not only by physical force but also through a "consensual submission of the very people who [are] dominated" (Litowitz 2000, p. 518). However this notion of hegemony has a long history and multi layers and it is important to unravel its complete meaning to understand its significance in Gramsci's adoption of the concept.

According to Raymond Williams the word *hegemony* probably comes from the Greek word *egemonia* whose root is *egemon*, meaning "leader, ruler, often in the sense of a state other than his own" (1976, p. 144). From the nineteenth century onward hegemony came to indicate a "political predominance, usually of one state over another" and subsequently described a "policy expressing or aimed at political predominance" (p. 144). In his *Antinomies of Antonio Gramsci* (1976), Perry Anderson points out the concept of *hegemony* or *gegemoniya* that had started to emerge in the writings of Georgi Valentinovich Plekhanov (1856–1918), a Marxist theoretician and founder of the Social Democratic movement in Russia, was subsequently used by the Russian Marxists as a central political slogan during the Russian Social Democratic movement from 1890s through the Bolshevik Revolution in 1917. Russian Marxists used hegemony to refer to the political struggle and leadership by the working class to overthrow the tsarist rule in Russia. This emphasis placed on the primacy of the working class to acquire hegemony in the bourgeois revolution in Russia was further devel-

oped by Vladimir Lenin especially in *What Is to Be Done*, written in 1902.

The notion of hegemony so far debated in the works of Russian theorists gained an international valence through the first two World Congresses (1919, 1920) of the Third International (1919) and emphasized the need for the proletariat to exercise hegemony in order to form alliance with other exploited groups to struggle against capitalism in the Soviet Union. However, according to Perry Anderson it was in the Fourth Congress (1922) of the Third International that hegemony for the first time also included the idea of "domination of the bourgeoisie over the proletariat, if the former succeeded in confining the latter to a corporate role by inducing it to accept a division between political and economic struggles in its class practice" (1976–1977, p. 18). It was this notion of hegemony brought forth in the Third International that seemed to have influenced most Gramsci's conceptualization of the term.

In accordance with the principles of the Third International, Gramsci defined hegemony as class alliance of the proletariat with other peasants to forge a common struggle against capitalism. This notion of hegemony included the need for certain "concessions" or "sacrifices" necessary on the part of the proletariat to be able to include the needs and interests of the group over which hegemony is to be exercised without resorting to win them over through violence.

However as Douglas Litowitz pointed out in his 2000 article, "Gramsci, Hegemony, and the Law," Gramsci's view of hegemony changed when he noticed that in Italy under the fascist dictatorship of Mussolini the very people who were exploited by fascism and capitalism willingly consented to their exploitation. Thus Gramsci concluded that domination could be exercised not only through physical force but also through persuasion, when the dominant group is able to disseminate its values through mediums such as church, schools, or popular culture. This consensual hegemony is not only economic but also political and cultural as well. In this conceptualization of hegemony as political and cultural, Gramsci was quite influenced by the Italian philosopher and politician Benedetto Croce's (1866–1952) work on the role of culture and consent in politics.

According to Gramsci hegemony always has its basis in economy and "must necessarily be based on the decisive function exercised by the leading group in the decisive nucleus of economic activity" (Hoare, Quintin, and Smith 1971, p. 161). However his concept of "economic" is different from Karl Marx's distinction between an economic base and a political and cultural superstructure and Marx's assertion that only if the base changes, superstructure will change as well. Gramsci argued that dominance in economic relations of production as well as means of production, although necessary, is not a sufficient condition for social dominance. Thus according to Robert Bocock (1986), by opposing the economic determinism of Marx, Gramsci emphasized the political and the cultural by including the state and the civil society as areas in which power is exercised and hegemony established.

Gramsci argued that while hegemony pertains to civil society, which is an ensemble of organizations, force/coercion belongs to the realm of the state. Within capitalism, state thus resorts to coercive domination to conform the popular mass to certain types of production and economy, while civil society exercises hegemony through cultural institutions such as the church, trade union, schools, media or through the print culture. Thus hegemony in this context refers to the cultural control or the "ideological subordination of the working class by the bourgeoisie, which enables it to rule by consent" (Anderson 1976–1977, p. 26). According to Anderson Gramsci has used this model to analyze the difference between Tsarist Russia and western Europe to imply that the tsars ruled by force while the British and French bourgeoisie by deception, flattery, and concessions.

This first model of hegemony by Gramsci underwent further mutations to give rise to a second model when hegemony is seen as being exercised not only by the civil society but by the state as well. Hegemony exercised by the state can be termed as political hegemony and the organs of political hegemony consists of executive, legislature and judiciary.

The third model of Gramsci erases the distinction between state and civil society so that "consent and coercion alike become co-extensive with the State" (p. 125). This was Gramsci's idea of an "integral state," a term he borrowed from the German philosopher Georg Wilhelm Friedrich Hegel (1770–1831). As Jeremy Lester (2000) noted, this concept of "integral state" encompasses a complex set of practices and activities through which the ruling class can not only dominate through force but obtain consensus as well. Thus State embodies not only coercion but cultural and ideological hegemony as well. Gramsci used this model to elucidate how bourgeois capitalism maintains its rule over the working class through consensus as well as coercion. In this third model Gramsci, alludes to Niccolò Machiavelli's conceptualization of "Centaur," which is half beast and half human and a combination of the dual traits of fox and lion that is deception and violence respectively. Gramsci thus argued that in order to dominate, the state must include the dual levels of force and consent, domination and hegemony, violence and civilization.

Thus hegemony—by constituting a synthesis of political, economic, and cultural meanings and values and experienced and internalized by people who are exposed to it—plays a pivotal role in the process of normalization where such values appear to be "common sense" to those who are subordinated and hegemonized by the ruling group.

SEE ALSO *Culture; Fascism; Gramsci, Antonio; Ideology; Machiavelli, Niccolò; Marx, Karl; Marxism; Mussolini, Benito; Propaganda; State, The*

BIBLIOGRAPHY

Anderson, Perry. 1976–1977. The Antinomies of Antonio Gramsci. *New Left Review* 100 (November–December): 5–78.

Bocock, Robert. 1986. Hegemony. In *Key Ideas*, ed. P. Hamilton. London and New York: Ellis Horwood Limited.

Hoare, Quintin, and Geoffrey Nowell Smith. 1971. *Selections from the Prison Notebooks of Antonio Gramsci*. 1st ed. New York: International Publishers.

Lester, Jeremy. 2000. *The Dialogue of Negation: Debates on Hegemony in Russia and the West*. London: Pluto Press.

Litowitz, Douglas. 2000. Gramsci, Hegemony, and the Law. *Brigham Young University Law Review* 2000 (Spring 2): 515–551.

Williams, Raymond. 1976. *Keywords: A Vocabulary of Culture and Society*. 2nd ed. London: Fontana.

Srabani Maitra

HEIDER, FRITZ
SEE *Equilibrium in Psychology.*

HEILBRONER, ROBERT
1919–2005

Robert Louis Heilbroner was an economist and public intellectual best known for his popular book *The Worldly Philosophers* (1953). In what became one of the best-selling books in the discipline, Heilbroner outlined the dramatic scenarios of the classical political economists, especially the work of Adam Smith (1723–1790), David Ricardo (1772–1823), Thomas Robert Malthus (1766–1834), Karl Marx (1818–1883), and John Stuart Mill (1806–1873), as well as Joseph Schumpeter (1883–1950), Thorstein Veblen (1857–1929), and John Maynard Keynes (1883–1946), whom he regarded as continuing the classical tradition of viewing the economy as historically and institutionally situated. The classical scenarios depict the almost inexorable movement of the capitalist economic system, with its "laws of motion," its systematic tendencies leading to some "future immanent in the present" (1992, p. 381). Underlying the system's movements were a variety of factors, both economic and noneconomic. In other words, the trajectory of the system is inseparable from both the wider sociopolitical context within which the economy is situated and the subjective drives and behavioral tendencies of historical agents, which both shape and are shaped by changing socioeconomic and political structures.

Heilbroner's initial fascination with the worldly philosophers' prognoses led to his own analyses of the economic, political, cultural, and sociopsychological drives, motivations, and propensities underlying production, distribution, and exchange. In these investigations, Heilbroner adopted his own versions of Schumpeter's (1954) notions of "vision" and "analysis." Whereas for Schumpeter, analysis had a kind of "cleansing" effect, which prevented the necessarily ideological nature of the "pre-analytical cognitive act" from tainting the scientific endeavor, for Heilbroner, economic theory is inescapably value-laden. Biases are always present, at times lurking just beneath the surface, but often emerging in the form of assumptions that determine the content of analytical categories and the direction of prognostications.

Although Heilbroner's explicit self-identification with a "hermeneutic" approach came relatively late, he had always emphasized that inquiry necessarily has an interpretive dimension. For Heilbroner, this meant that the very object of inquiry cannot be presumed self-evident. The "economy" is an abstraction from the social totality, and thus the defining of the subject matter of economics is a task that influences the nature and direction of analysis. Heilbroner long advocated "material provisioning"—the harnessing of society's material resources to provide for the needs and wants of its members—as the central problematic of the political economist. He thus argued against any notion of universal economic "laws," emphasizing the historical specificity of capitalism in human history. Heilbroner's historical approach, rejection of universal laws, and refusal to "read" markets back into precapitalist societies provide a welcome respite from the "economics imperialism" of modern neoclassical economics.

In later years, Heilbroner questioned whether, under present contemporary circumstances, worldly philosophy is still possible. He believed that scenarios and visions do not lend themselves to formal analytical procedures. More importantly, he held the position that the economic behaviors that set the system on its path have become less dependable, while political intervention has become more strategic. An "instrumental" approach, in his mentor Adolph Lowe's ([1965] 1977) sense, thus becomes more appropriate, with "blueprints depicting possible routes from present realities to desired destinations" replacing "scenarios depicting a future immanent in the present" (Heilbroner 1992, p. 381; Heilbroner and Milberg 1995, pp. 118ff; Forstater 1999).

Despite such skepticism, Heilbroner expressed the hope that the "irrelevant scholasticism" of contemporary neoclassical economics might be replaced with a reinvigorated political economy. Political economy may "perhaps [be] resurrected by a corps of dissenting economists," employing a framework that: "take[s] full cognizance of the sociopolitical realities of our time, whatever the difficulties they may pose for the construction of elegant models.... [A] rekindling of the tradition of political economy is within the realm of possibility. That would indeed be a happy ending to the teachings of the worldly philosophy." (Heilbroner 1996, p. 336).

BIBLIOGRAPHY

Forstater, Mathew. 1999. Working Backwards: Instrumental Analysis as a Policy Discovery Procedure. *Review of Political Economy* 11 (1): 5–18.

Heilbroner, Robert. 1953. *The Worldly Philosophers: The Lives, Times, and Ideas of the Great Economic Thinkers.* New York: Simon & Schuster.

Heilbroner, Robert. 1992. Is Worldly Philosophy Still Possible? *Review of Social Economy* 50: 374–382.

Heilbroner, Robert. 1996. *Teachings from the Worldly Philosophy.* New York: Norton.

Heilbroner, Robert, and William Milberg. 1995. *The Crisis of Vision in Modern Economic Thought.* Cambridge, U.K.: Cambridge University Press.

Lowe, Adolph. [1965] 1977. *On Economic Knowledge: Toward a Science of Political Economics.* Enl. ed. Armonk, NY: Sharpe.

Schumpeter, Joseph A. 1954. *History of Economic Analysis.* New York: Oxford University Press.

Mathew Forstater

HELL

The English word *hell* comes from *hel*, the abode of the dead and the underworld of Norse mythology. In the Bible, the Hebrew word *Sheol* and the Greek word *Hádēs* refer to the netherworld, a shadowy realm of the dead more than a place of torment (though some New Testament texts use *Hádēs* to refer to punishment or the dominion of death; see Luke 16:23, Matt. 16:18, and Rev. 6:8).

The biblical word for the state of postmortem punishment is *Gehenna*, from the Hebrew *ge-hinnōm*, an abbreviation for the "valley of the son of Hinnom," a place south of Jerusalem known for idolatry and human sacrifice (see 2 Kings 23:10 and Jer. 7:31–32). In Jewish apocalyptic and rabbinic literature, Gehenna often refers to a place of darkness, fire, and punishment for the wicked—a punishment variously conceived as everlasting, temporary, or ending in annihilation. In modern times, many Jews have rejected the concept of eternal damnation.

In the New Testament, Gehenna is used for the state of everlasting punishment and fire (see Matt. 5:22, Mark 9:43, and James 3:6), though the Greek word *Tartarus* does appear (see 2 Pet. 2:4). The concept of eternal punishment is expressed through images of "everlasting fire" (Matt. 18:8 and 25:41), "weeping and gnashing of teeth" (Matt. 8:12), "fire and brimstone" (Rev. 14:10), and a "pool of fire" (Rev. 19:20). People confined to the everlasting fire include those who despise the needy (Matt. 25:41–46), as well as "cowards, the faithless, the polluted, murderers, fornicators, sorcerers, idolaters and liars" (Rev. 21:8). In addition to damned humans, Satan and the fallen angels also receive everlasting punishment (see Jude 6, Matt. 25:41, and Rev. 20:10).

Christian theology developed an understanding of hell as everlasting punishment and exclusion from heaven. In the Middle Ages, temporary purifications after death (purgatory) were distinguished from the everlasting torments of hell, as was the state of *limbo*, in which the souls of unbaptized babies and virtuous non-Christians were deprived of the beatific vision but did not suffer the torments of hell. Dante Alighieri (1265–1321) gave poetic expression to limbo and the levels of hell in his *Inferno*, the first part of his *Divine Comedy*, which continues with *Purgatory* and *Paradise*.

Traditional Christians (whether Catholic, Orthodox, or Protestant) affirm hell as a true possibility, either for those who culpably reject the Christian Gospel or who die in a state of "mortal sin." The everlasting nature of hell, even after the resurrection of the body, was affirmed at various Church councils (e.g., the local synod of Constantinople of 543 and the Fourth Lateran Council of 1215). Some Christians hope for universal salvation, but most Christian denominations still affirm the possibility of eternal damnation. Many Christians today believe that sincere non-Christians, who are outside of the Church "through no fault of their own," might still achieve salvation (see *Catechism of the Catholic Church*, no. 847).

The ancient Greeks and Romans had multiple concepts of the underworld and the fate of the dead. In the mystery religions and fertility cults, *Hádēs* or the underworld played a prominent role in themes of death and rebirth. By the fifth century BCE (perhaps due to Egyptian and Persian influences), the Greeks had developed concepts of rewards and punishments after death, with *Tartarus*, the lower realm of *Hádēs*, as the place of punishment for the wicked. Platonism and Neoplatonism incorporated beliefs in reincarnation and the transmigration of

souls, which made purification from wrongdoing achievable over multiple lifetimes.

In the ancient world, the Egyptians and the Zoroastrians from Persia were most pronounced in their affirmations of rewards and punishments after death. Around 1750 BCE, the Egyptian *Book of Going Forth by Day* (or *Book of the Dead*) described how the soul or heart of the deceased person is weighed on a scale balanced by the "feather of truth." Rewards or punishments then follow (with complete destruction being one possibility).

The Persian religion of Zoroastrianism (from the prophet Zoroaster/Zarathustra, circa ninth or tenth century BCE) describes judgment after death as the crossing of the Chinvat Bridge toward Paradise. The souls of the wicked are tossed off the bridge into hell, whereas the righteous souls enter Paradise and other souls go to a state of limbo. At the end of time, the souls of the deceased are reunited with their bodies and experience a final judgment. The souls in limbo (and perhaps those in hell) then enter Paradise after a final purification. The evil spirit Angra Mainyu and other demons are, however, consigned to hell forever.

Islam, like Christianity and Zoroastrianism, affirms judgment after death and a future resurrection of the body, as well as rewards in heaven (paradise) and punishments in hell. Muslims believe that God (Allah) assigns certain angels to keep a record of human deeds, and this record will determine one's fate after death. After death, those who are wicked begin to experience the hellfire—even in the grave prior to the Day of Judgment and the resurrection of the body. The righteous souls, in turn, begin to experience the rewards of Paradise, which continue forever after the reunion with their bodies. Some Muslims, following 2:262 and 5:69 of the Qur'an, believe that followers of other religions can escape hell and enter Paradise. Others, following 4:56, believe severe punishments await those who deny the Qur'an as God's revelation.

Classical Chinese culture recognized some type of life after death, but a clear and consistent concept of hell never developed. Confucius (c. 551–479 BCE) was reluctant to talk about the afterlife, and Taoism tended toward a naturalism that denied personal survival after death.

Jainism, Hinduism, Buddhism, and Sikhism—the main religions originating in India—all affirm reincarnation and the transmigration of souls; moreover, Hindus and Buddhists recognize thousands of hells. Because of reincarnation, however, the possibility of eventual purification and deliverance is maintained, even if this liberation may require countless lifetimes.

The fear of hell remains a living reality among many people today, especially in Christian and Muslim circles. In modern secular societies, however, the word *hell* has assumed a largely metaphorical meaning. Situations of poverty, violence, and devastation are described frequently as "living hells." Many psychologists and sociologists understand hell as an archetype of the deepest fears of the human imagination, expressing the thoughts of torture, rejection, and abandonment that circulate within the human psyche.

SEE ALSO *Anxiety; Christianity; Heaven; Psychology; Religion*

BIBLIOGRAPHY

Badham, Paul, and Linda Badham, eds. 1987. *Death and Immortality in the Religions of the World.* New York: Paragon House Publishers.

Freedman, David Noel, ed. 2000. *Eerdmans Dictionary of the Bible.* Grand Rapids, MI: W. B. Eerdmans Publishing.

Johnston, Sarah Iles. 2005. Afterlife: Greek and Roman Concepts. In *Encyclopedia of Religion*, 2nd ed., Vol. 1, ed. Lindsay Jones, 163–166. Detroit, MI: Thomson Gale.

McKenzie, John L., S.J. 1965. *Dictionary of the Bible.* Milwaukee, WI: Bruce Publishing.

Smart, Ninian. 1989. *The World's Religions.* Englewood Cliffs, NJ: Prentice-Hall.

Turner, Alice K. 1993. *The History of Hell.* Orlando, FL: Harcourt Brace.

Robert Fastiggi

HERD BEHAVIOR

The term *herd behavior* derives from the observation that animals that form part of a group sometimes mimic actions of either a leader or each other apparently without thought. In economics and financial markets, this term describes situations in which a large number of agents appear to be making similar decisions. *Spurious* herding results when decisions are similar, but based on independent analysis by agents. *True* herding results when decisions are based only on public information about the behavior of others, and private information is neglected. Herd behavior can have a detrimental effect on economic efficiency. It stands in contradiction to the basic tenets of efficient markets and to the claim of the superiority of the market system; it undermines the reliance on rationality that requires that agents base their decisions on all information. Modeling of herd behavior has only recently begun to shed light on its motivations and consequences.

A form of herd behavior results when *information cascades* develop in markets characterized by the high cost of information collection. When information collection is costly, an agent may make the same decision as previous agents and not seek any private information. The situation is exacerbated by the presence of moral hazards.

Portfolio managers may herd when their performance is evaluated relative to the market, and herding behavior can also be observed in the international lending decisions of banks (see the discussion of international lending below). Agents may be forced to herd in situations where market sentiment will dictate outcome—regardless of the underlying economics. What is an investor to do when the market sentiment is that the stock market will rise? The sentiment itself will cause the market to rise—an individual investor who, perhaps rightly, believes that a bubble is forming cannot expect to gain from this information unless the timing of the collapse of the bubble can be predicted. The rational strategy for this investor would be to herd.

In the public policy arena, public support for or opposition to particular policy measures frequently derives from what are called *availability cascades*: the more available information is, the more it is considered reliable. Public opposition to smoking is often cited as an example of herding caused by availability cascades.

Herding may be rational behavior in the presence of external threats. Wild animals move together when threatened by a predator—in such cases, the optimal behavior for an individual member is to stay with the group. What is observed as herd behavior is really a consequence of individuals acting rationally.

Less rationally, social pressure may cause individuals to conform to what others are doing. Fads, manias, and fashions may be the consequences of herding resulting from social pressure. Individuals may also seek to safeguard their personal reputation by following the crowd rather than risk the consequences of standing out. Adolescents' behavior in high schools and conformity to politically correct language are examples of this latter type of herding.

INTERNATIONAL BANK LOANS AND INFORMATION CASCADES

International bank loans to developing countries from 1973 to 1982 provide a good illustration of how information cascades, managerial incentives, and moral hazard lead to herding. The oil price shocks of the 1970s left commercial banks from industrialized countries with large pools of recycled petrodollars and the developing countries with large current account deficits. Although the loan of excess bank liquidity to the developing countries would solve the imbalances for both groups at least temporarily, banks had limited knowledge regarding the credit risks of such loans. Some of the largest banks invested resources in developing the technology for risk assessment, but the large majority of the banks went along for the ride based solely on their observation that the larger banks were willing to lend their own funds to developing countries and were lead-managing multibillion-dollar syndicates to provide funds to these borrowers. For the smaller banks, the marginal cost of doing their own analysis was much higher than the cost of gathering public information. The banks also felt pressure from the stock markets, which compared a bank's earnings against those of others that were making what had become highly profitable loans (at least until the middle of 1982). The situation was not helped by the blessings given by the governments of Organisation for Economic Co-Operation and Development member states (who believed that recycled funds would support their exporters) and by international development organizations like the International Monetary Fund (which were unable to finance the developing countries' deficits on their own). Such blessings were taken as an implicit understanding that these governments would help the banks should the banks' lending behavior get them in trouble. Large commercial banks relied on an implicit protection inherent in their market power, believing that governments would not allow major banks to fail. Smaller banks may have herded for two reasons: (1) they could not replicate the information-gathering and analytic capabilities of the larger banks; and (2) they were sure that central banking authorities could not allow smaller banks to fail while saving the larger ones. Indeed all banks, large as well as small, were propped up after the Third World debt crisis began to unfold in August of 1982.

Herd behavior may be at least partly responsible for the Mexican crisis of 1994 and the East Asian crisis of 1997–1998. In both these situations, investment managers may have continued to invest in assets that had become excessively risky under the belief that markets would have penalized them if they failed to earn returns similar to their competitors.

Herd behavior, by encouraging overinvestment when things look good and mass exodus when that impression is reversed, adds to market volatility. It has, however, been difficult to develop tests that can establish either the presence or the impact of herding with some certainty. Future research in this field will have to focus on isolating real herding from mere similarity of outcomes.

SEE ALSO *Banking; Bubbles; Conformity; Developing Countries; Economic Crises; International Monetary Fund; Loan Pushing; Loans; Manias; Moral Hazard; Panics; Rationality; Stock Exchanges*

BIBLIOGRAPHY

Bikhchandani, Sushil, David Hirschleifer, and Ivo Welsh. 1992. A Theory of Fads, Fashions, Custom, and Cultural Change as Information Cascades. *Journal of Political Economy* 100: 992–1026.

Bikhchandani, Sushil, and Sunil Sharma. 2001. Herd Behavior in Financial Markets. *IMF Staff Papers* 47 (3): 279–310.

Darity, William, Jr., and Bobbie L. Horn. 1988. *The Loan Pushers: The Role of Commercial Banks in the International Debt Crisis.* Cambridge, MA: Ballinger Publishing Company.

Jain, Arvind K., and Satyadev Gupta. 1987. Some Evidence on 'Herding' Behavior by U.S. Banks. *Journal of Money, Credit, and Banking* 19 (1): 78–89.

Arvind K. Jain

HEREDITY

From a historical and biological perspective, heredity is the transfer of traits from a parent organism to its offspring. Traditional conceptualizations of heredity have focused on genes and the expression of genetic code that is transferred during reproduction. More recently and in response to knowledge about the limits of genetics in the human phenotypes and behavior, the conceptualization of heredity has been expanded to include the transfer of characteristics of the parent organism to offspring via a range of mechanisms, to include social institutions.

First described as animalcules and ultimately the basis of the school of scientists known as "spermists," early thinkers such as Anton van Leeuwenhoek recognized that there were microscopic parts of the human existence. Others went further to suggest that sperm contained little men who were small representations of adults. As such, heredity was determined by the male of the species, and the role of women in reproduction was simply to carry the homunculus that had been deposited by the male. As a reflection of societal values and the diminished value of women, this theory of heredity prevailed throughout the seventeenth century.

In a controversial and radical move forward, Gregor Mendel was credited for determining the rules associated with genetic transfer in the 1800s in a series of experiments using garden peas. He established patterns of inheritance by observing frequency of traits such as seed color and based on assumptions that the frequency was a direct function of specified patterns of genetic transmission. It was he who observed patterns and coined subsequent rules of genetics, notably the basis of modern genomic theories.

During this era science recognized that both the male and female contributed to heredity and that the ovum and sperm fused toward the development of a synergistic being. The mechanism of this transmission was later determined to be deoxyribonucleic acid (DNA), which was carried on chromosomes. From these seminal discoveries emerged the notion of the "central dogma" that indicates that DNA codes for ribonucleic acid (RNA) in transcription and RNA codes for proteins through a translational process. DNA was ultimately recognized as the blueprint in the direction of cellular activities, tissue and organ functions, and organismic activity and reproduction in both plants and animals.

The molecular structure of DNA was deduced in 1953 by James Watson and Francis Crick and has since served as the basis for understanding modern molecular and behavioral genetics. DNA is characterized as a polymeric double helix containing repeating nucleotide bases linked to phosphorylated sugars. These DNA molecules are arranged in linear or circular chromosomes, specific to species. In some organisms, chromosomes are circular and singular, but in most higher order organisms, chromosomes exist in linear and duplicate form. For example, humans have twenty-three pairs of chromosomes, where inheritance is derived from both mother and father. The sequence of repeating units that make up DNA determines the organism's genotype and, ultimately, phenotype. Genetic variation occurs when there is a change in the DNA sequence secondary to biological or environmental provocation.

We have grown to recognize that heredity significantly influences how we look and how we behave in, anticipate, and respond to our environmental context. This includes how and what we contract in terms of disease, how disease susceptibility is manifest in subsequent generations, and how wellness is defined. In a reciprocal fashion, our environmental context modifies the relationship between genotype and phenotype. Genotype influences phenotype but may produce several different phenotypes, depending on the environmental context. One example is phenylketonuria. This disease is caused by a genetic defect that results in a buildup of phenylalanine, which causes brain damage in children. However, if the affected child's diet contains low levels of phenylalanine, mental retardation is prevented. This environmental change prevents disease presentation, even though the genotype would otherwise predict disease and mental retardation.

Inheritance in humans is often difficult to study. First, all study methods outside the laboratory are observational; scientific ethics prevent us from forcing or selectively controlling mating in humans. Secondly, it is very difficult to study human heredity prospectively because we have very long generation times. As a consequence, a number of techniques have been discovered that uniquely and creatively provide insight into the human inheritance. These include the use of pedigree, twin, and adoption studies. Pedigree studies give scientists a long-term picture

of the inheritance of a given trait, or of several traits, by several generations of a given family. Specific rules regarding pedigrees allow researchers to determine the pattern of inheritance, such as whether a trait is autosomal dominant, autosomal recessive, X-linked dominant, X-linked recessive, or Y-linked. Dizygotic and monozygotic twins offer insight into the influence of environment on diseases with a significant genetic etiology. Since monozygotic twins share the same genetic makeup, it is expected that the manifestation of a genetic trait would be the same for the pair if they are in the same environment. Low concordance in monozygotic twins signals to investigators that environmental factors play a large role in the characteristic. Similarly, but from an environmental perspective, adoption studies also assist with determining the influence of environment and genetics on human functioning. Persons who are adopted often have few genes in common with their parents. However, they share the same environment for a number of years and often have health characteristics similar to those of their adoptive parents. Comparisons are made between adoptees and their adoptive parents, as well as between adoptees and one or both natural parents.

Inheritance is also of interest to those who study human behavior. For example, because of advances in statistical procedures and the use of twin methodologies in recent years, several researchers have begun evaluating the genetic influence of common psychiatric and personality traits, coping, and other behaviors. For example, using behavioral and molecular genetic analyses, Whitfield et al. (2006) recently reported that up to 35 percent of the variance in coping may be genetically mediated. This study suggests that genetics may provide a baseline for coping that is ultimately malleable and susceptible to learning and environmental influences. Similarly, Whitfield et al (2007) reported that 60 percent of individual smoking behavior was genetically mediated, with very few meaningful differences in the genes that determine or influence smoking behavior between racially classified social groups.

Studies like those reported above have been used by some to promote biological explanations for social phenomena and suggest genetic predispositions for favorable or unfavorable social outcomes. Notably, the prevailing scientific evidence strongly challenges genetic explanations in the etiology of social outcomes and suggests that societal inequities are much more salient than are genetic factors.

The recent growth of genomics as a science has frequently exceeded our planning and thinking on topics such as ethics, morals, and the law. Our physical capacity to disentangle the building blocks of human existence has not always been equaled by our appreciation for the impact of such knowledge. For example, should predispositions identified by genetic testing be reported to insurance companies as an acceptable factor in the calculation of risk and an influence on the cost of insurance premiums? Should our ability to manipulate phenotypic characteristic in humans (blond hair, blue eyes, tall, etc.) be used in a fashion representative of a modern-day extension of the concept of eugenics put forth by Francis Galton in the mid-1800s? The eugenics movement advocated selective breeding for the purpose of producing desirable human phenotypes. Should parents be able to preselect the characteristics of their children prior to birth? We will likely continue to develop reactive ethics, morals, and laws as the result of advances in the genomic sciences. We view the future of the study of heredity to include a range of social, psychological, biological, and genetic influences. Genetics serves as a necessary but insufficient factor to understand the scope of intergenerational stability and variation.

SEE ALSO *Darwin, Charles; Determinism, Biological; Determinism, Genetic; Disease; Evolutionary Psychology; Genomics; IQ Controversy; Nature vs. Nurture; Psychosomatics; Twin Studies*

BIBLIOGRAPHY

Edwards, C. L., K. Whitfield, S. Sudhakar, et al. 2006. Parental Substance Abuse, Reports of Chronic Pain, and Coping in Adult Patients with Sickle Cell Disease (SCD). *Journal of the National Medical Association* 98 (3): 420–428.

Gillham, Nicholas Wright. 2001. *A Life of Sir Francis Galton: From African Exploration to the Birth of Eugenics.* New York: Oxford University Press.

Whitfield, K. E., D. T. Brandon, E. Robinson, et al. 2006. Sources of Variability in John Henryism. *Journal of the National Medical Association* 98 (4): 641–647.

Whitfield, K. E., G. King, S. Moller, et al. 2007. Concordance Rates for Smoking among African-American Twins. *Journal of the National Medical Association* 99 (3): 213–217.

Christopher L. Edwards
Goldie Byrd

HERESY

SEE *Orthodoxy.*

HERMENEUTICS

Hermeneutics is a German word of Greek origin translated as *interpretation* in English. In the modern period it was originally used to refer to biblical interpretation and later to the general approach to literary and legal studies. In the past fifty years it has described an alternative to positivist approaches to the study of society. Positivist social science subscribes to methodological monism—the idea that there is a single scientific method, modeled after the natural sciences, that is the means for accumulating objective knowledge about the social and political world. As science, it looks to exclude normative and moral claims or evaluations about the social world. While acknowledging the importance of a scientific understanding of some aspects of the social world, hermeneutics rejects the methodological privilege that positivism ascribes to the natural sciences. Hermeneuticists argue that a more fundamental understanding and explanation of social life may be found in the meaning that action has for social and political actors. The emphasis on meaning implies that social behavior be construed as a text or text-analogue to be interpreted, according to Paul Ricoeur in *Hermeneutics and the Human Sciences* (1981), rather than as an object of scientific and technological understanding. In this respect hermeneuticists hold that the study of social life is more closely related to explanation and understanding of literary texts than to the objective study of physical objects or biological processes. Moreover, proponents argue that hermeneutics shows that the explanation of social life has a necessary moral or normative dimension to it.

Two of the earliest proponents of hermeneutics were Friedrich Schleiermacher (1768–1834) and Wilhelm Dilthey (1833–1911). Schleiermacher argued that the understanding of literary texts, legal documents, religious practices, or works of art require that one start with the object of interpretation and work backward to ascertain the intention of the author. Dilthey, building on Schleiermacher's work, argued that historical events as well as works of art are the meaningful embodiment of the subjective intention of social actors and authors. Both thinkers, according to Hans-Georg Gadamer (1900–2000) in *Truth and Method* (1989), strove to develop an approach to interpretation that would uncover the objective meaning of the object of inquiry.

Schleiermacher and Dilthey formed the basis of what became known as the hermeneutics of recovery. The hermeneutics of recovery presupposes that the task of social inquiry is to capture the original intention or meaning that motivates and informs social action. This presupposes that there is an original, intended meaning that is determinate of social behavior and institutions. This version of hermeneutics often presupposes that empathy is a primary requirement for understanding social action and that explanations are to be couched in the subjective beliefs and intentions of actors.

A second approach, the hermeneutics of suspicion, is grounded in the work of Friedrich Nietzsche

(1844–1900), Karl Marx (1818–1883), and Sigmund Freud (1856–1939), according to Ricoeur. It takes what proponents argue is a more critical approach to interpretation than found in the hermeneutics of recovery. The hermeneutics of suspicion maintains that the subjective intentions or conventional understanding of social actors is misleading and a distortion of social reality. Whether it is the conventional accounts of morality (Nietzsche), the ideology of the capitalist political economy (Marx), or the self-misunderstandings of individuals concerning the genuine motivations for their behavior and particularly their neuroses (Freud), the conscious, subjective, and prevailing understandings of society and social relations remain at the level of mere appearances and function to obscure and distort the reality that the social investigator needs to uncover to reveal the true meaning behind the apparent world.

More recently, two thinkers who have had the greatest impact on hermeneutics have been Martin Heidegger (1889–1976) and Ludwig Wittgenstein (1889–1951). Both Heidegger and Wittgenstein emphasize the priority of language for understanding human existence. For both, language is not just a tool that human beings possess. What is distinctive about human beings is that their experience of the world and their social relations are constituted by and expressed in language. Conversely, language gets its sense from the way of life (Wittgenstein) or the historical horizon (Heidegger) within which it evolves. Hence, there is a close connection between language and the social reality it helps to constitute and embody; the two are intertwined. The meaning of social action must be explained in terms of the linguistic tradition within which it is located, and the linguistic tradition in turn is explicated by reference to the meaningful behavior of social actors. This to-and-fro movement of interpretation is what is meant by the hermeneutic circle.

Heidegger and Wittgenstein have influenced a wide range of interpretive social scientists (Hiley, Bohman, and Schusterman eds. 1991). Perhaps the two most important are Hans-Georg Gadamer (1989; see also Malpas, Arnswald, and Kertscher eds. 2002) and Charles Taylor (b. 1931) (1985, 1995), both of whom go beyond the hermeneutics of recovery and of suspicion. Building on Heidegger's accounts of language and historicity, Gadamer argues that because human behavior and human understanding are historically and linguistically situated, a person's understanding of the world is always both enabled and constrained by the person's linguistic-historical tradition. This means that the prejudices or prejudgments of that tradition are an inescapable and necessary part of people's attempts to understand themselves as well as other historical traditions. This does not, however, mean that people are trapped in a prison of language. Rather, Gadamer argues that a dialogue with the other

encourages openness to the experience of other historical traditions. The result is a fusion of horizons that transcends previous understandings.

Taylor makes a similar point concerning language. Drawing on both Heidegger and Wittgenstein, he argues that language and the social practices in which it is embedded form a social imaginary that serves to express an understanding of the possibilities for human beings and for social and political life. Because that understanding is often inchoate, tacit, and imperfectly articulated, the goal of the social theorist is to give an expression to that social imaginary. Taylor ties this reformulation of the self-understanding of social life to the possibility of deep forms of moral and political evaluation and reflection on the part of social and political actors (Taylor 1985a, 1985b, 1995). Moreover, building on the work of Gadamer, Taylor argues that Gadamer's account of the fusion of horizons is pertinent not just for the understanding of other historical situations. It is also important in understanding other contemporary cultures and ways of life. The dialogical process that takes place in such efforts makes mutual understanding possible, though not guaranteed. Moreover, it makes greater reflective understanding of ourselves possible as well (Taylor in Malpas, Arnswald, and Kertscher 2002, 277–298)

The most recent significant development in hermeneutics is found in the work of Italian philosopher and social theorist Gianni Vattimo. In *Beyond Interpretation: The Meaning of Hermeneutics for Philosophy* (1997), Vattimo argues that taking the anti-essentialism of Nietzsche more seriously enables a more radical approach to hermeneutics and interpretation. He looks to challenge the distinction between the natural and the human sciences and to encourage a dialogue among science, art, religion, and ethics. Perhaps most important, along with Taylor he sees a more robust role for religion in the public sphere in what some hermeneuticists describe as a post-secular society.

CRITICISM OF HERMENEUTICS

Despite what proponents see as the promise of interpretive approaches to the study of social life, a number of criticisms have been offered of hermeneutics. One criticism continues to be advanced by conventional social scientists. Focusing on earlier forms of hermeneutics, they claim that empathic understanding may be a useful tool in formulating better hypotheses, but it does not exhaust the range of behavior that is of interest to social science. Moreover, it is not a criterion of verification in the research process, according to those committed to scientifically defined social inquiry.

A second criticism originates with critical theory and the work of Jürgen Habermas. In his debate with

Gadamer, Habermas argues that despite its importance for social inquiry, the hermeneutic emphasis on tradition, prejudices, and internal standards of rationality limits its critical leverage on prevailing ideologies that mask the social reality and specifically the exercise of power (Habermas 1987). Critical theorists maintain that this reflects an inherent, politically conservative bias.

A third criticism, from a perspective reminiscent of Michel Foucault (1926–1984), argues that hermeneutic/ interpretive theory is still committed to conventional conceptions of truth and the self that are constituted by dominant discursive practices of the self and politics. These, in turn, deploy categories and practices of identity and difference that privilege some forms of human beings and understanding and marginalize or disqualify others. Hermeneutics fails to acknowledge the extent to which it is implicated in prevailing notions of the self and politics.

Needless to say, interpretive theorists have responded to each of these criticisms. To the first they point out that the emphasis on language and its relation to social practice requires explanation that goes beyond empathic understanding. It involves the investigator in what the anthropologist Clifford Geertz (1987) calls depth interpretation. To the second and third criticisms, thinkers such as Gadamer and Taylor acknowledge the limitations of hermeneutics. Consequently, each argues that no historical prejudgments can be allowed to go unchallenged and that one needs to be aware of the ways that prevailing practices of politics and the self influence the possibilities of social explanation. What is perhaps most important, however, is not so much the specific responses of hermeneutics to its critics as the hermeneutic claim that because of the self-interpreting nature of human beings, social science is best understood as a form of practical reason analogous to Aristotle's fourth-century BCE discussion of practical wisdom in Book VI of the *Nicomachean Ethics*. This, according to Gibbons (2006), commits hermeneuticists to a dialogue with social actors and competing perspectives as the most promising response to theoretical contestation and pluralism.

SEE ALSO *Anthropology, Linguistic; Essentialism; Freud, Sigmund; Geertz, Clifford; Literature; Marginalization; Marx, Karl; Nietzsche, Friedrich; Philosophy; Positivism; Social Science*

BIBLIOGRAPHY

Aristotle. 2000. *Nicomachean Ethics*. Trans. and ed. Roger Crisp. Cambridge, U.K.: Cambridge University Press. (Orig. created fourth century BCE.)

Gadamer, Hans-Georg. 1989. *Truth and Method*. 2nd ed. Rev. Trans. Joel Weinsheimer and Donald G. Marshall. New York: Crossroad.

Geertz, Clifford. 1987. From the Native's Point of View: On the Nature of Anthropological Understanding. In *Interpreting Politics*, ed. Michael T. Gibbons, pp. 133–147. New York: New York University Press.

Gibbons, Michael T. 2006. Hermeneutics, Political Inquiry, and Practical Reason: An Evolving Challenge to Political Science. *American Political Science Review: Centennial Edition* 100 (4): 563–571.

Habermas, Jürgen. 1987. The Hermeneutic Claim to Universality. In *Interpreting Politics*, ed. Michael T. Gibbons, pp. 175–202. New York: New York University Press.

Hiley, David R., James F. Bohman, and Richard Shusterman, eds. 1991. *The Interpretive Turn: Philosophy, Science, Culture*. Ithaca, NY: Cornell University Press.

Malpas, Jeff, Ulrich Arnswald, and Jens Kertscher, eds. 2002. *Gadamer's Century: Essays in Honor of Hans-Georg Gadamer*. Cambridge, MA: MIT Press.

Ricoeur, Paul. 1981. *Hermeneutics and the Human Sciences: Essays on Language, Action, and Interpretation*, ed. and trans. John B. Thompson. Cambridge, U.K.: Cambridge University Press.

Taylor, Charles. 1985a. *Human Agency and Language*. Vol. 1 of *Philosophical Papers*. Cambridge, U.K.: Cambridge University Press.

Taylor, Charles. 1985b. *Philosophy and the Human Sciences*. Vol. 2 of *Philosophical Papers*. Cambridge, U.K.: Cambridge University Press.

Taylor, Charles. 1995. *Philosophical Arguments*. Cambridge, MA: Harvard University Press.

Vattimo, Gianni. 1997. *Beyond Interpretation: The Meaning of Hermeneutics for Philosophy*. Trans. David Webb. Stanford, CA: Stanford University Press.

Michael T. Gibbons

HERNANDEZ V. TEXAS

Brown v. Board of Education was not, as almost everyone assumes, the first decision in which the U.S. Supreme Court, newly unified under the leadership of Chief Justice Earl Warren, set to dismantling Jim Crow segregation. That distinction belongs to a jury exclusion case decided two weeks earlier, *Hernandez v. Texas*. *Hernandez* is not just the first case in which the Warren Court took on segregation; it is also the greatest early triumph in the Mexican American struggle for civil rights and the first Supreme Court case to extend to Latinos constitutional protection against discrimination, no small matter now that Hispanics constitute the largest minority group in the United States.

After a two-day trial and less than three hours of deliberation, an all-white jury in Jackson County, Texas, in 1951, convicted Pete Hernández of murder and sentenced him to life in prison. The jury's racial composition was not an aberration for the era. The county stipulated at trial that no person with a Spanish surname had served on a trial or grand jury in more than a quarter century; more than 6,000 jurors had been seated, but in a county over 15 percent Mexican American, none had been from that group. The League of United Latin American Citizens (LULAC), then the most prominent Mexican American civil rights group in the country, agreed to help represent Hernández's case before the Supreme Court.

A JIM CROW CASE

In deciding whether impermissible discrimination occurred, the Court considered a veritable catalog of Jim Crow oppressions. The Court noted that a restaurant in the county seat prominently displayed a sign saying "No Mexicans Served." In addition, Jackson County residents routinely distinguished between "whites" and "Mexicans." Business and civic groups almost entirely excluded Mexican American members. The schools were segregated, at least through the fourth grade, after which almost all Mexican Americans were forced out of school altogether. Finally, the opinion also recorded that on the Jackson County courthouse grounds there were two men's bathrooms. One was unmarked. The other said "Colored Men" and "Hombres Aquí," meaning, "Men Here."

Consider more fully the underlying claim of jury exclusion. All-white juries imperiled Mexican American defendants who, such as Hernández, risked conviction by hostile and biased juries. Moreover, the Mexican American community suffered because white juries rarely and reluctantly convicted whites for depredations against Mexican Americans. Finally, determined opposition to jury exclusion arose because of its symbolism. In the context of Texas race politics, putting Mexican Americans on juries was tantamount to elevating such persons to equal status with whites. The idea that "Mexicans" might judge whites deeply violated Texas's racial caste system. LULAC hoped *Hernandez* would help to topple a key pillar of Jim Crow: the belief that whites should judge all, but be judged by none but themselves.

FRUSTRATING A RACIAL ANALYSIS

Even though it challenged a Jim Crow practice, the Supreme Court did not decide *Hernandez* as a race case. The Court avoided a racial analysis because, strikingly, both parties argued that Mexican Americans were racially white.

As the evidence in *Hernandez* demonstrates, Anglos in Texas in the 1950s considered Mexicans an inferior race. This belief originated during the Anglo expansion into the Southwest in the early to mid-1800s that culminated in the expropriation of the northern half of Mexico. Initially, Mexicans in the United States, or at least the

community's leaders, resisted their racial subordination by constructing themselves as Mexican nationals and by envisioning an eventual return to Mexico. In the 1920s and 1930s, however, broad segments of the U.S. Mexican community came to see themselves as Americans. During this epoch Mexican community leaders embraced an assimilationist ideology; indeed, the label "Mexican American" emerges from this period and encapsulates the effort to both retain pride in the community's Mexican cultural origins and to express an American national identity. Inseparable from this new assimilationist identity, however, was an engagement with American racial logic: on this score the community leaders argued that Mexican Americans were white.

These ideas found clear expression in LULAC's arguments in *Hernandez v. Texas*. As in other cases, LULAC followed what it termed its "other white" legal strategy, protesting not segregation itself, but the inappropriate segregation of Mexican Americans as a white racial group. Thus, LULAC objected in its brief to the Supreme Court that, "while legally white," in Jackson County "frequently the term white excludes the Mexicans and is reserved for the rest of the non-Negro population" (Brief of Petitioner at 38, *Hernandez v. Texas*, 347 U.S. 475, No. 406). Hernández's lawyers did not argue principally that segregation was legally wrong, but that Mexican Americans were legally white.

Meanwhile, Texas also adopted the claim that Mexican Americans were white—though to preserve segregation. LULAC and others had brought at least seven challenges to jury exclusion in Texas before *Hernandez*. In the initial cases Texas courts relied on testimony that Mexican Americans were "ignorant" or "not intelligent enough" in ruling that no Mexican Americans were qualified for jury service. By the late 1940s, however, the Texas courts shifted to a new approach. Seeking to turn LULAC's arguments back against them, the courts began to hold that there was no discrimination because, like every jury member, Mexican Americans were white. As the decision under appeal in *Hernandez* reasoned, "Mexicans are white people.... The grand jury that indicted [Hernández] and the petit jury that tried him being composed of members of his race, it cannot be said ... that appellant has been discriminated against in the organization of such juries" [*Hernandez v. Texas*, 251 S.W.2d 531, 536 (Tex. Crim. App. 1951)].

PROTECTING SUBORDINATED GROUPS

Confronted with contending parties who nevertheless agreed that Mexican Americans were white, the Supreme Court jettisoned an explicitly racial analysis. The case, Warren said, did not turn on "race or color." However,

Warren did not then attempt to decide the case in terms of some other form of difference, for instance national origin, ancestry, or ethnicity. Rather, the Court approached this case as concerning group subordination generally. "Community prejudices are not static," Warren wrote, "and from time to time other differences from the community norm may define other groups which need [constitutional] protection." For Warren, a group's standing was "a question of fact," something that "might be demonstrated by showing the attitude of the community" (*Hernandez v. Texas*, 347 U.S. at 478, 479).

In considering whether the Fourteenth Amendment commanded the Court's intervention, Warren framed the core question as this: Are social practices based on notions of racial difference being used to subordinate? To answer this question, the Court cataloged the Jim Crow system that defined race relations in Jackson County. *Hernandez* struck down jury discrimination against Mexican Americans not because they were nominally a race, but because in the context of mid-century Texas, Mexicans were a subordinated group.

SEE ALSO Brown v. Board of Education, *1954; Civil Rights; Colonialism; Warren, Earl*

BIBLIOGRAPHY

Haney López, Ian. 1997. Race, Ethnicity, Erasure: The Salience of Race. *California Law Review* 85 (October): 1143–1211.

Haney López, Ian. 2003. *Racism on Trial: The Chicano Fight for Justice.* Cambridge, MA: Belknap Press of Harvard University Press.

Haney López, Ian. 2005. Race and Colorblindness after *Hernandez* and *Brown. Chicano-Latino Law Review* 25: 61–76.

Hernandez v. Texas, 251 S.W.2d 531 (Tex. Crim. App. 1952).

Hernandez v. Texas, 347 U.S. 475 (1954). http://caselaw.lp.findlaw.com/scripts/getcase.pl?court=us&vol=347&invol=475.

Olivas, Michael A., ed. 2006. *"Colored Men and Hombres Aquí": Hernandez v. Texas and the Emergence of Mexican American Lawyering.* Houston, TX: Arte Publico Press.

Ian F. Haney López

HERSKOVITS, MELVILLE J.
1895–1963

The American anthropologist Melville J. Herskovits spent his long academic career at Northwestern University, from 1927 until his death in 1963. There he established the first program in African studies at a major U.S. university.

Herskovits has been regarded as a pioneer for advocating the serious and respectful study of Africa and the African diaspora. In *The Myth of the Negro Past* (1941), perhaps his best-known book, he sought to document the strength of an African cultural heritage of which blacks in the United States could be proud; he felt that once this was known and respected, antiblack prejudice would diminish.

Herskovits was born in Ohio to European-Jewish immigrant parents. Briefly a student at Hebrew Union College in Cincinnati, he enlisted in the U.S. army during World War I (1914–1918). He later attended Columbia University, where he studied with Franz Boas (1858–1942), who was seen as the "father" of American anthropology. Herskovits did a library doctoral dissertation on the "cattle complex" of East Africa with a focus on culture areas, tracing the diffusion of cultural traits. (The "cattle complex" referred to the cultural meanings, economic functions, and politics associated with cattle in East African cultures.) He then undertook physical anthropological research among African Americans. With his wife and anthropological partner Frances S. Herskovits (1897–1972), he did ethnographic fieldwork in Africa, in Dahomey (1931), and among Afro-American groups in Suriname (1928 and 1929), Haiti (1934), Trinidad (1939), and Brazil (1941–1942), before turning his attention more fully to African societies and politics.

Beginning with his popular and professional writings in the 1920s, Herskovits sought to combat racism and nativism through the use of anthropology conceived of as a science. He furthered Boas's insistence on the plasticity of "race" by arguing that the "American Negro" was a racially mixed "amalgam" (Herskovits 1928, 1930). When he turned to the cultural anthropology of the African diaspora, Herskovits initially held that African Americans evinced "complete acculturation" to (white) U.S. mainstream culture (Jackson 1986). However, influenced by ethnologists and historians from Latin America and the Caribbean, African American intellectuals, and others, he soon redirected his scholarship to the study of what he called *Africanisms*, viewed as cultural elements of African provenance (Yelvington 2006). For Herskovits, in the acculturative context of African diaspora in the Americas, where culture contact occurred between African, European, Amerindian, and other cultures, Africanisms shaped the behavioral responses of what he called the "Negro in the New World," and were even to be found among whites and other groups (e.g., in cuisine and speech in the U.S. South). Africanisms, which could sometimes be identified by African ethnic origin, were conceived as cultural baselines, and they were thought to vary in intensity across the region and across cultural forms such as kinship, language, dance, and games—indeed, they could be charted on a "scale of intensity" continuum. They were found in folklore, but they were believed to be especially strong in religion (Baron 1994). In *Suriname Folk-Lore* (1936) the Herskovitses sought to demonstrate "correspondences" between Creole tales and tales of Old World origin; their work in Dahomey (Herskovits 1938a; Herskovits and Herskovits 1958) was concerned with the performance of narratives, creative expression, and the role of proverbs and riddles in enculturation, as well as with religion. In the 1930s Herskovits became interested in *acculturation,* or culture contact and culture change (Herskovits 1938b). In *Life in a Haitian Valley* (Herskovits 1937) he combined this interest with psychology, and introduced the idea of *socialized ambivalence* to describe what he saw as the conflict-ridden personalities that were the result of a dual cultural legacy. *Syncretism,* or the merging of two belief systems that still retain their identities, became important in Herskovits's conceptual lexicon at this time. These concepts were brought together in *The Myth of the Negro Past* (1941). With *Trinidad Village* (Herskovits and Herskovits 1947), the concept of reinterpretation was used to designate how Afro-Americans retained "inner" behavior while giving new meaning to acquired cultural forms (Baron 2003). Herskovits's promotion of cultural relativism and his mature ideas of cultural dynamics were elaborated most fully in *Man and His Works* (1948).

Herskovits was criticized by some such as Gunnar Myrdal (1898–1987), main author of the landmark *An American Dilemma* (1944), and African American sociologist E. Franklin Frazier (1894–1962) who, while joining with Herskovits's goal of eliminating racism, could not agree with his theoretical stance.

Herskovits garnered an international reputation within the disciplines of anthropology and African diaspora studies, holding many positions of influence (Gershenhorn 2004) and publishing more than 400 books and scientific papers (Merriam 1964). Meanwhile, he trained a cadre of doctoral students at Northwestern University. His writings have inspired cultural and identity politics. All of which means that Herskovits's work remains controversially relevant.

SEE ALSO *Anthropology, U.S.; Boas, Franz*

BIBLIOGRAPHY

PRIMARY WORKS

Herskovits, Melville J. 1928. *The American Negro: A Study in Racial Crossing.* New York: Alfred A. Knopf.

Herskovits, Melville J. 1930. *The Anthropometry of the American Negro.* New York: Columbia University Press.

Herskovits, Melville J. 1937. *Life in a Haitian Valley.* New York: Alfred A. Knopf.

Herskovits, Melville J. 1938a. *Dahomey, An Ancient West African Kingdom.* New York: J. J. Augustin.

Herskovits, Melville J. 1938b. *Acculturation: The Study of Culture Contact.* New York: J. J. Augustin.

Herskovits, Melville J. 1941. *The Myth of the Negro Past.* New York: Harper and Brothers.

Herskovits, Melville J. 1948. *Man and His Works: The Science of Cultural Anthropology.* New York: Alfred A. Knopf.

Herskovits, Melville J., and Frances S. Herskovits. 1936. *Suriname Folk-Lore.* New York: Columbia University Press.

Herskovits, Melville J., and Frances S. Herskovits. 1947. *Trinidad Village.* New York: Alfred A. Knopf.

Herskovits, Melville J., and Frances S. Herskovits. 1958. *Dahomean Narrative: A Cross-Cultural Analysis.* Evanston, IL: Northwestern University Press.

SECONDARY WORKS

Baron, Robert. 1994. Africa in the Americas: Melville J. Herskovits' Folkloristic and Anthropological Scholarship, 1923–1941. PhD diss., University of Pennsylvania.

Baron, Robert. 2003. Amalgams and Mosaics, Syncretisms and Reinterpretations: Reading Herskovits and Contemporary Creolists for Metaphors of Creolization. *Journal of American Folklore* 116 (459): 88–115.

Gershenhorn, Jerry. 2004. *Melville J. Herskovits and the Racial Politics of Knowledge.* Lincoln: University of Nebraska Press.

Jackson, Walter A. 1986. Melville Herskovits and the Search for Afro-American Culture. In *Malinowski, Rivers, Benedict, and Others: Essays on Culture and Personality*, ed. George W. Stocking, Jr., 95–126. Madison: University of Wisconsin Press.

Merriam, Alan P. 1964. Melville Jean Herskovits, 1895–1963. *American Anthropologist* 66 (1): 83–109.

Myrdal, Gunnar. 1944. *An American Dilemma: The Negro Problem and Modern Democracy.* New York: Harper and Brothers.

Yelvington, Kevin A. 2006. The Invention of Africa in Latin America and the Caribbean: Political Discourse and Anthropological Praxis, 1920–1940. In *Afro-Atlantic Dialogues: Anthropology in the Diaspora*, ed. Kevin A. Yelvington, 35–82. Santa Fe, N.M.: School of American Research Press.

Kevin A. Yelvington

HESSIAN MATRIX

The Hessian matrix was developed by Ludwig Otto Hesse (1811–1874), a German mathematician, though the term was first used by James Joseph Sylvester (1814–1897), an English mathematician who studied under Karl Gustav Jacob Jacobi (1804–1851). The Hessian is a square (the number of rows equal to the number of columns) and symmetric (if the rows are written as the columns, the same matrix is produced) matrix whose entries are second-order partial derivatives defined as $\dfrac{\partial^3 f}{\partial x_i \partial x_j}$. Since the Hessian is defined using second-order partial derivatives, the function must be continuous (smooth with no breaks or gaps) and differentiable (the derivative must exist at the point being evaluated).

The Hessian is used to characterize stationary or inflection points of a multivariable function, $f(x_1, x_2)$, as maximums or minimums. The identification as a maximum or minimum requires knowledge about the leading principal minor, $|H_k|$—the determinant of the principal submatrix of order k. For a stationary point to be a maximum, the leading principal minors must alternate in sign with $|H_1|$ being negative. If all the leading principal minors are positive, then the stationary point is a minimum. Failure to satisfy either of these conditions, which includes a leading principal minor of value zero, means characterization of the stationary point is inconclusive. The drawback of the Hessian is that calculating all the leading principal minors becomes laborious for an n-variable function with $n < 2$.

The Hessian, as defined, is used to characterize stationary points of unconstrained optimization problems, which are drawn from the theory of the firm. Goods are produced using capital (K) and labor (L) with the following production function, $f(L, K)$. Firms must decide the optimal combination to maximize profit. Applying the Hessian to such a problem generates a condition for profit maximization. For $|H_1|$ to be negative, the marginal product of labor must be diminishing—additional labor beyond the optimal choice decreases productivity, therefore, decreasing profit. The positive requirement of $|H_2|$ means that the marginal product of capital must also be diminishing. Without knowledge of these conditions, changes to the firm's production policy would result in inefficient use of resources and a decrease in social welfare. Therefore, the Hessian matrix is an important tool in the policy analysis of unconstrained choices.

SEE ALSO *Inverse Matrix; Jacobian Matrix; Matrix Algebra*

BIBLIOGRAPHY

Baldani, Jeffrey, James Bradfield, and Robert Turner. 2005. *Mathematical Economics*. 2nd ed. Mason, OH: Thomson/South-Western.

Chiang, Alpha C., and Kevin Wainwright. 2005. *Fundamental Methods of Mathematical Economics*. 4th ed. Boston: McGraw-Hill/Irwin.

Dowling, Edward T. 2001. *Schaum's Outline of Theory and Problems of Introduction to Mathematical Economics*. 3rd ed. Boston: McGraw-Hill.

Fuente, Angel de la. 2000. *Mathematical Methods and Models for Economists*. New York: Cambridge University Press.

Hoy, Michael, et al. 2001. *Mathematics for Economists*. 2nd ed. Cambridge, MA: MIT Press.

Jehle, Geoffrey A., and Philip J. Reny. 2001. *Advanced Microeconomic Theory*. 2nd ed. Boston: Addison-Wesley.

MacTutor History of Mathematics Archive. University of St. Andrews, Scotland. http://www-groups.dcs.st-and.ac.uk/~history/.

Silbergberg, Eugene, and Wing Suen. 2001. *The Structure of Economics: A Mathematical Analysis*. 3rd ed. Boston: McGraw-Hill/Irwin.

Simon, P. Carl, and Lawrence Blume. 1994. *Mathematics for Economists*. New York: Norton.

Varian, Hal R. 1992. *Microeconomic Analysis*. 3rd ed. New York: Norton.

Rhonda V. Sharpe
Idrissa A. Boly

HETERARCHY

Complex systems science is the study of dynamic nonlinear systems that are not in equilibrium and do not act in a predictable manner. Key features (integration, communication, history/initial conditions) in complex biophysical systems correspond with key features of social systems: the holistic nature of culture, knowledge sharing through the senses, and the formative power of traditions, structures and materials, strategies, and habits of mind.

While several areas of complex systems research have potential for the social sciences, one of the most promising is the concept of heterarchy, which treats the diversity of relationships among system elements and offers a way to think about systemic change in spatial, temporal, and cognitive dimensions. Definitions of heterarchy are remarkably consistent across disciplines, while the work they do is extraordinarily diverse. The earliest definition describes the mind's ability to hold conflicting values as a "heterarchy of values determined by the topology of nervous nets" (McCulloch 1945, p. 89). In artificial intelligence and computer design, the organization of computer sub-routines that can call one another is heterarchical (Minsky and Papert 1972, p. 2). A mathematician defines heterarchy as a program in which there is no highest level (Hofstadter 1979, p. 134). A sociologist who studies corporations defines heterarchy as "an emergent organizational form with distinctive network properties ... and multiple organizing principles" (Stark 2001, p. 71). A general purpose definition contrasts hierarchies, the elements of which are ranked relative to one another, with heterarchies, the elements of which are unranked, or possess the potential for being ranked in a number of different ways, depending on systemic requirements (Crumley 1979, p. 144).

Heterarchy does not stand apart from hierarchy; rather, the two forms are in a dialectical relationship. From a mathematical standpoint heterarchy is the more general category and subsumes hierarchy as a special case. The concept's versatility permits its use as a physical structure, as an abstract model, or in an historical narrative. Heterarchy meets requirements for robust social theory inasmuch as the concept can relate the micro (individual) level to the macro (social) level, the agency of social actors to the social structure in which they operate, and provide an explanation for discontinuous and fundamental changes in the social system as a whole.

Heterarchy is a corrective to the naturalized characterization of power relations, which conflates hierarchy with order (Crumley 1987, 2005; Ehrenreich 1995). Since archaeology's founding as a discipline, most interpretation has assumed a linear progression from small, early, "simple" societies to those that were more populous, later in time, and "complex." Such a definition of complex (having more administrative levels) is in contrast to the definition of complexity in nonlinear systems (more richly networked). Political systems were assumed to have greater stability the more they tended toward tiered hierarchies of power. Yet powerful forces can manifest entirely outside the framework of state hierarchies and beyond their control. In non-linear systems, this is chaos or surprise, and reflects the characteristic brittleness of very hierarchical societies rendered vulnerable by systemic barriers to information transfer and limited recognition of other dimensions of power.

Archaeological and ethnographic evidence indicates that hierarchies and heterarchies of power coexist in all human societies, including states. Thus biological diversity has a correlate in human societies: the toleration of difference in individuals and groups offers a reserve of knowledge for use in problem solving, just as genetic and biological diversity increases ecosystemic resilience. Similarly, organizational flexibility (economic, social, and political) enables societies to adjust to changed circumstances. As in ecology, researchers must remain aware of intensity, periodicity, and duration of relations; in human societies this might be thought of as the range of powers an individual, a group, or an institution has, and the regularity and duration of particular roles. Heterarchy is a fundamental principle of social organization.

SEE ALSO *Archaeology; Chaos Theory; Ethnography; Hierarchy; Networks; Political Economy; Power; Systems Theory*

BIBLIOGRAPHY

Crumley, Carole L. 1979. Three Locational Models: An Epistemological Assessment for Anthropology and Archaeology. *Advances in Archaeological Method and Theory,* vol. 2, 141–173.

Crumley, Carole L. 1987. A Dialectical Critique of Hierarchy. In *Power Relations and State Formation,* eds. Thomas C. Patterson and Christine Ward Gailey, 155–168. Washington, DC: American Anthropological Association.

Crumley, Carole L. 2005. Remember How to Organize: Heterarchy Across Disciplines. In *Nonlinear Models for Archaeology and Anthropology,* eds. Christopher S. Beekman and William S. Baden, 35–50. Aldershot, Hampshire, UK: Ashgate Press.

Ehrenreich, Robert M., Carole L. Crumley, and Janet E. Levy, eds. 1995. *Heterarchy and the Analysis of Complex Societies.* Archaeological Papers of the American Anthropological Association no. 6. Washington, DC: American Anthropological Association.

Hofstadter, Douglas. 1979. *Godel, Escher, Bach: An Eternal Golden Braid.* New York: Basic Books.

McCulloch, Warren S. 1945. A Heterarchy of Values Determined by the Topology of Nervous Nets. *Bulletin of Mathematical Biophysics* 7: 89–93.

Minsky, M., and S. Papert. 1972. *Artificial Intelligence Progress Report* (AI Memo 252). Cambridge, MA: MIT Artificial Intelligence Laboratory.

Stark, David. 2001. Ambiguous Assets for Uncertain Environments: Heterarchy in Postsocialist Firms. In *The Twenty-First-Century Firm: Changing Economic Organization in International Perspective,* ed. Paul DiMaggio, 69–104. Princeton, NJ: Princeton University Press.

Carole L. Crumley

HETEROGENOUS AGENTS
SEE *Principal-Agent Models.*

HETEROGLOSS
SEE *Anthropology, Linguistic.*

HETERONOMY
SEE *Kant, Immanuel.*

HETERONORMATIVITY

Coined in 1991 by Michael Warner, a social critic, the term *heteronormativity* refers to pervasive and invisible norms of heterosexuality (sexual desire exclusively for the opposite sex) embedded as a normative principle in social institutions and theory; those who fall outside this standard are devalued. The concept is useful in attempting to understand the assumptions upon which heterosexuality rests, and in showing how and why deviations from heterosexual norms are subject to social and legal sanctions. For example, heteronormativity assumes a belief in *dimorphic sexual difference* (there are two sexes), *biological essentialism* (male and female functions are essentially different), and *mimetic sex/gender relationship* (psychosocial traits follow anatomy). Those who deviate from these assumptions of the gender binary by openly preferring romantic partners of the same sex, by changing from one sex to another, or by violating heterosexual norms in other ways, are marginalized. They are considered by many societies to be mentally defective and morally inferior, and they are subject to street violence, discrimination in employment, and withdrawal of social acceptance. These sanctions force conformity to sexual norms.

The term *heteronormativity* is itself controversial because it suggests to some a condemnation of those who espouse heterosexuality, or of those who oppose nonheterosexual behavior based on religious or moral beliefs. Some have suggested that it is used to enforce liberal orthodoxy. This is correct to some extent, in that the concept of heteronormativity focuses on the exclusivity of heterosexual norms. Thus, the concept implies criticism of those social conservatives who disapprove of nonheterosexual behavior. This criticism is justified to some degree because it is often difficult for those in the majority, heterosexual culture to realize the extent to which their culture routinely pervades society and constantly creates and enforces norms that marginalize nonheterosexual behavior. Normative heterosexual culture pressures all to conform, or at least to hide their differences, because those outside the norms are perceived as "strange." The normative culture also erases the extent to which it makes heterosexuality an issue. Because heterosexuality is the order of things, it seems as if nonheterosexuals make an issue of their sexuality, but heterosexuals do not. The gay American writer and radio host Michelangelo Signorile writes about the pervasiveness and invisibility of heterosexual norms:

> These heterosexuals don't realize that they routinely discuss aspects of their own sexuality every day: telling coworkers about a vacation they took with a lover; explaining to their bosses that they're going through a rough divorce; bragging to friends about a new romance. Heterosexual reporters have no problem asking heterosexual public figures about their husbands, wives, girlfriends, boyfriends or children—and all these questions confirm and make an issue of heterosexuality. The ultimate example of making an issue of heterosexuality is the announcements in the newspapers every Sunday that heterosexuals are getting married. (Signorile 1993, xvii)

SEE ALSO *Gender; Sexual Orientation, Determinants of*

BIBLIOGRAPHY

Signorile, Michelangelo. 1993. *Queer in America: Sex, the Media, and the Closets of Power.* Madison: University of Wisconsin Press.

Warner, Michael. 1991. Introduction: Fear of a Queer Planet. *Social Text* 29 (4): 3–17.

Jillian T. Weiss

HETEROSKEDASTICITY

The classical statistical assumptions underlying econometric analysis refer to a set of requirements that need to hold in order for ordinary least squares (OLS) to yield the "best" estimator available for regression models. Heteroskedasticity violates the classical assumption that observations of the error term are drawn from a distribution that has a constant variance. Homoskedasticity, the assumption of constant variance for different observations of the error term, is not always realistic, because the larger an independent variable, the larger the variance of the associated disturbance.

In general heteroskedasticity is more likely to take place in cross-sectional models than in time-series models. However, heteroskedasticity can occur in time-series models with significant changes in the dependent variable. Heteroskedasticity can also occur in any model where the quality of data collection changes dramatically within the sample, or it can be caused by a model specification error.

When the violation of homoskedasticity takes place, ordinary least squares estimation of regression coefficient (β^{OLS}) remains unbiased, but it no longer has minimum variance among all linear unbiased estimators. Heteroskedasticity causes OLS to tend to underestimate the variances (and standard errors) of the coefficients. As a result, tests of statistical significance, such as the t-statistic and the F-statistic, cannot be relied on in face of uncorrected heteroskedasticity. In practice OLS usually turns up with higher t-scores than would be obtained if the error terms were homoskedastic, leading researchers to reject null hypotheses that should not be rejected.

There is no universally agreed-upon method of testing heteroskedasticity; econometric textbooks list as many as eight different methods for such testing. However, the visual inspection of residuals plotted against the suspected independent variable provide the first step for detecting the problem, and many computer packages can produce this graph. Some commonly used detection tests are the Goldfeld-Quandt test, the Glejser test, the Maximum Likelihood technique, the Park test, the White test, and the Bartlett's test. The majority of these tests use the residuals of an equation to test for the possibility of heteroskedasticity in the error terms. Certain disadvantages exist in every detection test, such as the computational cost (Maximum Likelihood technique) or the identification of a proper value for the best possible form of heteroskedasticity (Park test). It is worth mentioning, however, that an extensive Monte Carlo study of these techniques showed that the Maximum Likelihood approach is the most desirable.

The first step in correcting heteroskedasticity is to check for an omitted variable that might be causing impure heteroskedasticity. If the specification is as good as possible, then solutions such as the Weighted Least Squares (WLS) or the Heteroskedasticity-Corrected Standard Errors (HCSE) should be considered. The WLS involves dividing the main equation by whatever will make the error term homoskedastic and then rerunning the regression on the transformed variables; a disadvantage of this method is the identification of this proportionality factor. The HCSE is the most popular remedy for heteroskedasticity, and it takes a completely different approach to the problem. It focuses on improving the standard errors of the coefficients without changing the parameter estimates. One of the disadvantages of this technique is that it works best on large samples, and not all computer regression software packages calculate HCSE.

BIBLIOGRAPHY

Kennedy, Peter. 1987. *A Guide to Econometrics.* Cambridge, MA: MIT Press.

Studenmund, A. H. 2001. *Using Econometrics: A Practical Guide.* 4th ed. New York: Addison, Wesley, Longman.

Persefoni Tsaliki

HETEROTYPIC STABILITY

SEE *Stability, Psychological.*

HICKS, JOHN R.
1904–1989

Sir John R. Hicks, a British economist and author of twenty books, was knighted in 1964 and received the 1972 Nobel Prize for his contributions to general equilibrium theory and welfare economics. After graduating from Oxford University in 1925, he taught at the London School of Economics (LSE), where he formulated concepts on the elasticity of substitution, relative income shares of labor and capital, and liquidity. At LSE Hicks came under the influence of Lionel Robbins and Friedrich Hayek but broke away from their thinking in his book *The Theory of Wages* (1932), in which he considered unions as monopolies in the sense of rigid wages in a discrimination setting. He joined Cambridge University (1935–1938), where he was swayed by John Maynard Keynes's (1883–1946) writings. Afterward, he was chair of political economy at the University of Manchester. He became a fellow at Nuffield College, Oxford, in 1946 and was the Drummond Professor of Political Economy from 1952 until his retirement in 1965. Hicks continued his work in the areas of fixprice and flexprice markets, liquidity, and inventions.

Hicks's contributions stand out in the areas of applied economics, Keynesian economics, value theory, and technological progress. His method was to modify a theory to fit the facts. Facts are linked to events of the day and have a history that can become dramatic at times. According to Hicks, these dramatic facts are like blinkers waiting to be simplifed, theorized about, and selected to explain topical events. Hicks continually revised his theories because economic facts are less permanent and less repeatable than facts in the natural sciences.

Hicks viewed welfare economics as an application of demand theory, focusing on efficient and optimal cost and use of the social product. An efficiency test for welfare benefits tells us how to acquire more of one thing without having less of another thing. Demand theory makes sure that what we are getting more of is not detrimental. A welfare optimum may not be attained in a market with uniform prices, making room for cost-benefit analysis.

Hicks's IS and LL curves represent Keynes's ideas of equilibrium in the goods and money markets, respectively. Alvin Hansen later suggested the label LM for LL (Hansen 1953, p. 144). Darity and Young (1995, pp. 1–14, 26–27) clarified that Hansen's contribution emphasized one sector, while Hicks's contribution emphasized two sectors. Hicks developed a four-equation system representing liquidity preference, $M = L(r, Y)$; investment, $I = I(r, Y)$; savings, $S = S(r, Y)$; and saving-investment equilibrium, $S = I$, where M is money, I is investment, S is savings, Y is income, and r is the rate of interest. The first equation yields the LM curve. If the interest rate rises, the alternative cost of holding money relative to other assets becomes higher, lowering the demand for money. A rise in income will increase the demand for money. The other three equations yield the IS curve, which shows how income and interest rates adjust to make savings equal to investments. By making unsold inventories depend on the future, the model accommodates short period expectations. In the short term, such as a day, expectations do not change, so the condition for saving to equal investment in the model is achieved. The IS-LM curves can take on special shapes that would prevent automatic adjustments from occurring. Hicks later thought that the IS curve represents a flow concept, and the LM curve, a stock concept. In his *Capital and Growth* (1965), he proceeded to show that a stock equilibrium over a period would require a flow equilibrium over that period.

Hicks argued against the cardinal view, where utility is added, and for the ordinal view of value, where consumers rank their tastes and preferences. Alfred Marshal and the founders of the marginal revolution examined value with a given utility function. They required a utility surface for consumer maximization. Hicks's value theory examined "what adjustments in the statement of the marginal theory of value are made necessary by Pareto's discovery" (Hicks 1981, p. 7). Vilfredo Pareto postulated a scale of preferences concept, which represented value only by indifference curves. Hicks transformed the cardinal concept of total utility to the marginal rate of substitution between two commodities on an indifference curve. Similarly, he transformed the idea of diminishing marginal utility to diminishing marginal rate of substitution measured by the convex shape of the indifference curve. Following Hicks's work, comparative static analysis that allows prediction from demand analysis can be performed. One of his predictions states that if demand shifts from good 1 to good 2, then the relative price of 2 in terms of 1 would increase, except if 2 is a free good.

On the technology side, Hicks classified inventions as neutral, labor saving, or capital saving. When inventions change the marginal productivity of labor and capital in the same proportion, the invention is called neutral. Hicks predicted that if wages increase, labor's share of output would rise, and that would encourage inventions to replace labor, making them labor saving. In an analogous manner, the same can be argued for capital-saving inventions. In general, when changes in relative prices of factors occur, they induce inventions; otherwise inventions are autonomous. Autonomous inventions are likely to be randomly distributed, while induced inventions are likely to be labor saving.

SEE ALSO *Capital; Economics; Economics, Keynesian; Economics, Nobel Prize in; IS-LM Model;*

Technological Progress, Economic Growth; Utility, Subjective; Value; Value, Subjective; Welfare Economics

BIBLIOGRAPHY

Darity, W., and W. Young. 1995. IS-LM: An Inquest. *History of Political Economy* 27 (1): 1–41.

Hansen, Alvin H. 1953. *A Guide to Keynes.* New York: McGraw-Hill.

Hicks, John R. 1932. *The Theory of Wages,* 2nd ed. London: Macmillan, 1963.

Hicks, John R. 1937. Mr. Keynes and the Classics: A Suggested Simplification. *Econometrica* (April): 147–159.

Hicks, John R. 1939. *Value and Capital: An Inquiry into Some Fundamental Principles of Economic Theory,* 2nd ed. Oxford: Clarendon Press, 1946.

Hicks, John R. 1956. *A Revision of Demand Theory.* Oxford: Clarendon Press.

Hicks, John R. 1965. *Capital and Growth.* New York: Oxford University Press.

Hicks, John R. 1980. IS-LM: An Explanation. *Journal of Post Keynesian Economics* 3 (2): 139–154.

Hicks, John R. 1981. *Wealth and Welfare.* Vol. 1 of *Collected Essays in Economic Theory.* Oxford: Basil Blackwell.

Hicks, John R. 1982. *Money, Interest and Wages.* Vol. 2 of *Collected Essays in Economic Theory.* Oxford: Basil Blackwell.

Hicks, John R. 1983. *Classics and Moderns.* Vol. 3 of *Collected Essays in Economic Theory.* Oxford: Basil Blackwell.

Hicks, John R., and R. G. D. Allen. 1934. A Reconsideration of the Theory of Value. *Economica* 1: 52–76.

Lall Ramrattan
Michael Szenberg

HICKS-KALDOR COMPENSATION

SEE *Public Interest; Welfare Economics.*

HIDDEN PERSUADERS

The idea that there are subtle forces within the advertising industry that try to manipulate consumers' subconscious desires in order to sell products emerged in the first decades of the twentieth century. After World War II, debates about legitimate levels of consumer persuasion in advertising returned with a vengeance. In these years, Western societies' material wealth and choice of products increased dramatically, which led to ever more advertising being targeted at consumers, especially through the new medium of television. As the Cold War intensified, anxieties spread that governments could use some of the motivational and subliminal persuasion techniques developed by advertisers for political purposes.

These wide-ranging issues were coherently discussed and brought to a wider, non-academic audience by the journalist Vance Packard in his 1957 best-seller *The Hidden Persuaders*. Packard laid bare how the motivational researcher Ernest Dichter applied psychoanalytic techniques in a way that helped marketers understand and influence consumers' decision-making in the supermarket or automobile showroom. Packard also discussed the subliminal advertising techniques newly developed by the market researcher James Vicary, who in 1957 had designed an experiment in which split-second advertising messages for cola and popcorn were inserted into a movie. The short messages used in Vicary's movie experiment were as invisible to the conscious mind as the psychoanalytic techniques that Dichter developed for his clients, such as the use of subtle sexual imagery to make household products more attractive. Packard argued that motivational research, subliminal advertising, and the method of product placement defied the ideal of open and honest advertising and instead led to forms of "hidden" persuasion that undermined the rational autonomy of consumers and citizens, thus endangering the very basis of liberal democracy.

Similar arguments, though based on a more philosophical analysis of the normative nature of capitalism's political economy, were developed at the same time by the Harvard economist John Kenneth Galbraith. Galbraith's well-known 1958 book on *The Affluent Society* pointed out that advertising was not merely a means of selling products but, by its very ability to form people's anxieties and desires, a form of social power. In the eyes of Galbraith, traditional economic thought had ignored this fact and had therefore failed to acknowledge that market capitalism was anything but a set of institutions governed by rational decision makers.

Packard's much-discussed ideas reemerged in the 1970s when a new generation of critical journalists and social scientists launched attacks on the hidden persuaders in multinational corporations and governments. Most prominently, Wilson Bryan Key's 1973 book *Subliminal Seduction* and Stuart Ewen's 1976 publication *Captains of Consciousness* revived the idea that advertisers willingly applied manipulative and subliminal advertising techniques or images of sexually attractive, youthful, and ever-happy people in order to increase the sale of products. In the 1990s social psychologists approached the issue of consumer persuasion, and of subliminal advertising in particular, with far greater skepticism. While it needs to be acknowledged that advertisers do indeed attempt to influence consumer behavior through all possible means, psychologists have until today found no conclusive evidence

that subliminal advertising messages do actually have measurable and reproducible effects on consumers. As a result of this, the discussion of advertising's contested role in capitalist societies has slowly moved away from allegations of hidden psychological seduction or subliminal messages. Rather than looking for evidence of subliminal manipulation of consumers, authors have begun to criticize the often blatant conquest of public spaces and people's private lives by megabrands and the corporate interests behind them. This, in turn, has led to more debates about such things as advertising directed at children, and advertising's relation to potential health risks (associated with products such as cigarettes, alcohol, and fast food). Juliet Schor, for example, has shown how advertising for well-known car, fashion, food, and cosmetic brands determines what many consumers feel they ought to possess and parade in front of neighbors and peer-group members. This type of lifestyle advertising puts pressure on people to spend more time at work—instead of within families or communities—in order to be able to buy more luxury products.

SEE ALSO *Conspicuous Consumption; Subliminal Suggestion*

BIBLIOGRAPHY

Ewen, Stuart. 1976. *Captains of Consciousness: Advertising and the Social Roots of the Consumer Culture.* New York: McGraw Hill.

Galbraith, John Kenneth. 1958. *The Affluent Society.* Boston: Houghton Mifflin.

Key, Wilson Bryan. 1973. *Subliminal Seduction: Ad Media's Manipulation of a Not So Innocent America.* Englewood Cliffs, NJ: Prentice-Hall.

Klein, Naomi. 2000. *No Logo: Taking Aim at the Brand Bullies.* Toronto: Knopf Canada.

Packard, Vance. 1957. *The Hidden Persuaders.* New York: D. McKay.

Pratkanis, Anthony R., and Elliot Aronson. 1992. *Age of Propaganda: The Everyday Use and Abuse of Persuasion.* New York: W. H. Freeman.

Schor, Juliet B. 2004. *Born to Buy: The Commercialized Child and the New Consumer Culture.* New York: Scribner.

Stefan Schwarzkopf

HIERARCHY

A hierarchy is any ranking of objects into grades, orders, or classes of increasing dominance or inclusiveness. As a social phenomenon, hierarchy is a specific type of social organization in which members are divided by status or especially authority. Early use restricted the concept to sacred rankings of heavenly bodies (e.g., orders of angels) or ecclesiastical and religious rule. Indeed, in his masterwork *Economy and Society*, the German sociologist Max Weber (1864–1920) first distinguished between political and hierocratic organizations, limiting the latter to those entities with a monopoly of psychic coercion in distributing or denying religious benefits. Contemporary usage refers to any status or authority ranking based on traditional or religious beliefs and customs, formal-legal rules, or persistent inequalities.

Although contested, many scholars believe that humans, like other primates, are hierarchical animals who innately create social rankings within groups. Less contested is that humans throughout history have formed many social hierarchies, ranging from family, tribe, and clan groupings to genders, classes, and castes, to city-states, empires, and nation-states, to bureaucratic organizations including corporations, guilds, unions, political parties, and other civic associations.

Although particular forms differ, all hierarchies are comprised of relationships of superiority-inferiority or domination-subordination. On a daily basis, each individual in a modern society is likely to be a member of several distinct hierarchies with multiple and overlapping jurisdictions. One can simultaneously be a dominant member of a family from a "lower" class and a union leader, subject to the laws of the state in all these roles.

As these examples suggest, hierarchy is ubiquitous in social life. No definitive enumeration of types or forms is possible. At the same time, hierarchy is not universal. Many relationships are carried out between more or less equals, including interactions within peer or friendship networks, transactions in the marketplace, and diplomatic exchanges between great powers in international politics.

Hierarchy is not only varied but dynamic, evolving in form and extent. Although the historical trajectory has not been smooth and unidirectional, hierarchy appears to have deepened in scope and expanded in range over time, and especially in the modern era. With the rise of the nation-state as the encompassing form of hierarchy in the twentieth century, and the deepening of the division of labor within and between societies, greater areas of social life are now more clearly organized by rank and authority than in the past. This trend is challenged in the twenty-first century by globalization, the Internet, and various transnational social networks, all of which carry the potential for alternative, nonhierarchical forms of social organization. Whether these developments signal a long-term change in trajectory or merely a short-term oscillation in the degree of hierarchy remains a subject of debate.

Early understandings of the origins and rules of hierarchy were often functionalist, positing that hierarchies form to solve collective problems within societies. Perhaps best known among these early approaches is Robert Michaels's "iron law of oligarchy," which posited that the division of labor within organizations combines with the self-interest of organization elites to produce hierarchy even within bodies that pursue egalitarian goals ([1915] 1958). Subsequent scholars have rendered this "law" a contingent tendency, but the forces first identified by Michaels remain important in our understanding of hierarchy.

Contemporary theories of hierarchy can be grouped into three principal schools. Psychological theories ground the ubiquity of social hierarchy in human nature. Associated with the work of James Sidanius and his colleagues, social dominance theory is, perhaps, the most prominent psychological approach today, largely because its multilevel approach avoids many of the problems of strictly individual-level theories. Like authoritarian personality theory and other individual approaches, social dominance theory posits a social dominance orientation that, although universal, varies across the human population and expresses the value people place on hierarchically structured relationships among social groups. Social dominance orientation, in turn, interacts with context-specific institutions and ideologies to produce age, gender, and "arbitrary-set" hierarchies that take the form of clan, ethnic, caste, class or other socially constructed types of discrimination. Although providing a persuasive synthesis of a tendency towards hierarchy in all nonsubsistence societies, social dominance theory lacks a well-developed mechanism for explaining intra- and intersocietal differences in the degree of group-based hierarchy.

The other two main approaches to hierarchy seek to explain precisely the differences in the forms and extent of hierarchy. The contractual perspective dates most clearly from Oliver Williamson's path-breaking *Markets and Hierarchies* (1975). In a world of costly contracts that fail to specify obligations in all possible future states of the world, Williamson posited, self-seeking actors will tend to form hierarchies when one, but not both, of the parties to a recurring transaction possesses relationally specific assets—or assets that are worth considerably more within that relationship than in their next best use. An example would be a producer of specialized components for a particular brand of automobile. By placing the transactions under unified ownership, and subjecting them to administrative controls (dominance), the incentives of the parties to act opportunistically toward one another are greatly reduced. By internalizing transactions within a hierarchy, actors give up the information and discipline that is otherwise provided by market competition, but reduce the likelihood that they will be exploited by partners. Thus, Williamson and his many followers predict that the producer of specialized components will be subsumed within the automotive firm into a corporate hierarchy. In the absence of relationally specific assets or frequent exchanges, in contrast, actors will prefer to transact "at arm's length" in a market. When both parties have relationally specific assets, they hold "mutual hostages" and can coexist effectively in long-term, bilateral, and non-hierarchical relationships. This key insight on hierarchies as solutions to the problem of incomplete contracting in the presence of relationally specific assets has been extended from firms and economic exchange to bureaucracies and other managerial hierarchies, as well as to the analysis of empires, alliances, federal states, international organizations, and a variety of other institutions.

The distributional school lacks a single defining work, but generally understands hierarchies as emerging from initial inequalities between individuals or groups and, then, reinforcing those inequalities to produce an even more highly stratified society. Like the contractual approach, this school conceives of hierarchy as largely negotiated, albeit often under duress and possibly under threat of coercion, between actors who accept a subordinate status in exchange for access to the economic surplus possessed by the would-be superior. In the "big man" societies of Melanesia, for example, individuals acquire status and authority by using their comparative advantage in hunting, gardening, ritual knowledge, or violence to accumulate a material surplus, which they then redistribute to needy villagers. Often pressed to appeal to the big man by unexpected downturns in fortune, the supplicants become followers or subordinates in an informal village hierarchy. Over time, or once embedded into some religious or ideological frame, these relations of inequality become accepted or "normalized" into legitimate rule, with big men or perhaps their sons turning into "chiefs" at some later date. Similar hierarchies unfolded in early monarchies and empires, on the one hand, and in modern capitalist societies, on the other.

A contractual approach understands hierarchy as constructed to prevent possible opportunism, whereas the distributional approach posits that hierarchy emerges from actual inequality and exploitation. Despite this apparent tension, the two schools are actually complementary. Within the distributional approach, subordinates are understood to be locked into hierarchies by the material benefits provided by the superior; although perhaps driven by necessity to appeal to the dominant party for assistance, the subordinates are better off than they would be otherwise, absent that aid. In turn, the benefits of reduced opportunism provide the superior with the economic surplus necessary to assist subordinates while making himself better off as well. This exchange of goods for status and authority, what Herbert Spencer (1820–1903) first called "compulsory cooperation," provides the glue that holds social hierarchies together. Yet, to understand hierarchy as a bargain of sorts that leaves the parties to an agreement better off than they would otherwise be in an anarchic state of nature—where life would be, as Thomas Hobbes (1588–1679) famously described it, "short, nasty, and brutish"—is not to accept that inequalities of status or resources are fixed and immutable or cannot be made more equal. The history of social struggle is largely one of subordinates claiming a greater and possibly equal share of the social benefits produced by hierarchy. To the extent that hierarchy is an enduring feature of human life, social struggle will persist as well.

SEE ALSO *Caste; Community Power Studies; Elites; Michels, Robert; Oligarchy, Iron Law of; Power Elite; Psychology; Social Dominance Orientation; Spencer, Herbert; Stratification*

BIBLIOGRAPHY

Diehl, Michael W., ed. 2000. *Hierarchies in Action: Cui Bono?*. Occasional Paper 27. Carbondale: Center for Archaeological Investigations, Southern Illinois University.

Lake, David A. 1996. Anarchy, Hierarchy, and the Variety of International Relations. *International Organization* 50 (1): 1–33.

Michaels, Robert. [1915] 1958. *Political Parties: A Sociological Study of the Oligarchic Tendencies of Modern Democracy*. Trans. Eden Paul and Cedar Paul. Glencoe, IL: Free Press.

Miller, Gary J. 1992. *Managerial Dilemmas: The Political Economy of Hierarchy*. New York: Cambridge University Press.

Sidanius, Jim, and Felicia Pratto. 1999. *Social Dominance: An Intergroup Theory of Hierarchy and Oppression*. New York: Cambridge University Press.

Williamson, Oliver E. 1975. *Markets and Hierarchies: Analysis and Antitrust Implications*. New York: Free Press.

David A. Lake

HIGH BLOOD PRESSURE
SEE *Hypertension.*

HIGH-POWERED MONEY
SEE *Monetary Base.*

HIGH TECHNOLOGY
SEE *Microelectronics Industry.*

HILFERDING, RUDOLF
1877–1941

The economist Rudolf Hilferding was born in Vienna in 1877 to a liberal Jewish family. While studying medicine at the University of Vienna, Hilferding was influenced by his Marxian teacher Carl Grünberg (1861–1940). He abandoned medicine and, together with other Marxists, founded the *Marx-Studien* journal in 1904. He later moved to Berlin, where he became involved in politics and served twice as Germany's finance minister (1923, 1928–1929). In 1933 Hilferding fled Germany and settled in Paris, but he was later arrested and was murdered by the Gestapo in 1941.

Hilferding became noted for his criticism of the Austrian economist Eugen von Böhm-Bawerk (1851–1914) with the publication in 1904 of his book *Böhm-Bawerk's Criticism of Marx.* For Böhm-Bawerk, the market determines prices, and competition requires the freedom of capital and labor to yield equal profit rates. For Hilferding, in contrast, the market is conditioned by the relationship of surplus value to wages and its distribution among productive agents, while competition is a reciprocal relationship between products (Sweezy [1949] 1966, p. 191). For Böhm-Bawerk, labor is a disutility of work; for Hilferding, "labor is the social bond uniting an atomized society" (Sweezy [1949] 1966, p. 134).

Hilferding used Marxian schemata to criticize Böhm-Bawerk. He found different prices for each sector but the same total price and value for all sectors. To Hilferding, Böhm-Bawerk's position equates price as equal to value. Hilferding underscored that Marx had modified value in a definite way, where the law of value passes to the law of motion through commodities. In the labor theory of value, commodities are exchanged for their values. This is not a condition of exchange in general. Changing historical conditions modify exchanged value, and "all that is necessary is that we should understand the course of prices to be a modification of the pre-existing course of prices. … Böhm-Bawerk's mistake is that he confuses value with price" (Sweezy [1949] 1966, p. 156).

In *Finance Capital* (1910) Hilferding built on Marx's work in the areas of joint stock companies and cartels, crises, and imperialism. Hilferding argued that as capitalist industries develop, they form cartels to avoid competition. At the same time a concentration of banking evolves as banks come to encompass huge financial capacity. Thus, as the banks' capital is invested in industry, it becomes finance capital.

The high profits of cartels find their way into banks. Banks seek to export capital as investment opportunities decline at home and form general cartels. To foster exports, tariffs and protectionism are encouraged. As car-

tels and banks expand, finance capital becomes increasingly concentrated, creating a Marxian money-to-money circuit, $M - M'$. Hilferding's unique contribution is that shareholders no longer rely on profits. They can be money capitalists relying on interest. He referred to this gain as *promoter's profits*, $P = \dfrac{100Y}{d} - \dfrac{100Y}{p}$, where d is dividend, p is average profit, and Y is the yield of the enterprise. The formula shows a positive yield when a corporation transfers productive profit-yielding capital into interest-yielding capital (Hilferding [1910] 1981, pp. 114, 117).

Hilferding presented a crisis theory that is based primarily on proportionality between the capital-goods and the consumption-goods sectors. When a commodity plays the dual role of money (M) and commodity (C), a crisis is possible in the $C_1 - M - C_2$ circuit when money is hoarded. For Hilferding, "a crisis is simply the point at which the rate of profit begins to fall" (Hilferding [1910] 1981, p. 257). Marxian crises result from falling profits and underconsumption. Hilferding emphasized the disproportion in which commodities are produced and deemphasized the underconsumption theory. As the aggregate product is represented by the sum of constant capital, variable capital, and surplus value, the part of constant capital that is used up must be replaced, and if variable capital and surplus are consumed, proportionality is maintained, and production will be sustained.

Hilferding's finance capital is marked by the highest level of concentration of economic and political power. This is due to mergers of corporations, which eliminate trade, create substantial profits that strengthen a firm against downswings, and allow financial capital controlled by banks to enter industries. At this stage capitalism has withered but is not dead, and economic power is transformed into state control. State power breeds international conflicts, while internal conflicts increase with the concentration of capital. The proletariat's response to this imperialism is a demand for socialism. A country can maintain its capital only by increasing military operations. V. I. Lenin (1870–1924) considered this "a very valuable theoretical analysis" (Lenin [1917] 1973, p. 11). While in Lenin's version competition and monopoly are maintained, in Hilferding's version organized capitalism without competition and capitalist control ensues as in the socialist planned economy.

The American economist Paul Sweezy (1910–2004), a major critic of Hilferding (Sweezy [1942] 1970, p. 268), maintained that finance capital is a temporary phase, as many corporations obtain financing from their internal sources of funds, and that banks now have a less powerful role. In addition to pointing out that imperialism is not a necessary state of capitalism, the Austrian economist

Joseph Schumpeter (1883–1950) considered Hilferding's monetary theory to be old-fashioned (Schumpeter 1954, p. 881).

SEE ALSO *Austro-Marxism; Capital; Capitalism; Economics, Marxian; Lenin, Vladimir Ilitch; Marxism; Nazism*

BIBLIOGRAPHY

Hilferding, Rudolf. [1910] 1981. *Finance Capital: A Study of the Latest Phase of Capitalist Development*, ed. Tom Bottomore, trans. Morris Watnick and Sam Gordon. London: Routledge and Kegan Paul.

Lenin, V. I. [1917] 1973. *Imperialism: The Highest Stage of Capitalism*. Beijing: Foreign Language Press.

Schumpeter, Joseph A. 1954. *History of Economic Analysis*, ed. Elizabeth Boody Schumpeter. New York: Oxford University Press.

Sweezy, Paul M. [1942] 1970. *The Theory of Capitalist Development: Principles of Marxian Political Economy*. New York: Modern Reader.

Sweezy, Paul M., ed. [1949] 1966. *Karl Marx and the Close of His System, by Eugen von Böhm-Bawerk; and Böhm-Bawerk's Criticism of Marx, by Rudolf Hilferding*. New York: Kelley.

Lall Ramrattan
Michael Szenberg

HINDUISM

Hinduism embraces a great diversity of beliefs and forms of worship, and it has therefore been called a "family of religions" rather than one religion. Hindus form the majority population of India (approximately 82% of India's 1.25 billion people). About 45 million Hindus live outside of India, mostly in the neighboring countries of Nepal (where Hinduism is the state religion), Bangladesh, and Sri Lanka. About 2.5 million Hindus live in North America, where they have established dozens of temples.

British authors in the early nineteenth century coined the term "Hinduism" by adding "-ism" to the word *Hindu*, which had been used by the Ancient Persians to identify the inhabitants of the land beyond the Indus River. Hindus themselves had called their tradition *Vaidika dharma* (the Vedic Dispensation) or *Sanātana dharma* (the Eternal Law). The Vedic civilization arose in northwestern India around 4000 BCE, and the Indus civilization (c. 2500–1900 BCE) may have been part of it. When the settlements had to be abandoned around 2000 BCE, due to a major climate change, most moved east into the Yamunā-Ganges Doab, which became the new home of Vedic civilization, with Mathurā (on the Yamunā) and Vārāṇasī (on the Ganges) as main cultural centers.

Hinduism is closely tied to the land, and the *Mātrī-bhūmī* (Motherland) has a unique emotional appeal for Hindus. The physical features of the country are associated with Hindu gods and goddesses and with Hindu religious practices and eschatological expectations. The great rivers of India are not only important bodies of water; they are also sources of inspiration and ritual purification, as well as divinities to be worshipped. Many towns and cities along their banks are places where pilgrims congregate to obtain supernatural blessings. In addition, mountains such as the Himālayas, the Vindhyas, the Ghats, and the Nilgiri Hills are the abodes of gods. Hundreds of thousands of temples, small and large, embellish India's landscape, visibly transforming the country into the Hindu Holy Land.

SCRIPTURES AND RITUALS

Hindu scriptures have come down through the ages in two major streams: the *Vedas* and the *Āgamas*. The Vedas are the literature of the religious professionals, to be memorized and recited only by Brahmins. They comprise the four *Saṃhitās* (collections of hymns) and a large number of *Brāhmaṇas* (ritual texts), *Āraṇyakas* (forest treatises), and *Upaniṣads* (mystical writings). The Āgamas are the sacred literature of the people at large. The Great Epics, the *Rāmāyaṇa* and the *Mahābhārata*, are also important sources of Hindu religion.

Many Hindus consider the *Bhagavadgītā*, a section of the *Mahābhārata*, an epitome of their religion. The *Purāṇas*, bible-like compendia of Hindu lore, are widely read by Hindus from all classes. Numerous texts are considered to be revealed scriptures by the followers of specific worship traditions. They contain creation narratives, moral teachings, worship rituals, genealogies of kings and patriarchs, myths of gods and goddesses, edifying stories, and eschatological lore. Based on these texts, poets and playwrights such as Kālidāsa and Bāṇa (fifth or sixth century CE) produced dramatic literature of a high order in Sanskrit. Poet-saints such as Tulasīdāsa and Kamban (sixteenth century CE) created popular vernacular versions of the classics that continue to be performed, while countless "Bollywood" films take their stories from these books.

The language of the most ancient literary documents of Hinduism, "Vedic" is an archaic form of Sanskrit, the "refined language," standardized around 600 BCE by Pāṇini. Sanskrit was called *Deva-vāni*, or the "language of the gods." It became the language of Hindu scholarship and classical poetry as well as Hindu religious literature. All modern North Indian vernaculars are largely derived from Sanskrit.

Domestic and public rituals were a prominent feature of early Vedic culture and were considered indispensable for the well-being of individuals and society. In their performance, hundreds of intricate and interrelated rules had to be observed. The construction of the altars demanded the solution of difficult arithmetic and geometric problems, and the timing of sacrifices was based on precise astronomical observations. The change of seasons was accompanied by rituals, as were the various life stages. Public offerings ensured the fertility of fields and domestic animals, while home rituals accompanied birth, adolescence, marriage, and death. In later centuries *pūjā*, the worship of great gods like Viṣṇu and Śiva, became the predominant form of religion. But the performance of Vedic rituals continues to this very day. For example, Brahmins still recite Vedic hymns at *upanayana* (initiation), *vivāha* (marriage), and *antyeṣṭi* (last rites). Many Hindus participate in daily temple worship and partake of consecrated food (*prasāda*), and the major temple festivals are great public events for every village and town. Domestic rituals, such as offering food to the deity or waving lights before the image of the deity, are also still widespread in India.

SOCIAL ORGANIZATION

Traditional Hindu society functioned on the assumption that humans are not born equal and that their birth in different *varṇas* (classes) defines their specific rights and duties. According to the *Puruṣa Sūkta*, the Vedic creation myth, *Brahmins*, born from the Great Being's mouth, were the custodians of the Veda, the highest in rank. *Kṣatriyas* (or *Kshatriyas*), born from its chest, were rulers and warriors. *Vaiśyas* (Vaisyas), born from its belly—businesspeople, artisans, farmers and clerks—had to provide the necessities of life for society at large. *Śūdras* (Sudras), originating from its feet, were to serve the upper three *varṇas*. The three higher *varṇas* alone were entitled to receive the *saṃskāras* (sacraments) that made them *dvi-jātis* (twiceborn). *Ati-śūdras* (Ati-sudras), the people below the *Śūdras* (also called *Asprihyas* or untouchables) were outside the pale of Hindu society proper. They were relegated to doing work that was considered ritually polluting, such as skinning carcasses, cleaning latrines, and disposing of the dead. They were not allowed to dwell in the village proper and were not entitled to using amenities reserved for caste people. Each of the four *varṇas* consists of hundreds of *jātis* (birth lines, or subcastes) that also observe ranking among themselves.

Duties also varied with respect to stages in life. A twice-born male was to spend the first twelve years after initiation with a reputable teacher (*brahmacarya*). He then had to marry and to procreate children. After the children had grown up he was to live as a forest-dweller in a life of simplicity and meditation. Finally he was to enter the stage of renunciation, and as a homeless pilgrim he was to visit holy places until death relieved him of the burden of his body. While this schema was never literally carried out

on a large scale, it provided a value orientation that was widely respected.

Early in their history, Hindus developed principles of theory and practice of government (*rajya-dharma*). The *Mahābhārata* devotes long sections to this, and the Kauṭilīya *Arthaśāstra,* ascribed to the prime minister of Chandragupta Maurya (321–293 BCE), provides a detailed description of a well-ordered professional administration. One of the aims of the Hindu *jāgaran* (awakening) that began in the early twentieth century was to reestablish India as a Hindu nation. The Hindū Mahāsabhā, the first modern Hindu political party, was founded in 1909. It maintained that "Hindus have a right to live in peace as Hindus, to legislate, to rule themselves in accordance with Hindu genius and ideals and establish by all lawful and legal means a Hindu State, based on Hindu culture and tradition, so that Hindu ideology and way of life would have a homeland of its own" (Pattabhiram, p. 217). Vir Savarkar, one of its main ideologues, strove to unify Hindu-India under the banner of "Hindutva," a cultural Hindu identity. In 1926, K. V. Hedgewar founded the Rāṣṭrīya Svayamsevak Sangh (RSS) in order to counteract Muslim influence in Indian politics. The RSS leader M. S. Golwalkar was instrumental in creating the *Viśva Hindū Pariṣad* in 1964, which aims at unifying all Hindus across the different denominations. It vigorously promotes and defends Hindu interests both within India and abroad.

ANCIENT CHALLENGES

In the sixth century BCE, movements arose in India that challenged the necessity of rituals (especially the animal sacrifices) and the mediating function of Brahmins. Among the breakaway factions that survived the centuries are Jainism and Buddhism. Jīna Mahāvīra, the last reformer of a more ancient religion, declared *ahiṃsā* (nonkilling) to be the highest moral principle. Gautama Buddha, the latest of a long series of "Enlightened" ones, taught that ethical perfection, rather than birth, made a person a Brahmin. For several centuries the traditions based on the teachings of these sages, Jainism and Buddhism, respectively, were the majority religions in India. Under the Imperial Guptas (320–540 CE), the Brahmins launched a major campaign to lure people back to Hindu rituals. They built temples and encouraged the composition of popular religious books. After the disintegration of the Gupta Empire, many smaller kingdoms arose in various parts of India. Hindu culture also reached out to Southeast Asia as far as the Philippines, and the languages and arts of Southeast Asia still show a strong Indian influence. From the twelfth century onward, most of India came under the rule of Muslim invaders, who destroyed many Hindu temples and built mosques on their sites. These actions are still the cause of much friction between Hindus and Muslims today.

THE TRANSMISSION OF HINDUISM

Vedic religion was family based. Specific branches (*śākhas*) of the Veda were preserved in individual families, who held hereditary offices in public rituals. The home was also a center for religious practices, and the sacred hearthfire was not allowed to die out. Families were responsible for the life-cycle rituals, and husband and wife together had to perform the domestic rituals. Young boys moved into the families of gurus to be taught. The role of the guru reached great prominence when specific worship communities developed under the leadership of charismatic personalities, who often claimed to be the embodiment of a deity. These *ācāryas* (Masters) shaped mainstream Hinduism and still exercise great influence on Hindus at large, regulating the lives of their followers and reinterpreting scriptures and traditional teachings.

Pluralism was a hallmark of Hindu religion from its very beginning. Many gods and goddesses are invoked in Vedic hymns, and Hindus continue to worship a great variety of deities in their temples. There is no common creed to which all Hindus subscribe, nor is there a single doctrine or practice that is followed by all Hindus, except perhaps the nominal acceptance of the Veda as a revealed scripture and the belief in karma and rebirth. It is natural for Hindus with an inquiring mind to analyze and investigate the teachings of their traditions, and professional philosophers with a Hindu background also deal with religious issues in a philosophically meaningful way. Hindu philosophical systems (*darśanas*) are not mere abstract constructs, they are also paths for the realization of the highest purpose of life (*sādhanas*). Among the qualifications required for beginning philosophical study is the earnest desire to find liberation from the sufferings of the cycle of rebirths (*samsāra*), caused by ignorance concerning the true nature of reality.

Education was always a high priority for Hindus: the early life of Brahmins was devoted to study, and continued private study (*svādhayāya*) was one of their lifelong obligations. In addition to the private, tutorial-like teaching from guru to disciple, imparted in the guru's home, schools were attached to ashrams and temples from early on. The well-organized, ancient Indian universities, which were publicly as well as privately sponsored, taught not only the *Veda*, but also the "eighteen sciences," later supplemented by the "sixty-four arts." The basic curriculum included linguistics, arts and crafts, medicine, logic and spirituality. High ethical standards were expected both from students and teachers. The most famous of these universities were Takṣaśīla in the Punjab, and Nālandā and Mithilā in Bihar.

Hindus believe in a balance of values, expressed in the four aims of life (*puruṣārthas*): the acquisition of wealth (*artha*), the enjoyment of life (*kāma*), the practice of morality (*dharma*), and the search for final emancipation (*mokṣa*).

HINDU SCIENCE

The central ritual of Vedic culture was performed at astronomically fixed times on altars built with specifically produced bricks arranged in a prescribed geometric pattern. The altar was conceived as a symbol of the human body as well as of the universe: the 360 bricks of an altar represented the 360 days of the year and the 360 bones in the human body. The building of altars in different configurations, and their change in shape and volume, involved a sophisticated geometry. The *Śulva-sūtras* provided the rules for constructing a variety of shapes of altars and their permutations. Astronomical knowledge of a fairly high order was required to determine the right time for the performance of Vedic sacrifices. One of the auxiliary Vedic sciences, the *Jyotiṣa*, explains how to determine the positions of the sun and moon at solstices, and of the new and full moon in the circle of the twenty-seven *nakṣatras*. Geometry and other fields of Indian mathematics developed out of the requirements for the Vedic sacrifice. Algebra, in spite of its Arabic name, is an Indian invention, as are the concept of "zero," the decimal system, and "Arabic" numerals.

The *Atharvaveda* contains invocations relating to bodily and mental diseases. Its auxiliary *Āyurveda*, (life-science) was mainly oriented toward preventing diseases and healing through herbal remedies. Good health was not only considered generally desirable, it was viewed as a precondition for reaching spiritual fulfillment. Medicine as a "charity" was widely recommended and supported by Hindu rulers. Two Indian medical handbooks, the *Cāraka-saṃhitā* and the *Suśruta-saṃhitā*, were the result of centuries of development and became famous in the ancient world far beyond India. *Āyurveda* was also applied to animals and plants, and there is an ancient handbook for professional gardeners and a text for cattle veterinarians. Other works deal with veterinary medicine relating to horses and elephants. Ancient India had both hospitals and animal clinics, and *Gośālas*, places in which elderly cattle are provided for, are still popular in some parts of India. *Āyurveda* was the source of much of ancient Greek and Roman, as well as mediaeval Arabic medical knowledge. In modern times, Ayurvedic pharmacology has become recognized by major Western pharmaceutical companies and researchers.

In connection with the building of temples, Hindus developed a great architectural tradition. No village or city was deemed inhabitable without a temple. Professional handbooks like the *Manasāra* and the *Mayamata* provide artistic and religious canons for the architects and sculptors.

Adhyātma-vidyā, the science relating to *Brahman*, the Supreme Reality, was considered the highest branch of science. It rested on personal experience, a coherent epistemology, and the exegesis of revealed utterances. The ideas of the Upanishads were further developed into the systematic of Vedānta philosophy, mainly laid down in numerous commentaries on the *Brahma-sūtras* ascribed to Bādarāyaṇa (second century BCE). Beginning with Śaṅkara (eighth century CE), through Rāmānuja (eleventh century) to Madhva (thirteenth century), the greatest minds of India have endeavored to cultivate the science of the eternal spirit.

WHO IS A HINDU?

For many centuries, membership in the Hindu community was restricted to those who were born from Hindu parents and who had undergone the various prescribed rituals that made a Hindu a full member of the Hindu community. But even in ancient times, many foreigners who came to India adopted Hindu thought and culture. With the establishment of British rule in India and the advent of Christian missionaries, the interest of Hindus in spreading their religion abroad was awakened. Swami Vivekananda's much celebrated presentations at the World Parliament of Religions in Chicago in 1893, and his subsequent journey through the United States and England, resulted in the establishment of Vedanta Centers. Mahatma Gandhi, who led the Indian independence movement to success on the basis of the Hindu ideal of nonviolence, did much to gain worldwide respect for Hinduism. Sarvepalli Radhakrishnan, the president of India from 1962 to 1967, became the voice of the twentieth-century Hindu intelligentsia, representing Hinduism as the most advanced form of universal spirituality. The numerous Hindu swamis and gurus who came to the West beginning in the 1960s familiarized thousands with sectarian Hinduism and attracted many Westerners to joining Hindu religious communities. In the twenty-first century, many Hindu authorities have given up their reservations and freely accept Western converts to Hinduism.

SEE ALSO *Buddhism; Caste; Caste, Anthropology of; Jainism; Religion; Sikhism*

BIBLIOGRAPHY

Flood, Gavin, ed. 2003. *The Blackwell Companion to Hinduism.* Malden, MA: Blackwell Publishing.

Klostermaier, Klaus. 1998. *A Concise Encyclopaedia of Hinduism.* Oxford: Oneworld.

Klostermaier, Klaus. 2000. *Hinduism: A Short Introduction.* Oxford: Oneworld.

Klostermaier, Klaus. 2007. *A Survey of Hinduism.* 3rd ed. Albany: State University of New York Press.

Mittal, Sushil, and Gene Thursby, eds. 2004. *The Hindu World.* New York: Routledge.

Pattabhiram, Mohan, ed. 1967. *General Elections in India 1967.* Bombay: Allied Publishers.

Sharma, Arvind, ed. 2003. *The Study of Hinduism.* Columbia: University of South Carolina Press.

Klaus K. Klostermaier

HIP HOP

Hip hop is a bundle of cultural practices that coalesced during the 1970s. It was largely developed by black and Latino youth in the Bronx, a New York City borough particularly affected by urban blight, middle-class flight, and deindustrialization. *Hip hop* is often used interchangeably with the term *rap* to describe the musical dimension of the cultural movement. *Hip hop*, though, is an umbrella term that refers to four distinct cultural forms. *Graffiti* (or *bombing*) is an art form that was typically staged on New York City subway trains before it gained mainstream recognition in the early 1980s. The second cultural practice associated with the emergence of hip hop is *breakdancing* or *breaking* (as performed, for example, by the Rock Steady Crew). Breaking has obvious roots in earlier forms of dance within the United States and provided the inspiration for the term *b-boy*, a male break dancer. The remaining two elements—*deejaying* and *emceeing*—constitute the primary distinguishing characteristics of the musical idiom associated with hip hop culture. The first refers to the role of turntables in the making and mixing of rap music rhythms in the place of live musicians (in the traditional sense). The emergence of the emcee as a dominant figure reflects the role the spoken word plays in hip hop, distinguishing it from the genres of gospel, blues, and rhythm and blues, in which singing features prominently. With time, graffiti and break-dancing became less prominent and commodifiable, as the deejay and especially the emcee emerged as the genre's iconic representatives.

The three individuals most associated with the music's early development were Bronx residents Kool Herc, Afrika Bambaataa, and Grandmaster Flash. Herc is celebrated for his adaptation of the sound-system culture—bass and volume—of his native Jamaica to the parks and community centers of the Bronx. Afrika Bambaataa, the child of Caribbean immigrants, would contribute his eclectic taste and his willingness to use rock, reggae, soul, and jazz musical sources to create rap music. Grandmaster Flash, an immigrant from the Caribbean island of Barbados, is known as the pioneer in the realm of turntablism and for developing the art of mixing. At this early stage, the primary figures associated with the genre were all deejays. Their work, in the aggregate, provides evidence of the influence of Jamaican popular culture upon rap's emergence (for example, producers such as Lee Perry and King Tubby, and performers such as I-Roy and U-Roy).

Hip hop emerged as a prominent form of black popular culture outside of the New York area with the success of the Sugarhill Gang's "Rapper's Delight" (1979), which was released on an independent label owned by musician and producer Sylvia Robinson. Indeed, most of the music's pioneers did not consider rap to be commercially viable and, as a consequence, did not try to make and distribute recordings. The developing interest in these practices by the culture industries created new stars, such as Kurtis Blow, the Funky Four Plus One, and the Treacherous Three, along with older groups such as Grandmaster Flash and the Furious Five, Afrika Bambaataa and the Soul Sonic Force, and the Cold Crush Brothers. The genre also achieved crossover popularity through the work of pop groups such as Blondie ("Rapture," 1980). Up until this juncture, most observers saw rap as a novelty and most of the records were made for independent labels.

As a recorded medium, the first classic era of rap music was launched with the release in 1982 of Afrika Bambaataa and the Soul Sonic Force's "Planet Rock" and Grandmaster Flash and the Furious Five's "The Message." The former recording revealed a strong influence by the German electronic group Kraftwerk. The latter, with its relatively pointed social message, was recorded and released against the will and without the participation of most of the group's members (including Grandmaster Flash), and would signal the changing balance between deejays and emcees, with the turntablists gradually fading in prominence. Following in the wake of these canonical recordings was the work of New York–area artists such as Run DMC, LL Cool J, Boogie Down Productions, Eric B. & Rakim, and Public Enemy. As the music's influence spread beyond the inner city, suburban youth became involved as artists, including most prominently De La Soul and the Native Tongues movement. Hip hop's audience crossed boundaries with time, and it is suggested that at points as many as three-quarters of the consumers of the music were neither black nor Latino.

The effects of crack cocaine and its associated industries energized (and in some instances subsidized) new forms of rap music. The kinds of rap that emerged from the west coast of the United States (especially Los Angeles and Oakland) were distinguished from their counterparts in the Northeast not only by their linguistic innovations and source preferences (e.g., Parliament/Funkadelic and Zapp versus soul jazz and James Brown), but also, at least initially, by their moral economies. By the middle of the 1990s, these perspectives provided the dominant template for the making of rap music in the South (OutKast, Petey Pablo, and others, in the wake of Miami's 2 Live Crew), the West (N.W.A., Ice T, Ice Cube, Dr. Dre, Snoop Doggy Dogg, and Tupac), and the Northeast (the Notorious B.I.G., Jay-Z, and later 50 Cent).

The musical genre of rap has proved to be diverse in many respects. Nevertheless, throughout its history it has been a space that has privileged masculine perspectives and—in contrast to rhythm and blues, which is often cast as its feminized other—has featured few successful women practitioners (exceptions include Roxanne Shanté, MC Lyte, Queen Latifah, Lauryn Hill, L'il Kim, and Foxy Brown). Indeed, the genre as manifested in its lyrics, its publications, and in film became relatively misogynistic. Its boundaries would also—in contrast to other black music forms, such as house music—discourage the open participation of lesbians and gays with its often ritualistic deployment of homophobic discourse. Its successful practitioners have also been overwhelmingly black with few exceptions (e.g., Eminem). Hip hop music and culture have also had a great impact abroad throughout Europe, Africa, parts of Asia, and the Americas, and have generated new genres in response, including drum and bass, reggaeton, grime, and kwaito.

Hip hop defined the generation coming of age in the 1980s and afterward. Moreover, with its particular sartorial, linguistic, gender, and class inflections, it represents in the eyes of many a rejection of the aesthetics, values, and goals of the civil rights generation. It has also been used to market clothing, running shoes, and subsequently a wide range of consumer goods, as well as politics (most prominently in the form of the Hip Hop Action Network and the Vote or Die voter registration campaigns mounted during the 2004 American national elections).

BIBLIOGRAPHY

Forman, Murray, and Mark Anthony Neal. 2004. *That's the Joint! The Hip-Hop Studies Reader.* New York: Routledge.

Kitwana, Bakari. 2002. *The Hip Hop Generation: Young Blacks and the Crisis in African American Culture.* New York: Basic Civitas.

Rose, Tricia. 1994. *Black Noise: Rap Music and Black Culture in Contemporary America.* Hanover, NH: Wesleyan University Press.

Watkins, S. Craig. 2005. *Hip Hop Matters: Politics, Pop Culture, and the Struggle for the Soul of a Movement.* Boston: Beacon.

Richard Iton

HISPANICS

SEE *Latinos.*

HISTOGRAMS

SEE *Inference, Statistical.*

HISTORY, ECONOMIC

SEE *Cliometrics.*

HISTORY OF CONSCIOUSNESS

SEE *Consciousness.*

HISTORY, SOCIAL

Social history emerged as a discipline over the course of about twenty years at the conjunction of two seemingly contradictory schools of historical writing: English social history and the French Annales school.

Defined by George Macaulay Trevelyan (1876–1962) as "history with the politics left out," English social history sought to examine the "manners, morals and customs" of the English people within a disciplinary rubric that placed social history alongside political, economic, and, in some quarters, labor history as discrete subfields (Trevelyan 1942).

The Annales school, founded in 1929 by Marc Bloch (1886–1944) and Lucien Febvre (1878–1956) and named after the journal *Annales d'histoire economique and social,* sought quite the opposite. Bloch and Febvre intended a new "science of society" that would incorporate all domains of the human and social sciences. The two envisioned their project in diametric opposition both to Durkheimian sociology, which they felt merely rummaged history for support of its theories, as well as historical renderings that purported to render through a catalogue of facts an objective past. They and their colleagues sought at once to investigate the differentia of past presents and to come through these investigations to a fuller sense not only of how a given society came together in all its interrelated elements, but also human society as conceived as an entity in which all historical moments participate and elucidate. What was envisioned was a massive inductive project incorporating myriad local histories that would yield at an endlessly forestalled future time, a "history of society."

The first Annales school was enthusiastically received by what was known as the Communist Party Historian's Group in Britain (1946–1956). Though putatively an organ of the Communist Party, under the de facto leadership of the British journalist Dona Torr (1883–1957), the group enjoyed a free and open discussion. Its members included E. P. Thompson (1924–1993), Dorothy Thompson (1894–1961), Christopher Hill (1912–2003), Rodney Hilton (1916–2002), Eric Hobsbawm (b. 1917), and George Rudé (1910–1993), among other future notables of social history. The group's concerns maintained a tension between two poles that would inform the members' later work: at one end an interest in social transformation, specifically the transition from feudalism to capitalism, and at the other, an interest in the "manners, morals and customs" of the poor in relation to those transformations. The first roughly corresponded to discussion of Maurice Dobb's (1900–1976) *Studies in the Development of Capitalism* (1946) and the second to A. L. Morton's (1903–1987) *People's History of England* (1938).

In 1952, the group founded the journal *Past and Present*, which sought to give voice to these concerns and to engage with non-Marxist historians interested in similar lines of inquiry. In the first issue, Hobsbawm published his groundbreaking analysis of the machine breakers, which demonstrated that Luddite riots were not resistance to the machine as such, as has long been argued, but to the "machine in the hands of the capitalist" (Hobsbawm 1952). He argued that in the absence of organizational and political avenues, such protests should be read as "collective bargaining by riot." The theme was later expanded in a series of similarly pathbreaking studies by Rudé on the crowd. Meanwhile, Hill demonstrated that the "manners, morals and customs" of the poor were themselves a source of political struggle in his important essay "Puritans and the Poor," which examined the disciplinary techniques of the nascent English bourgeoisie (Hill 1952).

The group's twin concerns were on full display in E. P. Thompson's magisterial work *The Making of the English Working Class* ([1963] 1968), which brought to bear his understanding of culture as a "whole way of conflict." Thompson argued that class comes into being as a result of struggle; through this struggle, persons become conscious of their interests and themselves as a class over time. Thompson therefore rejected sociological definitions that sought to define class as distinct from historical struggle and, by extension, context. What resulted was a notion of class that Mikhail Bakhtin would call "novelistic," in that class designated an open-ended, dialogic "unity" which, through the ceaseless interpenetration of other voices and experiences, undoes and redoes its own provisional unity. From a methodological standpoint, Thompson's work was highly innovative, incorporating literature (from high to very low), folklore, local archives, and spy reports in a way that elucidated the complex moral and symbolic universe in which class struggle was imbricated. In *The Making of the English Working Class* and in later works dealing with grain riots, game laws, and time and its relation to work discipline, Thompson demonstrated a subtle understanding of human agency that did not recognize, for example, time or the law as necessarily instruments of ruling-class power (which they were initially, he allowed). Instead, he suggested that these created circumstances through their own claims to universality that permitted a defense (if only a weak one at first) on those very same grounds against the arbitrary actions of elites. Thompson presented his objects of study as situated in historical processes, the relative meanings of which were constituted through struggle and human agency.

Thompson inaugurated a new version of social history in the late 1960s and into the 1970s with mixed success. On the one hand, authors such as Eugene Genovese (b. 1930) and Herbert Gutman (1928–1985) produced subtle and far-reaching studies in the American context that recovered local knowledges and successfully mapped larger processes through them. On the other, there was a tendency to shrink back from the theoretical engagements of these authors, producing something closer to Trevelyan's "history with the politics left out" even in studies of working-class culture. It was against this trend that Hobsbawm wrote his important essay "From Social History to the History of Society," which appears in his collection *On History* (1997), urging a reconnection of such studies to larger historical processes.

While culturalist "advocacy" readings of the working class turned away from larger issues, the rise of historical sociology—with its use of demography, cliometrics, and other statistical tools inspired by the second and third waves of the Annales school—tended to efface culture and, with it, class conflict entirely. The twin recoil from the interventions of the Communist Party Historian's Group inspired important and often scathing critiques by Tony Judt, Elizabeth Fox-Genovese and Eugene Genovese, and Geoff Eley and Keith Nield.

CRISES

In the late 1970s and early 1980s, the field of social history found itself in another sort of crisis entirely. Feminists began calling into question the primacy of class in historical analysis, arguing that gender complicated and prob-lematized easy assumptions regarding the universality of the class experience, which they argued tended to be gendered male. While the worst of these arguments reproduced the atheoretical "advocacy" histories discussed above in the context of gender, the best of these critically engaged the concept of class and have significantly enriched contemporary understandings of past societies. The scholars Deborah Valenze and Barbara Taylor revisited Methodism (a religion founded by John Wesley in the eighteenth century) and Owenism (a theory developed by utopian socialist Robert Owen, often considered a precursor to Marxism) respectively, demonstrating the egalitarian promises and realities of each for women that E. P. Thompson had overlooked. Similarly, Christine Stansell examined gender and working-class formation in New York City in her delightful *City of Women* (1987). Judith Walkowitz produced an influential social history of Victorian prostitution on which Stansell drew, and she later expanded on these themes, drawing successfully on the work of Gareth Stedman Jones (b. 1942) and the literary scholar Coral Lansbury's (1933–1991) work to elucidate the physical and cultural landscape around the Jack the Ripper murders. The historians Sonya Rose and Anna Clark have sought more frontally to rehabilitate the concept of class while addressing what the latter views as its misogynist articulations and realities. Catherine Hall, first with Lenore Davidoff in *Family Fortunes: Men and Women of the English Middle Class, 1780–1850* (1987), engaged the deep intersections of class and gender in the formation of the English middle class, and later alone demonstrated the ways these were both deeply implicated in colonialism. Most suggestively, the literary scholar Mary Poovey has, like Hall, opened exciting avenues for examining the manner in which class, gender, and race influenced each other, inflecting every aspect of social life in the nineteenth century.

Coeval with the rise of feminist studies in social history arose what has come to be called the linguistic turn, which can be traced to Stedman Jones's 1982 essay "The Language of Chartism" (Chartism being a movement for the franchise on the part of the middle and working class, beginning formally in the late 1820s and continuing through the Reform Act of 1867). Stedman Jones argued that an examination of Chartist language revealed a fundamentally political movement that obscured rather than articulated working-class interests. The historians Patrick Joyce and James Vernon pushed Stedman Jones's observations still further, the former arguing that class should be replaced by what he feels to be a more fluid and soft term, *the people*. Drawing on the French sociologist Jean Baudrillard's (b. 1929) conception of *the mass*, Joyce has argued for a formless corpus whose solidarities are formed and mobilized through political speech, only to form anew in different configurations in different contexts.

Criticisms of Stedman Jones, Joyce, and Vernon have been many and often unhelpful, a situation exacerbated by the posturings of the latter two. Joan Scott has offered a successful critique of Stedman Jones, arguing that his somewhat literal reading of political discourse excises the gendered nature of that language (Scott 1988). Eley and Nield have argued that Joyce's formulations rely upon a straw man of a crudely economic, reductionist Marxism jettisoned from social history nearly from its inception. Joyce and Vernon's most sympathetic and formidable critic, James Epstein, has argued that their formulations fail to take into account the conditions of the production and dissemination of political speech, especially the crowds to whom that speech is addressed.

In some renderings, social history has been in crisis since it began. When it has been successful, it has embraced new ideas and domains of inquiry by holding these in creative tension with the analytical purchase of its past discoveries. It is only through these engagements variously with feminism, postcolonial studies, Marxism, anthropology, and, more recently, literary studies that it has achieved something like its foundational concern of a "history of society" articulated by Bloch and Febvre and reiterated variously by Hobsbawm and, later, Eley and Nield.

SEE ALSO *Marxism*

BIBLIOGRAPHY

Bloch, Marc. 1953. *The Historian's Craft*. Trans. Peter Putnam. New York: Knopf.

Clark, Anna. 1995. *The Struggle for the Breeches: Gender and the Making of the English Working Class*. Berkeley: University of California Press.

Davidoff, Lenore, and Catherine Hall. 1987. *Family Fortunes: Men and Women of the English Middle Class, 1780–1850*. Chicago: University of Chicago Press.

Dobb, Maurice. 1946. *Studies in the Development of Capitalism*. London: Routledge.

Eley, Geoff. 2005. *A Crooked Line: From Cultural History to the History of Society*. Ann Arbor: University of Michigan Press.

Eley, Geoff, and Keith Nield. 1980. Why Does Social History Ignore Politics? *Social History* 5 (2): 249–269.

Eley, Geoff, and Keith Nield. 1995. Starting Over: The Present, the Post-Modern and the Moment of Social History. *Social History* 20 (3): 355–364.

Eley, Geoff, and Keith Nield. 2000. Farewell to the Working Class? *International Labor and Working Class History* 57 (Spring): 1–30.

Epstein, James. 2003. *In Practice: Studies in the Language and Culture of Popular Politics in Modern Britain*. Stanford, CA: Stanford University Press.

Fox-Genovese, Elizabeth, and Eugene Genovese. 1976. The Political Crisis of Social History: A Marxist Perspective. *Journal of Social History* 10 (2): 205–220.

Genovese, Eugene. 1974. *Roll Jordan Roll: The World the Slaves Made*. New York: Pantheon Books.

Hall, Catherine. 1992. *White, Male, and Middle Class: Explorations in Feminism and History*. New York: Routledge.

Hall, Catherine. 2002. *Civilising Subjects: Colony and Metropole in the English Imagination, 1830–1867*. Chicago: University of Chicago Press.

Hill, Christopher. 1952. Puritans and the Poor. *Past and Present* 2 (1): 32–50.

Hill, Christopher. 1958. *Puritanism and Revolution: Studies in Interpretation of the English Revolution of the Seventeenth Century*. London: Secker & Warburg.

Hobsbawm, Eric. 1952. The Machine Breakers *Past and Present* 1: 57–70.

Hobsbawm, Eric J. 1997. *On History*. New York: New Press.

Joyce, Patrick. 1991. *Visions of the People: Industrial England and the Question of Class, 1848–1914*. Cambridge, U.K.: Cambridge University Press.

Joyce, Patrick. 1994. *Democratic Subjects: The Self and the Social in Nineteenth-Century England*. Cambridge, U.K.: Cambridge University Press.

Joyce, Patrick. 1995. The End of Social History? *Social History* 20 (1): 73–91.

Judt, Tony. 1979. A Clown in Regal Purple: Social History and the Historians. *History Workshop Journal* 7 (Spring): 66–94.

Lansbury, Coral. 1985. *The Old Brown Dog: Women, Workers, and Vivisection in Edwardian England*. Madison: University of Wisconsin Press.

Morton, A. L. 1938. *A People's History of England*. New York: Random House.

Poovey, Mary. 1988. *Uneven Development: The Ideological Work of Gender in Mid-Victorian England*. Chicago: University of Chicago Press.

Poovey, Mary. 1995. *Making a Social Body: British Cultural Formation, 1830–1864*. Chicago: University of Chicago Press.

Rose, Sonya O. 1992. *Limited Livelihoods: Gender and Class in Nineteenth-Century England*. Berkeley: University of California Press.

Scott, Joan Wallach. 1988. *Gender and the Politics of History*. New York: Columbia University Press.

Stansell, Christine. 1987. *City of Women: Sex and Class in New York, 1789–1860*. Urbana: University of Illinois Press.

Stedman Jones, Gareth. 1982. The Language of Chartism. In *The Chartist Experience: Studies in Working-Class Radicalism and Culture, 1830–1860*, eds. James Epstein and Dorothy Thompson. London: Macmillan Press.

Stedman Jones, Gareth. 1983. *Languages of Class: Studies in English Working-Class History, 1832–1982*. Cambridge, U.K.: Cambridge University Press.

Thompson, E. P. 1961a. The Long Revolution (Part I). *New Left Review* 1 (9): 24–33.

Thompson, E. P. 1961b. The Long Revolution (Part II). *New Left Review* 1 (10): 34–39.

Thompson, E. P. [1963] 1968. *The Making of the English Working Class*. Harmondsworth, U.K.: Penguin.

Thompson, E. P. 1975. *Whigs and Hunters: The Origin of the Black Act.* New York: Pantheon Books.

Thompson, E. P. 1978. *The Poverty of Theory and Other Essays.* New York: Monthly Review Press.

Thompson, E. P. 1991. *Customs in Common: Studies in Traditional Popular Culture.* New York: New Press.

Trevelyan, G. M. 1942. *English Social History: A Survey of Six Centuries, Chaucer to Queen Victoria.* London, New York: Longmans, Green.

Valenze, Deborah M. 1985. *Prophetic Sons and Daughters: Female Preaching and Popular Religion in Industrial England.* Princeton, NJ: Princeton University Press.

Vernon, James. 1994. Who's Afraid of the "Linguistic Turn"? The Politics of Social History and Its Discontents. *Social History* 19 (1): 81–97.

Walkowitz, Judith. 1980. *Prostitution and Victorian Society: Women, Class, and the State.* Cambridge, U.K.: Cambridge University Press.

Walkowitz, Judith. 1992. *City of Dreadful Delight: Narratives of Sexual Danger in Late-Victorian London.* Chicago: University of Chicago Press.

Christopher J. Lamping

HITE REPORT

SEE *Hite, Shere.*

HITE, SHERE
1942–

Author Shere Hite ignited nationwide discussion on the roles of gender and culture in sexuality with the publication of her controversial series of books known as the Hite Reports. Hite has been praised by some for advancing theories of human sexuality by incorporating concepts of societal influences on sex and by revealing the previously overlooked sexual experiences of women. However, she has been criticized by many social scientists for her research methods, which have been described as nonscientific and biased.

Hite was born Shirley Diana Gregory in Saint Joseph, Missouri, and was later adopted by her stepfather, Raymond Hite. She earned a bachelor's and a master's degree in history at the University of Florida and subsequently enrolled in a doctoral program at Columbia University from which she ultimately withdrew. The first book in Hite's series, *The Hite Report: A Nationwide Study of Female Sexuality*, was based on replies to a questionnaire distributed by Hite while she served as director of the Feminist Sexuality Project for the National Organization

for Women (NOW). This book, consisting primarily of verbatim responses from more than three thousand women, became a best seller when it was published in 1976. Contrary to the theories about female sexuality prevalent at that time, which were centered on vaginal penetration, the testimonies of women quoted in Hite's book demonstrated that almost all women could regularly achieve orgasm through clitoral stimulation. In contrast, only about 30 percent of women sampled reported achieving orgasm regularly through vaginal intercourse. Feminists embraced the book for presenting attitudes and experiences in the women's own words and for reporting findings that suggested that a woman's sexual enjoyment was not dependent on the presence of a male. Ultimately, the first Hite Report called for an expansion of the conceptualization of female sexuality to include desires, emotions, and cultural influences on expectations of sex, rather than the limited focus on biology and reproduction.

The inclusion of emotions and societal influences in sexuality theory was also prevalent in Hite's second publication, *The Hite Report on Male Sexuality* (1981). This work argued that male sexuality extended beyond the accepted model that men are solely interested in penetrative sex. Rather, men desire a diversity of sexual activities and are affected by cultural expectations regarding emotions and behavior. Hite has gone on to publish more than ten books generally focusing on sexuality and relationships.

Despite the commercial success of Hite's publications, her methods drew criticism from the scientific community. Although the sample for Hite's initial study of over three thousand women is seemingly large, it represents only 3 percent of the 100,000 women who were sent Hite's questionnaire. Such small response rates are generally indicative of a self-selecting bias, in that only the women who felt strongly enough about the material would be willing to complete the time-consuming survey, which consisted of about sixty open-ended essay questions. Thus, it is often those with the most extreme views who are willing to participate in these types of studies. Additionally, research methods for studies in which statistics are presented as an estimate of population value require the use of a randomly selected sample. However, Hite's survey was sent to a number of women's groups, many of which were considered to be feminist organizations. Hite continued to use similar methods for each of her studies and has repeatedly drawn criticism for presenting statistics and developing theories using samples that are not representative of the population.

SEE ALSO *Feminism; Gender; Sex and Mating; Sexuality*

BIBLIOGRAPHY

Asahina, Robert. 1981. Reading and Writing: Social-Science Fiction. *New York Times*, August 2: Sec. 7.

Hite, Shere. 1976. *The Hite Report: A Nationwide Study of Female Sexuality*. New York: Macmillan.

Hite, Shere. 1981. *The Hite Report on Male Sexuality*. New York: Knopf.

Adrienne A. Williams

HITLER, ADOLF
1889–1945

As the leader of Germany's Third Reich in the 1930s and 1940s, Adolf Hitler developed a totalitarian fascist state dedicated to imperialist expansion of a pure German race. Hitler and his anti-Semitic, supra-nationalistic National Socialist German Workers' Party (Nazi Party) was ultimately responsible for millions of deaths during the Holocaust and a massive refugee crisis in Central and Eastern Europe during World War II (1939–1945).

Hitler was born on April 20, 1889, in Braunau am Inn, Austria, and spent his younger years in Linz, Austria, and in Vienna. Hitler was not a good student; he left the *Gymnasium* without graduating and failed to be accepted as an art student at Vienna's Academy of Fine Arts. This failed career move left Hitler a lonely and distraught young man. While in Vienna in the years leading up to World War I (1914–1918), Hitler developed anti-Semitic tendencies, most likely fed by his envy of affluent Jewish citizens during his years of extreme poverty and destitution as well as the influence of Vienna's Lord Mayor who publicly supported anti-Semitic policies. In 1913 Hitler moved to Munich where he lived until the war broke out and he volunteered to serve in the German Army. During the war, Hitler was injured twice, once in 1916 and again in 1918, the second time as a victim of a gas attack. For his bravery and valor, he earned the Iron Cross twice and was promoted to the rank of corporal. Hitler returned to Munich after the war, dispirited, disillusioned, and angry over the Versailles settlement. Like many young returning soldiers, Hitler believed that Germany's new liberal government should not have signed the Treaty of Versailles. The Treaty forced Germany to accept full responsibility for starting the war, stripped Germany of its colonies, required that it pay heavy reparations to the Allied powers, demilitarized a large portion of its western territory, and reduced its military numbers substantially. Hitler believed that these terms unjustly punished Germany and joined the right-wing, nationalist German Workers' Party

in 1919, the forerunner of the National Socialist German Workers' Party, to work toward a reversal of the treaty.

By 1920 Hitler was the leader of propaganda of the growing German Workers' Party, and in 1921 he became the *führer* (leader) of the organization, now called the Nazi Party. The Nazis at this time were still a very small splinter party, but gained notoriety with their failed Munich Hall putsch in 1923, after which Hitler served nine months in prison. During his incarceration, Hitler wrote his famous memoir and political treatise *Mein Kampf* (My Struggle) where he condemned democratic systems and blamed Europe's Jewish population for what he considered to be Germany's crisis of morality and modernity. The issue of race and its intimate connection to political institutions that stood as symbols of a vanishing collective identity became the focal point of Hitler's theory of fascism. In the tradition of other "philosophers of race" such as Comte de Gobineau and H. S. Chamberlain, Hitler believed in the natural inequality of human races. The white race, he argued, was superior to all others, with the Teutonic race as the most civilized and advanced. Because Hitler believed that the demise of the human race begins with an intermingling of races that causes social instability through a crisis of identity, he called for social, political, economic, and cultural policy to protect the purity of German blood first and foremost.

This belief in ethnic community as the foundation of the nation led Hitler to be suspicious of the Jews' lack of a homeland. He referred to them as "parasites on other peoples" and fervently believed that their infiltration into European society needed to be halted immediately. Hitler was equally suspicious of liberal doctrines of "equality" and "liberty" because, he argued, they only allowed Jews to exploit Europe's gullibility about their true intentions to take over European society. Hitler pointed to the Jewish origins of many Soviet revolutionary leaders, their support of trade unionist activities, as well as their overarching presence in business, finance, banking, and stock market sectors as evidence of Jewish infiltration. Therefore, for Hitler and the Nazis, Jews represented the gravest threat to the Aryan race because of their prominent roles in the development of liberal capitalism and socialism, two modern ideologies that threatened Germans' collective identity. In this way, Hitler's brand of fascism was both anti-Marxist and anti-Semitic, for the two were inextricably intertwined in his mind. Hitler's race doctrine was thus used as an instrument of defense against the inescapable degeneration of Aryan civilization. Only through active destruction of racial inferiors, defined by Hitler to be primarily Jews but also included Slavs, Roma, homosexuals, political dissidents, and disabled people of all ethnicities, could Germany be saved. This dedication to action, outlined in *Mein Kampf*, provided the philosophical foundation for the Holocaust and was responsible for the deaths of approximately 6 million Jews and 3 million other "degenerates" during the Nazi era.

THE RISE OF HITLER'S NAZI PARTY

After his release from prison, Hitler worked throughout the 1920s and 1930s on building a mass political movement. Nazi Party propaganda publicized Hitler's ideas of a Jewish and socialist threat by arguing that both were responsible for Germany's inflationary crisis that was, in fact, due to the Republic's printing of monies to make reparations payments, a number of attempted coups, and the French occupation of the Ruhr. Between 1925 and 1928 alone, Nazi Party membership jumped from 27,000 to 108,000 active supporters. On the eve of the United States stock market crash of 1929, the National Socialists were active in parliamentary politics, earning 810,000 votes in the 1928 election and occupying twelve seats in the Reichstag.

The Nazis gained considerable momentum as economic crisis intensified with the onset of the Great Depression in the early 1930s. The major challenge for Hitler and the Nazis was to prevent unemployed workers from becoming socialist revolutionaries, and so their propaganda vilified trade unionism. Hitler further targeted socialists as enemies of the German nation because the Social Democratic and German Communist parties had voted against war credits during World War I and a revolutionary German socialist government had signed the armistice authorizing Germany's capitulation in 1918. Nazi propaganda became more openly anti-Semitic at this time too, with Hitler firmly blaming Jews for Germany's national crisis through their perpetuation of immoral capitalist practices. At the same time, Hitler pointed to the inability of Weimar's parliamentary system to respond adequately to the Depression. Disagreements between coalition factions and internal divisions in the Social Democratic Party, Germany's largest political party, led to a general paralysis in how to finance unemployment relief. Hitler promised voters the eradication of unemployment, the creation of a welfare state, and a nationalist program of industrial, agricultural and governmental cooperation. With this platform, Hitler succeeded in winning 6.4 million votes and 107 parliamentary seats in the 1930 election. Despite this incredible success, the Nazis still had yet to earn the support of disenchanted industrial workers. Most of their electoral support came from traditional right-wing voters—members of the petty bourgeoisie and agricultural workers—and young, new voters. Hitler successfully converted young Germans to National Socialism through the creation of youth organizations and events such as parades and political rallies that fostered a sense of national community and presented the Nazi Party as one that would unify Germans and resurrect a lost Germanic

empire. By 1931 industrialists responded en masse to Hitler's anti-Marxist platform and his assertions that what would be good for the German people would be good for German industry and joined the Nazi crusade. In the 1932 election, the Nazis won 230 Reichstag seats, the most seats ever held by a single political party in German history, though they still did not enjoy an electoral majority.

On January 30, 1933, President Paul von Hindenburg appointed Hitler the chancellor of Germany. The Reichstag fire on February 27, erroneously believed to have been set by representatives of the German Communist Party (KPD), allowed Hitler a further opportunity to warn Germans of an impending socialist revolution that would destroy the German Fatherland. With heavy pressure from Hitler, Hindenburg then issued an emergency decree "for the Protection of People and State" that restricted personal liberties, extended the government's legal ability to obtain warrants for house searches, confiscate private property, and monitor citizens' postal and electronic communications, and allowed all KPD Reichstag members and other leading anti-Nazis to be arrested. In March 1933, the Reichstag approved the implementation of the Enabling Act that granted Hitler dictatorial powers for four years and officially destroyed the Weimar constitution. A plebiscite in late 1933 confirmed the Nazis' control and, with Hindenburg's death in August 1934, Hitler became Germany's new *führer*.

THE DEVELOPMENT OF THE THIRD REICH

Throughout the mid-1930s Hitler successfully established a strong centralized government that exercised unlimited authority to direct the development of the Third Reich, as Hitler titled his new German empire. The state fulfilled its promises to solve Germany's national crisis by guaranteeing universal employment (with the caveat that all citizens must work), extending social welfare programs including old age pensions and economic protection of mothers and children, nationalizing industry, introducing land reform, and institutionalizing the creation of physical fitness programs to promote national health and vigor. The government also solidified its political power by controlling all forms of media, forming a national army, institutionalizing a "social contract" that emphasized the symbiotic dutiful relationship between state and citizen (not of individuals to one another as in the Marxist model) primarily through the heavy use of propaganda, parades, and other public displays of nationalism. In addition, the state re-aligned the education system's philosophical foundation to fuse "German" moral values of obedience and deference to authority with Hitler's race doctrine and developed a legal system that defended the Nazis' use of terror and coercion to create a totalitarian state.

The Nazi government also worked to expose and eradicate Jews from German society. The 1935 Nuremburg Laws, which included the Reich Citizenship Act and the Act for the Protection of German Blood and German Honor, enacted a number of anti-Semitic laws allowing only ethnically "pure" Germans citizenship rights. These acts categorically excluded Jews from civil and public service and prohibited Germans and Jews from marrying and forming other intimate relationships in order to preserve the Aryan blood line. The Nuremburg Laws were the first step in the eventual ghettoization and murder of millions of European Jews in concentration camps during World War II.

HITLER AND WORLD WAR II

After securing Germans' loyalty through his propaganda of equality and community, Hitler set out to expand Germany's borders through imperialist wars. First he instituted compulsory military service and re-militarized the Rhineland in blatant violation of the terms of the Versailles Treaty. He then began the process of uniting all Germanic peoples into a *Grossdeutschland* ("large Germany") with the annexation of Austria in early 1938. Participants of the Munich Conference in late 1938— Britain, France, and Italy—then allowed Hitler to annex the Sudetenland, the northwestern portion of Czechoslovakia, bringing the large German minority population there under Nazi control. Hitler's imperialist intentions became more apparent in early 1939 when he invaded Bohemia-Moravia and established a Nazi puppet state in Slovakia. Britain and France then realized that their policy of appeasement toward Germany was failing and prepared for war. World War II broke out in September 1939 when Hitler invaded Poland, a move the Western allies viewed as a blatant violation of Poland's right to national self-determination.

Hitler invaded Poland for what he called "*Lebensraum*" ("living space"). His goal was to expand Germany's empire through the annexation of Polish territory, the murder of Polish Jews and political dissenters, and the resettlement of the German *Volk* (the "people") into Poland. This expansion, Hitler argued, was an essential component of German national growth because it would allow the peasant class to maintain its identity as the foundation of the nation through successful cooptation of agricultural land that was untouched by the vagrancies of modernization. This policy of acquiring *Lebensraum* provided the practical justification for the Holocaust. Poland was an easy target for Hitler because it housed the largest Jewish population in Europe and repre-

sented a traditional subordinate territory of the two old German empires: the Prussian and the Habsburg.

In the early years of the war, Hitler succeeded in either conquering or establishing Nazi puppet states or allies on most of the European continent including France, Holland, Belgium, Denmark, Norway, Finland, Austria, Poland, Czechoslovakia, Hungary, Romania, Croatia, Yugoslavia, Bulgaria, Albania, and Greece. The United States' entry into the war in December 1941 as an ally of Britain and the Soviet Union turned the tides of battle and they succeeded in defeating Germany in May 1945. Recognizing Germany's imminent defeat, Hitler committed suicide in Berlin on April 30, 1945.

SEE ALSO *Aryans; Dictatorship; Ethnocentrism; Fascism; Genocide; Gobineau, Comte de; Holocaust, The; Jews; Nationalism and Nationality; Nazism; Racism; White Supremacy; World War II*

BIBLIOGRAPHY

Browning, Christopher R. 2004. *The Origins of the Final Solution: The Evolution of Nazi Jewish Policy, September 1939–March 1942*. Lincoln: University of Nebraska Press.

Flood, Charles Bracelen. 1989. *Hitler, the Path to Power*. Boston: Houghton Mifflin.

Hilter, Adolf. 1927. *Mein Kampf*. München: Zentralverlag der NSDAP.

Kershaw, Ian. 1987. *The "Hitler Myth": Image and Reality in the Third Reich*. New York: Oxford University Press.

Kershaw, Ian. 2000. *Hitler*. New York: W.W. Norton.

Payne, Robert. 1973. *The Life and Death of Adolf Hitler*. New York: Praeger.

Rosenbaum, Ron. 1998. *Explaining Hitler: The Search for the Origins of His Evil*. New York: Random House.

Snyder, Louis L. 1961. *Hitler and Nazism*. New York: Bantam Books.

Toland, John. 1976. *Adolf Hitler*. Garden City, NY: Doubleday Press.

Tracey A. Pepper

HIV

The human immunodeficiency virus (HIV) is part of a family of retroviruses that have the capacity of reproduction from RNA in the nucleus of a helping cell of the human immune system. Using enzymes—chemical substances in the human organism that enhance reactions without intervening in them—the virus breaks through the cell membrane to the nucleus, where it is reproduced. Infection with HIV leads to the disease known as AIDS.

The origin of HIV is unknown, but it is widely understood that it is a mutation of a similar retrovirus, such as the simian immunodeficiency virus. It is speculated that the virus developed the capacity to infect human beings through the practice of ingesting raw meat or blood in religious rituals in isolated parts of Africa. Even though the first AIDS cases were reported in Africa in the early 1980s, several known cases were before this date.

THE DISCOVERY OF HIV

At the beginning of the AIDS epidemic, the virus was initially called human T-lymphotropic virus type III (HTLV III) by the U.S. research group under the leadership of Robert Gallo. The virus was also discovered at about the same time by researchers at the Pasteur Institute of France under the leadership of Luc Montagnier, who named it lymphadenopathy-associated virus (LAV). Following an international controversy between the two researchers, who both claimed credit for the discovery, the name HIV was agreed upon.

By 1982 it had been established that HIV had caused the destruction of the immune system of numerous individuals, rendering them susceptible to infections that produced a combination of diseases, such as Kaposi sarcoma and pneumonia. This overall disease process was called acquired immunodeficiency syndrome (AIDS). By this time it had also been established that the virus was transmitted via body fluids, such as blood and semen.

A number of factors—including the migration of infected people to populated zones, overpopulation in certain communities, difficulties in access to medical care, and ignorance of the disease—led to the infection becoming a pandemic by the end of the 1980s. The first AIDS cases in the United States were reported in the summer of 1980, when the Centers for Disease Control and Prevention (CDC) reported several cases of young males with opportunistic infections and a compromised immune system. The number of reported AIDS cases then began to increase in a geometrical way through the entire world. According to the CDC, the cumulative estimated number of diagnoses of AIDS through 2003 in the United States was 929,985. Adult and adolescent AIDS cases totaled 920,566, with 749,887 cases in males and 170,679 cases in females. The remaining 9,419 cases had occurred in children under age 13. At the end of 2003, it was estimated that 1,039,000 to 1,185,000 persons in the United States were living with HIV/AIDS and that between 24 and 27 percent were undiagnosed and unaware of their condition.

TESTING FOR HIV

There is a test to detect the presence of HIV antibodies. A more specialized test, the polymerase chain reaction (PCR) test, can identify the virus, but it is only used for special cases or research due to its high cost. For the general public, the ELISA test is used, which only detects the presence of HIV antibodies. This test is highly sensitive for negatives, which is why it is commonly used for screening possible cases. But because of this sensitivity, ELISA tests that are positive must be confirmed with a more accurate test, called the Western blot. Both tests are readily available through public health services, and many health community-based organizations provide the test at outreach activities in the communities.

TREATMENT AND PREVENTION

As of 2007 there was no available vaccine for HIV. More than 95 percent of all new infections were in developing countries, making HIV/AIDS one of the most serious threats to global health and global development. Many believe that only a vaccine will stop the spread of the infection. Developing a vaccine will thus represent a huge milestone in the AIDS epidemic, and several clinical trials are being developed in different countries. However, the versatility of the virus and other concerns have made this a difficult task.

Due to the nature of HIV infection and the lack of a cure or vaccine, the only way to address the epidemic is by means of prevention. Primary prevention programs target vulnerable populations by means of culturally and competent interventions designed to help people avoid being infected. Because the virus is transmitted by contact with fluids, sharing infected needles for drug use, having sexual intercourse without protection, and mother-to-infant transmission are the main venues for the virus to be introduced to human beings. Important primary prevention interventions have been developed and evaluated in the United States and other industrialized countries, and these are being transferred to other communities around the world. These prevention programs include education about the virus, condom distribution, clean needle distribution for drug addicts, and peer counseling, and they have slowed the spread of HIV. The basic idea is that by learning the ways the virus is transmitted and by developing personal and social skills that protect and empower at-risk minority communities, it is possible to stop the spread of the infection.

Advances in treatment have yielded important new AIDS therapies, but the cost and complexity of their use put them out of reach for most people in the countries where they are needed the most. In industrialized nations, where the drugs are more readily available, side effects and increased rates of viral resistance have raised concerns about the long-term use of these therapies. Since the mid-1990s, HIV infection has spread most rapidly among women, children, and sexual minorities. Both in the United States and in developing countries, the incidence of HIV infection has had a disproportional impact on communities of color. Efforts at primary prevention must therefore take into consideration the social and cultural context and meanings of what are known as "high-risk behaviors."

It is also important of course to pay attention to those already living with HIV/AIDS, with the goal of providing them access to care and secondary prevention. By engaging people living with HIV/AIDS in appropriate treatment, the quality of life of these individuals can be enhanced. This level of treatment will also reduce the continuing transmission of the infection. For this to happen, the human rights of people living with HIV/AIDS need to be protected. This will encourage them to get tested and receive medical and social care.

THE STIGMA OF AIDS

Jonathan Mann, the founding director of the World Health Organization's Global Programme on AIDS, described the HIV epidemic as more than just a biological disease. It is also a social phenomenon that he identified as potentially explosive because it is an epidemic of social, cultural, economic, and political responses to the disease. This social epidemic is characterized above all by exceptionally high levels of stigma, discrimination, and at times collective denial.

The concept of *stigma* dates to ancient Greece, where it was used to describe persons who had been involved with certain bad deeds, for which they were distinguished from others by the application of bodily marks or tattoos. People so marked were to be avoided by the general populace. The concept has also been associated with an unnatural mark in the bodies of saints, a mark made with a hot iron on the flesh of slaves, a bad reputation, and even a physical dysfunction. Some authors have described stigma as a social construction associated with the recognition of a "difference" based on a specific characteristic, which is used to devalue the person who possesses that characteristic. All of these definitions share the idea that a stigma is the negative evaluation of a particular difference that may be identified in a person. The stigma associated with AIDS has become the biggest obstacle for HIV/AIDS prevention, because it hinders the possibility of dignity and access to care for people living with the infection.

SEE ALSO *AIDS; AIDS/HIV in Developing Countries, Impact of; Disease; Public Health; World Health Organization*

BIBLIOGRAPHY

Centers for Disease Control and Prevention. 1981. Kaposi's Sarcoma and *Pneumocystis* Pneumonia among Homosexual Men: New York City and California. *Morbidity and Mortality Weekly Reports* 30: 305–308.

Centers for Disease Control and Prevention. 1981. *Pneumocystis* Pneumonia: Los Angeles. *Morbidity and Mortality Weekly Reports* 30: 250–252.

Centers for Disease Control and Prevention. 2004. *HIV/AIDS Surveillance Report.* Vol. 15, *Cases of HIV Infection and AIDS in the United States, 2003.* Atlanta, GA: Author.

Goffman, Erving. 1963. *Stigma: Notes on the Management of Spoiled Identity.* Englewood Cliffs, NJ: Prentice-Hall.

Herek, Gregory M. 1999. AIDS and Stigma in the United States. *American Behavioral Scientist* 42 (7): 1106–1116.

Herek, Gregory M., and John P. Capitano. 1999. AIDS Stigma and Sexual Prejudice. *American Behavioral Scientists* 42 (7): 1130–1147.

HIV Vaccine Trials Network. "The Step Study": HVTN 502/Merck 023 A Merck/HVTN Proof-of-Concept Vaccine Trial. http://www.hvtn.org/science/step.html.

Joint United Nations Programme on HIV/AIDS (UNAIDS). 2003. *Report on the Global HIV/AIDS Epidemic, December 2003.* Geneva, Switzerland: UNAIDS.

Kalichman, Seth C. 1998. *Understanding AIDS: Advances in Research and Treatment.* Washington, DC: American Psychological Association.

José Toro-Alfonso

HMONG

Hmong society is based on outmarrying patriclans within which ideals of fraternal hospitality are maintained. Within clans, lineages are clustered around the worship of a common ancestor. Cultural divisions cut across clans to mark different groups of Hmong by dialect, female costume, and architecture. Shamanism, ancestor worship, and a belief in nature spirits form a profound religious complex. There is no traditional form of Hmong writing, but a missionary-invented romanized script is widely used.

Traditionally the Hmong were shifting cultivators of forest at altitudes of 3,000 to 5,000 feet in the mountains of southern China and the neighboring countries of Indochina, with an economy based on the production of dry rice, maize, and opium as a cash crop, some hunting, and animal husbandry. The household was the unit of production, and hamlets were often settled by members of the same local descent group. There was no hereditary position of political authority, nor any political authority higher than the village. Houses were built on the ground out of wood.

The Hmong form perhaps a third of the Miao national minority of China, which numbered 9.6 million in 2002. Although unknown in Chinese records under the *Hmong* ethnonym, under the name of *Miao* it is clear that their history in China is an ancient one, and was characterized by a series of violent clashes against centralized imperial authority.

During the last half of the nineteenth century, Hmong from China migrated into Burma (Myanmar), Thailand, and the northern parts of Laos and Vietnam, after the failure of rebellions in south China and increasing pressures on scarce land resources. In north Vietnam, the Hmong were caught up in the First Indochina War (1946–1954) and were instrumental in the Viet Minh victory against the French at the battle of Dien Bien Phu (1954).

During the civil wars in Laos from 1962 to 1973, Hmong were divided along clan and regional lines between support for the rightist parties and for the socialist Pathet Lao. As porters, guides, spies, and fighters, they were crucial to a war effort fought mostly in sensitive border regions; many became regular or irregular troops under General Vang Pao of the Royal Lao Army. Casualties were heavy.

With the fall of Laos in 1975, more than 100,000 Hmong fled Laos for Thailand, where they were housed in five refugee camps along the border, from which they have mostly been resettled in third countries. A large number refused resettlement because they were led to believe they would be needed to retake Laos, where a small resistance movement continues with variable support from elements of the old counterinsurgency military establishment. Formal recognition of their support for the American war effort in Indochina was won in the Hmong Veterans' Naturalization Act of 2000, which allows special consideration for irregular Hmong ex-soldiers.

A new culture emerged in the refugee camps as farming people with newfound leisure produced new forms of culture for sale to the outside world that told of their history and sufferings, such as embroidered story-cloths and the new music championed by the leader of a messianic movement. The Hmong came under increasing Christian influence in the camps, which has led to serious divisions in the community.

Outside China the Hmong have been estimated at 153,955 in Thailand, 315,000 in Laos, 787,604 in Vietnam, and perhaps 2,000 in Burma. Overseas population figures are estimated at 15,000 for France, 1,800 for Australia, 2,000 for French Guyana, 1,200 for Canada, 250 in Argentina, 92 in Germany, and 186,310 in the United States. Resettled Hmong have sought to regroup in areas of better economic opportunity and to join larger groups of Hmong. In the early 1990s, half the Australian Hmong population moved to North Queensland to farm bananas. By 2003, all 150 Hmong settled in New Zealand had joined the Australian Hmong. From 1981 to 1983, 20,000 Hmong arrived in the Central Valley of California, and some 20,000 moved again in 1998 from California to Minnesota.

American Hmong are concentrated in California, Minnesota, and Wisconsin. Particular cultural problems have been caused by ritual animal sacrifices in cases of illness and at funerals, which traditionally take place at home. Pressing social issues include the changing position of women, underage marriages, and the growing prevalence of youth gangs. Although the majority of Hmong refugees find unskilled work or remain on social welfare, there have been many success stories, with the emergence of Hmong singers and poets, publishers, academics, and politicians. The fragmentation of families between two or more countries remains an issue for most of the older generation. Clan organization has proved a vital adaptation mechanism, with lending pools and mutual help societies formed. Some return visits to Laos and Thailand have taken place, remittances are often sent home, and some brides have been sought from Thailand, Laos, or China. Overall there has been a huge change of consciousness as the Hmong recognize themselves as a global, albeit fragmented, community and adopt new forms of communication, such as the Internet and telephone, with facility.

BIBLIOGRAPHY

Fadiman, Anne. 1997. *The Spirit Catches You and You Fall Down: A Hmong Child, Her American Doctors, and the Collision of Two Cultures.* New York: Farrar, Straus, and Giroux.

Geddes, William R. 1976. *Migrants of the Mountains: The Cultural Ecology of the Blue Miao (Hmong Njua) of Thailand.* Oxford: Clarendon.

Tapp, Nicholas, Jean Michaud, Christian Culas, and Gary Yia Lee, eds. 2004. *Hmong/Miao in Asia.* Chiang Mai, Thailand: Silkworm Books.

Nicholas Tapp

HO CHI MINH
1890–1969

Ho Chi Minh played a pivotal role in the global processes of anticolonialism and decolonization that accompanied World Wars I and II. His leadership has become an enduring symbol of third world resistance to the West during the twentieth century.

Ho Chi Minh was born in on May 19, 1890, in central Vietnam. Biographers have estimated that he used over fifty aliases during his career. He was educated in the Confucian classics, instructed in three languages (Chinese, French, and romanized Vietnamese), exposed to a modern multidisciplinary curriculum, and steeped in Vietnamese history. In 1908 he was expelled from the National Academy for his involvement in a peasant demonstration.

In 1911 Ho Chi Minh resolved to leave Vietnam to experience life in France. He secured employment with a steamship company and traveled widely to ports in Europe, Africa, Asia, and the United States. He claimed to have lived in New York in 1912. In 1913 he moved to London, where he studied English, and in 1917 he returned to France.

In 1919 Ho Chi Minh gained notoriety when he presented to the major powers gathered at the Versailles peace conference a petition arguing that Woodrow Wilson's Fourteen Points should be applied to the colonial peoples in Indochina. This document was signed "Nguyen Ai Quoc," a pseudonym he used for the next quarter century. In 1920 Ho Chi Minh joined a breakaway faction of the French Socialist Party that joined the Communist Third International.

In 1923 Ho Chi Minh moved to Moscow and began a career as an agent of the Communist Third International (or Comintern). He was assigned to China in 1924. In February 1930 he presided over the founding conference of the Vietnam Communist Party. Ho Chi Minh's revolutionary career was interrupted by his arrest and detention by British authorities in Hong Kong (1931–1933). He resumed work with the Comintern in Moscow after his release, and in 1938 he was posted back to China.

In February 1941 Ho Chi Minh returned to Vietnam after an absence of three decades. In May of that year he founded the anti-Japanese Viet Minh Front. He was detained by Nationalist authorities in southern China the following year and released in 1943. While in China, he made his first contacts with U.S. officials. He professed admiration for President Franklin Roosevelt's anticolonial sentiments. In 1944 Ho Chi Minh reached an agreement with the Office of Strategic Services (OSS) in China. He agreed to supply intelligence and assist in the rescue of downed pilots in exchange for OSS assistance to and training of Viet Minh troops.

In August 1945 the Viet Minh seized power, and on September 2 Ho Chi Minh declared Vietnam independent, citing the opening words from the American Declaration of Independence. He used his OSS contacts to convey messages to President Harry Truman requesting support. In 1946 Ho Chi Minh twice offered the United States access to Cam Ranh Bay.

Ho Chi Minh led the Vietnamese people in a successful eight-year war to expel the French (1946–1954). From 1954 until his death on September 2, 1969, he held the twin positions of head of state and chairman of the party in North Vietnam. In reality power over domestic affairs was held by the party general secretary and senior members of the politburo. Increasingly he focused his energies on foreign affairs and national reunification.

Ho Chi Minh was both a Communist and a nationalist. His brand of communism was more pragmatic than doctrinaire, while his patriotism was uncompromising. In Ho Chi Minh's words, "Nothing is more precious than independence and freedom."

SEE ALSO *Anticolonial Movements; Communism; Domino Theory; Freedom; Nationalism and Nationality; Self-Determination; Vietnam War; World War I*

BIBLIOGRAPHY

Duiker, William J. 2000. *Ho Chi Minh: A Life*. New York: Hyperion.

Quinn-Judge, Sophie. 2002. *Ho Chi Minh: The Missing Years, 1919–1941*. Berkeley: University of California Press.

Carlyle A. Thayer

HOBBES, THOMAS
1588–1679

Thomas Hobbes was the first influential philosopher to apply the methods of Enlightenment science to politics. At the age of twenty, he was hired as a tutor for the son of William Cavendish (1640–1707), the first Earl of Devonshire, and he received support and employment from the Cavendish family throughout his life. In 1628 Hobbes published a translation of Thucydides' (c. 460–c. 401 BCE) *History of the Peloponnesian War*, and in various visits to the Continent he befriended and engaged in discussions about mathematics and science with the luminaries of the day, including Galileo Galilei (1564–1642), Pierre Gassendi (1592–1655), and Marin Mersenne (1588–1648).

He authored his first book, *Elements of Law* (1640), at age fifty-two. Sounding themes that would become familiar throughout his work, he declares that humanity's natural state is a state of war and that only by divesting themselves of their natural rights and transferring those rights to a sovereign can people ensure their physical safety. Shortly thereafter, in anticipation of the English Civil War (1642–1648), Hobbes fled to France, fearing that a treatise that justified the king's prerogatives would bring retribution from the parliamentarians.

While in France he tutored the future Charles II (1630–1685), critiqued René Descartes (1596–1650), wrote *De Cive* (an expanded version of the second part of *The Elements of Law*), and authored and published his most important work: *Leviathan* (1651).

In *Leviathan*, Hobbes asserts that humanity's natural condition is characterized by two kinds of equality. First, everyone has the ability to kill. Second, everyone is equally prone to believe that they are more wise than everyone else. This leads to competition, mistrust, and a desire for glory, which in turn makes people's natural condition a state of war. The state of war for Hobbes is as much a milieu as it is actual fighting and it is the background condition of all human relations.

The difficulties that attend people's natural condition, in combination with their natural desire for self-preservation, means that they have a natural right to anything and everything. However, reason (and experience) leads one to the conclusion that retaining this right can only lead to a life that is "solitary, poor, nasty, brutish, and short" (Hobbes 1994, p. 76).

The solution to the war of all against all is a social contract. By giving up their natural right to anything and everything, people create a sovereign who commands precisely that right: an absolute sovereign. Creating this sort of sovereign is the most effective way to ward off the state of nature because an absolute sovereign overawes those who might be tempted to reclaim their natural right. Indeed, the leviathan is, citing Job, "King of the Proud." In addition, a single decision maker eliminates the potential for internal disputes and undivided power prevents one sector of society or government from withholding resources from another.

The sovereign power is not itself party to the social contract because a covenant is only valid if it has the power of the public sword behind it. In effect, no subject can bring redress against the sovereign, because the sovereign itself is the only party to which redress can be brought. The sovereign is therefore not obligated to act in a way that is beneficial to the individuals who created it. Instead, having contracted their will to the sovereign, the decisions and punishments of the sovereign amount to decisions and punishments that a subject inflicts on him- or herself. However, the sovereign is obligated to protect the commonwealth from internal and external enemies (by making law and making war) and there are incentives for the sovereign to act in ways that are beneficial to subjects. Hobbes also suggests that the sovereign cannot expect individuals to literally kill themselves on command. The crucial point to keep in mind is that even a bad government is preferable to the state of war or a government prone to dissolution.

In *Leviathan* and in his other works, Hobbes uses the principles of science and mathematics to ascertain the fundamental basis of politics. This approach understands the world as composed of bodies in motion and requires developing and working from careful definitions of key concepts. The result is a mechanistic rendering of human relationships that imagines human bodies and desires in geometric relation to one another. This is not to say his works are gauged only for the scientific reader. Instead, Hobbes combines science and rhetoric in an attempt to affect the politics of his time.

In 1652 he returned to England, having offended Parisian royalists who took exception to his attack on Roman Catholicism. Hobbes envisioned a three-part description of political existence consisting of body, man, and government. *The Elements of Law* and *Leviathan* describe most of the salient features of the second and third parts of this scheme and *De Cive* is devoted exclusively to the third, but he set out to fully develop the first two parts, writing *De Corpore* (Of Body, 1655) and then *De Homine* (Of Man, 1658). He also wrote a history of the English Civil War, *Behemoth* (1668). His work was widely read and debated during his lifetime. Some of his mathematical assertions were successfully rebutted and his stated commitment to Christianity and God was and is a matter of dispute.

By grounding government in a contract between equals, as opposed to divine sanction, Hobbes initiates a discussion about the purposes and character of government that defines much of modern political thought. His most notable and direct influence was on John Locke and Jean-Jacques Rousseau, and his influence on certain forms of conservatism endures.

SEE ALSO *Locke, John; Rousseau, Jean-Jacques; Social Contract; State of Nature*

BIBLIOGRAPHY

Dietz, Mary G., ed. 1990. *Thomas Hobbes and Political Theory.* Lawrence: University Press of Kansas.

Hobbes, Thomas. [1651] 1994. *Leviathan, with Selected Variants from the Latin Edition of 1668.* Indianapolis, IN: Hackett.

Johnston, David. 1986. *The Rhetoric of Leviathan: Thomas Hobbes and the Politics of Cultural Transformation.* Princeton, NJ: Princeton University Press.

Dustin Ells Howes

HOBOS

The term *hobo* was used to describe homeless people who moved around in order to find temporary work in the United States during a cycle of depressions between 1879 and 1939. The term was often conflated with the terms *tramp* and *bum*. Contemporary uses of the word are rare. Similar people are now most often called homeless or migrant workers. The most famous definition of the hobo is said to originate from the Chicago anarchist Ben Reitman who stated that a hobo moves and works, a tramp moves and doesn't work, and a bum stays still and does not work. It is unclear from where the name originates. Some claim that it is derived from the name *hoe boy*—an agricultural worker. Another theory is that *hobo* is a derivation of the Latin *homa bonas* (good man).

Despite such attempts to differentiate hobos from tramps, contemporary observers tended to refer to the mobile homeless as tramps and hobos interchangeably. Most were male, white, and American-born, but there were significant numbers of black and female hobos as well. In 1911 one researcher suggested a population of 350,000 hobos. A 1906 estimate put the population at 500,000.

Hobos and tramps were most likely to travel alone either on freight trains or on foot. Because such train travel was illegal, it was also extremely dangerous. They would travel between, on top of, or underneath carriages. As they often had to get onto the train while it was moving, they were frequently injured or killed in the process. Railroad police were also known to deliberately throw hobos off moving trains. Estimates of annual death and injury to hobos and tramps ran as high as 5,000. Hobos most often worked in construction, agriculture, and mining. Indeed, the newly industrialized agriculture of the American West depended on the ability of migrant laborers to follow harvests from apples in Washington State to beets and grapes in California. Others followed the wheat harvest through the Midwest from Kansas to the Dakotas.

Between jobs hobos would gather on the outskirts of urban areas alongside railroad tracks in places known as hobo jungles. They would also use police stations, lodging houses, "flop houses" (a place offering very cramped, cheap lodging for transients, usually men), and missions. These would normally be located along an area called the Main Stem—a part of town associated with lodging for the homeless as well as employment agencies, cheap cafes, and soup kitchens.

Following the recession of 1879 hobos were subjects of a moral panic known as the tramp scare. They were generally represented as being foreign-born, lazy, and politically subversive. Newspapers called for them to be jailed, forced into work camps, sterilized, or even killed. Eugenicists believed them to be members of an "inferior"

racial group who favored a nomadic lifestyle. By World War II (1939–1945) the term *hobo* had been replaced by the term *migrant*, which had been used in the 1930s to refer to those displaced by the Great Depression and the Dust Bowl in the American South and Midwest. Since World War II people who would have been called tramps or hobos in the early part of the twentieth century have been referred to most often simply as the homeless. Indeed, the earlier figures of hobos and tramps became romantic figures. Charlie Chaplin, Jack Kerouac, and others used the hobo figure to question some of the assumptions about "normal" life in the United States.

BIBLIOGRAPHY

Anderson, Nels. 1998. *On Hobos and Homelessness.* Chicago: University of Chicago Press.

Cresswell, Tim. 2001. *The Tramp in America.* London: Reaktion Books.

Tim Cresswell

HOBSON, JOHN ATKINSON

SEE *Imperialism; Underconsumption.*

HOLISM

SEE *Anthropology.*

HOLLYWOOD

SEE *Culture; Entertainment Industry; Film Industry; Gone with the Wind; Romance.*

HOLOCAUST, THE

"The Holocaust" is the most common name for the systematic destruction of almost 6 million European Jews under German National Socialism between 1933 and 1945. *Holocaust*, from the Greek *holokauston*, means a burnt sacrifice or offering. Because the events of the Holocaust were no such thing, however, many prefer other terms, including the Hebrew Shoah (calamity) or "genocide of the European Jews." The term *genocide* (murder of an entire ethnic group) was coined during World War II (1939–1945) by the Polish exile lawyer Raphael

Lemkin to describe the murderous program Germany was carrying out, particularly in occupied central and eastern Europe; since then *genocide* has been used to refer to numerous other historical programs of mass ethnic-based extermination.

JEWS AND THE NAZI REGIME

The Nazi regime never made a secret of its anti-Semitism, if there is nevertheless substantial debate about how early, public, and explicitly murderous were its intentions to make Europe *Judenrein* (free of Jews). Vilification and scapegoating of Jews was certainly a central feature of Nazi rhetoric throughout the 1920s. Following the Nazi seizure of power in Germany in January 1933, the regime instituted a boycott of Jewish businesses. Soon thereafter Jews were dismissed from the civil service, and strict quotas were placed on Jewish presence in schools. In May 1933 libraries were purged of "decadent" materials, Jewish and otherwise, which were burned in great pyres in public squares.

As discrimination against Jews escalated in the following years, authorities felt the need for a more precise legal definition of "Jew," which they produced in the September 15, 1935, Nuremberg Laws for the Protection of German Blood and German Honor and the Law of the Reich Citizen. The Nuremberg Laws defined Jews as those having at least three Jewish grandparents; those with one or two Jewish grandparents were defined as *Mischlinge* (mixed breeds). The laws prohibited marriage between Jews and "Aryans" and declared civil and political rights only for "Germans." Despite many generations of patriotic commitment and a high degree of social integration, including often enthusiastic participation in the German military during World War I (1914–1918), Jews were no longer considered German.

A more vigorous stage of persecution began on November 9, 1938. Following the murder of a German diplomat in Paris by a Jew, the Nazi regime sponsored an enormous nationwide pogrom against Jews often referred to as *Kristallnacht* (Night of Broken Glass). In two days more than 7,000 Jewish-owned shops and businesses were destroyed, more than 1,500 synagogues (almost every synagogue in the country) were burned, more than 100 Jews were killed, and more than 30,000 other Jews were imprisoned in the so-called concentration camps that had been set up since the first days of the regime for holding political opponents and others.

World War II began on September 1, 1939, when the German army invaded Poland. With the progress of war and the occupation of vast portions of eastern Europe, the Nazis' murderous programs entered a new phase. Chancellor Adolf Hitler explicitly endorsed a large program of "euthanasia" for "undesirables," mainly the men-

tally and physically handicapped, though the definition of "undesirable" extended to include homosexuals, prostitutes, Jehovah's Witnesses, and Sinti and Roma peoples (Gypsies), among others. In July 1941 Hitler also explicitly discussed the so-called *Einsatzgruppen* (operational forces). These special units engaged in systematic, though cumbersome, mass murder of Jews and partisans in the occupied territories, often by machine-gunning large groups of people gathered to dig their own graves.

Nevertheless, given the stresses and expenses of such a program, Nazi planners sought other, more efficient means for killing large numbers of Jews as well as for disposing of their bodies in a more sanitary way. Experimentation thus continued with various forms of mobile death squads and subsequently with specially designed gas chambers as well as large-scale crematoria. The regime built and expanded camps to carry out these latter innovations. The extent of these practices was systematized and expanded following the Wannsee Conference of January 20, 1942, where Nazi leaders met and empowered such functionaries as Adolf Eichmann to coordinate the vast transport of Jews to the death camps, defining what they euphemistically called "the final solution to the Jewish problem." In July 1942 SS leader Heinrich Himmler ordered the evacuation of the many ghettos the Nazis had set up in eastern European cities to segregate and control Jewish populations. Most of these evacuations—most notoriously of the Warsaw ghetto—involved transport to "extermination camps" (*Vernichtungslager*) in such places as Auschwitz-Birkenau, Treblinka, Belzec, and Majdanek. Best estimates are that approximately three million Jews died in the death camps, in addition to the millions of others who died in concentration camps, by mass killings, and of disease, hunger, desperation, and murder.

SOCIAL SCIENCE AND THE HOLOCAUST

Most accounts from a social sciences perspective emphasize how sociologists, psychologists, and others have sought to explain the Holocaust as well as how social science was necessarily influenced and challenged by the ramifications of the Holocaust. In focusing on the role the Holocaust has played in social science, however, we overlook the role social science played in the Holocaust. For indeed social theory and research of various kinds was an important part of the intellectual milieu from which National Socialism arose. National Socialist ideologues drew explicitly on social Darwinism and eugenics, which were prominent themes across the political spectrum both in Germany and elsewhere in the first decades of the twentieth century. In Germany in particular social theory helped define a climate of "radical conservatism."

Prominent thinkers, such as Oswald Spengler, Werner Sombart, Arnold Gehlen, and others, helped define a mood of cultural discontent and suspicion of liberalism, which contributed to the failure of the Weimer Republic. Indeed many such figures remained in Germany throughout the Nazi years, some—for instance, Hans Freyer—even assuming positions of power in Nazi academe and beyond. Many of these intellectuals, as well as those trained under them during the Nazi period, were rehabilitated after the war and became prominent figures in postwar thought (e.g., Helmut Schelsky).

Given the predominance of both Marxism and Jews in German sociology during the 1920s, moreover, many falsely assume that the Nazis rejected the social sciences. That was not entirely the case. The Nazi regime used the social sciences for a variety of purposes, drawing great power from the advanced state, for instance, of German managerial science. In the early years of the regime, the Swiss psychoanalyst Carl Jung collaborated with Matthias Goering, brother of the Nazi propaganda minister and Hitler confidante Hermann Goering, on the formation of a German Psychoanalytic Society "free of Jewish influence." The sociologist Theodor Geiger's work was part of the discussion of Nazi sterilization and euthanasia programs. Social scientific work on regional planning was useful to the formation of occupation policy in the East, as were area specialists, who drew on and contributed to German *Ostforschung* (research on the East), which incorporated geographical, economic, and sociological approaches. Freyer, director of the German Scientific Institute in Budapest, and his assistant Schelsky contributed to cultural propaganda aimed at the Hungarian intelligentsia. The so-called *Inlandsnachrichtendienst* (Domestic Information Service) employed large numbers of social scientists to gather public opinion and other data. While the regime had chased large numbers of leading scholars into exile, remaining Nazi scholars sought to combine traditional social theory (*Gesellschaftslehre*) with a new racist anthropology (*Volkskundelehre*) into a "unified theory" (*Gesamtheitslehre*). As in law, medicine, literature, and other institutional spheres, then, portions of the social sciences as well as some of their members were associated with, were used by, and supported the Nazi regime, and the contemporary disciplines neglect examination of this legacy at their peril.

EXPLAINING THE HOLOCAUST

Social scientific efforts to explain the Holocaust directly have been few and far between. In the first place, the unprecedented scale of industrial killing the Nazis undertook as well as the unfathomable mass of cruelty they sponsored in some sense defy explanation and are grasped more readily in the philosophical vocabulary of radical evil. Indeed cultural theorists have often described the Holocaust as an event "beyond the limits," which include those of comprehensibility as well as representability. In the second place, sociology and political science, some have argued, are better suited to explaining conditions and structures rather than events, particularly events considered unique in a sense beyond the usual one in which all historical events are unique. But part of the reason is that the contemporary association of National Socialism and World War II with the Holocaust was not always as central as it is in the early twenty-first century. For at least twenty years after 1945, most social scientific and historical accounts saw the Judeocide as a consequence of rather than as the centerpiece of National Socialism.

To be sure, a wide variety of theory has sought to explain the rise of National Socialism in Germany and the extreme violence it produced. Two major axes of argument characterize most of this literature. The first is between theories that see National Socialism as a variety of "fascism," an extreme outgrowth of capitalism, milder versions of which can be found in all capitalist societies, and "totalitarianism," a form of radical authoritarianism characterizing both Nazi Germany and the Soviet Union. The second is between "intentionalists," who see Nazi aggression and the destruction of the Jews as the result of a master plan, and "functionalists," who see it as a sort of "industrial accident," the conditions for which could be found almost anywhere but combined in unusual ways in Germany. Intentionalists emphasize both the evil machinations of leaders as well as unique desires inherent in German culture, while functionalists emphasize Germany's delayed modernization, absent middle class, and polycratic (dis)organization. The social scientific and historical literatures thus range over a variety of causes and characteristics of the Nazi regime, including "massification," secularism, nihilism, consumerism, militarism, imperialism, evolutionism, and modernity itself. In most such accounts, however, the dependent variable is National Socialism, not the Holocaust. Theories associating radical Nazi anti-Semitism and the Holocaust with modernity generally—such as Max Horkheimer and Theodor Adorno's *Dialectic of Enlightenment* (written before the era of extermination camps, though it did not appear until 1944) and Zygmunt Bauman's *Modernity and the Holocaust* (1989)—are perhaps the most successful because they seek to draw meaning rather than determine causation.

Beyond the more macrohistorical efforts to explain National Socialism (which, again, confound the Judeocide with political authoritarianism and militarism), a number of sociological and social-psychological studies have sought to confront the cruelty and evil of National Socialism and the extermination camps as general problems of deviant behavior and social psychology, thus approaching the question equally as obliquely as the macrohistorical theorists. Adorno and colleagues conducted research into what they called "the Authoritarian Personality." During the war the psychiatrist Richard Brickner diagnosed a collective paranoia, as did Jung after the war, both arguing for an occupation policy modeled on therapy for a neurotic patient. The sociologist Everett Hughes framed Nazi brutality as a matter of "good people and dirty work." Similar to Hannah Arendt, who most famously described Nazi brutality as banal, not in the sense of being trivial but in the sense of being ordinary, the work of desk-chair perpetrators (*Schreibtischtaeter*), Hughes sought to understand the social processes that made ordinary people capable of extraordinary cruelty, just as theories of "differential association" and "socialization" explain other kinds of deviance. In a similar vein Christopher Browning's studies of police officers who served in death squads underscore the universal capacity of every person for brutality in the right circumstances. Most famously the psychologist Stanley Milgram designed a series of experiments in which ordinary people were led, under a variety of conditions, to administer increasingly painful and finally lethal electrical charges to fictional test subjects, illustrating the general tendency for human beings to be "obedient to authority."

Debates about the causes of National Socialism and of the centrality of the murder of the Jews are ongoing and frequently occasion public controversy. For instance, the political scientist Daniel Goldhagen's 1996 book *Hitler's Willing Executioners* attracted a great deal of public attention for its thesis that Germany exhibited a unique form of "eliminationist anti-Semitism" and that as a result ordinary Germans supported the extermination of the Jews. The consensus is that Goldhagen failed to establish the existence and operation of a uniquely "eliminationist" political culture. Goldhagen's charge that macrohistorical and macrosociological accounts have not adequately conceptualized the centrality of Jew hatred has received less attention.

From about the 1980s on a particularly interesting strand of social scientific work focusing directly on the Holocaust developed concepts of "collective memory" and "cultural trauma" to understand the aftereffects of the Holocaust in contemporary culture. In the first place, collective memory scholars have studied how nations have confronted and commemorated both their victimhood and their complicity in the crimes. For Germany, the question has been what kind of an identity a nation held responsible for what many consider to be the worst crime in human history can have after such knowledge.

Elsewhere the questions have centered on the fluid boundaries between complicity and resistance; in Poland and Israel questions of the centrality of victimhood to

contemporary identity have been key, and sociologists of memory have sought to understand the complex comparative dynamics of the different national cases. In the second place, theorists of trauma, both individual and cultural, have studied the problems of cultural and social transmission. For both survivors and perpetrators, scholars have identified unique legacies for the second and third generations, identifying both substantive problems from this particular history and general processes of intergenerational transmission. Finally, political sociologists have described the Holocaust as an interesting model for the "globalization" of memory, arguing that the civilizational dimensions of the Holocaust and its implied indictment of modernity are diagnostic of the present condition and serve as a model for commemorative forms elsewhere as well as for the pursuit of redress claims in a variety of cases.

SEE ALSO *Anti-Semitism; Arendt, Hannah; Concentration Camps; Eugenics; Genocide; Hitler, Adolf; Jews; Milgram, Stanley; Nazism; Neumann, Franz; World War II*

BIBLIOGRAPHY

Adorno, Theodor, and Max Horkheimer. 2002. *Dialectic of Enlightenment: Philosophical Fragments*. Ed. Gunzelin Schmid Noerr, trans. Edmund Jephcott. Stanford, CA: Stanford University Press.

Arendt, Hannah. 1963. *Eichmann in Jerusalem: A Report on the Banality of Evil*. New York: Viking.

Arendt, Hannah. 2004. *The Origins of Totalitarianism*. New York: Schocken Books.

Bauman, Zygmunt. 1989. *Holocaust and Modernity*. Cambridge, U.K.: Polity.

Browning, Christopher. 1992. *Ordinary Men: Reserve Police Batallion 101 and the Final Solution in Poland*. New York: HarperCollins.

Derks, Hans. 1999. Social Science in Germany, 1933–1945. *Germany History* 17 (2): 177–219.

Friedlaender, Saul, ed. 1992. *Probing the Limits of Representation: Nazism and the "Final Solution."* Cambridge, MA: Harvard University Press.

Gerson, Judith M., and Diane L. Wolf, eds. 2007. *Sociology Confronts the Holocaust: Memories and Identities in Jewish Diasporas*. Durham, NC: Duke University Press.

Hilberg, Raul. 1961. *The Destruction of the European Jews*. Chicago: Quadrangle Books.

Levy, Daniel, and Natan Sznaider. 2006. *The Holocaust and Memory in the Global Age*. Trans. Assenka Oksiloff. Philadelphia: Temple University Press.

Milgram, Stanley. 1974. *Obedience to Authority: An Experimental View*. New York: Harper and Row.

Muller, Jerry Z. 1987. *The Other God That Failed: Hans Freyer and the Deradicalization of German Conservatism*. Princeton, NJ: Princeton University Press.

Neumann, Franz. 1944. *Behemoth: The Structure and Practice of National Socialism, 1933–1944.* Toronto and New York: Oxford University Press.

Jeffrey K. Olick
Shannon Latkin Anderson

HOLY ROMAN EMPIRE

The foundation of the Holy Roman Empire is usually dated to the decision of Charlemagne (742–814), king of the Franks, to assume an imperial title on Christmas Day, 800. The exact reasons for this remain a matter of dispute, but were clearly related to Charlemagne's personal mission to establish Christian rule in western and central Europe. The original empire was partitioned in 843, with the eastern portion retaining the association with the Christian imperial mission. This assumed greater ideological significance with the coronation of Otto I (r. 936–973) in Rome in 962 as he consciously invoked not only continuity with Charlemagne's empire, but that of ancient Rome. The concept of "imperial translation" claimed that the empire was a direct continuation of that of ancient Rome in its final, Christian configuration, and so was the last of the four "world monarchies" prophesied in the Bible to rule over the earth before the Day of Judgment. Such ideas buttressed the emperor's claim to be the supreme overlord of all other Christian rulers and thus the secular arm of a single, universal Christendom, leading to a prolonged dispute with the papacy.

The Christianizing mission combined with internal population growth to push the empire across the river Elbe early in the twelfth century, making it the largest polity in Europe until the growth of the Russian Empire in the eighteenth century. This expansion was assisted by the relative continuity of three successive imperial dynasties: the Ottonians (919–1024), the Salians (1024–1125), and the Staufers (1138–1254). However, the growth of more distinct kingdoms in western Europe restricted the emperor's practical authority to the lands east of the Rhine and north of the Alps. Moreover, the emperor only ruled a small portion of the vast area directly, relying on a host of secular and spiritual lords, as well as autonomous cities to manage local and regional affairs. These lords (increasingly called "princes") and cities evolved as the "imperial estates" (*Reichsstände*) between the thirteenth and sixteenth centuries, each controlling a distinct territory within the empire, with their own subordinate clergy, nobility, towns, and rural communes.

The absence of a single imperial dynasty after 1254 assisted this process and led to an elective imperial title that became entrenched in Germany and could be assumed without papal participation. Following the demise of the Luxembourg dynasty (1347–1437), the title passed by election to the Habsburgs, who retained it with only a single break (1740–1745) until the end of the empire in 1806. The onset of prolonged warfare with France and the Ottomans coincided with the confessional strife of the Reformation, and social and economic change. These pressures forced constitutional change from the late fifteenth century, creating an elaborate web of written and customary rights intended to preserve the autonomy of the imperial estates and the corporate structure of central European society within a hierarchical political framework under the emperor's overall authority, but not his direct rule. The growth of Austria and Prussia as distinct European great powers undermined this structure from within and led to its collapse during the Napoleonic Wars when the last emperor abdicated in 1806.

SEE ALSO *Church, The*

BIBLIOGRAPHY

Arnold, Benjamin. 1997. *Medieval Germany, 500–1300: A Political Interpretation.* Basingstoke, U.K.: Macmillan.

Wilson, Peter H. 1999. *The Holy Roman Empire, 1495–1806.* Basingstoke, U.K.: Macmillan.

Peter H. Wilson

HOMELESSNESS

The National Law Center on Homelessness and Poverty indicates that, on any given day, approximately 840,000 people in the United States are homeless or living in temporary shelters. Approximately 3.5 million people in the United States will meet criteria for homelessness within a given year, and 1.35 million of them are children. It is estimated that 7.4 percent of U.S. residents, or as many as 13.5 million people in the United States, have been homeless at one point in their lives.

The majority of the homeless in urban areas are adult men of minority descent. In rural areas, however, the homeless are more likely to be Caucasian, and their genders and ages are less well known. Across both rural and urban settings, approximately 20 to 25 percent of the homeless adult population suffer from some type of severe and persistent mental illness. Although homelessness has been a historically significant phenomenon in the United States, it still remains difficult to cull reliable and comprehensive data about homeless individuals. Indeed given the difficulty of tracking and finding individuals who are homeless because of the variability in their locations, national data may significantly underestimate the incidence and prevalence of this social condition.

In 1987 the Stewart B. McKinney Homeless Assistance Act marked the first time the U.S. government acknowledged homelessness as a national crisis, despite its prevalence for decades prior to this event. In addition to designating federal money to help research and solve the problem of homelessness, the McKinney Act also provided a clear definition of *homeless*. According to the legislation, a "homeless" individual is one who lacks a fixed, regular, and adequate nighttime residence or has a primary nighttime residence that is a supervised publicly or privately operated shelter, an institution that provides temporary residence for individuals who will be institutionalized, or a public or private place not ordinarily used as regular sleeping accommodations for human beings.

The term *homeless* is inapplicable to individuals who are imprisoned or detained under congressional or state law. The concept as understood in the United States is largely based on an individual's physical living arrangements or accommodations. However, as the literature suggests, this definition may be inadequate and unable to capture the complexity of phenomena internationally. Indeed this U.S. definition of homelessness reduces the concept to an issue of "houselessness," which is a critical caveat to achieving an international understanding of the phenomenon.

The United Nations Centre for Human Settlements (Habitat) has refined homelessness and developed a more globally appropriate and responsive definition. The center also recognizes that definitions of homelessness vary widely and are influenced by geographic and socioeconomic factors. Most of what is known about homelessness, including an accepted definition of the construct, is based on the limited statistics and information available from European and North American countries and from the developing country of India. From this perspective, commonly held conceptualizations of homelessness include a consideration of social and familial relationships and sociodemographic factors.

Globally it is estimated that between 100 million and one billion individuals are homeless. Notably, however, homelessness data from developing countries are particularly sparse and difficult to collect. Across developed and developing countries, homelessness is often understood through both the narrow lens of accommodations, or lack thereof, and broader perspectives in an effort to inform services and interventions for those affected. For example, while some countries employ a typology based on characteristics of housing quality or on the length of time an individual is homeless, other countries may use a typology based on risk or potential of facing houseless conditions.

There are some emerging cross-cultural categories for understanding homelessness in an international arena. For example, *supplementation homelessness*, whereby an individual is homeless in response to migration, is quite different from *survival homelessness*, whereby individuals are homeless because they are searching for improved opportunities. *Crisis homelessness*, a precipitant of homelessness produced by a crisis (such as a storm, earthquake, or war) is quite different from the previous two. These categories focus more on the etiology for homelessness rather than on factors directly associated with the homeless individuals' culture, race, or premorbid socioeconomic status.

From a global perspective, much attention is given to homeless children and adolescents, often referred to as *street children*. It was estimated that there were 100 million street children worldwide in 1992, with 71 million of these children working and living on the streets full-time, 23 million working and living on the streets part-time, and approximately 7 to 8 million abandoned. While street children are considered among the homeless, the literature makes clear distinctions between homeless adults and homeless children. The most accepted definition of a *street child* is "any girl or boy for whom the street (in the widest sense of the word, including unoccupied dwellings, wasteland, etc.) has become his or her habitual abode and/or source of livelihood; and who is inadequately protected, supervised, or directed by responsible adults" (Glasser 1994, p. 54).

Such a definition addresses characteristics in addition to physical living arrangements with a broader consideration of a child's basic needs (that is, need for security and socialization). Similar to the various typologies used to understand global homelessness among adults, a typology has been developed by UNICEF that differentiates street children who live at home and those who do not, which is particularly relevant given that the majority of street children have some contact with their families.

Specifically the literature has found that there are experiential differences between street children who are deemed at high risk of homelessness (that is, the child spends some time in the streets), street children who are in the streets (for example, they spend most of their time in the streets, usually working), and street children who are *of* the streets (that is, the street is the child's home). As with the typologies used with homeless adults, these categories may be useful in determining the level and the type of services needed.

Homelessness is an international crisis. The understanding of who is most affected and under what conditions as well as the ability to programmatically remediate the social ills that promote this condition are further limited by the national definitions that are often internally valid but not well generalized internationally.

SEE ALSO *Children; Children's Rights; Hobos; Poverty; Slums; Vagabonds*

BIBLIOGRAPHY

Edgar, Bill, Joe Doherty, and Amy Mina-Coull. 1999. *Services for Homeless People: Innovation and Change in the European Union.* Bristol, U.K.: Policy.

Ennew, Judith, and Brian Milne. 1990. *The Next Generation: Lives of Third World Children.* Philadelphia: New Society Publishers.

Epstein, Irving. 1995. Dependency Served: Rhetorical Assumptions Governing the Education of Homeless Children and Youth. Paper delivered at the International Sociological Association Midterm Conference of the Sociology of Education Research Committee, Jerusalem, December 28.

Glasser, Irene. 1994. *Homelessness in Global Perspective.* New York: Macmillan.

Kuhn, Randall, and Dennis P. Culhane. 1998. Applying Cluster Analysis to Test a Typology of Homelessness by Pattern of Shelter Utilization. *American Journal of Community Psychology* 26: 207–232.

National Law Center on Homelessness and Poverty. 2004. *Homelessness in the United States and the Human Right to Housing.* National Law Center on Homelessness and Poverty. http://www.nlchp.org/Pubs/index.cfm?FA=7&TAB=0.

Speak, Suzanne. 2004. Degrees of Destitution: A Typology of Homelessness in Developing Countries. *Housing Studies* 19 (3): 465–482.

Springer, Sabine. 2000. Homelessness: A Proposal for a Global Definition and Classification. *Habitat International* 24 (4): 475–484.

United Nations Centre for Human Settlements. 1996. *An Urbanizing World: Global Report on Human Settlements.* Oxford: Oxford University Press.

U.S. Conference of Mayors. 2001. *A Status Report on Hunger and Homelessness in America's Cities.* Washington, DC: U.S. Conference of Mayors.

U.S. Conference of Mayors. 2005. *A Status Report on Hunger and Homelessness in America's Cities.* Washington, DC: U.S. Conference of Mayors. http://www.mayors.org/uscm/hungersurvey/2005/HH2005FINAL.pdf.

U.S. Department of Agriculture, Rural Economic and Community Development. 1996. *Rural Homelessness: Focusing on the Needs of the Rural Homeless.* Washington, DC: U.S. Department of Agriculture, Rural Housing Service, Rural Economic and Community Development.

Christopher L. Edwards
Crystal L. Barksdale

HOMEOSTASIS

SEE *Social System.*

HOMICIDE

SEE *Murder.*

HOMO ECONOMICUS

SEE *Theory.*

HOMO PSYCHOLOGICUS

SEE *Theory.*

HOMOSEXUALITY

SEE *Sexual Orientation, Determinants of.*

HOMOTYPIC STABILITY

SEE *Stability, Psychological.*

HOODOO

SEE *Vodou.*

HOOVER, J. EDGAR
1895–1972

John Edgar Hoover was born in Washington, D.C., on January 1, 1895, and died there on May 2, 1972. He served as director of the U.S. Bureau of Investigation (BOI)—known after 1935 as the Federal Bureau of Investigation (FBI)—from 1924 until his death. During his long tenure he greatly expanded the bureau, giving to it much of its modern identity, but he was also the focus of a great deal of controversy because of his autocratic leadership style and his frequent abuses of power in the name of fighting subversion.

After earning a law degree from George Washington University in 1917, Hoover joined the Justice Department during World War I (1914–1918), working in (and briefly heading) its Enemy Aliens Registration Section. Two years later he was chosen as head of the newly established General Intelligence Division of the Justice Department. In this capacity, he was involved in the Palmer Raids (1919–1920), during the course of which U.S. Attorney General A. Mitchell Palmer (1872–1936) ordered the arrest of thousands of radical political figures, violating their civil rights, and deporting hundreds who were not U.S. citizens. Hoover's role in this effort eventually led to his appointment by President Calvin Coolidge as the sixth director of the Bureau of Investigation in May of 1924.

As director of the BOI, Hoover expanded the bureau's staff. He also modernized its methods of conducting criminal investigations by, among other things, establishing what would become the FBI Laboratory and amassing, in the bureau's Identification Division, an enormous collection of criminal's fingerprints. The bureau rose to prominence during what is often referred to as the "lawless decade" of the 1920s, and during the 1930s it engaged in a number of high-profile battles with such famous criminals of the Depression era as John Dillinger, Alvin Karpis, Bonny Parker and Clyde Barrow, and Machine Gun Kelly. After its name change to the Federal Bureau of Investigation in 1935, the bureau became increasingly a part of the American vocabulary.

During World War II (1939–1945) the bureau played an important role in domestic surveillance, and its efforts led to the capture of a number of Nazi agents and saboteurs working undercover in the United States. In the years following the war, however, Hoover's war against subversion took a more controversial turn. During the late 1940s and early 1950s he became deeply involved in the anti-Communist movement known popularly as *McCarthyism*—after the reckless, witch hunt methods of Senator Joseph McCarthy of Wisconsin (1908–1957). In the name of rooting out Communist subversion, Hoover authorized illegal wiretapping and spying on thousands of suspected Communists. In the second half of the 1950s he expanded his area of concern to the emerging civil rights movement, which he also believed to be subversive in character. He sought to discredit the work of the early civil rights leader T. R. M. Howard (1908–1976), and later made similar efforts against Martin Luther King Jr.

Hoover served during the administrations of eight presidents, and while several of these individuals—especially Truman, Kennedy, Johnson, and Nixon—felt that he had grown too powerful, none was able or willing to remove him from office, due in part to his and the FBI's near-iconic status in the mind of the average American. Celebrations of the FBI in American popular culture that contributed to this status included a long-running radio program (*The FBI in Peace and War*, 1944–1958), a popular television series (*The F.B.I.*, 1965–1974), and a 1959 film, *The FBI Story*, starring the well-known Hollywood actor James Stewart. Hoover himself was the author of several books, among them the best-selling *Masters of Deceit: The Story of Communism in America and How to Fight It* (1958).

Hoover's management style at the bureau was highly autocratic, and he was greatly feared by those who worked for him. Following his death in 1972, Clyde Tolson (1900–1975), his longtime friend and associate FBI director, succeeded him as director.

In the years following Hoover's death the controversies surrounding his life and career have continued to grow. Among them, suggestions of homosexuality (in Anthony Summers's *Official and Confidential: The Secret Life of J. Edgar Hoover* [1993]) and possible African American ancestry (in Millie McGhee's *Secrets Uncovered: J. Edgar Hoover—Passing for White?* [2000]) have rendered particularly ironic Hoover's use of information regarding sexual orientation as a means of attacking or intimidating political opponents and his strong opposition to the postwar civil rights movement.

SEE ALSO *Civil Rights Movement, U.S.; Communism; Crime and Criminology; King, Martin Luther, Jr.; McCarthyism*

BIBLIOGRAPHY

Garrow, David J. 1981. *The FBI and Martin Luther King, Jr.: From "Solo" to Memphis.* New York: W. W. Norton.

McGhee, Millie L. 2000. *Secrets Uncovered: J. Edgar Hoover—Passing for White?* Rancho Cucamonga, CA: Allen-Morris.

Powers, Richard Gid. 1983. *G-Men: Hoover's FBI in American Popular Culture.* Carbondale: Southern Illinois University Press.

Summers, Anthony. 1993. *Official and Confidential: The Secret Life of J. Edgar Hoover.* New York: G. P. Putnam's Sons.

Theoharis, Athan G., and John Stuart Cox. 1988. *The Boss: J. Edgar Hoover and the Great American Inquisition.* Philadelphia: Temple University Press.

Scott Wright

HOPE

In an ancient Greek myth, Zeus was irate at humans for having stolen fire from the gods. In the spirit of revenge, he fashioned a young maiden named Pandora and, using reverse psychology, sent her to earth with a dowry chest, with the crucial instruction not to open it. Of course, her curiosity got the best of her, and she opened the lid. Out came a plague of evil forces. Panicked at what she had unleashed, Pandora tried to close the chest, only to find that hope was stuck on the lid. Hope could overcome the evil forces unleashed. Thus hope came into the world.

A young couple stood at the graveside of their two twin daughters, born prematurely, as a circle of family and friends sang the hymn, "Lead, Kindly Light, Amid the Encircling Gloom." Having their precious daughters buried near their great grandparents in a historic cemetery brought them comfort and hope in the face of perinatal loss (Callister 2006). Hopefulness in such situations is a personal, comforting, and life-sustaining belief that even in difficult times, life has meaning. Hope is also a belief that something favorable can happen for oneself or others in the future. P. S. Hinds (1984) defined hope as the human characteristic that allows an individual, irrespective of age, to transcend disappointments, pursue goals, and diminish the sense of the future as unbearable or futile. Hope is a force contributing to a person's will to live (Cousins 1989).

Detractors to hope exist. It is postulated that inside every person there is a spirit of hopefulness that can be influenced negatively or positively by others. Suffering and feeling alone or unappreciated, along with unaddressed spiritual needs, are some of the challenges to being hopeful.

James Averill and his associates (1990) asked people to describe circumstances in which they thought hope would be important. Responders described periods when they perceived some degree of personal control over their lives, and times when their life goals were important, had a reasonable chance of being reached, and were socially and morally acceptable.

Strategies that contribute to the strengthening of hope include believing in oneself, trusting in the good intentions of others, and feeling close to another person. For many people, faith and religious beliefs also contribute to hopefulness. Hope is vital for those who have been diagnosed with a serious, life-threatening, or terminal illness, as well as for their families. Those who lack hope find no meaning in life or find it difficult to persevere in troubling times. They may lack or lose a sense of well-being, and doubt the possibility of favorable outcomes. The components of hope include "positive thinking or optimism, reality-based and future oriented goals, positive future for self or others, and positive support systems" (Hendricks-Ferguson 1997, p. 76). Hope is essential to negotiating difficult life challenges. Knowing that others have hope for positive outcomes can foster hope in individuals.

On the other hand, hope may be perceived by others as evidence that individuals and families are unrealistically positive. Thus, hope may become simply "magic" when one has a wishful expectation that everything will "turn out all right" based on luck, fate, or the intervention of a higher power. Still, hope can be fostered by reflecting on positive outcomes and by formulating potential goals.

Hope thus becomes realistic as one recognizes the existence of limitations or conditions.

Multiple tools have been developed to measure hope, including the *adult hope scale* developed by C. R. Snyder and colleagues (1991). Eight items are ranked on an eight-point Likert scale from "definitely false" to "definitely true," with four agency items such as "I energetically pursue my goals." The higher the score, the higher the level of overall hope. A similar children's hope scale has also been developed.

Hope has been studied across the lifespan. Kaye Herth (1998) used interviews and drawings to study sixty homeless children who had lived through multiple losses. Themes included connectedness, internal resources, cognitive strategies, energy, and hope objects. The children used symbols in their drawings, most often trees or rainbows, which for them symbolized hope. As one homeless adolescent wrote, "a young tree is very fragile and in need of just the right amount of water and sunlight to grow; hope at first is very fragile but flourishes with care" (Herth 1998, p. 1057). Many of the children drew pictures of houses, with open doorways and flowers and favorite toys, indicating a longing to have a "real home." One child who drew a sad face explained, "sometimes you have to be sad before you can smile again" (Herth 1998, p. 1058). The adolescents shared stories of significant losses but demonstrated inner strength that sustained their hope. One favorite book at the shelter was *The Little Engine that Could,* with the hopeful refrain, "I think I can, I think I can."

Adela Yarcheski and associates (1994) studied ninety-nine high school students, finding statistically significant positive correlations between perceived hopefulness and social support, as well as hopefulness and general well-being. Hopefulness was fostered through social interaction, mutuality, attachment, intimacy, affirmation, encouragement, and a nurturing environment. Hopefulness in adolescents with cancer has also been studied and has been linked with improved quality of life and better health even in the face of chronic or terminal illnesses (Hendricks-Ferguson 1997).

Hope is experienced differently by those who are chronically ill than by those who are healthy. Dal Sook Kim and associates (2006) studied hope in chronically ill hospitalized patients and identified five life orientations related to hope:

- Externalism orientation—hope based on reliance on family, friends, or God.

- Pragmatic orientation—hope in the ability to accomplish small things in life.

- Reality orientation—hope manifested by realistically enjoying that which can be.

- Future orientation—hope focused on positive possibilities that may exist in the future, which may include a strong reliance on a higher power; for example, a person may say, "I feel hope in my faith in God" or "I feel hope when I realize that I am in God's hands."

- Internal orientation—hope oriented toward the self.

J. M. Morse and B. Doberneck (1995) studied patterns of hope exhibited in a variety of people undergoing different life experiences. Their subjects included breast cancer survivors, individuals waiting for heart transplants, unemployed mothers, and persons with spinal cord injuries. The presence and function of hope has also been studied in people with acute spinal cord injuries (Lohne and Severinsson 2004) and adults undergoing bone marrow transplants for leukemia (Ersek 1992). In Mary Ersek's study, factors associated with hope included "feelings of powerfulness or control, meaning or purpose in life, adequate social support, and positive self esteem" (1992, p. 883). Ersek identified the structure of hopefulness as:

- Appraising the illness in a nonthreatening manner (seeing it as a positive event).

- Cognitively managing the illness experience (including the practice of joking).

- Managing emotional responses to the illness.

- Managing a sense of control (either maintaining or relinquishing control).

- Taking a stance toward illness and treatment (fighting the illness or accepting it).

- Managing the uncertainty (minimizing or maximizing the uncertainty).

- Focusing on the future (living from day to day or focusing on the long term).

- Viewing the self in relation to the illness (minimizing the illness and maximizing personal strengths).

Further research is needed to increase our understanding of hope, including how to mediate the variables and strategies that enhance hope in individuals across the lifespan. Many experts assume that sources of hope include support from family and significant others, as well as spiritual beliefs (Hendricks-Ferguson 1997). How these sources of hope make a difference merits further inquiry.

BIBLIOGRAPHY

Averill, James R., George Catlin, and K. K. Chon. 1990. *Rules of Hope.* New York: Springer.

Callister, Lynn Clark. 2006. Perinatal Loss: A Family Perspective. *Journal of Perinatal and Neonatal Nursing* 20 (3): 227–234.

Cousins, Norman. 1989. *Head First: The Biology of Hope.* New York: Dutton.

Ersek, Mary. 1992. The Process of Maintaining Hope in Adults Undergoing Bone Marrow Transplantation for Leukemia. *Oncology Nursing Forum* 19 (6): 883–889.

Hendricks-Ferguson, Verna L. 1997. An Analysis of the Concept of Hope in the Adolescent with Cancer. *Journal of Pediatric Oncology Nursing* 14 (2): 73–80.

Herth, Kaye. 1998. Hope as Seen through the Eyes of Homeless Children. *Journal of Advanced Nursing* 28 (5): 1053–1062.

Hinds, P. S. 1984. Inducing a Definition of "Hope" through the Use of Grounded Theory Methodology. *Journal of Advanced Nursing* 9: 357–362.

Kim, Dal Sook, Suzie Kim Hesook, Donna Schwartz-Barcott, and Donna Zucker. 2006. The Nature of Hope in Hospitalized Chronically Ill Patients. *International Journal of Nursing Studies* 43: 547–556.

Kylma, Jari, and Katri Vehvilainen-Julkunen. 1997. Hope in Nursing Research. *Journal of Advanced Nursing* 25 (2): 364–371.

Lohne, Vibeke, and Elisabeth Severinsson. 2004. Hope and Despair: The Awakening of Hope Following Acute Spinal Cord Injury—An Interpretive Study. *International Journal of Nursing Studies* 41: 881–890.

Morse, J. M., and B. Doberneck. 1995. Delineating the Concept of Hope. *Image: Journal of Nursing Scholarship* 27 (4): 277–286.

Ritchie, Mary Ann. 2001. Self-esteem and Hopefulness in Adolescents with Cancer. *Journal of Pediatric Nursing* 16 (1): 35–42.

Snyder, C. R., Cheri Harris, John R. Anderson, et al. 1991. The Will and Ways: Development and Validation of an Individual-Differences Measure of Hope. *Journal of Personality and Social Psychology* 60: 570–585.

Yarcheski, Adela, Mary Ann Scoloveno, and Noreen Mahon. 1994. Social Support and Well-being in Adolescents: The Mediating Role of Hopefulness. *Nursing Research* 43 (5): 288–292.

Lynn Clark Callister

HOSTILITY

SEE *Personality, Type A/Type B.*

HOTELLING RULE

SEE *Resource Economics.*

HOT MONEY

Hot money may be defined in two ways. Currency traders define it as opportunistic funds seeking the highest short-term return in international markets, moving from one trend to the next—hence, its highly liquid or "hot" character. In more journalistic usage, the adjective refers to money whose ownership is concealed at least from the tax authorities and often from criminal prosecutors as well. This is done by creating corporate shells, and it is done increasingly legally, blurring the boundary between legal and illicit. Rather than countering the activity, European and American governments have promoted it and offered special tax advantages in order to attract this money.

The corrupt associations of "hot money" derive less from the activity itself than from the social status of its practitioners. It is disparaged when the funds come from dope dealing and arms trading or from small-fry falsifying their tax returns. But hot money is blessed and even given special tax subsidy when conducted at the top of the economic pyramid.

Early hot-money centers were Switzerland, Liberia, and Panama. Switzerland long refused to cooperate with foreign criminal prosecutors on the logic that its laws did not recognize tax avoidance as a crime. Liberia and Panama offered "flags of convenience" to the oil industry and refrained from imposing any income or sales taxes in a fiscal "race to the bottom." Oil companies avoided taxes by incorporating shipping affiliates in Panama and Liberia to buy crude oil at low prices from their branches in the producing nations and sell them at a high enough markup to their refineries in the consuming nations, so that neither oil wells nor refineries had reportable income.

By the 1960s these tax-avoidance centers inspired smaller versions throughout the Caribbean and other islands. These "offshore banking centers" specialized in legal "tax avoidance" as distinct from outright tax *evasion*. By far the major quantitative suppliers of funds in such centers are large multinational corporations, global money managers, and post-Soviet kleptocrats. Smaller fry simply have moved in their wake, facilitated by the international banks that have set up branches in these enclaves.

When the U.S. dollar came under pressure in the late 1960s, Congress voted to refrain from imposing the usual 15 percent income-tax withholding on interest paid to holders of Treasury bonds in these centers. Deeming it to be in the U.S. interest to attract tax-evasion money and the soaring sums of overtly criminal wealth to stabilize the balance of payments, the government encouraged U.S. banks to set up branches in these centers. Britain announced a similar rationale to permit its residents to conduct real estate and other transactions via the Channel Islands, along with the British West Indies and a few other imperial dependencies in the Caribbean. For continental Europe, Liechtenstein and more recently Cyprus have played a similar role, with Russian oligarchs and their counterparts in other parts of the former USSR favoring Cyprus.

The prize for banks in these centers is a volume of flight capital, tax-avoidance, and criminal money that took a quantum leap after the breakup of the Soviet Union in 1991. Capital flight from Russia alone is estimated at $25 billion annually since that time. Usually a "veil of tiers" is set up by lawyers using multiple offshore banking centers to make the funds more difficult to trace. The ultimate magnitude is reported regularly by central banks. The Federal Reserve Board reports U.S. deposits from offshore banking centers quarterly, segregating out deposits at U.S. bank branches. The Bank of England and the German Bundesbank publish similar quarterly reports in their central bank bulletins, and U.S. congressional committees periodically hold hearings to assess how the rising flow of hot money can best be tapped to serve U.S. national interests.

These statistics show the major role hot money has come to play in international banking. The United States has become the world's largest hot-money haven, followed by Britain. The Bank of Credit and Commerce International and Riggs Bank in Washington, D.C., and the Bank of New York and Citibank have been singled out for serving kleptocrats, dictators, and smaller crooks, highlighted by the uncovering in 2004 of secret accounts for former Chilean dictator Augusto Pinochet (1915–2006). An eight-year 1998–2006 FBI probe of money laundering focused on operations by Semion Mogilevich and other members of Russia's *mafiya* at the Bank of New York.

In sum, the growth of "legitimate" savings by multinational firms, government officials, and major vested interests makes any estimate of the magnitude of hot money fairly irrelevant. Different observers may draw the line at different points along the line from respected multinationals to small-time tax dodgers and crooks who use these centers to make their money invisible to the tax and police authorities.

SEE ALSO *Capital Flight; Corruption; Crime and Criminology; Drug Traffic; Money Laundering; Offshore Banking; Taxes*

BIBLIOGRAPHY

Naylor, R. T. 2004. *Hot Money and the Politics of Debt.* 3rd ed. Montreal: McGill-Queens University Press.

Michael Hudson

HOUSE UN-AMERICAN ACTIVITIES COMMITTEE

SEE *Civil Rights, Cold War; Cold War; McCarthyism.*

HOUSTON, CHARLES HAMILTON
1895–1950

Charles Hamilton Houston was born in 1895, one year before the U.S. Supreme Court's decision in *Plessy v. Ferguson*. In *Plessy*, the Court upheld laws requiring racially segregated public facilities, known as Jim Crow laws, ruling that "separate but equal" facilities for blacks and whites did not violate the U.S. Constitution. Charles Houston dedicated his life to destroying Jim Crow and ending racial segregation by law in the United States.

Houston believed that the law could be used to bring about social change and that black lawyers should be trained as social engineers. He attended law school at Harvard University, where he was the first black editor of the *Harvard Law Review*. In 1929 Houston was appointed head of the law school at Howard University, a historically black institution. Houston raised admissions standards, improved the faculty, strengthened the curriculum, and achieved accreditation for the school. His mission was to train a cadre of black lawyers that would successfully challenge government-sanctioned discrimination. One of Houston's students, Thurgood Marshall (1908–1993), went on to argue *Brown v. Board of Education* (1954) before the U.S. Supreme Court and later to serve as the Court's first black justice.

In 1935 Houston took a leave of absence from the law school to serve as special counsel to the National Association for the Advancement of Colored People (NAACP). Within a few months of joining the NAACP, Houston initiated a legal campaign to end racial discrimination in public education. The first step in Houston's strategy was to attack *Plessy's* "separate but equal" doctrine as it applied to graduate and professional schools. Most states offered legal education only to white students, thus failing to meet the "separate" requirement, and Houston brought test cases to challenge these policies. In *Murray v. Maryland* (1936) and *Missouri ex. rel. Gaines v. Canada* (1938), the Maryland Court of Appeals and the U.S. Supreme Court ruled that states must either admit black students to their established institutions or provide blacks with equal facilities for graduate and professional training.

Houston resigned as NAACP special counsel in 1938, but he remained active in civil rights litigation. He turned his attention to racial discrimination in labor and housing. In the *Steele* and *Tunstall* cases of 1944, Houston successfully challenged preferential hiring in the railroad industry, and in *Hurd v. Hodge* (1948), he took on restrictive covenants among homeowners and prevailed.

Houston also continued to advise Thurgood Marshall, who had taken over the education litigation. The next step was to challenge the separate graduate and professional schools created in the wake of *Murray* and *Gaines* and to show that equality was impossible, or at least too expensive, to achieve. In *Sweatt v. Painter* (1950) and *McLaurin v. Oklahoma* (1950), the NAACP argued that the education offered to black law and graduate students was substantially inferior to that available to white students, and the Supreme Court unanimously agreed.

Houston died of heart failure in 1950 and did not live to see the culmination of his strategy to overturn *Plessy v. Ferguson*. In *Brown v. Board of Education* (1954) and its companion cases, the Supreme Court was unanimous in striking down segregation in primary and secondary education, declaring that "in the field of public education the doctrine of 'separate but equal' has no place."

SEE ALSO Brown v. Board of Education, *1954; Marshall, Thurgood; National Association for the Advancement of Colored People (NAACP)*

BIBLIOGRAPHY

Klebanow, Diana, and Franklin L. Jonas. 2003. *People's Lawyers: Crusaders for Justice in American History.* Armonk, NY: Sharpe.

McNeil, Genna Rae. 1983. *Groundwork: Charles Hamilton Houston and the Struggle for Civil Rights.* Philadelphia: University of Pennsylvania Press.

Malia Reddick

HULL, CLARK
1884–1952

A leading American psychologist during the middle decades of the twentieth century, Clark Leonard Hull established an early reputation for carefully controlled research and formulated an influential version of neobehaviorist learning theory. His ambitious theoretical system was marked by quantitative precision and systematic exposition in terms of postulates and equations.

Hull was raised on a small farm in Michigan and attended Alma College in preparation for a career in engineering. But while convalescing from polio, he read

William James's *Principles of Psychology* (1890) and transferred to the University of Michigan to study psychology. He then entered graduate school at the University of Wisconsin, receiving a doctorate in 1918 with a thesis on concept formation under the direction of Joseph Jastrow (1863–1944).

Remaining at Wisconsin as an instructor, Hull pursued research in three areas. His study "The Influence of Tobacco Smoking on Mental and Motor Efficiency" (1924) produced mixed results but was noteworthy for implementing a placebo design in which blindfolded subjects smoked pipes that delivered either tobacco or heated, smoke-scented air. He also conducted quantitative studies of aptitude testing and carefully controlled research on hypnosis, eventually publishing well-received books on both topics. His *Hypnosis and Suggestibility* (1933) was a pioneering work in the scientific study of hypnotic phenomena.

In 1929 Hull received an appointment at Yale, where his interests shifted to behaviorist learning theory. Inspired by the works of the Russian physiologist Ivan Pavlov (1849–1936) and the American psychologist Edward Thorndike (1874–1949), he published a series of "miniature systems"—theoretical models of limited scope that applied to circumscribed domains of learned behavior. The systems made ingenious use of the explanatory constructs—such as pure stimulus acts and habit-family hierarchies—that would become standard devices for "Hullians" in the following decades. During the 1930s, Hull also designed and built robotic machines that could exhibit learned behavior, a practice that prefigured later uses of computers to model mental processes.

Meanwhile, Hull assumed a leadership role at Yale's Institute of Human Relations, which attracted talented young psychologists otherwise unemployed during the Great Depression. Hull's weekly seminars at the institute were devoted to applications of behavioral principles to phenomena of social learning, aggression, and psychopathology. His students and associates at Yale included such notables as Neal Miller, John Dollard, Eleanor Gibson, Charles Osgood, Robert Sears, and Kenneth Spence. As Hull's chief disciple, Spence trained scores of students in the Hullian tradition at the University of Iowa.

Elected president of the American Psychological Association in 1936, Hull furthered his standing with the 1943 publication of his masterwork *Principles of Behavior*. Consistent with the logical positivist philosophy of the time, the book adopted a hypothetico-deductive method in which theory was framed as postulates and theorems to be subjected to experimental verification. It quickly became the most cited work in experimental psychology and led to Hull's involvement in celebrated learning-

theory debates, notably with Edward Tolman (1886–1959) and Kurt Lewin (1890–1947), during the 1940s.

In *Essentials of Behavior* (1951), Hull revised the postulates of the *Principles* in light of anomalous findings, but his system became mired in the complexities of learned behavior. By the late 1960s, his influence had crested and many psychologists were turning to the simplified neobehaviorism of B. F. Skinner (1904–1990) or to cognitive approaches. Hull's efforts at grand theory are now largely regarded as failures, but his legacy of careful experimentation and domain-limited theoretical models remains influential.

BIBLIOGRAPHY

Amsel, Abram, and Michael E. Rashotte, eds. 1984. *Mechanisms of Adaptive Behavior: Clark L. Hull's Theoretical Papers, with Commentary.* New York: Columbia University Press.

Hilgard, Ernest R., and Gordon H. Bower. 1966. *Theories of Learning.* 3rd ed. New York: Appleton-Century-Crofts.

Hull, Clark L. 1952. Autobiography. In *A History of Psychology in Autobiography*, vol. 4, eds. Edwin G. Boring, Heinz Werner, Herbert S. Langfeld, and Robert M. Yerkes, 143–162. Worcester, MA: Clark University Press.

Laurence D. Smith

HUMAN CAPITAL

According to marginal analysis, each factor of production is paid according to its contribution to production, and the market constitutes a mechanism that establishes a moral rule of distributive justice in the society. This theory of marginal productivity was put forth around the turn of the twentieth century by the American economist John Bates Clark (1847–1938). In the neoclassical analysis of the labor market, the equilibrium wage is set at the point of intersection of the demand and supply curves of labor. The level of the equilibrium wage set by the intersection of the two curves guides the allocation of workers across firms in such a way that an efficient allocation of resources is achieved. The implication is that wages are equal to the value of the marginal product of labor, which is the same for all workers and every firm. To achieve this condition, firms and workers should operate in a perfectly competitive environment, anonymity for both sides should be present, and the allocation of labor to firms should be random. However, wage differentials are present in the labor market, and several attempts have been made to explain the reasons for these wage differentials.

Adam Smith (1723–1790) was the first economist to introduce the idea of wage differentials and attempt to offer reasons for its existence. According to Smith, one reason for wage differentials is the common idea that wages vary positively, everything else being held constant, with the disutility of labor. This argument was later formalized by William Stanley Jevons (1835–1882) and states that an individual is willing to offer more labor input only if the wage is higher; this is because leisure time gets scarcer and thus becomes more valuable to an individual. Another reason for relative wage differentials put forward by Smith is related to the concept of human capital, which has been introduced only recently into economic analysis. According to Smith, the cost of a person's education or training can be viewed as an investment in the individual's future earnings capacity, analogous to an investment in physical capital. To be economically justified, this investment must be recuperated over the lifetime of the student or trainee. Thus, those with education or training will generally earn more than those without. In recent years, this interpretation of wage differentials has given rise to numerous attempts to measure the rate of return on investment in education and training. In general, these efforts have sought to check whether such investments in education and training do, in fact, earn normal profits for an equally valuable capital.

Neoclassical theory has never abandoned the idea that wages tend to equal the net product of labor; in other words, the marginal productivity of labor rules the determination of wages. However, it has also been recognized that wages tend to retain an intricate, although indirect, relationship with the cost of rearing, training, and sustaining the energy of efficient labor. All these factors cause wage differentials, and they make up what is known as human capital in economic literature. Human capital, in mainstream economics, is similar to the physical means of production—for example, factories and machines—and is defined as the knowledge and skills possessed by the workforce that can be accumulated. Human capital, therefore, is a stock of assets that one owns and that allows one to receive a flow of income, similar to interest earned. In modern times, human capital is largely a product of education, training, and experience. Within this approach, investment in human capital is treated similarly to investment in physical capital and is considered, in many cases, as a principal factor for the observed differences in developmental levels between nations. It is argued that investment in human capital can take various forms, including improvements in health services, formal education, and training of employees, and it can help eliminate blockages in productivity enhancements. It is worth clarifying that the acquisition of more human capital is not related to the number in the workforce but to the improvement of labor services and the concomitant increase in labor productivity.

Today, new growth theorists put a lot of emphasis on human capital: "The main engine of growth is the accumulation of human capital—or knowledge—and the main source of differences in living standards among nations is a difference in human capital. Physical capital plays an essential but decidedly subsidiary role. Human capital takes place in schools, in research organizations, and in the course of producing goods and engaging in trade" (Lucas 1993, p. 270). Within this framework, a lot of emphasis is given to the policies promoting human capital, such as investment in education or health. More than that, according to the economists Theodore W. Schultz (1902–1998) and Anthony P. Thirlwall, it is argued that differences in the quality of human capital are the cause of the different levels of development among nations and that the improvement of human capital might reduce the need for physical capital.

In addition, literature about organizational behavior and human resource management has emphasized the role of human capital in promoting the development and implementation of national and corporate strategies. Hence, human capital is a very important asset and may serve as a useful link in the chain between employee and business performance; moreover, human capital, human-resources practices, and firm performance are areas that need to be explored together to design better corporate strategies.

MINCER'S WAGE EQUATIONS

Modern human capital theory was initiated by the work of Jacob Mincer, in which investment in human resources is considered similarly to other types of investments. In Mincer's first model (1958), individuals are assumed to be identical prior to any training, thereby forcing a differential wage to employment based on the length of the expected training period. The size of the compensating differential is determined by equating the present value of the future net earnings stream (gross earnings minus costs) with the different levels of investment. The formal presentation of Mincer's first simple model is:

$$lnw(s) = lnw(0) + rs$$

where $lnw(s)$ represents the log of the annual earnings of an individual with s years of education, $lnw(0)$ represents the log of the annual earnings of an individual with basic years of education, and r is the internal rate of return to schooling years s. According to the above equation, individuals with more training receive higher earnings. The difference between earning levels of individuals with different years of schooling is determined by the second term of the right-hand side of the equation. If one defines the internal rate of return to schooling as the discount rate that equates the lifetime earnings stream for different educational choices, then the internal rate of return to schooling can be estimated by the coefficient on years of schooling. This simple framework offers a number of interesting implications. However, the whole analysis relies on some unrealistic assumptions, which can be summarized as follows:

the individuals are all identical prior to making choices;

the age of retirement does not depend on years of schooling;

the only cost of schooling is foregone earnings;

earnings do not vary over the life cycle; and

there is no post-school on-the-job investment.

Mincer's second model (1974) allows for the on-the-job investment and yields an earnings specification that is similar to the first. To establish the relationship between potential earnings and years of labor-market experience, assuming that observed earnings are equal to potential earnings less investment cost, the following relationship for observed earnings is produced:

$$lnw(sx) = a_0 + \rho_s s + \beta_0 x + \beta_1 x^2$$

where *lnw(sx)* stands for the observed earnings, x is the amount of work experience, ρ_s is the rate of return on formal schooling, and s represents the years of education. The intercept term is the product of the log skill price and the initial ability of the individual. The coefficients β_0 and β_1 stand for the return to experience.

This second expression is called Mincer's standard wage equation, which regresses the log earnings on a constant term, on a linear term of the years of schooling, and on a quadratic term of the labor-market experience. Mincer's standard wage equation transforms a normal distribution of years of schooling into a log-normal distribution of earnings. Under the assumption that post-school investment patterns are identical across individuals and do not depend on the schooling level, Mincer shows that there is an important distinction between age-earnings profiles and experience-earnings profiles, where experience means years since leaving school. More specifically, he shows that the log-earnings-experience profiles are parallel across schooling levels and that log-earnings-age profiles diverge with age across schooling levels.

By the early 1970s, the estimation of the returns on schooling using Mincerian wage regressions had become one of the most widely analyzed topics in applied econometrics. The reason is that the human-capital earning function has several distinct characteristics that make it particularly attractive:

the functional form is not arbitrary, and the identity is based on the optimizing behavior of individuals as captured by the outcome of the labor-market process;

it converts immeasurables (the dollar cost of investment in human capital) into measurables (years of schooling and years of labor-market experience);

it can include instrumental variables to capture a dichotomous variable describing some characteristics such as race or sex; and

the coefficients of the regression equation may be attributed with economic interpretations.

While the human-capital literature has now been generalized to incorporate on-the-job training, it should be noted that the Mincerian wage regression equation is a representation of the statistical relationship between wages and experience (given schooling) for an exogenously determined rate of on-the-job training. The Mincerian wage regression disregards the endogeneity of post-schooling human-capital accumulation and treats schooling and training symmetrically. More precisely, Mincer's approach ignores the possibility that schooling may change the human-capital accumulation process that takes place on the job.

THUROW'S JOB-COMPETITION MODEL

C. Lester Thurow's job-competition model serves as an interesting counterpoint to the traditional models in explaining the distribution of earnings. In his book *Generating Inequality: Mechanisms of Distribution in the U.S. Economy* (1975), Thurow shows that for the period 1950–1970, changes in the educational attainments of white males 25 to 64 years old did not affect their earnings. He finds that educational distribution is equalized through the years while income distribution is not, and he notes that the expected arguments and results from marginal productivity are not fulfilled. To explain the distribution of wage earnings, Thurow rejects market imperfections as a possible explanation of unexpected observations in labor markets. In fact, he argues that individuals compete against one another for job opportunities based on their relative costs of being trained to fill a job position instead of based on wages they are willing to accept. He argues that wages are based on the marginal productivity of the job, not of the worker. Workers who compete for jobs offered at fixed wages determine the labor supply, and workers compete for relative positions based upon their training costs to employers rather than on wages. Hence, job competition prompts people to overinvest in formal education for purely defensive reasons. Moreover, technology, the sociology of wage determination, and the distribution of training costs determine the distribution of job opportunities.

Even though the advantages of education are frequently exaggerated in terms of their strictly economic results, there is no doubt that education is advantageous in earning a higher income and also teaches general skills that improve the quality of labor and, by extension, human capital. However, recent literature on issues related to human capital stresses the need to consider other dimensions of human identity that contribute to the formation of human capital. In fact, modern labor economics has criticized the simple approach that tries to explain all differences in wages and salaries in terms of human capital as a function of knowledge, skills, and education. The reason is that the concept of human capital can be infinitely elastic, including unmeasurable variables such as culture, personal character, or family ties. Many other factors, therefore, may contribute to wage differentials, such as gender or race. The existence of imperfections in labor markets implies mostly the existence of segmentation in labor that causes the return on human capital to differ between different labor-market segments. Similarly, discrimination against minority or female employees implies different rates of return on human capital. Most of these studies in their wage equations use the technique of instrumental (or dummy) variables to introduce specific characteristics of the labor segmentation that takes place. The statistical significance of these instrumental variables indicates their importance in forming human capital and the concomitant wage differentials. In addition, over the past few decades several writers, including Rhonda Williams (1991) and Howard Botwinick (1993), have begun to develop alternative approaches to the analysis of discrimination and wage differentials that are based on a more classical analysis of capitalist competition and accumulation.

HUMAN CAPITAL AND RELATED FIELDS

The theoretical discussion about the meaning of human capital is vast and extends into the fields of human development and human resource management. For instance, human-development literature often distinguishes between specific and general human capital, where the first refers to specific skills or knowledge that is useful only to a single employer, while the second refers to general skills, such as literacy, that are useful to all employers. Human-development theories also differentiate social trust (social capital), sharable knowledge (instructional capital), and individual leadership and creativity (individual capital) as three distinct forms of human participation in economic activity.

Indisputably, the term *human capital* is used everywhere in economic and business analysis in which labor has to count as an input in the production process. The term has gradually replaced terms such as *laborer, labor force,* and *labor power* in the relevant analysis, giving an impression that these traditional terms are socially degraded. Moreover, in the strict sense of the term, human capital is not really capital at all. The term was originally used as an illustrative analogy between, on the one hand, investing resources to increase the stock of ordinary physical capital (such as tools, machines, or buildings) in order to increase the productivity of labor and, on the other hand, investing in educating or training the labor force as an alternative way of accomplishing the same general economic objective. In both sorts of investment, investors incur costs in the present with the expectation of deriving future benefits over time. However, the analogy between human capital and physical capital breaks down in one important and very crucial respect. Property rights over ordinary physical capital are readily transferable by sale, whereas human capital itself cannot be directly bought and sold on the market. Human capital is inseparably embedded in the nervous system of a specific individual and thus it cannot be separately owned. Hence, at least in regimes that ban slavery and indentured servitude, the analogy between human capital and physical capital breaks down.

BIBLIOGRAPHY

Botwinick, Howard. 1993. *Persistent Inequalities: Wage Disparity under Capitalist Competition.* Princeton, NJ: Princeton University Press.

Gintis, Herbert, Samuel Bowles, and Melissa Osborne. 2001. The Determinants of Individual Earnings: Skills, Preferences, and Schooling. *Journal of Economic Literature* 39 (4): 1137–1176.

Lucas, Robert E., Jr. 1993. Making a Miracle. *Econometrica* 61: 251–272.

Mincer, Jacob. 1958. Investment in Human Capital and Personal Income Distribution. *Journal of Political Economy* 66 (4): 281–302.

Mincer, Jacob. 1974. *Schooling, Experience and Earnings.* New York: National Bureau of Economic Research.

Schultz, Theodore W. 1962. Reflections on Investment in Man. *Journal of Political Economy* 70: 1–8.

Thirlwall, Anthony P. 1999. *Growth and Development.* London: Macmillan.

Thurow, C. Lester. 1975. *Generating Inequality: Mechanisms of Distribution in the U.S. Economy.* New York: Basic Books.

Williams, Rhonda. 1991. Competition, Discrimination and Differential Wage Rates: On the Continued Relevance of Marxian Theory to the Analysis of Earnings and Employment Inequality. In *New Approaches to Economic and*

Social Analyses of Discrimination, eds. Richard R. Cornwall and Phanindra V. Wunnava. New York: Praeger.

Persefoni Tsaliki

HUMAN DEVELOPMENT

SEE *Developmental Psychology.*

HUMAN ECOLOGY

Human ecology, the study of the relationships between humans and their environments, is a field with a large scope and complex history. It arose out of multiple disciplines—animal biology, anthropology, geology, ecology, and sociology—in the early 1900s as scientists struggled to make sense of the impact of humans on the man-made and natural environment and the impact of environments on the social systems of humans. Human ecology is also viewed by many as a methodology or framework for studying human activities and social institutions, often in conjunction with the health and functioning of the natural environment.

HISTORY AND DEVELOPMENT

The earliest mention of human ecology can be found in the early 1900s among animal ecologists, who, as a result of studying population trends among plants and animals, suggested that ecological principles also applied to humans and their relationship to the natural environment. Later, biological ecologists and population scientists used similar concepts—such as ecosystem, environmental niche (the space occupied by an organism in which it can survive and reproduce), feedback loop, stability, and growth—to address issues of population growth and environmental destruction; this line of study became particularly prominent in the 1960s and 1970s, as in the 1973 work of Paul Erhlich, Anne Erhlich, and John Holdren. Also in the 1970s, Urie Bronfenbrenner (1979) developed an ecological model of human development to understand the reciprocal relationships between individuals and the multiple environments in which they live. Gerald Marten (2001) uses human ecology and complex systems theory as a framework to examine economic systems and other social institutions and their impact on the natural environment. In particular, he discusses human ecology as a tool for resolving issues of sustainable development and environmental problems by understanding the complex interrelationship between human social systems and the ecosystem.

Anthropologists used ecological concepts to study the history and culture of human groups and societies to explain their success, failure, or adaptation. The concepts of equilibrium, movement of resources, sustainable development (meeting present needs without compromising the ability of future generations to meet their own needs), and the adaptation of organizational systems have been applied to the study of families, communities, race relations, schools, workplaces, government agencies, and other social institutions. It was in the study of urban environments that the concepts of human ecology achieved prominence. Sociologists working in this area—Park and Burgess (1920s), Frazier and Sutherland (1930s), and Janowitz (1950s)—addressed key issues such as the impact of human settlement on land-use patterns (for example, traffic flow patterns, water and flood management), the intertwined history of industrial development and urban decay, race relations, and white flight to the suburbs—in other words, the components of urban and regional planning. The underlying issue is understanding how demands for space and resources influence the development of community and business organizations across rural and urban landscapes, and how the environment influences the structures and strictures imposed by human social systems.

The sociological approach to human ecology was epitomized by the Chicago School—an approach to research pioneered most famously by the Department of Sociology at the University of Chicago beginning in the 1920s and 1930s—which focused on using theory and field research methods to understand human behavior and organization in the urban environment. Beginning in the early 1920s, scholars such as Ernest Burgess and Robert E. Park employed ecological concepts to explain the development of cities and communities. For example, the POET model—population, organization, environment, and technology—was developed to address the complex relationships between humans, their social organizations, and their environments. One of the architects of sociological human ecology was Amos Hawley (b. 1910), a population specialist and professor at the University of North Carolina, Chapel Hill, who argued that human ecology was "the basic social science" (1944, p. 405). Hawley is known for his work on the conceptual and theoretical foundations of sociological human ecology (see Hawley 1986) and the associations among population, the social-political-economic environment, and change in developing nations.

THE ECOLOGY OF HUMAN DEVELOPMENT

Human development is a subfield within the larger field of human ecology. In the 1970s Bronfenbrenner developed the ecological theory of human development, which made use of the general principles of ecology, general systems theory, and human development to explain individual differences in cognitive, biological, and social-emotional development in context. Bronfenbrenner conceived of context as a series of concentric circles, with the individual at the center and each circle representing increasingly complex environments, from proximal to distal, that might affect the development of the individual. Lines of influence are viewed as reciprocal within and between environments. For example, the most proximal environment for a child is the family, represented by parent-child interactions, child-sibling interactions, and marital interactions, all of which may influence some aspect of the child's development. Just as humans do not live in isolation from nature, a family does not exist in isolation, but operates in a microsystem encompassing those individuals with whom children and parents have regular and ongoing interaction. The third circle represents larger societal institutions, such as schools, businesses, churches, and local government, and the outer circle (the exosystem, or societal institutions that form larger environments of family units) represents larger structural institutions such as state and federal government and international social systems whose polices and laws may affect families and their natural environments. This theoretical framework explicitly recognizes that individuals do not develop in isolation; interactions with families and social groups influence individual development across the lifespan and across generations.

HUMAN ECOLOGY AS A FIELD OF STUDY

As an academic discipline, human ecology has emerged around the world as a field that brings together various aspects of sociology, economics, home economics, anthropology, gender studies, community development, agronomy, and regional planning. The concepts of human ecology fit into the scientific framework of multiple disciplines, all of which examine some aspect of the interactions between humans and their multiple environments. In a 1994 article William Catton suggests that sociologists "must learn to see human social life ineluctably intertwined with other components of ecosystems" if human ecology is to understand and address the problems of human societies (p. 86). Although different, not always overlapping strains of human ecology have evolved in multiple disciplines, the central concepts are strikingly similar, whether pertaining to issues of urban and regional planning, the use of natural resources and sustainable development, or the study of individuals and families. Humans and their social systems, from small to large, must be viewed within their larger environments, including the natural environment, to trace the "chain of effects through ecosystems and human society, and by understanding more generally how people interact with ecosystems" (Marten 2001, p. xv).

Researchers and writers across multiple disciplines agree that human ecology is a valuable framework for studying and understanding the interrelationships between the social systems of humans and the systems of nature. The health of humans, their social systems, and their natural environments may depend on an understanding of this interdependency.

SEE ALSO *Anthropology; Anthropology, Urban; Cities; Development; Development Economics; Planning; Social Science; Sociology; Sociology, Rural; Sociology, Urban; Urban Studies; Urbanization*

BIBLIOGRAPHY

Bronfenbrenner, Urie. 1979. *The Ecology of Human Development: Experiments by Nature and Design*. Cambridge, MA: Harvard University Press.

Bronfenbrenner, Urie, and Pamela A. Morris. 1998. The Bioecological Model of Human Development. In *Theoretical Models of Child Development*, Vol. 1 of *Handbook of Child Psychology*, 5th ed., ed. William Damon, 993–1028. New York: John Wiley.

Catton, William R., Jr. 1994. Foundations of Human Ecology. *Sociological Perspectives* 37 (1): 75–95.

Ehrlich, Paul. R., Anne H. Ehrlich, and John P. Holdren. 1973. *Human Ecology: Problems and Solutions*. San Francisco: W. H. Freeman.

Hawley, Amos H. 1944. Ecology and Human Ecology. *Social Forces* 22 (4): 398–405.

Hawley, Amos H. 1950. *Human Ecology: A Theory of Community Structure*. New York: Ronald Press.

Hawley, Amos H. 1986. *Human Ecology: A Theoretical Essay*. Chicago: University of Chicago Press.

Marten, Gerald G. 2001. *Human Ecology: Basic Concepts for Sustainable Development*. London and Sterling, CA: Earthscan Publications.

Micklin, Michael, and Harvey M. Choldin, eds. 1984. *Sociological Human Ecology: Contemporary Issues and Applications*. Boulder, CO: Westview.

Katherine Jewsbury Conger

HUMAN EXPERIMENTATION
SEE *Experiments, Human.*

HUMAN GENOME PROJECT
SEE *Genetic Testing; Genomics; Race.*

HUMAN RIGHTS

The core conception underlying human rights rests on the following premises: (1) all humans have equal rights that derive from the dignity and inherent worth of every person; (2) all humans have rights to freedom and development; (3) the advance of human rights is inherent in the pursuit of world peace, social justice, democracy, and the rule of law; (4) vulnerable groups need special protections; (5) cultural diversity and pluralism affirm persons' identities; and (6) human rights must be linked with the promotion of sustainable communities and environments. This conception has formally evolved within the international framework of the United Nations, as well as the United Nations' specialized agencies—the International Labour Organization (ILO) and the United Nations Educational, Scientific, and Cultural Organization (UNESCO). Still, the roots of this conception are everywhere evident, in communities, in peoples' movements, and increasingly in state constitutions (for summaries see Howard 1995; An-Na'im 2002; Orend 2002; Felice 2003).

THE ORIGINS OF HUMAN RIGHTS

The international response to the Holocaust at the end of World War II (1939–1945) was swift and decisive, specifically, the founding of the United Nations in 1945, which in turn paved the way for the formal elaboration of human rights in terms of two distinct but related frameworks (Moore and Pubantz 2006). One framework deals with the most egregious violations, namely, humanitarian law, embodied in the 1949 Geneva Convention on the Prevention and Punishment of the Crime of Genocide, and subsequently in various treaties and statutes, including the 1998 statute that established the International Criminal Court (ICC), which tries individuals who commit crimes against humanity (Robertson 1999).

The second framework deals with fundamental human rights, initially enshrined in the 1948 Universal Declaration of Human Rights (UDHR). This document is extraordinary for many reasons, not the least of which is that it has been affirmed by all of the nearly two hundred member states of the United Nations. (The UDHR does not have treaty status, and therefore is not enforceable.) The philosophical premise, as stated in Article 1, is that "all human beings are born free and equal in dignity and rights. They are endowed with reason and conscience and should act towards one another in a spirit of brotherhood." The UDHR encompasses three main sorts of rights: (1) political and civil rights that historically evolved in Great Britain, Europe, and the United States; (2) socioeconomic rights and security rights, specifically those rights people have by virtue of being human, such as the right to a job, community and family, food, security, housing, and education; and (3) the rights of vulnerable persons and minority populations.

Subsequently, international treaties have been enacted that are designed to assist nation-states in advancing human rights. These treaties are:

> International Covenant on Civil and Political Rights
>
> International Covenant on Economic, Social, and Cultural Rights
>
> Convention on the Elimination of All Forms of Discrimination Against Women
>
> International Convention on the Elimination of All Forms of Racial Discrimination
>
> International Convention on the Protection of the Rights of All Migrant Workers and Members of Their Families
>
> Convention on the Rights of the Child
>
> Convention Against Torture and Other Cruel, Inhuman, or Degrading Treatment or Punishment

Additionally, the United Nations has promulgated other declarations and charters (without treaty status) dealing with human rights, some of which concern specific groups, such as indigenous peoples, the mentally disabled, and many others. The ILO and UNESCO also have standards for human rights in areas in which they have expertise and authority.

GLOBAL INTERDEPENDENCE AND HUMAN RIGHTS

Human rights take on new significance in an increasingly interconnected world in which the gaps in human welfare are widening and all humans are at increased risk owing to the proliferation of weapons, terrorism, and the deterioration of natural habitats (Singer 2004). Just as multinationals acquired the capacities in the 1980s to move their operations everywhere around the globe to find the cheapest labor (Amin 1997), the policies of the World Bank and the International Monetary Fund put the populations of many poor countries at risk (UNDP 2004). Aggravating these material inequalities, the world's "haves" are largely white, whereas the world's "have-nots" are largely non-white.

Another aspect of global interconnectedness is that declines in some national economies have spurred high rates of migration, while affluent countries have increasingly barred migrants' entry. Furthermore, the rate of decline of the planet's environment, climate, and biodiversity has accelerated. A sustainable habitat is also a basic human right, but environmental degradation, climate change, hazardous wastes, pesticides, and toxic products all threaten sustainability. On the positive side, the advance of communications has expanded peoples' own connectedness, which has fostered remarkable cooperation around shared objectives, such as poverty reduction.

HUMAN RIGHTS AS CONSCIENCE AND SOCIAL VALUES

As already implied, human rights are more than formal agreements. They rest on a set of ideals and values. All religious traditions, from the ancient Hindu Upanishads to contemporary religions, have emphasized the importance of duties and obligations, and continue to play an ongoing role in human rights, as do currents in philosophy and ethics (Lauren 2003). The U.S. civil rights movement and other social movements, such as those for gender equality, have played key roles in shaping peoples' conscience about equality of rights. Liberation struggles against colonial oppressors have also reshaped conscience. The Martinican-born political theorist Frantz Fanon (1925–1961) powerfully captures this in *The Wretched of the Earth*: "Independence is … an indispensable condition for the existence of men and women who are truly liberated, in other words who are truly masters of all the material means which make possible the radical transformation of society" (1963, p. 310).

CURRENT FRONTS FOR THE ADVANCE OF HUMAN RIGHTS

The advance of human rights is a vision that is increasingly shared by advocates for justice as well as by development specialists, and this is possible because people at the grassroots, community level have been increasingly successful in generating the infrastructures for local nongovernmental organizations (NGOs) that, in turn, form coalitions with international NGOs. In important ways, these relationships have fundamentally transformed development projects, from a top-down approach to complex, collaborative approaches. These coalitions are able to leverage governmental reforms, and sometimes can gain major concessions from local private-sector firms. For

example, the French NGO, Dignity International, collaborates with the Nairobi Hakijamii Centre for Economic and Social Rights to reduce poverty in Kenya, and this partnership also has developed models for development that it uses in international education.

Many NGOs already have consultative status with the United Nations, and such relationships are growing and intensifying as the United Nations has embarked on a new and expansive agenda to partner with these organizations, as well as local and state governments and private-sector organizations. The objective is to create layers of engagement, including grassroots engagement, to promote development, human rights, and peace and to stem the causes of human and environmental degradation (Annan 2005). A few examples of NGOs are: Global Rights; the Center for Economic and Social Rights (CESR); Choike-Latin America; Third World Network; and Amnesty International. Very often these NGOs function more as the conduits of expansive networks rather than as single-site organizations. The NGOs that work with the United Nations are also involved in the global World Social Forum, which is an amalgam of a peoples' social movement, an NGO, and a network of NGOs.

Recent interest centers on the importance of direct, participatory democracy as both a vehicle for governance and an expression of human rights (Beetham 1999; Green 1999). New electronic technologies make it possible for members of a community to participate in democratic self-governance, and the initial pilot projects have been remarkably successful (MacLean 2004). Another approach is based on the idea that credit is a human right. Bangladeshi economist Muhammad Yunus established the nonprofit Grameen Bank in 1976 to give microloans to the very poor in third world countries (Chowdhury 2001). By 2005 Grameen Bank had given out $4,896 million in loans, primarily to women, to start their own businesses. The repayment rate was a remarkable 98 percent. Microloans are not structural solutions for solving poverty, but nevertheless they help to transform the lives of poor women and indirectly benefit their communities.

THE UNITED STATES AND HUMAN RIGHTS

In spite of the great progress that has been made since the initial formalization of the principles of human rights in 1948, there are serious obstacles. A major one has to do with worldwide inequalities of resources, which can be traced to the long-term effects of colonialism, ongoing exploitation by multinationals, and authoritarian governments. Some states are too poor to implement human rights programs, and, besides, many poor states have not yet attained the kind of stable government structures that give people a voice to make demands for their rights. Yet, paradoxically, the world's most powerful and richest nation, the United States, has been one of the world's worst partners in the international human rights community.

The United States has remained on the margins of the world's human rights community. For example, it rejects the idea that socioeconomic security and cultural identity are human rights. In part, this grows out of ideological conflicts during the cold war; but it is also pragmatic, consistent with U.S. geopolitical ambitions (Tabb 2002). Another explanation is that human rights are not in synch with American values that stress competitive individualism (Blau and Moncada 2005). Indeed, the U.S. Constitution is one of the few in the world today that does not include provisions for socioeconomic rights (Blau and Moncada 2006). In addition, the world's richest nation does not support various treaties to slow the rate of environmental degradation and climate change (Low 1999; Kaul et al. 2003). The United States is one of only a few countries not party to the ICC and during the Iraq War violated the terms of the Geneva Convention, which it has ratified (Hooks and Mosher 2005).

Still, worldwide, the momentum of the human rights revolution has accelerated, possibly because of developments in communications and because of the increasingly grave conditions threatening humans and their habitats. The goal, as often stressed by UNESCO, is "to build peace in the minds of people," which resonates with the motto of the World Social Forum: "A Better World Is Possible."

Leading international human rights organizations, such as Amnesty International and Human Rights Watch, have been on the front lines defending peoples' rights against brutal oppressors and inhuman acts of violence. The very complex and challenging tasks involving securing positive rights, such as the right to a decent job, housing, food, health care, and the rights to a culture and to identity require social movements, the engagement of activists, and immense efforts by people in their workplaces and communities. People of color in the United States and elsewhere have played leading roles in such challenging tasks, including roles in the Civil Rights Movement, South Africa's anti-Apartheid struggle, the Zapatista Movement, the Brazilian Landless Movement, and the Malawian shaming campaign against neoliberal policies and foreign investors. In the United States it is significant that an African American, Gay McDougall, executive director of a leading human rights organization, Global Rights, was appointed to serve as UN independent expert on minority issues.

SEE ALSO *Civil Rights; Genocide; Natural Rights; Needs, Basic; United Nations*

BIBLIOGRAPHY

Amin, Samir. 1997. *Capitalism in the Age of Globalization: The Management of Contemporary Society.* London: Zed.

Amnesty International. http://amnesty.org/.

An-Na'im, Abdullahi A., ed. 2002. *Cultural Transformation and Human Rights in Africa.* London: Zed.

Annan, Kofi. 2005. In Larger Freedom: Towards Security, Development, and Human Rights for All. Report of the Secretary-General of the United Nations for Decision by Heads of State and Government in September 2005. http://www.un.org/largerfreedom/.

Beetham, David. 1999. *Democracy and Human Rights.* Cambridge, U.K.: Polity.

Blau, Judith, and Alberto Moncada. 2005. *Human Rights: Beyond the Liberal Vision.* Lanham, MD: Rowman and Littlefield.

Blau, Judith, and Alberto Moncada. 2006. *Justice in the United States: Human Rights and the U.S. Constitution.* Lanham, MD: Rowman and Littlefield.

Center for Economic and Social Rights (CESR). http://cesr.org/.

Choike-Latin America. http://choike.org/.

Chowdhury, Afsan. 2001. Local Heroes. *New Internationalist* 332: 22–23.

Dignity International. http://www.dignityinternational.org/.

Fanon, Frantz. 1963. *The Wretched of the Earth.* Preface by Jean-Paul Sartre. Trans. Constance Farrington. New York: Grove.

Felice, William F. 2003. *The Global New Deal: Economic and Social Human Rights in World Politics.* Lanham, MD: Rowman and Littlefield.

Global Rights. http://www.globalrights.org/.

Grameen Bank. http://www.grameen-info.org/.

Green, Judith M. 1999. *Deep Democracy: Community, Diversity, and Transformation.* Lanham, MD: Rowman and Littlefield.

Hooks, Gregory, and Clayton Mosher. 2005. Outrages against Personal Dignity: Rationalizing Abuses and Torture in the War on Terror. *Social Forces* 83 (4): 1627–1646.

Howard, Rhoda E. 1995. *Human Rights and the Search for Community.* Boulder, CO: Westview.

Human Rights Watch. http://www.hrw.org/.

International Labour Organization (ILO). http://www.ilo.org/.

Kaul, Inge, Pedro Conceição, Katell Le Goulven, and Ronald U. Mendoza, eds. 2003. *Providing Global Public Goods: Managing Globalization.* New York: UNDP.

Lauren, Paul Gordon. 2003. *The Evolution of International Human Rights: Visions Seen.* 2nd ed. Philadelphia: University of Pennsylvania Press.

Low, Nicholas, ed. 1999. *Global Ethics and Environment.* London: Routledge.

MacLean, Don, ed. 2004. *Internet Governance: A Grand Collaboration.* New York: United Nations Information and Communication Technologies Task Force.

Moore, John Allphin, Jr., and Jerry Pubantz. 2006. *The New United Nations: International Organization in the Twenty-first Century.* New York: Prentice-Hall.

Orend, Brian. 2002. *Human Rights: Concept and Context.* Peterborough, Ontario, Canada: Broadview.

Robertson, Geoffrey. 1999. *Crimes against Humanity: The Struggle for Global Justice.* London: Allen Lane.

Singer, Peter. 2004. *One World: The Ethics of Globalization.* 2nd ed. New Haven, CT: Yale University Press.

Tabb, William K. 2002. *Unequal Partners: A Primer on Globalization.* New York: New Press.

Third World Network (TWN). http://twnside.org.sg/.

United Nations. http://www.un.org/.

United Nations. 1948. Universal Declaration of Human Rights. www.un.org/Overview/rights.html.

United Nations Development Program (UNDP). 2004. *Human Development Report 2004: Cultural Liberty in Today's Diverse World.* New York: Author.

United Nations Educational, Scientific, and Cultural Organization (UNESCO). http://www.unesco.org.

United Nations Treaty Body Data Base. http://www.unhchr.ch/tbs/doc.nsf.

World Social Forum (WSF). http://www.forumsocialmundial.org.br/.

Judith Blau

HUMAN RIGHTS WATCH

SEE *Civil Liberties.*

HUMAN SACRIFICE

The practice of human sacrifice has been associated with religious beliefs, famine, and national pride. The term is generally approached with reference to the Aztecs and other Meso-American cultures. Yet human sacrifice has been in practice since the Stone Age and refers to ceremonial slaughter that is performed to achieve a benefit for society, albeit through grisly means.

Evidence of human sacrifice has been found in Denmark, Holland, and Germany. During the Iron Age in these areas, people would be ritually killed by hanging, bludgeoning, strangling, or by having their throats slit. The bodies would then be submerged in a peat bog, where their remains were preserved for centuries. Examples have been found that date back to 3500 BCE. "Bog bodies" have also been found in England. Anthropologists have noted that an overwhelming characteristic of the bodies found was physical deformity, such as extra or missing digits or shortened legs, and it has been postulated that these individuals were thought to have been "touched by the gods," making them fitting sacrifices.

Between 3100 BCE and 2890 BCE, there was mass human sacrifice in Egypt, for the pharaohs required servants to follow them to the grave. This was also prevalent in Mesopotamia, where servants, guards, and even musicians and grooms consumed poison to follow their kings into death. In the kingdom of Kerma, in Africa, huge pits have been discovered in which some 500 or more people were buried just outside their ruler's mausoleum. The same rituals occurred in China around the first to second centuries BCE.

Human sacrifice was also practiced in Ancient Greece. Archaeological evidence leading to this assumption has been found on the Isle of Crete. Skeletal remains of several individuals found near Knossos appear to have been put to death in ceremonial ways. One male approximately eighteen years old at the time of death, was trussed tightly, and a decorated dagger was found among his bones. He lay near a trough, which is thought to have been used to collect sacrificial blood, and the body of a woman lay spread-eagled in the southwest corner of the room. Further, what appears to be an altar was festooned with crop-filled vases, alluding to religious ritual.

The Celts also practiced human sacrifice for religious reasons, and their rites were documented in the work of Julius Caesar. According to Caesar, though this point might be contested, the Druids sacrificed murderers, as they believed that only a life offered in atonement for a life taken could appease the gods. Murderers were sometimes sentenced to enclosure in an immense human effigy, which was burned with the criminals inside. Thieves were also sentenced to this fiery death, and when not enough criminals were present to fill the container, innocent people were added to its contents. The Celts also allegedly applied decapitation, throttling, clubbing, or throat slitting, also accompanied by burial in a peat bog. They also killed men by striking them in the back with a sword, and they divined meaning from the ensuing death struggle. In her war against Roman occupation, the warrior queen Boudica impaled vanquished Roman soldiers to honor the gods.

Though the Romans thought these Celtic practices were barbaric, they had in fact carried out their own versions of human sacrifice, though they had ended the practice a century sooner. Yet they still practiced mass execution in the Coliseum during the gladiatorial games, and at a later time Christians would be fed to the lions. Vikings were sometimes buried with slave girls, who were thought to become their wives in Valhalla. Some scholars believe that the women were willing participants who asked for the honor of being ritually stabbed and then burned in the ship with their masters.

The practice of human sacrifice in Meso-America did not begin with the Aztec culture. In fact, evidence has been found that human sacrifice was part of religion as far back as the first known Meso-American civilization, the Olmecs. The Aztecs are certainly the most well known for their propensity for ritual killings, however. Many of their gods would only be appeased by the flow of human blood. Their most important god was Huitzilopochtli, the Sun God. Aztecs believed that if they did not ritually sacrifice to him regularly, the sun would not rise. In his honor, the high priest would lay a man over the sacrificial stone and cut the beating heart out of his chest, which would then be held up before the attending crowd.

Though this was the most prevalent type of sacrifice, the Aztecs had many gods to satisfy, and they each had prescribed rites. For Xipe Totec, or "Our Lord the Flayed One," victims were first tied to a tree, then shot with arrows. The ritual required that the victim be flayed so that the skin remained intact. The high priest would then don the skin to symbolize the "new skin" of springtime. For Tezcatlipoca, a young man would be selected and treated royally for one year. At the end of that time, he would be sacrificed. Though these practices seem horrific in modern times, Aztec sacrificial victims were honored to be chosen.

This was also true among the Mayas, who might sacrifice entire losing teams in a ritual ballgame. Criminals were weakened by hunger and then forced to play the game with healthy athletes. The criminal team was soundly routed, with decapitation as the end result. Mayans also sacrificed people to the water god, Chaak, over limestone sinkholes, which were believed to be doors to the underworld.

The Incas also practiced human sacrifice. Yet, unlike early European incidents, Incan sacrifices had to be pure and free of blemishes. Often, a child of the king's would be sacrificed to strengthen the bond between king and deity. Earthquakes, droughts, epidemics, or the death of kings were reasons for performing the sacrificial ritual, which entailed taking the child to the top of a mountain, where a stone mausoleum would be built. The boy or girl was given a drug to ease the pain, wrapped tightly in ceremonial garments, and buried with many honorific items surrounding the body. Evidence now points to the children receiving a blow to the head, but it is not certain whether it was simply to knock them unconscious or to kill them because the skull fractures found in all the Incan "mummies" are mild.

Though all of these civilizations found reason in what modern man would find a barbaric practice, each civilization had rules for which human sacrifice was required, as well as rules about who the victims would be. This relates to the work of the Italian philosopher Giorgio Agamben, who defines the role of *homo sacer* or "the citizen," which is an individual who exists in law as an exile without legal rights or identity. Though such persons can be killed, they may not be ritually sacrificed. Only "bare life," or individuals without inalienable rights (which relates to political prisoners stripped of citizenship), could be sacrificed by Roman Law. This was not always true in Meso-American civilization. In most cases, it was an honor to be chosen.

Some modern films, such as Mel Gibson's *Apocalypto* (2006), which is based on the Mayan civilization, can bring the horror and reality of human sacrifice to life. Though the process of the sacrifice is portrayed accurately in Gibson's film, other aspects of the practice are not. As stated above, most sacrificial victims went to their doom willingly, in repayment to their gods for life and abundance. To turn down such an offer, or to escape (as Gibson's character Jaguar Paw does in the film), would have been considered an effrontery to the gods and evoked their wrath upon their entire civilization.

Though the practice of human sacrifice died out after the Conquistadors conquered the New World, it continues in Asia in modern times. In India, a small percentage of followers of the religion Tantrism practice human sacrifice, though this is thoroughly illegal. In one tantric rite, a woman hacked a three-year-old to death to achieve the promise of limitless wealth. In another, a couple who could not have children were directed to murder a child and wash in its blood to assure conception. Though the police have apprehended some of those involved in such cases, it is uncertain whether the practice of human sacrifice will ever end.

SEE ALSO *Archaeology; Civilization; Death and Dying; Incas; Olmecs; Religion; Rituals*

BIBLIOGRAPHY

Caesar, Caius Julius. 2004. *"De Bello Gallico" and Other Commentaries*. E-book 10657. Salt Lake City, UT: Project Gutenberg. http://www.gutenberg.org/etext/10657.

Clark, Liesl. 1996. The Sacrificial Ceremony. Nova Online Adventure. http://www.pbs.org/wgbh/nova/peru/worlds/sacrifice1.html.

James, Susan E. 2002. Mimetic Rituals of Child Sacrifice in the Hopi Kachina Cult. *Journal of the Southwest* 44 (3): 337–356.

MacCulloch, J. A. 2005. *The Religion of the Ancient Celts*. E-book 14672. Salt Lake City, UT: Project Gutenberg. http://www.gutenberg.org/etext/14672.

Parker-Pearson, Mike. 2002. The Practice of Human Sacrifice. BBC History Online. http://www.bbc.co.uk/history/ancient/british_prehistory/human_sacrifice_01.shtml.

Stannard, David E. 1992. Genocide in the Americas: Columbus's Legacy. *The Nation*, October 19.

Winkelman, Michael. 1998. Aztec Human Sacrifice: Cross-Cultural Assessments of the Ecological Hypothesis. *Ethnology* 37 (3): 285–298.

Patricia Cronin Marcello

HUMANISM

In the widest sense, humanism is conceived as referring to an approach to understanding the world and of living in that world focused first and foremost on humans rather than on God or on nature. Although individualistic, never organized in the form of a movement, and highly variegated and including religious and nonreligious forms, humanisms have exhibited various combinations of freedom and responsibility, learning and observation, reason and values. The term itself only dates from the mid-nineteenth century. The descriptive term, *humanist*, however, gained wide currency from the late 1400s, and the advent of humanism in the West is usually associated with the classical revival of what has come to be known since the nineteenth century, now often contentiously, as the Italian Renaissance.

Humanists were particularly scholars of the Greek and Latin *literae humaniores* and engaged in teaching what Cicero (106–43 BCE) had termed *studia humanitatis* based on a liberal education, especially grammar, rhetoric, history, poetry, and philosophy. From early in the fourteenth century, they began to develop a periodization of history that, unlike the continuity experienced in the Middle Ages, was marked by a break with the civilizations of Greece and Rome. Thus in antiquity could be found alternative models for thought and life. Humanist scholars then, with Francesco Petrarca (Petrarch, 1304–1374) and his friend Giovanni Boccaccio (1313–1375) in the lead and establishing a model widely emulated, were engaged in the recovery of classical texts. Using a philological method, humanists further sought to establish the integrity and the original meaning of the classics in the context in which they were written.

Their passion for antiquity and the proclaimed break with the medieval world presented Renaissance humanists with the problem of reconciling Christian and pagan values in a new historical and intellectual climate. Humanists had attacked scholasticism and, instead of in Aristotle (384–322 BCE), eventually found more congenial philosophical bases in Plato (427–347 BCE). An associated question was that of an active versus contemplative life and the role of the scholar in public affairs. Lino Coluccio di Piero Salutati (1331–1406, chancellor of the Florentine Republic 1375–1406) and the generation of the first half of the fifteenth century tipped the balance toward civic virtue, *civic humanism*, and made Florence the center of humanist studies. The life and work of Leon Battista Alberti (1404–1472) epitomized humanism in the arts. Personifying the Renaissance ideal of the "universal man," he shared with many humanists a taste for archaeological studies and campaigned for a return to classical models. He advanced realistic representation, systematized perspective, advocated for principles of harmony and the social function of architecture, and put these into practice himself as an architect. The humanists' interests in perspective, anatomy, and the mathematical bases of proportion and harmony (including that of music) provided material groundwork for the development of the natural sciences as an autonomous domain of knowledge production.

Humanist thought and practice spread widely beyond the original center in Florence to other parts of Italy and, following the invasion of the Italian Peninsula in 1494, extended rapidly to the north as the *new learning*. Education, the key to the discovery of one's *humanitas*, was a fundamental element in the development of "humanism." Although the old universities remained in the grip of scholasticism, existing schools were revitalized and new ones established all over Europe to make available a classical education, at least to an elite, and humanist thought prospered in informal groups, correspondence networks, and academies.

While the violence and dislocations of the Wars of Religion of the late 1500s and the attacks on what was considered the heretical idea of personal freedom of thought in the Reformation and Counter-Reformation shook optimism and faith in fundamental human dignity, a renewed sense of confidence and the possibility of progress; a belief in freedom, including freedom of thought and expression, in reason, and in science; and especially an emphasis on a critical outlook marked the eighteenth-century Enlightenment. The corollary to the accent on emancipation and the individual was secularism, indeed an anticlericalism and atheism—different from the accommodation that had satisfied Renaissance humanists. However, the reaction to the French Revolution (1789–1799) offered a sharp rebuff to the way the Enlightenment *philosophes* had envisioned the world. The ineluctable reality of change brought forth contradictory attitudes toward the meaning of "progress" and was translated into the mutually exclusive politics—based on conflicting value sets—of conservatives and radicals. Nonetheless, a belief in the centrality of the human experience and the value of reason and education continued to color nineteenth-century attitudes.

During the late eighteenth century and early nineteenth century, humanism evolved in the Germanies with an emphasis on the individual (even to the detriment of social concerns), the pursuit of classicism in the arts, education reform, and the assertion of classical roots as a fundamental element in the establishment and development of the German state. In England in the early 1880s, the relative merits of the arts (especially schooling in the classics) and the sciences (and the unbiased "truths" they produced) in education were debated by Matthew Arnold (1822–1888), champion of "culture" and a "liberal of the future," and T. H. Huxley (1825–1895), Charles Darwin's (1809–1882) apologist. But their positions were not so far apart; both were needed. Indeed after mid-century, *liberal humanism* was characterized by a confidence in a future of incremental material and social progress, supported by the emerging social sciences, whose principle actor or "subject," however, was an autonomous, entrepreneurial, propertied white male. By the end of the century, the new liberalism had co-opted much of both the conservative and radical agendas, and the "common culture" espoused by Arnold was offered as a substitute for equality.

From the late nineteenth century, the European avant-garde contested realist representation (associated with a bourgeois establishment) and the positivist attitude by figuring an internal world, and the twentieth-century wars undermined confidence in an innate human decency and the improvements to be expected from scientific "progress." Furthermore, over the second half of the twentieth century, the humanist tradition was assailed in a series of developments in the production of knowledge itself. In 1946 Jean-Paul Sartre (1905–1980) extolled existentialism as a humanism, not the liberal/bourgeois humanism with its metaphysical assumptions but a humanism grounded in choice and commitment that linked the individual to the community. In 1947 Martin Heidegger (1889–1976) responded, rejecting humanism and existentialism as metaphysical; instead of the thinking subject, he placed the accent on "being."

The scope of critiques of the possibility of any universal humanism widened from the 1950s through the mid-1960s. Léopold Sédar Senghor (1906–2001) pronounced *négritude*, a direct attack on universalizing, Eurocentric culture at the world scale, to be a humanism. Alain Robbe-Grillet, speaking for the *nouveau roman* and in a debate with Sartre, pointed to the double-edged and paralyzing nature of existentialism that underwrote a hegemony of "man," a fundamental ideological pillar of modern thought. For Michel Foucault (1926–1984), conceding the influence of Friedrich Nietzsche (1844–1900), not only had humanism as a philosophy reached an end but "man," a concept of recent invention, would also have to be abandoned (Foucault 1966).

In response to the crisis on the left occasioned by the events of 1956—Hungary, Suez, Nikita Khrushchev's (1894–1971) secret speech—E. P. Thompson (1924–1993) promoted *socialist humanism*, which was "*humanist* because it places once again real men and women at the centre of socialist theory and aspiration … *socialist* because it re-affirms the revolutionary perspectives of Communism … faith in real men and women" (1957, p. 109). The movement, founded on the early Karl Marx (1818–1883), attracted wide support. In 1964 Louis Althusser (1918–1990) took the couplet to task, associat-

ing the terms *socialist* with science and *humanism* with ideology by singling out what he called Marx's break with "every theory that based history or politics on an essence of man" ([1965] 1986, p. 227). Althusser argued that Marx's "structural" account of social relations gave rise to *theoretical antihumanism*, which, however, did not rule out ethical commitments. Despite the many valid criticisms, Althusser's work was the primary source for what came to be known as *structuralist Marxism* and rendered "humanist" agendas on the left suspect.

By far the most far-reaching development was that of *structuralism*. Based on the work in linguistics of Ferdinand de Saussure (1857–1913), the structuralisms offered the promise of a new rigor and scientific status, nonreductionist and nonpositivist, for the human sciences. But the emphasis on "constructedness" spelled the end for any humanism founded in essentialist categories, whether human or material. Saussure insisted that languages, systems of signs that express meaning, should be studied not just in terms of their individual parts, diachronically as philologists had, but also in terms of the relationship between those parts, synchronically. The model rehabilitated a version of relational thinking and was appropriated by the social sciences and applied to nonlinguistic phenomena.

The term *secular humanism* is generally applied to those who embrace humanist principles and contend that these lead to secularism and who reject the supernatural, especially religious faith, while maintaining a belief in the inherent dignity of humankind. It has at times acquired a pejorative tonality, especially when used by religious conservatives to describe nonreligious opponents such as some scientists and intellectuals.

Edward Said (1935–2003) reclaimed the term *humanism* in a positive sense to describe a practice for what is in the end a defense against inhumanity: historical, rational, and critical thinking (which includes the philological method) informing responsible, activist social agency.

SEE ALSO *Althusser, Louis; Aristotle; Enlightenment; French Revolution; Hungarian Revolution; Plato; Poststructuralism; Revolution; Said, Edward; Schooling; Social Science; Socialism; Structuralism; Thompson, Edward P.*

BIBLIOGRAPHY

Althusser, Louis. [1965] 1986. *For Marx*. Trans. Ben Brewster. London: Verso.

Burckhardt, Jacob. [1855–1860] 1995. *The Civilization of the Renaissance in Italy*. 2 vols. Trans. S. G. C. Middlemore. Oxford: Phaidon.

Davies, Tony. 1997. *Humanism*. London: Routledge.

Dosse, François. 1997. *History of Structuralism.* 2 vols. Trans. Deborah Glassman. Minneapolis: University of Minnesota Press.

Foucault, Michel. [1966] 1973. *The Order of Things: An Archaeology of the Human Sciences.* New York: Vintage.

Said, Edward. 2004. *Humanism and Democratic Criticism.* New York: Columbia University Press.

Soper, Kate. 1986. *Humanism and Anti-Humanism.* London: Hutchinson.

Thompson, E. P. 1957. Socialist Humanism. *New Reasoner* 1 (1): 105–143.

Richard E. Lee

HUMBOLDT, ALEXANDER VON

SEE *Geography.*

HUME, DAVID
1711–1776

David Hume's work was crucial in the development of many important social scientific concepts like "the fact/value distinction," "ideology," and "economic equilibrium." Moreover, in a period when the "social sciences" did not yet exist, he envisioned the transformation of the ancient discipline of "moral philosophy" into a "science of man" through the "application of an experimental philosophy to moral subjects" (Hume 1739–1740, p. 4). Such a methodological transformation was essential for the creation of the social sciences.

Hume was born in Edinburgh on April 26, 1711, and he grew up at his family home in the Scottish Borderlands. He studied at the University of Edinburgh, and after rejecting a career as a merchant or a lawyer, he made his way in life as an intellectual and author. He joined a circle of Scottish Enlightenment thinkers, including Adam Smith and Lords Kames and Monboddo, who made Edinburgh the center of their social life. They kept a careful distance both from the Scottish Highlanders to the North—who were prone to violent rebellion against the "powers that be" in London—and the English establishment figures to the South—who were often hostile to ambitious Scots like themselves. Although his philosophical works did not win him fame and fortune, his multivolume *History of England* (published between 1754 and 1762) did. During his later years, between 1763 and 1768, he broke through the governmental "glass ceiling" for Scots and was appointed to a number of important

diplomatic posts, including charge d'affaires in the British Embassy in Paris and under-secretary of state for the Northern Department (which included Scotland). He died in Edinburgh on August 25, 1776.

Hume's writings spanned the genres from intricate philosophical studies to belletristic essays and historical narratives. In these texts, Hume created concepts and attitudes that pointed social investigations away from the formal, contractualist framework that dominated Enlightenment social thought and toward a dynamic, empirical approach to human nature.

Hume acerbically made a sharp distinction in the discourse concerning human affairs between "the usual copulations of propositions, is, and is not" and the propositions connecting subject and predicate with "ought" and "ought not." He insisted that one could not validly deduce "ought" propositions from those stating facts about human behavior alone, and that once "small attention" was paid to this fallacious reasoning, "all the vulgar systems of morality" would be "subverted" (Hume 1739–1740, p. 302). Indeed, the "is/ought" distinction became a starting point for the social sciences in the next century.

Along with this categorical revision of the social world, Hume cultivated in his readers a healthy skepticism for the application of crude causal categories in "the science of man." Just as Newton rejected the primacy of contact (push-pull) forces in natural philosophy and introduced relational forces—such as gravitational attraction, which operates instantaneously across huge distances—he also debunked the primacy of mechanical causation in the social realm and called for a deeper appreciation of tendential, correlational forces expressed in sympathy, convention, and habit.

Hume also rejected an atomistic conception of the self. He argued that the notion of a simple unified self is a fictional product of an ingrained "propensity to confound identity with relation." Hume's "science of man" guards against this propensity and seeks to uncover the complex relations and forces at play in the formation of a self, thus proposing one of the key research themes of the future social sciences. A century later, his recognition of the importance of fictions in social life was to be developed further with the notion of "ideology."

Hume also emphasized the importance of the precontractual basis of contractual societies by refusing to take the rational, contracting individual as the starting point of social thought. He noted that "two men, who pull the oars of a boat, do it by an agreement or convention, tho' they have never given promises to each other" (Hume 1739–1740, p. 315), and his new science gave primacy to this level of social cooperation and convention that makes promises and contracts possible.

Although Hume's work affected the methodology of the social sciences in general, his discourses on commerce, money, and the balance of trade had a major impact on economic thought, both directly and through his influence on Adam Smith.

Hume also recognized that the rules of property ownership and the use of money are "artificial," that they must be constructed both in an individual's life and humanity's history. Consequently, economic "laws," such as the quantity theory of money, do not automatically apply, but instead require the development of a state where money has "a universal diffusion and circulation" (Hume 1742–1752, p. 294). Moreover, in a fully monetarized society, Hume, like Isaac Newton, differentiated between steady states and accelerating changes of a system's basic quantities. Thus, he argued that though, in the long run, the price of commodities will be proportional to the quantity of money, "alterations in the quantity of money … are not immediately attended with proportionable alternations in the prices of commodities" (Hume 1742–1752, p. 288). For example, influxes of money, in some circumstances, can stimulate economic activity.

Hume observed that, in a commercial world, money moves across borders in an autonomous manner that makes mercantilist efforts to prevent a country's loss of specie (e.g., by prohibiting the export of bullion) nugatory and even counterproductive. As long as a nation "preserves its people and industry," its money supply will tend almost naturally toward an appropriate equilibrium level, just as "all water, wherever it communicates, remains always at a level" (Hume 1742–1752, p. 312).

Finally, although Hume was one of the first major European philosophers to oppose slavery, he was also one of the first to develop the rudiments of a modern race theory claiming to be based on science. His observations of plantation life in the British West Indies convinced him that wage labor was much more productive than slave labor, and that the threat of unemployment had much more disciplinary power for the free workers than the threat of the whip had for slaves (Hume 1742–1752, p. 390). However, since he also claimed to know of "no ingenious manufactures amongst [Africans], no arts, no sciences," either in Africa or among the freed African slaves in Europe, he was "apt to suspect the negroes to be naturally inferior to the whites" (Hume 1742–1752, p. 208). Thus, he was an influential founder of a biopolitical racism compatible with a regime of waged labor.

In many ways then, Hume is the most "postmodern" of Enlightenment thinkers. An appreciation for his subversive, paradoxical, and militantly secular attitudes and concepts has therefore grown among historians in search of alternative genealogies for the social sciences.

SEE ALSO *Equilibrium in Economics; Philosophy; Quantity Theory of Money; Smith, Adam*

BIBLIOGRAPHY

Baier, Annette. 1991. *A Progress of Sentiments: Reflections on Hume's Treatise*. Cambridge, MA: Harvard University Press.

Berry, Christopher J. 1997. *Social Theory of the Scottish Enlightenment*. Edinburgh: Edinburgh University Press.

Broadie, Alexander, ed. 2003. *The Cambridge Companion to The Scottish Enlightenment*. Cambridge, U.K.: Cambridge University Press.

Deleuze, Gilles. 1991. *Empiricism and Subjectivity: An Essay on Hume's Theory of Human Nature*. Trans. Constantin V. Boundas. New York: Columbia University Press.

Hume, David. 1739–1740. *A Treatise of Human Nature*. Ed. David Fate Norton and Mary J. Norton. Oxford, U.K.: Oxford University Press, 2000.

Hume, David. 1742–1752. *Essays Moral, Political, and Literary*. Ed. Eugene F. Miller. Indianapolis, IN: Liberty Fund, 1987.

Norton, David Fate, ed. 1993. *The Cambridge Companion to Hume*. Cambridge, U.K.: Cambridge University Press.

C. George Caffentzis

HUME PROCESS

The Scottish philosopher David Hume (1711–1776) made famous the argument that the balance of trade was not worth worrying about because any imbalance would be self-regulating. A trade surplus would lead to higher prices, then to an outflow of gold and silver—and vice versa for a trade deficit. This has come to be known as the *Hume process*. It is described in the following passage from Hume's "Of the Balance of Trade" (1748), which is one of the most frequently quoted and among the most influential essays in the history of economics:

> Suppose, that all the money of Great Britain were multiplied fivefold in a night, must not the contrary effect follow? Must not all labor and commodities rise to such an exorbitant height, that no neighboring nations could afford to buy from us; while their commodities, on the other hand, became comparatively so cheap, that, in spite of all the laws which could be formed, they would be run in upon us, and our money flow out; till we fall to a level with foreigners, and lose that great superiority of riches, which had laid us under such disadvantages? (Hume [1748] 1985, p. 311)

The popularity of the Hume process arose largely because it was seen as a death blow to the mercantilist fetish for accumulating bullion. Two points about the Hume process struck serious contemporaries. First, Hume assumes a sudden, large inflow of money to make his point. This is a very different thing from the small (relative to the money stock) and steady inflow advocated by the so-called mercantilists. Secondly, Hume assumes that this sudden inflow is met by an instantaneous adjustment in prices. Otherwise, if the change in, say, wages attracts more labor, there is no reason why the increased money supply could not lead to a greater output and thus avoid inflation. Hume's "new" result was obtained by (1) altering the substantive position in question from the effects of a steady inflow of gold to that of a sudden inflow, and (2) denying the standard mercantilist assumption of international labor mobility for skilled workers. Hume and the mercantilists differed in that they asked different questions and answered them under different assumptions. Indeed, two of Hume's correspondents, James Oswald (1715–1769) and the Reverend Josiah Tucker (1712–1799), each provided penetrating critiques and forced Hume to admit, in a later paper, that slow inflation may well help growth.

Hume's argument is simple and powerful; unfortunately, its implicit assumptions are not obvious. Three such assumptions may be noted. First, the use of the simple *quantity theory* by Hume, with metal as the sole medium counting as money, was a step backward since the Irish philosopher George Berkeley (1685–1753) had already emphasized the paramount importance of credit a decade earlier. Secondly, Hume assumed that individuals care only about real values, or what is called the *homogeneity of degree zero* in money and prices. Frank Hahn (1980) clearly points out that even if one grants this assumption for individuals, it does not follow that the economy as a whole will exhibit such homogeneity, unless general equilibrium is unique. Finally, William Darity (1987) showed how the endogeneity of money, which all Hume's contemporaries were aware of, could make the process neutral or even unstable and hence permit a continual adverse balance of trade. If the gold or silver mines provided metal with increasing returns, then the more prices rose in Spain, the more cheaply they could obtain more precious metal, so that it was actually "economical" for Spain to continue an unfavorable balance of trade. While the popular acclaim for Hume's argument is not doubted, it largely reflects the difference between an argument that is readily understood by the educated public and one acceptable to those who devote care to such issues.

SEE ALSO *Balance of Payments; Balance of Trade; Equilibrium in Economics; Hume, David; Quantity Theory of Money; Trade, Bilateral*

BIBLIOGRAPHY

Darity, William A., Jr. 1987. The Hume Process, Laws of Returns, and the Anglo-Portuguese Trade. *Southern Economic Journal* 54 (1): 119–133.

Hahn, Frank H. 1980. Discussion. In *Models of Monetary Economies: Proceedings and Contributions from Participants of a December 1978 Conference Sponsored by the Federal Reserve Bank of Minneapolis*, eds. John H. Kareken and Neil Wallace, 161–165. Minneapolis, MN: Federal Reserve Bank of Minneapolis.

Hume, David. [1748] 1985. Of the Balance of Trade. In *Essays: Moral, Political and Literary*, ed. Eugene F. Miller. Indianapolis, IN: Liberty Fund.

Rashid, Salim. 1984. David Hume and Eighteenth Century Monetary Theory: A Critical Comment on Recent Views. *Hume Studies* 10 (2): 156–164.

Rashid, Salim. 2000. Monetary Economics and Economic Development in Berkeley's *Querist*. In *The Querist* [1735–1737] by George Berkeley, 135–159. Düsseldorf, Germany: Verlag Wirtschaft und Finanzen.

Viner, Jacob. [1937] 1965. *Studies in the Theory of International Trade.* New York: Kelley.

Salim Rashid

HUMILIATION

The field of humiliation studies emerged in the early twenty-first century. In 2001 the Human Dignity and Humiliation Studies (HumanDHS) network (http://www.humiliationstudies.org) was founded as a global consortium of distinguished academics and practitioners with the aim to create a new multidisciplinary field that bridges academia with practice and incorporates scholarship from anthropology, history, philosophy, political science, social psychology, and sociology.

The phenomenon of humiliation is rapidly gaining visibility and significance. Expectations of equal dignity and opportunity rise as people come closer together, both physically and digitally, in a globalizing world. Coupled with the spread of the human rights message, any attempt to lower the expectations of any one group becomes a humiliating offense against all groups and humanity in general. The first sentence in Article 1 of the Universal Declaration of Human Rights reads, "All human beings are born free and equal in dignity and rights."

Few researchers have studied humiliation explicitly. In many cases the term *humiliation* has not been differentiated from other concepts. In the work of HumanDHS, in contrast, humiliation is addressed on its own and is differentiated from other concepts: humiliation is, for example, not regarded simply as a variant of shame. Shame is often accepted as prosocial humbling—human rights advocates, for instance, frequently use shaming techniques to make people abide by human rights—while humiliation describes a hurtful experience that typically is rejected as an illegitimate violation by the victim. (However, a special type of shame—unacknowledged and bypassed shame—as been described to be emotionally destructive.)

In today's mainstream language, the word humiliation is used threefold. First, the word humiliation signifies an act; second, a feeling; and third, a process: "I humiliate you, you feel humiliated, and the entire process is one of humiliation." This triple meaning of the word humiliation complicates its use; sometimes humiliation indicates the feeling of a victim, sometimes the act of a perpetrator, sometimes the entire process from act to feeling.

The core meaning of humiliation entails a downward push, down to the ground, to earth, as derived from the Latin word *humus*. This push can be perceived as a hurtful violation, or not, depending on the overall societal, cultural, and psychological framework. In human rights–based contexts being pushed down and held down is perceived as a violation that will lead to suffering and rage that may be turned inward or outward. Rage and fury turned inwards render feelings of depression, abandonment, anomie, and alienation. Rage and fury turned outward feed violence, including mass violence.

Yet, prior to the human rights movement, being put down was often embedded into a culture of ranking in which higher beings were expected to show lower beings their due lowly place. In that case being put down is not perceived as a violation and therefore does not elicit the same consequences as previously described. Human rights delegitimize such practices and empower the downtrodden to invoke humiliation.

In other words, the differentiations one uses today are historically recent. According to the Oxford English Dictionary, the earliest recorded use of *to humiliate*, meaning to mortify or to lower or to depress the dignity or self-respect of someone, did not occur until 1757. Up to 1757, the words *to humble* and *to humiliate* were used rather interchangeably. It is in tact with the emergence of human rights ideals of equal dignity for all that these two words move into diametrically opposed directions.

Humiliation is a complicated concept. Not always does a person witness a humiliator and a humiliatee. For example, help may humiliate. In that case there is a benevolent helper on one side and no ill-intentioned perpetrator at all. Or, neither actor nor victim may define a situation as humiliating, only a third party. The social worker wants to rescue the battered wife, but she claims that the beatings are her husband's way of loving her. Then, one may expect that humiliation is always avoided, however, some people seek it, for example in sadomasochism or religious rites. Thus, humiliation is an act,

an emotional state, and a social mechanism, with a broad relevance, from anthropology, sociology, philosophy, social and clinical psychology to political science.

Phenomena such as global terror may be explained as an outfall of global clashes due to humiliation rather than of clashes of civilizations. Global and local terror and violence may be linked to humiliation rather than to "unexplainable evil." Conflicts of interest over scarce resources, often identified as a source of violent conflict, may very well lead to cooperation. It may be precisely humiliation that hampers cooperation. Many people profess their love for peace, while being unaware that their fear of humiliation and their wish to resist humiliation may foreclose peace. A Somali proverb makes this point very clear, "A man deserves to be killed and not to be humiliated."

Adolf Hitler imagined future world domination and humiliation from the World Jewry (Weltjudentum), and the Holocaust was his atrocious attempt to "prevent" future humiliation. Also in Rwanda, it was imagined humiliation in the future that was "prevented" by genocide. Nelson Mandela, in contrast, made constructive use of the energy contained in the experience of humiliation brought about by apartheid. After twenty-seven years of humiliation in prison, he could have unleashed genocide on the white South African elite. However, he did not. He refrained from instigating cycles of humiliation and instead promoted constructive social change that included the perpetrators.

The solution is egalization, brought about in a Mandela-like fashion. *Egalization*, a word coined by Evelin Lindner in the context of HumanDHS, has been designed to match the word *globalization* and at the same time differentiate it from words such as *equality*, *equity*, or *egalitarianism*. The main point of egalization is the true implementation, beyond mere rhetoric, of equal dignity for everybody as stipulated in the Human Rights Convention. Only a world that combines globalization with egalization, and thus prevents and heals the violent outfalls from dynamics of humiliation, can be expected to be sustainable and decent.

SEE ALSO *Contempt; Genocide; Globalization, Social and Economic Aspects of; Holocaust, The; Peace; Rape; Recognition; Shame; Terrorism; Violence*

BIBLIOGRAPHY

Hartling, Linda M., and Tracy Luchetta. 1999. Humiliation: Assessing the Impact of Derision, Degradation, and Debasement. In *The Journal of Primary Prevention* 19 (5): 259–278.

Klein, Donald C. 1991. Spec. issue, The Humiliation Dynamic: Viewing the Task of Prevention from a New Perspective: Section I: The Humiliation Dynamic; Section II: Those at Risk of Humiliation; Section III: Systemically Related

Humiliation; Section IV: Dealing with Humiliation. *The Journal of Primary Prevention* 12 (2 and 3).

Lindner, Evelin Gerda. 2006. *Making Enemies: Humiliation and International Conflict.* Westport, CT: Praeger Publishers.

Margalit, Avishai. 1996. *The Decent Society.* Cambridge, MA: Harvard University Press.

Ury, William. 1999. *Getting to Peace: Transforming Conflict at Home, at Work, and in the World.* New York: Viking.

Evelin G. Lindner

HUNGARIAN REVOLUTION

The events in Hungary in October to November 1956 have been characterized both as an uprising and a revolution. The revolt was spontaneous, and its adherents came from diverse political and social backgrounds with disparate motivations. However, the speed with which the unrest spread across the country evidenced a commonly held and deep-seated bitterness over the nation's political and economic plight. Moreover, most of those involved blamed the crisis squarely on the Soviet-dominated regime that had been in place since 1949, and demanded the removal of Soviet forces from Hungary as well as the reintroduction of a multiparty political structure. The magnitude of popular opposition and the general objective of abolishing the existing system merit classifying the events of 1956 as a revolution.

Despite its failure, the revolution had significant effects. In the short term, it did result in greater consolidation of Soviet control over both Hungary and the region. With Moscow's backing, the newly installed leadership under János Kádár (1912–1989) violently quashed the rebellion, executing hundreds, including the reformist prime minister Imre Nagy (1896–1958), and imprisoning thousands, thus eliminating all overt political dissent. Regionally, the revolution forced Soviet leader Nikita Khrushchev to be more cautious in encouraging East European Communist rulers to pursue reforms. However, the long-term effects of the revolt were more significant. The crisis exposed the ideological bankruptcy of Soviet-led communism and the brutality of Moscow's methods, and served as a permanent symbol for the causes of self-determination and independence in the region.

Half a century later, scholarly debates persist about many aspects of the revolution, although the opening of archival records in recent years has helped to resolve important issues. In Hungary the scale of the revolt, the manner in which it unfolded, the behavior of various groups in different parts of the country, and the methods employed to fight the Soviets are all well known. Of particular interest among the new findings are records describing the actions of Nagy and his colleagues in the temporary government. Nagy emerges as a figure both complex and courageous, if ultimately inadequate to the task, who was thoroughly underestimated by both Moscow and Washington. The circumstances surrounding his fate are more fully understood as well: Kádár, not the Soviets, pressed for his execution, which finally took place in 1958.

The archives further explain a great deal about decision making in Moscow. Handwritten notes of Soviet Presidium meetings by Vladimir Malin, head of the General Department of the party, record key debates over whether to acquiesce to the changes in Hungary or to suppress the revolt. Khrushchev and his more moderate allies clearly hoped to avoid a major intervention, and the Kremlin appeared to be on the verge of ordering a troop withdrawal from Hungary (a public declaration to that effect appeared on October 30) when he suddenly reversed course a day later.

The U.S. role is also clearer. The revolution caught the White House by surprise, and the Eisenhower administration came under criticism from certain quarters for its passive reaction. Yet suspicions have lingered that the United States quietly undertook certain covert operations such as unleashing trained émigré units and providing weapons to the rebels. Recently declassified internal records from the Central Intelligence Agency make clear, however, that no such activities took place, nor did senior White House officials contemplate them. Furthermore, it is well established that President Eisenhower opposed any actions that might provoke a direct conflict with the Soviet Union.

Yet, a number of questions remain unanswered. Kádár is still a controversial figure in Hungary, and his exact motivations in accepting the role of the Kremlin's agent of repression are still in dispute. Scholars also continue to discuss the most contentious aspect of U.S. involvement—Radio Free Europe (RFE). RFE tapes from the period confirm that the organization broadcast statements that at the very least encouraged insurgents to take action. Although recent analyses downplay the impact of those broadcasts, there is some disagreement over whether U.S. officials authorized them and to what degree they were responsible for inciting Hungarians to risk their lives in the revolution.

Regarding the Soviet response, although we now know better which issues concerned Khrushchev—the descent into chaos inside Hungary, the Suez crisis, domestic political considerations and possibly China's views—it remains unclear exactly which of these, or what combination of these, ultimately changed his views. A related difference of opinion exists over whether and how the Suez crisis affected events in Hungary beyond influencing Khrushchev's thinking. Underlying these questions is the fascinating debate over whether the crushing of the revolt was inevitable or whether different choices by the rebels, Nagy, members of the Soviet leadership, or even the Americans might have averted the tragedy.

SEE ALSO *Berlin Wall; Cold War; Glasnost; Khrushchev, Nikita; Union of Soviet Socialist Republics; Warsaw Pact*

BIBLIOGRAPHY

Békés, Csaba. 1996. The 1956 Hungarian Revolution and World Politics. Cold War International History Project Working Paper no. 16. Washington, DC: Woodrow Wilson International Center for Scholars.

Békés, Csaba, Malcolm Byrne, and János Rainer. 2002. *The 1956 Hungarian Revolution: A History in Documents.* Budapest: Central European University Press.

Borhi, László. 2004. *Hungary in the Cold War, 1945–1956: Between the United States and the Soviet Union.* Budapest: Central European University Press.

Gati, Charles. 2006. *Failed Illusions: Moscow, Washington, Budapest and the 1956 Hungarian Revolt.* Stanford, CA: Stanford University Press and Woodrow Wilson Center Press.

Kovrig, Bennett. 1973. *The Myth of Liberation: East Central Europe in U.S. Diplomacy and Politics Since 1941.* Baltimore, MD: Johns Hopkins University Press.

Kovrig, Bennett. 1991. *Of Walls and Bridges: The United States and Eastern Europe.* New York: New York University Press.

Kramer, Mark. 1996. The "Malin Notes" on the Crises in Hungary and Poland, 1956. *Cold War International History Project Bulletin* 8/9 (Winter): 385–410.

Litván, György, János M. Bak, and Lyman H. Legters, eds. 1996. *The Hungarian Revolution of 1956: Reform, Revolt, and Repression, 1953–1963.* New York: Longman.

Orekhova, Elena D., Viacheslav T. Sereda, and Aleksandr S. Stykalin, eds. 1998. *Sovietskii Soiuz i Vengerskii Krizis 1956 Goda: Dokumenty* [The Soviet Union and the Hungarian Crisis in 1956: Documents]. Moscow: Rossiiskaya Politicheskaya Enciklopedia.

Rainer, János. 1996–1999. *Nagy Imre: Politikai életrajz* [Imre Nagy: A Political Biography]. 2 vols. Budapest: 1956-os Intézet.

Malcolm Byrne

HUNTER, FLOYD
1912–1992

Born into a farm family of meager means, Floyd Hunter came of age during the Great Depression and early on displayed populist tendencies. His experiences as a social worker and administrator heightened his wariness of business. Subsequent to receiving his undergraduate degree (1939) and his master's degree in social service administration (1941) from the University of Chicago, Hunter began work with the United Service Organizations. He came to Atlanta, Georgia, in 1943 and headed that organization's southeast office, shifting to work with the Atlanta Community Council from 1946 to 1948. Fired from the latter position as a controversial figure, Hunter had acquired an insider's understanding of how communities deal with social problems.

He next undertook graduate study in sociology at the University of North Carolina and returned to Atlanta for field research, completing his dissertation and then converting it into a reputation-establishing first book, *Community Power Structure: A Study of Decision Makers* (1953). A work about Atlanta, it inspired a surge of community leadership studies. Hunter's later research extended to state and national levels, but subsequent work never matched the pathbreaking impact of *Community Power Structure*. Within political science a pluralist school of thought attacked Hunter's approach, blunting its influence within this area of academia.

Some ambiguity is attached to the term *power structure*. It is often used simply to refer to a group deemed to be top leaders. True to his training in sociology, Hunter, however, coined the phrase to refer to stable relationships through which major policy decisions are made for the community. For Atlanta in the immediate postwar years, Hunter's central finding was that reality deviated sharply from the ideals of representative government, with policy making centered in arrangements around the city's top business leaders.

Critics attributed to Hunter the view that Atlanta was run by forty individuals. This, however, is an oversimplification of both his method and findings. Hunter relied on knowledgeable insiders to compile and refine a list of top leaders, ten from each of four sectors of community life. He then used a sociometric technique to identify patterns of interaction. For good measure, he added an examination of particular issues, and he did a separate analysis of leadership within the black subcommunity and how it related to Atlanta's white leadership. The logic of Hunter's research was not about determining a specific number of top leaders, but about examining the relations among different sectors and how those interrelations affect policy making for the community.

In contrast with Robert S. Lynd and Helen M. Lynd's (1929, 1937) earlier works on Middletown, in which business is accorded a pervasive form of influence based on the domination of business values, Hunter's study of Atlanta was specifically concerned with the ability of business-centered leadership to manage social change through a structured capacity to set the policy agenda. Atlanta's business leaders led lives quite insulated from the concerns faced by ordinary citizens, especially the poor. Nonetheless, Hunter found that through their control of economic assets, their central role in civic matters, and their ability to use informal channels of interaction among themselves to reach consensus, they formed a relatively closed leadership group.

Later works, including his follow-up study of Atlanta, *Community Power Succession: Atlanta's Policy-Makers Revisited*, were variations on this initial theme. Hunter taught at the University of North Carolina until 1960, then moved to California, mixing social-research consulting with numerous visiting faculty appointments. He died in 1992.

SEE ALSO *Community Power Studies; Pluralism; Power*

BIBLIOGRAPHY

PRIMARY WORKS

Hunter, Floyd. 1953. *Community Power Structure: A Study of Decision Makers*. Chapel Hill: University of North Carolina Press.

Hunter, Floyd. 1959. *Top Leadership, U.S.A.* Chapel Hill: University of North Carolina Press.

Hunter, Floyd. 1965. *The Big Rich and the Little Rich*. Garden City, NY: Doubleday.

Hunter, Floyd. 1980. *Community Power Succession: Atlanta's Policy-Makers Revisited*. Chapel Hill: University of North Carolina Press.

SECONDARY WORKS

D'Antonio, William V., Howard J. Ehrlich, and Eugene C. Erickson. 1962. Further Notes on the Study of Community Power. *American Sociological Review* 27, no. 6 (December): 848–853.

Herson, Lawrence J. R. 1961. In the Footsteps of Community Power. *American Political Science Review* 55 (December): 817–830.

Hunter, Floyd, Ruth Conner Schaffer, and Cecil G. Sheps. 1956. *Community Organization: Action and Inaction*. Chapel Hill: University of North Carolina Press.

Lynd, Robert S., and Helen M. Lynd. 1929. *Middletown: A Study in Contemporary American Culture*. New York: Harcourt, Brace.

Lynd, Robert S., and Helen M. Lynd. 1937. *Middletown in Transition: A Study in Cultural Conflicts*. New York: Harcourt, Brace.

Polsby, Nelson W. 1980. *Community Power and Political Theory: A Further Look at Problems of Evidence and Inference*. 2nd ed. New Haven, CT: Yale University Press.

Saunders, Peter. 1983. *Urban Politics: A Sociological Interpretation*. London: Hutchinson.

Stone, Clarence N. 1988. Preemptive Power: Floyd Hunter's "Community Power Structure" Reconsidered. *American Journal of Political Science* 32 (February): 82–104.

Wolfinger, Raymond E. 1960. Reputation and Reality in the Study of Community Power. *American Sociological Review* 25 (October): 636–644.

Clarence N. Stone

HUNTINGTON, SAMUEL P.
1928–

Samuel Phillips Huntington, born April 18, 1928, has contributed controversial insights to contemporary political debates. Huntington graduated from Yale University at the age of eighteen. After serving in the military, he graduated from Harvard University with a doctoral degree at twenty-three years of age. Huntington's most notable contribution to the field of political science is the book *The Clash of Civilizations and the Remaking of World Order*, an instantly controversial success. Originally conceived as an article contribution to *Foreign Affairs* magazine in 1993, the author expanded the piece due to popular demand. In this article, Huntington's primary focus is the decline of nation-centered unity. He argues that instead of focusing on nationalistic principles as had been the precedent before the end of the cold war, states have begun cooperating based on cultural orientation. The author predicts that distinct and violently competitive civilizations will emerge. According to Huntington, the countries of Europe and North America should learn to unite. Their cultural foundation is based on moral principles and a commitment to what he calls "Western" values: peace, freedom, and democracy. Should economic warfare divide European and North American countries, the author believes a shift in the geopolitical balance of power will take place. It is Huntington's belief that insofar as these democracies prevailed in the twentieth century, the "Chinese/Sinic/Confucian" and the militant Islamic world will dominate the twenty-first century. The polemical nature of Huntington's theses has opened his arguments to vituperative criticism. His critics label this "civilizations thesis" as single-minded and parochial.

In Huntington's judgment, the Hispanic community in the United States stands accused of a refusal to assimilate and of a wholesale rejection of America's English language, creeds, and values. In *Who Are We? The Challenges to America's National Identity*, published in 2004, the author asserts that Mexican Americans refuse to adopt American identities. To Huntington, this is of particular concern because of their high reproduction rate, which may result in a population that will divide America when it desperately needs cultural unity in the face of mounting international challenges. Huntington's premise is America's distinctiveness: the perception that the United States has triumphed in the past as a result of the maintenance of the Protestant work ethic and the religious unity originally instilled by the founders of the nation. An erosion of this commonality, he argues, bodes ill for the future.

Huntington also wrote *American Politics: The Promise of Disharmony*, published in 1981. In this monograph he argues that a divide exists between the political ideal and the political reality in American politics. Binding Americans together throughout U.S. history has been their love of freedom and their contempt for totalitarian dictatorships. Huntington believes that Americans revolt socially every third generation in protest of the bitter compromise of promoting freedom while supporting hierarchies of power to maintain national security. Asserting that protests will continue to grow in strength, he once again raises his central theme: In order to perpetuate democratic ideals and the spread of freedom, the United States must assert itself forcefully abroad to reassure the public at home of its morality and greatness.

In 2005 a new edition was published of Huntington's 1957 work, *The Soldier and the State: The Theory and Politics of Civil-Military Relations*. For Huntington, central to the politics of military affairs is the liberal double standard. Political liberals vociferously announce their intent to diminish violence, genocide, and the expansion of destructive armaments, according to his observations, but they contradict these objectives by seeking to restructure the U.S. military and weaken it from within. They seek to apply a civilian control over military matters, thereby reducing the ability to conduct wars effectively and to diminish threats to America. Huntington suggests that national security can only be ensured when conservative frameworks are applied to military affairs. This entails continuously maintaining a state of preparedness.

Huntington is the Albert J. Weatherhead III University Professor at Harvard University.

SEE ALSO *Civilization; Civilizations, Clash of; Communism; Coup d'Etat; Culture; Democratization; Essentialism; Fundamentalism; Fundamentalism, Christian; Fundamentalism, Islamic; Islam, Shia and Sunni; Political Culture; Radicalism; Totalitarianism*

BIBLIOGRAPHY

Huntington, Samuel P. [1957] 2005. *The Soldier and the State: The Theory and Politics of Civil-Military Relations.* Cambridge, MA: Belknap Press.

Huntington, Samuel P. 1981. *American Politics: The Promise of Disharmony.* Cambridge, MA: Belknap Press.

Huntington, Samuel P. 1993. The Clash of Civilizations? *Foreign Affairs.* 72 (3): 22–49.

Huntington, Samuel P. 1996a. *The Clash of Civilizations and the Remaking of World Order.* New York: Simon and Schuster.

Huntington, Samuel P., ed. 1996b. *The Clash of Civilizations? The Debate.* New York: Foreign Affairs.

Huntington, Samuel P. 2004. *Who Are We? The Challenges to America's National Identity.* New York: Simon and Schuster.

Kurtz, Stanley. 2002. The Future of "History": Francis Fukuyama vs. Samuel P. Huntington. *Policy Review* no. 113 (June 1): 43–59.

Wolfe, Alan. 2004. Native Son: Samuel Huntington Defends the Homeland. *Foreign Affairs* 83, no. 3 (May/June): 120–125.

Jonathan Jacobs

HURRICANE KATRINA
SEE *Disaster Management; Natural Disasters.*

HURSTON, ZORA NEALE
1891–1960

Zora Neale Hurston was born almost a decade earlier than she declared in her autobiography, *Dust Tracks on a Road* (1942); accordingly, to biographer Valerie Boyd, she was a woman "ahead of her time" (Boyd 2003, p. 17). Hurston is noted today for her contributions as a literary author, folklorist, and anthropologist. She stands as a "first" in many arenas, including as the first African American woman to graduate from Barnard College in 1928 at the nontraditional age of 37. As a Barnard student, Hurston was able to take classes at Columbia University, where she flourished. "Under the kind eye of the preeminent Franz Boas, considered the father of American anthropology, Hurston found support for her folklore research," wrote biographer Irma McClaurin (2000, p. 18). It was Boas who encouraged her to use "the clarifying monocle of anthropology" to salvage and analyze the superstitious stories and "down-home 'lies' " she remembered hearing as a child in Eatonville, Florida, an all-black town founded in 1887 near Orlando (Boyd 2003, p. 115). This thriving community of African Americans who supported and respected each other, according to Boyd, became a vital source of inspiration for Hurston, who lived there from the time she was almost two years old. Her father was elected mayor in 1897 and then again in 1912. Hurston eventually studied the rich folk culture of her hometown, recognizing the priceless contribution it could make to the field of cultural anthropology. Memories of the tales she heard on her neighbor Joe Clark's storefront porch influenced Hurston's fiction and are evident in stories like "Sweat" and "Possum or Pig," both published in 1926. That same year she also published *The Eatonville Anthology*, "an engaging amalgam of folklore, fiction, and Eatonville history" (Boyd 2003, p. 139).

A NEW DAY: THE HARLEM RENAISSANCE

There is some debate over when the Harlem Renaissance began. Some list 1919 as the starting date and its demise during the mid-1930s. Also, there is some question as to where it started since Hurston and other Renaissance writers, including Angelina Grimké (1805–1879), Jean Toomer (1894–1967), Sterling Brown (1901–1989), Richard Bruce Nugent (1906–1987), and William Waring Cuney (1906–1976), began meeting in Washington, D.C., in the early 1920s as members of "the Saturday Nighters" at the home of the poet Georgia Douglas Johnson (1886–1966). Into their midst came influential writers and scholars such as W. E. B. Du Bois (1868–1963), Alain Locke (1886–1954), and James Weldon Johnson (1871–1938), all of whom traveled between Washington, D.C., and New York City and had great influence in shaping the Renaissance. As a result of these interactions with "the gifted, the famous, and the wannabe famous," Hurston, who didn't arrive in Harlem until 1925, had no problem settling in and finding her place among the artists and writers who dubbed themselves "the Niggerati" (Boyd 2003, p. 116). It was not an easy time for a single black woman to establish herself as a writer; during the 1920s African American women were most often employed as domestic help or store clerks. "And so, in the 1920s," wrote McClaurin, "we must see Zora as a woman who lived against the grain, … perfect[ing] a hat-wearing, cigarette smoking, gun-toting persona that was tremendously at odds with the ideals and standards of traditional womanhood of the time—for both black and white women" (2003, p. 5).

RESEARCHING THE AFRICAN DIASPORA

From the start of her research, Hurston worked to gather perspectives from the African Diaspora—the scattering of African people throughout the Americas—collecting black folklore in the U.S. South, the Bahamas, Haiti, Jamaica, and the Honduras. Hurston believed that, despite slavery and its resulting social inequality, African-descended people retained and continued to create a rich canon of stories, myths, and "lies," all communicated through evocative language and performance—what she called "the greatest cultural wealth of the continent" (Kaplan 2001, p. xxiii). It was also Hurston who recognized the "logic" of studying the culture of blacks in the South and the Caribbean as part of a continuum. In fact, Hurston had a desire to create a field of study around the American Negro, as she wrote in a letter to the anthropologist Melville Herskovits (1895–1963): "You fully appreciate how much there is to be done when you realize that there is no real curricula for those Anthropologists who wish to study the Am. Negro [sic]. Papa Franz knows the Indian, etc, but there was nothing to help me in my study of the Negro.… Suppose we set out to create the same thing for the Negro at Northwestern as Boas has done for the Indian at Columbia" (Hurston 2002, p. 372). In 1936, Herskovits was not only unsupportive of Hurston's overtures, but he also tried to steer her away from conducting research in Jamaica and Haiti, where she eventually finished the manuscript for *Their Eyes Were Watching God*, published in 1937.

HURSTON AS DRAMATIST, ETHNOGRAPHER, AND WRITER

Funded by a grant from Carter G. Woodson's Association for the Study of Negro Life and History in 1927, and later a contract with white patron, Charlotte Osgood Mason (1854–1946), between 1927 and 1929 Hurston traveled to Florida, Alabama, Georgia, New Orleans, and the Bahamas in search of "authentic" Negro expressive folk culture (Kaplan 2001, p. xxii). She wrote to the author Langston Hughes (1902–1967) of her desire to write at least seven books based upon these ethnographic journeys, but she published only one, *Mules and Men*, in 1935. She also presented her patron, Mason, with a manuscript entitled "Negro Folk-tales from the Gulf States," published posthumously in 2001 as *Every Tongue Got to Confess*. Much of Hurston's folklore material from her 1920s fieldwork seems to have vanished, although some of the rich data surfaced in her collaboration with Hughes on the play *Mule Bone* in 1930.

The 1930s proved a prolific period for Hurston: She published "Hoodoo in America" in the *Journal of American Folklore* in 1931, conducted ethnographic research on West Indian Obeah practices in 1936 in Jamaica and Haiti under a Guggenheim fellowship, and wrote *Their Eyes Were Watching God* in seven weeks and published it in 1937. With her Guggenheim fellowship renewed for 1937, she continued to conduct research in Haiti, recording her field experiences of the previous year in Jamaica and Haiti in her only traditional ethnography, *Tell My Horse*, completed and published in 1938. In 1939 Hurston joined the Federal Writers Project (FWP), where she produced "consummate essays and commentary about Florida and folklore," demonstrating that she was "a serious anthropologist whose career had just hit its stride" (Bordelon 1999, p. x). During this time, according to biographer Carla Kaplan, she also staged folklore productions.

A TRAGIC ENDING

Numerous tragedies struck Hurston in the 1940s. The FWP project ended, as did her second marriage (1939–1943) to Albert Price III. For a brief time in 1944, Hurston was married to James Howell Pitts, and published "My Most Humiliating Jim Crow Experience." Always intrigued by the Diaspora, Hurston traveled to the British Honduras in 1947 to study black communities. While there she wrote *Seraph on the Suwanee*. Published in 1948, the novel contains excerpts taken from Hurston's "FWP field notes and placed … in the mouths of her novel's characters" (Bordelon 1999, p. x). In 1948, Hurston was accused of molesting a minor. Although the charges were dismissed a year later, the event took its toll.

Between 1950 and 1959, Hurston worked a series of odd jobs—journalist, librarian, maid, and substitute teacher—and published some memorable essays along the way, including the controversial "What White Publishers Won't Print" in the *Negro Digest* and her last published story, "The Conscience of the Court," in the *Saturday Evening Post*, both appearing in 1950. In the early part of 1959, Hurston suffered a stroke. By October she was forced to move into the St. Lucie County Welfare Home.

On January 28, 1960, the once-famous Hurston, noted anthropologist, folklorist, novelist, playwright, and preserver of black folk culture, died penniless. She was buried in an "unmarked grave in the Garden of Heavenly Rest, Fort Pierce" (Gates 1990, p. 311). Interest in Hurston revived in 1975 with the publication of Alice Walker's "In Search of Zora Neale Hurston" in *Ms.* magazine. In 2005 Hurston's novel *Their Eyes Were Watching God* became a television movie starring Academy Award–winning actress Halle Berry. Hurston held a consummate passion for and commitment to the preservation of African American folk culture. What she contributed to anthropology was a body of scholarship that sometimes challenged the literary, social science, and social conventions of her time but illuminated the "figurative capacity of black language" in a manner yet to be replicated (Gates 1990b, p. 212). Hurston's life, her strikes against social conventions, and her love for black language and black folk culture in all its expressive manifestations continue to inspire into the twenty-first century.

SEE ALSO *Anthropology, U.S.; Boas, Franz; Harlem Renaissance; Herskovits, Melville J.*

BIBLIOGRAPHY

PRIMARY WORKS

Hurston, Zora Neale. 1926. Sweat. *Fire!* 1 (1): 40–45.

Hurston, Zora Neale. 1926. The Eatonville Anthology. *Messenger* 8 (September–November): 261–262, 297, 319, 332.

Hurston, Zora Neale. 1926. Possum or Pig. *Forum* 76 (September): 465.

Hurston, Zora Neale. 1931. Hoodoo in America. *Journal of American Folklore* 44 (October–December): 317–418.

Hurston, Zora Neale. 1934. *Jonah's Gourd Vine*. Philadelphia: J. B. Lippincott.

Hurston, Zora Neale. 1935. *Mules and Men*. Philadelphia: J. B. Lippincott.

Hurston, Zora Neale. 1937. *Their Eyes Were Watching God*. Philadelphia: J. B. Lippincott.

Hurston, Zora Neale. 1938. *Tell My Horse: Voodoo and Life in Haiti and Jamaica*. Philadelphia: J. B. Lippincott.

Hurston, Zora Neale. 1942. *Dust Tracks on a Road*. Philadelphia: J. B. Lippincott.

Hurston, Zora Neale. 1944. My Most Humiliating Jim Crow Experience. *Negro Digest* 2 (June): 25–26.

Hurston, Zora Neale. 1948. *Seraph on the Suwanee*. New York: Scribner's.

Hurston, Zora Neale. 1950a. The Conscience of the Court. *Saturday Evening Post* (March 18): 22–23, 112–122.

Hurston, Zora Neale. 1950b. What White Publishers Won't Print. *Negro Digest* 8 (April): 85–89.

Hurston, Zora Neale. 1981. *The Sanctified Church: The Folklore Writings of Zora Neale Hurston*. Berkeley: Turtle Island.

Hurston, Zora Neale. 2001. *Every Tongue Got to Confess: Negro Folk-tales from the Gulf States*. New York: HarperCollins.

Hurston, Zora Neale, with Langston Hughes. 1991. *Mule Bone: A Comedy of Negro Life*, edited and with introductions by George Houston Bass and Henry Louis Gates Jr. (New York: HarperPerennial, 1991).

SECONDARY WORKS

Bordelon, Pamela, ed. 1999. *Go Gator and Muddy the Water: Writings by Zora Neale Hurston from the Federal Writers' Project*. New York: Norton.

Boyd, Valerie. 2003. *Wrapped in Rainbows: The Life of Zora Neale Hurston*. New York: Scribner's.

Gates, Henry Louis, Jr. 1990a. Afterword, Selected Bibliography, and Chronology. In *Jonah's Gourd Vine*, Zora Neale Hurston, 207–229. New York: Perennial Library.

Gates, Henry Louis, Jr. 1990b. Afterword, Selected Bibliography, and Chronology. In *Tell My Horse: Voodoo and Life in Haiti and Jamaica*, Zora Neale Hurston, 301–311. New York: Perennial Library.

Kaplan, Carla. 2001. Introduction. In *Every Tongue Got to Confess: Negro Folk-tales from the Gulf States*, Zora Neale Hurston. New York: HarperCollins.

Kaplan, Carla, ed. 2002. *Zora Neale Hurston: A Life in Letters*. New York: Doubleday.

McClaurin, Irma. 2000. Belle Lettres: "Dear Langston, Love Zora." *FlaVour: Black Florida Life and Style* (Autumn): 16–19.

McClaurin, Irma. 2003. The Politics of "Being"—Zora Neale Hurston. Unpublished Paper presented (with an interpretation by Tracey Graham) at the conference Jumpin' at the Sun: Reassessing the Life and Work of Zora Neale Hurston, Barnard College, October 3, 2003.

Walker, Alice. 1975. In Search of Zora Neale Hurston. *Ms.* (March): 74–79, 85–89.

Irma McClaurin

HURWICZ, LEONID
1917–

Leonid Hurwicz is among the leading mathematical economists of his generation. He utilized game theory, mathematical programming, dynamical systems, and topology, among many other fields of mathematics, contributing to the development of those fields and to their application to economic theory and policy. Hurwicz was born in Moscow to Polish Jewish parents in the year of the Russian Revolution. His parents therefore moved with him to Warsaw in 1918. Hurwicz shared the educational experience of all Jewish boys in Warsaw, likely attending a gymnasium, or high school, with further education in a yeshiva. He entered the University of Warsaw in 1933, graduating in 1938 with a degree in law, having concentrated in political economy. In 1938 Hurwicz traveled to Britain to study at the London School of Economics and Political Science under neo-Austrian economists Lionel Robbins (1898–1984) and Friedrich Hayek (1899–1992). Importantly for his subsequent career, a recent member of the faculty was Polish socialist refugee Oskar Lange (1904–1965), who had left the University of Krakow in 1935. In 1939 Hurwicz studied at the Postgraduate Institute of International Studies in Geneva, where he attended a seminar conducted by Jewish Austrian economist Ludwig von Mises (1881–1973).

At the suggestion of Lange, Hurwicz migrated to the United States in 1940. He went to Chicago, which had a large Polish immigrant population, and studied for two years at the University of Chicago, where Lange was on the economics faculty. In 1941, while a student at Chicago, Hurwicz also studied at Harvard University under Wassily Leontief (1906–1999), whom he met at the Cowles Commission conference in Colorado Springs in 1940.

In January 1942 Hurwicz was recruited to the staff of the Cowles Commission by research director Theodore O. Yntema (1900–1985). In this position, Hurwicz assisted Lange in statistical testing of business-cycle theories, and worked with Yntema and Joel Dean (1906–1979) as executive director of the project on wartime price controls of the Committee on Price Determination of the Price Conference of the National Bureau of Economic Research (NBER). He would remain on the commission staff until 1961.

In 1941 Hurwicz secured a research and teaching fellowship at the Massachusetts Institute of Technology. The following year, he taught mathematics and statistics to members of the U.S. Army Signal Corps at the Illinois Institute of Technology. Simultaneously, and continuing to 1944, he was hired as a faculty member of the Institute of Meteorology at the University of Chicago and an instructor of statistics in the Economics Department. He was awarded a Guggenheim Fellowship for the 1945–1946 period. From 1946 to 1949 he served as associate professor of economics at Iowa State University in Ames. From 1949 to 1951 Hurwicz served as professor of economics at the University of Illinois. He then became professor of economics and mathematics at the University of Minnesota Graduate School of Business, a position he retained until retiring around 1987.

In the 1940s and early 1950s Hurwicz presented several papers to professional associations in mathematics, statistics, and economics, and he published papers in the journals of these associations and in a book published by the Cowles Commission. Most of these papers were on statistics. His focus shifted to game theory in 1953, then in 1955 he began to focus explicitly on economics, publishing articles on resource allocation, including a review of Leontief's book on input-output analysis. In 1956 Hurwicz and Kenneth Arrow began a long collaboration that would continue beyond the 1970s. In 1958 Hurwicz and Arrow published an article on the stability of equilibrium in a general equilibrium system. Hurwicz's first book was published in 1958, when he was forty-one years old. It was a joint effort with Arrow and Hirofumi Uzawa.

In 1955 Hurwicz published a Cowles Commission discussion paper titled "Decentralized Resource Allocation," in which he initiated his research on economic information theory. In this paper, he was stimulated by Hayek's polemic with the socialists on the feasibility of calculating equilibrium prices and quantities in the absence of a market, due to the absence at the center of decentralized price information. Hurwicz's 1955 paper developed from the argument by Hayek and Mises that only a decentralized (i.e., market) system could manage a modern economy. His subsequent writings in this area represent extensions of this argument in different mathematical directions. Arrow and Hurwicz later observed that the Hayek-Mises position implied that information was not a costless resource, but that a perfectly competitive market minimized this cost.

Because solving a system of linear equations is simpler than solving a system of nonlinear equations, most macroeconomic models are specified as linear models. Hurwicz was a leader in research on estimating the parameters of the nonlinear model. The parameters were the prices at which demand equaled supply in each of hundreds of industries. His motivation for this research was not only theoretical, but stemmed from his work in the 1940s at the Cowles Commission, where he directed the program to study empirically, as well as theoretically, the wartime price-controls program, the nearest that the United States has ever come to comprehensive central economic planning.

Given a system of differential equations, several questions may be posed: Does a solution to the system exist? Is any given solution, once found, a stable solution? And what mathematical tools can be used to answer the first two questions? Hurwicz did not contribute to the literature on the existence problem. Between 1958 and 1960, he and Arrow published four articles and one book on the stability issue. In these publications, they attempted to extend the stability conditions for a single market to the general equilibrium case of multiple markets. Arrow and Hurwicz developed an analysis that economist Don Patinkin (1922–1995) called "stability in the large," defined as "the conditions that make it possible for the Walrasian *tâtonnement* to bring the economy to an equilibrium from any point whatsoever." They simplified this task by reducing the economy to a two-good economy (Hurwicz and Arrow 1958, p. 522). A recent answer to the third question is phase diagrams, which assist in solving systems of differential equations. Hurwicz did not use this technique in any publications through the 1970s.

Hurwicz's work in linear and nonlinear programming was done largely in the 1950s with Arrow. Most of this research focused on the development of the gradient method of finding a solution to the programming problem of optimizing a function under constraints. The gradient method was intended to solve concave functions, rather than linear functions. The project found that the gradient method was inferior to the simplex method, an algorithm developed by George Dantzig (1914–2005). This was so despite the fact that the simplex method had been developed to solve linear functions.

Hurwicz is considered the father of information theory in economics. He showed clearly that information and its distribution within economic institutions was critical to decision making in resource allocation. This work provided additional theoretical underpinnings for transfer pricing in state enterprises and large complex private corporations.

SEE ALSO *Cumulative Causation; Difference Equations; Differential Equations; Information, Economics of; Nonlinear Regression; Phase Diagrams; Programming,* *Linear and Nonlinear; Stability in Economics; Transfer Pricing*

BIBLIOGRAPHY

PRIMARY WORKS

Arrow, Kenneth, and Leonid Hurwicz, eds. 1977. *Studies in Resource Allocation Processes.* New York: Cambridge University Press.

Chipman, John S., Leonid Hurwicz, Marcel K. Richter, and Hugo S. Sonnenschein, eds. 1971. *Preferences, Utility, and Demand: A Minnesota Symposium.* New York: Harcourt.

Hurwicz, Leonid. 1955. Decentralized Resource Allocation. Cowles Commission Discussion Paper No. 2112.

Hurwicz, Leonid. 1973. The Design of Mechanisms for Resource Allocation: Richard T. Ely Lecture. *American Economic Review: Papers and Proceedings of the Eighty-fifth Annual Meeting of the American Economic Association* 63 (2): 1–30.

Hurwicz, Leonid, and Kenneth Arrow. 1958. On the Stability of the Competitive Equilibrium, I. *Econometrica* 26 (4): 522–553.

Hurwicz, Leonid, Kenneth Arrow, and Hirofumi Uzawa. 1958. *Studies in Linear and Non-Linear Programming.* Stanford, CA: Stanford University Press.

Hurwicz, Leonid, and Stanley Reiter. 2006. *Designing Economic Mechanisms.* New York: Cambridge University Press.

Hurwicz, Leonid, David Schmeidler, and Hugo Sonnenschein, eds. 1985. *Social Goals and Social Organization: Essays in Memory of Elisha Pazner.* Cambridge, U.K.: Cambridge University Press.

SECONDARY WORKS

Chipman, John, Daniel McFadden, and Marcel K. Richter, eds. 1988. *Preferences, Uncertainty, and Optimality: Essays in Honor of Leonid Hurwicz.* Boulder, CO: Westview.

Graves, Theodore, Roy Radner, and Stanley Reiter, eds. 1987. *Information, Incentives, and Economic Mechanisms: Essays in Honor of Leonid Hurwicz.* Minneapolis: University of Minnesota Press.

Julian Ellison

HUSSEIN, KING OF JORDAN
1935–1999

Hussein bin ("son of") Talal, the longest-ruling king of Jordan, was born in November 1935 in Amman, Transjordan. His grandfather, Abdullah (1882–1951), ruled as emir over a sparsely populated, impoverished principality formally under the British administration in neighboring Palestine. Abdullah came from the Hashemite family of Mecca, which led an Arab nationalist uprising against Ottoman Turkish rule during World War I (1914–1918). After the defeat of the Ottomans, Britain created Transjordan, installing Abdullah as its proxy ruler in the strategically important area. Abdullah later became king upon the country's formal independence in 1946. Significantly, Jordan fought against Israel during the first Arab-Israeli War of 1948. Although the war ended as a disastrous defeat for the Arabs generally, and the Palestinians particularly, Abdullah expanded his kingdom when in 1950 he formally annexed the portion of Palestine that came to be known as the West Bank.

Young Hussein bin Talal was close to his grandfather and became heavily imbued with his family's self-proclaimed legacy as the vanguards of Arab nationalism and protectors of the Palestinians. Educated in Britain, Hussein also adopted Abdullah's pro-Western orientation. Hussein was by Abdullah's side when the monarch was assassinated in Jerusalem by a disgruntled Palestinian in 1951. After the brief rule of his father, Talal (1909–1972), the seventeen-year-old Hussein formally became king in 1952, although he was not enthroned until reaching the age of eighteen in 1953.

Until his death in 1999, King Hussein's long rule was noteworthy both for Jordan's remarkable socioeconomic development and for the tremendous strategic challenges that buffeted the country. These included the powerful surge of anti-Western Arab nationalism in the 1950s and 1960s that nearly led to a military coup in 1957; the ongoing Arab-Israeli conflict, especially the disastrous Arab defeat in 1967 that saw Israel occupy the West Bank; and the subsequent rise of Palestinian nationalism and demands for an independent Palestinian state, free from both Israeli and Jordanian control. With its large Palestinian population, Jordan was particularly affected by the latter. The demands of Palestinian guerrillas for renewed war with Israel after 1967 and for the overthrow of Hussein led to the gravest crisis the king ever faced—open war in his country between the Jordanian army and Palestinian fighters in September 1970 and again in July 1971 that resulted in the Palestinians' defeat.

In this and other trials, King Hussein proved a consummate political survivor. Domestically he survived economic downturns and demands for greater democracy. As a monarch who reigned *and* ruled, Hussein both could clamp down hard on political opposition (as when he banned political parties and declared martial law in 1957) or liberalize the political system (as when he ended martial law and allowed the return of political parties and elections starting in 1989). In terms of foreign policy, he managed to weather threats from powerful neighbors and foes such as Syria, Iraq, the Palestine Liberation Organization (PLO), and Israel by cozying up to one or more of them at the expense of the others. Hussein's

maneuvering led him to a rapprochement with the PLO by the 1980s, a renunciation of claims to the West Bank in 1988, support for Iraq during the 1991 Gulf War, and a peace treaty with Israel in 1994.

King Hussein died of cancer in Amman in February 1999, and was succeeded by his eldest son from his first marriage, Abdullah.

SEE ALSO *Arab League, The; Arab-Israeli War of 1967; Arabs; Arafat, Yasir; Black September; Jews; Nationalism and Nationality; Palestine Liberation Organization (PLO); Palestinian Authority; Palestinians; Pan-Arabism; Peace Process; Zionism*

BIBLIOGRAPHY

Hussein bin Talal. 1962. *Uneasy Lies the Head: The Autobiography of His Majesty King Hussein I of the Hashemite Kingdom of Jordan.* New York: Bernard Geis.

Hussein bin Talal. 1969. *My "War" with Israel.* Trans. June P. Wilson and Walter B. Michaels. London: Peter Owen.

Hussein bin Talal. 1975. *Mon métier de roi.* Paris: R. Laffont.

Michael R. Fischbach

HUSSEIN, SADDAM
1937–2006

Saddam Hussein was born on April 28, 1937, in the northern town of Tikrit, Iraq, to a landless family. His mother was widowed and lost Hussein's older brother while she was pregnant with Saddam. After his mother remarried, the family moved to the tiny village of Uja, a few miles south of Tikrit, where they led an impoverished life. His mother had three more children with her new husband, and Hussein's stepfather preferred them over him. Being fatherless, Hussein was exposed to abuse on the part of the village's children. His parents did not want to send him to school, but when he turned ten he insisted on moving to Tikrit to stay with his maternal uncle, Khayr Allah Tilfah, and attended primary school there. In 1955 he moved with his uncle's family to Baghdad to attend high school, but before graduating he became involved in political activities, having joined the revolutionary underground Baath Party in 1957. Later, as an exile in Cairo, he completed his secondary education and took some classes in law. As vice president of Iraq, he took private lessons in law, but he never completed his formal education.

On July 14, 1958, General Abdul-Karim Qassem (1914–1963) toppled the monarchy in Baghdad and established a semibenevolent dictatorship. Within weeks it became clear that Qassem's approach to Arab unity was opposed to that of the Baath Arab Socialist Party, Hussein's chosen venue for political action. With the support of Iraqi communists, Qassem objected to unification with Gamal Abdel Nasser's (1918–1970) Egypt, and he placed a heavy emphasis on Iraqi identity and Iraqi interests, rather than on pan-Arab ideology and practice. In October 1959 Hussein participated in a failed assassination attempt on Qassem's life. Hussein and his collaborators managed to wound the Iraqi dictator, but Hussein himself was wounded in his thigh and one of his team was killed, apparently from bullets shot by their own colleagues. Hussein managed to escape to Syria, an odyssey that became the object of a heroic myth weaved by his media after he became president. In Damascus he met the founder and chief ideologue of the Baath Party, the Syrian Christian intellectual Michel Aflaq (1910–1989). Aflaq was impressed by Hussein's audacity and strength of character, and thereafter Hussein's position in the party was assured. Hussein soon left Damascus for Cairo, where he lived a modest life sponsored by Nasser.

BAATH PARTY COMES TO POWER

On February 8, 1963, the Baath Party, in collaboration with a few army officers, staged a coup d'état and killed Qassem. Hussein immediately left Cairo and arrived in Baghdad, where he became a midlevel internal security official. This was also when he married his maternal cousin, Sajidah Khayr Allah Tilfah. Qassem's downfall was apparently not the exclusive result of his mistake of denying the Communists weapons, nor of the Baath Party's talent for staging coups. According to reliable sources, the coup was supported, if not actually engineered, by the U.S. Central Intelligence Agency (CIA). Starting in 1959, the CIA identified Qassem as a sworn enemy of the United States and a staunch ally of the Soviet Union. Over this issue there were deep disagreements between the CIA and the Mossad, the Israeli intelligence agency. The Israeli analysts were convinced that Qassem was not a Communist, nor a Soviet satellite, and they had sufficient evidence that he was not an enemy of Israel. In fact, his rivalry with Nasser served Israel's purpose of separating Iraq from Egypt. In 1963 the CIA, if it was indeed involved, had the upper hand. The Baath regime under General Abdul Salam Arif (1920–1966) as a titular figurehead launched a bloody campaign against Iraqi Communists who, despite deep reservations, had supported Qassem. Within six months the regime managed to slaughter around ten thousand men, real or perceived Communists. This, however, was no victory for the United States, because the Baath regime was still seeking Soviet, not American, support.

During the nine months of Baath rule (February to November 1963), Hussein aligned himself with the centrist faction in the party that was also supported by Aflaq. Hussein found it easy to join this faction because the group's leader, General Ahmad Hasan al-Bakr (1914–1982), the prime minister under General Arif, was his distant relative and a childhood friend of Hussein's uncle. All three were members of the Albu Nasir tribe, al-Beigat section, and all originated from the Tikrit area. This connection to Bakr proved a crucial step in Hussein's rise to power.

In November 1963 Arif and the army, with the help of some Baath officers including Bakr, toppled the civilian Baath regime and took full control of the country. After a few months of collaboration with Arif, the Baath leaders, including Hussein and Bakr, were hunted down and imprisoned. In 1964 Hussein escaped from prison. Other party members were released, which enabled them in July 1968 to stage another coup and topple the Arif regime.

HUSSEIN BECOMES DICTATOR OF IRAQ

There are claims that the second Baath coup was also supported by the CIA, but these claims are less credible than those regarding the 1963 takeover. Whatever the case, the July 1968 "revolution" was almost bloodless, and Arif was sent abroad. Before the coup, Hussein had been deputy secretary-general of the Iraqi "Command" of the (clandestine) Baath Party and in charge of its internal security system. By August 1968 Hussein was already the czar of domestic security. Despite his young age and minimal period of party affiliation, Hussein quickly became the power behind President Bakr. Hussein surrounded the regime's luminaries and the senior command of the armed forces with bodyguards and internal security apparatchiks who hailed from his own town and tribe. Before they realized it, the party leaders and army officers alike, including President Bakr, became prisoners in golden cages.

In November 1969 Hussein became vice president and deputy chairman of the powerful Revolutionary Command Council. At first his internal security apparatuses destroyed the party's real and perceived enemies: Communists, radical Islamists, Nasserists, pro-Western politicians, and pro-Syrian officers; and they even hanged in a public square helpless young Jews to demonstrate their Iraqi and Arab patriotism. The next step, however, was to gradually eliminate Hussein's personal rivals within the party. On July 16, 1979, Hussein replaced Bakr as president. A few days later, he purged all those in the party and armed forces whom he considered a threat. Hundreds were shot by firing squads, and Hussein became an absolute dictator.

Upon taking power in 1968, the Baath Party adopted the most extreme and recalcitrant pan-Arab, anti-Israeli, and anti-imperialist (or anti-American) rhetoric and, to an extent, practice. They launched vitriolic attacks against all the Arab regimes, but mainly those that lost the Six-Day War against Israel in 1967. Animosity with Baathist Syria became a cornerstone in Baghdad's regional policy. Iraq promised to wage war for the liberation of Palestine and the annihilation of Israel within a year. Iraq also kept some twenty thousand soldiers in Jordan and Syria. Their slogan "everything for the [Palestine] battle" reflected their view that Iraq should be ready to sacrifice everything for the pan-Arab cause of liberating Palestine, from the Jordan River to the Mediterranean. This position changed dramatically during "Black September" of 1970. Rather than keeping their promise to help the Palestinian armed organizations to topple the Hashemite regime, Iraq's Baath leaders ordered the Iraqi forces in Jordan to stay put, and by July 1971 the last Iraqi soldier was withdrawn from Jordan and Syria.

PAN-ARABISM, OIL, AND THE POLICE STATE

During the next decade, Hussein was the driving force behind an about-face in the Baghdad-based Baath Party's definition of Pan-Arabism. From expressed readiness to sacrifice Iraq on the altar of the supreme pan-Arab causes, he steered party ideology and politics toward an Iraq-centered approach. He promised that Iraq would still liberate Palestine and unite all the Arabs, but only after it became all-powerful, and this could take a decade or two.

During the early 1970s, Hussein embarked on a secret military nuclear program. Detaching Iraq from the day-to-day struggle against Israel (with the brief exception of the 1973 Arab-Israeli War) did not change the rhetoric of the regime. With some exceptions due to overpowering political constraints, Israel and the United States served Hussein as reliable hate objects, matched only by Iran after 1980. By blaming on these three countries all the travails of the Arabs and Muslims, and by promising to rid the Arab world of U.S. influence and Israeli existence, Hussein's regime sought to gain support and legitimacy among the Shia, as well as in the broader Arab and Islamic worlds.

In the 1970s the concept of Arab unity, too, underwent a metamorphosis. Traditional Ba'thist doctrine was egalitarian in that it perceived all Arab states as equal, and integrative in that it visualized the united Arab world as an amalgam in which all the existing Arab states and peoples would melt together in a huge crucible. Hussein's Pan-Arabism, in contrast, was Iraq-centered and hegemonic. The Iraqi people and state were never to melt and disappear, and Arab unity was conceived as a large brotherly federation of Arab states and peoples, rather than a crucible. Iraq was the elder brother in the Arab family, destined to lead. By late 1978 this approach was fully formulated, and on the eve of the Gulf War of 1991, the party leadership defined the Iraqis as "the pearl of the Arab crown." The Iraqi people were seen as having a glorious future largely because they had a glorious past. History, Hussein and his intellectuals pointed out, began in Sumer some six thousand years ago, and the modern Iraqis are the contemporary cultural heirs and genetic offspring of the glory that was Mesopotamia.

This policy represented a very secular aspect of the Baath regime. At the same time, the party also introduced its version of socialism: They took more land from large landowners and gave it to more peasants than did their predecessors; they created many agricultural cooperatives in the countryside; they nationalized more institutions; and they increased substantially government spending on social projects and development. In the mid- to late 1970s, the country experienced a thrust in the development of infrastructure, industry, social security, and health and education services, and Iraqis saw a general rise in their standard of living. In that respect, Hussein's June 1972 decision to nationalize the property of the Iraq Petroleum (Oil) Company proved a brilliant gamble: When oil prices went up in 1973 as a result of the Arab oil embargo against the West, Iraq did not participate in the embargo and its revenues quadrupled by 1975. This enabled the regime to spend huge resources on its social and economic programs.

At the same time, the regime also allowed the creation of a large stratum of new millionaires, consisting of regime luminaries and private entrepreneurs who thrived as a result of patron-client relations with the ruling elite. This situation bred widespread corruption. Another part of the regime's understanding of socialism was the creation of a huge body of state officialdom. This new middle class, which was dependent on state salaries and thus very docile politically, gradually replaced the original Iraqi middle class of economic entrepreneurs. Another mechanism designed for the same purpose was the encouragement of tribalism, which contradicted every tenet of the Ba'thist faith. Through the promotion of tribal *shaykhs* with gifts of land, money, and weapons, Hussein managed to better control the countryside. This policy was given full exposure only in the 1990s.

Above all, the 1970s and 1980s saw the mushrooming of state security apparatuses that managed to penetrate almost every corner of society. With Hussein as president, Iraq became a harsh police state characterized by severe repression of all political opponents, real and perceived. Between 1969 and 1971 and again between 1978 and 1980, the Communists were repressed, and many were executed or disappeared in Hussein's prisons. Likewise, between 1977 and 1980, Shi'i religious activists were executed, jailed, or expelled from Iraq, and the religious universities of Najaf and Karbala were reduced to a shadow of what they had been.

WAR WITH IRAN

Indeed, once Ayatollah Ruhollah Khomeini (1900–1989) came to power in Tehran in 1979, the Shi'i religious threat to Hussein's regime explains to a large extent his decision to launch an offensive against Iran on September 22, 1980. Khomeini called upon the Iraqis to rise against Hussein's "infidel" regime, and with slightly more than 50 percent of Iraq's population consisting of Shia, Hussein regarded the Shia as a great threat. Considerations of balance of power and international circumstances also played a role. While Khomeini had destroyed his own armed forces through purges, the Iraqi army was well equipped and well organized. In addition, the United States had abandoned Iran completely after the hostage incident of November 1979, and it was unlikely to stop Iraq. Furthermore, after mid-1979, Iraqi-American relations began slowly to improve. When the Soviet Union invaded Afghanistan in December of that year, Hussein criticized it in no unclear terms, fearing similar Soviet support for Iraqi Communists. This common interest brought Iraq and the United States closer still.

But the straw that broke the camel's back was a slight to Hussein's sense of pride. In April 1980 a Shi'i activist made an attempt on the life of Tariq Aziz, Hussein's closest associate. Hussein considered it an Iranian affront, and decided to go to war. Following a few months of hectic preparations on September 22, 1980, Iraq invaded Iran with eleven out of its twelve army divisions. After six days Hussein declared victory, but the war lasted for eight more years. During that war, when religious fervor proved a source of power to the Iranian regime, many secular Iraqis, Sunni and Shia alike, returned to Islam. At first the regime tried to fight this development, but by the mid- to late 1980s, the Iraqi government started to pay far more rhetorical tribute to religion than before. This rediscovery of religion was accelerated by the regime in the 1990s as it tried to harness Islam to win public support under the harsh conditions of the international embargo. During this period, Hussein initiated a faith campaign involving compulsory Qur'an classes for millions, even party members, and an increase in the number of mosques and Islamic educational institutions. Hussein himself made every effort to portray himself as a pious Muslim. Occasionally he created the impression that he had really became a devout Muslim who expected God to reward him by extricating him from the accumulating disasters in which he had landed himself. In his last meeting with his army's high command before the American invasion of March 2003 he promised them victory because, as he put it, Iraq was the only country that was guided by true Islam.

By the time the Iraq-Iran War ended in a stalemate, the Iraqi economy was devastated. Iraq entered a dangerous period of economic stagnation that Hussein knew could result in serious civil disturbances. Hussein felt that his regime was again under threat, though for different reasons than in 1980, the year Iraq's oil revenues reached an unprecedented peak. In 1980 Hussein's regime was challenged by Khomeini's mesmerizing influence on the Iraqi Shia, but in 1990 Iraq faced a major crisis of socioeconomic expectations on the part of the Iraq population, which expected an economic boom after the eight-year war. Here too, there were additional incentives to go to war. Kuwait was weak militarily and the Soviet-American rivalry had ended, so an occupation of a country friendly to the United States could no longer be seen as part of the cold war. Hussein even believed that he could stay in Kuwait if he would guarantee the United States its basic needs: an undisturbed flow of oil from the Gulf at reasonable prices.

WARS WITH THE UNITED STATES

Hussein, however, again allowed his hurt pride to dictate a major strategic step. He saw Kuwait's overproduction of oil, and was offended by Kuwaiti reluctance to continue its financial support of Iraq and to lease to Iraq two strategic islands. Hussein interpreted these actions as expressions of ingratitude after Iraq had protected Kuwait and other Gulf states from Iran.

In this situation, as in 1980, Hussein was the incurable optimist. In 1980 he was certain that he could beat Iran and bring Khomeini down in a short blitzkrieg. In 1990 he was likewise convinced that the international community and the Arab world would, at worst, satisfy themselves with protests. Even with 500,000 American and international troops in Saudi Arabia, he still believed that the United States was bluffing, and that even if war broke out, Iraq's formidable army would stop them.

Following a ceasefire agreement with the Allied forces on February 28, 1991, that sealed Iraq's devastating defeat, a massive Shi'i revolt in the south and a Kurdish revolt in the north almost brought the regime down. The revolts were suppressed with a tremendous effort only because the United States decided to remain aloof. More than one million Kurdish refugees fled their homes for fear of a repeat of the chemical attack ordered by Hussein in 1988. The French, the British, and the United States were forced to establish for them a refuge in Iraqi Kurdistan. Hussein thus lost control over much of the Iraqi north. Iraq thereafter entered into years of weapons inspections and a devastating phase of international sanctions that lasted until 2003.

Following the terrorist attacks in the United States on September 11, 2001, the U.S. approach to "rogue states" changed radically. Hussein was so oblivious to the change that he allowed his media to gloat over the American tragedy. Again, even with 100,000 U.S. soldiers in Kuwait, he believed that President George W. Bush was bluffing when he threatened to invade Iraq. And again, Hussein was convinced that even if the Americans attacked, his army could stop them on the outskirts of Baghdad. He did not even plan for his own escape, nor did he establish safe houses in the Sunni provinces. Hussein was captured on December 13, 2003, by American soldiers as he hid in a spider hole near the Iraqi city of Adwar, ten miles south of Tikrit, a few hundred yards from the place where he had crossed the Tigris in 1959 in his escape to Syria after the failed attempt on Qassem's life. Following a public trial by an Iraqi court, he was found guilty of ordering the unlawful execution of 148 Shi'i inhabitants of Dujayl, a village north of Baghdad, in retaliation for an attempt on his life there in 1982. Hussein will never be tried for the mass murder of civilians in Kurdistan-Iraq in 1987 and 1988 and in the Shi'i south in 1991 because on December 30, 2006, he was hanged in Baghdad.

SEE ALSO *Arab-Israeli War of 1967; Arabs; Black September; Central Intelligence Agency, U.S.; Dictatorship; Gulf War of 1991; Iranian Revolution; Iran-Iraq War; Iraq-U.S. War; Islam, Shia and Sunni; Khomeini, Ayatollah Ruhollah; Nasser, Gamal Abdel; Pan-Arabism; Personality, Cult of; September 11, 2001; Union of Soviet Socialist Republics*

BIBLIOGRAPHY

Aburish, Saïd K. 2000. *Saddam Hussein: The Politics of Revenge.* London: Bloombury.

Al-Khalil, Samir (Kanan Makiya). 1989. *Republic of Fear: The Politics of Modern Iraq.* Los Angeles: University of California Press.

Baram, Amatzia. 1991. *Culture, History, and Ideology in the Formation of Ba'thist Iraq, 1968–89.* New York: St. Martin's Press.

Baram, Amatzia. 1996. Re-Inventing Nationalism in Ba'thi Iraq 1968–1994: Supra-Territorial and Territorial Identities and What Lies Below. *Princeton Papers* 5 (Fall): 29–56.

Bengio, Ofra. 1998. *Saddam's Word: Political Discourse in Iraq.* New York: Oxford University Press.

Farouk-Sluglett, Marion, and Peter Sluglett. 2001. *Iraq Since 1958: From Revolution to Dictatorship.* Rev. ed. New York: Tauris.

Marr, Phebe. 2004. *The Modern History of Iraq.* 2nd ed. Boulder, CO: Westview.

Tripp, Charles. 2000. *A History of Iraq.* Cambridge, U.K.: Cambridge University Press.

Amatzia Baram

HUTCHINSON AFFAIR
SEE *Franklin, Benjamin.*

HYBRIDITY

A basic definition of *hybrid* and its derivative *hybridity*, provided by the *Oxford English Dictionary*, is that it is a noun used to describe "a thing made by combining two different elements; a mixture." *Hybrid* can also be used as an adjective to describe something of "mixed character." The word *hybrid* originated in the early seventeenth century and was first used regularly in the nineteenth century to describe the offspring of two plants or animals of different species (in Latin the word meant the "offspring of a tame sow and wild boar"). The term was taken up in the mid-1800s by the Victorian extreme right to describe the offspring of humans of different races—races assumed to be of different species. *Hybridity* was later deployed by postcolonial theorists to describe cultural forms that emerged from colonial encounters. Its more recent adoption by social scientists—particularly those interested in migration, diaspora, transnationalism, and globalization—is varied and includes debates about its usefulness as a category. These debates stem, in part, from the term's historical usages.

During the nineteenth century, discussions about hybridity were shaped by racist assumptions about the human species. Given that a hybrid was defined as a cross between two species that should not, in theory, be able to reproduce with each other, debates about human hybrids hinged on questions of fertility and sexuality and reflected a widespread anxiety about sexual unions between different races (in particular, between blacks and whites; one early definition of hybrid is "child of a freeman and slave"). Although arguments that relied on evidence of infertility were difficult to sustain in the face of growing mixed-race populations, persistent efforts were made to fine-tune theories of biology that perpetuated ideologies of racial hierarchy and difference. Debates about hybridity took place not only in the natural sciences, but also in social sciences such as anthropology and sociology.

The subsequent use of *hybridity* in postcolonial studies was shaped by linguistic models that analyze culture as a process and a site of contestation. Particularly influential here has been the work of Mikhail Bakhtin, a pioneering linguist who theorized the political effects of hybridity in language. He used *hybridity* to refer to the way in which language, within a single utterance, can be double-accented—that is, it can contain two styles, belief systems, or social languages. While Bakhtin contends that "organic" hybridity (or ongoing mixing) is an important feature of the evolution of all languages, he is particularly interested in "intentional" hybridity, which he describes as a politicized process whereby one voice is able to unmask another's authorial one through a language that is double-accented.

This conceptual use of hybridity was extended by postcolonial scholars to analyze forms of resistance to colonialism. Homi Bhabha's work has been particularly significant; he uses the term *hybridity* to refer to the ways in which the power that colonial discourses attempt to exercise is disrupted in and through its very attempts to deny other knowledges, the traces of which shape colonial discourse and render it inherently double-voiced. *Hybridization* thus describes "the ambivalence at the source of traditional discourses on authority" (Bhabha 1994, pg. 112). Bhabha's work celebrates hybridity as subversive and as an "active moment of challenge and resistance against a dominant cultural power" (Young 1995, p. 23). By focusing on the production of meaning, postcolonial scholarship such as Bhabha's emphasizes representation and signification, and hence concentrates on analyzing discourse. Bhabha also argues, however, that transgressions can occur in a "third space" that includes forms of interaction and cultural difference that challenge dominant and totalizing norms.

These diverse histories of hybridity in biology, linguistics, and postcolonial studies have shaped its recent adoption by social scientists as well as debates about the term's usefulness. Scholars interested in migration, diaspora, transnationalism, and globalization have used the term to describe the identity of persons of mixed race or cultural origin or influence (such as migrants), the cultural production of "hybrid" persons (i.e., music, language, style), and/or processes of cultural mixing that shape identity formation and cultural production. *Hybridity* thus shares semantic terrain with terms such as *creolization, syncretism, bricolage, borderland, fusion,* and *cosmopolitanism.* Although *hybridity* has been used to describe a variety of phenomena, it is often mobilized with a common theoretical intent: That is, hybrid identities, cultural products, and/or practices are often seen as challenging, in novel and creative ways, essentialist norms of culture, race, and nation.

A number of criticisms have been made recently about this politicized usage of *hybridity*. One set of concerns flags the inherent epistemological contradictions of the term itself: For example, one critique is that the term can never be liberatory because it always implies a prior state of purity, even as it attempts to critique this idea; also, because it is shaped by organic and biological conceptions that are also heterosexist, it risks naturalizing essentialisms. Some further argue that it is an imprecise concept if one takes as axiomatic that all cultures are hybrid and that purity is a mythical construct.

A second set of critiques addresses dominant uses of *hybridity*. For example, some argue that it has come to delimit certain objects of inquiry in ways that elide questions of inequality. They contend that the concept is used in facile ways to impute to hybrid persons, products, and processes a politics of resistance solely based on their purported hybrid properties. A related critique is that it has been used in academia as an apoliticized celebration of difference in ways that dovetail with the capitalist project of commodifying diversity. Some also contend that hybridity has been reduced to the experience of the migrant in the metropole at the expense of understanding how broader transnational processes that lead to migrancy also impact populations who cannot travel; these scholars relatedly raise questions about who is or is not considered "hybrid" and thus fashionable to study.

More recently, many scholars are arguing that a useful way to study hybridity is by analyzing empirically how the term *hybridity* is used (who deploys the concept, with which kinds of understandings, from which contexts and locations, and with what effects). By doing so, we contextualize the concept (i.e., historically, geographically) rather than imputing to it an ahistoricized principle of resistance. We can thus understand the various usages to which the concept is put, its diverse modalities, and its effects, all of which can be multiple and not necessarily resistant (for example, scholars are showing how it can be tied to political projects such as nationalism and fascism).

SEE ALSO *Creolization; Culture; Identity*

BIBLIOGRAPHY

Bakhtin, Mikhail M. 1981. *The Dialogic Imagination.* Trans. Caryl Emerson and Michael Holquist. Austin: University of Texas Press.

Ballinger, Pamela. 2004. "Authentic Hybrids" in the Balkan Borderlands. *Current Anthropology* 45 (1): 31–60.

Bhabha, Homi. 1994. *The Location of Culture.* London and New York: Routledge.

Gilroy, Paul. 1987. *"There Ain't No Black in the Union Jack:" The Cultural Politics of Race and Nation.* Chicago: University of Chicago Press.

Hutnyk, John. 2005. Hybridity. *Ethnic and Racial Studies* 28 (1): 79–102.

Lavie, Smadar, and Ted Swedenburg, eds. 1996. *Displacement, Diaspora, and Geographies of Identity.* Durham, NC: Duke University Press.

Puri, Shalini. 2004. *The Caribbean Postcolonial: Social Equality, Post-Nationalisms, and Cultural Hybridity.* New York: Palgrave Macmillan.

Young, Robert. 1995. *Colonial Desire: Hybridity in Theory, Culture, and Race.* London: Routledge.

Falu Bakrania

HYGIENE

SEE *Sanitation.*

HYPERACTIVITY

The term *activity*, in regards to hyperactivity, generally refers to movement, particularly gross motor movement. Individuals' activity levels are variable and are affected by development, daily cycles, environmental demands, and internal states. After taking into account these factors, an individual may be considered hyperactive if his or her activity level is excessive compared to others. Since activity level, like height or weight, is continuous and can be characterized by a bell curve, *hyperactivity* is a term generally used to indicate those individuals on the high end of this continuum. *Hypoactivity* signifies those individuals on the low end of this continuum. Significant hyperactivity may impair an individual's ability to function across academic, occupational, social, and familial domains.

Multiple medical and psychological disorders are characterized by symptoms of hyperactivity. Perhaps the disorder that is most closely tied to hyperactivity is *attention deficit hyperactivity disorder* (ADHD). Hyperactivity, combined with impulsive symptoms, is one of the core behavioral symptom domains identified by current diagnostic nosology; inattention represents the other behavioral symptom domain. Most pediatric patients diagnosed with ADHD have hyperactive symptoms. Hyperactive symptoms of ADHD include fidgeting or squirming in one's seat, difficulty remaining seated, running about or climbing excessively, difficulty engaging in leisure activities quietly, acting as if "driven by a motor," and talking excessively. As exhibited by the patient with ADHD, these behaviors are purposeless. Patients are judged to have these symptoms if they exhibit these behaviors excessively compared to individuals of the same sex and age under similar circumstances.

The hyperactivity observed in patients with ADHD is generally not episodic. Several other disorders/diseases are defined by hyperactivity that is episodic or appears as discrete behavioral events. For example, Huntington's disease is a neurodegenerative disease that affects cognition,

memory, and mood. The hallmark of this disease is hyperactivity consisting of rapid, jerky motions with no clear purpose. Similarly, tic disorders (e.g., Tourette's disorder) are characterized by repeated and involuntary bodily movements or uncontrollable vocal sounds.

Across disorders with hyperactive features, the neurological causes of hyperactivity appear to be related to the brain's motor circuitry or dopaminergic abnormalities. The human brain has numerous functional regions, most of which are interconnected to constitute neural circuits. One neural circuit primarily involved in motor activity begins in the cerebral cortex, connects to basal ganglia, which connect to the thalamus, and finally loops to the motor cortex. Within this circuit, there are minicircuits with substantia nigra and the subthalamic nucleus. Further, there are both direct and indirect pathways that project through this circuitry. Irrespective of subcircuitry and pathways, the basal ganglia (i.e., caudate, putamen, and globus pallidus) exert a modulating effect on this neural circuit and thus affect the behavioral manifestation of movement. The basal ganglia are primarily innervated with dopaminergic neurons. Concordantly, ADHD, tic disorders, and Huntington's disease have all been associated either morphometric abnormalities (i.e., usually reductions) or dopaminergic abnormalities in basal ganglia regions.

Hyperactivity as manifested in disorders with episodic hyperactive symptoms, such as Huntington's or Tourette's, can often be assessed through observation. The mere presence of tics or choreiform movements may be considered pathological. Even at low frequencies, these abnormal episodic movements are usually indicative of disease presence. The hyperactivity associated with ADHD is less well defined. Because ADHD-related hyperactivity occurs along a continuum, the assessment of presence or absence of this hyperactivity relies heavily on clinical judgment of what is a clinically significant level of hyperactive behavior. Using all available information, a clinician must decide whether the hyperactive behavior exhibited by a patient falls outside the realm of normal behavior. Commonly utilized tools for helping to make this determination are parent and teacher rating scales for pediatric patients and self- and other-report rating scales for adult patients. Several rating scales exist for assessing ADHD behaviors, including the Vanderbilt Rating Scales, the DuPaul ADHD Rating Scale, and the Conners's Rating Scales. Ratings are scored according to several empirically derived factors. Most scales have a factor measuring hyperactivity. An individual's scores on the hyperactivity factors can be compared to derived age and sex norms to determine the severity of hyperactive behavior.

Other methods for assessing ADHD-related hyperactivity are the use of actometers and observation.

Actometers are mechanical devices that can be worn on a patient's limb or placed on a patient's chair. The actometer is designed to measure movement. Actometers attached to the patient's body can provide valuable information about cycles of movement throughout the day and night. Patient observation can be performed in a variety of formats. Most simply, a clinician can observe the ADHD patient during interviews or testing on the day of clinical evaluation. An alternative format is to have the patient engage in an analog task (e.g., perform an academic assignment) while an observer codes activity level using an observational coding system. One may increase the ecological validity of the observation procedure by observing the patient in his or her natural environment (e.g., school). Similarly, qualitative or quantitative methods could be utilized to describe the patient's activity level.

Evidence-based treatment of ADHD-related hyperactivity can be classified into either of two treatment strategies: medication or behavioral treatment. The most frequently used class of medications that target hyperactive symptoms among patients with ADHD are the stimulants. Stimulant medications exert their effect by increasing levels of extracellular dopamine in the brain. Stimulants wield their effects quickly and effectively. Other medications, such as atomoxetine, bupropion, and tricyclic antidepressants, have also been shown to decrease hyperactivity levels in patients with ADHD. In addition, behavioral treatment has been shown to be an effective treatment for patients with ADHD. Behavioral treatments primarily consist of consequating a patient's behavior with behavioral contingencies. Common behavioral techniques are token economies, response cost, or daily report cards. Behavioral therapy likely exerts its effect in children by increasing their awareness of their own maladaptive behavior by making environmental contingencies increasingly salient. Both medication and behavioral therapy have been shown to be effective treatments for improving hyperactivity symptoms in children with ADHD. However, medication does appear to have a more robust treatment effect when hyperactive symptomatology is used as the outcome measure.

SEE ALSO *Attention Deficit Hyperactivity Disorder; Psychotherapy; Psychotropic Drugs*

BIBLIOGRAPHY

Barkley, Russell, and Charles Cunningham. 1979. The Effects of Methylphenidate on the Mother-Child Interactions of Hyperactive Children. *Archives of General Psychiatry* 36 (2): 201–208.

MTA Cooperative Group. 1999. A 14-Month Randomized Clinical Trial of Treatment Strategies for Attention-Deficit/Hyperactivity Disorder. *Archives of General Psychiatry* 56 (12): 1073–1086.

Solanto, Mary. 2002. Dopamine Dysfunction in AD/HD: Integrating Clinical and Basic Neuroscience Research. *Behavioural Brain Research* 130: 65–71.

Jeffery N. Epstein

HYPERGAMY

SEE *Dowry and Bride Price.*

HYPEROPIA

SEE *Farsightedness.*

HYPERTENSION

Hypertension (high blood pressure) is a highly prevalent and largely symptomless chronic medical condition that affects almost one in three adults living in industrialized nations. Hypertension is more prevalent among blacks than whites, with prevalence rates of black Americans among the highest in the world. Among whites, hypertension is more prevalent among males than females until age sixty-five, when females with hypertension begin to outnumber males. Among blacks, hypertension becomes more prevalent among females in comparison to males much earlier, beginning at age forty-five. Although prevalence rates of hypertension typically increase with age in industrialized countries, inhabitants of nonindustrialized countries maintain stable blood pressures across their lifespan, suggesting that lifestyle factors associated with industrialization are associated with an increased propensity for developing hypertension. Prevalence rates for hypertension among Hispanic or Latino, Asian, and Native American populations are much lower than among white and black Americans.

There are two forms of hypertension: primary (or essential) hypertension and secondary hypertension. Essential hypertension represents the vast majority of cases and is characterized by chronically elevated blood pressure of unknown origin. In contrast, secondary hypertension is characterized by elevated blood pressures caused by another physiological abnormality, such as kidney disease, endocrine disturbances, or blockage of blood circulation. Regardless of form, hypertension is associated with increased risk for a number of diseases of the cardiovascular system, including coronary heart disease, stroke, peripheral artery disease, and congestive heart failure. Hypertension is therefore the primary cause of mortality in more than 10 percent of deaths among whites and more than 20 percent of deaths among blacks.

DIAGNOSING HYPERTENSION

The diagnosis of hypertension is typically made by a physician during a medical evaluation in a clinic setting. As part of this evaluation, measures of blood pressure are obtained by temporarily blocking blood flow in the brachial artery (upper arm) with an occluding cuff and listening to sounds of blood pulsations, called Korotkoff sounds, as arterial flow resumes. The first sound detected is associated with the magnitude of arterial pressure during cardiac contraction and is called systolic blood pressure (SBP). The disappearance of the Korotkoff sounds that occurs when blood flow returns to normal is associated with the magnitude of arterial pressure during cardiac refilling and is called diastolic blood pressure (DBP). Measures of SBP that are less than 120 millimeters of mercury (mm Hg) and DBP that are less than 80 mm Hg are considered within the normal range. SBPs and DBPs higher than these values are associated with increased risks for cardiovascular disease consequences in a linear fashion; a diagnosis of Stage 1 hypertension is assigned for patients with SBPs between 140 and 159 mm Hg or DBPs between 90 and 99 mm Hg, and a diagnosis of Stage 2 hypertension is assigned for patients with SBPs greater than 160 mm Hg or DBPs greater than 100 mm Hg.

It is well established that blood pressures measured by health care professionals in clinic settings often bear little correspondence to blood pressures that occur during daily life, creating diagnostic dilemmas for health care providers. In some cases, patients exhibit high blood pressures in the clinic but normal blood pressures in other settings, a condition called "white coat" hypertension from the presumption that these patients display physiological stress reactions while having their blood pressure measured. Another group of patients exhibits normal blood pressures in the clinic setting accompanied by elevated blood pressures throughout daily life. This condition has been termed "masked" hypertension, as both physician and patient are unaware of the elevated blood pressures unless sophisticated automated blood pressure devices, called ambulatory blood pressure monitors, are used to assess blood-pressure levels throughout a normal day. "White coat" hypertension is typically associated with lesser risk for cardiovascular disease, while "masked" hypertension is associated with risk profiles comparable to patients with untreated hypertension.

STRESS AND HYPERTENSION

It is widely recognized that an exposure to stressful life events, such as enduring natural or human-made disasters, being employed in a highly stressful job, or living in con-

ditions of socioeconomic deprivation, is associated with increased blood pressure. However, not all persons exposed to these types of stressful events or life situations develop hypertension. This suggests that individual difference factors exist that either increase or decrease vulnerability for developing hypertension. Individual difference factors associated with a risk for hypertension can be categorized into three types: demographic and historical developmental factors, modifiable psychological or behavioral factors, and modifiable social factors.

Demographic and historical developmental variables represent risk factors that cannot be modified by the individual. For example, it is well known that hypertension runs in families, suggesting a genetic contribution. A risk for hypertension associated with one's age, gender, or race represents other factors that are not modifiable by the individual. Specific medical conditions such as diabetes mellitus or obesity are also associated with an increased risk for hypertension.

Several modifiable lifestyle behavioral factors are associated with an increased risk for hypertension; foremost among these are physical inactivity and excessive consumption of alcohol or sodium. Three psychological characteristics have also been associated with hypertension. First, hypertensive patients often exhibit higher rates of symptoms of depression, anxiety, and anger than persons with normal blood pressure, leading researchers to hypothesize that a negative affect is associated with an increased risk for hypertension. Second, hypertensive patients have been shown to express anger less effectively than persons with normal blood pressure, either displaying more overt aggression during confrontation or suppressing the expression of anger entirely. Third, hypertensive patients exhibit higher rates of emotional defensiveness than persons with normal blood pressures, indicating that this tendency to be out of touch with their emotions may play a role in their condition.

A few modifiable social environment factors have also been implicated in establishing risk for developing hypertension. Families of hypertensive patients, for example, have been characterized as exhibiting less social skill than those of non-hypertensive patients, particularly when handling conflict. Further, as with many other chronic medical conditions, a lack of social support is strongly associated with an increased incidence of hypertension.

No single demographic, modifiable psychological, or social environmental individual difference variable explains entirely why stress leads to hypertension, suggesting that a combination of factors explains the association between stress and hypertension. For example, several individual difference variables have been hypothesized to explain the high prevalence of hypertension among black Americans. First, increased sodium retention in response to stress has been observed among black Americans that some social epidemiologists believe results from adaptive physiologies of African ancestors who survived the middle passage from Africa to America. Second, the psychological construct of John Henryism, described as effortful active coping in the face of extreme adversity, has been directly associated with blood-pressure levels in some black American samples, particularly those of low socio-economic status. Finally, an exposure to the racism and discrimination that is frequently experienced by many black Americans represents a social environmental factor that has been linked to higher blood pressure. Although consistent support linking each of these three individual difference variables to hypertension is lacking, there is sufficient evidence to suggest that each affects blood-pressure levels for some black Americans and is partly involved in explaining their increased prevalence of hypertension.

The physiological mechanisms through which psychological, behavioral, and social factors influence the risk for hypertension are unknown, although the autonomic nervous system is thought to be involved. Evidence from animal studies and from prospective trials on humans has revealed that participants who exhibit exaggerated blood-pressure responses to stress are more likely to develop hypertension later in life. According to this reactivity hypothesis, psychological factors, like the experience or inappropriate expression of anger, promote the onset of hypertension only inasmuch as they result in elevated blood-pressure responses to stress, which are presumably driven by the autonomic nervous system. Based upon this hypothesis, a considerable amount of research has linked various risk factors associated with hypertension to the magnitude of blood-pressure reactivity to stress. For example, healthy offspring of hypertensive parents exhibit greater blood-pressure reactions to stress than offspring of non-hypertensive parents. Similarly, both overt aggression and anger suppression are associated with heightened blood-pressure reactions to stress, in contrast to the appropriate expression of anger. Although the exact pathway through which psychosocial risk factors exert their influence on blood pressure–regulating organs is still unknown, the reactivity hypothesis has provided important clues regarding how a psychological construct like suppressed anger could lead to a physiological disturbance of blood-pressure regulation.

TREATMENT OF HYPERTENSION

Because of the high prevalence and lethal consequences of hypertension, a number of interventions have been developed to lower blood pressure. The primary treatment strategy for both lowering blood pressure and reducing the risk of cardiovascular disease associated with hypertension consists of a variety of antihypertensive medications. Although the various classes of medications operate through different physiological pathways, they all are potent blood pressure–lowering agents. Unfortunately, a large number of hypertensive patients do not take their medication as prescribed, partly because the side effects can be more noticeable than the condition of hypertension itself.

Several non-pharmacologic methods are known to lower blood pressure and have served as useful adjunct treatments for hypertensive patients and as primary preventive strategies for persons at risk for developing hypertension. Weight loss, typically achieved through a combination of dietary management and increased physical activity, can result in blood-pressure reductions comparable to antihypertensive medication. Sodium restriction and potassium supplementation also reduce blood pressures, particularly among patients who are sodium sensitive. Eliminating the consumption of alcohol is an effective means of lowering blood pressure among hypertensive patients who consume alcohol regularly.

Because psychological factors are linked to hypertension, the blood pressure–reducing properties of three psychological interventions have been examined: relaxation, biofeedback, and individualized stress-management programs. The magnitude of blood-pressure reductions observed with relaxation and biofeedback interventions is generally much lower than those observed with antihypertensive medication. Because stress-management approaches are individualized based upon the patient's unique psychological profile, larger reductions in blood pressure have been observed.

Hypertension is a chronic medical condition with no single cause. By considering both pharmacologic and non-pharmacologic interventions with respect to each individual patient, effective intervention and prevention programs will help eliminate hypertension as a public health problem.

BIBLIOGRAPHY

American Heart Association. 2004. *Heart Disease and Stroke Statistics—2005 Update*. Dallas, TX: American Heart Association.

Blumenthal, James A., Andrew Sherwood, Elizabeth C. D. Gullette, et al. 2002. Biobehavioral Approaches to the Treatment of Essential Hypertension. *Journal of Clinical and Consulting Psychology* 70 (3): 569–589.

Brondolo, Elizabeth, Ricardo Rieppi, Kim P. Kelly, and William Gerin. 2003. Perceived Racism and Blood Pressure: A Review of the Literature and Conceptual and Methodological Critique. *Annals of Behavioral Medicine* 25 (1): 55–65.

Chobanian, Aram V., George L. Bakris, Henry R. Black, et al. 2003. Seventh Report of the Joint National Committee on Prevention, Detection, Evaluation, and Treatment of High Blood Pressure. *Hypertension* 42 (6): 1206–1252.

Fields, Larry E., Vicki L. Burt, Jeffrey A. Cutler, et al. 2004. The Burden of Adult Hypertension in the United States 1999 to 2000: A Rising Tide. *Hypertension* 44 (4): 398–404.

Jorgensen, Randall S., Blair T. Johnson, Monika E. Kolodziej, and George E. Schreer. 1996. Elevated Blood Pressure and Personality: A Meta-analytic Review. *Psychological Bulletin* 120 (2): 293–320.

Larkin, Kevin T. 2005. *Stress and Hypertension: Examining the Relation between Psychological Stress and High Blood Pressure.* New Haven, CT: Yale University Press.

Kevin T. Larkin

HYPOGAMY

SEE *Dowry and Bride Price.*

HYPOTHESIS AND HYPOTHESIS TESTING

The scientific method is central to the identity of any self-described social science. Science is distinguished from nonscience not by the content or subject of study. Rather, the distinguishing characteristic of a science is the method of investigation. The scientific method relies on systematic, repeatable testing of expectations against the observed world. In their adoption of the scientific method, social sciences more closely resemble chemistry than its alchemical predecessors, which relied instead on the application of metaphysical rules to guide their work.

The physicist may use complex instruments to observe minute characteristics of subatomic particles. Similarly, the social scientist may use surveys to observe the characteristics of human behavior. The focus on observation as a method for testing expectations unites the physicist and the social scientist in their use of a common tool of the scientific method.

THE PURPOSE OF HYPOTHESES

Hypotheses are the central tool of scientific observation. Because the core method of scientific investigation is the comparison of expectations against observations of the world, scientists need to make clear statements about their expectations. A hypothesis is a concise, falsifiable statement that is subjected to observational testing as part of a scientific investigation.

Scientific research generally starts with a question about the observable world. In the social sciences research questions focus on human behavior—especially behavior related to groups (e.g., communities, countries, or soci-

eties). The scientific method says nothing about the origins of these research questions (just as it says nothing about the content of the areas of research). The scientific method simply requires that a scientist state an answer to this question (the hypothesis) that can be tested with observations (hypothesis testing).

There is a bewildering array of potential research questions—and thus hypotheses—in the domain of social science. Hypotheses can focus on expectations about voting behavior, the tendency of nations to go to war, or the factors that contribute to juvenile delinquency or to decisions about where to live (among many, many other hypotheses).

The purpose of the hypothesis is to ease the task of testing an expectation with observations of the world. A good hypothesis, then, is one that is easily tested. The ease of testing contributes to a second key aspect of the scientific method: reproducibility of testing. A clearly worded hypothesis can be tested repeatedly by a scientist and, maybe more important, by other scientists (King, Keohane, and Verba 1994, pp. 28–29).

Consider the following example. A social scientist may hypothesize that smaller class sizes in secondary schools will lead to higher performance on standardized tests. Because it is easy to observe the number of students in a class and the standardized tests scores are also easily observable (though there may be questions of the validity of the test as a measure of "intelligence" or even "academic achievement"), this hypothesis is easy to test. The test itself is also easy to replicate by the original social scientist or by other investigators. The hypothesis is sufficiently clear that any observer would be able to tell whether people in the smaller classes actually performed better on standardized tests. The judgment, then, is not a product of the specific observer but is instead independent of the identity of the scientist (a subject of some controversy that is discussed in a later section).

STRATEGIES OF HYPOTHESIS TESTING—QUANTITATIVE STRATEGIES

One of the major strategies for hypothesis testing is quantitative research. The focus of this approach is on the quantification of social science concepts for purposes of comparison and hypothesis testing. For example, a social scientist might ask whether the U.S. president's approval ratings have gone down over the past year. This could give some sense of the power the president might have in promoting his or her legislative agenda or the chances of the president's party in an upcoming election.

The hypothesis would be the social scientist's guess as to how the candidate will fare against the proposed opponent. A good hypothesis will be one that is well grounded in the available theory on elections and that is testable against observable data (in this case a survey). The hypothesis would predict whether the approval ratings of the president have gone down over the past year. It would provide a preliminary answer to the stated research question. More ambitious hypotheses that predict specific levels of support (that the president has lost 8 percent of support from the previous year) are possible, but these require highly developed theories. One can take as an example the basic hypothesis that the president's approval rating has gone down in the past year.

Armed with a hypothesis, the scientist will conduct a survey of a sample of potential voters to test the hypothesis. The scientist cannot, or would not want to, survey all citizens of the United States. Instead, the scientist will select a small sample out of the U.S. population. The scientist might send a survey to 1,000 citizens and see whether the hypothesis is correct within this sample of voters. The results of the survey will give the scientist a sense of the president's current approval rating for comparison to previous approval ratings (Babbie 1995, pp. 190–193).

Quantitative hypothesis testing—the comparison of numerically represented measurements for purposes of hypothesis testing—allows for some detailed comparisons. One can say, for the sake of argument, that the survey suggests 43 percent of respondents said they approved of the job the president was doing. The previous year's survey had reported that 47 percent of respondents had said they approved. At first glance, the evidence provides support for the hypothesis.

A number of questions remain about this test of the hypothesis. To what extent is the observed dip in approval indicative of a general trend in the U.S. population? To what extent is the dip indicative of a persistent change in approval? Tools of probability and statistics provide some opportunity to address these questions. Sampling theory provides some sense of how reliable the results are that come from a sample of a larger population (Babbie 1995, pp. 195–203). Such theory helps scientists describe the range of possible values in the population given the size of the sample surveyed. One could describe the probability that the actual approval rating was 47 percent (the previous rating) while the sample happened to be skewed toward lower approval ratings. In general, the larger the sample size, the lower the probability of these sorts of discrepancies. Such theory also provides insight into whether the variation one sees is relatively permanent or just part of the inherent variability in measuring people's approval of a public figure. It is the ability to assess these issues of sampling and fundamental uncertainty that have convinced many of the utility of quantitative hypothesis testing techniques.

STRATEGIES OF HYPOTHESIS TESTING—QUALITATIVE STRATEGIES

Many scholars pursue an alternative style of hypothesis testing. These scholars tend to be unsatisfied with the techniques of measurement for social concepts employed in many quantitative research projects. In lieu of quantitative measurements of large samples of observations, qualitative hypothesis testing involves the careful study of a smaller number of observations with detailed treatment of the context and meaning of the social concepts themselves.

A qualitative hypothesis testing strategy follows the basic procedure of hypothesis testing. The social scientist generates a hypothesis in response to a research question. The social scientist then compares his or her expectation against the observed world. The difference between the qualitative approach and the quantitative approach reviewed earlier is in the strategy for getting reliable observations of the world.

Qualitative hypothesis testing tends to focus on detailed histories and culturally sensitive accounts of the social systems that are being studied. The detail and contextual knowledge provide the qualitative hypothesis testing strategies leverage on the challenges of hypothesis testing in two ways. First, the detailed knowledge of the subjects under study allow for careful selection of cases for study. As opposed to the quantitative strategy of multiplying the number of observations to avoid the possibility of drawing the wrong lessons from a study, qualitative hypothesis testing involves carefully selecting a few observations to achieve the ideal contrast. Second, the detailed knowledge of the subjects also allows for greater attention to the measurement of variables. Proponents of qualitative research focus on the ability to really get to know the subjects as a means to understand the nuances of the proposed effects of policies (e.g., Brady and Collier 2004).

Qualitative research tends to investigate different types of hypotheses than quantitative research, though the barriers between the two have eroded somewhat since the late twentieth century. Whereas quantitative hypotheses tend to involve statements of correlation, qualitative hypotheses have tended to focus on issues of necessary and sufficient conditions. These hypotheses focus on the conditions whose presence guarantees that an effect will be present (a sufficient condition) or whose absence will guarantee that an effect will not be present (a necessary condition) (Goertz and Starr 2003).

Theda Skocpol's (1979) research on social revolutions exemplifies this approach. In *States and Social Revolutions: A Comparative Analysis of France, Russia, and China,* Skocpol studies the factors that are essential to the success of peasant revolutions in a selection of countries. To study complicated processes such as social revolution and its relation to the political structures of regimes, Skocpol focuses her attention on the contrast between France, Russia, and China. These detailed cases are contrasted with control cases such as England and Prussia. The control cases serve the comparative role of the prior approval ratings in the quantitative example given earlier. This approach allows Skocpol to study each of the cases in great detail and to have confidence in the measurement of such concepts as types of revolution and various aspects of regime structure. The result is a widely praised multidimensional account of the necessary conditions of success for peasant revolutions.

FUNDAMENTAL CONTROVERSIES IN HYPOTHESIS TESTING

While there is debate over the relative merits of qualitative and quantitative hypothesis testing, there are also more fundamental critiques of hypotheses testing. The quantitative and qualitative hypotheses are different strategies to accomplish the same goal. In both approaches observations are compared against hypotheses about the essential nature of the social world. In the qualitative example Skocpol is testing hypotheses about the underlying nature of social revolution. This assumes that there is an underlying nature of social revolutions. Some critics of the hypothesis testing contend that there is no singular underlying social nature. These authors, mostly associated with poststructuralism, argue that there is no singular structure of society about which one can generalize or that one can discover through repeated observation (for a famous statement of this argument, see Derrida 1978).

Other authors focus their criticism not on the absence of a stable world to observe, but instead on the tools that social scientists have to observe the world (assuming that such a stable world exists). These critics allege that social measurement is inherently filled with biases. Observation, these critics allege, is inseparable from the observer. If this is the case, especially given the importance of social values to humans, there is no such thing as neutral observation of the social world. The result is that all hypothesis tests are suspect. Many of these critics recommend exploring the social world through admittedly biased accounts and narratives rather than the "at-a-distance" observation implied by the typical hypothesis testing framework (Shank 2002).

SEE ALSO *Scientific Method; Social Science*

BIBLIOGRAPHY

Babbie, Earl. 1995. *The Practice of Social Research.* 7th ed. Belmont, CA: Wadsworth.

Brady, Henry E., and David Collier, eds. 2004. *Rethinking Social Inquiry: Diverse Tools, Shared Standards.* Lanham, NY: Rowman and Littlefield.

Derrida, Jacques. 1978. *Writing and Difference.* Trans. Alan Bass. Chicago: University of Chicago Press.

Goertz, Gary, and Harvey Starr, eds. 2003. *Necessary Conditions: Theory, Methodology, and Applications.* Lanham, MD: Rowman and Littlefield.

King, Gary, Robert O. Keohane, and Sidney Verba. 1994. *Designing Social Inquiry: Scientific Inference in Qualitative Research.* Princeton, NJ: Princeton University Press.

Shank, Gary D. 2002. *Qualitative Research: A Personal Skills Approach.* Upper Saddle River, NJ: Prentice Hall.

Skocpol, Theda. 1979. *States and Social Revolutions: A Comparative Analysis of France, Russia, and China.* New York: Cambridge University Press.

Scott E. Robinson

HYPOTHESIS, NESTED

The term *nested hypothesis* sometimes refers to a group of hypotheses—that is, tentative assumptions or hypothetical factors in an experimental model—and other times to a subordinate hypothesis within a group. A nested hypothesis is the same as its non-nested analogue, except that one or more of the parameters in the non-nested hypothesis is constrained or limited in the nested hypothesis. To be considered nested, then, a hypothesis must meet the following conditions. First, it must be one among a group of related hypotheses. Second, all of the hypotheses must have some ordering pattern to them. This ordering pattern causes some hypotheses to be logical subsets of other hypotheses. It is possible for all but one hypothesis to be a subset of another hypothesis. Any hypothesis that is a subset of another hypothesis is nested. Third, when the hypotheses are ordered, each hypothesis must completely contain all the hypotheses preceding it. This condition of containment or nesting is the source of the nested hypothesis's name.

Research programs sometimes are designed so that there are multiple groups of hypotheses. In these cases, each of the groups may consist of nested hypotheses, but none are nested with respect to any other group. This type of situation is sometimes referred to as *partially nested*. Also some research disciplines reverse the ordering so that the main hypothesis comes first and the nested hypotheses follow it. This situation usually occurs in written material and not when the hypotheses are stated mathematically.

A common situation in which nested hypotheses often occur is traditional hypothesis testing using an alternative null hypothesis. The null hypothesis is an alternative to the hypothesis being tested where the explanatory factors being researched have no impact on the situation under consideration. When the null hypothesis is simply the testing hypothesis with one of the parameters set at any constant, then nesting exists. If, for example, a researcher was looking for factors influencing voting decisions and one of the factors chosen was birth year, the null hypothesis would be that birth year is unimportant (and that parameter would be set to zero). In this case, the hypotheses are nested because the null hypothesis is completely included within the main hypothesis.

Nested hypotheses have been around as long as scientific research. It is both logical and easy to use a null hypothesis in cases where the factor being examined simply becomes unimportant. Nested hypotheses also frequently occur in the social sciences when researchers are investigating a primary hypothesis. Sometimes researchers will also examine secondary hypotheses (dependant on the primary one) as nested hypotheses. There are, however, conditions under which nested hypotheses should only be used with caution. Nested hypotheses are sometimes used solely for ease of computation, without any underlying research basis. Before using nested hypotheses, researchers should make certain that the question being researched provides a substantive logical reason for using nesting.

A significant problem that nested models have is deviance. As the number of parameters in a model is decreased, model deviance automatically increases. In instances where there is a significant amount of nesting, the deviance can rise substantially. The difference between the deviances of two models is the basis for comparing their reliability. Therefore if there are a significant number of parameter changes, there will automatically be a bias in favor of the more complicated model, irrespective of the real accuracy increase. According to some experts in statistics, when analysis techniques such as the log-likelihood are involved, it is impossible for a nested model to have a larger maximum than the associated non-nested model.

A lesser concern is that there are different ways of nesting hypotheses. Population groupings provide an example of this. These groupings can either be superordinated, such that one group is separated out in each nesting, or divided, in which case some of the constituent groups become one nested hypothesis and the remainder become the other hypothesis. These latter subgroups are both nested with respect to the main hypothesis but not with respect to each other. This is a different situation from the former grouping condition, where each new hypothesis is nested with respect to all preceding hypotheses. In order to compare the models and their results, it is necessary to know which approach was used. In cases where nested hypotheses are not appropriate or desirable, there are a number of Bayesian, categorical, generalized linear model, and likelihood data-analysis techniques that can be used in place of the traditional hypothesis/null hypothesis framework.

SEE ALSO *Hypothesis and Hypothesis Testing; Regression; Regression Analysis*

BIBLIOGRAPHY

Agresti, Alan. 1996. *An Introduction to Categorical Data Analysis.* New York: Wiley Inter-Science.

Agresti, Alan. 2002. *Categorical Data Analysis.* New York: Wiley Inter-Science.

Carlin, Bradley P., and Thomas A. Louis. 2000. *Bayes and Empirical Bayes Methods for Data Analysis.* 2nd ed. Washington, DC: Chapman and Hall/CRC.

Fox, John. 1997. *Applied Regression Analysis, Linear Models, and Related Methods.* London: Sage.

Long, J. Scott. 1997. *Regression Models for Categorical and Limited Dependent Variables.* London: Sage.

Weisstein, Eric W. 2002. *CRC Concise Encyclopedia of Mathematics.* 2nd ed. Washington, DC: Chapman and Hall/CRC.

David B. Conklin

I

IBM

SEE *Microelectronics Industry.*

IBN KHALDŪN
1332–1406

Ibn Khaldūn was born in Tunis in 1332 as the child of an influential and politically active family and died 1406 in Cairo. He had a traditional education, studying the Qur'an and Islamic law; later he also studied mathematics and philosophy. He held several official positions for different rulers in North Africa's Maghreb region, but as a consequence of political changes he lost his office in Fez and moved to Andalusia, where the sultan of Granada entrusted him with diplomatic negotiations with Pedro the Cruel, the king of Castile. Eventually Ibn Khaldūn quit the service of the sultan and moved back to the Maghreb, where he held several high political offices and lived with Berber tribes. During a three-year stay with one of these tribes he wrote the *Muqaddimah*, which he continued to edit for the rest of his life. In 1382 he moved to Cairo, where he spent the second part of his life, becoming a close counselor of Sultan Barquq, who appointed him professor and *qadi* (supreme judge)—an office that Ibn Khaldūn lost and regained several times. Aside from his scholarly works, he is known particularly for his encounter with the Mongolian conqueror Timur (Tamerlane) in 1401 during the latter's siege of Damascus. During their meeting Ibn Khaldūn discussed the history of the Arab world with Timur before the Mongolian army razed the city of Damascus, but spared Ibn Khaldūn's life.

Ibn Khaldūn's main work is his world history *Kitāb al-ʿIbar* (*Book of Examples*), a several-volume history of the known world incorporating a comprehensive introduction, the *Muqaddimah*, which is considered to be a singular achievement in his time. In the *Muqaddimah* Ibn Khaldūn develops the science of human civilization or culture (*ʿIlm al-ʿUmrān*) to describe and analyze the history of human society. The main concept he uses for this endeavor is the *ʿaṣabiyya*. This term has been translated as "group feeling," "solidarity," "blood ties," "esprit de corps," and even "national spirit." *Aṣabiyya* refers mainly to family ties, but Ibn Khaldūn also extends its meaning to alliances and clientships. It is conceived as a vitalizing force of group cohesion enabling its bearers to exert power. The strength of the *ʿaṣabiyya* plays a determining role in the rise and fall of patrimonial empires, particularly those following the reign of the caliphs (the four kings ruling after Muhammad's death). Rural tribesmen, or bedouins, are characterized as having a strong *ʿaṣabiyya*, in contrast to sophisticated urban dwellers, who have a weak *ʿaṣabiyya* but highly developed crafts and sciences. In the *Muqaddimah* Ibn Khaldūn distinguishes rural or tribal life (*badāwa*) from urban or civilized life (*ḥaḍāra*), and a rural economy based on sustenance from an urban economy in which human labor generates value, serving to make profit and accumulate capital. He analyzes urban life, examining in detail how growing cities develop and manage their commerce, law, and education. Cities are the locations of a growing division of labor, producing specialized crafts that require time and resources to be learned. Having specific requirements that can only be met by urban civilizations of sufficient size, the sciences develop in larger, longer-lasting urban civilizations. Ibn Khaldūn discusses sciences such as reading and interpreting the Qur'an, jurisprudence, mathematics, medicine, natural sciences, and occult sciences. Some sciences are criticized for their lack of religious faith (e.g., Greek philosophy) or for not adhering to historical facts (e.g., astrology and alchemy). Ibn Khaldūn argues that growing sophistication leads to decadence and corruption, weakening the *ʿaṣabiyya* and making urban civilization prone to attacks and destruction by tribes with a strong *ʿaṣabiyya*. These tribes in turn will settle down and become urbanized, generating a cycle of fall and decline of civilizations that contrasts starkly with later European conceptions of progressive development.

Ibn Khaldūn's work was repopularized by orientalists in nineteenth-century Europe. He has been regarded as a forefather of history, sociology, and political science, and his economic theory was seen as anticipating the political economic theories of both Adam Smith and Karl Marx, the former in his insistence on the importance of free markets and free trade, and both in his theory of value. In all of these disciplines there is debate about the extent to which Ibn Khaldūn directly or indirectly influenced classic European social scientists. His historical analysis was reapplied in different contexts by proponents of anticolonial movements. Accordingly, his work has been situated in many different contexts, and its interpretations range from carefully applied hermeneutics to political polemics.

BIBLIOGRAPHY

Ibn Khaldūn. 1958. *The Muqaddimah: An Introduction to History*. Trans. Franz Rosenthal. 3 vols. London: Routledge and Kegan Paul.

Simon, Róbert. 2002. *Ibn Khaldūn: History as Science and the Patrimonial Empire*. Trans. Klára Pogátsa. Budapest: Akadémiai Kiadó, 2002.

Spalding, Tim. Ibn Khaldun on the Web. http://www.isidore-of-seville.com/ibnkhaldun/.

Lars Frers

IBO

SEE *Negro.*

ICEBERG SLIM

SEE *Pimps.*

ID

SEE *Equilibrium in Psychology; Freud, Sigmund.*

IDEAL TYPE

An *ideal type* is a methodological construct developed by German sociologist Max Weber (1864–1920). Key to his formulation of ideal types is a focus on what motivates social action. Weber believed that we can understand human action by discovering the subjective meanings actors attach to their own behavior and to the behavior of others. For Weber, subjective meanings are important in understanding the laws and regularities that create and govern social structures. It is possible to discover these regularities because uniformity of social action is widespread; actions are frequently repeated by the same individual and they correspond to the subjective meaning the actors attach to them.

An ideal type serves as a way to determine similarities as well as deviations found in empirical cases. Ideal types do not refer to moral ideals or to statistical averages; they do not describe an individual course of action, or an ideal case, but a typical one. They are analytical constructs that enable the researcher to develop hypotheses linking the types with the conditions that brought about the event, phenomena, or social structure, or with consequences that follow from its emergence. Because they are composites of all the necessary features of an act or action, these types rarely appear in real life and do not represent the only possibility for a particular course of action. In other words, ideal types do not exhaust or fully reflect concrete reality. Rather they are analytical tools that allow the researcher to find features that are common among all the varied and unique social and historical realities in order to conduct comparative analyses. Classifying types of motivated action allows us to make systematic typological distinctions, such as between types of authority, while also providing a basis for investigating historical developments.

Weber distinguishes four basic ideal types to describe motivated social action: *zweckrational, wertrational, affectual,* and *traditional.* He organizes these types of action in terms of their rationality and irrationality. *Zweckrational* action is social action in which individuals rationally choose both goals and means. *Wertrational* action is characterized by striving for a goal, which in itself may not be rational, but which is nonetheless pursued rationally. Affectual social action is grounded in the emotional state of the actor, rather than in the rational weighing of means and ends. Traditional action is guided by customary habits of thought, by reliance on "the way it's always been done." Weber's concern is with modern European and North American society, where he saw behavior increasingly dominated by goal-oriented rationality, whereas earlier it tended to be motivated by tradition, affect, or value-oriented rationality.

The most understandable type, according to Weber, is *zweckrational* action because it determines rationally

INTERNATIONAL ENCYCLOPEDIA OF THE SOCIAL SCIENCES, 2ND EDITION organized and administered structures like bureaucracies. Bureaucratic organizations are characterized by depersonalization, routinization, predictability, and the rational calculation of costs and benefits. Using ideal types, Weber was able to argue that the characteristic form of modern institutional organizations, such as the state, the corporation, the military, and the church, is bureaucratic.

SEE ALSO *Bureaucracy; Weber, Max*

BIBLIOGRAPHY

Weber, Max. 1946. *From Max Weber: Essays in Sociology.* Trans. and eds. Hans Gerth and C. Wright Mills. New York: Oxford University Press.

Weber, Max. 1947. *Max Weber: The Theory of Social and Economic Organization.* Ed. Talcott Parsons; trans. Talcott Parsons and A. M. Henderson. New York: Free Press.

Weber, Max. 1978. *Economy and Society: An Outline of Interpretive Sociology.* Eds. Guenther Roth and Claus Wittich; trans. Ephraim Fischoff et al. Berkeley: University of California Press.

Deborah L. Rapuano

IDEALISM

In philosophy, *idealism* designates a variety of historical positions since Plato (c. 428–348 or 347 BCE). The general characteristics of idealism derive from its historical examples. In metaphysics, *idealism* stands for a general belief about the nature of reality. In epistemology, it represents the belief that only a certain kind of reality is intelligible to the human mind. In Plato, whose idealism is influenced by the pre-Socratic philosopher Parmenides (born c. 515 BCE), the metaphysical and the epistemological aspects of idealism are combined in such a way that only ideas (or Forms) are fully real and only ideas are fully intelligible (compare Plato, *Phaedo* 65A–67B, and *Republic* 506B–518D). All forms of idealism hold that intelligible structures ("ideas") are part of the world itself rather than merely interpretations or constructs of the mind. As a result, idealist philosophers assume either a partial or a complete identity between intelligible structures and reality itself. In the most extreme case—namely, that of the Irish philosopher George Berkeley (1685–1753)—ideas and minds are said to be the only reality there is.

Furthermore, all forms of idealism hold that intelligible structures rather than matter or physical bodies constitute the foundation of reality. In this sense, idealism is opposed to materialism and physicalism in metaphysics or ontology. Idealists also generally hold that what is known or knowable about the world are ideal entities (e.g., conceptual structures, laws, principles, values) that are either inherent in things as their essence or that function as their normative archetypes. In this sense, idealism is opposed to realism in epistemology.

Among the major idealist philosophies after Plato are the rationalist idealism of Gottfried Wilhelm Leibniz (1646–1716), according to whom reality consists of infinitely many ideal entities called monads ("metaphysical atoms"); Berkeley's empirical or psychological idealism ("to be is to be perceived"); the transcendental or critical idealism of Immanuel Kant (1724–1804), who in the *Critique of Pure Reason* (first edition, 1781) states that "the conditions of the *possibility of experience* in general are likewise conditions of the *possibility of the objects of experience*" (A 158); German idealism represented primarily by Johann Gottlieb Fichte (1762–1814), Friedrich Wilhelm Joseph Schelling (1775–1854), and Georg Wilhelm Friedrich Hegel (1770–1831); the British idealism of Thomas Hill Green (1836–1882), Francis Herbert Bradley (1846–1924), and Bernard Bosanquet (1848–1923); and the American idealism of Josiah Royce (1855–1916).

Idealism achieved its most highly developed form and its most comprehensive and ambitious expression in post-Kantian German idealism and in Hegel's system in particular. Although insisting that he remained perfectly true to the spirit of Kant's philosophy, Fichte made the first decisive step beyond Kant by abandoning the thing-in-itself as well as the dualism of concept and intuition in favor of a unified first principle, the absolute ego. In this way, he very much set the agenda for post-Kantian German idealism's drive toward a holistic system based on a monistic principle. Scholarship since the 1950S has pointed out that a rivaling realist tendency with dualistic aspects continued to be an ingredient in post-Kantian idealism, as can be seen in the philosophies of the later Fichte and Schelling.

Hegel's strict monism conceived of the totality of reality or "the absolute" as a self-determining system exhibiting the structure of a self-referential, self-conscious subject called spirit. Spirit unfolds in human history and achieves complete self-recognition in Hegel's speculative idealism. The conceptual structure of spirit is that of the Concept or the Idea: "The Absolute is the universal and One Idea" (Hegel 1831, §213). At the heart of Hegel's system, for which the *Phenomenology of Spirit* (1807) initially served as an introduction, is the three-part *Science of Logic*. In three books titled *Being* (1812), *Essence* (1813), and *The Concept* (1816), the *Logic* develops the categories ("thought-determinations") that are supposed to provide the intelligible structure of spirit's external existence as nature, subjective, objective, and absolute spirit. These forms of spirit in externality comprise a philosophy of nature, a philosophy of mind (soul, consciousness, self-consciousness), a moral and political philosophy, and a philosophy of religion, the arts, and philosophy itself. The categories of the *Logic* are derived by means of the dialectical method through which concepts are shown to generate an opposite that is nonetheless also their necessary complement (e.g., no ground without a grounded) and must therefore be combined in a new concept in order to capture the whole of which they are merely a part. The dialectical process continues until an all-inclusive concept (the "absolute Idea") is reached. Hegel claims that the categories are generated autonomously by thought itself and have objective validity. His *Logic* is thus an epistemology just as much as it is an ontology. According to Hegel, it replaces traditional metaphysics.

Idealism is also used to characterize basic approaches in ethics, aesthetics, social ethics, and political science, where it is referred to as *practical idealism*. Idealism has been criticized for being inherently teleological in that it typically focuses on the consummation of the process of cognition in an ideal state of total (self-)knowledge or in the achievement or eschatological projection of an "end of history" (both tendencies are manifest primarily in Fichte, Schelling, and Hegel). This seems to contradict the open-endedness of the process of cognition as well as that of history. The future seems either closed or predetermined. Both assumptions contradict our normal intuitions as well as scientific rationality. Idealism's attempt to overcome dualisms such as appearance and reality, nature and spirit, mind and matter, concept and intuition has also been criticized for making the mind, self, thought, or spirit the only true reality, thus abandoning the realistic element that normally accounts for the content of knowledge. Thus in Hegel the object or "other" turns out to be the self in disguise and genuine otherness seems to have disappeared. All cognition becomes self-cognition and reality a self-manifestation of reason. A charitable reading of idealist philosophies will point out, however, that to the extent that all knowledge is mediated by concepts or acts of interpretation, an ideal element in all cognition remains an irreducible factor. Thus this criticism must be directed primarily at those idealist positions that leave no room for ontological otherness.

SEE ALSO *Epistemology; Hegel, Georg Wilhelm Friedrich; Materialism; Philosophy of Science*

BIBLIOGRAPHY

Ameriks, Karl, ed. 2000. *The Cambridge Companion to German Idealism.* Cambridge, U.K.: Cambridge University Press.

Ewing, Alfred Cyril, ed. 1957. *The Idealist Tradition: From Berkeley to Blanshard.* Glencoe, IL: Free Press.

Hegel, G. W. F. 1990. *Encyclopedia of the Philosophical Sciences in Outline, and Critical Writings,* ed. Ernst Behler. New York: Continuum.

McDowell, John. 1994. *Mind and World.* Cambridge, MA: Harvard University Press.

Sandkühler, Hans Jörg, ed. 2005. *Handbuch Deutscher Idealismus.* Stuttgart: J. B. Metzler.

Vesey, Godfrey, ed. 1982. *Idealism, Past and Present.* Cambridge, U.K.: Cambridge University Press.

Klaus Brinkmann

IDENTIFICATION, RACIAL

Racial identification occurs when individuals consider themselves to be a part of an imagined conglomerate of people who are presumed to share certain physical, cultural, intellectual, and moral traits. This identification can be made for cultural, social, legal, or political purposes, and it involves both self-identification and categorization. *Self-identification* is the choice individuals make when confronted with racial choices. The options usually offered in the U.S. context are white, black, Asian, and Native American. *Categorization* refers to the way that people are racially identified by others. Economic analysis shows that racial-identification norms arise from the simultaneous processes of self-identification, which is achieved via within-group altruism, and categorization, which is achieved via between-group altruism. The relative payoffs to social interactions are influenced by and contribute to intergroup differences in wealth and power. It is of no small import that the categories one may racially identify with or be categorized with today are a colonial invention, created to justify the enslavement of Africans and the genocide of Native Americans (see Allen 1994).

The idea of "race" involves the notion that all of the people in the world can be divided into discrete categories, based on shared physical and cultural traits. A key notion in the idea of race is that not only can inferences be made about people's moral, intellectual, or social value on the basis of physical characteristics such as skin color or hair texture, but also that these same traits are expected to be passed down to offspring. In the United States, as Ashley Montagu points out in *Man's Most Dangerous Myth* (1997), to accept the idea of race is to accept the notion that races are populations of people whose physical differences are innately linked with significant cultural and social differences, and that these innate hierarchical differences can be measured and judged. Thus, when people are asked to identify with one or more racial categories on survey forms, they are really being asked to report where they fall within this colonial hierarchy. And when one categorizes people in this way, one is, in effect, placing them within this same hierarchy.

Although race is an invented categorization scheme, the idea that race is real and important has become hegemonic in the United States, where people have been trained to identify others by race. If people in the United States see someone and don't know "what they are," they often get inquisitive or begin to feel uncomfortable. As Eduardo Bonilla-Silva points out in "The Essential Social Fact of Race" (1999), race is about "what you are," while ethnicity is about "where you are from." Thus to be unable to racially identify others can create confusion about "what they are."

It may be surprising that, although people seem to view racial categories as fixed and based on fact, these classifications have changed quite a bit over the course of U.S. history. In fact, the racial classifications used by the U.S. Census have changed each time the Census has been carried out. In 1880, the U.S. Census categories were: White, Black, Mulatto, Chinese, and Indian. A decade later, Quadroon, Octoroon, Japanese, Samoan, Other Asian, Other Pacific Islander, and Some Other Race were added, only to be taken out again, along with mulatto, in 1900. Mexican was added temporarily in 1930. After many changes, the Census categories used in 2000 were White; Black, African American, or Negro; American Indian or Alaska Native; Asian Indian; Chinese; Filipino; Japanese; Korean; Vietnamese; Native Hawaiian; Guamanian or Chamorro; Samoan; Other Asian; Other Pacific Islander; and Some Other Race. In addition, in 2000, people were given the option of checking off as many of these options as they wished, thereby greatly increasing the number of racial choices available to people.

Notably, people were given the opportunity to identify themselves multiracially in 2000 because of a political campaign to allow people more than one choice on Census forms. This is just one of many campaigns that have altered the ways racial classifications are used. There is also a strong movement to dissolve the use of race in public policy altogether. This has resulted in the passage of Proposition 209 in California in 1996 and the adoption of Proposition 2 in Michigan in 2006. Both of these propositions prohibit all state and local government entities from using race, ethnicity, color, gender, or national origin to make decisions about public employment, public education, or government contracting. California also witnessed another movement to remove racial and ethnic identifications from data collection efforts, in the form of Proposition 54, the Classification by Race, Ethnicity, Color and National Origin Initiative.

Following the defeat of this proposition in 2003, the American Sociological Association (ASA) issued a statement about the importance of being able to collect data on racial identifications. The ASA also published a statement in 2002 arguing that, although racial categories are socially constructed, it is important to ask people to give their racial self-identification in data collection efforts, insofar as this provides vital information about inequalities in educational, labor market, health care, and other outcomes. In other words, as long as a social meaning is given to race, it is important to know how people identify themselves racially and how this identification affects their prospects for success.

The creation of the Hispanic category was also the result of political campaigns, primarily in the 1960s. Hispanics or Latinos/as are currently the largest and fastest-growing minority group in the United States. However, according to the regulations used by the U.S. Census, Hispanic is an ethnic, not a racial category. Thus, Hispanics, just like non-Hispanics, are asked to choose between the various racial categories on the Census form. Other data collection efforts, such as those used by some educational institutions in the United States, include Hispanic as an option, although these classification schemes are often designated as racial or ethnic self-identification. Hispanic, in many ways, functions as a racialized category in the United States, insofar as people use physical cues to determine whether or not someone is Hispanic. However, the category Hispanic, like the categories Arab or Middle-Eastern, is a result of a different set of historical processes than those through which the categories White, Black, Asian, and Native American were created. European scholars writing in the seventeenth century generally restricted themselves to these latter four categories in their pseudo-scientific work on the characteristics of the human races.

Despite this tainted history, racial identification cannot be seen solely as an act of dominance, for it can also be an act of resistance. By identifying themselves racially, as opposed to ethnically, some Hispanics may be resisting white privilege and expressing solidarity with other people of color. Indeed, there is evidence that Latinos who experience discrimination are more likely to racially identify as Latino than those who have not experienced discrimination.

Racial identifications are thus social, cultural, political, and legal categories that are the result of particular historical processes, and that continue to be subject to changing ideas about the reality of race. As social categories, they are related to various social outcomes such as educational attainment and wages. As cultural categories, they are imbued with meaning and associated with certain cultural characteristics, such as language, dialect, or musical preferences. As political categories, they can be used to mobilize people behind a common agenda. And as legal categories, they have been used to prevent miscegenation, to enforce segregation, and to maintain racial slavery.

SEE ALSO *Formation, Racial; Hierarchy; Identity; Identity, Social; Latino National Political Survey; Multidimensional Inventory of Black Identity; Politics, Identity; Race; Racial Classification; Racism; Self-Classification; Self-Identity; Stratification*

BIBLIOGRAPHY

Allen, Theodore W. 1994. *The Invention of the White Race: Racial Oppression and Social Control.* New York: Verso.

Bonilla-Silva, Eduardo. 1999. The Essential Social Fact of Race. *American Sociological Review* 64 (6): 899–906.

Dalmage, Heather. 2000. *Tripping on the Color Line: Black-White Multiracial Families in a Racially Divided World.* New Brunswick, NJ: Rutgers University Press.

Darity, William, Jr., Patrick L. Mason, and James B. Stewart. 2006. The Economics of Identity: The Origin and Persistence of Racial Norms. *Journal of Economic Behavior and Organizations* 60 (3): 283–305.

Martín-Alcoff, Linda. 2006. *Visible Identities: Race, Gender, and the Self.* Oxford: Oxford University Press.

Montagu, Ashley. 1997. *Man's Most Dangerous Myth: The Fallacy of Race.* 6th ed. Walnut Creek, CA: AltaMira Press.

Sanjek, Roger. 1996. The Enduring Inequalities of Race. In *Race,* eds. Steven Gregory and Roger Sanjek. New Brunswick, NJ: Rutgers University Press.

Smedley, Audrey. 2007. *Race in North America: Origin and Evolution of a World View.* 3rd ed. Boulder, CO: Westview Press.

Tanya Maria Golash-Boza

IDENTIFICATION PROBLEM

The identification problem is a deductive, logical issue that must be solved before estimating an economic model. In a demand and supply model, the equilibrium point belongs to both curves, and many presumptive curves can be drawn through such a point. We need prior information on the slopes, intercepts, and error terms to identify the true from the presumptive demand and supply curves. Such prior information will give a set of structural equations. If the equations are linear, and the error terms are normally distributed with zero mean and constant variance, then a model is formed for estimation.

A typical identification process may fix the demand curve and shift the supply curve, cutting the demand curve at many points to trace it out. By the zero mean assumption of the error term, half the observations are expected above and half below the demand curve. In the same way, the supply curve can be identified. This method originated with Ragnar Frisch (1938) and Trygve Haavelemo (1944). Tjalling Koopmans evolved the order and rank conditions for identifying linear models (1949). Franklin Fisher's work was the first major textbook on the subject (1966), and Charles Manski extended it to the social sciences (1995).

The order condition is the most used technique for identifying a model. Each equation in the model has a predetermined variable that is either given from outside of the model (exogenous) or determined in the model (endogenous) but fitted with a lag. A standard exogenous variable for the supply curve is technology, T, and for the demand curve it is income, Y. A two-function model with $Q = f(P, Y)$ for the demand and $Q = f(P, T)$ for the supply, where P is price and Q is quantity, meets the order condition for identification by excluding technology from the demand curve, and by excluding income from the supply curve. The number of excluded variables EV is one in each equation. The order condition requires that EV equal the number of exogenous variables M, less one. An equation is exactly identified if $EV = M - 1$, overidentified if $EV > M - 1$, and underidentified otherwise. In the two-function model above, the equations are exactly identified because the exogenous variables P and Q yield $M - 1 = 1$, and each equation has only one excluded variable, Y or T.

The rank condition guarantees that the equations can be solved. Econometric texts often create a spreadsheet to demonstrate the rank condition. For the model above, the column is labeled with the variables Q, P, Y, T, and the rows contain information on the equations. Each cell has either a 0 for an excluded variable or a 1 for an included variable. For the demand function above, the entry for the row vector is [1, 1, 1, 0] and for the supply function [1, 1, 0, 1]. To identify the demand curve for the order condition, first locate the zero in its vector, then pick up the corresponding number in the supply vector. The picked-up number, which is 1, should be equal to $M - 1$, which is also 1. With many equations, the numbers that we pick up will array into many rows and columns. The general rank test requires one to find $M - 1$ rows and $M - 1$ columns in that array whose elements are not all zeros, because such a $(M - 1)(M - 1)$ spreadsheet will make the model solvable.

SEE ALSO *Frisch, Ragnar; Koopmans, Tjalling; Structural Equation Models*

BIBLIOGRAPHY

Fisher, Franklin M. 1966. *The Identification Problem in Econometrics.* New York: McGraw-Hill.

Frisch, Ragnar. 1938. Statistical Versus Theoretical Relations in Economic Macrodynamics. League of Nations memorandum. Geneva, Switzerland: League of Nations.

Haavelmo, Trygve. 1944. The Probability Approach in Econometrics. *Econometrica* 12 (July): 1–115.

Koopmans, Tjalling C. 1949. Identification Problem in Economic Model Construction. *Econometrica* 17: 15–144.

Koopmans, Tjalling C., Herman Rubin, and R. B. Leipnik. 1950. Measuring the Equation Systems of Dynamic Economics. In *Statistical Inference in Dynamic Economic Models*, ed. Tjalling C. Koopmans, 53–237. New York: Wiley.

Manski, Charles F. 1995. *Identification Problems in the Social Sciences*. Cambridge, MA: Harvard University Press.

Lall Ramrattan
Michael Szenberg

IDENTITIES, DEADLY

"Deadly identities" is the literal translation of the title of Amin Maalouf's nonfiction *Les identités meurtrières* (1998), which examines the issues and problems surrounding individuals having multiple social identities. Maalouf (b. 1949) is a Lebanese-born Catholic Arab novelist who has lived in Paris since 1977, writes in French, and is the 1993 winner of the Goncourt Prize, France's most prestigious literary award. For Maalouf, the term *identity* is a "false friend." "It starts by reflecting a perfectly permissible aspiration, then before we know where we are it has become an instrument of war" (Maalouf [1998] 2000, p. 32). The meaning of *identity* here is that of social identity, which results from our identification with others in social groups according to shared religion, ethnicity, nationality, gender, age, occupation, place of residence, and so forth. Social identities generate violence when social groups are in conflict, and their respective members behave antagonistically toward each other, though they may have no animosity toward one another as individuals. Such conflicts have become more common in the age of globalization, Maalouf believes, because of an ever-accelerating intermingling between peoples. For many, then, the dilemma this often creates is a choice between a complete loss or a vigorous assertion of traditional identities—between the disintegration of identity and fundamentalism.

But Maalouf argues that this choice is an illusion, because people do not have just one social identity, which is then their individual identity; rather, they have many social identities, the specific combination of which gives each person a unique individual identity. This is the concept of *complex identity*, and it is not unchanging, but changes over a person's lifetime, as do a person's associa-

tions and experiences. Maalouf offers several interpretations of complex identity. One is the idea of a limiting concept: the "more ties" one has, the "rarer and more particular" one's identity becomes (Maalouf 1998 [2000], p. 18). Alternatively, an individual's complex identity develops continuously over a lifetime as new characteristics are acquired "step by step" (p. 25). The meaning, however, that most directly targets the problem of violence is complex identity as that which individuals assemble and arrange for themselves out of their different social identities (p. 16), since this presupposes a capacity for reflection about one's social identities, which Maalouf sees as the best protection against the insanity of murder and butchery in the name of some "tribal" identity.

In this respect, Maalouf is close in his thinking to that of the 1998 Nobel laureate in economics, Amartya Sen (2006), who has also argued that individuals can appraise their identities rather than be captives of them. Both writers, then, closely associate individual identity with this reflective capacity. Their understanding of what it means to be an individual contrasts with the view in much of social science that takes individuals to be unconsciously responsive to a variety of motives, drives, and desires.

SEE ALSO *Ethnic Fractionalization; Ethnicity; Identity; Identity Matrix; Politics, Identity; Religion; Sen, Amartya Kumar; Tribalism; Violence*

BIBLIOGRAPHY

Maalouf, Amin. 1998. *Les identités meurtrières*. Paris: Grasset. Translated into English by Barbara Bray. 2000. *In the Name of Identity: Violence and the Need to Belong*. London: Harvill.

Sen, Amartya. 2006. *Identity and Violence: The Illusion of Destiny*. New York: Norton.

John B. Davis

IDENTITY

Identity is a pervasive concept in popular culture. Broadly speaking, *identity* refers to the overall character or personality of an individual or group. For example, a young mother might define her identity as that which reflects the essence of who she is (such as being a woman, spouse, and parent) and how she got to be that way. A business can have its own identity, perhaps defined by its unique corporate culture or its advertising history. Significant historical events like wars, natural disasters, or surges in immigration can play important roles in helping to define a nation's identity.

On the one hand, the defining features of identity frequently entail elements that must be "found" by an individual or group. For example, a musical group or the cast of a television show might have to work together for a long period of time before its performances flow smoothly and effortlessly and it is able to establish its own voice or overall character. Adolescents as well as adults can pass through *identity crises* that refer to periods of personal uncertainty or confusion. When a sports coach talks about his or her team finding its identity, this may refer to the development or recognition of a consistent way of playing or performing.

On the other hand, individuals or groups can also "lose" their identity through a variety of events or circumstances. For example, when politicians, celebrities, or other public figures engage in controversial behavior, those individuals must frequently work to reclaim or redefine their identities. A company that has made poor business decisions might be referred to as having lost its corporate identity. The modern phenomenon of *identity theft* is another example of identity loss, although it is more accurate to refer to this phenomenon as *identification* or *ID* theft. The popularity of the *identity theft* label suggests that an important part of lay definitions of individual identities are the public, demographic, and commercial means of identification.

As the previous examples illustrate, the popular boundaries of the identity concept are quite broad. This concept is similarly pervasive and broad in the theories and research of the social sciences and humanities. *Self* and *identity* are frequently used interchangeably by such theorists and researchers. In fact, sometimes writers will combine the terms into concepts such as *self-identity* or *ego-identity*. Within the social sciences and humanities, different disciplines emphasize different components of the concept. Thus, it is useful to consider how different fields define and operationalize identity.

Social science theorists and researchers distinguish a large number of different kinds of identity. Examples of identity types include racial, ethnic, group, social, religious, occupational, gender and sex role, cultural, physical and bodily, musical, athletic, academic, and so forth. Among these different identity types, a common distinction is made between *personal* and *social* identities. Personal identity usually refers to the unique characteristics of a person, including personality traits, personal values, opinions and preferences, physical characteristics, and career and lifestyle choices. In other words, these refer to aspects of a person's identity that are distinct and different from other people. Social identity usually refers to one's social roles, such as gender, racial, religious, political, ideological, and national group memberships. Typically, these roles involve ways that a person's identity is similar to others, such as sharing a physical characteristic, speaking a common language, having a similar social class or

socioeconomic status, practicing the same religion, or living in a common region.

Regardless of whether one focuses on personal or social facets, identity development involves a sense of sameness, continuity, and unity. Philosophically speaking, personal identity refers to the extent that an individual's characteristics are the same over time. That is, identity establishes the conditions that define a person's stable uniqueness. This can refer to the physical, psychological, and social aspects of the person. Thus, most social scientists agree that identity is something that develops over time and requires organization and integration, often achieved through the resolution of personal or social conflicts or crises. The failure to achieve some degree of identity coherence is thought to be a symptom of psychological, social, or cultural problems.

Identity also entails an individual commitment to a set of values and goals associated with specific characteristics. For example, much of personal identity involves identifying one's unique features and determining the value of those features and how they relate to a person's short-term and long-term goals. Social identity supposes an awareness of one's group memberships, as well as some level of commitment, closeness, or emotional attachment to those groups. People who highly value their social identities are more likely to act in ways that are consistent with those roles than people who do not value their social identities. Identity development is, therefore, tied to how people think about themselves and how they decide which aspects of their experience are most important as they define themselves. In other words, the development of identity involves personal and social processes of definition, construction, and negotiation.

HISTORY OF THE IDENTITY CONCEPT

The pervasiveness of identity-related concerns is a relatively recent cultural and historical phenomenon. The psychologist Roy Baumeister (1986) described several influential social trends in European and American societies running from about 1500 to 1800. During these centuries, a variety of social, cultural, and economic changes corresponded with a shift in how philosophers, artists, writers, and the lay public viewed personhood and identity. Since the Middle Ages, there has been a weakening of the importance of a person's geographical home and of the institutions of marriage and job in defining one's identity. At the same time, the formerly important roles of one's family of ancestry, social rank, gender, and religion have been at least somewhat trivialized. Thus, traditions and institutions that had previously defined people's identity lost importance and influence.

These changes corresponded with new views on what constituted a person's identity. For example, people began to consider the possibility that there is a hidden self; that individuality is important; that there is a separation of their public, social lives from their private lives; and that children develop and have their own potentialities worthy of attention. In other words, the boundaries of identity became increasingly broad and malleable. Baumeister (1986) argued that these trends continued through the twentieth century, reflecting an age of mass consumption, greater occupational choices, dramatic technological changes, and the marketing of both products and people. The net effect of these social, cultural, and economic changes is that people in industrialized societies are now plagued with difficulties in defining their identities. Because of the loss of traditional ways of knowing who one is, the more abstract, elusive sense of identity makes it increasingly difficult to define. Much more than was the case one hundred or two hundred years ago, people must work to find or uncover who they are, in order to resolve the dilemmas of modern personhood.

Contemporary identity requires choice, achievement, and frequent self-redefinitions as opposed to the passive assignment of identity of the past. With the widespread desire for establishing and determining one's individuality and uniqueness comes greater difficulty, choice, and effort in achieving this. For instance, modern identity can be constructed out of one's personality traits, material possessions, personal accomplishments, group memberships, and activities and organizations. For these reasons, various writers have labeled identity as "empty," "saturated," and "overburdened," and as reflecting "an epidemic of role distance" (Hoyle et al. 1999, p. 49). Some writers argue that European and American culture's extreme preoccupation with an inner, independent identity leads to a devaluing or ignoring of the social world and the potential negative effects of contemporary social arrangements. This causes a seeking out of experiences and material possessions in order to avoid feelings of worthlessness or identity confusion.

TREATMENTS OF IDENTITY IN THE SOCIAL SCIENCES

Identity is a topic of extensive theory and research for many of the social sciences. Two disciplines that have devoted a great deal of attention to identity are sociology and psychology. Sociologists generally define the overall self as consisting of multiple identities tied to the different roles a person plays in the social world. Early twentieth-century sociologists such as Charles Horton Cooley (1864–1929) and George Herbert Mead (1863–1931) emphasized how other people provide "reflected appraisals" that encourage the understanding and establishment of a sense of identity. In his 1959 book *The Presentation of Self in Everyday Life*, the sociologist Erving Goffman (1922–1982) brought a dramaturgical approach to social identity. Goffman theorized that people play social roles like actors on a stage, claiming and becoming committed to a particular public or group identity. Part of this identity includes a public "face" that a person claims and then defends in social interaction. In later writings, Goffman presented the idea of a "spoiled" identity, in which a person can be stigmatized as a result of deviant behaviors or personal characteristics.

More recently, the symbolic interactionist perspective has assumed a prominent role in the sociological approach to identity. Contemporary versions of symbolic interactionism examine how a person's identity is affected by the elements of social structure, in particular the social positions or roles that one plays and the meanings and expectations associated with those roles (Stets and Burke 2003). Role identities may differ in number, prominence, salience, and value to an individual, and sociologists have conducted a great deal of research on these aspects of role identity. For example, a greater number of role identities have been associated with greater resistance to stress and more positive mental health, particularly when those identities are voluntary or freely chosen ones rather than when they are conferred or obligatory.

The meaning of a role identity is something that a person must determine and negotiate. As such, it can be affected by the reactions of others. Over time, there can be changes in a role, as well as in the identity associated with that role. For example, when a person takes on a new role of being a spouse in a married couple, specific behaviors associated with that role must be defined and may change over time. In addition, the definition and boundaries of the spouse identity can change. Thus, the taking on, development, internalization, and changing of multiple roles comprise the most important features of identity from a sociological perspective.

Within psychology, the best-known treatment of identity comes from Erik Erikson's (1902–1994) psychosocial stages of development across the lifespan (Erikson 1968). When and how does a coherent sense of identity develop? Research suggests that identity concerns are especially prominent among late adolescents and early adults. This seems to be due to the fact that it is only by this time that young people become physically and sexually mature, are competent in abstract thought, show increased emotional stability, and have a certain amount of freedom from parental and peer constraints. Younger children are typically not assumed to have an identity (at least in the overall coherent and stable sense of the term). However, aspects of identity (e.g., age, sex, and race) have been shown to be important to the self-perceptions and self-definitions of younger, preadolescent children. Understanding how a person is similar to and different from others is an important part of identity formation. In this regard, significant others can help to define the developing sense of identity.

In Erikson's theory, adolescence is a time of increased power and responsibility and also a time when young adults must determine who they are and where they fit into their culture and society. Thus, the struggle for a sense of identity and the formation of a "philosophy of life" seems to be especially intense during this period. There are several different ways that young adults might deal with their identity struggles (Marcia 1980). For example, a person might show identity *foreclosure*. This can occur when people prematurely commit to and unquestioningly adopt the beliefs, values, or roles prescribed by parents rather than going through the process of developing their own beliefs, values, and career choices. Second, people may delay commitment in order to try out alternative identities, beliefs, roles, or behaviors. In this situation, called an identity *moratorium*, such people are actively caught up in the throes of the identity struggle and are striving to resolve it. However, they have yet to develop a coherent and stable identity.

A third possible outcome of the young adulthood identity crisis is called identity *diffusion*. This refers to an unwillingness to confront the challenge of charting a life course and a failure to achieve a stable and integrated sense of self. Unlike in the moratorium, such people show little concern or effort to resolve their self-doubt, apathy, and passivity. Finally, people can arrive at a sense of self and direction and form an integrated image of themselves as unique persons. This is called identity *achievement*. Such individuals have passed successfully through the identity crisis and are now able to make a commitment to a career objective and a personally meaningful set of beliefs and values. For Erikson and other identity theorists, adequate identity formation is the foundation of sound psychological health in adulthood. Identity confusion can interfere with important developmental transitions during the adult years.

More recent psychological approaches to identity include the idea that self-narratives or life stories serve as central features in the creation of a person's identity. Psychological research also shows that people engage in a wide variety of behaviors to construct, test, and confirm their identities. For example, social psychologists have studied the processes by which people present specific identity aspects to others and manage the impressions that others form of them. What makes particular identity characteristics salient is likely to be tied to the social setting or context. Psychologists are also interested in studying how organized cognitive structures (or schemata) serve to maintain a person's identity. For instance, cognitive structures can filter out competing or inconsistent information or lead to other forms of biased information processing that serves to protect or maintain one's identity.

Whereas sociologically based identity theories focus more on the different roles that constitute a person's identity, psychologically based social identity theory deals with how membership in groups is associated with self-categorization and social identities. For example, those who belong to the same group are seen as *ingroup* members, whereas nonmembers or those who belong to different groups are seen as *outgroup* members. A large amount of research has shown that such ingroup-outgroup categorization (sometimes based on arbitrarily defined group membership) results in ingroup favoritism and outgroup discrimination. Thus, it appears that merely belonging to a group can create meaningful social identities with strong attitudinal (e.g., prejudice) and behavioral (e.g., discrimination) implications.

Other disciplines within the social sciences and humanities also have utilized the identity concept in their theories and research. For example, political scientists are interested in the role of identity as a source of people's political beliefs or political party affiliation. They are also interested in how identity is affected by isolation, alienation, anomie, and social injustices in modern society and how these problems impact social structure, political party affiliation, political action, and international relations. As such, the identity concept is one of many factors that can affect political actions and larger social conflicts.

Political scientists sometimes focus on how membership in particular groups is associated with a specific identity that may have implications for social movements, community mobilization, and other forms of collective behavior. That is, through the identification or construction of a collective identity, groups may be able to increase pride and consciousness, mobilize resources, and bring about societal changes. In other words, groups may strive to expand the range of a particular identity characteristic into a political force with accompanying social and legislative reforms. This process is referred to as *identity politics*. Examples of identities that fall into this category include religion, race, ethnicity, gender, and physical disability. Critics have argued that politicizing an identity component can be counterproductive to the goal of social change. For example, by calling attention to a specific identity, a group may find it more difficult to address the social injustices associated with it. Or there may be broader social or cultural backlashes directed toward a group identity.

Anthropologists and other social scientists have explored the processes of cultural identification and cultural variations in identity construction. A popular distinction relates to identity differences that are based on independent (or individualistic) and interdependent (or collectivistic) cultural construals. Educational researchers consider the development of academic identity and the relationship of various identity facets to academic achievement. Business and marketing researchers examine the mechanisms and processes associated with developing a corporate or brand identity in consumers. Within the humanities, a great deal of attention has been devoted to cultural and historical trends in the construction and management of identity (e.g., identity politics) and how identity is represented in and affected by works of art, music, theater, and literature.

Some of the current issues related to the identity concept include how to best measure the different kinds of identities and how multiple identities (and conflicts among these) affect behavior in specific situations. In addition, the development of different kinds of identities and how they interrelate from childhood through adulthood has received little research attention. How do multiple identities overlap and affect individual and group behavior? This is a particularly important question when considering broad social, cultural, or nationalistic actions, where several different identities may combine or conflict. For example, adopted or biracial children may experience unique issues as they attempt to develop their racial or cultural identity. More broadly speaking, one of the effects of an increasingly multicultural world is that the establishment of one's identity may become more difficult or complicated. One interesting domain for identity theorists and researchers concerns how technological changes, particularly those associated with the Internet, affect identity processes. For example, the social scientist Sherry Turkle (1995) has shown that exploration of new, alternative, and multiple identities has become significantly easier and more varied through online communities, multiuser domains, role-playing games, and fantasy worlds.

In summary, identity is a very broad and influential concept in the social sciences and humanities. It has proven to be remarkably fluid and malleable, with different disciplines able to define identity in ways that best suit their purposes and emphases. The cultural and historical trends that led to changes in identity over the past several centuries are likely to continue to provide new challenges to identity formation in the future. Increasing globalization, industrial development, scientific advances, and technological innovations will mean that difficulties in defining identity will be a worldwide phenomenon.

SEE ALSO *Adolescent Psychology; Cyberspace; Economics, Behavioral; Economics, Stratification; Erikson, Erik; Ethnicity; Gender; Goffman, Erving; Groups; Hybridity; Identity Crisis; Identity Matrix; Identity, Social; Internet; Nation; Nationalism and Nationality; Performance; Personality; Politics, Gender; Politics, Identity; Popular Culture; Psychology; Race; Representation; Role Theory; Self-Classification; Self-Representation; Social Science; Sociology; Stages of Development; Values*

BIBLIOGRAPHY

Baumeister, Roy F. 1986. *Identity: Cultural Change and the Struggle for Self.* New York: Oxford University Press.

Erikson, Erik H. 1968. *Identity, Youth, and Crisis.* New York: Norton.

Hoyle, Rick H., Michael H. Kernis, Mark R. Leary, and Mark W. Baldwin. 1999. *Selfhood: Identity, Esteem, Regulation.* Boulder, CO: Westview.

Marcia, James E. 1980. Identity in Adolescence. In *Handbook of Adolescent Psychology*, ed. Joseph Adelson, 159–187. New York: Wiley.

Stets, Jan E., and Peter J. Burke. 2003. A Sociological Approach to Self and Identity. In *Handbook of Self and Identity*, eds. Mark R. Leary and June Price Tangney, 128–152. New York: Guilford.

Turkle, Sherry. 1995. *Life on the Screen: Identity in the Age of the Internet.* New York: Simon and Shuster.

Thomas M. Brinthaupt

IDENTITY, SOCIAL

Social identity is defined as an individual's identification *with* others. In contrast, the concept of personal identity can be understood as an individual's identity *apart* from others. At the same time, social identity and personal identity are clearly related. Furthermore, whereas individuals are usually thought to have a single personal identity, they have many social identities associated with the many different collections of other individuals with whom they identify. These different collections of other individuals are usually thought of as social groups, though there are different ways to understand the idea of a social group, explain its boundaries, and account for the attachment individuals have to social groups. For example, individuals might identify with others by race, gender, nationality, and religion (very large social groups or social categories), with those in their workplaces and communities (intermediate size social groups), and with friends and family members (small social groups). In all cases, social identity provides a social basis for how individuals see themselves—a *sense of self* or *self-image*—that depends on their seeing themselves as being much like a reflection of those others with whom they identify.

There are two broad approaches to understanding social identity: the social identity approach (particularly in the form of self-categorization theory) and the sociological approach to identity (Hogg, Terry, and White 1995). The social identity approach derives principally from the work of Henri Tajfel and John Turner, who explain social identity in terms of the individual's knowledge that he or she belongs to certain social groups, combined with the emotional and value significance this membership imparts. Self-categorization theory concerns the cognitive processes by which individuals come to identify with others and embrace membership in social groups. In experimental research, individuals exhibit in-group favoritism and out-group biases for arbitrarily constructed social identities. This can be understood as an "accentuation effect" of group membership, whereby once individuals believe a particular social category applies to them, they perceptually "accentuate" both the similarities among stimuli falling within that category and the differences between stimuli from that and other categories (Tajfel 1959). Tajfel argued that the accentuation effect helps explain such phenomena as stereotyping, prejudice, and ethnocentrism.

The sociological approach to identity derives from the symbolic interactionist thinking of George Mead, and assumes there to be a reciprocal relation between the self and society or between the self and individuals' social identities (Stryker 1980). Social groups are seen as being structured in terms of different roles, and individuals accordingly have different types of relationships to social groups depending on the roles they occupy in those groups (Stets and Burke 2000). Roles can be paired with counter-roles (such as parent and child), or in more complicated group and institutional settings (such as in business firms) where roles are more highly differentiated, they can exhibit a variety of interconnections with one another. On the assumption that there is a reciprocal relation between the self and society, roles are subject to interpretation and negotiation, while at the same time individuals generally seek to match their own self-conceptions or self-images with social expectations of their roles. Thus, whereas social identity theory focuses on in-group and out-group relationships with respect to particular social groups, the sociological approach focuses on how individuals' social identity relationships are structured and negotiated within social groups.

Neither the social identity approach nor the sociological approach to identity pays significant attention to the relationship between social identity and personal identity. Yet the meaning of social identity as "identification with others" implies that there is a separate someone who identifies with others, and thus that individuals have an identity apart from or over and above their social identification with others. Also, the idea that an individual has many social identities implies some concept of personal identity, if only because it assumes the existence of a single subject to whom those multiple identities belong. Thus, the concepts of social identity and personal identity are related to one another, and need ultimately to be explained jointly to give a full understanding of either concept. Unfortunately, little has been done to develop this more comprehensive kind of explanation.

SEE ALSO *Collective Wisdom; Communication; Gender; Groups; Groupthink; Identification, Racial; Identity; Identity Matrix; Mead, George Herbert; Prejudice; Race; Role Theory; Self-Classification; Self-Identity; Social Cognitive Map; Social Psychology; Society; Sociology; Symbols*

BIBLIOGRAPHY

Hogg, Michael A., Deborah J. Terry, and Katherine M. White. 1995. A Tale of Two Theories: A Critical Comparison of Identity Theory with Social Identity Theory. *Social Psychology Quarterly* 58 (4): 255–269.

Stets, Jan E., and Peter J. Burke. 2000. Identity Theory and Social Identity Theory. *Social Psychological Quarterly* 63 (3): 224–237.

Stryker, Sheldon. 1980. *Symbolic Interactionism: A Social Structural Version*. Menlo Park, CA: Benjamin/Cummings.

Tajfel, Henri. 1959. Quantitative Judgment in Social Perception. *British Journal of Psychology* 50: 16–29.

John B. Davis

IDENTITY CRISIS

"Identity versus Identity Confusion" is the fifth of Erik Erikson's eight psychosocial stages of development, which he developed in the late 1950s. Adolescence is the most salient time for defining identity, the process of determining the meaning, purpose, and direction of one's inner, unique core of self—while also maintaining some sense of sameness and continuity with one's past and of comfort within the context of one's culture. An identity crisis is "a necessary turning point, a crucial moment, when development must move one way or another, marshaling resources of growth, recovery, and further differentiation" (Erikson 1968, p. 16). The most common use of the term *identity crisis* refers to normative psychosocial development during the periods of adolescence and emerging adulthood. This concept of crisis, however, has been applied quite broadly, at times being used to include not only healthy individual growth but also other issues of individual therapy and reconsiderations of what it means to be part of a reconstituted nation in the process of rapid historical change.

Based on Erikson's epigenetic principle, each of the other seven psychosocial stages has implications for the quality of identity resolution. Along a continuum within each stage, a person will express healthier psychosocial development if that stage's crisis is resolved with more positive (syntonic) outcomes. Ideally, for example, one develops reasonable trust in the world, autonomy, initiative, efficacy, identity, interpersonal desire, worth, and finally with stage eight, satisfaction. The results of ego syntonic or dystonic outcomes may include viewing one's self as either protected or vulnerable in the world, self-controlled or disordered and dependent, ambitious or evasive, competent or incapable at tasks, committed or lacking conviction, loving or reclusive, productive and caring or not valued, and a success or a failure. Unsatisfactory aspects of one's identity in these areas (i.e., being more dystonic) may lead to crisis, in which one must rework a previous stage and seek a different outcome.

James Marcia has provided the most influential empirical framework for identity formation. He has focused on a behavioral expression of identity by investigating the processes of exploration of alternatives and commitment to values, beliefs, and goals in various life domains, such as career and ideologies. From the dimensions of exploration and commitment, he derived four identity statuses: Achievement (exploration resulting in commitment), Moratorium (present exploration with the intention of achieving a commitment), Foreclosure (ascribed commitment with no exploration), and Diffusion (no commitment whether exploration has taken place in the past or not). Moratorium is the status of "crisis" or exploration, defined by the need to arrive at a self-definition, which is actively propelled by the individual. In 1990 Alan Waterman described an important goal of identity exploration as the identification of potential talents, the development of which can lead to feelings of personal expressiveness. It is the responsibility of significant others to aid the individual in learning the process of exploration and to provide information that may help the individual to arrive at a commitment that is exemplified by continuity, "goodness of fit" within self, and appropriateness within one's social contexts. While each individual should find unique domains of importance, individuals identified as being in a state of long-term Diffusion, without meaningful self-definition in any domains of significance, may be perceived especially as being in need of counseling. These individuals approach the task of identity with passivity or perhaps apathy, and they have poor resolution of at least some of the other psychosocial stages of development.

Working within Erikson's psychosocial theoretical perspective, decades of research have emerged from Marcia's empirical framework focused on development in numerous and varied contexts (e.g., Marcia 1966; Kroger 2007). Examples of other contemporary approaches to identity and its measurement include the structural stage perspective, which focuses on internal structures that provide meaning making, and the sociocultural perspective, which focuses on the roles and status granted by one's society. These and other frameworks are described and critiqued by Jane Kroger in *Identity Development: Adolescence through Adulthood* (2007).

Mixed societal demands are particularly problematic for identity formation and its refinement at a time when one is seeking continuity or looking to find a sense of one's uniqueness yet still fit within one's societal parameters over time. In those instances in which one is part of a minority (e.g., by race, ethnicity, or sexual orientation), or if one has identifications with multiple groups (e.g., by being biracial), or if one is pulled by conflicting messages (e.g., those coming from the media and the family), an identity crisis is likely to emerge. Respect for diversity of self would go a long way in allowing people to be "uniquely themselves" while belonging to a community. Healthy "crisis" or exploration can afford people the opportunity to knowledgeably investigate choices in which there is positive meaning with regard to where they have come from, where they presently exist, and where they envision their future to be.

SEE ALSO *Ethnicity; Identity; Self-Concept; Self-Identity*

BIBLIOGRAPHY

Archer, Sally L., ed. 1994. *Interventions for Adolescent Identity Development.* Thousand Oaks, CA: Sage.

Erikson, Erik. 1950. *Childhood and Society.* New York: Norton.

Erikson, Erik. 1968. *Identity, Youth, and Crisis.* New York: Norton.

Kroger, Jane. 2007. *Identity Development: Adolescence through Adulthood.* Thousand Oaks, CA: Sage.

Marcia, James E. 1966. Development and Validation of Ego Identity Status. *Journal of Personality and Social Psychology* 3: 551–558.

Marcia, James E., Alan S. Waterman, David R. Matteson, et al. 1993. *Ego Identity: A Handbook for Psychosocial Research.* New York: Springer-Verlag.

Waterman, Alan S. 1990. Personal Expressiveness: Philosophical and Psychological Foundations. *Journal of Mind and Behavior* 11 (1): 47–74.

Sally L. Archer
Jeremy A. Grey

IDENTITY MATRIX

The identity matrix I_n is an $n \times n$ matrix with 1s along the main diagonal and 0s in the off-diagonal elements. It can be written as $I_n = diag\,(1,\,1....1)$. For instance, for $n = 3$, the matrix looks like

$$I_3 = \begin{bmatrix} 1 & 0 & 0 \\ 0 & 1 & 0 \\ 0 & 0 & 1 \end{bmatrix} = diag\,(1,1,1)$$

The columns of the identity matrix are known as the *unit vectors*. For the above example, these are $e_1 = (1\ 0\ 0)'$, $e_2 = (0\ 1\ 0)'$, and $e_3 = (0\ 0\ 1)'$. If the dimension of the matrix is 1×1, the matrix reduces to the scalar 1.

The identity matrix has the following properties:

1. It is square, that is, it has the same number of rows and columns.

2. It is symmetric, that is, transposing rows with columns (or vice versa) we obtain the matrix itself, that is, $I = I'$ where I' is the transpose matrix.

3. It is idempotent, that is, $I^2 = I$; in the scalar case this is equivalent to $I^2 = 1$.

4. For any $n \times n$ matrix A, multiplication by the identity matrix delivers the matrix A itself, that is, $AI = A$; in the scalar case this is equivalent to $a \times 1 = a$.

5. It has the commutative property, that is, for any $n \times n$ matrix A, $AI = IA = A$; in the scalar case, this is equivalent to $a \times 1 = 1 \times a = a$.

6. For any nonsingular $n \times n$ matrix A, there exists a matrix A^{-1} such that $AA^{-1} = A^{-1}A = I$ where A^{-1} is called the inverse matrix of A. In the scalar case, this property is equivalent to the inverse operation of multiplication (or division), that is, $a \times \frac{1}{a} = \frac{1}{a} \times a = 1$.

7. It has full rank; the n columns (or the n rows) of the matrix are linearly independent vectors and consequently the determinant is different from zero. The only symmetric, idempotent, and full rank matrix is the identity matrix.

8. Because I is a diagonal matrix, its determinant is equal to the product of the elements in the main diagonal, which in this case is equal to 1 regardless of the dimension of the matrix. A positive determinant is a necessary and sufficient condition for the identity matrix to be a positive definite matrix. The trace of the identity matrix is $tr\,I_n = n$, which is the sum of the elements in the main diagonal.

9. The n eigenvectors of the identity matrix are the unit vectors, and all the n eigenvalues are equal to 1.

Matrix algebra is a fundamental tool for the econometric analysis of general regression models. Classical estimation methodologies such as Ordinary Least Squares (OLS), Nonlinear Least Squares, Generalized Least Squares, Maximum Likelihood, and the Method of Moments rely on matrix algebra to derive their estimators and their properties in an elegant and compact format. The identity matrix shows up in several technical proofs. For instance, the identity matrix is an integral part of a projection matrix. In the OLS regression of y on X with a sample of size n, the projection matrix is $P \equiv (I_n - X(X'X)^{-1}X')$. It is important because when P is applied to a vector such as y, the result is the fitted values of y through the regression, that is, $\hat{y} = Py$.

BIBLIOGRAPHY

Strang, Gilbert. 1980. *Linear Algebra and Its Applications.* 2nd ed. New York: Academic Press.

Gloria González-Rivera

IDEOLOGY

The previous edition of this *Encyclopedia* contains two entries devoted to *Ideology*, one on its concept and function by Edward Shils, the other on "Ideology and the Social System" by Harry M. Johnson, which taken together well illustrate the difficulties involved in achieving a common understanding of the term's meaning. Shils's contribution is quite stipulative and opinionated. After distinguishing ideologies from "outlooks and creeds, systems and movements of thought, and programs" (p. 66), it asserts that "all ideologies—whether progressive or traditional, revolutionary or reactionary—entail an aggressive alienation from the existing society," that "participation in the routine life of the civil political order is alien to the ideological spirit" (p. 68), and that no great ideology has ever considered itself obliged to respect the modern, scientific spirit in its quest for truth (p. 73). Johnson, while apparently agreeing to some extent with this final assertion of Shils's and offering some important observations about the historical role of the concept, is most concerned to explore the role of ideologies within the theoretical framework developed by Talcott Parsons. Nevertheless, however unscientific it may be thought to be, the term *ideology* has come to play a very prominent role in the discourses of virtually all of the social sciences, so that it is essential to attempt to clarify its meaning(s).

ORIGINAL MEANING

The simple original sense of the term, first deployed by Antoine Destutt de Tracy, was, parallel with the Greek-based names of so many academic disciplines, the study of ideas. Tracy's intention, as a materialist philosopher, was systematically to map the material origins or causes of the ideas in people's heads, and to this end he directed the short-lived Institut de France where such research was undertaken. It briefly enjoyed the favor of Napoleon Bonaparte, who later turned against it. Upon returning from his defeat in Russia in 1812, Napoleon denounced ideology, in an address to the Conseil d'Etat, as a dark metaphysics, dedicated to a subtle search for first causes upon which to base laws. Rather, he urged, laws should be based on a knowledge of the human heart and on the lessons of history. Ideology, he concluded, was responsible for all the misfortunes that had befallen "our beautiful France" ("*notre belle France*"). In other words, for Napoleon the problem with ideology—quite paradoxically, in light of some contemporary conceptions of it—was that it was based on an excessively scientific philosophy. Since that time, the term *ideology* has never entirely escaped the pejorative connotations that Napoleon imposed upon it.

Karl Marx and his lifelong colleague Friedrich Engels wrote a lengthy, highly polemical manuscript entitled *The German Ideology* in which this pejorative sense predominated. Although it was to be the better part of a century before this product of the mid-1840s was published in full, its core notion of ideology was reflected in other works of theirs, such as *The Communist Manifesto* (1848), and thus became a part of the broad Marxist tradition. According to this notion, ideologies are large thought-systems (e.g., metaphysics, morality, and religion) that in reality have their basis in human beings' material life-processes, but that mistakenly come to be regarded as independent of the latter and as having a superior life of their own, as supposedly eternal verities. Just such an assumption had been central to the thinking of Hegel, the most influential philosopher during Marx's early years, who saw history itself as the work and self-realization of a supra-material reality that he called *Absolute Spirit*, and who tried to show in some detail just how this was so. For Marx and Engels, ideologies typically have the conservative effect of justifying existing relationships of dominance and subordination; thus, according to them, it was not surprising to find contemporary "bourgeois ideologists" defending the capitalist system as the highest and best possible, or in Hegel's terms as "the end of history." However, at a time of crisis, which they declared their own era to be, a certain segment of the bourgeois ideologists are able correctly to grasp the movement of history and go over to the side of the subordinate class, the proletariat. In this way, readers might infer, members of this enlightened group (among whom they obviously included themselves) succeed in overcoming and getting beyond ideology.

AMBIGUITIES

But there is sufficient ambiguity in *The German Ideology* to explain why some of Marx's intellectual heirs—especially so-called "orthodox Marxists" of the Soviet era—could employ the word *ideology* in a more positive sense, even referring uncritically to "Marxist ideology" in official textbooks of dialectical materialism. Louis Althusser, a French Marxist theorist who exerted considerable influence during a brief period in the 1960s, regarded ideology as an all-pervasive, inescapable phenomenon, one that is closely connected with Freud's notion of the "Unconscious": Ideology, for Althusser, is the mechanism by which, through their imaginations, individuals relate themselves to human existence in different historical epochs. At the same time, Althusser distinguished ideology from science—the latter being, for him, a set of objective concepts detached from interests, the brilliant discovery of which within the domain of history he located in the later work of Marx. (In a very interesting anticipation of what is essentially the same idea—to wit, that there is a strong conceptual contrast to be drawn between science and what others have called ideology—Thorstein Veblen, when discussing the increasingly dominant role of science in the modern world, had also suggested that the continued coexistence, along with science, of more romantic and dramatic as well as pragmatic ways of thinking may be a human necessity.)

By contrast, in his writings of the 1920s and 1930s the Marxist psychologist and psychoanalyst Wilhelm Reich, at once an admirer and a strong critic of Freud, continued to treat ideologies as predominantly negative, repressive phenomena. At the margins of Marxist thinking later in the twentieth century, the French poststructuralist Michel Foucault rejected Althusser's science/ideology dichotomy and increasingly distanced himself from "ideology critique" in favor of minute, detailed examinations of actual disciplinary and other practices in which there are uneven distributions of power. According to Foucault, relations of dominance and subordination cannot be explained primarily in terms of what neo-Marxist partisans of ideology critique, such as Reich, like to call "false consciousness."

This same basic ambiguity has also pervaded much of the non-Marxist literature on the subject. Max Weber, clearer than most in this respect, identified two senses of *ideology*, the first consisting of a reflection of the dominant thought of a given time, the other being the pejorative sense of a manipulative distortion of reality. Johnson, in his previously mentioned *Encyclopedia* article, makes a small, parenthetical concession to this tradition of ambiguity by explaining that, while from his standpoint the expression *ideological distortion* is strictly speaking redundant (because all ideology is for him distortive), nevertheless he would continue to use the full expression, "since this technical meaning of 'ideology' is not universally established" (p. 77).

Among treatments of ideology that have been of greatest importance for the social sciences is that of Karl Mannheim, who, in *Ideology and Utopia* (1929), asserted that, in addition to the "particular" concept of ideology—which equates ideology with a "phenomenon of deception," or what Mannheim's Marxist contemporary Georg Lukács called "the reified mind" or more recent thinkers such as Herbert Marcuse often call "false consciousness"—we must also recognize the rise, in modern times, of a "total," more or less universal concept of it, which sociologists of knowledge can explore across various societies and social groups in an historically "relativizing," value-neutral way. Mannheim's advocacy of this kind of theoretically rigorous, scientific, but very broad inquiry seems ultimately to have had the unintended effect of generalizing and "de-fanging" the notion of ideology to such an extent that its contours have become extremely vague and open-ended in much of the more recent literature.

THE "END OF IDEOLOGY"

This tendency was well illustrated in the controversy, which reached its height in the early 1960s, over the alleged "end of ideology." These words constituted the title of a book by Daniel Bell; other, mainly but not exclusively American, political scientists and sociologists, including Seymour Lipset and Edward Shils, also came to be associated with this idea, which came popularly to be regarded as a literal statement about the then-contemporary historical situation. But, as Shils himself makes quite clear at the end of his *Encyclopedia* article, neither Bell nor Shils nor most other "end of ideology" scholars intended to make a blanket statement about the demise of ideology in general, as distinguished, at best, from the demise of certain types of ideological thought such as Marxism. This point is particularly well expressed by the fiercely anti-Marxist Raymond Aron at the end of his preface to the new edition of his 1955 book *The Opium of the Intellectuals*. Aron admits to having previously evoked the end of the age of ideology, and then adds: "But if I detest ideological fanaticism, I like little better the indifference which sometimes succeeds it. … Ten years ago, I thought it necessary to fight ideological fanaticism. Tomorrow it will perhaps be indifference which seems to me to be feared. The fanatic, animated by hate, seems to me terrifying. A self-satisfied mankind fills me with horror" (pp. xv–xvi).

Thus it would appear that social scientists will be unable to dispense with the highly elusive concept of ideology for the foreseeable future, and that, if they ever come to feel that they can, this will probably signify something historically catastrophic.

SEE ALSO *Althusser, Louis; Mannheim, Karl; Marxism*

BIBLIOGRAPHY

Althusser, Louis. 1971. *Lenin and Philosophy and Other Essays.* Trans. Ben Brewster. New York: Monthly Review Press.

Aron, Raymond. [1955] 1962. *The Opium of the Intellectuals.* Trans. Terence Kilmartin. 2nd ed. New York: Norton Library.

Cohen, Ira H. 1982. *Ideology and Consciousness: Reich, Freud, and Marx.* New York: New York University Press.

Lichtheim, George. 1965. "The Concept of Ideology." *History and Theory* 4 (2): 164–195.

Mannheim, Karl. [1936] 1986. *Ideology and Utopia.* Trans. Louis Worth and Edward Shils. San Diego, CA: Harcourt Brace Jovanovich.

Marx, Karl, and Friedrich Engels. 1976. *The German Ideology.* Moscow: Progress Publishers.

Rosen, Michael. 1996. *On Voluntary Servitude: False Consciousness and the Theory of Ideology.* Cambridge, MA: Harvard University Press.

William L. McBride

IGNORANCE, PLURALISTIC

Pluralistic ignorance is a psychological phenomenon in which people think they feel differently from everybody else, even though they are behaving similarly. Consider the following case of pluralistic ignorance: On most college campuses, alcohol use is widespread, and students drink, some to excess, at most social functions. Surveys reveal that most students have misgivings about heavy drinking, particularly when it interferes with schoolwork. Nevertheless, they do not act on these misgivings; instead, they publicly conform to campus norms that prescribe a liberal attitude toward drinking and tolerance for drunkenness. These circumstances give rise to pluralistic ignorance: Students take their peers' behavior at face value, assuming that everybody else is much more comfortable with heavy drinking than they are.

The study of pluralistic ignorance originated with Floyd Allport, who coined the term in 1928 to describe the situation in which virtually all members of a group privately reject the group's norms and yet believe that virtually all members of the group privately accept them. In the intervening eighty years, pluralistic ignorance has been linked empirically to a wide variety of collective phenomena, including the failure of bystanders to intervene in emergency situations, groupthink, the spiral of silence, and the perpetuation of unpopular and deleterious social norms and practices. Once a behavior achieves a high degree of uniformity within a group, pluralistic ignorance fuels its perpetuation.

Pluralistic ignorance often originates in widespread conformity to social norms, driven by a desire both to gain peers' approval (normatively based conformity) and to do the right thing (informationally based conformity). When this conformity produces consensual behavior that belies private misgivings, pluralistic ignorance is frequently the result. People recognize that their own actions are driven by a desire to be in step with their peers, but assume that everybody else's actions reflect their private convictions. This dynamic has been shown to produce pluralistic ignorance in a wide variety of attitudinal domains, including students' attitudes toward alcohol use on campus, nurses' attitudes toward their jobs, racial attitudes during the civil rights movement, and the opinions of board members about the declining performance of their firm.

Pluralistic ignorance also arises when uniform behavior is driven by other social motives. Consider, for example, the plight of two individuals trying to initiate a romantic relationship. Their interest in each other is mingled with fear of being rejected, and as a consequence, neither is willing to make the first move. Yet, even though both are behaving similarly, they interpret this behavior differently: They see their own inaction as driven by fear of rejection and the other's inaction as driven by lack of interest. In this case, it is not conformity that produces consensual behavior but rather common fears and anxieties. Pluralistic ignorance results from people's failure to recognize just how common their fears and anxieties are. This dynamic has been shown to produce pluralistic ignorance in a variety of interpersonal settings, including interactions between potential romantic partners, interracial contact situations, college classrooms, and public emergencies.

SEE ALSO *Conformity; Genocide; Groupthink; Herd Behavior; Lynchings; Milgram, Stanley; Psychology*

BIBLIOGRAPHY

Miller, Dale T., and Deborah A. Prentice. 1994. Collective Errors and Errors about the Collective. *Personality and Social Psychology Bulletin* 20 (5): 541–550.

O'Gorman, Hubert J. 1986. The Discovery of Pluralistic Ignorance: An Ironic Lesson. *Journal of the History of the Behavioral Sciences* 22 (4): 333–347.

Deborah A. Prentice

ILLEGITIMACY
SEE *Births, Out-of-Wedlock.*

ILLUMINATI, THE

Although many groups have referred to themselves as "the Illuminati," or "enlightened ones," the term most commonly refers to the Order of Illuminists, an organization founded by Adam Weishaupt (1748–1830), a law professor at the University of Ingolstadt in Bavaria, and four of his friends on May 1, 1776. The Order's stated mission was "to encourage a humane and sociable outlook; to inhibit all vicious impulses; to support Virtue, wherever she is threatened or oppressed by Vice, to further the advance of deserving persons and to spread useful knowledge among the broad mass of people who were at present deprived of all education" (Johnson 1983, p. 45). While these aims appear moderate, they were in fact a proposal for sweeping social change. The Illuminati and their goals so threatened Bavaria's political and religious authorities that Karl Theodor, the prince-elector and duke of Bavaria (r. 1724–1799), banned the group in 1787.

The Illuminati emerged as a reaction to the social and political environment of Bavaria in the late eighteenth century. Its institutions were dominated by the Church, and the Jesuits controlled university education. Weishaupt was frustrated by their interference in the university curriculum, particularly their resistance to the dissemination of ideas of the French Enlightenment (Billington 1980). That frustration moved him to create the Illuminati, which he hoped would spread Enlightenment philosophy and put it into practice.

Weishaupt was convinced that a secret society was the most effective way to accomplish these goals, and he utilized his experience with the Jesuits and Freemasons to create his new organization. Although he viewed the Jesuits as his enemies and the Freemasons as conservative and apolitical, he admired their secrecy, discipline, and organization, as well as their capacity to pursue their own interests even (in his view) at the expense of the interests of society as a whole (Roberts 1972). Weishaupt deliberately recruited Freemasons and used the organization's structure and symbolism as a model for the Illuminati. Members took pseudonyms (Weishaupt became Spartacus) and utilized Zoroastrian symbols to describe themselves and their ceremonies. Initiates read classical political philosophy, and as they moved through the movement's ranks they were gradually exposed to the Illuminati's true purpose: to spread the Enlightenment ideas of rationalism and egalitarianism. Only those within the movement's inner circle, the Areopagus, were told of its related political goals. The Illuminati members were to infiltrate the social and political institutions of Bavaria and initiate a peaceful revolution. Bavaria would be freed from the tyranny of the Church, and reason and equality would flourish.

Membership in the Illuminati proved tremendously appealing to members of the Bavarian middle and upper classes. From its origins in Ingolstadt, the movement grew rapidly. By 1779, it had members in at least four other Bavarian cities, and by the time it was banned in 1787, its membership numbered between two and four thousand (Roberts 1972).

Although the Order of the Illuminists was short-lived, it had considerable influence. Cloaked in secrecy and symbols, the real substance of the Illuminati was its propagation of Enlightenment ideas. Theodor could declare that anyone caught recruiting new members would be executed and thus ensure the effective end of the organization, but he could not stop the influence of Enlightenment ideas on those who had come into contact with them. The Order's members were scattered across the upper echelons of Bavarian society, and many were well placed to influence others. Its membership included doctors, lawyers, judges, professors, and government officials. Their exposure to Enlightenment philosophy affected the way they approached politics and probably also influenced those with whom they came into contact. Theodor attempted to purge the Illuminati from positions of power, but military force cannot, in the end, stop the spread of ideas. Illuminism became a source of inspiration for revolutionaries on both the left and right of the political spectrum (Billington 1980).

Weishaupt's greatest genius may have been his transformation of the secret-society model into an effective political instrument. In devising the Order's structure and doctrine, he made two important innovations. First, he deliberately created the Order of Illuminists as a political organization. He understood that secrecy could be not only an end in itself but also a political strategy. Second, he used existing secret organizations—namely, the Freemasons—for his own ends. In doing so, he created a network of secret societies that could be used for his own political purposes. While these achievements furthered his immediate goals, they also insured the Illuminati a place of particular importance in the history of conspiracy theories.

Conspiracy theories—expressing the belief that some covert power with malicious intent is directing world affairs—became a popular mode of political explanation in the early twentieth century, and they remained popular into the twenty-first century. Typically, conspiracy theories emerge during times of social change; they provide believers with a sense of certainty in uncertain times. The Illuminati play a pivotal role in many of the most influen-

tial modern conspiracy theories; the organization is, for example, believed in league with forces as diverse as aliens, Jewish financial power, and the individuals behind the events of September 11, 2001. Most scholars argue that the Order of Illuminists does not control history in this way. While political conspiracies have certainly existed—secrecy is often an element of political strategy—human beings exist in a contingent world and are limited in their ability to control history.

The Order of Illuminists therefore remains relevant today. It is most effectively understood as an eighteenth-century model of the power of secrecy and the use of allies in executing political strategy.

SEE ALSO *Politics; Secrecy*

BIBLIOGRAPHY

Billington, James H. 1980. *Fire in the Minds of Men: Origins of the Revolutionary Faith.* New York: Basic Books.

Johnson, George. 1983. *Architects of Fear: Conspiracy Theories and Paranoia in American Politics.* Los Angeles: J. P. Tarcher.

Pipes, Daniel. 1997. *Conspiracy: How the Paranoid Style Flourishes and Where It Comes From.* New York: The Free Press.

Roberts, J. M. 1972. *The Mythology of the Secret Societies.* London: Secker and Warburg.

Martha F. Lee

IMITATION

SEE *Social Learning Perspective.*

IMMIGRANTS, ASIAN

Asian migrations to the United States form one aspect of a dynamic, global social process that has seen peoples from Asian nations create new communities in such diverse destinations as the United States, Cuba, Canada, Mexico, Peru, the United Kingdom, East Africa, South Africa, and nation-states in Europe. This demographic movement happened over a long period of time and it continues to this day. The U.S. chapter of this worldwide story is both emblematic of these processes and singular in its own right.

When one speaks of Asian migrations to the United States one must underscore the diversity of these movements. Before World War II (1939–1945), Asian migration flows came from five major streams originating from particular regions in China, Japan, Korea, the Philippines, and India. After World War II, and especially after 1965 and 1975, Asian flows diversified to include South Asia and Southeast Asia. From the former came entrants from Pakistan, India, the Maldives, Nepal, Bhutan, Bangladesh, and Sri Lanka. From the latter came Vietnamese, Hmong, Laotian, Cambodian, and Thai contributors to modern Asian America.

The long roots of Asian migration can be traced as far back as 1763, when shipworkers from the Philippines, "the Manila men," established themselves as a community in what is today Louisiana. Other pioneer Asian arrivals came earlier than the better-known migrations to California in the 1840s, and they showed up on the Atlantic Coast, not the Pacific. In 1785 a ship with a crew of "Chinese, Malays, Japanese, and Moors" arrived in Baltimore, and South Asians worked in Massachusetts and Pennsylvania as indentured servants in the 1790s. By 1856 an estimated 150 Chinese lived in lower Manhattan in New York, working such jobs as sailors, ship workers, cooks, and stewards. These forgotten early Asian settlers on the Atlantic Coast preceded the Asians and Pacific Islanders who were lured to California by the gold rush of the late 1840s.

Chinese settlements produced political and social reactions in the United States, particularly in California after 1850. This agitation continued and grew in force until it culminated in the 1880s with Congress passing the first Chinese laborer suspension act, thus creating the Chinese exclusion system. From 1882 to 1904 the U.S. Congress passed at least seven major amendments that continued and amplified the Chinese exclusion statutory regime. Ostensibly promulgated to suspend Chinese laborer migration for a period of time, the laws had the overall social and legal effect of controlling the movements of Chinese-derived persons, both across the Pacific and across the United States.

Although exclusion was technically limited to the Chinese, the logic of the exclusion laws could be applied to other Asian immigrants and their communities. That logic found its most powerful expression in the legal idea of ineligibility for citizenship. Based on a judicial decision in 1879 that declared Chinese to be ineligible for U.S. naturalization, various federal judges applied the same racially based rule to other Asian groups and individuals. As a result, state governments barred persons ineligible to be citizens from owning property and pursuing a range of occupations. This logic was adopted by the Supreme Court in two decisions in 1922 and 1923 that successively denied U.S. naturalization to those of Japanese descent and those of "Hindu" or South Asian origins.

As exclusion grew, so did the territorial reach of the United States. When the United States made its foray as a world power after defeating Spain in the Spanish American War in 1898, it asserted control over Spain's for-mer Pacific possession, the Philippine Islands, thus precipitating another stream of Asian migration. Filipinos moved to the United States to work in California agriculture in the 1920s and 1930s, or to take up university scholarships provided by the government. At the same time, exclusionary rules were being applied to Chinese living in the Philippines. In addition to the Philippines being included under Chinese exclusion, would-be migrants from other areas of the Pacific, East Asia, and the Near East fell under exclusionary bans inspired by the Chinese exclusion precedent. On February 5, 1917 the U.S. Congress banned the entry of aliens from a large segment of the world marked off as the "Asiatic Barred Zone," an area that included Indochina, India, Burma, Thailand, the Malay States, the East Indian Islands, Asiatic Russia, the Polynesian Islands, and parts of Arabia and Afghanistan. With the exception of teachers, merchants, and students, no one from the zone was eligible for U.S. entry

The U.S. involvement in World War II was a watershed era for all Asian-derived communities in the United States. Chinese exclusion came to a formal end in December 1943 when the U.S. Congress repealed it in an attempt to bolster China as a wartime ally. Korean Americans living in the United States, along with other Asian-derived Americans, joined the U.S. armed forces. Filipinos benefited from an improved public image due to their homeland's resistance to the Imperial Japanese Army. During the war, South Asians were emboldened to seek U.S. citizenship rights, and both Filipinos and South Asians received U.S. naturalization rights in 1946. Although these communities gained from the U.S. involvement in the war, Japanese Americans were forcibly evacuated and interned. From 1942 until the war's end, 110,000 Japanese who resided in Oregon, Washington, and California, most of whom were native-born U.S. citizens, were ousted from their homes and livelihoods on the U.S. west coast and sent to relocation camps in the country's interior. This involuntary removal, unmatched in history in terms of its scale and scope, was in effect a mass incarceration.

After World War II, cold war immigration patterns reshaped both the United States and that of Asian America. Those patterns benefited from the halting yet persistent reform trends set in motion by the repeal of Chinese exclusion in the mid-1940s. Twelve years after the repeal, Congress enacted the 1952 McCarran-Walter Act, which brought forward the reform trends of 1943 to 1946 but also set new limits to Asian migration. The 1952 law allowed U.S. citizenship and naturalization for all Asian-derived individuals, thus removing a key disability, but it also replaced the Asiatic Barred Zone with the "Asia Pacific Triangle," a provision that simultaneously provided new entry quotas for twenty Asian nations and stipulated an overall low ceiling on how many Asians were eligible to enter. It was not until the civil rights era that the most important immigration law to shape modern Asian Pacific America came to be. In 1965 Congress undid the restrictive immigration laws that had hampered non-Chinese Asian migration since 1917 by passing the Immigration Act of 1965, allowing for greater numbers of Asian immigrants. The act was passed at the juncture of the civil rights movement and the beginning of the U.S. ground war in Vietnam. Ten years later, the U.S. military and political presence in Vietnam ended. In spring 1975 U.S.-backed regimes in Southeast Asia fell, thus inaugurating flows of Vietnamese, Cambodian, and Laotian refugees to the United States. The diversity of Southeast Asian migrations from 1975 to 1980 and thereafter is as striking as any of the pre–World War II migration flows from Asia.

Although the mid-1960s saw civil rights and immigration reforms for Asian-derived communities, the same era also burdened all Asian Pacific American communities with a new stereotype—Asians as the "model minority." On its surface this was an improvement over exclusion-era denigrations, but the "model minority" label actually obscures the lived realities of many Asian American individuals and communities by claiming that Asians have overcome all the barriers faced by exclusion-era Asians. Although the harshest aspects of exclusion have ended, and many Asian American communities and individuals have moved beyond the stereotypic urban niche occupations of laundry work, the model minority claim is really myopic. The label obscures and sidesteps the realities of Asian Pacific American experience: continued poverty; the historical and social conditions that privilege, in some Asian communities, the immigration of already trained professionals who enter more readily into middle-class positions; and the hidden costs of extra work and long hours that enable the middle-class attainments of home ownership and better education for children. Also kept out of view is the glass ceiling that limits and frustrates professional advancement. In the end, the model minority notion is never about actually lived Asian American lives; it is always about the conceit of holding onto beliefs that celebrate ideals about social mobility in the United States.

Asian migrations did not stop with the end of the cold war. The flow of people from every imaginable Asian starting point continues, and the vibrancy of Asian American communities throughout the United States is impressive. These contemporary Asian migrations build upon the legacies of earlier movements. Although separated by different historical experiences, these communities all share the legacy of persistence and survival that characterize the long sweep of Asian American history.

SEE ALSO *Assimilation; Chinese Americans; Chinese Diaspora; East Indian Diaspora; Immigration; Incarceration, Japanese American; Japanese Americans; Model Minority; Politics, Asian-American; World War II*

BIBLIOGRAPHY

Chan, Sucheng. 1991. *Asian Americans: An Interpretive History.* Boston: Twayne.

Hing, Bill Ong. 1993. *Making and Remaking Asian America through Immigration Policy, 1850–1990.* Palo Alto, CA: Stanford University Press.

Kashima, Tetsuden. 1997. *Personal Justice Denied: Report of the Commission on Wartime Relocation and Internment of Citizens.* Seattle: University of Washington Press.

Lai, Eric, and Dennis Arguelles, eds. 2003. *The New Face of Asian Pacific America: Numbers, Diversity, and Change in the 21st Century.* Los Angeles: UCLA Asian American Studies Center Press.

Odo, Franklin, ed. 2002. *The Columbia Documentary History of the Asian American Experience.* New York: Columbia University Press.

Okihiro, Gary Y. 2001. *The Columbia Guide to Asian American History.* New York: Columbia University Press.

Takaki, Ronald. 1989. *Strangers From a Different Shore.* Boston: Little, Brown.

Victor Jew

IMMIGRANTS, BLACK

The black population in the United States has always been diverse in terms of national origins. A sizeable influx of black immigrants from the Caribbean, Latin America, and sub-Saharan Africa added to that diversity in the second half of the twentieth century. Significant differences in the factors that stimulated migration, characteristics of the migrants, and the contexts they encountered make it possible to speak of two generations of black immigrants: the pre–World War II wave that arrived primarily between 1900 and 1930, and the post-1965 wave that swelled after the Hart-Celler Act (Immigration Reform Act of 1965) and other immigration-policy changes in the United States and Europe.

THE FIRST GENERATION OF BLACK IMMIGRANTS

Although the number of black immigrants historically has been quite small, their presence in the United States dates back to the turn of the last century. According to Ira A. Reid, at a time when U.S. immigration was at its peak (between 1880 and 1930), foreign-born blacks comprised only 1 percent of the total black population (Reid 1939). By the end of this era of mass migration, nearly 28 million immigrants had entered the United States; of that number approximately 100,000 persons were socially defined as "Negro immigrants."

The first generation of black immigrants came primarily from the Caribbean region, Canada, and the Cape Verde Islands (a Portuguese colony off the west coast of Africa). The forces that prompted and sustained the migrant flows were fundamentally political and economic. In the British or anglophone Caribbean, oppressive colonial policies, economic distress, and natural disasters, together with opportunities abroad, occasioned mass migration to the Panama Canal zone, to sugar plantations in the Dominican Republic and Cuba, and most notably to the industrializing United States. Similarly, Cape Verdeans fleeing drought, famine, and a lack of rewarding employment migrated to southeastern New England in search of lucrative, short-term employment.

The immigrants were mostly males in their wage-earning years; over 36 percent were between the ages of sixteen and thirty-seven years old; and the majority was not married. Many had been skilled artisans, bankers, merchants, colonial civil servants, and professional persons in their countries of origin. Because immigrant laws selected for literacy, more than 98 percent were literate when they arrived and, with the exception of less than 2 percent, they spoke English. Although the migrants represented a select segment of their home societies, in general they were future male industrial workers and female domestic servants.

These foreign-born blacks tended to settle in urban areas—especially New York, Miami, and Boston, which served as primary ports of entry. Cambridge and New Bedford, Massachusetts, Tampa, and Detroit also had sizeable black immigrant populations. Cigar manufacturing in Florida pulled migrants to Tampa; and black immigrants found work fishing, whaling, and, later, in the cranberry industry in New Bedford. Where certain groups settled had as much to do with the economic opportunities there as how they were located or perceived in the social hierarchies of each city or region. Notably, with the exception of Florida, few black immigrants settled in the U.S. South.

For the black immigrants who arrived at the turn of the last century, their hyperracialization as blacks had the most profound impact on their experiences. For the most part, distinctions of color, language, education, economic status, religious practice, and nationality mattered little in a society with a racial hierarchy held together by an ideology of biological inferiority. Whether or not they lived their lives as Haitians, Jamaicans, Nigerians, West Indians, or Africans, what the historian F. James Davis calls "the one-drop rule" of racial classification consigned black people of all classes to the bottom of the social ladder and was the basis for their exclusion from economic and educational opportunities (Davis 1991). Not only did they suffer from the same rigid segregation and blanket discrimination as native-born black Americans, in addition, they were rarely considered as part of the British or Portuguese immigrant communities. In a seminal essay, Roy S. Bryce-Laporte argued that for black immigrants, incorporation into the larger African American community generated an additional layer of social marginality; they were invisible both as blacks and as immigrants (Bryce-Laporte 1972).

BLACK IMMIGRANTS TODAY

The visibility of black immigrants has dramatically increased since the 1970s. In the ten years following the Hart-Celler Act, the number of black immigrants exceeded the total from the previous seventy years. Black immigration continued to grow in volume after that. Demographer John Logan and his colleagues show that black immigrant groups are growing faster than well-established ethnic minorities such as Cubans and Koreans (Logan 2003).

Unlike the first generation of black immigrants, the post-1965 wave is much more diverse in terms of both country of origin and type. In addition to the 1,393,000 newcomers from the Caribbean (primarily Jamaica, Haiti, and Trinidad and Tobago), in 2000 there were nearly 600,000 African immigrants living in the United States. (Notably, there is no consensus in the scholarship about how to count black immigrants. The U.S. Census and the Immigration and Naturalization Service report the foreign-born by place of birth. Because not all African immigrants are black—consider the case of Egyptians or South Africans—and a considerable number of Latin American immigrants—from Cuba or Puerto Rico, for instance—identify as black, all enumerations of the population of black immigrants are estimates. The estimates reported here are based on sample data from the U. S. Census Bureau for the foreign-born population born in all nations of the Caribbean except Cuba and Dominican Republic, eastern Africa, and western Africa.)

The end of World War II produced significant political changes in many African countries, and in some cases political instability, economic mismanagement, and civil unrest in the wake of independence triggered migration. The main sources of African immigration are Nigeria, Ghana, Cape Verde, and more recently, the Horn of Africa—including Ethiopia, Eritrea, Somalia, and the Sudan.

According to John Arthur's *Invisible Sojourners: African Immigrant Diaspora in the United States* (2000), post-1965 migration created a brain drain from Africa—

an exodus of the educated, the professional class, and civil servants. This perspective mirrors that of earlier scholars who argued that black immigrants were more successful than native-born blacks because migrants represent a select segment of the populations of their countries of origin (Reid 1939). Across racial groups, immigrants tend to be self-selected with respect to human capital characteristics, such as education and occupational status. However, because the immigration reforms facilitated family reunification, those with relatives or contacts abroad could more easily migrate despite having lower skills and levels of education. Further, civil war and famine in northeast Africa have added a large flow of political refugees and asylum seekers to the number of voluntary migrants who come to the United States for educational and economic opportunities. The diversity of languages spoken and reasons for migrating combine to further dilute the selectivity of the contemporary wave of foreign-born blacks.

The level of geographic dispersion among black immigrants today is unique. Destinations such as Miami, New York City, and Boston continue to attract large numbers, but the residential landscape of post-1965 foreign-born blacks is decidedly metropolitan; that is, immigrant ports have expanded beyond the central cities. Rather than settling exclusively in urban areas, black immigrants have also formed communities in suburban and rural areas. African immigrants are concentrated in the Washington, D.C., Atlanta, and Minneapolis–St. Paul metropolitan areas.

SOCIAL AND ECONOMIC EXPERIENCES

Comparison to African Americans has been a constant feature of the social scientific literature on black immigrants. Since the publication of Reid's pioneering work in 1939, scholars have been most concerned with what the experiences of black immigrants tell us about race in the United States. One noteworthy debate concerns the relative importance of race and ethnicity in determining socioeconomic success.

As Table 1 summarizes, contemporary immigrant blacks seem to fare better than native-born blacks on a number of socioeconomic indicators (Logan 2003): They have higher education and income levels, and a substantially lower percentage are unemployed or below the poverty line. Analyses of U.S. Census data also reveal that in the metropolitan areas where they live in largest numbers, black immigrants tend to reside in neighborhoods with higher median incomes, higher education levels, and higher proportions of homeowners than do African Americans. Some researchers have used such indicators to argue that race and discrimination are no longer significant determinants of life chances.

Moreover, recent research shows that the representation of blacks with immigrant-origins at selective colleges and universities is roughly double their share in the population (Massey et al 2007). Whereas only 13 percent of all black Americans between the ages of 18–19 were either foreign-born or the children of migrants, sociologist Douglas Massey and his colleagues found that among the black college freshman entering selective institutions in 1999, 27 percent were first- or second-generation immigrants. Their research, along with previous work which suggests favoritism toward black immigrants by white employers, calls into question, not only the efficacy of affirmative action programs, but also whether black immigrants are the appropriate beneficiaries of such policies in

Table 1. Socioeconomic Characteristics of Major Race and Ethnic Groups by Nativity, 2000

		U.S. Citizen	Speak Only English	Years of Education	Median Household Income	Unemployed	Below Poverty
White	Native	100.0%	96.5%	13.5	$52,000	3.9%	8.5%
	Immigrant	60.8%	43.9%	13.4	$51,000	3.7%	11.4%
Black	Native	100.0%	97.5%	12.5	$33,200	10.0%	24.4%
	Immigrant	46.9%	57.8%	13.2	$42,000	6.5%	15.9%
Hispanic	Native	100.0%	35.3%	12.1	$38,000	8.3%	21.7%
	Immigrant	28.4%	4.3%	9.7	$37,200	5.8%	22.0%
Asian	Native	100.0%	60.2%	14.5	$67,000	5.9%	10.4%
	Immigrant	52.3%	12.7%	13.8	$62,500	4.5%	12.7%

SOURCE: Logan, John. 2003 America's Newcomers.

Table 1

education and employment designed to ameliorate the past exclusion of native-born, African Americans.

However, beneath the apparent differences between the majority of blacks with historical origins in slavery and in the rural South and black immigrants from the Caribbean and Africa is a shared experience of race-based discrimination. The relative success of foreign-born blacks is partly due to the size of the black immigrant population: Even with the current rate of growth, they comprise less than 1 percent of the total population of the United States and only 6 percent of the non-Hispanic black population. For this reason, it is important to note how black immigrants are doing relative to whites and other immigrants. Compared to Asian immigrants, for instance, foreign-born blacks have appreciably lower median household incomes ($42,000 compared to $62,500), higher rates of unemployment (6.5% and 5.8%, respectively), and a larger proportion living in poverty (15.9% compared to 12.7%). Moreover, black immigrants, like African Americans, are highly segregated from whites; and regardless of nativity, non-Hispanic blacks live in worse neighborhoods than do non-Hispanic whites. With respect to academic achievement on college campuses, black students of all backgrounds do not perform as well as whites with similar characteristics. So far, the empirical evidence suggests that institutional and societal processes have a differential effect on black immigrants, compared to native-born blacks, not that there are discernible cultural differences at work. As Mary Waters concluded in *Black Identities: West Indian Immigrant Dreams and American Realities* (1998), race still shapes everyday life for black immigrants and their offspring.

THE FUTURE FOR BLACK IMMIGRANTS

Black immigrant communities will continue to be part of the U.S. ethnic mosaic. Contemporary black immigrants encounter a U.S. context that is more diverse, with considerably more recognition of the diverse national origins of blacks than ever before. According to Philip Kasinitz (1992), the racial structure of the United States prevented cultural self-determination and self-representation among black immigrants for most of the twentieth century. Within the black community, attempts by black immigrants to distinguish themselves from the native-born were considered divisive and ethnocentric. Today, the larger numbers of black immigrants, the uninterrupted flow of newcomers, and the new U.S. context have created a space for the consolidation of distinct black ethnic communities, subjectivities, and social identities.

SEE ALSO *Blackness; Caribbean, The; Discrimination, Racial; Immigrants to North America;*

Marginalization; Migration; Mobility; Mobility, Lateral; Model Minority; Race; Racism

BIBLIOGRAPHY

Arthur, John A. 2000. *Invisible Sojourners: African Immigrant Diaspora in the United States.* Westport, CT: Praeger.

Bryce-Laporte, Roy S. 1972. Black Immigrants: The Experience of Invisibility and Inequality. *Journal of Black Studies* 3: 29–56.

Davis, F. James. 1991. *Who Is Black? One Nation's Definition.* University Park, PA: Penn State University Press.

Kasinitz, Philip. 1992. *Caribbean New York: Black Immigrants and the Politics of Race.* Ithaca, NY: Cornell University Press.

Logan, John. 2003. America's Newcomers. Lewis Mumford Center for Comparative Urban and Regional Research. University at Albany, State University of New York. http://mumford.albany.edu/census/NewComersReport/NewComer01.htm.

Massey, Douglas, Margarita Mooney, Kimberly Torres, and Camille Z. Charles. 2007. Black Immigrants and Black Natives Attending Selective Colleges and Universities in the United States. *American Journal of Education* 113: 243–271.

Reid, Ira D. A. 1939. *The Negro Immigrant: His Background, Characteristics and Social Adjustment, 1899–1937.* New York: Columbia University Press.

Waters, Mary C. 1998. *Black Identities: West Indian Immigrant Dreams and American Realities.* New York: Russell Sage Foundation.

Regine O. Jackson

IMMIGRANTS, EUROPEAN

Humans migrated to European regions from Africa approximately 40,000 years ago and have been moving ever since. Europeans seem to be highly related to the same northeastern Africans who settled much of Asia and the Middle East, or Eurasia. Thus, it is hypothesized that there were numerous movements of tribes and peoples both eastward and westward across Eurasia in the years before the early middle ages. Knowledge of their movements is more accurate around 2000 BCE, once Europeans started keeping track of their history through books and oral traditions. As archaeologists and geneticists complete more studies, more precise details of migration patterns from more than 2,000 years ago may come to light.

EUROPEAN MIGRATION, 1000–1800

Some historians believe that migration movements were common in the early middle ages, but solitary migrations were rare and people tended to move in midsize groups.

Later this reversed, and migrations of solitary individuals or small groups became more common. Still, voluntary immigration movements were rarer in the few centuries after the fall of the Roman Empire than they are today. Travel around Europe was difficult, slow, and dangerous, and mostly restricted to merchants, ambassadors and envoys, and pilgrims. Before 1000 CE, traveling from Italy to Constantinople, for instance, could take at least seven months, although travel times gradually became shorter over the centuries. A few people migrated to parts outside of Europe, but this was rare and involved mostly people engaged in embassy work or associated with religious institutions. A notable exception, however, was the settlement Vikings established in Newfoundland around the year 1000, although it was abandoned after only a few years.

What was more common was involuntary migration in the form of the transportation of slaves. Slaves, with no choice in the matter, could walk long distances and even carry things for their owners. Most individuals became slaves through a slave raid on their community or as a result of military action. In the early middle ages, many slaves came from towns along the Mediterranean coast and in the eastern "Slavic" parts of central Europe. Arab raiders liked to find their potential slaves in southern European coastal villages, and Frankish tribes found many of their slaves first in England and later in the East. Slaves could be sold at many organized markets, most of which were located in the European and Arab parts of the Mediterranean world.

Several main immigrations to places outside of Europe occurred between the tenth and fifteenth centuries. Victorious armies or raiders continued to capture and enslave people, who ended up typically in the Mediterranean area where slaves were extensively used, which included northern Africa and the Ottoman and Arab/Muslim world. Secondly, in the thirteenth and fourteenth centuries, under Mongol protection, some Italian missionaries made it to Asia on the heels of Venetian traders such as Marco Polo. In addition, crusaders from Europe invaded the Holy Land in 1099; some integrated into society or settled in other places such as Constantinople, but many of their descendants moved back to Europe once Turkish and Kurdish rulers claimed Jerusalem in 1187. Thereafter, pilgrims still visited but did not usually settle in the Holy Land.

As in the early middle ages, merchants, traders, sailors, and government and religious officials all were more likely to venture beyond the borders of Europe. Significant group migrations also took place in this time period. In the thirteenth and fourteenth centuries Jews were expelled from many parts of Europe, and some ventured to eastern parts of the continent. Others, including many of the Sephardic Jews of Iberia, left in 1492 for parts of the Ottoman Empire, including Palestine, Syria, Tunis, Egypt, Morocco, and Constantinople. During the same period, the Spanish and Portuguese also placed restrictions on the commercial and religious practices of Muslims, who were eventually completely expelled from the Iberian Peninsula by the mid-seventeenth century. Many of them left for communities in the Ottoman Empire.

By the 1400s Europeans were using better ships and navigational technology and were sailing farther away from their continent. Portuguese explorers made inroads in sailing around Africa and eventually all the way to parts of Asia, while the Italian explorer Christopher Columbus, funded with Spanish money, made it to Central America. Thereafter, it was a race for European nations to settle and claim different parts of North, Central, and South America, Africa, parts of Asia, and Australia and New Zealand. The search for colonial possessions lasted until the twentieth century.

The Portuguese were prodigious in establishing trading stations on the coastlines of Africa and Asia along with the settlements in Brazil, and all of this required a lot of manpower. From the sixteenth until the eighteenth centuries large numbers of Portuguese left their homeland to serve in various roles, as soldiers, settlers, and missionaries. Even though Spain was colonizing large parts of the Americas, during this period more people left Portugal than Spain.

Nations that created settlements or colonies provided destinations for their countrymen who wanted to leave Europe; trading networks that emerged between Europe and new settlements provided the necessary transportation for migrants. Before 1800, for example, Britain at different points in time had claim to Australia, New Zealand, the American colonies, Canada, some Caribbean islands, and British Guyana, among others; later, for periods of time it controlled various African areas including Egypt, Rhodesia, Nigeria, and South Africa. France at one point claimed parts of present-day Canada, various Caribbean islands, French Guiana, Cambodia, Vietnam, and a host of African countries. In addition, Belgium, Denmark, Germany, Italy, the Netherlands, Portugal, and Spain also exercised their imperial ambitions and operated various colonies at some point.

Most of these colonies no longer exist, but their existence influenced the patterns of European settlement from the sixteenth to the twentieth centuries. As British colonies, Australia and New Zealand, for instance, became a major settlement for British and Irish emigrants. In Africa, many British emigrants settled where the British had set up colonies, including South Africa and Rhodesia. French emigrants settled in French colonies such as Quebec; likewise, many Portuguese emigrants settled in

Brazil, and numerous Spaniards in Spanish settlements throughout the Americas. The various Dutch colonies attracted thousands of Dutch emigrants, particularly to the East Indies. Those with ambition but no financial assets could sign on as soldiers or for work with companies such as the Dutch East India Company. Colonies needed laborers and thus provided ways for impoverished individuals to emigrate from Europe. Until the 1830s a very common way to migrate to the British colonies in North America was by way of indentured servant contracts, which provided prepaid passage in exchange for future years of labor services.

1800 TO THE PRESENT

Emigration from Europe increased remarkably in the nineteenth century, partly as a result of increases in population growth along with changes in emigration policies. Before the nineteenth century Europe's population doubled approximately every 1,000 years, but by the nineteenth century population growth had increased tremendously, such that Europe's population doubled in less than 100 years during the nineteenth century. In addition, the Vienna Congress in 1815 extended the right to emigrate to many more Europeans. The period after 1815 thus saw a tremendous increase in the numbers of people who left Europe permanently and voluntarily. Between 1815 and 1930 more than 52 million Europeans left Europe for overseas destinations. About two-thirds went to the United States, and most of the rest to South America: Approximately 12 percent went to Argentina, 8 percent to Brazil, and 7 percent to Australia. Over this period, 11 and 10 million of these European emigrants left from Britain and Italy, respectively. Other countries that lost more than 2 million individuals include (in order of largest to smallest) Austria-Hungary, Germany, Spain, Russia, and Portugal.

Emigration rates—the percent of the population at home that leaves—differed tremendously across different countries. If a country had a small population overall, it could lose a small number of individuals to emigration movements but still have a high emigration rate. This was the case for Ireland: Until 1900, Irish emigration rates were the highest by far of all European nations. During several decades annual Irish emigration rates reached 14 per 1,000 of the home population; the next highest annual rates occurred in the 1880s with Norway losing 10 per 1,000 and Scotland 7 per 1,000. In the years after 1900 emigration rates were still high for Scotland, but also very high for Italy and Spain. Although a high emigration rate often reflected poor economic conditions within certain regions of a country, it also could signify a late or slow demographic transition, or an arduous adjustment from an agricultural economy to an industrial one that left many

without viable livings as farmers or craftsmen. Some areas suffered terrible exogenous events such as the potato famine of the 1840s, which occurred throughout much of Europe but hit Ireland especially hard.

In the nineteenth century it was not always the case that European emigrants were the very poorest. The fact that moving overseas was an expensive proposition meant that many potential emigrants without a remittance of some sort did not leave Europe because they could not afford to do so. In many regions both the richest and the poorest stayed home, the former because they had no interest in leaving and the latter because they could not afford to do so. That many emigrants ended up depending on family or friends who had moved before them for financial assistance or advice to achieve their goals meant that many emigrants left from the same European villages or regions; in other regions such chain migration connections did not evolve, and these areas experienced much less emigration.

Improvement of one's standard of living was of primary concern for many European emigrants over the centuries, but many moved for religious or political reasons. Various Christian groups settled in North America, including Pietists, Calvinists, Mennonites, Amish, and others. Jews from various parts of Europe, but especially those who suffered the nineteenth-century pogroms of Russia, sought new homes overseas. Political uprisings in Europe such as the Revolutions of 1848 encouraged at least a few individuals to leave Europe permanently. Colonial powers also found their new territorial possessions convenient as dumping grounds for the convicts they wanted to get rid of in the home country.

Traveling by sailing ship was the norm until the latter half of the 1850s, when steamships were introduced, dramatically changing the nature of migration. Whereas a voyage from England to New York could take six to eight weeks by sailing ship, steamships cut the time down to less than two weeks. This meant less time out of work while en route and a smaller probability of contracting a disease on board. The less arduous traveling conditions and the gradual drop in passage fares (in real terms) over time made both seasonal and return migration more possible. Emigrating from Europe to overseas destinations in the era of the sailing ship had mostly involved permanent moves, but this new technology and lower passage prices changed that.

The years before the 1920s were the golden age for European immigrants as most destination countries granted them access without much reservation. During the 1920s many of the popular destination countries passed legislative measures establishing restrictions on the number of annual immigrants. Today, most countries practice immigration regulations based on national-origin quotas and limits on the total numbers of annual immigrants.

BIBLIOGRAPHY

Baines, Dudley. 1995. *Emigration from Europe, 1815–1930.* Cambridge, U.K.: Cambridge University Press.

Cameron, Rondo. 1993. *A Concise Economic History of the World.* 2nd ed. Oxford: Oxford University Press.

Canny, Nicholas, ed. 1994. *Europeans on the Move: Studies on European Migration, 1500–1800.* Oxford: Clarendon Press and Oxford University Press.

Galenson, David. 1984. The Rise and Fall of Indentured Servitude in the Americas. *Journal of Economic History* 44 (1): 1–26.

Hoerder, Dirk. 2002. *Cultures in Contact: World Migrations in the Second Millennium.* Durham, NC: Duke University Press.

Kleinschmidt, Harald. 2003. *People on the Move: Attitudes toward and Perceptions of Migration in Medieval and Modern Europe.* Westport, CT: Praeger.

McCormick, Michael. 2001. *Origins of the European Economy: Communications and Commerce, AD 300–900.* Cambridge, U.K., and New York: Cambridge University Press.

Olsen, Steve. 2002. *Mapping Human History: Discovering the Past Through Our Genes.* Boston: Houghton Mifflin.

Simone A. Wegge

IMMIGRANTS, LATIN AMERICAN

Immigration from Latin America closely tracks several factors: U.S. foreign policy, both economic and political; U.S. domestic economic policy; and political and economic crisis in the home countries. In some cases, the arrival of Latin Americans to the U.S. mainland is less "immigration" of foreign nationals than "migration" of U.S. citizens from, for example, Puerto Rico.

U.S. economic pressures play a major role in Latin American migration. Business interests desire the low-cost labor that immigrants represent. Labor leaders, immigration-opponent organizations, and individuals argue that immigrants undercut the wages of U.S. workers and cost taxpayers in the form of public services. Immigration advocates defend their presence and advocate for the humane treatment of immigrants; they argue that without immigrants, U.S. industry would come to a standstill. Virtually voiceless are the immigrants themselves, who are unable to exert political pressure.

From the standpoint of the sending Latin American countries, emigration often represents an escape mechanism, with employment opportunities not available at home. In addition, remittances sent back to home countries through wire transfers allow individual families and communities necessities they would otherwise forego.

In terms of foreign policy, U.S. immigration policy is generally determined by whether the home country is seen as a threat to the U.S. way of life.

THEORETICAL FRAMEWORKS

Social scientists have applied various theoretical frameworks to immigration. The melting pot, or assimilation perspective, in which newcomers to the country blended into one "America," seems to have fallen short of the mark when it came to Latinos in the United States, who maintain their cultural identity even after several generations.

Another theoretical framework that gained favor in the 1970s was the internal colonization model. Subscribers to the internal colonization model noted that the "melting pot" did not apply to people of color. Mario Barrera, for example, noted that internal colonization is especially discernable in particular in areas where the colonized are in the majority, but not in control (1979).

Latino immigrants, like immigrants from other continents, often straddle their home countries and their new countries. In this pattern of settlement, sometimes referred to as "transnationalism," immigrants maintain close ties to their homelands and, in fact, send remittances to sustain family ties. In "diasporic citizenship," immigrants maintain such close ties to their home countries that they are able to effect occurrences there while also exercising some power in their new countries.

MEXICAN MIGRANTS

Mexican migration offers the most salient and large-scale story of U.S. immigration policy, due to the countries' shared history and their common 2,000-mile border. Mexicans made up 30.7 percent of the foreign-born persons living in the United States in 2005, the largest nationality by far. To understand the relationship of Mexican immigrants to the United States, one must consider that in 1848 Mexico lost the U.S.-Mexico War and was forced to sell to the United States for $15 million what is now California, New Mexico, Nevada, and part of Colorado and Arizona.

Mexican immigrants have felt the brunt of U.S. immigration policy changes. For instance, during the Great Depression an estimated 200,000 Mexicans returned voluntarily to Mexico, but between 1931 and 1932, an estimated half-million people were deported to Mexico. Later, when the United States faced a labor shortage during World War II, the U.S. and Mexican governments signed an agreement for the importing of *braceros*, agriculture and railroad workers. The Bracero program was renewed annually, until it was terminated in 1964; in 1965, Operation Wetback deported thousands of Mexicans.

PUERTO RICANS

Spain conquered Puerto Rico in 1493, when Columbus landed there on his second voyage to the New World. Although the Spanish-American War of 1898 was fought over Cuba, the treaty that was signed in Paris in December 1898 also gave the United States control over some of Spain's other possessions, including Puerto Rico, Guam, and the Philippines, which were sold to the United States for $20 million.

The first migration of Puerto Ricans to the U.S. mainland lasted from 1900 until 1945, and the main destination was New York City. By the end of World War II Puerto Ricans numbered 135,000 in New York City. A second large migration lasted from 1946 to 1964. In the mid-1960s Operation Bootstrap lured industry to Puerto Rico with the promise of low wages, tax-free operations, and duty-free exports to the mainland. Although the program was saluted as a success, one negative effect was that rural Puerto Ricans abandoned their homes for the promise of jobs in the cities. When there were not enough jobs, Puerto Ricans left home and arrived in the mainland. By 1980 more than 80 percent of Puerto Ricans lived outside of the island.

Puerto Rico has a nonvoting commissioner representing the island in the U.S. Congress. Puerto Ricans may not vote in national elections, but they are eligible to participate in party primaries. A continuing and persistent debate for Puerto Ricans is whether to continue the status quo as a possession of the United States, or to advocate for statehood, or to demand independence. The writer Juan Gonzalez notes that the Puerto Rican migrant experience is "the contradiction of being at once citizens and foreigners" (Gonzales 2000, p. 82).

CUBAN IMMIGRANTS

The Cuban immigrant population dates back to the late 1880s, and has included waves of people who vary in educational and class backgrounds. The first groups settled in New York City, Philadelphia, Tampa, and Key West. Cuban immigrant cigar makers created Ybor City, outside of Tampa, as early as 1886.

In 1898 an explosion aboard the U.S.S. *Maine* in the port of Havana prompted the United States to step in on the conflict that had raged between Spain and Cuba for thirty years. Spanish forces were quickly squelched in what became known as the "Spanish-American War," and the Treaty of Paris ending the war was signed by the United States and Spain—without the participation of Cubans. The United States governed Cuba until May 20, 1902.

The story of contemporary Cuban immigration begins after 1959, when Fidel Castro (b. 1926) and revolutionaries ousted Fulgencio Batista (1901–1973) from power. Cuba's elite arrived in the United States immediately, expecting that the United States would oust Castro quickly. This first group of exiles supported military intercession. Thousands underwent U.S.-sponsored training in Central America, and on April 17, 1961, armed exiles invaded Cuba at the Bay of Pigs, expecting U.S. air cover, which never materialized. Sixty-eight people were killed and the Castro government took 1,209 exiles prisoner. They were released in December 1962 in exchange for $53 million in medical supplies, food, and money.

The Cuban exodus included more than 14,000 unaccompanied minors who arrived between December 1960 and October 1962. After Castro announced his allegiance to communism, middle-class Cubans, fearful of the future, put their children on U.S.-bound flights to be met by relatives or, sometimes, by strangers participating in what later became known as "Operation Peter Pan."

A third wave of Cuban immigrants came after hundreds of Cubans sought asylum at the Peruvian embassy in April 1980. Castro announced that whoever wanted to leave could do so—provided someone arrived to take them from the port of Mariel. Those émigrés came to be called *Marielitos*. A fourth wave, in the mid-1990s, was prompted by the continuing deterioration of Cuba's economy. These people were known as *balseros*, after the small boats and homemade rafts they used to navigate the 90-mile journey to the Florida Keys. Between August 5 and September 10, 1994, the U.S. Coast Guard picked up 30,305 *balseros*.

The United States, in an attempt to weaken the Cuban regime, has made considerable efforts to help Cuban immigrants, calling them "refugees" fleeing communism and making available various federal programs to smooth their adjustment. Federal funds were allocated for resettlement, monthly relief checks, health services, job training, adult-educational opportunities, and surplus food. The federal government also provided grants to Florida colleges and universities to train Cuban teachers. Other aid included a loan program for Cuban college students.

Cubans have transformed south Florida. María Cristina García (1996), referring to the strong anti-Castro sentiment, notes that residents of Miami joke that Florida is the only state in the union with its own foreign policy. At times, anti-Castro fervor has led to violence against those who want a normalizing of relations with Cuba. As the numbers of Cubans in Florida has grown, a public backlash has occurred. In Dade County in 1980 voters repealed the 1973 Bilingual-Bicultural Ordinance, so county funds can no longer be used for programs supporting any language other than English, or for promoting any culture other than that of the United States.

CENTRAL AMERICAN IMMIGRANTS

Most of the immigrants from Central America have come from three nations: Nicaragua, El Salvador, and Guatemala. The difference in the treatment of refugees from the three countries was particularly stark in the late 1980s, when Nicaraguans were fleeing a Marxist government, and the Salvadorans and Guatemalans were fleeing conservative governments and civil war: The U.S. government granted asylum to only 2.6 percent of Salvadorans and only 1.8 percent of Guatemalans, but 25 percent of the Nicaraguan requests for political asylum were approved.

SEE ALSO *Assimilation; Citizenship; Cold War; Cuban Revolution; Diaspora; Immigrants, New York City; Immigration; Latinos; Mexican Americans; Migrant Labor; Migration; Operation Bootstrap; Prejudice; Racism*

BIBLIOGRAPHY

Acuña, Rodolfo. 1988. *Occupied America: A History of Chicanos.* 3rd ed. New York: HarperCollins Publishers.

Bach, Robert L. 1990. Latin America and the Caribbean. In *Immigration and U.S. Foreign Policy,* eds. Robert W. Tucker, Charles B. Keely, and Linda Wrighley, 123–149. Boulder, CO: Westview Press.

Barrera, Mario. 1979. *Race and Class in the Southwest: A Theory of Racial Inequality.* Notre Dame, IN: University of Notre Dame Press.

García, María Cristina. 1996. *Havana USA: Cuban Exiles and Cuban Americans in South Florida, 1959–1994.* Berkeley: University of California Press.

Gonzalez, Juan. 2000. *Harvest of Empire: A History of Latinos in America.* New York: Viking.

Pedraza, Silvia. 1996. Cuba's Refugees: Manifold Migrations. In *Origins and Destinies: Immigration, Race, and Ethnicity in America,* eds. Silvia Pedra and Rubén G. Rumbaut. Belmont, CA: Wadsworth.

Rodriguez, Clara E. 1989. *Puerto Ricans: Born in the U.S.A.* Winchester, MA: Unwin Hyman.

Maggie Rivas-Rodriguez

IMMIGRANTS, NEW YORK CITY

For most countries, immigration constitutes an engine of transformation. For the United States, New York City serves as a symbol of the many peoples from all over the globe who have arrived in the country. It also serves as a microcosm of the complex cultural, political, and socioeconomic issues that immigration gives rise to.

By the time the first Europeans sailed into what is today New York City in the early sixteenth century, the migration of indigenous people into the region had been occurring for thousands of years. The Lenape—who spoke the Algonquin language—populated the area at the time. The influx of European immigrants was slow at first. It was not until the third decade of the seventeenth century that the first major wave of European immigrants settled in the New York City area. The largest immigrant groups were of northern and western European background. Dutch immigrants were the first to locate in what is now Manhattan, founding a settlement they called New Amsterdam. African populations also made an early appearance in the region. On September 15, 1655, the ship *Witte Paert* brought 300 African slaves to New Amsterdam. By 1664, the black population was estimated at between 20 and 25 percent of the total.

In the summer of 1664, New Amsterdam fell to the British. In 1674, the colony was granted to James, the Duke of York, giving New York its name. The Dutch remained the largest immigrant group throughout the seventeenth and eighteenth centuries, followed by French Huguenots. Over 60,000 people resided in the city in 1800.

Immigration into New York greatly expanded in the period between 1815 and 1880, which became known as the Old Immigration era. The immigrant flow from northern and western Europe continued, but from different countries. Hundreds of thousands of Irish and German immigrants moved into the city, followed by English and Scots. By 1860, New York City had 813,669 residents, out of which 383,717 were foreign-born, including 203,740 Irish and 118,292 Germans.

IRISH AND GERMAN IMMIGRANTS

The Irish migration to the United States in the nineteenth century was motivated by a wide array of forces. The American economy had been expanding rapidly and was an attractive source of jobs. New York City itself was booming as a result of the opening of the Erie Canal, which allowed transportation of goods along the Hudson River all the way to the Great Lakes. At the same time, what is now Ireland had become the most densely populated part of Europe, with hundreds of thousands of young workers desperately looking for employment, some in the United States. Immigration peaked in the 1850s, when close to a million Irish moved to America. This migration surge was a result of sharply deteriorating economic conditions in Ireland. In 1845, a fungal disease viciously attacked Irish potato fields, leaving crops almost entirely destroyed. Famine and disease followed, with more than a million people dying and many others fleeing to the United States and other countries in the ensuing decade.

Many of the Irish immigrants were poor and unskilled. They lived in tenements, which were large, cramped, multifamily housing units with scant plumbing, heating, or lighting. They were often discriminated against and vilified for taking employment opportunities from U.S.-born Americans. Nativist groups, whose ideology was that the immigrants were hurting the American economy, society, and culture, campaigned against Irish immigrants, often spreading bigoted views of the Irish. Like other immigrant groups, the Irish were initially marginalized from the city's social and political mainstream. Historians such as Noel Ignatiev and David R. Roedinger find that these immigrants were considered racial minorities at the time, not part of the white population of the city. This poverty and social exclusion exploded in the draft riots of 1863. In July, as the names of thousands of Civil War draftees were announced, many poor Irish who could not pay the $300 draft waiver ran into the streets of the city in protest, burning buildings, looting stores, and assaulting and killing thousands of people. Black residents of the city came under savage attacks that were fueled not just by prejudice but also by the rioters seeking a scapegoat, blaming blacks for their many miseries, including the Civil War draft, low wages, and lack of employment opportunities.

Despite the initial barriers, Irish immigrants gradually progressed in the economy and in society. Because of their growing numbers, they were able to exert considerable political influence in New York City's government institutions, especially through the Democratic Party. Indeed, from being considered a disenfranchised racial minority, the Irish eventually became part of the ethnic white majority population of the city.

Although most German immigrants in the nineteenth century moved to America for the same reason as the Irish—economic opportunity—they had very different origins. They tended to be highly skilled and were able to avoid poverty. From piano production and rubber manufacturing to finance, Germans dominated many high-income sectors of the New York City economic structure. Despite its comparative wealth, the German community in New York—called Kleindeutschland—became highly segregated from the rest of the population. This was partly the result of language differences, but it also reflected the reproduction of German institutions within the community.

THE NEW IMMIGRATION

The ethnic composition of immigrants to New York City changed drastically in the period from 1880 to 1920, when it shifted toward immigrants of southern and east-

ern European background. This immigrant wave, consisting of Italians, Russian Jews, Poles, and Greeks, among others, became known as the New Immigration. Many of these immigrants passed through the immigrant reception center at Ellis Island in the New York City harbor, which opened January 2, 1892.

Like many other mass migration movements, this one followed a chain migration process, by which the initial flow of migrants self-sustains and expands over time. The earlier immigrants sent information about employment opportunities back home, then provided social, economic, and cultural support to later migrants. Between 1880 and 1920, more than 4.1 million Italian immigrants arrived in the United States. Many of these stayed in New York City. Although only 14,000 Italian immigrants resided in New York City in 1880, by 1920 there were almost 400,000. Similarly, the city's Russian Jewish immigrant community grew from 14,000 in 1880 to over half a million in 1920, becoming the largest foreign-born population.

The reasons for this mass migration episode are many. In the early nineteenth century, travel from Europe to the United States could take months. By the late nineteenth century, however, the growth of steamship and railroad travel had made the global movement of people both faster and cheaper. Economic dislocations in southern and eastern Europe, particularly those associated with the decline of agriculture, had generated populations of workers eager to seek opportunities elsewhere. A large share of Italian immigrants, for example, came from southern Italy, especially Sicily and the Mezzogiorno, regions that had stagnated relative to north. Many of these immigrants were unskilled and obtained relatively low-paying jobs in America, including construction (for men) and the garment industry (for women). The mass migration of Russian—and other—Jews to America in the period from 1880 to 1920 was triggered not just by economic forces but also by the resurgence of anti-Semitism, pogroms, and other restrictive laws in many parts of central and eastern Europe. This led them to seek refuge in America. Many of these migrants were skilled workers who became artisans, craftsmen, traders, and financiers.

The late 1920s saw immigration to New York City decline sharply. One reason was the Great Depression, which started in 1929 and lasted through the 1930s. In New York City, unemployment rates reached as high as 25 percent, discouraging potential migrants from moving to America. But economic distress was not the only reason for the drop in immigration. Until the 1920s, the United States had virtually no immigration restrictions. Although border checkpoints had been introduced at twenty-four seaports and popular border crossings such as Ellis Island beginning in the early 1890s, the only restrictions were to exclude sick persons, known criminals, and the like. The

Group	Population In 2000	Income per Capita	Poverty Rate (%)	Unemployment rate (%)	% with less than high school
New York City	8,008,278	$24,010	19.1	6.0	27.7
White	2,801,267	37,391	9.7	3.3	15.3
Black	1,962,154	15,367	23.6	8.9	28.7
Asian	783,058	19,533	18.2	4.3	30.5
Hispanic/Latino	2,160,554	12,500	29.7	9.0	46.6
Immigrants	2,871,032	18,718	19.9	4.9	34.6
Dom. Republic	369,186	10,417	30.3	8.0	56.0
China	261,551	16,228	21.6	3.7	44.6
Jamaica	178,922	18,360	14.6	5.7	30.4
Mexico	145,012	9,790	30.4	5.8	64.8
Guyana	130,647	16,271	13.4	5.4	34.4
Ecuador	114,944	11,964	21.6	6.2	47.7
Haiti	95,580	14,122	18.4	6.1	30.9

SOURCE: 2000 U.S. Census of Population, author's tabulations.

Table 1

one country that faced sharp restrictions was China; the 1882 Chinese Exclusion and Immigration Act effectively barred Chinese immigration until the 1940s. But the Immigration and Naturalization Act of 1924 ended this lax immigration policy. The law imposed the first permanent quotas on immigration, although Western Hemisphere migrants were exempted. It also created a system of immigration preferences that gave an advantage to western and northern Europe. The 1930s saw further restrictive immigration policy initiatives; immigrants were seen as taking jobs from Americans in a period of severe unemployment.

ASSIMILATION

Immigration began to rebound in the 1940s and 1950s, and it surged again after 1965. In that year, legislation that repealed the quota system established in the 1920s was signed into law. The result was a sharp increase in immigration, especially from developing nations. The proportion of New Yorkers born outside the United States had declined from 34 percent in 1924 to a low of 18 percent in 1970, but by 2000 the proportion had risen back to 36 percent. Most of these immigrants were not from Europe but from Latin America, the Caribbean, and Asia. Out of the 2,871,032 immigrants counted by the 2000 U.S. Census of Population, 53 percent were born in Latin America and the Caribbean and 24 percent in Asia. Table 1 shows the population of the largest immigrant groups in 2000. The countries of origin where the largest number of immigrants originated were the Dominican Republic, China, Jamaica, Mexico, and Guyana. Most of these migrants had an economic reason for moving to the city, motivated by huge wage differences between their home

countries and a New York City economy that has displayed renewed and resilient strength since the early 1980s. Indeed, recent immigrants have generally been able to raise their families' standard of living, sending billions of dollars back to their home countries in the form of remittances. But their social and economic progress in the United States has not been without challenges.

Assimilation refers to the process of absorption or fusion of immigrant groups and their descendants into American culture or society. Robert E. Park and the Chicago school of sociology were among the first social scientists to study the process of assimilation in Chicago, New York, and other cities, beginning in the 1920s. Their analysis suggested that for the European immigrant groups entering America in the late nineteenth and early twentieth centuries, assimilation did gradually occur over time. From the acquisition of English to a successful accommodation to the labor market, the immigrants and their descendants (second and third generations) were becoming an integral part of American civil society. This became known as the melting pot view of American society.

But concern has been expressed by some social scientists about the process of assimilation of recent immigrants, particularly those from Latin America and the Caribbean. For instance, political scientist Samuel P. Huntington, in his book *Who Are We? The Challenges to American Cultural Identity* (2004), claims that, unlike previous immigration flows, recent immigrants from Latin America and the Caribbean have not assimilated into mainstream American society. Other social scientists have also expressed concerns that recent immigrants may face difficulties assimilating to the American labor market. The evidence on these issues is not clear-cut.

CHALLENGES FOR IMMIGRANTS

Recent New York City immigrants struggle in an economy that is increasingly unequal and that rewards skills and schooling above anything else. For immigrants from Latin America and the Caribbean, whose level of schooling is substantially below the average, this leads to comparatively low income levels and high poverty rates. Table 1 displays basic indicators of socioeconomic status for various New York City populations. The data are from the 2000 U.S. Census of Population. As can be seen, the annual income per person in the average New York City household was $24,010. But for Dominican migrants, the largest immigrant group in the city, the average income per capita of $10,417 was less than half the average for the city and less than one-third the income per capita of the white population. Poverty rates among immigrants also tend to be higher than among the overall city population. For example, according to the 2000 census, about 30 percent of both Dominican and Mexican immigrants in New York had income below the poverty line, much higher than the citywide poverty rate of approximately 20 percent. The struggle of immigrants in and around New York City is poignantly portrayed by Dominican writer Junot Diaz in his novel *Drown* (1996).

Table 1 shows that the lower socioeconomic status of New York immigrants is not linked to high unemployment. The unemployment rates among immigrants are not that different from those of other New Yorkers. But wages are much lower, an outcome connected in part to lower educational attainment. As Table 1 depicts, the percentage of immigrants twenty-five years of age or older who had not completed a high school education in 2000 was much higher than for the rest of the city's population; for Dominicans it was 56 percent, more than twice the average citywide.

Some recent immigrants are also undocumented workers and face even more serious socioeconomic challenges. Estimates for 2005 suggest that as many as 10 million undocumented workers may be residing in the United States, with half a million in the New York City area. Recent immigration policy initiatives have led to more stringent U.S. immigration enforcement efforts, especially after the September 11, 2001, World Trade Center attacks. As a consequence, many undocumented workers—whether from China, Mexico, or Ecuador—are forced further underground, fearing deportation after many years of residence in the country. Entry into the United States from many developing countries has also become much tougher for both documented and undocumented immigrants.

But the social and economic struggles of the new immigrants are not new. Unskilled immigrants have historically struggled in the New York City economy. Even

social scientists who proposed the melting pot theory noted that immigrant assimilation took several generations and that immigrants themselves often remained embedded in ethnic enclaves with limited linguistic, political, and economic incorporation into American society, whether in the form of a Kleindeutschland or a barrio. Some find that America, particularly urban America, was not and probably never will be culturally homogenous. For instance, Nathan Glazer and Daniel Patrick Moynihan concluded in *Beyond the Melting Pot* (1963) that in New York City cultural diversity and ethnic identity remain even after many generations, a conclusion shared more recently by sociologists Victor Nee and Richard Alba. At the same time, some immigrant groups have historically been able to make the transition from being marginalized racial and ethnic minorities to being considered as part of the country's majority white population while others have not. Social scientists such as Milton M. Gordon and John Ogbu have argued that discrimination and social exclusion may delay or permanently stall any processes of assimilation of stigmatized immigrant groups. The "racialization" of these immigrants may not, however, run along simple black-white racial lines. As sociologists Jennifer Hochschild, Clara Rodriguez, and Mary Waters have noted recently, racial formation for recent immigrants may evolve complex constructions, involving perhaps multiple racial identities. In addition, the recent waves of migrants to New York City include many who move back and forth between their source countries and the United States. This transnationalization, which makes the new immigration different from the old European immigration waves of the nineteenth and early twentieth centuries, generates new opportunities but also challenges for the migrants. Sociologists Hector Cordero-Guzman, Robert C. Smith, and Ramon Grosfoguel summarize these issues and discuss the work of the authors mentioned above in their edited volume *Migration, Transnationalization, and Race in a Changing New York* (2001).

National opinion surveys suggest that most recent immigrant groups and their children, including those from Latin America and the Caribbean, wish to succeed in American society in a way similar to their earlier cohorts. As in the past, despite serious challenges, many immigrants remain the strongest advocates of the American Dream. Sharply improved standards of living relative to the situation in source countries, as well as positive expectations of future economic progress and social mobility, are behind these opinions. But various populations in the United States—from blacks and Chinese to Puerto Ricans and Mexicans—have faced severe and persistent barriers to their socioeconomic progress. Recent immigrants are not immune from these forces, and they are well aware of the difficulties. For instance, the 2003 Pew Hispanic

Center National Survey of Latinos found that over 90 percent of immigrants from Latin America and the Caribbean believe that it is very important (for most, essential) that their children receive a college education in order to succeed in American society. But the same survey found that these immigrants are also seriously concerned about the quality of the high schools their children attend, the rising cost of college tuition, and similar issues.

Particularly worrisome is the condition of undocumented immigrants. In 2006, tens of millions of undocumented immigrants and other concerned groups peacefully marched in New York City, Los Angeles, and many other cities to encourage policy makers to adopt policies that will allow the immigrants to emerge from the underground labor markets in which they work. As in the past, appropriate economic, social, and immigration policies that facilitate immigrant socioeconomic mobility will be required to ensure that the new immigrants achieve their goals.

SEE ALSO *African Americans; American Dream; Assimilation; Caribbean, The; Citizenship; Diaspora; Disease; Ethnicity; Famine; Great Depression; Huntington, Samuel P.; Immigrants to North America; Immigration; Latinos; Melting Pot; Migration; Mobility, Lateral; Naturalization; Nuyoricans; Ogbu, John U.; Park School, The; Segregation, Residential; U.S. Civil War*

BIBLIOGRAPHY

Binder, Frederick M., and David M. Reimers. 1995. *All the Nations Under Heaven: An Ethnic and Racial History of New York City.* New York: Columbia University Press.

Burrows, Edwin G., and Mike Wallace. 1998. *Gotham: A History of New York City to 1898.* New York: Oxford University Press.

Cordero-Guzman, Hector, Robert C. Smith, and Ramon Grosfoguel, eds. 2001. *Migration, Transnationalization, and Race in a Changing New York.* Philadelphia: Temple University Press.

Diaz, Junot. 1996. *Drown.* New York: Riverhead Books.

Foner, Nancy. 2000. *From Ellis Island to JFK, New York's Two Great Waves of Immigration.* New Haven, CT: Yale University Press.

Glazer, Nathan, and Daniel Patrick Moynihan. 1963. *Beyond the Melting Pot: The Negroes, Puerto Ricans, Jews, Italians and Irish of New York City.* Cambridge, MA: MIT Press and Harvard University Press.

Hernandez, Ramona, and Francisco L. Rivera-Batiz. 1997. *Dominican New Yorkers: A Socioeconomic Profile.* New York: Dominican Research Monograph, City College Dominican Studies Institute.

Huntington, Samuel P. 2004. *Who Are We? The Challenges to American Cultural Identity.* New York: Simon and Schuster.

Kasinitz, Philip, John H. Mollenkopf, and Mary C. Waters. 2004. *Becoming New Yorkers: Ethnographies of the Second Generation.* New York: Russell Sage Foundation.

Portes, Alejandro, and Ruben Rumbaut. 2006. *Immigrant America: A Portrait*, 3rd ed. Berkeley: University of California Press.

Rivera-Batiz, Francisco L. 2004. NewYorktitlan: The Socioeconomic Status of Mexican New Yorkers. *Regional Labor Review* 6 (1): 33–45.

Smith, Robert. 2005. *Mexican New York: Transnational Lives of New Immigrants.* Berkeley: University of California Press.

Francisco Rivera-Batiz

IMMIGRANTS TO NORTH AMERICA

An immigrant is a migrant who crosses an international boundary in the process of entering a new country and eventually establishing residence there. Immigrants differ from tourists because they eventually settle in the foreign country, whereas tourists eventually return home without establishing any settlement. The individual does not have to enter the country with the intention of settling, nor does the individual have to permanently settle. In some cases the migrant may move back and forth between one or more countries and the home country. Although in this case the migration is not permanent, the individual is considered a migrant. In contrast, an emigrant is a migrant who crosses an international boundary in the process of leaving a country with the intention of establishing residence elsewhere. A person who crosses an international boundary and enters a new country without establishing a new residence is a tourist or a visitor.

In every international migration, a migrant is simultaneously an immigrant and an emigrant. A key element in the definition of an immigrant is the establishment of a permanent residence in the new country. This usually means residence in the country of destination of at least one year, and is referred to as "long-term immigration." The number of long-term immigrants in the world has increased steadily in recent decades, from 75 million in 1965, to 120 million in 1990 (Martin 2001), to 190 million in 2006 (United Nations 2006). Approximately 3 percent of the world's population in 2006 was composed of long-term immigrants.

The motivations for immigration vary, but the most common is economic. Migrating for economic reasons is particularly important for persons moving from less developed countries to more developed countries (defined as all the countries of Europe and North America, plus the countries of Australia, New Zealand, and Japan). Most immigration is to the more developed countries. Of the 190 million long-term immigrants in the world in 2006, 115 million resided in more developed countries (United Nations 2006).

Regarding the net gain or loss of international migrants, between 1995 and 2000 the United States had a net gain (immigrants minus emigrants) of more than 6.2 million immigrants, far surpassing the nearly 2 million net gain received by Rwanda, the country with the second-largest number. China experienced the largest net loss of immigrants during the period 1995 to 2000, with almost 2 million more emigrants than immigrants. Mexico had the second-highest net loss, more than 1.5 million more emigrants than immigrants (United Nations 2003).

CROSS-NATIONAL PERSPECTIVES

There are push and pull conditions facilitating migration in all countries of the world. In order for an individual or group to decide to migrate there typically needs to be a "push" from the mother country and/or a "pull" to the receiving country. These factors can be occupational, financial, or a variety of personal reasons. Other than these individual factors that encourage immigration, there are also contextual factors that pull migrants to the receiving countries. Once in these countries many migrants are pulled into so-called ethnic enclaves (Borjas and Tienda 1987). Such communities help individuals transition into life as immigrants by providing support and environments much like those in their mother countries.

Migration is most likely to happen between countries that are geographically close together. For the United States this means that most immigration comes from Mexico and Central America, due to proximity. Recently, however, a large number of migrants have come to the United States from China. Even though China is geographically distant from the United States, making migration difficult and expensive, the push and pull factors of China and the United States are strong.

THE AMERICAN IMMIGRANT

More than 98 percent of the residents of the United States are immigrants or the descendants of immigrants. In the United States in 2000, only 4.3 million people, or 1.5 percent, identified themselves as American Indians or Alaska Natives (Ogunwole 2006). Native Americans and Alaska Natives have resided in North America for as many as 40,000 years before the arrival of the first immigrants. They populated areas throughout North and South America, and many coexisted with European settlers until the eighteenth century, when most were eliminated through either disease or war. These conflicts continued

through the late 1800s, when only a fraction of Native Americans remained (Purcell 1995).

In 1598 Spanish settlers first came to the United States for the purpose of colonization. They exploited the land and the indigenous peoples, but differed from earlier explorers in that most remained permanently in the United States. They settled mainly in the present-day southwestern United States and throughout Florida (Purcell 1995).

The first major influx of European immigrants to the United States was from England, with settlement mainly along the east coast in the present state of Virginia (Purcell 1995). The first permanent English settlement was Jamestown in Virginia, established in 1607. These early immigrants mainly lived off the profits from tobacco crops. Tobacco proved to be a profitable but labor-intensive pursuit and eventually spearheaded the immigration of British indentured servants and African slaves. Indentured servants usually came voluntarily to escape the economic downturns in England. The landing of the pilgrims on Plymouth Rock in 1620 marked the beginning of a great influx of English migrants who came to settle in the New World for religious freedom (Purcell 1995). These early immigrant groups "of the 1600s and 1700s established the basic context of American society. English was the dominant language in America; English legal and government documents were the norm; and culture was for two centuries copied after English literature, drama, and art" (Purcell 1995, p. 5). This early British model of American society would serve as the basis for future discrimination and exclusion of some immigrants over the next two centuries.

The forced migration of hundreds of thousands of Africans as slaves also occurred during this period. The first African slaves in the United States were purchased in Jamestown in 1619. This initial forced migration of Africans included only twenty persons, and the slavery of Africans was slow to develop in the colonies because of the use of Native Americans and white indentured servants for slave labor. However, by 1690 there were more African slaves in the United States than white indentured servants (Purcell 1995). The exploitation of African slaves in early America enabled the United States to compete in and eventually dominate the world market. The slave trade ended in 1807, but slavery persisted in the United States until the end of the Civil War (1861–1865). However, the system of racism upon which slavery was founded is engrained in the United States and remains a hurdle for African Americans and other racial and ethnic minorities in the United States.

The Dutch came to America in the 1600s and claimed much of present-day New York (Purcell 1995). Swedish immigrants also came to the New World during this era, but were less successful than the British and Dutch settlers. These early European settlers created a stable life in America, which eased the immigration of others from Europe.

Scotch-Irish immigrants came to America for economic reasons and settled mainly in Pennsylvania. The seventeenth century also saw an influx of German immigrants who were largely motivated by war in Germany. The Germans were the largest non-British and non-English-speaking immigrant group to come to America, and they retained much of their culture. These cultural differences made the Germans one of the first European immigrant groups to experience discrimination from earlier settlers.

Before 1830 the contribution of immigration to population growth in the United States was small. Between 1821 and 1825, for example, the average number of immigrants every year was only about 8,000. This figure increased to almost 21,000 between 1826 and 1830. From 1841 to 1845 immigrants to the United States each year numbered more than 86,000. In the eight years between 1850 and 1857, the total number of immigrants to the United States was 2.2 million. In sum, between 1790 and 1860 the total number of immigrants to the United States was almost 5 million, and most of these were from Europe (Taeuber and Taeuber 1958).

The combination of pro-immigration campaigns and the reduced cost and ease of transcontinental transportation increased immigration drastically during this period. There was a second influx of German and Irish immigrants. German immigrants came to the United States and found work in established industry, aiding in the overall development of U.S. commerce. Irish immigrants, mostly Catholics, suffered severe discrimination that reached a peak in the mid-1850s with the emergence of the Know-Nothings, an anti-Catholic organization dedicated to maintaining the dominance in the United States of Anglo-Saxon Protestants. The end of the nineteenth century also saw immigration from Scandinavian countries. These immigrants sought land for farming and developed the mostly unsettled Midwest.

Chinese first entered the United States shortly after the beginnings of the California Gold Rush in 1849. An estimated 288,000 Chinese entered the United States during this period, although many returned to China before 1882 (Black 1963). Like most immigrants, the Chinese first came to the United States as laborers in search of work and wages. The port of entry for most Chinese immigrants during this first period was San Francisco, and to this day the Chinese name for San Francisco is *Jiu Jin Shan*, or "Old Gold Mountain." The Chinese were subjected to hostile discrimination because many American workers were threatened by the low wages the Chinese

were willing to take. With the passing of the Chinese Exclusion Act of 1882, Chinese immigration tapered off, eventually halting by the end of the twentieth century (Pedraza and Rumbaut 1996).

Overlapping with early Chinese immigration was increased immigration from eastern and southern Europe. These immigrants were not as welcome as the previous European immigrants because the "old" immigrants thought these "new" immigrants would take their jobs (Purcell 1995). The "new" immigrants were Italians, Greeks, Poles, and Slavs who spoke different languages and had slightly different physical features than western Europeans. They were subjected to discrimination, but were able to assimilate into white American culture with passing generations.

Currently the largest numbers of immigrants to the United States are from Asia and Mexico. These immigrants come to the United States for many of the same reasons the European immigrants came in earlier years. Population booms and increased industrialization combined with the economic opportunities of the United States created the push and pull factors that increased emigration from Asia. The Asian immigrants are able to move into ethnic enclaves where they find jobs and homes among people from their countries of origin. They are often criticized for not assimilating into "mainstream" white American culture (Portes and Rumbaut 1990).

The end of the twentieth century to the beginning of the twenty-first century has seen the immigration of millions of Mexicans to the United States. Like many newcomers to the United States, Mexicans come to find work and higher wages. Mexican migrants are subjected to the same discrimination as earlier immigrants groups (Hay 2001). Americans of Mexican descent vary in their levels of assimilation, based mostly on how long they or their forebears have been in the United States.

IMMIGRATION POLICY

Immigration was not a concern in early America, and no laws or policies regulated it on a national level, but the new U.S. Constitution did deal with the issue of naturalization, that is, the process by which an individual becomes a citizen (Purcell 1995). The Articles of Confederation allowed aliens to naturalize as American citizens after two years in the United States, something that was not previously allowed under British rule (Gabaccia 2002). These policies, however, did not apply to white indentured servants or to blacks. This was especially reflected in the Aliens Acts of 1798, which required aliens to register and allowed the president to deport any individuals deemed dangerous. The laws expired in 1801 when Thomas Jefferson took office, and the citizenship waiting period increased to five years (Purcell 1995).

Restrictions on certain groups based on race, ethnicity, or national identity continue to influence immigration policy in the United States even today.

One of the most notable laws restricting immigration to the United States was the Chinese Exclusion Act of May 6, 1882, which reflected the public concern about the large numbers of Chinese who had come to the United States to provide inexpensive labor for the construction of the transcontinental railroad. This law suspended the immigration of Chinese laborers for ten years; permitted Chinese who were in the United States as of November 17, 1880, to stay, travel abroad, and return; prohibited the naturalization of Chinese; and created the so-called "Section 6 exempt status" for Chinese teachers, students, merchants, and travelers, who were admitted on the presentation of certificates from the Chinese government.

The next significant exclusionary legislation was the Act to Prohibit the Coming of Chinese Persons into the United States of May 1892, better known as the Geary Act. It allowed Chinese laborers to travel to China and reenter the United States, but its provisions were otherwise more restrictive than preceding immigration laws. The Geary Act required Chinese to register and to secure a certificate as proof of their right to be in the United States; those who failed to do so could be put into prison or deported. Other restrictive immigration acts affecting citizens of Chinese ancestry followed (King and Locke 1980). The Chinese Exclusion Act and later exclusionary laws were the first to use the concept of an "illegal alien" (Pedraza and Rumbaut 1996).

The next major policy relating to immigrants was the Immigration Act passed in 1917 that increased the head tax on immigrants to $8.00 and required incoming immigrants to pass literacy tests. The Immigration Act also "established several new categories for exclusion, including vagrants, alcoholics, and the psychopathically inferior" (Purcell 1995, p. 82). This law required the potential immigrant to be able to read a passage in English or another language. It also extended the exclusion of Chinese and Japanese to all Asians.

In 1921 further restrictions were passed setting quotas based on nation of origin. In 1924 Congress took this one step further by passing the National Origins Act, which restricted the total number of immigrants to 150,000; the division of the quotas reflected the American population enumerated in the 1890 census. This was done in an effort to restrict immigration mainly to those from Great Britain, Scandinavia, and Germany while reducing immigration from all Asian countries and severely restricting the immigration of Italians, Slavs, Jews, Greeks, and other southern and eastern Europeans (Purcell 1995).

From the 1920s to the 1950s immigration in the United States changed. The Great Depression and World War II (1939–1945) ushered in a period of slow, and sometimes negative immigration, resulting in a net loss. The only significant immigration was from Mexico under the Bracero Program, which admitted Mexican male workers while Americans were overseas. In 1952 the Immigration and Naturalization Act was passed, maintaining most of the quotas set forth by the National Origins Act of 1924 (Hay 2001).

The next major law regarding immigration policy was the Immigration and Naturalization Act of 1965, which became law in 1968. This act ended the national origins quota and allowed the immigration of family members of those already living in the United States, as well as individuals in certain occupations. It also ended the restrictions on Asian immigration and limited immigration from the Western Hemisphere as a whole to 120,000 (Hay 2001). The change in law produced an influx of immigrants from previously unrepresented countries such as many in Southeast Asia and the Middle East.

EXPERIENCES OF IMMIGRANTS

Immigrants have been subjected to discrimination from individuals and from institutions in the United States (Feagin and Eckberg 1980) that have limited their access to the means of success in the United States. "Because patterns of discrimination—individual and institutional—served to exclude some groups from full participation in the society, their access to the historical moments of opportunity that presented themselves over time also varied" (Pedraza and Rumbaut 1996, p. 17). The experiences of discrimination that immigrants have endured vary by race, ethnicity, nationality, and time of immigration.

Assimilation is the process by which individuals become a part of the greater American culture. In order to succeed in America, common thought has dictated that individuals must assimilate into the dominant culture, thought to be composed of white, Protestant individuals of European descent. Cultural pluralism, or multiculturalism (Gordon 1964), the accepted notion of assimilation in the United States today, entails that all groups retain their uniqueness but come together to form a diverse and distinct American culture. However, immigrants are not given the same opportunities to assimilate based on their ethnicity, race, or the circumstances surrounding their immigration. In the early centuries of the United States, assimilation into white dominant culture was an easier task because of the racial, ethnic, and national similarities that were shared among immigrants from Europe. Their transitions into the dominant culture were not necessarily effortless or quick, but were less difficult than those of later generations of foreign immigrants.

In many ways, immigration to the Americas introduced the concept of whiteness and what it meant to be considered white or nonwhite. "[T]he founding fathers drew a boundary around the nation and its citizens" with unequal access to naturalization by race and nationality (Gabaccia 2002, p. 60). The distinction between whites and nonwhites was evident and was even spelled out in government documents. Nonwhites were said to be biologically inferior to whites, and "scientific" arguments were developed to show that whites were smarter, healthier, and altogether stronger. The dominant culture held that Africans, Jews, Italians, and Slavs were inferior to British, German, and Scandinavian immigrants from earlier generations (Gabaccia 2002). Unfortunately, this sentiment was very popular throughout the United States during the end of the 1800s and into the 1900s, and groups such as the Immigration Restriction League in 1894 helped to bring these ideas to the American public. Subsequent laws restricting the immigration of certain groups were not surprising given the racist attitudes of the time.

Some believe that immigrants can have negative impacts on their receiving countries, although a considerable literature shows the opposite (Bean and Stevens, 2003). Immigrant workers sometimes affect the wages of natives (Engerman and Jones 1997): Generally, immigrants are willing, or are forced, to work for lower wages than natives. Accordingly, some lower-prestige occupations disproportionately hire immigrants for lower wages rather than pay natives the higher wages they demand. These issues have the greatest impact in areas of high ethnic concentration (Borjas and Tienda 1987). Immigrants since the 1970s tend to have lower levels of education than previous generations of immigrants, and educational achievement is not likely to increase substantially with time because immigrants typically need to concentrate on earning income rather than education (Martin and Taylor 1998).

From the African slaves working on farms, to the Chinese immigrants building the railroad and working in the gold mines, to the European immigrants participating in the development of American industry, the contribution of immigrants is evident in every aspect of American life. Although their contribution is undisputable, much immigration policy is still founded on the restriction and exclusion of different groups. U.S. immigration has increased steadily over time, with immigration from European countries declining, and immigration from Asian and Latin American countries increasing. Presently, U.S. immigration legislation deals largely with issues of undocumented immigrants and refugees. Efforts to control immigration during the past three decades have included the 1986 Immigration Reform and Control Act, which aimed to control undocumented immigrants, and the second Immigration Reform and Control Act of 1990, which reduced the numbers of family-related admissions and focused on immigration for those in professional occupations, such as doctors, professors, and other highly edu-

cated individuals. In 2006 laws were proposed to stop and control undocumented immigration, mostly from Mexico. The study of immigration shows clearly the undeniable role that immigration has had on America and American culture. The contribution of immigrants is a major foundation of the United States and will continue to be important in every aspect of American life.

SEE ALSO *Assimilation; Colonialism; Migration; Xenophobia*

BIBLIOGRAPHY

Bean, Frank D., and Gillian Stevens. 2003. *America's Newcomers and the Dynamics of Diversity*. New York: Russell Sage.

Black, Isabella. 1963. American Labour and Chinese Immigration. *Past and Present* 25: 59–76.

Feagin, Joe R., and Douglas Lee Eckberg. 1980. Discrimination: Motivation, Action, Effects and Contact. *Annual Review of Sociology* 6:1–20.

Gabaccia, Donna R. 2002. *Immigration and American Diversity: A Social and Cultural History*. Malden, MA: Blackwell.

Gordon, Milton. 1964. *Assimilation in American Life*. New York: Oxford University Press.

Hay, Jeff, ed. 2001. *Immigration*. San Diego, CA: Greenhaven.

Jones, Maldwyn Allen. 1992. *American Immigration*. 2nd ed. Chicago: University of Chicago Press.

King, Haitung, and Frances B. Locke. 1980. Chinese in the United States: A Century of Occupational Transition. *International Migration Review* 14: 15–42.

Martin, Susan F. 2001. Global Migration Trends and Asylum. *Journal of Humanitarian Assistance*. Working paper 41, October 30. http://www.jha.ac/articles/u041.htm.

Massey, Douglas S. 1981. Dimensions of the New Immigration to the United States and the Prospects for Assimilation. *Annual Review of Sociology* 7: 57–85.

Ogunwole, Stella U. 2006. We the People: American Indians and Alaska Natives in the United States. Washington, DC: U.S. Census Bureau. http://www.census.gov/prod/2006pubs/censr-28.pdf.

Pedraza, Sylvia, and Ruben G. Rumbaut. 1996. *Origins and Destinies: Immigration, Race, and Ethnicity in America*. Belmont, CA: Wadsworth.

Portes, Alejandro, and Ruben G. Rumbaut. 1990. *Immigrant America: A Portrait*. Berkeley: University of California Press.

Purcell, L. Edward. 1995. *Immigration: Social Issues in American History*. Phoenix, AZ: Oryx.

Taeuber, Conrad, and Irene B. Taeuber. 1958. *The Changing Population of the United States*. New York: Wiley.

United Nations. 2003. *World Population Prospects: The 2002 Revision*. New York: United Nations.

United Nations. 2006. *International Migration 2006 Wallchart*. New York: United Nations.

Rachel Traut Cortes
Dudley L. Poston Jr.

IMMIGRATION

Immigration studies have yet to reach a consensus on which kinds of human movements constitute immigration. This entry uses the term in its broadest sense, referring to people's temporary or permanent movements and geographic relocation or displacement across political boundaries.

INTERNATIONAL IMMIGRATION

Throughout history, immigration has been an important social force shaped by the world as well as shaping it. In *Global Transformations* (1998), David Held et al. delineate three phases of migration: premodern, modern, and contemporary migration. In the premodern societies, mass migration was instrumental to the formation of states, particularly in Asia but also in other parts of the world. Modern migration started from the fifteenth century and occurred in three major immigrant flows: (1) European settlers, or the first mass migrants, primarily sponsored by the states, to North America; (2) chattel slaves from Africa to North America, the largest forced migration in human history; and (3) indentured Asian laborers, or the coolie system, which replaced chattel slavery in the latter half of the nineteenth century. Contemporary migration is said to have started after World War II (1939–1945). In the contemporary era, major migration flows were not only to North America but also to Europe, Australasia, and the Middle East. Among the immigrant populations of the contemporary era were increasing numbers of refugees as a result of wars, localized poverty, and political persecution.

Many scholars, including Joaquin Arango (2004) and Stephen Castles and Mark J. Miller (2003), also note that immigration since the 1970s has taken on distinct features. First, nation-states have exercised more control over immigration, drawing an increasingly more pronounced line between desired and undesired immigrants. On the one hand, there is state-engineered competition for skilled labor, particularly among traditional destination countries such as Australia, Canada, and the United States. On the other hand, border controls, mainly directed at immigrants deemed illegal, have been intensified. Despite the increased border control, however, human trafficking has become more salient. The second character of the latest immigration movements is the increasing number of actors shaping immigration flows. Attempts to manage international immigration have been coming from different levels of society, ranging from transnational immigrant communities to the United Nations. The third feature of the current migration trends is the changing demography of immigrants. Asians, Africans, and Latin Americans have gradually replaced the Europeans as the major immigrant population. In addition, the gendered composition of immigrants has changed. Women now account for around 50 percent of the total immigrant population. As well, more women than before move as independent immigrants. Whereas this change remains merely a statistical fact to many scholars, it has compelled others to try to bring women back into the history of immigration, which has largely been written in a gender-neutral or genderless tradition. A good example is the book *Women, Gender, and Labour Migration: Historical and Global Perspectives* (2001), edited by Pamela Sharpe, which offers perspectives on immigration that take gender into account.

THEORIZING IMMIGRATION

The complex social phenomenon of human movements has spurred much theorizing about the causes and consequences of immigration. The three major theoretical approaches informing immigrant studies are the economic equilibrium approach, the historical-structural approach, and the migration system theory.

The economic equilibrium approach, also known as the push-and-pull theory, is the dominant perspective in the literature of immigrant studies, according to Castles and Miller. The major tenet of this approach is that immigration is the summation of human agency and an outcome of people's rational cost-and-benefit calculations. Factors pushing immigrants to leave typically include poverty and political repression; factors pulling immigrants away from their origins are often better economic opportunities and political freedom. George Borjas (1989) presents a modern version of the equilibrium approach. He proposes a conception of an immigrant market wherein immigrants, instead of commodities, are exchanged. According to Borjas, individual people are "utility maximizers" responsive to the call of an immigrant market. That is, immigration is regarded as a mechanism through which an optimum distribution of land, labor, capital, and natural resources can be achieved and the social-economic equilibrium of different places can be established.

Whereas the equilibrium approach takes individuals' decisions as its units of analysis, the historical-structural approach locates the reasons and results of immigration in the macroeconomic and political structures of the world. As Castles and Miller point out, this approach is informed by Marxist political economy and the world system theory. It posits that contemporary immigration is a social process that mobilizes cheap labor for capital and thereby helps to sustain the capitalist mode of production in the era of globalization. From the perspective of the world system theory, immigration is considered a new link between developed and developing nations, which were previously connected through colonial occupation or other forms of domination. As the new link, immigration perpetuates the asymmetrical power relationship between the two.

The migration system theory is an attempt to capture all factors affecting the movements of people. A migration system is constituted by two or more countries involved in people's movements. This theory directs researchers' attention to the micro, macro, and meso aspects of migration, as well as historical conditions contributing to migration. Similar to the historical-structural approach, it suggests that prior links between immigrant sending and receiving countries, such as colonial domination, military occupation, trade, and investment, all help to lead to people's migration movements between these countries. At the macro level, international relations, interstate relations, and immigration and other state policies are important incentives or disincentives to migration. At the meso level, the migration system theory is interested in the roles of individuals, groups, or institutions that mediate people's movements. At the micro level, the theory addresses informal networks such as family and community connections that facilitate immigration. In recent years, the new links between transnational communities, in particular, have given rise to a new area of study on transnationalism, according to Castles and Miller.

CRITIQUE OF IMMIGRATION THEORIES AND FUTURE DIRECTIONS OF RESEARCH

While insightful, each of the approaches proposed has significant limitations. A major critique of the equilibrium approach comes from Charles Wood (1982). Wood points out that, first of all, immigration movement has not brought about the anticipated social-economic equilibrium. Rather, recent decades have witnessed increased disparities in regional development. Second, the ahistorical nature of the approach is problematic. The notion of a free market, on which the whole approach is based, is not the empirical truth in all societies at all historical moments. Finally, with a sole focus on micro-level decision making, this approach misses the large social conditions conducive to the movements of people.

In contrast, the historical-structural approach is mainly criticized for failing to explain how the immigration decision comes about for individual actors, as discussed by Wood and also by Castles and Miller. As well, the consequences of immigration as proposed in the historical-structural approach are uni-dimensional and deterministic. Movements of people may not necessarily lead to deprivation in one country and capitalization in the other. Immigrants may bring multiple effects on both the sending and receiving countries. The central problem with this approach is that it reduces people to labor caught up in the capitalization process on a global scale, rather than treating them as human beings with diverse needs and interests.

Epistemologically, the above two approaches are distinct from each other; whereas the former is functionalist in nature, seeing immigration as a means to social harmony, the latter construes immigration as a force adding to social inequalities and conflicts. Despite the differences, there is no doubt that both approaches illuminate some facets of immigration while disregarding others. For instance, neither of them has addressed the facilities and material conditions that contribute to or contain the movements of people. The migration system theory is advantageous to the others in that it focuses on all key dimensions of immigration. However, despite its promise for a holistic understanding of immigration, the migration system theory does not offer a means of interpretation.

In addition to the problems associated with each approach, there are significant issues related to how the phenomenon of immigration is approached in general. First of all, immigration is often considered an aberration that needs to be corrected or a problem that needs to be addressed. The fact that immigration is an integral part of human history has not been registered in the conceptual underpinning of studies on immigration. Second, studies tend to focus on why people move instead of why few people move or why the majority of human populations are not free to move, according to Arango. Posing the alternative questions makes it necessary to critically consider the roles that nation-states play in controlling or restraining people's movements, which have yet to be deeply interrogated. Third, immigration studies mainly center on labor migration. Refugees and the so-called illegal and undesired immigrants remain at the margin of immigrant research. Finally, while immigration studies have started to address the issue of gender, insufficient attention has been paid to how the increasing presence of immigrant women engenders political, economic, and cultural changes in both sending and receiving countries.

SEE ALSO *Immigrants to North America; Immigrants, Asian; Immigrants, Black; Immigrants, European; Immigrants, Latin American; Immigrants, New York City; Migration; Refugees; Settlement; Transnationalism*

BIBLIOGRAPHY

Arango, Joaquin. 2004. Theories of International Migration. In *International Migration in the New Millennium: Global Movement and Settlement*, ed. Danièle Joly, 15–35. Burlington, VT: Ashgate Publishing.

Borjas, George. 1989. Economic Theory and International Migration. *International Migration Review* 23 (3): 457–478.

Castles, Stephen, and Mark J. Miller. 2003. *The Age of Migration: International Population Movements in the Modern World*. 3rd ed. New York: Guilford Press.

Held, David, Anthony G. McGrew, David Goldblatt, and Jonathan Perraton. 1998. *Global Transformations: Politics, Economics and Culture.* Stanford, CA: Stanford University Press.

Sharpe, Pamela, ed. 2001. *Women, Gender, and Labour Migration: Historical and Global Perspectives.* New York: Routledge.

Wood, Charles. 1982. Equilibrium and Historical-Structural Perspectives on Migration. *International Migration Review* 16 (2): 298–319.

Hongxia Shan

IMMIGRATION AND NATURALIZATION ACT OF 1965

SEE *Chinese Americans.*

IMMIGRATION REFORM ACT, 1965

SEE *Immigrants, Black.*

IMMISERIZING GROWTH

Immiserizing growth occurs if a technological improvement or an increase in the availability of a factor of production makes people more miserable in that it actually decreases the real output of an economy. It is often modeled as occurring because of structural rigidities in a model with international trade. Early exceptions, where immiserizing growth had domestic causes, come from classical and, perhaps, Marxist theories (Marx 1863–1883). David Ricardo (1817) introduced this possibility in a chapter entitled "On Machinery" that he added to his last edition of *The Principles of Political Economy and Taxation.* He provided an example where a technological improvement would reduce equilibrium output in the short run. In the long run, however, real output would rise (see Hicks 1969; Samuelson 1988; Shields 1989). Marx also discussed the possibility of economic crises brought on by a falling rate of profits and a rising rate of exploitation (see Shaikh and Tonak 1994).

In the neoclassical tradition, immiserizing growth is seen as a result of either policy distortions or market failures. The policy distortions might be domestic distortions such as distorted factor prices (Bhagwati 1969) or trade distortions such as tariffs (Johnson 1967). The most discussed possibility of immiserizing growth, both in the short run and in the long run, was developed and discussed by Jagdish Bhagwati (1969). It involves a decrease in the country's terms of trade resulting from this growth, which is of sufficient magnitude to reduce the country's real income. A country will export goods using its abundant factor. If the supply of this factor increases, the country will produce and export more of these export goods and produce less of other goods (the Rybczynski Theorem). Immiserizing growth can occur if this expansion in exports causes the prices for the country's export goods to deteriorate enough to make it worse off with the increase in production. Whether or not a country might be likely to suffer from immiserizing growth depends on three conditions. First, the country must be driven to export. Second, changes in these exports need to have a large impact on the good's price, and the foreign demand for these exports needs to be inelastic so that a rise in exports leads to a decline in export earnings. Third, the country must be highly dependent on exports, and exports must be a high proportion of gross national product.

The export pessimism underlying the concept of immiserizing growth is an extreme form of the pessimism behind the structuralism of Raúl Prebisch (1964) and others. It implies some unlikely behavior of the exporting country. It implies no endogenous reaction to these declining terms of trade (Clarete and Whalley 1994). To see why this type of immiserizing growth is unlikely to occur, consider the situation of the major oil exporters such as Saudi Arabia and Kuwait. They seem to satisfy the conditions for immiserizing growth. They are clearly driven to export oil, as it dominates the economies of these countries. In addition, the countries are sufficiently important as suppliers that an increase in their exports will drive oil prices down. Since the demand for oil is highly inelastic, this increase in supply would dramatically reduce oil revenues. However, long-term immiserizing growth seems unlikely for these countries.

The very reason immiserizing growth may be unlikely for these countries is the very reason it is such a threat. It would be foolish for any supplier to do nothing in the face of dramatically declining terms of trade. The inelasticity of demand provides an incentive for suppliers to exercise monopoly power and to try to organize other suppliers into a cartel. Indeed this is what happened with the formation of the Organization of Petroleum Exporting Countries (OPEC). Far from being competitive suppliers with no power to control prices, the major oil exporters, individually and collectively, have considerable price control. They did not dramatically increase production when prices were low in a desperate but fruitless attempt to increase declining revenues.

Structuralists such as Prebisch and neo-Marxists (see Prebisch 1964; Frank 1967) emphasize that growth for small, less developed countries might harm these countries even if the demand for their country's exports is highly elastic. Collectively, they may be selling into a market with inelastic demand. While it may seem to be in the interest of each country to expand its exports, collectively they may drive the price down to an extent that immiserizing growth occurs.

SEE ALSO *Bhagwati, Jagdish; Distortions; Exports; Heckscher-Ohlin-Samuelson Model; Machinery Question, The; Organization of Petroleum Exporting Countries (OPEC); Prebisch, Raúl; Prebisch-Singer Hypothesis; Ricardo, David; Rybczynski Theorem; Technological Progress, Economic Growth; Terms of Trade; Trade*

BIBLIOGRAPHY

Bhagwati, Jagdish N. 1969. Optimal Policies and Immiserizing Growth. *American Economic Review* 59 (December): 967–970.

Clarete, Raymond L., and John Whalley. 1994. Immiserizing Growth and Endogenous Protection. *Journal of Development Economics* 45 (October): 121–133.

Frank, Andre Gunder. 1967. *Capitalism and Underdevelopment in Latin America.* New York: Monthly Review Press.

Hicks, John. 1969. *A Theory of Economic History.* Oxford: Clarendon.

Johnson, Harry G. 1967. The Possibility of Income Losses from Increased Efficiency or Factor Accumulation in the Presence of Tariffs. *Economic Journal* 77 (March): 151–154.

Marx, Karl. 1863–1883. *Capital: A Critique of Political Economy,* ed. Frederick Engels. New York: International Publishers 1967.

Prebisch, Raúl. 1964. *Towards a New Trade Policy for Development: Report by the Secretary-General of the United Nations Conference on Trade and Development.* New York: United Nations.

Ricardo, David. 1817. *The Principles of Political Economy and Taxation.* London: Aldine Press for Dent, 1965.

Samuelson, Paul A. 1988. Mathematical Vindication of Ricardo on Machinery. *Journal of Political Economy* 96 (April): 274–282.

Shaikh, Answar M., and E. Ahmet Tonak. 1994. *Measuring the Wealth of Nations: The Political Economy of National Accounts.* New York: Cambridge University Press.

Shields, Michael P. 1989. The Machinery Question: Can Technological Improvements Reduce Real Output. *Economica* 56 (May): 215–224.

Michael P. Shields

IMPEACHMENT

Shortly before the House Judiciary Committee met in October 1973 to debate proposed articles impeaching President Richard Nixon (1913–1994), a then-unknown Democratic congresswoman from Texas momentarily caught the public's attention. Barbara Jordan (1936–1996) announced that she felt bound to go to the U.S. National Archives to put her fingers on the constitutional text that delegated to the House of Representatives the power to vote articles of impeachment. To many, hearing Jordan's sonorous retelling of her experience, the impression must have been that by reading the constitutional language dealing with the impeachment and removal of "the President, Vice President and all civil Officers of the United States" (Art. I Sec. 2 (5), Sec. 3 (6–7); Art. II Sec. 2 (1), Sec. 4), Jordan would know exactly what the rules were that governed the process. In fact, the Constitution's language on impeachment is as difficult to interpret as pharaoh's dreams.

Impeachment dates to the thirteenth century. Those who would frame and ratify the U.S. Constitution were familiar with the process. In England, it allowed the king's ministers to be punished even though the king himself could do no wrong. By the mid-eighteenth century, however, despite the publicity that attended the impeachment in 1787 of Warren Hastings (1732–1818), the first governor-general of British India, the process had pretty much disappeared. Hastings was charged with corruption during his tenure in India. His trial began in 1788; he was finally acquitted in 1795. It had never been transplanted to the colonies. In England, its decline paralleled the growth of ministerial responsibility to Parliament and the need of a ministry to have "the confidence of Parliament" and not simply the approbation of the monarch.

IMPEACHMENT IN AMERICA

Despite its rarity in contemporary England, both the Virginia and New Jersey plans provided for impeachment, although both gave the power to members of the judiciary. Only as the Constitutional Convention was winding down in 1787 was the power to impeach and remove vested in the House and Senate, with the chief justice of the Supreme Court involved as the presiding officer only at the trial of an impeached president. The Constitution also clearly distinguished how impeachment would be used in the United States as opposed to England by providing that conviction was limited to removal from office and possibly disqualification from holding public office in the future. In contrast, in England, Parliament could vote for criminal punishments, including death for those found guilty of "high crimes and misdemeanors." The U.S. Constitution also explicitly limited the president of the United States from pardoning those impeached and convicted.

Although generally referred to as *impeachment*, the process has two distinct steps. The first involves impeachment, a task assigned to the House, where a simple majority vote is required to approve articles of impeachment. Persons impeached are then tried before the Senate, with the House designating the prosecutors. A two-thirds vote of the Senate is required for conviction. Two presidents—Andrew Johnson (1808–1875) and William Jefferson Clinton (1946–)—have been impeached. Nixon resigned before the full House voted on the impeachment articles adopted by the Judiciary Committee.

More common have been impeachment proceedings against federal judges. Thirteen have been impeached; seven were convicted, four were acquitted, and two resigned with no further Senate action. One U.S. senator and one cabinet member were also impeached. Senator William Blount (1749–1800) of Tennessee was the first individual impeached. The Senate expelled Blount in 1797 and then voted that it did not have jurisdiction to vote on the impeachment articles. Blount was charged with seeking to incite Indians to assist the British in driving the Spanish from west Florida. U.S. Secretary of War William Belknap (1829–1890) resigned in 1876 after being impeached for receiving bribes; the Senate failed to muster the required two-thirds vote to convict.

DISPUTED LANGUAGE

Despite the number of times impeachment has been initiated there remains much controversy as to its exact parameters. Republican House Minority Leader (later president) Gerald Ford (1913–2006), in leading the effort to impeach Justice William O. Douglas (1898–1980) (Ford and fellow Republicans were concerned both about the Justice's increasingly erratic lifestyle and the possibility that some of his business dealings were illegal), famously quipped that an impeachable offense was "whatever a majority of the House [concludes it] to be …; conviction results from whatever offense or offenses two-thirds of the other body considers to be sufficiently serious." Given the continuing scholarly debate, Ford's statement has much to recommend it. Among the debated issues is the nature of "high crimes and misdemeanors," the famously imprecise language taken from British practice and enshrined by the Framers in the fourth section of Article II: whether Congress members can be impeached and whether judges can be removed for lack of "good behavior;" whether those removed can have recourse to judicial review; and, finally, whether there are other constitutionally permissible means by which officials can be removed from office.

One set of scholars argues that "high crimes" is limited to indictable offenses. This was argued by Richard

Nixon's attorney, James St. Clair (1920–2001), and by law professor Raoul Berger (1901–2000). In contrast, Michael Gerhardt (2000) claims this is too narrow a reading of the English precedents and would have meant for much of early American history that there were few if any grounds for impeachment, since there were few if any federal crimes for which an individual could be indicted. His argument is that the term embraces any activity that would threaten the nation or bring the office into grave disrepute.

Others have claimed that offenses must relate to the office the person holds. This view is generally rejected with the frequently cited example being that of a hypothetical public official who commits a murder totally unrelated to his or her public responsibilities.

Supporting the argument that the standard, particularly regarding presidents, should be high is the claim that removing a president should be a very rare occurrence, since in doing so the Congress would be setting aside the will of the people. Critics of the impeachment of President Clinton argue that this action was almost akin to a congressional coup d'état and that the underlying act, a tryst with a White House intern, was a purely private act. Supporters of the impeachment argue that Clinton's grand jury perjury and his sullying of his office were more than sufficient to justify his removal and that his successor, Vice President Al Gore, had also been elected by the people, a situation quite unlike the nineteenth-century case of President Andrew Johnson.

The impeachment of Senator Blount can be used to argue both that members of Congress can be removed and that they cannot. The dominant view is that there is no basis to include members of Congress under the phrase "all civil Officers."

The first official removed from office (Blount was expelled by the Senate, acting under its powers under Article I, section 5), John Pickering (1738–1805), a U.S. district court judge who was impeached in 1803, clearly committed no crime. He was probably mentally ill and frequently drunk. Like many subsequent impeachments, the vote was along party lines. Pickering's impeachment leads some to argue that since judges serve "during good behavior" (referring to Article III, Section 1 of the Constitution, which concerns a judge's life tenure), the fact of bad behavior on the part of judges constitutes additional grounds for removal. The weight of historical evidence is opposed to this position.

Very much in dispute is whether the Constitution allows Congress to fashion other means to remove officials, particularly someone like Pickering who commit no crime and whose behavior would not serve to bring the government into disrepute. The Senate has, since the 1930s, provided that the trial can be conducted by a committee reporting to the full Senate. Several proposals have been advanced in Congress by which federal judges could be removed short of impeachment. The Twenty-fifth Amendment provides a means by which an incapacitated president can be removed. Whether a similar amendment to remove disabled judges is necessary or whether there can be a statutory solution is not clear.

Finally, impeachment appears to be one of the few issues that might fall within the steadily shrinking orbit of nonjusticiable "political questions." In a case arising from the 1989 impeachment for perjury of Judge Walter Nixon Jr., the Supreme Court, by dismissing his appeal, appeared to indicate that judicial review, after conviction, was not an option. However, like nearly every other aspect of the impeachment process, this statement too is subject to dispute.

SEE ALSO *Clinton, Bill; Nixon, Richard M.; Politics*

BIBLIOGRAPHY

Berger, Raoul. 1974. *Impeachment: The Constitutional Problems.* Enl. ed. Cambridge, MA: Harvard University Press.

Black, Charles L. 1974. *Impeachment: A Handbook.* New Haven, CT: Yale University Press.

Brant, Irving. 1972. *Impeachment: Trials and Errors.* New York: Knopf.

Gerhardt, Michael J. 2000. *The Federal Impeachment Process: A Constitutional and Historical Analysis.* 2nd ed. Chicago: University of Chicago Press.

Labovitz, John R. 1978. *Presidential Impeachment.* New Haven, CT: Yale University Press.

Posner, Richard A. 1999. *An Affair of State: The Investigation, Impeachment, and Trial of President Clinton.* Cambridge, MA: Harvard University Press.

Rehnquist, William H. 1992. *Grand Inquests: The Historic Impeachments of Justice Samuel Chase and President Andrew Johnson.* New York: Morrow.

U.S. House Committee on the Judiciary. 1973. *Impeachment: Selected Materials.* 93rd Cong., 1st Sess. October 1973. Washington, DC: U.S. Government Printing Office.

U.S. House Committee on the Judiciary. 1975. *Impeachment of Richard M. Nixon, President of the United States: The Final Report of the Committee on the Judiciary, House of Representatives, Peter W. Rodino, Jr., Chairman.* New York: Viking.

U.S. House Committee on the Judiciary. 1998. *Impeachment of William Jefferson Clinton, President of the United States: Report of the Committee on the Judiciary, Together with Additional, Minority, and Dissenting Views to Accompany H. Res. 611.* 105th Cong., 2nd Sess. December 16, 1998. Washington, DC: U.S. Government Printing Office.

Walter Nixon v. United States, 113 S.Ct. 732 (1993).

Francis Graham Lee

IMPERFECT COMPETITION

SEE *Competition, Imperfect.*

IMPERIALISM

Imperialism as a distinct set of ideas can be traced to the second half of the nineteenth century; it refers primarily to a political system based on colonies governed from an imperial metropolitan center for direct or indirect economic benefit. Commonly associated with the policy of direct extension of sovereignty and dominion over noncontiguous and often distant overseas territories, it also denotes indirect political or economic control of powerful states over weaker peoples. Regarded also as a doctrine based on the use of deliberate force, imperialism has been subject to moral censure by its critics, and thus the term is frequently used in international propaganda as a pejorative for expansionist and aggressive foreign policy.

IMPERIALISM IN THE NINETEENTH CENTURY

Although the term *empire* (Latin: *imperium*), inhering in the idea of supreme command or authority, is regarded as part of a universal human political experience since the rise of polities in antiquity, *imperialism* is more narrowly dated to the era of colonial empires of the eighteenth and nineteenth centuries. During this era the economic and military advantages of mercantile, industrialist, and capitalist countries were translated into a more or less systematic and formal policy of conquest, annexation, and administration of the world outside of Europe and the Americas. Between 1880 and 1914 much of this world was partitioned in territories under the direct rule of European countries, or subjected to their political influence. Led by Great Britain, France, Germany, the Netherlands, Belgium, and the United States, and later followed by Russia and Japan, principal powers of the world divided Asia into informal zones of influence, and carved up the Pacific and Africa into new territorial, and mostly colonial, units. The expectation of asymmetrical and iniquitous distribution of political-economic gains was complemented by the roughly contemporaneous idea that the world was inhabited by advanced and backward races and nations, and that imperial expansion was also in part the preponderance of those who were fit and thus destined to rule. In the 1890s many contemporary observers associated imperial expansionism with a new phase in the development of international capitalism, one that succeeded the era of free competition and economic liberalism of the mid-nineteenth century. This particular use of the term *imperialism* has often been attributed to V. I. Lenin, the architect of the Russian Revolution. John A. Hobson (1858–1940) noted the heightened currency of the term in the late nineteenth century, both in political discussion and common speech. Whether they were influenced by Karl Marx's theories or not, contemporaries were aware of the economic roots of this new version of imperial expansion, which they identified with the territorial division of the world among major European powers into formal or informal colonies and spheres of influence. Such claims among European military and economic rivals were nowhere more evident than at the Berlin Conference of 1884, hosted by the German chancellor Otto von Bismarck (1815–1898), who had come to the conclusion that an Africa divided along colonial lines by mutual agreement among the European empires would safeguard markets and raw materials. This move led to the proclamation of a number of protectorates and colonies, known as the "scramble for Africa," and the eventual partition of the entire continent.

The ties between mercantile capital, empire-building, and colonial ventures had already been secured by the late eighteenth century. Capital invested in the triangular trade between England, Africa, and the Caribbean had a profound impact on New World Iberian colonies. The African slave trade, for example, provided the labor for Brazilian and Caribbean plantations that produced sugar for much of western Europe and North America. During the early nineteenth century, settler colonies were also becoming important, both commercially and politically, best articulated perhaps in the context of Upper and Lower Canada by John Lambton, Lord Durham (1792–1840) in his *Report on the Affairs of British North America* (1839). While drawing up the report he was ably assisted by Edward Gibbon Wakefield (1796–1862) and Charles Buller (1806–1848), both of whom were well known for their progressive and radical views on social reform. The Durham Report, which effectively safeguarded British influence over a divided Canada, advocated responsible government through graduated constitutional change, while at the same time recognizing the value of commerce and investment. It also delineated imperial trade and foreign policy, and the regulation of colonial settlement through a careful distribution of public lands by the British government.

Already by the 1840s colonies had assumed heightened importance as welcome outlets, not only for criminals and outcasts, but also for increasingly large numbers of migrants who could not secure adequate employment and resources in the mother country. There were many theorists and advocates of settler colonialism, among them the radical Wakefield, who called for a "systematic colonization" of the Australian continent, arguing that a successful transference depended on the compatibility of capital and labor, and economic opportunity to create harmony between the different classes of settlers. The absorption of "redundant people" in the colonies, Wakefield pointed out in his *View of the Art of Colonization* (1849), would result in increased supply of food and raw materials for manufacture for the inhabitants of the empire at home. Wakefield clearly anticipated the importance of empire for the accumulation of capital and investment overseas.

It was Bruno Bauer (1809–1882), the German philosopher, historian, and theologian, and also onetime leader of the left-Hegelians, who advanced the idea of imperialism as a powerful and disruptive global political force. The entry of Russia as a world power, he predicted, would usher in a new era of transnational imperial rivalry. According to Bauer, this was the result of the contradictions that had arisen between the demands of modern mass society and the political absolutism of the state, a symptom of the crisis of the old European liberal order (Bauer 1882). Thus, for example, in Bismarck's model of state-based socialism in Germany, economic production was subjected to close political control, driven by the need to rein in the unruly forces of capitalism. In Benjamin Disraeli's England, in contrast, political leaders sought a mass mandate for imperial policies in order to shore up and bolster a paternalist monarchy whose institutional basis had been eroded by the force of economic change. Bauer's verged on an apocalyptic vision, portending heightened imperial rivalry across the world, resulting in a war among the leading nations.

Imperialism and nationalism had long been regarded as kindred forces. At the turn of the century, among theorists who challenged this commonly accepted idea was the British liberal economist John A. Hobson, who argued in his influential *Imperialism: A Study* (1902) that the drive for imperialist expansion in Europe could not be fully explained by the rise of patriotic nationalism. From the vantage point of an entire nation and its people, the policy of imperial expansion did not result in long-term and tangible economic benefits; the costs of wars of expansion far outweighed the returns, and indeed, necessary social reforms that would have benefited the economically disadvantaged sections of the population were often set aside in favor of imperial adventurism. Such policies, however, served the financial interests of capitalists and their representative political groups, who were, according to Hobson, custodians of the "imperial engine." Periodic congestion of capital in manufacturing, resulting from uneven distribution of income, falling demand, and excess goods and capital inside a given nation-state, urged the search for investment outlets overseas, thus driving the search for new markets and opportunities for investment in foreign markets, including distant colonies and dependencies. This process was further propelled through the practices of larger firms and financial groups operating in trusts and combines that sought restrictions on output in order to avert loss through overproduction. Hobson's study, which focused on business cycles, behavior of financial groups, and patterns of overseas investment, directly influenced Marxist thinkers in their analysis of imperialism.

IMPERIALISM AND ITS CRITICS: THE TWENTIETH CENTURY AND BEYOND

During the early decades of the twentieth century there were many radical critics on the Left who saw the rise of imperialism as a historical force intimately tied to the worldwide expansion and consolidation of finance capital. As Lenin in his introduction to Nikolai Bukharin's tract *Imperialism and World Economy* (1917 [1972]) noted succinctly: "The typical ruler of the world became finance capital, a power that is peculiarly mobile and flexible, particularly intertwined at home and internationally, peculiarly devoid of individuality and divorced from the immediate process of production, peculiarly easy to concentrate" (p. 11). Much of the debate centered on Marx's prediction about the concentration of capital. Rudolf Hilferding in *Finance Capital* (1910 [1981]) and Otto Bauer in *Die Nationalitätenfrage und die Sozialdemokratie* (The Nationalities Question and the Social Democracy, 1907), extending Marxian ideas of capital accumulation, argued that the sectors of banking and finance had increasingly started to exert pressure on industrial production, leading to the formation of monopolies and cartels, the quest for protection of markets, and ultimately to economic imperialism, international rivalry, and war. Similarly, Rosa Luxemburg, the Polish-born German revolutionary and founder of the Polish Social Democratic Party and the Spartacus League (which later became the German Communist Party), forcefully argued in her 1913 tract *Die Akkumulation des Kapitals* (The Accumulation of Capital) that imperialism was the direct result of the dynamic and aggressive inroad of capitalism into the less economically advanced parts of the world.

Bukharin and Lenin, stalwarts of Bolshevism and veterans of the October Revolution, took these ideas further, advancing that imperialism was not a contest for world domination among rival races such as Slavs and Teutons, but the direct result of a particular form of capitalism marked by the changing structure of financial investment and relations of production. Colonial expansion and imperial wars were indeed signs of a developing global economy. Bukharin saw the global expansion of finance capital as a historic phenomenon tied to new national rivalries, fiscal competition, and imperial conquest.

Lenin penned a small tract, "Imperialism: The Highest Stage of Capitalism" (1917 [1970]), which soon became one of the most influential of all Marxist studies on the subject. Lenin saw imperialism as closely tied to the normal functions of an advanced capitalism that had already undergone profound changes along with the development of modern European nation-states. More importantly, monopoly capitalism had already edged out an earlier form of competitive capitalism marked by the free entry and exit of small and large-scale industries and businesses. Toward the end of the nineteenth century, an advanced stage of capital was already in progress where open economic competition and production of commodities were replaced by predatory monopolies and cartels. For Lenin, a good example of this process was the changed role of banks as financial intermediaries to monopolistic interest groups, merging readily with industry and leading to the domination of finance capital and the unprecedented concentration of production. As a result, a fundamental and historic feature of capitalism had been altered: What was once characterized by the separation of ownership of capital from the process of production was now marked by a separation of finance capital from industrial capital. Lenin held that new finance capital had outpaced commodities in reaching far corners of the world, heightening actual divisions and rivalry between trading groups and nations. New segments of the world market were thus being appropriated by monopoly capital, with the merging of corporations—such as conglomerates in the oil industry—to weed out competition.

Lenin saw the division of the world among colonial and imperial powers as closely associated with the transformative power of finance capital. Thus the scramble among powerful nations for colonial expansion was largely fueled by the drive for raw materials and markets. Lenin famously proclaimed imperialism as the "highest stage" in the development of capitalism. As monopoly interest groups sought to divide the world into arenas of economic exploitation, they unleashed new rivalries over markets and raw materials among both advanced and less advanced capitalist nations. The uneven economic development of nations, including imperial and colonial powers, further intensified economic competition and political conflict.

Lenin was vehement in his opposition to other theorists of imperialism, especially his contemporary Karl Kautsky (1854–1938), one of the most influential voices among German Social Democrats before World War I. Kautsky in "Die Internationalität und der Krieg" (Imperialism and the War, 1914) argued that imperialism was indeed the logical outcome of capitalism, but was beset by its own fatal contradictions. Kautsky predicted that World War II would lead to the demise of imperialism as an international policy along with its global-industrial order, and rather than a worldwide communist revolution, it would create a new and peaceful consortium among advanced nations along with a cosmopolitan global economy free of imperialistic militarism.

This theory—that political, military, and ideological aspects of imperialism during the late nineteenth and early twentieth centuries were essentially manifestations of deep-seated economic causes, especially the rise of monopolistic finance capital fueling the drive for overseas colonies and global markets—is often referred to as the "Lenin-Hobson thesis." Although some of the basic premises of the thesis have been questioned in light of subsequent history—for instance, the relationship between militarism and economic gain and also between colonialism and the expansion of finance capital—aspects of it continue to be influential. Critics of Lenin and Hobson, and of Marxist theories of imperialism in general, question the assertion that wars of colonial expansion or imperial rivalry were fought for solely economic reasons and that capitalism was the primary engine of colonial and imperial expansion. Some have argued that imperialism was an ideology inherently antithetical to the logic of capitalism and market economy, and as such, a relic of the past; others have sought its origins in the rise of mass politics and fascism (Arendt [1951] (1973)).

More recently, historians following Ronald Robinson and John Gallagher (1961) have questioned the very premise that the high tide of imperialist expansion in the late nineteenth century was a new or unprecedented phenomenon, arguing instead for an extended period of free-trade imperialism bridging the era of mercantilist empires that developed during the fifteenth to the eighteenth centuries and the nineteenth-century wars of imperial annexation. In this intermediate stage, European political and commercial interests were extended through indirect means, without the administrative responsibility of direct colonial rule. Relying largely on the history of the British Empire in Asia and Africa and the expansion of British financial interests in Latin America, such critics view imperialism as a long-unfolding process in which imperial occupation and commercial exploitation are the results of long-term, informal economic relationships between European commercial agents and local regimes, which in themselves were active participants in the process of empire building. Such formulations underscore the role of political regimes that eventually succumbed to European empires, and their subjects who resisted or became unequal partners in colonial economic expansion. They also emphasize the vital role played by newly independent Latin American countries such as Argentina, Bolivia, and Chile as substantial markets, and as part of an extended informal empire (Hopkins 1994). These markets were crucial to British industrial production and finance capital in the late nineteenth and early twentieth centuries,

and more generally to the global economy dominated by the United States and western Europe, without directly being part of the colonial system.

Despite such revisions, critics of imperialism still ascribe it to the direct or indirect manifestation of the march of global capitalism from the nineteenth century to the present. Sociologists such as Immanuel Wallerstein (1979, 1988) and economists such as Andre Gunder Frank (1966, 1967) consider European imperial expansion as part of a much larger history of the expansion of capitalism as a world-system, in which shifting economic cores and peripheries are mutually constituted through abiding asymmetric economic and political relationships. Others emphasize imperialism not so much as an economic but as a cultural and ideological force associated with European hegemony. In this wider and more general sense, imperialism has been related to post-Darwinian biological theories of race, theories of western industrial and technological superiority, militant nationalism, orientalism, and also modern-day environmentalism. Subject to such wide-ranging usage, imperialism is harder to define in the present context as a specific set of ideas. Rather, it is more accurately described as an all-purposive political orientation, no longer focused on the extension of the sovereignty of the European nation-states beyond their internationally recognized boundaries, but much more on the political condition of a collective present (Hardt and Negri 2000) marked by a post-European global hegemony of displaced and multilocal capitalism.

SEE ALSO *Capital; Capitalism; Colonialism; Decolonization; Determinism, Biological; Empire; Frank, Andre Gunder; Hegelians; Hilferding, Rudolf; Jingoism; Lenin, Vladimir Ilitch; Luxemburg, Rosa; Marx, Karl; Nationalism and Nationality; Neocolonialism; Neoimperialism; Racism; Underconsumption; Wallerstein, Immanuel; World-System*

BIBLIOGRAPHY

Adas, Michael. 1990. *Machines As the Measure of Men: Science, Technology, and Ideologies of Western Dominance.* Ithaca, NY: Cornell University Press.

Arendt, Hannah. [1951] 1973. *Origins of Totalitarianism.* San Diego: Harvest Books.

Bauer, Bruno. 1882. *Disraelis Romantischer und Bismarcks Sozialistischer Imperialismus* (Disraeli's Romantic and Bismarck's Socialist Imperialism). Chemnitz, Germany: E. Schmeitzer.

Bauer, Otto. 1907. *Die Nationalitätenfrage und die Sozialdemokratie* (The Nationalities Question and the Social Democracy). Vienna: Verlag der Wiener.

Bukharin, Nikolai. [1917] 1972. *Imperialism and World Economy.* London: Merlin.

Durham, John George Lambton, Earl. 1839. *Report on the Affairs of British North America.* London: Ridgways.

Frank, Andre Gunder. 1966. *The Development of Underdevelopment.* Boston, MA: New England Free Press.

Frank, Andre Gunder. 1967. *Capitalism and Underdevelopment in Latin America; Historical Studies of Chile and Brazil.* New York: Monthly Review Press.

Grove, Richard. 1996. *Green Imperialism: Colonial Expansion, Tropical Island Edens and the Origins of Environmentalism, 1600–1860.* New York: Cambridge University Press.

Hardt, Michael, and Antonio Negri. 2000. *Empire.* Cambridge, MA: Harvard University Press.

Hilferding, Rudolf. [1910] 1981. *Finance Capital*, ed. and trans. Tom Bottomore. London: Routledge and Kegan Paul.

Hobson, John A. 1902. *Imperialism: A Study.* New York: James Pott.

Hopkins, A. G. 1994. Informal Empire in Argentina: An Alternative View. *Journal of Latin American Studies* 26: 469–484.

Kautsky, Karl. 1914. Die Internationalität und der Krieg (Imperialism and the War). Trans. William E. Bohn. *International Socialist Review* (November).

Lenin, Vladimir I. [1917] 1970. Imperialism: The Highest Stage of Capitalism. *Lenin Selected Works*, Vol. 1, 667–766. Moscow: Progress Publishers.

Luxemburg, Rosa. 1913. *Die Akkumulation des Kapitals* (*The Accumulation of Capital*). Berlin: Buchhandlung Vorwärts Paul Singer.

Robinson, Ronald, and John Gallagher. 1961. *Africa and the Victorians: The Official Mind of Imperialism.* London: Macmillan.

Shumpeter, Joseph. 1951. *Imperialism and Social Classes.* Trans. Heinz Norden; ed. and intro., Paul M. Sweezy. New York: Kelley.

Wakefield, Edward Gibbon. 1849. *View of the Art of Colonization.* London: John W. Parker.

Wallerstein, Immanuel. 1979. *The Capitalist World-Economy: Essays.* Cambridge, U.K.: Cambridge University Press.

Wallerstein, Immanuel. 1988. *The Modern World System III: The Second Era of Great Expansion of the Capitalist World-Economy, 1730-1840s.* New York: Academic Press.

Weaver, Frederick Stirton. 2000. *Latin America in the World Economy: Mercantile Colonialism to Global Capitalism.* Boulder, CO: Westview.

Sudipta Sen

IMPORT PENETRATION

The export ratio and import penetration rate are important concepts in considering a country's trade structure. A search of the American Economic Association's EconLit, a leading database of economics literature, resulted in 142 articles (as of April 2006) that have been published since 1969 and use the term *import penetration*. The oldest of these is by James Hughes and A. P. Thirlwall (1977).

The relationship between domestic output, represented by Y, and domestic demand, represented by D, can be expressed as follows: $Y = D + EX - IM$, with EX representing exports, and IM, imports.

The export ratio is the percentage of domestic output that is exported—in other words, EX/Y. The import penetration rate (IP), on the other hand, is the percentage of domestic demand fulfilled by imports (OECD 2003):

$$IP = \frac{IM}{D} = \frac{IM}{Y - EX + IM}$$

To illustrate, if domestic television sales during a year amount to two million units, and the number of televisions imported totals 800,000, the import penetration rate would be calculated as follows:

$$\frac{80}{200} \times 100 = 40(\%)$$

The concept of the import penetration rate is important in relation to particular industries, as well as to the entire macroeconomy, and it has been a focus of much research. Representative studies were performed by Howard Marvel (1980) and Stephen Rhoades (1984), who analyzed the relationship between concentration and the import penetration rate for its potential as a way to integrate industrial organization and international economics, and Avinash Dixit (1989), who researched the relationship between the import penetration rate and exchange rate pass-through.

From a macroeconomic perspective, a country that produces manufactured goods with a high degree of international competitiveness will see increasing exports and decreasing imports. Under these circumstances, the export ratio will rise and the import penetration rate will fall. Conversely, a country that produces manufactured goods with a low degree of international competitiveness will see decreasing exports and increasing imports. In this case, the export ratio will fall and the import penetration will rise. It must be noted, however, that the relationship described here does not always hold. Two factors—import barriers and transaction costs—may interfere with it. If a country has established import barriers, another country's comparatively better manufactured goods will have little impact on its imports, and its import penetration rate will not rise. Likewise, if transportation and other transaction costs are extremely high for traded goods, differences in international competitiveness may not be reflected in the import penetration rate.

At the industry level, the export ratio and import penetration rate reflect a country's industrial structure. In the case of a developing country, for example, there is a

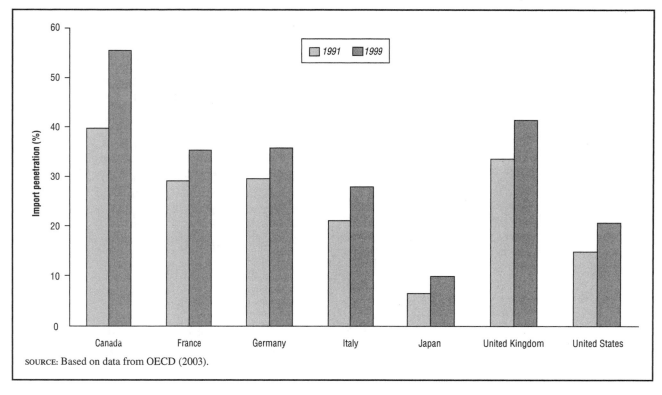

Figure 1: Import Penetration Rates.

tendency to export a significant volume of primary goods and to import large quantities of industrial goods. As a result, developing countries often have high export ratios for primary goods and high import penetration rates for industrial goods. Industrialized countries, in contrast, export significant volumes of industrial goods and import large quantities of primary goods. Industrialized countries, therefore, often have high export ratios for industrial goods and high import penetration rates for primary goods.

It must be noted that low (high) import penetration rates do not necessarily mean that there are high (low) import barriers. In actuality, a low import penetration rate may reflect a particular set of industrial characteristics that are unfavorable for international trade (e.g., high transportation costs). Furthermore, the combination of a high export ratio and low import penetration rate may be an indicator of the high competitiveness of domestic companies. When the export ratio and import penetration rate are both high for a particular industry, it may very likely be that such factors as intra-industry trade have resulted in a high degree of internationalization.

Figure 1 shows the changes in the import penetration rates of the Group of Seven (G7) countries (Canada, France, Germany, Italy, Japan, the United Kingdom, and the United States) between 1991 and 1999. As this graph clearly indicates, import penetration rates in all of the G7 countries rose

during this period. This may reflect an increasing degree of internationalization over these nine years.

SEE ALSO *Exchange Rates; Export Penetration; Export Promotion; Import Substitution; Imports; Trade*

BIBLIOGRAPHY

Dixit, Avinash K. 1989. Hysteresis, Import Penetration, and Exchange Rate Pass-Through. *Quarterly Journal of Economics* 104: 205–228.

EconLit: The American Economic Association's electronic bibliography of economics literature. http://www.econlit.org/.

Hughes, James J., and A. P. Thirlwall. 1977. Trends and Cycles in Import Penetration in the U.K. *Oxford Bulletin of Economics and Statistics* 39: 301–317.

Marvel, Howard P. 1980. Foreign Trade and Domestic Competition. *Economic Inquiry* 18: 103–122.

Organization for Economic Cooperation and Development (OECD). 2003. *Science, Technology, and Industry Scoreboard 2003: Towards a Knowledge-Based Economy.* http://www1.oecd.org/publications/e-book/92-2003-04-1-7294/.

Rhoades, Stephen A. 1984. Wages, Concentration, and Import Penetration: An Analysis of the Interrelationships. *Atlantic Economic Journal* 12: 23–31.

Shigeyuki Hamori

IMPORT PROMOTION

Import-promotion policies are measures intended to increase the volume of a country's imports from a particular trading partner or group of trading partners. Such policies may include bilateral agreements, bureaucratic directives, import subsidies, or procedures to improve foreign exporters' information about domestic market opportunities. Many countries have used trade policy to spur development of their own domestic industries, either by restricting competition from imports (import substitution) or by expanding exports (export promotion). Import promotion, which has the effect of *increasing* the foreign competition faced by domestic firms, is much less common.

Among major trading countries, import promotion has been employed to defuse political tensions arising from large bilateral trade imbalances, particularly the record trade surpluses of Japan and other East Asian countries during the 1980s. Voluntary import expansion (VIE) agreements between the United States and Japan set numerical targets for Japanese imports of specific U.S. products including semiconductors, automobiles, and auto parts. The United States later negotiated VIEs for rice and beef with South Korea, another country running a large bilateral surplus on trade with the United States.

VIEs, along with the more common voluntary export restraints (VERs), are results-oriented trading arrangements in which politically acceptable trade *outcomes* are negotiated bilaterally, in contrast to rules-based relationships, in which underlying economic conditions determine trade flows and trade balances given those rules. Results-oriented bilateral agreements, which were negotiated outside the General Agreement on Tariffs and Trade (GATT), failed to satisfy the GATT's most-favored-nation (MFN) principle—that a country should not discriminate among its trading partners. By promoting imports from one specific source, VIEs allowed imports from the favored source to displace lower-cost exports from other countries (trade diversion). VERs likewise diverted trade, with higher-cost goods from other sources replacing exports from the restricted supplier. Bilateral trade commitments also weakened competition among suppliers of affected products, thus raising their profits. Moreover, because compliance with negotiated commitments required coordination of purchases or sales, VIEs facilitated collusion among affected importing firms; VERs likewise facilitated collusion among exporting firms.

More recently, advanced countries have used import-promotion policies to assist potential exporters in developing and transition economies. For example, import-promotion agencies in a number of European countries supply information about market opportunities, organize trade fairs for small and medium-sized firms in developing and transition countries, and offer technical assistance to potential exporters. These efforts complement the Generalized System of Preferences (GSP), which allows manufactured exports of lower-income countries preferential access to the markets of industrialized nations, and broader programs offering duty-free market access to most exports from the least-developed countries. In contrast to negotiated bilateral arrangements, these import-promotion efforts are a form of development assistance that is extended to a large class of countries. The aim is to improve efficiency by overcoming informational gaps that would otherwise prevent smaller firms in poor countries from penetrating export markets. Affected exporters are likely to benefit through increased sales abroad as well as higher prices for their products. However, as with VIEs, these policies discriminate among potential trading partners and thus run the risk that the imports promoted will displace lower-cost products from ineligible exporting nations.

SEE ALSO *Export Promotion; General Agreement on Tariffs and Trade; Import Penetration; Import Substitution; Imports; Trade Surplus*

BIBLIOGRAPHY

Bergsten, C. Fred, and Marcus Noland. 1993. *Reconcilable Differences? United States–Japan Economic Conflict.* Washington, DC: Institute for International Economics.

European Commission. Export HelpDesk for Developing Countries. http://exporthelp.europa.eu/.

Rachel McCulloch

IMPORT QUOTA
SEE *Wage and Price Controls.*

IMPORT SUBSTITUTION

Import substitution, also referred to as import substitution industrialization (ISI), is a set of policies that addresses the developmental concerns of structurally deficient economic countries. As the name suggests, the ultimate goal of ISI is to promote a country's economic industrialization by encouraging domestic production and discouraging imports of consumer goods.

The dependency theorists were the first to formally devise import substitution as a viable economic strategy. Inspired by Karl Marx and Friedrich Engels's writings on imperialism, the dependency theorists characterize the international system as divided between countries of the core and those of the periphery. In contrast to the industrialized nations of the core, the peripheral countries are poor and lag behind technologically. Another trait of the countries of the periphery, according to this school of thought, is their inability to influence economic outcomes in the international realm. The asymmetry in power relations between core and peripheral countries is borne out of the unfavorable economic exchanges that developing countries have with the developed world. This theory asserts that developed nations utilize their economic superiority to influence, and often intervene in, the peripheral countries' economic, diplomatic, and military interests.

The dependency theorists contend that developing nations are bound to experience balance of payments problems due to declining terms of trade; that is, their ability to use earnings from agricultural (or other primary) exports to pay for industrialized (and high value-added) imports from developed nations is likely to diminish (Hirschman 1971). Hence, they argue that developing countries can enhance their international strategic position by reducing, or eliminating, their trade dependence on wealthy nations if they substitute their industrialized imports for goods manufactured domestically.

Besides the theory that inspires ISI policies, past international crises have forged a consensus among developing countries for the need to promote their local industries. The Great Depression and the two world wars were devastating for developing countries, whose industrialized imports from the developed economies were drastically interrupted. The economic success of the Soviet Union during the first half of the twentieth century also inspired policy makers throughout the developing world, including proponents of capitalism, who were persuaded by the apparent efficacy of a centrally planned economy. Indeed, the political and economic elites of peripheral countries were convinced that the state had to lead the crucial task of promoting domestic industry. Policy makers believed that a well-conceived and coordinated state intervention in the economy would eventually enable peripheral countries to catch up economically to the developed nations, which had the historical advantage of being the first ones to achieve industrial development.

In a nutshell, import substitution is a government-led, tightly staged economic strategy aimed at promoting industrialization by offering a package of subsidies to its local industries (which are oftentimes government owned) and by insulating infant industries from foreign competition. Two important tasks of a successful ISI strategy are to persuade domestic consumers to buy locally produced goods and to encourage domestic producers to participate in the country's industrialization project. ISI policy tools include:

1. High import tariffs on consumer goods
2. Low or negative tariffs on imports of machinery and intermediary inputs
3. Cheap credit (frequently at negative real interest rates) to industrial firms
4. Preferential exchange rates for industrial producers
5. Public investment in infrastructure (e.g., transportation and power) and in so-called basic industries, such as steel (Weaver 1980)

One important feature of ISI is the tendency to transfer income from agricultural exports to industrial development. Countries that adopt this economic strategy in effect penalize their agricultural sectors, even though most of these countries enjoy significant comparative advantages in agricultural production. Michael Lipton (1977) denounces this practice as "urban bias," namely, policies that favor urban industrial producers and labor at the expense of farmers and workers in rural areas. Some of the policies that characterize urban bias are overvalued real exchange rates, which penalize the export sector; price controls on domestic sales of locally produced agricultural goods as a means to subsidize food consumption in urban centers; and heavy taxation on agricultural exports. Therefore, one could argue that import substitution results in economic autarky.

ECONOMIC PROBLEMS ATTRIBUTED TO ISI

Despite widespread enthusiasm in the 1940s and 1950s, levels of economic success among governments that pursued ISI policies tend to vary across regions and countries. Nevertheless, a common pattern exists among the ISI countries that achieve material domestic industrialization: They all tend to have large domestic markets. In Latin America, for example, some of the countries with relatively successful ISI experiences include Argentina, Brazil, and Mexico, the three largest countries in the continent. Scholars believe that import substitution cannot succeed as a development strategy without the support of a fairly large domestic market. Such markets are necessary to encourage local production.

Unfortunately, import substitution has left a devastating legacy in Africa, where most ISI economies have experienced stagnant or declining production in their agricultural sectors. Since 70 percent or more of the African population earns its income from agriculture, the urban bias that characterizes import substitution has resulted in a reduction in the real income of those who are among the poorest in the region (World Bank 1981).

Some of the other economic problems attributed to ISI include:

1. An increase in state bureaucracy and in administrative inefficiency, in part because of the government's excessive intervention in the economy;

2. Increased fiscal deficits, which are primarily caused by governmental investments in heavy industry despite the lack of public resources;

3. Chronic real exchange rate misalignments resulting from the maintenance of overvalued exchange rates;

4. A shortage of foreign exchange, mostly due to the countries' poor trade performance;

5. An increase in foreign debt because ISI economies tend to borrow heavily from international capital markets to finance their development strategies;

6. An increase in income inequality, especially between rural and urban workers; and

7. An increase in balance of payments problems due to poor export performance and the rise in the importation of heavy machinery by domestic industry.

Of all the problems associated with import substitution, arguably the latter is the most ironic. A reduction in trade dependency on developed nations is precisely one of the main objectives in the pursuit of ISI strategy. Since the late 1980s there has been little support for import substitution among scholars. However, the economic nationalism that motivated much of this economic strategy has not completely gone out of fashion.

SEE ALSO *Balance of Trade; Economic Growth; Export Promotion; Industrialization; Infant Industry; Protectionism; Trade*

BIBLIOGRAPHY

Hirschman, Albert O. 1971. *A Bias for Hope: Essays on Development and Latin America.* New Haven, CT: Yale University Press.

Lipton, Michael. 1977. *Why Poor People Stay Poor: Urban Bias in World Development.* Cambridge, MA.: Harvard University Press.

Weaver, Frederick Stirton. 1980. *Class, State, and Industrial Structure: The Historical Process of South American Industrial Growth.* Westport, CT.: Greenwood.

World Bank. 1981. *Accelerated Development in Sub-Saharan Africa: An Agenda for Action.* Washington, DC: World Bank.

Monica Arruda de Almeida

IMPORTS

Imports are products or services shipped from producers in one country to users who are located in another country. While many import transactions involve a distinct buyer and seller, not all imports involve a market transaction, since some imports arise when a producer in one country ships its products to an associate or affiliate abroad.

The pattern of import demand—whether a country imports shoes, electronics, and oil, or some other bundle of goods and services, for example—is partially determined by international differences in comparative advantage. Such differences are driven by cross-country differences in the relative endowments of capital, labor, and other resources or by cross-country differences in productivity across products. Import patterns are also influenced by customer desire for variety. Since expanding product varieties generally requires firms to make fixed-cost investments in the development of new varieties as well as the construction of new production facilities, producers in different countries specialize in distinct varieties of a product, and a limited range of varieties are available from each country. Thus, when individuals prefer a particular car, chocolate, or cheese that is not produced at home, they may import their preferred variety from the country that produces their preferred variety or brand.

Multinational firms—firms whose plants, offices, and facilities are located in more than one country—play an important role in the movement of imported goods, since multinational firms' networks of overseas affiliates both

---

Multinational firms and the composition of U.S. goods trade in 2003: Each cell reports the percentage of trade conveyed by multinational companies (MNCs).

	MNC Trade	Intrafirm MNC Trade
U.S. imports of goods		
U.S.–owned nonbank MNCs	37%	15%
Majority-owned nonbank U.S. affiliates of foreign-owned firms	28%	23%
Total imports conveyed by MNC firms	65%	38%
U.S. exports of goods		
U.S.–owned nonbank MNCs	57%	22%
Majority-owned nonbank U.S. affiliates of foreign-owned firms	21%	10%
Total exports conveyed by MNC firms	78%	32%

SOURCE: U.S. Bureau of Economic Analysis; Zeile 2005, Table 7; Mataloni 2005, Table 2; Nephew et al. 2005, Table A.

---

create and support international import transactions. To demonstrate the importance of multinational firms in the mediation of trade, Table 1 shows the percentage of U.S. import value in 2003 that involved a multinational firm at the shipping or receiving end of the transaction. For example, of the $1,257 billion in goods imported into the United States in 2003, 65 percent of the transactions involved multinational firms. Similarly, noting that U.S. exports become another country's imports, 78 percent of the $725 billion of U.S. goods exported in 2003 involved multinational firms. In each of these examples, there were two potential avenues for engagement by multinational firms: the first avenue involved American-owned multinational firms, while the second involved foreign-owned affiliates operating in the United States.

The networks and presence of multinational firms were also notable in the conduct of services trade. Data from the U.S. Bureau of Economic Analysis show that other countries imported $769 billion of services from the United States in 2003, 62 percent of which involved the participation of U.S. service affiliates located overseas (Nephew, Koncz, Borga, and Mann 2005). Similarly, 63 percent of U.S. service imports in 2003 were conducted via the U.S.-based affiliates of foreign-owned firms (Nephew, Koncz, Borga, and Mann 2005).

While countries differ in the percentage of their imports handled by multinational firms, a portion of each country's trade is likely to involve multinational firms. At the most basic level, firms often enter into operation as a multinational when they set up an overseas affiliate dedicated to the distribution of their products in foreign countries. Over time, the multinational firm's presence in the foreign country may allow it to expand its foreign sales, and consequently the imports of the foreign country, since affiliate operations help firms to learn which of their products best match local tastes. If the local demand is sufficiently different and the foreign market is sufficiently large, the foreign affiliate may enable the multinational firm to tailor its products or services to the specific nature of foreign customer demands.

While the international networks of multinational firms often stimulate import flows, the operation of foreign affiliates may reduce import volumes. This outcome is especially likely when the multinational firm uses the output of its foreign subsidiary to serve its foreign customers, rather than having the foreign customers import the firm's product. This type of substitution is especially likely when import tariffs are high, or international transportation costs are large, since the multinational firm maximizes its profits by producing in a foreign subsidiary, rather than engaging in international trade in its products. In contrast, when the cost of creating a new plant in a foreign location is large, the profit-maximizing multinational

will be more inclined to produce in a more limited number of locations, or even a single location, thus requiring foreign customers to import their products. Since the cost of creating a new production facility does not vary dramatically across countries, this suggests that the displacement of imports by subsidiary production will be greatest for countries with large markets, where the variable cost savings due to lower transportation costs and tariffs more than compensate for the added fixed costs of building a new production plant overseas.

Production by a multinational firm's overseas affiliates stimulates demand for imported intermediate inputs that are used in the foreign affiliate's production. In many instances, these transactions give rise to intrafirm imports, where the multinational firm is both the shipper and recipient in the import transaction. For example, the production of cars in Toyota's U.S. assembly plants generates intrafirm imports when Toyota's U.S. assembly plants import engines from Toyota-owned production facilities in Japan. As Table 1 shows, 38 percent of U.S. imports and 32 percent of foreign imports of U.S. goods represented intrafirm transactions, which placed the same multinational firm as the shipper and receiver of the imported goods.

More broadly, increasing vertical specialization in international trade allows production to be decomposed across countries, as each country contributes to some elements of the production process. The international trade incentives for engaging in vertical specialization are identical to the motives driving the demand for imports of final products. However, in vertical production relationships, comparative advantage determines which stages of production are conducted in each country along the production process. For a broad range of countries, David Hummels, Jun Ishii, and Kei-Mu Yi (2001) estimate that vertical specialization, involving the trade of both affiliated and unaffiliated firms, represented 20 percent of all trade by 1990, and that the growth of vertical specialization was responsible for 30 percent of the growth in trade between 1970 and 1990. As tariff and transportation costs continue to decline, and technologies for international communication and coordination improve, vertical specialization imports should grow further yet.

SEE ALSO *Balance of Payments; Balance of Trade; Exchange Rates; Exports; Trade*

BIBLIOGRAPHY

Hummels, David, Jun Ishii, and Kei-Mu Yi. 2001. The Nature and Growth of Vertical Specialization in World Trade. *Journal of International Economics* 54 (1): 75–96.

Markusen, James R. 2002. *Multinational Firms and the Theory of International Trade.* Cambridge, MA: MIT Press.

Mataloni, Raymond J., Jr. 2005. U.S. Multinational Companies Operations in 2003. *Survey of Current Business* 85 (7): 9–29. http://www.bea.gov/bea/ARTICLES/2005/07July/0705_MNCs.pdf.

Nephew, Erin, Jennifer Koncz, Maria Borga, and Michael Mann. 2005. U.S. International Services: Cross-Border Trade in 2004 and Sales Through Affiliates in 2003. *Survey of Current Business* 85 (10): 25–77. http://www.bea.gov/bea/ARTICLES/2005/10October/1005_xborder.pdf.

Yi, Kei-Mu. 2003. Can Vertical Specialization Explain the Growth of World Trade? *Journal of Political Economy* 111 (1): 52–102.

Zeile, William J. 2005. U.S. Affiliates of Foreign Companies Operations in 2003. *Survey of Current Business* 85 (8): 198–214. http://www.bea.gov/bea/ARTICLES/2005/08August/0805_Foreign_WEB.pdf.

Deborah L. Swenson

IMPOSSIBILITY THEOREM

SEE *Arrow Possibility Theorem.*

IMPRESSION MANAGEMENT

SEE *Survey.*

IMPRISONMENT

Imprisonment is a political act. Until early-nineteenth-century reforms, lockups most often confined people awaiting trial. Earlier political elites, kings and queens for example, locked away their opposition, critics, or competitors in dungeons or, in the case of enemies of the English Crown, the Tower of London. Common criminals were often executed, were banished, or received corporal punishment. The concept of the European and North American prison as a primary form of punishment was a reform advocated by individuals such as the Italian jurist Cesare Beccaria (1738–1794) and the American reformer Jeremy Bentham. Early American prisons in Pennsylvania and New York were thought to provide a more reasonable alternative than previous practices, which reformers believed were too often cruel and capricious.

Imprisoning offenders provides a rational means of punishment because the length of incarceration can be tied to the severity of the offense or offenses. Which crimes people will be imprisoned for and for how long are decisions that are made in political arenas. In the late twentieth century the Soviet Union, South Africa, and the United States were the nations with the largest portions of their populations in custody. With the collapse of the Soviet Union and the subsequent release of political prisoners, the demise of apartheid and the consequent liberation of democracy advocates and freedom fighters, the United States moved into the lead. Since then, the war on drugs and other "get tough" practices have led to a quadrupling of the number of American inmates. Officials of both major political parties have supported such practices because they want to run for reelection on "get tough on crime" platforms, and they fear being painted as "soft on crime" by the opposition. Thus, the consequences for criminal acts, including length of incarceration, are essentially outcomes of the political process, involving politicians, public interest groups, and advocates.

Decisions have been made against a backdrop of two competing visions of the role of prisons. Is their primary purpose punishment or rehabilitation? Estimates of recidivism rates frequently have surpassed two-thirds when corrections officials were concerned about rehabilitation *and* when punishment was stressed. With such limited success with either philosophy, legislatures often "reform" and alter sentencing and imprisonment policies based on what will garner votes, rather than a rational penology.

PRISON SYSTEMS IN AMERICA AND ABROAD

Evidence of the political and economic underpinnings of imprisonment in the United States can be seen in the history of race and American incarceration. Prior to the Civil War very few blacks were ever confined in prison. Most African Americans lived in southern states and most were slaves. Freedmen found guilty of crimes were frequently re-enslaved. Bondsmen who were thought to violate the law were more likely to be punished by their owners and not imprisoned (even though white offenders might be locked up), because to do so deprived southern elites of workers. After the demise of Reconstruction in the late 1870s the prisoner lease system was instituted in the South. This system of "renting" convicts (which included more blacks, now that they were not enslaved) to work on plantations, in mines, on railroads, and in other laborious or dangerous industries provided cheap labor, but it also buttressed the Jim Crow racial caste structure that emerged. Although Jim Crow laws no longer exist in the United States, an argument among researchers remains: What role does race play in the rates of imprisonment, and what percentage of minority imprisonment can be justly accounted for by minorities' higher levels of involvement in crime?

In societies with heterogeneous populations race and ethnicity are important determinants of imprisonment. Michael Tonry's *Ethnicity, Crime, and Immigration* (1997) presents studies of race, immigration, crime, and criminal justice practices in Europe, Australia, Canada, and the United States. The countries included, with the exception of Australia, do not have the oppressive domestic racial history of the United States or its level of racial disparity in imprisonment. In Australia the treatment of Aboriginal people has been racist. Nevertheless, studies included by Tonry document important shifts in criminal justice practices as the number of people defined as "outsiders" grows. Within the United States, the debate continues to be not about whether racial unfairness results in disproportionate confinement of African Americans and Latinos, but how much of observed racial disparities in imprisonment are due to unwarranted, discriminating treatment. As European nations develop more diverse populations it is likely that they too will have growing disparity in imprisonment and debates that parallel those in the United States. Europeans will have to consider what portion of racial and ethnic imprisonment disparities result from higher criminal involvement among "others"—probably in part a result of their political, economic, and social disadvantages within the society—and what portion are consequences of the politics of imprisonment.

Nations still use prisons to stifle political dissent: Amnesty International regularly publishes lists of nations that use prisons to violate human rights. Litigation resulting from U.S. policies that lock up "criminal combatants" in the "war on terror," with neither constitutionally guaranteed due process nor supposed Geneva Convention protections, is likely to continue for decades in either American or international courts.

EFFECTS ON ECONOMY AND COMMUNITY

There are two additional important aspects of imprisonment: its differential economic effects and its effects on communities. In 2004 Bruce Western and his colleagues showed that racial and class inequalities have been maintained, in part, by U.S. imprisonment patterns. For example, their research shows that the reduced number of unemployed African Americans is a consequence of the increased number of blacks who are held in confinement rather than as a result of any improving economic fortune; they have simply been removed from both the labor market and the unemployment roles. When eventually released, they will then have considerably poorer employment prospects than before their incarceration.

The massive increase in U.S. imprisonment has also been detrimental to communities. In 1998 Dina Rose and Todd Clear demonstrated that when large numbers of people are forcibly removed from communities by incarceration, the social structure is destabilized, opening the door for social problems, including increased crime. Also, released inmates tend to return to the same neighborhoods they lived in prior to imprisonment. They bring back their increased social and economic disadvantage and social stigma. When the released are concentrated in already disadvantaged neighborhoods, they further destabilize those communities.

Few argue that imprisonment is not a better form of punishment than the arbitrary and frequently cruel practices that it replaced, and even fewer will suggest that incarceration is not a necessary practice in complex societies. Too often, however, there is little recognition of the political nature of imprisonment and the social and economic consequences of incarceration.

SEE ALSO *Deterrence; Prisons*

BIBLIOGRAPHY

Pettit, Becky, and Bruce Western. 2004. Mass Imprisonment and the Life Course: Race and Class Inequality in U.S. Incarceration. *American Sociological Review* 69 (2): 151–169.

Rose, Dina R., and Todd R. Clear. 1998. Incarceration, Social Capital, and Crime: Implications for Social Disorganization Theory. *Criminology* 36 (3): 441–479.

Tonry, Michael. 1997. *Ethnicity, Crime, and Immigration.* Chicago: University of Chicago Press.

Western, Bruce, Meredith Kleykamp, and Jake Rosenfeld. 2004. Crime, Punishment, and American Inequality. In *Social Inequality*, ed. Kathryn M. Neckerman. New York: Russell Sage.

Robert D. Crutchfield

IN VIVO TRANSFERS

In vivo transfers are gifts living parents give to their adult children. In other words, in vivo transfers can be likened to bequests, the main distinction being that with an in vivo transfer, the transfer occurs between two living persons. According to the life-cycle permanent income hypothesis (Kotlikoff 2001), an individual saves and borrows in order to smooth consumption in the face of income fluctuations. Like bequests, in vivo transfers affect the utility and budget constraints of individuals who are concerned about the future welfare or happiness of their children. This theory of consumption further predicts that changes in tax structure may influence consumption patterns over time.

Any change in fiscal policy, uncertainty, costs, preferences, and the like provides an incentive for individuals concerned with the future happiness of their children to change their consumption, saving, and wealth-accumulation behavior and provide in vivo transfers. An obvious incentive provided by a tax on transfers of wealth at death is for taxpayers to arrange to transfer wealth before dying by making gifts to their heirs. As such, the gift tax is the government's response to such efforts to avoid inheritance taxes. In short, according to the life-cycle permanent-income hypothesis, tax policy may have important implications for in vivo transfers and bequests.

Joseph Altonji, Fumio Hayashi, and Laurence Kotlikoff (1997) test whether in vivo transfers are motivated by altruistic concern by individuals for their children. They find that parents increase their transfer by a few cents for each extra dollar of current or permanent income they have, which in itself is consistent with altruism. Interestingly, they also find that parents reduce their transfer for every increase in their children's income. Using French data, Luc Arrondel and Anne Laferrere (2001) also report evidence that transfer behavior is responsive to changes in the fiscal system. In contrast to Altonji, Hayashi, and Kotlikoff, Arrondel and Laferrere find no support for altruism. In their view, no legal or fiscal system is so strong and so detailed as to determine family behavior, but some individuals seem to use the tax system to optimize their transfers. They find strong behavioral responses to tax incentives. The empirical tests do not validate a single model of intergenerational transfers. They conclude that altruism seems to be involved at the time in the life-cycle when children are young adults, but the gifts are of comparatively small amounts. Altruism is harder to detect from the study of total in vivo gifts.

Ernesto Villanueva (2005) found some evidence that public help may displace in vivo transfers. Tentative estimates suggest that in West Germany, an extra dollar of public help displaces between 8 and 12 cents of parental transfers. Those results are somewhat smaller than corresponding estimates from the United States reported by Robert Schoeni (2000). That is, following a cut in unemployment benefits, individuals who have access to private help are less likely to see their standard of living affected by the change. Comparing in vivo transfers in size and incidence between ethnic groups, using data from the mid- to late-1980s, Mark Wilhelm (2001) found that annually whites had a higher likelihood of receiving a transfer and that it was on average a larger amount for whites than non-whites. The average amount received was $2,824 for whites and $805 for non-whites. The average incidence of receipt was 20 percent for whites and 17.8 percent for non-whites.

Using U.S. data, David Joulfaian and Kathleen McGarry (2004) examine the responsiveness of in vivo transfers to changes in tax laws. They find that many wealthy individuals do not take full advantage of the ability to make in vivo transfers free of estate and gift taxes, as long as the gift is less than approximately $40,000 per year, and those who do make in vivo transfers do so only on a one-off basis. Further, they find that there are sizable shifts in the timing of giving in response to tax changes, but the wealthy do not make sizable in vivo transfers over time.

In summary, there is considerable evidence that taxes and specifically estate and gift taxes appear to influence decisions to make in vivo transfers.

SEE ALSO *Altruism; Bequests; Family Functioning; Inequality, Wealth; Inheritance; Inheritance Tax; Intergenerational Transmission; Life-Cycle Hypothesis; Permanent Income Hypothesis; Policy, Fiscal; Taxes*

BIBLIOGRAPHY

Altonji, Joseph G., Fumio Hayashi, and Laurence J. Kotlikoff. 1997. Parental Altruism and In Vivos Transfers: Theory and Evidence. *Journal of Political Economy* 105: (6): 1121–1166.

Arrondel, Luc, and Anne Laferrere. 2001. Taxation and Wealth Transmission in France. *Journal of Public Economics* 79 (1): 3–33.

Cox, Donald. 1987. Motives for Private Income Transfers. *Journal of Political Economy* 95 (3): 508–546.

Joulfaian, David, and Kathleen McGarry. 2004. Estate and Gift Tax Incentives and Inter Vivos Giving. *National Tax Journal* 57 (2, pt. 2): 429–444.

Kotlikoff, Laurence J. 2001. *Essays on Saving, Bequests, Altruism, and Life-Cycle Planning.* Cambridge, MA: MIT Press.

Schoeni, Robert. 2000. Does Unemployment Insurance Displace Familial Assistance? Rand Labor and Population Program, Working Paper No. 00-05. http://www.rand.org/pubs/drafts/DRU2289/.

Villanueva, Ernesto. 2005. Inter Vivos Transfers and Bequests in Three OECD Countries. *Economic Policy* 20 (43): 505–565.

Wilhelm, Mark O. 2001. The Role of Intergenerational Transfers in Spreading Asset Ownership. In *Assets of the Poor: The Benefits of Spreading Asset Ownership*, ed. Thomas M. Shapiro and Edward N. Wolff, 132–164. Ford Foundation Series on Asset Building. New York: Russell Sage Foundation.

Mark Rider

INADA CONDITIONS

Economists usually posit that production can be represented by a mathematical function that relates output to input factors. One assumes that aggregate production (Y) depends on the two input factors capital (K) and labor (L). Formally, the process relating output to the inputs is described by the function $F(K, L) = Y$, where more input raises output. The function $F(\cdot)$ is assumed to be linearly homogenous, so that production can be written as $Y = L \cdot F(K/L, 1)$, stating that raising capital and labor by a certain amount leads to a proportional rise of production. Given this property, production per labor input, $y = Y/L$, can be written as $y = f(k)$, with $k = K/L$ capital per labor. The function $f(\cdot)$ is increasing in k continuously, meaning that jumps are excluded, and it is continuously differentiable, implying that the derivative of the function exists and is itself a continuous function.

In addition, $f(k)$ satisfies the following conditions, called the Inada conditions, which are ideal assumptions about its shape:

The value of the function at 0 is zero, $f(0) = 0$

The function is strictly increasing in k, $f'(k) > 0$, with ' denoting the derivative

The derivative of the function is decreasing so that the function is strictly concave, $f''(k) < 0$

The limit of the derivative approaches plus infinity when k goes to zero, $\lim f'(k) = \infty$, for $k \to 0$

The limit of the derivative approaches zero when k goes to infinity, $\lim f'(k) = 0$, for $k \to \infty$

These conditions were named after the Japanese economist Ken-Ichi Inada (1925–2002), who wrote a number of important papers on welfare economics, economic growth, and international trade.

The Inada conditions guarantee that a unique steady state in the neoclassical growth model exists and is stable. The Inada conditions are purely technical assumptions and are hardly relevant for empirical economics. The neoclassical growth model is described by the differential equation $dk(t)/dt = s \cdot f(k(t)) - (n + \delta) \cdot k(t)$, where s is the constant savings rate, n is the growth rate of labor, δ is the depreciation rate of capital, and t denotes time. This equation states that the change in capital per labor equals savings per labor in the economy, which are equal to investment, minus that part of capital per labor that is used up due to depreciation and due to the growth of the labor force. A steady state is defined as a situation with $dk(t)/dt = 0$ so that capital per labor is constant over time. Total investment, $I(t)$, in the economy then equals $(n + \delta) \cdot K(t)$, so that the total capital stock grows at the same rate as labor. Given the Inada conditions, there exists a unique value $k^* > 0$ solving $dk(t)/dt = 0$, because $s \cdot f(\cdot)$ is larger than $(n + \delta) \cdot k$ for values of $k < k^*$, and it is smaller for values of $k > k^*$. Figure 1 illustrates the situation graphically. In addition, $k < k^*$ is stable because for $k < k^*$ capital per labor rises, $dk(t)/dt > 0$, and for $k > k^*$ capital declines, $dk(t)/dt < 0$.

SEE ALSO *Neoclassical Growth Model; Production Function; Returns, Diminishing*

BIBLIOGRAPHY

Inada, Ken-Ichi. 1963. On a Two-Sector Model of Economic Growth: Comments and a Generalization. *The Review of Economic Studies* 30 (2): 119–127.

Alfred Greiner

INCARCERATION

SEE *Imprisonment.*

INCARCERATION, JAPANESE AMERICAN

From 1885 to 1924 approximately 200,000 Japanese immigrated to Hawaii, and 180,000 Japanese immigrated to the mainland United States. This first generation of immigrants (Issei) built a vibrant community, raising families, starting churches, and forming social and business organizations. Their success met with prejudice and an anti-Japanese movement. Discriminatory laws prevented Issei from becoming naturalized U.S. citizens. They were barred from owning land, marrying whites, and sending their children to schools attended by whites. In 1924 Congress passed the Immigration Act, which barred any further immigration from Japan. The second generation (Nisei) also faced discrimination. Even though they were born in the United States, spoke English like other Americans, and often did well in school, these U.S. citizens of Japanese ancestry faced discrimination in employ-

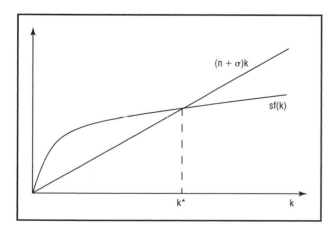

Figure 1

ment, housing, public settings (restaurants, stores, hotels, swimming pools, etc.), and social and civic activities.

ARREST OF COMMUNITY LEADERS

On December 7, 1941, Japan attacked U.S. military bases in Pearl Harbor, Hawaii. More than 3,500 American servicemen and civilians were killed or wounded. In the hours following the attack, the FBI arrested over 1,200 Japanese immigrant men: businessmen, Buddhist priests, Japanese language teachers, and other community leaders.

More than 5,500 Issei men were eventually picked up and held as potential threats to national security. Most of these men were taken first to Immigration and Naturalization Service (INS) detention stations and then to Department of Justice (DOJ) internment camps to undergo hearings. Officially, these internment cases were given individual legal review, but in practice the majority of Issei were imprisoned without evidence that they posed any threat to national security. Internees were not allowed legal representation. Approximately 1,700 were "released" to War Relocation Authority (WRA) concentration camps after these hearings, but most were transferred to U.S. Army internment camps.

MASS REMOVAL OF U.S. CITIZENS

On February 19, 1942, President Franklin D. Roosevelt (1882–1945) signed Executive Order 9066, which authorized military commanders to designate military areas from which any person could be excluded. Congress supported the executive order by authorizing a prison term and fine for a civilian convicted of violating the military order. General John L. DeWitt (1880–1962), Western Defense Command, then issued over one hundred military orders that only applied to civilians of Japanese ancestry living in the West Coast states. Thus the president and Congress authorized the removal and incarceration of over 110,000 people based solely on race without charges, hearings, or evidence of wrongdoing. More than two-thirds of those incarcerated were U.S. citizens—over half were children.

Ironically, over 150,000 people of Japanese ancestry in Hawaii were not removed or incarcerated. General Delos Emmons (1888–1965), who became commanding general in Hawaii shortly after the bombing of Pearl Harbor, treated the Issei and Nisei as loyal to the United States. Although there were many false stories of Japanese American spies, General Emmons repeatedly rejected anti-Japanese pleas for mass removal of Japanese ancestry from Hawaii. He knew there was no evidence of Japanese American espionage or sabotage. In fact during World War II (1939–1945) no Japanese American in the United States, Hawaii, or Alaska—citizen or immigrant—was ever convicted of espionage or sabotage.

DISPERSAL TO DETENTION SITES THROUGHOUT THE UNITED STATES

The general public, through books, movies, and school lessons, is most familiar with the ten WRA concentration camps, such as the Manzanar "relocation center" near Independence, California. The full extent of the imprisonment, however, included approximately sixty other government facilities: temporary "assembly centers," immigration detention stations, federal prisons, and internment camps. Italian and German immigrants, Alaskan natives, Japanese Latin Americans, and Japanese Hawaiians were also sent to live at these sites.

Which detention facility a person entered depended on several factors, including citizenship status, perceived level of threat, geography, degree of cooperation or protest, and sheer chance. For the most part the DOJ and U.S. Army camps interned first-generation men who were arrested by the FBI, while the WRA concentration camps incarcerated both U.S. citizens and immigrants affected by the exclusion order.

SOME LEAVE CAMPS: "DISLOYALS" TRANSFERRED TO TULE LAKE

As early as April 1942, even before inmates were transferred from the temporary "assembly centers" to concentration camps, the WRA recognized that Japanese Americans eventually would have to reenter society. Thus the WRA enacted a policy of granting short-term or indefinite leave for college or work to Japanese Americans who were U.S. citizens and who could find sponsors. Additionally, thousands of Nisei men enlisted in the military and served in combat.

To help administer the military draft and work-release program, the U.S. Army and the WRA produced "loyalty questionnaires" for all WRA inmates seventeen years of age and older. Two questions caused confusion and controversy for inmates. They were asked if they were willing to serve in the armed forces and to forswear loyalty to Japan. Answering "yes" left the Issei stateless, as they could not be U.S. citizens and the wording falsely assumed the American-born Nisei were loyal to Japan. Despite serious problems with the meaning and purpose of the questions, government officials and others considered those who answered "no" to these two questions to be "disloyal" to the United States, and they were transferred to the Tule Lake concentration camp in northern California, which was designated a segregation camp. "Yes" answers to these questions qualified inmates for service in the U.S. Army, and some became eligible for release and resettlement in areas outside of the West Coast exclusion zones.

GOVERNMENT ENDS WEST COAST EXCLUSION

In December 1944 the U.S. Supreme Court ruled in the case brought by Mitsuye Endo, a Nisei contesting her incarceration, that a loyal U.S. citizen could not be held in a WRA concentration camp against his or her will. While the case was being heard, federal officials recognized that the continuing incarceration was not legally defensible and began preparations to close the concentration camps. In addition the exclusion orders were rescinded, and persons of Japanese ancestry were allowed to return to the West Coast. On March 20, 1945, the last WRA concentration camp, Tule Lake, was closed. The DOJ internment camps remained open longer. The last internment camp to close was the DOJ camp in Crystal City, Texas, in January 1948.

Upon release the majority of those who had been incarcerated were given $25 and one-way transportation. Many of the freed Japanese Americans returned to discover that their homes and farms had been vandalized and their belongings stolen. Even Nisei military veterans returning home in their uniforms from combat duty endured racist insults. Starting over was especially hard for the Issei, who were entering their senior years with little to show for a lifetime of work.

ADMISSION OF WRONGDOING: APOLOGY FROM THE GOVERNMENT

In the late 1960s community activists started a movement to petition the government to look into potential wrongdoings. Classified information was uncovered that showed that the exclusion order and incarceration were based on racism and falsehoods. In February 1980 Congress passed an act forming the Commission on Wartime Relocation and Internment of Civilians (CWRIC). This commission conducted hearings in 9 cities, heard testimonies from over 750 witnesses, and examined over 10,000 documents. In 1983 the CWRIC issued its report, which concluded that military necessity was not the cause of the mass imprisonment. Rather, "the broad historical causes which shaped these decisions were race prejudice, war hysteria and a failure of political leadership" (Commission on Wartime Relocation and Internment of Civilians 1983, p. 18).

Acting upon the recommendations of the commission, Congress passed the Civil Liberties Act of 1988, and President Ronald Reagan (1911–2004) signed it into law. This law required payment and apology to survivors of the incarceration caused by Executive Order 9066. Two years later President George H. W. Bush presented the first apologies along with payments of $20,000 to each of the oldest survivors.

SEE ALSO *Civil Liberties; Civil Rights; Discrimination, Racial; Japanese Americans; Reparations; Roosevelt, Franklin D.*

BIBLIOGRAPHY

Burton, Jeffery F., Mary M. Farrell, Florence B. Lord, and Richard W. Lord. 2002. *Confinement and Ethnicity: An Overview of World War II Japanese American Relocation Sites.* Seattle: University of Washington Press.

Commission on Wartime Relocation and Internment of Civilians. 1983. *Personal Justice Denied: Report of the Commission on Wartime Relocation and Internment of Civilians.* Washington, DC: U.S. Government Printing Office. Repr. Seattle: University of Washington Press, 1997.

Kashima, Tetsuden. 2003. *Judgment without Trial: Japanese American Imprisonment during World War II.* Seattle: University of Washington Press.

Niiya, Brian, ed. 2001. *Japanese American History: An A-to-Z Reference from 1868 to the Present.* Updated ed. New York: Facts on File.

Tom Ikeda

INCAS

The Inca Empire was the last and greatest of several civilizations that existed in South America prior to the arrival of Europeans in the sixteenth century. The Incas began as one of many small, warring chiefdoms in central Peru. At its height in 1532 CE, the empire stretched from central Ecuador to south central Chile, and encompassed high altitude grasslands, coastal deserts, and tropical forests.

The dates for the Inca Empire are under debate. From study of Spanish documents, the late John Rowe, professor of anthropology at University of California, Berkeley, determined that the Incas began their expansion out of the region of Cuzco, their capital, around 1438 CE. Although archaeological work has suggested that the expansion actually began before that, the fact remains that the Incas created their empire in a remarkably short time, less than two centuries.

The success of the Incas was based on two main factors, a large and well-disciplined army and an effective administrative system. The Inca army was made up of a core of seasoned troops augmented by a large number of part-time soldiers, all led by a group of outstanding generals. The Inca army was successful also because of an effective infrastructure. The Incas built or expanded earlier road systems to make up more than 40,000 kilometers of roads. At regular intervals were major centers where provisions were collected from conquered people.

The Incas required labor, but little else, from their subjects. A conquered group had their land divided into three parts: one part each for the use of the Inca state and Inca religion, the third part remaining for the people's use. One labor obligation was working the Incas' parts first. Every household was also required to provide labor service, called *mit'a*, for a certain period each year. This labor might entail warfare, craft production, carrying messages, or building activities. The Incas provided all the food and materials for the *mit'a* labor. They also moved communities all over the empire to maximize food production and for political reasons. In this way, the Incas created an agricultural base and vast labor pool for both expanding their empire and creating the material and luxury goods that were needed to run it.

The Incas never developed a writing system, but used a knotted cord device called a *quipu* to keep track of goods and labor. Specially trained individuals, called *quipucamayocs*, were in charge of maintaining these records. The Inca administrative system was a hierarchical one, and was based on a decimal system of counting. The empire was ruled by the king, and consisted of four unequal parts, called *suyus*, that originated at Cuzco. Each *suyu* was made up of provinces, which were ideally divided into two or three *sayas*, units of 10,000 families. The *sayas* might correspond to a conquered ethnic group, or be a combination of smaller ones. *Suyus*, provinces, and *sayas* all had separate leaders. Within each *saya*, households were organized into a series of progressively smaller administrative units, led by local *curacas*, or leaders. There were *curacas* in charge of 5,000, 1,000, 500, 100, 50, and 10 families. Their jobs were to organize labor and lead their units' troops in battle. They were rewarded with gifts for jobs well done, and punished for doing poorly. Most of the *curacas* were local leaders who were incorporated into the lower levels of the social hierarchy. At the top of the hierarchy were the Inca nobility, those who could claim ancestry from any of the original kings, and allied ethnicities, called "Inca-by-privilege," who were granted Inca status. These two groups filled the highest administrative posts in the empire.

As with many ancient civilizations, Inca politics were intimately related to their religion. The Incas worshiped a host of deities of the earth and sky. In addition, the Incas revered a line of divine kings and held sacred any place that was considered imbued with supernatural power (*huacas*). Both the Incas and their subjects lived in fear of the displeasure of gods and *huacas*, and so carried out many different rituals. Although most of these involved only offerings of food or llamas, extremely important events, such as the accession of a new ruler, or a major calamity such as an earthquake, could require human sacrifice. Some of the most important Inca gods required human sacrifices as well. These sacrifices were always physically perfect children, from all over the empire. The remains of such sacrifices have been found on many of the highest peaks in the Andes.

The daily work of a person depended on his or her age, gender, and status. Conquered children watched a family's herds of llamas and alpacas. When children of both sexes achieved puberty and married, they took on other roles such as parents, warriors, and craftspeople. A boy would usually take the occupation of his father, and both males and females participated in agricultural work. Inca nobility probably had fewer domestic chores and more duties related to the empire than did their subjects. Some women served special duties in the empire as *acllyacuna*, or "chosen women." They were taken from their homes at an early age and taught domestic arts, and then worked in the empire's service at administrative centers. They made textiles and other crafts and performed many services.

Despite controlling a population estimated to be more than 10 million, the Inca Empire fell to a group of about 170 Spaniards led by Francisco Pizarro (c. 1475–1541). This conquest was achieved as a result of three things: a civil war between two rivals to the throne, European diseases that were introduced from Mexico, and the quick capture of the last Inca king. The latter event allowed the Spaniards to rule through the king for several months before they executed him and marched to Cuzco. A rebellion by the Incas four years later nearly succeeded, but was finally suppressed. The Spaniards introduced many new institutions, foods, and Catholicism to Andean people, yet much of the indigenous way of life still exists in regions remote from major cities.

BIBLIOGRAPHY

D'Altroy, Terence N. 2002. *The Incas*. Malden, MA: Blackwell.

Morris, Craig, and Adriana Von Hagen. 1992. *The Inca Empire and Its Andean Origins*. New York: American Museum of Natural History.

Moseley, Michael E. 2001. *The Incas and Their Ancestors. The Archaeology of Peru*. Rev. ed. New York: Thames and Hudson.

Rowe, John H. 1946. Inca Culture at the Time of the Spanish Conquest. In *The Handbook of South American Indians*, vol. 2: *The Andean Civilizations*, ed. Julian H. Steward, 183–330. Smithsonian Institution Bureau of American Ethnology Bulletin 143.

Michael A. Malpass

INCENTIVES

SEE *Value, Subjective*.

INCEST TABOO

SEE *Oedipus Complex.*

INCOME

Income is often defined as the amount of money received during a given period of time by a person, household, or other economic unit in return for services provided or goods sold. Although this is certainly a serviceable definition, working economists need a more precise one. Many economists use a comprehensive definition of income attributed to Robert Haig and Henry Simons, that *income* is equal to a person's (household's) consumption plus the increase in his or her net worth (Haig 1921, p. 7; Simons 1938, p. 50). The two definitions differ in several respects; most notably, the informal definition refers to money received, whereas the Haig and Simons concept refers to changes in net worth.

There are important distinctions between money received, as in the informal definition of income, and changes in net worth, as in the Haig and Simons definition. For example, person A may give person B a dozen eggs for performing a service, and suppose person B uses the eggs to make breakfast. Because no money has changed hands in this example, there is no income according to the informal definition of income. In terms of Haig and Simons's definition, however, person B's income has changed his consumption; therefore, his income has increased by the value of the eggs. In other words, barter income is included in Haig and Simons's income. To take another example, suppose a person buys a stock for $100 and its value increases to $150; unless he sells the stock, no money is received and his income from this asset is

zero ($0.00). In terms of Haig and Simons's income, however, his or her net worth has increased by $50, and thus there is income of $50 though no money has changed hands. In other words, accrued capital gains are included in Haig and Simons's income.

It is useful for analytical purposes to distinguish between sources of income. Thus, economists, journalists, and policy makers often talk about wage income, dividends and interest income, transfer payments, and so on. Labor income is the income generated from working for a set wage, including tips and fringe benefits. Financial income is the income obtained from financial markets, which includes accrued capital gains, interest income, dividends, and retained earnings. Retirement income refers to pensions and retirement transfers. Government income refers to government transfers such as social insurance payments. Other sources of income include bequests, prizes and awards, and alimony payments received.

EMPIRICAL SIGNIFICANCE

Defining income is important to the analysis of public policy. Using a measure that is not comprehensive could alter the outcome of the policy, and as such may result in poor decision making. For example, if a tax administration such as the U.S. Internal Revenue Service taxes only wage income at a single rate, then the burden of such a tax would take a higher proportion of the total income of low-income households than high-income households, because low-income households obtain a greater share of their income from wages than do high-income households. Another area of research is in the distribution of income and income inequality.

Table 1 shows the distribution of income by source for a variety of countries. The similarities in the shares of income by source among these countries are noteworthy.

2005 Gross Income by Source

	Gross income from employment	Tax and social security contributions	Gross income from investments	Gross income from benefits	Gross income from other sources
Canada	62.75%	18.49%	5.46%	10.87%	2.43%
China	64.52%	14.91%	1.63%	17.78%	1.16%
France	46.86%	25.03%	5.49%	22.26%	0.36%
Germany	47.25%	25.04%	10.51%	14.99%	2.21%
India	75.61%	4.36%	2.67%	3.97%	13.39%
Italy	47.04%	22.03%	13.83%	14.98%	2.12%
Japan	59.82%	22.43%	1.80%	12.48%	3.48%
Mexico	58.97%	6.67%	4.65%	6.20%	23.51%
Russia	67.55%	13.63%	5.69%	11.62%	1.51%
Spain	56.56%	23.52%	6.84%	9.85%	3.22%
United Kingdom	52.52%	22.55%	6.38%	14.94%	3.61%
United States	62.49%	15.29%	12.00%	6.28%	3.94%

SOURCE: http://stacks.gsu.edu:2422/womdas/

Although there appears to be considerable variation in income from employment, which varies from a low of 46.86 percent in France to a high of 75.61 percent in India, income from employment and taxes and social security contributions (payroll taxes) shows much less variation, with the smallest share being 65.64 in Mexico and the highest share being 82.25 percent in Japan. Many economists believe that tax policy may explain the relative shares of gross income from benefits. Because benefits such as contributions to retirement accounts and health insurance are generally not taxable, one would expect that people living in high-tax countries such as France would prefer to receive income in the form of untaxable benefits rather than taxable sources such as wages; in contrast, in low-tax countries such as India, people would prefer to receive income as wages. This pattern is borne out in the table.

SEE ALSO *Inequality, Income; Interest Rates; National Income Accounts; Policy, Fiscal; Profits; Stocks and Flows; Taxes; Wages*

BIBLIOGRAPHY

Birdsall, Nancy. 2006. Rising Inequality in the New Global Economy. *International Journal of Development Issues* 5 (1): 1–9.

Haig, Robert M. 1921. The Concept of Income: Economic and Legal Aspects. In *The Federal Income Tax*, ed. R. M. Haig. New York: Columbia University Press.

Piketty, Thomas, and Emmanuel Saez. 2006. The Evolution of Top Incomes: A Historical and International Perspective. *American Economic Review* 96 (2): 200–205.

Simons, Henry C. 1938. *Personal Income Taxation.* Chicago: University of Chicago Press.

Taylor, Lester D. 1971. Saving Out of Different Types of Income. Brookings Papers on Economic Activity 2: 383–407.

Mark Rider

INCOME DISTRIBUTION

Income distribution captures the proportion of total income accruing to different individuals that accounts for the total income distributed among them during a certain time period. If the unit of analysis is the country, the income distribution for a certain year would show how much of the country's yearly income went to each person. It may be of interest to capture the country's distribution of income within and across groups of individuals as well. Groups can be formed according to many criteria, depending on the issue under analysis. Criteria can include geographic (cities or states), gender, social, and ethnic considerations, to name a few. When groups of individuals are considered, it is typically of interest to distinguish between the income distribution within and across groups. For example, how much of a country's income goes to the urban and to the rural population corresponds to the across-group distribution of income. How much went to each person living in rural areas and how much went to each person living in urban areas is a measure of the distribution of income within groups.

Income distribution can be represented in different ways. It can be represented by an (income) density function, $f(y)$, where y stands for income; $f(y)dy$ gives the number of individuals earning income in the $[y, y + dy]$ interval. Integrating the income-density function to infinity yields the total population, N, while integrating $yf(y)$ gives total income, Y. Mean income, μ, is given by Y/N.

A plot of the income-density function would be the most comprehensive way of representing income distribution, but this is rarely possible in practice if the unit of analysis is a country. Histograms may provide an approximation, but these representations are not usually used when analyzing the dispersion in the distribution of income. The most widely used graphic representation of income distribution—while by no means the only one possible—is the Lorenz curve. To construct a Lorenz curve, individuals are first ranked by income in ascendant order: $y_i \leq y_{i+1}$, $i = 1, \ldots, N$. Then, the cumulative income up to rank j is computed: $s_j = y_1 + y_2 + y_j$, $j = 1, \ldots, N$. The Lorenz curve corresponds to the plot of $(j/N, s_j/Y)$, $j = 1, \ldots, N$. That is, it shows on the horizontal axis the cumulative population share (from 0 to 1) and on the vertical axis the corresponding income share (also from 0 to 1). It enables the determination of the share of income going to each quartile, quintile, decile, or centile—or any other breakdown of the population.

The Lorenz curve gives a visually compelling idea of the extent of inequality in the distribution of income. The line of perfect equality corresponds to the 45-degree line that goes from the origin to (1,1). That is, the poorest 10 percent of the population have 10 percent of income, then the poorest 20 percent have 20 percent of income, and so forth. The Lorenz curve lies always on or below the line of perfect equality, with "perfect inequality" (all income going to the richest individual) corresponding to the line that makes the lower and right-hand side of the square that encompasses the line of perfect inequality. That is, the shares of income going to all the shares of the population are zero, and 100 percent of income goes to the single individual at the top. Thus, the closer the Lorenz curve is to the line of perfect equality, the more equal the distribution of income; the farther it is, the higher the level of inequality.

Thus, intuitively, the area that lies between the line of perfect equality and the Lorenz curve provides an indication of the extent of inequality. If this area is very small, the Lorenz curve is very close to the area of perfect equality, and inequality is low. If this area is large, then the Lorenz curve is further away from the line of perfect equality, and inequality is high. The ratio of this area to the area of the triangle limited by the lines of perfect equality and perfect inequality is a number that falls always between zero (when the Lorenz curve coincides with the line of perfect equality) and one (when the Lorenz curve coincides with the line of perfect inequality and the area under the Lorenz curve is exactly the same as the area of the triangle). This number is the *Gini coefficient*, one of the most widely used measures of inequality—and one of the many possible summary measures of income distribution, whereby distribution is summarized by a single number.

While intuitively appealing, the Gini coefficient has a major drawback. As noted, in studies of inequality there is often an interest in grouping individuals and determining the shares of inequality that correspond to asymmetries in the distribution of income across and within groups. It is possible to decompose the Gini coefficient into within-group and between-group components, but this decomposition is not "perfect," in the sense that the components do not add up to total inequality—a third term, a *residual*, is typically required to be added to the other two terms to get to total inequality. The only summary measures of inequality that are perfectly decomposable correspond to a class known as *entropy-based* measures of inequality, which were pioneered by the Dutch econometrician Henri Theil (1924–2000). He drew inspiration from the entropy-based analysis of information, and thus the name of this class of measures.

The most widely used entropy-based measure of inequality is the Theil index. It is bound between zero and the natural logarithm of the size of the population (and not by one, like the Gini coefficient). The Theil index is the weighted sum of the natural logarithm of the ratio of the income shares to the population shares, where the weights are income shares. When applied to measure inequality across individuals, the "population share" is merely $1/N$, so the Theil index is the weighted sum of the natural logarithm of the ratio of each individual's income, y_i/Y, to $1/N$, where the weights are y_i/Y. When individuals are grouped, the between-group component of the Theil index is the weighted sum of the natural logarithm of the ratio of each group's income, Y_j/Y, to that group's population share, n_j/N, where the weights are Y_j/Y (n_j and Y_j are, respectively, the group's j population and total income). The within-group component of total inequality is given by the weighted sum of the within-group Theil index for each group, where the weights are the income

shares, Y_j/Y. Total inequality measured using the Theil index is the sum of the between-group and within-group components.

SEE ALSO *Economic Growth; Gini Coefficient; Inequality, Income; Inequality, Political; Justice, Distributive; Kuznets Hypothesis; Lorenz Curve; Theil Index; Wealth*

BIBLIOGRAPHY

Alison, P. D. 1978. Measures of Inequality. *American Sociological Review* 43 (December): 865–880.

Bourguignon, François. 1979. Decomposable Income Inequality Measures. *Econometrica* 47 (4): 901–920.

Cowell, Frank A. 1980. On the Structure of Additive Inequality Measures. *Review of Economic Studies* 47 (3): 521–531.

Sen, A. 1997. *On Economic Inequality.* Oxford: Clarendon Press.

Shorrocks, A. F. 1980. The Class of Additively Decomposable Inequality Measures. *Econometrica* 48 (3): 613–626.

Theil, Henri. 1967. *Economics and Information Theory.* Chicago: Rand McNally and Company.

Theil, Henri. 1996. *Studies in Global Econometrics.* Dordrecht, the Netherlands: Kluwer Academic Publishers.

Pedro Conceição

INCOME MAINTENANCE EXPERIMENTS

The income maintenance experiments in the United States and Canada were tests of a welfare program known as a *negative income tax*, which was designed to assist families in need while preserving their incentives to work. The negative income tax is the most important proposal in the history of welfare reform and has been a major object of study in the social sciences.

ORIGIN OF THE EXPERIMENTS

The idea of the negative income tax is generally associated with the Nobel laureate, conservative economist Milton Friedman (1962, chap. 12), although liberal economists Robert J. Lampman (1920–1997) and James Tobin (1918–2002) were also early developers. Friedman's proposal had both liberal and conservative elements. On the liberal side, he proposed that all families with low incomes receive an unrestricted grant from the government, leading to what some others termed a *guaranteed annual income*. However, Friedman noted that such a grant threatens to reduce work incentives by providing income support to families even if they are not employed. To counter that disincentive, Friedman proposed that families be given a financial incentive to work by means of a "tax rate" that would result in higher income if they worked. For example, if the tax rate were 50 percent, a nonworking family with a monthly grant of $500 who went to work and earned $100 would experience a grant reduction of $50 (50 percent of earnings) to $450. The family's total income would rise to $550, the sum of $100 of earnings and a grant of $450, providing the desired financial incentive. The lower the tax rate, the smaller the benefit reduction that would occur and hence the greater the work incentives.

In 1967 the federal government decided to conduct a social experiment to determine whether a guaranteed, unrestricted grant for nonworkers would induce working families to quit work and whether a low tax rate would counter that disincentive (Greenberg et al. 2003). To test the negative income tax, the government proposed to select a group of poor families, to randomly assign them to an "experimental" group and a "control" group, to give the experimental group the negative income tax, and then to later observe how many families in each group were working. The difference in the work levels of the two groups would be taken to be the effect of the negative income tax.

Four experiments were designed and implemented in the United States and one in Canada. They were located in New Jersey and Pennsylvania; South Carolina and Iowa; Gary, Indiana; Seattle, Washington, and Denver, Colorado; and in Manitoba, Canada (Greenberg and Shroder 2004). The first began in 1968 and the last ended in 1979. Most were designed as described previously, but with one variation: different families in the experimental groups were given different guaranteed grant amounts and different tax rates, allowing a test of the effect of the levels of the guaranteed income amount and the tax rate on work effort.

RESULTS OF THE EXPERIMENTS

The first question was whether offering families a guaranteed income if they did not work would reduce work effort. The answer from all the experiments was an unequivocal "Yes." The work levels of experimental families were almost always less than those of control families (Burtless 1986; Greenberg et al. 2003; Greenberg and Shroder 2004; SRI International 1983). For example, in the Seattle-Denver experiment, married men in the experimental group were five percentage points less likely to work during the year than those in the control group; the corresponding figures for married women and for single mothers were eleven percentage points and seven percentage points, respectively. Further, the comparisons of work levels across families with different experimental plans

revealed that families who were offered more generous grant amounts did, in fact, work less.

The second question was whether Friedman's idea of giving families a financial incentive to work with a reasonably low tax rate countered this disincentive. The answer to this question was much more ambiguous. Overall, the data from the experiments showed a mixed pattern of effects of this kind (e.g., SRI International 1983, Table 3.9). Why a stronger work response to financial incentives was not found generated a great deal of research over the subsequent years, with some arguing that statistical flaws in the experiments' design led to this result. But the leading explanation is that a reduction in the tax rate expands the generosity of the program, relative to the existing welfare program, and tends to bring new families onto welfare who had not received benefits previously. The work reductions of these families partially or wholly offset the positive work effects for those families initially on welfare.

The researchers conducting the experiments also gathered data on other aspects of behavior. For example, families in the experimental group had slightly greater expenditures on housing and increases in homeownership, stayed in school longer, and had greater increases in test scores among children in lower grades (Greenberg et al. 2003; Hanushek 1986). On the other hand, in the Seattle-Denver experiment, there was a surprising increase in the rate of marital dissolution, a controversial result that was not anticipated by policymakers or researchers. The negative income tax had been predicted to increase marital stability because it extended benefits to two-parent families compared to the current welfare system.

The political impact of the results of the income maintenance experiments was modest at best because political events moved too quickly (Moynihan 1973). President Richard Nixon (1913–1994) proposed a negative income tax to the U.S. Congress in 1969, long before the experiments had been completed. The plan passed the House of Representatives but failed in the Senate in 1972. Although the results of the experiments were used by the Jimmy Carter administration in formulating its welfare reform program, no negative income tax plan was ever seriously considered by Congress thereafter. When the results of the experiments were later published, the evidence of significant work reductions reinforced this lack of interest in a pure negative income tax (Greenberg et al. 2003).

LEGACY OF THE EXPERIMENTS

While the negative income tax in its idealized form has never been implemented in the United States or Canada, the idea of providing financial incentives to work has proved to be a powerful one and has led to many welfare reforms having such features. Much subsequent research has provided stronger evidence that some families, typically those with the lowest levels of earnings, work more if given a financial incentive to do so, thereby giving more support to this idea than did the experiments. In the 1990s, many U.S. states added financial incentives to their welfare programs.

The primary alternative to financial work incentives is the idea of simply requiring work of anyone who receives benefits, a policy often characterized as using a "stick" to encourage work rather than a "carrot" of financial incentives. Such work requirements were introduced in the United States in the 1990s and have been introduced on a more limited scale in Canada in more recent years, and can be seen as directly addressing the work disincentives from unrestricted grants to nonworking families that were shown to occur in the experiments. Critics of work requirements argue that they eliminate benefits for some families who are in need but cannot work. However, a second alternative policy is an "earnings subsidy" that offers little or no grant support to nonworkers but gives a grant to those who work, possibly only those who work full-time, to provide work incentives. The U.S. Earned Income Tax Credit is the major existing policy of this type. Earnings subsidies, while providing incentives to work, also provide no support to nonworking families, who are usually in greater need. The debate on these issues continues.

The income maintenance experiments have also had a major legacy by introducing the idea of randomized trials as a method of social policy evaluation, which was a radically new idea in 1967. Since the 1970s, there have been over 250 subsequent experiments with various social policies (Greenberg and Shroder 2004). Most of these experiments have been less ambitious and of a much smaller scale than those testing the negative income tax, but they nevertheless have used the same core methodology.

SEE ALSO *Negative Income Tax; Welfare*

BIBLIOGRAPHY

Burtless, Gary. 1986. The Work Response to a Guaranteed Income: A Survey of Experimental Evidence. In *Lessons from the Income Maintenance Experiments: Proceedings of a Conference Held at Melvin Village, New Hampshire, September 1986*, ed. Alicia H. Munnell, 22–52. Boston: Federal Reserve Bank of Boston.

Friedman, Milton. 1962. *Capitalism and Freedom.* Chicago: University of Chicago Press.

Greenberg, David, Donna Linksz, and Marvin Mandell. 2003. *Social Experimentation and Public Policymaking.* Washington, DC: Urban Institute Press.

Greenberg, David, and Mark Shroder. 2004. *The Digest of Social Experiments.* 3rd ed. Washington, DC: Urban Institute Press.

Hanushek, Eric. 1986. Non-Labor-Supply Responses to the Income Maintenance Experiments. In *Lessons from the Income Maintenance Experiments: Proceedings of a Conference Held at*

Melvin Village, New Hampshire, September 1986*, ed. Alicia H. Munnell, 106–121. Boston: Federal Reserve Bank of Boston.

Moynihan, Daniel P. 1973. *The Politics of a Guaranteed Income: The Nixon Administration and the Family Assistance Plan.* New York: Vintage.

SRI International. 1983. *Final Report of the Seattle-Denver Income Maintenance Experiment.* Vol. 1: *Design and Results.* Washington, DC: U.S. Department of Health and Human Services, 1983.

Robert A. Moffitt

INCOME POLICY

SEE *Inflation; Wage and Price Controls.*

INCOME TAX, CORPORATE

The corporate income tax is levied on the profits of incorporated businesses. Taxable income is defined as the gross income of a corporation minus its costs of doing business. Whereas the costs of labor and raw materials as well as interest payments are deducted from taxable income at the time they are incurred, the costs of capital assets are recovered only over time in the form of deductions for depreciation. To assess their tax liability, corporations apply a statutory tax rate to their taxable income and then subtract any deductions and other credits. The corporate income tax is mainly a central (federal) government tax, but subnational governments also apply the tax in many countries, although at a lower rate.

INCIDENCE

The effective tax rate differs from the statutory rate mainly because of the treatment of depreciation and interest payments. The effective tax burden is smaller the shorter the recovery period is and the more accelerated the rate of depreciation is. The effective burden is smaller the greater the use of debt relative to equity in financing investment is because interest payments, unlike dividend payments, are expensed. The extent of the "double taxation" of dividends, first as part of corporate taxable income and then as income received by individual taxpayers, and how to address it is subject to theoretical and empirical debate.

Because labor costs are excluded in calculating taxable income, the corporate income tax generally is viewed as a tax on capital income. However, some of the tax burden can be shifted from firms to consumers through higher prices or to workers through lower wages, depending on the structure of the product and labor markets. The closer such markets are to competitive conditions, the harder it is for firms to shift the tax burden. The empirical literature is inconclusive about the extent of that shifting.

EFFECTS

The corporate income tax can influence economic growth through its impact on economic behavior, including saving and investment. The effect on saving is ambiguous in both the theoretical and the empirical literature. The tax could affect the level and composition of capital formation by raising the cost of capital and imposing a relatively higher burden on equity versus debt financing. It also may induce firms to organize in unincorporated forms (which are not subject to corporate income tax) that may not be the economically optimal forms of organization apart from tax considerations. Moreover, tax compliance and the tax planning that businesses undertake to minimize tax liabilities, such as transfer pricing, and entail costs. The estimated costs of the distortions associated with the U.S. corporate tax fall in a wide range of one-quarter to nearly two-thirds of revenues. The tax can influence income distribution directly because taxes on capital income tend to be progressive relative to taxes on labor income and indirectly through its impact on the cost of capital.

THE CORPORATE INCOME TAX IN MAJOR INDUSTRIAL COUNTRIES AND DEVELOPING COUNTRIES

In 2003 revenue from the corporate income tax averaged around 3.5 percent of gross domestic product (GDP) among Organisation for Economic Cooperation and Development (OECD) countries. The top statutory tax rate varied substantially from 12.5 percent to 41 percent. Among developing countries that revenue averaged around 3 percent of GDP. Over the last decade or so there has been a general tendency for countries to reduce the statutory tax rate. Some countries offer corporate tax incentives in an effort to attract investment. The effectiveness of those incentives is open to debate, but incentives that provide for faster recovery of investment costs generally are considered preferable to those involving the tax rate.

SEE ALSO *Capital; Corporations; Distortions; Government; Income Distribution; Investment; Savings Rate; Taxes*

BIBLIOGRAPHY

Auerbach, Alan. 2006. Who Bears the Corporate Tax? A Review of What We Know. In *Tax Policy and the Economy*, vol. 20, ed. James M. Poterba, 1–40. Cambridge, MA: MIT Press.

Bernheim, B. D. 2002. Taxation and Saving. In *Handbook of Public Economics*, vol. 3, eds. Alan J. Auerbach and Martin Feldstein, 1173–1249. Amsterdam and New York: Elsevier.

Congressional Budget Office. 2005. *Corporate Income Tax Rates: International Comparisons*. Washington, DC: Author.

Gordon, Roger M., and Jeffrey H. MacKie-Mason. 1995. Why Is There Corporate Taxation in a Small Open Economy? The Role of Transfer Pricing and Income Shifting. In *The Effects of Taxation on Multinational Corporations*, eds. Martin Feldstein, James R. Hines, Jr., and R. Glenn Hubbard, 67–91. Chicago: University of Chicago Press.

Gravelle, Jane. 1994. *The Economic Effects of Taxing Capital Income*. Cambridge, MA: MIT Press.

Harberger, A. C. 1966. Efficiency Effects of Taxes on Income from Capital. In *Effects of the Corporate Income Tax*, ed. M. Krzyaniak, 107–117. Detroit: Wayne State University Press.

International Monetary Fund. Various years. *Government Finance Statistics*. Washington, DC: Author.

Musgrave, Richard A., and Peggy B. Musgrave. 1989. *Public Finance in Theory and Practice*, 5th ed. New York: McGraw-Hill.

Tanzi, Vito, and Howell Zee. 2000. Tax Policy for Emerging Markets: Developing Countries. *National Tax Journal* 53 (2): 299–328.

Zee, H., J. Stotsky, and E. Ley. 2002. Tax Incentives for Business Investment: A Primer for Policy Makers in Developing Countries. *World Development* 30 (9): 1497–1516.

Vivek Arora

INCONGRUITY EFFECT

SEE *Person Memory.*

INCREMENTALISM

Rejecting the rational, comprehensive model of decision-making that called for careful articulation of all goals and full consideration of all alternatives, Charles Lindblom's essay, "The Science of 'Muddling Through'" (1959), inaugurated a new approach to understanding public policy. While Lindblom used the term *successive limited comparison* rather than *incrementalism*, this new approach argued that: (1) means and ends are decided simultaneous, not sequentially; (2) comparisons are restricted to marginal changes in existing policy, and are not made among all possible alternatives; and (3) the appropriate test of good policy is simply the ability to make a decision. Based on both the cognitive limitations of decision makers and widespread conflicts over values in policymaking, Lindblom argued that it simply was not rational to try to make rational, comprehensive decisions.

Lindblom's insight provided the theoretical foundation of Aaron Wildavsky's (1930–1993) *The Politics of the Budgetary Process* (1964) and his later empirical modeling of U.S. appropriations decisions (Davis et al. 1966). As Wildavsky noted,

> Budgeting is incremental, not comprehensive. The beginning of wisdom about an agency budget is that it is almost never actively reviewed as a whole every year in the sense of reconsidering the value of all existing programs as compared to all alternatives. Instead, it is based on last year's budget with special attention given to a narrow range of increases or decreases. (Wildavsky 1964, p. 15)

Given this understanding of budget decision making, Wildavsky (1978) argued that a succession of budget reforms designed to introduce elements of rational, comprehensive choice into the appropriations process—such as President Lyndon Johnson's (1908–1973) planning-programming-budgeting system or President Jimmy Carter's zero-based budgeting—would inevitably fail.

The Lindblom-Wildavsky model of incrementalism was remarkably successful in inspiring a generation of research on public policymaking in general and budgeting in particular. But it also attracted considerable criticism even in its heyday. John Wanat (1974), for example, argued that the budget results reported by Wildavsky could be adequately accounted for by the prevalence of mandatory budgetary increases without reference to constraints on individual decision making or the need to coordinate decisions among political actors. John Gist (1982) then suggested that the level of competition within the budget process depended very much on the level of the budget examined. At lower levels, budgets change far more than might be expected given incremental decision making. And perhaps most telling of all, the very concept of incrementalism was characterized by considerable drift as various authors operationalized the concept in markedly different ways. Indeed, after identifying at least twelve different meanings of incrementalism used in research on public policy ranging from the "use of simple decision rules" through "smallness of ultimate change" to "absence of competition," William Berry (1990) argued that the concept had become so broad that it should be abandoned. But none of these criticisms really slowed the pace of research on incrementalism, in large part, perhaps, because none really identified an alternative theory that could account as well for the empirical regularities reported by those working within the incremental paradigm.

Such an alternative finally appeared after renewed attention to periods of rapid policy change. Wildavsky

and his colleagues (Davis et al. 1974) certainly acknowledged that, at least on occasion, policies and budgets change rapidly. But they were more attentive to the longer periods of stability than to the rarer episodes of change. But John Kingdon's *Agendas, Alternatives, and Public Policies* (1984) drew renewed attention to the importance of episodes of sudden, dramatic change in fundamentally shaping public policy. Kingdon's attention to nonincremental policy change was further developed by Frank Baumgartner and Bryan Jones in *Agendas and Instability in American Politics* (1993). Their punctuated equilibrium model of public policy purported to account for why we observe both short, rapid episodes of policy change and long-term stasis between such periods. Explaining how their model accounts for the former goes beyond the scope of an essay on incrementalism. But while Jones and Baumgartner's (2005) explanation for the periods of relative stasis in policy between periods of sharp change accounts for Wildavsky's findings, it also differs from his understanding of incrementalism. That is, rather than explaining stability by the need of politicians to find consensus in order to make any decision in the face of widespread conflict over values and the ultimate goals of public policy, the punctuated equilibrium model explains episodes of limited policy change by reference to both the government's inability to attend to more than a few major issues at any given time and the stickiness of political institutions that inhibits rapid change. When government attention is drawn to an issue and that stickiness breaks down as veto points are overcome by political momentum, significant policy change is likely.

Has the theory of incrementalism founded on the work of Lindblom and Wildavsky really been surpassed? It is clear that the theoretical analysis used to account for observations of incremental behavior has shifted from attention to the limited cognitive capacities of individuals and the necessity of politicians to make decisions in the face of conflicting values to the stickiness of political institutions and institutional limits on the size of policy agendas. And it is also true that scholars are now more attentive to the importance of periods of rapid change that are observed in most policy areas over time. In these senses, the theory of incrementalism has been surpassed by Baumgartner and Jones's theory of punctuated equilibrium. But in other respects, incrementalism is alive and well. Baumgartner and Jones's attention to periods of punctuation is important largely because most policymaking, most of the time, is incremental in the sense used by Wildavsky in the quotation presented at the beginning of this essay. Most policy decisions are not reexamined every year against all possible alternatives. The backdrop of punctuations is as important as the punctuations themselves. Even more importantly, neither Kingdon's policy agendas model nor Jones and Baumgartner's punctuated equilibrium model represents a return to the model of rational, comprehensive decision making so strongly rejected by Lindblom and Wildavsky.

SEE ALSO *Decision-making; Economics; Lindblom, Charles; Marginalism; Pluralism; Policy Analysis; Punctuated Equilibrium*

BIBLIOGRAPHY

Baumgartner, Frank, and Bryan D. Jones. 1993. *Agendas and Instability in American Politics.* Chicago: University of Chicago Press.

Berry, William D. 1990. The Confusing Case of Budgetary Incrementalism: Too Many Meanings for a Single Concept. *The Journal of Politics* 52 (1): 167–196.

Davis, Otto A., M. A. H. Dempster, and Aaron Wildavsky. 1966. A Theory of the Budgetary Process. *American Political Science Review* 60: 529–547.

Davis, Otto A., M. A. H. Dempster, and Aaron Wildavsky. 1974. Towards a Predictive Theory of the Government Expenditure: US Domestic Appropriations. *British Journal of Political Science* 4 (4): 419–452.

Gist, John R. 1982. "Stability" and "Competition" in Budgetary Theory. *American Political Science Review* 76: 859–872.

Jones, Bryan D., and Frank Baumgartner. 2005. *The Politics of Attention: How Government Prioritizes Problems.* Chicago: University of Chicago Press.

Kingdon, John W. 1984. *Agendas, Alternatives, and Public Policies.* Boston: Little Brown. 2nd ed., 2003. New York: Longman.

Lindblom, Charles E. 1959. The Science of "Muddling Through." *Public Administration Review* 19: 79–88.

Wanat, John. 1974. Bases of Budgetary Incrementalism. *American Political Science Review* 68: 1221–1228.

Wildavsky, Aaron. 1964. *The Politics of the Budgetary Process.* Boston: Little Brown. 4th ed., 1984.

Wildavsky, Aaron. 1978. A Budget for All Seasons: Why the Traditional Budget Lasts. *Public Administration Review* 38 (6): 501–509.

David Lowery

INDENTURED SERVITUDE

SEE *Servitude.*

INDEPENDENT VOTERS

SEE *Political Parties.*

INDEPENDENTLY AND IDENTICALLY DISTRIBUTED

SEE *Inference, Statistical.*

INDIAN NATIONAL ARMY

The Indian National Army (INA) was formed in 1942 by Indian prisoners of war captured by the Japanese in Singapore. It was created with the aid of Japanese forces. Captain Mohan Singh became the INA's first leader, and Major Iwaichi Fujiwara was the Japanese intelligence officer who brokered the arrangement to create the army, which was to be trained to fight British and other Allied forces in Southeast Asia. The Japanese had sent intelligence agents to Southeast Asia from the late 1930s onward, and they made contact with the considerable population of South Asians resident in Malaya, Singapore, Thailand, Burma, and other parts of the region. The Japanese aim was to use and benefit from the nationalism of Asian peoples in constructing what they called their "Greater East Asia Co-Prosperity Sphere."

With the opening victories in the war, from December 1941 through the early months of 1942, the Japanese captured large numbers of Indian prisoners, particularly in their victory at Singapore in February 1942. Some 40,000 to 50,000 men were recruited for a training corps of South Asian residents in Southeast Asia.

With the help of Rash Behari Bose, an Indian nationalist long resident in Japan, the civilian Indian Independence League (IIL) was formed to support the INA and push for Indian independence. This organization provided vital support for the INA throughout the war period. For example, one member in Burma traded liquor for medical supplies desperately needed by the INA.

Tensions developed in late 1942 between Mohan Singh and the Japanese over terms of cooperation. The Japanese were determined to exercise control over the INA that Mohan Singh was not willing to accept. He was relieved of command and imprisoned. Rash Behari Bose was still in good standing with the Japanese, but he had no popular following. A more charismatic leader was needed. In May 1943 Subhas Chandra Bose, a leading Congress nationalist from Bengal who had been working in Germany, arrived in Southeast Asia via a German and then a Japanese submarine, and he provided the leadership that was needed. He became commanding officer of the INA and also set up a provisional government of free India, which was recognized by the Axis powers. The main training camp of the INA was in Singapore, and young women from the South Asian community in Southeast Asia were recruited for the women's regiment, called the Rani of Jhansi Regiment. It was headed by a young medical doctor, Lakshmi Swaminathan, who also became minister for women's affairs in the provisional government. Bose worked carefully to get soldiers from all communities—Hindus, Muslims, and Sikhs—to cooperate for the greater good of Indian independence.

In late 1943, Bose persuaded the Japanese to attempt an invasion of India from Burma, with the INA as a small force working alongside the Japanese's main invading force. This effort succeeded in breaking into India near Imphal in 1944. However, the Japanese overextended their supply lines and had no air cover. In their opening victories of the war, the Japanese had good air cover and succeeded in capturing British supplies as they advanced, but now the battles in the Pacific and elsewhere had deprived them of most of their air force. The Allied forces, headed by General William Slim of Great Britain, retreated at first, by design, but then attacked and drove the Japanese and the INA from India and back through Burma. Both the Japanese and the INA suffered greatly from disease and starvation as they retreated. Though the INA fought bravely overall, some men surrendered, and the remaining troops were eventually captured as the British, Indian, and American forces triumphed in Southeast Asia in the spring and summer of 1945.

Subhas Bose attempted to escape to Manchuria and was in a Japanese plane that crashed after take-off in Taiwan in August 1945. The evidence shows that he died of his burns and was cremated there. There was one Indian survivor of the plane crash, Habibur Rahman, and several Japanese survivors, in addition to the doctor who treated him, all of whom testified on several occasions to the story of the crash and his death. However, some Indians chose for decades not to believe the account for personal and political reasons. His ashes were taken to Tokyo and lodged in a Buddhist temple where they remain.

Three officers of the INA, Shah Nawaz Khan (a Muslim), Prem Sahgal (a Hindu), and G. S. Dhillon (a Sikh), were tried for offenses against the King-Emperor in 1945–1946 in the Red Fort in Delhi. The British miscalculated by putting an individual from each religious community on trial, however, and there were massive demonstrations throughout India. As a result, although they were convicted and sentenced to transportation for life, they were soon released. The support the public showed for these rebel military men was one factor in the British government's decision to grant independence to India in 1947.

SEE ALSO *Anticolonial Movements; Bose, Subhas Chandra and Sarat Chandra; Decolonization; Imperialism;* *Indian National Congress; Liberation Movements; Nazism; Resistance; World War II*

BIBLIOGRAPHY

Ghosh, Kalyan K. 1969. *The Indian National Army.* Meerut, India: Meenakshi Prakasthan.

Gordon, Leonard A. 1990. *Brothers Against the Raj: A Biography of Indian Nationalists Sarat and Subhas Chandra Bose.* New York: Columbia University Press.

Lebra, Joyce C. 1971. *Jungle Alliance: Japan and the Indian National Army.* Singapore: Asia Pacific Press.

Toye, Hugh. 1959. *The Springing Tiger: A Study of a Revolutionary.* London: Cassell.

Leonard A. Gordon

INDIAN NATIONAL CONGRESS

Founded in 1885, the Indian National Congress (INC) was at the forefront of the nationalist movement in India before 1947. After India's independence in that year, the Congress emerged as the ruling party, and it maintained power uninterrupted for three decades (1947–1977). Since then, the party has been in and out of power.

In the first three decades of its existence the Congress was an elite organization dominated by English-educated, urban middle-class Indians. The organization was much like a debating society, but Mohandas K. Gandhi, who assumed its leadership in 1920 and remained its spiritual leader until his death in 1948, transformed the Congress into a mass movement and a political institution with an organizational structure that paralleled the colonial administration. Gandhi expanded the membership and appeal of the Congress by mobilizing the rural population, especially the lower castes and outcastes of the Hindu social hierarchy—the *sudras*, or "untouchables." The Congress became the sole representative of the national cause, leading three campaigns between 1920 and 1947: the noncooperation movement (1920–1922), the civil disobedience campaign (1931–1932), and the "Quit India" movement (August 1942). The Congress won seven of the eleven provinces in the 1937 elections, which were held under British rule following the provisions of the Government of India Act of 1935, and it formed a government in those provinces.

After independence the Congress, hitherto an all-embracing national movement, was transformed into a political party. Under the leadership of Jawaharlal Nehru, India's first prime minister (1947–1964), it retained the character of an eclectic political organization with a wide range of positions. The Congress controlled 70 percent of seats in parliament and held power in most states between 1951 and 1967. This period of one-party dominance has been referred to as the Congress "system" in Indian politics. However, the power struggle between Indira Gandhi (Nehru's daughter, who was prime minister from 1966 to 1977 and 1980 to 1984) and the Congress organization led to the party split in 1969. The majority followed Mrs. Gandhi to her "New Congress" or "Congress (R)" (*R* for "ruling"), which was recognized by the election commission as the "real" INC. Mrs. Gandhi's leadership of the Congress led to the deinstitutionalization of the party as she undermined the federal character of the party by stopping party elections and concentrating power in her own hands.

The Congress lost its dominant position for the first time in ninety years with its defeat in the 1977 elections, held after the unpopular Emergency Rule Mrs. Gandhi had imposed in 1975. Faced with criticism of her leadership, Mrs. Gandhi split the party a second time, in 1978, and formed the breakaway Congress (I) (*I* for "Indira"). The Congress (I) returned her to power in 1980, but she was assassinated in 1984. Mrs. Gandhi was succeeded by her older son Rajiv Gandhi (1944–1991), who lost power in the 1989 elections. When Rajiv Gandhi was assassinated in 1991, the party presidency was offered to his widow, Sonia Gandhi (b. 1946), who declined the offer. Although the party held power from 1991 to 1996, the Congress was in decline as a national party due primarily to the lackluster leaderships of P. V. Narasimha Rao (1921–2004) and Sitaram Kesri (1919–2000). In 1998 Sonia Gandhi was elected party president and started rebuilding the party, especially by expanding its support base among Muslims and the poor. Her leadership did not help the party win the 1999 elections, and a small number of Congress (I) leaders led by Sharad Pawar (b. 1940), who questioned the likelihood of foreign-born Gandhi becoming prime minister, formed a breakaway party in 1999 (the Nationalist Congress Party). Nevertheless, Gandhi's leadership energized and revitalized the Congress (I) Party. In the 2004 parliamentary elections the Congress won enough seats to form a coalition government with the support of about a dozen center-left parties. Gandhi, however, declined to become prime minister; instead she remained the party president, and Manmohan Singh (b. 1932) became prime minister. The Congress expects that Rajiv and Sonia's son Rahul Gandhi (b. 1970), who won a parliamentary seat in 2004, will play a significant role in the party in the near future.

SEE ALSO *Anticolonial Movements; Civil Disobedience; Congress Party, India; Democracy; Gandhi, Indira; Gandhi, Mohandas K.; Indian National Army*

BIBLIOGRAPHY

Brass, Paul. 2006. *The Politics of India since Independence.* 2nd ed. Cambridge, U.K.: Cambridge University Press.

Kochanek, Stanley. 1968. *The Congress Party of India.* Princeton, NJ: Princeton University Press.

Mitra, Subrata, Mike Enskat, and Clemens Spiess, eds. 2004. *Political Parties in South Asia.* Thousand Oaks, CA: Sage.

Seal, Anil. 1968. *The Emergence of Indian Nationalism.* Cambridge, U.K.: Cambridge University Press.

Sunil Sahu

INDICATIVE PLANNING
SEE *Convergence Theory.*

INDICATORS, LAGGING, LEADING, AND COINCIDENT
SEE *Lagging, Leading, and Coincident Indicators.*

INDICES, PRICE
SEE *Price Indices.*

INDICES OF POVERTY
SEE *Poverty, Indices of.*

INDIFFERENCE CURVES
SEE *Ordinality.*

INDIFFERENCE PRINCIPLE
SEE *Ordinality.*

INDIGENISMO

Broadly defined, *indigenismo* (Spanish, "indianism") refers to the representation of indigenous peoples (*indígenas* in

Spanish) in Latin America by outsiders (called *indigenistas*). It is a uniquely American phenomenon, and its origins are inextricably bound together with debates on the question of how colonized indigenous peoples should be treated. Its importance as a philosophical aspect of Latin American thought dates to the beginnings of European attempts to subdue the aboriginal inhabitants of the American continent in the late fifteenth century. It reached its high point in the early twentieth century in countries with high concentrations of indigenous peoples, particularly Mexico and Peru. Although its characteristics changed over time, *indigenismo* always presented a critique of indigenous issues from an elite, educated, urban perspective rather than from that of the indigenous peoples.

The Dominican priest Bartolomé de las Casas (1484–1566) presented the earliest articulate defense of indigenous rights from a European perspective. But he retained loyalty to the Catholic Church and to the Spanish Crown, and ultimately the purpose of his efforts was for the conversion of indigenous peoples to Christianity and their assimilation into the Spanish kingdom.

Modern *indigenismo* first emerged in the nineteenth century and was characterized by romantic and humanitarian impulses. This *indigenista* discourse came to be dominated by intellectuals who were strongly influenced by Spencerian positivist thought meant to assimilate the surviving indigenous peoples in the Americas into a dominant Spanish or Portuguese culture. *Indigenismo* particularly gained strength in Mexico in the aftermath of the 1910 revolution because it embraced the country's glorious indigenous past while assimilating their descendants into a unified *mestizo* nation.

By the 1920s *indigenismo* had become a form of protest against the injustices that Indians faced. Political parties, especially populist ones, began to exploit *indigenista* ideologies for political gain. *Indigenismo* flourished in the 1930s, particularly in Peru and Mexico, and in the 1950s it was institutionalized in the Guatemalan and Bolivian revolutions. With officialization, *indigenismo* lost its revolutionary potential to improve the lives of Indians. Elite *mestizo* intellectuals and leftist political leaders led this movement, which they often used only to advance their own political agendas.

Indigenismo often emerged out of anthropological and archaeological studies. Manuel Gamio (1883–1960) was both a pioneer anthropologist and *indigenista* in Mexico who reconstructed archaeological sites for tourists, including Teotihuacán north of Mexico City. Although *indigenistas* proudly championed the ancient Aztec and Inca civilizations, they often ignored or discounted their present-day descendants.

Peruvian Marxist José Carlos Mariátegui is one of the best-known *indigenista* intellectuals. In *Seven Interpretive Essays on Peruvian Reality* (1928), Mariátegui criticized various strategies that others had employed to improve the lives of indigenous peoples, including humanitarian campaigns, administrative policies, and legal reforms. He argued that their problems were rooted instead in the nature of the land-tenure system, and that only through fundamental economic change and land reform would social improvements be possible. Mariátegui was an *indigenista* in the classical sense in that he was an urban *mestizo* intellectual who had little contact with Peru's indigenous peoples, but he did not portray the worst elements of paternalism and assimilation common to *indigenismo*.

Indigenismo was also represented in literature, particularly in well-known novels such as Jorge Icaza's *Huasipungo* (1934) in Ecuador or Rosario Castellanos's *Balún-Canán* (1957) in Mexico. Typically, such novels focused on the oppression of poor indigenous agricultural workers at the hands of large landholders, depicting *indígenas* as primitive and ignorant people who are unable to improve their lives without outside assistance. The solution, when one is offered, is that through education they might be elevated and assimilated into the dominant culture; rarely are indigenous cultures recognized as valuable and worthy of protection. In art, the paintings by the Mexican artists Frida Kahlo (1907–1954) and Diego Rivera (1886–1957) utilized indigenous themes to advance their leftist political ideologies.

In 1940 the Mexican president Lázaro Cárdenas (1895–1970) organized the First Inter-American Indigenist Congress at Pátzcuaro in the state of Michoacán. Delegates were anthropologists and sociologists as well as religious workers and high government officials such as John Collier, the architect of Franklin D. Roosevelt's Indian policy in the United States. The Pátzcuaro Congress broke from colonialist thought, but its tone was still integrationist. The Instituto Indigenista Interamericano (III, Inter-American Indigenist Institute) that emerged out of the Pátzcuaro Congress was based in Mexico City, and Gamio served as its first director. The III held congresses about every five years, and *indigenistas* formed national branches in many of the American republics. In addition to publishing the journals *América Indigenista* (later renamed *Anuario Indigenista*) and *Boletín Indigenista*, the III became an official organ of the Organization of American States (OAS).

In 1971 eleven anthropologists gathered in Barbados for the Symposium on Inter-Ethnic Conflict in South America. Their Declaration of Barbados demanded the liberation of indigenous peoples from colonial domination, specifically calling for the defense of indigenous culture and territory, the establishment of economic, social, educational, and health assistance, and support for a native-led pan–Latin American movement for self-government.

As indigenous peoples began to build their own organizations, they presented a sustained critique of *indigenismo* as a construction of the dominant culture, a paternalistic impulse designed to stop liberation movements. Indigenous peoples criticized academics who studied their cultures without returning any political benefits to their communities. Rather than letting outsiders appropriate indigenous cultures and concerns for their own purposes, indigenous leaders insisted that they could represent themselves. Particularly strong indigenous political movements emerged in countries with relatively weak *indigenista* traditions such as Ecuador and Guatemala. By the end of the twentieth century indigenous leaders had created a *neoindigenismo* that advanced their own political agendas.

SEE ALSO *Indigenous Rights; Natives*

BIBLIOGRAPHY

Bonfil Batalla, Guillermo. 1996. *Mexico Profundo: Reclaiming a Civilization.* Austin: University of Texas Press.

Castellanos, Rosario. [1957] 1992. *Balún-Canán* [Nine guardians]. Trans. Irene Nicholson. London: Readers International.

Dawson, Alexander S. 2004. *Indian and Nation in Revolutionary Mexico.* Tucson: University of Arizona Press.

Díaz Polanco, Héctor. 1997. *Indigenous Peoples in Latin America: The Quest for Self-Determination.* Boulder, CO: Westview.

Graham, Richard, ed. 1990. *The Idea of Race in Latin America, 1870–1940.* Austin: University of Texas Press.

Icaza, Jorge. [1934] 1973. *Huasipungo* [The Villagers]. Trans. Bernard Dulsey. Carbondale: Southern Illinois University Press.

Mariátegui, José Carlos. [1928] 1971. *Seven Interpretive Essays on Peruvian Reality.* Austin: University of Texas Press.

Marc Becker

INDIGENOUS RIGHTS

Indigenous rights are those legal and moral rights claimed by indigenous peoples. But what is meant by "indigenous peoples," and in what sense are their rights peculiar to them? From what source do these rights flow? Are they legal rights granted by the state, or are they moral rights that have yet to be established in law? Or are they human rights, derived from those basic rights ascribed to human beings everywhere? The situation of indigenous peoples also raises further questions about the nature of these rights: Are they individual rights or group rights, social and political rights or cultural rights? And finally, against whom or what are they claimed? The state within which they live, or the international community as a whole—or both?

INDIGENOUS RIGHTS AND THE HISTORY OF COLONIZATION

But first, who counts as an indigenous people? This is a complex and politically loaded question, both in domestic and international contexts. First of all, there are disputes over who or what counts as "indigenous." Secondly, there are disputes over who counts as a "people" in international law, especially when it comes to ascribing and distributing the right to self-determination. There are two basic approaches to the question of indigeneity. First, one can link indigeneity to literal first residency or occupation of a particular territory. Contemporary indigenous peoples in this case would be descendants of the earliest populations living in that area. Second, one can tie indigeneity to those peoples who lived in that territory before settlers arrived and the process of colonization began. This relativizes the definition to prior occupation rather than first occupation. Although there is enormous diversity among the many different indigenous nations in the world, another common dimension to their self-description as indigenous is the connection to land; as James Anaya has put it, they are indigenous in the sense that "their ancestral roots are embedded in the lands in which they live ... much more deeply than the roots of more powerful sectors of society living on the same lands" (Anaya 1996, p. 3). Still, the term remains unsettled in international law and domestic practice. Given the diversity of peoples in question and the complexity of circumstances in which the claims are being made (for example, not just in the Americas and Australasia, but also in South and Southeast Asia), many have argued that indigeneity should be interpreted in as flexible and "constructivist" a manner as possible (Kingsbury 1998; 2001).

From the perspective of indigenous peoples at least, it is important to distinguish their claims from the claims of other minority groups, such as migrants or refugees, because they are challenging the extent to which their incorporation into the state (and its subsequent consequences) was just. The question of legitimacy looms much larger with regard to indigenous peoples than it does with other minority groups. Often precisely because their claims are distinct in this way they are controversial. They challenge liberal conceptions of distributive justice and the underlying conceptions of equality and individual rights that tend to presuppose the legitimacy question is moot. Although they challenge these conceptions, it is not clear that the claims of indigenous peoples are fundamentally incompatible with them (Kymlicka 1989, 1995; compare Barry 2001, Alfred 1999). However, the historical experience of indigenous peoples in the course of the development of liberal democracy in the Americas and Australasia suggests that the challenges they face are profound. Hence the ambiguity surrounding the appeal to the language of rights.

The history of European colonization and its impact on the indigenous inhabitants of the Americas and Australasia is by now depressingly familiar. Indigenous populations were displaced and removed from their traditional lands; they were dramatically reduced in size and strength through disease, war, and the consequences of European settlement and forced removals; and their legal and moral rights to exercise self-government over their territories were subsumed under the authority of the newly established states. In the United States, for example, although Justice John Marshall in a series of landmark cases in the nineteenth century recognized the limited sovereignty of the American Indian nations (as "domestic dependent nations"), they still were ultimately subject to the plenipotentiary power of Congress. Thus, although Native American tribes in the twenty-first century are able to exercise various forms of jurisdiction and claim ownership over some of their (much reduced) tribal lands, they remain subject to both state and federal law in significant respects. Similarly, in Canada, Australia, and New Zealand, although within a different jurisprudential framework, indigenous nations are able to exercise only limited forms of self-government (if any), and are able to claim ownership ("aboriginal" or "native" title) over an extremely small proportion of their former territories. In all of these places, indigenous people also tend to suffer from appalling social and economic hardship; they are amongst the poorest, sickest, most unemployed, and most incarcerated members of the population. They tend to have higher infant mortality rates and shorter life spans, and to suffer disproportionately from the effects of alcohol and drug abuse and domestic violence. In many cases, indigenous children were at various times either forcibly removed from their families or enrolled into residential schools, where often they suffered from abuse. And yet, despite this legacy of historical and enduring injustice, indigenous cultures and communities, as well as indigenous political activism, has persisted, in both domestic and international contexts. And indeed, one of the tools they have turned to, not without ambiguity, is the language and practice of rights.

WHAT KIND OF RIGHTS ARE INDIGENOUS RIGHTS?

Legal rights are those rights embedded in and enforced by an established legal framework. Moral rights are those rights that are grounded either in some purportedly valid moral claim, or with reference to some broader moral framework, but which are not necessarily established in law. We often appeal to moral rights in order to criticize existing practices and laws. Indigenous rights are asserted in both senses. Indigenous people argue that their rights are not merely derivative from the state, but rather are jus-

tified in relation to their own political theories and practices and more general moral arguments. This is distinct from the claim that in order to become effective, rights must eventually be recognized and enforced by the state, or some other effective set of legal and political institutions.

Rights are not self-justifying. They are used to mark out certain crucial interests or capacities of individuals (and sometimes groups) that it is thought deserves special kinds of moral and legal attention. But claims about the interests or capacities they refer to must be justified, and that means drawing on potentially controversial moral claims, which are often subject to change over time as societies and attitudes change. A challenge facing anyone defending indigenous rights is in making clear what work the modifier "indigenous" is doing. To what interests or capacities do these rights refer? One the one hand, one can appeal to the historical, cultural, and political specificity of the interests at issue—to indigenous difference, in other words. This might also lead one to emphasize the distinctive source of indigenous legal and moral rights— the hundreds of treaties that were signed between the various indigenous nations and European settlers in the Americas, for example, from the fifteenth century onward. The treaties themselves, as well as the normative framework of recognition, negotiation, and consent that they supposedly represent, offer both a legal and moral framework then for justifying and clarifying the rights of indigenous peoples (Tully 1995; Williams 1997). The danger, however, of appealing exclusively to historical agreements as the source of rights is that the agreements themselves might be morally problematic in various ways: The terms of the agreements might be morally unacceptable and the conditions under which they were struck deeply unfair. But it also risks tying the recognition and content of such rights to a sense of their radical otherness from Anglo-European law. This can sometimes work against indigenous claims, at least in law, because often courts will limit the recognition of indigenous rights to those practices or norms that were in place at the time of European settlement, or just before. This can limit the ability of indigenous nations to expand and modernize those activities they see as integral to their ongoing ways of life. It can also serve to depoliticize their claims, as when courts choose to emphasize the recognition of "lifestyle rights" over more explicitly political ones such as self-government.

A second approach, then, is to appeal to more general rights, and especially human rights, and to argue that indigenous rights are a species of these kinds of claims. Thus they refer to interests or capacities that everyone, indigenous or not, deserves to have protected or promoted. Reference to *indigenous* rights here is a pragmatic move; it is intended to extend to indigenous peoples those rights to which they have always been entitled, but denied for contingent historical and political reasons.

Of course, these two approaches overlap and are often combined. For example, the Canadian Royal Commission on Aboriginal Peoples (1996), charged with outlining a new vision for relations between Canada's "First Nations" and the state, drew on a normative vision they associated with the historical practice of treaty making. According to this argument, indigenous rights draw on a body of inter-societal law and practice based on those rights originally recognized between aboriginal nations and European powers at the time of European settlement, as well as more general moral and political claims to do with equality and freedom.

INDIVIDUAL RIGHTS, GROUP RIGHTS, AND COLLECTIVE RIGHTS

A fundamental question about the nature of indigenous rights is the extent to which they include not only individual rights but also group rights. To be sure, some individual rights enable or promote collective activities and public goods; for example, the right to freedom of association, or to religious freedom, or to a democratic say in government. And some individual rights can be distributed on the basis of group membership; these can be seen as "personal" collective rights, or "membership rights" (Appiah 2005).

Do indigenous peoples have collective rights in this sense, or in terms of a right possessed by the group or nation as a whole, as opposed to the individual members? Part of the concern is that promoting or protecting individual rights might not offer enough protection from the harms indigenous peoples have suffered from over the years, and might not suit the distinctive kinds of interests they seek to protect. Indigenous land rights, for example, are often thought of as a group right because "aboriginal title" inheres in the group as opposed to the individual members, given the distinctive conceptions of land within indigenous worldviews (although the relation between the collective title and individual entitlements under it are complex). The right to self-determination is also sometimes conceived as a group right, just insofar as it can only be exercised jointly by the group as a whole. If indigenous peoples have a moral and legal right to self-determination—as has been proposed in the Draft Declaration of Indigenous Rights (1993)—and the right to self-determination is a basic human right, then arguably there is at least one collective human right. But the right to self-determination is itself a deeply unsettled and contested doctrine in international law and normative political theory (Buchanan 2004). The best justification of the right to self-determination is one that embeds it within the constraints of broader individual human rights, as well as

detaching it from any necessary association with statehood. In fact, the political activism of indigenous peoples in international fora has helped to promote new thinking about the nature of self-determination more generally (Kingsbury 2001). It is the creative use of the practice of rights by indigenous peoples that is most striking about the emergence of "indigenous rights." They have used it to gain access to political debates and exert their political agency. And they have managed to turn around a discourse that was once used mainly to discriminate against them into one of the key tools of their struggle against enduring injustice.

SEE ALSO *Cultural Rights; Experiments, Human; Natives; Nativism*

BIBLIOGRAPHY

Alfred, Taiaiake. 1999. *Peace, Power, Righteousness: An Indigenous Manifesto.* Don Mills, Ontario: Oxford University Press.

Anaya, James. 1996. *Indigenous Peoples in International Law.* Oxford: Oxford University Press.

Appiah, Anthony. 2005. *The Ethics of Identity.* New York: Oxford University Press.

Barry, Brian. 2001. *Culture and Equality: An Egalitarian Critique of Multiculturalism.* Cambridge, MA: Harvard University Press.

Borrows, John. 2002. *Recovering Canada: The Resurgence of Indigenous Law.* Toronto: University of Toronto Press.

Buchanan, Alan. 2004. *Justice, Legitimacy, and Self-Determination: Moral Foundations for International Law.* Oxford, U.K.: Oxford University Press.

Ivison, Duncan, Paul Patton, and Will Sanders, eds. 2001. *Political Theory and the Rights of Indigenous Peoples.* Cambridge, U.K.: Cambridge University Press.

Kingsbury, Benedict. 1998. "Indigenous Peoples" in International Law: A Constructivist Approach to the Asian Controversy. *American Journal of International Law* 92 (3): 414–457.

Kingsbury, Benedict. 2001. Reconciling Five Competing Conceptual Structures of Indigenous Peoples' Claims in International and Comparative Law. *New York University School of Law Journal of International Law and Politics* 34: 189–250.

Kymlicka, Will. 1989. *Liberalism, Community, and Culture.* Oxford, U.K.: Oxford University Press.

Kymlicka, Will. 1995. *Multicultural Citizenship.* Oxford, U.K.: Oxford University Press.

Royal Commission on Aboriginal Peoples. 1996. Restructuring the Relationship. Vol. 2 of *Royal Commission on Aboriginal Peoples.* Ottawa, Canada: Ministry of Supply and Services.

Tully, James. 1995. *Strange Multiplicity: Constitutionalism in an Age of Diversity.* Cambridge, U.K.: Cambridge University Press.

United Nations Commission on Human Rights. 1993. *Draft Declaration of the Rights of Indigenous Peoples.* New York: Author.

Williams, Patricia J. 1991. *The Alchemy of Race and Rights.* Cambridge, MA: Harvard University Press.

Williams, Robert A. 1990. *The American Indian in Western Legal Thought: The Discourses of Conquest.* New York: Oxford University Press.

Williams, Robert A. 1997. *Linking Arms Together: American Indian Treaty Visions of Law and Peace, 1600–1800.* New York: Oxford University Press.

Duncan Ivison

INDIRECT RULE

Within colonial discourse, *indirect rule* designates a British system of African governance through indigenous chiefs, usually contrasted with French *assimilation*, a more centralized policy of transforming colonial subjects into replicas of European citizens. Historically, indirect rule can be understood in several ways: as an expedient of all modern colonial regimes; as an explicit British doctrine; and as the political dimension of a twentieth-century colonial syndrome that included the social sciences.

Although *indirect rule* might describe any exercise of imperial power through the agency of local authorities, the concept best applies to the colonialism that emerged with the establishment of British and Dutch rule in India and Indonesia during the latter 1700s. In these situations, a relatively small number of European officials took charge of territories with populations consisting of indigenous peoples rather than immigrant settlers or slaves. Most such governments, whether in Asia or Africa, would be "indirect" to some degree, that is, heavily dependent upon local auxiliaries. In no cases (except the very tiny French colonies that survived British conquest before 1815) were efforts made to assimilate the entire population to European culture and political status. In the larger colonial territories (including later-acquired French ones), the only choices were between the proportion and status of native auxiliaries who would either be co-opted from existing structures of authority or created anew via European schooling. Even these distinctions were not always clear: hereditary rulers could be given a European education or assigned a new role (as were provincial landlords in eighteenth-century Bengal and twentieth-century Uganda) based on European precedents. Moreover, all colonial administrations depended heavily upon European-educated clerks and interpreters, who held very low formal positions.

The British doctrine of indirect rule emerged in Africa during the early 1900s when the conqueror of Northern Nigeria, Lord Frederick Lugard (1858–1945), incorporated the local Sokoto caliphate into his new regime. Both Lugard and later historians linked this mode of administration to the already-established practices of upholding princely states in India. However, the major princely states, which remained separate for at least internal administrative purposes from British India, were far larger and more powerful than even the Sokoto caliphate, unique in tropical Africa for its degree of bureaucratic development. Moreover, indirect rule was extended throughout British Africa to much less articulated states and chiefdoms, even including, in the 1920s and 1930s, *joint native authorities* based on village councils. In contrast to the princely states (which might better be compared to protectorates of the short-lived League of Nations mandates established by the French and British throughout the Middle East), indirect rule involved continuous intrusion by European administrators into the internal affairs of local rulers through such standardized and highly transparent institutions as native treasuries and native courts.

Indirect rule rested upon a combination of conservatism and paternalist liberalism. Its overseas political goal—which ultimately failed—was to slow and "traditionalize" movements toward decolonization. Among European administrators and their domestic audience it became the center of a new colonial orthodoxy (even France abandoned assimilation for the more vague *association*). The "native," rather than economic gain, was to be the center of concern and was approached with a degree of cultural relativism. Mid-nineteenth-century India here became an anti-model in which aggressive British policies had produced both the Revolt of 1857 and a more enduring class of European-educated *babus* (actual or would-be native government employees). Reluctance to undermine any more indigenous rulers or landlords was one result of this retreat from direct rule/assimilation, but so was withdrawal of support for indigo planters in Bengal, new ideas about education, and programs of village-based anthropological research. All these concepts extended into newer colonies in Africa and (to a lesser extent) the Pacific and Southeast Asia.

Indirect rule, beliefs in peasant versus plantation economies, adapted education, and anthropology all came together in the International Institute for African Languages and Cultures (IIALC, now the International African Institute), founded in 1926. Lugard and similarly minded French and Belgian colonial administrators served as directors of the IIALC. The other founders were missionaries who joined with colonial officials in blocking white settler ascendancy in British East Africa. The most immediate concern for missionaries, however, was education, which they believed had to be less "literary" and European and undertaken in African languages (the anticlerical French Third Republic balked on the language issue, producing a key difference between the two colonial heritages).

The rising new school of functionalist social anthropology used the IIALC's journal *Africa* as a platform to publish its research, assert its relevance to indirect rule and related policies, and launch a successful campaign for funding from the U.S. Rockefeller Fund. In reality, most of the ethnography used to implement indirect rule in Africa (as had been the case earlier in India) was done by administrators and missionaries. Indirect rule was thus more important for the development of social science (in France as well as Britain) than academic anthropology proved to be for colonialism.

SEE ALSO *Colonialism; Decolonization; Neocolonialism; Postcolonialism*

BIBLIOGRAPHY

Cell, John W. 1999. Colonial Rule. In *The Twentieth Century*. Vol. 4 of *The Oxford History of the British Empire*, eds. Judith M. Brown and William Roger Louis, 232–254. Oxford: Oxford University Press.

Dimier, Véronique. 2004. *Le gouvernement des colonies: Regards croisés franco-britanniques*. Brussels: Editions de l'Université de Bruxelles.

Stocking, George W. 1995. *After Tylor: British Social Anthropology, 1888–1951*. Madison: University of Wisconsin Press.

Ralph A. Austen

INDIVIDUALISM

The term *individualism* covers a range of ideas, philosophies, and doctrines that emphasize the unlimited freedom of the individual and the individual's right to protect his or her own interests against those of society. The French liberal writer Alexis de Tocqueville (1805–1859) coined the word to characterize individual selfishness—a value system that predisposes human beings to be concerned only with themselves and their small circle of family and friends. Arising in reaction to the collectivist spirit of the Enlightenment and the French Revolution, its original meaning tended to be rather negative and controversial, implying that individualism was a source of social atomism, anarchy, and public disorder. Thus, while praising the individualism of nineteenth-century America, Tocqueville at the same time cautioned against its threat to public life through the weakening of social bonds and obligations.

LIBERAL INDIVIDUALISM

Today the term is often employed to describe a political and social philosophy—sometimes referred to as "liberal individualism" or "laissez-faire individualism"—that stresses the primacy of the individual and the importance attached to individual freedom, self-reliance, privacy rights, and individual choice. In its full-fledged form, it emerged first in Britain with the spread of the laissez-faire ideas of Adam Smith (1723–1790) and the utilitarianism of Jeremy Bentham (1748–1832) in economic and political theory. In the Anglo-Saxon world, liberal individualism became a catchword for free enterprise, free markets, limited government, and unrestricted economic freedom, as well as for the individualistic attitudes, forms of behavior, and aspirations that sustain the idea of "self-made man." One influential version of this usage was U.S. president Herbert Hoover's campaign speeches in 1928 celebrating "rugged individualism" in America. Above all, individualism came to signify a preference for a minimal government role in social, economic, and religious affairs, as exemplified by the slogan "That government that governs least governs best"—though not in matters of public morality or law and order—as opposed to the more collectivist ideals of socialism.

Individualism is frequently contrasted with collectivism, a social philosophy in which the collective or common weal rather than the individual good is considered paramount. Man is seen in the Aristotelian tradition as a social animal, whose very nature, wants, and capacities are to a very large extent the product of society and its institutions—running the gamut from the family through the workplace and all kinds of voluntary associations to the nation-state and the global market. For example, the famous Enlightenment philosopher Jean-Jacques Rousseau (1712–1778) advocated subordinating the individual will to the collective will, a view that is in fundamental opposition to the philosophy of individualism. Rousseau's popular treatise *Social Contract* (1762) maintains that each individual is under an implicit contract to submit his or her will to the "general will" of the entire citizenry (*volonte generale*), although the "general will" need not be the will of absolutely all citizens (*volonte de tous*).

In his major work *Democracy in America* (1835, 1840), Tocqueville himself took a rather ambiguous stand about individualism, at times giving it a distinctly pejorative flavor. He was torn between his admiration for the individualism of American democracy and his anxiety about its political implications, such as the danger of widespread social conformism. He pointed to two major aspects of the individualistic character of American society—on the one hand, a faith in individual reason as the sole basis of public opinion, and, on the other, a self-centered, self-interested preoccupation with private concerns.

This second aspect of American individualism manifested itself in pervasive egoism, a widespread tendency to withdraw from public affairs and to focus on the material welfare of the family as the most important purpose in life. This egoism was evident in unrestrained personal ambition and atomistic competition. In a society where the scramble for power and possession was widely thought to be open to all—and failure could not be ascribed to disadvantages of birth or any other privilege—the contest was bound to be fierce and uncompromising. Tocqueville believed that individualism could pose a threat to liberty, because individualistic attitudes encourage individual subservience to public opinion and conformism. U.S. democracy found its source of intellectual authority in prevailing public opinion based on the idea of the moral equality of all individuals. The conformity to generally held attitudes and social standards was thus the result of the imposition of social sanctions by one's peers. When Tocqueville asked why there were no professed atheists in the United States, his answer was that atheists would not get any jobs or customers. When faced with the opinion of the majority, the individual felt powerless: If the majority of one's equals is always right, then a dissenting opinion must be always wrong. For Tocqueville, this conformist attitude was an assault on individual liberty—a "new kind of despotism" over isolated individuals too afraid of public opinion to object, too absorbed in private concerns to participate in public activity, too aware of the economic value of public order to threaten protest and disorder. Such "tyranny of the majority," the Frenchman warned, would weaken not only liberty but the very will to liberty.

Tocqueville's warnings about the paradoxical contradictions of individualism have been echoed numerous times in modern social and cultural criticism. The philosophy of liberal individualism has been criticized for creating a culture of what Canada's most eminent political theorist, C. B. Macpherson (1911–1987), called "possessive individualism," a theory of human nature that is rooted in the seventeenth century and is based on "a conception of the individual as essentially the proprietor of his own person or capacities, owing nothing to society for them" (Macpherson 1962, p. 3). Such a society, according to Macpherson, where individual skills are a commodity to be bought and sold on the open market, demonstrates a selfish and unrestricted thirst for private consumption that is celebrated as the very essence of human nature. The American sociologist Robert Bellah (1985) has similarly warned that individualism is becoming so pervasive and excessive in the United States that it is destroying the integrity and moral foundations of American society.

During the nineteenth century and the early twentieth century, economic individualism in the form of laissez-faire capitalism came into conflict with political individualism in the form of representative democracy, as the newly enfranchised working-class voters increasingly came to demand government intervention in the marketplace far beyond the mere enforcing of economic contracts. The rise of militant labor unions and the mass socialist parties built upon them made free-market economic policies morally untenable and politically risky, especially after the 1917 Bolshevik Revolution in Russia. The worldwide Great Depression of the 1930s and the governmental response to it based on the interventionist theories of John Maynard Keynes (1883–1946), the preeminent British economist who revolutionized the science of economics by advocating active state involvement in the capitalist economy, ushered in the collectivist-inspired "social-welfare state" and also seemed to sound the death knell for the discredited doctrines of economic individualism. But the waning of western social democracy and the decline and eventual downfall of Soviet-style "state socialism" in the late twentieth century led to the revival of the ideas of laissez-faire capitalism—first during the era of Thatcherism in the United Kingdom and Reaganism in the United States, and later with the neoliberal policies of "globalization capitalism." The anti-Keynesian and anti-statist writings of Ludwig von Mises (1881–1973), Friedrich von Hayek (1899–1992), Milton Friedman (1912–2006), and their followers have also contributed to restoring the previously tattered intellectual reputation of economic individualism.

METHODOLOGICAL INDIVIDUALISM

In another widespread, although thematically separate usage, the so-called "methodological individualism" in the social sciences refers to the position adopted by those who argue that groups (collectivities) are nothing more than their individual members. In this view, there are no properties of groups that are not reducible to individual properties. Not only must scientists study individuals, but also the explanations of the social phenomena they study—phenomena such as social class, power, the political system, and so on—must be formulated as, or be reducible to, the characteristics of individuals. While not denying that groups exist, the individualist does deny that they have any independent status and that they are more than the sum of their parts. As former British prime minister Margaret Thatcher famously declared, "There is no society, only individuals."

This individualistic position stands in marked contrast to the so-called "methodological holism," the theoretical principle that each social entity (group, institution, society) has a totality that is distinct and cannot be understood by studying merely its individual component elements. There are emergent group properties that are not reducible and, therefore, groups (collectivities) are more than the sum of their parts. For example, the famous

French sociologist Émile Durkheim (1858–1917) claimed that collective phenomena are not reducible to the individual actor or psyche; hence, social facts can be investigated and explained independently of the individual. The debate over methodological individualism versus methodological holism in the social sciences reflects an underlying ideological tension about the relationship between the individual and society, recognizing that these two analytical levels are distinct and may have to be explicated separately.

SEE ALSO *Altruism; Bentham, Jeremy; Bolshevism; Choice in Psychology; Collectivism; Competition; Conformity; Constructivism; Durkheim, Émile; Elite Theory; Elites; Enlightenment; Freedom; French Revolution; Friedman, Milton; Great Depression; Hayek, Friedrich August von; Keynes, John Maynard; Laissez-faire; Libertarianism; Liberty; Microanalysis; Microeconomics; Mises, Ludwig Edler von; Party Systems, Competitive; Philosophy; Philosophy, Political; Political Theory; Reductionism; Rousseau, Jean-Jacques; Smith, Adam; Social Contract; Sociology, Micro-; Thatcher, Margaret; Tocqueville, Alexis de; Tyranny of the Majority; Utilitarianism; Welfare State*

BIBLIOGRAPHY

Bellah, Robert N., Richard Madsen, William M. Sullivan, et al. 1985. *Habits of the Heart: Individualism and Commitment in American Life.* Berkeley: University of California Press.

Brodbeck, May. 1958. Methodological Individualism: Definition and Reduction. *Philosophy of Science* 25 (1): 1–22.

Hayek, Friedrich A. von. [1948] 1976. *Individualism and Economic Order.* Chicago: University of Chicago Press; London: Routledge and Kegan Paul.

Lukes, Steven. 1973. *Individualism.* Oxford: Blackwell.

Macpherson, Crawford B. 1962. *The Political Theory of Possessive Individualism: Hobbes to Locke.* Oxford: Clarendon Press.

O'Neill, John, ed. 1973. *Modes of Individualism and Collectivism.* London: Heinemann.

Tocqueville, Alexis de. [1835, 1840] 1994. *Democracy in America.* New York: Knopf.

Rossen Vassilev

INDUSTRIAL ORGANIZATION

SEE *Industry.*

INDUSTRIAL SLAVERY

SEE *Slavery Industry.*

INDUSTRIALIZATION

Industrialization refers to a broad process through which industry displaces agriculture and assumes a dominant role in a society's economy. It involves the extension of commodity production on a large scale and the emergence of wage labor as the principle mechanism for the organization of work.

Historically, this shift has often come with a number of concomitant changes, including the formation of a united territory, where the state either created a legal system to protect property rights or directed the industrialization process itself; an increase in agricultural productivity, allowing a surplus population move into industry; the diffusion of scientific knowledge and technological know-how; the creation of a workforce socialized into an ethos of time discipline; and a willingness of investors or the state to commit large funds to industry rather than to speculation, plunder, or military expenditure.

EARLY THEORIES OF INDUSTRIALIZATION

Industrialization began in Britain at the end of the eighteenth century, and it soon spread throughout Europe, North America, and Japan. However the process was profoundly uneven, particularly as countries combined elements copied from the more advanced regions with their own traditional social practices. In his classic 1969 account of the French "paradox," Tom Kemp argued that while the Revolution of 1789 created the most favorable legal conditions for capitalist development, it also, ironically, allowed the peasantry to stay more rooted to the land and gave small-scale preindustrial forms of capitalism new opportunities for commercializing agricultural products. On a more general level, Alexander Gerschenkhron claimed that backwardness (essentially defined as a divergence from the British model) led to a "tension" that was only resolved when larger institutions such as banks intervened to mobilize scarce capital for an industrialization project. In the case of Germany, for example, the banks helped create an "organized capitalism," through which investment was concentrated in coal mining, iron and steel-making, electrical and general engineering, and chemical plants. Earlier industries that had played a key role in Britain's development, such as textiles, were of fringe interest because the banks strategically concentrated on new lead industries.

The pressure to industrialize, when combined with a scarcity of capital and a lack of domestic markets, also led to the intervention of another key player: the state. For Adam Smith and the neoclassical school, the only role assigned to the state was that of the famous "night watchman," who patrolled the perimeter of the economy guaranteeing property rights and security. Subsequently, many writers have questioned this minimalist role. For Ernest Gellner, writing in the 1980s, the very social and geographical mobility that industrialization required forced the state to take measures to standardize the cultural outlook of its population through the introduction of national curricula in schools. Gerschenkhron went further, arguing that a stronger state role might be needed to break the barriers of stagnation. Merely providing the promise of rewards for entrepreneurial efforts might not be enough. Writing in a decade when China was still an impoverished rural society, he noted that "capitalist industrialization under the auspices of socialist ideologies may be, after all, less surprising a phenomenon than would appear at first sight" (Gerschenkkhron 1952, p. 25).

In what the American economist Paul Krugman has called the period of "high development theory," in the late 1940s and 1950s, there was a consensus that a "visible hand" was necessary to propel a country towards industrialization. The Polish economist Paul Rosenstein-Rodan noted in 1943 that balanced growth and a "big push" were also required. Balanced growth was needed so that a complementarity of demand would reduce risk in investment. When investment occurred on a wide front, new producers could become each other's customers, thus reducing the risk of not finding a market. In addition, the state had a key role to play in developing infrastructure and training a workforce. While the concept of "balanced growth" was questioned by Albert Hirschman in 1958, the consensus was that industrialization would emerge from increased savings directed by the government to industry.

DEPENDENCY THEORY

Outside the field of conventional economics, a more radical critique of Smith's neoclassical model also developed. Starting with Raul Prebisch, who led the United Nations Economic Commission for Latin America and the Caribbean (ECLAC) from 1948 to 1963, this critique emphasized the wider structural relationships into which poorer countries were inserted. Prebisch and the other dependency theorists claimed that the nations on the periphery were often forced to supply primary produce to metropolitan countries in return for industrial and consumer goods. Far from gaining a comparative advantage by specializing in exporting products where they had natural advantages, however, they had to produce ever more primary goods to obtain the same quantity of manufactured goods. The solution, according to Prebisch, was import substitution, through which tariffs are imposed on goods from industrialized countries so that a space can be created for domestic manufacturers to produce simple consumer goods.

Dependency theory took on a more radical direction in the hands of Paul Baran and Andre Gunder Frank. For Baran, dependency was characterized by a dual economy comprised of a large agriculture sector with extremely low productivity and a small industrial enclave that could not find a domestic market for its goods. Shifting Marx's paradigm, Baran argued that a surplus was extracted from the peasantry and appropriated by landowners, moneylenders, merchants, and a mainly foreign capitalist class. These groupings had little interest in development and often functioned as a "comprador class," siphoning off the surplus to foreign capital and gaining privileges as a result. The only solution was extensive state intervention to promote national development.

Frank agreed that the cause of underdevelopment was the extraction of a surplus by metropolitan countries. This, however, occurred primarily through trade itself, rather than through a dualistic structure of the economy. The trading relationship with the metropolis affected all sectors of society and led to the draining away of resources. There was no original state of underdevelopment from which such countries had to incubate; they were underdeveloped through coming into contact with the metropolitan powers. The route to development lay, therefore, in delinking from the world economy.

Not everyone, however, shared this pessimism about the dual-sector model in underdeveloped countries. For W. Arthur Lewis, who won the Nobel Prize in Economics in 1979, the dual-sector economy meant that the modern capitalist sector could draw on a relatively unlimited supply of labor from the more traditional sectors without having to raise wages significantly. This meant that it could expand until the absorption of surplus labor was complete. Adopting a pragmatic approach to the use of public and private enterprise in the modern sector, he argued that it could give a positive feedback to the traditional sector by, for example, creating markets for its commodities.

EXPORT INDUSTRIALIZATION AND OTHER APPROACHES

The demise of dependency theory coincided with the emergence of a number of newly industrializing countries, particularly the "Asian Tigers" of South Korea, Singapore, Taiwan, and Hong Kong. By seeking a niche in the world economy and opening their economies to foreign investment, these nations appeared to overcome the obstacles to development through adopting an export industrialization program. As a result, contact with the global economy did not intensify underdevelopment, but instead allowed them to rapidly industrialize.

As the process of industrialization has spread, however, some older predictions are also being questioned.

According to Simon Kuznets's famous hypothesis, economic inequality should increase during the early stages of industrialization because an income gap will grow between those in rural and urban areas. Over time, however, this inequality should decrease as mass education opens the possibility of a more meritocratic society. Yet while this may appear to have been the case up to the 1970s, there has been a return to growing levels of inequality since then. As outlined by Robert Pollin in *Contours of Descent* (2003), evidence from the United States indicates that the share of wealth held by the top 10 percent of the population has grown, and that the difference between the pay of the average CEO and that of the average employee has multiplied considerably.

DEINDUSTRIALIZATION

Current debates also focus on deindustrialization. According to Robert Rowthorn and Ramana Ramaswarmy, the share of employment in industry in the twenty-three most advanced countries declined from 28 percent of the workforce in 1970 to 18 percent in 1994. The growth in services and the development of a "knowledge society" has led many to argue that the transition to a postindustrial society has already occurred. However, this ignores the fact that modern societies continue to rely heavily on mass-produced goods, and it fails to explain how most foreign direct investment (FDI) is still going to the advanced industrial economies, rather than to those with an abundance of cheap labor. The rise in employment in services may, in fact, be the result of the relatively slower growth of labor productivity in that sector when compared to manufacturing. The process of industrialization, therefore, appears to still have a long way to go.

SEE ALSO *Dependency Theory; Developing Countries; Development Economics; Economic Growth; Frank, Andre Gunder; Industry; Knowledge Society; Lewis, W. Arthur; Modernization; Prebisch-Singer Hypothesis; Terms of Trade; Unequal Exchange*

BIBLIOGRAPHY

Baran, Paul. 1957. *The Political Economy of Growth.* New York: Monthly Review Press.

Frank, Andre Gunder. 1967. *Capitalism and Underdevelopment in Latin America.* New York: Monthly Review Press.

Gellner, Ernest. 1983. *Nations and Nationalism.* Ithaca, NY: Cornell University Press.

Gerschenkron, Alexander. 1962. *Economic Backwardness in Historical Perspective.* Cambridge, MA: Belknap Press.

Hirschman, Albert O. 1958. *The Strategy of Economic Development.* New Haven, CT: Yale University Press.

Kemp, Tom. 1969. *Industrialization in Nineteenth-Century Europe.* London: Longmans.

Krugman, Paul. 1992. Toward a Counter-Counter-Revolution in Development Theory. In *Proceedings of World Bank Annual Conference on Development Economics,* 15–38. New York: Oxford University Press.

Kuznets, Simon Smith. 1965. *Economic Growth and Structure.* New York: Norton.

Lewis, W. Arthur. 1954. Economic Development with Unlimited Supplies of Labour. *The Manchester School of Economic and Social Studies* 22 (May): 139–191.

Lewis, W. Arthur. 1979. The Dual Economy Revisited. *The Manchester School of Economic and Social Studies* 47 (3): 211–229.

Pollin, Robert. 2003. *Contours of Descent: U.S. Economic Fractures and the Landscape of Global Austerity.* London: Verso.

Rosenstein-Rodan, Paul. 1943. Problems of Industrialization of Eastern and Southern Europe. *Economic Journal* 53: 210–211.

Rowthorn, Robert, and Ramana Ramaswarmy. 1997. Deindustrialization: Causes and Implications. IMF Working Paper. Washington, DC: International Monetary Fund.

Roxborough, Ian. 1979. *Theories of Underdevelopment.* Atlantic Highlands, NJ: Humanities Press.

Kieran Allen

INDUSTRY

Industry refers to the organization of the economy around a particular set of products or related activities. For practical purposes, researchers may wish to compare the structures of different product or country markets either simultaneously or over a defined time period. To meet this need, government statistical agencies have developed standardized systems for classifying the activities of firms into industries. The NACE classification system, which is a French acronym for General Industrial Classification for Economic activities within European Communities, is used in the European Union, while in the United States, Canada, and Mexico, the North American Industry Classification System (NAICS, pronounced "nakes") is used. These systems broadly classify business establishments according to their primary activity.

Unlike standard microeconomic analysis, the study of industrial organization takes as its starting point the view that markets are less than perfect. "Actually existing capitalism" does not operate according to price competition alone, but promotes a variety of business strategies. These are affected by the way that markets for industries are "embedded" in a particular institutional climate. There are also barriers to entry in markets that can result in minimizing the full force of competition.

The study of industrial organization focuses on the link between market structure and business conduct in determining market performance. Market structure can vary from conditions of near full competition to oligopolies with high barriers to entry. A key feature of any particular market is the degree of concentration in a small number of firms. The level of concentration can be measured by a Lorenz curve that plots the cumulative percentage of market output against the cumulative percentage of firms from smallest to largest. The market structure can affect business conduct in terms of pricing, research and development, or branding strategies. Finally, this leads to measures of business performance in terms of dynamic or product efficiency, profitability, or growth. Writers from the early Harvard school placed primary emphasis on market structure, whereas those from the Chicago school have attempted to use traditional price theory in their analysis of industrial performance.

The historical pattern by which particular countries industrialized can also have an important influence on the structure of its industries. In Europe, for example, the reliance of Britain on the markets of its empire inclined firms toward labor-intensive, simple, and cheap products. This led to a weakness in manufacturing after World War II (1939–1945), and today Britain has one of the highest rates of deindustrialization in the world. By contrast, the late industrialization of Germany, combined with a close interaction with the banks, led to an emphasis on technological sophistication and cost containment, which led to greater success for German manufacturing.

Industrial development can also be affected by different modes of regulation, defined as complexes of institutions, norms, and regulating networks that affect the behavior of firms. Among these complexes are the structure of bargaining over the wage-effort contract, the institutional compromises at the level of the state, the relationship between industry and finance, and the international trade regime. The mode of regulation can evolve though sociopolitical conflict, which eventually has an impact on industry.

SEE ALSO *Agricultural Industry; Automobile Industry; Aviation Industry; Banana Industry; Banking Industry; Bauxite Industry; Cattle Industry; Coffee Industry; Copper Industry; Cotton Industry; Diamond Industry; Drug Traffic; Energy Industry; Entertainment Industry; Film Industry; Fishing Industry; Flower Industry; Gold Industry; Industrialization; Infant Industry; Insurance Industry; Microelectronics Industry; Mining Industry; Peanut Industry; Petroleum Industry; Pharmaceutical Industry; Prison Industry; Railway Industry; Recording Industry; Shipping Industry; Silver Industry; Slavery Industry; Sports Industry; Steel Industry; Sugar Industry; Tea Industry; Telecommunications Industry; Textile Industry; Tobacco Industry; Tourism Industry; Transportation Industry; Vanilla Industry; Weapons Industry*

BIBLIOGRAPHY

Baumol, William J., John C. Panzar, and Robert D. Willig. 1982. *Contestable Markets and the Theory of Industry Structure.* New York: Harcourt Brace Jovanovich.

Davies, S., B. Lyons, H. Dixon, and P. Geroski, eds. 1988. *Economics of Industrial Organisation.* Harlow, U.K.: Longman.

Pickering, J. F. 1974. *Industrial Structure and Market Conduct.* London: Martin Robertson.

Scherer, Frederic M. 1970. *Industrial Market Structure and Economic Performance.* Chicago: Rand McNally.

Kieran Allen

INDUSTRY, OIL
SEE *Petroleum Industry.*

INEGALITARIANISM

There have been many defenses of inequality, several of which are rooted in moral or religious views (as in Hinduism) or in peculiar views of human nature (as in the teachings of Aristotle). Counter to such views, it is commonly presumed today that equality is preferable to inequality but that it should be balanced against other considerations that may causally trade off with it. Standard micro-level functional arguments in favor of inequality assert that inequality enhances production either because unequal incentives or unequal power (as in a hierarchy) are needed to organize the production of beneficial goods, both personal and collective, or because the productively efficient division of labor entails inequality.

These arguments generalize to macro-level claims about the organization of society. First, equality entails reduced incentives to those who are especially productive and leads to a trade-off between equality and the efficiency of production (Rawls 1971, Okun 1975). Second, hierarchy, and therefore inequality, is virtually necessary for achieving many desirable social goals. Finally, the division of labor is generally necessary in a modern society (Smith [1776] 1976; Durkheim [1893] 1933). At the societal level at least three further trade-offs undercut support for equality. First, the political power to achieve equality entails the power to do much else, including very undesirable things such as suppression of thought and dissent. Second, equality in a single society requires autarky and risks the selective emigration of the especially productive; both of these effects are likely to be economically crippling. Finally, in many areas, those who have greater resources than others can be trailblazers who support innovations that eventually benefit almost everyone (Hayek 1960, p. 44).

Each of these relationships involves a trade-off of equality for something else: productivity, successful organization, lack of suppression, economic viability, or innovation. In each of these cases, although there might be disagreements about the scale of the trade-off of equality that a society should bear, there will probably be little disagreement that some trade-off is desirable or even necessary. Again, inequality in these arguments is functional in that it leads to greater production, prosperity, and liberty.

Gender inequality may have arisen from or been reinforced by the efficiency of a gendered division of labor, with women specialized in childbearing, childrearing, and other home-oriented activities while men specialized in fieldwork. Racial and ethnic inequality seem unlikely to have resulted from their overall efficiency. They must generally follow from normative spurning of an out-group or from taking advantage of the subordinate group by making them do subordinate jobs. The push for equality of these groups and women is commonly from normative claims for the equality of all. But equality for all typically only means that the subordinate groups' members and women should face opportunities comparable to those of the rest of society, as unequal as those may generally be.

Major defenses of general social inequality in our time are functionally based in causal relations and have general significance beyond any idiosyncratic ethnic, gender, moral, or religious view. On these arguments there are reasons to think inequality either good or at least better than its implicit costs in an alternative.

Each of the arguments in favor of inequality in society might have a counterpart at the level of small groups or organizations; indeed, they are all expressed through actions at the micro level. However, relatively little attention has been paid to some of these effects at the micro level. The issues are especially important in macro contexts of developing economies and in micro contexts of differential power of the groups, such as those defined by gender and ethnicity, to which individuals belong and through which they are commonly identified.

Notions of inequality play a significant role in pragmatic political debates about democracy. James Madison (1751–1836), leader of the Constitutional Convention of 1787, and many others writing at the time of the drafting and adoption of the U.S. Constitution were deeply worried that democracy would lead to the expropriation of property. Given the vote, the large majority who were rel-

atively poor in comparison to Madison, Thomas Jefferson (1743–1826), George Washington (1732–1799), and other holders of grand estates might choose to levy heavy taxes on property and block its simple inheritance. Or they might simply seize property. This is what happened in many socialist nations, except that the appropriation was done by dictatorial, not democratic governments. It is perhaps ironic that liberal democracy is now thought to be a safeguard of property and is therefore associated with substantial inequality of wealth. The central difference between the liberal democracies and the socialist autocracies is that the former have relatively weak governments while the latter have very strong governments. While a strong government does not guarantee egalitarian policies, a weak government probably does lead to inegalitarian outcomes. But, again, a potential cost of the strong government that is necessary for egalitarianism is the capacity to intervene in lives in many ways other than merely economically.

SEE ALSO *Capitalism; Division of Labor; Durkheim, Émile; Equality; Hierarchy; Imperialism; Inequality, Gender; Inequality, Racial; Norms; Organizations; Productivity; Property, Private; Rawls, John; Slavery; Smith, Adam; Washington, George*

BIBLIOGRAPHY

Durkheim, Émile. [1893] 1933. *The Division of Labor in Society*. New York: Macmillan.

Hayek, Friedrich A. 1960. *The Constitution of Liberty*. Chicago: University of Chicago Press.

Okun, Arthur M. 1975. *Equality and Efficiency: The Big Tradeoff*. Washington, DC: The Brookings Institution.

Rawls, John. 1971. *A Theory of Justice*. Cambridge, MA: Harvard University Press.

Smith, Adam. [1776] 1976. *An Inquiry into the Nature and Causes of the Wealth of Nations*. Oxford: Clarendon Press.

Russell Hardin

INEQUALITY, GENDER

In the 1968 *International Encyclopedia of Social Sciences*, there is no entry for gender inequality. In 2006, thirty-eight years later, Carolyn Hannon, director of the United Nations Department of Economic and Social Affairs, Division for the Advancement of Women, stated: "It is difficult to say with certainty what a world truly based on gender equality would look like, since we are still so far from achieving it" (2006, p.1). This statement shows how awareness of gender as an analytical category and gender inequality as a lived phenomenon has grown since the late

1960s. The world is deeply divided and organized by *gender*, defined as a set of socially constructed practices linked to biological sex that shape how individuals understand the categories of woman and man. Gender as a process is historically and culturally specific; manifestations of women's subordination are highly varied yet intricately connected. Not only does the form and extent of women's oppression vary from country to country, but it is also always shaped by relations of power based on race, class, ability and sexual orientation. Gender inequality is recognized as a persistent and detrimental aspect of all human societies.

While there is debate about the origins of gender inequality, the material effects of it are easily identifiable. According to the Women's Environment and Development Organization, "Women work two-thirds of the world's working hours. They also produce half of the world's food. However, women earn only ten percent of the world's income, and own less than one percent of the world's property" (2005, p.1). Poverty itself has been feminized: approximately 70 percent of the people living on less than one dollar a day are women or girls. The differential treatment of men and women is evident in material conditions and supported by ideological practices. Men are numerically dominant in key global and national decision-making positions such as international organizations, governments, and boards of directors of private enterprise. Men, therefore, greatly control access to resources and are the key architects of social, economic, and political policies. Gender inequality requires the daily exercise of power to be maintained. Further, the work of men is more highly paid and is accorded greater status than the work of women, which is often unpaid and not recognized as work. Joni Seager and Ann Olson in *Women in the World: An International Atlas* note, "Everywhere women are worse off than men: women have less power, less autonomy, more work, less money, and more responsibility. Women everywhere have a smaller share of the pie; if the pie is very small (as in poor countries), women's share is smaller still. Women in rich countries have a higher standard of living than do women in poor countries, but nowhere are women equal to men" (1986, p. 7).

In most regions of the world, gender relations were transformed in the twentieth century by the globalization of economies, technological developments, changes in how work is organized, warfare, and organized resistance movements (feminist, anticolonial, and civil rights). In the year 1900, the vast majority of women in the world had no formal legal rights, had extremely limited employment options, and were starting to gain access to higher education. Although the specificity of gender inequality in the global North (the world's wealthier nations, located predominantly in the northern hemisphere) and the South (the world's poorer nations largely of the southern hemisphere) may differ, women across the globe have worked together to effect systemic, lasting changes to improve the material conditions of women's lives. To be able to build an effective feminist movement, Chandra Mohanty has argued that women must work from a framework that highlights "mutuality, accountability and the recognition of common interests as the basis for relationships among diverse communities" (2003, p. 7). The notion of common interests between women of the South and North is important because it disrupts the construction of women of the North as liberated and women of the South as victims in need of rescue.

ISSUES OF GENDER INEQUALITY IN WORK

To understand gender issues and work, it is important to note that work has been largely conceptualized in the social sciences as activities performed for wages outside of the home, in the productive or public sphere. This is the work that men predominantly perform. Work done in the home by women—unwaged reproductive work that provides essential services for the functioning of the public sphere such as producing food for the family and childcare—is not considered to be part of the economy and has been rendered invisible in global accounting systems. According to Marilyn Waring in *Counting for Nothing: What Men Value and What Women are Worth* (1999), economic indicators such as the gross domestic product (GDP) and gross national product (GNP) do not include "activities that lie outside the production boundary—that is, in every notion, the great bulk of labour performed by women in an unpaid capacity" (p. 58). Since GDP and GNP are used to set policy priorities and measure the economic performance of a nation, the omission of women's work has far-reaching consequences. Women's contributions are not included in the calculation of major economic indicators thus rendering women's work invisible and naturalizing the belief that women do not contribute to the economy. Waring argued that the recognition of the unpaid work of women would necessarily lead to changes in social policy.

Women and girls perform the vast majority of work done in the home. This work is unpaid, devalued, and unrecognized as legitimate work and the sharp gendered division of labor is often justified by the argument that the activities of housework are a natural extension of women's biology. In Japan, for example, women reported that they spent twenty-nine hours per week doing housework; the average for men was only four hours. A survey conducted in India in 1999 found that women cooked for fifteen hours a week, had five minutes per day for leisure, slept two hours less per night than men, and spent ten times longer on household work than men. Men indicated that they cooked for less than one hour per week and had, on average, two hours per day of leisure time (Seager, 2003, p. 70). In households where both partners work outside the home for wages, the division of labor within the home is disproportionately performed by women.

Entry into the waged labor market has been seen as a route to greater autonomy for women and since the 1970s the participation of women in the labor market has increased dramatically. In most countries, women now form at least 40 percent of waged workers. In 1999, 83 percent of women in Burundi, Mozambique, and Rwanda worked for wages. However, it is critical to examine the working conditions, wages, and occupational segregation faced by women. Women form approximately 75 percent of the world's part-time workforce and are often employed on short temporary contracts without health benefits, job security, or protection against job-related health problems.

Women tend to be clustered in occupations in the service sector, in nurturing roles such as teaching and nursing as well as industrial assembly work on the global assembly line. These occupations receive lower levels of pay and social status. Even for identical work performed by women and men, work is valued differently depending on who performs the work. For example, in the United States in 1998, compared to the earnings of white men for the same work, white women earned seventy-three cents on the dollar, African American women earned sixty-three cents, and Hispanic American women earned fifty-three cents. The gender gap in earnings also varies by race. Even when women have the education and experience, they are often not able to break into the highest levels of management. According to Seager, in Canada and the United States in 1999, only thirteen of the largest one thousand corporations had women chief executive officers and only 4 percent of the senior management positions were filled by women.

FORMAL RIGHTS AND POLITICAL POWER

Women have made significant progress with respect to formal legal rights since the mid-nineteenth century. There has been a growing awareness of gender inequality in formal power and legal systems. Across the globe, women have fought for rights to make their status equal to that of men in areas of universal suffrage, property rights, and access to education. As of 2006, there is only one country, Kuwait, in which women do not have the same voting rights as men. Although the struggle for universal suffrage began in the mid-nineteenth century in many countries, the extension of voting rights was unevenly applied over a period of years to different groups of women. For example, in Canada, white women were first granted the right to vote in federal elections in 1918

yet it was not until 1960 that everyone in Canada regardless of gender or race was allowed to vote.

The extension of voting rights to women has not significantly changed the face of political representation and the exercise of political power. As of 2006 there is no country where women comprise 50 percent of elected representatives in government. In 1990 when women held, on average, 12 percent of all seats in national houses of parliament, the United Nations Economic and Social Council recommended that nations should aim to achieve a level of 30 percent representation by women by 1995. As of 2005 women's political participation as a global average increased to 16 percent; only 19 countries met or exceeded the 30 percent target, according to the United Nations Statistical Division. The votes that women fought so hard for do not seem to have translated into direct political power for women as a group. Gender inequality is also prevalent in religious institutions. In all mainstream religious traditions (Christianity, Islam, Judaism, Hinduism, Buddhism) women are either forbidden from participating in leadership roles or sharply limited in what roles they can assume.

Feminists have argued that women and men are born with equal human capacity to learn, develop, and contribute to shaping the world. It is through the social organization of gender and gender roles that limit the potential of women to contribute to their full ability. Since 1960 there have been many positive developments, such as increased participation of women in political leadership roles and increased access for women and girls to education. One significant indicator of the success of feminist organizing is how an awareness of gender inequality as manifested in violence against women and reproductive health issues has been moved to the center of national and global discussions. Gender inequality has become a key focus of the United Nations. In 1975, the first World Conference on Women was held in Mexico with 133 governments participating in the discussions. Since 1975 there have been four additional conferences (Copenhagen, 1980; Nairobi, 1985; Beijing, 1995; New York, 2005) with participation increasing with each meeting. In 1995 more than 47,000 women and men participated in the creation of the Beijing Declaration and the Platform for Action. The Platform clearly stated that the empowerment of women and gender equality were critical to international development, peace, and human rights. One hundred eighty-nine countries endorsed the Platform, giving gender inequality a new profile in the formation of national policies and legislation.

Equality between women and men will not be achieved only by the implementation of legal reforms that position men and women as the same; there remains much work to be done beyond the achievement of formal legal rights. The elimination of global gender inequality will require a fundamental transformation of social relations between women and men.

SEE ALSO *Discrimination, Wage, by Gender; Female-Headed Families; Feminism; Feminism, Second Wave; Gender; Gender Gap; Gender Studies; Inequality, Income; Inequality, Political; Inequality, Racial; Inequality, Wealth; Matriarchy; Patriarchy; Social Movements; Women's Movement; Work and Women*

BIBLIOGRAPHY

Enloe, Cynthia. 1989. *Bananas, Beaches and Bases: Making Feminist Sense of International Politics*. Berkeley: University of California Press.

Hannon, Carolyn. 2006. *A New World: A Vision for Gender Equality and Empowerment of Women: Address to the Contemporary Woman Program At Brescia University*. United Nations Department of Economic and Social Affairs. http://www.un.org/womenwatch/daw/news/speech2006/Bres cia%20University%20Kentucky%20FINAL%206%20April %202006.pdf.

hooks, bell. 1984. *Feminist Theory: From Margin to Center*. Boston: South End Press.

Mohanty, Chandra Talpade. 2003. *Feminism without Borders: Decolonizing Theory Practicing Solidarity*. London: Duke University Press.

Seager, Joni. 2003. *The Penguin Atlas of Women in the World*. New York: Penguin Books.

Seager, Joni, and Ann Olson. 1986. *Women in the World: An International Atlas*. London: Pan Books.

Waring, Marilyn. 1999. *Counting for Nothing: What Men Value and What Women Are Worth*. Toronto: University of Toronto Press.

Women's Environment and Development Organization. 2005. *Shortchanging Women: How U.S. Economic Policy Impacts Women Worldwide*. http://www.wedo.org.

Bonnie Slade